Lecture Notes in Computer Science 8107

Commenced Publication in 1973
Founding and Former Series Editors:
Gerhard Goos, Juris Hartmanis, and Jan van Leeuwen

Editorial Board

Ana Moreira   Bernhard Schätz Jeff Gray
Antonio Vallecillo   Peter Clarke (Eds.)

Model-Driven Engineering Languages and Systems

16th International Conference, MODELS 2013
Miami, FL, USA, September 29 – October 4, 2013
Proceedings

 Springer

Volume Editors

Ana Moreira
Universidade Nova de Lisboa, Caparica, Portugal
E-mail: amm@fct.unl.pt

Bernhard Schätz
fortiss / Technische Universität München, Germany
E-mail: schaetz@fortiss.org

Jeff Gray
University of Alabama, Tuscaloosa, AL, USA
E-mail: gray@cs.ua.edu

Antonio Vallecillo
Universidad de Málaga, Spain
E-mail: av@lcc.uma.es

Peter Clarke
Florida International University, Miami, FL, USA
E-mail: clarkep@cis.fiu.edu

ISSN 0302-9743   e-ISSN 1611-3349
ISBN 978-3-642-41532-6   e-ISBN 978-3-642-41533-3
DOI 10.1007/978-3-642-41533-3
Springer Heidelberg New York Dordrecht London

Library of Congress Control Number: 2013950213

CR Subject Classification (1998): D.2, F.3.2-3, D.3, K.6.3, I.6.3-5, C.4

LNCS Sublibrary: SL 2 – Programming and Software Engineering

© Springer-Verlag Berlin Heidelberg 2013

Typesetting: Camera-ready by author, data conversion by Scientific Publishing Services, Chennai, India

Printed on acid-free paper

Springer is part of Springer Science+Business Media (www.springer.com)

Preface

Welcome to the proceedings of the ACM/IEEE 16th International Conference on Model Driven Engineering Languages and Systems (MODELS 2013). This year's MODELS edition took place in the "Magic City" of Miami, a renowned region for education and research. As the MODELS community celebrated its 16th birthday, this major hub for culture, entertainment, arts, and fashion offered a unique stage for hosting the international diversity of participants who attended MODELS.

Since its beginnings, the use of models has always been a core principle in computer science. Recently, model-based engineering has gained rapid popularity across various engineering disciplines. The pervasive use of models as the core artifacts of the development process, and model-driven development of complex systems, has been strengthened by a focus on executable models and automatic transformations supporting the generation of more refined models and implementations. Software models have become industrially accepted best practices in many application areas. Domains like automotive systems and avionics, interactive systems, business engineering, games, and Web-based applications commonly apply a tool-supported, model-based, or model-driven approach toward software development. The potential for early validation and verification, coupled with the generation of production code, has been shown to cover a large percentage of implemented functionality with improved productivity and reliability.

This increased success of using models in software and systems engineering also opens up new challenges, requiring collaborative research across multiple disciplines, ranging from offering suitable domain-specific modeling concepts to supporting legacy needs through models. The MODELS conference is devoted to model-based development for software and systems engineering, covering all types of modeling languages, methods, tools, and their applications. MODELS 2013 offered an opportunity for researchers, practitioners, educators, and students to come together, to reflect on and discuss our progress as a community, and to identify the important challenges still to be overcome.

The MODELS community was challenged to demonstrate the maturity and effectiveness of model-based and model-driven engineering, and to explore their limits by investigating new application areas and combinations with other emerging technologies. This challenge resulted in papers submitted to the MODELS 2013 Foundations and Applications Tracks.

The program of MODELS 2013 had a strong mix of research and application papers that demonstrate the advances in this thriving field, anchored by three keynote sessions. Our first keynote speaker was Charles Simonyi from Intentional Software, who talked about "The Magic of Software." Charles is a well-known high-tech pioneer, philanthropist, and space traveler. He was the chief architect of Microsoft Word, Excel and other widely-used application programs. He left Microsoft to found Intentional Software, which aims to develop and market computer software for knowledge processing. His passion for science and for space has led him to travel into space twice aboard the Soyuz spacecraft, becoming the fifth space tourist and the first ever to fly twice. Despite this, we found that his opinions are practical and down to earth!

Our second keynote speaker was Constance Heitmeyer, who leads the Software Engineering Section of the Naval Research Laboratory's (NRL.s) Center for High Assurance Computer Systems. She talked about "Model-Based Development of Software Systems: A Panacea or Academic Poppycock?" Her talk was an interesting view of software modeling from the perspective of transitioning research results to software practice. Among other things, she is the chief designer of NRL's SCR (Software Cost Reduction) toolset, a set of tools for modeling, validating, and verifying complex software systems, which has been transferred to over 200 industry, government, and university groups.

We were also honored with a keynote presentation by Professor Bernd Brügge, a renowned expert and well-known speaker from the Technische Universität München and Carnegie Mellon University. He discussed a challenging topic in his talk "Creativity vs. Rigor: Informal Modeling Is OK," showing how it is possible to include informal modeling techniques in project courses with real customers involving a large number of students at the sophomore and even freshmen level, without compromising the ideas of model-driven software development.

The Foundations Track papers provide significant contributions to the core software modeling body of knowledge in the form of new ideas and results that advance the state of the art. Two categories of Foundations Track papers are included in these proceedings: *Technical Papers*, describing original scientifically rigorous solutions to challenging model-driven development problems, and *Exploratory Papers*, describing new, non-conventional modeling research positions or approaches that challenge the status quo and describe solutions that are based on new ways of looking at software modeling problems.

The Applications Track papers demonstrate the relevance and effectiveness of the model-based paradigm of engineering. They include two categories of papers: *Application Papers*, providing a realistic and verifiable picture of the current state of the practice in model-based engineering and explore the problems encountered by the industrial adoption of model-based techniques, and *Empirical Evaluation Papers*, evaluating existing problem cases or scientifically validated proposed solutions through empirical studies, experiments, case studies, or simulations.

Following the successful format initiated in 2012, we used a Foundations Program Committee and an Applications Program Committee to evaluate all the papers. A separate Program Board (PB) also convened to help ensure that all reviews received by the authors provided constructive feedback, and to check that the selection process was as rigorous and fair as possible. In the 2013 review process each paper was reviewed by at least three members of the Program Committees; the reviews were monitored by a PB member assigned to the paper.

Each paper was extensively discussed at the online Program Committee (PC) meeting, giving due consideration to author responses. A physical PB meeting was held as a satellite event of ICSE 2013, in San Francisco, during May 24–25, 2013, to finalize the selection of papers by making acceptance decisions on those papers for which online PC discussions did not converge on a clear decision.

For MODELS 2013, we received a total of 180 full papers from the 236 abstracts submitted. From these, 130 papers were submitted to the Foundations Track and 50 to the Applications Track. Out of the 130 papers, the PC and PB accepted 30 papers and invited four for resubmission. Of the 50 Applications Track papers, 12 were accepted and one was invited to be improved and resubmitted. All five papers invited for resubmission were accepted after a second round of evaluations. This results in a total number of 47 papers accepted, with a 26% acceptance rate.

The PC chairs also conducted an author survey to obtain feedback on the quality of reviews. We received 112 responses from authors of Foundations Track papers and 44 responses from Applications Track authors. Authors were asked to evaluate the usefulness of the reviews. Over 76% of the respondents indicated that their reviews were either useful or very useful. Feedback like this helps us determine the effectiveness of the MODELS review process and we greatly appreciate the effort of the authors who submitted completed survey forms.

In addition to the invited talks and technical sessions, MODELS 2013 featured the traditional set of satellite events which this year included 18 workshops, ten tutorials, two sessions dedicated to tool demonstrations, one panel on "Abstraction Challenges," and one evening session devoted to posters of emergent ideas. The Educators and Doctoral Symposia also occurred again at MODELS 2013, providing the premier venue for both educators and doctoral students working on topics related to model-driven engineering. For the first time in its history, MODELS hosted the ACM Student Research Competition (SRC), sponsored by Microsoft Research. The ACM SRC is a forum for undergraduate and graduate students to showcase their research, exchange ideas, and improve their communication skills while competing for prizes at MODELS 2013.

Organizing MODELS 2013 involved the considerable effort of over 100 hard-working members of the Organizing Committee and the various selection committees. A list of the Organizing Committee and selection committees for the satellite events can be found on the MODELS 2013 website (http://www.modelsconference.org/). We thank them all for their expertise, time, and commitment across several years of planning and coordination.

We are particularly grateful to the Foundations PC, the Applications PC and the PB for their continued observance in maintaining the quality of the MODELS program. We also thank the additional reviewers who contributed to the MODELS 2013 review process. We extend special thanks to Gregor Engels (MODELS Steering Committee Chair) and all the other members of the Steering Committee for their support during the planning and execution of MODELS 2013. We appreciate the helpful assistance from Geri Georg, who served as the

MODELS Steering Committee Chair during the early phases of the MODELS 2013 formation.

Our special gratitude goes to the local Miami team at Florida International University, including the excellent group of student volunteers, for their hard work behind the scenes to make this conference happen. Organizing a conference represents almost two years of hard work and complete dedication.

We thank all the authors who submitted papers to MODELS, and we congratulate those authors whose papers appear in these proceedings. These papers reflect the quality of the current state of the art in software modeling research and practice.

A special word of gratitude is due to Richard van de Stadt for his CyberChair support. He went far beyond the call of duty in providing innovative responses to the many challenges presented him and was a tireless collaborator and companion on this exciting journey.

No conference would be viable without sponsors. We sincerely thank all of our generous supporters, especially our gold sponsors CEA-List and Microsoft Research, silver sponsors Intentional Software, Tata Consulting Services and Siemens, and the rest of the contributing and supporting companies and organizations including the OMG, Springer, CEUR, Greater Miami Convention and Visitors Bureau, and society sponsors IEEE, IEEE Computer Society, ACM and ACM SIGSOFT.

We are convinced that everyone had both an exciting and stimulating time in Miami, and left with new ideas and enthusiasm to broaden the MODELS community and strengthen the application of models in the engineering of software systems.

August 2013   Ana Moreira
                                                          Bernhard Schätz
                                                                Jeff Gray
                                                        Antonio Vallecillo
                                                             Peter Clarke

Organization

General Chairs

Jeff Gray   University of Alabama, USA
Antonio Vallecillo   Universidad de Málaga, Spain

Foundations Track Program Chair

Ana Moreira   Universidade Nova de Lisboa, Portugal

Applications Track Program Chair

Bernhard Schätz   Fortiss, and Technische Universität München,
Germany

Local Chair

Peter Clarke   Florida International University, USA

Industry Liaison

Magnus Christerson   Intentional Software, USA

Workshop Chairs

Fabio Costa   Universidade Federal de Goiás, Brazil
Eugene Syriani   University of Alabama, USA

Tutorial Chairs

Jordi Cabot   École des Mines de Nantes/Inria, France
Jörg Kienzle   McGill University, Canada

Panel Chairs

Silvia Abrahão   Universitat Politècnica de València, Spain
Isidro Ramos   Universitat Politècnica de València, Spain

Demonstration Chairs

Yan Liu   Concordia University, Canada
Steffen Zschaler   King's College London, UK

Poster Chairs

Benoit Baudry   Inria/IRISA, France
Sudipto Ghosh   Colorado State University, USA

ACM Student Research Competition Chairs

Ethan Jackson   Microsoft Research, USA
Davide Di Ruscio   Università dell'Aquila, Italy

Publicity Chairs

James Hill   IUPUI, USA
Martina Seidl   Johannes Kepler University, Austria

Social Media Chairs

Ralf Lämmel   Universität Koblenz-Landau, Germany
Vadim Zaytsev   CWI, The Netherlands

Publications Chair

Manuel Wimmer   Vienna University of Technology, Austria

Educators' Symposium Chairs

Perdita Stevens   University of Edinburgh, UK
Timothy Lethbridge   University of Ottawa, Canada

Doctoral Symposium Chair

Martin Gogolla   University of Bremen, Germany

Student Volunteers Chair

Jonathan Corley   University of Alabama, USA
Raymond Chang Lau   Florida International University, USA

Web Chair

Robert Tairas   Vanderbilt University, USA

Program Board

Lionel Briand   SnT Centre, Université du Luxembourg,
                                     Luxembourg
Jean-Michel Bruel   CNRS/IRIT, Université de Toulouse, France
Krzysztof Czarnecki   University of Waterloo, Canada
Jürgen Dingel   Queen's University, Canada
Gregor Engels   University of Paderborn, Germany
Robert France   Colorado State University, USA
Martin Gogolla   University of Bremen, Germany
Jean-Marc Jézéquel   IRISA, France
Richard Paige   University of York, UK
Dorina Petriu   Carleton University, Canada
Bernhard Rumpe   RWTH Aachen University, Germany
Jon Whittle   Lancaster University, UK

Program Committee: Foundations Track

Vasco Amaral   Universidade Nova de Lisboa, Portugal
Daniel Amyot   University of Ottawa, Canada
João Araújo   Universidade Nova de Lisboa, Portugal
Colin Atkinson   University of Mannheim, Germany
Mira Balaban   Ben-Gurion University, Israel
Benoit Baudry   INRIA, France
Nelly Bencomo   INRIA Paris-Rocquencourt, France
Xavier Blanc   Université Bordeaux, France
Ruth Breu   University of Innsbruck, Austria
Jordi Cabot   École des Mines de Nantes/Inria, France
Alessandra Cavarra   University of Oxford, UK
Siobhán Clarke   Trinity College Dublin, Ireland
Jane Cleland-Huang   DePaul University, USA
Juan de Lara   Universidad Autónoma de Madrid, Spain
Alexander Egyed   Johannes Kepler University, Austria
Rik Eshuis   Eindhoven University of Technology,
                                     The Netherlands
Lidia Fuentes   Universidad de Málaga, Spain
Alessandro Garcia   PUC-Rio, Brazil
Geri Georg   Colorado State University, USA
Sébastien Gérard   CEA List, France

Holger Giese   Hasso Plattner Institute,
                                   University of Potsdam, Germany
John Grundy   Swinburne University of Technology, Australia
Øystein Haugen   SINTEF, Norway
Zhenjiang Hu   National Institute of Informatics, Japan
Heinrich Hussmann   Ludwig-Maximilians-Universität München,
                                   Germany
Gerti Kappel   Vienna University of Technology, Austria
Gabor Karsai   Vanderbilt University, USA
Ingolf Krueger   UC San Diego, USA
Thomas Kühne   Victoria University of Wellington, New Zealand
Yvan Labiche   Carleton University, Canada
Philippe Lahire   University of Nice, France
Yves Le Traon   University of Luxembourg, Luxembourg
Hong Mei   Peking University, China
Dragan Milicev   University of Belgrade, Serbia
Raffaela Mirandola   Politecnico di Milano, Italy
Pierre-Alain Muller   University of Haute-Alsace, France
Gunter Mussbacher   Carleton University, Canada
Ileana Ober   IRIT Université de Toulouse, France
Alfonso Pierantonio   Università degli Studi dell'Aquila, Italy
Gianna Reggio   DIBRIS - University of Genoa, Italy
Gustavo Rossi   LIFIA, Argentina
Pete Sawyer   University of Lancaster, UK
Andy Schürr   Technische Universität Darmstadt, Germany
Arnor Solberg   SINTEF, Norway
Friedrich Steimann   Fernuniversität in Hagen, Germany
Gabriele Taentzer   Philipps-Universität Marburg, Germany
Dániel Varró   Budapest University of Technology
                                   and Economics, Hungary
Michael Whalen   University of Minnesota, USA
Tao Yue   Simula Research Laboratory, Norway
Steffen Zschaler   King's College London, UK

Program Committee: Applications Track

Silvia Abrahão   Universitat Politènica de València, Spain
Alfred Aue   Cap Gemini, Germany
Balbir Barn   Middlesex University, UK
Brian Berenbach   Siemens AG, USA
Fernando Brito e Abreu   DCTI, ISCTE-IUL, Portugal
Tony Clark   Middlesex University, UK
Alessandro Garcia   PUC-Rio, Brazil
Andreas Graf   itemis AG, Germany
Pavel Hruby   CSC, Denmark

Jürgen Kazmeier	Siemens AG, Germany
Cornel Klein	Siemens AG, Germany
Tihamer Levendovszky	Vanderbilt University, USA
Pieter Mosterman	MathWorks, USA
Oscar Pastor	Universitat Politècnica de València, Spain
Isabelle Perseil	INSERM, France
Rob Pettit	The Aerospace Corporation, USA
Alexander Pretschner	Technische Universität München, Germany
Wolfram Schulte	Microsoft, USA
Bran Selic	Malina Software Corporation, Canada
Ketil Stølen	SINTEF, Norway
Stephan Thesing	Eurocopter Deutschland GmbH, Germany
Juha-Pekka Tolvanen	MetaCase, Finland
Mario Trapp	Fraunhofer IESE, Germany
Markus Völter	independent/itemis, Germany

Steering Committee

Gregor Engels (Chair)	University of Paderborn, Germany
Lionel Briand (Vice Chair)	University of Luxembourg, Luxembourg
Silvia Abrahão	Universitat Politènica de València, Spain
Jean Bézivin	University of Nantes, France
Ruth Breu	University of Innsbruck, Austria
Jean-Michel Bruel	IRIT, France
Krzysztof Czarnecki	University of Waterloo, Canada
Laurie Dillon	Michigan State University, USA
Jürgen Dingel	Queen's University, Canada
Geri Georg	Colorado State University, USA
Jeff Gray	University of Alabama, USA
Øystein Haugen	SINTEF, Norway
Heinrich Hussmann	University of Munich, Germany
Thomas Kühne	Victoria University of Wellington, New Zealand
Ana Moreira	Universidade Nova de Lisboa, Portugal
Pierre-Alain Muller	University of Haute-Alsace, France
Oscar Nierstrasz	University of Bern, Switzerland
Dorina Petriu	Carleton University, Canada
Rob Pettit	The Aerospace Corp., USA
Gianna Reggio	University of Genoa, Italy
Bernhard Schätz	Technical University of Munich, Germany
Wolfram Schulte	Microsoft Research, USA
Andy Schürr	Technical University of Darmstadt, Germany
Steve Seidman	Texas State University, USA
Jon Whittle	Lancaster University, UK

Gold Sponsors

Silver Sponsors

Organizational Sponsors

Additional Reviewers

Mathieu Acher
Saeed Ahmadi Behnam
André Alexandersen Hauge
Abeer Al-Humaimeedy
Shaukat Ali
Anthony Anjorin
Nesa Asoudeh
Thomas Baar
Ankica Barisic
Bruno Barroca
Amel Bennaceur
Gregor Berg
Gábor Bergmann
Alexander Bergmayr
Thomas Beyhl
Erwan Bousse

Petra Brosch
Fabian Büttner
Juan Cadavid
Franck Chauvell
Bruno Cafeo
Emanuela Cartaxo
Fernando Castor
Dan Chiorean
Antonio Cicchetti
Harald Cichos
Elder Cirilo
Mickael Clavreul
Roberta Coelho
Philippe Collet
Arnaud Cuccuru
Duc-Hanh Dang

Frederik Deckwerth

Andreas Demuth

Johannes Dyck

Maged Elaasar

Brian Elvesæter

Gencer Erdogan

Claudiu Farcas

Emilia Farcas

João Faria

Kleinner Farias

Ali Fatolahi

Adrián Fernández

Nicolas Ferry

Martin Fleck

Frédéric Fondement

László Gönczy

Sebastian Gabmeyer

Nadia Gámez

Achraf Ghabi

Cláudio Gomes

Miguel Goulão

Stefanie Grewenig

Everton Guimarães

Annegret Habel

Evelyn Haslinger

Regina Hebig

Ábel Hegedüs

Christopher Hénard

Stephan Hildebrandt

Ákos Horváth

Florian Hölzl

Emilio Insfran

Muhammad Zohaib Iqbal

Martin Johansen

Teemu Kanstren

Jacques Klein

Uira Kulesza

Leen Lambers

Arnaud Lapitre

Marius Lauder

Yan Li

Malte Lochau

Azzam Maraee

Tanja Mayerhofer

Hossein Mehrfardx

Massimiliano Menarini

Zoltán Micskei

Dongyue Mou

Tejeddine Mouelhi

Stefan Neumann

Phu Nguyen

Alexander Nöhrer

Toacy Oliveira

Aida Omerovic

Ana Paiva

Marc Palyart

Mike Papadakis

Sven Patzina

Gilles Perrouin

Hendrik Radke

Isidro Ramos

István Ráth

Daniel Ratiu

Alexander Reder

Filippo Ricca

Alessandro Rossini

Jesús Sánchez Cuadrado

Nicolas Sannier

Fredrik Seehusen

Filippo Seracini

Luis Silva

Bjornar Solhaug

Daniel Strüber

Arnon Sturm

Wuliang Sun

Sabine Teufl

Alessandro Tiso

Juha-Pekka Tolvanen

Damiano Cosimo Torre

Catia Trubiani

Sara Tucci-Piergiovanni

Gergely Varro

Steffen Vaupel

Thomas Vogel

Shuai Wang

Sebastian Wilms

Manuel Wimmer

Ernest Wozniak

Qin Zhang

Xiang Zhang

Keynote Abstracts

The Magic of Software

Charles Simonyi

Intentional Software, USA

Abstract. Software allows for many models of computation. We create models to understand and reason about these computations (e.g., did the aircraft change its course because there was a hill in front of it or because a model indicated the presence of a hill?). As computers and software become more and more ubiquitous, the tangible world and computer models of the world are merging. We are re-designing our basic systems from networks, cars and aircrafts, to financial and health systems to reduce their costs and increase their effectiveness using software that, by necessity, must incorporate a model of the environment and its characteristics. Models can also take us outside of this reality and let us explore alternative timelines — what we call simulation. Today, programming languages are the primary way to communicate our intentions of these systems in software. Notation, syntax and semantics make the mental programming language models concrete for us as humans. But the computer does not really need the notation, syntax and semantics models of the software in the same way as we humans do. In this talk, we will trace the magic of software that enabled this progression from Moore's law, through computer languages, to the Digital Artifacts of today. We will investigate it carefully and come to some surprising conclusions that question the mainstream thinking around software models. What if we let go of some of our learned beliefs about software models and think differently about models of instructing computers?

Model-Based Development of Software: A Panacea or Academic Poppycock

Constance Heitmeyer

Center for High Assurance Computer Systems
Naval Research Laboratory, USA

Abstract. In recent years, the use of models in developing complex software systems has been steadily increasing. Advocates of model-based development argue that models can help reduce the time, cost, and effort needed to build software systems which satisfy their requirements and that model-based approaches are effective not only in system development but throughout a system's life-time. Thus the problem addressed by researchers in software and system modeling encompasses not only the original construction of a complex system but its complete life-cycle. This talk will address significant issues in model-based system and software development, including: What is the current and future role of models in software system development? What benefits can we obtain from the use of models not only in development but throughout the system life-cycle? What are the barriers to using models in software system development and evolution? What are the major challenges for system and software modeling researchers during the next decade?

Creativity vs Rigor:
Informal Modeling is OK

Bernd Brügge

Technische Universität München, Germany

Abstract. Single large project courses with clients from industry have been established as capstone courses in many software engineering curricula. They are considered a good way of teaching industry relevant software engineering practices, in particular model-based software development.

One particular challenge is how to balance between modeling and timely delivery. If we focus too much on modeling, the students do not have enough time to deliver the system ("analysis paralysis"). If we focus too much on the delivery of the system, the quality of the models usually goes down the drain. Another challenge is the balance between informal models intended for human communication and specification models intended for CASE tools. I argue that teachers often put too much weight on the rigor of the models, and less on the creative and iterative aspects of modeling. Modeling should be allowed to be informal, incomplete and inconsistent, especially during the early phases of software development. I have been teaching capstone courses for almost 25 years, initially at the senior and junior level. During this time excellent automatic build and release management tools have been developed. They reduce the need for heroic delivery efforts at the end of a course, especially if they are coupled with agile methods, allowing the teacher to spend more time on the creative aspects of modeling. I will use several examples from my courses to demonstrate how it is possible to include informal modeling techniques in project courses with real customers involving a large number of students at the sophomore and even freshmen level without compromising the ideas of model-driven software development.

Table of Contents

Tool Support 2

Testing

Semantics Evolution 1

Verification

Domain-Specific Modeling Languages

Models@RT

Design and Architecture

Model Transformation

Model Analysis

System Synthesis

Industrial Adoption of Model-Driven Engineering: Are the Tools Really the Problem?

Jon Whittle[1], John Hutchinson[1], Mark Rouncefield[1],
Håkan Burden[2], and Rogardt Heldal[2]

[1] School of Computing and Communications, Lancaster University, Lancaster, UK
[2] Computer Science and Engineering,
Chalmers University of Technology and University of Gothenburg,
Gothenburg, Sweden

Abstract. An oft-cited reason for lack of adoption of model-driven engineering (MDE) is poor tool support. However, studies have shown that adoption problems are as much to do with social and organizational factors as with tooling issues. This paper discusses the impact of tools on MDE adoption and places tooling within a broader organizational context. The paper revisits previous data on MDE adoption (19 in-depth interviews with MDE practitioners) and re-analyzes the data through the specific lens of MDE tools. In addition, the paper presents new data (20 new interviews in two specific companies) and analyzes it through the same lens. The key contribution of the paper is a taxonomy of tool-related considerations, based on industry data, which can be used to reflect on the tooling landscape as well as inform future research on MDE tools.

Keywords: model-driven engineering, modeling tools, organizational change.

1 Introduction

When describing barriers to adoption of model-driven engineering (MDE), many authors point to inadequate MDE tools. Den Haan [1] highlights "insufficient tools" as one of the eight reasons why MDE may fail. Kuhn et al. [2] identify five points of friction in MDE that introduce complexity; all relate to MDE tools. Staron [3] found that "technology maturity [may] not provide enough support for cost efficient adoption of MDE." Tomassetti et al.'s survey reveals that 30% of respondents see MDE tools as a barrier to adoption [4].

Clearly, then, MDE tools play a major part in the adoption (or not) of MDE. On the other hand, as shown by Hutchinson et al. [5,6], barriers are as likely to be social or organizational rather than purely technical or tool-related. The question remains, then, to what extent poor tools hold back adoption of MDE and, in particular, what aspects – both organizational and technical – should be considered in the next generation of MDE tools.

The key contribution of this paper is a taxonomy of factors which capture how MDE tools impact MDE adoption. The focus is on relating tools and their technical features to the broader social and organizational context in which they are

A. Moreira et al. (Eds.): MODELS 2013, LNCS 8107, pp. 1–17, 2013.

used. The taxonomy was developed by analyzing data from two separate studies of industrial MDE use. In the first, we interviewed 19 MDE practitioners from different companies. In the second, we interviewed a further 20 MDE practitioners in two different companies (10 per company). The two studies complement each other: the first is a broad but shallow study of MDE adoption across a wide range of industries; the second is a narrower but deeper study within two specific companies with different experiences of applying MDE. Neither study was limited to tooling issues; rather, they were both designed to capture a broad range of experiences related to MDE use and adoption and, in both, we used qualitative methods to allow key themes to emerge from the data. We focus in this paper only on emergent themes related to MDE tools.

The literature has relatively little to say about non-technical factors of MDE tooling. There have been a number of surveys of MDE tools (e.g., [7,8,9]) but they focus on classifying tools based on what technical functionalities they provide. More recently, Paige and Varró report on lessons learned from developing two significant (academic) MDE tools [10]. Again, however, very little is said about understanding users' needs and the users' organizational context: the authors simply state "Try to have real end-users; they keep you honest" and "Rapid response to feedback can help you keep your users."

Indeed, there is a distinct lack of knowledge about how MDE tools are actually adopted in industry and what social and organizational, as well as technical, considerations need to be in place for a tool to succeed. This paper makes a first attempt to redress the balance. Section 2 discusses existing literature on tools, with a focus on understanding users' needs and organizational context. Section 3 describes the methodological details of our studies. Section 4 presents our taxonomy, based on emerging themes from our first study of MDE adoption. Section 5 discusses our second study and relates its findings to the taxonomy. Finally, the paper discusses how the taxonomy can be used to advance research and development of MDE tools (Section 6).

2   Context and Related Work

Tools have long been of interest to those considering the use of technology in industrial settings. In research on computer supported cooperative work (CSCW), there have been two distinctive approaches. On the one hand there are those interested in how individuals use tools and, in particular, how to design tools that are intuitive and seamless to use. This reflects a Heideggerian difference between tools that are 'ready to hand' (they fade into the background) and 'present at hand' (focus is on the tool to the detriment of the 'real' issue) [11] [12, p. 109]. In contrast, another approach, exemplified by Grudin [13] and Brown [14], considers how organizations use tools and argues that failure can be attributed to: a disparity of benefit between tool users and those who are required to do unrecognized additional work to support tools; lack of management understanding; and a failure by designers and managers to recognize their limits. In a comment that might cause some reflection for MDE tool developers, Brown [14] suggests that (groupware) tools are generally useful in supporting existing everyday organizational processes, rather than radical organizational change.

The issue of how software development should be organized and supported has long been discussed and remedies have often, though not always, included particular tools, techniques, and practices. For example, whilst Merisalo-Rantanen et al. [15] found that tools facilitated fast delivery and easy modification of prototypes, amongst the core values of the 'agile manifesto' was a focus on "individuals and interactions over processes and tools" and a number of studies [16] emphasized the importance of organizational rather than technical factors.

However, when considering MDE tools there is little in the way of systematic evaluation. Cabot and Teniente [9] acknowledge MDE tools but suggest that they have several limitations regarding code generation. Selic [17] talks about the important characteristics of tools for the success of MDE, suggesting that some MDE tools "have now reached a degree of maturity where this is practical even in large-scale industrial applications". Recently, Stahl et al. [18] have claimed that MDE does not make sense without tool support. Two studies [19,2] identify the impact of tools on processes and organizations, and vice versa, but the main focus is on introducing MDE in large-scale software development.

There have been two recent, and very different, studies about the experience of developing and deploying MDE tools. Paige and Varró [10] conclude that: "using MDD tools – in anger, on real projects, with reported real results, is now both feasible and necessary." However, it is significant that this study is about academic MDE tools. In contrast, Clark and Muller [20] use their own commercial experiences to identify lessons learned about tool development, in cases that might be considered technical successes but were ultimately business or organizational failures: "The last decade has seen a number of high profile commercial MDD tools fail . . . these tools were expensive to produce and maintain . . . there are number of open-source successes but it is not clear that these systems can support a business model". In terms of specific lessons with regard to tools, this one stands out: "ObjeXion and Xactium made comparable mistakes. They were developing elegant tools for researchers, not pragmatic tools for engineers".

3   Study Method

The key contribution of the paper is a taxonomy of MDE tool-related issues. The taxonomy has been developed based on two sets of interviews: a set of 19 interviews from 18 different companies carried out between Nov 2009 and Jul 2010, and a set of 20 interviews carried out in two companies between Jan and Feb 2013. Our method was to use the first set to develop the taxonomy; the second to validate the taxonomy. The two sets are complementary: the first provides broad, shallow coverage of 10 different industrial sectors; the second provides narrow, deep coverage of two companies.

Our first set of interviews is the same set used in earlier publications [5,6]. However, prior publications gave a holistic view of the findings and did not include data on tools. The procedure for selecting and carrying out the interviews

has been described elsewhere [6]. All interviewees came from industry and had
significant experience of applying MDE in practice. The interviews were semi-
structured, taking around 60 minutes each, and all began with general questions
about the participant's background and experience with MDE. All interviews
were recorded and transcribed. In total, we collected around 20 hours of conversation, amounting to over 150,000 words of transcribed data.

The second set consists of 10 interviews at Ericsson AB and 10 interviews
at Volvo Cars Corporation. The interviewees at Ericsson came from the Radio
Base Station unit, which has been involved in MDE since the late 1980s while
the interviewees at Volvo represent a new unit that has just started to use MDE
for in-house software development for electrical propulsion. The interviews cover
more than 20 hours of recorded conversation and were conducted in the same
semi-structured fashion as the first set.

Analysis of the interview transcripts was slightly different in each case. The
first set was used to develop the taxonomy. Each transcript was coded by two
researchers. The initial task was to simply go through the transcripts looking
for where the respondents said anything about tools; these fragments were then
coded by reference to particular ideas or phrases mentioned in the text – such
as 'cost' or 'processes'. The average reference to tool issues per transcript was
11 with 3 being the lowest and 18 being the highest. Inter-coder reliability was
computed using Holsti's formula [21], dividing the number of agreements by the
number of text fragments. For this research, the average inter-coder agreement
was 0.86 (161/187). The researchers then grouped the initial coding into broad
themes relating to 'technical', 'organizational' and 'social' issues.

The second set was used to validate the taxonomy. Researchers read the transcripts looking for tool-related issues and then mapped those to the proposed
taxonomy. Any deviations from the taxonomy were noted.

4   A Taxonomy of MDE Tool Considerations

This section presents the taxonomy, developed from the first set of interviews.
Our analysis process resulted in four broad themes, each broken into categories at
two levels of detail: (i) Technical Factors – where interviewees discussed specific
technical aspects of MDE tools, such as a missing feature or technical considerations of applying tools in practice; (ii) Internal Organizational Factors – the
relationship between tools and the way a company organizes itself; (iii) External
Organizational Factors – influences from outside the company which may affect
tool use and application; (iv) Social Factors – issues related to the way people
perceive MDE tools or tool stakeholders.

Tables 1-4 form the taxonomy. Each category is briefly defined in the tables,
and an example of each sub-category is given. Numbers in brackets are the
number of interviewees who commented on a particular sub-category (max. 19).
Care should be taken when interpreting these numbers – they merely reflect
what proportion of our participants happened to talk about a particular issue.
They do not necessarily indicate relative importance of sub-categories because

one interviewee may have talked in depth about a sub-category whereas another may have mentioned it only briefly. A deeper analysis would be required to produce sub-category weightings. The reader should also avoid the temptation to make comparisons between factors based on the table.

The following subsections present highlights from each theme: we have picked out particularly insightful or relevant experiences from the interview transcripts. We quote from the transcripts frequently; these are given italicized and in quotation marks. Quotes are taken from the transcripts verbatim. Square brackets are used to include contextual information.

The taxonomy is a data-driven, evidence-based description of issues that industrial MDE practitioners have encountered in practice when applying or developing MDE tools. We make no claim that the taxonomy covers all possible tool-related issues; clearly, further evidence from other practitioners may lead to an extension of the taxonomy. We also do not claim that the sub-categories are orthogonal. As will be seen later, some examples of tool use can be classified into multiple sub-categories. Finally, we do not claim that this is the 'perfect' taxonomy. It is simply one way of structuring the emerging themes from our data, and the reader is welcome to re-structure the themes into an alternative taxonomy which better fits his/her purposes.

The taxonomy can be used in a variety of ways. It can be used as a checklist of issues to consider when developing tools. It can be used as a framework to evaluate existing tools. Principally, however, we hope that it simply points to a range of technical, social and organizational factors that may be under-represented in the MDE research community.

4.1 Technical Factors

Table 1 presents the set of categories and sub-categories that relate to technical challenges and opportunities when applying MDE tools. There are six categories.

Category Descriptions. The first, Tool Features, details specific tool functionalities which interviewees felt impacted on project success. These include support for modeling system behavior, architectures, domain-specific modeling, and flexibility in code generation. Code Generation Templates, for example, refers to the ability to define one's own code generation rules, whereas Scoped Code Generation refers to an incremental form of code generation where only model changes are re-generated. The second category, Practical Applicability, contains issues related to how tools can be made to work in practice. The issues range from tool support for very large models (scaleability), to the impact of using multiple tools or multiple versions of tools together, to the general maturity level of tools and how flexibly they can be adapted into existing tool chains. The third category concerns Complexity, which includes Accidental Complexity, where the tools introduce complexity unnecessarily. The fourth category is Human Factors and includes both classical usability issues but also bigger issues such as whether the way tools are designed (and, in particular, the kinds of abstractions they use) match the way that people think. The final two categories

Table 1. Technical Categories

Category	Sub-Category
Tool Features *Specific functionalities offered in tools*	- Modeling Behavior (1) - Action Languages (1) - Support for Domain-Specific Languages (6) - Support for Architecture (3) - Code Generation Templates (6) - UML Profiles (1) - Scoped Code Generation (2) - Model Analysis (5) - Reverse Engineering Models (3) - Sketching Models (1) - Refactoring Models (1)
Practical Applicability *Challenges of applying tools in practice*	- Tool Scaleability (1) - Tool Versioning (1) - Chaining Tools Together (2) - Industrial Quality of Generated Code (8) - Flexibility of Tools (3) - Maturity of Tools (1) - Dealing with Legacy (2)
Complexity *Challenges brought on by excessive complexity in tools*	- Tool Complexity (4) - Language Complexity (5) - Accidental Complexity Introduced by Tools (1)
Human Factors *Consideration of tool users*	- Whether Tools Match Human Abstractions (4) - Usability (4)
Theory *Theory underpinning tools*	- Theoretical Foundations of Tools (1) - Formal Semantics (2)
Impact on Development *Impact of tools on technical success criteria*	- Impact on Quality (2) - Impact on Productivity (4) - Impact on Maintainability (3)

concern the way that the lack of formal foundations leads to sub-optimal tools and the reported perceptions about how tools impact quality, productivity and maintainability.

Observations. One very clear finding that comes out of our analysis is that MDE can be very effective, but it takes effort to make it work. The majority of our interviewees were very successful with MDE but all of them either built their own modeling tools, made heavy adaptations of off-the-shelf tools, or spent a lot of time finding ways to work around tools. The only accounts of easy-to-use, intuitive tools came from those who had developed tools themselves for bespoke purposes. Indeed, this suggests that current tools are a barrier to success rather than an enabler and *"the fact that people are struggling with the tools... and succeed nonetheless requires a certain level of enthusiasm and competence."*

Our interviewees emphasized tool immaturity, complexity and lack of usability as major barriers. Usability issues can be blamed, at least in part, on an over-emphasis on graphical interfaces: "... *I did an analysis of one of the IBM tools and I counted 250 menu items.*" More generally, tools are often very powerful, but it is too difficult for users to access that power; or, in some cases, they do not really need that power and require something much simpler: "*I was really impressed with the power of it and on the other hand I saw windows popping up everywhere... at the end I thought I still really have no idea how to use this tool and I have only seen a glimpse of the power that it has.*"

These examples hint at a more fundamental problem, which appears to be true of textual modeling tools as well: a lack of consideration for how people work and think: "*basically it's still the mindset that the human adapts to the computer, not vice-versa.*" In addition, current tools have focused on automating solutions once a problem has been solved. In contrast, scant attention has been paid to supporting the problem solving process itself: "*so once the analyst has figured out what maps to what it's relatively easy... However, what the tools don't do is help the analyst figure out what maps to what.*"

Complexity problems are typically associated with off-the-shelf tools. Of particular note is accidental complexity – which can be introduced due to poor consideration of other categories, such as lack of flexibility to adapt the tools to a company's own context. One interviewee described how the company's processes had to be significantly changed to allow them to use the tool: a lack of control over the code generation templates led to the need to modify the generated code directly, which in turn led to a process to control these manual edits. Complexity also arises when fitting an MDE tool into an existing tool chain: "*And the integration with all of the other products that you have in your environment...*" Despite significant investment in providing suites of tools that can work together, this is clearly an area where it is easy to introduce accidental complexity.

It is ironic that MDE was introduced to help deal with the essential complexity of systems, but in many cases, adds accidental complexity. Although this should not be surprising (cf. Brooks [22]), it is interesting to describe this phenomenon in the context of MDE. For the technical categories, in almost every case, interviewees gave examples where the category helped to tackle essential complexity, but also other examples where the category led to the introduction of accidental complexity. So, interviewees talked about the benefits of code generation, but, at the same time, lamented the fact that "*we have some problems with the complexity of the code generated... we are permanently optimizing this tool.*" Interviewees discussed how domain-specific languages (DSLs) should be targeted at complex parts of the system, such as where multiple disciplines intersect ("*if you have multiple disciplines like mechanical electronics and software, you can really use those techniques*") whilst, at the same time realizing that the use of DSLs introduces new complexities when maintaining a standard DSL across a whole industry: "*their own kind of textual DSL [for pension rules]... And they went to a second company and the second company said no our pension rules are totally different.*" Clearly, as well known from Brooks, there is no silver bullet.

Table 2. Internal Organizational Categories

Category	Sub-Category

Processes
Adapting tools to processes or vice-versa
	- Tailoring to a Company's Existing Processes (5)
	- Sustainability of Tools over the Long Term (3)
	- Appropriating Tools for Purposes
	    They Were Not Designed For (3)
	- Issues of Integrating Multiple Tools (6)
	- Migrating to different tool versions (3)
	- Offsetting Gains: Tools bring gains
	    in one aspect but losses in another (2)
	- Whether Maintenance is carried out
	    at the Code or Model Level (3)

Organizational Culture *Impact of cultural attitudes on tool application*	- Tailoring to a Company's Culture (4) - Inertia: Reluctance to Try New Things (1) - Over-Ambition: Asking Too Much of Tools (1) - Low Hanging Fruit: Using Tools on Easy Problems First (6)
Skills *Skills needed to apply tools*	- Training Workforce (11) - Availability of MDE Skills in Workforce (4)

4.2 Internal Organizational Factors

Category Descriptions. Table 2 gives the set of internal organizational categories. The first, Processes, relates to how tools must be adapted to fit into existing processes or how existing processes must be adapted in order to use tools. Tailoring to Existing Processes concerns the former of these; the remaining sub-categories the latter. Sustainability of tools concerns processes for ensuring long term effectiveness of tools, taking into account changes needed to the tools as their use grows within the organization. Appropriation is about how tool use changes over time, often in a way not originally intended. Integration Issues are where new processes are needed to integrate MDE tools with existing tools. Migration Issues are about migrating from one tool to another or from one tool version to another. Offsetting Gains is where a tool brings benefits in one part of the organization but disadvantages in another part of the organization. Maintenance Level is about processes that either mandate model-level changes only, or allow code-level changes under certain constraints. The Organizational Culture category relates to the culture of an institution: to what extent tools need to be adapted to fit culture (Tailoring to Existing Culture), cultural resistance to use new tools (Inertia), a lack of realistic expectations about tool capabilities (Over Ambition), and attitudes that look for quick wins for new tools to prove themselves (Low Hanging Fruit). The third category concerns Skills — both training needs (Training) and how existing skills affect adoption (Availability of Skills).

Observations. Our interviews point to a strong need for tailoring of some sort: either tailor the tool to the process, tailor the process to the tool, or build your own tool that naturally fits your own process. Based on our data, it seems that, on balance, it is currently much easier to do the latter. Some tool vendors actively prohibit tailoring to the process, but rather a process is imposed by the tool for business reasons: "... *the transformation engines are used as services... we don't want to give our customers the source code of the transformation engines and have them change them freely. That's a business question.*"

When introducing MDE tools, one should think carefully *where* to introduce them. One company reported, "*We needed to find a way to let them incrementally adopt the technology.*" The solution was to first introduce reverse engineering of code into models, as the first part of a process of change management. Another company introduced MDE tools by first using them only in testing. The 'perfect' MDE tool may not always be necessary. For example, one company used MDE where the user interface was not so critical: "*cases which are internal applications ... where the user interface is not such an issue ... that's where you get the maximum productivity from a tool like ours.*"

There is a danger, though, in believing that one "killer application" of an MDE tool leads to another: "*prior to that they had used the technology successfully in a different project and it worked and they were very happy, so they thought, ok, this could be applied to virtually any kind of application.*" It is not easy to identify which applications are appropriate for MDE tools and which are not. Apart from obvious industries where MDE has been applied more widely than others (cf. the automotive industry), we do not have a fine-grained way of knowing which MDE tools are appropriate for which jobs.

A curious paradox of MDE is that it was developed as a way to improve portability [23]. However, time and again issues of migration and versioning came up in our interviews: "*[XX] have burned a lot of money to build their own tool which they stopped doing because they lost their models when the [YY] version changed.*"

This migration challenge manifests itself slightly differently as 'sustainability' when considering strategies for long-term tool effectiveness. It was often remarked by our interviewees that an MDE effort started small, and was well supported by tools, but that processes and tools broke down when trying to roll out MDE across a wider part of the organization: "*the complexity of these little [DSL] languages started to grow and grow and grow... we were trying to share the [code generation] templates across teams and versioning and releasing of these templates was not under any kind of control at all.*" One of our interviewees makes this point more generally: "*One of the things people forget about domain specific languages is that you may be able to develop a language that really is very well suited to you; however, the cost of sustaining just grows and it becomes eventually unacceptable because a language requires maintenance, it requires tooling, it requires education.*"

Table 3. External Organizational Categories

Category	Sub-Category
External Influences *Factors which an organization has no direct control over*	- Impact of Marketing Issues (1) - Impact of Government/Industry Standards (4)
Commercial Aspects *Business considerations impacting on tool use and application*	- Business Models for Applying MDE (3) - Cost of Tools (5) - How to Select Tools (2)

4.3   External Organizational Factors

Category Descriptions. External organizational factors (Table 3) are those which are outside the direct control of organizations. External Influences include the impact of government or industry-wide standards on the way tools are developed or applied, as well as ways in which marketing strategies of the organization or tool vendors impact on the use and application of tools. Commercial Aspects include how the cost of tools affects tool uptake, how selection of tools can be made based on commercial rather than technical priorities, and how the use of tools relates to a company's business model.

Observations. External influences clearly have an impact on whether tools – any kind of tool, not just MDE – are adopted in an organization. Our interviews show that the tool market is focused only on supporting models at an abstraction level very close to code, where the mapping to code is straightforward. This is clearly somewhat removed from the MDE vision. Unfortunately, there is also a clear gap in the way that vendors market their tools and their real capabilities in terms of this low-level approach. As a result, many MDE applications fail due to expectations that have not been managed properly.

Data on the impact of the cost of tools seems to be inconclusive. Some interviewees clearly found cost of tools to be a prohibitive factor. In one case, the high cost of licenses led a company to hack the tool's license server! For the most part, however, companies do not seem to point to tool costs as a major factor: the cost of tools tends to be dwarfed by more indirect costs of training, process change, and cultural shift: *"... it takes a lot of upfront investment for someone to learn how to use the tools and the only reason I learnt how to use them was because I was on a mission."*

Government or industry standards can both positively and negatively affect whether tools are used or not. MDE tools can help with certification processes: *"they looked at the development method using the modeling tools and said, well, it's a very clear and a very comprehensive way to go and they accepted that."* In other cases, interviewees reported that MDE tools can make certification more difficult as current government certification processes are not set up to deal with

Table 4. Social Categories

Category	Sub-Category
Control *Impact of tools on whether stake- holders feel in control of their project*	Ways of Interacting with Tool Vendors (2) Subverting Tools: Workarounds Needed to Apply Them (1)
Trust *Impact of trust on tool use and adoption*	Trust of Vendors (4) Engineers' Trust of Tools (6) Impact of Personal Career Needs (1)

auto-generated code. Sometimes, external legal demands were a main driver for the use of MDE tools in the first place: *"with the European legal demands, it's more and more important to have traceability."*

4.4   Social Factors

Category Descriptions. When it comes to MDE tools, social factors (Table 4) revolve around issues of trust and control. Tool vendors, for example, have different business models when it comes to controlling or opening up their tools (Interacting with Tool Vendors). Subverting Tools is when a company looks for creative solutions to bring a tool under its control. The data has a lot to say about Vendor Trust, or how perceptions of vendors influence tool uptake. Engineers' Trust also affects tool success: typical examples are when programmers are reluctant to use modeling tools because they do not trust code generated. Career Needs refers to how the culture of the software industry may disadvantage MDE: an example is the ubiquitous use of consultants who are not necessarily inclined to take the kind of long term view that MDE needs.

Observations. At a very general level, our data points to ways in which different roles in a development project react to MDE tools. One cannot generalize, of course, but roughly speaking, software architects tend to embrace MDE tools because they can encode their architectural rules and easily mandate that others follow them. Code 'gurus', or those highly expert programmers in a project, tend to avoid MDE tools as they can take away some of their control. Similarly, 'hobbyist programmers', those nine-to-fivers who nevertheless like to go home and read about new programming techniques, also tend to avoid MDE because it risks taking away their creativity. Managers respond very differently to MDE tools depending on their background and the current context. For example, one manager was presented with a good abstract model of the architecture but took this as a sign that the architects were not working hard enough!

One much-trumpeted advantage of MDE is that it allows stakeholders to better appreciate the big picture. Whilst this is undoubtedly true, there are also cases where MDE tools can cloud understanding, especially of junior developers:

"we'd been using C and we were very clear about the memory map and each engineer had a clear view... But in this case, we cannot do something with the generated code so we simply ask the hardware guys to have more hard disc."

Similar implications can arise when companies become dependent on vendors. Vendors often spend a lot of time with clients customizing tools to a particular environment. But this can often cause delays and cost overruns and takes control away from the client: *"And suddenly the tool doesn't do something expected and it's a nightmare for them. So they try to contact the vendor but they do not really know what's going on, they are mostly sales guys."*

MDE asks for a fundamental shift in the way that people approach their work. This may not always be embraced. One example is where MDE tools support engineers in thinking more abstractly, and, in particular, tackling the harder business problems. But engineers may not feel confident enough to do this: *"when you come to work and you say, well, I could work on a technical problem or I could work on this business problem that seems not solvable to me, it's really tempting to go work on the technical stuff."* MDE tools require up-front investment to succeed and the return on this investment may not come until the tool has been applied to multiple projects. There is a tension here with the consultancy model which is often the norm in MDE: *"So they felt that, let me do my best in this one project. Afterwards, I am moving into some other project... [in a] consultancy organization, you measure yourself and you associate yourself with things in a limited time."*

5   A Study of MDE Practice in Two Companies

This section presents insights from our second set of data: 20 additional interviews in Ericsson AB and Volvo Cars. Interviewees at Ericsson were users of Rational Software Architect RealTime Edition (RSA/RTE). At Volvo Cars, interviewees used Simulink. This set of interviews was carried out independently of the development of the taxonomy. The taxonomy was used in coding the second set of transcripts but any deviations from the taxonomy were noted.

5.1   Technical Factors

The second study clearly shows that MDE tools can both reduce and increase complexity. Ericsson employees found benefits of using RSA/RTE because of the complex aspects of the radio base station domain, such as synchronous/ asynchronous message passing: *"It takes care of these things for you so you can focus on the behavior you want to have within a base station."* Interestingly, this interviewee has now moved to a new project where all development is done using C++ and a lot of time is spent on issues that were dealt with by the tool before. And it is a constant source of error. On the other hand, *"I don't think you gain advantage in solving all kinds of problems in modeling."* There is a danger of over-engineering the solution: *"You would try to do some smart modeling, or stuff and you would fail. After a while you would end up in a worse place than if you had done this in C++".*

5.2   External Organizational Factors

Both companies illustrate how external organizational factors impact on MDE success. The functionality of Ericsson's radio base stations is accessed by Telecoms companies such as AT&T through an API. The API is developed using RSA/RTE by 7-8 software engineers. The changes to the API are managed by a forum which is responsible for ensuring that the accepted changes are consistent and that they make sense for the customers: *"We do have a process for how to change it and we review the changes very carefully. For new functions, we want it to look similar, we want to follow certain design rules and have it so it fits in with the rest."* This example illustrates how MDE can be effectively used to manage external influences: in this case, Ericsson models the API as a UML profile and manages it through MDE.

At Volvo, the automotive standard AUTOSAR[1] has made the choice of development tool a non-issue; Simulink is the standard tool: *"...a language which makes it possible to communicate across the disciplinary borders. That the system architect, the engineer and the tester actually understand what they see."*

5.3   Internal Organizational Factors

One Ericsson employee notes the importance of internal organizational support for MDE tools: *"Tool-wise I was better off five years ago than I am today...then we had tool support within the organization. And they knew everything. Today, if I get stuck there is no support to help me."* The quote comes from a system architect at Ericsson who concludes that the tools are difficult to use since they are so unintuitive. The threshold for learning how to produce and consume models can be overcome but it requires an organization where developers are not exposed to different tools between projects.

According to another employee at Ericsson, it is necessary to change the existing processes and culture in order to make the most out of MDE tools: *"I think actually that the technology for doing this [MDE] and the tools, as the enablers, they are more advanced than the organizations that can use them ...Because the organizations are not mature to do it there are few users of those tools and then the usability is poor."*

At Volvo a substantial effort has been made in order to enable the transition from Simulink as a specification and prototype tool into a code generation tool; due to the properties of the code generator different design rules are suitable for readability versus code generation. Migrating from one tool to another also requires that old processes are updated: *"When it comes to TargetLink – a competitor to Simulink – we have the knowledge of good and bad design patterns. For Simulink, that is something we are currently obtaining, what to do and not, in Simulink models."*

---

[1] AUTomotive Open System ARchitecture; www.autosar.org/

5.4 Social Factors

It seems that the effort put into tailoring the tools to the existing organization has paid off at Volvo since the domain experts trust the tools to deliver: *"I do like it. In quite a lot of ways. Especially for the kind of software we are developing. It's not like rocket science, really. It's like systems where you have a few signals in, you should make a few decisions, make some kind of output. It is not that difficult applications. There are no complex algorithms... And for that I think Simulink is very sufficient... I like it."*

At Ericsson, interviewees commented that the main difference between working with RSA/RTE and code is that the latter is well-documented on the web: *"You can find examples and case studies and what not in millions."* But when searching for tool-specific help on UML, *"you basically come up empty-handed."*

5.5 Taxonomy Validation

The study at Ericsson and Volvo is in itself revealing about MDE practice. However, for the purposes of this paper, it serves primarily to validate our taxonomy. In only one case did we find that an extension to the taxonomy was necessary. This was on the role that an open community can play in supporting MDE. As discussed in Section 5.4, the lack of online support forums for MDE can lead to feelings of isolation and, in turn, lack of engagement with MDE. We therefore extend our taxonomy to reflect this – by adding a new category, Open Community, with sub-category, Developer Forums, in Table 4. The other issue is that it can be difficult to pick a single sub-category to which a statement applies. Often, a single statement overlaps multiple sub-categories. This, however, was not unexpected. Issues of MDE adoption and tool use are complex and involve many dependencies, so it would be unrealistic to expect a taxonomy with completely orthogonal sub-categories.

6 Discussion and Conclusions

Through two separate studies of MDE practitioners, comprising a total of 39 interviews, we have developed a taxonomy of technical, social and organizational issues related to MDE tool use in practice. This taxonomy serves as a checklist for companies developing and using tools, and also points to a number of open challenges for those working on MDE tool development. We now discuss some of these challenges, which have emerged from the data.

Match tools to people, not the other way around. Most MDE tools are developed by those with a technical background but without in-depth experience of human-computer interaction or business issues. This can lead to a situation where good tools force people to think in a certain way. We recommend that the MDE community pay more attention to tried-and-tested HCI methods, which can help to produce more useful and usable tools. There is empirical work on studying MDE languages and tools, but this is rarely taken into account.

Research should avoid competing with the market. The research community should focus on issues not already tackled by commercial vendors. Our study found that the majority of tools support the transition from low level design to code. However, many bigger issues of modeling – such as support for early design stages and support for creativity in modeling – are relatively unexplored.

Finding the right problem is crucial. Our studies suggest that finding the right place for applying MDE is a crucial success factor. However, there is very little data about which parts of projects are good for MDE and which are not. Nor is there data about which tools are right for which jobs. In general, even the research community has not clearly articulated how to decide what to model and what not to model, and what tools to use or not to use.

More focus on processes, less on tools. The modeling research community focuses a lot on developing new tools and much less on understanding and improving processes. A particular case is the importance of tailoring. Very little research has been carried out on how best to tailor: what kinds of tailoring go on, how tools can or cannot support this, and how to develop simpler tools that can fit into existing processes with minimal tailoring.

Open MDE Communities. There is a distinct lack of open MDE developer forums. Those who do take the plunge with MDE are left feeling isolated, with nowhere to go to get technical questions answered or to discuss best practice. There are few examples of 'good' models online which people can consult, and efforts towards repositories of such models (cf. [24]) have achieved limited success. There is a chicken-and-egg dilemma here: if MDE is widely adopted, developer communities will self-organize; if it is not, they will not.

The big conclusion of our studies is that MDE can work, but it is a struggle. MDE tools do not seem to support those who try. We need simpler tools and more focus on the underlying processes. MDE tools also need to be more resilient: as with any new method, MDE is highly dependent on a range of technical, social and organizational factors. Rather than assuming a perfect configuration of such factors, MDE methods and tools should be resilient to imperfections.

For the most part, our sub-categories are already known and have been noted either in the literature or anecdotally. France and Rumpe [25], for example, point out that "Current work on MDE technologies tends to focus on producing implementation... from detailed design models". Aranda et al. [19] found that tailoring of processes is critical for MDE. Similarly, Staron found that organizational context has a huge impact on the cost effectiveness of MDE [3]. Indeed, many of our observations about organizational aspects of MDE adoption are not necessarily specific to MDE but are true of technology adoption generally. However, the contribution of the taxonomy is that it brings all of the factors – both technical and non-technical – together in one place to act as a reference point.

This paper began with the question: "Are tools really the problem?" The answer appears to be both yes and no. MDE tools could definitely be better. But good tools alone would not solve the problem. A proper consideration of people and organizations is needed in parallel. As one of our interviewees noted: *"Wait a second, the tools are really interesting, I agree, but to me it's much more about what is the process and the technique and the pattern and the practice."*

Acknowledgments. The authors would like to thank all those who took part in the interviews, including those who facilitated the study at Ericsson and Volvo.

References

1. Den Haan, J.: 8 reasons why model-driven approaches (will) fail (2008), http://www.infoq.com/articles/8-reasons-why-MDE-fails
2. Kuhn, A., Murphy, G.C., Thompson, C.A.: An exploratory study of forces and frictions affecting large-scale model-driven development. In: [26], pp. 352–367
3. Staron, M.: Adopting model driven software development in industry – a case study at two companies. In: Wang, J., Whittle, J., Harel, D., Reggio, G. (eds.) MoDELS 2006. LNCS, vol. 4199, pp. 57–72. Springer, Heidelberg (2006)
4. Tomassetti, F., Torchiano, M., Tiso, A., Ricca, F., Reggio, G.: Maturity of software modelling and model driven engineering: A survey in the Italian industry. In: Baldassarre, M.T., Genero, M., Mendes, E., Piattini, M. (eds.) 16th International Conference on Evaluation & Assessment in Software Engineering, EASE 2012, Ciudad Real, Spain, May 14-15, pp. 91–100. IET - The Institute of Engineering and Technology (2012)
5. Hutchinson, J., Rouncefield, M., Whittle, J.: Model-driven engineering practices in industry. In: [27], pp. 633–642
6. Hutchinson, J., Whittle, J., Rouncefield, M., Kristoffersen, S.: Empirical assessment of MDE in industry. In: [27], pp. 471–480
7. Pérez-Medina, J.L., Dupuy-Chessa, S., Front, A.: A survey of model driven engineering tools for user interface design. In: Winckler, M., Johnson, H. (eds.) TAMODIA 2007. LNCS, vol. 4849, pp. 84–97. Springer, Heidelberg (2007)
8. de Sousa Saraiva, J., da Silva, A.R.: Evaluation of MDE tools from a metamodeling perspective. In: Principal Advancements in Database Management Technologies, pp. 105–131. IGI Global (2010)
9. Cabot, J., Teniente, E.: Constraint support in MDA tools: A survey. In: Rensink, A., Warmer, J. (eds.) ECMDA-FA 2006. LNCS, vol. 4066, pp. 256–267. Springer, Heidelberg (2006)
10. Paige, R.F., Varró, D.: Lessons learned from building model-driven development tools. Software and System Modeling 11(4), 527–539 (2012)
11. Chalmers, M.: A historical view of context. Computer Supported Cooperative Work 13(3), 223–247 (2004)
12. Dourish, P.: Where the action is: the foundations of embodied interaction. MIT Press, Cambridge (2001)
13. Grudin, J.: Why CSCW applications fail: Problems in the design and evaluation of organization of organizational interfaces. In: Greif, I. (ed.) CSCW, pp. 65–84. ACM (1988)
14. Brown, B.: The artful use of groupware: An ethnographic study of how Lotus Notes is used in practice. Behavior and Information Technology 19(4), 263–273 (1990)
15. Merisalo-Rantanen, H., Tuunanen, T., Rossi, M.: Is extreme programming just old wine in new bottles: A comparison of two cases. J. Database Manag. 16(4), 41–61 (2005)
16. Robinson, H., Sharp, H.: The social side of technical practices. In: Baumeister, H., Marchesi, M., Holcombe, M. (eds.) XP 2005. LNCS, vol. 3556, pp. 100–108. Springer, Heidelberg (2005)

17. Selic, B.: The pragmatics of model-driven development. IEEE Software 20(5), 19–25 (2003)
18. Stahl, T., Völter, M., Bettin, J., Haase, A., Helsen, S.: Model-driven software development - technology, engineering, management. Pitman (2006)
19. Aranda, J., Damian, D., Borici, A.: Transition to model-driven engineering - what is revolutionary, what remains the same? In: [26], pp. 692–708
20. Clark, T., Muller, P.-A.: Exploiting model driven technology: a tale of two startups. Software and System Modeling 11(4), 481–493 (2012)
21. Holsti, O.R.: Content Analysis for the Social Sciences and Humanities. Addison-Wesley Publishing Company, Reading (1969)
22. Brooks Jr., F.P.: The mythical man-month – essays on software engineering, 2nd edn. Addison-Wesley (1995)
23. Kleppe, A.G., Warmer, J., Bast, W.: MDA Explained: The Model Driven Architecture: Practice and Promise. Addison-Wesley Longman Publishing Co., Inc., Boston (2003)
24. France, R.B., Bieman, J.M., Mandalaparty, S.P., Cheng, B.H.C., Jensen, A.C.: Repository for model driven development (ReMoDD). In: Glinz, M., Murphy, G.C., Pezzè, M. (eds.) 34th International Conference on Software Engineering, ICSE 2012, Zurich, Switzerland, June 2-9, pp. 1471–1472. IEEE (2012)
25. France, R.B., Rumpe, B.: Model-driven development of complex software: A research roadmap. In: Briand, L.C., Wolf, A.L. (eds.) International Conference on Software Engineering, ICSE 2007, Track on the Future of Software Engineering, FOSE 2007, Minneapolis, MN, USA, May 23-25, pp. 37–54 (2007)
26. France, R.B., Kazmeier, J., Breu, R., Atkinson, C. (eds.): MODELS 2012. LNCS, vol. 7590. Springer, Heidelberg (2012)
27. Taylor, R.N., Gall, H., Medvidovic, N. (eds.): Proceedings of the 33rd International Conference on Software Engineering, ICSE 2011, Waikiki, Honolulu, HI, USA, May 21-28. ACM (2011)

Generic Model Assist

Friedrich Steimann and Bastian Ulke

Lehrgebiet Programmiersysteme
Fernuniversität in Hagen
D-58084 Hagen
steimann@acm.org, Bastian.Ulke@feu.de

Abstract. Model assist is a feature of modelling environments aiding their users with entering well-formed models into an editor. Current implementations of model assist are mostly hard-coded in the editor and duplicate the logic captured in the environment's validation methods used for post hoc checking of models for well-formedness. We propose a fully declarative approach which computes legal model assists from a modelling language's well-formedness rules via constraint solving, covering a large array of assistance scenarios with only minor differences in the assistance specifications. We describe an implementation of our approach and evaluate it on 299 small to medium size open source models. Although more research will be needed to explore the boundaries of our approach, first results presented here suggest that it is feasible.

1 Introduction

Code assist is considered a major asset of integrated development environments such as Eclipse [4] or Visual Studio [29]: while the developer types a name, the environment computes a list of declared entities to which the name could refer, and suggests corresponding completions of the typing. This assistance goes as far as suggesting names before the typing has begun — for this, code assist collects from all declared entities the names of those that may occur in the place of the cursor without making the code ill-formed, and presents the resulting list to the developer, who is to make a selection. Where code is already ill-formed, code assist provides a list of possible corrections (in Eclipse referred to as quick fixes), from which the developer can select.

Model assist as we define it here (but see Section 6 for how it has been defined differently) is code assist applied to models: whenever the modeller is to make reference to some existing model element, the modelling environment will present a choice from which the modeller can select. Just like for code assist, for model assist to be maximally useful it should not offer choices that make a model ill-formed, and should be able to propose fixes for ill-formed models.

Contemporary modelling environments such as EMF [5], IBM RSA [10], or Papyrus [18] extract type information from the modelling language's metamodel to restrict model elements that can be referenced at a given position. For instance, where

A. Moreira et al. (Eds.): MODELS 2013, LNCS 8107, pp. 18–34, 2013.

the metamodel requires a class, the modelling environment will present the list of all classes that are currently defined by the model. However, more involved well-formedness rules, for instance that the generalization relationship of classifiers must not be circular, are either ignored when collecting the candidates presented for selection, or are hard-coded into the model editor, causing an untoward duplication of validation logic which is not only tedious, but also prone to inconsistencies and errors.

To improve on this situation, we have devised and implemented a uniform framework for computing well-formed *model completions, changes, and fixes* (here collectively referred to as *model assists*) from the well-formedness constraints specified with the metamodel. Our approach works by representing the subjects of assists (usually — but not limited to — references to other model elements) with constraint variables, and by letting a constraint solver *solve* the constraints that a well-formedness checker would merely check. Because constraint solving is undirected in the sense that every constraint variable can serve as input as well as as output, our approach is generic in that a single specification of well-formedness serves the implementation of all model completions, changes, and fixes constrained by this specification.

The remainder of our paper is organized as follows. In Section 2, we motivate our work by presenting various different model assistance scenarios all governed by the same conditions of well-formedness, suggesting that devising a toll for each scenario individually is indeed undesirable. In Section 3, we describe the theoretical basis of our approach to generic model assist, whose implementation in the Refacola constraint language and framework we sketch in Section 4. Section 5 presents the results of a systematic evaluation on 299 open source models. A discussion of related work concludes.

2   Motivation

To motivate our work, we use the example of sequence diagrams that must be well-formed with respect to the class diagram of Figure 1. The class diagram defines two (unrelated) classes, C_1 and C_2, each defining operations (methods; o_1, o_2, and o_3).

A sequence diagram can *refer to*, or *use*, the elements of a class diagram as follows:

1. A lifeline (representing an object and depicted as a vertical line) can refer to a class as the classifier of the object.
2. A message sent to an object (depicted as an arrow pointing to the object's lifeline) can refer to an operation that is associated with the message.

For a sequence diagram to be well-formed, the operation associated with a message must be owned[1] by the classifier associated with the lifeline to which the message is directed.

---

[1] It could also be inherited. However, we do not deal with inheritance here; the reader interested in how it can be handled using the same means as we will be using is referred to [28].

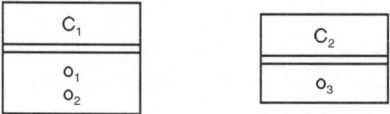

Fig. 1. Class diagram used for model completion

2.1   Model Completion

Based on the class diagram of Figure 1, Figure 2 depicts four different completion scenarios for sequence diagrams:

SCENARIO 1: A message is sent to a lifeline using class C_1 as its classifier. This restricts the operations that can be associated with the message to the operations of C_1. Specifically, when the modeller completes the model by selecting an operation (currently represented by the question mark), a choice has to be made between o_1 and o_2 (the operations of C_1; cf. Figure 1).   ◆

SCENARIO 2: A message associated with o_2 is sent to a lifeline with unspecified classifier. To complete this model, a selection from $\{C_1, C_2\}$ (the only two available classes in Figure 1) needs to be made. Since only C_1 owns operation o_2, model completion should present only C_1 for selection.   ◆

SCENARIO 3: A message with as yet unspecified operator is sent to a lifeline whose classifier is also not yet specified. This model is completed by choosing from a set of pairs of operators and classifiers, namely $\{(o_1, C_1), (o_2, C_1), (o_3, C_2)\}$.   ◆

SCENARIO 4: For a message associated with o_2, the target lifeline needs to be selected. Correct model completion can offer only the lifeline associated with classifier C_1 for selection, since it is the only one that has operation o_2 available.   ◆

While model completion for each of the above scenarios is easily conceived and implemented, doing so for each scenario separately may lead to maintenance problems (e.g., when the language specification changes) and inconsistent behaviour, and doing it for all scenarios in one requires complex case analyses and is therefore error-prone.

2.2   Controlled Model Change

Change of a model is also subject to well-formedness conditions. We call a change that is guaranteed to preserve well-formedness a *controlled change*, and add controlled changes to the portfolio of functions to be offered by model assist.

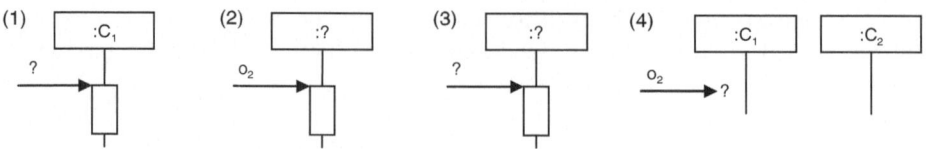

Fig. 2. Four scenarios of completing a sequence diagram. Question marks mark as yet missing entries (references with open target) subject to completion.

While simply checking whether an intended change leaves a model well-formed is trivial, we strive for assistance enabling intended changes that require other, *secondary* changes to keep the model well-formed. The following scenarios illustrate this.

SCENARIO 5: Consider that after the completion of Scenario 2, the modeller decides to call operation o_3, rather than o_2, on the object represented by the lifeline. Alone, this change would make the model ill-formed. However, if complemented by a change of the classifier associated with the lifeline, C_1, to C_2, well-formedness is restored.   ♦

SCENARIO 6: Starting again from the completed Scenario 2, consider that the modeller decides to change the classifier of the lifeline receiving the message, C_1, to C_2. As above, this change would make the model ill-formed. However, if complemented by a move of message o_2 to classifier C_2, well-formedness is preserved.   ♦

The alert reader will have noticed that the above scenarios complement each other in that each one offers a solution that the other one lacks: in case of Scenario 5, an alternative solution would be to move o_3 to C_1, and in case of Scenario 6, an alternative solution would be to replace the call of o_2 with a call of o_3. Indeed, specifying the mechanics of each scenario of controlled change separately likely leads to inconsistency.

2.3   Model Fixing

If a model is ill-formed, the modelling environment usually associates ill-formedness with a single property[2] of a single model element. A simple fix procedure healing ill-formedness is then to treat the property as "to be completed" and proceed as for model completion. However, the cause of the error may equally lie in other properties involved in the violated well-formedness condition, as suggested by the following scenario.

SCENARIO 7: Assume that in Scenario 4, the message is sent to the object represented by the right lifeline (with classifier C_2) so that the model is ill-formed (C_2 has no operation o_2; cf. Figure 1). This can be fixed by changing the operation associated with the message to o_3, or by moving o_2 to C_2, or by changing the classifier of the right lifeline to C_1, or by redirecting the message to the left lifeline.   ♦

Although all four fixes possible for this scenario differ fundamentally from a user perspective (and indeed amount to rather different models), they are all motivated by the same well-formedness condition. As for model completion and controlled changes, implementing them separately is tedious and error-prone.

---

[2] In both UML and OCL, a property is either an attribute or a reference [15, 16] (the latter also being referred to as an *opposite association end* in [16]).

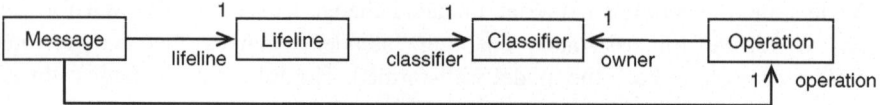

Fig. 3. Metamodel underlying well-formedness rule (1)

2.4   Combining Completions and Fixes with Controlled Changes

The number of possible completions and fixes can be increased by combining them with controlled changes. For instance, in Scenario 1, all three operations can be offered for completion, provided that the completion procedure is allowed to change the classifier of the lifeline from C_1 to C_2. Even though we will use this in our evaluation in Section 5, generally granting model completion and fixing arbitrary changes will lead to excessive numbers of choices to select from.

3   A Declarative Approach to Model Assist

We introduce our approach to generic model assist using the example of model completion, generalizing it to controlled model changes and fixes along the way.

3.1   Deriving Model Completions from Well-Formedness Rules

The well-formedness condition informally introduced above is formally expressed as

$$\forall\, m \in \mathsf{Message} : m.operation.owner = m.lifeline.classifier \qquad (1)$$

meaning that the owner of the operation associated with every message m of a model must be the classifier of the lifeline to which the message is directed (see Figure 3 for the underlying metamodel).[3] An obvious way to compute legal model completions is therefore to first generate all possible completions exploiting the type information of Figure 3 and then to exclude from these those violating (1). However, for large models and more than one well-formedness rule involved, this generate-and-test procedure will become prohibitively expensive, especially when more than one reference is to be completed (as in Scenario 3). A more goal directed procedure is therefore needed.

As it turns out, using (1) and the model to be completed, the legal completions can be directly inferred. For instance, in case of Scenario 1, we have

---

[3] Other works, including [6, 8, 11], rely on name-based binding, here meaning that a name is attached to the message and requiring that this name equals the name of some operation (establishing the binding through equality of names). The same could also be done for binding a classifier to a lifeline. However, we have chosen to represent the binding through an explicit link (a reference) here, since this conforms more closely to the UML metamodel [15].

$$\frac{m_1.\text{lifeline} = l_1 \qquad l_1.\text{classifier} = C_1}{m_1.\text{lifeline.classifier} = C_1} \qquad \text{[Figure 2 (1)]}$$

$$\frac{m_1.\text{operation.owner} = m_1.\text{lifeline.classifier}}{m_1.\text{operation.owner} = C_1} \cdot \qquad \text{[Eq. (1)]}$$

$$\frac{o_1.\text{owner} = C_1 \quad o_2.\text{owner} = C_1 \quad o_3.\text{owner} = C_2}{m_1.\text{operation} = o_1 \lor m_1.\text{operation} = o_2} \qquad \text{[Figure 1]}$$

where m_1 denotes the message and l_1 denotes the lifeline in Figure 2 (1). Analogous inferences can be performed for the other completion scenarios (but have been omitted here for a lack of space); they produce precisely the required solutions.

3.2   Model Completion as Constraint Solving

The above derivations of legal model completions are easily done on paper, yet for a tool they need to be automated. As we will see, this can be trusted to a constraint solver. For this however, we must translate well-formedness rules to constraints accepted by a constraint solver first.

An expression of the form e.r (such as m_1.operation), where e is a model element and r is a property (a reference or an attribute; cf. Footnote 2) of e, directly translates to a constraint variable v whose domain is that of e.r. An expression of the form e_1.r = e_2 (such as m_1.operation = o_2) directly translates to a constraint v = e_2, fixing the value of the constraint variable v (representing e_1.r) to e_2. Note that only constraint variables whose values are not fixed can be assigned new values by the constraint solver (and can thus be the subject of completion).

An expression of the form $e.r_1.r_2$ represents an indirection (or, in modelling terms, a navigation path) that cannot be translated directly to a constraint variable. The reason for this is that which (whose model element's) reference $e.r_1.r_2$ represents depends on the value (target) of the constraint variable v representing $e.r_1$. Following [25, §4.2], however, we can translate a well-formedness rule such as (1) involving indirection (here: two indirections) into one without, in case of (1) to

$$\forall\, m \in \text{Message} \; \forall\, o \in \text{Operation} \; \forall\, l \in \text{Lifeline} : \qquad (2)$$
$$(m.\text{operation} = o \land m.\text{lifeline} = l) \rightarrow o.\text{owner} = l.\text{classifier}$$

Applying (2) to the model defined by Figure 1 and Figure 2, Scenarios 1–3, where we have that Operation = $\{o_1, o_2, o_3\}$ and Lifeline = $\{l_1\}$, we get the constraint set (by unrolling the quantifiers)

$$\{(m_1.\text{operation} = o_1 \land m_1.\text{lifeline} = l_1) \rightarrow o_1.\text{owner} = l_1.\text{classifier},$$
$$(m_1.\text{operation} = o_2 \land m_1.\text{lifeline} = l_1) \rightarrow o_2.\text{owner} = l_1.\text{classifier}, \qquad (3)$$
$$(m_1.\text{operation} = o_3 \land m_1.\text{lifeline} = l_1) \rightarrow o_3.\text{owner} = l_1.\text{classifier}\}$$

which contains no indirections. When complemented by the constraints fixing the targets (values) of references as provided by the model to be completed, a constraint solver will compute all legal model completions. For instance, for Scenario 1, the constraint set (3) is complemented by the set

$$\{o_1.\text{owner} = C_1, o_2.\text{owner} = C_1, o_3.\text{owner} = C_2, m_1.\text{lifeline} = l_1, l_1.\text{classifier} = C_1\}$$

for which the solver computes the solutions $m_1.operation = o_1$ and $m_1.operation = o_2$. For Scenario 2, $l_1.classifier = C_1$ is replaced by $m_1.operation = o_2$; for Scenario 3, both are dropped. For Scenario 4, (2) unrolls to 6 constraints (3 for l_1 and 3 for l_2) to which the fixing constraints must be added. Thus, a simple transformation to constraints amenable to constraint solving lets us compute all legal model completions.

Mapping well-formedness rules involving indirection (navigation paths) may be simple, yet it introduces considerable complexity to the constraint solving process, by introducing disjunctions (in the form of implications) and by increasing the number of constraints. However, we maintain that navigation is at the heart of modelling, and any implementation of model assist that does not support it will be of limited value. In particular, all systems that are limited to the completion of (value-typed) attributes (as opposed to references; cf. Section 6) fall into this category.

Constraint generating and solving as described above also solves the problems of controlled model changes and fixes. The only difference lies in specifying which properties of a model are to be changed (either to user-provided new values or to values computed by the constraint solver) and which are to remain constant.

3.3   Specifying Model Assists: Intended and Allowed Changes

In modelling, properties can be optional, meaning that they may, but need not be provided. For instance, in a meta-model like that of Figure 3, attaching a classifier to a lifeline l could be optional, in which case "target not specified" would be represented by $l.classifier = null$. However, even if the modeller chooses to *not* provide a classifier, she still has made a choice. This is to be distinguished from "target not *yet* specified" or "to be completed", for which no special value exists. Therefore, the subjects of model completion must be specified explicitly as input to the completion process.

For controlled model changes and fixes this is not sufficient. A controlled change involves and *intended change* of a property which is to be specified by the user. However, as suggested by Scenarios 5 and 6, for an intended change to be feasible the solver must be allowed to change the values of other properties, the so-called *allowed changes* [24]. If the allowed changes are not limited, the solver will produce too many solutions (most of which — even though correct — will appear far-fetched); it they are too limited, they may prevent intended changes that the user would want to see. For model fixing, the situation is roughly analogous: although it has no intended change, it requires the allowed changes to be specified, to limit the fix proposals to the ones accepted by the user as reasonable. Section 5 will provide examples of this.

3.4   Generating the Constraints

Once it is clear which properties are to be changed and which are to be kept constant, all constraints constraining the variable properties need to be generated. A simple approach here is to generate all constraints from a model; however, this solution may not only be prohibitively expensive both in terms of time and space, it may also lead to an unsolvable constraint system, namely when the model is ill-formed in another place than the one in which the completion, change, or fix is to be applied. Therefore, the constraint generation process must be carefully crafted.

4   Implementation

To utilize previous work on constraint generation, we implemented constraint-based model assist as described here on top of our refactoring constraint language and framework Refacola [24]. The Refacola language allows the specification of constraint-generating rules based on a specification of the target language (e.g., Java or UML; see Section 5 for details), while the Refacola framework takes over generation of the constraints from an artefact in the target language (a program or a model), their submission to a constraint solver, and the writing back of the solution (new values of properties) to the artefact. The constraint generation algorithm of Refacola takes care that only the constraints needed for a specific problem are created, by first generating all constraints directly constraining the initial changes (the refactoring intent in case of refactoring and the properties to be completed, changed, or fixed in our current setting), and then recursively generating all constraints further constraining the allowed changes constrained by the previous generations of constraints [24]. To reduce the depth of recursion, the generator performs a form of constraint propagation (arc consistency basically) combined with an evaluation of constraints at generation time where possible [26]. Both means are especially effective when the constraint variables have small domains, particularly when indirection is involved.

Interestingly, to adapt Refacola to model assist as described here, we had to introduce null as a possible value of references (see above), which was not needed for program refactoring. Null values are problematic because they may appear in navigation paths (indirections), where they would cause a runtime error (the equivalent of a null pointer exception), a notion foreign to constraint solving. To avoid this, we adopted the Null Object pattern [30] and set the value of null.r to null for all references r.

Table 1. Statistical data describing the 299 models from [1] used in our evaluation

NUMBER OF:	CLASSES	REFERENCES	OPPOSITES	CONTAINMENTS
average	48	50	23	14
standard deviation	102	91	37	28
maximum	699	778	222	250
total	14335	15005	6772	4327

5   Evaluation

We deemed that an evaluation of our approach required its systematic application to

1. a significant number of open source models and
2. a significant number of non-trivial well-formedness rules applying to the open source models.

We demanded openness of models to allow others to repeat our experiments. Significant numbers of both models and well-formedness rules are required to lower the bias towards the concrete instances selected. Non-trivial well-formedness rules are needed to show the power of our approach.

```
public boolean validateEReference_ConsistentOpposite(EReference eReference, …) {
  EReference eOpposite = eReference.getEOpposite();
  if (eOpposite != null) {
    if (eReference.getEContainingClass() != null) {
      EReference oppositeEOpposite = eOpposite.getEOpposite();
      if (oppositeEOpposite != eReference) {
        return false; // this.eOpposite.eOpposite is not this reference
      }
      EClassifier eType = eReference.getEType();
      if (eType != null) {
        EClass oppositeEContainingClass = eOpposite.getEContainingClass();
        if (oppositeEContainingClass != null && oppositeEContainingClass != eType) {
          return false; // this.opposite is not a feature of the type of this ref.
        }
      }
    }
  …
  }
  return true;
}
```

Fig. 4. Ecore validation method comprising two well-formedness rules (from [5]; slightly edited for clarity of presentation)

Much to our disillusionment, however, satisfying these constraints proved difficult. Open source model portals such as ReMoDD [21] or The Open Model Initiative [17] do not provide machine-readable models in sufficient numbers, and in the few cases in which models used different diagram types, the corresponding views were not integrated, providing no opportunities for model assist of the kind suggested by the scenarios of Section 2. In terms of availability, the situation is better when turning to the metamodelling level: for instance, the AtlanMod Metamodel Zoo [1] contains some 300 metamodels[4] expressed in the EMF metamodel Ecore [5] (which serves as a meta-metamodel here). However, metamodels, which are structural by nature, consist of class diagrams only, so that class diagrams need to be completed against themselves. Due to a lack of alternatives, we nevertheless decided to perform our evaluation using these; some relevant measures of the size of the models are given Table 1.

A closer analysis of the 54 well-formedness rules of Ecore (implemented in 37 non-empty validation methods) revealed that most deal with trivial conditions for which our model assist cannot demonstrate its power, such as the well-formedness of strings, the uniqueness of names, or the consistency of multiplicities ([20] reports similar findings). In fact, only 5 of the 54 well-formedness rules constrained references (rather than attributes). These rules dealt with opposite references (implementing bi-directional relationships) and containment.

The implementation of two of the rules constraining opposite references in Ecore is shown in Figure 4. The two rules are comprised in one validation method, where each rule is defined as the path leading to one return of false. The implementation is based on the metamodel shown in Figure 5, using getter methods to access the references.

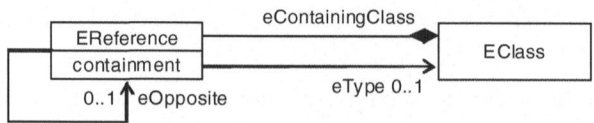

Fig. 5. Excerpt of the Ecore metamodel as used by the validation method of Figure 4.

---

[4] 302 as of Nov. 29, 2012; 3 of these could not be loaded into EMF.

```
language ecore
kinds
    EStructuralFeature <: ENTITY { eType, lowerBound, upperBound }
    EReference <: EStructuralFeature { eOpposite, eContainingClass, containment }
    EClass <: ENTITY
properties
    eType : EClass
    eLowerBound, eUpperBound : Integer
    eOpposite : EReference
    eContainingClass : EClass
    containment : Boolean
queries
    owner(EReference, EClass)
    has-type(EReference, EClass)
    all-references(EClass, EReference)
rules
    "consistent opposite 1"
        for all
            eReference : EReference  eOpposite : EReference  eContainingClass : EClass
        if
            owner(eReference, eContainingClass)
        then
            (eReference.eOpposite = eOpposite and eReference.eOpposite != null) ->
                (eContainingClass != null -> eReference = eOpposite.eOpposite)
    "consistent opposite 2"
        for all
            eReference : EReference  eOpposite : EReference
        always
        (eReference.eOpposite = eOpposite and eOpposite != null
            and eReference.eType != null) -> (eOpposite.eContainingClass = null
                or eOpposite.eContainingClass = eReference.eType)
    "consistent opposite 4"
        for all
            r : EReference  q : EReference
        always
            (r.eOpposite != null and r.eOpposite = q)
            -> not (q.containment and r.containment)
    "consistent containment"
        for all
            r, r2, q : EReference    r_eContainingClass, r_referenceType : EClass
        if
            owner(r, r_eContainingClass), has-type(r, r_referenceType),
            all-references(r_referenceType, r2)
        then
            (r.containment and r_eContainingClass != null) ->
                (r2.eOpposite = r or r2.eOpposite = null or r2.lowerBound = 0 or
                    (r2.eOpposite = q -> not q.containment))
    "opposite must not be self"
        for all r : EReference    always r.eOpposite != r
```

Fig. 6. Transcription of Ecore validation rules to constraint rules in Refacola

The transcriptions of 4 of the 5 Ecore well-formedness rules into Refacola constraint rules are shown in Figure 6. This includes the two rules of Figure 4, in Figure 6 labelled "inconsistent opposite 1" and "2". The 5th Ecore rule was irrelevant for our endeavour; instead, we added a rule "opposite must not be self" to conform to a validation rule implemented in the Ecore editor alone (cf. Section 5.5).

The constraint rules (listed in the rules section of Figure 6) are preceded by a language specification of Ecore in Refacola declaring the relevant kinds of model elements together with their properties and their domains (note the analogy to a metamodel), as well as a list of queries used by the rules. Each rule has a name (for identification only) and is introduced by the declarations of the variables representing the model elements to which the rule applies. The rule itself is either an axiom (introduced by always) or has a head (introduced by if) and a body (then). The head consists of queries binding the variables to concrete model elements and the body lists the constraints to be generated for the model elements bound by the queries. For instance, rule "consistent opposite 1" will instantiate the constraint in its body with every triple (r, r′, c) of two references and a class such that owner(r, c).

5.1   Checking Well-Formedness

Since our goal is to replace current validation methods and the logic implemented by various forms of model assist by a single well-formedness specification, we first checked whether our Refacola implementations could replace Ecore's built-in validation methods. For this, we generated all constraints constraining each property of each model element, and checked whether the constraints were satisfied if and only if the validation method for this property passed (60,020 checks in total). We found that both approaches identified the same 462 violations in the 299 metamodels, meaning that for the given models, the constraint rules of Figure 6 and Ecore's validation methods are equivalent.

5.2   Fixing Ill-Formed Models

To fix existing violations, we defined the following fix specifications (cf. Section 3.3) to be applied to every reference r for which ill-formedness has been detected:

- *fix inconsistent opposite*   allow change of r.eOpposite.eOpposite to arbitrary references, allow change of r′.eOpposite to null for all r′ ∉ {r, r.eOpposite}, and allow change of r.eOpposite.eType to arbitrary type
- *fix inconsistent containment*   allow change of r.containment and, if r.eOpposite is not null, of r.eOpposite.containment

The number of applications of each fix specification, how often application was successful (i.e., whether the model could be fixed using it), the average number of properties changed per fix, the average number of alternative solutions per successful application, the average number of constraints generated, and the average times for both generating and solving the constraints are shown in Table 2. As can be seen, fixing inconsistent opposite, if possible, always had a unique solution. Fixing inconsistent containment was always possible, with either 3 (8 times) or only 1 solution.[5]

---

[5] Fixing inconsistent opposite was impossible when the opposite reference was defined in a superclass of the class serving as the type of the original reference. Automatically fixing these situations would require changeability of eType or of eContainingClass, but this would lead to numerous fix alternatives in the cases easily fixed. Similarly, the number of alternative fixes for fixing inconsistent containment can be increased by allowing the change of the containment flags of the opposites of the other references to false. Generally, however, offering complex fixes like this to the modeller must be carefully traded against the cognitive load imposed on her by proposing solutions that are difficult to reconstruct, and that are rarely demanded.

Table 2. Performance of computing fixes, completions, and controlled changes

ASSIST	APPLI CATIO NS	SUCC ESSFU L	if successful			CONSTRAINTS GENERATED		TIME [MSEC]*			
			SOLUTIONS		Δ			generating		solving	
			Ø	σ	Ø	Ø	σ	Ø	σ	Ø	σ
fix incons. opposite	144	138	1	0	1.22	1080	465	655	534	2.9	7.3
fix incons. containm.	318	318	1.05	0.31	1.04	0.80	0.4	202	290	0.3	2.0
complete opposite	8232	711	2.8	2.5	2	914	764	2406	3370	124	62
compl. opp. and type	14335	3081	2.7	4.2	3	667	644	1531	2168	9	30
change opposite	6772	5597	1	0	5.3	3	1	345	251	62	37
change containment	2713	1894	1	0	1.7	0	0	216	189	0	0

Δ : number of changes made in the model; Ø : average; σ : standard deviation

* timed on a contemporary laptop with Windows 7 operating system and Intel i7 CPU clocked at 2.8 GHz, using the Choco constraint solver [3]

As can be seen, the number of constraints generated for fixing inconsistent opposites (1080) is rather large. This is so because *inconsistent opposites* includes the case in which a reference is the declared opposite of more than one other reference, in which case fixing requires selection of one of these references, and setting eOpposite of the remaining to null. Since the constraint generation process starts from the first reference for which the violation is reported, without knowledge of the other violations related to it, constraints for all references need to be generated. However, despite the large number of constraints, the times required for generating and solving them stayed within reasonable bounds (0.7 s on average; the maximum time required for a fix was 3.3 s). The very low numbers of constraints generated for fixing *inconsistent containment* (0.8 on average) is due to the algorithm employed for constraint generation (see Section 4); this "shift of duty" is reflected in the (by comparison) long times required to generate the constraints (200 ms vs. 2 ms on average).

5.3   Completing Incomplete Models

Unlike ill-formedness, incompleteness is not a property that can be derived from a model (cf. Section 3.3). Therefore, we have to simulate incompleteness of the models used in our evaluation. For this, we define two simulated completion scenarios:

- *complete opposite.*   A reference's opposite that is currently null is assumed as being "to be completed". For completion, we allow changes of further references' opposites currently null so that they can oppose the reference to be completed (otherwise, we would get no candidates for a well-formed completion).
- *complete opposite and type of new reference.*   A new reference is inserted in a class, with its opposite and type to be completed. As possible targets of the completion, we allow references whose opposite is null, and allow the change of this opposite to target the new reference. To further restrict the opposites, we require that their type is the host class of the new reference.

We applied the first completion scenario to each reference whose opposite was null, and the second scenario to each class in each of the 299 models fixed as above. The results are also shown in Table 2. As can be seen, the success rate of both completions, as well as the number of alternatives available for completion ("solutions") is rather low, which is however owing to the construction of the completion scenarios and does not reflect a limitation of our approach. That the number of constraints generated does not rise quadractically when compared to fixing *inconsistent opposite* (as one might expect because of the "active" indirection) is due to the restriction of the change of r.eOpposite.eOpposite to r, which the constraint generation algorithm sketched in Section 4 exploits. As above, this is reflected in the time required for generating the constraints, which averages at 2.4 s and 1.5 s, respectively; although both times appear too long for practical use, profiling showed that on average, approx. 80% of the time needed for generating the constraints was spent on querying the model (and that the number of queries issued to generate the constraints grows quadratically with the number of references in a model). However, our current implementation of querying has considerable unexploited potential for optimization.

5.4   Well-Formedness Preserving Change of Models

To probe the feasibility of controlled model changes as described in Section 2.2, we define the following two evaluation scenarios:

- *Change opposite to a reference that has no or a different opposite* We change the target of r.eOpposite, t, to a new target, t'. For this to work, r.eType, t'.eOpposite, and t'.eType must be changeable. To account for the fact that old opposites must be set to null, eOpposite may be changed to null for all other references than r or t'.
- *Change containment* We toggle the containment flag for references for which it is currently false. To enable this change, we allow the change of lowerBound attributes to 0 (rule "consistent containment" in Figure 6).

We applied the first change to all 6772 references of the 299 models that had an opposite assigned, using a randomly chosen reference as its new opposite, and the second change to all 2713 references whose containment flag was set to false. The results are again shown in Table 2.

The intended changes were possible in 83% and 70% of all cases, resp., and always had a single solution. The numbers of additional (allowed) changes necessary to maintain well-formedness ranged between 1 and 6 and 1 and 4, resp., clearly demonstrating the utility of this assist. The numbers of constraints generated are small throughout, as are the times required for constraint generation and solving. This is due to the effective absence of indirection in both scenarios (the "middle" variables are fixed).

5.5   Discussion

Our evaluation shows that the same constraints used for well-formedness checking can indeed be used to compute fixes, completions, and controlled changes of a model.

Where no changes of "middle" references in a navigation expression are required, our approach is fast; otherwise, the disjunctions (cf. Section 3.2) take their toll.

Compared to the cost incurred by duplicate implementation, the overhead that comes with adding a constraint solver to a modelling environment should quickly pay. Indeed, we found that where the Ecore editor considers the conditions of well-formedness implemented in the Ecore validation methods, it uses its own implementation. For instance, when changing the target of an eOpposite in the EMF editor, the eOpposite of the old opposite, and eOpposite of the new opposite's old opposite, are automatically set to null[6]. In our approach, this necessary change is computed by the constraint solver, using the same constraint rules that are used for well-formedness checking. Apart from the initial and maintenance effort required by duplication, the separation between editor and well-formedness checking can also lead to inconsistencies: for instance, we found that the Ecore model editor prevents r.eOpposite from referring to r, whereas no validation rule exists that flags this condition in a model that is, for instance, loaded from a file (reported as https://bugs.eclipse.org/401313).

The boundaries of our approach appear to be the boundaries of constraint solving. To save the translation of OCL well-formedness rules into the constraint rules of Refacola (cf. [2] for a similar undertaking), we are currently exploring the mechanics of generating solver constraints from OCL expressions directly. However, this means porting the elaborate constraint generation algorithms of Refacola to a different environment, which means a major investment.

6   Related Work

As has been noted in [13], work on model assist is surprisingly rare. Model completion for domain-specific model editors as proposed in [22, 23], like our own work, relies on the metamodel of a language, and on solving the constraints provided to specify well-formedness of its instances. However, given that it can create new model elements by itself, it seems that the work's true scope is model synthesis[7], which is rather different from our intent, namely to assist the modeller in making the next atomic modelling step (which is either to enter a missing property value or to change an existing one or to locally fix a problem). To the best of our knowledge the work does not cover indirection, and has not been evaluated on real models; given the combinatorial complexity of the endeavour (especially when indirection is involved), performance figures provided for small examples suggest that it will not scale.

Janota et al. show how a class diagram backed by constraints can be instantiated by presenting the user with a continuous stream of computed edit options in such a way that all well-formed instances can be generated [11]. While the systematic rigour of the approach is intriguing, it requires a start-up processing step that could be considered prohibitively expensive (NP-hard [11]). Also, we maintain that the typical modelling process will be discontinuous, that is, model elements will be added and

---

[6] org.eclipse.emf.ecore.provider.EReferenceItemProvider.addEOppositePropertyDescriptor(.)
[7] This goal is shared by other works, including [8, 9, 11, 12, 13, 14, 19].

changed in different diagrams (and diagram types) in no specific order, even invalidating well-formedness temporarily. This will only be supported by more flexible model assistance, as for instance offered by [8, 13]. The former uses a Prolog representation of the model for computing next possible edit operations in the context of multiple partial specifications; although no performance problems are reported, it is not clear why the approach should not suffer from the same combinatorial explosion as others, particularly since no special measure to counter it are described. The latter uses hyperedge replacement grammars to compute possible connections between the edges of a hypergraph representing an incomplete model. However, since the sizes of the computed completions (which may involve the introduction of new nodes) are not limited per se, a maximum size has to be provided to remain reasonably efficient. To our knowledge, the approach has also not been evaluated on realistic model completion scenarios.

Egyed et al. present an approach to the generation of changes fixing inconsistencies in a UML model, without introducing new ones [7]. Basically, their fixes are computed using a generate-and-test approach, which is made feasible by profiling the evaluation of consistency rules [6], enabling them to determine directly which constraints are affected by each possible fix. In our approach, this step is replaced by the "smart" constraint generation process described in [24, 26] which makes sure that starting from a number of properties to be changed, only those constraints that — directly or indirectly (through additional changeable properties) constrain these properties are generated. Any change satisfying all generated constraints (i.e., any change suggested by a constraint solver) is thus guaranteed to not introduce new inconsistencies. The number of possible fixes is reduced by fix specifications, constraining the (kinds of) properties that may be changed by a fix.

Badger [20] uses regression planning to compute a sequence of actions resolving one or more inconsistencies in a model. Like our own approach, Badger utilizes standard well-formedness rules and does not require the writing of special resolution rules. However, the inconsistencies the evaluation of Badger relies on involve no indirections (which present a hard problem) so that the results are not comparable. The Beanbag language [31] allows the extension of OCL-like consistency relations with fixing behaviour specifying how changes leading to model inconsistencies are to be compensated with other, repairing changes. This is somewhat similar to our controlled changes. However, as noted in [20], the extensions "pollute" well-formedness rules with resolution information, making them single purpose. Neither Beanbag nor Badger suggest whether and how their approaches extend to model completion.

Model assist is also related to model refactoring in that like model assist, model refactoring must not make a model ill-formed. However, model assist differs from model refactoring in that it contributes to, or changes, the meaning of a model, while refactoring preserves it. Model assist may thus be considered a reduced form of model refactoring in which the goal of meaning preservation has been relaxed to the (weaker) goal of well-formedness preservation [25, 27].

7   Conclusion

We have shown how the well-formedness rules of a modelling language, if formulated as constraint generating rules, cannot only be used for well-formedness checking, but also for providing various forms of assistance to the modeller. Due to a shortage of publically available models that utilize different diagram types, we have evaluated our proposal on 299 metamodels taken from the AtlanMod Ecore Metamodel Zoo [1], using 6 different model assist scenarios relating to the definition of bidirectional relationships. Results indicate that our approach is practically feasible.

Acknowledgments. This work has been supported by the Deutsche Forschungs-gemeinschaft (DFG) under grant STE 906/4-2.

References

1. AtlanMod Ecore Metamodel Zoo, http://www.emn.fr/z-info/atlanmod/index.php/Ecore
2. Cabot, J., Clarisó, R., Riera, D.: UMLtoCSP: A tool for the formal verification of UML/OCL models using constraint programming. In: Proc. of ASE, pp. 547–548 (2007)
3. CHOCO Team choco: an Open Source Java Constraint Programming Library (Research Report 10-02-INFO, Ecole des Mines de Nantes, 2010)
4. Eclipse, http://www.eclipse.org
5. EMF Metamodel Version 2.8.1, http://www.eclipse.org/modeling/emf
6. Egyed, A.: Instant consistency checking for the UML. In: Proc. of ICSE, pp. 381–390 (2006)
7. Egyed, A., Letier, E., Finkelstein, A.: Generating and evaluating choices for fixing inconsis-tencies in UML design models. In: Proc. of ASE, pp. 99–108 (2008)
8. Hessellund, A., Czarnecki, K., Wąsowski, A.: Guided development with multiple domain-specific languages. In: Engels, G., Opdyke, B., Schmidt, D.C., Weil, F. (eds.) MODELS 2007. LNCS, vol. 4735, pp. 46–60. Springer, Heidelberg (2007)
9. Hill, J.H.: Measuring and reducing modeling effort in domain-specific modeling languages with examples. In: Proc. of ECBS, pp. 120–129 (2011)
10. IBM Rational Software Architect, http://www-01.ibm.com/software/rational/products/swarchitect/
11. Janota, M., Kuzina, V., Wąsowski, A.: Model construction with external constraints: An interactive journey from semantics to syntax. In: Czarnecki, K., Ober, I., Bruel, J.-M., Uhl, A., Völter, M. (eds.) MODELS 2008. LNCS, vol. 5301, pp. 431–445. Springer, Heidelberg (2008)
12. Kuschke, T., Mäder, P., Rempel, P.: Recommending auto-completions for software modeling activities. In: Moreira, A., Schätz, B., Gray, J., Vallecillo, A., Clarke, P. (eds.) MODELS 2013. LNCS, vol. 8107, pp. 170–186. Springer, Heidelberg (2013)
13. Mazanek, S., Maier, S., Minas, M.: Auto-completion for diagram editors based on graph grammars. In: Proc. of VL/HCC, pp. 242–245 (2008)
14. Nechypurenko, A., Wuchner, E., White, J., Schmidt, D.C.: Applying model intelligence frameworks for deployment problem in real-time and embedded systems. In: Kühne, T. (ed.) MoDELS 2006. LNCS, vol. 4364, pp. 143–151. Springer, Heidelberg (2007)

15. Object Management Group Unified Modeling Language Superstructure Version 2.3, http://www.omg.org/spec/UML/2.3/Superstructure
16. Object Management Group Object Constraint Language Version 2.2, http://www.omg.org/spec/OCL/2.2
17. http://www.openmodels.org
18. Papyrus UML Editor, http://www.eclipse.org/papyrus/
19. Pati, T., Feiock, D.C., Hill, J.H.: Proactive modeling: auto-generating models from their semantics and constraints. In: Proc. of DSM, pp. 7–12 (2012)
20. Pinna Puissant, J., Van Der Straeten, R., Mens, T.: Badger: A regression planner to resolve design model inconsistencies. In: Vallecillo, A., Tolvanen, J.-P., Kindler, E., Störrle, H., Kolovos, D. (eds.) ECMFA 2012. LNCS, vol. 7349, pp. 146–161. Springer, Heidelberg (2012)
21. ReMoDD, http://www.cs.colostate.edu/remodd
22. Sen, S., Baudry, B., Vangheluwe, H.: Domain-specific model editors with model completion. In: Giese, H. (ed.) MODELS 2008. LNCS, vol. 5002, pp. 259–270. Springer, Heidelberg (2008)
23. Sen, S., Baudry, B., Vangheluwe, H.: Towards domain-specific model editors with automatic model completion. Simulation 86(2), 109–126 (2010)
24. Steimann, F., Kollee, C., von Pilgrim, J.: A refactoring constraint language and its application to Eiffel. In: Mezini, M. (ed.) ECOOP 2011. LNCS, vol. 6813, pp. 255–280. Springer, Heidelberg (2011)
25. Steimann, F.: Constraint-based model refactoring. In: Whittle, J., Clark, T., Kühne, T. (eds.) MODELS 2011. LNCS, vol. 6981, pp. 440–454. Springer, Heidelberg (2011)
26. Steimann, F., von Pilgrim, J.: Constraint-based refactoring with foresight. In: Noble, J. (ed.) ECOOP 2012. LNCS, vol. 7313, pp. 535–559. Springer, Heidelberg (2012)
27. Steimann, F.: From well-formedness to meaning preservation: Model refactoring for almost free. SoSyM (in print)
28. Tip, F., Fuhrer, R.M., Kiezun, A., Ernst, M.D., Balaban, I., De Sutter, B.: Refactoring using type constraints. ACM Trans. Program. Lang. Syst. 33(3), 9 (2011)
29. Visual Studio, http://www.microsoft.com/visualstudio/
30. Woolf, B.: Null Object. In: Pattern Languages of Program Design, vol. 3. Addison-Wesley (1998)
31. Xiong, Y., Hu, Z., Zhao, H., Song, H., Takeichi, M., Mei, H.: Supporting automatic model incon-sistency fixing. In: Proc. of ESEC/SIGSOFT FSE, pp. 315–324 (2009)

Adding Spreadsheets to the MDE Toolkit

Mārtiņš Francis, Dimitrios S. Kolovos,
Nicholas Matragkas, and Richard F. Paige

Department of Computer Science, University of York,
Deramore Lane, York, YO10 5GH, UK
{mf550,dimitris.kolovos,nicholas.matragkas,
richard.paige}@york.ac.uk

Abstract. Spreadsheets are widely used to support software development activities. They have been used to collect requirements and software defects, to capture traceability information between requirements and test cases, and in general, to fill in gaps that are not covered satisfactorily by more specialised tools. Despite their widespread use, spreadsheets have received little attention from researchers in the field of Model Driven Engineering. In this paper, we argue for the usefulness of model management support for querying and modifying spreadsheets, we identify the conceptual gap between contemporary model management languages and spreadsheets, and we propose an approach for bridging it. We present a prototype that builds atop the Epsilon and Google Drive platforms and we evaluate the proposed approach through a case study that involves validating and transforming software requirements captured using spreadsheets.

1 Introduction

Spreadsheets are arguably one of the most versatile and ubiquitous tools in the software world. In software development, spreadsheets are often used to collect requirements [1] and software defects, to capture traceability information between requirements and test cases, and in general to fill in gaps not covered by other components of typical engineering tool-chains. Although one can reasonably argue that using spreadsheets instead of more sophisticated task-specific tools is more often than not a sub-optimal choice, their use in practice is too widespread to ignore. Despite their popularity among practitioners, spreadsheets have received little attention from researchers in the field of Model-Driven Engineering (MDE).

In this paper we propose an approach for treating spreadsheets as *first-class models* in MDE processes, by providing support for seamlessly integrating them in MDE workflows alongside traditional models (e.g. EMF-based models). Our approach enables engineers to perform a range of model management operations on spreadsheets including model (cross-) validation, model-to-model transformation and code generation. We evaluate the proposed approach on a case study in which requirements captured in a spreadsheet are validated for their correctness

A. Moreira et al. (Eds.): MODELS 2013, LNCS 8107, pp. 35–51, 2013.

and used to generate requirements graphs. By doing so, we demonstrate that it is feasible, practical and beneficial to treat spreadsheets and (metamodel-based) models uniformly using the same set of tools.

The remainder of the paper is organised as follows. Section 2 provides a discussion on the background and motivation of this work. Section 3 discusses the challenges involved in bridging spreadsheets and contemporary OCL-based model management languages, and proposes a language-independent solution to the problem. Section 4 illustrates a prototype that implements the proposed solutions and enables the model management languages of the Epsilon platform to query and modify Google Spreadsheets; this in turn enables a range of model management operations (including transformations) to be carried out. Section 5 evaluates the usefulness of the proposed approach using a comprehensive case study, Section 6 provides an overview of related work, and Section 7 concludes the paper and provides directions for further work.

2   Background and Motivation

MDE elevates models to first-class artefacts of the software development process, and proposes the use of automated model management (code generation, model transformation etc.) to try to enhance both the productivity of developers and the quality of the produced artefacts. While MDE is conceptually not restricted to a particular type of models, over the last few years approaches to MDE have converged on the automated management of models adhering to 3-layer metamodeling architectures, and most notably on models captured using the facilities provided by the the Eclipse Modelling Framework [2].

The majority of contemporary model management languages - including languages such as Acceleo, ATL, Kermeta, QVT and OCL - provide built-in support for EMF-based models. Using EMF as a de facto modelling framework has reduced unhelpful diversity and enhanced interoperability between MDE tools. However, in our view, for MDE tools to appeal to a wider audience of developers, they need to provide first-class support for other types of structured artefacts that developers commonly use to store meta-information. We first made this argument in [3], where we argued that providing support for schema-less XML documents would be beneficial for the wider adoption of MDE among software development practitioners. Our rationale is two-fold: first, meta-information description formats that do not require 3-layer architectures are generally simpler to learn and adopt, and can be used as a stepping stone for moving on to more powerful modelling architectures (e.g. EMF) once developers are convinced of the benefits of MDE. Second, there is already a significant amount of legacy meta-information captured in such formats for MDE researchers and tool providers to ignore.

Following this argument, in this work we have focused on providing support for integrating spreadsheets in MDE processes. Our intention is to enable engineers to use spreadsheets in the context of automated model management operations (such as model validation, transformation and code generation) in a *conceptually uniform manner to models*, i.e., that does not artificially impose transforming from/to an intermediate representation format (e.g. transforming behind the scenes spreadsheets to EMF models and vice versa).

The first challenge of providing support for managing spreadsheets with contemporary model management tools and languages lies in the different metaphors used by the two. Model management languages – influenced by 3-layer metamodelling architectures – typically provide an object-oriented syntax for manipulating information organised in terms of objects and relationships, whereas spreadsheets are structured in terms of worksheets, rows and columns. For spreadsheets to be manipulable by contemporary model management tools and languages, this gap needs to be bridged.

The other challenge is related to efficient querying of spreadsheets. Spreadsheet management tools typically provide highly efficient built-in query functionality (e.g. find all rows in worksheet X where the value of the second column is larger than Y) which need to be reused in model management languages. The alternative – encoding spreadsheet queries using naive iterations and comparisons in model management languages – is undesirable (in terms of reimplementation effort) and likely inefficient.

3 Querying and Modifying Spreadsheets Using OCL-Based Languages

In this section we propose an approach for addressing these challenges at a conceptual level. Our approach comprises two separate aspects: querying and modifying spreadsheets. As such, it is in principle applicable both to side-effect free languages such as OCL and to transformation languages such as ATL [4], Kermeta [5], QVTo and EOL [6].

3.1 Querying Spreadsheets

Spreadsheets are organised into multiple tabular worksheets. Each worksheet typically has a name and a theoretically unbounded number of rows (numbered from 1 to ∞) and columns (titled incrementally using letters of the latin alphabet i.e. $A, B, \ldots, AA, AB \ldots, AAA, \ldots$). To bridge the gap between this data organisation paradigm and the object-oriented style of OCL-based model management languages we propose using worksheet names as (meta-)class names, and the values of the first cell of each column (e.g. A1, B1 etc.) as property names. Using only these assumptions, the spreadsheet illustrated in Figure 1, [1] can in principle be unambiguously queried using the following OCL expression to retrieve all students over the age of 25.

```
Student.allInstances->select(p:Student|p.age > 25)
```

---

[1] In this section, for simplicity, we use an artificial example to demonstrate the challenges and the proposed solutions for bridging the gap between spreadsheets and OCL-based languages. In the evaluation section, we demonstrate using the proposed approach with a requirements traceability spreadsheet.

	A	B	C	D	E	F
1	id	firstname	lastname	age	supervisor	modules
2	jd501	Joe	Thompson	23	mt506	MSD,RQE
3	jd502	Jane	Smith	22	mt506	MSD,HCI
4						

Student | Staff | Module | Mark

	A	B	C	D	E
1	id	firstname	lastname	teaches	
2	mt506	Matthew	Thomas	MSD,RQE	
3	dj512	Daniel	Jackson	HCI	

Student | **Staff** | Module | Mark

	A	B	C	D
1	id	title	term	
2	MSD	Modelling and System Design	Autumn	
3	RQE	Requirements Engineering	Spring	
4	HCI	Human Computer Interaction	Spring	

Student | Staff | **Module** | Mark

	A	B	C	D	E
1	student	module	mark		
2	jd501	TPOP	62		
3	jd502	ICAR	74		

Student | Staff | Module | **Mark**

Fig. 1. Spreadsheet comprising 4 worksheets: *Staff, Student, Module* and *Mark*

While using the first cell of each column as its name is straightforward if the engineer has control of the layout of the spreadsheet, it may not be an option for existing spreadsheets with a fixed layout. In terms of support for datatypes, most spreadsheet software support defining datatypes (*formats*) at the level of individual cells. When capturing data organised in a manner similar to that of Figure 1, it is useful to be able to specify the data types of entire columns (e.g. values in column D of the Student worksheet should be integers).

To enable engineers to decorate spreadsheets with such complementary information (column names, types etc.) that cannot be captured on the spreadsheet itself, we propose using an optional configuration model which conforms to the metamodel of Figure 2.

Spreadsheet configuration models can be constructed manually to complement/override the information (worksheet names, column names) already provided in spreadsheets of interest, or to generate automatically from object-oriented specifications (e.g. UML class diagrams or Ecore metamodels) via model-to-model transformation. The following paragraphs briefly discuss the roles, features and relationships of the concepts that comprise the spreadsheet configuration metamodel of Figure 2.

Worksheet. Each worksheet can have an optional name (if a name is not provided, the name of the worksheet on the spreadsheet is used) and acts as a container for *Column* elements.

Column. Each *Column* needs to specify its index in the context of the worksheet it belongs to, and optionally, a *name* (if a name is not provided, the one specified in its first cell is used as discussed above), an *alias*, a *datatype*, a *cardinality*, and

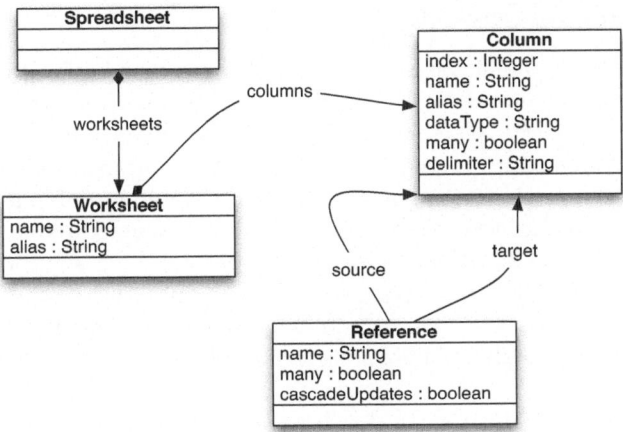

Fig. 2. Spreadsheet Configuration Metamodel

in case of columns with unbounded cardinality, the *delimiter* that should be used to separate the values stored in a single cell (comma is used as the default delimiter).

Reference. In a configuration model engineers can specify ID-based references to capture relationships between columns belonging to potentially different worksheets. Each reference has a *source* and a *target* column, an optional *name* (if a name is not specified, the name of the source column is used to navigate the reference), a cardinality (*many* attribute), and specifies whether updates to cells of the target column should be propagated automatically (*cascade Updates* attribute) to the respective cells in the source column to preserve referential integrity.

For the spreadsheet illustrated in Figure 1, a single-valued reference can be defined between the contents of the *supervisor* column of worksheet *Student* and the *id* column of worksheet *Staff*, and a multi-valued reference can be defined between the *modules* column of the *Student* worksheet, and the *id* column of the module worksheet. Navigating a single-valued reference should return a row (or null), while navigating a multi-valued reference should return a non-unique ordered collection of rows to facilitate concise navigation over the spreadsheet data. Under these assumptions, to find all students whose supervisor name is *Thomas*, the following OCL query can be used.

```
Student.allInstances->select
    (s:Student|s.supervisor.firstname = "Thomas")
```

On a more complicated example, to find all modules taught by a member of staff called *Daniel*, the following query can be used.

```
Module.allInstances->select(m:Module|
    Staff.allInstances->exists(s:Staff|
        s.firstname="Daniel" and s.teaches->includes(m)))
```

3.2   Modifying Spreadsheets

While OCL itself is side-effect-free, many languages that build atop it – techni-cally or conceptually – (such as QVTo, Kermeta, ATL and EOL) need to produce side-effects to support tasks such as model transformation and refactoring. In the context of supporting the requirements of such programs, three types of edit operations are required: creating and deleting rows, and modifying the values of individual cells. In this section we assume that languages capable of producing side-effects provide an additional assignment operator (:=), support for defining typed variables (e.g. through a *var* keyword), support for instantiating meta-types (e.g. through a *new* keyword) and deleting model elements (e.g. through a *delete* keyword), and built-in operations for modifying the contents of collections (e.g. add(), remove()).

Creating Rows. As discussed above, in the proposed approach worksheets are treated as meta-classes and rows as their instances. As such, to create a new row in the Student worksheet, the meta-class instantiation capabilities of the action language can be used as follows. Creating a new row should not have any other side-effects on the spreadsheet.

```
var student : new Student;
```

Deleting Rows. To delete a row from a worksheet, the respective syntax for deleting model elements in the action language can be used. When a row is deleted, all the rows that contain cells referring to it through cascade-update references also need to be recursively deleted.

```
var student = Student.allInstances->select(s:Student|s.id = "
    js502")->first();
delete student;
// deletes row 2 of the Student worksheet
// also deletes row 3 of the Mark worksheet
```

Modifying Cell Values. If a cell is single-valued, a type-conforming assign-ment can be used to edit its value. For example, the following listing demon-strates modifying the age and the supervisor of a particular student.

```
var student : Student = ...;
var supervisor : Staff = ...;
student.age := 24;
student.supervisor := supervisor;
```

If on the other hand the cell is multi-valued, then its values should be handled as a collection. For example to move a module between two members of staff, the module row would need to be retrieved first, so that it can be removed/added from/to the *teaches* collections of the appropriate members of staff.

```
// Moves a module between two members of staff
var from : Staff := ...;
var to : Staff := ...;
var module : Module := ...;
from.teaches->remove(module);
to.teaches->add(module);
```

Updating the value of a cell can have side effects to other cells that are linked to it through cascade-update references to preserve referential integrity. For example, updating the value of cell A3 in the Module worksheet, should trigger appropriate updates in cells D2 and F2 of the Staff and Student worksheets respectively[2].

3.3 Efficient Querying

Using what has been discussed so far, to find all adult students in our spreadsheet, the following OCL query would need to be constructed and evaluated.

```
Student.allInstances->select(s:Student | s.age > 17);
```

Evaluating this query in a naive manner would involve iterating through all the rows of the Student worksheet, retrieving the value of the third cell of each row, casting it to an integer and comparing it against the predefined value. For large spreadsheets, this would be sub-optimal, particularly given that most spreadsheet management systems provide built-in search capabilities. For example, the OCL query above can be expressed in the Google Spreadsheet query language as follows:

```
https://spreadsheets.google.com/feeds/list/tb-
<student-worksheet-guid>/od6/private/full?sq=age>17
```

To support efficient execution of simple queries, we propose detecting optimisable patterns and rewriting them as native queries instead where possible (one such pattern is displayed below). The potential for optimisation through rewriting and the details of the rewriting process predominately depend on the expressiveness and the operators supported by the native query language.

```
X.allInstances->select(x:X | x.p1 = y)
```

4 Prototype

To evaluate the feasibility and practicality of the proposed approach, we have implemented a prototype that adds support for managing Google Spreadsheets to the Epsilon platform of model management languages [3]. Below, we briefly discuss the relevant Epsilon infrastructure and then illustrate the Google Spreadsheets extension.

---

[2] We intentionally refrain from any further discussion on cascade-update algorithms as this is a trivial and well-understood topic.

[3] The prototype is available under
http://epsilon-emc-google-spreadsheet-driver.googlecode.com/

4.1 Epsilon

Epsilon [7] is a mature family of interoperable languages for model management. Languages in Epsilon can be used to manage models of diverse metamodels and technologies (detailed below). The core of Epsilon is the Epsilon Object Language (EOL) [6], an OCL-based imperative language that provides additional features including model modification, multiple model access, conventional programming constructs (variables, loops, branches etc.), user interaction, profiling, and support for transactions. EOL can and has been used as a general-purpose model management language (e.g. for operational model transformation). It is primarily intended to be reused in task-specific model management languages. A number of task-specific languages have been implemented atop EOL, including: model transformation (ETL), model comparison (ECL), model merging (EML), model validation (EVL), model refactoring (EWL) and model-to-text transformation (EGL). These languages reuse EOL in different ways, e.g. by acting as a preprocessor, or by using EOL to define behaviour of rules.

Epsilon is designed to be technology agnostic - that is, the same Epsilon program can be used to manage models from different technologies: the concepts and tasks of model management are independent of how models are represented and stored. To support this, Epsilon provides the Epsilon Model Connectivity (EMC) layer[4], which offers a uniform interface for interacting with models of different modelling technologies. New technologies are supported by adding a *driver* to EMC. Currently, EMC drivers have been implemented to support EMF [2] (XMI 2.x), MDR [8] (XMI 1.x), pure XML, and Z [9] specifications in LaTeX using CZT [10] Also, to enable users to compose complex workflows that involve a number of individual model management tasks, Epsilon provides ANT [11] tasks and an inter-task communication framework discussed in detail in [12].

The technical architecture of Epsilon is illustrated in Figure 3.

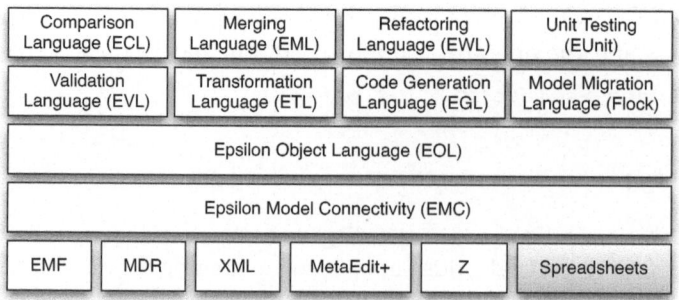

Fig. 3. Overview of the architecture of Epsilon

---

[4] http://www.eclipse.org/epsilon/doc/emc

As mentioned earlier, EMC enables developers to implement *drivers* – essentially classes that implement the `IModel` interface of Figure 4 – to support diverse modelling technologies. The work in this section illustrates the design and implementation of a new driver (in addition to the existing drivers for managing EMF, MDR and Z, XML models) for interacting with Google Spreadsheets.

In addition to abstracting over the technical details of specific modelling technologies, EMC facilitates the concurrent management of models expressed with different technologies. For instance, Epsilon can be used to transform an EMF-based model into an MDR-based model, to perform inter-model validation between a Z model and an EMF model, or to develop a code generator that consumes information from an EMF-based and a Google Spreadsheet model at the same time.

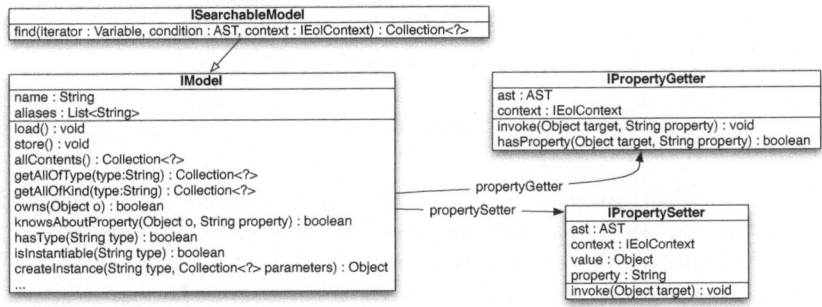

Fig. 4. Epsilon Model Connectivity (EMC) Layer Interfaces

4.2   The EMC Google Spreadsheet Driver

As illustrated in Figure 5, support for Google Spreadsheets has been implemented as a driver conforming to the EMC interfaces. More specifically, the *GSModel* class acts as a wrapper for Google Spreadsheets and implements methods such as *getAllOfType(String type)* which returns all the rows of a particular worksheet (type), and *createInstance(String type)/deleteElement(Object element)* which can create and delete rows respectively. Classes *GSPropertyGetter* and *GSPropertySetter* on the other hand are responsible for retrieving and setting property values of rows.

As displayed in Figure 5, we have used an additional level of abstraction between the EMC interfaces and their Google Spreadsheet implementations which capture spreadsheet-specific but Google Spreadsheet-independent logic and which can be reused to implement support for additional types of spreadsheets (e.g. Microsoft Excel or Open Office spreadsheets).

The Google Spreadsheet driver adopts a lazy approach to retrieving data from remote spreadsheets instead of attempting to construct an in-memory copy of the entire contents of the spreadsheet upon initialisation. Also, all side-effects produced on spreadsheets are propagated directly to the remote spreadsheet to avoid the problem of working with stale data.

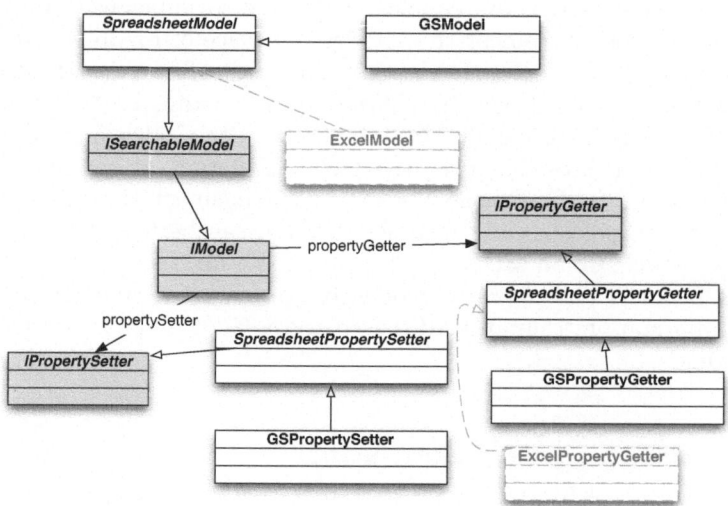

Fig. 5. Google Spreadsheet EMC Driver Design

With regard to spreadsheet configuration models, we have opted for an XML-based concrete syntax in an effort to enable engineers to use this driver with minimal effort (using EMF-based configuration models would be a technically more sound approach but would require engineers to become familiar with EMF). The supported datatypes in the spreadsheet configuration models are: *integer*, *boolean*, *String*(default), *real* and *double*. Using this XML-based format, the configuration model for the spreadsheet of Figure 1 is illustrated below.

```
<spreadsheet>
  <worksheet name="Student">
    <column name="age" datatype="integer"/>
  </worksheet>
  <worksheet name="Mark">
    <column name="mark" datatype="integer"/>
  </worksheet>
  <worksheet name="Staff">
    <column name="teaches" many="true" delimiter=","/>
  </worksheet>
  <reference source="Student->supervisor"
        target="Staff->id"/>
  <reference source="Staff->teaches"
        target="Module->id" many="true"/>
  ...
</spreadsheet>
```

With regard to performing efficient queries on spreadsheets, *GSModel* implements the *ISearchableModel* interface provided by EMC, and implements its *find(Variable iterator, AST condition)* method in which it rewrites optimisable conditions as native Google Spreadsheet queries at runtime as discussed in

Section 3. The rewriter employs a recursive descent algorithm, and fully exploits the capabilities of the Google Spreadsheet query language (numeric and string comparisons as well as composite queries consisting of more than one and/or clauses). Non-optimisable conditions in *find* cause the driver to fail gracefully. The following listing demonstrates using the *find* operation to perform queries on the spreadsheet of Figure 1.

```
// Collects all the first names
// of students with marks < 50
M->find(m:Mark | m.mark < 50)->
  collect(m:Mark | m.student.firstname);

// Fails gracefully as the condition involves
// a two-level property navigation and cannot be
// rewritten as a native query
M->find(s:Student |
  s.supervisor.firstname = "Daniel");
```

By providing a Google Spreadsheet driver for EMC, all languages that build atop EOL can now interact with such spreadsheets. For example, the EVL constraint below checks that no member of staff teaches more than 4 modules. This is illustrated further in the case study that follows.

```
context Staff {
  constraint NotOverloaded {
    check: self.teaches->size() <= 4
    message: "Member of staff" + self.firstname +
      " " + self.lastname + " is overloaded"
  }
}
```

5 Case Study

In this section we demonstrate the proposed approach by applying it to representative case study. This case study is provided in the official SysML documentation [13], and is based on a specification published by the National Highway Traffic Safety Administration (NHTSA).

5.1 Hybrid SUV Example

The case study illustrates the application of the proposed approach for the development of a Hybrid gas/electric powered Sport Utility Vehicle (SUV). It is interesting in that it consists of a complex requirements hierarchy which can be captured efficiently using spreadsheets. The example focuses mainly on the requirements engineering phase of the development process and how this can benefit from treating spreadsheets as models. A significant benefit comes from the seamless integration of spreadsheets with downstream MDE tasks.

In this case study, the various system requirements are captured in a spreadsheet comprising four worksheets. These requirements concern the operation and performance of the vehicle. Figure 6 illustrates an excerpt of the requirements spreadsheet of the Hybrid SUV. In the first worksheet the system requirements are captured. The first column captures the unique requirement identifiers. These identifiers have a fixed format and they conform to the dot notation. The subsequent columns capture the name of a requirement, whether a requirement is derived from another requirement and finally the requirement's text.

	A	B	C	D
1	id	name	derived	text
2	REQ-0	HSUV Specification		
3	REQ-0.1	Performance		The HSUV shall have...
4	REQ-0.2	Capacity		The HSUV shall have the capacity...
5	REQ-0.1.1	Braking		The HSUV shall have the braking...
6	REQ-0.1.2	Fuel Economy		The HSUV shall have fuel economy...
7	REQ-0.1.3	Acceleration		The vehicle should have a 0-30 mph...
8	REQ-0.1.4	OffRoad Capability		The HSUV shall have the offroad capability...
9	REQ-0.3	Regenerative Breaking	REQ-0.1.1,REQ-0.1.2	Regenerative braking should not adversely impact...
9	REQ-0.4	Power	REQ-0.1.3,REQ-0.1.4	The power of the engine...
10	...	...	...	...
Requirement	Problems	Rationale	TestCase	

Fig. 6. Hybrid SUV requirements spreadsheet

5.2   Managing Requirements Spreadsheets with Epsilon

In this section, we illustrate how the proposed approach can be used in the context of the Hybrid SUV case study. More specifically, we show three scenarios: how we can query the spreadsheet, how we can validate the correctness of the information captured in the spreadsheet and, finally, how we can generate textual artefacts from it. The spreadsheet configuration model for this spreadsheet follows.

```
<spreadsheet>
    <reference source="Requirement->derived"
        target="Requirement->id"/>
    <worksheet title="Requirement">
      <column title="derived" many="true" delimiter=","/>
    </worksheet>
</spreadsheet>
```

Querying Requirements Spreadsheets. In the first usage scenario, the engineer wishes to retrieve all the children in the requirement hierarchy for a given requirement. By doing this, the engineer wishes to understand the rationale behind a given composite requirement and how this composite requirement is decomposed. In the proposed approach, to do this the engineer has to define an EOL operation, which returns a collection with all the children elements of the hierarchy for a given requirement. This operation is illustrated in Listing 1.1.

```
operation Requirement getChildren() : Sequence {
  var children : new Sequence;
    //iterates all requirements, and checks if their id
    //starts with the id of the parent
    for(r in Requirement.all) {
       if((r.id+'.').startsWith(self.id+'.')){
          children.add(r);
       }
    }
    //returns a set with all the requirements
    //in the hierarchy
    return children;
}
```

Listing 1.1. getChildren() EOL operation

To identify the child requirements, the operation relies on the requirement ids and the convention that all the requirement identifiers have to conform to the dot notation. Therefore, this operation assumes that all the requirements in the spreadsheet have a valid id. In the following we will demonstrate how an engineer could check if these assumptions hold.

Validating Requirements Spreadsheets. To validate the contents of the requirements spreadsheet the engineer can specify a set of EVL constraints. These constraints are illustrated in Listing 1.2; if the constraints hold, all the requirements have an id and they all have a valid format. To simplify the expression of these constraints, we also write an EOL operation (Listing 1.3), which encapsulates the functionality that checks the correctness (using a regular expression) of an id's format.

```
// For all requirements
context Requirement {
  //Checks whether the requirement has an id
  constraint HasId {
    check: self.id.isDefined()
    message: 'Requirement ' + self.name + 'does not have an id.'
  }
  //Checks whether the requirement has a a valid id
  constraint HasValidId {
    check: self.hasValidId()
    message: 'Requirement ' + self.name + 'does not have a
        valid id.'
  }
}
```

Listing 1.2. EVL constraints for requirements spreadsheets

```
// This operation uses a regular expression to
// test whether the requirement id has a valid format
operation Requirement hasValidId() : Boolean {
  return self.id.matches("REQ-[0-9]+(\\.([0-9]+))*"));
}
```

Listing 1.3. Requirement ID validation operation

Generating Textual Artefacts. Once the requirements are well understood and well-formatted they can be used as first-class citizens in the MDE development process. For instance, a requirements derivation graph such as the one displayed in Figure 7 can be generated automatically using GraphViz [14] and the EGL model-to-text transformation below.

```
digraph G {
  [%for (r in Requirement.all) { %]
  [%for (derived in r.derived) { %]
  "[%=r.id%]" -> "[%=derived.id%]";
  [%}%]
  [%}%]
}
```

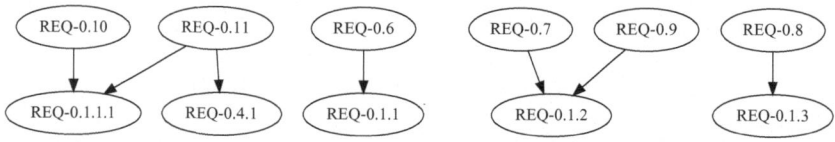

Fig. 7. Hybrid SUV requirements derivation graph

Additional MDE tasks and operations can now easily be carried out, e.g. model-to-model transformations to more structured formats (such as EMF models), or update-in-place transformations to correct any 'bad smells' [15] that can be identified.

6   Related Work

Although spreadsheets are widely used in software engineering for supporting numerous development activities (such as collecting system requirements, monitoring project process and capturing traceability information) there is little research on using them formally in a software engineering lifecycle. The majority of the literature focuses mainly on how to use software engineering principles to support the development of high quality spreadsheets. There are two main approaches to spreadsheet engineering - constructive and analytical [17]. The purpose of the former is to ensure that spreadsheets are correct by construction, while the latter aims to detect errors after a spreadsheet has been created.

Two representative examples of an analytical approach are [18] and [19]. The former uses data flow adequacy criteria and coverage monitoring to test spreadsheets, while the latter is an extension which employs fault localisation techniques to isolate spreadsheet errors. In [20] user-provided assertions about cell ranges are used to identify errors in formulas. The FFR (formulae, formats, relations) model [21] abstracts the structure and fundamental features of spreadsheets without paying attention to the detailed semantics of operations and functions. Anomalies in the structure of the model (for example breaking areas) highlight possible errors. In [15], analogies to code 'smells' are specified and analysed against spreadsheets and worksheets to identify flaws and design errors; their experiments show that numerous errors can be automatically identified.

ClassSheet [17] is the most popular constructive approach. This approach introduces a formal higher-level object-oriented model which can be used to automatically generate spreadsheets. Given the formal nature of this model a number of typical errors associated with spreadsheets can be prevented, as the spreadsheets will be correct by construction. A more recent constructive approach to spreadsheet engineering is *MDSheet* [22]. This is a model-driven approach and it is based on *ClassSheet*. *MDSheet* relies on a bi-directional transformation framework [23] in order to maintain spreadsheet models (i.e. *ClassSheet* models) and their instances synchronized.

The focus of the aforementioned research work is quite different from the focus of the proposed approach. As mentioned previously, past research focuses on how to ensure the correctness of spreadsheets. On the other hand, this paper proposes an approach whose focus is on the seamless integration of spreadsheets in the MDE development process, as well as their elevation to first-class models. In our approach spreadsheets are considered just another type of model in an MDE process. As such, spreadsheets can be queried, validated or even transformed to other artefacts using MDE techniques and concepts.

7   Conclusions and Further Work

In this paper, we have argued for the importance of adding support for spreadsheets to the MDE toolkit and in particular to enable their support in OCL-based model management languages. We have presented an approach that bridges the conceptual gap between the tabular nature of spreadsheets and the object-oriented nature of contemporary modelling technologies and model management languages, which also addresses the problem of efficiently querying spreadsheets from within such languages. We have evaluated this approach by constructing a prototype Google Spreadsheet driver on top of the model connectivity framework of Epsilon. We have also presented a case study that demonstrates the practicality and usefulness of managing spreadsheets with model management languages.

In future iterations of this work, we plan to extend the spreadsheet driver to target additional types of spreadsheets, and construct transformations that can generate spreadsheet configuration models from object-oriented specifications such as UML class models and Ecore metamodels. We also intend to use model refactoring languages and tools (particularly EWL) to support spreadsheet and worksheet refactoring to automatically eliminate so-called 'bad smells' [15,24].

References

1. Firesmith, D.: Common requirements problems, their negative consequences, and industry best practices to help solve them. Journal of Object Technology 6, 17–33 (2007)
2. Steinberg, D., Budinsky, F., Paternostro, M., Merks, E.: EMF: Eclipse Modelling Framework, 2nd edn. Eclipse Series. Addison-Wesley Professional (December 2008)
3. Kolovos, D.S., Rose, L.M., Williams, J., Matragkas, N., Paige, R.F.: A lightweight approach for managing xml documents with mde languages. In: Vallecillo, A., Tolvanen, J.-P., Kindler, E., Störrle, H., Kolovos, D. (eds.) ECMFA 2012. LNCS, vol. 7349, pp. 118–132. Springer, Heidelberg (2012)
4. Jouault, F., Kurtev, I.: Transforming Models with ATL. In: Bruel, J.-M. (ed.) MoDELS 2005. LNCS, vol. 3844, pp. 128–138. Springer, Heidelberg (2006)
5. Muller, P.-A., Fleurey, F., Jézéquel, J.-M.: Weaving executability into object-oriented meta-languages. In: Briand, L.C., Williams, C. (eds.) MoDELS 2005. LNCS, vol. 3713, pp. 264–278. Springer, Heidelberg (2005)
6. Kolovos, D.S., Paige, R.F., Polack, F.A.C.: The Epsilon Object Language (EOL). In: Rensink, A., Warmer, J. (eds.) ECMDA-FA 2006. LNCS, vol. 4066, pp. 128–142. Springer, Heidelberg (2006)
7. Eclipse Foundation. Epsilon Modeling GMT component, http://www.eclipse.org/gmt/epsilon
8. Sun Microsystems. Meta Data Repository, http://mdr.netbeans.org
9. Woodcock, J., Davies, J.: Using Z: Specification, Refinement, and Proof. Prentice Hall (March 1996)
10. Community Z Tools, http://czt.sourceforge.net
11. The Apache Ant Project, http://ant.apache.org
12. Kolovos, D.S., Paige, R.F., Polack, F.A.C.: A Framework for Composing Modular and Interoperable Model Management Tasks. In: Proc. Workshop on Model Driven Tool and Process Integration (MDTPI), ECMDA, Berlin, Germany (June 2008)
13. OMG, Systems Modeling Language, SysML (2012), http://www.omg.org/spec/SysML/1.3/PDF/
14. Graphviz - Graph Visualization Software, Official Web-Site, http://www.graphviz.org
15. Hermans, F., Pinzger, M., van Deursen, A.: Detecting and visualizing inter-worksheet smells in spreadsheets. In: ICSE, pp. 441–451. IEEE (2012)
16. Raymond, R.: Panko. Spreadsheet Errors: What We Know. What We Think We Can Do. In: Proceedings of the Spreadsheet Risk Symposium, European Spreadsheet Risks Interest Group (EuSpRIG) (July 2000)
17. Engels, G., Erwig, M.: Classsheets: automatic generation of spreadsheet applications from object-oriented specifications. In: Proceedings of the 20th IEEE/ACM International Conference on Automated Software Engineering, ASE 2005, pp. 124–133. ACM, New York (2005)
18. Rothermel, G., Burnett, M., Li, L., Dupuis, C., Sheretov, A.: A methodology for testing spreadsheets. ACM Trans. Softw. Eng. Methodol. 10(1), 110–147 (2001)

19. Prabhakararao, S., Cook, C., Ruthruff, J., Creswick, E., Main, M., Durham, M., Burnett, M.: Strategies and behaviors of end-user programmers with interactive fault localization. In: Proceedings of the 2003 IEEE Symposium on Human Centric Computing Languages and Environments, HCC 2003, pp. 15–22. IEEE Computer Society, Washington, DC (2003)

20. Burnett, M., Cook, C., Pendse, O., Rothermel, G., Summet, J., Wallace, C.: End-user software engineering with assertions in the spreadsheet paradigm. In: Proceedings of the 25th International Conference on Software Engineering, ICSE 2003, pp. 93–103. IEEE Computer Society, Washington, DC (2003)

21. Sajaniemi, J.: Modeling spreadsheet audit: A rigorous approach to automatic visualization. Journal of Visual Languages & Computing 11(1), 49–82 (2000)

22. Cunha, J., Fernandes, J.P., Ribeiro, H., Saraiva, J.: Mdsheet: A framework for model-driven spreadsheet engineering. In: 34th International Conference on Software Engineering (ICSE), pp. 1395–1398 (June 2012)

23. Cunha, J., Fernandes, J.P., Ribeiro, H., Saraiva, J.: A bidirectional model-driven spreadsheet environment. In: 2012 34th International Conference on Software Engineering (ICSE), pp. 1443–1444 (June 2012)

24. Cunha, J., Fernandes, J.P., Ribeiro, H., Saraiva, J.: Towards a catalog of spreadsheet smells. In: Murgante, B., Gervasi, O., Misra, S., Nedjah, N., Rocha, A.M.A.C., Taniar, D., Apduhan, B.O. (eds.) ICCSA 2012, Part IV. LNCS, vol. 7336, pp. 202–216. Springer, Heidelberg (2012)

Model-Driven Extraction
and Analysis of Network Security Policies

Salvador Martínez[1], Joaquin Garcia-Alfaro[3], Frédéric Cuppens[2],
Nora Cuppens-Boulahia[2], and Jordi Cabot[1]

[1] AtlanMod, École des Mines de Nantes - INRIA, LINA, Nantes, France
`{salvador.martinez_perez,jordi.cabot}@inria.fr`
[2] Télécom Bretagne, LUSSI Department Université Européenne de Bretagne, France
`forename.surname@telecom-bretagne.eu`
[3] Télécom SudParis, RST Department CNRS Samovar UMR 5157, Evry, France
`joaquin.garcia_alfaro@telecom-sudparis.eu`

Abstract. Firewalls are a key element in network security. They are
in charge of filtering the traffic of the network in compliance with a
number of access-control rules that enforce a given security policy. In
an always-evolving context, where security policies must often be updated to respond to new security requirements, knowing with precision
the policy being enforced by a network system is a critical information.
Otherwise, we risk to hamper the proper evolution of the system and
compromise its security. Unfortunately, discovering such enforced policy
is an error-prone and time consuming task that requires low-level and,
often, vendor-specific expertise since firewalls may be configured using
different languages and conform to a complex network topology. To tackle
this problem, we propose a model-driven reverse engineering approach
able to extract the security policy implemented by a set of firewalls in
a working network, easing the understanding, analysis and evolution of
network security policies.

1 Introduction

Firewalls, designed to filter the traffic of a network with respect to a given
number of access-control rules, are key elements in the enforcement of network
security policies.

Although there exist approaches to derive firewall configurations from high-
level network policy specifications[18,4], these configuration files are still mostly
manually written, using low-level and, often, vendor-specific rule filtering languages. Moreover, the network topology, that may include several firewalls
(potentially from different vendors), may impose the necessity of splitting the
enforcement of the global security policy among several elements. Due to the
complexity of the process, it is likely that we end up with differences between
the implemented policy and the desired one. Moreover, security policies must be
often updated to respond to new security requirements, which requires evolving
the access-control rules included in the firewall configuration files.

A. Moreira et al. (Eds.): MODELS 2013, LNCS 8107, pp. 52–68, 2013.

Therefore, there is a clear need of an easy way to represent and understand the security policy actually enforced by a deployed network system. At the moment, this still requires a manual approach that requires, again, low-level and vendor-specific expertise. Given a network system consisting in several firewalls configured with hundreds of rules, the feasibility of this manual approach could be seriously questioned. While the security research community has provided a plethora of works dealing with the reasoning on security policies, succeeding at providing a good analysis and verification of the low-level firewall rules, we believe they fail at obtaining a comprehensive solution as they do not provide a high-level, easy to understand and manage representation nor take, generally, networks composed by several heterogeneous firewalls into account. Moreover, the extraction step is often neglected and the solution presented over synthetic rules without providing the means to bridge the gap between them and the real configurations.

In this sense, we believe that an integrated solution is missing. We believe such a solution must have the following features. First, it has to provide independence from the concrete underlying technology, so that the focus can be put into the security problem and not in implementation mechanisms like chains, routing tables, etc. Second, it has to provide a higher-level representation so that the policy becomes easier to understand, analyse and manipulate. Third, the solution, to be comprehensive, must take into account the contribution of each policy enforcing element (firewall) to the global policy, as the partial picture given by isolated firewalls does not provide enough information to understand the network policy.

In this joint work between the modeling and the security communities, we propose a model-driven approach aimed at covering this gap. Our approach, first, extracts and abstracts the information of each firewall configuration file to models conforming to a Platform-independent metamodel specially tailored to represent network-access control information in an efficient and concise way. Then, after performing structural verification of the information in the individual models, it combines these models to obtain a centralised view of the security policy of the whole network. Finally, this global network access-control model can be analysed and further processed to derive useful information. As en example, we analyse the structure of its contents to derive the network topology the firewalls operate on. Then, we provide a mapping to obtain a representation of the policy in XACML, a standardised access-control model, enabling the (re)use of the many tools developed to work with the standard.

We validate the feasibility of our approach by providing a prototype implementation working for firewalls using the netfilter iptables and Cisco PIX rule filtering languages. Our prototype can be easily extended to work with any other packet-filtering languages.

The rest of the paper is organized as follows. Section 2 presents a motivating and running example of a network. In Section 3 we present and detail our approach whereas in Section 4 we present some application scenarios. In 5 we discuss a prototype implementation. Section 6 discusses related work. The paper finishes in Section 7 with some conclusions and future works.

2 Motivation

In order to motivate our approach, we present here a network example that will be used through the rest of the paper.

Let us consider we have a De-Militarized Zone (DMZ) network architecture like the one depicted in Figure 1. This is a very common architecture used to provide services both to a local network and to the public untrusted network while preventing the local network to be attacked. It is composed by the following elements:

- An intranet composed by a number of private hosts where one of the private hosts acts as an administrator of certain services provided by the network system.
- A DMZ that contains two servers. A DNS server and a multiserver providing the following services: HTTP/HTTPS (web), FTP, SMTP (email) and SSH.
- Two firewalls controlling the traffic towards and from the DMZ. The first firewall controls the traffic between the public hosts (the Internet) and the services provided by the DMZ. The second firewall controls the traffic between the intranet and the DMZ.

The two firewalls in charge of enforcing the security policy of our example network, could be of the same kind. However, following the *defense in depth*[1] security strategy, it is highly recommended, to use two different firewalls so that a possible vulnerability does not affect the whole network. In our example, the *firewall 1* is a linux iptables packet-filtering firewall whereas *firewall 2* is a Cisco firewall implementing Cisco PIX filtering.

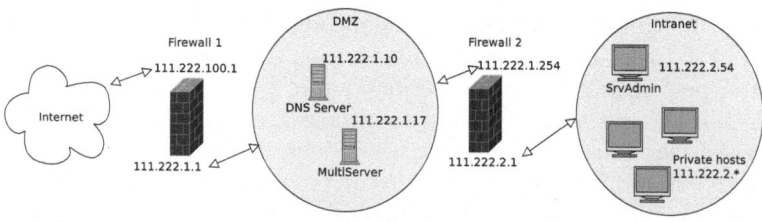

Fig. 1. Network example

In Listing 1.1 we show an excerpt of the configuration file of *firewall 1* wrt the HTTP and SMTP services. It controls the traffic from the public hosts to the services provided in the DMZ. This sample configuration uses the netfilter iptables[19] rule language. Note that this configuration file is written using the iptables *custom chains* feature, which allows the user to define exclusions to rules without using drop or deny rules.

First, it states in the first three lines that the global policy for the firewall is the rejection of any connection not explicitly allowed. Then, the first chain controls the outcoming SMTP messages towards the public host. It allows them for every hosts but for the host in the local network. The second chain controls the incoming SMTP messages to the server. If the request is done through one machine belonging to the local network, it is rejected while it is allowed for any other machine. The third rule controls the HTTP requests from the public hosts. Again, connections are allowed for any host but for the local ones.

Listing 1.1. Firewall 1 netfilter configuration

```
iptables -P INPUT DROP
iptables -P FORWARD DROP
iptables -P OUTPUT DROP

iptables -N Out_SMTP
iptables -A FORWARD -s 111.222.1.17 -d 0.0.0.0/0 -p tcp --dport 25 -j Out_SMTP
iptables -A Out_SMTP -d 111.222.0.0/16 -j RETURN
iptables -A Out_SMTP -j ACCEPT

iptables -N In_SMPT
iptables -A FORWARD -s 0.0.0.0/0 -d 111.222.1.17 -p tcp --dport 25 -j In_SMTP
iptables -A In_SMTP -s 111.222.0.0/16 -j RETURN
iptables -A In_SMTP -j ACCEPT

iptables -N NetWeb_HTTP
iptables -A FORWARD -s 0.0.0.0/0 -d 111.222.1.17 -p tcp --dport 80 -j NetWeb_HTTP
iptables -A NetWeb_HTTP -s 111.222.0.0/16 -j RETURN
iptables -A NetWeb_HTTP -j ACCEPT
```

Firewall number 2 controls the traffic from the private hosts to the services provided in the DMZ. Listing 1.2 shows the rules that control the access to the SMTP and HTTP services. It is written in the Cisco PIX language that does not provide support to a feature like the iptables *custom chains*.

Rules one to six, control the SMTP requests to the server. They are all allowed for the hosts in the private zone discarding only the administrator host, identified by the IP address 111.222.2.54, and for a free-access host, identified by IP address 111.222.2.53. Rules seven to twelve do the same for the HTTP requests. Again, HTTP requests are allowed for all the hosts in the private zone discarding only the administrator host and the free-access host.

Listing 1.2. Firewall 2 Cisco PIX configuration

```
access-list eth1_acl_in  remark Fw2Policy 0 (global)
access-list eth1_acl_in deny tcp host 111.222.2.54 111.222.1.17 eq 25

access-list eth1_acl_in remark Fw2Policy 1 (global)
access-list eth1_acl_in deny tcp host 111.222.2.53 111.222.1.17 eq 25

access-list eth1_acl_in remark Fw2Policy 2 (global)
access-list eth1_acl_in permit tcp 111.222.2.0 255.255.255.0 111.222.1.17 eq 25

access-list eth1_acl_in remark Fw2Policy 4 (global)
access-list eth1_acl_in deny tcp host 111.222.2.54 111.222.1.17 eq 80

access-list eth1_acl_in remark Fw2Policy 5 (global)
access-list eth1_acl_in deny tcp host 111.222.2.53 111.222.1.17 eq 80

access-list eth1_acl_in remark Fw2Policy 3 (global)
access-list eth1_acl_in permit tcp 111.222.2.0 255.255.255.0 111.222.1.17 eq 80

access-group eth1_acl_in in interface eth1
```

2.1   Example Evaluation

Faced with this example, a security expert willing to understand the enforced access control rules will have to directly review the configuration files of the firewalls in the system (disregarding the low-level and often incomplete management tools provided by the firewall vendors, obviously only valid for the firewalls of that vendor), which in this case, involves two different rule languages. Not even the topology picture of the network, provided here with the purpose of easing the discussion, can be taken for granted but instead needs to be derived from the configuration files themselves.

Therefore, we can see that the task of extracting the global access control policy enforced by the set of rules in these two firewalls (that are just minimal excerpts of what a full configuration policy would be) requires expert knowledge about netfilter iptables and Cisco PIX. Its syntax along with its execution semantics would have to be mastered to properly interpret the meaning of the configuration files. Moreover, the information from the two configuration files and the default policies would have to be combined as they collaborate to enforce the global policy and can not be regarded in isolation.

In corporate networks potentially composed by up to a thousand firewalls, composed by hundreds of rules and potentially from different vendors using different configuration languages and execution semantics, the task of manually extracting the enforced access control policy would become very complex and expensive, seriously hampering the analysis and evolution tasks the dynamic environment of corporations impose. This is the challenge our approach aims to tackle as described in the next sections.

3   Approach

This section details our MDE approach to generate a high-level platform-independent model providing a global view of all access-control rules in a set of firewall configurations files.

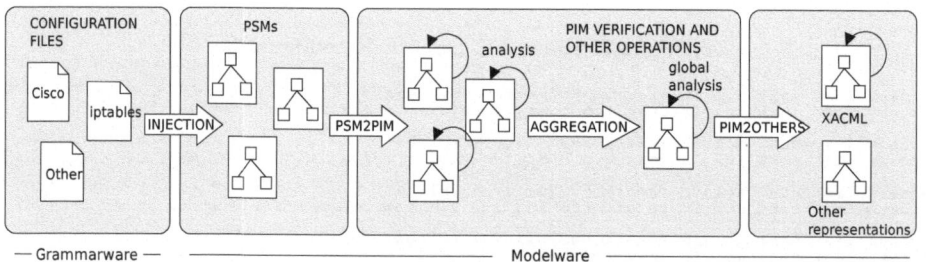

Fig. 2. Extraction approach

Our model-driven reverse engineering approach, that extends the preliminary one in [14], is summarized in Figure 2. It starts by injecting the information contained in the firewall configuration files into platform-specific models (PSMs). Afterwards, each PSM is translated into a different network access-control PIM and an structural analysis to detect misconfigurations is performed. These PIMs are then aggregated into a global model, representing the access-control policy of the whole network. Operations are also performed over this global model to classify the information in "locally" or globally relevant.

3.1   Injection

The first step of our approach constitutes a mere translation between technical spaces where the textual information in the configuration files is expressed in terms of models. A PSM and a parser recognizing the grammar of each concrete firewall rule-filtering language present in the network system is required. In Listing 1.3 we excerpt a grammar for *CISCO PIX* whereas in Section 5, we show how we use it to obtain the corresponding parser and PSM. Due to space limitations, we do not show here the grammar for the *linux Iptables* filtering language (it is available on the web of the project [2]). The integration of any other language will follow the same strategy.

Listing 1.3. Cisco grammar excerpt

```
Model:
    rules += Rule*;
Rule:
    AccessGroup | AccessList;
AccessGroup:
    'access-group' id=ID 'in' 'interface' interface=Interface;
Interface:
    id=ID;
AccessList:
    ('no')? 'access-list' id=ID decision=('deny' | 'permit') protocol=Protocol
    protocolObjectGroup=ProtocolObjectGroup
    serviceObjectGroup=ServiceObjectGroup
    networkObjectGroup=NetworkObjectGroup;
ProtocolObjectGroup:
    (pogId=ID)? sourceAddress=IPExpr sourceMask=MaskExpr;
ServiceObjectGroup:
    targetAddress=IPExpr targetMask=IPExpr;
NetworkObjectGroup:
    operator=Operator port=INT;
Operator:
    name=('eq' | 'lt' | 'gt');
Protocol:
    name= ('tcp'| 'udp' | 'ip');
IPExpr:
    INT '.' INT '.' INT '.' INT;
```

Note that this step is performed without losing any information and that the obtained models remain at the same abstraction level as the configuration files.

3.2   Platform-Specific to Platform-Independent Model

The second step of our approach implies transforming the PSMs obtained in the previous step to PIMs so that we get rid off the concrete details of the firewall technology, language and even writing style. Central to this step is the definition of a Network access-control metamodel able to represent the information contained in the PSMs. In the following we present and justify our proposal for such a metamodel.

Generally, firewall access-control policies can be seen as a set of individual security rules of type $R_i : \{conditions\} \rightarrow \{decision\}$, where the subindex i specifies the ordering of the rule within the configuration file, *decision* can be accept or deny and *conditions* is a set of rule matching attributes like the source and destination addresses, the used protocol and the source and destination port.

Such a policy representation presents several disadvantages. First of all, the information is highly redundant and disperse, so that the details relevant to a given host or zone may appear, unassociated, in different places of the configuration file (potentially, containing up to several hundreds of rules). Metamodeling and model-driven technologies contain a big potential to reduce this issues, however, a proper representation must be chosen in order to maximize its benefits.

Second, this representation is not suited for representing the firewall policy in a natural and efficient way. Although firewall policies could be written by only using positive or negative logic (what leads however to over-complicated and not natural rule sets, impacting legibility and maintainability) a firewall access-control policy is better explained by expressing just rules in one sense (either negative or positive) and then exceptions (see [10] for a detailed study of the use of exceptions in access control policies) to the application of these rules. This way, in a close policy environment (where everything not explicitly accepted is forbidden) it is very common to define a security policy that accepts the traffic from a given zone and then denies it only for some elements of the zone.

Native support for the representation of exceptions simplifies the representation and management of network policies while decreasing the risk of misconfiguration. The *custom chains mechanism*, recently provided by the linux iptables filter language, evidences the need for such a native support.

3.2.1 Network Access-Control Metamodel

The platform independent network access-control metamodel we propose here (see Figure 3) provides support for the representation of rules and exceptions. Moreover, our reverse engineering approach is designed to recover an exception-oriented representation of network security policies from configuration files disregarding if they use a good representation of exceptions like in the iptables example in Section 2, or not, like in the Cisco PIX example in the same section.

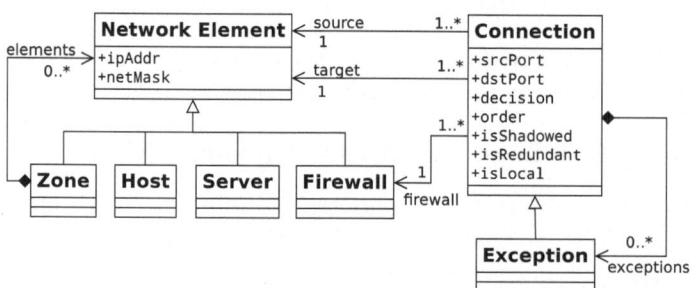

Fig. 3. Filter PIM excerpt

Our metamodel proposal contains the following elements (note that, for simplicity, some attributes and references are not represented in the image):

- *Network Element.* Represents any subject (source of the access request) or object (target of the access request) within a network system. It is characterised by its ip address and its network mask.
- *Zone, Host, Server and Firewall.* Several different types of *Network Element* may exist in a network environment. For the purpose of this paper, the relevant ones are: *Host, Zone* which in turn, contains other Network Elements,

Server and *Firewall*. However, the list of elements can be extended to manage different scenarios, like the presence of routers, intrusion detections systems (IDSs), etc.

- *Connection.* Represents a connection between Network Elements. Apart from its source and target Network Elements, it is characterized by the following attributes: source and destination port, identifying the requested service; decision, stating if the connections is accepted or denied (our metamodel can represent open, close and mixed policies); order, reflecting the rule ordering in the corresponding configuration file; firewall, that identifies the firewall from where the connections were extracted; isLocal that tells is the connection is only locally relevant, isShadowed that identifies the connection as not reachable and finally, isRedundant, stating that the connection can be removed without affecting the policy.
- *Exception.* A connection may contain several exceptions to its application. These exceptions are connections with opposite decisions matching a subset of the elements matched by the containing connection.

3.2.2   PSM-to-PIM Transformation

Our PIM metamodel provides the means for representing network access-control policies in a concise and organised way. However, a proper processing of the information coming from the configuration files is required in order to fully exploit its capacities (a policy could be represented by using only *Connections* without using the *Exception* element). Therefore, the process of populating the PIM model from a PSM model is composed by two sub-steps.

The first sub-step fills our PIM with the information as it is normally found in configuration files, i.e., in the form of a set of rules representing exceptions with mixed positive and negative logic. However, this representation can lead to policy anomalies and ambiguities. Concretely, as defined in [8], a firewall rule set may present the following anomalies:

Rule shadowing: a rule R is shadowed when it never applies because another rule with higher priority matches all the packets it may match.

Rule redundancy: a rule R is redundant when it is not shadowed and removing it from the rule set does not change the security policy.

Rule irrelevance: a rule R is irrelevant when it is meant to match packets that does not pass by a given firewall.

Thus, the second sub-step, refines the initial PIM model and improve its internal organization to deal with the aforementioned problems. More specifically, this step applies the following algorithm on the PIM model (we describe the process for closed policies with exceptions, however, a version adapted to open policies would be straightforward):

1. Collect all the *Connection* elements C whose decision is *Accept*.
2. For each retrieved *Connection* C_i, get *Connections* C_j with the following constraints:
   (a) C_j decision is *Deny*
   (b) C_j conditions match a subset of the set matched by the conditions of C_i.
   (c) C_j ordering number is lower than the C_i ordering number (if not, mark C_j as shadowed).
   Then, for each retrieved C_j create an *Exception* element and aggregate it to the C_i. Remove the C_j *Connection*.
3. For each remaining *Connection* element C_j whose decision is *Deny* and is-Shadowed equals *false*:
   – mark C_j as isRedundant

The algorithm we have presented is a modification of the one presented in [9], e.g. to drop the requirement of using as input policy one free of shadowing and redundancy. On the contrary, it is meant to work on real configurations and helps to discover these anomalies: *shadowed* deny rules and *redundant* deny rules. The security expert can retrieve them easily from the PIM as any left *Connection* in the PIM with decision *Deny* is an anomaly and as such is marked as *isShadowed* or as *isRedundant*.

This algorithm can be complemented by a direct application of additional algorithms described in [8] to uncover other less important anomalies. Note that the correction of these anomalies will often require the segmentation and rewriting of the rules, therefore we consider the correction as an optional step to be manually triggered by the security expert after analysing the detected anomalies.

3.3   Aggregation of Individual PIMs

At the end of the previous step we get a set of PIM's (one per firewall in the network). Clearly, an individual firewall gives only a partial vision of the security policy enforced in the whole network. In our example, analyzing one firewall will yield that the public host can access the SMTP server, however, this server can be also accessed by the private network with some exceptions. Thus, in order to obtain a complete representation of the network policy the individual PIM models have to be combined into one global network access-control model. Note that as we keep information regarding which firewall contains a given *Connection* element and the ordering with respect to the original configuration file, this step would be reversible, so that the individual policies may be reproduced from the global model.

We obtain the global model by performing a model union operation between the individual models, so that no *Network Element* or *Connection* is duplicated. Then, as an extra step, a refining transformation is performed to assign the proper type to the *Network Elements*. This step is performed by analysing the *ip* addresses and the incoming and outgoing connections. This way, we are able to establish if a network element is a zone or being an individual network element behaves as a host or a server (a unique firewall element is created upon the initialization of each PIM model in order to represent the firewall the rules come from). Once we have obtained the global model, some operations become available.

First of all, local *Exceptions* and *Connections*, i.e., *Exceptions* and *Connections* that only make sense in the context of a concrete firewall, can be identified (so that they can be filtered out when representing the global policy.). Local exceptions are usually added due to the mechanisms used to enforce the global policy. As en example, in the Listing 1.1 the elements in the network zone 222.111.0.0 are not allowed to send or receive smtp messages. However, elements in 222.111.2.0 are allowed to send them regarding the configuration Listing 1.2. This contradiction is due to the enforcing architecture that imposes the traffic to pass through a certain firewall (in this case, hosts in the local network are meant to access the DMZ through the second firewall). The algorithm to detect local *Exceptions* and *Connections* works as follows:

1. Collect all the *Exceptions* E in the aggregated model.
2. For each *Exception* E_i, L is a set of *Connections* C with the following constraints:
   (a) C_i is retrieved from a firewall different that the one containing E_i
   (b) C_i conditions , are subset (or equal) of E_i conditions.
   If the obtained set of *Connections* L is not empty:
   - Mark E_i as local.
   - For each C_i in L, mark C_i as local if it has not been already marked.

This will be also useful when extracting a representation of the network topology covered by the firewalls (see next section).

4   Application Scenarios

Once all the access-control information is aggregated in our final PIM, we are able to use the model in several interesting security application scenarios.

Metrics and Advanced Queries. First of all, having the access-control information of a network represented as a model, enables the reutilization of a plethora of well-known, off-the-shelf MDE tools. Editor generators, model transformation engines, etc. become automatically available. An immediate application would be the use of the well-known OCL query language to calculate interesting metrics on the model and perform some advanced queries on the rules represented in it. In the following example, we query our model (in the example, the context of *self* is the root of our PIM) for the existence of any connection allowing the administrator host (111.222.2.54) to connect to the server (111.222.1.17):

```
Evaluating:
self.connections->exists(e | e.source.ipAddr='111.222.2.54' and e.target.ipAddr
    ='111.222.1.17')
Results:
false
```

Forward Engineering. Our PIM model extracts and abstracts information from working networks. Nevertheless, the PIM is still rich enough to be able to be used as starting point for the regeneration of the configuration files if necessary (e.g. after modifications on the PIM to update the security policy of the network according to the new requirements). In that sense, some existing forward engineering efforts[18,4] that produce firewall configurations from high level representations can be reused.

Visualization of the Topology. Our PIM can also be used to derive the topology of the network, i.e., the arrangement of components and how the information flow through them. For this purpose, a model-driven visualization tool like Portolan[1] can be used. A transformation from our aggregated PIM towards the Portolan Cartography model (Portolan is able to graphically represent any model corresponding to its Cartography metamodel) has been written. This transformation analyzes the global PIM to first, extract the *Firewall* elements and represent them as nodes. Then, represent the other *Network Elements* also as nodes and the local containment of *Zones*. Finally, it extracts the *Connections* and build the links between each *Connection* source *Network Element* to the corresponding *Firewall* element and from the *Firewall* element to the target *Network Element*.

In Figure 4 we show the visualization the tool provided. In the figure, servers (element 111.222.1.17), firewalls, zones and contained elements are easily identifiably as well as the enabled connections between them. If we compare this figure with the figure 1 presented in section 2, we can see that the topology is accurately represented.

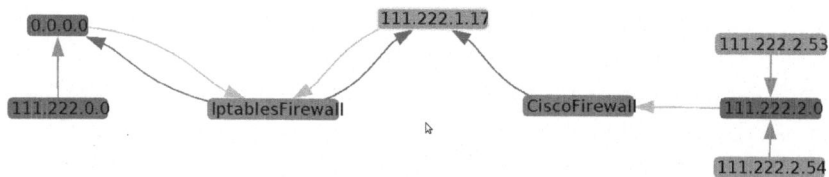

Fig. 4. Extracted network topology

Network PIM to XACML. Our proposed network access-control PIM is a specific representation specially tailored to the network domain. We consider that a translation from our PIM towards a more generic access-control representation will complement our approach by enabling reusing tools and results that work on the general access-control model have produced.

XACML [13] is an OASIS standard for the specification of access-control policies in XML and is ABAC[23] and RBAC[20] (two of the most successful access-control models) capable. Its flexibility to represent multiple policies for

---

[1] http://code.google.com/a/eclipselabs.org/p/portolan/

the same system and the fact of counting with a reference implementation, along with the increasing adoption by industry and academy, makes XACML a good choice for a generic access-control representation. Indeed, some works in the model-driven community already chose XACML as a target language as in [3] and [16].

In the following, we briefly introduce the XACML policy language and the mapping from our PIM.

XACML policies are composed by three main elements *PolicySet*, *Policy* and *Rule*. A *PolicySet* can contain other *PolicySets* or a single *Policy* that is a container of *Rules* (Policy and PolicySet also specify a rule-combining algorithm, in order to solve conflicts between their contained elements). These three elements can specify a *Target* that establishes its applicability, i.e., to which combination of *Subject*, *Resource* and *Action* the *PolicySet*, *Policy* and *Rule* applies. *Subject*, *Resource* and *Action* identifies subjects accessing given resources to perform actions. These elements can hold *Attribute* elements, that represent additional characteristics (e.g., the role of the subject). Optionally, a *Rule* element can hold a *Condition* that represents a boolean condition over a subject resource or action. Upon an access request, these elements are used to get an answer of the type: permit, deny or not applicable.

The translation from our network access-control metamodel to XACML follows the mapping summarized in Table 1. In Listing 1.4 we excerpt the XACML representation of a PIM *Connection*.

Table 1. PIM to XACML Mappings

XACML	PIM Metamodel
PolicySet	A PolicySet containing a Policy is created for each firewall in the PIM
Policy	All the Connections and Exceptions belonging to a given firewall
Rule	A single connection or Exception
Subject	Source NetworkElement address and source port of a given Connection or Exception
Resource	Target NetworkElement address and target port a given Connection or Exception
Action	Not mapped. The action is always the ability of sending a message.
Condition	Protocol field

With this translation, the utilisation of a wide range of tools and research results based in the standard become enabled. Between the more interesting ones, we can reuse the several formalizations of the language as provided by [7,11]. Reusing these formal approaches, operations like automatic policy comparison and change impact analysis can be performed.

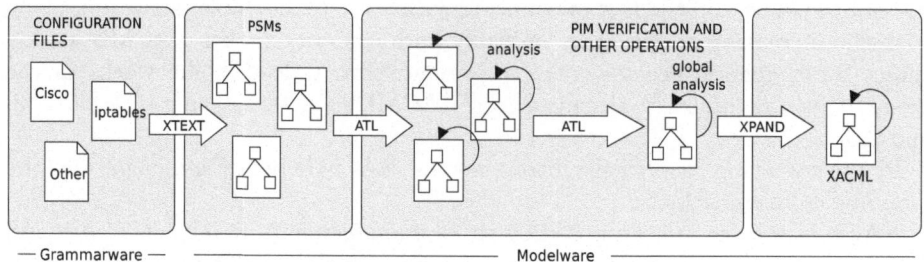

Fig. 5. Extraction approach implementation

Listing 1.4. Firewall rule in XACML

```
<Rule Effect="Deny" RuleId="1">
  <Target>
    <Subjects>
      <Subject>
        <SubjectMatch MatchId="...function:ipAddress-regexp-match">
          <AttributeValue
            DataType="...XMLSchema#string">(111)\.(222)\.(2)\.([0-9][0-9]?[0-9]?)
          </AttributeValue>
          <SubjectAttributeDesignator
            SubjectCategory="...subject-category:access-subject"
            AttributeId="...:subject:subject-id"
            DataType="....data-type:ipAddress"/>
          ...
    <Resources>
      <Resource>
        <ResourceMatch MatchId="...function:ipAddress-regexp-match">
          <AttributeValue
            DataType="...XMLSchema#string">(111)\.(222)\.(1)\.(17)</AttributeValue>
          <ResourceAttributeDesignator AttributeId="...resource:resource-id">
            DataType="...data-type:ipAddress"/>
          ...
  </Target>
  <Condition>
    <SubjectAttributeDesignator AttributeId="protocol"
      DataType="...XMLSchema#string" />
    ...
</Rule>
```

5 Implementation

In order to validate the feasibility of our approach, a prototype tool[2], able to
work with two popular firewall filtering languages *Linux Iptables* and *Cisco PIX*,
has been developed under the Eclipse[2] environment. Figure 5 summarizes the
steps and technological choices we made for the prototype development.

The tool implements the first step of our approach (the injection process) with
Xtext [3], an Eclipse plugin for building domain specific languages. As an input
to this tool we have written simple yet usable grammars for the two languages
supported by our tool. By providing these two grammars the Xtext tool creates
for us the corresponding metamodels depicted in Figures 6 and 7 along with the
parser and the injector needed to get models out of the configurations files.

The transformations from the PSMs to the PIM along with the detection of
anomalies have been written using the model transformation language ATL[12],

---

[2] http://www.eclipse.org/
[3] http://www.eclipse.org/Xtext/

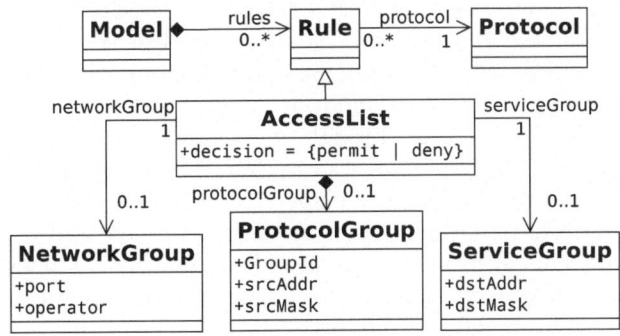

Fig. 6. Cisco Metamodel excerpt

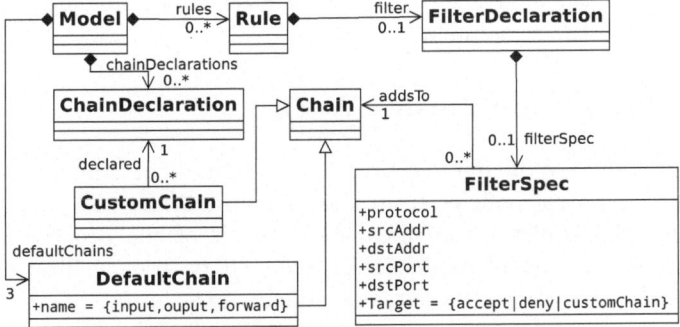

Fig. 7. Iptables Metamodel excerpt

both in its normal and in-place (for model refining[21]) modes. Same for the PIM's aggregation process. The visualization of the topology relies on Portolan and the translation from our PIM to XACML policies has been developed using Xpand[4], a model-to-text tool.

6 Related Work

Several other works tackle the problem of extracting access control policies from network configurations but they either are limited to analyzing one single firewall component or focus on a specific analysis task and thus they do not generate a usable representation of the firewall/s under analysis. Moreover, these latter works require as an additional input the network topology, instead we are able to calculate it as part of the process.

More specifically, [22] proposes a technique that aims to infer the higher-level security policy rules from the rules on firewalls by extracting classes (types) of

---

[4] http://wiki.eclipse.org/Xpand

services, hosts and protocols. However, it takes only one firewall into account for the process. In [15] and [17] a method and tool to discover and test a network security policy is proposed. The configuration files along with the description of the network topology are used to build an internal representation of the policy that can be verified by the user through queries in ad-hoc languages. Unfortunately, no explicit model of the recovered security policy is provided and thus, the extracted policy can not be globally inspected without learning complex query languages. [5] proposes a bi-directional method to enforce and reverse engineer firewall configurations. It promotes the use of an intermediate policy representation but does not provide a model for such representation nor specific processes to perform the enforcement and the discovery tasks.

Some other works provide a metamodel for representing firewall configurations like [18], [24] and [6]. Nevertheless, a reverse engineering process to populate those models from existing configuration files is not provided, and in our opinion, the abstraction of the models level is still too close to the implementation details, therefore limiting their usability.

7   Conclusions and Future Work

We have presented a model-driven reverse engineering approach to extract network access-control policies from the network information included in the network's firewall configuration files. As a result of the process, a platform-independent access control model is created. Apart from facilitating the comprehension and analysis of the network policies to security experts, this model can also be the basis for further applications like the visualization of the (implicit) network topology or the generation of an equivalent XACML-like model ready to be processed by specialized security reasoning tools.

As a future work we plan to extend our approach to take into account other network elements that may take part in the enforcement of a security policy like routers, VPN tunnels and intrusion detection systems. We consider also that giving precise semantics to the proposed metamodel concepts constitutes a necessary next step. Moreover, given that the own XACML defines extensibility mechanisms for this standard, we believe it would be useful to work on a network-specific extension that facilitates the representation and analysis of this kind of firewall access-control policies. Finally, we plan to apply our approach on real network configurations to test the scalability of the approach.

References

1. Building secure software: how to avoid security problems the right way. Addison-Wesley Longman Publishing Co., Inc., Boston (2002)
2. Firewall Reverse Engineering project web site (2013), http://www.emn.fr/z-info/atlanmod/index.php/Firewall_Reverse_Engineering
3. Alam, M., Hafner, M., Breu, R.: Constraint based role based access control in the sectet-framework: A model-driven approach. J. Comput. Secur. 16(2), 223–260 (2008)

4. Bartal, Y., Mayer, A., Nissim, K., Wool, A.: Firmato: A novel firewall management toolkit. ACM Trans. Comput. Syst. 22(4), 381–420 (2004)

5. Bishop, M., Peisert, S.: Your security policy is what?? Technical report (2006)

6. Brucker, A.D., Brügger, L., Kearney, P., Wolff, B.: Verified firewall policy transformations for test-case generation. In: Third International Conference on Software Testing, Verification, and Validation (ICST), pp. 345–354. IEEE Computer Society, Los Alamitos (2010)

7. Fisler, K., Krishnamurthi, S., Meyerovich, L.A., Tschantz, M.C.: Verification and change-impact analysis of access-control policies. In: Proceedings of the 27th International Conference on Software Engineering, ICSE 2005, pp. 196–205. ACM, New York (2005)

8. Garcia-Alfaro, J., Boulahia-Cuppens, N., Cuppens, F.: Complete analysis of configuration rules to guarantee reliable network security policies. Int. J. Inf. Secur. 7(2), 103–122 (2008)

9. Garcia-Alfaro, J., Cuppens, F., Cuppens-Boulahia, N.: Aggregating and deploying network access control policies, pp. 532–542. IEEE Computer Society, Los Alamitos (2007)

10. Garcia-Alfaro, J., Cuppens, F., Cuppens-Boulahia, N.: Management of exceptions on access control policies. In: Venter, H., Eloff, M., Labuschagne, L., Eloff, J., von Solms, R. (eds.) SEC. IFIP, vol. 232, pp. 97–108. Springer, Boston (2007)

11. Hughes, G., Bultan, T.: Automated verification of access control policies using a sat solver. Int. J. Softw. Tools Technol. Transf. 10(6), 503–520 (2008)

12. Jouault, F., Kurtev, I.: Transforming models with ATL. In: Bruel, J.-M. (ed.) MoDELS 2005. LNCS, vol. 3844, pp. 128–138. Springer, Heidelberg (2006)

13. Lockhart, H., Parducci, B., Anderson, A.: OASIS XACML TC (2013)

14. Martínez, S., Cabot, J., Garcia-Alfaro, J., Cuppens, F., Cuppens-Boulahia, N.: A model-driven approach for the extraction of network access-control policies. In: Proceedings of the Workshop on Model-Driven Security, MDsec 2012, pp. 5:1–5:6. ACM (2012)

15. Mayer, A., Wool, A., Ziskind, E.: Fang: A firewall analysis engine. In: Proceedings of the 2000 IEEE Symposium on Security and Privacy, SP 2000, pp. 177–187. IEEE Computer Society, Washington, DC (2000)

16. Mouelhi, T., Fleurey, F., Baudry, B., Le Traon, Y.: A model-based framework for security policy specification, deployment and testing. In: Czarnecki, K., Ober, I., Bruel, J.-M., Uhl, A., Völter, M. (eds.) MODELS 2008. LNCS, vol. 5301, pp. 537–552. Springer, Heidelberg (2008)

17. Nelson, T., Barratt, C., Dougherty, D.J., Fisler, K., Krishnamurthi, S.: The margrave tool for firewall analysis. In: Proceedings of the 24th International Conference on Large Installation System Administration, LISA 2010, pp. 1–8. USENIX Association, Berkeley (2010)

18. Pozo, S., Gasca, R.M., Reina-Quintero, A.M., Varela-Vaca, A.J.: Confiddent: A model-driven consistent and non-redundant layer-3 firewall acl design, development and maintenance framework. Journal of Systems and Software 85(2), 425–457 (2012)

19. Russell, R.: Linux 2.4 packet filtering howto (2002), http://www.netfilter.org/documentation/HOWTO/packet-filtering-HOWTO.html

20. Sandhu, R., Ferraiolo, D., Kuhn, R.: The nist model for role-based access control: towards a unified standard. In: Proceedings of the Fifth ACM Workshop on Role-based Access Control, RBAC 2000, pp. 47–63. ACM, New York (2000)

21. Tisi, M., Martínez, S., Jouault, F., Cabot, J.: Refining Models with Rule-based Model Transformations. Rapport de recherche RR-7582, INRIA (2011)
22. Tongaonkar, A., Inamdar, N., Sekar, R.: Inferring higher level policies from firewall rules. In: Proceedings of the 21st Conference on Large Installation System Administration Conference, LISA 2007. LISA 2007, pp. 2:1–2:10. USENIX Association, Berkeley (2007)
23. Yuan, E., Tong, J.: Attributed based access control (abac) for web services. In: Proceedings of the IEEE International Conference on Web Services, ICWS 2005, pp. 561–569. IEEE Computer Society, Washington, DC (2005)
24. Zaliva, V.: Platform-independent firewall policy representation. CoRR, abs/0805.1886 (2008)

SafetyMet: A Metamodel for Safety Standards

Jose Luis de la Vara and Rajwinder Kaur Panesar-Walawege

Certus Centre for Software V&V, Simula Research Laboratory
P.O. Box 134, 1325 Lysaker, Norway
{jdelavara,rpanesar}@simula.no

Abstract. In domains such as automotive, avionics, and railway, critical systems must comply with safety standards to allow their operation in a given context. Safety compliance can be an extremely demanding activity as practitioners have to show fulfilment of the safety criteria specified in the standards and thus that a system can be deemed safe. This is usually both costly and time consuming, and becomes even more challenging when, for instance, a system changes or aims to be reused in another project or domain. This paper presents SafetyMet, a metamodel for safety standards targeted at facilitating safety compliance. The metamodel consists of entities and relationships that abstract concepts common to different safety standards from different domains. Its use can help practitioners to show how they have followed the recommendations of a standard, and particularly in evolutionary or cross-domain scenarios. We discuss the benefits of the use of the metamodel, its limitations, and open issues in order to clearly present the aspects of safety compliance that are facilitated and those that are not addressed.

Keywords: safety standard, metamodel, safety compliance, safety assurance, safety certification, SafetyMet, OPENCOSS.

1   Introduction

Safety-critical systems are those whose failure can cause injury or death to people or harm to the environment in which they operate. These systems are subject to rigorous safety assurance and assessment processes, which are usually based on some safety standards upon which the system is to be certified [34]. System suppliers have to show that a system (and/or its lifecycle) has fulfilled the requirements of the safety standard so that the system can be deemed safe for operation in a given context.

Examples of safety standards include IEC61508 [24] for systems that combine electrical, electronic, and programmable electronic systems, DO-178C [45] for the avionics domain, the CENELEC standards (e.g., EN50128 [8]) for the railway domain, and ISO26262 [26] for the automotive industry. Companies can also adopt recommended practices (e.g., [14]) or defined company-specific practices as a part of their own, internal safety procedures.

Demonstration of safety compliance is usually costly and time-consuming [16], and can be very challenging [33, 34]. Firstly, system suppliers have to collect evidence of compliance such as hazard specifications, test results, and activity records. This can be hindered because of difficulties in understanding safety

A. Moreira et al. (Eds.): MODELS 2013, LNCS 8107, pp. 69–86, 2013.

standards, in determining the evidence, or in gaining confidence in evidence adequacy. Secondly, practitioners usually have to manage large quantities of evidence and structure it to show how a system complies with a standard. If the evidence is not structured properly, its sheer volume and complexity can jeopardize safety certification.

Demonstration of compliance with safety standards becomes even more difficult when a system evolves [13]. For example, recertification of a system requires a completely new set of evidence since changes to the system will have invalidated previously existing evidence. There can be re-use of evidence only if it is possible to accurately assess how the changes have impacted the existing evidence. Consequently, industry needs approaches that enable evidence reuse and support evidence change impact analysis.

If aiming to reuse an already-compliant system in another domain, practitioners have to demonstrate compliance with other standards. This is currently an important concern in industry [4]. Although correspondence between regulations has been addressed in other fields (e.g., [19]), the situation in safety compliance is more complex. No perfect match usually exists between safety standards, and system suppliers usually have their own interpretations and thus usage of a standard. As a result, compliance with a new standard is never straightforward, and means to facilitate this activity are necessary.

All the challenges above can lead to certification risks [3]. In other words, a system supplier might not be able to develop a safe system, show system safety, or make a third party gain confidence in system safety.

To tackle these issues we propose the use of model-based technologies. Several proponents of these technologies have argued their suitability for mitigating the complexity of and thus facilitating safety compliance (e.g., [41]). However, the current model-based approaches for safety compliance have been targeted at specific standards or domains, thus they do not provide generic solutions that can be applied in contexts of cross-domain use or where multiple standards are required in the same domain.

This paper aims to fill this gap by presenting SafetyMet, a metamodel for safety standards. This metamodel aims to support practitioners when having to deal with safety compliance, especially in situations in which a system evolves or must comply with several standards. The metamodel is part of our contribution to OPENCOSS (http://www.opencoss-project.eu/), a European research project whose goal is to devise a common certification framework for the automotive, avionics, and railway domains. The metamodel has been developed in close collaboration with industry.

SafetyMet is a generic metamodel that includes concepts and relationships common to different safety standards and to different domains. It addresses safety compliance from several perspectives, explicitly dealing with information related to the process, data, and objectives that are necessary to demonstrate compliance. The metamodel is a part of an overall approach for model-based safety compliance that encompasses both standard-specific and project-specific aspects.

Apart from supporting demonstration of safety compliance in general, use of the metamodel can help practitioners to structure and reuse evidence, assess its adequacy, and deal with evidence traceability and change. Nevertheless, some compliance needs such as human aspects are out of the scope of SafetyMet and its application.

The rest of the paper is organised as follows. Section 2 introduces the background of the paper. Section 3 presents SafetyMet, whereas Section 4 discusses its benefits and limitations. Finally, Section 5 summarises our conclusions and future work.

2   Background

This section introduces the OPENCOSS project and reviews related work.

2.1   OPENCOSS

OPENCOSS is a large-scale FP7 European project that aims to (1) devise a common certification framework that spans different vertical markets for railway, avionics, and automotive industries, and (2) establish an open-source safety certification infrastructure. The ultimate goal of the project is to bring about substantial reductions in recurring safety certification costs and at the same time reduce certification risks through the introduction of more systematic safety assurance practices. The project deals with: (1) creation of a common certification conceptual framework; (2) compositional certification; (3) evolutionary chain of evidence; (4) transparent certification process, and; (5) compliance-aware development process.

SafetyMet can be regarded as a part of the common certification framework. More details about the framework and the role and usage of SafetyMet are presented below. It must also be mentioned that this paper presents our current vision of the framework, thus it might not reflect the final vision of the entire OPENCOSS consortium.

2.2   Related Work

Related work can be divided into three main streams: models for compliance or assurance in general, models for safety assurance, and models for safety compliance. When mentioning models in this section, we refer to both models and metamodels, understood as sets of concepts and the relationships between them, independently of the graphical or textual languages used for their representation.

Models for compliance or assurance in general have been proposed in order to facilitate demonstration of fulfilment or alignment with different requirements or criteria. This topic has received great attention in the requirements engineering and business process management communities. Systematic reviews on compliance from a requirements engineering and business process perspective can be found in [17, 48].

The requirements engineering community has provided insights into issues such as regulatory compliance in practice [36], correspondence between regulations [19], regulation formalization [47], argumentation [25], and component selection [35]. Examples of aspects related to business process compliance that have been addressed are compliance patterns [43], compliance management [1], and compliance with reference models [28], context [12], contracts [20], and control objectives [46].

Most of the models proposed (e.g., [15, 18]) are generic. An especially relevant example is the just published first version of SACM (Structure Assurance Case

Metamodel; [39]). It is an OMG specification and includes an argumentation and an evidence metamodel. Other models have been developed for compliance with non-safety-specific standards (e.g., CMMI [32]).

Apart from not targeting system evolution, the main weaknesses of these models is that they do not support safety standards-specific needs such as having to show alignment with the many varied criteria of the standards (activities, artefacts, techniques, requirements, criticality levels, etc.).

Models for safety assurance can be regarded as a refinement of the models presented above. They aim at supporting analysis of safety-related system aspects such as traceability between requirements and design [37], process assurance [23], or dependability [5]. Broader traceability models for safety-critical systems can also be found in the literature (e.g., [9, 27, 52]). In the context of graphical modelling of safety argumentation, metamodels for GSN (Goal Structuring Notation) (e.g., [11]) and a model of evidence for safety cases [51] have been proposed.

In general, these models can be regarded as closer to the domain of project-specific aspects than to the domain of safety standards. For example, they do not include means to explicitly model and analyse the requirements of a safety standard and thus to show how they have been fulfilled by means of the execution of some activity or the creation of some artefact.

During the past few years, several **models for safety compliance** have been presented in order to support demonstration of fulfilment of the criteria of a safety standard. This has been usually presented in the scope of some specific standard. Examples of safety standards for which models have been proposed include ISO26262 [29], IEC61508 [30, 42], and DO-178B [54]. A model that combines ISO26262 and SPICE can be found in [2]. In some cases, these models have focused in specific parts of the standards such as quality-related aspects [31], faults [49], and testing [50]. These models are not generic but standard-specific, thus they cannot be directly applied when, for instance, aiming at demonstrating compliance with another standard. These models can be regarded as SafetyMet instances.

Other related works are those that have proposed models for impact analysis (e.g., [7]) or for system evolution (e.g., [53]). However, they have not explicitly addressed how these aspects are related to safety compliance.

In summary, since the models reviewed have purposes different to SafetyMet, they do not fit its needs. In this sense, SafetyMet aims to extend the state art by providing a metamodel that (1) supports safety compliance in a generic way that can be adapted to different regulatory contexts, and (2) facilitates evidence change management and cross-standard/domain compliance. Consequently, the metamodel aims to generalize and widen the scope of past proposals (e.g., [42]).

3   Metamodel for Safety Standards

This section introduces SafetyMet, the metamodel that we propose for safety compliance. The metamodel includes a number of key relationships that exist between the different pieces of information that are managed for safety compliance. Showing these relationships is a prerequisite to demonstrating compliance [40].

For the purpose of compliance, there are two main sources of information: the standard to be complied with and the product for which compliance is sought. Related to the product we have information regarding the process used in its construction, the evidence that contributes to gaining confidence in system safety, and the argumentation to justify system safety. Argumentation can be presented implicitly (e.g., [42]) or explicitly (e.g., [21]). These three aspects must match the process, data, and objectives prescribed by the safety standard. In addition, it is necessary to understand the vocabulary (i.e., terms) used in the standard and usually map it to the vocabulary that exists in the domain in which the product is being developed.

Based on these relationships and the need to abstract the relevant information from the vast amount of data that is created during system lifecycle, we advocate for the creation of models that represent both the compliance and product-specific information. The models must also be structured in a specific manner in order to perform useful analyses with them. To this end, we propose the use of metamodels to which all the models must conform [6].

The following subsections present more details about the context and purpose of SafetyMet, its concepts and relationships, and how it has been validated.

3.1   Scope and Purpose

In general, safety compliance is not based on just one standard. Minimally there are at least the safety standard mandated by a particular industry and then the internal working procedures of the specific system supplier. These procedures are a mix of internal best practices and geared towards aiding compliance to the applicable safety standard. In other cases a system is to be certified to multiple standards used in different parts of the world, and finally there may be the case of using components (or systems) that have been certified in one domain in another. Hence a component certified to one standard may have to be re-certified to another. There exist also other specific needs when a system evolves [13], such as managing evidence change impact. We propose SafetyMet in order to aid compliance in these various scenarios.

The metamodel captures the abstract notions that can be used to describe the information that needs to be collected to show compliance to safety standards and manage system change. Specifically, SafetyMet corresponds to a unified metamodel that will aid in the creation of models for compliance.

SafetyMet is an element of a set of metamodels and corresponds to a metamodel for safety standards (Fig. 1). The models resulting from these metamodels will capture the information necessary for showing compliance in specific projects (safety compliance models). The rationale for developing such models is to create a consistent interpretation of the standard being used and link this to the product being certified. The need for a consistent interpretation stems from the fact that safety standards are textual documents amenable to subjective interpretation. By creating a model we do not avoid subjectivity but aid in a shared, consistent interpretation.

Regarding the actual product being certified, the metamodels will also include the concepts and relationships necessary for modelling and managing project-specific information. This information needs to be recorded regardless of the safety standards being followed (e.g., confidence in evidence). There are metamodels for modelling:

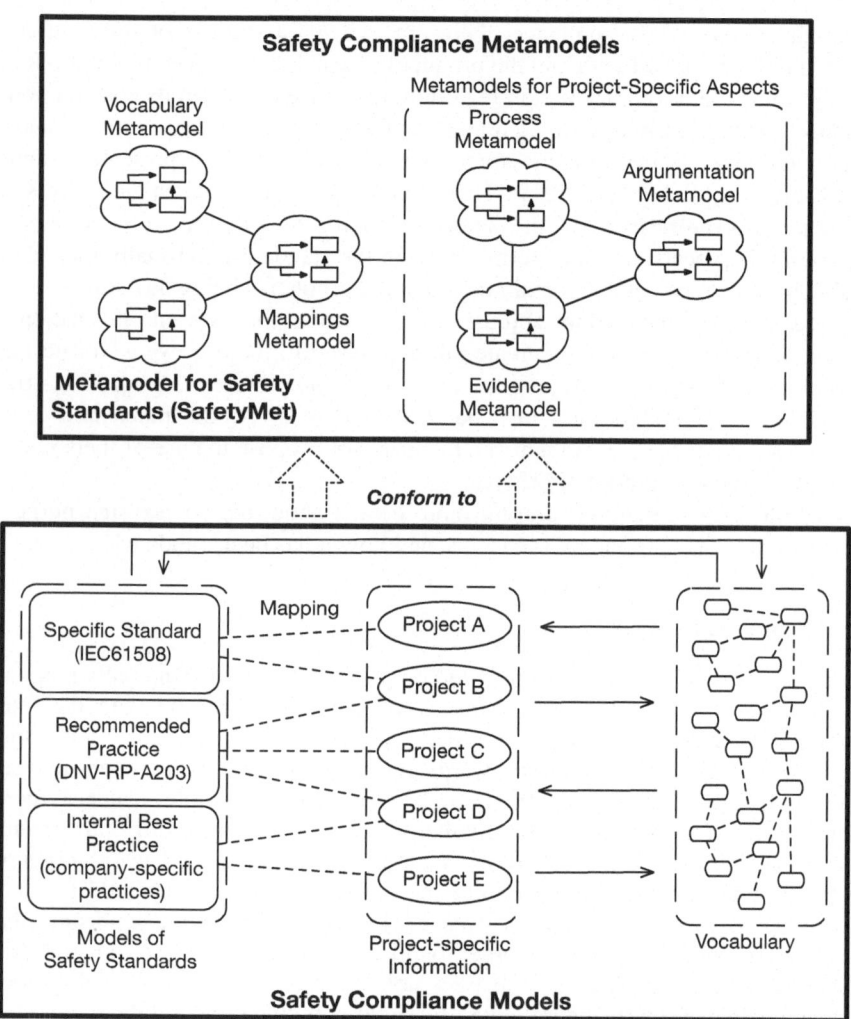

Fig. 1. Overall approach for safety compliance

- The actual process used to create a product, which is important as assurance artefacts are produced as a result of process activities and it must be shown that the activities materialise the process mandated by safety standards;
- The argumentation that will be used to justify key safety-related decisions taken during the project and must be in line with the objectives of safety standards, and;
- The specific information that needs to be kept about the concrete artefacts that will be used as evidence of compliance and that thus must materialise those types of artefacts prescribed by safety standards.

Two other metamodels are proposed, which may be considered the 'glue' that connects the others. The vocabulary metamodel is a means to define and record the terms and concepts used to characterize reusable assets such as evidence, argumentation, and process assets. When multiple standards are used for compliance purposes (e.g., certification of a system for another domain), mappings will be created between the vocabulary terms of one standard and those of another. The mappings will then allow engineers to use this information in order to make informed decisions about the appropriateness and implications of reusing a given asset that was created for compliance to a particular safety standard in the context of another standard.

Finally, there is a metamodel for mappings. We have already mentioned mappings in the context of the vocabulary used in one standard to the vocabulary used in another standard. Another use of mappings will be for associating the assurance information gathered during a project to the safety criteria of a standard. This is a means of showing compliance to the standard. We discuss the mappings further when describing the actual models created using the metamodels proposed. Mappings between models of safety standards can also exist.

It must be noted that although we refer to them as a set of metamodels, a single metamodel aimed at supporting several aspects of safety compliance will be created. Relationships will exist between the concepts of the metamodels, such as the evidence (evidence metamodel) used for argumentation (argumentation metamodel) or the mapping (mappings metamodels) of project artefacts (evidence metamodel) to the types of artefacts of some safety standards (metamodel for safety standards).

The metamodels will be used to create the actual models that will be used for showing compliance. This is depicted in the bottom part of Fig. 1. The metamodel for safety standards is used to create the models of the relevant safety standards and the project-specific models are created using the process, argumentation, and evidence metamodels. As these models are being created, the vocabulary metamodel is used to capture the relevant vocabulary terms, such as the vocabulary used in the standards as well as that used in the project.

Mappings from the project assets to the assets mandated by the standard need to be created in order to demonstrate compliance. Doing so, we can show clearly how a particular asset created during a project complies with a particular standard. When a project needs to comply with multiple standards, then the vocabulary can aid in mapping the assurance assets created in the project for compliance with one standard to those required by another standard. In this case not all assets may be reusable, some new assets may need to be created, and some assets might have to be modified [13].

This overall approach for safety compliance aims to enable reuse of certification assets. As further discussed below, the models of safety standards and the vocabulary will be used from one project to another and will be valuable assurance assets in a company. The use of mapping provides a clear traceable link between the assets of a project and the standard to be complied with. This is a link very difficult to show and maintain using textual documents but can be more easily managed using models.

3.2   SafetyMet

The metamodel is shown in Fig. 2 in the form of an Ecore diagram [22]. We have modelled it this way in order to quickly generate model editors for validation purposes. The metaclasses of which SafetyMet consists are defined as follows.

- *Safety Standard* is used to hold information about the safety regulation(s) modelled.
- *Criticality Level* corresponds to the categories of criticality that a safety standard defines and that indicate the relative level of risk reduction being provided (e.g., *SIL 1, 2, 3,* and *4* in IEC61508).
- *Applicability Level* represents the categories of applicability that a safety standard defines (e.g., a given technique is *mandated* in EN50128).
- *Activity Type* is targeted at modelling the activities (i.e., the units of behaviour [42]) that a safety standard defines for system lifecycle and must be executed to demonstrate compliance. An activity type can be decomposed in others.
- *Role* represents the types of agents [42] that execute activity types, either explicitly defined in a safety standard or required to be defined by the supplier.
- *Artefact Type* represents types of units of data that a safety standard prescribes to be created and maintained during system lifecycle. Artefact types are materialised in projects by means of concrete artefacts [38]. This means that these artefacts have the same or a similar structure (syntax) and/or purpose (semantics) [9]. Artefact types can be required or produced by activity types, and some can determine the criticality level in a project (e.g., risks [14]).
- *Artefact Type Property* is used to model the characteristics [38] of an artefact type.
- *Artefact Relationship Type* aims to model the existence of a relationship between two artefact types (source and target of the artefact type relationship) [38, 44]. An artefact relationship type is materialised by relating two artefacts of a project, and characterizes those artefact relationships that have the same or similar structure (syntax) and/or purpose (semantics) [9]. Such a relationship can be recorded in an artefact if the relationship itself is used as evidence (e.g., DO-178C explicitly requests the provision of traceability information). An artefact type relationship can be created as a result of executing some activity type.
- *Technique* corresponds to specific ways to create an artefact type and that can be utilised in some activity type. Specific techniques are defined in many standards.
- *Requirement* represents the criteria (e.g., objectives) that a safety standard defines (or prescribes) to comply with it. Requirements are fulfilled by executing activity types, and are the aim of artefact types (i.e., the reason why they are necessary).
- *Requirement Decomposition* corresponds to the contribution of several requirements to the fulfilment of another requirement.
- *Criticality Applicability* represents the assignation, in a safety standard, of an applicability level for a given criticality level to its requirements or techniques.

Two enumerations have also been included, one for specifying how a requirement can be decomposed (*Decomposition Type*) and another for specifying the *Change Effect* of the target of an artefact type relationship on the source.

Although at first sight some relationships might seem redundant (e.g., *Activity Type* utilizes *Technique* and *Artefact Type* results from *Technique*), they all are necessary in order to allow different and alternative ways to model a safety standard. For example, an activity type might produce several artefact types, and several activity types might produce an artefact type. Therefore, it might be necessary to link *Technique* with both *Activity Type* and *Artefact Type* in order to be able to determine what technique is used in a specific activity type to produce a given artefact type.

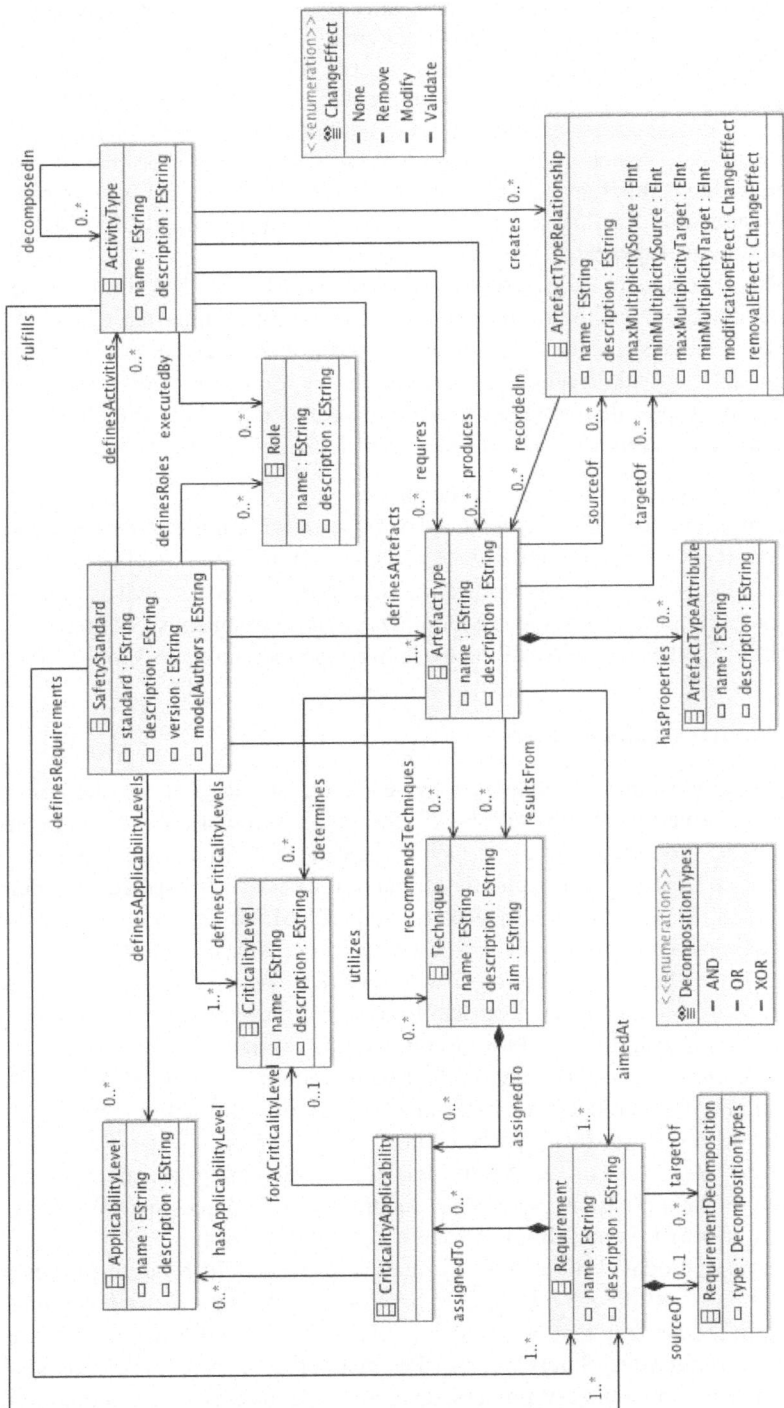

Fig. 2. Metamodel for safety standards

Further details about the classes, their attributes, their relationships, and their constraints are not provided due to page limitations.

As can be noted, SafetyMet includes concepts related to process (e.g., *Activity Type*), data (e.g., *Artefact Type*), and objectives (e.g., *Requirement*) for safety compliance. In essence, the metamodel is targeted at modelling those elements of a safety standard with which correspondence must be shown in a project in order to demonstrate safety compliance. These elements are also necessary to compare and map safety standards. In this sense, it is very important to know the objectives of activity and artefact types when comparing standards.

SafetyMet also aims to be generic and flexible, in order to allow different ways to model a standard. For example, the metamodel does not assume the existence of a given number of levels (i.e., decompositions) of requirements and activities types, and provides modellers with freedom to determine the granularity of artefact types. Nonetheless, and especially for the latter aspect, we plan to provide guidelines.

Some aspects of SafetyMet to be further studied and developed in the future are:

- Specification of more attributes for the classes
- Further support for change impact analysis by specifying more change effects
- Provision of a set relationships between types of artefacts (i.e., inclusion of classes that specialise *ArtefactTypeRelationship*, as proposed in works such as [44])
- Inclusion of more links between requirements and between activity types
  Decisions upon these aspects will be made once the metamodel is further validated.

3.3   Preliminary Validation

We have initially validated SafetyMet by analysing its support for the necessary compliance information of several specific software safety standards and thus by modelling them. More concretely, we have validated SafetyMet with: DO-178C [45] (although not specifically and explicitly targeted at safety, it is used for this purpose [33]); EN50128 [8]; ISO26262 [26] (Part 6), and; IEC61508 [24] (Part 3). This set of standards corresponds to both objective-based and process-based safety standards.

In Table 1 we show examples of how SafetyMet classes correspond to specific information from the standards. More details and examples are not shown due to page limitations. Although all the standards do not include explicit information about some elements (e.g., *Role*), this information is usually required. For other concepts, the standards might not explicitly include such pieces of information, but it can be specified as a result of their interpretation. For example, DO-178C objectives correspond to *Requirement* in SafetyMet, and their analysis can lead to the specification of other requirements that decompose the objectives. We have not included this information in Table 1 to keep it as small as possible.

We have also validated SafetyMet by analysing if it could be used to create the models for safety compliance reviewed in Section 2.2. We have determined that it is possible, despite the fact that no model includes all the information that can be specified with SafetyMet. SafetyMet can be regarded as a metamodel for all these models, addressing modelling of process, data, and objectives for safety compliance.

Table 1. Examples of SafetyMet elements from several safety standards

SafetyMet Element	Safety Standard			
	DO-178C	EN50128	ISO26262	IEC61508
Criticality Level	Software Level A, B, C, D, E	SIL 0,1, 2, 3, 4	ASIL A, B, C, D	SIL 1, 2, 3, 4
Applicability Level	Satisfied, Satisfied With independence	M, HR, R, NR, -	+, ++, o	R, HR, NR, -
Activity Type	Software Development Processes	Component Design	Software Unit Design and Implementation	Software Design and Development
Role	(Specified by the supplier)	Designer	Designer	(Specified by the supplier)
Artefact Type	Input: Software Requirements Data; Output: Design Description	Input: Software Design Specification; Output: Software Component Design Specification	Input: Softw. Architectural Design Specification; Output: Software Unit Design Specification	Input: Softw. Architecture Design Description; Output: Software System Design Specification
Artefact Type Property	Approval Status	Author	Version	Date of Revision
Artefact Type Relationship	Design Description *satisfies* Software Requirements Data	Software Component Design Specification *links to* Software Component Test Specification	Software Unit Design Specification *links to* Software Requirements and *specifies* Software Unit Implementation	Software System Design Specification *derived from* Softw. Architecture Design and Hardware Architecture Design Descriptions
Technique	(Specified by the supplier)	Modelling	Semi-formal notations	Semi-formal methods
Requirement	(A-4.8) Software architecture is compatible with high-level requirements.	(7.4.4.1) For each component, a Software Component Design Specification shall be written, under the responsibility of the Designer, on the basis of the Software Design Specification.	(8.4.3) The specification of the software units shall describe the functional behaviour and the internal design to the level of detail necessary for their implementation.	(7.4.5.3) The software should be produced to achieve modularity, testability, and the capacity for safe modification.
Criticality Applicability	Software Level A, Satisfied with Independence	SIL 2, HR	ASIL D, ++	SIL.2, HR

An instance of SafetyMet must be regarded as an interpretation of how a project can comply with a safety standard and of how evidence traceability and change will be managed. For the latter two aspects, this is the reason why, for instance, Artefact Type Relationship has attributes related to multiplicity and change effect.

4   Discussion

In this section we discuss the benefits, limitations, and open issues of the application of SafetyMet.

4.1   Application and Benefits of SafetyMet

Several benefits of SafetyMet have been outlined throughout the previous sections, such as the creation of a shared, common, and consistent interpretation of safety standards. We now present further details about the most novel and salient benefits, which come from three usage aspects of the safety compliance metamodels in general and of SafetyMet in particular: the mapping between safety standard models and project information, the reuse of safety standards models, and the relationship with the vocabulary. Other benefits of applying model-driven engineering for safety compliance such as the generation of electronic evidence repositories or the provisions of support for compliance planning have been discussed in [41]. For compliance with several standards, one model for all the standards or one model for each standard can be created, and thus associated to a project.

4.1.1 Mapping between Safety Standard Models and Project Information
Fig. 3 shows how SafetyMet elements (bottom part of the figure) can be mapped to elements of project-specific metamodels (top part). In this example, *ArtefactType* is mapped to *Artefact*.

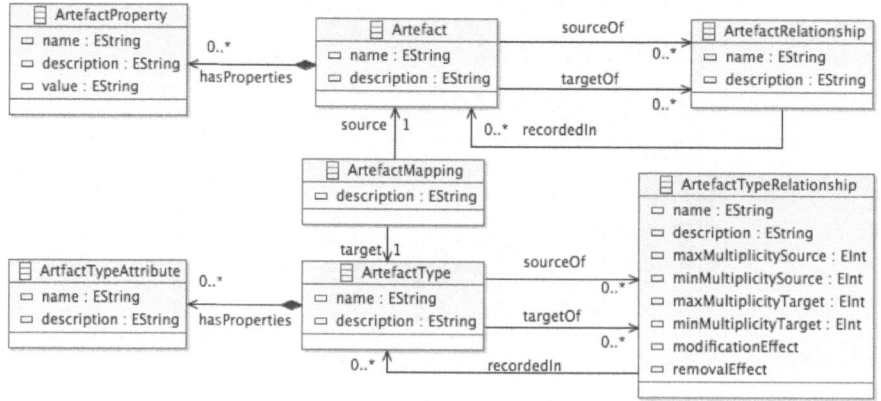

Fig. 3. Example of mapping with SafetyMet

The possibility of establishing this mapping between these two elements provides a specific way of structuring the artefacts of a project according to how a safety standard requires them. At the same time, this allows identification of missing artefacts or artefact relationships. For example, if two artefact types are related in a safety standard model and it is specified that the artefact type relationship must exist for one of the artefacts types, it may be possible to detect that some artefact relationship is missing in a project.

In summary, a safety standard model provides what is usually referred to in the literature as conceptual schema [38] or traceability information model [10]. This can help practitioners to know if, for instance and in relation to the artefacts of a project, the set of artefacts is complete and consistent, thus allowing safety compliance according to a given safety standard model.

Another benefit from this usage is evidence reuse between projects. Once an artefact has been mapped to an artefact type, such a mapping and thus the use of the artefact as evidence of compliance with the corresponding safety standard can be reused. Finally, evidence change impact analysis can also be facilitated. By specifying change-related information in artefact type relationships, such information can be used to analyse change impact in the related artefacts (i.e., evidence).

4.1.2 Reuse of Safety Standards Models

Although project-specific information usually varies among projects, safety standard models can be reused in several projects. Therefore, all the benefits indicated in the previous section can apply to any project targeted at compliance with a given safety standard (i.e., its model). An existing safety standard model could also be used as the source for creating another model, thus reducing the effort for this task.

Furthermore, if mappings are specified between safety standards and thus between their models, it can be possible to determine how project assets mapped to a given safety standard model correspond to the elements of another safety standard model.

4.1.3 Relationship with the Vocabulary

In relation to the vocabulary, it is possible to both store information (i.e., terms) from a safety standard model in the vocabulary and also name the elements of a safety standard model according to the information stored in the vocabulary. Consequently, SafetyMet, in conjunction with the vocabulary, allows term reuse.

Another advantage of this reuse is related to terminology alignment. Once the terms of a safety standard have been stored in the vocabulary, they can be reused. Therefore, it is possible to guarantee that the terminology used in another safety standard model is aligned with that previously stored.

Finally, if mappings between the terminologies of different safety standard exist, and in line with the discussion in the previous section, terminology and the related compliance assets can be reused for compliance with several safety standards.

4.2   Limitations of SafetyMet and Its Application

Despite the argued benefits of SafetyMet, we also acknowledge that it has some limitations. Compliance with safety standards is a very complex activity, thus a metamodel alone cannot address all its needs and possible challenges. In this sense, OPENCOSS aims to mitigate many challenges in safety compliance by proposing new, systematic ways to address system assurance and certification. Nonetheless, some aspects are out of the scope of the project (e.g., analysis of the correctness of a fault tree), and some aspects cannot be fully addressed by means of new technology because of their nature (e.g., aspects in which a human has to make some judgement).

Two main areas have been identified in relation to the limitations of SafetyMet: certification risks and human aspects of safety compliance. Limitations arising from the validation performed so far (e.g., model creation for a limited set of standards) are not discussed but are regarded as aspects to be addressed in future work.

4.2.1   Certification Risks

Application of SafetyMet does not guarantee that certification risks will not arise in a project. In essence, there is no way to completely avoid these risks by means of model-based approaches, despite the fact that they can support and facilitate safety assurance and certification.

Although a project conforms to a safety standard model it is still possible that:

- Someone does not develop a safe system (e.g., because a hazard was missed).
- System safety cannot be demonstrated (e.g., someone might present inconsistent evidence, such test cases linked to requirements that the cases do not test).
- A third party does not agree upon the demonstration of safety compliance (e.g., there are aspects related to argumentation are out of the scope of SafetyMet).

4.2.2   Human Aspects of Safety Compliance

When dealing with safety compliance, many aspects cannot be fully supported by models and tools, automated, or automatically verified. Humans play a major role in safety compliance, and they will always be responsible for deciding upon safety.

Although this limitation cannot be avoided, we think that SafetyMet can help both suppliers and assessors in making informed decisions about system safety. It can help them to find the information that they need to gain confidence in system safety by providing traceability between the criteria of a safety standard and the assets managed in a project. SafetyMet can also support, for instance, verification of the existence of traceability between requirements and test results.

4.3   Open Issues

Last but not least, we have identified the following open issues regarding SafetyMet.

What sort of tool support and user interaction should be created to facilitate the use of SafetyMet? The practitioners who are expected to use SafetyMet (e.g., safety engineers and assurance managers) might not be familiar with the creation of graphical models and hence alternative representations may need to be investigated. Another aspect to study regarding tool support is how to present the large amount of information necessary to model a safety standard.

To what extent can the generation of safety standard models be automated? Given the size of safety standards, creation of the models can be very time-consuming. Therefore, the advantages and suitability of automatically generating the models from the textual standards could be studied.

Is there a correspondence between SafetyMet and the results of the OMG Software Assurance Task Force? The OMG has been working on the development of several specifications related to SafetyMet (e.g., SACM [39]). It is necessary to analyse in depth how SafetyMet relates to them in order to allow their integration.

How can SafetyMet be promoted in industry? A challenge for SafetyMet (and its tool support) is that it needs to be accepted by practitioners as a suitable way to deal with safety compliance. Further validation with industry and probably adjustments according to its needs will be necessary.

Which concepts should be in SafetyMet and which should be in the vocabulary of the overall safety compliance approach? An aspect about which we are not completely sure yet is the extent to which some safety standard-related information should be considered in SafetyMet or regarded as elements of the vocabulary. For example, some safety standards define enumerations for the values of the attributes of its artefact types. This has to be discussed with practitioners.

5   Conclusion

This paper has presented SafetyMet, a metamodel for safety standards. SafetyMet is part of an overall approach for safety compliance in evolutionary situations. The approach distinguishes between safety compliance metamodels and safety compliance models, as well as between safety standard-related information and project-specific information. The correspondence between these two aspects is not always clear, direct, or straightforward, and mappings must be defined.

SafetyMet includes the concepts necessary for enabling the demonstration of safety compliance in general, and in scenarios in which a system evolves or must be certified to different standards in particular. The metamodel aims to be generic and to allow flexibility in its use. It allows modelling of information related to process, data, and objectives for safety compliance. All these aspects can be necessary when having to demonstrate compliance with safety standards, and omission of the information can result in certification risks.

Industry can benefit from the application of SafetyMet by creating models of safety standards, mapping these models to project-specific models, reusing safety standard models, and relating the models and the vocabulary of the overall approach for safety compliance. Nonetheless, practitioners must be aware of the limitations of applying the metamodel. Certification risks cannot be completely avoided, and some decisions on safety compliance have to be made by humans. In this sense, SafetyMet can support and facilitate but not guarantee safety assurance and certification. In addition, there exist several open issues regarding SafetyMet and its use that must be studied.

As future work, we plan to address the open issues discussed above and to continue working on the specification and link of the rest of the safety compliance metamodels. SafetyMet also needs to be further validated, especially beyond the text of safety standards. Data from industrial projects will be used for this purpose.

Acknowledgments. The research leading to this paper has received funding from the FP7 programme under the grant agreement n° 289011 (OPENCOSS) and from the Research Council of Norway under the project Certus-SFI. We also thank the OPENCOSS partners who have provided input and feedback on the metamodel, especially Katrina Attwood, Philippa Conmy, Huascar Espinoza, Tim Kelly, Jerome Lambourg, Sunil Nair, and Alejandra Ruiz.

References

1. Syed Abdullah, N., Sadiq, S., Indulska, M.: A Compliance Management Ontology: Developing Shared Understanding through Models. In: Ralyté, J., Franch, X., Brinkkemper, S., Wrycza, S. (eds.) CAiSE 2012. LNCS, vol. 7328, pp. 429–444. Springer, Heidelberg (2012)
2. Adedjouma, M.: Requirements engineering process according to automotive standards in a model-driven framework. PhD thesis, University of Paris Sud XI (2012)
3. Alexander, R., Kelly, T., Gorry, B.: Safety Lifecycle Activities for Autonomous Systems Development. In: 5th SEAS DTC Technical Conference (2010)
4. Baufreton, P., et al.: Multi-domain comparison of safety standards. In: ERTS 2010 (2010)
5. Bernardi, S., et al.: A dependability profile within MARTE. SoSyM 10(3), 313–336 (2011)
6. Bézivin, J.: On the unification power of models. SoSyM 4(2), 171–188 (2005)
7. Briand, L.C., et al.: Automated impact analysis of UML models. Journal of Systems and Software 79(3), 339–352 (2006)
8. CENELEC: Railway applications - Communications, signalling and processing systems - Software for railway control and protection systems - EN 50128 (2011)
9. Cleland-Huang, J., et al. (eds.): Software and Systems Traceability. Springer (2012)
10. Cleland-Huang, J., Heimdahl, M., Huffman Hayes, J., Lutz, R., Maeder, P.: Trace Queries for Safety Requirements in High Assurance Systems. In: Regnell, B., Damian, D. (eds.) REFSQ 2011. LNCS, vol. 7195, pp. 179–193. Springer, Heidelberg (2012)
11. Denney, E., Pai, G., Pohl, J.: AdvoCATE: An assurance case automation toolset. In: Ortmeier, F., Daniel, P. (eds.) SAFECOMP Workshops 2012. LNCS, vol. 7613, pp. 8–21. Springer, Heidelberg (2012)
12. de la Vara, J.L., Ali, R., Dalpiaz, F., Sánchez, J., Giorgini, P.: COMPRO: A Methodological Approach for Business Process Contextualisation. In: Meersman, R., Dillon, T.S., Herrero, P. (eds.) OTM 2010. LNCS, vol. 6426, pp. 132–149. Springer, Heidelberg (2010)
13. de la Vara, J.L., Nair, S., Verhulst, E., Studzizba, J., Pepek, P., Lambourg, J., Sabetzadeh, M.: Towards a Model-Based Evolutionary Chain of Evidence for Compliance with Safety Standards. In: Ortmeier, F., Daniel, P. (eds.) SAFECOMP Workshops 2012. LNCS, vol. 7613, pp. 64–78. Springer, Heidelberg (2012)
14. DNV: Qualification of New Technology - DNV-RP-A203 (2012)
15. Emmerich, W., et al.: Managing Standards Compliance. IEEE TSE 25(6), 826–851 (1999)

16. Falessi, D., et al.: Planning for safety evidence collection. IEEE Softw. 29(3), 64–70 (2012)
17. Ghanavati, S., Amyot, D., Peyton, L.: A systematic review of goal-oriented requirements management frameworks for business process compliance. In: RELAW 2011 (2011)
18. Giblin, C., et al.: Regulations Expressed As Logical Models (REALM). In: JURIX 2005 (2005)
19. Gordon, D.G., Breaux, T.D.: Reconciling multi-jurisdictional requirements. In: RE 2012 (2012)
20. Governatori, G., Milosevic, Z., Sadiq, S.W.: Compliance checking between business processes and business contracts. In: EDOC 2006 (2006)
21. Graydon, P.J., et al.: Arguing Conformance. IEEE Software 29(3), 50–57 (2012)
22. Gronback, R.C.: Eclipse Modeling Project. Addison-Wesley (2009)
23. Habli, I., Kelly, T.: A Model-Driven Approach to Assuring Process. In: ISSRE 2008 (2008)
24. IEC: Functional safety of electrical / electronic / programmable electronic safety-related systems (IEC 61508) (2005)
25. Ingolfo, S., et al.: Arguing regulatory compliance of software requirements. Data & Knowledge Engineering (accepted paper) (2012)
26. ISO: International Standard Road vehicles — Functional safety - ISO/DIS 26262 (2011)
27. Katta, V., Stålhane, T.: A Conceptual Model of Traceability for Safety Systems. In: CSDM 2011 (2011)
28. Koschmider, A., de la Vara, J.L., Sánchez, J.: Measuring the Progress of Reference Model-Based Business Process Modeling. In: BPSC 2010 (2010)
29. Krammer, M., Armengaud, E., Bourroihh, Q.: Method Library Framework for Safety Standard Compliant Process Tailoring. In: SEAA 2011 (2011)
30. Kuschnerus, D., et al.: A UML Profile for the Development of IEC 61508 Compliant Embedded Software. In: ERTS 2012 (2012)
31. Mayr, A., Plösch, R., Saft, M.: Towards an Operational Safety Standard for Software: Modelling IEC 61508 Part 3. In: ECBS 2011 (2011)
32. Musat, D., Castaño, V., Calvo-Manzano, J.A., Garbajosa, J.: MATURE: A Model Driven bAsed Tool to Automatically Generate a langUage That suppoRts CMMI Process Areas spEcification. In: Riel, A., O'Connor, R., Tichkiewitch, S., Messnarz, R. (eds.) EuroSPI 2010. CCIS, vol. 99, pp. 48–59. Springer, Heidelberg (2010)
33. Nair, S., et al.: The State of the Practice on Evidence Management for Compliance with Safety Standards. Simula Research Laboratory, Technical Report (2013)
34. Nair, S., et al.: Classification, Structuring, and Assessment of Evidence For Safety: A Systematic Literature Review. In: ICST 2013 (2013)
35. Ncube, C., Maiden, N.A.M.: PORE: Procurement-Oriented Requirements Eng. Method for the Component-Based Systems Engineering Development Paradigm. In: CBSE 1999 (1999)
36. Nekvi, M. R.I., Madhavji, N.H., Ferrari, R., Berenbach, B.: Impediments to Requirements-Compliance. In: Regnell, B., Damian, D. (eds.) REFSQ 2011. LNCS, vol. 7195, pp. 30–36. Springer, Heidelberg (2012)
37. Nejati, S., et al.: A SysML-Based Approach to Traceability Management and Design Slicing of Safety Certification. Information & Software Technology 54(6), 569–590 (2012)
38. Olivé, A.: Conceptual Modeling of Information Systems. Springer (2007)
39. OMG: Structured Assurance Case Metamodel (SACM) – Version 1.0 (2013), http://www.omg.org/spec/SACM/ (accessed March 3, 2013)

40. Panesar-Walawege, R.K., et al.: Characterizing the Chain of Evidence for Software Safety Cases: A Conceptual Model Based on the IEC 61508 Standard. In: ICST 2010 (2010)
41. Panesar-Walawege, R.K., et al.: Using Model-Driven Engineering for Managing Safety Evidence: Challenges, Vision and Experience. In: WOSOCER 2011 (2011)
42. Panesar-Walawege, R.K., et al.: Supporting the verification of compliance to safety standards via model-driven engineering. Info. Softw. Technol. (accepted paper, 2013)
43. Papazoglou, M.P.: Making Business Processes Compliant to Standards & Regulations. In: EDOC 2011 (2011)
44. Pohl, K.: Requirements Engineering. Springer (2010)
45. RTCA: DO-178C - Software Considerations in Airborne Systems and Equipment (2012)
46. Sadiq, W., Governatori, G., Namiri, K.: Modeling Control Objectives for Business Process Compliance. In: Alonso, G., Dadam, P., Rosemann, M. (eds.) BPM 2007. LNCS, vol. 4714, pp. 149–164. Springer, Heidelberg (2007)
47. Sannier, N., Baudry, B.: Toward multilevel textual requirements traceability using model-driven engineering and information retrieval. In: MoDRE 2012 (2012)
48. Shamsaei, A., Amyot, D., Pourshahid, A.: A Systematic Review of Compliance Measurement Based on Goals and Indicators. In: Salinesi, C., Pastor, O. (eds.) CAiSE Workshops 2011. LNBIP, vol. 83, pp. 228–237. Springer, Heidelberg (2011)
49. Sojer, D., Knoll, A., Buckl, C.: Synthesis of Diagnostic Techniques Based on an IEC 61508-aware Metamodel. In: SIES 2011 (2011)
50. Stallbaum, H., Rzepka, M.: Toward DO-178B-compliant Test Models. In: MoDeVVa 2010 (2010)
51. Sun, L., Kelly, T.: Elaborating the Concept of Evidence in Safety Cases. In: SSS 2013 (2013)
52. Taromirad, M., Paige, R.: Agile Requirements Traceability Using Domain-Specific Modelling Languages. In: XM 2012 (2012)
53. Wenzel, S.: Unique identification of elements in evolving software models. SoSyM (accepted paper) (2013)
54. Zoughbi, G., Briand, L., Labiche, Y.: Modeling safety and airworthiness (RTCA DO-178B) information. SoSyM 10(3), 337–367 (2011)

A Generic Fault Model for Quality Assurance

Alexander Pretschner[1], Dominik Holling[1],
Robert Eschbach[2], and Matthias Gemmar[2]

[1] Technische Universität München, Germany
{pretschn,holling}@in.tum.de
[2] itk Engineering, Germany
{robert.eschbach,matthias.gemmar}@itk-engineering.de

Abstract. Because they are comparatively easy to implement, structural coverage criteria are commonly used for test derivation in model- and code-based testing. However, there is a lack of compelling evidence that they are useful for finding faults, specifically so when compared to random testing. This paper challenges the idea of using coverage criteria for test selection and instead proposes an approach based on fault models. We define a general fault model as a transformation from correct to incorrect programs and/or a partition of the input data space. Thereby, we leverage the idea of fault injection for test assessment to test derivation.

We instantiate the developed general fault model to describe existing fault models. We also show by example how to derive test cases.

1 Introduction

Partition-based testing [23] relies on the idea of partitioning the input domain of a program into blocks. For testing, a specified number of input values is usually drawn randomly from each block. The number of tests per block can be identical, or can vary according to a usage profile. Sometimes, the blocks of the partition are considered to be "equivalence classes" in an intuitive sense, namely in that they either execute the same functionality, or are likely to provoke related failures. Code coverage criteria, including statement, branch and various forms of condition coverage, naturally induce a partition of the input domain: in a control flow graph, every path from the entry to the exit node (or back to the entry node) of a program represents all those input data values that, when applied to the program, lead to the respective path being executed. Since this same argument also applies to different forms of condition coverage, coverage-based testing can be seen as an instance of partition-based testing.

More than twenty years ago, Weyuker and Jeng have looked into the nature of test selection based on input domain partitions [25]. They contrasted partition-based testing to random testing; more specifically, to test selection that uniformly samples input values from a program's input domain. To keep the model simple, their criterion to contrast these two forms of testing measures the probability of detecting at least one failure.

They show that depending on how the failure-causing inputs are distributed across the input domain, partition-based testing can be better, the same, or worse

A. Moreira et al. (Eds.): MODELS 2013, LNCS 8107, pp. 87–103, 2013.

than random testing. By means of example, let us assume an input domain of 100 elements out of which 8 are failure causing. Let us assume a partition of two blocks, and that we can execute two tests.

1. Assume the failure causing inputs are uniformly distributed across the input domain. Assume two blocks of the partition of size 50, each of which contains 4 (uniformly distributed) failure-causing inputs. Drawing one test from each block as opposed to sampling two tests from the entire domain yields the same likelihood of catching at least one failure-causing input: partition-based testing and random testing have the same effectiveness.
2. Assume one block of 8 elements, all of which are failure-causing. The probability of detecting at least one failure with partition-based testing then is 1, certainly more effective than random testing.
3. Assume one block with just 1 element which is not failure-causing, and a second block with 99 elements, out of which 8 are failure-causing. Intuitively, we are wasting one test in the small block; partition-based testing is less effective than random testing.

As we have seen, code coverage criteria induce a partition of the input space. However, in general, we do not know which of the cases (1)-(3) this induced partition corresponds to. In other words, in general, we simply do not know if test selection based on coverage criteria defined over a program's syntax will outperform random sampling. Worse, it may even be less effective than random testing! It is then questionable if this coverage-based approach to test selection can be justified.

Note that limit testing—the idea of picking tests from the "boundaries" of ordered data types—seems to contradict this reasoning. In fact, the contrary is true: limit testing is based on empirical (or at least anecdotal) evidence that things "do go wrong" more often at the ends of intervals than in other places. Therefore, partition-based testing based on limit analysis precisely increases the probability that a failure will be caused by an element of the limit blocks, which puts this scenario, on average, in the context of scenario (2) described above.

Also note that we are careful to distinguish between different methodological usages of coverage criteria. Zhu et al. speak of adequacy criteria that can be used as selection, stopping, or test suite assessment criteria [26]. If tests are *derived* using whatever magic selection criterion but *assessed* using coverage criteria, then coverage criteria have empirically been shown to lead to better quality: they point the tester to parts of the code that has not, or insufficiently, been tested yet [20,17]. However, if an organization uses any kind of metric for assessment, then there always is the risk that this metric is optimized. In other words, it is possible that after some time, the magic selection criterion will be substituted by the coverage criterion used for test assessment.

Goal. The above remark on limit testing motivates the research presented in this paper. Limit testing relies on a fault model—an intuitive or empirically justified idea that things "go wrong" at the limits of intervals. If partition-based selection criteria are to be useful, then they must be likely to induce partitions with blocks that have a high likelihood of revealing failures (or have a comparatively high failure rate). Our goal is (1) to precisely capture a general notion of fault models; (2) to show its applicability by instantiating the generic fault model to fault models known from the literature; and (3) to use these instantiated fault models for the derivation of tests that, by construction, have a high likelihood of revealing potential faults—or at least a higher likelihood than random testing.

Contribution. Both in testing practice and in the academic literature, many fault models have been presented. Yet, we are not aware of a unifying understanding of what a fault model, in general, is. This paper closes the gap. It formally defines a general fault model and shows how various fault models from the literature can be seen as instances of our generic fault model. We consider our work to yield a different viewpoint on fault models, partition-based testing and fault injection.

Structure. The structure of this paper is as follows: Section 2 puts our work in context. In Section 3 we introduce our general fault model; Section 4 presents fault models found in the literature and illustrates how they are instances of our general fault model. Section 5 concludes.

2 Related Work

Fault Models. Fault models are a common concept in the field of software and hardware testing. Many fault models have been described in the literature (among others, those of Section 4). These fault models usually describe what the fault is and how to test for it, or provide a method to define the input part of the test cases. Although the descriptions exist, we are not aware of a comprehensive definition that encompasses all existing fault models, and enables their unified instantiation. Martin and Xie state that a fault model is "an engineering model of something that could go wrong in the construction or operation of a piece of equipment, structure, or software [18]." Harris states that a fault model associates a potential fault with an artifact [12]. Both definitions are rather abstract and describe faults of any activity during the software engineering process or even during deployment. However, the aforementioned descriptions are too general to allow an operationalization of fault models in quality assurance. In contrast, the definition by Bochmann et. al. [4] is related to testing. It says that a fault model "describes a set of faults responsible for a failure possibly at a higher level of abstraction and is the basis for mutation testing." This definition is similar to our definition of α in the general fault model (see Section 3).

Effectiveness of Partition-Based Testing. Gutjahr observed that the assumption of fixed failure densities (number of failure causing inputs divided by number of elements in the respective block) in Weyuker's and Jeng's model is rather unrealistic [11]: It seems impossible to state for a given program and a given partition what the failure rates of the single block are. He suggests to rather model failure rates as random variables. To do so, he picks one fixed specification and a corresponding input space partition, and considers a (hypothetical) class of programs written to that specification. On the grounds of knowledge w.r.t. developers, organizations, programming language, implemented functionality, etc., it appears then possible to state, for each block of the partition, what the distribution of failure rates for the programs of the hypothetical class would be. This then gives rise to *expected* failure rates for each block of the partition. Using this construction, he can show that under specific assumptions, if the expected failure rate for all blocks is the same, then partition-based testing is, in general, better than or the same as random testing. While we consider the assumption of equal expected failure rates to be inacceptably strong in practice, we will use Gutjahr's construction as a pillar for defining fault models.

In the same paper, Gutjahr also formulates shortcomings of the model of Weyuker and Jeng. This includes "at least one detected failure" to be a questionable criterion for comparing testing strategies. He suggests alternatives that relate to faults rather than failures and to their severity, and can show that his results are not impacted by these modifications. For simplicity's sake, we stick to the model of Weyuker and Jeng here when assessing the effectiveness of fault models, and leave the formally precise generalization to future work.

Random Testing. It is important not to misread the results of Weyuker and Jeng to be advocating uniform random testing; for a recent discussion, see the work of Arcuri et al. [2,1]. In addition, the quality of tests is not only determined by their probability of detecting faults or failures, but also by their cost. This cost includes many factors, one of which is the effort of determining the fault that led to a failure. In our experience [24,8], failures provoked by random tests are particularly hard to analyze because the way they execute a program does not follow any "intuitive" logic.

Coverage Criteria. In spite of the above argument, one cannot overlook that coverage criteria for test case selection are popular. We conjecture there are two main related reasons. The first is that standards like DO-178B require coverage (MC/DC coverage) for a specific class of software, even though there is little evidence that MC/DC increases the quality of tests in terms of failure detection [13,9]. Secondly, code (and model) coverage criteria naturally lend themselves to the automated generation of test cases, which then appears a promising field of research and development. We are also aware that coverage criteria provide numbers which are, from a management perspective, always useful. We would like to re-iterate that a-posteriori usages of coverage criteria have been shown to be useful [20,17].

3   A Generic Fault Model

3.1   Preliminaries

Behavior Descriptions and Specifications: Programs, models, and architectures all are behavior descriptions. We assume they are developed w.r.t. another behavior description (BD), a so-called specification. Syntactic representations of BDs form the set $\mathcal{B}$; syntactic representations of specifications form the set $\mathcal{S}$.

Of course, $\mathcal{B}$ and $\mathcal{S}$ are not necessarily disjoint. Given universal input and output domains I and O, both BDs and specifications give rise to associated semantics $[\![\cdot]\!] : I \to 2^O$.

Correctness of Behavior Descriptions: A BD $b \in \mathcal{B}$ is *correct* w.r.t. or satisfies a specification $s \in \mathcal{S}$ iff $\mathrm{dom}([\![b]\!]) \supseteq \mathrm{dom}([\![s]\!])$ and $\forall i \in \mathrm{dom}([\![s]\!])$: $[\![b]\!](i) \subseteq [\![s]\!](i)$. This is denoted as $b \models s$.

Faults and Failures: *Faults* are textual (or graphical) differences between an incorrect and a correct BD. Faults may or may not lead to *failures* in the semantics of BDs, which are observable differences between specified and actual behaviors. We do not consider *errors* here, that is, incorrect states of a BD.

Faults as Textual Mutations; Fault Classes: Because faults are defined as textual or graphical differences between incorrect and correct BDs, we may assume that there is a textual or graphical transformation $\alpha : \mathcal{B} \to 2^{\mathcal{B}}$ that maps a BD that is correct w.r.t. a specification s into the set of all BDs that are not correct w.r.t. specification s. These latter incorrect BDs in the codomain of α may contain one or multiple faults; these faults may or may not lead to failure; and some of the faults in one BD may be of the same class (see below).

Furthermore, we assume for a subset of all BDs that parts of α can be characterized w.r.t. a set of recurring problems. α_K describes textual or graphical transformations on $\mathcal{B}$ w.r.t. a *fault class* K. Examples for fault classes include textual problems ("> where $\geq$ would have been correct") and typical faults such as problems at the boundaries of loops or ordered data types. Note that this definition does not say how to define K or α_K—it is possible (yet arguably not too useful) to have K capture all possible faults.

$$B_K^s = \bigcup_{b \in \{b' \in \mathcal{B} : b' \models s\}} \alpha_K(b)$$

is the set of all BDs, written to specification s, that contain instances of fault class K. Note that B_K^s is of a hypothetical nature, similar to the construction used by Gutjahr [11]. The elements in $\alpha_K(b)$ may contain one or multiple instances of fault class K.

Failure Domains and Induced Failure Domains: BDs have failure domains. Let a BD b be written to a specification s. The *failure domain* of b, $F^{b,s} \subseteq \mathrm{dom}([\![s]\!])$, consists of precisely those inputs that cause incorrect outputs, $i \in F^{b,s}$ iff $i \in \mathrm{dom}([\![s]\!]) \wedge [\![b]\!](i) \not\subseteq [\![s]\!](i)$.

$$\varphi(\alpha_K, s) = \bigcup_{b \in B_K^s} F^{b,s}$$

then defines the failure domain induced by fault class K on specification s. Note that the induced failure domain is independent of any specific BD but rather defined by specification s and fault class K (or rather α_K which is needed for the computation of $F^{b,s}$). $\varphi(\alpha_K, s)$ is the set of all those inputs that potentially provoke a failure related to a fault of class K for *any* BD written to s. The failure domain of every specific BD is a subset of this $\varphi(\alpha_K, s)$, and this failure domain may very well be empty or contain only very few elements of $\varphi(\alpha_K, s)$.

3.2 Fault Models

Fault Models: Intuitively, a fault model is the understanding of "specific things that can go wrong when writing a BD." In a first approximation, we define fault models to be descriptions of the differences with correct BDs that contain instances of fault class K. More precisely, for a class of specifications $S \subseteq \mathcal{S}$, we define a fault model for class K to be descriptions of the computation of α_K. Sometimes, α_K cannot be provided but the respective induced failure domain can, using the definition of $\tilde{\alpha}_K$ (see below). A *fault model* for class K therefore is a description of the computation of α_K or a direct description of the failure domains induced by α_K, $\varphi(\alpha_K, s)$ for all $s \in S$.

Approximated Fault Models: In general, a precise and comprehensive definition of the transformations α_K or the induced failure domains $\varphi(\alpha_K, s)$ is not possible and can only be approximated. For a given BD b and a specification s, let $\tilde{\alpha}_K$ describe an approximation of α_K, and let $\tilde{\varphi}$ describe an approximation of the computation of failure domains. They are approximations in that $\text{dom}(\alpha_K) \cap \text{dom}(\tilde{\alpha}_K) \neq \emptyset$ and $\exists b \in \mathcal{B} : \alpha_K(b) \cap \tilde{\alpha}_K(b) \neq \emptyset$. This formal definition is rather weak. The intuition is that $\tilde{\alpha}_K$ should be applicable to *many* elements from $\text{dom}(\alpha_K)$ and that, for a *large class of BDs* B', the result of applying $\tilde{\alpha}_K$ to $b' \in B'$ coincides largely with $\alpha_K(b')$. Similar to α_K, $\tilde{\alpha}_K$ gives rise to a partition of the input domain of every BD w.r.t. fault class K. Because $\tilde{\alpha}_K$ is an approximation, these induced partitions may or may not be failure domains w.r.t. the considered specification.

Example: Approximations $\tilde{\alpha}_K$ can be over-approximations that may contain mutants that do not necessarily contain faults or even are equivalent to the orginal BD; under-approximations that yield fewer mutants due to the omission of some transformations; or a combination of both. As an example, consider the class of off-by-one faults k, where a boundary condition is shifted by one value due to a logical programming mistake. For off-by-one faults an exemplary α_k transforms a relational operator into a different one or transforms the afterthought of a loop such that the loop is executed once too often. To demonstrate over-approximation, $\tilde{\alpha}_k$ transforms the BD b with the fragment "if (x<=50) { if (x==50) {" into a set of BDs. This set includes the BD b', in which only the aforementioned fragment was transformed into "if (x<=50) { if (x>=50) {". b' is semantically equivalent to b and not faulty. Thus, the set of BDs created by $\tilde{\alpha}_k$ is larger than the set of BDs created by α_k (which by definition, contain faults of class k). To demonstrate under-approximation, one possibility is to limit $\tilde{\alpha}_k$ to consider only relational operators and not afterthoughts. Then, the set of BDs created by $\tilde{\alpha}_k$ is smaller than the set of BDs created by α_k.

Approximated Induced Failure Domains and Test Selection Strategies: The intuition behind the input space partitions induced by an approximated $\tilde{\alpha}_K$

is that it computes hypotheses about input blocks with associated failure rates that, overall, lead to good test effectiveness (formally defined below). While φ implicitly computes two blocks for every BD—one where every input is potentially causing a failure related to class K, and another one where every input certainly is not—the approximations of φ, called $\tilde{\varphi}$ in the sequel, may compute multiple of these blocks. In order to capture relevant fault models from the literature, we augment the definition by stipulating that $\tilde{\varphi}$ computes a number of tests to be drawn from each block (if this number is not known, a constant number n of tests may be assumed for every block). $\tilde{\varphi}$ then is a test selection strategy.

Formally, for the set $\mathcal{J}$ of index sets and appropriate $J \in \mathcal{J}$, we require $\tilde{\varphi}_K : \mathcal{B} \to (J \to 2^I \times \mathbb{N})$ to define a partition of the input domain of a BD together with the number of tests to be drawn from each block.

3.3   Effective Fault Models

Comparing Fault Models: So far, fault models describe anything that *could go wrong*. They arguably are more useful if they capture problems that *do go wrong* in practice. In order to define useful fault models, we will simplify matters: We will compare testing strategies w.r.t. the likelihood of detecting at least one failure. We can now use the model introduced by Weyuker and Jeng that we described in Section 1. When randomly (uniformly) sampling n elements from the input space of a BD b written to specification s, the probability of causing at least one failure with n tests (with redrawal) is [25]

$$P_{rnd}(b, s, n) = 1 - \left(1 - \frac{|F^{b,s}|}{|\mathrm{dom}(\llbracket b \rrbracket)|}\right)^n.$$

Let $\downarrow_1()$ and $\downarrow_2()$ denote the left and right projections on pairs. Again using the model introduced in Section 1, in terms of partition-based testing, if possibly different numbers of tests are drawn from each block defined by a given selection strategy $\tilde{\varphi}_K(b) = \pi$ with $\pi : J \to 2^I \times \mathbb{N}$ for some index set $J \in \mathcal{J}$, then the likelihood of detecting at least one failure is [25]

$$P_{prt}(b, s, \pi) = 1 - \prod_{j=1}^{|\mathrm{dom}(\pi)|} \left(1 - \frac{|F^{b,s} \cap \downarrow_1(\pi(j))|}{|\downarrow_1(\pi(j))|}\right)^{\downarrow_2(\pi(j))}$$

because $\frac{|F^{b,s} \cap \downarrow_1(\pi(j))|}{|\downarrow_1(\pi(j))|}$ is the failure rate of the j-th block of the partition.

Effectiveness: Not every class of faults is relevant for every set of specifications. For instance, rounding issues are unlikely to occur in text processing contexts. We therefore characterize effective fault models for a domain-, company- or technology-specific set of specifications $S' \subseteq S$ by using a (hypothetical) set of BDs $B_{S'} \subseteq \mathcal{B}$ written to these specifications. We want to capture the fact that a fault model $- \tilde{\alpha}_K$ and the induced $\tilde{\varphi}$, or some provided $\tilde{\varphi} -$ is useful. We do this by defining when a fault model is applicable in the sense that the respective fault class typically happens in practice. When comparing partition-based testing to random testing, it is reasonable to overall use the same number of test cases, i.e., $n = \sum_{j \in \mathrm{dom}(\pi)} \downarrow_2 (\pi(j))$.

$$n_{S'} = \left| \left\{ s \in S' : \left| \{ b \in B_{S'} : P_{prt}(b, s, \tilde{\varphi}_K(b)) \gg P_{rnd}(b, s, n) \} \right| \right. \right.$$
$$\left. \left. \gg \left| \{ b \in B_{S'} : P_{prt}(b, s, \tilde{\varphi}_K(b)) \not\gg P_{rnd}(b, s, n) \} \right| \right\} \right|$$

is the number n'_S of specifications from S' for which the number of BDs that can effectively be tested using partition-based testing via $\tilde{\varphi}_K$ is significantly higher than the number of BDs for which random testing is performing equally well or better. If $\tilde{\varphi}_K$ is defining a fault model or is induced by some α_K, the respective specifications are those to which the fault model is applicable. A fault model is effective if this number is high.

In order to define an effective fault model, we say that $n_{S'}$ must be far larger than the number of specifications from S' to which the fault model is not applicable:

$$n_{S'} \gg \left| \left\{ s \in S' : \left| \{ b \in B_{S'} : P_{prt}(b, s, \tilde{\varphi}_K(b)) \gg P_{rnd}(b, s, n) \} \right| \right. \right.$$
$$\left. \left. \not\gg \left| \{ b \in B_{S'} : P_{prt}(b, s, \tilde{\varphi}_K(p)) \not\gg P_{rnd}(b, s, n) \} \right| \right\} \right|.$$

Remark I: This definition of fault models is based on the intuition that a fault model is "better" if it is more generally applicable, that is, if many realistic BDs potentially contain an instance of the respective fault class. If used retrospectively, this notion is thus ideally based on empirical evidence that a specific fault class is relevant in a specific setting. However, it is noteworthy that this idea of a fault model can, without any modifications, also be used prospectively for *one BD* and therefore without empirical evidence about *many BDs*: If it is decided that an instance of a fault class *may* be present in a specific BD, then this fault class can be tested for. The effectiveness of this model is then based on a notion of likelihood that is not based on frequency in the past ("typical fault") but rather on the possibility that the fault may occur. This insight could have been gained on the grounds of a hazard analysis, for instance.

Remark II: We could model failure rates as random variables, in the spirit of Gutjahr's work [11]. We could then compute their expectations, and also the expectations of the probabilities. We do not do this here. Note, however, for the *characterization* of the effectiveness of fault models, it does not really matter which precise numbers we use—the point is rather about comparing the cardinality of different sets of specifications and BDs.

4 Instantiation

To demonstrate the usefulness of our general fault model, we now show existing fault models to be an instance of it. We performed a literature survey and considered existing fault models explicitly stated as such. This list is not intended to be exhaustive but to demonstrate the instantiation process using examples.

The instantiationsare described using the respective α, φ, and their approximations. $\tilde{\alpha}$ describes a fault as a (possibly higher order) mutant. $\tilde{\varphi}$ defines possible input space partitions induced by $\tilde{\alpha}$. We assume that the BDs are correct w.r.t. their specification before the transformation $\tilde{\alpha}$ and incorrect afterwards. Intuitively, this reflects a transformation of *specifications* rather than BDs and can be seen as a transformation of the system model in a model-based engineering approach: test case derivation is then performed at the level of the models. By using our definition of specification, both the correct and incorrect BD can be derived.

Since the failure domain varies due to functions applied to the input before the faulty part of the BD is executed, no general partition of the input space can be given. However, a general schema to derive the partition can be given. The generic definition of φ will partition the input space into one block of inputs for which the output is different after the application of α, and one block for which this is not the case. In practice, the applied functions may only be approximated using the approximation $\tilde{\varphi}$.

α and $\tilde{\alpha}$ are set-valued functions. Let α' and $\tilde{\alpha}'$ denote modifications of these functions that pick one arbitrary element from the codomain of α and $\tilde{\alpha}$, respectively. If α' or $\tilde{\alpha}'$ occur more than once in one definition, then each instance is supposed to pick the same element.

4.1   Stuck-At

The stuck-at fault model [19] is known for automated test pattern generation in the hardware industry. It assumes that a manufacturing defect is present in one or multiple logic gates or subcircuits such that regardless of their input, their output is always the same. The transformation α for stuck-at is the transformation of one circuit into another circuit where one subcircuit is replaced by 1 or 0. For our purposes, this replacement can equivalently be performed at the level of logical formulas f that represent equivalent circuits. For each application of α, that is, each element that is picked by α', φ then creates one block of inputs $\{i : [\![f]\!](i) \neq [\![\alpha'(f)]\!](i)\}$ and one block of inputs $\{i : [\![f]\!](i) = [\![\alpha'(f)]\!](i)\}$ (and it does this for each element of the codomain of α that is picked by α'). Consequently, $\tilde{\varphi}(f) = \{1 \mapsto (\{i : [\![\alpha'(f) \text{ XOR } f]\!](i) == 1\}, n_1), 2 \mapsto (\{i : [\![\alpha'(f) \text{ XOR } f]\!](i) == 0\}, n_2)\}$ where the overall number n of tests is assumed to be fixed, $n = n_1 + n_2$ and $n_1 = n$ if $n \leq |\{i : [\![\alpha'(f) \text{ XOR } f]\!](i) == 1\}|$ and $n_1 = |\{i : [\![\alpha'(f) \text{ XOR } f]\!](i) == 1\}|$ otherwise. Operationally, depending on the formalism used, a SAT solver is adequate to compute $\tilde{\varphi}$ for a specific circuit.

As an example, assume a function (a circuit) $f = (a \wedge b) \vee (b \wedge c)$. As one exemplary stuck-at-0 fault, α introduces a permanent output of 0 for the subformula (the gate) $b \wedge c$, that is, $\alpha'(f) = (a \wedge b) \vee 0$. It is easy to verify that the first block of the input partition is $(a = 0, b = 1, c = 1)$ with one test to be drawn, and the second block of all remaining valuations with $n - 1$ tests to be drawn.

4.2   Division by Zero

Division by zero is a classic fault in many BDs. It typically happens if developers do not perform input sanitization (i.e. check for a value of 0 for the divisor) prior to a division, or when the value 0 for the divisor was not assumed possible in the BD's context. Let us concentrate on the former case (and this in itself is an example of how to under-approximate α by some $\tilde{\alpha}$). The transformation $\tilde{\alpha}$ removes the sanitization mechanisms from BD p and induces two blocks of inputs for $\tilde{\varphi}$. The first block of inputs is $\{i : [\![p]\!](i) \neq [\![\tilde{\alpha}'(p)]\!](i)\}$ and the second block is $\{i : [\![p]\!](i) = [\![\tilde{\alpha}'(p)]\!](i)\}$. Note that for the first block of inputs the divisor will be 0 at the point of the division, while for the second it will be different from 0. Thus, $\tilde{\varphi}(p) = \{1 \mapsto (\{i : [\![p]\!](i) \neq [\![\tilde{\alpha}'(p)]\!](i)\}, n_1), 2 \mapsto (\{i : [\![p]\!](i) = [\![\tilde{\alpha}'(p)]\!](i)\}, n_2)\}$ where the overall number n of tests is assumed to be fixed, $n = n_1 + n_2$ and $n_1 = n$ if $n \leq |\{i : [\![p]\!](i) \neq [\![\tilde{\alpha}'(p)]\!](i)\}|$ and $n_1 = |\{i : [\![p]\!](i) \neq [\![\tilde{\alpha}'(p)]\!](i)\}|$ otherwise.

For a BD p_d with input parameter i and $p_d = f_x(i)/f_y(i)$ developed to divide two integers, let $\tilde{\alpha}'(p_d) = f_x(i)/f_z(i)$ be the replacement of the function f_y including some sanitization mechanism by an f_z without sanitization. Then $\tilde{\varphi}(p_d) = \{1 \mapsto (\{i : [\![f_z^{-1}]\!](i) == 0\}, 1), 2 \mapsto (\{i : [\![f_z^{-1}]\!](i) \neq 0\}, n-1)\}$ where the overall number n of tests is assumed to be determined. Operationally, depending on the formalism used, a symbolic execution tool is an adequate tool to compute some $\tilde{\varphi}$ for a specific BD and a specific set of mutation operators.

4.3   Mutation Testing

While mutation testing aims at assessing test suites and targets small syntactic faults, mutation operators do describe fault models that we can use for our purposes (for instance, Ma et al. provide several direct relationships between some mutation operators and faults [16] where the coupling hypothesis appears immediately justified). Mutation operators are intuitively captured by our transformation α—in fact, we see α as a reasonable higher order mutation operator. Since α is applied to a program, the general considerations of Section 4.2 with the two blocks $\{i : [\![p]\!](i) \neq [\![\alpha'(p)]\!](i)\}$ and $\{i : [\![p]\!](i) = [\![\alpha'(p)]\!](i)\}$ also apply here. Consequently, symbolic execution tools are promising for computing φ.

As an example, take a program p_m with input parameter x and $p_m = 1$ if $x < 10$ and $p_m = 0$ otherwise. Using a mutation that transforms $<$ to $\leq$, let $\alpha'(p_m) = 1$ if $x \leq 10$ and $\alpha'(p_m) = 0$ otherwise. Then $\tilde{\varphi}(p_m) = \{1 \mapsto (\{10\}, 1), 2 \mapsto (I - \{10\}, n-1)\}$ for the input domain I.

4.4   Finite State Machine Testing

In finite state machine (FSM)-based testing, typical fault models are based on output and transfer faults. As one typical example that easily generalizes, let us consider BDs in the form of deterministic Mealy machines $\mathcal{M}$ such that each $M \in \mathcal{M}$ is a sextuple $(\Sigma, \Gamma, S, s_0, \delta, \gamma)$ where Σ and Γ are input and output alphabets, S is the set of states, $s_i \in S$ is an initial state, $\delta : S \times \Sigma \to S$ is the transfer and $\gamma : S \times \Sigma \to \Gamma$ the output function.

Output faults occur when a transition yields a different output than specified in the output function. This deviation is the result of the transformation $\alpha_o :$ $(S \times \Sigma \to \Gamma) \to 2^{S \times \Sigma \to \Gamma'}$ which models faults in the same way as in the stuck-at fault model (see Section 4.1: for a given transition, the correct output is mapped to another, incorrect output from a set $\Gamma' \supseteq \Gamma$). Analogously, transfer faults lead the FSM into a different state than specified in the transfer function, $\alpha_t : (S \times \Sigma \to S) \to 2^{S \times \Sigma \to S'}$ with $S' \supseteq S$ since the destination state of a transfer fault may be a new state not in the design of the original FSM [4]. In the following, we assume that the definitions of α_o and α_t are lifted to entire machines in the obvious way, that is, α_o and α_t are of type $\mathcal{M} \to 2^{\mathcal{M}}$. In the remainder of this paragraph, α refers to both α_o and α_t.

Finite traces $[\![M]\!] \in \Sigma^* \to \Gamma^*$ for a $M \in \mathcal{M}$ are pairs of (input, output) sequences that we assume to respect the transfer and output functions in an intuitive way (that is, they induce state changes that are captured by δ, and they model γ). φ then defines two blocks of input sequences. The first block, $\{i \in \Sigma^* : [\![M]\!](i) \neq [\![\alpha'(M)]\!](i)\}$, defines all those traces that are different in M and $\alpha(M)$ – these are the traces that exhibit faults. The second block is the set of traces for which no difference can be observed: $\{i \in \Sigma^* : [\![M]\!](i) = [\![\alpha'(M)]\!](i)\}$.

Generally speaking, model checkers and dedicated algorithms on graphs are adequate tools for computing approximations $\tilde{\varphi}$.

Several related fault models have been described in the area of object-oriented testing [3] that model objects as finite state machines. One of them is sneak path, which describes that a message (i.e. a composite input) is accepted although it should not be. In the notion of an FSM, a sneak path is a an additional transition in the transfer function and can be modeled by $\alpha_t : (S \times \Sigma \to S) \to 2^{S \times \Sigma \to S'}$ as described above.

Similarly, a trap door is the acceptance of an undefined message (i.e. a new letter in the alphabet), which causes the system to go to an arbitrary state. Intuitively, $\alpha_t : (S \times \Sigma \to S) \to 2^{S \times \Sigma' \to S'}$ reflects a trap door by introducing a new character to the alphabet $\Sigma' \supseteq \Sigma$ and a new transition leading to a possibly new state in $S' \supseteq S$.

4.5   Object-Oriented Testing

In addition, there are fault models catering to subtyping and polymorphism [22] in object-oriented programming. These are, for example, state definition anomalies (pre or post conditions are possibly violated by subtypes) or anomalous construction behaviors (i.e. the subtype shadows variables used by the constructor of the supertype). The general considerations for both fault models can be described by using transformations similar to α from Section 4.2, but at the level of pre- and post conditions rather than at the level of code.

For a state definition anomaly, let a class C contain a method $p_{sda}^C(x) = f(x)$; $s := x\{s \neq NULL\}$; with post condition $s \neq NULL$ for some instance variable s, and a method $q_{sda}^C(x, z) = p_{sda}^C(x)$; $if\ z\ then\ \{s \neq NULL\}\ g(s)$; where the precondition of function g is assumed to require the argument to be different from $NULL$. Class C' is a subclass of C where $p_{sda}^{C'}(x) = p_{sda}^{C}(x); h(x)\{true\}$; overrides method p_{sda}^{C} in C'. If the post condition of h in the definition of $p_{sda}^{C'}(x)$ does not imply $s \neq NULL$, then the inherited $q_{sda}^{C'}(x,z) = p_{sda}^{C'}(x); if\ z\ then\ \{s \neq NULL\}\ g(s)$; causes problems if the precondition of g is not met.

There are many different ways of violating pre or post conditions, and it seems unlikely that these can be comprehensively captured by patterns of textual modifications of code. However, the modification of *explicitly provided or inferred pre- or postconditions* can be specified using α, the domain of which is inherited functions only; in our example, $q_{sda}^{C'}(x)$ is the only one. One possibility then is that $\alpha'(q_{sda}^{C'}(x))$ computes to $p_{sda}^{C}(x); if\ z\ then\ \{s == NULL\}\ g(s)$; by modifying the precondition of function g. Intuitively, this models the possibility that an inherited function leads to a state where the specified precondition of g *cannot* be satisfied. If they exist, test cases representing the second block of $\tilde{\varphi} = \{1 \mapsto (\{(x \mapsto i, z \mapsto false) : i \in \mathbb{N}\}, n-1), 2 \mapsto (\{(x \mapsto i, z \mapsto true) : i \in \mathbb{N}\ and\ s == NULL\ before\ g\ is\ executed\ from\ within\ q_{sda}^{C'}(x))\}, 1)\}$ would then provoke a failure when applied to method $p_{sda}^{C'}$ of an object of class C'. Possible technology for computing $\tilde{\varphi}$ includes symbolic execution.

4.6   Aspect-Oriented Testing

The use of AOP has been shown to induce specific faults [6]. One such fault model concerns the failure to establish expected post-conditions and preserve state invariants. The post-conditions and state invariants introduced in the basic functionality are contracts that should be preserved in the weaved code. This fault is analogous to object-oriented testing where it can be caused by inheritance (see Section 4.5).

A second fault model consists of incorrect changes in the exceptional control flow. Whenever features having their own exception handling are introduced, an exception may trigger the execution of a different catch block than the one intended by the basic functionality. For this fault model, let $p_a = try\{f_x(x);\}$ catch (Exception e)$\{f_e(e);\}$ try$\{f_y(x);\}$ catch (Runtime− Exception ex)$\{f_{ex}(ex);\}$ with input parameter x be a program with exception handling f_e for the original functionality f_x and exception handling f_{ex} of an introduced feature f_y. Also let $\tilde{\alpha}'(p_a) = \{try\{f_x(x); f_y(x);\}$ catch (RuntimeException ex$\{f_{ex}(ex);\}$ catch (Exception e)$\{f_e(e);\}\}$ be the transformation of p_a, which merges both try/catch blocks and extends the exception handling. Then, the first block of $\tilde{\varphi}$ must contain inputs triggering a runtime exception (or one of its subtypes) in f_x to let f_x use exception handling f_{ex} instead of the intended f_e. The second block contains all other inputs.

4.7   Performance Testing

One fault model—there are multiple others—for performance testing [21] describes one or multiple hardware component failures or malfunctions causing the BD to have a degraded performance. Such failures or malfunctions could be related to hard drive, network or memory problems. If we model the hardware and software as an FSM, then the transformation α can simulate a malfunction by removing states and transitions to these states. Thus, α requires the system to take more transitions thereby taking more steps for the same computation or blocks the system from ever reaching its desired state causing a failure. Precisely this modification of the transfer function is shown in the FSM fault model in Section 4.4.

4.8   Concurrency Testing

Fault models used in testing concurrent systems regard atomicity and order violations [15], in addition to deadlock and livelock problems. For an atomicity violation the developer did not implement a monitor (or implemented it in the wrong way). Let m be a monitor and $p_{atom} = $ monitor_lock$(m); f_x(x);$ monitor_unlock(m); ||monitor_lock$(m); f_y(x);$ monitor_unlock(m); with input parameter x be a program using this monitor and $f||g$ be defined as the execution of f and g in parallel. Also let $\alpha'(p_{atom}) = f_x(x); ||f_y(x);$ be a transformation of p_{atom} removing its usage of monitors. With the usage of concurrency, the semantics of the program are also influenced by the schedule of execution. An atomicity violation typically changes the output of the program when using different schedules while the input remains the same. Thus, the input space must be extended by adding the schedule to the input vector. Then, the first block of $\tilde{\varphi}$ contains those inputs for which the output is different when only using a different schedule. The second block contains all other inputs.

For order violations the developer made a wrong assumption about the order of execution of statements. No α is required as the developer assumed an execution order s_0, but did not enforce it. Thus, the first block of φ aims to break the assumption by executing all schedules different from s_0 and checking whether the semantics have changed. Thus, the first block of $\tilde{\varphi}$ contains all inputs for which the output is different when only a different schedule is used. The second block contains all other inputs.

4.9   Security Testing

In security testing, one approach to find faults w.r.t. given security properties (e.g. confidentiality and integrity) using a formal system model is presented by Büchler et al. [5]. The transformation α is reflected in semantic mutation operators (see Section 4.3) for a model of the system. These operators modify the model such that an assumed vulnerability in the respective implementation is present. α is therefore described by these mutation operators. The idea to induce the input space partition φ is to have a sequence of actions (i.e. a trace) that violate the security property. Practically, this is performed by using a model checker to find this trace τ and executing τ on the implementation of the system. Since the model checker may not return all traces in useful time, φ must be approximated by $\tilde{\varphi}$ and the first block of $\tilde{\varphi}$ also contains these unknown traces. Thus, $\tilde{\varphi}$ can be constructed in the same way as in Section 4.4.

4.10   Limit Testing

The well-known fault model of boundary value analysis (based on the category partition method [23]) is underlying limit testing and, like the fault model of Section 4.5, differs from the rest of the introduced fault models in that the transformation α is unknown (or, analogously, models all those possibilities to get a BD's treatment of limit values wrong). It is, however, possible to create the partition of the input space φ. This creation requires a partition γ, which can use control flow or data flow-based criteria for example. φ then takes the blocks of γ and splits them such that a new block is created for each block boundary including its closest inputs.

An integer block containing the number 1 to 100 would, for example, be split into 3 blocks. The first block contains 0 and 1, the second block contains the number 2 to 98 and the third block contains 99 and 100. Note that, in some cases -1 and 101 are included in the first and last block respectively. This fault model is considered useful, as there is anecdotal evidence that the failure causing inputs are more likely to be in the first and third blocks.

4.11   Combinatorial Testing

The fault model of combinatorial, or n-wise, testing [14] states that only a combination of 2, 3 or n parameters causes a failure, but not all possible combinations of parameters. It thus provides a test selection criteria requiring fewer test cases than exhaustive testing (i.e. all combinations). The transformation α is again unknown, but the partition of the input space $\tilde{\varphi}$ (i.e. the partition of the 2-way, 3-way or n-way interactions) can be derived by adhering to the parameter combinations. $\tilde{\varphi}$ can be computed using known algorithms on the grounds of Latin squares, for instance. One block of the partition will contain a minimal set of test cases covering all 2-way, 3-way or n-way interactions and the other block will cover all other possible interactions. Note that there are multiple possible partitions and an arbitrary minimal partition can be selected (e.g. in the case of 3 parameters with 3 values and all 2-way interactions to be tested, there exist 12 possibilities to select the minimal number of test cases being 9).

As an example, reconsider function f from Section 4.1. One exemplary set of inputs testing all pairwise combinations for f is (0,0,0), (0,1,1), (1,0,1), (1,0,0). This set of inputs would find, but is not limited to, the faults described by the stuck-at fault model.

5   Conclusion

The contribution of this paper is a general characterization of fault models that encompasses fault models found in practice and the literature. The aim of using fault models in testing is to derive good test cases. We consider a test case to be good if it detects a potential, or likely, fault.[1] Our fault models consist of

---

[1] In fact, it should do so with good cost effectiveness, including debugging cost, but this is not the subject of this paper.

syntactic transformations (higher-order, or semantic, mutants), and/or an input space partition. Using several different technologies, this allows us to derive test cases that address the potential faults. We have instantiated our generic fault model to several fault models found in the literature. We do not claim that we capture all fault models but consider our choice to be representative.

By defining fault models with a transformation that is essentially a cleverly chosen higher order mutant, we connected the notion of using fault injection for test case assessment to using mutants for test case derivation. In addition, we introduced an experience model creating a relationship between classes of systems and class of faults, which we consider helpful in creating adequate fault models, improving risk assessment and test derivation for fault tolerance mechanisms.

Although we have not evaluated the effectiveness of operationalized fault models yet, we see multiple advantages with respect to risk assessment in testing. Coverage criteria and random testing are unable to state whether the system still contains a class of faults after testing. The use of fault models can increase the probability of a particular targeted class of faults to not be present in the system after testing. In addition, fault tolerance can be evaluated by using fault models that target faults handled by the fault tolerance systems. It is also noteworthy that classes of faults in fault models can be associated with the impairment of quality attributes in the system. Thereby, testing using these fault models can reduce the risk of impairment in the final product. Lastly, when using fault models with an inherent transformation, the fault localization effort can be estimated and reduced since the transformations describe what to look for and where. The cost effectiveness of fault models cannot be determined *in general* as it varies from instance to instance. The cost factors involved, however, can be named and are the test level, class of systems (including its context) and the likely class of faults.

We elaborated fault models in testing, but have not limited our general definition to it. Fault models may also be used in other quality assurance techniques such as reviews or inspection performed on non-executable artifacts. Because specifications are BDs themselves, it is straightforward to generalize the transformation α to the level of specifications, thereby allowing it to transform requirements, architecture and design artifacts among others.

We do not believe that the use of fault models is the silver bullet. By its very definition, faults for which no model exists cannot be targeted with our approach. However, for a class of recurring and typical faults in specific contexts, we consider our work to be useful in practice.

Future Work. Our current research focuses on creating a prototype to (semi-) automatically generate test cases using underlying fault models, using the different mentioned technologies. In the future we wish to complete this prototype and to empirically evaluate our introduced fault models with it. In addition, we are also exploring the sources of experience data for fault models. We see many promising areas inside and outside software testing. A promising method to gain knowledge common faults in software testing is orthogonal defect classification [7]. Using this method faults can be classified according to criteria, which in turn can be leveraged to select faults to test for. We also plan to investigate whether

fault models can be created from faults found during reviews and inspections
[10]. This investigation will particularly focus on the comparison of effectiveness
of quality assurance techniques per created fault model.

References

1. Arcuri, A., Briand, L.: Formal analysis of the probability of interaction fault detection using random testing. IEEE Transactions on Software Engineering 38(5),
   1088–1099 (2012)
2. Arcuri, A., Iqbal, M.Z., Briand, L.: Random testing: Theoretical results and practical implications. IEEE Transactions on Software Engineering 38(2), 258–277 (2012)
3. Binder, R.V.: Testing Object-Oriented Systems: Models, Patterns, and Tools. Object Technology Series. Addison-Wesley (1999)
4. Bochmann, G.v., Das, A., Dssouli, R., Dubuc, M., Ghedamsi, A., Luo, G.: Fault
   models in testing. In: Proceedings of the IFIP TC6/WG6.1 Fourth International
   Workshop on Protocol Test Systems IV, pp. 17–30. North-Holland Publishing Co.,
   Amsterdam (1992), http://dl.acm.org/citation.cfm?id=648126.747577
5. Büchler, M., Oudinet, J., Pretschner, A.: Semi-automatic security testing of web
   applications from a secure model. In: 2012 IEEE Sixth International Conference
   on Software Security and Reliability (SERE), pp. 253–262 (2012)
6. Ceccato, M., Tonella, P., Ricca, F.: Is aop code easier or harder to test than oop
   code? In: On-line Proceedings of the First Workshop on Testing Aspect-Oriented
   Programs (WTAOP 2005) (March 2005)
7. Chillarege, R., Bhandari, I.S., Chaar, J.K., Halliday, M.J., Moebus, D.S., Ray, B.K.,
   Wong, M.Y.: Orthogonal Defect Classification-A Concept for In-Process Measure-
   ments. IEEE Trans. Softw. Eng. 18(11), 943–956 (1992),
   http://dx.doi.org/10.1109/32.177364
8. Ciupa, I., Pretschner, A., Oriol, M., Leitner, A., Meyer, B.: On the number and
   nature of faults found by random testing. Softw. Test. Verif. Reliab. 21(1), 3–28
   (2011)
9. Dupuy, A., Leveson, N.: An empirical evaluation of the mc/dc coverage criterion on
   the hete-2 satellite software. In: Proceedings of the 19th Digital Avionics Systems
   Conference, DASC 2000, vol. 1, pp. 1B6/1–1B6/7 (2000)
10. Fagan, M.E.: Design and code inspections to reduce errors in program development.
    IBM Syst. J. 15(3), 182–211 (1976), http://dx.doi.org/10.1147/sj.153.0182
11. Gutjahr, W.J.: Partition testing vs. random testing: The influence of uncertainty.
    IEEE Trans. Softw. Eng. 25(5), 661–674 (1999),
    http://dx.doi.org/10.1109/32.815325
12. Harris, I.G.: Fault models and test generation for hardware-software covalidation.
    IEEE Des. Test 20(04), 40–47 (2003),
    http://dx.doi.org/10.1109/MDT.2003.1214351, doi:10.1109/MDT.2003.1214351
13. Heimdahl, M., Whalen, M., Rajan, A., Staats, M.: On mc/dc and implementa-
    tion structure: An empirical study. In: IEEE/AIAA 27th Digital Avionics Systems
    Conference, DASC 2008, pp. 5.B.3–1–5.B.3–13 (2008)
14. Kuhn, D.R., Wallace, D.R., Gallo Jr., A.M.: Software fault interactions and impli-
    cations for software testing. IEEE Trans. Softw. Eng. 30(6), 418–421 (2004)

15. Lu, S., Park, S., Seo, E., Zhou, Y.: Learning from mistakes: a comprehensive study on real world concurrency bug characteristics. In: Proceedings of the 13th International Conference on Architectural Support for Programming Languages and Operating Systems, ASPLOS XIII, pp. 329–339. ACM, New York (2008), http://dx.doi.org/10.1145/1346281.1346323

16. Ma, Y.-S., Kwon, Y.-R., Offutt, J.: Inter-class mutation operators for java. In: ISSRE, pp. 352–366 (2002)

17. Malaiya, Y., Li, M., Bieman, J., Karcich, R.: Software reliability growth with test coverage. IEEE Transactions on Reliability 51(4), 420–426 (2002)

18. Martin, E., Xie, T.: A fault model and mutation testing of access control policies. In: Proceedings of the 16th International Conference on World Wide Web, WWW 2007, pp. 667–676. ACM, New York (2007), http://dx.doi.org/10.1145/1242572.1242663

19. McCluskey, E., Clegg, F.W.: Fault equivalence in combinational logic networks. IEEE Transactions on Computers C-20(11), 1286–1293 (1971)

20. Mockus, A., Nagappan, N., Dinh-Trong, T.T.: Test coverage and post-verification defects: A multiple case study. In: Proceedings of the 2009 3rd International Symposium on Empirical Software Engineering and Measurement, ESEM 2009, pp. 291–301 (2009)

21. Nagaraja, K., Li, X., Bianchini, R., Martin, R.P., Nguyen, T.D.: Using fault injection and modeling to evaluate the performability of cluster-based services. In: Proceedings of the 4th Conference on USENIX Symposium on Internet Technologies and Systems, USITS 2003, vol. 4, p. 2. USENIX Association, Berkeley (2003), http://dl.acm.org/citation.cfm?id=1251460.1251462

22. Offutt, J., Alexander, R., Wu, Y., Xiao, Q., Hutchinson, C.: A fault model for subtype inheritance and polymorphism. In: Proceedings of the 12th International Symposium on Software Reliability Engineering, ISSRE 2001, pp. 84–95. IEEE Computer Society, Washington, DC (2001), http://dl.acm.org/citation.cfm?id=851028.856258

23. Ostrand, T.J., Balcer, M.J.: The category-partition method for specifying and generating fuctional tests. Commun. ACM 31(6), 676–686 (1988), http://dx.doi.org/10.1145/62959.62964

24. Pretschner, A., Prenninger, W., Wagner, S., Kühnel, C., Baumgartner, M., Sostawa, B., Zölch, R., Stauner, T.: One evaluation of model-based testing and its automation. In: Proceedings of the 27th International Conference on Software Engineering, pp. 392–401 (2005)

25. Weyuker, E., Jeng, B.: Analyzing partition testing strategies. IEEE Transaction on Software Engineering 17(7), 703–711 (1991)

26. Zhu, H., Hall, P.A.V., May, J.H.R.: Software unit test coverage and adequacy. ACM Comput. Surv. 29(4), 366–427 (1997)

Towards an Operationalization of the "Physics of Notations" for the Analysis of Visual Languages

Harald Störrle[1] and Andrew Fish[2,*]

[1] Dept. of Informatics and Applied Mathematics, Technical University of Denmark
hsto@dtu.dk
[2] School of Computing, Engineering and Mathematics, University of Brighton, UK
Andrew.Fish@brighton.ac.uk

Abstract. We attempt to validate the conceptual framework "Physics of Notation" (PoN) as a means for analysing visual languages by applying it to UML Use Case Diagrams. We discover that the PoN, in its current form, is neither precise nor comprehensive enough to be applied in an objective way to analyse practical visual software engineering notations. We propose an operationalization of a part of the PoN, highlight conceptual shortcomings of the PoN, and explore ways to address them.

1 Introduction

Motivation. The Software Engineering domain uses many visual notations like the ones defined in the Unified Modeling Language (UML). Being visual is frequently quoted as a major advantage of such notations, but previous research [6] has indicated substantial problems with UML as a visual notation. The concrete syntax of UML has received significantly less research attention than the abstract syntax, semantics, and pragmatics of the UML.

Whilst diagrams, when used appropriately, can support human perceptual and thought processes [15], and good layout of UML diagrams benefits model understanding [22,23], there is currently no systematic way of assessing the perceptual quality of a visual notation. Therefore, Moody's recent proposal of the "Physics of Notations" (PoN) [16] has been greeted with enthusiasm. In this paper, we study the PoN with a view to turning it from a mere theory into a practical tool that can be used to assess visual notations of practical relevance.

Approach. We pursue this project by applying PoN to UML Use Case Diagrams (UCDs). The decision for this particular case study is motivated by three considerations. First, we observe that UCDs are the second most commonly used of the UML notations, and the most highly used when clients are involved [5]. Thus UCDs can have high impact on a project, and hence require a high degree of usability. Thus, analyzing (and possibly improving it) through the application of the PoN is a goal of great practical merit.

* Thanks to UK EPSRC for support via grant EP/J010898/1.

A. Moreira et al. (Eds.): MODELS 2013, LNCS 8107, pp. 104–120, 2013.

Second, UCDs are perceived to be one of the simpler notations among those defined by UML. Using it should minimize the issues that arise from this particular notation rather than from the difficulty of operationalizing the PoN, which is our primary objective.

Third, *analyzing* a language is supposedly one of the simpler tasks the PoN claims to support (Moody characterizes it as a Gregor Type I-theory, see [12]). The 'higher' purposes of this theory need to build upon this basic capability. Since there have not yet been many attempts to use the PoN, we start at the most basic purpose that the PoN claims to address.

Contributions. Prior to this research, we expected to find a degree of freedom in exactly how to operationalise the PoN. However, during our analysis, we were surprised by the number and the fundamental nature of the issues with the PoN: (1) some of the principles are ambiguous and there is a large number of alternative assumptions which influence the outcome considerably; (2) many criteria are postulated without quantifying or relating them to each other, and there is no existing empirical knowledge to fill this gap; (3) assumptions are made and preconditions imposed which are unreasonable in that they cannot be expected from practical notations. We surmise that the PoN in its current form is not yet a tool that allows repeatable and falsifiable assessments of practical visual notations.

The main contribution of this paper is to make progress in developing the PoN into such a tool, facilitating its application in a repeatable and objective manner. Of course, we will not be able to achieve complete objectivity, since the application of a procedure such as the PoN by humans will always involve some degree of judgment. However, we aim to reduce the number of choices as far as possible, making the options and decisions clear and understandable. This will help to leverage the usefulness of the PoN.

Related Work. In the 1980's Green, Petre, and Blackwell [11,10,3] developed the Cognitive Dimensions of Notations framework (CD). It has been widely used for usability assessments and has proved to be a pragmatic and lightweight (or 'broad-brush') approach. However, CD was not originally designed to be formal, and so allows different interpretations. CD has been applied to an early version of UML in [14], but this analysis compares only simple sequence and communication diagrams, disregards secondary notation (e.g., layout), and is mainly concerned with calibrating CD against empirical results on diagram understanding. New avenues for CD research have recently been considered [9], and there are some empirical validations of the benefit of developing formal definitions of a usability framework based on CD [19]. In [16], Moody classifies CD as unfalsifiable, and thus pre-scientific, identifying it as a Gregor Type I-theory (see [12]).

Possibly the earliest systematic approach to studying the concrete syntax of UML is found in [6] where the authors transfer notions like "free ride" [20] or "cheap ride" [13] from diagrammatic theory to the concrete case of UML. They also develop novel notions like "derived meaning" and "symbol overload" for the analysis of the UML concrete syntax, deriving suggestions for improvement of UML from a visual languages point of view.

A similar, though more structured approach, was presented under the name "Physics of Notations" (PoN) in [16]. The PoN consider a wider scope of cognitive aspects of visual notations which makes it applicable to a wider range of notations. However, the UML examples contained in the PoN articles are not all convincing (e.g., see [16, Fig. 13, Tab. 1]). The follow-up article [17] adds only minor clarifications. Since the PoN is a recent achievement, there are not many publications utilising it for the study of visual notations. One is [4], where some criteria of the PoN that can be quantified easily are utilised in the assessment of visual language for robots that the authors developed. Genon et al. have applied the PoN to Use Case Maps and BPMN (see [7,8]), but it is not clear how they have computed the numeric values they provide for the various PoN criteria (e.g., semiotic clarity).

2   UML Use Case Diagrams (UCDs)

A UCD is a diagram for specifying requirements of a system, with key concepts of actors, use cases and subjects (see [18, p. 603]). See Fig. 1 for a sample UCD and Fig. 2 for an overview of the concepts represented in UCDs. The UML goes to great lengths to define the abstract syntax (i.e., the modelling concepts) for its notations, whilst the concrete syntax is much less diligently defined. We take the graphemes of UCDs to be those shown in Fig. 2 that have no patterned background.

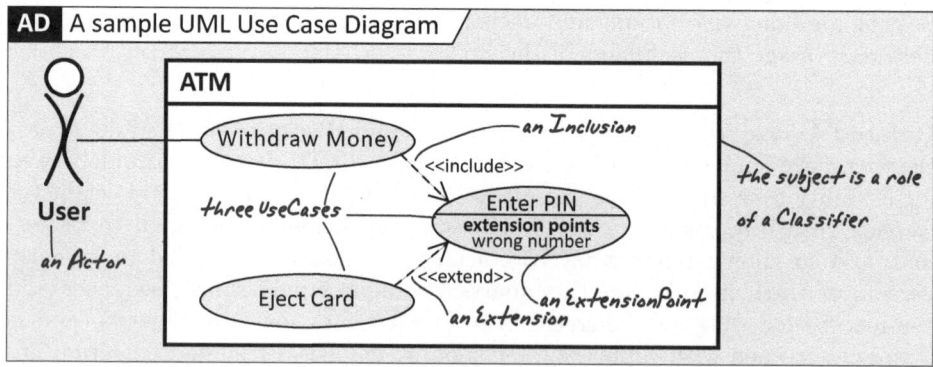

Fig. 1. A sample UML Use Case Diagram (UCD). The red 'handwritten' annotations explain the UML concepts represented.

Precision. The description is *informal*, offering only prose and a few examples to explain the syntax, usage, and constraints of UCDs. The UML also provides a list of the graphemes (see [18, Fig. 16.1, pp. 617]), but that list is informal and incomplete. We ignore the alternative notation of ExtensionPoint, since this

Grapheme ("Symbol")	Meta Class ("Concept")	Informal Meaning	Alternative Notations
(actor figure) <Name>	Actor 16.3.1	role played by a user or any other system interacting with the subject	<<actor>> <Name> (icon) <Name> any icon
(box) <Name>	subject (Classifier) 16.3.2 (7.3.8)	set of instances with common features	<Name>
(oval) <Name>	UseCase 16.3.6	specification of a set of actions performed by a system	<Name> ○ (oval) <Name>
extension points <ep name>	ExtensionPoint 16.3.4	describes tuples of references to instances	<Name> ○ extension points <ep name> : in <state>
/	Association 7.3.3	describes tuples of references to instances	none
↗	Generalization 7.3.20	holds between a more general and a more specific classifier	none
<<include>> ↗	Include 16.3.5	defines that a use case contains the behavior defined in another use case	none
<<extend>> ↗	Extend 16.3.3	how/when the extending use cases behavior can be inserted into the extended use case	<<extend>> ↗ condition: <state> extension point: <ep name>
(note symbol)	Comment 7.3.9	a textual annotation that can be attached to a set of elements	none
/·/	undefined 7.3.9 (notation)	may be used to specify the model element to which a comment refers	none

Fig. 2. The concepts and notations of UCD: the contents of columns 3 and 4 are taken directly from the UML standard, the respective chapters are indicated in column 2. The alternative notations with patterned background are not considered here.

is really not an alternative for ExtensionPoint, but a combination of the one grapheme for extension point with the alternative notation of UseCase.

Focus. The description of the notation is *split across* several places in Chapter 16, with some aspects and examples explained for individual concepts (e.g. the last subsections in each of Sections 16.3.1–16.3.6), and some for diagram type (e.g. Section 16.4), which gives rise to inconsistency and incompleteness in the descriptions. Moreover, the description of the notational elements are scattered over the whole UML standard: five out of ten concepts commonly used in UCDs are defined in other chapters (e.g. Comments, Classifiers and Associations). Since the relevant standard document is 752 pages long, it is difficult to obtain a comprehensive view of UCDs. Also, the standard does not define some graphemes at all, e.g., any icon may be used to represent Actors; we exclude the notation "any icon".

Comments. the PoN indicates that one should disregard secondary notation such as layout and naming conventions when analysing a visual notation. In particular, it considers UML comments as secondary notation that *"will [erroneously] be interpreted as constructs"* (cf. [16, p. 762]). However, within the context of practical UML modelling, comments are not simply meta-level annotations, but they are frequently used as ad-hoc extensions to the modelling notation adding significant detail such as OCL constraints or specifications of extension points (see p. 617, [18]). Also, there is a meta class "Comment" in the UML meta model, so comments *are* proper model elements in UML. Therefore, we include comments as "first class modelling constructs" in the community of model elements. We exclude the alternative notation in Fig. 2, because it is just a combination of the graphemes for Extend and a Comment with a structured text, and the PoN does not cover textual annotations of this kind.

Layout. The PoN offers no concept that allows us to differentiate between different placements of inscriptions on graphemes, as used in the alternative notation for UseCases in Fig. 2. Thus we exclude this grapheme in our considerations.

In order to apply the PoN to UCDs, we have to make interpretations and place restrictions on the UCD notation, which we will describe as we progress. Similar restrictions will likely have to be applied for the analysis of other UML notations, and, possibly, most other practically relevant notations. This means the first step of applying the PoN in a realistic setting must be to ensure its applicability, possibly documenting all restrictions and assumptions about the notation to be analysed. In fact, we expect it to be necessary to first provide a description of the notation in a standardized and precise way before the PoN can be applied at all. Currently, this is not part of the PoN. One might argue that this is a shortcoming of the languages in question, but if the PoN is to be useful in a practical setting, it must itself be adapted to fit into such a setting.

3   Physics of Notations

The PoN attempts to lay a scientific foundation for analysing and constructing visual notations in software engineering by drawing on existing knowledge from Psychophysics, Cognitive Psychology, and Graphic Design. PoN postulates nine principles that decompose into 25 criteria (see Fig. 3). Due to lack of space we examine only the first two of the PoN principles (A and B) in this paper. Even so, these account for almost two fifths of the PoN criteria.

We address these criteria individually, identifying any assumptions and choices made in the process of operationalisation. Aiming for conceptual simplicity we adopt 'symmetric definitions' for metrics wherever possible (e.g., duality within concepts should lead to duality in metric definitions; see metrics SR and SO below). We provide adjustable weights for metrics to accommodate future empirical findings (e.g., the relative weight of visual variables). All metrics are normalised to range from 0 to 1, and stable in the sense that small changes in a notation will lead to relatively small changes in the assessment.

3.1   A: Semiotic Clarity

Semiotic clarity is the degree to which a notation achieves a one-to-one mapping between its concepts and symbols. It is assessed through four criteria: symbol

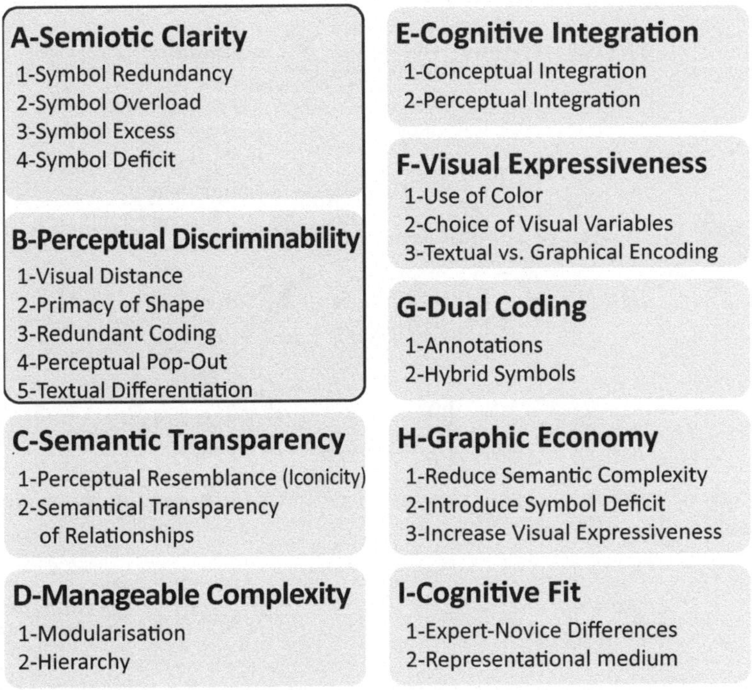

A-Semiotic Clarity	E-Cognitive Integration
1-Symbol Redundancy 2-Symbol Overload 3-Symbol Excess 4-Symbol Deficit	1-Conceptual Integration 2-Perceptual Integration

A-Semiotic Clarity

1-Symbol Redundancy
2-Symbol Overload
3-Symbol Excess
4-Symbol Deficit

B-Perceptual Discriminability

1-Visual Distance
2-Primacy of Shape
3-Redundant Coding
4-Perceptual Pop-Out
5-Textual Differentiation

C-Semantic Transparency

1-Perceptual Resemblance (Iconicity)
2-Semantical Transparency
   of Relationships

D-Manageable Complexity

1-Modularisation
2-Hierarchy

E-Cognitive Integration

1-Conceptual Integration
2-Perceptual Integration

F-Visual Expressiveness

1-Use of Color
2-Choice of Visual Variables
3-Textual vs. Graphical Encoding

G-Dual Coding

1-Annotations
2-Hybrid Symbols

H-Graphic Economy

1-Reduce Semantic Complexity
2-Introduce Symbol Deficit
3-Increase Visual Expressiveness

I-Cognitive Fit

1-Expert-Novice Differences
2-Representational medium

Fig. 3. The PoN principles and their criteria; this paper covers principles A and B

redundancy (multiple graphemes are used for one construct), symbol overload (multiple constructs use the same grapheme), symbol excess (graphemes representing no constructs), and symbol deficit (constructs without representation). We formalise these criteria.

A visual notation N is a triple $\langle C, G, \sigma \rangle$, where C and G are the sets of concepts and graphemes used in N, respectively (with $C \cap G = \emptyset$), and $\sigma \subseteq C \times G$ is the relation associating concepts and graphemes. The PoN uses the name "constructs" for concepts, but in the UML this corresponds to the meta-classes whose instances may occur in a diagram of given type. We write C_N to indicate the concept C from a notation N, and we use G_N and σ_N similarly, omitting N if it is clear from the context. We write $\sigma(c)$ to denote $\{g \in G \mid \langle c, g \rangle \in \sigma\}$, the image of $c \in C$ under $\sigma(c)$, and similarly $\sigma^{-1}(g)$ denotes $\{c \in C \mid \langle c, g \rangle \in \sigma\}$. Let

$$visualized(C) := \{c \in C \mid \sigma(c) \neq \emptyset\}$$
$$meaningful(G) := \{g \in G \mid \sigma^{-1}(g) \neq \emptyset\}$$

denote the sets of concepts with at least one associated grapheme, and the set of graphemes with at least one associated concept, respectively. We frequently lift functions from elements to sets of elements. The degree of symbol redundancy of a notation N is

$$SR(N) := \frac{1}{|visualized(C_N)|} \sum_{c \in C_N} redundancy(c)$$

where

$$redundancy(c) := \begin{cases} 0 & \text{if } \sigma(c) = \emptyset, \\ 1 - \frac{1}{|\sigma(c)|} & \text{otherwise.} \end{cases}$$

Analogously, the degree of symbol overload of N is

$$SO(N) := \frac{1}{|meaningful(G_N)|} \sum_{g \in G_N} overload(g)$$

where

$$overload(g) := \begin{cases} 0 & \text{if } \sigma^{-1}(g) = \emptyset, \\ 1 - \frac{1}{|\sigma^{-1}(g)|} & \text{otherwise.} \end{cases}$$

The degrees of symbol excess and symbol deficit of a notation N are defined in parallel as

$$SE(N) := 1 - \frac{|meaningful(G_N)|}{|G_N|}, \quad \text{and} \quad SD(N) := 1 - \frac{|visualized(C_N)|}{|C_N|}.$$

The only data these metrics require as input are the sets of concepts and graphemes and their relationships, as defined by the notation.

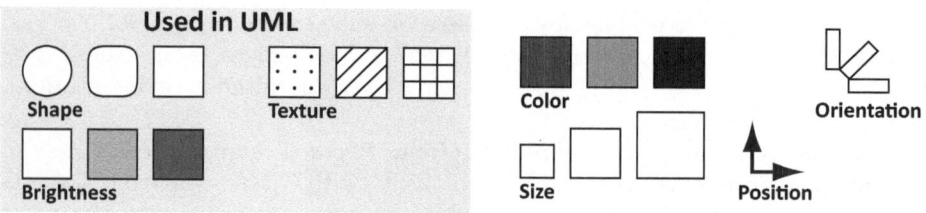

Fig. 4. Bertin's eight visual variables (position has two dimensions): only shape, texture, and brightness are used in UML

3.2   B: Perceptual Discriminability

The PoN defines the principle of perceptual discriminability of two graphemes as *"the ease and accuracy with which [they] can be differentiated from each other"*. Moody decomposes this principle into five criteria: visual distance, primacy of shape, redundant coding, perceptual pop-out, and textual differentiation. Since the PoN builds on Bertin's notion of visual variables [2,1], shown in Fig. 4, one can simply assign to each grapheme a tuple of the values according to these visual variables. We call this tuple the *visual vector* of a grapheme. By convention, we use the variables g and h for graphemes in a given visual notation, $v(g)$ for the visual vector of g, and $v_i(g)$ for the i-th component of the visual vector of g.

Grapheme ("Symbol")	Meta Class ("Concept")	Visual Variables			Textual Differentiation
		Shape	Texture	Brightness	
 (stick figure) <Name>	Actor	Stick Figure	Solid	White	-
(terminal icon) <Name>	Actor	Terminal	Pattern1	Grey1	-
<<actor>> <Name>	Actor	Rectangle	Solid	White	<<actor>>
<Name>	Classifier as subject				-
<Name>	Classifier as subject	Combination1 2 rectangles	Solid	White	-
(comment box)	Comment	Combination2 rectangle, triangle	Solid	White	-
(<Name>)	UseCase	Ellipse	Solid	White	-
<Name>	UseCase	Combination3 2 rectangles, ellipse	Solid	White	-
extension points <ep name>	ExtensionPoint	Line	Solid	-	extension points
	Association				-
(dashed line)	attachment of comment	Line	Dashed	-	-
(arrow)	Generalization	Arrow1	Solid	White	-
<<include>>	Inclusion	Arrow2	Dashed	-	<<includes>>
<<extend>>	Extension				<<extends>>

Fig. 5. Assessment of Bertin's 8 visual variables for the graphemes of UML UCDs

B.1: Visual Distance. We interpret visual vectors as points in 8-dimensional space. Classic results from Psychophysics indicate the range of values we can expect humans to easily discriminate (c.f. [2,21]). For instance, humans can easily distinguish 6-7 different values for brightness (i.e. shades of grey), and 2-5 different textures, whilst the number of different shapes we can distinguish is virtually unlimited. Brightness is on an ordinal scale (for simplicity, we assume equidistance), whilst textures and shapes are on nominal scales. We compute the values utilized within the semiotic clarity principle, comprising of the visual variables (shape, texture, brighness), following Bertin, and the additional textual discrimination (used in Fig. 5 below).

Shape provides the richest variations and the highest impact on visual discriminability. Assuming shapes to be a homogeneous set would be the simplest option, only observing shapes as either the same or different. However, a more refined measure would provide a notion of similarity of shape, indicating that a rectangle is more closely related to an ellipse than a stick figure, for example. For definiteness, we postulate three basic groups of shapes (lines, icons, and regions), and we decompose regions into two types: simple (e.g., rectangles and ellipses) and complex (e.g., a combination of two rectangles and an ellipse, as in the alternative grapheme of UseCases). We assume that elements in different groups are less similar than elements in the same group. Fig. 6 shows the basic shapes in UCDs, and our proposed shape groupings.

One may postulate that there are gradations of similarities between circles, ellipses, roundtangles (a rectangular shape with rounded corners), and rectangles for instance (e.g. circles are closer to ellipses than to rectangles, and roundtangles are as similar to rectangles as to ellipses). However, since such gradations are relatively subtle in comparison with the fundamental differences between the shape groups, we do not refine the shape groups further here. Empirical evidence testing for similarity of shapes appears appropriate before further hypothesis and subsequent examination to see if intra-group differences are significant. We assume a visual shape distance (abbreviated to *vsd*) of 0.5 between elements of the same basic group (line, icon, simple, complex), 1 between elements of different main groups (line, icon, region), and 0.75 between different subgroups (simple and complex regions).

Bertin seems to interpret texture mainly for areas (see [16, Fig. 7]), but the PoN also applies it to lines (cf. "*solid and dashed*" [16, p. 769]). UCDs (and, in fact, UML) only use solid fill for areas, and solid or dashed lines. Icons are assigned a unique "pattern" value. For other notations, different textures may have to be distinguished; the PoN proposes to use 2-5 different values.

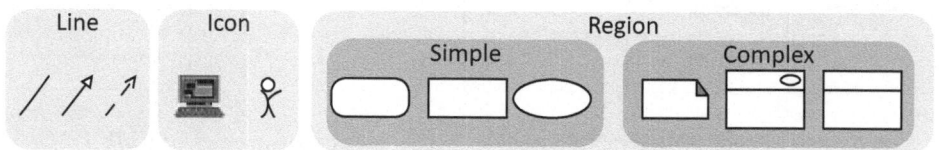

Fig. 6. Visual distance between any two shapes depends on their relative grouping

For our evaluation, we took the brightness of a grapheme to be the brightness of the largest area contained in the grapheme ("undefined" if there is no such area); the PoN proposes to use 6-7 different values of grey. Clearly, high visual distance would contribute to high perceptual discriminability. However, for the criteria of semiotic clarity, low values amount to high quality. In order to permit a unified interpretation of the results, we invert the scale for visual distance so that small values represent high quality. The same will be done below for the criteria B.2 and B.4.

B.2: Primacy of Shape. The PoN emphasises that "*shape should be the primary visual variable*"; that is, the distance between two visual vectors is affected more strongly by shape differences than other visual variable changes. However, the PoN does not quantify the impact of shape (or make any judgement on its impact relative to variation in several other visual variables).

We implement the primacy of shape criterion by attaching a specific weight to the visual vectors when determining their distance. This weight can easily be adjusted when empirical results are obtained which provide evidence for the perceptual distances involved. Since empirical results are not yet available, we propose an initial model in which the weight for shape distance is as high as all of the other weights combined (taking weight 1 for the seven other variables, and weight 7 for shape). We define the visual variable difference function vvd, for visual variables a, b, as follows:

$$vvd(a,b) := \begin{cases} 0 & \text{if } a = b \text{ or both are undefined} \\ \frac{|a-b|}{c} & \text{if } a \neq b \text{ on ordinal scale with capacity } c \\ 0.5 & \text{if } a \neq b \text{ are shapes in same basic group} \\ 0.75 & \text{if } a, b \text{ are shapes in different subgroups} \\ 1 & \text{if } a, b \text{ are shapes in different main groups} \\ & \text{or } a \neq b \text{ on a nominal scale (except shape)} \\ & \text{or exactly one of } a \text{ or } b \text{ is undefined} \end{cases}$$

where the capacity is the maximal number of perceptual steps of a scale. The visual distance between graphemes is:

$$vd(g,h) := \frac{1}{||w||} \sum_{i=1}^{d} w_i \cdot vvd(v_i(g), v_i(h))$$

where $||w|| = \sum_{i=1}^{d} w_i$, d is the number of visual dimensions (i.e. 8 according to Bertin's theory), and $w = \langle w_1, \ldots, w_d \rangle$ is a weight vector used to calibrate the measure. For a notation N, we obtain the following metric for its average visual distance (including the primacy of shape):

$$VD(N) := 1 - \frac{1}{|G_N|^2} \sum_{g,h \in G_N} vd(g,h).$$

B.3: Redundant Coding. The PoN indicates that multiple variables should be used to distinguish between any two graphemes in an attempt to reduce perceptual errors through visual redundancy. We make use of the number of visual variables in which two graphemes g and h from G_N differ:

$$vr(g,h) := \frac{1}{d} \sum_{i=1}^{d} [v_i(g) \neq v_i(h)]$$

where $[\phi]$ denotes 1 if the predicate ϕ is true, and 0 otherwise. Thus, the PoN recommendation is that for the visual vectors of any two graphemes g, h in a visual notation, $vr(g, h) \geq 2/d$ should hold. For a notation N we obtain the following measure for redundant coding:

$$RC(N) := \frac{1}{|G_N|^2} \sum_{g,h \in G_N} vr(g, h).$$

B.4: Perceptual Pop-out. The PoN recommends that each grapheme of a visual notation has a unique value in one visual variable so that it may be identified by that unique value as opposed to requiring a combinations of values to discriminate. Thus, for any two graphemes g and h in a given visual notation, there is an i with $0 < i \leq d$ such that $g \neq h \implies v_i(g) \neq v_i(h)$. For a grapheme g, within a set of graphemes G, we define its perceptual pop-out as

$$ppo(G, g) := \begin{cases} 1 & \text{if } \exists 0 < i \leq d \text{ such that } \forall h \in G \\ & \quad g \neq h \implies v_i(g) \neq v_i(h) \\ 0 & \text{otherwise.} \end{cases}$$

The perceptual pop-out of a set of graphemes G_N is:

$$PPO(N) := 1 - \frac{1}{|G_N|} \sum_{g \in G_N} ppo(G_N, g).$$

B.5: Textual Differentiation. Notational elements can also be differentiated by textual annotations: two different graphemes g and h, can have the same values on all visual variables, so that $v(g) = v(h)$, but may have additional textual annotation which enables discrimination. The PoN recommends not permitting this option because it is a cognitively inefficient procedure (reducing the role of perceptual processing). An example of textual differentiation are the includes- and extends-relationships of UCDs, which are visually identical except for the textual annotations "includes" and "extends".

We define the degree of textual differentiation for the vocabulary G as the proportion of graphemes whose appearance only differs by a textual annotation.

$$TD(N) := \frac{|\{g \in G_N \,|\, \exists g' \in G_N : g \text{ and } g' \text{ differ only by text}\}|}{|G_N|}$$

4   Semiotic Clarity of UCDs

Based on the UCD, as defined in Fig. 2, the criteria contained in the PoN principle of semiotic clarity can be computed objectively, yielding the values shown in Fig. 7 (top). Observe that the UML does mention the use of colour in diagrams as an option to highlight individual model elements, but this is not a normative part of the standard: UML explicitly abstains from semantic interpretation of colour, size, position, and orientation. That is to say, any two graphemes defined by UML will be indistinguishable with respect to these visual dimensions.

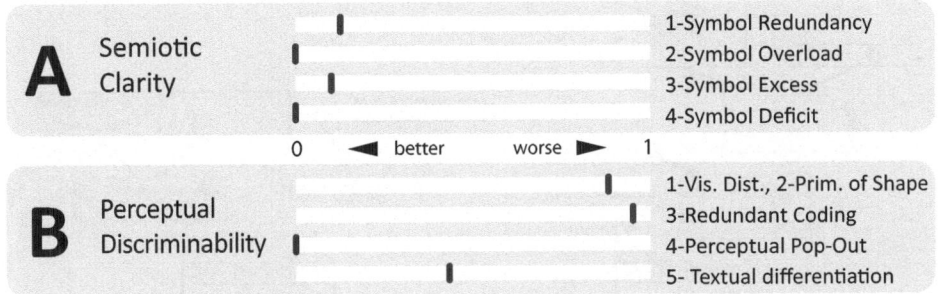

Fig. 7. The assessment of the criteria of the first two PoN principles according to our formalization and assumptions; scales for criteria B1 through B4 have been reversed as compared to the original definition in the PoN for increased clarity

We see that UCDs have neither symbol deficit, nor symbol overload. The values for symbol excess and symbol redundancy appear to be small. However, the PoN does not provide any indication of relative size or thresholds, and there is no comparable data for other notations.

The impact of alternatives in our operationalisation provide more insight into the PoN. We have argued that UCDs shall contain comments as a proper concept. Dropping this assumption, i.e., removing both the concept and the associated graphemes from the language definition, symbol excess drops from .071 to 0, while symbol redundancy climbs from 0.185 to 0.208. Again, due to a lack of comparable data, we cannot judge the magnitude of these differences.

Also, the measure of semiotic clarity very much depends on the definition of the notation vocabulary; making different assumptions for UCDs influences the outcome of the analysis. Consider for example the graphemes for Actor. If we drop our assumption and accept that any *"other icons [...] may also be used [Actors]"* as the UML standard declares [18, p. 606], we have $|\sigma(\texttt{Actor})| = \infty$. Then, symbol redundancy climbs to 1 (assuming $1/\infty = 0$), while the other metrics remain constant.

Finally, the PoN does not offer a concept of graphemes as compounds of other graphemes, such as the first alternative notation of UseCase in Fig. 2. Here, a compartmented box (which in turn could be considered as a combination of two rectangles), is combined with a small ellipse. The result may again be combined with the grapheme for ExtensionPoint, as shown in the parse tree in Fig. 8 (left). However, there may be alternative grapheme compositions, as in Fig. 8 (right), and so it is not clear what the base graphemes should be.

The PoN does not offer concepts which are useful for capturing syntactical structures, except for compounds of a grapheme and a piece of text ("textual differentiation"). The PoN does not appear to distinguish between constant pieces of text (such as stereotypes) which carry semantic meaning on the type level, and variable pieces of text (such as names) which only carry meaning at the instance level. Likewise, the PoN does not differentiate between the content of a piece of text and its formatting (e.g., bold, italics, underlining), see [16, p. 763].

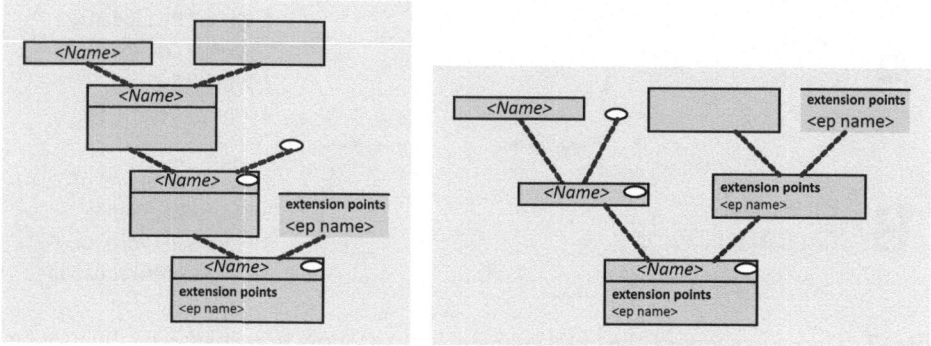

Fig. 8. Graphemes can be understood as compounds

In this paper, we consider all graphemes as individuals rather than compounds. It is clear, however, that this will lead to an explosion in the number of graphemes if a language systematically uses compounds, as the UML does (see [6]). Thus, the application of the PoN to larger parts of the UML will be very difficult without a method for dealing with compound graphemes.

5 Perceptual Discriminability of UCDs

Computing perceptual discriminability of UCDs yields the values shown in Fig. 7 (bottom). We see that UCDs enjoy maximal perceptual pop-out, and close to minimal redundant coding and visual distance, including primacy of shape.[1] Again, we lack guidance from the PoN and previous work, so we have no means of assessing the significance of the value of these metrics.

We have assumed a certain structure of the distances of shapes (see Fig. 6), but do not yet have empirical evidence to support our assumption. If we vary our assumption, however, the visual distance metric decreases from 0.222 (our original assumption), to 0.221 (no difference between simple and complex shapes), and 0.218 (equidistance between all shapes). Thus, the visual distance decreases as we take fewer differences into account. Consider also the "any icon" alternative notation for actors which we have excluded in Section 2. Observe that we could not assess its perceptual discriminability here, simply because the grapheme is undefined.

Almost all UCD graphemes have a unique value in one visual variable (shape), thus affording perceptual pop-out. The exceptions to this rule are: (1) the includes- and extends-relationships which have identical values in all of their visual variables, and (2) the first alternative notation for Actor which is visually identical to Classifier (i.e. subject).

---

[1] Recall that maximal corresponds to 0 here, and minimal to 1.

6   Discussion

The PoN aspires to be a theory *"to evaluate, compare, and improve existing visual notations [for SE] as well as to construct new ones."* (cf. [16, p. 756]). We apply it to UCDs, a relatively simple visual notation, so as to reduce issues arising from the UCD notation rather than those arising from the PoN, whose formalisation is our primary objective.

This case study resulted in an operationalization of the first part of the PoN in a traceable and verifiable way. In this process, we exhibited shortcomings and deficiencies in the PoN, also highlighting weaknesses in the description of the concrete syntax of UML UCDs along the way. Most of all, however, it became clear that it will take a major additional effort to achieve a complete operationalization of the PoN. We will now discuss the obstacles we have identified for this effort.

Grapheme Structure. While the PoN seems to maintain that graphemes are atomic and small in number, they are in fact structured and numerous, at least for practical languages such as UML or BPMN. First, even the most basic graphemes may be built up from smaller, orthogonal graphical primitives, which gives rise to alternative decompositions (see Fig. 8 for an example).

Second, UML and similar languages frequently utilise nesting of graphemes to express semantic relationships, e.g., nesting a UseCase within a Classifier as in Fig. 1. If we consider such a combination to constitute a new grapheme, visual notations would generally have a very large number of graphemes, which makes no sense. However, nesting a small ellipse in the top right corner of a rectangle representing a UseCase does constitute a new grapheme (see the alternative notation for UseCase in Fig. 2), although visually, there is only little difference between them. In order to make a difference, we would have to consider internal grapheme structure (i.e., compartments) as well as relative size and position.

Third, there are subtle interactions between the internal structure of graphemes constituting a single concept, and the combination of graphemes that each represent individual concepts, at least in UML.

Text and Diagram Structure. The PoN focuses almost exclusively on graphical symbols, and summarizes all forms of text as "textual annotation". However, these annotations are rich in structure, too, at least in UML. For instance, the text structure (e.g., presence of ':' or '/' in a name), and format (e.g., bold, italic, underline) are meaningful, and there are constant and variable annotations (e.g., stereotypes and names, respectively), that add information at the levels of concept and instance, respectively.

Similarly, the PoN rejects the idea of considering diagram layout as a means of communication, even though it is clear that the quality of the layout of a UML diagram contributes quite significantly to the understanding of, and performance with, a model (see [22]). The PoN also does not consider notions for relative size and/or position of graphemes.

Empirical Foundation. the PoN collects 25 criteria organised into nine principles, but does not clearly state their relative weight. For many of these criteria, it is not clear how they should be evaluated and measured. For instance, in Section 3.2 we discussed alternatives for the visual distances between shapes. However, the PoN does not provide such information; empirical studies would be needed to determine these factors. Furthermore, the PoN provides no guidance as to what the results of any operationalization would mean, i.e., what values should be considered good or bad.

7   Conclusion

The PoN compiles a great number of valuable insights from cognitive psychology that might inform the analysis and design of visual notations, and have otherwise been underestimated or downright ignored. However, even in its first two principles, we miss precision and detailedness in the PoN that would be needed for an unambiguous operationalization. In order to apply the PoN various choices about the notation in question must be made: what are the base graphemes, how are they combined into compounds, what weight shall be assigned to them and so on. Subsequent to the production of metrics for the entire set of principles of the PoN, we envisage the production of a standard form providing guidance on exactly what choices need to be made before analysis, separating the generically required choices from any required for the specific metrics developed.

In this paper, we have begun the process of systematically operationalising the principles of the PoN. Space restrictions clearly prohibit the complete analysis, but we observe that some of the other principles do not apply to the consideration of a single notation, without dialects, and some require a basis in cognitive science models. It makes sense to develop measures for single diagram types and then to extend to consider multiple diagram types. For example, the cognitive integration principle only applies in the context of multiple diagrams, so this is not relevant to UCDs alone. Measures to reflect the intent will require some basis in cognitive theories to try to capture notions of conceptual and perceptual integration and this may be highly complex to define for arbitrary diagram types. Similarly, the principle of cognitive fit will not apply to UCDs alone since it relates to the use of different dialects for different tasks and problem solver skills; the operationalisation will require the development of metrics to distinguish dialects and differentiate between features appropriate to distinctions between expert and novices, making use of current cognitive theories of expert-novice differences, for example.

References

1. Bertin, J.: Graphics and Graphic Information- Processing. Verlag Walther de Gruyter (1981)
2. Bertin, J.: Semiology of Graphics: Diagrams, Networks, Maps. Univ. Wisconsin Press (1983)

3. Blackwell, A., Green, T.R.G.: Notational systems–the cognitive dimensions of notations framework. In: HCI Models, Theories and Frameworks: Toward a Multidisciplinary Science, pp. 103–134 (2003)
4. Diprose, J.P., MacDonald, B.A., Hosking, J.G.: Ruru: A spatial and interactive visual programming language for novice robot programming. In: Costagliola, G., et al. (eds.) Proc. IEEE Symp. Visual Languages and Human-Centric Computing (VL/HCC 2011), pp. 25–32. IEEE Computer Society (2011)
5. Dobing, B., Parsons, J.: How UML is used. Com. ACM 49(5), 109–113 (2006)
6. Fish, A., Störrle, H.: Visual qualities of the Unified Modeling Language: Deficiencies and Improvements. In: Cox, P., Hosking, J. (eds.) Proc. IEEE Symposium on Visual Languages and Human-Centric Computing (VL/HCC 2007), pp. 41–49. IEEE Computer Society (2007)
7. Genon, N., Amyot, D., Heymans, P.: Analysing the Cognitive Effectiveness of the UCM Visual Notation. In: Kraemer, F.A., Herrmann, P. (eds.) SAM 2010. LNCS, vol. 6598, pp. 221–240. Springer, Heidelberg (2011)
8. Genon, N., Heymans, P., Amyot, D.: Analysing the Cognitive Effectiveness of the BPMN 2.0 Visual Notation. In: Malloy, B., Staab, S., van den Brand, M. (eds.) SLE 2010. LNCS, vol. 6563, pp. 377–396. Springer, Heidelberg (2011)
9. Green, T.R.G., Blandford, A., Church, L., Roast, C., Clarke, S.: Cognitive Dimensions: achievements, new directions, and open questions. J. Visual Languages and Computing 17(4), 328–365 (2006)
10. Green, T.R.G., Petre, M.: Usability analysis of visual programming environments: A 'cognitive dimensions' framework. J. Visual Languages and Computing (7), 131–174 (1996)
11. Green, T.: Cognitive dimensions of notations, pp. 443–460. Cambridge University Press (1989)
12. Gregor, S.: The Nature of Theory in Information Systems. MIS Quarterly 30(3), 611–642 (2006)
13. Gurr, C.: Effective Diagrammatic Communication: Syntactic, Semantic and Pragmatic Issues. J. Visual Languages and Computing 10, 317–342 (1999)
14. Kutar, M., Britton, C., Barker, T.: A comparison of empirical study and cognitive dimensions analysis in the evaluation of uml diagrams. In: Proc. 14th Psychology of Programming Interest Group (2002)
15. Larkin, J., Simon, H.: Why a diagram is (sometimes) worth ten thousand words. Cognitive Science 11, 65–99 (1987)
16. Moody, D.L.: The Physics of Notations: Toward a Scientific Basis for Constructing Visual Notations in Software Engineering. IEEE Trans. Software Engineering 35(6), 756–779 (2009)
17. Moody, D., van Hillegersberg, J.: Evaluating the Visual Syntax of UML: An Analysis of the Cognitive Effectiveness of the UML Family of Diagrams. In: Gašević, D., Lämmel, R., Van Wyk, E. (eds.) SLE 2008. LNCS, vol. 5452, pp. 16–34. Springer, Heidelberg (2009)
18. OMG: OMG Unified Modeling Language (OMG UML), Superstructure, V2.4 (ptc/2010-11-14). Technical report, Object Management Group (January 2011)
19. Roast, C.R., Khazaei, B.: An Investigation into the Validation of Formalised Cognitive Dimensions, pp. 109–122. Springer (2007)
20. Shimojima, A.: Inferential and Expressive Capacities of Graphical Representations: Survey and Some Generalizations. In: Blackwell, A.F., Marriott, K., Shimojima, A. (eds.) Diagrams 2004. LNCS (LNAI), vol. 2980, pp. 18–21. Springer, Heidelberg (2004)

21. Stevens, S.S.: Psychophysics. J. Wiley & Sons (1975)
22. Störrle, H.: On the Impact of Layout Quality to Unterstanding UML Diagrams. In: Costagliola, G., et al. (eds.) Proc. IEEE Symp. Visual Languages and Human-Centric Computing (VL/HCC 2011), pp. 135–142. IEEE Computer Society (2011)
23. Störrle, H.: On the Impact of Layout Quality to Unterstanding UML Diagrams: Diagram Type and Expertise. In: Costagliola, G., Ko, A., Cypher, A., Nichols, J., Scaffidi, C., Kelleher, C., Myers, B. (eds.) Proc. IEEE Symp. Visual Languages and Human-Centric Computing (VL/HCC 2012), pp. 195–202. IEEE Computer Society (2012)

Teaching Model Driven Engineering
from a Relational Database Perspective

Don Batory[1], Eric Latimer[1], and Maider Azanza[2]

[1] University of Texas at Austin, Austin, TX 78712 USA
batory@cs.utexas.edu, e@utexas.edu
[2] University of the Basque Country (UPV/EHU), San Sebastian, Spain
maider.azanza@ehu.es

Abstract. We reinterpret MDE from the viewpoint of relational databases to provide an alternative way to teach, understand, and demonstrate MDE using concepts and technologies that should be familiar to undergraduates. We use (1) relational databases to express models and metamodels, (2) Prolog to express constraints and M2M transformations, (3) Java tools to implement M2T and T2M transformations, and (4) OO shell-scripting languages to compose MDE transformations. Case studies demonstrate the viability of our approach.

1 Introduction

Model Driven Engineering (MDE) is a standard technology for program specification and construction. We believe it is essential to expose undergraduates to MDE concepts (models, metamodels, M2M, M2T, T2M transformations, constraints, and bootstrapping), so that they will have an appreciation for MDE when they encounter it in industry. Our motivation was experience: unless students encounter an idea (however immature) in school, they are less likely to embrace it in the future. *Further, teaching MDE is intimately related, if not inseparable, to the tools and languages that make MDE ideas concrete.*

Our initial attempt to do this (Fall 2011) was a failure. We used the Eclipse Modeling Tools[1] and spent quite some time creating videos for students to watch, both for installation and for tool usage. For whatever reason, installation for students was a problem. A version of Eclipse was eventually posted that had all the tools installed. The results were no better when students used the tools. A simple assignment was given to draw a metamodel for state diagrams (largely something presented in class) using Eclipse, let Eclipse generate a tool for drawing state diagrams, and to use this generated tool to draw particular state diagrams. This turned into a very frustrating experience for most students. 25% of our upper-division undergraduate class got it right; 50% had mediocre submissions, and the remaining just gave up. Another week was given (with tutorial help) to allow 80% to "get it right", but that still left too many behind. The whole experience left a bitter taste for us, and worse, our students. *We do not know if this is a typical situation or an aberration, but we will not try this again.*

---

[1] Specifically EMT, Graphical Modeling Tooling Framework Plug-in, OCL Tools Plug-in, and Eugenia for Eclipse 3.6.2.

A. Moreira et al. (Eds.): MODELS 2013, LNCS 8107, pp. 121–137, 2013.

In retrospect we found many reasons, but basically Eclipse MDE tools are the problem. (1) The tools we used were unappealing—they were difficult to use even for trivial applications. (2) The tools fostered a medieval mentality in students to use incantations to solve problems. Point here, click that, something happens. From a student's perspective, this is gibberish. Although we could tell them what was happening, this mode of interaction leaves a vacuum where a deep understanding should reside. (3) With the benefit of years of hindsight, we concluded that the entry cost of using, teaching, and understanding these tools was too high for our comfort. (Whether students agree with this or not is the subject of an empirical study targeted for this fall). We sought an alternative and light-weight way to understand and demonstrate MDE, *leveraging tools and concepts undergraduates should already know.*

In this paper, we present an evolutionary rather than revolutionary approach to understand and teach core MDE concepts (models, metamodels, M2M, M2T, T2M transformations, constraints, and bootstrapping). We tried this approach with a new class of undergraduates in Fall 2012 with many fewer problems. (Again, we carefully avoid words like "better" or "more successful" until the results of our empirical study are in; the appropriate word to use is "interesting"). This paper concentrates on the technology we used and the case studies in its evaluation). It is our hope that others in MDE may benefit from the simplicity of our approach.

2 MDE Models and MetaModels

MDE can be understood as an application of relational databases. Although MDE is usually presented in terms of graphs (as visual representations of models or metamodels), all graphs have simple encodings as a set of normalized tables.

Consider a metamodel for *finite state machines (FSMs)* in Figure 1a, consisting of nodes and edges. The schemas of the underlying relational tables (using manufactured identifiers, denoted by *node#* and *edge#*) are shown in Figure 1b.

An instance of a FSM populates these tables with tuples. The FSM of the first author's eating habits and its tuples are given in Figure 1c-d.

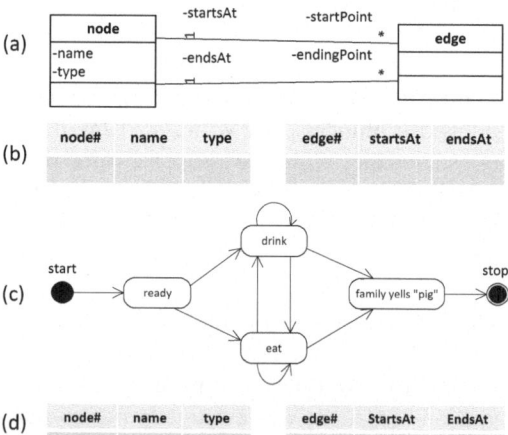

Fig. 1. A State Machine and its Tables

Manufactured tuple identifiers eliminate virtually all of the complexities of relational table design (*c.f.* [8,12]). There are only five simple rules to map metamodels to table definitions and one rule for tuple instantiation:

1. Every metaclass maps to a distinct table. If a metaclass has k attributes, the table will contain *at least* $1 + k$ columns: one for the identifier and one for each attribute.
2. $n : m$ associations are valid in metamodels [17], but not in ours. Every association must have an end with a 0..1 or 1 cardinality. Figure 2 shows how $n : m$ associations are transformed into a pair of $1 : n$ and $1 : m$ associations with an explicit association class. The reason for this is the next rule.

Fig. 2. Transformation That Removes $n : m$ Associations

3. Each association is represented by a single attribute on the "0 : 1" or "1" side of the association. Usually an association adds an attribute to both tables that it relates. The "n" side would have a set-valued attribute which is disallowed in normalized tables. The "1" side has a unary-valued attribute (a tuple identifier) which is permitted. As both attributes encode exactly the same information, we simply drop the set-valued attribute. Figure 3a illustrates the application of the last three rules: the *dept* table has two columns (# and *name*) and the *student* table has three (#, *utid*, and *enrolledIn*). Column *enrolledIn*, which contains a *dept*# value, represents the *student − dept* association. The mapping of Figure 1a to 1b is another example.

Fig. 3. Diagram-to-Table Mapping

4. For classes that are related by inheritance, all attributes of superclasses are propagated into the class tables. The identifier of the root class is shared by all subclasses. Tables need not be produced for abstract classes. See Figure 4.
5. Only objects of a class that are not instances of subclasses populate the tuples of a table. This rule is is discussed in more detail in Section 4.
6. Tuple identifiers can manufactured (*e.g.* $e1$ and $e3$ in Figure 1d) or they can be readable single-column keys (*e.g.* *nReady* and *nDrink*). Keys are preferred for handwritten assignments; manufactured identifiers are preferred in tools.

Note that relational tables have always been able to encode data hierarchies. We see the elegance of normalized or "flat" tables to be an important conceptual simplicity.

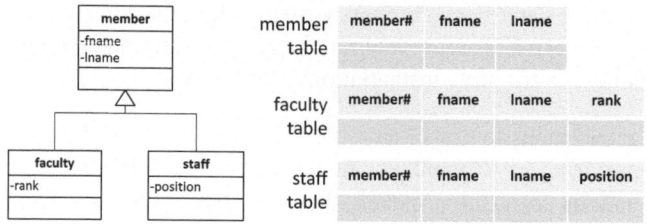

Fig. 4. Inheritance Diagram-to-Table Mapping

3   Model Constraints

OCL is the standard language for expressing model constraints. Given the connection to relational databases, we can do better. Prolog is a fundamental language in *Computer Science (CS)* for writing declarative database constraints. It is Turing-complete and is a language that all CS students should have exposure. Figure 5a shows how to express tuples of a relational table as Prolog facts. The first fact in Figure 5a defines the schema of the *node* table of Figure 1b: it has three columns {*id*, *name*, *type*}.

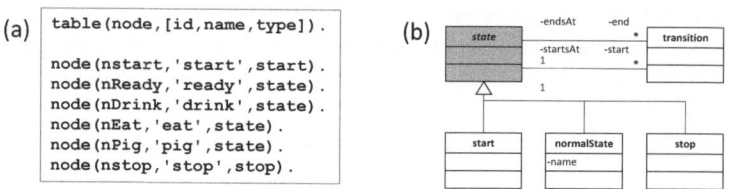

Fig. 5. A Prolog Table and Target MetaModel

Here are three constraints to enforce on a FSM:

*c*1   All states have unique names,
*c*2   All transitions must start and end at a state, and
*c*3   There must be precisely one start state.

Their expression in SWI-Prolog [19] is given below; *error(Msg)* is a library call that reports an error. *allConstraints* is true if there are no violations of each constraint.

```
c1 :- node(A,N,_),node(B,N,_),not(A=B),error('non-unique names').
c2 :- edge(_,S,E), ( not(node(_,S,_)) ; not(node(_,E,_)) ), error('bad edge').
c3a :- not(node(_,_,start)), error('no start state').
c3b :- node(A,_,start),node(B,_,start),not(A=B),error('multiple start states').
allConstraints :- not(c1),not(c2),not(c3a),not(c3b).
```

4   Model-to-Model Transformations

Fundamental activities in MDE are *model-to-model (M2M)* transformations. Instead of using languages that were specifically invented for MDE, Prolog can be used to write database-to-database (or M2M) transformations declaratively.

Suppose we want to translate the database of Figure 1d to a database that conforms to the metamodel of Figure 5b. (We shade abstract classes to make them easier to recognize.) The Prolog rules to express this transformation are:

```
start(I,A) :- node(I,A,start).
stop(I,A) :- node(I,A,stop).
normalState(I,A) :- node(I,A,state).
transition(A,B,C) :- edge(A,B,C).
```

Another example: The tuples of the *staff* and *faculty* tables of Figure 4 do not appear in the *member* table. To propagate tuples from subclass tables into superclass tables, the following transformations can be used:

```
newMember(I,F,L) :- member(I,F,L).
newMember(I,F,L) :- staff(I,F,L,_).
newMember(I,F,L) :- faculty(I,F,L,_).
newStaff(I,F,L,R) :- staff(I,F,L,R).
newFaculty(I,F,L,P) :- faculty(I,F,L,P).
```

As Prolog is Turing-complete, database transformations can be arbitrarily complex.

Observations. There is an intimate connection between database design and metamodel design. Presenting MDE in the above manner reinforces this connection. Further, students *do not* have to be familiar with databases to understand the above ideas. Normalized tables are a fundamental and simple conceptual structure in CS. Undergraduates may already have been exposed to Prolog in an introductory course on programming languages. (When one deals with normalized tuples and almost no lists, Prolog is indeed a simple language). We chose Prolog for its obvious database connection, but suspect that Datalog, Haskell, Scala, or other functional languages might be just as effective.

5   Model-to-Text Transformations

A key strength of MDE is that it mechanizes the production of boiler-plate code. This is accomplished by *Model-to-Text (M2T)* transformations. There are many text template engines used in industry. Apache Velocity is a particularly easy-to-learn and powerful example [4]. We made two small modifications to Velocity to cleanly integrate it with Prolog databases. Our tool is called *Velocity Model-2-Text (VM2T)*.

First, we defined Velocity variables for tables. If the name of a table is "*table*" then the table variable is "*tableS*" (appending an "*S*" to "*table*"). This enables a Velocity *foreach* statement to iterate over all tuples of a table:

```
#foreach($tuple in $tableS)
    ...
#end
```

Second, a Velocity template directs its output to standard out. We introduced markers to redirect output to different files during template execution. The value of the *MARKER* variable defines the name of the file to which output is directed; reassigning its value redirects output to another file. An example of *MARKER* is presented shortly.

Figure 6a shows a metamodel for classes. Two instances of this metamodel, *city* and *account*, are shown in Figure 6b. The database containing both instances is Figure 6c.

Figure 7a is a VM2T template. When the non-*MARKER* statements are executed, Figure 7b is the output. Perferably, the definition of each class should be in its own file. When all statements are executed, the desired two files are produced (Figure 7c).

Given VM2T, it is an interesting and straightforward assignment to translate the FSM database of Figure 1d to the code represented by the class diagram of Figure 8.

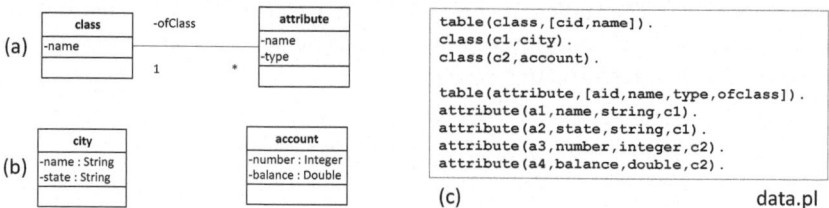

Fig. 6. A Class Metamodel, a Model, and its Prolog Database

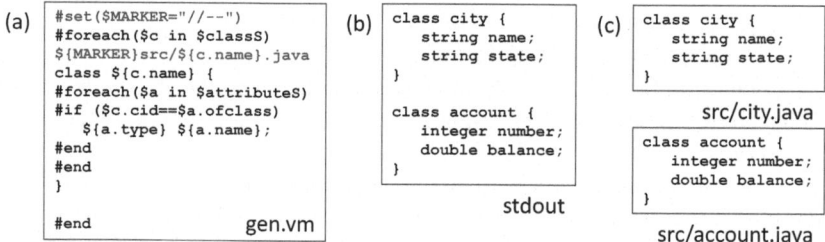

Fig. 7. A VM2T Template and Two Outputs

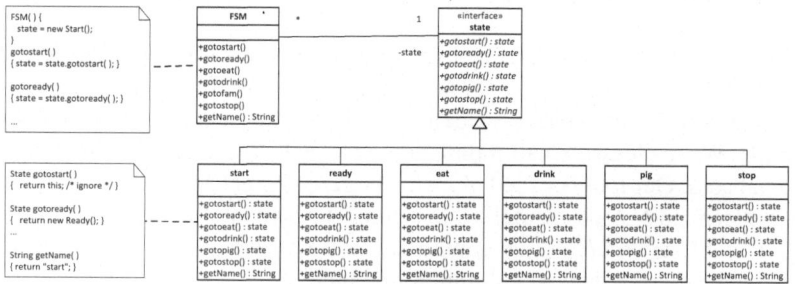

Fig. 8. Class Diagram of FSM Code Output

Observations. The benefits of Velocity seem clear: students use an industrial tool that is not-MDE or Eclipse-specific; it is stable, reasonably bug-free, and has decent documentation. In our opinion, it is easy to learn and relatively painless to use.

6   Text-to-Model Transformations

Given the above, it is not difficult for students to understand Figure 9: an application engineer specifies a FSM using a graphical tool, the tool produces a set of tables, the tables are transformed, and VM2T produces the source code for the FSM.

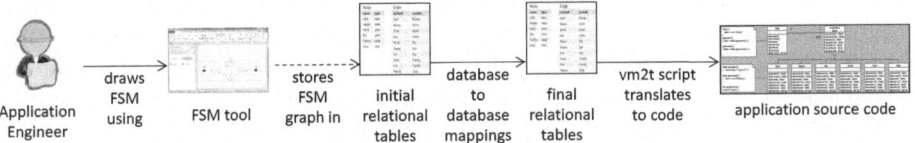

Fig. 9. FSM Application Engineering in MDE

What is missing is a *Text-to-Model (T2M)* transformation (the dashed arrow in Figure 9) that converts grossly-verbose XML output of a graphics tool into a clean set of Prolog tables. It is easy to write a simple Java program that reads XML, parses it, and outputs a single text file containing a Prolog database. Using a more general tool that parses XML into Prolog may be preferable, but loses the advantage a hands-on understanding of the inner workings of T2M transformations.

Finding suitable *graphical editor $\mathcal{GE}$* is a three-fold challenge:

(a) its XML must simple to understand,
(b) its XML is stable, meaning its XML format is unlikely to change anytime soon, and
(c) its palette[2] is customizable.

MS Visio is easy to use and its palette is easily customizable, but its XML files are incomprehensible and MS periodically modifies the format of these files. Simpler $\mathcal{GE}$s, such as Violet [21], yUML [22], UMLFactory [20], satisfy (a) and (b); it is not difficult to write T2M tools for them.

We have yet to find a $\mathcal{GE}$ that satisfies all three constraints. Violet is typical: all palettes are hardwired—there is one per UML diagram. One cannot define a set of icons (with graphic properties) to draw customized graphs. All one can do is to translate XML documents that were specifically designed for a given UML diagram to Prolog tables. This isn't bad; it just isn't ideal. Until a flexible $\mathcal{GE}$ is found, bootstrapping MDELite (to build customized $\mathcal{GE}$s for target domains, a key idea in MDE) is difficult to demonstrate. More on this in Section 9.

Observations. MDE tools (such as the FSM tool) could be structure editors. That is, a tool should immediately label incorrect drawings or prevent users from creating incorrect drawings. $\mathcal{GE}$s can be stupid—they let you draw anything (such as edges that connect no nodes). To provide immediate feedback would require saving a design to an XML document, translating the document into Prolog tables, evaluating Prolog constraints, and displaying the errors encountered. Modifying existing tools to present this feedback could be done, but this is not high-priority.

---

[2] The icons/classes that one can drag and drop onto a canvas to create instances.

7   MDELite and Its Applications

MDELite is a small set of tools (SWI Prolog, VM2T) that are loosely connected by a tiny Java framework that implements the ideas of the prior section. An *MDELite application* uses this framework and is expressed as a category [5,16]. A *category* is simply a directed multigraph; nodes are *domains* and arrows are functions (transformations) drawn from the function's domain to its codomain. Many of the interesting ideas about categories, like functors and natural transformations, are absent in the MDE applications of this paper, so there is nothing to frighten students. Nonetheless, it is useful to remind students that categories are a fundamental structure of mathematics, they are a core part of MDE formalisms (e.g., [9]), and they define the structure of an MDE application.[3]

As an example of an MDELite application, consider the tool chain that allows users to draw FSMs and generate their corresponding Java source (Figure 9). This tool chain is a category with four domains (Figure 10): the domain of XML documents that are output by the FSM tool, a domain of database instances that a T2M tool creates, another domain of database instances that results from a restructuring of T2M-produced databases, and a domain of Java Source Code whose elements are FSM programs.

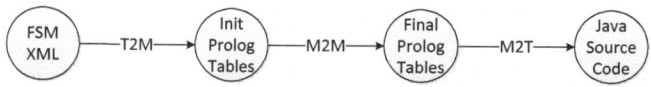

Fig. 10. Category of a FSM Tool

When this category is written in Java, each domain is a class and each arrow is a method (see Figure 11a). Unlike most UML class diagrams, MDELite designs typically have no associations, but can have inheritance relationships.

To perform an action of the FSM tool (*i.e.* a method in Figure 11a), one writes a straight-line script to invoke the appropriate transformations and checks. Figure 11b shows the sequence of method calls in an MDELite program to translate an FSMXML file—an XML file produced by the FSM drawing tool—into a Java program. Any error encountered during translation or conformance test simply halts the MDELite application with an explanative message.

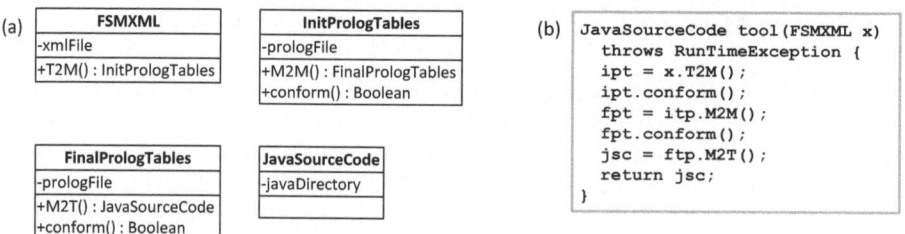

Fig. 11. MDELite Encoding of the Category of Figure 10

---

[3] Also known as *megamodels* [7] and *tool chain diagrams* [15].

Observations. *MDE lifts metamodel design to the level of* metaprogramming—*programs that build other programs.* The objects of MDE are programs (models) and the methods of MDE are transformations that yield or manipulate other programs (models). The elements of each domain are file system entities—an XML file, a Prolog file that encodes a database, or a directory of Java files—not typical programming language objects [6]. Each MDELite method is literally a distinct executable: a T2M or M2T arrow is a Java program and an M2M arrow (and conformance test) is a Prolog program. Perhaps MDELite needs to be written in an OO shell scripting language, such as Python. We used Java to implement the MDELite framework (and may reconsider this decision—we figured Prolog is enough for undergraduates to absorb). MDELite is clearly a multi-lingual application.

8   Evaluation: A Case Study of MDELite

Our first application of MDELite was quite instructive. We found several free UML tools that we wanted to (i) draw UML class diagrams, (ii) apply the ideas of the previous sections, and (iii) integrate.

The integration of the Violet, UMLFactory, and yUML tools (as they existed in June 2012) is expressed by the category of Figure 12a.[4] We could draw UML class diagrams in each of these tools and have them displayed in any other tool. So a script that translated a Violet class diagram into a yUML class diagram is Figure 12b and vice versa is Figure 12c. Figure 13 shows the translation of a specific Violet class diagram (an XML file) into an *SDBPL* database and then into a yUML class diagram (a yUML file).

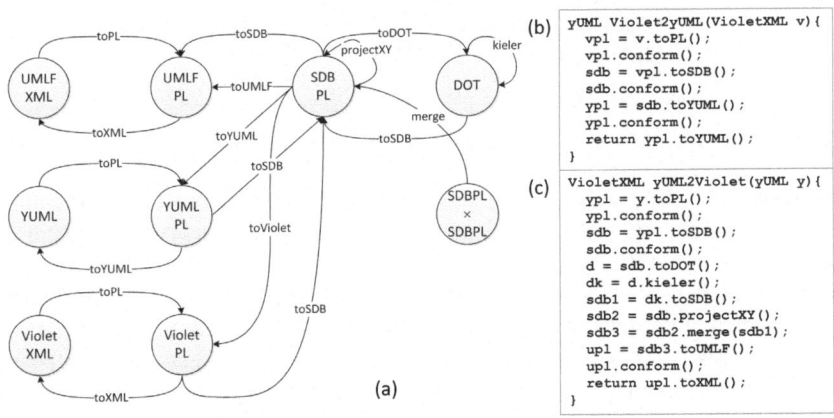

Fig. 12. A Category for an MDELite Application

The category of Figure 12a is produced by a process that is similar to global schema design in databases that integrates database schemas of different tools [10]. Each tool

---
[4] The only oddity of Figure 12a is the domain *SDBPL* × *SDBPL*, which is the cross-product of the *SDBPL* domain with itself. The *merge* arrow composes two *SDBPL* databases into a single *SPBPL* database (*i.e. merge* : *SDBPL* × *SDBPL* → *SDBPL*).

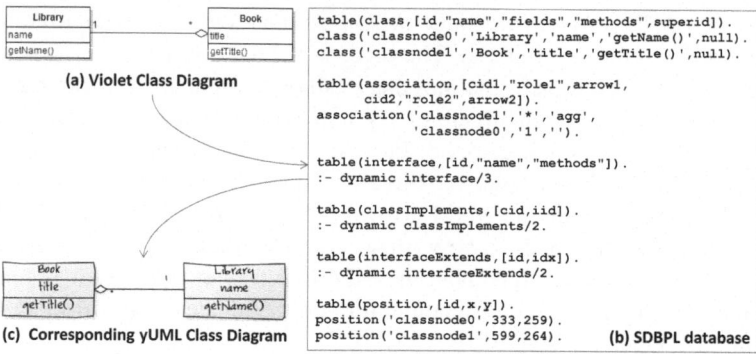

```
table(class,[id,"name","fields","methods",superid]).
class('classnode0','Library','name','getName()',null).
class('classnode1','Book','title','getTitle()',null).

table(association,[cid1,"role1",arrow1,
                  cid2,"role2",arrow2]).
association('classnode1','*','agg',
           'classnode0','1','').

table(interface,[id,"name","methods"]).
:- dynamic interface/3.

table(classImplements,[cid,iid]).
:- dynamic classImplements/2.

table(interfaceExtends,[id,idx]).
:- dynamic interfaceExtends/2.

table(position,[id,x,y]).
position('classnode0',333,259).
position('classnode1',599,264).
```

(a) Violet Class Diagram

(c) Corresponding yUML Class Diagram   (b) SDBPL database

Fig. 13. A Violet Diagram mapped to an *SDBPL* database mapped to a yUML Diagram

exports and imports a distinct data format (read: database). A global schema (a Prolog database, *SDBPL*, to which all tool-specific databases are translated) stores data that is shared by all tools. The hard part is manufacturing data that is not in the global database that is needed for tool-specific displays. An example is given shortly.

This application required all kinds of T2M, M2T, and M2M transformations. Figure 14 shows the size of MDELite framework and this application in lines of Prolog, Velocity, and Java code. As the tables indicate, the framework is tiny; the application numbers indicate the volume of "code" that was needed to write this application.

Concern	LOC Prolog	LOC Velocity	LOC Java Java
MDELite Framework	84	0	581
MDELite Application	506	654	2532
Total	590	654	3093

Fig. 14. Size of MDELite Framework and Application: Lines of Prolog, Velocity, and Java Code

Observations. You can try this for any set of tools that satisfies constraints (a) and (b) of Section 6. Doing so, you will likely discover that your set of selected tools were never designed for interoperability. Ideally, interoperability should be transparent to users. Unfortunately, this is not always achievable. We found UMLFactory to be flakey; most tools had cases that we simply couldn't tell if they worked correctly. Hidden dependencies lurked in XML documents about the order in which elements could appear and divining these dependencies to produce decent displays was unpleasant (as there was no documentation). But it is a great lesson about the challenges of tool interoperability, albeit on a small-scale.

Interesting technical problems also arise. A yUML spec for Figure 13c is:

```
[Library|name|getName()]
[Book|title|getTitle()]
[Book]<>*-1[Library]
```

Translating a yUML spec to the XML document of another tool requires graphical (x,y) positioning information about each class (*i.e.* where each class is to appear on a canvas).

yUML computes this information, but never returns it. Lacking positioning information, Violet simply draws all the classes on top of each other, yielding an unreadable mess. We looked for tools to compute node positioning information for a graph and found the Kieler Web Service [13]. We translated an SDBPL database into a DOT graph, transmited the DOT file to the Kieler server, and it returned a new DOT graph with the required positioning information. A simple T2M tool mapped the positioning information to a Prolog table, and this table was merged with a SDBPL database that lacked positioning information (as indicated in the Figure 12c script). Only then was a usable Violet file produced. Figure 15a shows the generated DOT file, Figure 15b the DOT file returned by the Kieler server, and Figure 15c the T2M extracted *position* table.

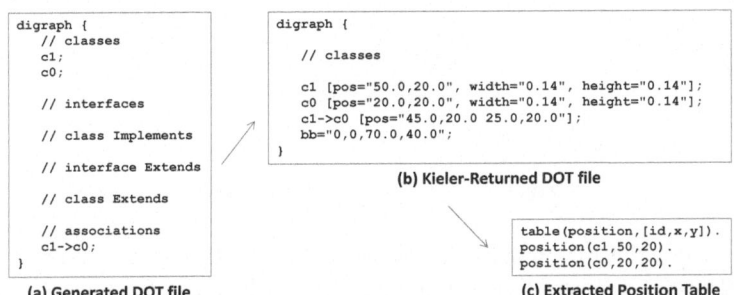

(a) Generated DOT file

(b) Kieler-Returned DOT file

(c) Extracted Position Table

Fig. 15. DOT File Transformations

9   Towards Bootstrapping

Although we have not fully bootstrapped MDELite for reasons discussed earlier, there are two basic steps to produce the FSM tool or any other domain-specific MDE tool.

First, we need to specify how metaclass instances are to be drawn by the $\mathcal{GE}$. The simplest way is to allow the $\mathcal{GE}$ to set properties of each metaclass to provide the necessary information. For example, Figure 16 uses stereotypes to declare that a *State* is to be drawn as an oval, except a *Start* state is a solid-circle and a *Stop* state is a double-circle (c.f. Figure 1). Other ways to encode this information are also possible.

Second, look at Figure 17. A FSM domain architect would (1) draw the FSM metamodel using a *Metamodel Drawing Tool (MDT)*, which mecha-

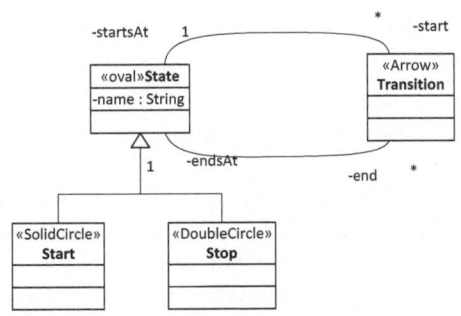

Fig. 16. FSM Metamodel with Graphical Stereotypes

nizes the rules of Section 2 to produce Prolog table definitions for the input metamodel and a palette of icon-metaclass pairings to customize the $\mathcal{GE}$, (2) write the Prolog metamodel constraints, the Prolog M2M transformations, and a Velocity M2T file, and (3) run a build script that integrates these inputs with a *MDE Tool Shell* to generate the FSM tool.

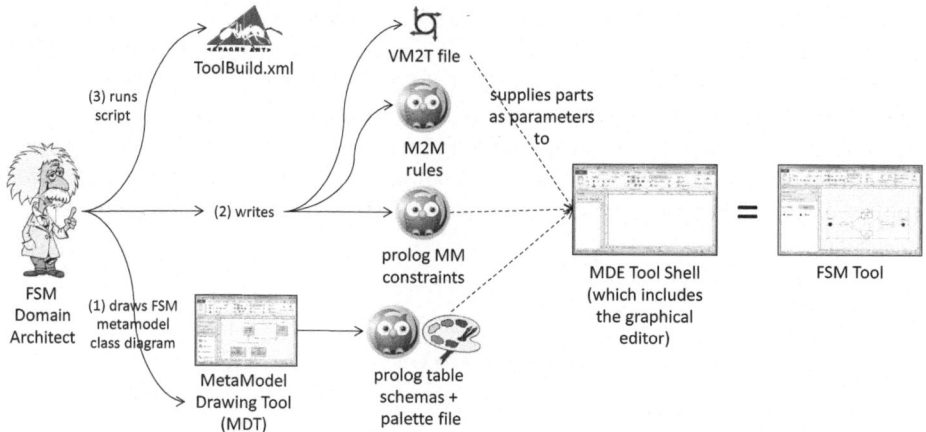

Fig. 17. Generating a MDE FSM Tool

To bootstrap MDELite requires an MDE$\mathcal{G}$od to build the two tools (*MDT* and *MDE Tool Shell*) and script (*ToolBuild.xml*) that a Domain Architect (Einstein) invokes (see Figure 17). Specifically, MDE$\mathcal{G}$od writes the *ToolBuild.xml* script and purchases or outsources the writing of the *MDE Tool|Shell* (which includes the $\mathcal{GE}$). Initially the MDE$\mathcal{G}$od hacks a *MetaModel Drawing Tool (MDT)*. MDE$\mathcal{G}$od then relies on a fundamental MDE constraint that the MDELite meta-meta-model must be an instance of itself. So, the MDE$\mathcal{G}$od plays the role of a MetaModel Domain Architect, replacing Einstein in Figure 17 with him/herself. MDE$\mathcal{G}$od (1) draws the metamodel of all class diagrams, (2) writes its Prolog metamodel constraints, Prolog M2M transformations, and a VM2T file (which produces Prolog table schemas and a palette for drawing class diagrams from the Prolog database), (3) runs the build script to produce the *MDT* to complete the bootstrap, thereby building an *MDT* to replace the hacked *MDT*. Again, all of this hinges on finding a palette-customizable $\mathcal{GE}$.

10   Personal Experiences, Insights, and a Small Second Case Study

We created MDELite as an alternative to Eclipse MDE tools to understand and teach MDE concepts. Our work begs for an empirical study to evaluate the benefits of teaching MDELite; we intend to conduct such a study later this year. MDELite is an interesting technical contribution in its own regards, and that is what we focus on in this paper.

We used MDELite in a Fall 2012 undergraduate course on "Introduction to Software Design", giving an assignment more ambitious than what we tried in Fall 2011. Specifically, we asked students to:

1. Given a simple metamodel of class diagrams, manually produce the schemas of the metamodel's underlying Prolog tables;

2. Write a T2M transformation in Java using Java reflection to extract information about classes, methods, and fields from .class files and present this information as tuples in their tables;
3. Write Prolog constraints to evaluate the correctness of the tables they produced;
4. Write a Velocity M2T transformation that maps their tables into stubbed Java source;
5. Write another T2M transformation that converts Java reflection information to produce a yUML specification, which is then translated into a Violet diagram by MDELite; and
6. Extend the MDELite category (Figure 12) with the domains and arrows of Figure 18 by implementing the required classes and methods to script their transformations.

We can report many fewer difficulties with this assignment than the simpler assignment of the previous year that used Eclipse MDE tools. Still, there are some practical difficulties that we are obliged to alert readers.

Fig. 18. Additional Domains and Arrows to Figure 12

Multi-Paradigm Programming. We are Java programmers and novices to Prolog. Prolog and Java have two very different mind-sets, and flipping between paradigms can be confusing. Trivial things like Prolog rules ending in (Java) semicolons instead of (Prolog) periods was a mistake we constantly made. Prolog inequalities ($=<$) are syntactically reversed in Java ($<=$). In SWI-Prolog, when something is mistyped, a question-mark prompt (?) is produced and the usual Windows/Linux character escapes to reset to the command prompt simply do not work. Problems like these disappear once familiarity with Prolog sets in—they clearly are not fundamental, but are jolting to students in a first, quick immersion into Prolog. For this reason, recommend that MDELite be a pair-programming project: one person concentrating on Prolog, the other on Java, to minimize cross-world confusion.

Many-Columned Tables. When there are many columns, it can be daunting in Prolog to correctly reference a table and account for each of its columns in a predicate. In such cases, one can M2M transform such tables into RDF 3-tuple format of (*tupleid, columnName, value*) or a 4-tuple format (*tableName, tupleid, columnName, value*) for easy attribute referencing.

Transformation Debugging. MDELite provides a microcosm of the challenges of debugging transformations. Even though a transformation takes an object (a model) as input and produces an object (a model) as output, objects are Prolog databases that are not simple

Fig. 19. Debugging Transformation Scripts

values and can have complex structures. *Writing transformations in any language is not simple*—it is easy to forget a case or miss-write a translation. Our hunch is that the simpler a transformation's specification, the easier it will be to track down errors. This remains, however, a conjecture.

A technique that we found useful—perhaps motivated by the "shape" of the category of Figure 12a—was to define a transformation τ and then its inverse τ^{-1}, so that we could test whether $\tau \cdot \tau^{-1}$ was an identity or an equivalence.[5] This helped, but obviously did not eliminate all bugs.

Nonetheless, the fundamental challenge in debugging transformations becomes clearly evident: an error is detected in a database (far right of Figure 19). Upon examination, we discovered that the transformation that produced it was correct, but its input database was incorrect. This unwinds backwards until we discover a correct database that was input to a transformation that produced an incorrect database. Surely results on debugging Prolog programs and debugging database transactions—studied long ago—might be useful to MDELite. This too remains a conjecture.

Preparatory M2M Transformations. When Velocity templates have many loops and *if* statements, it is easy to lose track of loop and if-then-else boundaries, thereby creating incorrect templates. One reason why loops and if-statements are used is to join tables. For example, consider the following Class table rows, where class *Customer* is connected to class *Address* via a $* \rightarrow^1$ association:

```
class(c1,'Customer','','','').
class(c2,'Address','','','').
association(c1,'*',none,c2,'1',arrow).
```

In a M2T transformation, the class table must be joined (twice) with the association table to convert class identifiers (*c*1 and *c*2) into class names (*Customer* and *Address*). Similarly, other computations can arise to convert atoms (like '*arrow*' above) into rendering text (in this case, the character '>' to denote an arrow). Such translations significantly complicate Velocity templates—it would not be so bad if one could indent Velocity statements to pair up the start and end of loops and if-statements:

```
#forall($a in $associationS)
    #forall($c in $classS)
        #if ($a.id = $c.id)
            #set($classname=$c.name)
        #end
    #end
#end
```

Indenting, however, generates extra spaces, which is not always desirable. The alternative is to produce a table of association declarations that render Velocity printing trivial:

```
yumlAssociation('Customer','*','','Billing Address','1','>').
```

---

[5] Two documents d_1 and d_2 can differ in whitespace, ordering of declarations, etc. and still represent equivalent class diagrams.

Using M2M transformations can reduce the size (read: complexity) of Velocity files substantially. Although this is not a hard-and-fast heuristic, our experience is that keeping Velocity templates as simple as possible is worth the extra stage in Prolog translation.

11 Related Work

A paper by Favre inspired our work [11]. He warned against adding complex technologies on top of already complex technologies, and advocated a back-to-basics approach, specifically suggesting that MDE be identified with set theory and the use of Prolog to express MDE relationships among models and their meta-model counterparts.

In searching the literature, we found many papers advocating Prolog-database interpretations of MDE. For lack of space, we concentrate on the most significant, although we feel none are quite as compact or as clean as MDELite. Almendros-Jiménez and Iribarne advocated Prolog to write model transformations and model constraints [2,3]. The difference between our work and theirs is orientation: our goal is to find a simple way to demonstrate and teach MDE to undergraduates. Their goal is to explore the use of logic programming languages in MDE applications. For example, PTL is a hybrid of the Atlas Transformation Language and Prolog for writing model transformations [1]. In another paper, OWL files encode MDE databases and OWL RL specifies constraints in terms of Description Logics. For teaching undergraduates, the use of OWL and Description Logic is overkill and obscures the simplicity of MDELite. How M2T transformations are handled and MDE applications (categories) are encoded are not discussed.

Störrle's Model Manipulation Toolkit uses unnormalized (set-valued) relational tables as the basic Prolog data representation and uses Prolog to query these tables [18]. Although M2M transformations seem not to be discussed, the obvious implication is present. MDELite goes beyond this work also integrating M2T and T2M transformations, as well as exposing the bigger picture of MDE applications as categories.

Oetsch et. al. advocate *Answer-Set Programming (ASP)* to express a limited form of MDE [14]. Entity-Relationship models represent meta-models (drawn using Eclipse MDE tools); and their tool allows one to enter ASP facts (similar to Prolog facts) manually that conform to the input meta-models; ASP queries are used to validate meta-model constraints expressed in the ER model.[6] MDELite is more general than this: M2M, M2T, and T2M mappings need to be defined in addition to model constraints. Further, how MDE applications are defined (as in MDELite categories) is not considered.

12 Conclusions

MDELite reinterprets MDE from the viewpoint of relational databases. A model is a database of tables; (meta-)model constraints and M2M transformations are expressed by Prolog. M2T and T2M transformations rely on simple Java programs. Categories, a

---

[6] The Eclipse OCL tool plugin is similar in that one has to manually enter tuples beforehand before OCL queries can be executed. This is impractical, even for classroom settings.

fundamental structure in mathematics, integrates these concepts to define MDE applications. MDELite leverages (and maybe introduces or refreshes) core undergraduate CS knowledge to explain, illustrate, and build MDE applications without the overhead and complexity of Eclipse MDE tools. Our case studies indicate MDELite is feasible; a user study to evaluate the benefits of MDELite in teaching is a next step in our work.

We believe MDELite is a clarion way to explain MDE to undergraduate students. It is our hope that others may benefit, and indeed improve, our ideas. MDELite is available at http://www.cs.utexas.edu/schwartz/MDELite.html

Acknowledgements. We am indebted to Salva Trujillo (Ikerlan), Oscar Diaz (San Sebastian), and Perdita Stevens (Edinburgh) for their insightful comments on earlier drafts of this paper. We also thank Robert Berg, Eric Huneke, Amin Shali, and Joyce Ho for VM2T. We also appreciate the help given to me by Miro Spönemann on the Kieler graph layout tools and Ralf Lämmel his invaluable help answering questions about Prolog. We gratefully acknowledge support for this work by NSF grants CCF 0724979 and OCI-1148125.

References

1. Almendros-Jiménez, J.M., Iribarne, L.: A model transformation language based on logic programming. In: van Emde Boas, P., Groen, F.C.A., Italiano, G.F., Nawrocki, J., Sack, H. (eds.) SOFSEM 2013. LNCS, vol. 7741, pp. 382–394. Springer, Heidelberg (2013)
2. Almendros-Jimenez, J., Iribarne, L.: A framework for model transformation in logic programming (2008)
3. Almendros-Jimenez, J., Iribarne, L.: Odm-based uml model transformations using prolog (2011)
4. Apache Velocity Project, http://velocity.apache.org/
5. Batory, D., Azanza, M., Saraiva, J.: The Objects and Arrows of Computational Design. In: Czarnecki, K., Ober, I., Bruel, J.-M., Uhl, A., Völter, M. (eds.) MODELS 2008. LNCS, vol. 5301, pp. 1–20. Springer, Heidelberg (2008)
6. Batory, D.: Multilevel models in model-driven engineering, product lines, and metaprogramming. IBM Syst. J. (July 2006)
7. Bezivin, J., Jouault, F., Valduriez, P.: On the need for megamodels. In: Proc. of the OOPSLA/GPCE Workshop on Best Practices for Model-Driven Software Development (2004)
8. Dehayni, M., Féraud, L.: An approach of model transformation based on attribute grammars. In: Masood, A., Léonard, M., Pigneur, Y., Patel, S. (eds.) OOIS 2003. LNCS, vol. 2817, pp. 412–423. Springer, Heidelberg (2003)
9. Diskin, Z.: Algebraic models for bidirectional model synchronization. In: Czarnecki, K., Ober, I., Bruel, J.-M., Uhl, A., Völter, M. (eds.) MODELS 2008. LNCS, vol. 5301, pp. 21–36. Springer, Heidelberg (2008)
10. Elmasri, R., Navathe, S.: Fundamentals of Database Systems. Addison-Wesley (2010)
11. Favre, J.M.: Towards a basic theory to model model driven engineering. In: Workshop on Software Model Engineering, WISME 2004 (2004)
12. Hainaut, J.-L.: The transformational approach to database engineering. In: Lämmel, R., Saraiva, J., Visser, J. (eds.) GTTSE 2005. LNCS, vol. 4143, pp. 95–143. Springer, Heidelberg (2006)
13. Kieler Web Service Tool,
   http://trac.rtsys.informatik.uni-kiel.de/trac/kieler/wiki/Releases/Tools

14. Oetsch, J., Pührer, J., Seidl, M., Tompits, H., Zwickl, P.: VIDEAS: A development tool for answer-set programs based on model-driven engineering technology. In: Delgrande, J.P., Faber, W. (eds.) LPNMR 2011. LNCS, vol. 6645, pp. 382–387. Springer, Heidelberg (2011)
15. Oldevik, J.: Umt: Uml model transformation tool overview and user guide documentation (2004), http://umt-qvt.sourceforge.net/docs/
16. Pierce, B.: Basic Category Theory for Computer Scientists. MIT Press (1991)
17. Sprinkle, J., Rumpe, B., Vangheluwe, H., Karsai, G.: Metamodelling: state of the art and research challenges. In: Proc. of the 2007 Dagstuhl Conference on Model-Based Engineering of Embedded Real-time Systems (2010)
18. Störrle, H.: A prolog-based approach to representing and querying software engineering models
19. SWI-Prolog, http://www.swi-prolog.org/
20. UML Factory, http://www.umlfactory.com/
21. Violet UML Editor, http://alexdp.free.fr/violetumleditor/page.php
22. yUML Beta, http://yuml.me/

Big Metamodels Are Evil

Package Unmerge — A Technique for Downsizing Metamodels

Frédéric Fondement, Pierre-Alain Muller,
Laurent Thiry, Brice Wittmann, and Germain Forestier

MIPS, Université de Haute Alsace,
12, rue des frères Lumière, 68093 Mulhouse cedex, France
{frederic.fondement,pierre-alain.muller,
laurent.thiry,brice.wittmann,germain.forestier}@uha.fr

Abstract. While reuse is typically considered a good practice, it may also lead to keeping irrelevant concerns in derived elements. For instance, new metamodels are usually built upon existing metamodels using additive techniques such as profiling and package merge. With such additive techniques, new metamodels tend to become bigger and bigger, which leads to harmful overheads of complexity for both tool builders and users. In this paper, we introduce «package unmerge» - a proposal for a subtractive relation between packages - which complements existing metamodel-extension techniques.

1   Introduction and Motivation

In the domain of software engineering, reuse is typically achieved by sharing reusable software parts in so-called libraries. From reusable procedures or structures, those parts evolved into fully fledged components [1]. Components are pieces of software that can be combined together to build up new software systems. Research related to this topic showed that it is of paramount importance to define precisely contracts for components, upon which both component makers and component users can rely [2]. Interface specification, which indicates what messages can be treated or sent by a component, is only the very first step towards the definition of a contract [3]. Of course, any component claiming to implement a contract must fulfill it completely.

Programming languages are another mean for helping software reuse. Indeed, languages abstract away details of platforms while still making it possible to describe expected behavior of a software system. Examples of platforms' details abstracted by many languages are the instruction set of a processor, and available interruptions of an operating system. A compiler can automatically infer details abstracted away from code so that an executable program can be delivered, as long as the code conforms to the expected programming language. This way, the same source code could be used by different compilers made for the same programming language, but targeting different platforms, e.g. different processors or operating systems. Model driven engineering (MDE) pushes the same idea a step further: abstracting away details of platforms while offering simple constructs in a modeling language, with compilers being replaced by

A. Moreira et al. (Eds.): MODELS 2013, LNCS 8107, pp. 138–153, 2013.

model transformations. In addition to model transformations, a given model can be manipulated by a constellation of tools, thus following a data-centric architectural style.

Examples of such tools for modeling are textual or graphical model editors, model verifiers, model checkers, model serializers, model interpreters, and model transformation engines. All of them need to be able to manipulate one (or more) model(s). Following the example of compilers handling programs written in a well-defined language, tools for modeling handle models with a well defined structure. The model structure is most of the time specified by a metamodel. In this realm, metamodels are to modeling tools, what contracts were to components.

One typical problem with this data-centric architectural style, is that tools might not all have the same capabilities. If some tools may handle all of the possible modeling constructs of a language (as defined in a metamodel), some other tools may only work on a given subset of those constructs [4]. An example is UML code generators, which are usually able to generate code for class diagrams, or state chart diagrams, yet discarding any information provided by use case diagrams or timing diagrams. It does not necessarily mean that such tools, which cover only part of a modeling language, should be blamed: usually, discarded information is just useless within the perspective of the intent of the tools [5]. However, it might make tools' users feel that the contract of the tool is not fulfilled as parts of the metamodel are ignored.

A similar situation happens when it comes to defining a new language by reusing an existing metamodel. To reuse an existing metamodel, one usually extends it by defining additional concepts and relations. To extend a metamodel, one possible solution is to use an annotation mechanism such as profiles [6 - section 18]. However, this approach is an additive-only technique, making the resulting metamodel bigger than the extended metamodel. Thanks to (or because of) this additive nature, tools for the extended language can still work on models of the new language, yet ignoring all information that could be included in the model thanks to the extension. As an example, if someone extends UML with a profile, UML code generators will be still able to generate code for profiled UML models, but information carried by the profile application will be merely ignored, usually without even a warning.

From the modeling tools' users point of view, the only way to know whether an element of a model will be ignored or not is to read documentation written in natural language, or to try and see either nothing happening, or an error message raised while invoking the tools. This situation can be compared to a compiler not considering the complete program code without clearly stating which part of the code is considered. By indicating formally the subset of the metamodel that is actually covered, a tool could be made more precise regarding handled models, i.e. regarding its contract. One could thus check his/her models in order to know exactly what information is to be ignored by a given tool. Moreover, by supplying a real and clear interface (i.e. metamodel) of handled elements, modeling tools could be more easily selected, verified, or assembled, following the advanced practices of the software component community.

While metamodel extension has deserved significant interest, reduction has not yet gained the same exposure. As a consequence, the more a metamodel is built by reusing other metamodels, the more it is likely to contain irrelevant constructs from the perspective of a given tool. In other words, metamodels contain too many features, one reason for that being that it is currently impracticable to identify and remove unneeded parts.

In this paper, we examine how reduction of metamodels could be expressed in an explicit way, basically by describing package unmerge mechanism, built as a counterpart of the existing package merge metamodel additive extension mechanism as defined in [7 - section 11.9.3].

The paper is organized as follows: after this introduction, section 2 presents three dominant techniques for metamodel extension, section 3 presents our proposal for reduction (which we call package unmerge relation), section 4 describes the package unmerge algorithm, section 5 provides more in depth examples, section 6 gives a short overview of the tool support we propose for package merge and unmerge, section 7 compares our approach to others, and section 8 concludes and presents future directions.

2   Extending Metamodels

Typical mechanisms for controlling metamodel extension include UML profiles, package merge relations, and aspect weaving.

Profiles [6 - section 18] became popular as UML promoted them as a lightweight approach for language extension. Profiles define extension points (called stereotypes) for the metaclasses of a (MOF [8]) metamodel. Stereotypes can insert additional properties or constraints to the metaclass they extend. Stereotypes work as decorations, do not modify the decorated metamodels, and can be removed or swapped at any moment in the lifecycle of a model. Therefore, models remain conform to their original metamodels (regardless of profiles).

Package merge relations [7 - section 11.9.3], as opposed to profiles, are considered an heavyweight extension mechanism, since they impact directly the metamodel elements. Package merge relations are available both in the UML standard and in the MOF metalanguage. Package merge relations combine the contents of two packages into a single one, following a recursive union-like copy approach. In case of name conflicts, conflicting elements are merged together into the same element in the resulting package. Package merge relations make the core of the modularization technique of the UML metamodel. An illustrating example is the definition of UML compliance levels. Compliance levels define the modeling concepts that must be supported by tools. A tool with compliance level L1 must support class diagrams and use case diagrams, while L2 compliance level also requires to support profiles. Since UML modeling elements are distributed across a set of packages in the UML metamodel, the L1 compliance level is formalized by a package that is merely built by merging those packages that define the necessary concepts for class and use case diagrams. Similarly, L2 compliance level is also defined by a package that merges L1 package and the package that formalizes the profile concepts (among others).

Aspect weaving was originally proposed in the context of programming [9]. Generally speaking, aspects define extension points (often called join points) where elements (often called advices) may be injected (woven in aspect-oriented terminology).

Join points are conveniently specified by pointcuts, which can target different join points using a single pattern. More recently, aspect weaving has been used to alter models, and by extension metamodels [10]. Many different formalisms have been studied so far, including UML class diagrams [11]. As MOF is also based on class diagrams, MOF metamodels may also be woven with aspect models in order to be extended.

To summarize, profiles provide a lightweight approach, that makes some meta-modeling capabilities available at modeling time. Package merge relations focus on meta-modeling time. Aspect weaving, is used at modeling time, but can be used at meta-modeling time as well, since any metamodel is also a model.

3   Unmerging Metamodels

A metamodel may be seen as a hierarchical set of information about the structure of conforming models. For metalanguages such as MOF and Ecore, such structure is defined using a set of meta-classes and relations between meta-classes; a model can thus be seen as a set of related instances. By altering those meta-classes and relations, it is possible to restrict the range of conforming models. Typical modifications include removing class properties and strengthening constraints such as multiplicities.

To identify those specific removal points, i.e. elements that should be dropped from a to-be-reduced metamodel, we found convenient to use the same metalanguage in which the to-be-reduced metamodel is expressed. Meta-elements to be pruned in a to-be-reduced metamodel are identified in a reduction metamodel: the elements to be cut are duplicated in the unmerge metamodel using the same name and included in a matching hierarchy. Thus, prune points are identified as leaves of the reduction me-tamodel. Corresponding elements in the to-be-reduced metamodel can thus be identi-fied as to be removed. In addition, all elements part of the hierarchy of removed element should also be removed, even if not explicitly designated by the reduction metamodel. Since the pruning points are matched with elements of the to-be-reduced metamodel according to their name, and since the metamodeling language is directly used to define a change in a metamodel, the mechanism looks like package merge. As we aim at reducing a metamodel rather than extending it, we decided to name this approach «package unmerge».

In order to unmerge metamodels in a deterministic way, we had to define a compo-sition hierarchy of concepts and matching rules. Hierarchy and matching rules depend on the metalanguage used to define metamodels. This hierarchy is defined as follows:

- the root is a package,
- a package may contain other packages and classes,
- a class may contain properties and invariant constraints,
- properties and invariant constraints do not contain other elements.

An element in the reduced metamodel will match an element in the unmerge meta-model if they both have:

- the same name,

- the same metaclass (i.e. packages can only match packages, classes can match only classes, etc.),
- matching owners.

Constraints can be either strengthened or relaxed. If a leaf element has a stronger constraint, then the matching element appears in the final metamodel (i.e. is not removed) but updated with this stronger constraint. Elements that hold constraints are the following:

- classes, that can be either concrete or abstract; an abstract class being more constrained than a concrete class,
- properties, that may define multiplicities; a property with a smaller multiplicity range is considered more constrained than a property with a larger multiplicity range.

Invariant constraints also have to be updated according to pruning action performed on the metamodel-to-be-reduced. In the case of package unmerge, any invariant constraint depending on a pruned element (e.g. a metaclass or a property) should also be marked to be unmerged, otherwise the package unmerge definition would be illegal. In this, we follow our guideline to define package merge as the pure counterpart of package unmerge that can add new invariant constraints (but not relax existing ones).

Finally, the name of the metamodel resulting from the unmerge transformation is the name of the unmerge metamodel.

Package unmerge proceeds the following way. All the elements of the to-be-reduced metamodel that match leaf elements of the package unmerge metamodel are recursively removed from the original metamodel. Removing a class C also removes properties whose type is C (see UC3 in Table 1 below). Moreover, if a C class inherits from a B class to be removed, and if B inherits from classes A1 and A2 to be kept, then C class in the reduced metamodel will inherit from classes A1 and A2 directly (see UC7 in Table 1 below). Leaf elements from the unmerge metamodel that do not match any element in the metamodel to be unmerged are ignored.

Table 1 shows a set of simple example use cases which illustrate the main aspects of package unmerge. First column shows the to-be-reduced metamodel together with an unmerge metamodel, and second column shows the reduced metamodel obtained after unmerging, together with the merge metamodel necessary to get the original to-be-reduced metamodel back. This latter part is more extensively explained in the next section.

4   Unmerge Algorithm

As shown in Figure 1, the outcome of an unmerge is the reduced version of the original metamodel (L--). While the unmerging transformation removes some elements from a metamodel, the dual package merge transformation adds elements to a metamodel. Interestingly, package merge and unmerge transformations can also generate the counterparts which may be used later to undo the effect of either merge or unmerge. Hence, in addition to the resulting metamodel, the transformation may reference all those concepts that were removed from the metamodel to be unmerged (L) in an extension taking the shape of a package merge (M).

Table 1. Unmerge use cases

Unmerge use cases	Results and merge counterparts
UC1 - Unmerging package P	
UC2 - Removing package P	
UC3 - Removing class C	
UC4 - Removing class P::C	
UC5 - Removing attribute C.p1	
UC6 - Removing reference C.d	
UC7 - Removing class C in hierarchy	
UC8 - Removing referenced class D	

Table 1. (*Continued*)

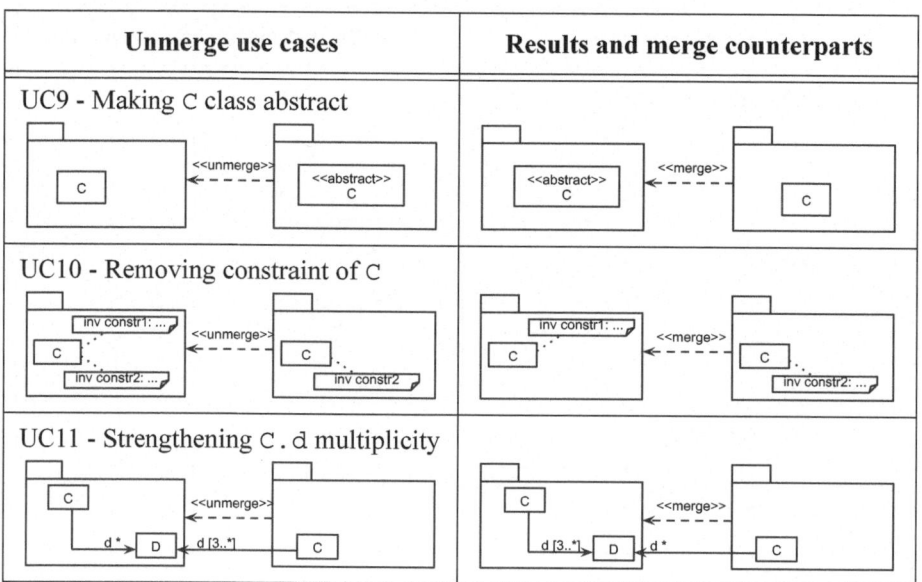

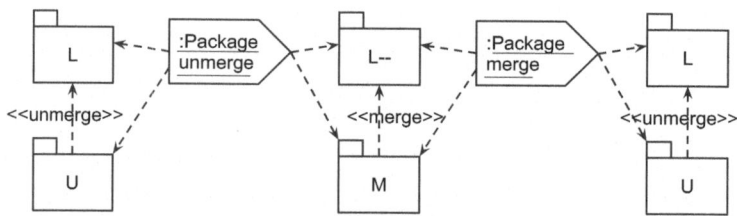

Fig. 1. Reversibility of the package merge and package unmerge transformations

To go back to the unmerged metamodel (L), one just needs to perform a package merge transformation on the unmerged version (L– –) driven by the previously generated merge (M). Thus, the generated merge (M) plays the role of the trace of the unmerge transformation: it makes it possible to control what happened during the unmerge, and to reverse the unmerge process. It also allows to reflect any eventual change in L-- or M back to L or U. Symmetrically, the package merge transformation can be extended to generate the unmerge counterpart, so that any addition to the merged metamodel (L– –) is referenced in a generated unmerge counterpart (U). As such, the package unmerge transformation is the inverse transformation of the package merge transformation.

The algorithm for unmerging a metamodel is defined here with the same formalism as in [4]. The algorithm relies on structure shown in Figure 2 for metamodels (MM, MM_u, MM_t, and MM_m), though it could be adapted to other class-oriented structures.

`elements` is an operation returning recursively all composed elements from `Package`, and `removeElement` an operation that removes an element from a package wherever it occurs in the hierarchy of the package. For sake of space and readability, opposite properties and re-affectation of properties type is not discussed in this paper.

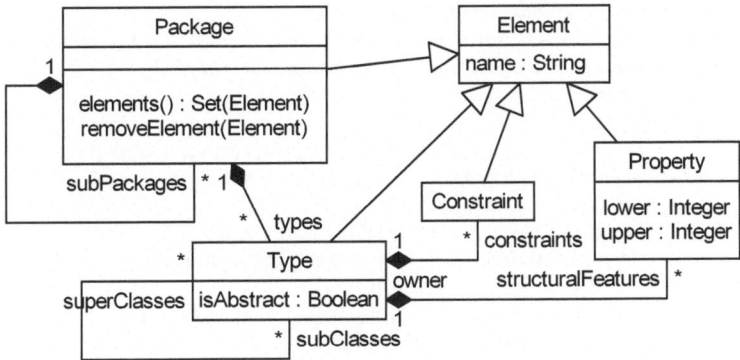

Fig. 2. Expectations on an unmerged metamodel

Algorithm to find a matching element
```
match(MM, e): elt
      elt ← ∅
    MM.elements().each{ ue |
          e.name = ue.name
              && e.metaType = ue.metaType
              && match(MM, e.owner) = ue.owner
      ⇒ elt ← ue}
```

Algorithm to unmerge a metamodel MM with an unmerge metamodel MM$_u$
```
packageUnmerge(MM,MM_u) : MM_t,MM_m
```
1. Copies source meta-model MM into target metamodel MM$_t$ and its merge MM$_m$
```
    MM_t ← MM,  MM_m ← MM,   E_req ← {},  E_merge ← {}
```
2. Checking types
```
MM_t.types.each{ t |
```
 2.1 Types are kept in MM$_m$ and removed from MM$_t$ (as C in UC3), except if...
```
    match(MM_u, t) ≠ ∅ ⇒ E_merge ← E_merge ∪ {match(MM_m, t)}
```
 2.1.a it is abstract in MM$_u$ while not in MM (as C in UC9)
```
    if !t.isAbstract && match(MM_u,t).isAbstract then
          E_req ← E_req ∪ {t}, t.abstract = true
```
 2.1.b it does not remove all properties/constraints (as C in UC5/UC10)
```
    elsif match(MM_u,t).structuralFeatures ≠ ∅
          || match(MM_u,t).constraints ≠ ∅ then
          E_req ← E_req ∪ {t}
```
 2.1.c If a class is removed (as C in UC7), its sub-classes (as D in UC7)
```
    else
          - are kept in merge (as D in MM_m in UC7)
          E_merge ← E_merge ∪ t.subClasses.each{ mme |
                match(MM_m,mme) }
```

- inherit from its super-class (D inherits A1 and A2 in UC7 MM$_t$)

```
t.subClasses.each{ s | s.superClasses ←
              (s.superClasses / {t}) ∪ t.superClasses}
end if
```
2.2 Types not in unmerge are kept only in target meta-model (as D in UC3)
```
match(MMu, t) = ∅ ⇒ Ereq ← Ereq ∪ {t} }
```

3. Checking properties and constraints
```
MMt.types.structuralFeatures ∪ MMt.types.constraints).each{ p |
```
    3.1 Properties and constraints from MM$_u$ are kept in MM$_m$
    and removed from MM$_t$ (as C.p1 in UC5), except if...
```
match(MMu, p) ≠ ∅
     ⇒ Emerge ← Emerge ∪ {match(MMm,p), match(MMm, p.owner)}
```
    3.1.a the element is a property with a different multiplicity (as C.d in UC11)
```
p ∈ p.owner.structuralFeatures
     && ( p.lower ≠ match(MMu, p).lower
       || p.upper ≠ match(MMu, p).upper))
     ⇒ (Ereq ← Ereq ∪ {p}, Ereq ← Ereq ∪ {p.owner},
         p.lower ← max(p.lower, match(MMu, p).lower),
         p.upper ← min(p.upper, match(MMu, p).upper))
```
    3.2 Elements that are not in unmerge are kept only in target meta-model
```
match(MMu, p)= ∅ ⇒ Ereq ← Ereq ∪ {p} }
```

4. sub-packages
```
MMt.subPackages.each{ sp |
```
    4.1 Packages in unmerge are kept in merge
    and removed from target metamodel (as P in UC2), except if...
```
match(MMu, sp) ≠ ∅ ⇒ Emerge ← Emerge ∪ {match(MMm, sp)}
```
    4.1.a it removes not all contents (as P in UC4)
```
match(MMu, sp).types ≠ ∅
     ⇒ ((spu, spm) ← packageUnmerge(sp, match(MMu, sp)),
         Ereq ← Ereq ∪ {spu}, Emerge ← Emerge ∪ {spm},
         MMt ← (MMt / {sp}) ∪ spu, MMm ← MMm ∪ {spm})
```
    4.2 Packages that are not in unmerge are kept only in target meta-model
```
match(MMu, sp) = ∅ ⇒ Ereq ← Ereq ∪ {sp} }
```

5.Remove non-required elements in target meta-model
(elements include sub-packages, types, and constraints)
```
MMt.elements().each{ e | e ∉ Ereq ⇒ MMt.removeElement(e)}
```
6.Remove non-required elements in merge meta-model
```
MMm.elements().each{ e | e ∉ Emerge ⇒ MMm.removeElement(e)}
```

5   Example

This section shows how the package merge and unmerge relations may be used to build a metamodel by reusing other metamodels. The overall context is model-based testing of SysML models, and the example is borrowed from the VETESS project [12]. The goal is to generate a set of test cases from a behavioral model of the system under test.

    The available tooling for test generation is based on a dialect of the UML language (called UML4MBT, UML for Model Based Testing), and a model transformation may be used to translate UML models to UML4MBT models (which is out of the scope of this example).

The same scheme is implemented for SysML models. A dedicated SysML dialect (called SysML4MBT, SysML for Model Based Testing) has been defined. A model transformation has been written to translate SysML4MBT models to UML4MBT models, thus allowing direct reuse of the tooling for test generation as explained in [13]. Figure 3 describes this transformation chain.

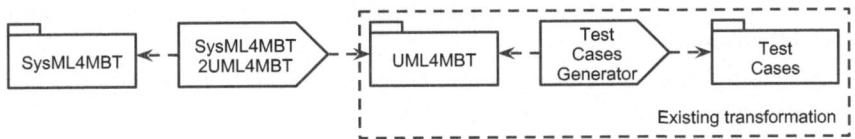

Fig. 3. VETESS tool chain for SysML

SysML4MBT and UML4MBT are good examples of languages which are more or less similar. They share a lot of commonalities, but diverge on some parts. To specify a model transformation between SysML4MBT and UML4MBT, it is convenient to explicitly state how these two languages compare, and how they can be built from each other.

Figure 4 shows how SysML4MBT can be derived from UML4MBT. Constructions to be removed are represented in the package unmerge metamodel while parts to be added are specified in the package merge metamodel.

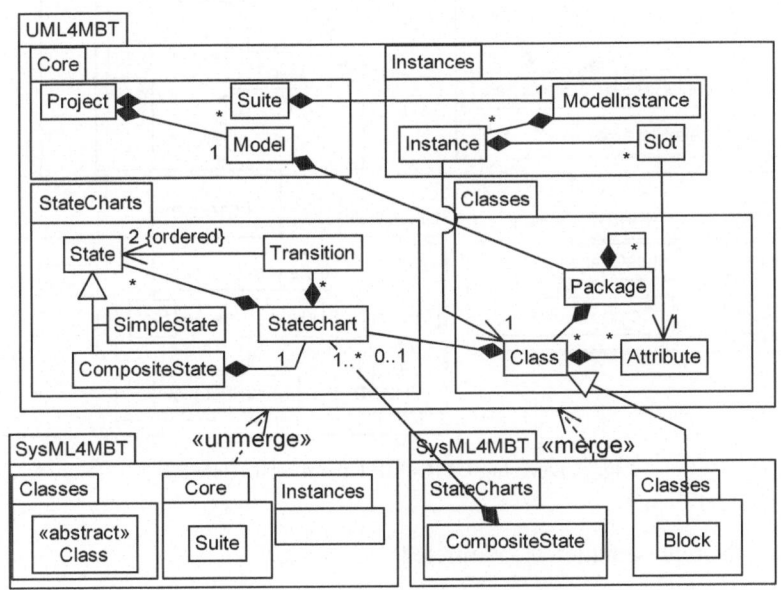

Fig. 4. Deriving SysML4MBT from UML4MBT

The representation is interpreted as follows:

- The `Instances` package has to be removed, including all contained elements.
- The `Core::Suite` metaclass has to be removed. The containing `Core` package will not be removed, but references to `Suite` will be dropped (in our case `Core::Project.suite`).
- `Class` is made abstract (by the unmerge) and `Block` is added as a concrete subclass (by the merge). Notice here that merging could not be used to set `Class` as abstract, because the merge semantics state that merging concrete with abstract yields concrete.
- The multiplicity of the composition relation between `CompositeState` and `Statechart` is set to 1..* (by the merge).

As explained earlier, package merge and package unmerge can be used either to trace their effect each other, or to undo their effect. We will illustrate this last point in the following lines. Figure 5 shows how to build UML4MBT from SysML4MBT, by merging and unmerging the respective counterparts.

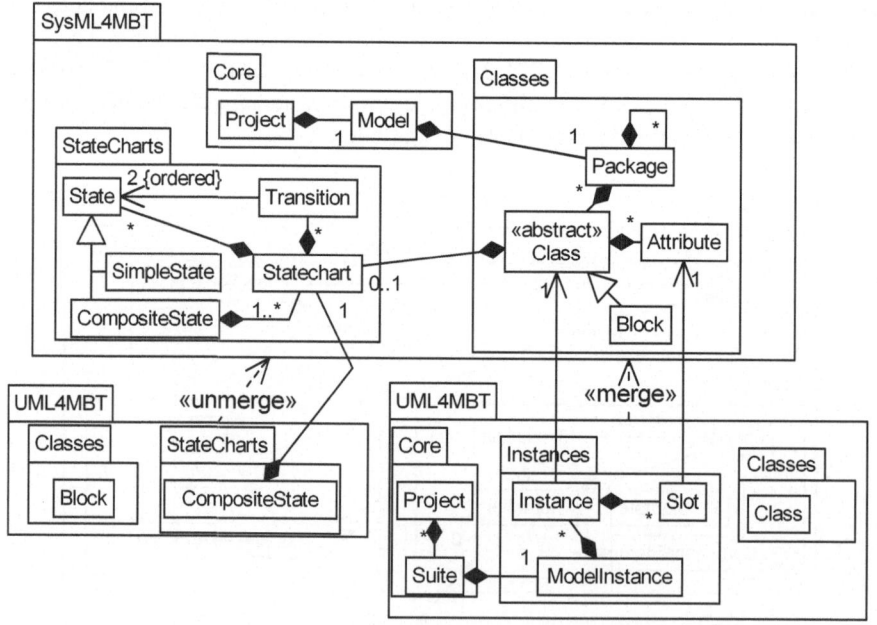

Fig. 5. Deriving UML4MBT from SysML4MBT

Again, the representation is interpreted as follows:

- The unmerge part states that `Classes::Block` should be removed, and that the `StateCharts::CompositeState::StateChart` multiplicity should be strengthened to 1..1.

- The merge part redefines `Instances` and its components, which are equivalent to those dropped from UML4MBT, re-introduces the `Core::Suite` construct (including incoming and outgoing references), and makes the `Classes::Class` metaclass concrete.

Package merge and package unmerge, along with the respective counterparts, can be used to go back and forth from one metamodel to another. From this point, it becomes possible to automate, at least partially, the translation from SysML4MBT to UML4MBT (and conversely from UML4MBT to SysML4MBT). Indeed, because of the way SysML4MBT is produced from UML4MBT, those two metamodels expose many similarities. In the SysML4MBT to UML4MBT transformation, those similarities take the shape of "copy" rules: `SysML4MBT::Project` elements create `UML4MBT::Project` elements, `SysML4MBT::Model` create `UML4MBT::Model`, etc. Finally, any information whose structure in SysML4MBT was kept from UML4MBT is merely copied to the resulting UML4MBT model.

6   Implementation

An open-source prototype implementation for both package merge and package unmerge as it is defined in this paper is available on the project website[1]. This implementation takes the shape of an Eclipse plug-in. A set of tutorials, corresponding to Table 1., is also available from the VETESS website[2].

The transformation can be invoked on an ecore file holding serialization for a package unmerge metamodel. The metamodel to be unmerged is referenced in an annotation of the package unmerge metamodel. Once invoked, the file name for serializing the unmerged metamodel is given and the transformation happens. The outcome is another ecore file for the unmerged metamodel plus an additional ecore file representing the merge counterpart. We developed a similar transformation for package merge, which also produces the merged metamodel and the corresponding unmerge counterpart.

While experimenting UML metamodel unmerge, we found it a very repetitive and error-prone task to eliminate invariant constraints (i.e. UML well formedness rules) that depend on an element that was pruned in the unmerged metamodel. That is why we included in the prototype a drop mechanism that discards from the unmerged metamodel any invariant constraint on which a type checking could not succeed.

In order to exchange models, we also developed automatic model transformation so that a model conforming to an unmerged metamodel can be transformed into a model conforming the metamodel that was unmerged. We also made the reverse transformation that removes information from a model of a metamodel that was unmerged so that it becomes a model of the unmerged metamodel. These two transformation make it possible to reuse existing models and interact with a tool defined for working on a metamodel subset defined in terms of package merge.

---

[1] https://sourcesup.cru.fr/projects/vetess/

[2] http://bit.ly/1itERM

7   Related Works

As mentioned in section 1, reducing metamodels was paid much less attention than extending. However, one interesting proposal was made by Sen et al. [4]. They identify four reasons to motivate the reduction of a metamodel and thus avoid over-specification:

- clearly state what are the input/output domains of a model transformation,
- avoid chaining transformations with inconsistent input/output domains,
- avoid generating input data models with unused concepts when testing transformations,
- avoid confusing a model designer.

They also propose an algorithm for reducing a metamodel. This algorithm requires the set of all interesting elements in a metamodel; those elements are kept in the resulting metamodel, including their dependencies in a transitive way. However, they do not state how interesting constructs can be identified. Our approach rather identifies elements that must not appear in the reduced metamodel. Indeed, identifying all interesting parts may require an effort as important as defining a metamodel from scratch. Moreover, we state how those "uninteresting elements" can be identified using the metalanguage in which the metamodel-to-be-reduced is defined. Finally, thanks to the symmetry that exists between the merge and unmerge relations, we are able to create the reverse definition to highlight what the reduction actually did. To sum up, our approach fits better when a lot of top elements are to be removed, and when complex operations are necessary (such as removing a class from an inheritance hierarchy, or making a class abstract). Otherwise, approach of [4] fits better when only a few elements are to be kept in a metamodel, all of them being well identified.

Some few aspect-oriented modeling techniques, whose purpose is to weave changes into a (meta)model, provide means for deleting modeling constructs as a "removal" advice. One example is MATA [11] for class diagram-like models. A strength of these techniques is that they can designate various elements in a metamodel using a single rule. Such multiple designation rules could easily be integrated in package unmerge (and package merge), e.g. by introducing more sophisticated pattern matching constructs. Compared to aspect-oriented modeling, package merge and unmerge clearly separate the notions of adding information from removing information in two distinct specifications. Another difference is that package unmerge is one simple additional relationship construct to be added to metamodeling languages, unlike aspect-oriented modeling which requires completely new languages, even if aspect languages are defined as extensions to the languages to which aspects are to be applied. Such extensions include additional concepts to the base language (like pointcuts, a set of designators, and different categories of advice). Those extensions could be described by means of package merge and unmerge.

Metamodel matching and differencing [14] is another field related to our work. Metamodel matching compares two given metamodels and outputs a mapping that can be used to specify or generate a model alignment transformation [15]. Differences can be shown in a difference model (such as an AMW model [16]) that would represent the equivalent for our package unmerge model. First, package merge and unmerge could be used as alternative models to represent this mapping while emphasizing commonalties and differences. Second, the difference model usually references the compared (meta)models. As such, it is not possible to compute one metamodel from the other as both need to exist. However, instead of merely relying on a named elements hierarchy, package merge and package unmerge could benefit from metamodel matching techniques to match elements of the package (un)merge with elements of the package-to-be-(un)merged.

(Meta)model slicing [17] is a technique taking its roots in program slicing and graph decomposition. It makes it possible to extract from a model (and thus a metamodel) a sub-model containing elements depending on a set of elements of interest. The set of elements to be kept is computed from transitive dependencies of the elements of interest, and finally, only those elements that are not related to the elements of interest are discarded. Package unmerge rather identifies elements to be removed, and all contained elements are also removed, even if a dependency exists between an element to be kept and an element to be removed. An example found in section 5 was the `Core::Suite` that had to be dropped even though `Core::Project` had to be kept. Purpose of model slicing is more about model understanding and impact analysis while purpose of package unmerge is metamodel reuse.

Steel et al. [18] define rules for comparing two metamodels. This way model transformations may declare their input and output domains, so as to check that a given model can actually "enter" a transformation. As such, they check that a model which conforms to a given metamodel also conforms to another metamodel. Unfortunately, a model conforming to a reduced metamodel may not always conform to the metamodel-to-be reduced. This stems from the properties of the merge transformation. As pointed out in [19], a model conforming to a metamodel-to-be-merged may not conform to the merged metamodel. As the counterpart of package merge, package unmerge may thus not preserve model typing. A concluding remark is that extending the perimeter of a language is not the only possibility of package merge; symmetrically, reducing the perimeter of a language may not be done only by package unmerge.

8   Conclusion

This work is a contribution to the field of metamodel reuse, in the context of language engineering. We have presented here a new mechanism for controlling metamodel reduction, based on the definition of counterparts to package merge relations, that we call «package unmerge». Package merge and package unmerge can be considered a dual approach to metamodel engineering, by which the effect of one can be traced and reversed by the other. Used together, package merge and unmerge allow fine tuning of metamodel reuse.

We have developed a tool which implements both package merge and unmerge, and which provides assistance to determine the subset of a metamodel that a given tool effectively implements. The tool also automates the generation of package counterparts for package merge and unmerge. This tool is open-source, and can be downloaded from `http://sourcesup.cru.fr/projects/vetess/`.

Package unmerge, due to its definition as the package merge counterpart, inherits its strengths and drawbacks from package merge. It designates clearly what is to be removed, which may be an advantage (no unexpected removal) or a drawback (different pruning points all have to be designated). Moreover, as package merge is not the only mechanism for composing metamodels, the package unmerge we propose here is not be the only approach to metamodel pruning. For example, in [20], beside metamodel merge (corresponding to the approach taken by package merge approach) are identified metamodel interfacing, class refinement, and template instantiation. Counterparts for some of these approaches might also be possible and deserve to be explored and compared to, now package unmerge is proposed a definition.

We consider a metamodel too big when it is used by a tool that does not handle all of the concepts it declares. Making clear what actual metamodel is used by modeling tools would make tools' behavior clearer, as metamodel of manipulated models is part of tools' contract. A problem with many tools is that they do not fulfill their contract, because they declare a metamodel that is often too big, especially for metamodels constructed by reuse. One solution for this problem is to be able to alter extended metamodels using subtractive techniques as the one we propose in this paper. Thus, we consider metamodel reduction as step towards what one could call «component-based model engineering», where modeling tools could be selected, verified or assembled according to their contract. Hopefully, shifting to component-based paradigm could change the nature of MDE as components changed the nature of software [21].

References

1. Szyperski, C.A.: Component software - beyond object-oriented programming. Addison-Wesley-Longman (1998)
2. Meyer, B.: Object-Oriented Software Construction, 1st edn. Prentice-Hall (1988)
3. Beugnard, A., Jézéquel, J.-M., Plouzeau, N.: Making components contract aware. IEEE Computer 32(7), 38–45 (1999)
4. Sen, S., Moha, N., Baudry, B., Jézéquel, J.-M.: Meta-model pruning. In: Schürr, A., Selic, B. (eds.) MODELS 2009. LNCS, vol. 5795, pp. 32–46. Springer, Heidelberg (2009)
5. Muller, P.-A., Fondement, F., Baudry, B., Combemale, B.: Modeling modeling modeling. Software and System Modeling 11(3), 347–359 (2012)
6. Object Management Group, Unified Modeling Language (UML), superstructure, version 2.4.1. OMG Document formal/2011-08-06 (August 2011)
7. Object Management Group, Unified Modeling Language (UML), infrastructure, version 2.4.1. OMG Document formal/2011-08-05 (August 2011)
8. Object Management Group, Meta-Object Facility (MOF) core, v2.4.1. OMG Document formal/2011-08-07 (August 2011)
9. Kiczales, G., Lamping, J., Mendhekar, A., Maeda, C., Lopes, C., Loingtier, J.-M., Irwin, J.: Aspect-oriented programming. In: Akşit, M., Matsuoka, S. (eds.) ECOOP 1997. LNCS, vol. 1241, pp. 220–242. Springer, Heidelberg (1997)

10. Schauerhuber, A., Schwinger, W., Retschitzegger, W., Wimmer, M., Kappel, G.: A survey on aspect-oriented modeling approaches. tech. rep., Vienna University of Technology (October 2007)
11. Whittle, J., Jayaraman, P.K., Elkhodary, A.M., Moreira, A., Araújo, J.: MATA: A unified approach for composing UML aspect models based on graph transformation. T. Aspect-Oriented Software Development VI 6, 191–237 (2009)
12. Lasalle, J., Peureux, F., Fondement, F.: Development of an automated MBT toolchain from UML/SysML models. ISSE 7(4), 247–256 (2011)
13. Lasalle, J., Bouquet, F., Legeard, B., Peureux, F.: SysML to UML model transformation for test generation purpose. In: UML&FM 2010, 3rd IEEE Int. Workshop on UML and Formal Methods, Shanghai, China, pp. 1–8 (2011)
14. Lopes, D., Hammoudi, S., de Souza, J., Bontempo, A.: Metamodel matching: Experiments and comparison. In: ICSEA, p. 2. IEEE Computer Society (2006)
15. Falleri, J.-R., Huchard, M., Lafourcade, M., Nebut, C.: Metamodel matching for automatic model transformation generation. In: Czarnecki, K., Ober, I., Bruel, J.-M., Uhl, A., Völter, M. (eds.) MODELS 2008. LNCS, vol. 5301, pp. 326–340. Springer, Heidelberg (2008)
16. Didonet, M., Fabro, D., Bézivin, J., Valduriez, P.: Weaving models with the Eclipse AMW plugin. In: Eclipse Modeling Symposium, Eclipse Summit Europe (2006)
17. Kagdi, H.H., Maletic, J.I., Sutton, A.: Context-free slicing of UML class models. In: ICSM, pp. 635–638. IEEE Computer Society (2005)
18. Steel, J., Jézéquel, J.-M.: On Model Typing. Journal of Software and Systems Modeling (SoSyM) 6, 401–414 (2007)
19. Dingel, J., Diskin, Z., Zito, A.: Understanding and improving UML package merge. Journal of Software and Systems Modeling (SoSyM) 7, 443–467 (2008)
20. Emerson, M., Sztipanovits, J.: Techniques for metamodel composition. In: The 6th OOPSLA Workshop on Domain-Specific Modeling, OOPSLA 2006, pp. 123–139. ACM Press (2006)
21. Herzum, P., Sims, O.: Business Component Factory: A Comprehensive Overview of Component-Based Development for the Enterprise. Wiley (1999)

Integrating Modeling Tools
in the Development Lifecycle with OSLC: A Case Study

Maged Elaasar and Adam Neal

IBM Canada Ltd., Rational Software, Ottawa Lab.
770 Palladium Dr., Kanata, ON. K2V 1C8, Canada
{melaasar,adam_neal}@ca.ibm.com

Abstract. Models play a central role in a model driven development process. They realize requirements, specify system design, abstract source code, drive test cases, etc. However, for a modeling tool to be most effective, it needs to integrate its data and workflows with other tools in the development lifecycle. This is often problematic as these tools are usually disparate. OSLC is an emerging specification for integrating lifecycle tools using the principles of linked data. In this paper, we describe how OSLC can be used to integrate MOF-based modeling tools with other lifecycle tools. We demonstrate this in a case study involving an EMF-based modeling tool. We show how we made the tool conform to the OSLC specification and discuss how this enabled it to integrate seamlessly with other lifecycle tools to support some key end-to-end development lifecycle workflows.

Keywords: Model, Lifecycle, OSLC, Semantic Web, OWL, RDF, UML, MOF.

1   Introduction

Software development is an inherently complex endeavor. While there is no silver bullet [1], the complexity can often be mitigated with a set of specialized tools. Such tools support different activities in the software development lifecycle like specifying requirements, creating models, developing source code, defining test cases, managing builds, assigning work items, etc. However, in many cases, these tools are designed as silos that have weak or no integration between each other, which hampers their combined value.

One approach to integrate development tools is to design them on the same platform creating an integrated development environment (IDE). For example, this is the approach taken by the Eclipse IDE [2]. This approach helps integration because tools follow the platform's guidelines (on UI, process, extensibility, etc.) and use common components. For example, the Eclipse Modeling Framework (EMF) [3] allows a modeling tool and a requirements tool to define their structured data and cross-reference each other's artifacts using a common infrastructure.

However, this approach does not help integrate tools built on different platforms. For example, it does not help integrate an Eclipse-based modeling tool with a web

A. Moreira et al. (Eds.): MODELS 2013, LNCS 8107, pp. 154–169, 2013.
© Springer-Verlag Berlin Heidelberg 2013

based requirements tool. It also does not ensure that data and API used to integrate tools are flexible enough to cope with tool evolution. For example, changing a metamodel used by a modeling tool may break references to model elements made by a requirements tool. Similarly, changing the API (e.g., by adding an extra parameter) for displaying a modeling diagram could break a tool trying to display a linked modeling diagram. Furthermore, as tools become more and more networked (cloud or web based), integrating them using traditional platforms becomes harder and less maintainable.

Recently, a set of specifications for integrating software development tools, called the Open Services for Lifecycle Collaboration (OSLC) [4], has emerged. The specifications allow conforming tools to integrate their data and workflows in support of end-to-end lifecycle scenarios. OSLC does not standardize the behavior of any tool or class of tools. Instead, it specifies a minimum amount of protocol to allow tools to work together relatively seamlessly. OSLC also tries to accommodate a wide variety of tool implementation technologies.

Furthermore, OSLC defines two primary techniques for integrating tools. The first is linking data in a scalable platform-independent way using web technologies. This is where OSLC uses the linked data method [5] to represent some information on tool artifacts as RDF [6] resources identified by HTTP URIs. OSLC also provides a common protocol for manipulating those resources in a RESTful [7] way using HTTP CRUD (Create, Read, Update, Delete) operations [8]. Finally, artifact linking is achieved by embedding the URI of one resource in the representation of another.

The second technique is linking data via a HTML user interface. This is where OSLC specifies a protocol that allows a tool to invoke fragments of web-based user interface (e.g., selection dialog) of another tool. This enables a tool to exploit the user interface and business logic in other tools when integrating their data and processes.

In this paper, we focus on integrating MOF-based modeling tools with other lifecycle tools using OSLC. MOF [9] is a standard by the Object Management Group (OMG) for defining modeling languages like UML [10] and BPMN [11]. We present an approach for allowing a MOF-based modeling tool to publish its models generically according to the OSLC specification. We demonstrate our approach in a case study involving a server extension of the EMF-based Rational Software Architect (RSA) modeling tool called Design Manager (DM) [12]. RSA DM supports a number of standard MOF-based modeling languages. We use examples from of the UML class diagram whenever relevant. We also show how OSLC enables a modeling tool, like RSA DM, to integrate its UI with other lifecycle tools, like those in the Collaborative Lifecycle Management tool suite [13], to support some key development workflows (e.g., traceability, impact analysis and link preview). We conclude that OSLC is a light-weight and practical approach for integrating independent lifecycle tools.

The remainder of the paper is organized as follows: Section 2 gives an overview of the OSLC specification; a case study showing how OSLC can be implemented by a MOF-based modeling tool, along with how this can help the tool integrate with other lifecycle tools to support key development workflows is given in Section 3; Section 4 discusses the case study and highlights some remaining gaps; a review of related work is provided in Section 5; Finally, Section 6 concludes and outlines future work .

2   Overview of Open Services for Lifecycle Collaboration

Open Services for Lifecycle Collaboration (OSLC) [4] is a set of specifications for integrating development lifecycle tools. The specifications are organized as a Core specification and a set of domain specifications (e.g., configuration management, quality management, requirements management and architecture management) that build on it. Core specifies the primary integration techniques for lifecycle tools. This consists mostly of standard rules and patterns for using HTTP and RDF. The Core specification is not meant to be used by itself, but rather in conjunction with one or more of the domain specifications. Together, they describe the specification set implemented by a domain tool. For example, a modeling tool would implement both Core and Architecture Management (AM) specifications. In this section, we overview some concepts from these specifications referred to by the case study in section 3.

2.1   Service Provider

The Core specification defines the concept of a Service Provider that enables provider tools to expose resources and allows consumer tools to navigate to these resources and create new ones. A service provider is itself defined as a RDF resource (Figure 1) with a given URI (line 2). It associates itself with one of the OSLC domains (e.g., the AM domain, line 5) and defines two properties: a `creation` URL (line 8) to do HTTP POST on to create new resources, and a `queryBase` URL (line 11) to do HTTP Get on to get a list of existing resources in the provider. That list is represented as an RDF container resource with the existing resources as its members (Figure 2, lines 3-5).

```
01    @prefix oslc: <http://open-service.net/ns/core#>.
02    <http://abc.com/toolA> a oslc:ServiceProvider;
03        oslc:service
04            [a oslc:Service;
05                oslc:domain <http://open-services.net/ns/am#>;
06                oslc:creationFactory
07                    [a oslc:CreationFactory;
08                        oslc:creation <http://abc.com/toolA/contents>];
09                oslc:queryCapability
10                    [a oslc:QueryCapability;
11                        oslc:queryBase <http://abc.com/toolA/contents>]
12            ].
```

Fig. 1. Sample service provider resource

```
01    @prefix rdfs: <http://www.w3.org/2000/01/rdf-schema#>.
02    <http://abc.com/toolA/contents>
03        <rdfs:member> <http://abc.com/toolA/resource/000>;
04        # … 998 more triples here …
05        <rdfs:member> <http://abc.com/toolB/resource/999>.
```

Fig. 2. Sample query base resource

2.2   Resource

An OSLC resource is contained by an OSLC service provider and has a URI and a type (e.g., `oslc_am:Resource`) that is defined by an OSLC domain specification. This makes an OSLC resource type an RDF class. A resource must also have its state represented in RDF/XML (beside other possible representations) and defined by a set of common RDF properties to support OSLC integration between tools. These common properties (such as label, description, creator, last-modification-time and priority) have common names defined by standards like RDFS [6] (e.g., `rdfs:type`) and Dublin Core [14] (e.g., `dcterms:title`), although some are defined by OSLC itself (e.g., `oslc:usage`). These properties may also have alias names (coming from the providing tool) in the same resource (e.g., `uml:NamedElement_name` is used as an alias to `dcterms:title` when the resource is a UML named element).

Furthermore, OSLC adopts an *open world* assumption about a resource state. Although it defines some standard types and properties for integration, it also assumes that any given resource may have many more types and properties than are defined in the specification. Properties in an OSLC resource maybe have values that are either literals typed by one of the standard RDF data types (e.g., Boolean and Integer) or references to some resources. OSLC generally avoids constraining the range of a reference property to be a type from another specification. This allows OSLC to evolve independently of other specifications and also allows tools that have slightly evolved to smoothly interoperate with each other.

2.3   Resource Shape

OSLC generally adopts the open world assumption that implies that there is no single authority on the validity of a given resource. However, OSLC also recognizes that there is a category of tools that still operates with a *closed world* assumption. This is why OSLC allows the definition of a Resource Shape, for a given resource type, with a list of properties having allowed types and values. In other words, a resource shape specifies the constraints that a resource must satisfy. To help illustrate how a resource shape is defined, consider the example resource shape in Figure 3. It partially describes a UML Class resource (line 8) by defining three of its properties. The first is a standard Dublin Core `dcterms:title` property, which represents optional strings (lines 9-15). The second is a property called `uml:NamedElement_visibility`, which applies to a UML class (according to the UML metamodel) and can have one of four allowed values (lines 16-26). The third is `uml:Class_superClass` property, which also applies to a UML class and represents optional references to its super classes (lines 27-34). Such a resource shape can be retrieved from a modeling tool that is an OSLC service provider to help construct, update, interpret or validate linked UML class resources.

```
01    @prefix oslc: <http://open-service.net/ns/core#>.
02    @prefix xsd: <http://www.w3.org/2001/XMLSchema#>.
03    @prefix dcterms: <http://purl.org/dc/terms/>.
04    @prefix uml: <http://www.omg.org/spec/UML/2011070#>.
05    <http://acme.com/toolA/UMLClassShape>
06          a oslc:ResourceShape;
07          dcterms:title "Shape of resources of type UML Class";
08          oslc:describes: uml:Class;
09          oslc:property [
10                a oslc:Property;
11                dcterms:title "details for dcterms:title property";
12                oslc:propertyDefinition dcterms:title;
13                oslc:name "title";
14                oslc:occurs oslc:Zero-or-many;
15                oslc:valueType xsd:String ];
16          oslc:property [
17                a oslc:Property;
18                dcterms:title "details for visibility property";
19                oslc:propertyDefinition uml:NamedElement_visibility;
20                oslc:name "visibility";
21                oslc:occurs oslc:Zero-or-one;
22                oslc:valueType oslc:Resource;
23                oslc:allowedValue uml:VisibilityKind::public;
24                oslc:allowedValue uml:VisibilityKind::private;
25                oslc:allowedValue uml:VisibilityKind::protected;
26                oslc:allowedValue uml:VisibilityKind::package ];
27          oslc:property [
28                a oslc:Property;
29                dcterms:title "details for superClass property";
30                oslc:propertyDefinition uml:Class_superClass;
31                oslc:name "superClass";
32                oslc:occurs oslc:Zero-or-many;
33                oslc:valueType oslc:Resource;
34                oslc:range uml:Class ].
```

Fig. 3. Sample resource shape

2.4 Data Integration Protocols

So far we have seen how a service provider tool provides URLs that can be used by a consumer tool to perform resource creation (HTTP POST) and retrieval (HTTP GET). Similarly, update (HTTP PUT) and delete (HTTP DELETE) operations can be performed on resources directly using their URLs. In addition, OSLC allows two query mechanisms to find specific information in resources. The first mechanism allows adding a list of properties as a parameter to a resource URI to only get triples using those properties from a resource. For example, performing a HTTP GET on the URL   http://abc.com/toolA/resource/001?oslc.properties=dcterms:title, uml:NamedElement_visibility of a UML class resource gets the triples that use the *title* and *visibility* properties only. The other mechanism allows an OSLC query to be added as a parameter to a service provider's queryBase URI to filter the list of member resources to get. For example, performing a HTTP GET on the URL `http://abc.com/toolA?oslc.where=dcterm:title="Class1"` gets all resources whose title is Class1 in a modeling tool A.

2.5   User Interface Integration Protocols

While the data integration protocols of OSLC are useful, using them might not be sufficient in all cases. For example, when a user of a UML modeling tool wants to create or select defects, in a defect tracking tool, and link them to UML resources, it would be much better tool integration to delegate to the defect tracking tool's own (web based) creation/selection dialogs rather than redefining them in the modeling tool. OSLC provides a protocol that allows a UI provider tool (the defect tracking tool in this case) to define these dialogs and declare them in its service provider resource, such that a consumer tool (the modeling tool in this case) can embed them, using HTML and Javascript, in its web or rich client UI. The consumer tool would invoke and initialize these dialogs then get notified by the consumer tool of the resource URLs created or selected. More details can be found in the OSLC specification [4].

Another UI integration protocol by OSLC allows preview of linked resources. The protocol is often invoked when a user hovers over a link to another resource in the UI and a popup box appears showing the preview of the resource. This protocol allows a consumer tool to perform a HTTP GET on a resource with a special media type. The provider tool would then return a small amount of information about the resource (e.g., title, icon, description and URL) for the purpose showing the preview. More information on UI integration protocols can be found in the OSLC specification.

3   Case Study: Publishing MOF-Based Models as OSLC Resources

In section 2, we provide an overview of the concepts of resource linking in OSLC. In this section, we show in a case study how a MOF-based modeling tool can use those concepts to publish its models in a way that allows linking with other development lifecycle artifacts. We use the OSLC support in RSA DM tool as a running example to demonstrate those ideas. We then follow by describing some key workflows for using this integration in the development lifecycle.

3.1   Running Example

Rational Software Architect (RSA) is a MOF-based modeling tool developed on the Eclipse platform. RSA uses the Eclipse Modeling Framework (EMF) [3] as its MOF infrastructure. Since XMI [15] is the native interchange format supported by MOF/EMF, RSA models are natively stored as XMI files, as shown in Figure 4.

Furthermore, RSA provides no linking capabilities between its models and other lifecycle artifacts. In order to bridge this gap, a Design Management (DM) extension was added to RSA resulting in the RSA DM tool. The extension allows RSA to provide a collaborative approach to modeling (out of scope for this paper) [16] and to link its models with artifacts of other lifecycle tools, using OSLC, thereby facilitating new features such as cross-lifecycle traceability, impact analysis, and link preview (these features are discussed in Section 4).

The DM (OSLC AM) extension consists of four components, as shown by the black boxes in Figure 4. The first component is a DM server, which is responsible for: a) converting the XMI-based models into RDF resources, b) providing the RDF resources as OSLC resources such that other OSLC enabled tools are able to link to them, and c) providing other expected OSLC resources and services. We focus on these capabilities in the following sub-sections. The second component is an import engine that allows periodic publishing of RSA model files to the server. The third component is a rich client, which is an extension to RSA that allows it to load file-based models to the server and manipulate server-based models consistently with the file-based ones. The fourth component is a web client that allows some manipulation (e.g., editing of properties) of server-based models from a web browser, in addition to resource linking and collaborative features (e.g., markup, comment and review).

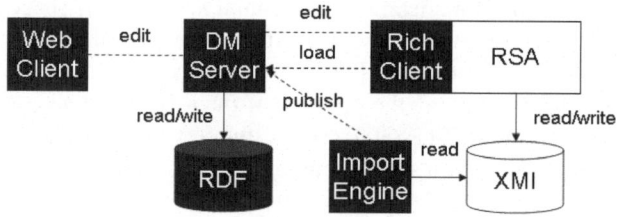

Fig. 4. Architecture of RSA DM

3.2   Converting XMI Models to RDF Resources

Recall from Section 2 that one of the basic principles of OSLC is to represent data as RDF resources with HTTP URIs. Therefore, when converting MOF-based models to OSLC resources, several operations have to take place: a) mapping the XMI data to RDF triples, b) grouping the RDF triples into RDF graphs, and c) assigning unique HTTP URIs to the RDF resources.

3.2.1   Mapping XMI Data to RDF Triples

One approach to convert the XMI data to RDF triples is to use some mapping between their schemas. While XMI data is defined using a MOF metamodel, RDF triples are defined using a RDFS/OWL [17] ontology. RSA DM provides a mapping between MOF to OWL. For example, every MOF `Package` is mapped to an OWL `Ontology`. Every `Class`, `Datatype` and `Property` in a package is mapped to corresponding `rdfs:Class`, `rdfs:Datatype` and `rdfs:Property` in an ontology. UML profiles are also mapped to ontologies and their stereotypes to classes. Furthermore, instance model mapping is based on metamodel mapping. Every model element maps to an RDF individual typed by classes that correspond to the element's type (and any applied stereotypes) in the model. This is possible since RDF supports multi-classification. Every property value (including on stereotype applications) maps to a triple that uses the property as a predicate.

3.2.2   Grouping the RDF Triples into RDF Graphs

The second operation is to group the resulting RDF triples into RDF graphs. A graph is a set of triples with a unique namespace (URL). One simple way to accomplish that is to group triples based on models they map from. However, while a model might be fragmented into multiple files (RSA supports this feature), it is very common for a model to be monolithic (i.e., all the contents are stored in a single model). Mapping such model to a monolithic graph has major consequences (edit locks and complex merge sessions) in a team environment where multiple users collaborate on the model.

One way around that problem is to specify an automatic fragmentation strategy for RDF graphs (sets of triples). In other words, define the granularity of grouping triples into graphs. The way to accomplish that is by annotating some classes in the ontology as "graph type", i.e., a type whose resources (model elements) have their own graphs that contains their triples and those of their contained resources. For example, RSA DM specifies the graph granularity of the UML metamodel by annotating the `Package`, `Classifier`, `Attribute` and `Operation` classes as graph types. This selection was based on feedback from users on the most suitable unit of fragmentation (hence collaboration). This makes model elements typed by those classes map to their own RDF graphs automatically upon conversion, and regardless of the actual model fragmentation before the conversion. Note that annotating every class in the metamodel as a graph type may result in too many created graphs, which would benefit collaboration but may adversely affect performance. The balance in practice depends on the domain author's preference and the physical limits of the tool.

3.2.3   Assigning Unique HTTP URIs to RDF Resources

OSLC requires that every OSLC resource is identified by a unique HTTP URI. When mapping model elements to RDF resources, unique URIs have to be produced and assigned to each element. An HTTP URI is typically made of three parts: base, id and optional fragment (`base/id<#fragment>`). The base in this case is typically the URL of the server that the OSLC resources are published to (e.g., `http://www.abc.com/`). The id in this case is that of an RDF graph. Recall that upon conversion from XMI to RDF, some model elements (those that are instances of graph types) are mapped to their own RDF graphs, while others are mapped to resources nested within their ancestors' graphs. There are alternative approaches for producing a unique id for an RDF graph. One approach is to derive the id from the model element. This could either be the XMI id or the fully qualified name of the element (e.g., `http://www.abc.com/P1_C2_op3`). Another approach is to assign a unique resource number on the server (e.g., `http://www.abc.com/resources/123`). RSA DM uses qualified names when mapping metamodels to OWL ontologies since those names tend to be more stable as changing them have dire consequences on instance models. On the other hand, RSA DM uses resource numbers when mapping instance models to RDF since element names tend to frequently change. The XMI id is not used in both cases since in RSA DM's case it is typically a non-user friendly GUID.

Furthermore, the fragment of the URI is only required for those RDF resources that map from non-graph model elements, i.e., those that are nested within other graphs. The fragment is typically derived in this case from the model element, either its XMI id or its qualified name up to the ancestor corresponding to the graph (e.g., `http://www.abc.com/P1_C2_op3#param4`). RSA DM uses the qualified names in this case. It is important to notice that elements with fragments in their URIs cannot be recognized as separate OSLC resources since such URIs are not distinguishable from their graph URIs when CRUD operations are performed using HTTP.

3.3   Providing the RDF Resources as OSLC Resources

Once RDF resources are produced from XMI data via mapping, they can be provided as OSLC resources. The process involves adding the expected OSLC types and attributes to the resources. Specifically, an OSLC type (e.g., `oslc_am:Resource` for the AM domain) is added as another type for an RDF resource. This is possible due to RDF's support of multi-classification. Then, values for all relevant OSLC properties for the type (e.g., `dcterms:title` and `dcterms:creator`) are added to the resource. These values are either derived from the resource when properties have aliases in the domain (e.g., `uml:NamedElement_name` is an alias property for `dcterms:title` in UML) or based on the info persisted in the RDF repository (e.g., the resource creator).

Another step in the process involves filtering all RDF types and properties that are not intended to be exposed to OSLC consumers. These types and properties can be annotated in their ontologies as OSLC private. Filtering a type leads to ignoring all triples involving instances of that type when publishing resources. If a type was a graph type then all graphs corresponding to resources of that class (which may include nested resources) are also ignored.

Furthermore, OSLC resources may have links to other OSLC resources. An OSLC link is a triple that relates two OSLC resources, a source and a target, with a known predicate thus providing traceability between them. An OSLC link triple may be contained in the graph of one of the linked resources or in a totally separate graph. The OSLC specification does not predefine link predicates; rather it is up to the OSLC service provider to define them. An example of a predicate that is supported by RSA DM is `<http://jazz.net/ns/dm/linktypes#derives>` that is often used to link a model element to a requirement defined in a requirement management tool.

3.4   Providing Other OSLC Resources and Services

In order to facilitate collaboration with other OSLC-enabled tools, a modeling tool provides a Service Provider resource (Section 2.1). That resource contains a URL of a `queryBase` HTTP service that provides RDF resources in the format defined by the OSLC specification. It also contains a URL of a `creationFactory` HTTP service that provides CRUD operations for OSLC resources.

In addition, a modeling tool may publish OSLC resource shapes (RSA DM does not support them in v4.01), which are type definitions for OSLC resources. Recall (from Section 2.3) that a resource shape describes a set of properties that may exist for a given type of OSLC resource. This set can be derived from OWL ontologies defining that type (which in turn were generated from MOF metamodel). Specifically, OWL ontologies are queried for all OWL properties that have as a domain a class that is either the same or a super class of the shape's described type. For each one of those properties, all information needed to construct a property definition in a resource shape can be derived. For example, the `oslc:name` value is derived from   the property's `rdfs:label` triple, the `oslc:occurs` value is derived from `owl:minCardinality` and `owl:maxCardinality` restrictions on the property, the `oslc:valueType/oslc:range` value is derived from the property's `rdfs:range`, and the `oslc:allowedValue` values are derived for an enumeration from its `owl:oneOf` list members. We do not describe the full details of the derivation here for brevity.

Finally, an OSLC-enabled modeling tool may provide a service that provides web UI to link to OSLC modeling resources. This service allows users of other OSLC consumer tools to open a dialog (Figure 5 right) and pick a resource in order to add a link between the two artifacts and thus provide some traceability between them. A modeling tool can also provide a service that returns compact information about a given OSLC resource to help construct a preview window (Figure 5 left) for the resource in another lifecycle tool.

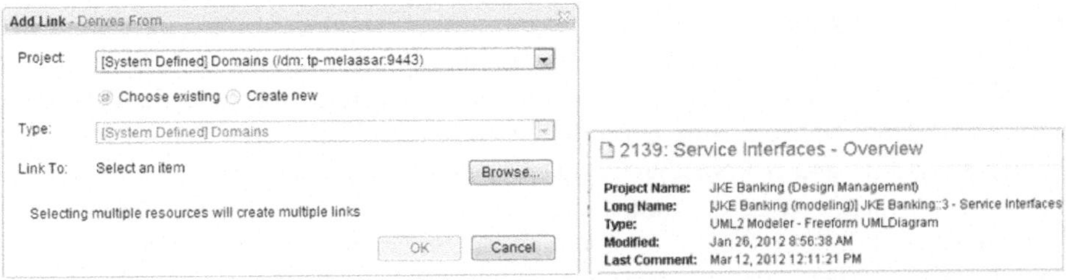

Fig. 5. An OSLC add link dialog (left) and an OSLC preview window (right)

3.5   Enabling Key Development Workflows with OSLC

So far, we described how modeling tools can conform to the OSLC specifications, by implementing the required services and exposing their models in an OSLC compliant way, in order to integrate with other lifecycle tools. The benefits of this integration can be seen in enabling several key development workflows between related tools in the lifecycle. For example, when a design needs to change, it would not be wise to change it without analyzing the impact of such change on derived source code. Also, when one is trying to understand a design, it would help to check the requirement satisfied by the design. Moreover, it would be easier to understand a design if its linked artifacts can be previewed without actually navigating to their defining tool, since trying to use another tool's UI might be hard.

In this section, we describe at a high level of abstraction key lifecycle development workflows, such as traceability, impact analysis and link preview, that have actually been implemented in RSA DM as an OSLC AM tool. The workflows demonstrate integration with other OSLC tools for change management (CM), requirement management (RM) and quality management (QM), which are all part of the Collaboration Lifecycle Management (CLM) tool suite [13].

3.5.1   Traceability
Traceability refers to the ability to link artifacts in one tool to another. The type of link (i.e., the predicate used in the link triple) allows a user to understand the meaning

of the link. For example, RSA DM provides a set of out of the box link types ('Elaborates', 'Derives From', etc) that facilitate linking artifacts from multiple OSLC compliant tools (Figure 6). Typically, specific link types are used on specific artifacts, although the tool does not enforce any rule. To give an example of how modeling tool traceability fits into a lifecycle workflow, consider this scenario:

A developer, Bob, has a change request, defined in a CM tool, which identifies a problem with some behavior of the code. The code has been generated from a specific UML state chart diagram in an AM tool. Bob opens the change request and chooses to create a new OSLC link to the specific state chart diagram, which models this behavior. Bob creates an 'Elaborated by' link in the CM tool and is immediately prompted to find and select the state chart diagram of interest, using a selection dialog provided by the AM tool. Bob assigns the change request to Al, an architect, and leaves a comment, in the CM change request, asking him to remodel the behavior based on the change request.

Al opens the change request, and clicks on the 'Elaborated By' link, which immediately opens up the state chart in question. Al inspects the state chart diagram and finds a 'Derives From' link that points to a requirement, defined in an RM tool. Al clicks this link and is immediately taken to the requirement. After reviewing the requirement's description, Al jumps back to the state chart, in the AM tool, by following a back link in the RM tool, so that he can update the behavior accordingly. Once updated, Al navigates a link, in the AM tool, from the state chart to the change request and assigns it back to Bob who regenerates the code and closes the request.

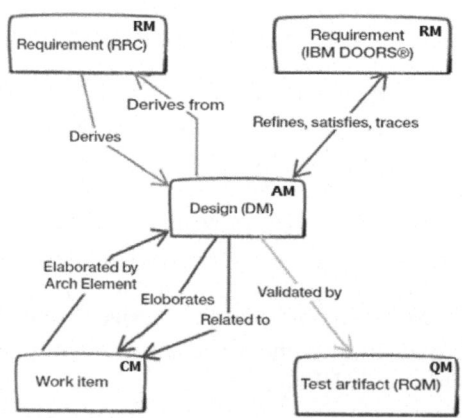

Fig. 6. Possible OSLC links between RSA DM and other CLM tools

3.5.2   Impact Analysis

Impact Analysis is method of traversing incoming and outgoing links to a particular resource. As such, it can aid an architect in identifying the impact of a change to a given resource. The theory and behavior of impact analysis is not something new, and in the modeling world it is commonly used during refactoring actions in order to identify all the resources which are required to change. However, once we include

OSLC into the equation, and consider the traceability information, we find that impact analysis gets even more powerful. Consider the following scenario:

Al, the architect, wants to change the signature of operation *sendMessage(buffer)* in a UML model and needs to determine the impact of this change. Al runs a multi-level (i.e., involving multiple link levels) impact analysis on the operation to find outgoing and incoming links to/from the operation (Figure 7). He sees an outgoing link (`Operation::ownedParameter`) to the operation's input parameter *buffer*, which in turn has an "Elaborates" link to a change request (*need return buffer*). He understands that he has to inspect the change request, in the CM tool, to verify that he does not invalidate it with the proposed change. He also sees an incoming link (`Class::ownedOperation`) to the operation's class *MessageProtocol*, which in turn has a 'Derives From' link to a requirement (*Define Message Protocol*). He checks the requirement and realizes that he will need to update it in the RM tool. Finally, he sees an outgoing link (`Operation::method`) to an interaction *Notify User*, which in turn has a 'Validated By' link to a test case (*Verify User notification*). He reads the test case, in the QM tool, and discovers that he will also need to rerun the test to validate the interaction after the change. As we can see, the traceability links can now play a vital role in impact analysis as well, since the impact is now stretching past the model boundaries and into the realm of other lifecycle artifacts.

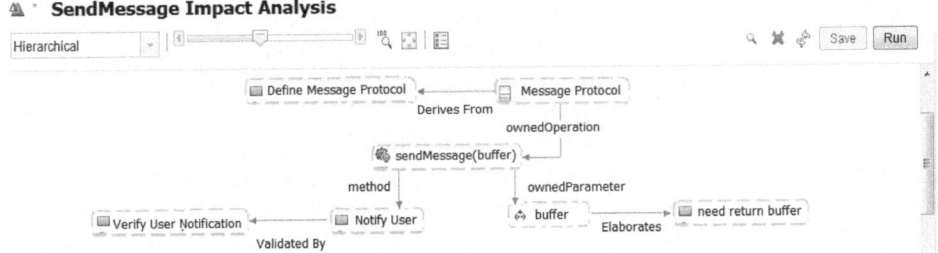

Fig. 7. Impact analysis diagram of SendMessage operation

3.5.3   Link Preview

The rich hover feature plays a complimentary role to traceability and impact analysis. Rich hover allows a user to inspect the contents of the linked resource in a convenient way without having to fully navigate a link. Consider the impact analysis case again:

When Al views the impact analysis results with the multitude of links, he is able to simply hover over the links of interest and get presented with a convenient, compact rendering (i.e., preview) of the target resource of the link. For example, hovering over the interaction shows a sequence diagram so Al can quickly understand the meaning of that interaction without having to leave the results of the impact analysis. Similarly, hovering over the related requirement provides Al with a quick view of the requirement text, as well as showing some additional outgoing links to other design artifacts. He now knows that updating this requirement will potentially affect other linked design resources, and now he needs to focus on those resources to ensure that any changes made in the requirement are carried out through out the design model.

4   Discussion

Based on our experience using OSLC, presented in this paper as a case study, we would like to discuss a few points. The first point is the use of resource shapes for resource validation, which allows collaborating tools to check each other's expectations on resources. Recall from Section 2.3 that a resource shape provides a description of OSLC resources of a given type, in terms of possible properties used on these resources, their types, multiplicities and allowed values. It could be argued that an OWL ontology can also provide this information and hence a new concept, like a resource shape, is not needed. However, on a closer look, the open world assumption (what is not known to be false is true) made by OWL works against it being used for validation (the purpose of type definitions). For example, when you have a property isMarriedTo defined in an OWL ontology with its domain and range being class Person, and when you have two resources, Joe of type Person and ET of type Robot, then a triple stating that ET isMarriedTo Joe would not be invalid according to the ontology. This is because an OWL reasoner performing consistency check (the closest operation to validation) would simply infer that ET is also of type Person, instead of complain that class Robot does not have property isMarriedTo. This ability to infer new truth goes against validation, which makes a closed world assumption. Therefore, we see that resource shapes are indeed a needed feature of OSLC. Other related discussion on this topic can be found in [18].

The second point concerns where an OSLC link between resources managed by different tools should be owned. Two approaches exist, which have been implemented in the context of RSA DM. The first approach is to make the tool owning the source resource be the owner regardless of which tool creates the link. For example, a 'Derives From" link between a model element (in RSA DM) and a requirement (in the RM tool of CLM) is always owned at the RSA DM side regardless of which tool created it because a RSA DM resource is always the source of such link. The target tool may still find out about the link by sending an OSLC query to the source tool. A second approach is to store bi-directional links, i.e., add a back link in the target tool as well. For example, when creating an 'Elaborates' link from a model element (in RSA DM) to a work item (in the CM tool of CLM), a back link 'Elaboated By' is also created and owned by the CM tool. However, this approach complicates the synchronization of both links. A third possible approach (not implemented yet in RSA DM) is to let the tool that defines the link, which could be a third tool, own it. However, in the case of a third tool, the source and target tools would not know about the link.

The third point concerns the behavior of OSLC linking when the integrated tools use different configurations of the same resources. For example, RSA DM supports the ability to define multiple n-dimensional configurations for resources (e.g., for a UML design model of cars, the dimensions could be the make, model and year).

A resource in this case may still have the same URI. The question becomes which configuration of the resource is actually linked when an OSLC link involves such a resource? One approach to answer this question is to include a configuration id to the linked resource URI through an HTTP `context` parameter. For example, when `configuration1` of a model element is linked, then the URI of the corresponding OSLC resource becomes `<baseURI>?context=configuration1`. The support of configurations is on the list of future work for upcoming reversions of OSLC.

5   Related Works

Application Lifecycle Management (ALM) [19] is a continuous process of managing the life of an application through governance, development and maintenance. Such process is being realized by RSA DM's integration with the various tools in the CLM suite. OSLC plays a central role in this integration by enabling linking across the development artifacts and integration of UI (via delegated dialogs and link preview).

Furthermore, some platforms provide tools that are horizontally integrated, i.e., tools that work together on one of the three aspects of ALM. For example, the Eclipse platform [2] and the Microsoft Visual Studio [20] platform provide tools that integrate together by following the platforms' guidelines and sharing common components. Yet tools should be integrated not just horizontally but also vertically, helping organizations make connections across the three ALM aspects. For instance, RSA DM and CLM allow a configuration and change management tool (the governance aspect) to be integrated with requirement, development and architecture management tools (the development aspect), which are also connected to a quality management tool (the maintenance aspect).

Another solution that supports ALM is Microsoft Visual Studio coupled with Team Foundation Server [21]. The solution supports linking between lifecycle artifacts for the purpose of traceability [22]. It also supports UI integration (through selection and creation dialogs) of the various lifecycle tools. However, it is not clear to what extent these features are possible due to the development of these tools on the same platform, as opposed to due to standard tool integration protocols like those offered by OSLC. While it is true that RSA DM and CLM are built on the same platform, i.e., Jazz [23], the integration approach relies more heavily on OSLC as explained in this paper. In fact, there exist examples of tool integration through OSLC where the tool is not Jazz-based (e.g., the DOORS requirements tool [24]).

6   Conclusion and Future Work

Integrating a modeling tool with other lifecycle tools gives a synergetic boost to the development process that cannot be underestimated. Tool integration has historically been poor or non-existent due to various technologies used to develop these tools and the high cost of producing point to point integrations. OSLC is an emerging specification for integrating development lifecycle tools. It standardizes a set of data expectations and protocols that can be implemented by compliant tools to ease their integration. In this paper, we overviewed OSLC, highlighting its main concepts and protocols, and presented a case study for using it to integrate MOF-based modeling tools with other lifecycle tools. We showed how such integration can be generalized for any MOF domain but used examples from the UML domain to demonstrate it. We also used our RSA DM tool, which conforms to the OSLC AM specification, as an example modeling tool. Moreover, we showed the value proposition of such approach by highlighting key development lifecycle scenarios that would be enabled thanks to OSLC integration of a modeling tool into the lifecycle. Finally, we discussed three points: a) the need for OSLC shapes, b) the owner of OSLC links and c) the handling of multiple resource configurations, which arose in the case study.

Going forward, we plan to continue to leverage OSLC to tightly integrate RSA DM with other lifecycle tools including those in the CLM suite. A new revision of OSLC (reversion 3) is currently being developed and promises to address other integration issues including incremental (partial) updating of OSLC resources, discovery of OSLC services of a given tool, and coordinated reporting on OSLC linking errors. We plan to report on implementing these features in the future. Furthermore, we plan to report on industrial case studies of using RSA DM, along with CLM, to define an integrated development process.

References

1. Brooks, F.: No Silver Bullet; Essence and Accidents of Software Engineering. Computer Journal 20(4), 10–19 (1987)
2. Eclipse platform, http://www.eclipse.org
3. Steinberg, D., Budinsky, F., Paternostro, M., Merks, E.: EMF: Eclipse Modeling Framework, 2nd edn (2009)
4. Open Services for Lifecycle Collaboration (OSLC), http://open-services.net/
5. Heath, T., Bizer, C.: Linked Data: Evolving the Web into a Global Data Space, 1st edn. Synthesis Lectures on the Semantic Web: Theory and Technology, vol. 1(1), pp. 1–136. Morgan & Claypool
6. RDF Primer, http://www.w3.org/TR/2004/REC-rdf-primer-20040210/
7. Richardson, L., Ruby, S.: RESTful Web Services. O'Reilly (2007)
8. Martin, J.: Managing the Data-base Environment, p. 381. Prentice-Hall (1983)
9. Meta Object Facility (MOF) v2.0, http://www.omg.org/spec/MOF/2.0/
10. Unified Modeling Language (UML) v2.2, http://www.omg.org/spec/UML/2.2/
11. Business Process Model and Notation (BPMN) v2.0,
    http://www.omg.org/spec/BPMN/2.0/
12. Rational Software Architect Design Manager,
    https://jazz.net/products/design-management/
13. Collaborative Lifecycle Management (CLM), https://jazz.net/products/clm/
14. Dublin Core Metadata Initiave, http://dublincore.org/
15. MOF 2.0 / XMI Mapping v2.1.1, http://www.omg.org/spec/XMI/2.1.1/
16. Elaasar, M., Conallen, J.: Design Management: a Collaborative Design Solution. In: Van Gorp, P., Ritter, T., Rose, L.M. (eds.) ECMFA 2013. LNCS, vol. 7949, pp. 165–178. Springer, Heidelberg (2013)
17. Web Ontology Language (OWL), http://www.w3.org/TR/owl-features/

18. Ryman, A.: Linked Data, RDF, and OSLC Resource Shapes: Define REST API Contracts for RDF Resource Representations (to appear soon in Developer Works)
19. Chappell, D.: What is Application Lifecycle Management?, http://www.davidchappell.com/WhatIsALM-Chappell.pdf
20. Microsoft Visual Studio, http://www.microsoft.com/visualstudio/
21. Microsoft Team Foundation Server, http://tfs.visualstudio.com/
22. Microsoft Visual Studio. Link Work Items and Objects to Support Traceability. MSDN, http://msdn.microsoft.com/en-ca/library/vstudio/dd293534.aspx
23. The Jazz Platform, https://jazz.net/
24. Rational DOORS, http://pic.dhe.ibm.com/infocenter/doorshlp/v9/topic/com.ibm.doors.install.doc/topics/r_oslc_services.html

Recommending Auto-completions
for Software Modeling Activities

Tobias Kuschke, Patrick Mäder, and Patrick Rempel

Department of Software Systems, Ilmenau Technical University
{tobias.kuschke,patrick.maeder,patrick.rempel}@tu-ilmenau.de

Abstract. Auto-completion of textual inputs benefits software developers using IDEs. However, graphical modeling tools used to design software do not provide this functionality. The challenges of recommending auto-completions for graphical modeling activities are largely unexplored. Recommending such auto-completions requires detecting meaningful partly completed activities, tolerating variance in user actions, and determining most relevant activities that a user wants to perform. This paper proposes an approach that works in the background while a developer is creating or evolving models and handles all these challenges. Editing operations are analyzed and matched to a predefined but extensible catalog of common modeling activities for structural UML models. In this paper we solely focus on determining recommendations rather than automatically completing activities. We demonstrated the quality of recommendations generated by our approach in a controlled experiment with 16 students evolving models. We recommended 88% of a user's activities within a short list of ten recommendations.

1 Introduction

Automating tasks of a software engineering process is a state-of-the-art way to increase the quality of a software product and the efficiency of its development. Auto-completion of textual inputs, as it exists in source code editors of modern integrated development environments, supports developer's work without the need to interrupt code writing and triggering menu functions, making its usage very efficient.

However, when designing a system in a graphical modeling environment no such support is currently available. The challenges that arise when recommending auto-completions for such modeling activities are largely unexplored. Though, there are plenty of opportunities for supporting recurring activities during model-driven architecture and design. For example, Arlow and Neustadt [1] describe typical activities that have to be carried out when refining an initial UML analysis model into a design model for a system. Furthermore, many of Fowler's [2,3] well-known source code refactorings impact the structure of a system and can as well be executed on a class model perspective of a system.

Recommending relevant auto-completions during graphical modeling requires handling challenging aspects accompanied with the problem such as:

A. Moreira et al. (Eds.): MODELS 2013, LNCS 8107, pp. 170–186, 2013.

C1 *Detect Partly Performed Activities.* Complex modeling activities are described by a set of editing operations with mutual dependencies. Detecting partly performed activities requires to match arbitrary incomplete subsets of editing operations while tolerating dependencies to unavailable information.

C2 *Tolerate Modeling Variances.* Modeling activities need to be detected in a variety of combinations of editing operations establishing the same activity. Not only can different orders of the same operations establish an equal activity, but different types and counts of operations can also establish the same activity.

C3 *Be Unintrusive.* A successful approach requires processing without noticeable system response delays.

C4 *Recommend Valid and Relevant Activity Completions.* Detected partial activities are not necessarily completable, i.e., not all are valid as recommendations. Furthermore, high numbers of valid recommendations have to be reduced to a limited set of most relevant completions for being useful.

C5 *Be Extensible for New Activities and Platforms.* A successful approach needs to be extensible to new activities and adaptable to other development tools.

We present an approach that handles these five challenges. The focus of this paper is determining and ranking relevant recommendations. In a follow-up publication we will focus on the auto-completion of a recommendation accepted by a user. Our paper is organized as follows. Section 2 reviews relevant related work on recognizing modeling activities, recommending modeling activities, and on auto-completion of modeling activities. In Section 3 we introduce our catalog of common modeling activities for structural UML models. Our approach for computing relevant recommendations of activity completions is introduced and discussed in Section 4. In Section 5 we evaluate the approach and assess its capabilities, followed by Section 6 where we discuss the results. Finally, Section 7 concludes our work and outlines future research.

2   Related Work

Our approach consists of three main stages: i) recognizing partial modeling activities, ii) recommending modeling activities, and iii) auto-completing modeling activities. In the following, we discuss previous research in these three areas.

Recognizing Modeling Activities. Sun et al. [4,5] suggest model transformations based on pattern matching. A repository holds model transformation patterns, which can be extended through live-demonstrations of the user. Developers can select these patterns when modeling. The system then calculates and presents all automatically executable transformations where pattern preconditions match the current state of model objects. This approach provides a simple and comfortable way to define transformation patterns and to share them with others. However, detecting partly executed transformations for automatic completion is not supported. Furthermore, the performance and usability of the approach is limited due to very high numbers of occurring transformation pattern matches.

Filtering and ranking matched transformations is not considered. The Eclipse framework *VIATRA2* by Rath et al. [6] presents another approach for live model transformation. *VIATRA2* can incrementally synchronize a target model to editing operations carried out on a source model. The authors employ an efficient RETE-based pattern matching technique [7]. Their transformation language supports incremental transformation rules as well as complex graph transformations. While this language could be used to express modeling activities, *VIATRA2* is not designed to detect partly performed states of activities. However, our approach uses similar concepts for the recognition of partly performed activities.

Recommending Modeling Activities. Several authors developed approaches to assist users of development tools with recommendations. Murphy-Hill et al. [8] recommend Eclipse commands. The applied data mining algorithms are efficient for recommending single commands, but are unsuitable for recognizing multi-step modeling activities. Recommendation ranking is based on user history, which could also be beneficial for modeling activities once long-term context information is available. *Strathcona* by Holmes et al. [9] recommends source code examples for using APIs. The user selects a source code fragment within Eclipse and starts the tool. Structural and context facts are extracted from the code and sent to a server. Based on four predefined heuristics the server matches the queried fact set to the stored examples trying to find structurally similar source code. The 10 most relevant examples are returned and presented. Other recommender approaches focus on business process modeling [10],[11].

Auto-completion of Modeling Activities. Forster et al. [12] proposed *WitchDoctor* for detecting and completing source code refactorings while observing developers writing source code. Their approach matches editing operations of the code to a list of refactorings with every keystroke of a developer. Upon a match, the complete refactoring is being calculated and displayed as gray-colored suggestion within the editor. Similar to our approach, the authors capture atomic editing operations and match them against predefined patterns of operation sequences. However, the authors do not discuss how to extract valid and relevant recommendations within a set of detected activities. This becomes crucial when recommending a number of different modeling activities consisting of similar editing operations. Mazanaek et al. [13,14] studied auto-completions for model and diagram editors in general. Based on graph grammars, their approach calculates all possible completions for incomplete model graphs. Although, the approach recommends correct structural completions for the current graph state, it does not support the completion of complex modeling activities within structural UML models. As such activities contain specific conditions regarding structural aspects and object property values it would be a difficult task to express them by a general graph grammar. Furthermore, it is impracticable to calculate and present all completions for a complex structural UML model. Sen et al. [15] propose a similar approach. A domain-specific modeling language and a partial instance of an appropriate model are transferred into an Alloy constraint model. This Alloy model is taken as input for a SAT solver that generates possible completed models. The system is triggered by the user and presents recommendations in graphical form. It is mainly designed to support small modeling languages and computes its results within seconds up to minutes. The approach shows similar limitations as the previous. Furthermore, there are approaches [16,17] that deal with user assistance in keeping models consistent and well-formed. Similarly, these approaches also calculate editing operations that are presented to the user. In contrast to our work, the focus of those works is changing a model in a minimal way in order to fix local inconsistencies rather than predicting a user's intent in performing complex modeling activities.

Summarizing, prior approaches that focused on recommending or on auto-completing activities within textual or graphical development environments all show limitations concerning the challenges identified in Section 1. In this paper, we present a novel approach for recommending valid and relevant completions of structural UML modeling activities while they are performed by a developer. Our contributions comprise the following aspects: 1) detecting partly performed complex modeling activities while observing developers editing a model, 2) tolerating variable editing operation combinations that establish the same activity, 3) recommending relevant modeling activity completions with every model editing operation that is carried out by a developer, 4) filtering and ranking the most relevant activity completions from a large number of possible recommendations, 5) processing without noticeable system response delays, 6) being extensible for defining new complex activities, and 7) being platform-independent to support different editors especially industrial modeling tools like Sparx Enterprise Architect [18] and IBM Rational Software Architect [19].

3   Modeling Activities and Illustrating Example

The basis for our approach is a catalog of predefined modeling activities for structural UML models that we created for our *traceMaintainer* approach [20,21]. *traceMaintainer* recognizes meaningful modeling activities within incremental editing operations to traced UML models and semi-automatically updates impacted traceability relations. The activity catalog has been used and improved during several studies and experiments. Activities in the catalog are declared as patterns $AP = (ap_1, \ldots, ap_n)$ that describe a set of expected editing operations $EO = (eo_1, .., eo_i)$ each. The catalog comprises a set of 19 activity patterns with 67 alternative editing operation sequences to carry them out. These patterns cover 38 modeling activities. Examples of defined activity patterns are:

- Replacing an association between two classes by an interface realization (ap_6)
- Extracting an attribute into an associated class (ap_{13})
- Specializing an element inheriting to an sub element (ap_{17})

We introduce a simple modeling example and use it throughout the paper. A developer wants to enhance a small embedded system containing a *Control Unit* and a *Communication Adapter* for sending and receiving messages (see

Figure 1, left). As part of the enhancement, two types of communication protocols shall be supported by the *Communication Adapter*: universal asynchronous
receiver/transmitter (UART) and serial peripheral interface (SPI). Furthermore,
an exchanged message shall identify its sender and receiver allowing adding additional communicating units. A possible realization is shown in Figure 1 (right).

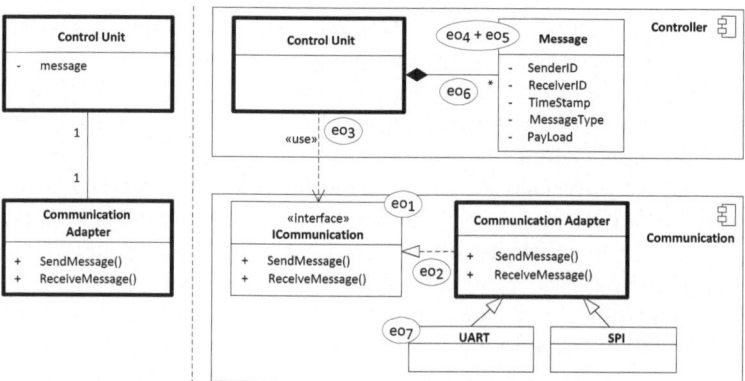

Fig. 1. Model of the illustrating example. On the left hand side the initial model state
is show, while the right hand side depicts a possible enhancement.

As first step, the developer converts the association between *Communication
Adapter* and *Control Unit* into an interface. Figure 2 shows from left to right
the temporal progress of performed editing operations to implement the desired
interface. First, she adds a new interface *ICommunication* (eo_1). One minute
later, she adds a realization-dependency between *Communication Adapter* and
the new interface *ICommunication* (eo_2). Another minute later, she adds a use-
dependency between *Control Unit* and the new interface *ICommunication* (eo_3).

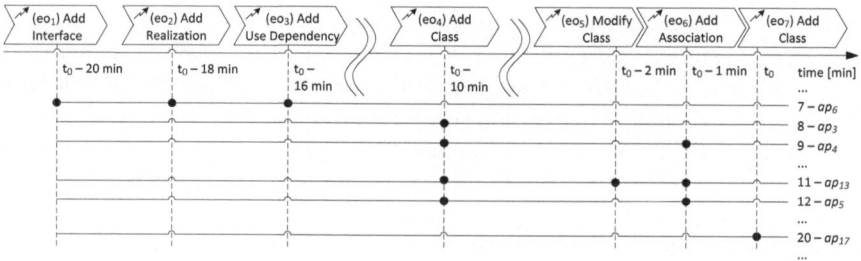

Fig. 2. Visualization of incoming events for the editing operations of the illustrating
example, there temporal order, and a subset of matched activity patterns

After a five minute break for planing the next step, the developer decides
to extract the attribute message from the *Control Unit* into a separate class in

order to extend it with additional properties. She starts this activity by adding a new class to the model (eo_4). At this time she gets interrupted by a phone call that takes 15 minutes. She continues by modifying the new class (eo_5) and by associating it to the *Control Unit* class (eo_6). Eventually, she creates a new class *UART* (eo_7). Our example stops at this point, which we will refer to as t_0 in the remaining text.

4   Approach

In this paper, we propose an approach for recommending valid and relevant completions of modeling activities for structural UML models while a developer is editing a model. In order to address the challenges identified in Section 1, we propose the following four step process. Each step is discussed in detail in the following four subsections.

Step 1: *Recognizing partly performed modeling activities.* While a developer is modeling within a tool, each editing operation is triggering an event containing detailed information of the change. Incoming events are matched against predefined activity patterns AP in order to detect partly performed modeling activities. The resulting set of activity candidates $AC = (ac_1, \ldots, ac_n)$ serves as input to the following process step.

Step 2: *Filtering invalid activity candidates.* All activity candidates that cannot be completed within the user's model are treated as invalid and filtered from the set AC.

Step 3: *Ranking activity candidates by relevance.* The filtered set AC is then ranked in relation to the relevance of each candidate for the user. Relevant are activities that the user wants to perform. Three ranking criteria are used to estimate relevance.

Step 4: *Presenting recommendations.* Finally, the filtered and ranked activity candidates in AC are reduced to a comprehensible number of recommendations and presented within the modeling environment.

4.1   Step 1: Recognizing Partly Performed Modeling Activities

We previously developed a traceability maintenance approach called *traceMaintainer* [21]. By recognizing modeling activities within incremental editing operations to traced UML models, *traceMaintainer* performs required updates to impacted traceability relations semi-automatically. While the goal of recognizing activities is similar to the approach presented here, there are fundamental differences in terms of required event processing. The need for matching partly performed activities required us to adopt a more advanced event processing. While our previous activity patterns contained designated trigger operations that had to occur in order to start the matching process, we required for this approach a mechanism that could match activity patterns starting from the first incoming event that contributed to them. Within the following paragraphs we introduce the redesigned recognition process.

First, each editing operation triggers an event of type *add, delete,* or *modify,* which carries the properties of the edited model element (see Figure 3, left). Second, events are matched against a set of predefined activity patterns *AP*. Each activity pattern ap_x defines a set of expected editing operations $EO = (eo_1, .., eo_i)$ that have to be performed in order to complete a modeling activity. The definition of an expected editing operation comprises conditions that have to be fulfilled by an incoming event to be matched. For example, the event for editing operation eo_5 in Figure 3 (left) would be matched by the definition $E3$ in the activity pattern (right), if all conditions can be evaluated to true. Thus, the completion of an activity would be recognized if a sequence of incoming events matches all editing operations *EO* of an activity pattern.

We decided to implement our matching process on a RETE-based rule engine [7]. This is a well-known technique for the kind of problem we had to solve. RETE translates and merges all complex pattern descriptions into a network of condition checking nodes. The technique reaches high execution performance for large numbers of received events, because checking results are temporarily cached in the network. Paschke et al. [22] published a survey on rule-based event processing systems and identified the freely available RETE-based Drools platform [23] as being very efficient for complex event processing (CEP). Drools's implementation is mature and the rule declaration language is highly expressive. Furthermore, the platform allows to retract inserted events and to output all matched subsets of events.

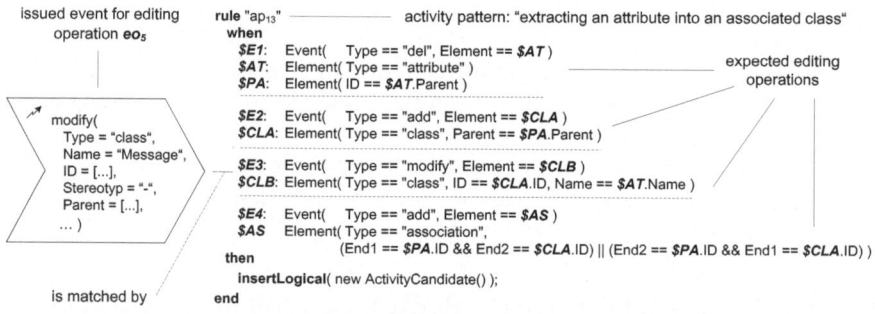

Fig. 3. Event for the editing operation eo_5 of the illustrating example (left) and the Drools rule declaration for activity pattern ap_{13} (right)

To integrate Drools in our solution, the activity patterns of *AP* with all their possible alternatives had to be declared using Drools's rule language. Figure 3 (right) shows a simplified Drools rule matching the ap_{13} activity pattern. The definition of an expected editing operation eo_x is separated into conditions for a matching event and for the edited model element. Cross-references between element properties are highlighted in bold. In order to recognize partly performed activities, all possible permutations of the expected editing operations in *EO* are declared within separate rules. Each fully matched Drools rule generates an activity candidate ac_x in *AC*, which defines the remaining editing operations for completing the modeling activity. As different modeling activities can contain similar definitions of editing operations it is not possible to declare these activity patterns without partly overlapping each other, i.e., incoming events can be matched to multiple patterns in AP. Furthermore, an activity pattern can be recognized multiple times, because the RETE algorithm matches all possible event combinations that fulfill the pattern's conditions. Accordingly, the raw output AC of the activity recognition step requires post-processing steps to generate relevant recommendations for a user. In the second column of Table 1 we show the raw output AC produced for our illustrating example. A total number of 21 activity candidates has been matched based on the last triggered event at t_0 and all previously incoming events.

4.2   Step 2: Filtering Invalid Activity Candidates

Recommended activity candidates need to be completable. We call a candidate that fulfills this condition "valid". To explain what a valid activity candidate is, we take a closer look at the recognized activity pattern candidate for ap_5 in our example (see Figure 2). The ap_5 activity pattern describes the transformation of an association with association class into a model structure consisting of a class and two associations. The transformation can be realized by adding a new class, by transferring all properties of the association class into the new class, by associating the class to both ends (classes) of the original association, and finally by deleting the original association including the connected association class. Figure 2 shows that the activity candidate for $ap5$ has got two allocated events *Add Class* and *Add Association*. Two more editing operations would be required to complete the activity, the deletion of the original association with association class and the creation of another association. Figure 1 shows the final state of our model and it is visible that no association with association class is contained. That means that the activity candidate for ap_5 cannot be completed, it is invalid and will be filtered.

To realize the filtering we derive model queries from activity candidates that are applied to the repository of the modeling environment. These queries verify the existence of model elements required to complete a partly matched activity. Queries are executed for all activity candidates after each incoming event on the current state of the model. The concrete content of a query depends on the completeness of an activity candidate as each event allocation may add new conditions related to the required model state. Similarly, each editing operation may validate or invalidate existing activity candidates. Accordingly, queries for all activity candidates are derived and executed upon each incoming event.

4.3   Step 3: Ranking Activity Candidates by Relevance

The previous filtering step results in a set of valid activity candidates. In order to present useful recommendations, activity candidates need to be ranked according their relevance for a developer. This ranking requires criteria that are able to characterize the relevance of an activity candidate. Based on available information about activity candidates, on related work and on our own industrial modeling experiences, we identified three ranking criteria.

α_{ac} – Average age of allocated events of an activity candidate
β_{ac} – Average period between allocated events of an activity candidate
γ_{ac} – Completeness of an activity candidate

We do not claim that these three criteria are the only possible, but we will demonstrate their effectiveness within the evaluation section. It will be a future exercise to further explore the area for other criteria. The following paragraphs describe each criterion in detail and demonstrate their influence on the ranking of activity candidates. Table 1 shows the ranking results after performing edit operation eo_1 – eo_7 in the prototype. For our example we know the three carried out modeling activities and highlighted them within the columns.

Table 1. Visualization of the influence of the identified ranking criteria on the set of activity candidates $AC(t_0)$ after executing editing operation eo_1 to eo_7 (see Figure 1) in the prototype. The second column shows the order of activity candidates as delivered by the rule engine. The third to fifth column rank these candidates based on a single ranking criterion each. Finally, column six shows the resulting list ranked by combining all three criteria. Cells within the table reflect the activity pattern type ap of a recognized candidate ac and the value calculated for the criterion.

Rank	Non-ranked	Ranked based on			
		α_{ac}	β_{ac}	γ_{ac}	$\frac{\alpha_{ac}+\beta_{ac}+\gamma_{ac}}{3}$
1	ap_3	ap_3 (1.00)	ap_5 (1.00)	ap_6 (0.75)	ap_5 (0.87)
2	ap_4	ap_4 (1.00)	ap_6 (0.99)	ap_{13} (0.75)	ap_{13} (0.70)
3	ap_{10}	ap_{10} (1.00)	ap_{13} (0.34)	ap_{10} (0.50)	ap_6 (0.69)
4	ap_{13}	ap_{13} (1.00)	ap_3 (0.00)	ap_{17} (0.50)	ap_5 (0.52)
5	ap_{17}	ap_{17} (1.00)	ap_4 (0.00)	ap_{10} (0.50)	ap_{10} (0.38)
6	ap_5	ap_5 (1.00)	ap_{10} (0.00)	ap_{17} (0.50)	ap_{17} (0.38)
7	ap_6	ap_7 (0.98)	ap_{13} (0.00)	ap_5 (0.50)	ap_7 (0.37)
8	ap_3	ap_5 (0.96)	ap_{17} (0.00)	ap_5 (0.50)	ap_3 (0.31)
9	ap_4	ap_{13} (0.71)	ap_5 (0.00)	ap_7 (0.50)	ap_4 (0.31)
...	...	...	...	...	...
11	ap_{13}	ap_3 (0.20)	ap_4 (0.00)	ap_{17} (0.50)	ap_5 (0.31)
...	...	...	...	...	...
15	ap_7	ap_6 (0.03)	ap_7 (0.00)	ap_5 (0.25)	ap_{17} (0.13)
...	...	...	...	...	...
20	ap_{17}	ap_{17} (0.00)	ap_{17} (0.00)	ap_{13} (0.25)	ap_{13} (0.06)
21	ap_5	ap_5 (0.00)	ap_5 (0.00)	ap_5 (0.25)	ap_5 (0.06)

Average age of allocated events. Based on our experience, we assume that a human developer can only work on a limited number of tasks in parallel. Thus, modeling is rather continuous and started modeling activities will be completed within a restricted period of time. Accordingly, it is more likely that a developer is actually working on a younger activity candidate than one that has been recognized a longer time ago. To address this fact, we define the current age of an event e_y as the time span between the occurrence of the last triggered event t_0 and its own occurrence t_{e_y}:

$$a_{e_y}(t_0) = t_0 - t_{e_y}. \tag{1}$$

The average age of all n allocated events of an activity candidate ac_x is determined as:

$$\bar{a}_{ac_x}(t_0) = \frac{\sum(a_{e_1}, \dots, a_{e_n})}{n}. \tag{2}$$

Let $A = (\bar{a}_{ac_1}, \dots, \bar{a}_{ac_m})$ be the set of average ages for all m activity candidates at t_0. The ranking criterion α_{ac} of an activity candidate ac_x is defined as:

$$\alpha_{ac_x}(t_0) = 1 - \frac{\bar{a}_{ac_x} - min(A)}{|max(A) - min(A)|}. \tag{3}$$

The formula means that an increasing average age of an activity candidate decreases its likeliness of being relevant. Values of α_{ac} are normalized on a scale between zero and one. The candidate with the smallest average age receives a value of 1.0, while the one with the largest average age receives a value of 0. This is done to assess proportions between activity candidates rather than absolute values to ensure comparability over time. The influence of α_{ac} on the ranking for the our example is illustrated in Table 1.

Average period between allocated events. Not only the average age but also the period between the allocated events influences the relevance of an activity candidate. We assume that events establishing the same modeling activity more likely occur within a limited period of time. Even if the completion is interrupted, see the phone call in our running example (Section 3), most editing operations are carried out as a contiguous sequence. Thus, an activity candidate is more likely to be irrelevant if its allocated events occurred with long periods in between. To assess a candidate ac_x for this criterion, we calculate the average period between its allocated events as the time span from the first (t_{first}) to the last (t_{last}) allocated event divided by the total number of allocations n minus one:

$$\bar{p}_{ac_x} = \frac{t_{first_x} - t_{last_x}}{n - 1} \tag{4}$$

Let $P = (\bar{p}_{ac_1}, \dots, \bar{p}_{ac_m})$ be the set of average periods for all m activity candidates. The ranking criterion β_{ac} of an activity candidate ac_x is defined as:

$$\beta_{ac_x} = 1 - \frac{\bar{p}_{ac_x} - min(P)}{|max(P) - min(P)|} \tag{5}$$

An increasing average period for an activity candidate decreases its likeliness of being relevant. Values of β_{ac} are normalized on a scale between zero and one. The candidate with the smallest average period in the set of current activity candidates receives the value 1.0, while the one with the largest average period receives the value 0. The influence of β_{ac} on the ranking for the example is illustrated in Table 1.

Completeness. Activity candidates are detected by comparing events against specified activity patterns. We assume that the relevance of detected activity candidates increases with each additional allocated event, i.e., with its completeness. The completeness of an activity candidate ac_x is assessed by calculating the ratio of its currently allocated events (n_{alloc}) to the total number of expected editing operations (n_{total}) establishing the corresponding activity:

$$\gamma_{ac_x} = \frac{n_{alloc_x}}{n_{total_x}} \qquad (6)$$

The influence of γ_{ac} on the ranking for the example is illustrated in Table 1. Figure 2 shows the completeness of recognized activities and that the activity candidates ap_6 and ap_{13} should be ranked to the top of the list regarding that criterion.

Combining ranking criteria. Finally, the described ranking criteria need to be combined into an overall probability value for each activity candidate. Without history data about the interplay of the identified ranking criteria, a possible way for combining single criteria is to average them, treating each criterion as equally important. The last column of Table 1 shows this probability for our example. However, in order to maximize the quality of recommendations, history data should be used to compute an optimized statistical model that treats the influence of the ranking criteria individually. This approach has been used for the computation of our experimental results in Section 5.

4.4   Step 4: Presenting Recommendations

By filtering (Step 2) and ranking (Step 3), an ordered list of relevant activity candidates has been created. Although, candidates representing relevant activities are ranked topmost, the set likely contains many additional valid but less relevant entries. Reed's [24] experiments with humans memorizing list entries suggest a relation between the number of entries and a subject's comprehension. Hence, we hypothesize that it is necessary to limit presented recommendations to a useful number. Holmes et al. [9] also identified that need and refer to a list of ten entries as useful. For the computation of our experimental results (see Section 5), we follow that suggestion, but also explore a more sophisticated method that takes into account the overall probability of recommendations.

5   Evaluation

We evaluated our approach according to the challenges C1 to C4 described in Section 1. Challenges C1 and C2 require the ability to recognize partly performed activities, which forms the basis of our approach. Thereby, the system has to handle user variability such as different orders of editing operations to perform the same modeling activity. We evaluated the tolerance of modeling variations of our approach within Experiment 1. A crucial aspect of user acceptance for a recommendation approach is its performance. We evaluated the performance of our approach with Experiment 2, which refers to challenge C3. Challenge C4 addresses the quality of generated recommendations. We evaluated this aspect within the extensive Experiment 3. The extensibility of our approach (Challenge C5) was not evaluated for this paper. We are enhancing the recommender system with auto-completion functionality within the ongoing research work and we will demonstrate its usage on different platforms and with an extended catalog of activity patterns as future work.

5.1 Experimental Setup

We implemented our recommender system as plug-in for the commercial modeling environment Sparx Enterprise Architect [18]. The prototype embeds the Drools 5.5 rule engine. All experiments were performed on a system with an Intel i7 2.7GHz processor, 4GB RAM, and a 64-bit Windows Microsoft 7 OS.

Our experiment is using recorded data sets of an experiment with 16 subjects that performed modeling tasks over a period of approximately two hours each. The experiment was originally conducted to evaluate our *traceMaintainer* approach [21]. In the original experiment we were purely interested in the quality and efficiency of traceability maintenance possible for the modeling tasks performed by a subject . However, we also logged all editing operations performed by the subjects and use that data to evaluate our recommendation approach.

A medium size model-based development project of a mail-order system was used. This project comprised various UML diagrams on three levels of abstraction: requirements, design, and implementation. Subjects had to perform three maintenance tasks on the mail-order system. First, the system's functionality had to be enhanced to distinguish private and business customers and to handle foreign suppliers. Second, the system layers view and data had to be extracted into separate components. And third, the system's functionality had to be enhanced to handle additional product groups and to categorize products according to content categories. Tasks were described in general terms in order to acquire a wide spread of different solutions. The experiment was performed by 16 computer science students that were either in the fourth or fifth year of their university studies. All students were taking a course on software quality and had advanced experience in model-based software engineering and UML. The 16 acquired data sets contained recorded events describing each performed editing operation. As we kept the event notation consistent with our previous approach, data could directly be used for our evaluation. All experimental material is available in [20].

5.2 Experiment 1: Modeling Variance Toleration

Experiment 1 was conducted to evaluate the toleration by the recognition part of our approach for modeling variances in performing the same activity pattern. The approach must recognize the same activity patterns within different permutations of the same event sequences. Therefore, we replayed 100 randomly generated permutations of the recorded events and compared the computed recognition result with the original recognitions. To validate alternative ways for executing activities, the experiment was conducted for all 16 different subjects. All generated experiment results contained exactly the same set of activity recognitions as their corresponding original, but in different orders according to the permutation of events.

5.3   Experiment 2: Performance

We measured the execution time across all processing steps, i.e., from the occurrence of an event triggered by an editing operation to the fully presented recommendation set within Sparx Enterprise Architect. This time is independent of the model size but depends on the number of processed events and the number of activity patterns defined in the catalog. We computed the average execution time $\bar{t}_{P_x}$ and the maximum execution time $\hat{t}_{P_x}$ across all performed editing operations of the 16 subjects for a number of 5, 10 and 19 defined activity patterns in the catalog. Results are discussed in Section 6:

$$\bar{t}_{P_x} = \frac{\bar{t}_{S_1 P_x} + \ldots + \bar{t}_{S_{16} P_x}}{16} \qquad \bar{t}_{P_5, P_{10}, P_{19}} = \{104ms, 131ms, 186ms\} \quad (7)$$

$$\hat{t}_{P_{19}} = max(\hat{t}_{S_1 P_{19}}, \ldots, \hat{t}_{S_{16} P_{19}}) \qquad \hat{t}_{P_{19}} = 257ms \quad (8)$$

5.4   Experiment 3: Quality of Recommendations

In this experiment we evaluated the quality of generated recommendations for the user. First, we determined for each editing operation that a subject had performed all activity candidates that she/he started at this point and that she/he completed during the remaining modeling session. These identified activity candidates comprised a golden master of relevant activities per editing operation of a subject. We compared this golden master with the actual recommendations of our approach and evaluated the relevance of recommendations with the averaged common metrics recall, precision, and average precision. Mean recall (MR) measures shown relevant recommendations in relation to all relevant recommendations across all editing operations made by a subject. Mean precision (MP) measures the amount of relevant recommendations in relation to all shown recommendations across all editing operations made by a subject. Finally, mean average precision (MAP) measures the precision of recommendations at every position in the ranked sequence of recommendations across all editing operations of a subject. This metric evaluates the ranking performance of our approach.

We determined an optimized weighting function for the three ranking criteria by performing a binominal regression based on our evaluation data (see Section 4.3). Due to the limited amount of subjects performing the experiment, we applied a leave-one-out cross-validation strategy [25] across the acquired 16 data sets. We fitted 16 generalized linear models, every time using 15 out of 16 data sets. These models were then used to rank the recommendations of the 16th data set. Results are shown in Table 2. We applied three threshold strategies to cut the list of available recommendations to a comprehensible number (see Section 4.4).

Table 2. Quality of computed recommendations measured as mean recall (MR), mean precision (MP), and mean average precision (MAP) at three different thresholds (th)

Subject	$th_{max} = 10, th_{prob} = /$ MAP	MR	MP	$th_{max} = /, th_{prob} = 0.02$ MAP	MR	MP	$th_{max} = 10, th_{prob} = 0.02$ MAP	MR	MP
1	100.00%	100.00%	13.40%	100.00%	100.00%	37.08%	100.00%	100.00%	37.08%
2	71.61%	98.82%	34.92%	71.84%	100.00%	33.51%	71.61%	98.82%	37.11%
3	65.55%	100.00%	48.06%	67.88%	89.56%	48.40%	67.88%	89.56%	48.40%
4	56.47%	62.02%	15.74%	45.55%	80.05%	16.42%	56.47%	62.02%	18.42%
5	55.59%	76.69%	11.83%	50.13%	86.72%	10.20%	55.59%	76.69%	12.19%
6	60.72%	99.34%	21.46%	65.33%	83.11%	15.19%	65.33%	83.11%	19.92%
7	82.15%	92.58%	12.83%	79.32%	93.75%	11.94%	82.12%	90.23%	14.30%
8	71.94%	100.00%	10.00%	71.94%	100.00%	10.10%	71.94%	100.00%	12.87%
9	60.45%	64.89%	17.31%	59.00%	77.43%	24.75%	66.45%	54.50%	22.88%
10	77.26%	100.00%	15.11%	77.26%	100.00%	17.74%	77.26%	100.00%	18.38%
11	77.40%	100.00%	12.14%	77.70%	98.60%	10.98%	77.70%	98.60%	14.78%
12	57.32%	52.87%	17.46%	49.24%	59.62%	25.15%	76.96%	31.20%	23.83%
13	89.84%	100.00%	17.81%	89.52%	96.88%	21.37%	89.52%	96.88%	25.91%
14	48.12%	61.22%	16.67%	41.20%	83.84%	14.04%	48.12%	61.22%	17.17%
15	97.74%	100.00%	16.76%	97.74%	100.00%	15.42%	97.74%	100.00%	18.78%
16	82.93%	100.00%	17.03%	82.93%	100.00%	24.41%	82.93%	100.00%	25.54%
Average	72.19%	88.03%	18.66%	70.41%	90.60%	21.04%	74.23%	83.93%	22.97%

Columns 2–4 show the three metrics for a fixed cutoff of 10 recommendations. Columns 5–7 show the metrics for a dynamic cutoff at probability 0.02. Finally, columns 8–10 show the metrics for a cutoff at probability 0.02 or at 10 recommendations, whatever occurs earlier.

6   Discussion

In Experiment 1, we evaluated the tolerance of the approach for possible variations in a developer's flow of editing operations. We found that we recognized the same set of modeling activities across 100 permutations of the editing operations performed by each subject. This result shows that our event processing and activity pattern matching implementation is independent of the order of events and tolerates variances in the way a developer performs a modeling activity.

In Experiment 2, we studied the performance of the approach and found that the generation of recommendations after an editing operation consumed on average 186ms with a maximum of 257ms for a set of 19 activity patterns. We consider these values as unintrusive for a user. However, computation time of the activity pattern matching depends on the number of patterns defined in the catalog and on the number of events kept in the matching process. The results show that computation time rises linearly with the number of defined patterns. Our subjects performed on average 219 editing operations during the experiment. Drool's implementation is known as very efficient and the algorithm itself as the state of the art for complex event processing. However, it might be necessary to limit the event history for models with many editing operations in order to guarantee a certain computation time. We are planning a more substantial performance evaluation regarding those facts as part of a future industrial study.

In Experiment 3, we studied the quality of recommendations generated by our approach (see Table 2). Focusing on the first threshold strategy, which always presents the ten most relevant recommendations to the user, we recommended across all 16 subjects 88% (MR) of the activities that a user was actually working on. These relevant recommendations comprised 19% (MP) of all recommendations. The value of 72% for the MAP metric shows that we rank relevant recommendations close to the top of the list. All three values are very promising and show that we were able to recommend the majority of activities performed by the user in a list of ten elements. The other two thresholding strategies show similar promising results. Whether these results are good enough to get acceptance is a research question for ongoing work, which will be evaluated once the whole auto-completion approach is available.

Concluding, the results of our evaluation show that the proposed approach meets the challenges C1–C4 discussed in Section 1. However, our evaluation is limited in several regards. The studied modeling activities were carried out over a relatively short period of two hours and all subjects were solving the same tasks. However, this experiment ensured that we captured manifold editing operation sequences with similar goal and evaluated the tolerance for developer variances. The computed regression models that combined individual ranking criteria are based on the data of other subjects performing the the same modeling tasks, this approach might have biased our results positively. We clearly identify the need for more empirical and industrial evaluation to draw general conclusions about the applicability of our approach.

7   Conclusions and Future Work

We presented an approach for recommending auto-completions of modeling activities performed on structural UML-models. We identified five challenges that had to be handled for making a recommendation approach useful to a user. The developed approach addresses these challenges. It works in the background while a developer is creating or evolving a model. Editing operations are analyzed and matched to a predefined but extensible catalog of common modeling activities for structural UML models. We evaluated our approach in a controlled experiment with 16 students evolving models. We recommended 88% of the activities that the subjects wanted to perform within a short list of ten recommendations.

We are currently working on an auto-completion mechanism for selected recommendations to complement our approach. Once both approaches are available, we are planning an industrial study to gain more empirical data on performed modeling activities, user preferences, and the discussed ranking criteria.

Acknowledgment. We are supported by the German Research Foundation (DFG): Ph49/8-1 and the German Ministry of Education and Research (BMBF): Grant No. 16V0116.

References

1. Arlow, J., Neustadt, I.: UML and the unified process: practical object-oriented analysis and design, 2nd edn. Addison-Wesley (2006) ISBN 0-321-32127-8
2. Fowler, M.: Refactoring: improving the design of existing code, 19th edn. Addison-Wesley (2006) ISBN 0-201-48567-2
3. University of Illinois at Chicago: Optimizing the object design model: Course notes for object-oriented software engineering, http://www.cs.uic.edu/~jbell/CourseNotes/OO_SoftwareEngineering/MappingModels.html (accessed March 15, 2013)
4. Sun, Y., White, J., Gray, J.: Model transformation by demonstration. In: Schürr, A., Selic, B. (eds.) MODELS 2009. LNCS, vol. 5795, pp. 712–726. Springer, Heidelberg (2009)
5. Sun, Y., Gray, J., Wienands, C., Golm, M., White, J.: A demonstration-based approach to support live transformations in a model editor. In: Cabot, J., Visser, E. (eds.) ICMT 2011. LNCS, vol. 6707, pp. 213–227. Springer, Heidelberg (2011)
6. Ráth, I., Bergmann, G., Ökrös, A., Varró, D.: Live model transformations driven by incremental pattern matching. In: Vallecillo, A., Gray, J., Pierantonio, A. (eds.) ICMT 2008. LNCS, vol. 5063, pp. 107–121. Springer, Heidelberg (2008)
7. Forgy, C.L.: Rete: A fast algorithm for the many pattern/many object pattern match problem. Artificial Intelligence 19(1), 17–37 (1982)
8. Murphy-Hill, E., Jiresal, R., Murphy, G.C.: Improving software developers' fluency by recommending development environment commands. In: Proceedings of the ACM SIGSOFT 20th International Symposium on the Foundations of Software Engineering, FSE 2012, pp. 42:1–42:11. ACM, New York (2012)
9. Holmes, R., Walker, R., Murphy, G.: Approximate structural context matching: An approach to recommend relevant examples. IEEE Transactions on Software Engineering 32(12), 952–970 (2006)
10. Koschmider, A., Hornung, T., Oberweis, A.: Recommendation-based editor for business process modeling. Data & Knowledge Engineering 70(6), 483–503 (2011)
11. Hornung, T., Koschmider, A., Oberweis, A.: Rule-based autocompletion of business process models. In: CAiSE Forum, vol. 247 (2007)
12. Foster, S.R., Griswold, W.G., Lerner, S.: Witchdoctor: Ide support for real-time auto-completion of refactorings. In: 2012 34th International Conference on Software Engineering, ICSE 2012, pp. 222–232. IEEE Press, Piscataway (2012)
13. Mazanek, S., Maier, S., Minas, M.: Auto-completion for diagram editors based on graph grammars. In: IEEE Symposium on Visual Languages and Human-Centric Computing, VL/HCC 2008, pp. 242–245 (2008)
14. Mazanek, S., Minas, M.: Business process models as a showcase for syntax-based assistance in diagram editors. In: Schürr, A., Selic, B. (eds.) MODELS 2009. LNCS, vol. 5795, pp. 322–336. Springer, Heidelberg (2009)
15. Sen, S., Baudry, B., Vangheluwe, H.: Towards domain-specific model editors with automatic model completion. Simulation 86(2), 109–126 (2010)
16. Reder, A., Egyed, A.: Computing repair trees for resolving inconsistencies in design models. In: Proceedings of the 27th IEEE/ACM International Conference on Automated Software Engineering, ASE 2012, pp. 220–229. ACM, New York (2012)
17. Steimann, F., Ulke, B.: Generic model assist. In: Moreira, A., Schätz, B., Gray, J., Vallecillo, A., Clarke, P. (eds.) MODELS 2013. LNCS, vol. 8107, pp. 18–34. Springer, Heidelberg (2013)

18. Sparx Systems: Enterprise architect: A model driven uml tool suite, http://www.sparxsystems.com (accessed March 15, 2013)
19. IBM: Rational software architect: Colaborative systems and software design, http://www-01.ibm.com/software/rational/products/swarchitect (accessed March 15, 2013)
20. Mäder, P.: Rule-based maintenance of post-requirements traceability. MV Verlag (2010)
21. Mäder, P., Gotel, O.: Towards automated traceability maintenance. Journal of Systems and Software 85(10), 2205–2227 (2012)
22. Paschke, A., Kozlenkov, A.: Rule-based event processing and reaction rules. In: Governatori, G., Hall, J., Paschke, A. (eds.) RuleML 2009. LNCS, vol. 5858, pp. 53–66. Springer, Heidelberg (2009)
23. Red Hat: Drools 5: An integrated platform for rules, workflows and event processing, http://www.jboss.org/drools (accessed March 15, 2013)
24. Reed, A.V.: List length and the time course of recognition in immediate memory. Memory & Cognition 4(1), 16–30 (1976)
25. Arlot, S., Celisse, A.: A survey of cross-validation procedures for model selection. Statistics Surveys 4, 40–79 (2010)

Automatically Searching
for Metamodel Well-Formedness Rules
in Examples and Counter-Examples

Martin Faunes[1], Juan Cadavid[2], Benoit Baudry[2],
Houari Sahraoui[1], and Benoit Combemale[2]

[1] Université de Montréal, Montreal, Canada
{faunescm,sahraouh}@iro.umontreal.ca
http://geodes.iro.umontreal.ca
[2] IRISA/INRIA, Rennes, France
{benoit.baudry,benoit.combemale}@irisa.fr
http://www.irisa.fr/triskell

Abstract. Current metamodeling formalisms support the definition of
a metamodel with two views: classes and relations, that form the core
of the metamodel, and well-formedness rules, that constraints the set of
valid models. While a safe application of automatic operations on models requires a precise definition of the domain using the two views, most
metamodels currently present in repositories have only the first one part.
In this paper, we propose to start from valid and invalid model examples
in order to automatically retrieve well-formedness rules in OCL using Genetic Programming. The approach is evaluated on metamodels for state
machines and features diagrams. The experiments aim at demonstrating
the feasibility of the approach and at illustrating some important design
decisions that must be considered when using this technique.

1 Introduction

Metamodeling is a key activity for capitalizing domain knowledge. A metamodel
formally defines the essential concepts of an engineering domain, providing the
basis for the automation of many operations on models in this domain (*e.g.,*
analysis, simulation, refactoring, transformation, visualization). However, domain engineers can benefit from the full power of automatic model operations
only if the metamodel is precise enough to effectively specify and implement
these operations, as well as to ensure a safe application. Current metamodeling techniques, such as EMF[1], GME [13] or MetaEdit+[2], impose to define a
metamodel as two parts: a *domain structure*, which captures the concepts and
relationships that can be used to build models in a specific domain, and *well-
formedness rules*, that impose further constraints that must be satisfied by all

---

[1] Eclipse Modeling Framework, cf. http://www.eclipse.org/modeling/emf/
[2] cf. http://www.metacase.com

A. Moreira et al. (Eds.): MODELS 2013, LNCS 8107, pp. 187–202, 2013.

models in the domain. The domain structure is usually modeled as a class diagram, while well-formedness rules are expressed as logical formula.

When looking at the most popular metamodel repositories (*e.g. [1]*, we find hundreds of metamodels which include only the domain structure, with no well-formedness rules. The major issue with this is that it is possible to build models that conform to the metamodel (*i.e.*, satisfy the structural constraints imposed by concepts and relationships of the domain structure), but are invalid with respect to the domain. For example, considering the class diagram metamodel without well-formedness rules, it is possible to build a class diagram in which there is a cyclic dependency in the inheritance tree (this model would be valid with respect to the domain structure but invalid with respect to the domain of object-oriented classes). From an engineering and metamodel exploitation perspective, the absence of well-formedness rules is a problem because it can introduce errors in operations that are defined on the basis of the domain structure. For example, operations that rely on automatic model generation might generate wrong models or compatibility analysis (*e.g.* to build model transformation chains) can be wrong if the input model is considered as conforming to the domain structure while it does not fully conform to the domain.

The intuition of this work is that domain experts know the well-formedness rules, but do not explicitly model them and some operations may consider them as assumptions (i.e., hidden contract). We believe that experts know them in the sense that, if we show them a set of models that conform to the domain structure, they are able to discriminate between those that are valid with respect to the domain and those that are not. However, we can only speculate about why they do not formalize them. Given the importance of well-formedness rules, we would like to have an explicit model of these rules to get a metamodel as precise as possible and get the greatest value out of automatic operations on models.

In this work, we leverage domain expertise to automatically generate well-formedness rules in the form of OCL (*Object Constraint Language*) invariants over a domain structure modeled as a class diagram with MOF. We gather domain expertise in the initial domain structure and a set of models that conform to the domain structure, in which some models are valid with respect to the domain and some models are invalid. Starting from this input, our technique relies on Genetic Programming [12] to automatically generate well-formedness rules that are able to discriminate between the valid and invalid models.

We validate our approach on two metamodels: a state machine metamodel and a feature diagrams metamodel. For the first metamodel our approach finds 10 out of 12 well-formedness rules, with *precision* = *recall* = 0.83. For the second metamodel we retrieve seven out of 11 well-formedness rules with a *precision* = 0.78 and *recall* = 0.64.

The contributions of this paper are the following:

- formalizing the synthesis of well-formedness rules as a search problem;
- a set of operators to automatically synthesize and mutate OCL expressions;
- a series of experiments that demonstrate the effectiveness of the approach and provide a set of lessons learned for automatic model search and mutation.

The paper is organized as follows. Section 2 provides the background and, defines and illustrates the problem addressed. Section 3 details the proposed approach using Genetic Programming to derive well-formedness rules, and Section 4 reports our experiments to evaluate the approach. Section 5 surveys related work. Finally, we conclude and outline our perspectives in Section 6.

2   Problem Definition

This section precisely defines what we mean by metamodeling and illustrates how both the domain structure and well-formedness rules are necessary to completely specify a metamodel. Then we illustrate how the absence of well-formedness rules can lead to situations where models conform to the domain structure but are invalid with respect to the domain.

2.1   Definitions

Definition 1. *Metamodel. A metamodel is defined as the composition of:*

- *Domain structure. This part of the metamodel specifies the core concepts and attributes that define the domain, as well as the relationships that specify how the concepts can be bound together in a model.*
- *Well-formedness rules. Additional properties that restrict the way concepts can be assembled to form a valid model.*

The method we introduce in this work can be applied to any metamodel that is specified according to this definition. Nevertheless, for this work we had to choose concrete formalisms to implement both parts. Thus, here, we experiment with domain structures formalized with MOF and well-formedness rules formalized with the Object Constraint Language (OCL).

2.2   Illustration of Precise Metamodeling

Here we illustrate why both parts of a metamodel are necessary to have a specification as precise as possible and avoid models that conform to the metamodel but are invalid with respect to the domain. The model in Fig. 1 specifies a simplified domain structure for state machines. A StateMachine is composed of several Vertexs and several Transitions. Transitions have a source and a target Vertex, while Vertexs can have several incoming and outgoing Transitions. The model distinguishes between several different types of Vertexs.

The domain structure in Fig. 1 accurately captures all the concepts that are necessary to build state machines, as well as all the valid relationships that can exist between these concepts. However, valid models can also exist, of this structure, that are not valid state machines. For example, the metamodel does not prevent the construction of a state machine in which a join pseudostate has only one incoming transition (when it should have at least 2). Thus, the sole

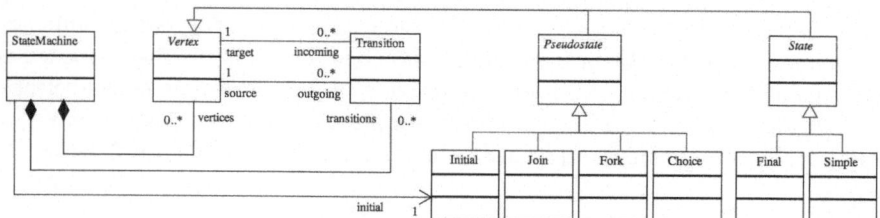

Fig. 1. State machine metamodel

domain structure of Fig. 1 is not sufficient to precisely model the specific domain
of state machines.

The domain structure needs to be enhanced with additional properties to capture the domain more precisely. The following well-formedness rules, expressed
in OCL, show some mandatory properties.

1. $WFR1$: Join pseudostates have one outgoing transition

   (**context** Join **inv** : self.outgoing->size() = 1))

2. $WFR2$: Fork pseudostates have at least two outgoing transitions

   (**context** Fork **inv** : self.outgoing->size() > 1)

2.3   Problem Definition

The initial observation of this work is that most metamodelers build the domain
structure, but do not specify the well-formedness rules. The absence of these
rules allows the creation of models that conform to the metamodel (only domain
structure) but are not valid with respect to the domain. For example, if we ignore
the well-formedness rules illustrated previously, it is possible to build the two
models of Fig. 2a and Fig. 2b. Both models conform to the structure of Fig. 1,
but the model of Fig. 2b is an invalid state machine.

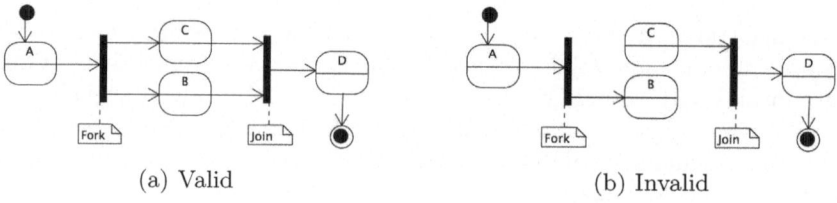

(a) Valid   (b) Invalid

Fig. 2. Example of state machines

The intuition of this work is that, given a domain structure without well-
formedness rules, it is possible (i) to generate models (*e.g.*, using test model
generation techniques [2]) and (ii) to ask domain experts to sort these models
between valid and invalid. Then, our objective is to automatically retrieve a set

of well-formedness rules. The retrieved well-formedness rules are not meant to be exactly those sought (that are unknown), but shall be a good approximation. In particular, they should be able to properly discriminate models beyond those provided in the learning process, *i.e.*, they should generalize the examples.

3   Approach Description

3.1   Approach Overview

The problem, as described in Section 2, is complex to solve. The only inputs to our derivation mechanism are the sets of examples of valid (positive) and invalid (negative) models. Hence, our goal is to retrieve the minimal set of well-formedness rules that better discriminate between the two sets of models.

From a certain perspective, well-formedness rule sets could be viewed as declarative programs that take as input a model and produce as output a decision about the validity of this model with respect to the domain. This observation motivates the use Genetic Programming (GP) as a technique to derive such rule sets. Indeed, GP is a popular evolutionary algorithm which aims at automatically deriving a *program* that approximates a *behaviour* from examples of inputs and outputs. It is used in a scenario where manually writing the program is difficult. In our work, the examples of inputs are the models and the outputs are their validity. As we will show later in this section, to guide the derivation process, well-formedness rules should be evaluated on the example models. To this end, the rules to search for are implemented as OCL invariants[3,4].

The boundaries of our derivation process are summarized in Fig. 3. In addition to example models, the derivation process takes as input a metamodel for which the invariants are sought. It produces as output fully operational OCL invariants that represent an approximation to the sought invariants.

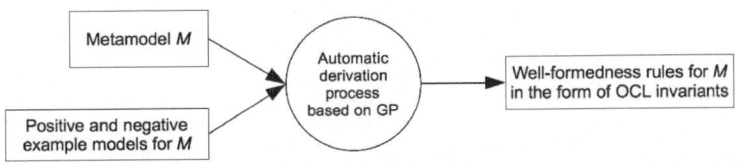

Fig. 3. Approach overview

In the next two sub-sections, first, a brief introduction to the GP technique is given and then its use to solve specifically the problem of well-formedness rule derivation is described.

---

[3] http://projects.eclipse.org/projects/modeling.mdt.ocl

[4] In the remainder of this section, we use the term "invariant" (resp. "invariant set") to designate a well-formedness rule (resp. rule set).

3.2   Genetic Programming

The most effective way to understand GP is to look to the typical GP process (cycle), sketched in Fig. 4. Step 1 of a GP cycle consists of creating an initial population of randomly-created programs. Then, in step 2, the fitness of each program in the current population is calculated. This is typically done by executing the programs over the example inputs and comparing the execution results with the expected outputs (those given as example). If the current population satisfies termination criteria in step 3, *e.g.*, a predefined number of iterations or a target fitness value, the fittest program met during the evolution is returned (step 7); otherwise, in step 4, a new population is created (it is also called *evolving* the current population). This is done by selecting the fittest programs of the current population and reproducing them. Although, the selection process favors the programs with the highest fitness values, it still gives a chance to any program to avoid local optima. Reproduction involves three families of genetic operations: (i) *elitism* to directly add top-ranked programs to the new population, (ii) *crossover* to create new programs by combining *genetic material* of the old ones, and (iii) *mutation* to alter an existing program by randomly adding new *genetic material*. Once a new population is created, it replaces the current one (step 5) and the next iteration of the GP cycle takes place, *i.e.*, steps 2 to 5. Thus, programs progressively change to better approximate the behaviour as specified by the inputs/outputs.

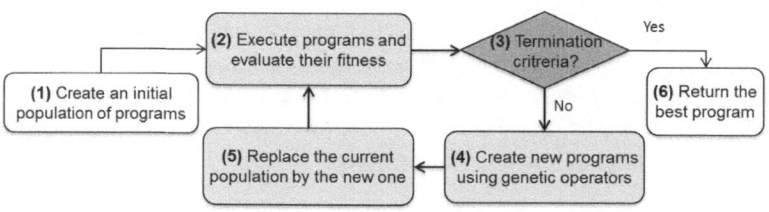

Fig. 4. A typical GP cycle

3.3   Using GP to Derive Well-Formedness Rules

To adapt GP to our problem, we have to produce a set of positive and negative models (base of examples). Then, we need to define a way to encode a set of invariants and to create the initial population of them. Another action consists in selecting a mechanism to execute sets of invariant on the provided models to calculate their fitness. Finally, proper genetic operators should be defined to evolve the population of candidate sets. In the rest of this section, these adaptations are described in details.

Input/output encoding: The base of examples E is a set of pairs $e = (m, v)$ where m is a model (conforming to the considered metamodel M) and v, a *boolean*, is the model validity stating if m satisfies the invariants or not. We refer to the example model as e_m and to the example model validity as e_v. Each model m conforms to the ECORE [16] metamodel M.

Invariant set encoding: In GP, a population of programs is initially created and evolved to search for the one which better approximates the behavior specified by the examples of inputs and outputs. In our adaptation, a program is a set p that contains OCL invariants i_j, $p = \{i_1, i_2, ..., i_n\}$. A model m, to be valid given an invariant set p, has to satisfy each invariant $i_j \in p$. To encode an OCL invariant i_j, we use the format provided by the Eclipse OCL framework. An OCL invariant is seen as a tuple (c, t) where c is the context, *i.e.*, a main metamodel class, and t is a tree that combines logical operators, comparison operators, functions, metamodel elements, and constants according to OCL syntax. Metamodel elements can be class attributes or class relationships (called references). In such a tree, the leave nodes are metamodel elements and constants, and the leave-node parents are comparison operators and functions. Any node on top of these two levels is a logical operator. In our implementation, we use the logical operators $\{and, or, not, implies\}$, comparison operators $\{>, <, =, \geq, \leq, \neq\}$, and other operations like $\{isKindOf, forAll, includesAll, size, allInstances, etc.\}$. These operations are generally enough to encode a wide range of OCL invariants.

Random invariant set creation: The first phase of the well-formedness rule derivation process is the random generation of the initial population, consisting of n invariant sets. In theory, there is an infinity of possible invariants that can be generated for a given metamodel. However, Cadavid et al. [3] showed empirically, *i.e.*, by analyzing dozens of metamodels from the standard community, academia, and industry, that there is a limited number of recurrent invariant patterns (20), whose instances are used individually or combined to create complex invariants. A pattern example is *CollectionSizeEqualsOne*, which states that the size of a collection *col*, contained in a class A, should be equal to 1:

```
context A inv : col->size() = 1
```

Such a pattern could be instantiated for any collection that can be found in a class, regardless of its type. Two possible instantiations for the state-machine metamodel in Fig. 1, could be the following:

```
context Fork inv : self.incoming-> size() = 1
context Fork inv : self.outgoing-> size() = 1
```

In our random generation process, we first automatically produce all the possible instances of the above-mentioned 20 basic patterns for the considered metamodel. This results in a large number of rules, lots of them are wrong, some of them are too simple or with wrong parameter values and thus it is still necessary to explore, combine and mutate this initial space of rules in order to produce the right set. To this end, for each invariant set to create, we randomly pick some of of the generated instances to produce simple invariants or complex ones by

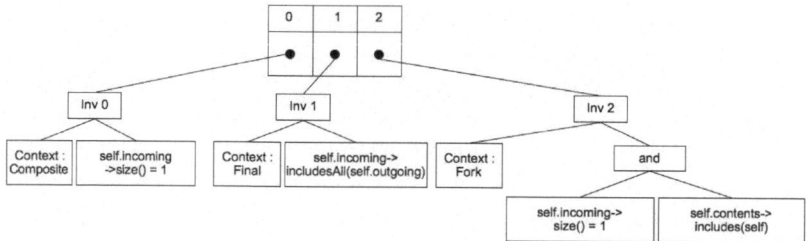

Fig. 5. An example of a randomly-created invariant set

combining the chosen instances with logical operators. Simple invariants can be combined if they share the same context. Fig. 5 shows an example of a set with three invariants. The two first invariants are simple and contain respectively an instance of the pattern *CollectionSizeEqualsOne* and an instance of the pattern *CollectionIsSubset*, *i.e.*, a collection that shoud be included in another one. The third invariant is the conjuction of an instance of *CollectionSizeEqualsOne* with an instance of *CollectionIncludesSelf*, *i.e.*, if a class contains a collection typed with itself, an instance of this class also makes part of this contained collection.

The number of instances to select as well as the number of combinations to perform to produce complex invariants (tree depths) are decided randomly during the creation of each set. The pattern instances are syntactically (w.r.t the OCL syntax) and semantically (w.r.t the metamodel structure) correct as they are their combinations. However, this does not mean that they are good invariants. This is decided by the fitness function.

Fitness calculation: In our implementation, OCL invariants are evaluated on the example models using the Eclipse OCL engine. The fitness function f assesses how well an invariant set p discriminates the models contained in the base of examples E with respect to the expert-based classification. f is a weighed function of two sub-functions f_1 and f_2. The first component, f_1, measures the rate of example models in E that are well classified by p. A model e_m is well classified if $v(e_m, p)$, the evaluation of p on e_m, is equal to e_v. f_1 is defined as:

$$f_1(p, E) = \frac{\sum_{e \in E} I(v(e_m, p) = e_v)}{|E|} \rightarrow [0, 1] \tag{1}$$

Function $I(a)$ returns 1 if $a = true$ and 0 otherwise. The evaluation of a set of invariants p on a model m , $v(m, p)$, is defined formally as:

$$v(m, p) = u(m, i_1) \wedge u(m, i_2) \wedge ... \wedge u(m, i_z) \rightarrow Boolean; \forall i_k \in p \tag{2}$$

Here, $u(m, i)$ is a boolean function that returns *true* if m satisfies the invariant i and $false$ otherwise.

Component f_1 allows to evaluate the set of invariants as a whole. However, it could penalize candidate sets that include good invariants but a few ones.

To reward good invariants individually, we defined a second component, f_2, of the fitness function. f_2 is calculated by counting the invariants $i \in p$ that are able to find at least α true positives T_p and at least β true negatives T_p. We then divide by the number of invariants $|p|$ to normalize the result between 0 and 1:

$$f_2\left(p, E\right) = \frac{\sum_{e \in E} I\left(T_p(i, E) \geq \alpha \ \wedge T_n(i, E) \geq \beta\right)}{|p|} \rightarrow [0, 1] \qquad (3)$$

Here, a true positive (resp. negative) is a model $e \in E$ classified as valid (resp. invalid) and that satisfies (resp. not satisfies) the invariant $i \in p$:

$$T_p\left(p, E\right) = \sum_{e \in E; e.v} I\left(u\left(e, i\right)\right); T_n\left(p, E\right) = \sum_{e \in E; \neg e.v} I\left(\neg u\left(e, i\right)\right) \qquad (4)$$

Now that we can generate an initial population and evaluate each of the invariant sets, the next step consists in selecting invariant sets to use them to produce a new population by applying crossover and mutation operators.

Selection method: To determine which sets of invariants will be reproduced to create the new population, the *Roulette-wheel* selection method is used in this work. This technique assigns to each invariant set in the current population a probability of being selected for reproduction that is proportional to its fitness. This selection strategy favours the fittest invariant sets while still giving a chance to the others.

Genetic Operators : The crossover operator consists of producing new invariant sets by combining the existing genetic material. After selecting two parent sets for reproduction, two new invariant sets are created by exchanging invariants of the parents. For instance, consider the two invariant sets $p_1 = \{i_{11}, i_{12}, i_{13}, i_{14}\}$ having four invariants and $p_2 = \{i_{21}, i_{22}, i_{23}, i_{24}, i_{25}\}$ with five invariants. If a cut-point is randomly set to 2 for p_1 and another to 3 for p_2, the offspring obtained are invariant sets $o_1 = \{i_{11}, i_{12}, i_{24}, i_{25}\}$ and $io_2 = \{i_{21}, i_{22}, i_{23}, i_{13}, i_{14}\}$. Because each parent invariant is syntactically and semantically correct before the crossover, this correctness is not altered for the offspring. Crossover is applied with high probability.

Mutation allows to randomly inject new genetic materiel in the population. It is applied with a low priority to offsprings after a crossover or to the selected parents when the crossover is not applied. In our adaptation of GP, we implemented 10 mutation operators that modify an invariant set at many levels. Every operator preserves the sibling correctness, syntactically and semantically. The first three operators are defined at the set level. One allows to add a new invariant, produced randomly according to the procedure used in the initial population generation. The second operator simply picks one of the existing invariants in the set and removes it. If we consider the set of Fig. 5 , we could have, for instance, the following mutations, corresponding respectively to the two operators:

```
Add: context Orthogonal inv : self.outgoing->includesAll(self.incoming)
Remove: context Fork inv : self.incoming-> size() = 1
```

The third operator at the set level selects two invariants, simple or complex, having the same context, and combines them using the "implies" operator. The remaining operators are defined at the invariant level. For one invariant of the considered set, some mutations consist in replacing respectively a comparison or a logical operator by a new one. For example, "=" in "Inv 0" of Fig. 5 could be replaced by ">". Similarly, "and" in "Inv 2" could become "implies". Incrementing/decrementing a numerical constant and replacing an attribute or a reference by a new one that is of the same type and that belongs to the same context, also are possible mutations, *e.g.*, replacing 1 by 0 or "incoming" by "outgoing" in "Inv 0". Another used mutation is the replacement of an operand (sub-tree) of a logical operator or a comparator by a randomly generated one. For example, the operand "self.contents->includes(self)" in "Inv 2" could be replaced by "self.outgoing->size() = 0". The final mutation is the negation of a node that returns a boolean value (a logical operator, a comparison operator or a boolean function). For instance, "Inv 1" could be mutated to "not self.incoming ->includesAll(self.outgoing)".

All the decisions made during the mutation, including the selection of the mutation operator, the invariant to change, and the replacement elements, are determined randomly.

4   Evaluation

4.1   Research Questions

The evaluation of our approach addresses the two following research questions:

1. To which extent our approach is able to derive well-formedness rules that properly discriminate between valid and invalid models?
2. Are the produced well-formedness rules those that are expected?

The first questions aims at assessing the validity of the approach from the quantitative perspective while the second considers the qualitative perspective.

4.2   Experimental Setting

Method. To answer both research questions, we conduct an experiment in which we evaluate our approach over two different metamodels. The evaluation is performed in a semi-real environment in which we know a priori the well-formedness rules sought (OCL invariants provided with the metamodels). The example models are randomly created using Alloy [9]. The creation with Alloy takes into account the known invariants. The number of positive models that are created (those that satisfy all the invariants) is equal to five times the number of known invariants. An identical number of negative models is also created. To create negative models, we randomly negate one or more invariants to force Alloy to violate them. The positive and negative model examples are then given as input to the derivation process, but not the known invariants.

To answer the first question, we first calculate the classification correctness of the best found invariant set, *i.e.*, proportion of models in the example base that are correctly classified (f_1 in the fitness function). Then, considering the stochastic nature of our approach, *i.e.*, different executions may lead to different results, we take a sample of executions and compare it with another sample obtained by a random technique. To have a fair comparison, we defined the random technique as the selection of the best from $n \times m$ randomly–generated sets, where n and m are respectively the size of a population and the number of iterations in our approach. In other words, both our approach and the random technique explore the same number of invariant sets. The comparison of the two samples is done using an independent-sample t-test (or Mann-Whitney test if f_1 values are not normally distributed in the two execution samples). The tests are performed with a significance at the level of $\alpha = 0.05$, *i.e.*, a probability of less than 5% that the difference between the two samples is obtained by chance.

To answer the second research question, we analyzed the invariants of the best derived solution and compare them with the known invariants. The comparison produces four sets: invariants found that match the expected ones (FOU), invariant found that are subsumed (less general) by the expected ones (SUB), invariants that are not expected (INC), and expected invariants not found excluding the subsumptions (MIS). Ideally, all the found invariants should be in FOU and MIS should be empty. Solutions with all the invariants in FOU but a few in SUB are also acceptable. We defined two versions of precision and recall depending on the acceptance of subsumed invariants (relaxed) or not (strict), as follows:

$$precision_{strict} = \frac{|FOU|}{|FOU|+|SUB|+|INC|} \text{ and } recall_{strict} = \frac{|FOU|}{|FOU|+|SUB|+|MIS|}$$
$$precision_{rel} = \frac{|FOU|+|SUB|}{|FOU|+|SUB|+|INC|} \text{ and } recall_{rel} = \frac{|FOU|+|SUB|}{|FOU|+|SUB|+|MIS|}$$

Data. The first metamodel used is the one of state machines (see Fig. 1). We selected 12 OCL invariants related to the incoming and outgoing transitions depending on the state types. As mentioned earlier we created 60 positive and 60 negative models (5×12 for each set).

The second metamodel that we consider represents the feature diagrams [11] (see Fig. 6). For this metamodel, we selected 11 OCL invariants covering the interdependencies between the feature types and the relation types. We created accordingly 55 positive and 55 negative example models.

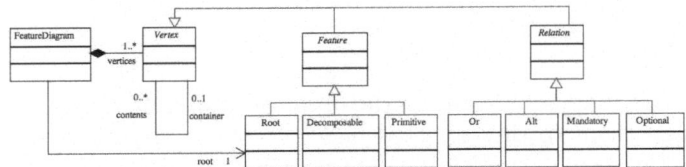

Fig. 6. Feature diagram metamodel

Algorithmic Parameters. GP, being a meta-heuristic algorithm, it depends on many parameters. The population size was fixed to 100 invariant sets and the evolution was performed with a maximum of 1000 iterations. To ensure that the best invariant sets will be kept during the evolution, we used an elitism strategy that consists in automatically adding the 10 fittest sets of each generation to the next one. For the evolution operator, the crossover probability was set to 0.9. We used the same probability for mutation. Unlike classical genetic algorithms, having a high mutation probability is not unusual for GP algorithms (see, for instance, [14]). For the fitness function we give equal weights to f_1 and f_2 (0.5), and the parameter α of f_2 was set to 1. Finally, the probability of creating complex invariants vs. simple ones during the random creation is set to 0.1, *i.e.*, each time an invariant has to be generated, it has nine chances to be simple and one to be complex. This probability is recursively applied to the operands of the logical operators when a complex invariant is created.

4.3   Results

Question 1. Given the stochastic nature of the GP, we performed a sample of executions and took the best found set. For the state machine metamodel the optimal best set was found before reaching the maximum number of iterations (after 537 iterations). This set perfectly discrimnates the positive models from the negative ones ($f_1 = 1$). For the feature digram metamodel, the best set missclassified 10 from the 110 models ($f_1 = 0.91$). The second step was to assess if the GP-based derivation performs better, in terms of discrimination power, than random generation. We performed a Kolmogoriv-Smirnov test that revealed that the f_1 values are normally distributed in both GP-based and random execution samples. This allows us to perform an independent-samples t-test with the null hypothesis that there is no difference in f_1 between the two derivation techniques. As illustrated in Table 1, the GP-based derivation performs clearly better than the random technique (~ 0.9 compared to ~ 0.25) and this difference in f_1 is statistically significant with $p < 0.001$ for both metamodels.

Table 1. Comparison with random generation (Question 1)

Metamodel	Average f_1 for GP	Average f_1 for Random	Sig.
State machines	0.96	0.22	< 0.001
Feature diagrams	0.88	0.25	< 0.001

Question 2. We manually analyzed the obtained invariants for each metamodel and compared them to the expected ones[5]. Table 2 summarizes the analysis results. For state machines, 12 invariants were found. 10 of them exactly matches

---

[5] Full results at http://geodes.iro.umontreal.ca/en/projects/MOTOE/MODELS13

Table 2. Precision and recall for invariant determination (Question 2)

Metamodel	$precision_{strict}$	$recall_{strict}$	$precision_{rel}$	$recall_{rel}$
State machines	0.83	0.83	0.83	0.83
Feature diagrams	0.78	0.64	0.89	0.73

expected invariants, 2 are incorrect and 2 are missing. This led to a precision and a recall (strict an relaxed) of 0.83. The missing and incorrect invariants are:

```
Missing invariants
  context Initial inv : self.incoming->size() = 0
  context Final inv : self.outgoing->size() = 0
Incorrect invariants
  context Initial inv : self.outgoing->includesAll(self.incoming))
  context Final inv : self.incoming->includesAll(self.outgoing))
```

We expected invariants enforcing that the set of incoming (respectively outgoing) transitions is empty for initial (respectively final) states. Our algorithm, based on the examples, finds invariants that evaluate to true, as empty sets are always included in other sets, but do not represent the correct semantic.

For the feature diagrams, the results were slightly worse. Indeed, 9 invariants were derived. 7 of them are good invariants whereas one is subsumed and one is incorrect. 3 expected invariants were not recovered. Consequently, the strict precision is 0.78 and the strict recall 0.64, whereas, the relaxed ones are increased respectively to 0.89 and 0.73. The concerned invariants are:

```
Missing invariants
  context Or inv : contents->forAll(v:Vertex | v.oclIsKindOf(Feature))
  context Optional inv : contents->forAll(v:Vertex | v.oclIsKindOf(Feature))
  context PrimitiveFeature inv : self.contents->size() = 0
Incorrect invariant
  context PrimitiveFeature inv : self.container->includesAll(self.contents))
Subsumed invariant
  Expected: context DecomposableFeature inv : self.contents->size() > 1
  Found: context DecomposableFeature inv : self.contents->size() > 0
```

The incorrect invariant correspond to the same case discussed for the state machines, *i.e.*, inclusion of an empty set. The subsumed invariant is explained by the fact that in all the positive models, the contents of a *DecomposableFeature* includes more than one element with lead to the condition ">1" instead of the expected ">0". Finally, two invariants with the iterator *forAll* were not found.

4.4 Threats to Validity and Performance Issues

As for any experimental evaluation, some threats could affect the validity of our findings. Conclusion validity could be affected by the stochastic nature of our approach. To address this threat, we conducted statistical tests on a sample of executions to show that the difference in correctness between our approach and random generation is large and statistically significant. Another related threat concerns the influence of the algorithmic parameters on the obtained results. We set some of the parameters to standard or consensual values (crossover probability, population size, and number of iterations). For the others, we tested different combinations (fitness function weights and mutation probability). Mutation probability, in particular, is certainly the parameter that has the most influence on the results. Indeed, when the initial population does not contain invariants that are close the ones sought, many mutations are necessary to converge towards the optimal invariant set (see for example, [14,7]).

We identified two potential threats to the external validity. First, the models used as examples were automatically generated taking into account the sought invariants rather than collected and classified by experts as valid/invalid. To ensure that the produced models cover well the modeling space, we forced Alloy to perform the generation with different parameter values such the number of class instances in each model. In the future, we plan to conduct new experiments with more real settings to circumvent this threat. The second threat concerns the used metamodels. Although these metamodels describe different domains, the investigation of more metamodels is necessary to draw better conclusions. The manual comparison made by the authors to answer *Question*2 could represent a threat to the internal validity. Deciding for the exact invariant matches and subsumptions could be error-prone and affected by the experimenter expectancies. To prevent this threat, we conducted this comparison rigorously and diligently. We expect to use independent subjects to write/classify the models and evaluate the invariants in our future experiments.

Several implementation iterations were necessary to obtain an efficient version of our algorithm. We reused many elements that affect the performance of our algorithm, Eclipse OCL engine, Alloy model generator, and Alloy to ECORE transformer. These elements are used for each invariant set in the population and repeated trough the different evolution iterations. To obtain an acceptable performance, we first parallelized the GP process to calculate the fitness function of each invariant set in a population in separated threads. After, many trials, we created one thread per invariant set when evaluating a population. A second change, which improved considerably the performance, is the pre-calculation of the component $u(e,i)$ that is used in f_1 and f_2, *i.e.*, we pre-calculate the validity of each example model for each invariant present in the population. As many invariants are shared by many sets, and their validity is used in f_1 and f_2, the improvement was considerable. The two optimizations allowed us to run the algorithm over a input size 20 time bigger.

5   RelatedWork

In this section we analyze the related works to our approach from two different perspectives. The first one is the derivation of invariants, as rules learned from an underlying artifact, either models or programs. In the second perspective, we cite other works using learning techniques to derive useful information for MDE stakeholders. For the first perspective, the main referent in the derivation of invariants in software engineering is Daikon [6]. Taking a program as input, it analyzes the computed values and detects likely invariants that can be used for program understanding and documentation and verification of formal specifications among other tasks. The machine learning technique used is an inference engine based on a generate-and-check algorithm. This approach was later notoriously complemented with Sam Ratcliff's work [14]. Demonstrating that evolutionary search can consider a very wide amount of program invariants, the need for a filtering mechanism was imposed. The given solution was the use of mutation testing, enabling thus the approach to sort out invariants that are not interesting for the user. Zeller investigates the idea of specification mining[17], where he intends to leverage on repositories of software specifications, in order to reuse this knowledge into actionable recommendations for today's developers of formal specifications. The main technique for achieving specification mining is the generation of test cases covering a wide range of possible program executions - the "execution space". Test cases which lead to undesired program executions, or so-called *illegal states*, are used to enrich specifications [4].

For the second perspective, in the field of Model-Driven Engineering, machine learning techniques have been used successfully. [5] uses formal concept analysis to learn patterns of model transformation rules from a set of examples. Another application is the reverse engineering of metamodels, also known as metamodel recovery. In [10] the authors propose a mechanism to learn a metamodel from a set of models, by using techniques inspired by grammar inference. In the same fashion, [8] proposes a process for pattern extraction from deployable artifacts in order to recover architecture models. Learning of metamodels has also been presented as *bottom-up metamodeling*. In [15], authors present an approach to build metamodels from partial object models, annotated with information to build abstractions. These abstractions are refined iteratively, in order to obtain an *implementation* metamodel ready to use for MDE activities. Although this approach does not actually use search-based techniques, it does highlight the importance of guiding domain experts in the difficult task of metamodeling.

6   Conclusions

In this paper, we propose an approach to automatically derive well-formedness rules for metamodels. Our approach uses positive and negative example models as input and it is based on a Genetic Programming that evolves a population of random created rules, guided by a fitness function that measures how well the rules discriminate the models used as example. Once finished, the process returns the best set of well-formedness rules ever created during the process. We validate the approach over two different metamodels coming from different domains: a state machines, and feature diagrams. As a result, our approach automatically derives most of the expected well-formedness rules. This results shows the feasibility of our approach and defines a starting point for our future works. Future work includes investigating the support of more complex invariants, and alternatives in the way to obtains model examples. We are also extending our experiments to address the threats to validity mentioned in this paper. In particular, we explore the application of the approach on other various metamodels, including ones coming from industry.

References

1. Metamodel zoos, http://www.emn.fr/z-info/atlanmod/index.php/Zoos
2. Cadavid, J., Baudry, B., Sahraoui, H.: Searching the boundaries of a modeling space to test metamodels. In: Proceedings of the International Conference on Software Testing, verification and validation (ICST) (April 2012)
3. Cadavid, J., Combemale, B., Baudry, B.: Ten years of Meta-Object Facility: an Analysis of Metamodeling Practices. Tech. report RR-7882, INRIA (2012)
4. Dallmeier, V., Knopp, N., Mallon, C., Hack, S., Zeller, A.: Generating test cases for specification mining. In: Proceedings of the 19th International Symposium on Software Testing and Analysis, pp. 85–96. ACM (2010)
5. Dolques, X., Huchard, M., Nebut, C., Saada, H., et al.: Formal and relational concept analysis approaches in software engineering: an overview and an application to learn model transformation patterns in examples (2011)
6. Ernst, M., Perkins, J., Guo, P., McCamant, S., Pacheco, C., Tschantz, M., Xiao, C.: The daikon system for dynamic detection of likely invariants. Science of Computer Programming 69(1-3), 35–45 (2007)
7. Faunes, M., Sahraoui, H., Boukadoum, M.: Generating model transformation rules from examples using an evolutionary algorithm. In: Proceedings of the 27th IEEE/ACM International Conference on Automated Software Engineering, pp. 250–253. ACM (2012)
8. Favre, J.: Cacophony: Metamodel-driven software architecture reconstruction. In: Proceedings of the 11th Working Conference on Reverse Engineering, pp. 204–213. IEEE (2004)
9. Jackson, D.: Alloy: a lightweight object modelling notation. ACM Transactions on Software Engineering and Methodology (TOSEM) 11(2), 256–290 (2002)
10. Javed, F., Mernik, M., Gray, J., Bryant, B.: MARS: A metamodel recovery system using grammar inference. Information and Software Technology 50(9-10), 948–968 (2008)
11. Kang, K.C., Cohen, S.G., Hess, J.A., Novak, W.E., Peterson, A.S.: Feature-oriented domain analysis (foda) feasibility study. Technical report, DTIC Document (1990)
12. Koza, J., Poli, R.: Genetic programming. In: Search Methodologies (2005)
13. Ledeczi, A., Maroti, M., Bakay, A., Karsai, G., Garrett, J., Thomason, C., Nordstrom, G., Sprinkle, J., Volgyesi, P.: The generic modeling environment. In: Workshop on Intelligent Signal Processing, Budapest, Hungary, vol. 17 (2001)
14. Ratcliff, S., White, D., Clark, J.A.: Searching for invariants using genetic programming and mutation testing (2011)
15. Sánchez-Cuadrado, J., de Lara, J., Guerra, E.: Bottom-up meta-modelling: An interactive approach. In: France, R.B., Kazmeier, J., Breu, R., Atkinson, C. (eds.) MODELS 2012. LNCS, vol. 7590, pp. 3–19. Springer, Heidelberg (2012)
16. Steinberg, D., Budinsky, F., Paternostro, M., Merks, E.: EMF: Eclipse Modeling Framework, 2nd edn. Addison-Wesley (2008)
17. Zeller, A.: Specifications for free. In: Bobaru, M., Havelund, K., Holzmann, G.J., Joshi, R. (eds.) NFM 2011. LNCS, vol. 6617, pp. 2–12. Springer, Heidelberg (2011)

Testing M2T/T2M Transformations

Manuel Wimmer[1] and Loli Burgueño[2]

[1] Business Informatics Group, Vienna University of Technology, Austria
wimmer@big.tuwien.ac.at
[2] GISUM/Atenea Research Group, Universidad de Málaga, Spain
loli@lcc.uma.es

Abstract. Testing model-to-model (M2M) transformations is becoming a prominent topic in the current Model-driven Engineering landscape. Current approaches for transformation testing, however, assume having explicit model representations for the input domain and for the output domain of the transformation. This excludes other important transformation kinds, such as model-to-text (M2T) and text-to-model (T2M) transformations, from being properly tested since adequate model representations are missing either for the input domain or for the output domain. The contribution of this paper to overcome this gap is extending Tracts, a M2M transformation testing approach, for M2T/T2M transformation testing. The main mechanism we employ for reusing Tracts is to represent text within a generic metamodel. By this, we transform the M2T/T2M transformation specification problems into equivalent M2M transformation specification problems. We demonstrate the applicability of the approach by two examples and present how the approach is implemented for the Eclipse Modeling Framework (EMF). Finally, we apply the approach to evaluate code generation capabilities of several existing UML tools.

1 Introduction

Much effort has been put into the establishment of model-to-model (M2M) transformation testing techniques in the past years [1,28]. Several approaches have been developed for defining contracts for M2M transformations that act as specifications for model transformation implementations [6,13], as oracle functions to validate the output of transformations [13,15], and as drivers for generating test cases [14]. In particular, constraints for input models, output models and for the relationship between both may be specified.

Besides M2M transformations, model-to-text (M2T) and text-to-model (T2M) transformations are of major importance in Model-driven Engineering [4,8]. M2T transformations are typically used to bridge the gap between modeling languages and programming languages by defining code generations but may be employed in a generic manner to produce text from models such as documentation or textual representations of a model's content. T2M transformations are typically used for reverse engineering [5], e.g., transforming legacy applications to models in the case of model-driven software modernization. However, these kinds of transformations have not gained much attention when it comes to testing.

A. Moreira et al. (Eds.): MODELS 2013, LNCS 8107, pp. 203–219, 2013.

In this paper we adopt current techniques for testing M2M transformations to the problem of testing T2M and M2T transformations. The prerequisite of using existing M2M transformation techniques is to have metamodels for the input and output of the transformations. However, for the side that is dealing with "just" text, no metamodels are usually available. Even more problematic, when considering T2M and M2T transformations, a set of metamodels and T2M parsers may be required as a prerequisite. For instance, consider Web applications where in addition to a general purpose programming language several other languages may be employed where some of the languages are even embeddable in other languages. Thus, developing metamodels and T2M parser support for such complex settings may introduce a huge overhead.

To alleviate the burden from T2M and M2T transformation developers, we introduce a generic approach that may be used for any transformation task where text is involved as input or output of the transformations. The main mechanism we employ is to represent text within a generic metamodel in order to transform M2T and T2M transformation specification problems into equivalent M2M transformation specification problems. The proposal is combinable with any contract-based M2M transformation approach, but in this paper we demonstrate its application with Tracts [13].

The structure of the paper is as follows. The next section introduces Tracts, a M2M transformation testing approach, by example. Section 3 shows how to represent text-based artifacts as models to allow for reusing the M2M transformation testing approaches. Section 4 demonstrates how Tracts are defined for M2T and T2M transformations and gives details about the implementation of the approach. Section 5 presents an evaluation of the approach, in particular to explore its capabilities to find shortcomings in code generations delivered by current UML tools. In Section 6 we present related work, and in Section 7, we conclude the paper with an outlook on future work.

2   Tracts for Testing Model-to-Model Transformations

Let us shortly introduce the formalism used in this paper, namely Tracts, for specifying M2M transformation contracts. As we shall see, this formalism assumes to have metamodels for the input and for the output of the transformation as all other existing contract specification approaches do.

Tracts were introduced in [13] as a specification and black-box testing mechanism for model transformations. They provide modular pieces of specification, each one focusing on a particular transformation scenario. Thus every model transformation can be specified by means of a set of tracts, each one covering a particular use case—which is defined in terms of particular input and output models and how they should be related by the transformation. In this way, tracts allow partitioning the full input space of the transformation into smaller, more focused behavioural units, and to define specific tests for them. Basically, what we do with the tracts is to identify the scenarios of interest to the user of the transformation (each one defined by a tract) and check whether the transformation behaves as expected in these scenarios. Another characteristic of Tracts is that we do not require complete proofs, just to check that the transformation works for the tract test suites, hence providing a *light-weight* form of verification.

In a nutshell, a tract defines a set of constraints on the *source* and *target* metamodels, a set of *source-target* constraints, and a tract *test suite*, i.e., a collection of source

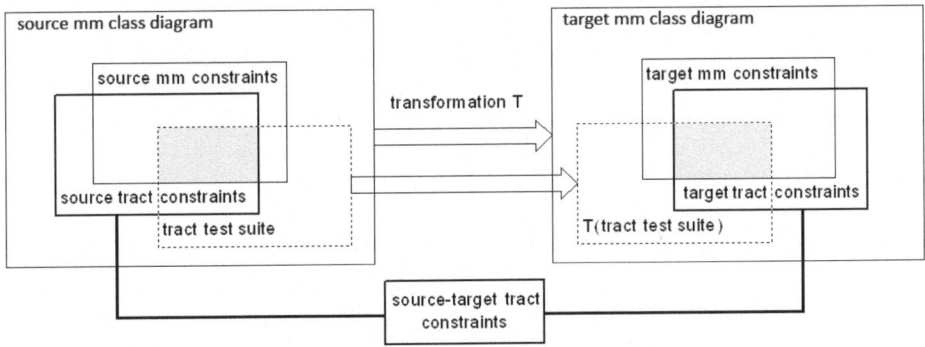

Fig. 1. Building blocks of a tract

models satisfying the source constraints. The constraints serve as "contracts" (in the sense of contract-based design [21]) for the transformation in some particular scenarios, and are expressed by means of OCL invariants. They provide the *specification* of the transformation.

In Figure 1 more details about the tracts approach are presented. The necessary components the approach rely on are the source and target metamodels, the transformation *T* under test and the transformation contract, which consists of a tract test suite and a set of tract constraints. In total, five different kinds of constraints are present: the source and target metamodels are restricted by general constraints added to the language definition, and the tract imposes additional source, target, and source-target tract constraints for a given transformation.

If we assume a source model *M* being an element of the test suite and satisfying the source metamodel and the source tract constraints given, the tract essentially requires that the result *T(M)* of applying transformation *T* satisfies the target metamodel and the target tract constraints and the tuple <*M, T(M)*> satisfies the source-target tract constraints.

For demonstrating how to use Tracts, we introduce the simple transformation example *Families2Persons*.[1] The source and target metamodels of this transformation are shown in Figure 2. For this example, a set of tracts is developed to consider only those families with exactly four members (mother, father, daughter, son):

```
-- C1: SRC_oneDaughterOneSon
 Family.allInstances->forAll(f|f.daughters->size=1 and f.sons->size=1)
-- C2: SRC_TRG_Mother2Female
 Family.allInstances->forAll(fam|Female.allInstances->exists(f|
    fam.mother.firstName.concat('␣').concat(fam.lastName)=f.fullName))
-- C3: SRC_TRG_Daughter2Female
 Family.allInstances->forAll(fam|Female.allInstances->exists(f|
    fam.daughters->exists(d|d.firstName.concat('␣').concat(fam.lastName)
      =f.fullName)))
-- C4: SRC_TRG_MemberSize_EQ_PersonSize
 Member.allInstances->size=Person.allInstances->size
-- C5: TRG_PersonHasName
 Person.allInstances->forAll(p|p.fullName<>'' and
    not p.fullName.oclIsUndefined())
```

---

[1] The complete example is available at our project website
http://atenea.lcc.uma.es/index.php/Main_Page/Resources/Tracts

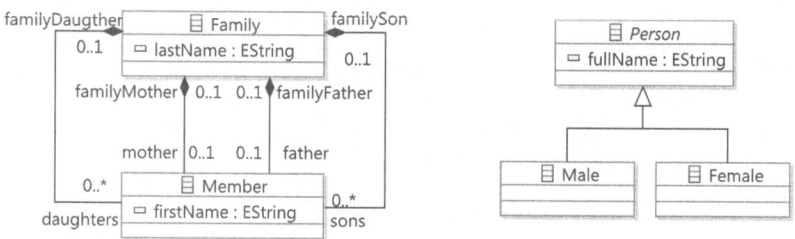

Fig. 2. The Family and Person metamodels

Concerning the kinds of the shown Tracts, C_1 represents a pre-condition for the transformation, C_2–C_4 define constraints on the relationships between the source and target models, i.e., constraints that should be ensured by the transformation, and finally, C_5 represents a post-condition for the transformation. Note that this approach is independent from the model transformation language and platform finally used to implement and execute the transformation.

3   A Generic Metamodel for Text

In order to reuse M2M transformation specification and testing approaches, we have to transform the M2T or T2M transformation specification problem into a M2M transformation specification problem. For this, the text artifacts residing in the input or output domain of the transformations under study have to be injected to the model engineering technical space [18].

For realizing this goal, there are several options. We may either decide to go for a specific format conforming to a specific grammar or to use a generic format that is able to represent any text-based artifact. In case there is already a metamodel available for the specific grammar, then this metamodel may be a good choice anyway. However, for most transformation scenarios involving text at one side there are no metamodels available, because metamodels are often not required at all. Just consider the case of generating documentation from models. Although there is no generalized and fixed structure, it may be necessary to check certain requirements of the transformation. This is why we have decided to use the second option, which allows us to save upfront the effort required when developing M2T or T2M transformations in general. Furthermore, using a generic metamodel to represent the text artifacts also reflects best practices in the development of M2T transformations, where no metamodel is used for the text artifacts. For example, consider template-based M2T transformation languages[2]. Usually, template-based approaches are used to generate that text. Finally, even if there is a T2M parser, this is again a transformation that may have to be specified and tested. Thus, our generic approach may be used to test the specific approach.

---

[2] http://www.omg.org/spec/MOFM2T/

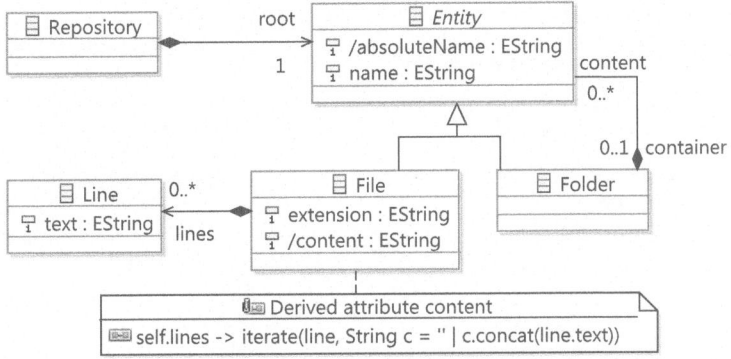

Fig. 3. Metamodel for representing text artifacts and repositories

Fig. 4. Exemplary folder structure and corresponding text model

Apart from this, there is a second aspect that needs to be considered when dealing with text-based artifacts. The artifacts are normally organized in a hierarchical folder structure, which should be taken into account. For instance, the output of a M2T transformation may not be just a single file but several, which should be also arranged in a certain folder structure. Thus, our approach has to cover concepts for describing the structure of a repository that contains the input or output artifacts of a transformation.

Figure 3 shows the metamodel for representing text artifacts stored in repositories using certain folder structures. Meta-class Repository represents the entry point to the root folder containing folders and files or to a file if only one single artifact is used. While folders just contain a name, files have in addition an extension as well as a content. The content of files is represented by lines that are sequentially ordered. A derived attribute content is used to allow easy access to the complete content of a file.

Figures 4 and 5 present an instance of the text metamodel coming from a Java code repository. On the left hand side of the figures, the repository's folder structure as well as the content of a Java file are shown, while on the right hand side an excerpt of the corresponding text model (shown in the EMF tree browser) is illustrated.

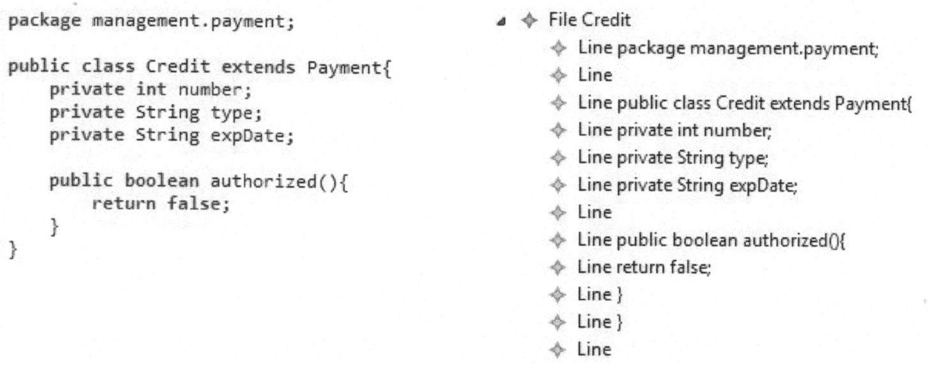

```
package management.payment;

public class Credit extends Payment{
    private int number;
    private String type;
    private String expDate;

    public boolean authorized(){
        return false;
    }
}
```

◢ ✧ File Credit
  ✧ Line package management.payment;
  ✧ Line
  ✧ Line public class Credit extends Payment{
  ✧ Line private int number;
  ✧ Line private String type;
  ✧ Line private String expDate;
  ✧ Line
  ✧ Line public boolean authorized(){
  ✧ Line return false;
  ✧ Line }
  ✧ Line }
  ✧ Line

Fig. 5. Exemplary file content and corresponding text model

4 M2T/T2M Transformation Testing By-Example

This section shows how the metamodel for describing text artifacts can be used in conjunction with tracts for M2T and T2M transformation testing.

4.1 M2T Example: UML to Java

For illustration purposes, let us apply our approach to a given case: the transformation that converts UML class models into the corresponding Java classes—which are text files that should be stored in folders inside a code repository. Figure 6 shows the subset of the UML metamodel that we will consider in this scenario. It is assumed that all meta-classes directly or indirectly inherit from NamedElement. The target metamodel is the one that we described above for speficying text artifacts, and that was shown in Figure 3.

The specification of such a transformation is composed of a set of tracts, each one focusing on a particular property that we want to ensure. As illustrative examples we have chosen 10 tracts, which are described below. Notice that in some of them we have used auxiliary operations such as toFirstUpper and toString to clarify the code. We have also introduced the operation matchesRE to deal with regular expressions in OCL. How these auxiliary operations are defined as an user-defined library in OCL is explained in Subsection 4.3.

The first tract states that nested UML packages should be transformed into nested folders. This is specified by the following constraint:

```
-- C1: Nested packages are transformed into nested folders
Package.allInstances() -> forAll(p| Folder.allInstances()->
  exists(f| f.name = p.name and p.subPackages->
    forAll(subp | f.folders()->exists(subf | subf.name = subp.name))))
```

The second tract states that Java packages should be imported when associations occur between elements contained in different UML packages.

```
-- C2: Import of packages when associations are crossing package borders
  Association.allInstances -> select(a |
```

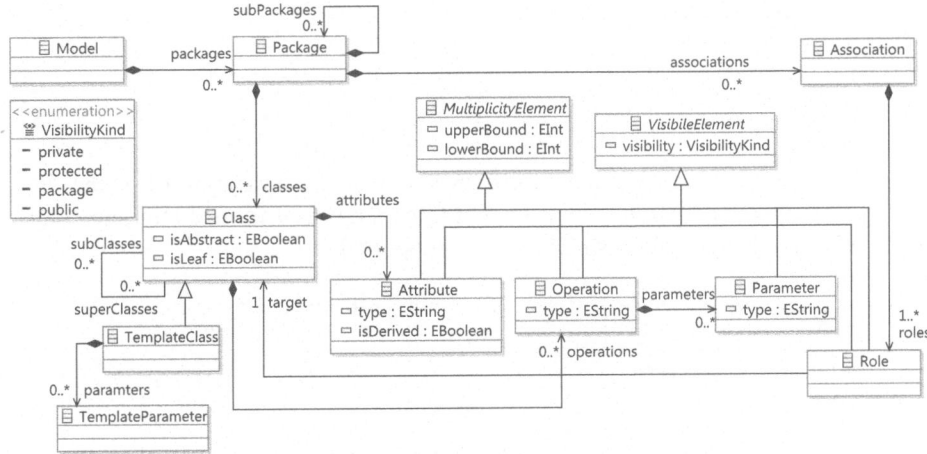

Fig. 6. A simplified metamodel for UML class diagrams

```
a.roles->at(1).target.package <> a.roles->at(2).target.package )
-> forAll(a| File.allInstances->exists(f |
    f.name = a.roles->at(1).target.name and f.extension = 'java' and
    f.content().matchesRE('import.*'+ a.roles->at(2).target.name))))
```

We should also ask for a precondition in order not to allow that any class inherits
from a leaf class.

```
-- C3: No leaf class as superclass
Class.allInstances() -> forAll(c| c.isLeaf implies c.subClasses->isEmpty())
```

Another precondition should check that there is no multiple inheritance in use in the
UML model (multiple inheritance is not allowed in Java).

```
-- C4: Only one superclass allowed in Java
 Class.allInstances()->forAll(c | c.superClasses->size()<=1)
```

We also include here some tracts to specify how particular elements in the UML
model should be transformed. For example, derived attributes can not be modified in
Java, and therefore only getter methods are generated for them.

```
-- C5: Derived attributes only have a getter method
Class.allInstances->forAll(c| File.allInstances
  ->exists(f | f.name = c.name and f.extension = 'java' and
    c.attributes->select(a | a.isDerived)->forAll(a |
    not f.content().matchesRE(a.type+'.*?'+a.name+'.*?;') and
    f.content().matchesRE(a.type+'\\s+get'+ toFirstUpper(a.name)))))
```

Similarly to the tract above, the following tract specifies how the visibility of attributes should be handled by the transformation.

```
-- C6: Visibility of attributes is considered
Package.allInstances->forAll( p|
  p.classes->forAll(c | File.allInstances->exists(f |
    f.name = c.name and f.extension = 'java' and
    f.container.name = p.name and
    c.attributes->select(a | not a.isDerived)->forAll(a |
      f.content().matchesRE(toString(a.visibility)
        +'.*?'+a.type+'.*?'+a.name+'.*?;')))))
```

And the same for association ends:

```
-- C7: Visibility of roles is considered
Association.allInstances->forAll(a | File.allInstances->exists(f |
  f.name = a.roles->at(1).target.name and f.extension = 'java' and
  f.content().matchesRE(toString(a.roles->at(2).visibility)+
    '.*?'+a.roles->at(2).target.name+'.*?'+a.roles->at(2).name+'.*?'))))
```

Finally, three further constraints specify that there are no Java keywords in the UML models, that the names of the elements and folders are well formed (e.g., no control characters) and that generic UML classes are supported.

```
-- C8: No keywords as name in UML model
NamedElement.allInstances()->forAll(ne | not Set{'abstract',
  'extends','implements','class','public','private','protected',....}
  .includes(ne.name))
-- C9: Well-formed names
NamedElement.allInstances()->forAll(ne |
    ne.name.matchesRE('[a-zA-Z_][a-zA-Z0-9_]*'))
-- C10: Generic classes are supported
TemplateClass.allInstances->forAll(c | File.allInstances->exists(f |
    f.name=c.name and f.extension='java' and
    f.content().matchesRE('class\\s+'+c.name+'\\s+<.*?>.*?{'))))
```

Of course, further constraints can be defined to deal with other requirements on the transformation. We have included here the tracts above in order to show examples of the expressiveness of our approach in the case of an M2T transformation. We do not try to claim completeness of full coverage of our specifications for the UML to Java case.

4.2   T2M Example: USE to UML

To illustrate the applicability and usage of our proposal in the case of T2M transformations, we have focused on a transformation between textual USE [12] specifications of structural models, and its corresponding UML specifications. USE features for representing models are similar to the ones defined in UML: classes, attributes, associations and operations. For example, the following USE code corresponds to a simple model of persons owning cars.

```
class Person
    attributes
        name : String
        birthDate: Integer
    operations
        age() : Integer
end
abstract class Vehicle
    attributes
        brand : String
end
class Car < Vehicle
    attributes
        licenceNumber : String
end
association Person_Car between
    Person [0..1] role owns
    Car [*] role owner
end
```

The following set of constraints are examples to show how different requirements on the transformation from USE to UML can be stated.

The first constraint specifies that the USE model should reside in only one file.

```
-- D1: Only one file per transformation run allowed
   File.allInstances()->size() = 1
```

The second constraint states that every USE class will correspond to one UML class with the same name.

```
-- D2: Every USE class should result in UML class
   Line.allInstances()->select(l | l.text.matchesRE('^\\s*class'))->
      forAll(l|Class.allInstances->exists(c|l.text.matchesRE(c.name)))
```

The third one specifies how USE inheritance relationships (cf. '<' symbol in the USE example) are transformed into UML inheritance relationships.

```
-- D3: less-than sign has to open an inheritance relationship
Line.allInstances()->select(l | l.text.matchesRE('\\s*class.*<'))->
   forAll(l|Class.allInstances->exists(c | l.text.matchesRE(c.name) and
   c.superClasses->exists(superClass|l.text.matchesRE(superClass.name))))
```

Similarly, the last three constraints allow to specify that USE abstract classes are transformed into UML abstract classes, USE attributes into UML attributes, and USE associations into UML associations.

```
-- D4: USE abstract classes to UML abstract classes
Line.allInstances()->select(l|l.text.matchesRE('abstract\\s+class'))->
   forAll(l|Class.allInstances->
   exists(c|l.text.matchesRE(c.name) and c.isAbstract))
-- D5: USE attributes to UML attributes
Class.allInstances()->forAll(c|c.attributes->
   forAll(a|File.allInstances->any(f | f.content().
   matchesRE('class\\s*'+c.name+'\\s*(<\\s*[A-Za-z0-9]+)?\\s*attributes.*?'
   +a.name+'\\s*:\\s*'+a.type+'.*?(end|operations)'))))
-- D6: USE associations to UML associations
Association.allInstances->forAll(a |
File.allInstances->any(f | f.content().matchesRE(
   a.roles->iterate(r; s : String =
      '(association|composition)\\s+[A-Za-z0-9_]+\\s+between.*?' |
      s.concat(r.target.name+'.*?role_'+r.name+'.*?')))))
```

4.3 Tool Support

In order to provide tool support for our proposal, we have developed a *injector* (parser) that converts the content of a repository, i.e., files, folders, and their structure, into a model that conforms the Text metamodel shown in Figure 3, and an *extractor* that takes models conforming to the Text metamodel and produces text organized in folders.

In order to check that a given M2T transformation fulfils a set of constraints (such as the ones shown in Section 4.1), we run the transformation with the set of models defined by the tract test suite (these input models have not been shown before for the sake of simplicity) and then use the injector with the output text (organized in folders) resulting from the transformation to generate the corresponding output models conforming to the Text metamodel. Then we are in a position to check the validity of the constraints as in the case of tracts defined for M2M transformations with our TractsTool [28]. The TractsTool evaluates the defined constraints on the source and target models by a transparent translation to the USE tool [12].

The case of testing T2M transformations is similar. Here the test suite is defined by the tract as a set of repositories, which need to be transformed first into a model-based representation by our injector component to check the source constraints. When the source constraints are fulfilled, the content of the repository is transformed by the T2M transformation under test to produce the output models. The models produced from the repository and their corresponding output models can then be validated by the TractsTool against the tracts.

For easing the formulation of the OCL constraints, we have also enriched USE with a set of libraries and operations to deal with Strings. For instance, to deal with regular expressions in OCL we have introduced the matchesRE operation shown above that checks whether a given sequence matches a regular expression or not. Furthermore, we have also introduced some auxiliary functions that are currently provided by M2T transformation languages such as toFirstUpper to end up with more concise OCL constraints than just using the standard OCL String operation library.

The TractsTool for testing M2T/T2M transformations is available at our project website[3] with several examples.

5   Evaluation

Most UML tools provide code generation facilities to produce source code from UML models. In order to evaluate the usefulness of using contract-based specifications for code generators, we tested a selected set of currently available UML tools by checking a set of tracts.

5.1   Selected Tracts and Test Models

For the evaluation, we used the constraints defined by the tracts presented in Section 4.1, which represent some of the most essential requirements that any UML to Java code generator has to fulfil. These constraints are described below, together with their type ('Scr' for source constaints and 'ScrTrg' for source-target constraints), as well as one example of the test suite models that was used to check the tracts.

C_1 SrcTrg: Nested packages are transformed into nested folders. Minimal test model: two nested packages in a UML model.

C_2 SrcTrg: Import of packages supported. Minimal test model: two packages, each one having one class and both connected by an association.

C_3 Src: Inheritance of a leaf class is not allowed. Minimal test model: a class inheriting from a leaf class.

C_4 Src: Only single inheritance is used in UML. Minimal test model: one class having two superclasses.

C_5 SrcTrg: Derived attributes only result in getter method. Minimal test model: one class having one derived attribute.

C_6 SrcTrg: Visibility of attributes mapped to Java. Minimal test model: one class having one public, one private, one package, and one protected attribute.

C_7 SrcTrg: Visibility of roles mapped to Java. Minimal test model: two classes related by three associations, whose association ends have different visibilities (public, private, package, and protected).

---

[3] http://atenea.lcc.uma.es/index.php/Main_Page/Resources/Tracts

C_8 Src: No Java keywords are allowed as names in UML models. Minimal test model: one class with name "class", one attribute with name "public", and one operation with name "implements".

C_9 Src: Names in UML model have to be valid Java identifiers. Minimal test model: one class with name "-", attribute with name "+", and operation with name "?".

C_{10} SrcTrg: Generic classes mapped to Java. Minimal test model: one generic class with two parameters.

5.2 Selected Tools

We selected six UML tools from industry that claimed to support code generation from UML class diagrams into Java code. The selected sample covers both commercial tools and open-source projects.

- **Altova UModel** (http://www.altova.com/umodel.html) is a UML 2.0 tool for software modeling. We evaluated Altova UModel Enterprise Edition 2013.
- **ArgoUML** (http://argouml.tigris.org) is a modeling tool supporting UML 1.4 diagrams. It is an open source project and distributed under the Eclipse Public License (EPL). Currently there is only one edition of ArgoUML available. We evaluated version 0.34.
- **BOUML** (http://www.bouml.fr) is a UML 2.0 diagram designer which also allows for code generation. We evaluated version 4.22.2.
- **EnterpriseArchitect** (http://www.sparxsystems.com) is a commercial modeling tool supporting UML 2.4.1 and is distributed by SparxSystems. We evaluated the professional edition, version 10.
- **MagicDraw** (http://www.nomagic.com) is a commercial modeling tool supporting UML 2.0 and is distributed by NoMagic. We evaluated the enterprise edition, version 16.8.
- **Poseidon for UML** (http://www.gentleware.com) is a modeling tool supporting UML 2.0, distributed by Gentleware. We evaluated the community edition of Poseidon for UML, version 6.0.2.

5.3 Evaluation Procedure

We defined reference test models based on the UML metamodel shown in Figure 6. Subsequently, we re-modelled the reference test models in all of the selected tools. Having the models within the specific tools allowed us to run the validation support and code generators of the specific tools. The validation support is related to the evaluation of support for the *Src* constraints that should act as filter for the code generator, i.e., only valid models should be transformed to code. Thus, we validated all test models in case validation support is available in a specific tool and checked if validation errors or at least warnings are reported for the negative test models associated to the *Src* constraints. For checking the *SrcTrg* constraints, we translated the output of the code generators to Text models and evaluated the resulting output in combination with the input models, i.e., the reference models, using the testing approach described in this paper. The reference models as well as examples of generated Java code and its corresponding text models are available at our project website.

Table 1. Evaluation results

Constraint / Tool	C_1	C_2	C_3	C_4	C_5	C_6	C_7	C_8	C_9	C_{10}
Altova UModel	×	✓	✓	✓	×	✓	✓	✓	✓	✓
ArgoUML	✓	✓	×	×	-	✓	✓	×	×	✓
BOUML	×	✓	-	✓	×	✓	✓	×	✓	✓
EnterpriseArchitect	✓	✓	✓	×	×	✓	✓	×	×	✓
MagicDraw	✓	✓	✓	✓	×	✓	✓	×	✓	✓
Poseidon	✓	×	×	✓	×	✓	✓	×	✓	-

It has to be mentioned that the UML tools are delivered with standard configurations for the code generators. Some tools also allow to tweak the code generation capabilities by configuring certain options using specific wizards before running the code generation. Others also allow to edit the code generation scripts, enabling further possibilities to customize the code generation facilities beyond the possibilities offered by the wizards. In this sense, we evaluated first the standard code generation features the tools offer, and after that we tried to tweak the tools by using the wizards to fulfill additional constraints that were not fulfilled in the standard configuration. However, the customization possibilities based on the wizards could not enhance further the evaluation results for the given constraints.

5.4   Results

Table 1 shows the results of the evaluation. In the table, a tick symbol (✓) means that the test passed for that tract and a cross symbol (×) means that the tract test failed. Some of the tests were not available for a given tool, e.g., a particular modeling feature is missing, and were not performed. This is indicated by a dash (-).

In the first place, constraint C_1 did not hold for some tools. In the case of BOUML and Altova UModel, the code generation requires that UML elements are manually associated to certain artifacts for which a path must be specified. Thus, the user has to specify the folders and Java files that should be generated. All other tools work well with packages in an automated way.

Concerning associations that cross package borders (C_2), Poseidon is the only tool that does not take this feature into account in the code generation process.

Precondition C_3 checks that no class inherits by another class marked as leaf. BOUML does not include the option to set a class as leaf. Poseidon fails because it allows that a class inherits from a leaf class. ArgoUML passes the test and gives a warning during the model validation only when the superclass is marked as leaf before the creation of the generalization relationship.

C_4 checks that the UML model does not use multiple inheritance, because it cannot be used in Java. ArgoUML and MagicDraw fail because they do not check this constraint, and they both create a Java class which does not even compile.

Concerning C_5, ArgoUML does not allow to define derived features. The rest of the tools do, but derived features are ignored in the code generation process. An expected solution would create derived attributes into their corresponding getter methods.

All tools work well with the transformation of the visibility of attributes and roles (constraints C_6 and C_7).

Most tools fail with constraints C_8 and C_9 (use of Java keywords and invalid names in Java). Tools do not seem to conduct any validation check before the code generation starts. Although many tools allow several kinds of validation checks on the UML models, most of these tests only deal with UML constraints. A few tools also allow the development of user-defined validation checks, but they do not seem to have been defined for the code generation facilities they support. The best results in this respect are achieved by Altova UModel, which raises a warning if non-valid Java identifiers or Java keywords are used as names for UML elements.

Finally, generic classes are supported and correct Java code is generated by all UML tools (constraint C_{10}) except Poseidon, which does not allow to define generic classes.

In summary, the results show that code generators have to fulfill several properties that should be specified at a higher level for allowing their validation. In particular, we found that no tool performs well even with respect to the basic UML to Java code generation requirements. Furthermore, we discovered that several tools produced incorrect Java code, even not compilable in some situations. In this sense, the tracts representing the basic requirements could be used as the initial components of a benchmark for future improvements and developments of UML-to-Java code generators.

6   Related Work

The need for systematic verification of model transformations has been documented by the research community by several publications outlining the challenges to be tackled [2,3,9,25]. As a response, a plethora of approaches ranging from lightweight certification to full verification have been proposed to reason about different kinds of properties of M2M transformations [1,28]. However, as mentioned before, transformations involving text on one side have not been extensively studied.

Several kinds of works apply contracts for M2M transformation testing using different notations for defining the contracts. In the following, we divide them into two main categories. First, contracts may be defined on the *model level* by either giving (*i*) complete examples of source and target model pairs, or (*ii*) giving only model fragments which should be included in the produced target models for given source models. Second, contracts may be defined on the *metamodel level* either by using (*iii*) graph constraint languages or (*iv*) textual constraint languages such as OCL.

A straight-forward approach is to define the expected target model for a given source model which acts as a reference model for analyzing the actual produced target model of a transformation as proposed in [10,17,19,20]. Model comparison frameworks are employed for computing a difference model between the expected and the actual target models. If there are differences then it is assumed that there exists an error either in the transformation or in the source/target model pair. Analogously, one could employ text comparison frameworks to reason about an expected text artefact and an computed text artefact. However, reasoning about the cause for the mismatch between the expected and actual text artefact solely based on the difference model is challenging. Several elements in the difference model may be effected by the same error, however, the transformation engineer has the burden to cluster the differences by herself.

A special form of verification by contract was presented in [22]. The authors propose to use model fragments (introduced in [24]) which are expected to be included in a target model which is produced from a specific source model. Using fragments as contracts is different from using examples as contracts. Examples require an equivalence relationship between the expected model and actual target model, while fragments require an inclusion relationship between the expected fragments and the actual target model. Using our text metamodel, one is able to define such fragments even for M2T/T2M transformations, but they still only define the oracle for one particular input model.

In previous work [15] we proposed a declarative language for the specification of visual contracts for defining pre- and post-conditions as well as invariants for model transformations. For evaluating the contracts on test models, the specifications are translated to QVT Relations which are executed in check-only mode. In particular, QVT Relations are executed before the transformation under test is executed to check the preconditions on the source models and afterwards to check relationships between the source and target models as well as postconditions on the target models. This approach may be used as an alternative syntax for our presented approach. Further alternative text-based approaches for defining oracles are presented in [6,7,10,11,16], however, they do not discuss how to apply their approaches for text artefacts.

The most closely related work is presented in Tiso et al. [27] where the problem of testing model-to-code transformations is explicitly mentioned. The authors enumerate two possibilities for such tests. First, they briefly mention a static approach which evaluates if certain properties are fulfilled by the transformation target code. However, they do not describe the details of this possibility. Second, they discuss a dynamic approach based on checking the execution of the transformation target, which is subsequently elaborated in their paper. In particular, they model, in addition to the domain classes, test classes that execute certain operations and check for given post-conditions after the operations have been executed. While we propose a generic and static approach to test M2T/T2M transformations in general, Tiso et al. propose an approach for testing a specific model-to-code transformation, namely from UML class diagrams to specific Java code and using JUnit tests that are also derived from a model representation. Furthermore, in our approach we have the possibility to directly test M2T/T2M transformations. However, in Tiso et al. [27] the execution output of the generated application has to be analyzed to trace eventual errors back to the M2T transformation.

Finally, an approach for testing code generators for executable languages is presented in [26]. The authors present a two-folded approach. On the one hand, first-order test cases that represents the models which are transformed into code are distinguished. On the other hand, second-order test cases are introduced representing tests that are executed on models as well as on the derived implementation, i.e., on the generated code. The output of the code execution is compared with the output of the model execution. If these outputs are equivalent, it is assumed that the code generators works as expected. Compared our proposal, we provide an orthogonal approach for testing the syntactic equivalence by checking certain constraints, i.e., how to define oracles for the first-order test cases. Combining a syntactical with a semantical approach seems to be an interesting subject for future work.

7   Conclusions and Future Work

This paper presented a language-agnostic approach for testing M2T/T2M transformations. Agnostic means independent from the languages used for the source and target artifacts of the transformations, as well as to the transformation language used for implementing the transformations. By extending OCL with additional String operations, we have been able to specify contracts for practical examples and evaluated the correctness of current UML-to-Java code generators offered by well-known UML tools. This evaluation showed a great potential for further improving code generators and documents the real need for an engineering discipline to develop M2T/T2M transformations.

There are several lines of work that we would like to explore next. In the first place, we plan to investigate how current Architecture Driven Modernization (ADM)[4] modeling standard such as Knowledge Discovery Metamodel (KDM) [23] may be used for defining contracts that are programming language independent and reusable for a family of code generators. For example, the presented contracts may be platform independently expressed and reused for testing UML-to-C# code generators. Secondly, the TractsTool we have used is a prototype whose limits need to be explored and improved. The models defined in the Tracts' test suites are normally of reasonable size (less than one or two thousand elements) because this is usually enough for checking the Tract constraints. However, we have discovered that large models (with several thousands of model elements) are hard to manage with the tools that we currently use. In this sense, looking for internal optimizations of the tool is something we also plan to explore next. Finally, we are working on the development of a benchmark for UML-to-Java code generators that could be useful to the community, based on a modular approach such as Tracts and on the proposal presented in this paper.

Acknowledgements. This work is partially funded by Research Project TIN2011-23795. We would like to sincerely thank the *Bremen Database Systems Group* led by Prof. Martin Gogolla, in particular to Lars Hamann, for their excellent support and help with their tool USE.

References

1. Amrani, M., Lúcio, L., Selim, G., Combemale, B., Dingel, J., Vangheluwe, H., Traon, Y.L., Cordy, J.R.: A Tridimensional Approach for Studying the Formal Verification of Model Transformations. In: Proceedings of the 1st International Workshop on Verification and Validation of Model Transformations (VOLT 2012) @ ICST, pp. 921–928. IEEE (2012)

---

[4] http://adm.omg.org

2. Baudry, B., Dinh-Trong, T., Mottu, J.M., Simmonds, D., France, R., Ghosh, S., Fleurey, F., Traon, Y.L.: Model transformation testing challenges. In: Proceedings of International Workshop on Integration of Model Driven Development and Model Driven Testing (IMDD-MDT 2006) @ ECMDA (2006)

3. Baudry, B., Ghosh, S., Fleurey, F., France, R., Traon, Y.L., Mottu, J.M.: Barriers to Systematic Model Transformation Testing. Commun. ACM 53(6), 139–143 (2010)

4. Brambilla, M., Cabot, J., Wimmer, M.: Model-Driven Software Engineering in Practice. Morgan & Claypool Publishers (2012)

5. Bruneliere, H., Cabot, J., Jouault, F., Madiot, F.: MoDisco: a generic and extensible framework for model driven reverse engineering. In: Proceedings of the 25th International Conference on Automated Software Engineering (ASE 2010), pp. 173–174. ACM (2010)

6. Cariou, E., Belloir, N., Barbier, F., Djemam, N.: OCL contracts for the verification of model transformations. ECEASST 24 (2009)

7. Cariou, E., Marvie, R., Seinturier, L., Duchien, L.: OCL for the specification of model transformation contracts. In: Proceedings of the International Workshop on OCL and Model Driven Engineering @ MODELS (2004)

8. Czarnecki, K., Helsen, S.: Feature-based survey of model transformation approaches. IBM Systems Journal 45(3), 621–646 (2006)

9. France, R.B., Rumpe, B.: Model-driven Development of Complex Software: A Research Roadmap. In: Proceedings of the 29th International Conference on Software Engineering (ISCE 2007) - Future of Software Engineering Track, pp. 37–54. IEEE Computer Society (2007)

10. García-Domínguez, A., Kolovos, D.S., Rose, L.M., Paige, R.F., Medina-Bulo, I.: EUnit: A Unit Testing Framework for Model Management Tasks. In: Whittle, J., Clark, T., Kühne, T. (eds.) MODELS 2011. LNCS, vol. 6981, pp. 395–409. Springer, Heidelberg (2011)

11. Giner, P., Pelechano, V.: Test-Driven Development of Model Transformations. In: Schürr, A., Selic, B. (eds.) MODELS 2009. LNCS, vol. 5795, pp. 748–752. Springer, Heidelberg (2009)

12. Gogolla, M., Büttner, F., Richters, M.: USE: A UML-based specification environment for validating UML and OCL. Science of Computer Programming 69, 27–34 (2007)

13. Gogolla, M., Vallecillo, A.: Tractable Model Transformation Testing. In: France, R.B., Kuester, J.M., Bordbar, B., Paige, R.F. (eds.) ECMFA 2011. LNCS, vol. 6698, pp. 221–235. Springer, Heidelberg (2011)

14. Guerra, E.: Specification-driven test generation for model transformations. In: Hu, Z., de Lara, J. (eds.) ICMT 2012. LNCS, vol. 7307, pp. 40–55. Springer, Heidelberg (2012)

15. Guerra, E., de Lara, J., Wimmer, M., Kappel, G., Kusel, A., Retschitzegger, W., Schönböck, J., Schwinger, W.: Automated verification of model transformations based on visual contracts. Autom. Softw. Eng. 20(1), 5–46 (2013)

16. Kolovos, D., Paige, R., Rose, L., Polack, F.: Unit testing model management operations. In: Workshop Proceedings of the IEEE International Conference on Software Testing Verification and Validation (ICSTW 2008), pp. 97–104. IEEE Computer Society (2008)

17. Kolovos, D.S., Paige, R.F., Polack, F.A.: Model comparison: a foundation for model composition and model transformation testing. In: Proceedings of the International Workshop on Global Integrated Model Management (GaMMa 2006) @ ICSE, pp. 13–20. ACM (2006)

18. Kurtev, I., Bézivin, J., Akşit, M.: Technological spaces: An initial appraisal. In: Proceedings of the Confederated International Conferences (CoopIS, DOA, and ODBASE), Industrial track (2002)

19. Lin, Y., Zhang, J., Gray, J.: Model comparison: A key challenge for transformation testing and version control in model driven software development. In: Proceedings of the Workshop on Best Practices for Model-Driven Software Development @ OOPSLA, pp. 219–236 (2004)

20. Lin, Y., Zhang, J., Gray, J.: A testing framework for model transformations. In: Beydeda, S., Book, M., Gruhn, V. (eds.) Model-Driven Software Development – Research and Practice in Software Engineering, pp. 219–236. Springer (2005)
21. Meyer, B.: Applying design by contract. IEEE Computer 25(10), 40–51 (1992)
22. Mottu, J.M., Baudry, B., Traon, Y.L.: Model transformation testing: oracle issue. In: Workshop Proceedings of the IEEE International Conference on Software Testing Verification and Validation (ICSTW 2008), pp. 105–112. IEEE Computer Society (2008)
23. Pérez-Castillo, R., de Guzmán, I.G.R., Piattini, M.: Knowledge Discovery Metamodel-ISO/IEC 19506: A standard to modernize legacy systems. Computer Standards & Interfaces 33(6), 519–532 (2011)
24. Ramos, R., Barais, O., Jézéquel, J.M.: Matching Model-Snippets. In: Engels, G., Opdyke, B., Schmidt, D.C., Weil, F. (eds.) MODELS 2007. LNCS, vol. 4735, pp. 121–135. Springer, Heidelberg (2007)
25. Van Der Straeten, R., Mens, T., Van Baelen, S.: Challenges in Model-Driven Software Engineering. In: Chaudron, M.R.V. (ed.) MODELS 2008. LNCS, vol. 5421, pp. 35–47. Springer, Heidelberg (2009)
26. Stürmer, I., Conrad, M., Dörr, H., Pepper, P.: Systematic testing of model-based code generators. IEEE Trans. Software Eng. 33(9), 622–634 (2007)
27. Tiso, A., Reggio, G., Leotta, M.: Early Experiences on Model Transformation Testing. In: Proceedings of the 1st Workshop on the Analysis of Model Transformations (AMT 2012) @ MODELS, pp. 15–20. ACM (2012)
28. Vallecillo, A., Gogolla, M., Burgueño, L., Wimmer, M., Hamann, L.: Formal Specification and Testing of Model Transformations. In: Bernardo, M., Cortellessa, V., Pierantonio, A. (eds.) SFM 2012. LNCS, vol. 7320, pp. 399–437. Springer, Heidelberg (2012)

An Approach to Testing Java Implementation against Its UML Class Model

Hector M. Chavez[1], Wuwei Shen[1], Robert B. France[2], and Benjamin A. Mechling[1]

[1] Department of Computer Science, Western Michigan University, USA
[2] Department of Computer Science, Colorado State University, USA
{wuwei.shen,h6chavezchav,b5mechling}@wmich.edu,
france@cs.colostate.edu

Abstract. Model Driven Engineering (MDE) aims to expedite the software development process by providing support for transforming models to running systems. Many modeling tools provide forward engineering features that automatically translate a model into a skeletal program that developers must complete. Inconsistencies between a design model and its implementation can result as a consequence of manually-added code. Manually checking that an implementation conforms to the model is a daunting task. Thus, there is a need for MDE tools that developers can use to check whether an implementation conforms to a model, especially when generated code is manually modified. This paper presents an approach for testing that an implementation satisfies the constraints specified in its design model. We also describe a prototypical tool that supports the approach, and we describe how its application to two Eclipse UML2 projects uncovered errors.

Keywords: UML, Class diagram, Java, Model checking.

1   Introduction

Software design models are abstract forms of a solution that can be used to analyze design choices and to partially generate implementations. In many cases, inconsistencies arise between a design model and its implementation when implementations evolve independently of the model from which it was generated. Checking conformance between a design model and its implementation is extremely important if the models are to continue to serve as contracts and blueprints for the implementation as it evolves. Conformance checking can assist in the understanding of a program implementation, strengthen the communication between designers and programmers, and extend the utility of models beyond initial generation of programs. In some domains, such as embedded software systems, mature conformance checking technologies exist because of the close relationship between a modeling language and an implementation language. For example, Reactis can automatically check whether a C program conforms to a Simulink model [1].

Object-oriented software development has become a dominant methodology in software development. The Unified Modeling Language (UML) [2], as a standard

A. Moreira et al. (Eds.): MODELS 2013, LNCS 8107, pp. 220–236, 2013.

modeling language, is a popular language for expressing design models. In particular, UML class diagrams are widely used to describe software designs. On the programming side, Java has been extensively used as an object-oriented implementation language. Many MDE tools can automatically generate Java skeletal programs from class diagrams to expedite the software development process. Developers often need to manually add method implementations to generated skeletal programs. Unfortunately, the completed implementation may not be consistent with the original class diagram. In addition to simple programmer errors, programmer misunderstanding of the generated structure in a skeletal program can lead to inconsistencies; the programmer would be implementing a software system based on a faulty interpretation of the generated code. Consequently, conformance checking that determines whether properties and constraints specified in a design model hold in the final implementation is needed.

The inclusion of constraints in a design model has become an indispensable step toward building a high quality software system. Although class diagrams are well designed to describe the structural relationships between objects, they are limited in describing logical relationships that must be maintained and many constraints cannot be diagrammatically expressed in class diagrams. For example, consider the relationship between the classes, *Association* and *Property*, in the UML metamodel [2] p.32. The diagram itself cannot show that "*the number of memberEnds must be exactly 2 if the aggregation kind is different than none*". As a result, the UML metamodel contains numerous constraints, or well-formedness rules, expressed in another language, the Object Constraint Language (OCL) [3].

In this paper, we focus on conformance checking that determines whether OCL constraints are violated in a Java implementation. To this end, we first define a translation schema that assumes (1) a UML class diagram with some OCL constraints is given, and (2) a Java skeletal program generated from the class diagram using a forward engineering tool is available. The translation schema Φ consists of two parts. The first part is concerned with the generation of Java skeletal code from a model. This part uses the Rational Software Architect (RSA) [4] translation schema, which is based on the following rules: (1) Each UML Class is mapped to a Java class with the same name, (2) each property is mapped to a class field with setter and getter methods, where both property and class field have the same name while their setter and getter methods names are prefixed with *set* and *get* respectively, and (3) each UML operation[1] is mapped to a Java method with the same name. The second part of the translation schema Φ is concerned with the generation of a Java Boolean method, from an OCL constraint. This method is referred to as a *post-method*. This part is based on the generation approach described in the OCL book by Warmer and Kleppe (Chapter 4) [5].

A Java method satisfies its corresponding UML method in terms of Φ if the following is true: *For every pre-state (the heap configuration) corresponding to a valid object diagram of the class diagram via the translation schema Φ, if the method is*

---

[1]   We will refer to UML operations as *methods* throughout the rest of the paper.

called on the pre-state and a post-state is generated, then the post-method derived from OCL method specification associated with the UML method returns true when invoked on the post-state. Otherwise, the method in the Java class does not satisfy its UML counterpart with respect to Φ. Consequently, the Java class does not conform to its UML class with respect to Φ. Likewise, if a Java class does not conform to its UML class with respect to Φ, then the Java implementation does not conform to its UML class diagram with respect to Φ. For brevity, we skip "with respect to Φ" throughout the paper.

Based on the above, the testing problem addressed by the approach described in this paper can be stated as follows: *Given a design model consisting of a class diagram with OCL constraints, and a Java implementation, automatically generate a set of high-quality test cases to explore execution paths of the implementation to reveal behavior that is not consistent with the behavior specified in the design model.*

In this paper we propose a novel automated test-based approach, called the CCUJ approach, which supports conformance checking between a UML design and a Java implementation. The approach checks whether a Java implementation is consistent with the OCL specifications associated with the design class diagram. CCUJ uses branch-coverage criteria and efficiently prunes the test input space by means of Universal Symbolic Execution [6]

The rest of the paper is organized as follows. Section 2 presents relevant background on software testing. Section 3 illustrates our approach using a simple example. Section 4 discusses the implementation of CCUJ approach. Section 5 presents empirical results. Section 6 discusses related work and draws a conclusion.

2   Background

Conformance checking between a UML class diagram and its Java implementation can be done either with formal verification or *testing-based* validation techniques. While formal verification has made some progress in past decades, they often do not scale effectively to real-world applications due to the complexity that arises with the increasing size of software. Thus, we adopt *testing-based* validation to support conformance checking. Specifically, we use a *model-based* testing approach, which characterizes by leveraging a program's model information for the generation of test cases. In general, a static defect in the software is called a *software fault* [7]. The software whose implementation needs to be tested is called the *software under test*. The *input values/pre-state* necessary to complete some execution of the software under test are called *test case values*. A *test oracle* specifies the *expected results/post-state* for a complete execution and evaluation of the software under test. A test case consists of test case values and *test oracles* for the software under test.

In the case of conformance checking between a UML class diagram and its Java implementation, the software under test is the method that we want to test so the method is called the *method under test*. A *post-condition* of a method in a class diagram is converted to a Java method, called a *post-method*, which serves as a *test oracle* for the corresponding Java implementation. The *pre-conditions* of a method in a class diagram are used to eliminate invalid test case values. In addition to satisfying *pre-conditions*, a test case value must also be a valid object diagram, i.e. it must satisfy all constraints given in the class diagram such as navigability and multiplicities. The goal of conformance checking is to find a fault in a method such that the *post-condition* is violated, i.e. returns false, after the method under test is called on a valid test case value. Every method specification (*pre-* and *post-conditions*) in a class includes all class invariants specified in a class diagram, that is, every class invariant in a class can be used as a *pre-* and *post-condition* for a method.

Program testing has been widely studied in the past decades and advances have been made recently. However, traditional program testing suffers two major obstacles with respect to conformance checking. First, most testing techniques, including symbolic execution techniques, do not consider *pre-* and *post-conditions* of a program under test, and they assume that the execution of a faulty statement can expose a software fault. Thus, most testing techniques adopt different coverage criteria to cover all statements including the faulty statements. Unfortunately, many errors in a program cannot be revealed based on this assumption. If a program does not have an asserting statement, then it is possible not to reveal an error even when a faulty statement is reached. Consider the example introduced by Ammann et al. [7] p.12 in which a method *numZero(int[] x)* calculates the number of zeros in array *x*. In its implementation, a programmer forgot to check the first element of the array in the for loop (instead of *for(int i=0;...)*, the program has *for(int i=1;..)*). When *numZero()* is invoked with test case [2,7,0], no error is revealed when the faulty statement *(i=1)* is executed.

Second, most testing techniques flip the condition branches during the execution in order to reach different statements. However, in MDE, some advanced forward engineering tools translate a class diagram to a program that has auxiliary information. For instance, on the Eclipse Modeling Framework (EMF) [8], the attribute *eContainerFeatureID* is an integer used to identify a container and specify whether it is a navigable feature or not by assigning a positive (navigable) or negative value. If the value of *eContainerFeatureID* is altered to cover a different execution path, as done by most testing techniques, a false positive that is not a real error can be reported. To avoid this issue, CCUJ only tracks fields that are directly derived from the program's class diagram.

3   An Illustrative Example

Consider the simple class diagram in Fig. 1 (a) which is excerpted from the *Royal and Loyal* system example [5] An OCL constraint is attached as a *post-condition* to method *earn()*. The code generated by Rational Software Architect (RSA) [4] is partially shown in Fig. 1 (b), where each property is mapped to private class fields with the setter and getter methods. We show how CCUJ can be used to check whether the implementation of *earn()* shown in Fig. 2 (a) conforms to the class diagram shown in Fig. 1 (a). Specifically, we check if the implementation satisfies the only OCL constraint in the class diagram. In short, CCUJ takes as input a class diagram that includes method *earn()* and its OCL *post-condition*, shown in Fig. 1 (a), and its implementation, as shown in Fig. 2 (a).

As a first step, CCUJ parses the class diagram to extract the corresponding OCL *post-condition* for the method under test, and it automatically generates the Boolean Java *post-method post_earn()* shown in Fig. 2 (b). Next, CCUJ uses the class diagram and the translation schema Φ, to match elements between the diagram and implementation, to produce a test case value for method *earn(i:Integer)*. Recall from Section 2 that every test case value should correspond to an object diagram. The correspondence relation between a *pre-state* and an object diagram is given by a heap configuration. Note that in the Java runtime environment, every created object is allocated a space in the heap area. Here, the equivalence between a test case value and an object diagram means that every object in the diagram has a space starting with address s_o, allocated in the heap area; and each value for an attribute of an object should be assigned the corresponding value via Φ in the corresponding heap location of the space allocated for an object's attribute.

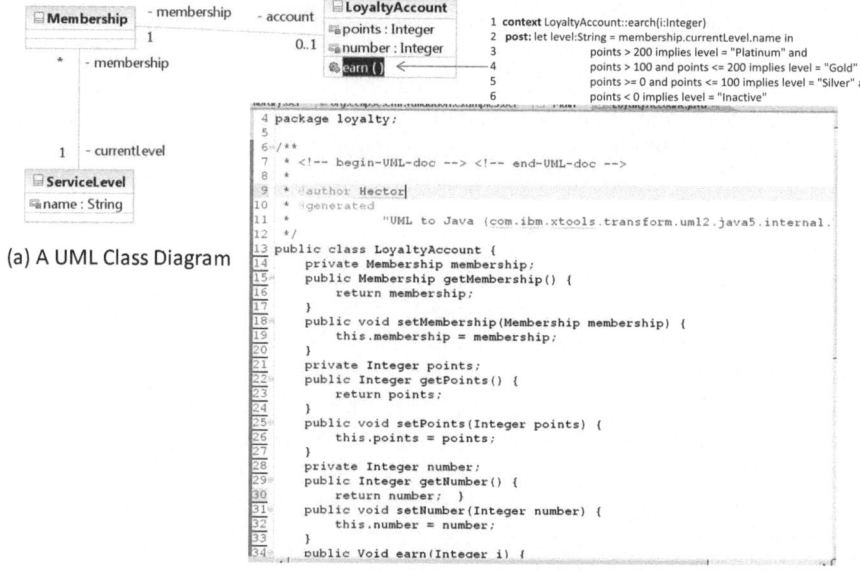

(a) A UML Class Diagram

(b) A program generated by RSA for CD in (a)

Fig. 1. Forward engineering feature supported by RSA

To generate an object diagram of Fig. 3 (a), CCUJ uses Φ to produce the program shown in Fig. 3 (b). The execution of the program produces the first test case *value/pre-state*. Next, CCUJ calls method *earn()* on the test case value and employs symbolic execution to guide the generation of further test case values. To tailor symbolic execution for the conformance checking, CCUJ tracks all object references, class fields, and method parameters derived from a class diagram.

During symbolic execution, each statement updates the symbolic memory or the path condition based on previous symbolic values in the symbolic memory. The initial symbolic memory of *earn()* is obtained by executing the program in Fig. 3 (b) and the path condition is initialized to true. Next, we show how CCUJ can reveal an error in method *earn()*:

- Trace I (Fig. 4):
  - The first execution based on the test case value, shown in Fig. 3 (b), starts with the execution of statement 2 at *earn* (Fig. 2 (a)).
  - As a result, CCUJ updates the symbolic memory by creating symbolic variable $3 for parameter *i* and updating $0.points to $0.points + $3 where $0 denotes the object of *LoyaltyAccount* (row 1 in Table 1).
  - Next, the execution takes the *else* branch of the first *if* statement (line 3 of *earn()*) and the *then* branch of the second *if* statement (line 6 of *earn()*). Thus, the path conditions for *earn()*, denoted by $pc_{earn()}$, is ¬($0.points + $3 > 100) ∧ $0.points + $3 >= 0.
  - Next, CCUJ continues to call the *post-method post_earn()* and the *then* branch of the first *if* statement (line 4 of *post_earn()*) is taken. Thus, the path condition of *post_earn()*, denoted by $pc_{post\_earn()}$, is $0.points + $3 <= 200 ∧ $0.points +$3 <= 100 ∧ $0.points + $3 >=0 ∧ $2.name = "Silver".

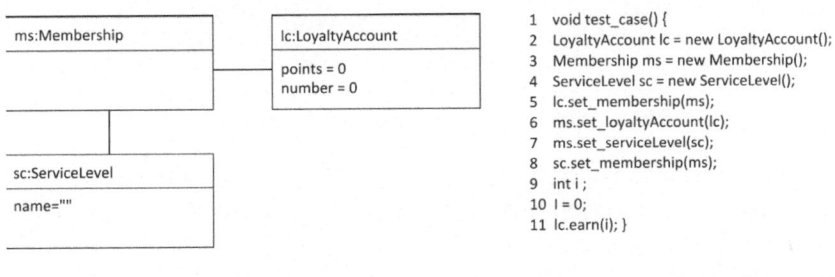

```
1  public void earn(Integer i) {          1  public boolean post_earn(int i) {
2    points += i;                          2    String level = this.getMembership().getCurrentLevel().getName();
3    if(points > 100) {                     3    boolean r0 = false;
4      membership.getCurrentLevel().setName("Gold");   4    if ((!(this.getPoints() > 200) || level == "Platinum")
5    } else {                               5        && (!(this.getPoints() > 100 && this.getPoints() <= 200) || level == "Gold")
6      if(points >= 0) {                    6        && (!(this.getPoints() >= 0 && this.getPoints() <= 100) || level == "Silver")
7        membership.getCurrentLevel().setName("Silver");  7        && (!(this.getPoints() < 0) || level == "Inactive"))
8      } else {                             8          { r0 = true; }
9        membership.getCurrentLevel().setName("Inactive");  9    return r0; }
10   } } }
```

(a) An implementation of the *earn* method   (b) Java method generated from *earn* OCL *post-condition*

Fig. 2. An implementation of the *earn* method and *post-condition*

```
ms:Membership            lc:LoyaltyAccount         1   void test_case() {
                                                   2   LoyaltyAccount lc = new LoyaltyAccount();
                         points = 0                3   Membership ms = new Membership();
                         number = 0               4   ServiceLevel sc = new ServiceLevel();
                                                   5   lc.set_membership(ms);
                                                   6   ms.set_loyaltyAccount(lc);
                                                   7   ms.set_serviceLevel(sc);
sc:ServiceLevel                                    8   sc.set_membership(ms);
                                                   9   int i ;
name=""                                            10  i = 0;
                                                   11  lc.earn(i); }
```

(a) A simple object diagram   (b) Code to generate the object diagram on (a)

Fig. 3. Test case values generation

If method *post_earn()* returns false, then CCUJ reports that a software fault is found. Otherwise, CCUJ calls the SAT solver to find whether $pc_{earn()} \rightarrow pc_{post\_earn()}$ is a tautology. If the implication relationship is a tautology, then all test case values satisfying $pc_{earn()}$ do satisfy $pc_{post\_earn()}$ and take the same path in *earn()* and *post_earn()*.

Thus, CCUJ looks for another test case value, i.e. another valid object diagram, by calling the SAT solver. In Trace I *post_earn()* returns true and $pc_{earn()} \rightarrow pc_{post\_earn()}$ is a tautology so CCUJ searches for another test case value as follows:

- Trace II (Fig. 4):
  - CCUJ calls the SAT solver to find a new test case value satisfying $\neg(\$0.points + \$3 > 100) \land \neg(\$0.points + \$3 >= 0)$, to enforce a different execution path. Here CCUJ uses a *last-input-first-output* stack to store the path conditions collected during execution following a back-tracking approach. Thus, $\$0.points + \$3 >= 0$ is popped and flipped. In this case, the SAT solver returns an assignment that is used to generate the test value $\$0.points = 0$ and, $\$3 = -1$.
  - Next, CCUJ generates another simple object diagram with $\$0.points = 0$ and $\$3 = -1$, and uses Φ to produce a new test case.

During this execution, CCUJ collects the two path conditions from the execution of *earn()* and *post_earn()*, i.e. $\neg(\$0.points + \$3 > 100) \land \$0.points + \$3 < 0$, denoted by $pc_{earn()}$, and $\$0.points + \$3 <= 200 \land \$0.points + \$3 <= 100 \land \$0.points + \$3 < 0 \land \$2.name = "Inactive"$, denoted by $pc_{post\_earn()}$ respectively.

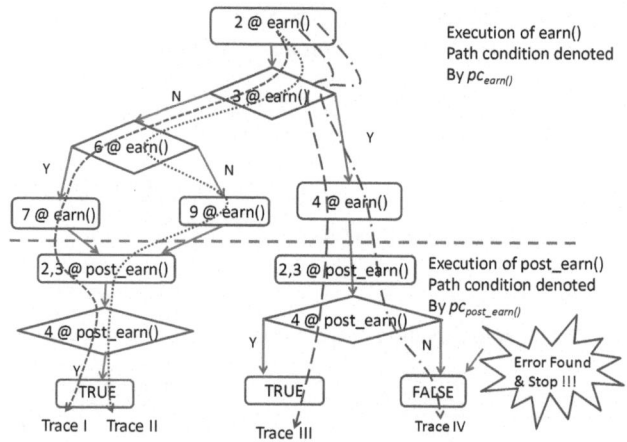

Fig. 4. Different execution paths explored by CCUJ

Again *post_earn()* returns true and $pc_{earn()} \rightarrow pc_{post\_earn()}$ is found to be a tautology by the SAT solver. CCUJ tries to find another test case value to alter the execution path of *earn()* as follows:

- Trace III (Fig. 4):
  - CCUJ next flips the first sub-path condition to $\$0.points + \$3 > 100$ and sends it to the solver. The solver returns ($\$0.points = 0$, $\$3 = 150$), and CCUJ generates another set of test values, and calls method *earn()* again.
  - The two path conditions collected by CCUJ for *earn()* and *post_earn()* are $\$0.points + \$3 > 100$, denoted by $pc_{earn()}$, and $\$0.points + \$3 <= 200 \land \$0.points + \$3 > 100 \land \$0.points + \$3 >= 0 \land \$2.name = "Gold"$, denoted by $pc_{post\_earn()}$.

While *post_earn()* returns true, the SAT solver finds that $pc_{earn()} \rightarrow pc_{post\_earn()}$ is not a tautology for Trace III. Therefore some test values that satisfy $pc_{earn()}$, following the same execution path of *earn()* in Trace III, do not follow the same execution path of *post_earn()* in Trace III. So, a different execution path of *post_earn()* should be explored to check whether false can be possibly returned. Thus, CCUJ attempts to find a test case value which alters the execution path of *post_earn()* as follows:

- Trace IV (Fig. 4):
  - CCUJ sends $pc_{earn()} \wedge \neg pc_{post\_earn()}$ to the SAT solver which returns (*$0.points = 0, $3 = 220*) and a new test case value is found and generated by CCUJ.
  - Finally, method *post_earn()* returns false on this test case, which means method *earn()* does not satisfy the *post-condition* defined in the class diagram. So a fault is found.

Table 1. Symbolic memory and path condition after first execution

Line No	Stmt	Symbolic Memory	Path Condition
2@earn()	points+=i	lc->$0; ms->$1;sc->$2;$0.membership->$1;$1.loyaltyAccount->$0;$1.serviceLevel->$2;$2.membership->$1; this->$0;i-> $3; $0.points->$0.points+$3	True
3@earn()	If(points>100)	Same as the above	!($0.points +$3 > 100)
6@earn()	if (points >= 0)	Same as the above	!($0.points +$3 > 100) and $0.points +$3 >=0
7@earn()	membership.getCurrentLevel().setName("Silver");	lc->$0; ms->$1;sc->$2;$0.membership->$1;$1.loyaltyAccount->$0;$1.serviceLevel->$2;$2.membership->$1; this-> $0; i-> $3; $0.points->$0.points+$3; $2.name->"Silver"	Same as the above
2,2@post_earn()	String level = this.getMembership().getCurrentLevel().getName(); r0=false	lc->$0; ms->$1;sc->$2;$0.membership->$1;$1.loyaltyAccount->$0;$1.serviceLevel->$2;$2.membership->$1; this-> $0; $0.points->$0.points+$3; $2.name->"Silver"; level-> $4; r0->$5;$5->false	True
4-7@post_earn()	If(!(this.getPoints()>200 ||...)	Same as the above	($0.points+$3) <=200 and ($0.points +$3) <=100 and ($0.points +$3) >=0 and $2.name="Silver"
8@post_earn()	return r0;	Same as the above	Same as the above

4   CCUJ Algorithm

Conformance checking in CCUJ requires a UML class diagram containing OCL constraints and a Java implementation of the diagram. The OCL constraints are extracted from the model and translated into a Java *post-method*. The program including both the methods under test and their post-methods is instrumented for symbolic execution. Each method under test is tested separately, but with the same procedure. For the first execution, only a minimal necessary set of objects is created. The method under test is executed concretely with concurrent symbolic execution from which a symbolic path condition is collected. The method's *post-method* is executed in the same manner to collect a *post-method's* return value and symbolic path condition. If an error is not found, new test case values are generated to exercise a different path condition than the previously collected. The testing process is repeated with the new calculated test case values until all reachable branches have been covered or an error is found. This testing process is described in the pseudocode below and explained in more detail in the following sections.

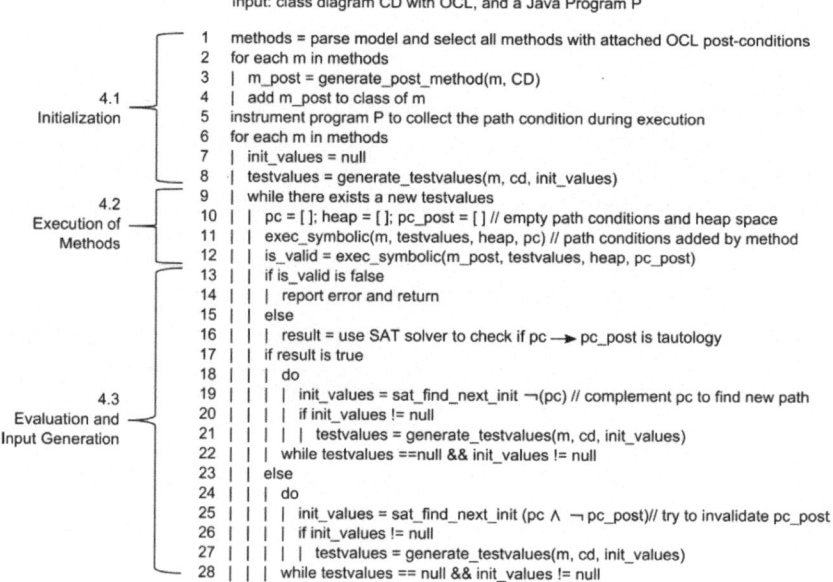

Input: class diagram CD with OCL, and a Java Program P

4.1
Initialization
```
1   methods = parse model and select all methods with attached OCL post-conditions
2   for each m in methods
3   |   m_post = generate_post_method(m, CD)
4   |   add m_post to class of m
5   instrument program P to collect the path condition during execution
6   for each m in methods
7   |   init_values = null
8   |   testvalues = generate_testvalues(m, cd, init_values)
```

4.2
Execution of
Methods
```
9   |   while there exists a new testvalues
10  |   |   pc = [ ]; heap = [ ]; pc_post = [ ] // empty path conditions and heap space
11  |   |   exec_symbolic(m, testvalues, heap, pc) // path conditions added by method
12  |   |   is_valid = exec_symbolic(m_post, testvalues, heap, pc_post)
```

4.3
Evaluation and
Input Generation
```
13  |   |   if is_valid is false
14  |   |   |   report error and return
15  |   |   else
16  |   |   |   result = use SAT solver to check if pc ⟶ pc_post is tautology
17  |   |   if result is true
18  |   |   |   do
19  |   |   |   |   init_values = sat_find_next_init ¬(pc) // complement pc to find new path
20  |   |   |   |   if init_values != null
21  |   |   |   |   |   testvalues = generate_testvalues(m, cd, init_values)
22  |   |   |   |   while testvalues ==null && init_values != null
23  |   |   else
24  |   |   |   do
25  |   |   |   |   init_values = sat_find_next_init (pc ∧ ¬ pc_post)// try to invalidate pc_post
26  |   |   |   |   if init_values != null
27  |   |   |   |   |   testvalues = generate_testvalues(m, cd, init_values)
28  |   |   |   |   while testvalues == null && init_values != null
```

Fig. 5. CCUJ algorithm

4.1   Initialization of CCUJ

To translate OCL expressions to Java code we adopt the OMG OCL 2.3.1 specification [3] and use the translation schema introduced by Warmer et al. [5]. To perform the translation, CCUJ takes as input a class diagram and the method under test with its corresponding OCL *post-condition* expression. Using the Eclipse Model Development Tools OCL project (MDT OCL) [9], the OCL expression is parsed and returned as an abstract syntax tree. CCUJ traverses the tree to form an equivalent Boolean Java method and adds it to the class where the method under test resides (Fig. 5, line 3-4).

To allow for concurrent concrete and symbolic program execution the Java program is compiled and the resulting class files are instrumented using the ASM Java bytecode manipulation and analysis framework [10] Instrumentation at the bytecode level allows for fine-grained replication of the concrete memory in symbolic memory. (Fig. 5, line 5)

Initially, CCUJ attempts to generate the simplest valid test case values. Null is used for all reference type method parameters, and primitives are given default values. The current implementation does not consider floating point numbers due to limitations of SAT solvers. The UML diagram is parsed to determine what minimal set of object relationships are required. Recall a test case value denotes a heap configuration equivalent to a valid object diagram. If the method under test is an instance method then an object of the class is instantiated and all its related associations are evaluated. Associations that require one or more instances of another class must also be instantiated and their respective associations must be evaluated recursively. As with the input parameters, non-required references are set to null and primitive fields are assigned default values. Upon completion of the process, a simplest test case value corresponding to a minimal heap configuration that conforms to the UML class model should be produced.

4.2   Execution of Methods

Once a test case value has been created with the input parameters set, the method under test is called. First, the method under test is called with an empty symbolic object heap (Fig. 5, line 11). The symbolic execution of a method identifies all discovered values as inputs and builds its memory representations from these values and the program constants. During execution, the path conditions evaluated on branches are collected and added to the symbolic path condition. More explanation of the symbolic execution process is provided below.

The execution of the *post-method* is slightly different in that it is given the symbolic memory constructed during the test method execution. Using this common memory allows the path conditions collected by the *post-method* to be expressed in terms of the same inputs (Fig. 5, line 12). During the execution of both methods program constants and discovered inputs are tracked. New values derived from them are tracked as expressions over these inputs. Like the method under test, the *post-method* collects a symbolic path condition.

The symbolic execution approach shown in Table 1 is based heavily on the idea of Universal Symbolic Execution [6]. For each concrete value found during the execution of the method under test, a symbolic value is assigned. The *execute_symbolic* method's parameter *params* shown in Fig. 6 is a list of known symbolic values for the method's parameters. The heap parameter is a mapping of known objects and object fields to symbolic values. The *pc* variable is a list of path condition expressions to which this method will add. The *pc* is expected to be empty when the method under test is started. (Line numbers in the remainder of section 4.2 refer to Fig. 6.)

For each monitored method in the call stack, a list of symbolic values is associated with the local variables (line 1). An expression stack (line 1) is used to evaluate runtime expressions. If no symbolic values are known for the input parameters (line 2), then new symbolic values are created (line 4) and added to the heap if not recognized (lines 5-6). Otherwise, the supplied values are associated with the corresponding local variables (lines 7-9).

Each instruction in the method under test, and possibly its subroutines, is mimicked in symbolic memory. Each time a local variable or object field is read (lines 11, 13) its symbolic value is pushed onto the expression stack (lines 12, 14). Conversely, when a value is assigned to local variable or object field (lines 15, 17), the value is popped off the stack and stored in the appropriate data structure (lines 16, 20). If an object value is not recognized, it is added to the heap (lines 18-19).

Expression execute_symbolic(method, params, heap, pc)

```
1    locals = [ ], expStack = []                          17  |   else if (insn == write field of object)
2    if params is empty then // implying unknown input    18  |   |  if (heap(object) is empty)
3    |   for each concrete parameter p                     19  |   |   |  heap(obejct) = new value
4    |   |  create new symbolic value                      20  |   |  heap(object+field) = expStack.pop
5    |   |  if (p is object) heap(p) = value               21  |  else if (insn == method return)
6    |   |  locals[p] = value                              22  |   |  return expStack.pop
7    else                                                  23  |  else
8    |   for each element of params p                       24  |   |  operands = [ ]
9    |   |  locals[p] = params[p]                           25  |   |  for each operand op
10   for each instructuion insn in method                  26  |   |   |  operands.add(expStack.pop)
11   |   if (insn == read local var)                       27  |   |  if (insn == stack operation with result)
12   |   |  expStack.push(locals[var])                      28  |   |   |  expStack.push(new Expression(
13   |   else if (insn == read field of object)            29  |   |   |   |  operands, operator, result))
14   |   |  expStack.push(heap(object+field))              30  |   |  else if (insn == method call)
15   |   else if (insn == write local var)                 31  |   |   |  expStack.push(execute_sysmbolic(
16   |   |  locals[var] = expStack.pop                      32  |   |   |   |  called method, params, heap, pc))
                                                           33  |   |  else if (insn == branch)
                                                           34  |   |   |  pc.add(new Expression(
                                                           35  |   |   |   |  operands, operator, result))
```

Fig. 6. Symbolic execution pseudocode

Stack operations, branches, and method calls, can have multiple operands. These operands are popped off of the stack (lines 24-26). For stack operations and branches, they are used to build a symbolic expression (lines 28-29, 34-35). Method calls are evaluated recursively (lines 31-32). If the called method is instrumented, it will be transparent to the process since its operations will be evaluated using given symbolic inputs and shared heap memory. The results of stack operations and method calls are pushed onto the stack (lines 28-29, 31-32). Branching expressions are added to the path condition (lines 34-35). Finally, at the end of the method (line 21) the remaining value on the expression stack is popped off and returned to the caller (line 22).

4.3   Evaluation of Results and Input Generation

As a result of executing the method under test and the *post-method*, a symbolic path condition (*pc*), *post-method* Boolean return value (*is_valid*), and *post-method* path condition (*pc_post*) have been collected. From these three values CCUJ can determine the next course of action.

In the simplest case, *is_valid* is false (Fig. 5, line 13) indicating that the model's OCL constraint on the method under test has been violated by the test case value. If this occurs then the error is reported and the process terminates.

If the *post-method* returns true, then the test case value does not violate the constraint, but that does not mean that another input on the same path could not cause a violation. To test for this possibility CCUJ tests the path conditions collected with a SAT solver, called Sat4j [11], a Boolean satisfaction and optimization library in Java (Fig. 5, line 16). If the SAT solver finds that $pc \rightarrow pc\_post$ is a tautology, that is $\neg(\neg pc \lor pc\_post)$ is not satisfiable, then all test case values satisfying the same path condition will satisfy the post-path condition as well and, thus, will satisfy the model's constraint. If this is the case, then CCUJ attempts to find a different test case value that would execute a different execution path in the method under test. To do so,

CCUJ uses back-tracking technique to negate one sub-condition of *pc* and sends the new formula to Sat4j. The returned assignments by Sat4J are stored in *init_values*. (Fig. 5, line 18-22)

If $pc \rightarrow pc\_post$ is not a tautology, that is $\neg(\neg pc \vee pc\_post)$ is satisfiable, then there exists a test case value that follows the same path in the method under test, but not in the *post-method*. Therefore, CCUJ tries to generate such a set of test values by solving the formula $pc \wedge \neg pc\_post$ via the back-tracking technique with Sat4j (Fig. 5, line 24-28). If a solution is found, CCUJ uses it to generate new possible test case values and repeats the testing process until no further test case values can be found.

5   Experiments

In order to validate the CCUJ approach, we conducted two kinds of experiments. First is the effectiveness experiment. Effectiveness can be observed by the ability of CCUJ to find real faults confirmed by developers in some industrial-strength software systems. The other type of experiment is concerned with evaluating the efficiency of CCUJ by comparison with some more established approaches.

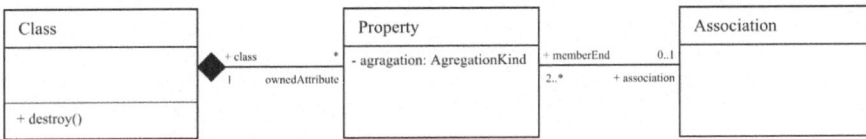

Fig. 7. Class diagram fragment of the UML specification

5.1   Effectiveness

When we studied the UML specification [2], we found that many existing approaches that claimed to recover UML composition by reverse engineering from a Java program do not strictly follow the semantics of UML composition [2,13,14]. The UML specification requires that *"... If a composite is deleted, all of its parts are normally deleted with it. Note that a part can (where allowed) be removed from a composite before the composite is deleted, and thus not be deleted as part of the composite..."* p. 41 [2]. However, many existing approaches require that all part objects cannot be accessed by any object except for its owner object. In fact, this is not the case. For instance, the class diagram excerpted from the UML specification in Fig. 7 shows that an object of class *Property*, which is owned by an object of class *Class*, can be accessed by an object of class *Association*. Therefore, when an owner object does not exist, all of its owned objects should not exist. Namely, all the links to the owned objects from other live objects should be removed. Assume method *destroy()* intends to implement the deletion of an owner object, Fig. 8 (a) shows the property as a *post-condition* after method *destroy()* is called on an owner object.

```
context Class::destroy() : Boolean              context Property::isAttribute(p: Property) : Boolear
post: self.ownedAttribute@pre->forAll(p |       post: result = Classifier.allInstances->exists(c |
    p.association@pre.memberEnd->excludes(p))        c.attribute->includes(p))
```

| (a) *Post-condition* for *destroy* method | (b) *Post-condition* for *isAttribute* method |

Fig. 8. UML meta-model OCL *post-conditions*

After the above observation, we tried CCUJ on one of the UML2 projects, i.e. the UML2 v1.1.1 implementation. CCUJ did detect the implementation error of all fields derived from UML composition and was confirmed with one of UML2 project members. The root cause of the implementation error is that the *destroy()* method iteratively checks each object contained in the resource, which is supposed to contain all the instantiated objects, and remove their links to the owned objects being destroyed. But the resource object, as part of EMF metamodel, did not automatically store all instantiated owned objects in the resource object appropriately.

Table 2. The comparison based on the Royal and Loyal and Binary Tree examples

Test	No. Classes	Number of Test Cases			
		CCUJ	Finitazation	Glass Box	Black Box
BinaryTree::orderChildren()	2	4	3	27	19683
		4	4	64	262144
		4	5	125	1953125
LoyaltyAccount::earn(i: Integer)	9	4	3, 2 *	54	39366
		4	4, 2 *	128	524288
		4	5, 2 *	250	3906250

* Object and integer finitization

We also applied CCUJ to the UML2 project v4.0.2 checking some OCL constraints in the UML specification [2]. CCUJ detected an error on the implementation of the method *isAttribute()* in class *Property*. The OCL post condition (p. 125[2][2]) for the method is shown in Fig. 8 (b). The problem was caused by the implementation only checking *non-navigable* inverse references to property *p*, this is, references in which an object (*obj1*) can access *p*, but *p* cannot directly access the object *obj1*. Since the reference *attribute* in class *Classifier* is a *navigable* inverse reference, it was ignored, and the method failed to return *true* when *c.attribute->includes(p)* is *true*. The problem was confirmed and fixed[2] by the developers.

---

[2] https://bugs.eclipse.org/bugs/show_bug.cgi?id=407028 [accessed 7-June-2013].

Table 3. UML specification test case generation comparison

Test	No. Classes	Number of Test Cases			
		CCUJ	Finitazation	Glass Box	Black Box
Classifier::maySpecializeType()	4	3	3	3	6561
	4	3	4	4	65536
	4	3	5	5	390625
StateMachine::ancestor()	8	10	3	27	6561
	8	10	4	64	65536
	8	10	5	125	390625
Classifier::isTemplate()	4	6	3	108	2916
	4	6	4	256	16384
	4	6	5	500	62500
Element::destroy()	3	3	3	27	531441
	3	3	4	64	16777216
	3	3	5	125	244140625

5.2   Efficiency

To determine the efficiency, we compare CCUJ with a glass box testing approach [15] and Korat [16], which are two prominent approaches, in terms of the number of generated test cases. One reason for this selection is that these two approaches consider different methods to generate test case values. The number of test cases determines the number of times that the method under test must be executed. Since CCUJ achieves branch coverage, the smaller the number of necessary test cases, the greater the efficiency. Our approach achieves a good efficiency without sacrificing coverage criteria. The glass box approach, similar to CCUJ, considers the generation of test case values based on the execution of the method under test. In the case of Korat, only an invariant method, *repOk()*, is considered in the generation of test case values. Both of Korat and the glass box testing approach use finitization to limit the number of values that can be assigned to a field. Thus, the number of possible test case values can be reduced. Furthermore, both Korat and the glass box prunes the fields not touched during the execution so the test case values can be further reduced. In order to run Korat, we converted the multiplicity and navigability constraints into the invariant method *repOk()* in each class. Table 2 shows the results of the three approaches in terms of the number of test case values being generated for the *Royal and Loyal* example and Binary tree example.

Likewise, we compared the three approaches based on the UML specification. We studied the partial metamodel, given in Fig. 15.2 and 7.9, in the UML2 Specification [2], and considered the methods *maySpecializeType()*, *ancestor()*, *isTemplate()*, and *destroy()*, on pages 54, 565 [2]. Because both Korat and the glass box approaches generate a large number of test case values quickly, we only considered a small number of classes related to these four methods. Table 3 shows a comparison result of these approaches in the UML specification.

6   Related Work and Conclusions

Various techniques have been proposed to support *model-based* testing. Most approaches consider the generation of test cases from a behavioral model of a system. These approaches can be further classified into two categories. In state-based approaches the system behavior is described by state machines. Abdurazik et al. proposed an approach to generate test cases based on UML state machines [17]. The other category uses scenario-based descriptions of interactions between different system entities. Roychoudhury et al. proposed a new notation, called symbolic message sequence charts, that generates test cases for process classes [18]. However, as far as we know, no prior work has been proposed to support conformance based testing of programs against UML class diagrams.

Testing UML associations, which is considered in our experiments, in a Java program has aroused some interest due to MDE. Akehurst et al. [19] discussed a variety of concepts related to associations such as subset in Java5 in detail. As for composition, the authors proposed to apply weak Java references to ensure all links to a part object have been removed but the authors failed to give the specific code to achieve this requirement. Other work by Gueheneuc et al. [14] and Milanova et al. [20] recovers UML composition from a program based on the non-accessibility property. However, this property is not required by the UML specification. So, their approach would fail to detect the errors found in UML v1.1.1 where a part object is leaked to a third-party object.

The KeY system [21] is a verification tool for Java employing a novel theorem prover for the first-order Dynamic Logic for Java with a user-friendly graphical interface. The KeY system considers OCL and JML as an assertion language to specify the *pre-* and *post-condition*s of a Java program under test. However, traditional program verification is often intractable for large software systems and that is why software testing techniques remain the most widely used method for software reliability.

While CCUJ considers Java as an implementation language, some other object-oriented programming languages such as C# can also use the CCUJ approach. In this case, CCUJ should be adjusted to accommodate the changes in a new programming language that is different from Java, such as, the generation of the *post-method* in a different target language, and the use of a different instrumentation API and symbolic execution tool. The most important contribution of CCUJ is still its approach for efficiently checking the conformance between a UML class diagram and implementation in an object-oriented language.

In conclusion, CCUJ was able to effectively and efficiently perform conformance checking between UML and Java. As future work we plan to extend our approach to consider floating point number during the test case generation by simulating the continuous values with the use of step functions.

Acknowledgments. We thank the MODELS anonymous reviewers for their constructive and detailed comments, as well as our colleagues Tao Xie and Zijiang Yang for their support and discussion during the early stages of the project.

References

1. Systems, R.: Software Testing and Validation with Reactis (2013),
   http://www.reactive-systems.com/ (accessed June 7, 2013)
2. Omg: OMG Unified Modeling Language (OMG UML), Superstructure Specification
   (Version 2.4.1). Tech. rep., Object Management Group (2011),
   http://www.omg.org/spec/UML/2.4.1/ (accessed June 7, 2013)
3. Omg: OMG Object Constraint Language (OCL) Version 2.3.1. Tech. rep (2012),
   http://www.omg.org/spec/OCL/2.3.1/ (accessed June 7, 2013)
4. IBM: IBM Rational Software and Systems Delivery (2013),
   http://www-01.ibm.com/software/rational/ (accessed June 7, 2013)
5. Warmer, J., Kleppe, A.: The Object Constraint Language: Getting Your Models Ready for
   MDA, 2nd edn. Addison-Wesley Longman Publishing Co., Inc., Boston (2003)
6. Kannan, Y., Sen, K.: Universal Symbolic Execution and its Application to Likely Data
   Structure Invariant Generation. In: Proceedings of the 2008 International Symposium on
   Software Testing and Analysis, New York, NY, USA, pp. 283–294 (2008)
7. Ammann, P., Offutt, J.: Introduction to Software Testing, 1st edn. Cambridge University
   Press, New York (2008)
8. Foundation, T.: Eclipse Modeling - MDT - Home (2013),
   http://www.eclipse.org/modeling/mdt/ (accessed June 7, 2013)
9. Foundation, T.: Eclipse Modeling - MDT - OCL (2013),
   http://www.eclipse.org/modeling/mdt/downloads/?project=ocl
   (accessed June 7, 2013)
10. Consortium, O.: ASM Home Page (2013), http://asm.ow2.org/ (accessed June 7,
    2013)
11. Le Berre, D., Parrain, A.: The Sat4j Library, Release 2.2. Journal on Satisfiability, Boolean
    Modeling and Computation 7, 59–64 (2010)
12. Barbier, F., Henderson-Sellers, B., Le Parc-Lacayrelle, A., Bruel, J.-M.: Formalization of
    the Whole-Part Relationship in the Unified Modeling Language. IEEE Trans. Softw.
    Eng. 29(5), 459–470 (2003)
13. Boyapati, C., Liskov, B., Shrira, L.: Ownership Types for Object Encapsulation. In: Pro-
    ceedings of the 30th ACM SIGPLAN-SIGACT Symposium on Principles of Programming
    Languages, New York, NY, USA, pp. 213–223 (2003)
14. Guhneuc, Y.-G., Albin-Amiot, H.: Recovering Binary Class Relationships: Putting Icing
    on the UML Cake. In: Proceedings of the 19th Annual ACM SIGPLAN Conference on
    Object-oriented Programming, Systems, Languages, and Applications, New York, NY,
    USA, pp. 301–314 (2004)
15. Darga, P., Boyapati, C.: Efficient Software Model Checking of Data Structure Properties.
    In: Proceedings of the 21st Annual ACM SIGPLAN Conference on Object-oriented Pro-
    gramming Systems, Languages, and Applications, New York, NY, USA, pp. 363–382
    (2006)
16. Boyapati, C., Khurshid, S., Marinov, D.: Korat: Automated Testing Based on Java Predi-
    cates. In: Proceedings of the 2002 ACM SIGSOFT International Symposium on Software
    Testing and Analysis, New York, NY, USA, pp. 123–133 (2002)
17. Abdurazik, A., Offutt, J.: Using UML Collaboration Diagrams for Static Checking and
    Test Generation. In: Proceedings of the 3rd International Conference on The Unified Mod-
    eling Language: Advancing the Standard, Berlin, Heidelberg, pp. 383–395 (2000)

18. Roychoudhury, A., Goel, A., Sengupta, B.: Symbolic Message Sequence Charts. ACM Trans. Softw. Eng. Methodol. 12, 12:1–12:44 (2012)
19. Akehurst, D., Howells, G., McDonald-Maier, K.: Implementing associations: UML 2.0 to Java 5. 0 to Java 5. Software & Systems Modeling 6(1), 3–35 (2007)
20. Milanova, A.: Precise Identification of Composition Relationships for UML Class Diagrams. In: Proceedings of the 20th IEEE/ACM International Conference on Automated Software Engineering, New York, NY, USA, pp. 76–85 (2005)
21. KeY Project: Integrated Deductive Software Design (2013), http://www.key-project.org/ (accessed June 7, 2013)

Automated Test Case Selection Using Feature Model: An Industrial Case Study

Shuai Wang[1,2], Arnaud Gotlieb[1], Shaukat Ali[1], and Marius Liaaen[3]

[1] Certus Software V&V Center, Simula Research Laboratory, Norway
[2] Department of Informatics, University of Oslo, Norway
[3] Cisco Systems Inc., Norway
{shuai,arnaud,shaukat}@simula.no,
marliaae@cisco.com

Abstract. Automated test case selection for a new product in a product line is challenging due to several reasons. First, the variability within the product line needs to be captured in a systematic way; second, the reusable test cases from the repository are required to be identified for testing a new product. The objective of such automated process is to reduce the overall effort for selection (e.g., selection time), while achieving an acceptable level of the coverage of testing functionalities. In this paper, we propose a systematic and automated methodology using a Feature Model for Testing (FM_T) to capture commonalities and variabilities of a product line and a Component Family Model for Testing (CFM_T) to capture the overall structure of test cases in the repository. With our methodology, a test engineer does not need to manually go through the repository to select a relevant set of test cases for a new product. Instead, a test engineer only needs to select a set of relevant features using FM_T at a higher level of abstraction for a product and a set of relevant test cases will be selected automatically. We applied our methodology to a product line of video conferencing systems called Saturn developed by Cisco and the results show that our methodology can reduce the selection effort significantly. Moreover, we conducted a questionnaire-based study to solicit the views of test engineers who were involved in developing FM_T and CFM_T. The results show that test engineers are positive about adapting our methodology and models (FM_T and CFM_T) in their current practice.

Keywords: Test Case Selection, Product Line, Feature Model, Component Family Model.

1 Introduction

Product line engineering (PLE) is a systematic process to capture commonalities and variability across a set of products belonging to a product line [1, 2]. PLE has demonstrated several benefits in both academia and industry including: reducing development time and cost, speeding up product time-to-market and reducing required modeling effort for Model-based Testing (MBT) through the mechanism of reuse [3, 4].

Test case selection is important for product line testing since the number of all possible products derived from the product line is very huge and it is difficult to

A. Moreira et al. (Eds.): MODELS 2013, LNCS 8107, pp. 237–253, 2013.

obtain a set of relevant test cases for a specific product [5]. Efficient test selection strategies can reduce the effort (i.e., selection time) and at the same time improve the coverage for required testing functionalities [6, 7]. In recent years, more and more researchers have spent significant effort on fully automated strategies for test case selection, which have proven to be efficient as compared to manual strategies [8].

Our industrial partner in the context of this work is Cisco Systems, Inc, Norway [9], which develops high quality product lines of Videoconferencing Systems (VCSs) [10]. The current test case selection practice at Cisco is to select test cases manually from a repository of test cases, whenever a new VCS is to be tested. Due to the increasing complexity of functionalities and diversity of VCS products, manual selection poses several challenges [11]. First, manual test case selection requires a lot of time, which reduces the efficiency of testing; Second, the manual selection process is mainly driven by the expertise of test engineers and hence it is not an objective and repeatable process (i.e., different test engineers may select different sets of test cases for the same product). Third, manual selection may result in a set of test cases that has low coverage for testing functionalities (i.e., all required testing functionalities may not be covered by the selected test cases), because a focus has been placed on the testing of specific functionalities. Finally, no guideline or methodology is provided to train recently hired engineers to select test cases. This means the current practice of test selection largely depends on the expertise of test engineers and is not scalable when more VCSs are developed and are to be tested.

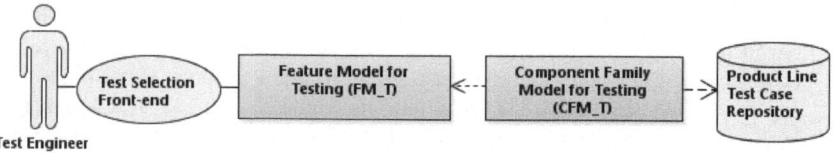

Fig. 1. An overview of the proposed methodology

To cope with the above-mentioned challenges, we propose a product line modeling methodology to support automated test case selection systematically. As shown in Fig. 1, we developed a *Feature Model for Testing* (FM_T) to capture commonalities and variabilities of a product line and a *Component Family Model for Testing* (CFM_T) to capture the overall test structure of test cases in the repository. Test engineers are only required to perform selection through the *Test Selection Front-end* for FM_T and the related test cases will be chosen automatically, based on the links built between FM_T and CFM_T, and between CFM_T and the *Product Line Test Case Repository*. To compare with the current manual practice at Cisco, our methodology is systematic and significantly reduces the complexity of selection for test cases since a test engineer doesn't need to know the implementation level details of a test case, thereby reducing the required selection effort (e.g., selection time).

The rest of the paper is organized as follows: Section 2 provides a background to Feature Model and Component Family Model. Section 3 describes the running example used to exemplify our methodology. Section 4 proposes our methodology using FM_T and CFM_T. Section 5 discuss the tool support. Section 6 presents evaluations. Section 7 discusses the related work and Section 8 concludes the paper.

2   Background

In this section, we briefly introduce feature model (Section 2.1), followed by related background of component family model (Section 2.2).

2.1   Feature Model (FM)

Feature modeling is a hierarchical modeling approach for capturing commonalities and variabilities in product line [1, 12]. FM can be represented as a 2-*tuple (features, constraints)* with four types of features, namely *mandatory, optional, alternative* and *or*. A *mandatory* feature means it must be included if its father feature is included in the current selection. The selection of an *optional* feature is optional even if its father feature is included. A father feature with a set of *alternative* features describes that only one of the *alternative* features can be included if their father feature is included. A father feature with a set of *or* features means at least one of the *or* features is included if their father feature is included. In addition, FM contains cross-tree constraints which are supplementary relations among unrelated features. There are two kinds of such constraints, namely *require* and *mutually exclusive* constraints. A *require* relation among two features (a source and a target) means if the source feature is included into the current selection, the targeted feature must also be included. A *mutually exclusive* relation has the opposite meaning, saying that if the source feature is included then the target feature cannot be included into the current selection [11].

2.2   Component Family Model (CFM)

A CFM is used to represent how products are assembled and generated in a product line by modeling relations among software architectural elements [13]. CFM can be represented as *a 4-tuple (components, parts, source elements, restrictions)*. *Components* are named entities organized into a tree-like structure that can be of any depth. Each *component* represents one or more functional elements of the products in product line (e.g. C functions, Java classes). *Parts* are named and typed entities. Each *part* belongs to a *component* and contains one or more *source elements*. A *part* can be associated with given programming language features, classes or objects, but it can also be associated with other key elements. A *source element* is an unnamed but typed entity. *Source elements* are usually used to determine how the source code for the specified element is generated. *Restrictions* specify conditions under which a *component, part* or *source element* may be excluded from a final selection [13, 14].

3   Running Example

In this section, we present a running example that will be used to exemplify our methodology (Section 4). The running example is a simplified version of the Saturn product line of Cisco with a set of products (e.g., C20, C40, C60, and C90).

The core functionality of a VCS is to establish a videoconference and the Saturn supports the following two types of videoconferences: Multi-way and Multi-site.

A Multi-way call in VCS products means one VCS can dial at most to only one End-point (EP1) and put the current call on hold to dial to another Endpoint (EP2). The VCS can then switch between EP1 and EP2, but can have only one active call at a time. Compared with a Multi-way call, a Multi-site call allows users to make calls to more than one Endpoint simultaneously. In the current VCSs, some of them, e.g., C20 only supports Multi-way calls and others, e.g., C60 and C90 support Multi-site calls. Among products supporting Multi-site call, there is also a possibility of transmitting presentations in parallel to a videoconference using VCS products. Presentations can be sent only by one conference participant at a time and all others receive it. The Saturn supports two protocols for videoconference: H323 and SIP.

To test Saturn, a testing repository including more than 2000 test cases is developed for various functionalities. For instance, the test case "Multi-way call test—max bandwidth" is designed and implemented to test the bandwidth of Multi-way call. Notice that each product is associated with a subset of test cases from the repository since it may not consist of all functionalities. Moreover, whenever a new functionality is introduced in the product line, new test cases are added into the repository.

4   Methodology

In this section, we present our methodology that is based on Feature Model (FM) and Component Family Model (CFM) for automated test case selection. Since our context is related with product line testing, we will call our FM as FM for Testing—FM_T and CFM as CFM for Testing—CFM_T. More specifically, FM_T is first presented to capture the commonalities and variabilities of a product line (Section 4.1) followed by CFM_T to capture the overall test structure of test cases (Section 4.2). Afterwards, we present how we perform test case selection for a product (Section 4.3).

4.1   Feature Model for Testing (FM_T)

In this section, we first present how to model testing functionalities of a product line using FM_T followed by how to model relations among testing functionalities using FM_T. Finally, we provide the statistics of the current FM_T for Saturn.

Modeling Testing Functionalities Using FM_T. Testing functionalities of a product line P can be represented as $FM\_T = \{f_1, f_2, f_3, ..., f_{nf}\}$, where nf is the total number of features for P. As shown in Fig. 2, each testing functionality is associated with a feature f_i in FM_T. For instance, the feature *Multi-way* is used to test the Multi-way call during conference meetings, and the *Multi-site* used to test the Multi-site call. Notice that the types of features in FM_T can be *mandatory*, *optional*, *alternative* and *or* as discussed in Section 2.1. For instance, as shown in Fig. 2 (Exclamation marks represent *mandatory* features, question marks represent *optional* features, double-arrow marks represent *alternative* features and cross-line marks represent *or* features), the feature *Call* is *mandatory* feature since each product must support call functionality and the feature *Presentation* is *optional* because not all products support the presentation functionality (e.g., C90 supports while C20 does not). The features *Multi-way* and *Multi-site* are *alternative* features since one product can only choose to support either Multi-way call or Multi-site call. *SIP* and *H323* features are *or* features because one product can support at least one protocol for videoconference. Moreover, based on the expertise, testing of a VCS product requires the following information:

- Testing states such as "Ready" and "Standby". The "Ready" state tells that a system is ready to be tested and "Standby" describes that the system needs some conditions or operations to wake up and transit into the "Ready" state;
- Testing functionalities such as "Multi-way" and "Multi-site";
- Testing parameters such as "SIP", "H323".

In order to meet the VCS testing domain, our FM_T represents testing states, testing functionalities, and testing parameters as different dimensions of features, which describe testing states of VCS products, functionalities needed to be tested and parameters needed to be configured. Hence, FM_T in our context consists of three parent features, namely, *Testing Sates* (F_{TS}), *Testing Features* (F_{TF}) and *Testing Parameters* (F_{TP}), respectively, i.e., FM_T can be divided into three parts $M_T = \{F_{TS}, F_{TF}, F_{TP}\}$. Each part consists of a list of relevant features: $F_{TS} = \{f_{ts1}, f_{ts2}, f_{ts3}, ..., f_{nts}\}$ such as the features *Ready* and *Standby*, $F_{TF} = \{f_{tf1}, f_{tf2}, f_{tf3}, ..., f_{ntf}\}$ such as the features *Video Call* and *Presentation* and $F_{TP} = \{f_{tp1}, f_{tp2}, f_{tp3}, ..., f_{ntp}\}$ such as the feature *Protocol* (Fig. 2), where nts, ntf, ntp are the numbers of features belonging to F_{TS}, F_{TF} and F_{TP}, respectively, and $nts + ntf + ntp = nf$. Notice all the features are identified and created together with the test engineers based on the domain knowledge and system information.

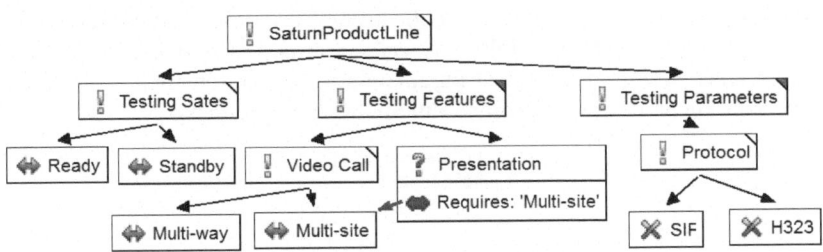

Fig. 2. An excerpt of FM_T

Modeling Relations Using FM_T. A set of cross-tree constraints is added to the FM_T since testing functionalities may be related to each other. All the constraints can be represented as $CONS = \{cons_1, cons_2, cons_3, ..., cons_{ncons}\}$, where $ncons$ is the number of constraints. Each $cons_i$ can be either *require* or *mutually exclusive*, i.e., $cons_i$ can be represented as $cons_i = require\ (f_m, f_n)$ or $cons_i = exclusive\ (f_m, f_n)$, where f_m is the source feature and f_n is the target feature (Section 2.1). For instance, the *Presentation* feature requires the *Multi-site* feature since one product cannot support the presentation functionality unless it supports the Multi-site call, then the constraint $cons_k = require\ (Presentation, Mult - site)$ is assigned from the source feature *Presentation* to the target feature *Multi-site* (Fig. 2). Notice that these cross-tree relations are also identified and built together with the test engineers in Cisco.

Summary for FM_T. The various products can be configured by performing different selections of the features in FM_T, i.e., a specific product can be represented as a subset of features. Together with test engineers of Cisco, we developed the FM_T for Saturn, which contains 134 features (44 *mandatory*, 38 *optional*, 25 *alternative* and 27 *or*) and 35 *require* constraints in total. Besides, according to our discussion with test engineers, we need to mention that building FM_T is one-time manual effort since the functionalities of Saturn doesn't change significantly.

4.2 Component Family Model for Testing (CFM_T)

In this section, we first present how to model the structure of all test cases in the repository using CFM_T followed by how to link FM_T and CFM_T using restrictions. Finally, we provide the statistics about CFM_T developed for Saturn.

Modeling Test Structure Using CFM_T. Test plans are usually composed of many test cases and test engineers spend significant amount of time organizing test cases within these plans. In order to model the structure of test cases and automatically obtain relevant test cases for test plans, we proposed a CFM_T to capture the overall structure of test cases in the repository.

First of all, we investigated the test structure in the context of Saturn. Based on the domain knowledge, we found that the test structure in VCS testing is composed by test tasks and test cases. A test task is a collection of test cases that has a common test resource requirement such as "Multi-way call" task and "Multi-site call" task. Each test case is a test script with a set of parameters for execution such as required software/hardware resources, which can be run on different products.

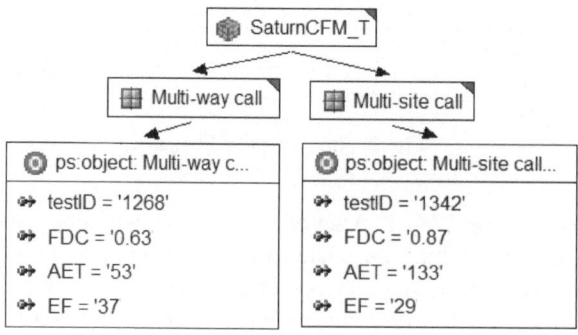

Fig. 3. An excerpt of CFM_T

Our CFM_T is represented as $CFM\_T = \{c_1, c_2, c_3, ..., c_n\}$ comprising of a set of components, where n is the number of components. Each component represents a test task and can be hierarchically decomposed into parts representing various test cases

$c_i = \{pa_{i1}, pa_{i2}, pa_{i3}, ..., pa_{in}\}$, where in is the number of parts belonging to c_i. Fig. 3 shows two components *Multi-way call* and *Multi-site call* in the CFM_T representing two test tasks "Muti-way call" and "Multi-site call". Each component includes a set of parts, which represent relevant test cases. Fig. 3 also shows two parts *Multi-way call test—max bandwidth* and *Multi-site call test—max bandwidth* belonging to the two components, which represent two test cases "Multi-way call test—max bandwidth" and "Multi-site call test—max bandwidth" belonging to the two test tasks (the names of two parts in CFM_T are not completely shown in Fig. 3 due to space).

Meanwhile, each part consists of a set of attributes representing different information for testing: $A\_pa_{ij} = \{a_{ij1}, a_{ij2}, a_{ij3}, ..., a_{ijn}\}$, where ijn is the number of attributes belonging to pa_{ij}. In particular, each part pa_{ij} in our current CFM_T consists of four attributes (Fig. 3), which can be categorized as two groups: 1) Attributes for tracing, more specifically, testID is used to identify and trace test cases between CFM_T and the repository; and 2) Attributes for test minimization, i.e., *fault detection capability* (FDC), *average execution time* (AET) which is recorded by seconds and execution frequency (EF) which is recorded per week. For instance, AET and EF for the test case "Multi-way call test—max bandwidth" is 53 and 37, respectively, showing the average execution time of the test case is 53 seconds and the test case is executed 37 times per week on average. Moreover, FDC is defined as the success rate of a test case in a week. For instance, the FDC of the part *Multi-way call test—max bandwidth* is 0.63 (Fig. 3), which means the test case "Multi-way call test—max bandwidth" executes successfully by 63% in a week. Using FDC, the number of selected test cases for testing a product obtained by our methodology can be further minimized based on their fault detection capability using different mechanisms such as genetic algorithms [15]. All the information for attributes is available (they can be generated from the test database in Cisco automatically) and can be used for different purposes. Notice that we only focus on the test case selection using CFM_T in this paper but our CFM_T can be adapted for more testing purposes via assigned attributes, e.g., minimizing the number of test cases for testing a product [15].

Linking FM_T and CFM_T Using Restrictions. Afterwards, restrictions are assigned to components or parts, which constrain relations between components or parts in CFM_T and features in FM_T. Notice that each component c_i or part pa_{ij} can be linked with one or more features in FM_T via restrictions (i.e., Each component or part can have any number of restrictions). A component or part cannot be included into the final selection for a product unless its restrictions evaluate to true. For instance, we assigned a restriction to the part *Multi-way call test—max bandwidth* to link this part with the feature *Multi-way* in the FM_T since the test case "Multi-way call test—max bandwidth" is developed to test the bandwidth of Multi-way call, i.e., during test case selection, the test case cannot be included into the final selection unless the feature *Multi-way* is in the selection set of features.

Summary for CFM_T. An initial version of CFM_T was built together with test engineers at Cisco so that test engineers can get familiarized with the notations of CFM_T. Later on, we developed a tool called Import Plugin and Transformation

(IPT) that can build CFM_T automatically (Section 5) in the context of Cisco. Following the test structure of Saturn, a CFM_T was built automatically using the tool IPT. In general, 143 test tasks with 2374 test cases in the repository are modeled as 143 components including 2374 parts with 9496 attributes (test ID, FDC, AEC and EF) in the CFM_T. Meanwhile, 7386 restrictions are assigned to relevant components or parts in the CFM_T, which are used to link with related features in the FM_T.

4.3   Process to Select Test Cases for a Product

Test case selection for a product has the following two steps: 1) Based on the expertise knowledge and system information, test engineers analyze the test requirements for the product; 2) According to the analyzed requirements, test engineers select a set of relevant features in FM_T. Afterwards, related components and parts in CFM_T will be selected automatically, i.e., a set of relevant test cases in the repository will be chosen automatically.

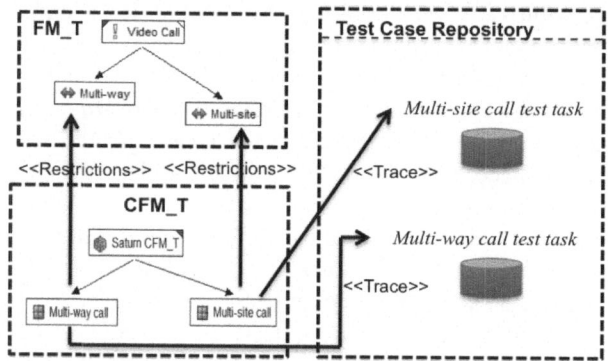

Fig. 4. An example of test case selection process for a product

Fig. 4 shows an example of test case selection process for a product and it has the following three main parts: 1) An excerpt of FM_T; 2) An excerpt of CFM_T and 3) Two associated test tasks including a set of test cases respectively. For FM_T, there are *alternative* two features, namely *Multi-way* and *Multi-site*. Each product can only support either Multi-way call or Multi-site call. In CFM_T, the component *Multi-way call* and *Multi-site call* are linked with the feature *Multi-way* and *Multi-site* in FM_T via restrictions at the same time the corresponding test tasks are associated with the related components in CFM_T. For instance, since C90 supports the Multi-site call, test engineers need to select the *Multi-site* feature in FM_T and then the component *Multi-site call* will be selected automatically via restrictions defined in CFM_T. Meanwhile, the test task "Multi-site call" will be chosen automatically from the repository for testing the functionality Multi-site call.

5   Automation

In this section, we present the tool support for our proposed methodology. Our tool is implemented as Eclipse plugin in Java.

In our methodology, a CFM_T is required to be built to maintain all the links to the repository of test cases and to a FM_T. The process of building a CFM_T can be automated or manually. In our current industrial application (i.e., Cisco), the repository updates very frequently (e.g., new test cases are developed and existing test cases are modified) thereby it is not practical to build a CFM_T manually. Meanwhile, building CFM_T with a large number of restrictions requires too much effort (Section 4.2).

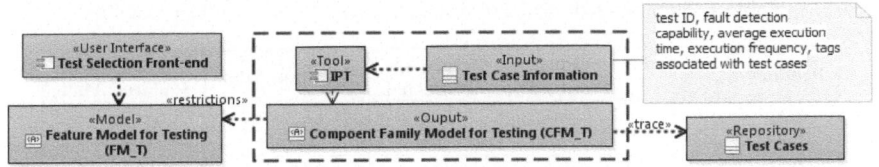

Fig. 5. Tool support architecture for the proposed methodology

To address such problem, the tool IPT is developed shown as Fig. 5, which automatically builds a CFM_T to capture the structure of a large number of test cases in the repository. The input of IPT is test case information such as test ID, fault detection capability, average execution time, execution frequency and tags associated with test cases. Such information can be automatically obtained as an xml file from the repository in Cisco. The *Test Selection Front-end* interface allows a test engineer to perform selection of features as discussed in Section 4.1. Notice that tags are used to identify testing functionalities of test cases. For instance, the test case "Multi-way call test—max bandwidth" with test id 1268 (Fig. 3) is developed for testing the bandwidth of Multi-way call so that one tag named "Multi-way" is integrated into the test case to identify that the Multi-way call is tested by such test case. Based on the tag, a restriction can be built to link the part *Multi-way call test—max bandwidth* in CFM_T with the feature *Multi-way* in FM_T. Using tags information associated with test cases, our tool can build all relevant restrictions from CFM_T to FM_T automatically.

6   Evaluation

In this section, we evaluate our methodology via: 1) reporting an industrial case study to demonstrate the benefits of applying our methodology in an industrial setting; and 2) reporting results of a questionnaire-based survey in Cisco with the objective of investigating the adoption of FM_T and CFM_T.

6.1   Industrial Case Study

Our case study is the Saturn product line developed in Cisco [9]. The Saturn family consists of various hardware codecs ranging from C20 to C90. C20 is the lowest end product with minimum hardware and has lowest performance while C90 is the highest end product with advanced hardware and highest performance.

Saturn family consists of 20 subsystems such as audio and video subsystems. Each subsystem can run in parallel to the subsystem implementing the core functionality that deals with establishing videoconferences. To test such product line family, a large number of test cases (more than 2000) have been developed for various products. Each test case can be scheduled and executed on different platforms. All these test cases are stored in the Saturn repository for test cases. When a specific product comes into play, it is required to choose a subset of relevant test cases from the repository and put them into execution after scheduling.

Table 1. Summarized results of test case selection for various products

Product	Selected Features	Selected Test Cases	Percentage of Selected	Selection Time	Percentage of Reduced Time
C20	17	238	10.0	2.5 hours	92
C40	25	367	15.5	3 hours	91
C60	32	592	24.9	4.5 hours	86
C90	43	739	31.1	6 hours	81

Table 1 summarizes the results of test case selection for various products in Saturn using our proposed methodology. The *Selected Features* column indicates the number of selected features in FM_T for each product. The *Selected Test Cases* column shows the number of selected test cases by our proposed methodology. The *Percentage of Selected* column describes the percentage of selected test cases for a product among all the test cases in the repository. The *Selection Time* and *Percentage of Reduced Time* columns show the required time for selection and the percentage of reduced time by our proposed methodology as compared with the current manual process.

Abstraction and Automation. FM_T captures various testing functionalities within the product line in a systematic way, whereas CFM_T provides an additional layer of abstraction on top of the low level details of the test cases in the repository. This additional layer of abstraction hides implementation of test scripts, test settings for execution (test setting files), and test files capturing required software/hardware resources from test engineers (test resource files). In the current practice, test engineers are required to go through all the test scripts, test setting files, and test resource files, to select a set of relevant test cases for a product. Using our methodology, a test engineer only selects a set of relevant features in FM_T for a product and corresponding test cases will be obtained from the repository automatically, which greatly reduces the complexity of the whole test case selection process in product lines. Notice CFM_T with restrictions is hidden from test engineers and built automatically by the IPT tool.

Reduced Selection Effort and Test Coverage. Through discussions with test engineers in Cisco, we have learnt that: 1) The current practice of manual test selection takes at minimum of two days; 2) Typically, two test engineers are involved in test selection; and 3) There is no systematic way to determine how many of testing functionalities are covered by the selected test cases.

From the *Percentage of Selected* column in Table 1, we can see that the percentage of relevant test cases for each product is low, e.g., 10% for C20. This means that significant effort is reduced since test engineers do not need to go through 90% of the test cases. Even for C90 that is the most advanced VCS in the Saturn, the percentage of relevant test cases is around 31%. Meanwhile, from the *Percentage of Reduced Time* column (the percentage of reduced time is calculated as: $\left(1 - \frac{the\ selection\ time\ by\ our\ methodology}{2\ working\ days * 2\ persons}\right) * 100\%$ where 2 working days * 2persons = 2 * 8 *2 = 32 hours (assuming minimum time required for test case selection using the current practice), we can see that the time required for test case selection using our methodology is reduced significantly, e.g., 92% time for selection is reduced for C20 ((1- 2.5/32) * 100* = 92%). In total, 87.5% time for selection is reduced as compared to the current manual process ((1 - 4 hours on average/32) * 100% =87.5%). Notice that effort and time saved is at the expense of creating FM_T and CFM_T, but as we discussed in Section 4.1, developing FM_T is one time effort and CFM_T is built automatically in our context.

With our methodology, selecting a set of relevant features in FM_T for a product ensures that all required testing functionalities are covered at least once with the selected corresponding test cases. However, in the current practice, there isn't any way to ensure such coverage for testing functionalities.

Less Reliance on Domain Expertise. The current test select practice largely depends on domain expertise of test engineers. This means that different groups of test engineers may obtain different sets of test cases based on their understanding for the same product. Moreover, most of test engineers in Cisco have been working for years in the testing group and thus understanding of testing functionalities and test cases in the repository is inside minds of several test engineers. Therefore, the current process lacks a unified understanding of testing functionalities and test cases in the repository. Because of this, when old test engineers leave, domain expertise of test selection is lost and training new test engineers require significant amount of effort. In contrast, using our methodology, FM_T captures all domain expertise for testing (testing functionalities) in a systematic way since it is built together with all the test engineers. Even training new test engineers is just limited to train them FM_T notations and the test engineers do not need to understand CFM_T.

Reduced Maintenance Effort. In the current practice, there is no systematic way to maintain the functionalities and test cases for the product line. Whenever a new functionality is introduced to the product line, the corresponding test cases are developed and added into the repository and when a testing functionality is removed, the corresponding test cases are not deleted from the repository. When a functionality is modified, the affected test cases are not deleted rather new test cases in the repository are added. Using FM_T and CFM_T, we provide a systematic way to maintain testing functionalities and test cases and maintaining them is straight forward. For FM_T, a new feature is added into the FM_T when a new functionality is introduced to the product line, an old feature is removed from the FM_T when a testing functionality is removed and the related feature is refined in case the current functionality is modified. For CFM_T, in case of any addition, deletion, or modification of test cases, the CFM_T can be rebuilt using IPT automatically. In summary, if existing products evolve, only the affected parts in the FM_T need to be updated and CFM_T is updated automatically with our IPT tool. Notice that the links from test cases to our CFM_T is also automatically done by our IPT tool (Section 5).

Adaption in Other Contexts. To adapt our methodology in other contexts, FM_T and CFM_T are required to be built. FM_T can be built based on the domain expertise and system information for other product lines. Notice that building FM_T is one time effort and once it is build, it doesn't require significant changes once new features are introduced in a product line. Similarly, CFM_T can be built manually or automatically. For example, in our industrial application, the tool IPT is developed to build CFM_T with restrictions automatically. In other contexts, it may not be feasible to build CFM_T with restrictions automatically. Therefore, a CFM_T with restrictions may have to be built manually, which is also one-time effort for a product line.

Limitations of the Methodology. Our methodology at its current stage has several limitations. Some of these are: 1) the current FM_T may not be complete since more detailed information for a product line is required to be added as features or cross-constraints into FM_T. However, notice that FM_T is for a product line and it will keep on evolving as more products are introduced into the product line; 2) in our current case, the restrictions between FM_T and CFM_T are determined by the integrated tags in the test cases. So the quality of test case selection largely depends on how well test engineers add relevant tags into the corresponding test cases; and 3) our methodology cannot deal with test case selection when test cases are bound to requirements and/or components at early stage (e.g., design and development), which requires further investigation for our proposed methodology.

6.2   Questionnaire-Based Study

We conducted a questionnaire-based study to solicit the views of the test engineers who were directly involved in the development of FM_T and CFM_T based. The questionnaire was conducted based on the reporting template defined by Wohlin [16].

Planning and Design. The FM_T and CFM_T have been designed together with the test engineers, and CFM_T can be built automatically using the IPT tool (CFM_T may be built manually in other contexts). So it is essential to solicit opinions from the industrial people about their experience for the FM_T and CFM_T, which is the main objective of this questionnaire. This questionnaire consists of two parts (i.e., FM_T and CFM_T) and the questions here were either multiple choices or required responses on a five-point Likert Scale. Notice that all relevant four people from the current testing team working with us have participated and filled out the questionnaire. Among the four participants, two of them are test managers and the other two are test engineers. Moreover, three of them have been working on Saturn for more than 5 years (the other one has been working for 2 years) and all of them have been involved into the discussion of our proposed methodology for at least five meetings.

Results and Analysis for FM_T. The objective of this section is to solicit the views of the participants on FM_T based on questions QA1-QA5 (Table 2).

Table 2. Responses to the questions related with FM_T*

Question	Strongly agree	Agree	No opinion	Disagree	Strongly disagree
QA1	0	4	0	0	0
QA2	1	3	0	0	0
QA3	2	2	0	0	0
QA4	2	2	0	0	0
QA5	2	1	1	0	0

*QA1: It is easy to understand the notations of FM_T. *QA2:* FM_T is sufficient to represent all functionalities of a VCS product line. *QA3:* It is easy to understand and use the provided tool for building FM_T. *QA4:* It is easy to build and revise a FM_T for a VCS product line. *QA5:* The functionalities of a VCS product line do not change significantly.

The objective of QA1 was to assess the difficulty of understanding the notations of FM_T since industrial people are not usually familiar with modeling notations. For QA1, all four participants agreed. QA2 was asked to determine the sufficiency of FM_T notations for capturing the variabilities for Saturn. For QA2, 1 participant strongly agreed and 3 participants agreed. QA3 and QA4 were designed to solicit the opinions of participants in terms of required effort for building and maintaining the FM_T using a provided commercial tool called Pure::Variants (P::V). For QA3 and QA4, 2 participants strongly agreed and 2 participants agreed. The objective of QA5 was to confirm whether the frequency of changes in functionalities of the Saturn since the FM_T is built manually and frequent and significant changes in functionalities do not warrant the use of FM_T. For QA5, 2 participants strongly agreed, 1 participant agreed and 1 participant had no opinion.

Based on the above results, we conclude that the test engineers have already good understanding of FM_T notations and it is agreed the notations are sufficient to model testing functionalities of Saturn. Moreover, the FM_T is easy to build and maintain. Notice that a version of FM_T has already been used by the test engineers in Cisco.

Results and Analysis for CFM_T. This section consisted of four questions QB1-QB4 (Table 3), which were designed to solicit the participants' views about CFM_T.

QB1 and QB2 were asked to determine if notations of CFM_T is easy to understand and if the notations are sufficient to represent test case structure of the repository. For QB1 and QB2, 1 participant strongly agreed and 3 participants agreed. QB3 and QB4 were asked to assess the easiness of obtaining the input (Section 5) for the IPT tool to build CFM_T with restrictions automatically. For QB3 and QB4, two participants strongly agreed, 1 participant agreed and 1 participant had no opinion.

Based on the above results, we can conclude that test engineers find the notations of CFM_T sufficient to represent test case structure of the repository. Notice that in our current context, it may not be important for test engineers to know the notations of CFM_T since it is built automatically. However, in other contexts, a CFM_T may not be built automatically and then it would be important to know the opinions of test engineers about the notations of CFM_T. The results also show that the CFM_T can be built easily using the tool IPT and the test engineers are positive about adopting CFM_T in their current practice for test case selection.

Table 3. Responses to the questions related with CFM_T*

Question	Strongly agree	Agree	No opinion	Disagree	Strongly disagree
QB1	1	3	0	0	0
QB2	1	3	0	0	0
QB3	2	1	1	0	0
QB4	2	1	1	0	0

*QB1: It is easy to understand the notations of CFM_T for VCSs. *QB2:* A CFM_T is sufficient to represent test case structure. *QB3:* It is easy to obtain the XML file from test database for representing the overall test case structure. *QB4:* It is easy to obtain and add tags information into the XML file representing the overall test case structure.

Threats to Validity. One of the main external threats to validity of our questionnaire-based survey is that there were only four participants and thus the results cannot be generalized. However, it is important to mention that the testing group we are working comprises of four people and all of them answered the questionnaire. Of course, to generalize our results and methodology, we need to adopt our methodology to other testing groups in Cisco. Notice that our FM_T and the tool IPT are already being used by the current testing group working with us in Cisco.

7   Related Work

Software product line testing is a relatively new, but intense field of research since product line engineering has shown significant benefits [5, 17-19]. McGregor [5] presented a set of activities, which can be used to address testing individual assets and testing artifacts. Muccini [17] proposed associating regression testing with product line by comparing code execution with the architectural design. However, these works only provide guidelines and suggestions and do not provide any systematic and automated test case selection process.

Comparing our work with regression testing, regression test selection aims at identifying a set of relevant test cases when changes are made to existing software [8]. Various types of such techniques are proposed in the literature, but mostly around the following two aspects: selection based on code changes [20-22] and selection based on specification changes [23, 24]. In addition, several thorough survey papers have been published in the literature [7, 8]. Although techniques for regression test selection have been evaluated in many previous works [25-27], there is no enough evidence to prove that these techniques still work well if being adapted in the context of product line. In our process, effort is spent on building reasonable models for product line and the structure of test cases, and making links between them. In contrast to regression testing, where focus is on testing changed functionality of an existing software system, our work is applicable when a new product is to be tested.

Our main objective is to perform test case selection automatically thereby reducing the selecting effort using FM and CFM in the context of product line. To the best of our knowledge, existing works have not covered such an objective: applying FM and CFM in product line for supporting automated selection of test cases in practice.

8   Conclusion and Future Work

In this paper, we proposed a product line modeling methodology for automated test case selection with the aims of reducing selection effort at the same time covering all required test functionalities. The methodology consists of the following main parts: 1) defining a Feature Model for Testing (FM_T) to model a product line for testing; 2) defining a Component Family Model for Testing (CFM_T) to model the test structure of test cases in the repository; and 3) linking CFM_T and FM_T via restrictions. With our methodology, test engineers only need to perform selection of features in FM_T and the related test cases can be chosen automatically from the repository.

We evaluated our methodology with two means. First, we applied our methodology to the Saturn product line of Videoconferencing Systems developed by Cisco Systems, Inc, Norway and performed test case selection for its four products. The results showed that the effort such as selection time can be reduced significantly at the same time all required testing functionalities can be covered for testing a product as compared with the current manual process at Cisco. Second, we conducted a questionnaire-based study to solicit the views of our proposed methodology from test engineers at Cisco. The results showed that the test engineers are very positive about adapting our methodology in their current practice.

In the future, we plan to evaluate our methodology in other product lines. We also want to conduct a thorough effectiveness analysis for test case selection between our methodology and current manual process. Moreover, we plan to link FM_T with behavior models (e.g., UML state machines) to generate new test cases that have high fault detection.

Acknowledgements. The work reported in this paper is funded by the Norwegian Research Council under the research-based innovation scheme (SFI) in the Certus Center hosted by Simula Research Laboratory. We would like to thank Marius Christian Liaaen and his group (Cisco Systems, Inc. Norway) for providing us the detailed case study and thorough discussions.

References

1. Benavides, D., Segura, S., Cortés, A.R.: Automated analysis of feature models 20 years later. A literature review. Information Systems (35), 615–636 (2010)
2. Czarnecki, K., Kim, C., Kalleberg, K.: Feature models are views on ontologies. In: Proceedings of the International Software Product Line Conference, pp. 41–51 (2006)
3. Ali, S., Yue, T., Briand, L.C., Walawege, S.: A product line modeling and configuration methodology to support model-based testing: an industrial case study. In: Proceedings of the ACM International Conference on Model Driven Engineering Languages and Systems (MODELS), pp. 726–742 (2012)
4. Wang, S., Ali, S., Tao, Y.: Product Line Modeling and Configuration Methodology using Feature Model for Supporting Model-Based Testing. Simula Research Laboratory. Technical Report 2012-24 (2013)
5. McGregor, J.: Testing a Software Product Line. Technical Report. CMU/SEI-2001-TR-022. Software Engineering Institute, Carnegie Mellon University, Pittsburgh, Pennsylvania (2001)
6. Engström, E.: Regression Test Selection and Product Line System Testing. In: Proceedings of Third International Conference on Software Testing, Verification and Validation (ICST), pp. 512–515 (2010)
7. Engström, E., Runeson, P., Skoglund, M.: A systematic review on regression test selection techniques. Information and Software Technology (IST) 52(1), 14–30 (2010)
8. Yoo, S., Harman, M.: Regression testing minimization, selection and prioritization: a survey. Software: Testing, Verification and Reliability 22(2), 67–120 (2012)
9. http://www.cisco.com
10. Cisco Systems: Cisco telepresence codec c90, Data sheet (2010), http://www.cisco.com
11. Wang, S., Gotlieb, A., Liaaen, M., Briand, L.C.: Automatic selection of test execution plans from a Video Conference System Product Line. In: Proceedings of the ACM MODELS Workshop VARiability for You (VARY 2012), pp. 32–37 (2012)
12. Beuche, D., Papajewski, H., Schröder-Preikschat, W.: Variability management with feature models. Science of Computer Programming 53(3), 333–352 (2004)
13. Pure systems GmbH: Variant management with pure:variants. Technical white paper (2006), http://web.pure-systems.com
14. Pure systems GmbH: Pure:Variants User's Guide (2011), http://web.pure-systems.com
15. Wang, S., Ali, S., Gotlieb, A.: Minimizing Test Suites in Software Product Lines Using Weighted-based Genetic Algorithms. Simula Research Laboratory. Technical Report 2012-25 (2013)
16. Wohlin, C., Runeson, P., Host, M., Ohlsson, M.C., Regnell, B., Wesslen, A.: Experimentation in Software Engineering. Springer (2012)
17. Muccini, H., Van Der Hoek, A.: Towards Testing Product Line Architectures. Electronic Notes in Theoretical Computer Science 82(6), 99–109 (2003)
18. Uzuncaova, E., Garcia, D., Khurshid, S., Batory, D.: Testing software product lines using incremental test generations. In: Proceedings of the IEEE International Symposium on Software Reliability Engineering (ISSRE), pp. 249–258 (2008)
19. Nebut, C., Le Traon, Y., Jézéquel, J.M.: System Testing of Product Lines: From Requirements to Test Cases. Software Product Lines. In: Research Issues in Engineering and Management, pp. 447–477. Springer (2006)

20. Chen, Y.F., Rosenblum, D.S., Vo, K.P.: Test tube: a system for selective regression testing. In: Proceedings of IEEE International Conference on Software Engineering (ICSE), Los Alamitos, CA, USA, pp. 211–220 (1994)
21. Hartmann, J., Robson, D.J.: Techniques for selective revalidation. IEEE Software 7(1), 31–36 (1990)
22. Harrold, M.J., Souffa, M.L.: An incremental approach to unit testing during maintenance. In: Proceedings of IEEE International Conference on Software Maintenance (ICSM), pp. 362–367 (1988)
23. Orso, A., Harrold, M.J., Rosenblum, D., Rothermel, G., Soffa, M.L., Do, H.: Using component metacontent to support the regression testing of component-based software. In: Proceedings of IEEE International Conference on Software Maintenance (ICSM), pp. 716–725 (2001)
24. Chen, Y., Probert, R.L., Sims, D.P.: Specification-based regression test selection with risk analysis. In: Proceedings of Conference of the Centre for Advanced Studies on Collaborative Research. IBM Press (2002)
25. Bible, J., Rothermel, G., Rosenblum, D.S.: A comparative study of coarse- and fine-grained safe regression test-selection techniques. ACM Transactions on Software Engineering and Methodology 10(2), 149–183 (2001)
26. Graves, T.L., Harrold, M.J., Kim, J.M., Porter, A., Rothermel, G.: An empirical study of regression test selection techniques. ACM Transactions on Software Engineering and Methodology 10(2), 184–208 (2001)
27. Mansour, N., Bahsoon, R., Baradhi, G.: Empirical comparison of regression test selection algorithms. The Journal of Systems and Software 57(1), 79–90 (2001)

Customizable Model Migration Schemes for Meta-model Evolutions with Multiplicity Changes*

Gabriele Taentzer[2,1], Florian Mantz[1], Thorsten Arendt[2], and Yngve Lamo[1]

[1] Høgskolen i Bergen, Norway
{fma,yla}@hib.no
[2] Philipps-Universität Marburg, Germany
{arendt,taentzer}@informatik.uni-marburg.de

Abstract. Modeling languages tailored to specific application domains promise to increase the productivity and quality of model-driven software development. Nevertheless due to, for example, evolving requirements, modeling languages, and their meta-models evolve which means that existing models have to be migrated accordingly. In our approach, such co-evolutions are specified as related graph transformations ensuring well-typed model migration results. Model migrations are specified by transformation rules that can be automatically deduced from given meta-model evolution rules and further customized to special needs. Up to now, meta-model constraints have not been taken into account. In this paper, we extend our approach to handle multiplicity constraints and illustrate this extension using several examples.

Keywords: meta-model evolution, model migration, graph transformation.

1 Introduction

Model-driven engineering [10] (MDE) is a software engineering discipline which raises the level of abstraction by using models as primary artifacts. In particular, domain-specific modeling languages (DSMLs) promise to increase productivity and quality of software development. Developers can focus on their essential tasks while repetitive and technology-dependent artifacts are automatically generated by transformations specified by experts in these areas. To keep this high level of abstraction, modeling languages have to evolve together with the evolving practice and understanding of target domains. However, this often causes problems since existing models and further language-dependent documents need to co-evolve with their languages (see. Fig. 1).

This migration challenge has been studied in different approaches to (partially) automate the tedious and error-prone process of model co-evolution, that

---

* This work was partially funded by NFR project 194521 (FORMGRID).

A. Moreira et al. (Eds.): MODELS 2013, LNCS 8107, pp. 254–270, 2013.

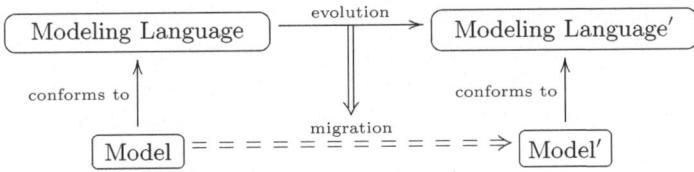

Fig. 1. Model co-evolution: Modeling language evolution and model migration

is, meta-model evolution together with the migration of all their instance models, see for example [7,12,22], and [26]. However, constraints have been mostly neglected.

In this paper, we present an approach to model co-evolution that can deal with multiplicity changes and with the insertion of obligatory classes and associations. We show how rule-based model migration specifications can be deduced from meta-model evolutions such that multiplicity constraints are not violated. While the deduction of rule-based migration specifications with respect to structural meta-model evolutions has been considered in our earlier works [26,19,18], we focus on multiplicity changes here. However, a complete model migration specification may cover structure and type migrations followed by specification parts that solve multiplicity constraint violations. All specification parts are rule-based: While structure and type migrations of models are performed first, multiplicity constraint violations are solved thereafter step-by-step. Model migrations with respect to multiplicity changes do not have to be developed manually in general, but can be generated. However, we will illustrate by an example that generated migration rules are not always optimal and may be subject to customization.

Allowing arbitrary multiplicity changes, it can happen that the multiplicities of an evolved meta-model are not finitely satisfiable, i.e. that there is no finite instance model satisfying all multiplicity constraints of its meta-model. To check finite satisfiability of meta-models, we can automatically generate a system of inequalities from all the given multiplicity constraints and can check if it is solvable. Each inequality assertion formulates the possible range of objects allowed in a given role. If an system of inequalities is not finitely satisfiable after a meta-model evolution, a subsequent model migration does not make sense, hence the developer should change corresponding meta-model evolution steps such that finite satisfiability can be preserved. It has been shown in [25] that each finite instance model of a given meta-model can be generated in finitely many transformation steps if the meta-model is finitely satisfiable. We use this fundamental result to argue that model migrations are also possible in finitely many steps resulting in models without multiplicity violations. Furthermore, we show how such consistency-preserving migration specifications can be automatically deduced from meta-model evolutions.

Throughout a meta-model evolution, it can happen that associations are refined by associations having subclasses as types of their ends. MOF [20] offers the feature "subsets" for this purpose. Dealing mainly with multiplicity changes here, we have to clarify how multiplicity constraints at "super" associations may be refined to constraints at "sub" associations. The deduction of model migration specifications has to be adapted to handle such association inheritance since this feature will require a new kind of multiplicity constraints. If association inheritance is not expressible in a chosen meta-model approach such as EMOF (used by the Eclipse Modeling Framework [8]), such constraints have to be specified in a different way, e.g. by OCL [21].

The rest of this paper is structured as follows: The next section introduces a small example evolution scenario based on activity models. Section 3 explains our approach to co-evolution handling multiplicity changes. We conclude with a consideration of related work and final remarks.

2   An Example Evolution Scenario

In the following, a concrete evolution scenario that focuses on multiplicity changes is given: We start with a simple activity meta-model (see Figure 2) where the only constraint is that each transition has one source and one target activity. Then we refine this meta-model to produce a meta-model that ensures well-structured activity models. However, models conforming to the resulting meta-model can still be ill-structured with respect to additional constraints.

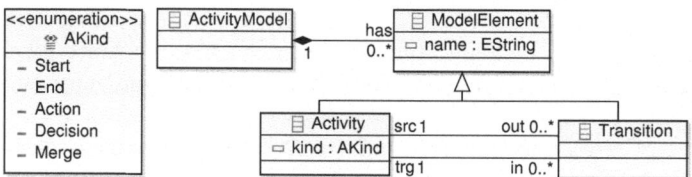

Fig. 2. A meta-model for simple activity models

In Figure 3, the following evolution steps have been performed: The enumeration AKind (activity kind) has been replaced by 5 subclasses of Activity. Associations between Activity and Transition are refined for all introduced subclasses of activity using association inheritance (indicated by subsets of roles). New associations start and end have been introduced to make Start and End activities explicitly navigable from the ActivityModel.

Due to space limitations, we do not go into details with respect to these evolution changes but refer to meta-model evolution rules and model migrations changes presented in our earlier work [26,19,18]. Furthermore, the following multiplicity changes on associations have been performed:

1. The minimal ActivityModel consists of a Start and an End activity with a Transition in between. Therefore the lower bound of the role has is changed to 3 model elements.

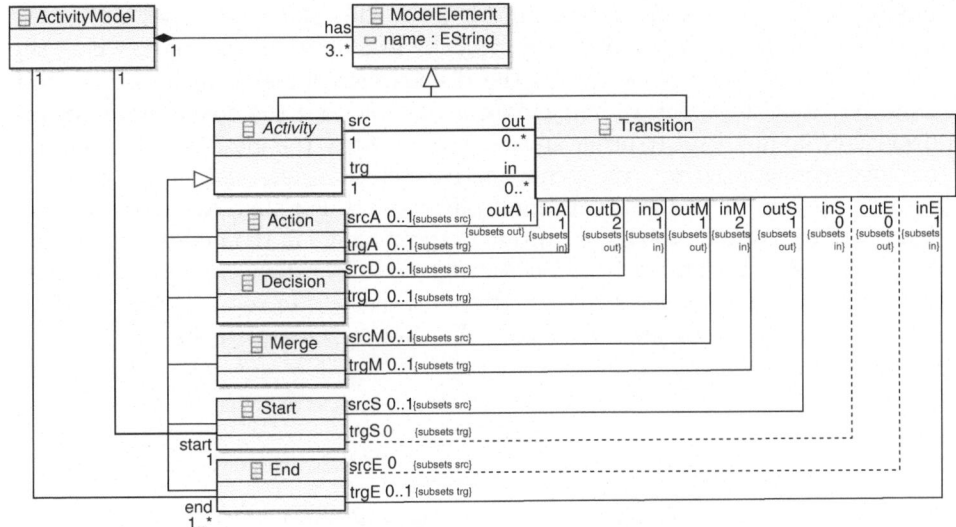

Fig. 3. Evolved meta-model for activity models

2. Association end start gets multiplicity [1..1] so that each ActivityModel requires exactly one Start activity. Association end end gets multiplicity [1..*] so that each ActivityModel has at least one end activity.
3. Class Activity becomes abstract.
4. All multiplicities ending at Transition or a subclass of Activity are refined. Due to multiplicity changes, Start activities are not allowed to have incoming transitions, and respectively, End activities are not allowed to have outgoing transitions anymore. Incoming and outgoing transitions of Action, Decision, and Merge activities are required to be exactly one or two. Multiplicities of refined src and trg roles are generalized to [0..1] to allow transitions to still be binary.

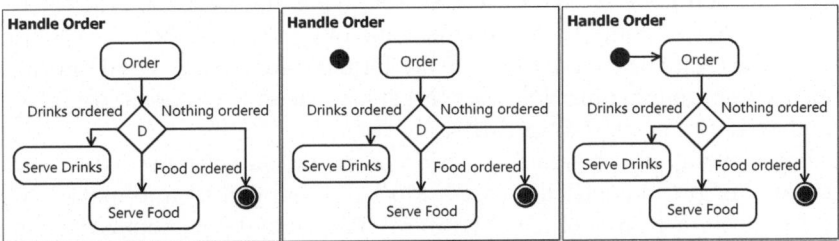

Fig. 4. An example activity model before (left), model after the first (center), and after the second migration (right)

Model migration is performed by the stepwise application of migration rules. Figure 4 shows two migration steps of a simple example activity model. The left model conforms to the meta-model in Figure 2. This model describes how orders are placed in a restaurant. A waiter typically asks waiting customers what they like to drink. After he has served the drinks, customers typically order food. However, sometimes the waiter arrives at a table and the customers have not decided or do not want to order anything more. After the meta-model evolution, activity models need to have a **Start** activity since a new association with role "start" has been introduced with multiplicity [1..1]. For this reason, the missing **Start** activity is added to the restaurant activity model in the middle of Figure 4. Furthermore, associations between **Activity** and **Transition** are refined and the multiplicity of outS' is set to [1..1]. Hence, the newly introduced **Start** activity needs to have an outgoing transition. We choose "Order" to be the target of this new transition since it is the only activity that does not have any incoming transition yet.

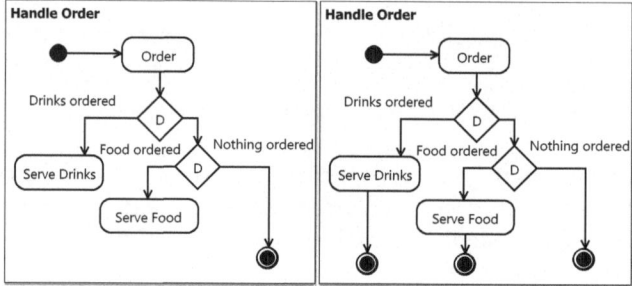

Fig. 5. An example activity model after the fourth migration (two snapshots)

Furthermore, all activity kinds are replaced by subclasses and models are re-typed accordingly. (Since all migrations are shown at the concrete syntax only, these changes relating the abstract syntax only, are not shown.) Finally, all associations running between these new subclasses and class **Transition** are refined. In particular, **Decision** activities are allowed to have two outgoing transitions only. If a new **Decision** node is introduced, several transitions can be redirected (see Figure 5). Since outgoing transitions become obligatory for **Action** activities in addition, it is required that actions "Serve Drinks" and "Serve Food" need to be extended by outgoing transitions. As targets for these transitions, we introduce new **End** activities since they suit best.

In the following, we present a selection of migration rules needed to perform the example migrations just discussed. Most of them can be automatically generated from the meta-model (see Figure 6). They may be customized to special needs. Migration rules may be equipped with priorities to perform a simple control flow on rule applications. Usually, customized rules get a higher priority than directly deduced ones. Note that all these migration rules are denoted in concrete syntax where bold parts indicate newly created elements. Two kinds of application conditions are used: The non-existence of patterns is denoted by the pattern preceded by "NOT" while all-quantified formulas are introduced by "FORALL". Each all-quantified formula has a premise and a conclusion introduced by "EXISTS".

Rule "Increase lower bound has" is a deduced migration rule to handle a lower bound violation. Throughout the evolution, the lower bound of association end has has been increased to 3. The rule creates a new Start activity if there are not already three model elements in the model. Similar rules are needed to create other kinds of activities. On the right of Figure 6, rule "Increase lower bound outD" adds one outgoing transition (without activity) if its Decision node does not have two outgoing transitions already. Rule "Decrease upper bound outD" handles the upper bound violation. Decision nodes are restricted to exactly two outgoing transitions. If a Decision node has three outgoing transitions, one is detached. On the left of Figure 6, the rule "Decrease upper bound outD 2" is shown being customized and added by the migration designer. It specifies a Decision node being added so that an equivalent structure of Decision nodes is produced. Therefore, two transitions are moved to a newly connected Decision node. Such migration rules that introduce equivalent structures, cannot be deduced automatically but have to be added manually to the derived rule set. Manually added rules are assigned a higher priority since they should be preferred over automatically deduced ones. In the bottom of Figure 6, two further migration rules that ensure lower bounds are shown. The left one adds an outgoing transition to each Action activity not having one. The right rule adds an End activity such that a transition gets a target. Their application conditions check that new elements are added only if there are no other "free" transitions or End activities available.

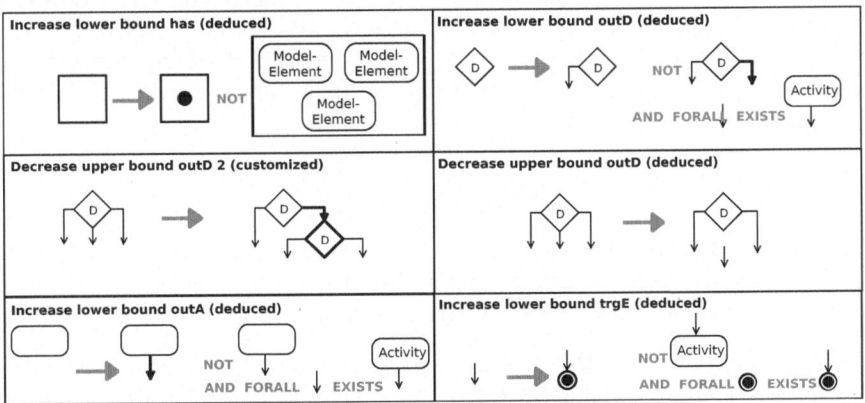

Fig. 6. Example migration rules

3   Co-evolutions with Multiplicity Changes

In the following, we present an approach to meta-model evolution that can deal with type structure evolutions as well as with multiplicity-related changes. We consider multiplicity-related meta-model evolutions, their deduced migration specifications as well as potential customizations in detail. If the evolved meta-model is finitely satisfiable, the deduced model migration specifications can migrate models in finitely many steps resulting in correctly typed models satisfying all multiplicity constraints.

3.1   Finitely Satisfiable Meta-model with Multiplicities

Allowing meta-models with arbitrary multiplicities, it may happen that multiplicities are chosen such that no finite model can fulfill them. In the literature [6,4], it is shown that this kind of finite satisfiability of meta-models can be checked by solving a system of in-equalities. After a meta-model evolution that may include multiplicity changes, we first have to check that the resulting meta-model is still finitely satisfiable. For the resulting meta-model, we deduce corresponding model migration schemes. To check if a meta-model has finite models, we use a reasoning technique for UML class diagrams [6,4]. This technique deduces a linear system of inequalities from all multiplicities. (We restrict attention to binary associations here.) A meta-model MM with multiplicities is called *finitely satisfiable* if the following condition is satisfied:

Given a meta-model MM, an system of inequalities is built over C, A, and R being variable sets for all classes, associations, and roles in MM correspondingly named. For all association variables a in A with role variables $r1, r2 \in R$, function $rtype : R \to C$ yields the class variable of each role variable and $mult : R \to (\mathbb{N} \times \mathbb{N} \cup \{*\})$ is defined by $mult(r1) = [k, l]$, and $mult(r2) = [m, n]$ with $k, m \in \mathbb{N}$, $l, n \in \mathbb{N} \cup \{*\}$, $k < l$, and $m < n$ according to MM. Then, we get the following equations in I

$$i \times rtype(r) \leq assoc$$

$$assoc \leq j \times rtype(r) \text{ if } j \neq *$$

$\forall (i, j, r, assoc) \in \{(k, l, r1, a), (m, n, r2, a), (k, l, r1, \sum_{a_s \in A_s}), (m, n, r2, \sum_{a_s \in A_s})\}$ with A_S being the variable set of association a and all associations subsetting it. I has to be solvable such that all variables in $C \cup A$ are positive.

Example 1. We now show the system of inequalities for the final meta-model in our evolution scenario given in Figure 3. Since associations are not named explicitly, their names are assembled by concatenating explicitly given role names. For example, the multiplicities of has require that an activity model must have at least 3 model elements. It is translated to inequality assertion $has \geq 3ActModel$. Note that the last two equations below are included due to association inheritance.

$$ModelElem = has \geq 3ActModel$$
$$Start = start = ActModel$$
$$End = end$$
$$Start = srcSoutS \leq Transition$$
$$End = trgEinE \leq Transition$$

$$Action = srcAoutA \leq Transition$$
$$Action = trgAinA \leq Transition$$
$$2Decision = srcDoutD \leq Transition$$
$$Decision = trgDinD \leq Transition$$
$$Merge = srcMoutM \leq Transition$$
$$2Merge = trgMinM \leq Transition$$

$$Transition = srcout + srcSoutS + srcAoutA + srcDoutD + srcMoutM$$
$$Transition = trgin + trgEinE + trgAinA + trgDinD + trgMinM$$

The complexity to solve such a system of inequalities is EXPTIME-complete in general. However, the exponentiality depends on the maximum number of classes involved in the same generalization hierarchy which is typically not very large (see also [6]).

3.2 Model Migration Process

Our approach comprises the deduction of rule-based model migration specifications from meta-model evolution rules applied to given meta-models. Meta-model evolution rules may contain changes of the type structure as well as multiplicity changes. Correspondingly, a model migration specification may cover type adaptations followed by specification parts that solve multiplicity constraint violations. In [27,18] a variety of evolution rules are presented being concerned with type adaptations e.g. inserting new classes, moving properties, and merging of classes. First, such type adaptations are performed in parallel on all occurrences in a given model yielding a model that conforms to the new meta-model (wrt. typing and structure). Thereafter, all multiplicity constraints of the evolved meta-model are checked and violations are solved by applying model transformations step-by-step. (See Figure 7 for an overview.)

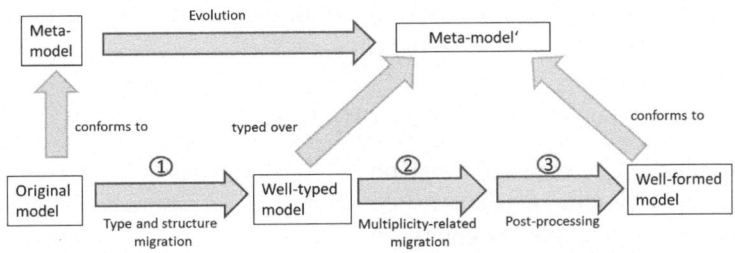

Fig. 7. Three phase approach to model migration

Model migration respecting multiplicity changes can be performed by the following process:

1. *Type and structure migrations* are performed without considering multiplicity constraints. In [26,18], we formalize meta-model and model co-evolutions

by co-transformations based on algebraic graph transformation [9] and show that migrated models are always well-typed over the evolved meta-model (not taking any multiplicity constraint into account).

2. *Model migration with respect to multiplicity changes* are performed. In the following, we will show for each migration rule that resulting models fulfill upper bounds but not necessarily lower bounds. If custom migration rules are added, they have to satisfy well-formed properties to ensure that the whole rule system terminates and leads to models fulfilling upper bounds. These well-formedness properties comprise the following: Given a custom rule, its right-hand side fulfills all upper bounds and does not introduce a new match of a migration rule applied in this phase. Custom rules are prioritized with respect to deduced migration rules. It can be shown that the application of the whole rule set terminates and solves all upper bound violations.

3. *Post-processing with respect to all lower bounds* of the given meta-model shall yield migrated models that fulfill all bounds. Given a model that fulfills all upper bounds, post-processing rules are applied as long as possible. We will argue that post-processing terminates and resulting models satisfy all lower bounds. In [25], an instance-generation algorithm is presented that takes a meta-model with arbitrary multiplicities (but without association inheritance) and generates instance models that conform to this meta-model. The generation process is performed by three layers: (1) creation of objects, (2) creation of links such that lower bounds are fulfilled, and (3) generation of further links such that upper bounds are still fulfilled. In this post-processing phase, we apply the rules of layer (2) as long as possible to produce models fulfilling all lower bounds. To argue that resulting models fulfill all lower bounds we first have to show that models before post-processing can be created by rules of layers (1) and (2). In layer (1), all objects of such a model are created. Since all upper bounds are satisfied in models before post-processing, rules of layer (2) are enough to create the necessary links. If rules of layer (2) are still applicable, not all lower bounds are fulfilled. In Theorem 1 in [25], it is shown that after having finished layer (2), all multiplicity constraints are fulfilled.

3.3   Increase Lower Bound of Multiplicity

Having decided to increase the lower bound of a multiplicity, dependent models have to be checked again and potentially extended. In Figure 8, a corresponding meta-model evolution rule is depicted in concrete syntax. All characters can be considered as parameters to be instantiated by concrete names and values. The meta-model evolution rule increases lower bound k to $k + x$.

Default model migration rules are shown in Figure 9. They are presented at the abstract syntax level where again all characters have to be considered as parameters to be set. Migrations can go in different directions: The conservative solution looks for a B-object that does not yet have more than n links going to A-objects. In that case, this object can be used as a target for a missing link. The corresponding migration rule can be found on the left of Figure 9. Alternatively, a new B-object is created and linked, as shown on the right of Figure 9. Both rules (and further ones later on) are presented in a visual syntax being similar to the visual syntax of Henshin [3], a model transformation language for EMF models. The left and right-hand sides of a rule are integrated in one graph where the left-hand side consists of all preserved and deleted objects and links while the right-hand side contains all preserved and newly created items. Two kinds of application conditions are shown: In the left rule, it is forbidden that n A-objects are already linked to a considered B-object. In the right rule, we check if all B-objects are already linked to n A-objects. (Note that containment links are not created for new objects, since they do not directly belong to the migration. Instead, they are created by post-processing rules that take care of lower bounds.)

These migration rules are designed such that upper bounds are not violated. Moreover, the application of these rules terminates when enough new links from A-objects to new or existing B-objects have been created, i.e. all A-objects are connected to at least $k + x$ B-objects. Since one more of such links is available after each rule application and since the number of A-objects in a given model is finite and not increased by these rules, the rule application terminates. (However, the lower bounds with respect to B-objects might not be always fulfilled. Such violations are solved in the post-processing phase.) If custom migration rules shall be used, well-formedness properties have to be shown also for them (see above).

Fig. 8. Meta-model evolution rule "Increase lower bound"

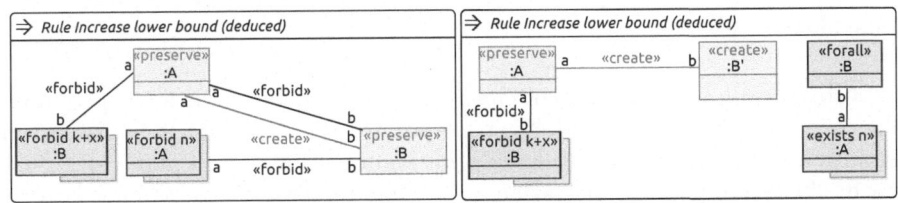

Fig. 9. Default model migration rules "Increase lower bound"

After having applied all migration rules as long as possible, lower bounds of further links may be violated. Hence, similar rules have to be applied to cover also those cases. The only difference is that lower bounds of other roles have not changed, hence we have $x = 0$ in those cases. These rules are called post-processing rules, since they do not perform the proper migration but complete it such that all multiplicity constraints are fulfilled after migration. (For further information on post-processing rules see Section 3.7.)

Example 2. In our example scenario (see Section 2), the lower bound of the multiplicity of role has is increased to 3 meaning that an activity model has to have at least three model elements, namely a Start and an End activity as well as a Transition in between. Generated migration rules create new model elements and add them to a given activity model if it has less than 3 elements. The rule selection is non-deterministic in general meaning that model elements of any kinds may be created. See e.g. the migration rule in Figure 10 where a new Start activity is added to an activity model if it does not already have three activities. Note that this migration rule is an instantiation of the right rule in Figure 9 where "A" corresponds to ActivityModel, "B" corresponds to ModelElement, "B' " corresponds to Start, $k = 0$, and $k + x = 3$. (It is not exactly the abstract syntax rule of the one in the upper left corner of Figure 6 since the second pre-condition shown in Fig. 10 is missing there. However, since Start activities without container are not allowed from the very beginning, the second condition is not important and is left out in the concrete version). Two similar rules are deduced for "B' " equal to Transition and End. We may want to define priorities for rule applications: E.g. a Start activity shall be created and added if the activity model does not already have one. Moreover, lower bound constraints for outgoing transitions may be preferably solved by End activities since no new constraint violations are inserted. Since any sequence of rule applications does terminate and fulfill upper bounds, as argued above, such a priority does not change this result.

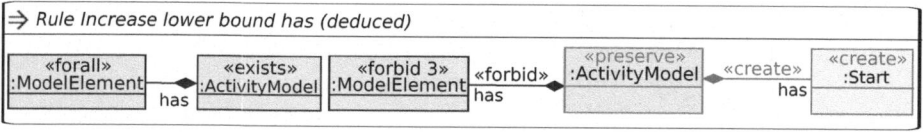

Fig. 10. Rule "Increase lower bound has" in abstract syntax (corresponding rule in concrete syntax in Figure 6)

Another example migration rule increasing a lower bound is shown in upper right corner of Figure 6, called "Increase lower bound outD". It is also an instantiation of the right-hand side rule in Figure 9 for $k = 0$ and $k + x = 2$. Two further examples for migration rules that increase lower bounds, are the two deduced migration rules in the bottom of Figure 6. In the left rule, Actions without outgoing transition are completed by a transition and in the right rule, a Transition without target is completed by an End activity. These two deduced migration rules increase the lower bounds of outA and of trgE.

3.4 Decrease upper Bound of Multiplicity

"Decrease upper bound" is another meta-model evolution that changes multiplicities and requires model migration. Figure 11 shows the corresponding meta-model evolution rule in concrete syntax. Again, characters have to be considered as parameters to be set. A special case is when the original multiplicity is $[i..*]$, i.e. does not specify an upper bound. Then, the evolution rule introduces a new upper bound constraint.

The default model migration is specified by the model migration rule in Figure 12. This rule is presented in abstract syntax where again all characters are meant to be parameters. This migration rule preserves l links and just deletes a link if there are more than l links. If the deduced rule does not suit well, there is the opportunity to specify custom migration rules with higher priority. All these migration rules are supposed to be applied as long as possible to finally fulfill the upper bound constraint. The application of the deduced migration rule terminates since it deletes links from A-objects as long as there are too many and does not create new ones to existing A-objects. Hence, the new upper bound of l is reached after finitely many steps. A custom rule fulfills the well-formedness properties, if it contains an upper bound violation on the left-hand side being solved on the right-hand side. As with deduced rules, we have to check that custom rules do not introduce new matches of themselves and of deduced migration rules. Then, the customized migration process would also terminate and would solve the corresponding upper bound violations. Thereafter, post-processing rules may be applied as long as possible to fulfill all lower bounds.

Fig. 11. Meta-model evolution rule "Decrease upper bound"

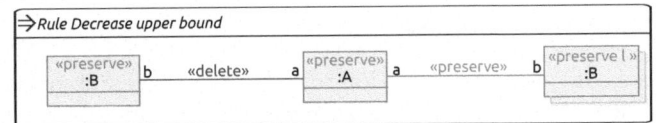

Fig. 12. Default model migration rule "Decrease upper bound"

Example 3. Figure 13 shows an instantiation of the deduced migration rule "Decrease upper bound" applied to role outD (that can be found in the meta-model shown in Figure 3). In this case, class "A" is bound to Decision, class "B" is bound to Transition, "b" is bound to outD, and $l = 2$. However, this solution is not optimal for our example meta-model since information would be lost. Automatically deduced migration rules may not show the desired result since the generator considers meta-model changes only. Therefore, a custom migration rule is needed here. The optimal one is shown in Figure 14. It divides a decision with three outgoing transitions into a cascade of two binary decisions. This rule fulfills the well-formedness properties since it shows an upper bound violation on the left and a solved situation on the right. Moreover, new matches of this rule and the deduced ones are not introduced. Similar rules can be deduced and customized for upper bound violations with respect to inD, outM, inM, outA, and inA.

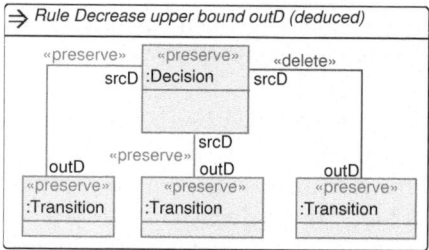

Fig. 13. Generated migration rule for decreasing the upper bound of outD (corresponding rule in concrete syntax in Figure 6)

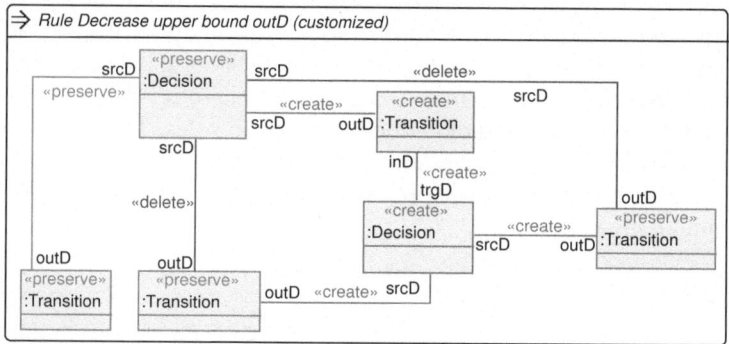

Fig. 14. Custom migration rule for decreasing the upper bound of outD (corresponding rule in concrete syntax in Figure 6)

3.5 Add Obligatory Association

Figure 15 shows a meta-model evolution rule that adds a new association between two existing classes. If its multiplicities have lower bounds larger than 0, this meta-model change causes model migrations. The deduced migration rule in Figure 16 creates a new link between an A-object and an object of type B if the A-object is not already linked to k B-objects and if the B-object is not already linked to n A-objects in corresponding roles. A second migration rule is needed which is analogous, replacing k by l and n by m (not shown). Moreover, it can happen that no more B-objects are allowed to be linked to an existing A-object, and vice versa. In these cases, two more migration rules are needed where one looks very similar to the right one in Figure 9 replacing $k + x$ by k.

Fig. 15. Meta-model evolution rule "Add obligatory association"

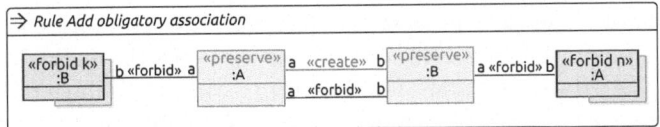

Fig. 16. Migration rule "Add obligatory association"

The other one handles the analogous case that no more A-objects may be linked to an existing B-object (not shown). These four rules are applied as long as possible. Since each of them creates a link, the number of links between A and B-objects increases until all A- and B-objects have enough links. Hence, there is only a finite number of applications possible. It has been shown in [25] that lower bounds can always be reached if the meta-model is finitely satisfiable. (Note that new A- and B-objects created during this migration phase might not have enough links to other objects. They have to be created in the post-processing phase.)

Example 4. In Figure 17, the migration rule in Fig. 16 is instantiated to activity models by setting "A" equal to ActivityModel, "B" to Start, "b" equal to start, and $k = n = 1$. Setting $l = m = 1$ would lead to the same instantiation.

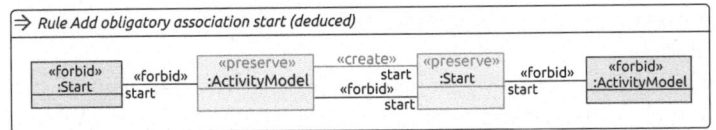

Fig. 17. Rule "Add obligatory association start" in abstract syntax

3.6 Further Multiplicity-Related Meta-model Evolutions

If lower and upper bounds of multiplicities are weakened, models are still well-formed and do not have to be migrated. This applies to the operations "Decrease lower bound" and "Increase upper bound". Furthermore, the operation "Add obligatory class" introduces a new multiplicity constraint, this operation is very similar to the operation "Add obligatory association". We do not go into details of these kinds of multiplicity-related co-evolutions. Furthermore, multiplicity changes at association loops are not considered explicitly in this paper.

3.7 Post-processing

After handling all upper bound violations, post-processing rules are applied to solve all remaining lower bound violations. Post-processing rules are very similar to the migration rules for "Add obligatory association"', i.e. four post-processing rules are deduced for each bound that differs from 0 and *. Since post-processing rules do not introduce any new upper bound conflict and the meta-model is finitely satisfiable, the post-processing phase always terminates and all lower bounds are fulfilled. If a super-association has more restricting multiplicity constraints than its sub-associations, additional pre-conditions have to be added to the post-processing rules. For example, a rule that creates a new trg-link between an existing Transition and an existing Action activity needs a negative application condition that forbids a trg-link from this transition to any activity, due to the [1..1]-multiplicity of role trg.

4   Related Work

The problem of co-evolving models and meta-models has been studied by several authors [24,12,7,22,26,19,16], surprisingly none of these works considers multiplicity constraints, except as pre-conditions that are checked before applying model transformation rules [17,12]. In [16], König et.al. use multiplicity constraints to decide which model elements shall be merged during model migration. In Flock [22], upper bound violations may be automatically handled by forgetting such links. Lower bound violations must be handled manually. In COPE [12], multiplicity constraints are used to e.g. check if an attribute can be moved along a reference. There is no further special support for model migrations in the context of multiplicity constraints.

Some work has been done on model transformations that respect constraints [23,17,5]. However, none of these approaches considers how to co-evolve models and meta-models.

Instance generation for meta-models has been considered using a variety of approaches, namely different kinds of grammars [1,13,14,25] or SAT/SMT solvers e.g., [11,15,2]. However, they have not been applied to model and meta-model co-evolution meaning that instance models are not deduced from scratch but have to be adapted to changed constraints. To migrate instances of the evolved meta-model we adapt the algorithm for instance-generating graph grammars that respects multiplicity constraints given in [25]. By our knowledge, this is the first work that deduces migration specifications for multiplicity changes, argues for their correctness in the sense of well-formed migration results, and allows customizations that preserves the validity of models.

5   Conclusion and Further Work

In this paper, we present a rule-based approach to model and meta-model co-evolution that respects multiplicity constraints. Several multiplicity-related meta-model changes with corresponding model migrations are considered. We show how migration rules can be automatically deduced from meta-model evolution rules such that they do not create new upper bound violations. Moreover, we argue that applying migration rules as long as possible leads to models satisfying all upper bounds. In a post-processing phase, further rules are applied to obtain models that also satisfy all lower bounds. An important assumption for this approach is the finite satisfiability of meta-models that ensures the existence of well-formed instance models. To allow flexible customizations without loosing the assurance that models are migrated to well-formed ones, we propose well-formedness properties for the customizing migration rules. The customization of migration rules is easier if they are presented on the abstract level. Since all migration rules are deduced along a fixed strategy, however, we assume that our approach can directly scale to larger models (which has to be evaluated in future work).

Model migration is specified by transformation rules, the given rules can be specified in the model transformation language Henshin [3]. In the future, a generator for rule-based migration specifications shall be developed to conduct larger case studies. Moreover, systematic case studies should be performed to get a clearer understanding of the potentials and limitations of this approach.

References

1. Alanen, M., Porres, I.: A relation between context-free grammars and meta object facility metamodels. Tech. Rep. 606, TUCS Turku Center for Computer Science (March 2003)
2. Anastasakis, K., Bordbar, B., Georg, G., Ray, I.: Uml2alloy: A challenging model transformation. In: Engels, G., Opdyke, B., Schmidt, D.C., Weil, F. (eds.) MOD-ELS 2007. LNCS, vol. 4735, pp. 436–450. Springer, Heidelberg (2007)
3. Arendt, T., Biermann, E., Jurack, S., Krause, C., Taentzer, G.: Henshin: Advanced Concepts and Tools for In-Place EMF Model Transformation. In: Petriu, D.C., Rouquette, N., Haugen, Ø. (eds.) MODELS 2010, Part I. LNCS, vol. 6394, pp. 121–135. Springer, Heidelberg (2010), http://www.eclipse.org/modeling/emft/henshin
4. Berardi, D., Cali, A., Calvanese, D., Giacomo, G.D.: Reasoning on UML Class Diagrams. Artifical Intelligence 168, 70–118 (2005)
5. Büttner, F., Bauerdick, H., Gogolla, M.: Towards Transformation of Integrity Constraints and Database States. In: DEXA 2005, pp. 823–828. IEEE (August 2005)
6. Cadoli, M., Calvanese, D., Mancini, T.: Finite satisfiability of UML class diagrams by Constraint Programming. In: Proc. of the 2004 International Workshop on Description Logics (DL 2004), vol. 104. CEUR-WS.org (2004)
7. Cicchetti, A., Di Ruscio, D., Eramo, R., Pierantonio, A.: Automating Co-evolution in Model-Driven Engineering. In: EDOC 2008, pp. 222–231. IEEE (2008)
8. Eclipse Modeling Framework: Project Web Site, http://www.eclipse.org/emf/
9. Ehrig, H., Ehrig, K., Prange, U., Taentzer, G.: Fundamentals of Algebraic Graph Transformation. Monographs in Theoretical Computer Science. Springer (2006)
10. Fowler, M.: Domain-Specific Languages. Addison-Wesley Professional (2010)
11. Gogolla, M., Bohling, J., Richters, M.: Validating UML and OCL Models in USE by Automatic Snapshot Generation. Software and Systems Modeling 4(4), 386–398 (2005)
12. Herrmannsdoerfer, M., Vermolen, S., Wachsmuth, G.: An Extensive Catalog of Operators for the Coupled Evolution of Metamodels and Models. In: Malloy, B., Staab, S., van den Brand, M. (eds.) SLE 2010. LNCS, vol. 6563, pp. 163–182. Springer, Heidelberg (2011)
13. Hoffmann, B., Minas, M.: Defining models - meta models versus graph grammars. ECEASST 29 (2010)

14. Hoffmann, B., Minas, M.: Generating instance graphs from class diagrams with adaptive star grammars. ECEASST 39 (2011)
15. Jackson, D.: Alloy: a lightweight object modelling notation. ACM Trans. Softw. Eng. Methodol. 11(2), 256–290 (2002)
16. König, H., Löwe, M., Schulz, C.: Model Transformation and Induced Instance Migration: A Universal Framework. In: Simao, A., Morgan, C. (eds.) SBMF 2011. LNCS, vol. 7021, pp. 1–15. Springer, Heidelberg (2011)
17. Lengyel, L., Levendovszky, T., Charaf, H.: Constraint Validation Support in Visual Model Transformation Systems. Acta Cybernetica 17(2), 339–357 (2005)
18. Mantz, F., Taentzer, G., Lamo, Y.: Well-formed Model Co-evolution with Customizable Model Migration (to appear in ECEASST)
19. Mantz, F., Taentzer, G., Lamo, Y.: Co-Transformation of Type and Instance Graphs Supporting Merging of Types with Retyping. In: GCM 2012, pp. 47–58 (September 2012), gcm2012.imag.fr/proceedingsGCM2012.pdf
20. Object Management Group: Meta-Object Facility Specification (January 2006), http://www.omg.org/spec/MOF/2.0/
21. Object Management Group: Object Constraint Language Specification (May 2006), http://www.omg.org/spec/OCL/2.0/
22. Rose, L., Kolovos, D., Paige, R.F., Polack, F.A.C.: Model Migration with Epsilon Flock. In: Tratt, L., Gogolla, M. (eds.) ICMT 2010. LNCS, vol. 6142, pp. 184–198. Springer, Heidelberg (2010)
23. Rutle, A., Rossini, A., Lamo, Y., Wolter, U.: A formal approach to the specification and transformation of constraints in MDE. JLAP 81(4), 422–457 (2012)
24. Sprinkle, J., Karsai, G.: A Domain-Specific Visual Language for Domain Model Evolution. Journal of Visual Languages and Computing 15(3-4), 291–307 (2004)
25. Taentzer, G.: Instance generation from type graphs with arbitrary multiplicities. ECEASST 47 (2012)
26. Taentzer, G., Mantz, F., Lamo, Y.: Co-Transformation of Graphs and Type Graphs With Application to Model Co-Evolution. In: Ehrig, H., Engels, G., Kreowski, H.-J., Rozenberg, G. (eds.) ICGT 2012. LNCS, vol. 7562, pp. 326–340. Springer, Heidelberg (2012)
27. Taentzer, G., Mantz, F., Lamo, Y.: Co-Transformation of Graphs and Type Graphs with Application to Model Co-Evolution: Long Version. Tech. rep., Dep. of Mathematics and Computer Science, University of Marburg, Germany (2012), www.uni-marburg.de/fb12/forschung/berichte/berichteinformtk

Fine-Grained Software Evolution
Using UML Activity and Class Models

Walter Cazzola[1], Nicole Alicia Rossini[1],
Mohammed Al-Refai[2], and Robert B. France[2]

[1] Computer Science Department, Università degli Studi di Milano, Italy
[2] Computer Science Department, Colorado State University, USA

Abstract. Modern software systems that play critical roles in society's infrastructures are often required to change at runtime so that they can continuously provide essential services in the dynamic environments they operate in. Updating open, distributed software systems at runtime is very challenging. Using runtime models as an interface for updating software at runtime can help developers manage the complexity of updating software while it is executing. In this work we describe an approach to updating Java software at runtime through the use of runtime models consisting of UML class and activity diagrams. Changes to models are turned into changes on Java source code, which is then propagated to the runtime system using the JavAdaptor technology. In particular, the presented approach permits in-the-small software changes, i.e., changes at the code statement level, as opposed to in-the-large changes, i.e., changes at the component level. We present a case study that demonstrates the major aspects of the approach and its use.

1 Motivation

The ability to perform updates on running systems is becoming a requirement for many software systems that play critical roles in society. Emerging cyberphysical systems such as smart grids, next-generation air-traffic control systems, and intelligent transportation systems must evolve after they are deployed if they are to continue to perform effectively in dynamically changing environments. Shutting down these systems to make a change is often not an option because loss or interruption of provided services could have a detrimental effect on the parts of society that rely on the services. Updating software at runtime is challenging and models that provide effective abstractions of runtime phenomenon can be used to manage the complexity [2].

Research on Models@RunTime (M@RT) is concerned with how abstractions of software implementations can be used at runtime to manage the complexity of making changes to software at runtime [2]. Current M@RT work tends to focus on how models can be used to support runtime adaptation in autonomous systems (i.e., in self-* systems) [19,12]. While M@RT research is dominated by work in the self-adaptation area, runtime models can be used to support other forms of runtime system evolution. In particular, runtime models can be interfaces for

A. Moreira et al. (Eds.): MODELS 2013, LNCS 8107, pp. 271–286, 2013.
© Springer-Verlag Berlin Heidelberg 2013

effecting changes on a software system while it is executing [8]. For example, a developer can modify a runtime model consisting of a class diagram to make changes in object attributes and references.

Runtime models can potentially be used to present the aspects of a running system that can be changed using abstractions that are understandable by a developer or that are more easily processed by a software change mechanism [8]. In many model-based self-adaptation approaches (e.g., see [1,6,9]) the models present the running system as a configuration of runtime components, and adaptation is often restricted to changes that can be effected by reconfiguring the component structure. We consider these approaches to be coursegrained because changes are restricted to adding and removing components and links between components. More fine-grained adaptation of a running system is limited by a lack of support in mainstream program development technologies (e.g., C/C++, C#, Java technologies) for dynamic update actions that involve dynamic object schema changes and substitution of an object of a class by a corresponding object of the modified class during execution (such substitution is typically treated as type mismatch and thus is not allowed in mainstream technologies).

In this contribution we describe a M@RT approach that supports runtime updates of Java programs by developers. In the approach, runtime models consisting of class and activity diagrams describe the aspects of the runtime structure and behavior that can be modified by a developer at runtime. Changes in the runtime models are formally related to changes in the running system, and thus changes to the models can be propagated to changes in the running system. This use of runtime models requires more fine-grained descriptions of changes than those typically used to support self-reconfiguration of running systems. In the proposed approach, JavAdaptor [18], a tool that provides support for performing dynamic update of Java programs at runtime, and that overcomes the limitations of the Java platform in this respect, provides the required fine-grained code changing facilities. Changes to the models are transformed to changes in the Java source code which are then effected on the running system using JavAdaptor.

In Sect. 2 we give an overview of how runtime updates are performed using the approach. A more detailed account of the model change operators and their mappings to code level change operators is given in Sect. 3 and 4 respectively. A demonstration case study is provided in Sect. 5, and results from an initial evaluation of the approach are described in Section 6. Related work is presented in Section 7, and we conclude with a discussion on further work in Section 8.

2   Architecture and Overview

Imagine we have a program running on a standard JVM and we need to update it without stopping it. The *Fine-Grained Adaptation* (FiGA) framework allows a developer to adapt his application by modifying UML diagrams and propagating the model changes to the source code. The change process is kept separate from

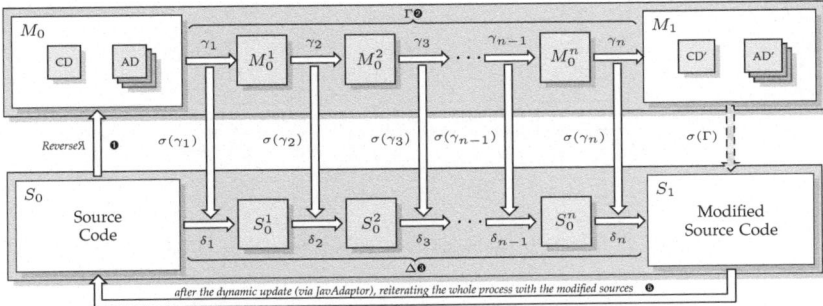

Fig. 1. Overview of the FiGA Approach

the running instance until the changes are ready to be compiled and loaded into the Java virtual machine, so as not to compromise the application service.

The FiGA approach is based on the JavAdaptor [18] tool, which can update a Java program during its execution without stopping it. JavAdaptor works at a low level, requiring a compiled version of the class to update as an input and a connection to the Java virtual machine in which the program is executing. Therefore, changes to the Java source code drive the application update. FiGA extends the JavAdaptor approach by replacing the source code with UML diagrams to drive the updating process. The process —depicted in Fig. 1— consists of five steps which can be repeated whenever the application needs to be updated.

Step 1: Model Generation. At the right abstraction level, models can be used to present aspects of a software program that can be changed in a manner that shields a developer from extraneous details in the source code, and thus helping them to better focus their development effort. The models, to drive the code modification, need to be as faithful as possible to the code and evolve with the code [3]. ReverseЯ [3] is used to generate —via reverse engineering driven by code annotations— the UML diagrams from the baseline source code. This ensures that the model used to make changes is a faithful representation of the running program at any time. Models are also generated the first time a change is made to the running system to avoid the well-known abstraction gap between design models and code [15] whose presence would jeopardize the feasibility of the whole approach. As a side effect, the use of ReverseЯ makes the FiGA approach usable when design models are not available.

Step 2: Model Modification. Models provide a view on the application that can be used to run the adaptation; a human operator will change the model to trigger the evolution process. Changes are expressed as a sequence of elementary operations —where the elementary term refers to the extent each change has on the model. Examples of elementary operations are an operation for removing a field in a class diagram and an operation for adding an action node in an activity diagram. More complex changes are yielded by applying several elementary operations. An elementary change does not necessarily leave the system in a consistent state. Checking consistency of the system is left to the human

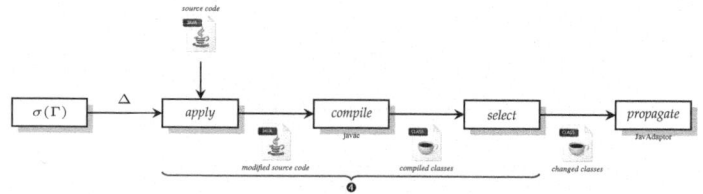

Fig. 2. How the Adaptation Takes Place in FiGA

operator exactly as it is left to the developer when writing code. These operators just describe the semantics of the change and are used to univocally map the model changes to code changes; all the model changes are performed via the preferred modeling tool[1] and mapped onto the change operators via modeling differencing [23,13].

Step 3: Adaptation Process. Let S_0 represent source code for a running Java program and M_0 its UML model. Let M_1 represent the model you get after adapting M_0 and S_1 represent the application source code we get after propagating model changes to S_0.

Let be $\boxplus$ the *change sequencing operator*: $M_1 = M_0 \boxplus \Gamma$, where Γ is a composition of change operations expressed with model operators γ_i, each representing an elementary change such that $\Gamma = \gamma_1 \boxplus \gamma_2 \boxplus \cdots \boxplus \gamma_i \boxplus \cdots \boxplus \gamma_n$. A detailed definition of the γ_i operators is given in Sect. 3.

Similarly, we define Δ as those changes necessary to adapt the source code to the system modeled by M_1 such that $S_1 = S_0 \boxplus \Delta$ where Δ is obtained by composing the single changes (δ_i) on the code: $\Delta = \delta_1 \boxplus \delta_2 \boxplus \cdots \boxplus \delta_i \boxplus \cdots \boxplus \delta_n$.

So Γ and Δ represent the same set of changes but expressed on two different layers of abstraction: the former on the model, the latter on the source code. The σ function maps the changes on the model to the corresponding changes on the code, such that $\Delta = \sigma(\Gamma)$, that is, it contains $\delta_i = \sigma(\gamma_i)\ \forall i \in [1, n]$. Therefore, we have $S_1 = S_0 \boxplus \sigma(\Gamma)$.

Figure 1 shows the described architecture. S_0 is the source code of the running application and M_0 is the model for S_0 extracted with ReverseЯ (Step 1). In Step 2, each γ_i is applied to the model M_0^{i-1} and turned into M_0^i ($M_0^i = M_0^{i-1} \boxplus \gamma_i$), where M_0 is considered as M_0^0. Similarly, each change on the model must be applied to the source code as well: $S_0^i = S_0^{i-1} \boxplus \delta_i$ where the code changes are derived from model changes thanks to the σ mapping as seen before.

The last model M_0 obtained by applying the last change γ_n models a new (and consistent) version of the application and is denoted by M_1. Likewise, after applying the last change δ_n we obtain the new sources S_1.

Step 4: Propagating Changes to the Application. Changes in the model are not immediately applied to the source code and thus they are not immediately

---

[1] Currently we support the IBM Rational Software Architecture (RSA) but the approach is general enough to be ported to any other modeling tool.

propagated to the running application. The translation process is triggered by the developer after the last change in a sequence of model changes is performed, i.e., when M_0 is turned into M_1. The sequence of model changes is determined by model differencing [23,13] between M_0 and M_1 and mapped into calls to the change operators (γ_i) with the proper parameters necessary to call them (Γ); such a sequence of change operators is turned into code changes via the σ mapping to form a script (Δ) used to update the source code (S_0). The modified source code is then compiled, and the modified classes are selected as input for the JavAdaptor tool, which is triggered in the last step. Finally, the new source code is passed to ReverseЯ to produce a new set of models that will be used in the next adaptation cycle. Figure 2 shows this workflow. This approach avoids the application of useless do/undo change patterns possible when the model is updated, and does not allow the running application to move into an inconsistent state, provided the developer triggers the update process only when all the diagrams have been updated and checked for consistency.

Step 5: Updating the Running Application. This steps is completely delegated to the JavAdaptor tool that not only take care of deploying the changes to the running applicaiton without stopping it, but also for preserving its state. Details on how the JavAdaptor tool works can be found in [18].

3   Operators for Model Adaptation

The operators represent elementary changes on the models. Since we are interested in the mapping between model and code changes the change operators are defined only for those model changes that affect the code as well. In the rest of the section, we will show the model changing operators and their syntax for class and activity models. Other types of models will be included in future work.

3.1   Class Model Operators

Class models describe the static structure of the running application. All structural changes are performed on the class model in FiGA. Operators for class models capture changes to various elements, including classes, interfaces, fields, constructors and methods. Two kinds of operations are defined: the *insertion* operations ($\oplus_{CD}$) and the *removal* operations ($\ominus_{CD}$). Given the differences among the class model elements, these operators are specialized to classes ($\oplus_{class}$ and $\ominus_{class}$), interfaces ($\oplus_{interface}$ and $\ominus_{interface}$), fields ($\oplus_{field}$ and $\ominus_{field}$), constructors ($\oplus_{constructor}$ and $\ominus_{constructor}$) and methods ($\oplus_{method}$ and $\ominus_{method}$). Moreover the operators $\triangleright$ and $\not\triangleright$ represent a change in the class hierarchy. Each specialization is associated with element-specific parameters.

3.2   Activity Model Operators

Activity models describe the behavior of methods. They provide an uncluttered but detailed description of method bodies, which makes them suitable for fine-grained adaptations of behavior. Change operators on activity models need to be as fine grained as possible to guarantee such a control level.

The activity model elements considered in FiGA are: action nodes, decision nodes, initial and final nodes, and input and output pins. Transition elements cannot be considered in isolation because they are tightly coupled with the elements they connect and therefore they do not have any associated change operator; their modification is captured by the change to the coupled element. In FiGA each activity model describes a single method where: i) each model has a single initial node and a single final node; ii) there is no other flow termination but the final node; and iii) the flow is continuous, it starts from the initial node and terminates in the final node.

As with class models, there are insertion ($\oplus_{AD}$) and removal ($\ominus_{AD}$) operators associated to the various activity diagram elements. The $\oplus_{AD}$ and the $\ominus_{AD}$ operators are specialized as follows:

$\ominus_{action}$(block label)
$\ominus_{test}$(block label)
$\ominus_{loop}$(block label)
$\ominus_{statement}$(block label, line no)

$\oplus_{action}$(method, label, flow, after)
$\oplus_{test}$(method, label, flow, after, type, branches no, condition)
$\oplus_{loop}$(method, flow, after, type, condition)
$\oplus_{statement}$(block label, line no, text)

$\oplus_{action}$ captures the creation of an empty action node in the activity diagram; in particular the flow parameter captures where in the flow (mainly, in which branch or in the main flow —identified by 1) it occurs. The $\oplus_{statement}$ operator captures the change to the statements the action describes. The $\oplus_{test}$ and $\oplus_{loop}$ operators capture changes to a decision node but their transitions are modeled according to the desired control structure. Obviously, their dual operators capture the removal of the corresponding structures.

To conclude the overview on the supported models, sequence diagrams are supported as well in FiGA [4] but since the code adaptations they permit largely overlaps with those supported via changes on the activity diagrams we do not present them in this work for lack of space.

4   From Model to Code Changes

To complete the description of how the FiGA approach works, we describe how model changes captured by model change operators $(\gamma_i)^2$ are mapped to source code changes (δ_i), that is, we define the σ function.

Mappings for Class Model Operators. A class model change represents a structural change that is directly reflected in the source code and thus they are easily (and without ambiguity) mappable on source code changes.

The $\oplus_{CD}$ family of operators adds the given element into classes or interfaces. How it affects the code is quite straightforward and can be easily explained

---

[2] For a more flowing style, in this section, we merge the change to the model with the operator capturing it without losing clarity, e.g., we say «the $\oplus_{class}$ operator adds a new class» instead of «the $\oplus_{class}$ operator captures the introduction of a new class».

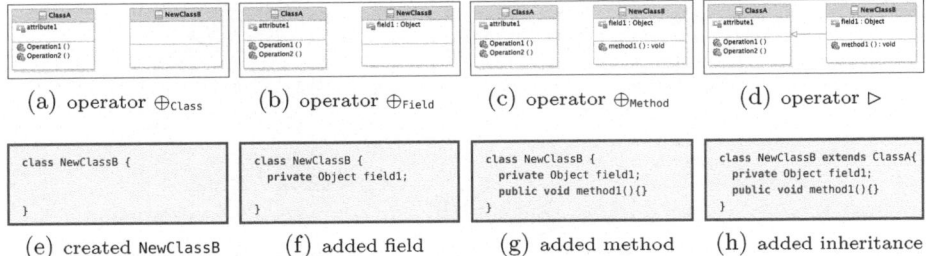

(a) operator $\oplus_{Class}$ (b) operator $\oplus_{Field}$ (c) operator $\oplus_{Method}$ (d) operator $\triangleright$

(e) created NewClassB   (f) added field   (g) added method   (h) added inheritance

Fig. 3. Change to the class diagram and its impact on the code

through an example. Figure 3 (in the top) shows the elementary changes necessary to add a new class (NewClassB) with a method and a field that extends an existing class; Fig. 3 (in the bottom) shows how the changes affect the code. In Fig. 3(a), the $\oplus_{class}$ is used to add a NewClassB to the system. The operation $\oplus_{class}$(NewClassB, **public**) corresponds to change shown in Fig. 3(e). Similarly, The $\oplus_{interface}$ operator adds an interface to the application code. In Fig. 3(b) a field (field1) is added to the model and its effect on the code $(\sigma(\oplus_{field}))$ is shown in Fig. 3(f); we chose to maintain the unwritten convention that all fields are added at the beginning of the class declaration so the new field is added as the first statement. The $\oplus_{method}$ (Fig. 3(g)) behaves similarly; it introduces a method declaration in the class (Fig. 3(c)). New methods are added at the end of the class declaration. The same operator can be used to add method prototypes into interfaces. Note that the method body is added through changes to the corresponding activity diagram. Finally, the $\triangleright$ operator creates a generalization or implementation relationship between a new classifier (class or interface) and an existing classifier (Fig. 3(d)). At the code level this could be mapped to the **extends** or the **implements** keyword depending on the kind of hierarchy relationship. In our case we have an inheritance relationship since both containers are classes (Fig. 3(h)). Similar mappings are defined for the removal $\ominus_{CD}$ family of operators. The removal operators are defined to be minimalistic and thus are not cascading, that is, they do not remove contained elements. Since a more detailed explanation of the mapping for these operators would not add to the discussion we will not discuss them further.

Mappings for Activity Diagram Operators. The FiGA framework —via ReverseЯ (see Sect. 2)— generates a detailed activity model for each method in the application. Given that, a new behavior or a behavior adaptation is described via progressive changes to an existing activity diagram. When a $\oplus_{method}$ operator adds a method to a class FiGA also produces an empty activity diagram, that is, a diagram composed only of the initial and final node connected by a transition. The work of ReverseЯ [3] is driven by @Java [5] annotations decorating the code and each operator acting on the activity diagram affects the code and the annotations as well.

We now describe how the changes represented by activity model change operators are mapped to code changes, and how the code consistency is preserved

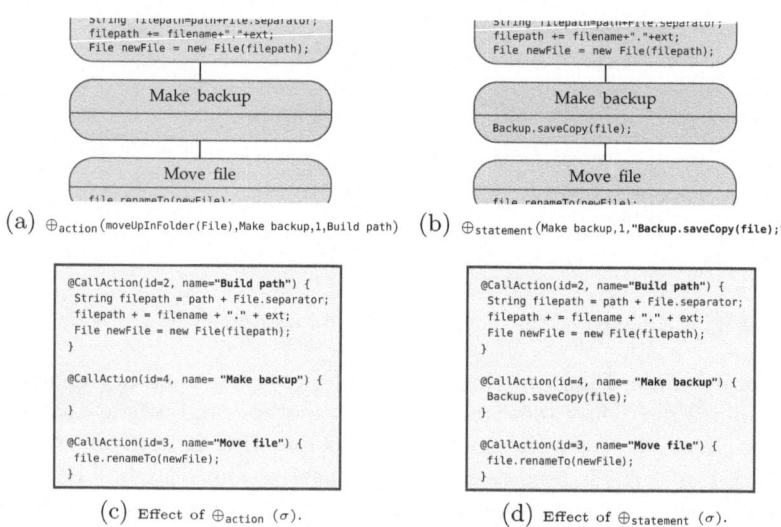

(a) $\oplus_{\mathtt{action}}$(moveUpInFolder(File),Make backup,1,Build path)   (b) $\oplus_{\mathtt{statement}}$(Make backup,1,"**Backup.saveCopy(file);**")

(c) Effect of $\oplus_{\mathtt{action}}$ (σ).   (d) Effect of $\oplus_{\mathtt{statement}}$ (σ).

Fig. 4. Activity diagram changes and the corresponding code changes

to support the model changes. A new action node is added by the $\oplus_{\mathtt{action}}$ operator. Action nodes provide an abstraction on the code —they are used to group a portion of code representing a semantic concept— so they do not have a direct representation unit in the code but such information must be available to rebuild the activity diagram. To this regard $\sigma(\oplus_{\mathtt{action}})$ will add the proper @CallAction annotations in the specified transaction line after the specified node; Fig. 4(c) shows the effect in the code of adding a new empty action, the red one, in the activity diagram (Fig. 4(a)). When a model is still empty, the node is added as the first block while the value of the **after** parameter —that denotes the action after which node should be inserted— is 0 (look at Sect. 3.2 for the details). The action label is passed to the @CallAction annotation as a parameter. The $\oplus_{\mathtt{statement}}$ adds a statement to an action, its mapping $\sigma(\oplus_{\mathtt{statement}})$ is straightforward and simply introduce the given statement in the code block corresponding to the action (see Fig. 4(d)). Lines are numbered locally to the action and their offset refers to the first line of the block they are inserted into. This will help to deal with movements of code blocks, i.e. action nodes, when these advanced features (copy and paste of nodes) are added to FIGA.

The mapping for conditionals and loops is more complicated because they can be mapped to several different statements and it is necessary to cope with such a variety. $\oplus_{\mathtt{test}}$ adds a decision node and a number of branches according to the type of decision that is added. This operator can be mapped into two types of conditional structures: **if-then-else** —where the condition evaluates on boolean values— or **switch** statements —where the condition evaluates to many values. In the former case $\sigma(\oplus_{\mathtt{test}})$ adds a whole statement as in Fig. 5 and insert the hooks for the transactions (the branches of the **if** statement) this block has created. The mapping always inserts a full **if** structure with both the

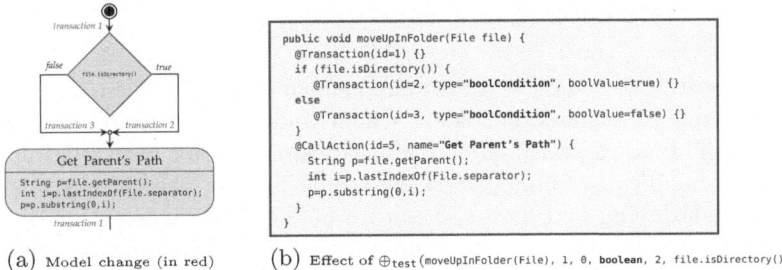

(a) Model change (in red)   (b) Effect of $\oplus_{test}$(moveUpInFolder(File), 1, 0, **boolean**, 2, file.isDirectory())

Fig. 5. Effect of conditional introduction in model and code

then and the **else** block, also when only one of the two blocks is used, in order to let the change agent to add blocks in both branches. The operator creates only the structure, it does not insert any code into the **if** branches because such code is part of an action node that should be added via an application of the $\oplus_{action}$ operator. In the latter case, the introduced conditional must specify the variable used in the test and each transitiont must be labeled with the value such a variable must assume in order to select the corresponding transition. Such a model change will be mapped into a **switch** statement with so many cases as transitions and the value of the cases value are after the label of the transitions. In both cases, the condition is supplied with the operator: a string representing a boolean test or an expression valuating on a primitive type respectively.

The $\oplus_{loop}$ model change can map into two kinds of loops: a **while** or a **do-while** structure. Such model changes are directly mapped into the corresponding control structures. In both cases the transaction labels determine the annotations to add in the code for the body and the position of the transaction labeled with true permit to distinguish the two cases. From the point of view of the model the **for** loop looks as the **while** loop but this is not true for the code and we need to distinguish them at model level as well to have a unique mapping. To do that we use UML stereotypes to mark the loop elements; the stereotypes to use are:

- on an action node «**for:dclr**» will represent the variable declaration (initialization) used in a **for** loop (usually **int** i=0);
- on a decision node «**for:stmnt**» will represent the **for** loop condition; and
- on an action node «**for:incr**» will specify the kind of increment we want to operate onto the variable (usually i++).

The declaration node must be placed exactly before the decision node, and the increment node will be the last action node of the loop. Stereotypes allow us to define nodes with special meaning. Marking the three nodes guarantees that these are exactly the variable declaration (or initialization) and increment that we need to build the **for** statement, as other increments might appear inside the loop and then we cannot define a mapping.

5   Demonstration Case Study

The case study considers a train management system (TMS) where the TMS is an example of a non-stop system which could benefit from runtime adaptation. The TMS is responsible for trains tracking and for coordinating the train transit: it handles the policy of every traffic light of the railway system. Due to the non-stopping and high risk nature of the TMS, it is highly desired that any adaptation be done on the running system without any perceived service delay. Given a running TMS, the considered adaptation consists of adding support for railroad segments that include intersections with roads. In the changed model, a segment is associated with zero or one road intersection. The extension is supported by introducing a new class `IntersectionSegment` representing a segment that intersects a road; it will be a subclass of the existing `Segment` class. An `IntersectionSegment` has an intersection traffic light to coordinate (1) the transit of cars through the intersection, and (2) the opening/closing of the intersection barriers at the intersection. The `IntersectionSegment` class has two main methods: `closeIntersection()` turns red the intersection traffic light and then closes the intersection barriers, and `openIntersection()` opens the intersection barriers and then turns green its traffic light.

From the point of view of the FiGA framework, the insertion of the new `IntersectionSegment` class is straightforward (see in Sect. 4) and thus we do not describe it any further. We instead focus on the changes to the behavior of the system. Due to space limitations, we describe only one adaptation of the `updateTrainPosition()` method of the class `TMSSystem`. Such a method already exists in the original source code prior but it needs to cope with the new concept of intersections. In particular it has to:

- permit the road traffic through the intersection (i.e., the traffic light is turned green and the barriers are opened) once the train leaves the segment, and
- forbid the road traffic through the intersection (i.e., the traffic light is turned red and the barriers are closed) when a train is approaching, i.e., the train is in the next segment.

In the adapted system, the segment state is changed to JustLeftSegment when a train leaves it, i.e., the track segment is empty and its intersection with a road (if any) can be safely opened.

Supporting the Segment Opening.   Figures 6(a) and 6(c) show, respctively, the portion of the activity diagram for the `updateTrainPosition()` method and the corresponding Java code that will be affected to support the opening of an intersection segment.

In this work, each activity diagram corresponds to a specific method of a specific class in the source code. The binding between them are preseverved by a set of `@CallAction` code annotations where each `@CallAction` groups a block of statements and represents an action node in the diagram. A `@CallAction` annotation is identified by a unique tag name within the scope of its method and this tag name labels also the corresponding action node. In other words,

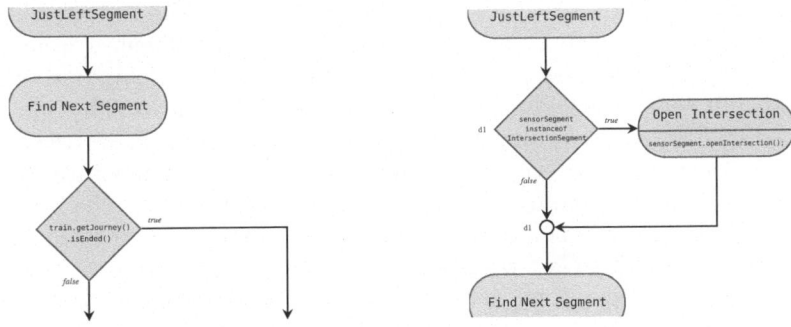

(a) View on `updateTrainPosition()` AD.   (b) Supporting the barrier opening.

```
@CallAction(id=7,name="Set JustLeftSegment") {
  train.setJustLeftPosition(sensorSegment, time);
}




@CallAction(id=9, name="Find Next Segment") {
  Segment nextInJourney = train.getNextPositionInJourney();
}
```

```
@CallAction(id=7,name="Set JustLeftSegment") {
    train.setJustLeftPosition(sensorSegment, time);
}

if (sensorSegment instanceof IntersegmentSegment) {
  @Transaction(id=6){}
    @CallAction(id=8, name="Open Intersection") {
      sensorSegment.openIntersection();
    }
  }
}
@CallAction(id=9, name="Find Next Segment") {
  Segment nextInJourney = train.getNextPositionInJourney();
}
```

(c) corresponding source code.   (d) effect of the change on the code.

Fig. 6. Model and code changes to support the opening of the intersection

```
Changes related  to  Activity2<Activity>::TMSSystem.updateTrainPosition()<Activity Diagram>
  Diff1. Add d1: sensorSegment instanceof IntersectionSegment<Decision Node> to Activity2<Activity>.children : Node
  Diff2. Add Open Intersection<Opaque Action> to Activity2<Activity>.children : Node
  Diff3. Add d1_end<Merge Node> to Activity2<Activity>.children : Node
  Diff4. Add (Set JustLeftSegment<Opaque Action>) (d1: sensorSegment instanceof IntersectionSegment<Decision Node>)
         <Control Flow> to TMSSystem.updateTrainPosition()<Diagram>.edges : Edge
  Diff5. Add (d1: sensorSegment instanceof IntersectionSegment<Decision Node>)
         (Open Intersection<Opaque Action>)True<Control Flow> to
         TMSSystem.updateTrainPosition()<Diagram>.edges : Edge
  Diff6. Add (d1: sensorSegment instanceof IntersectionSegment<Decision Node>)
         (d1<Merge Node>)False<Control Flow> to TMSSystem.updateTrainPosition()<Diagram>.edges : Edge
  Diff7. Add (Open Intersection<Opaque Action>)(d1_end<Merge Node>)<Control Flow> to
         TMSSystem.updateTrainPosition()<Diagram>.edges : Edge
  Diff8. Add (d1_end<Merge Node>)(Find Next Segment<Opaque Action>)<Control Flow> to updateTrainPosition()<Diagram>.edges: Edge
  Diff9. Delete (Set JustLeftSegment<Opaque Action>)(Find Next Segment<Opaque Action>)<Control Flow> from
         TMSSystem.updateTrainPosition()<Diagram>.edges : Edge
```

Fig. 7. Differences between Fig. 6(a) and Fig. 6(b)

each action node and its corresponding @CallAction annotation share the same tag name. If you look at Fig. 6(a) and Fig 6(c) this association should be evident, e.g., the node labeled by «Find Next Segment» finds a correspondence in the code annotation named in the same way. Figures 6(b) and 6(d) show, respectively, the changes (in red) to the activity diagram and to the code in order to support the opening of the barriers at the intersections.

The model updating is manually done through the Rational Software Architect (RSA). After the updating, the next step is to determine the differences between the two versions of the model in order to exploit the presented mapping (σ) to update the source code. RSA can automatically generate the differences as a set of additions and removals that permit to turn the old model into the new one when applied. Figure 7 shows the differences between the activity diagrams in Fig. 6(a) and Fig. 6(b) as generated by RSA. Such differences are used to determine which model change operators (γs) capture the changes in order to automatically adapt the code according to the model changes. The operations generated by RSA are quite similar to those considered in the FiGA architecture and the abstraction gap is overcome thanks to the described annotation mechanism used by ReverseЯ and by some label conventions, therefore, the translation is quite straightforward once the resulting file is correctly interpreted. To give the correct interpretative key we describe a couple of entries in Fig. 7 and their interpretation as γ operators. Diff1[3] states that a new decision node labeled «d1» and whose condition is «sensorSegment **instanceof** IntersectionSegment» is added to the activity diagram; this maps onto the $\oplus_{test}$ operator. Diff2 states that a new action node with tag name «Open Intersection» is added to the diagram and it is mapped to the $\oplus_{action}$ operator. Diff4 to Diff8 provides the information about where in the diagram these changes have been done and how the new elements interact with those already in the diagram; all these diffs do not have a direct mapping on model change operator but provide necessary data to istantiate them. Follows the detailed operators instatiation from Fig. 7.

- $\oplus_{test}$(TMSSystem.updateTrainPosition(), 1, Set JustLeftSegment, bool, 2, sensorSegment **instanceof** IntersectionSegment)
- $\oplus_{action}$(TMSSystem.updateTrainPosition(), Open Intersection, **true**, sensorSegment **instanceof** IntersectionSegment)
- $\oplus_{statement}$(Open Intersection, 1, **"sensorSegment.openIntersection();"**)

As explained in Sect. 4, from these γs operators and the σ mapping the FiGA framework can adapt the running source code to achieve the version in Fig. 6(d) and then apply the change to the running application via JavAdaptor.

Supporting the Segment Closing. As to support the barriers opening at the intersection, we need to do similar changes to close them when the train is approaching. Figure 8(a) shows a different portion of the updateTrainPosition() activity diagram that will be affected by the changes as depicted in Fig. 8(b). Figures 8(c) and 8(d) show the corresponding portion of code before and after the adaptation respectively whereas Fig. 9 shows the differences between the activity diagram in Fig. 8(a) and the one in Fig. 8(b) and since their discussion will not add any detail we just report their mapping on the change operators:

- $\oplus_{test}$(TMSSystem.updateTrainPosition(), **false**, train.getJourney().isEnded(), bool, 2, nextInJourneySeg **instanceof** IntersectionSegment)
- $\oplus_{action}$(TMSSystem.updateTrainPosition (), Close Intersection, **true**, nextInJourneySeg **instanceof** IntersectionSegment)
- $\oplus_{statement}$(Close Intersection, 1, **"nextInJourney.closeIntersection();"**).

6   Discussion

In the proposed approach, developers use graphical UML models, rather than the source code to make changes to running software. The models can be used

---

[3] Please note that the labels Diff have been manually added to ease their description.

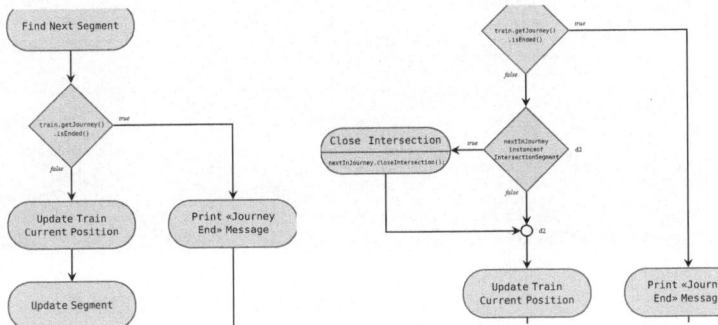

(a) View on `updateTrainPosition()`.   (b) Supporting the barrier closing.

```
if train.getJourney().isEnded() {
  @Transaction(id=7){}
  @CallAction(id=10, name="Print «Journey End» Message") {
    Out.println(train.getId()+"reached the end of its journey")
  }
} else {
  @Transaction(id=8){}




  @CallAction(id=12, name="Update Train Current Position") {
    train.setCurrentPosition(nextInJourney);
  }
}
```

```
if train.getJourney().isEnded() {
  @Transaction(id=7){}
  @CallAction(id=10, name="Print «Journey End» Message") {
    Out.println(train.getId()+"reached the end of its journey")
  }
} else {
  @Transaction(id=8){}
  if (nextInJourney instanceof IntersectionSegment) {
    @Transaction(id=9){}
    @CallAction(id=11, name="Close Intersection") {
      nextInJourney.closeIntersection();
    }
  }
  @CallAction(id=12, name="Update Train Current Position") {
    train.setCurrentPosition(nextInJourney);
  }
}
```

(c) corresponding source code.   (d) effect of the change on the code.

Fig. 8. Model and code changes to support the closing of the intersection

to present a running system in terms of UML constructs that present essential aspects of the coded structure and behavior, while shielding the developer from source code and process-level details. Making changes on the models in many cases can involve fewer steps than making corresponding changes on the source code. For example, if a developer wants to remove a bi-directional association between two classes in source code, she would have to remove the references in the related classes and the get and set methods associated with the references. The same change at the design class model level simply involves removing the association between the classes; removal of the association at the model level infers removal of corresponding get and set methods at the source code level. The change operators we provide represent the smallest units of change that a user can make using the FiGA approach. We do not claim the set to be complete with respect to all possible changes that a developer may need to make, but right now we have not yet identified any design level changes that cannot be expressed in terms of the units of changes we currently support. The automatic propagation of model changes to runtime changes is a key feature of the FiGA approach. A user can make changes at the model-level and be assured that changes on the source-code level and on the running system will be faithfully performed. In addition, the use of the reverse engineering mechanism to generate the

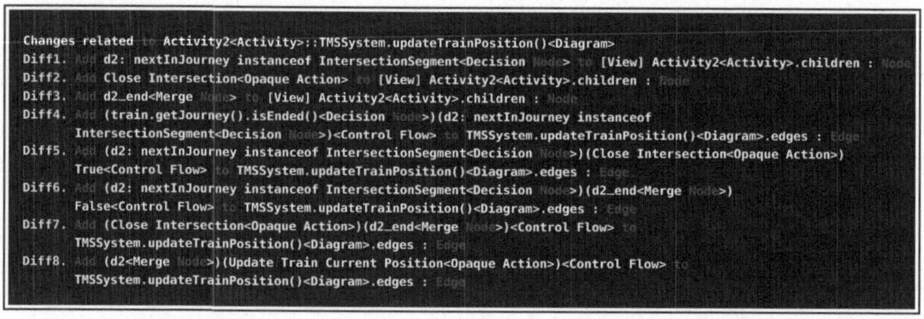

```
Changes related to Activity2<Activity>::TMSSystem.updateTrainPosition()<Diagram>
Diff1.   Add d2: nextInJourney instanceof IntersectionSegment<Decision Node> to [View] Activity2<Activity>.children : Node
Diff2.   Add Close Intersection<Opaque Action> to [View] Activity2<Activity>.children : Node
Diff3.   Add d2_end<Merge Node> to [View] Activity2<Activity>.children : Node
Diff4.   Add (train.getJourney().isEnded()<Decision Node>)(d2: nextInJourney instanceof
         IntersectionSegment<Decision Node>)<Control Flow> to TMSSystem.updateTrainPosition()<Diagram>.edges : Edge
Diff5.   Add (d2: nextInJourney instanceof IntersectionSegment<Decision Node>)(Close Intersection<Opaque Action>)
         True<Control Flow> to TMSSystem.updateTrainPosition()<Diagram>.edges : Edge
Diff6.   Add (d2: nextInJourney instanceof IntersectionSegment<Decision Node>)(d2_end<Merge Node>)
         False<Control Flow> to TMSSystem.updateTrainPosition()<Diagram>.edges : Edge
Diff7.   Add (Close Intersection<Opaque Action>)(d2_end<Merge Node>)<Control Flow> to
         TMSSystem.updateTrainPosition()<Diagram>.edges : Edge
Diff8.   Add (d2<Merge Node>)(Update Train Current Position<Opaque Action>)<Control Flow> to
         TMSSystem.updateTrainPosition()<Diagram>.edges : Edge
```

Fig. 9. Differences between Fig. 8(a) and Fig. 8(b)

models ensures that the models accurately describe the running system. To support automatic propagation of model changes to the source code we have to bridge the abstraction gap between the models and the source code [15,3,21]. This is a necessary pre-requisite for reliable propagation of changes across the abstraction gap. This challenge is handled in the FiGA approach through a well-defined mapping between model and source code elements embodied in the elementary model change operators we define, and in the reverse engineering mechanism we use to produce the models from the source code and associated meta-data in the source code (described as Java annotations). This tight connection between the models and the source code enables co-evolution of these artifacts. To make the approach more easy to use the model change operator are automatically derived from the changes the user perform on the diagrams by using model differencing [23,13]. JavAdaptor [18] is used to automatically propagate the changes to the runtime system. Many dynamic software updating approaches (e.g., see [24]) focus on the definition of states where the application can safely migrate from its original form to its evolved one. This is not our concern because we rely on JavAdaptor to replace each class while keeping its state intact: no data is lost and each object in the new version immediately starts running with its old state. JavAdaptor also determines when to freeze the class for the reloading operation also in a multi-threaded environment.

7   Related Work

Architecture-based software adaptation approaches focus on supporting automated coarse-grained reconfiguration of software structure at runtime (for example, see [7,9,10,14,16,22]). In these approaches, the running system is structured to facilitate the use of component-based runtime models that are causally connected to the running system. Each component is a coarse-grained abstraction that represents a logically encapsulated part of the running system. Runtime modifications are restricted to adding and removing components and links between components. The approach described in this paper provides support for finer-grained modifications at the Java program class level. Unlike the architecture-based approaches, our fine-grained approach does not constrain the structure of Java programs that can undergo runtime modifications. On the other hand, our approach currently supports manual changes, that is, humans manually modify the runtime models rather than the system itself. We will investigate how the approach can be extended to support self-adaptation.

Research on dynamic software updates (DSU) [11,17,20] aims to produce mechanisms that allow developers to change a running system without stopping and restarting the running system. Code level changes are submitted to these mechanisms, which are then effected on running systems. JavAdaptor [18] is one such mechanisms but with support for performing a finer granularity of changes. Unlike other work on dynamic software updates, FiGA, which is built on top of JavAdaptor, focuses on using models to raise the level of abstraction at which changes are presented to the running system. We are not aware of any DSU that uses models as an interface for making changes to a running system.

8 Conclusion

We presented the FiGA framwork, a model based approach to software evolution that supports expressing and propagating fine-grained changes to a running application without the need to stop the system. The UML models used in the approach can be viewed as model@runtime that are the means of expressing and then propagating changes to the running system. Developers change the models and these changes are automatically mapped to model change operators whose effect on code is known; the application of these operators, therefore, propagates the changes to the source code. In this way is possible to co-evolve the model and the source code; finally the planned evolution is effectively applied to the running application through the JavAdaptor framework [18] without stopping the application. The FiGA framework does not make any assumptions about the kind of changes that might occur and about which parts of the running application will be affected by the change. The current set of supported models allows us to express all the changes we anticipate. In this current version of the work we aim to demonstrate the feasibility of the approach and provide a solid base upon which we can build a more extended evolutionary engine. In the future we plan to support the full range of UML diagrams at various levels of abstraction.

References

1. Barais, O., Cariou, E., Duchien, L., Pessemier, N., Seinturier, L.: TranSAT: A Framework for the specification of Software Architecture Evolution. In: Proc. of WCAT 2004, Oslo, Norway, pp. 31–38 (June 2004)
2. Blair, G., Bencomo, N., France, R.: Models@run. time. IEEE Computer 42(10), 22–27 (2009)
3. Cazzola, W., Pini, S., Ghoneim, A., Saake, G.: Co-Evolving Application Code and Design Models by Exploiting Meta-Data. In: Proc. of SAC 2007, South Korea (2007)
4. Cazzola, W., Rossini, N.A., Bennett, P., Pradeep Mandalaparty, S., France, R.B.: Fine-Grained Semi-Automated Runtime Evolution. In: MoDELS@Run-Time. LNCS. Springer, Heidelberg (2013)

5. Cazzola, W., Vacchi, E.: @Java: Annotations in Freedom. In: Proc. of SAC 2013, Coimbra, Portugal, pp. 1691–1696. ACM Press (March 2013)
6. Costa-Soria, C., Hervás-Muñoz, D., Pérez Benedí, J., Carsí Cubel, J.: A Reflective Approach for Supporting the Dynamic Evolution of Component Types. In: Proc. of ICECCS 2009, Potsdam, Germany, pp. 301–310 (June 2009)
7. Floch, J., Hallsteinsen, S., Stav, E., Eliassen, F., Lund, K., Gjørven, E.: Beyond Design Time: Using Architecture Models for Runtime Adaptability. IEEE Software 23(2), 62–70 (2006)
8. France, R., Rumpe, B.: Model-Driven Development of Complex Software: A Research Roadmap. In: Proc. of FoSE 2007, pp. 37–54. IEEE, Minneapolis (2007)
9. Garlan, D., Cheng, S.-W., Huang, A.-C., Schmerl, B., Steenkiste, P.: Rainbow: Architecture-Based Self Adaptation with Reusable Infrastructure. IEEE Computer 37(10), 46–54 (2004)
10. Georgas, J., van der Hoek, A., Taylor, R.: Using Architectural Models to Manage and Visualize Runtime Adaptation. IEEE Computer 42(10), 52–60 (2009)
11. Hicks, M., Nettles, S.: Dynamic Software Updating. ACM Trans. on Progr. Languages and Systems 27(6), 1049–1096 (2005)
12. Kramer, J., Magee, J.: Self-Managed Systems: an Architectural Challenge. In: Proc. of FoSE 2007, pp. 259–268. IEEE, Minneapolis (2007)
13. Maoz, S., Ringert, J., Rumpe, B.: ADDiff: Semantic Differencing for Activity Diagrams. In: Proc. of ESEC/FSE 2011, Szeged, Hungary, pp. 179–189 (September 2011)
14. Morin, B., Barais, O., Jézéquel, J.-M., Fleurey, F., Solberg, A.: Models@ Run.time to Support Dynamic Adaptation. IEEE Computer 42(10), 44–51 (2009)
15. Murphy, G., Notkin, D., Sullivan, K.: Software Reflexion Models: Bridging the Gap between Design and Implementation. Trans. Softw. Eng. 27(4), 364–380 (2001)
16. Oreizy, P., Medvidovic, N., Taylor, R.: Architecture-Based Runtime Software Evolution. In: Proc. of ICSE 1998, pp. 177–186. IEEE, Kyoto (1998)
17. Orso, A., Rao, A., Harrold, M.: A Technique for Dynamic Updating of Java Software. In: Proc. of ICSM 2002, pp. 649–658. IEEE, Montréal (2002)
18. Pukall, M., Kästner, C., Cazzola, W., Götz, S., Grebhahn, A., Schöter, R., Saake, G.: JavAdaptor - Flexible Runtime Updates of Java Applications. Software-Practice and Experience 43(2), 153–185 (2013)
19. Salehie, M., Tahvildari, L.: Self-Adaptive Software: Landscape and Research Challenges. Trans. on Autonomous and Adaptive Systems 4(2), 14:1–14:42 (2009)
20. Stoyle, G., Hicks, M., Bierman, G., Sewell, P., Neamtiu, I.: Mutatis Mutandis. ACM Trans. on Progr. Languages and Systems 29(4) (August 2007)
21. Ubayashi, N., Akatoki, H., Nomura, J.: Pointcut-based Architectural Interface for Bridging a Gap between Design and Implementation. In: RAM-SE 2009, Italy (2009)
22. Vogel, T., Giese, H.: Adaptation and Abstract Runtime Models. In: Proc. of SEAMS 2010, pp. 39–48. ACM, Cape Town (2010)
23. Xing, Z., Stroulia, E.: Differencing Logical UML Models. Automated Software Engineering 14(2), 215–259 (2007)
24. Zhang, J., Cheng, B.: Model-Based Development of Dynamically Adaptive Software. In: Proc. of ICSE 2006, pp. 371–380. ACM, Shanghai (2006)

Supporting the Co-evolution of Metamodels and Constraints through Incremental Constraint Management

Andreas Demuth, Roberto E. Lopez-Herrejon, and Alexander Egyed

Institute for Systems Engineering and Automation
Johannes Kepler University (JKU)
Linz, Austria
{andreas.demuth,roberto.lopez,alexander.egyed}@jku.at

Abstract. Design models must abide by constraints that can come from diverse sources, like metamodels, requirements, or the problem domain. Modelers intent to live by these constraints and thus desire automated mechanism that provide instant feedback on constraint violations. However, typical approaches assume that constraints do not evolve over time, which, unfortunately, is becoming increasingly unrealistic. For example, the co-evolution of metamodels and models requires corresponding constraints to be co-evolved continuously. This demands efficient constraint adaptation mechanisms to ensure that validated constraints are up-to-date. This paper presents an approach based on constraint templates that tackles this evolution scenario by automatically updating constraints. We developed the Cross-Layer Modeler (XLM) approach which relies on incremental consistency-checking. As a case study, we performed evolutions of the UML-metamodel and 21 design models. Our approach is sound and the empirical evaluation shows that it is near instant and scales with increasing model sizes.

Keywords: Co-evolution, metamodeling, consistency-checking.

1 Introduction

In *Model-Driven Development (MDD)* [1], metamodels play a key role as they reflect real-world domains and define the language of models as well as the constraints these models must satisfy. Over the past years, a trend has emerged that calls for design tools with adaptable metamodels – to customize the tool to a particular discipline, domain, or even application under development. Indeed, those metamodels must evolve continuously; for example, to reflect changes of a domain or to meet new business needs. Refactorings that improve a metamodel's structure and usability are also common. Nowadays, a range of "flexible" design tools with adaptable metamodels are available to support such scenarios (e.g., [2,3]).

Co-evolution of models denotes the process of concurrently evolving metamodels and their models – a process that is non trivial since inconsistent

A. Moreira et al. (Eds.): MODELS 2013, LNCS 8107, pp. 287–303, 2013.
© Springer-Verlag Berlin Heidelberg 2013

co-evolution may cause models and metamodels to drift apart. Several incremental approaches have been proposed to support this process (e.g., [4]).

However, metamodels also impose constraints onto models. When the metamodels evolve, so must the constraints – a scenario that has been largely overlooked so far. For example, the *Unified Modeling Language (UML)* [5] is supported by hundreds of well-formedness rules and the community augmented these with even more consistency rules. Moreover, *UML Profiles*, which may also include consistency rules, are commonly used to extend the UML and adapt it to specific domains [6]. Modifying the UML metamodel thus impacts these constraints. Previously semantically and syntactically correct constraints may become incorrect after structural or semantic metamodel changes; or new constraints may appear. It is crucial to extend the notion of co-evolution to include the continuous maintenance of constraints such that only correct constraints are enforced on design models. Of course, it is also crucial to have available a consistency checker that is not only able to react to design model changes but also to metamodel/constraint changes. Generating and adapting constraints incrementally as well as checking them incrementally are thus pre-requisites to ensure that designers are always given instant and reliable feedback on the validity of their modeling work.

State-of-the-art consistency checkers are commonly employed to validate constraints and determine whether a model is consistent with respect to its metamodel. Most consistency checkers rely on an existing set of constraints for performing the validation [7, 8]. It is common to write these constraints manually, typically in a standardized language such as the *Object Constraint Language (OCL)* [9]. Often, constraints are also "hard-coded" into modeling tools. Although the automatic co-evolution of metamodels and models has become an active field of research, the issue of co-evolving constraints is not well addressed. Incremental consistency checkers typically do not support the live updating of constraints and little support for updating outdated constraints is available.

This paper describes an approach for the co-evolution of metamodels and their constraints that uses constraint templates and a template engine to automatically and incrementally manage constraints – it is an extension of a previously published idea-paper [10]. New contributions include the in-depth illustration and discussion of the approach and a prototype implementation (the *Cross-Layer Modeler (XLM)* [11]) that leverages from our previous work on the Model/Analyzer [8], an efficient incremental consistency checker. Moreover, we evaluated our approach by using the XLM for automating the generation of constraints that ensure the structural integrity of UML models and by performing sample evolutions of the UML metamodel. Tests were performed on 21 large industrial UML models of up to 36,205 model elements. While the UML is not the primary motivation for our approach (it changes occasionally only), it is like any modeling language in that it must adhere to a metamodel and imposes constraints. UML metamodel changes thus impose the same kind of challenges. The fact that the UML language is far from trivial and we have available large-scale, industrial models thus make it a very suitable environment to test the scalabil-

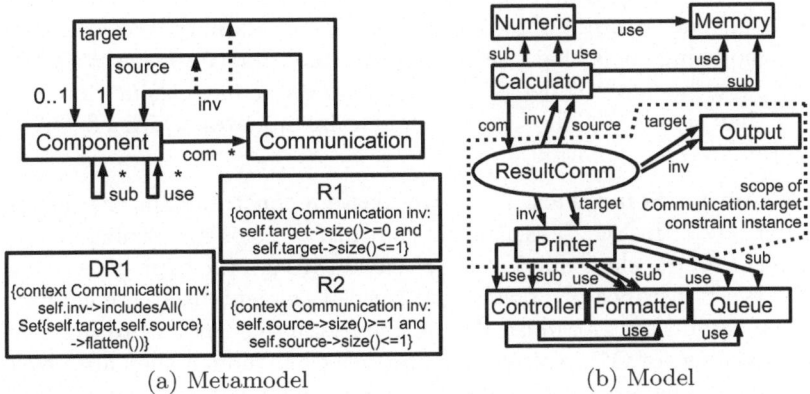

(a) Metamodel   (b) Model

Fig. 1. Metamodel and model of component-based system with constraints

ity of our approach and the XLM tool. The results show that our approach is correct and works efficiently even as model sizes increase.

2   Example and Motivation

We use an excerpt of a simple metamodel, shown in Fig. 1a, to illustrate our work. The metamodel consists of two elements: Component and Communication. Every Component can include an arbitrary number of sub-components and can directly use an undefined number of other components. A Communication expresses a data exchange from a source to at most one target component. Components can have an arbitrary number of open communications (com).

For building this metamodel, we used a simple metametamodel consisting of the elements: Class, Reference, DerivedReference. References between classes are drawn as arrows with an assigned name and a defined cardinality. Multiple references can be combined to a single *derived reference* which we draw without cardinality values and with dashed arrows to the references from which it is composed. For example, a derived reference is used to retrieve the components that are involved in a communication (inv).

For MDD to be effective, it is crucial to work with valid models that conform to their metamodels. That is, that such models adhere to the constraints specified in the following sources:

I: Metamodel Directly. First, we use intuitive constraints that check the cardinality of references. For each reference, we create a constraint (e.g., R1 or R2 in Fig. 1a) that ensures that every instance of the owning element is connected to the specified number of elements in a model (e.g., every instance of Communication must be connected to exactly one Component instance through a connection named source). We use the term *connected* in models to avoid ambiguity with *references* in the metamodel. Connections are depicted as named arrows in model diagrams. Constraints for references with unrestricted cardinalities (e.g., com) are not shown in Fig. 1a for readability reasons. Note that common modeling tools that use the *Eclipse Modeling Framework (EMF)* [12] for example either do not derive such constraints or have them "hard-coded", meaning that changes cannot lead to constraint updates which effectively disables automated co-evolution.

II: Metamodel Semantics. Next, we create a constraint for the derived reference (e.g., $DR1$ in Fig. 1a) to ensure that instances of the owning element are connected to all the elements that are reached through the aggregated references (e.g., for every instance of Communication, all elements that are connected to it via source and target must also be connected via inv). Note that our constraints make use of OCL collection iterations even though they are invoked on single objects. The issues arising because of the distinction between single and multi-object values in OCL have been discussed and identified in literature as a problem especially during evolution [13]. For the sake of generality, we use a consistency checker with an OCL interpreter that allows collection operations being used with single objects by performing the necessary conversions automatically.

III: Domain Knowledge. While the first two kinds of constraints could be generated automatically, constraints of the third type cannot be derived from the metamodel automatically with traditional approaches. An example would be a constraint that restricts direct usage of components based on component hierarchies. We omit a detailed description of such a constraint because of space restrictions.

As depicted in Fig. 1b, the metamodel from Fig. 1a is used to create a small model of a calculator system. The Calculator component has two sub-components that are used directly: Memory and Numeric. The Numeric component also uses the component Memory. A Printer has three sub-components: Formatter, Queue, and Controller. It uses the Queue to store print jobs and informs the Controller, which retrieves data from the Queue and runs the Formatter before printing. Finally, there is an Output component to display information to the user. The Calculator uses a Communication element called ResultComm to send its results to the Printer and the Output components.

As indicated by the encircled area in Fig. 1b, the two target connections of ResultComm are causing an inconsistency because only one target is allowed according to the metamodel. Note that any consistency checking approach could detect inconsistencies in the model according to the constraints we defined above.

2.1 Incremental Consistency Checking

As the model size increases, so does the effort to check its consistency. Checking consistency in an entire model can easily become a time consuming task. Incremental consistency checking addresses this limitation by looking only at a subset of an entire model, namely the elements that change as a model evolves [14]. This set of elements can be either directly observed or calculated from differences between model versions [8,15]. The existing approach automatically defines

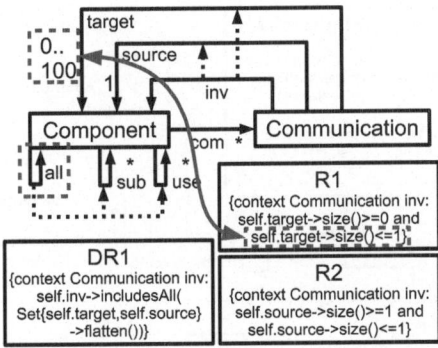

Fig. 2. The evolved metamodel

constraint instances that validate whether specific model elements violate a given constraint [14]. The change impact *scope* of a constraint instance is the set of model elements that are used for calculating the constraint instance's validation result which are also computed automatically. For example, Fig. 1b shows a *constraint instance* of the Communication metaclass constraint $R1$ that requires communications to have exactly one target. The scope of this constraint instance consists of the two elements that are reached through the target reference to Printer and Output. Changes falling within scope of a constraint instance, like removing a target, would lead to a re-validation of the constraint instance. The Model/Analyzer automatically creates, re-evaluates, and destroys constraint instances according to changes in the model in Fig. 1b. However, if the metamodel were to change, consistency checkers would continue to validate the now-potentially-outdated design rules.

2.2 Co-evolution Examples

Let us consider what happens when a metamodel changes. For instance, if the number of maximum targets of a Communication rises from 1 to 100 because new technologies allow multicasting of messages between components. Additionally, a new derived reference all is introduced to combine the sub and use references of a Component. These two changes are encircled with dashed lines in Fig. 2. These changes have the following consequences:

– Constraint $R1$ becomes incorrect. The upper bound checked by $R1$ (1), is no longer equal to the actual upper bound value of the reference (100).
– An additional constraint is needed for the new derived reference all.

In the first case, $R1$ must be adapted by replacing the upper limit value 1 with literal 100. Without this adaptation, the corresponding constraint instance, circled in Fig. 1b, would still incorrectly try to enforce an upper bound of 1. In the second case, the inconsistency that neither Calculator nor Printer have

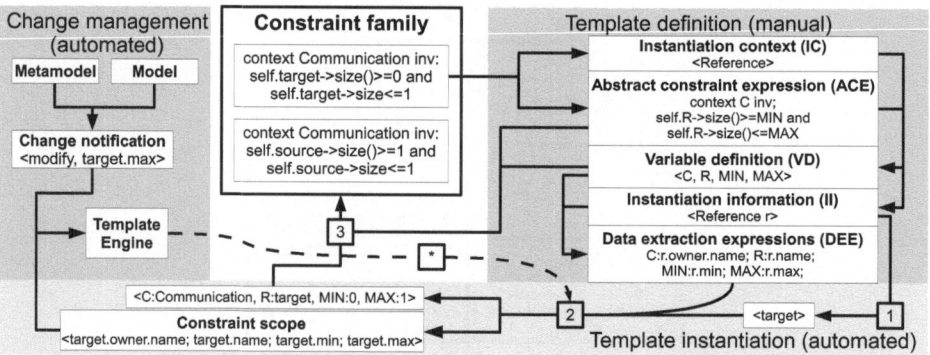

Fig. 3. Example of steps performed during template definition, instantiation, and change management

the required connection `all` in our model is missed. To address this problem, a constraint that checks the derived reference `all` needs to be added.

A common way of dealing with co-evolution is to manually re-write the constraints after performing a metamodel modification. Although this approach can work in our example because of its small size and simple constraints, manually identifying and adapting affected constraints in more complex models is both time consuming and error-prone.

3   Constraint Templates and Template Engine

We propose the use of constraint templates to automate the co-evolution of models and their constraints. These templates are based on the metamodel and constraints we want to evaluate. Basically, templates contain the static aspects that constraints have in common (e.g., fragments of an OCL constraint string) and define the points of variability. As models evolve, the templates are filled with specific data – to reflect the model evolution – and instantiated to automatically generate or update the constraints.

Next, we illustrate how constraint templates can be derived and how they are managed by a template engine to automate constraint generation and updating.

3.1   Template Definition

Templates are written manually by metamodel authors who are also in charge of maintaining and evolving metamodels. Before discussing the authoring process in detail, we discuss the structure of a template, as shown in Table 1, and the information it requires. The *instantiation context (IC)* defines for which elements, or combinations thereof, a template should be instantiated. The *abstract constraint expression (ACE)* is used to define the *family of constraints* generated from the template. A constraint family consists of constraints that share some

Table 1. Template structure

Instantiation context (IC)
Abstract constraint expression (ACE)
Variable definition (VD)
Instantiation information (II)
Data extraction expressions (DEE)

static aspects (e.g., the structure) and have some variable parts that differ for each constraint. Thus, the ACE captures the static parts of the constraint family and also identifies the locations of variability which are also defined explicitly in the *variable definition (VD)*. The VD declares which parts of the ACE are interpreted as variables. To bind specific values to these variables, data has to be read from specific elements that are available when the template is instantiated. These elements are specified in the *instantiation information (II)*. How the values for the variables are extracted from the elements is declared in *data extraction expressions (DEE)*. Let us now show how we can write a template $T1$ for the constraint family of $R1$ and $R2$.

Template for Cardinalities. The top-right section "Template definition" in Fig. 3 illustrates the steps we perform next. The remainder of the figure depicts template instantiation and change management processes we discuss later. Template $T1$, shown in Table 2, creates a constraint for every instance of `Reference`, for example when the reference `target` is added to the class `Communication` during the initial modeling of our sample metamodel. Therefore, we define the IC of our template to be `<Reference>`. This means that we provide an instance of `Reference` to the template in order to create a new constraint. Note that templates are reusable for other metamodels that conform to the same metametamodel. We define the ACE by using the desired expression of one sample constraint of the constraint family (e.g., an OCL statement) and replacing all concrete values that are specific for a single instance with variables. In our example, we take the expression from the constraint $R1$ for the reference `Communication.target` in Fig. 1a:

Table 2. Definition of template T1

```
IC:   <Reference>
ACE: context C inv:
     self.R->size()>=MIN and
     self.R->size()<=MAX
VD:  <C, R, MIN, MAX>
II:   <Reference r>
DEE: <C:r.owner.name, R:r.name,
     MIN:r.min, MAX:r.max>
```

Table 3. Definition of template T2

```
IC:   <DerivedReference>
ACE: context C inv:
     self.DR-> includesAll(
     REFS->collect(x|self.{x}))
VD:  <C, DR, REFS>
II:   <DerivedReference dr>
DEE: <C:dr.owner.name, DR:dr.name,
     REFS:dr.refs->collect(name)>
```

```
context Communication inv:
self.target->size()>=0 and
self.target->size()<=1
```

And replace the two values 0 and 1 with MIN and MAX for the minimum and maximum number of connected elements, the context Communication with C for the checked class, and the two occurrences of target with R for the used reference. The result is the abstract constraint expression:

```
context C inv:
self.R->size()>=MIN and
self.R->size()<=MAX
```

as defined in Table 2 with the variable parts (VD) being <C, R, MIN, MAX>. As shown in Fig. 3, the instantiation information of $T1$ is <Reference r>.

Desired constraints are built by reading the min, max, and name values of the passed reference r as well as the name of the class that owns the reference owner.name. The data extraction expressions can then be written as r.min, r.max, r.name and r.owner.name. In the DEEs, the variable to which the read data should be assigned is written before each DEE followed by a colon. Note that because of the single element instantiation context (i.e., we instantiate the template for every instance of that type), only one element is available as instantiation information, making both the II itself and the use of a prefix (i.e., "r") for the DEEs redundant. However, if more complex patterns were used in the IC, the II would contain more than one element from which DEEs read data. For example, we could have used the pattern <Class,Reference> as IC for $T1$ to generate a constraint for each reference that is actually added to a class. Then, distinguishing the class and the reference in the II and using prefixes in DEEs becomes necessary. We have now completed the template definition for $T1$.

Template for Derived References. We use the same process to write template $T2$, as shown in Table 3, based on the constraint $DR1$ as an example for the constraint family that checks derived references.

As a simplification, we replaced the set of references (Set{self.source, self.target}->flatten()) from $DR1$ in Fig. 1a with a construct (collect(x|self.{x})) that allows us to aggregate the results of different references – based on a set of reference names – dynamically. When the template is instantiated for the derived reference Communication.inv, the resulting constraint is:

```
context Communication inv:
self.inv->includesAll(
Set{''target'', ''source''}->collect(x|self.{x}))
```

The expression Set{''target'', ''source''}->collect(x| self.{x}) then collects all the elements returned by the expressions self.target and self.source.

Now that the templates $T1$ and $T2$ are written, let us discuss how templates are instantiated automatically to generate constraints.

3.2   Template Instantiation

To enable a template, it is passed to the template engine that observes a specific model and handles template instantiation and updating. We will now discuss how the template $T1$ for checking reference cardinalities is instantiated when it is applied to the metamodel in Fig. 1a.

For each occurence of the IC `<Reference>`, the template is instantiated once. In Fig. 1a there are five references and thus $T1$ is instantiated five times. However, we focus on a detailed discussion of the instantiation process for the reference `Communication.target`, as illustrated in the bottom box "Template instantiation" in Fig. 3. The process starts with the instantiation information (1). In this case, it containts the reference `target`. The data extraction expressions are applied to the element to retrieve the names (i.e., `Communication` and `target`) and the cardinality values (i.e., 0 and 1). This is shown in Fig. 3(2). In order to allow later updates of the generated constraints, the *constraint scope* is built automatically during the execution of the DEEs in step (2). This scope constains all elements that are accessed by the DEEs. The scope for the constraint $R1$ is therefore `<target.owner.name, target.name, target.min, target.max>`. The variables in the ACE are then replaced with these values to generate the constraint (3).

After applying our templates $T1$ and $T2$ to the initial version of our example metamodel from Fig. 1a, template $T1$ was instantiated once for every reference (i.e., five times in total), template $T2$ was instantiated once to generate the constraint for the only derived reference `inv` in the metamodel.

At this point we have shown how templates are written and how they are instantiated. We have seen that a template captures the static and the variable parts of a family of constraints. Typically, a single constraint template is written for every constraint family in the system. Combining templates is only necessary in the rare cases where different constraint families should be merged into one. If such a merge is required, template authors can build the corresponding template by writing a template for the merged constraint families. Next, we will illustrate how automatic constraint updates are performed.

3.3   Change Management

In Section 2 we discussed the effects of two metamodel evolutions on the correctness of constraints. We will now present how such metamodel evolutions are handled automatically by the template engine.

Metamodel Evolution. After every modification of the metamodel, the template engine is notified, as shown in the top-left box "Change management" in Fig. 3. The change notification includes information about the changed metamodel elements which the engine uses to determine the actions that are required to adapt the set of current constraints to the new version of the metamodel.

After the addition of metamodel elements, the engine looks for templates that can be instantiated (i.e., the types of the added model elements match the instantiation context). When metamodel elements are deleted, constraints that are based on these elements (i.e., their scope contains a removed element) are also removed. A metamodel element modification triggers the update process and the template engine uses the modified model element and the constraint scopes to calculate the set of affected constraints that need updating.

As an example, consider the metamodel version shown in Fig. 2. We first replaced the upper bound value 1 of the constraint $R1$ with the value 100. The change notification that is passed to the engine indicates that the metamodel element `target.max` was modified. Since the scope of the constraint $R1$ contains the modified element, as discussed above, the engine detects that this constraint is affected by the modification. Because there are no other constraints that include the modified model element in their scope, $R1$ is identified as the only constraint that needs to be updated.

The update is performed by executing the data extraction expressions that added the modified metamodel element to the constraint's scope, as depicted by step (*) in Fig. 3, and replacing the outdated values in the constraint expression with the newly retrieved ones. In our example, `target.max` now returns the value 100. Replacing the old value results in the new constraint expression

```
context Communication inv:
self.target->size()>=0 and
self.target->size()<=100
```

And the constraint co-evolution was successfully completed. Note that currently we delete the existing constraint and re-instantiate the template to generate an updated constraint. The update of single values or logical fragments in the existing constraints will be addressed in future work.

The second metamodel modification we have to consider is the addition of the new derived reference `all` to `Component`. When the template engine is informed that a derived reference has been added, it automatically discovers that this element matches the instantiation context of template $T2$. Therefore, template instantiation is triggered and the instantiation information `<all>` is used by the data retrieval expressions to retrieve the values that are then used to replace the variables in $T2$ in order to produce the required constraint.

Finally, let us consider what would happen if we remove the derived reference `Communication.inv` in another evolution step. In that case, the template engine would identify $DR1$ as the only constraint that includes the removed element in its scope. Therefore, it would remove the no longer needed constraint $DR1$ from the metamodel automatically.

Model Evolution. As we have discussed in Section 2.1, changes of a model typically lead to a re-validation of affected constraint instances. With our approach, such changes can affect the scopes of generated constraint instances. For example, imagine the addition of a new component as a `target` of `ResultComm` in Fig. 1b. Indeed, this may affect the consistency status of a constraint instance of $R1$. However, since such changes are handled entirely by the employed consistency checker, we omit a detailed discussion here and refer to [8].

4   Evaluation and Analysis

We evaluated the applicability and the performance of our approach with a case study that was done using a prototype implementation.

4.1   Prototype Implementation

For the evaluation, we developed the *Cross-Layer Modeler (XLM)* [11]. This tool allows working with models and their metamodels at the same time, which means that manipulations of the metamodel have immediate effects on the conformance of the model. The XLM leveraged from our previous work on the Model/Analyzer [8, 14] which supports efficient and scalable incremental consistency checking of arbitrary design constraints.

We extended the Model/Analyzer by adding an incremental template engine and the corresponding infrastructure to support the incremental creation, deletion and modification of constraints (based on meta model changes) which the Model/Analyzer then incrementally validates against model changes. Ten sample templates from different domains are available at the tool website [11].

4.2   Case Study: UML

As our case study, we used templates and the Cross-Layer Modeler tool to automate constraint generation and updates for the UML. We chose UML as the subject because it is a well known and commonly used language for modeling software systems. We argue that its size and high level of complexity make it ideal for our purposes because the sample evolutions we performed simulate typical evolutions of metamodels in general. Additionally, numerous industrial software models are available [16]. We ran tests with 21 models with sizes from 3,077 to 36,205 model elements (i.e., instances of UML elements) and with different characteristics for our experiments. Every test was performed 100 times on an Intel Core i5-650 machine with 8GB of memory running Windows 7 Professional. The median and average values were used for analysis.

We used templates to automatically create constraints that check the structural integrity of UML model elements (e.g., modeled classes). Structural integrity is given if a model element provides the structural features as defined in the UML metamodel. Our constraints are based on the *ECore* metamodel and check the number of assigned elements as well as the assigned elements' types for every reference and attribute in the UML (e.g., every instance of NamedElement must have exactly one String object assigned as its name). We classify the changes in our study in three categories.

Category I. Metamodel Evolution. Different metamodel modifications and common refactorings have been discussed in literature [4, 17–21]. During most common metamodel evolutions, references or attributes are added, removed, or are modified (e.g., the cardinality of an attribute is changed or an attribute is moved to another class). Therefore, we performed these kinds of evolutions

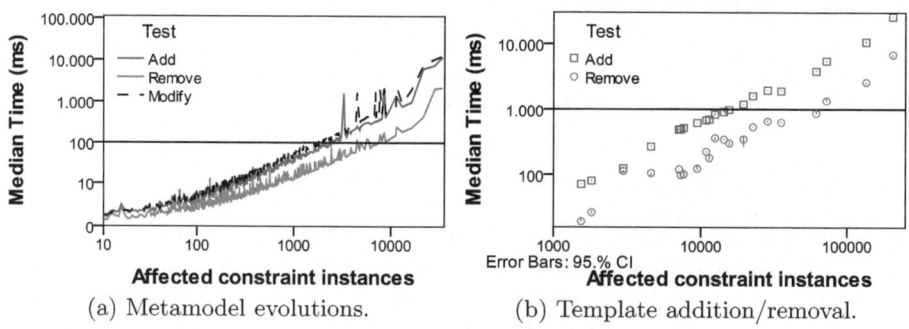

(a) Metamodel evolutions.   (b) Template addition/removal.

Fig. 4. Evaluation results

with the UML metamodel. From this point on we will use the term *property* for
references and attributes alike.

Scenario 1. Add new property. In the first scenario, a new property was added
to every single element of the UML metamodel, which required the generation of
a new constraint (as we discussed in Section 2.2 where we added a new derived
reference to our sample metamodel). We investigated the total time required for
performing the metamodel change, the required co-evolutions and the validation of the model with the new constraint. Note that for our statistics we only
considered those changes that created constraints that could actually be validated with at least one model element (e.g., we ignored the addition of a new
reference to UseCase if the model did not include any use cases). Fig. 4a shows
the required processing times for changes that affected different numbers of constraint instances. 99% of all modifications took less than 166ms to finish and only
0.15% of all performed changes took more than 500ms. On average, changes took
12.5ms and the generated constraint was validated with 201 constraint instances
in the model. For the addition of elements in this test we observed a Pearson
correlation coefficient of 0.845 between the required time and the number of
required validations. The correlation between T and the model size S, $P(T, S)$
was 0.099, which indicates that the processing time strongly depends on the
validation effort needed for the new constraint and that it is independent from
the model size.

Scenario 2. Remove existing property. In the second scenario, each test run
started with the unmodified UML metamodel and exactly one property was
removed, meaning that exactly one constraint became obsolete and was removed
from the consistency checker. Again, only changes of metamodel elements that
were actually used in the model were captured. 99% of all modification took
less than 38.5ms. Only 0.1% of the modifications took longer than 250ms. On
average, element removal took 4.5ms and 202 constraint instances were removed
with the obsolete constraint. Fig. 4a shows that property removal is always faster
than addition because there is no need for validating any constraint instances.

Scenario 3. Modify existing property. For these tests, the cardinality as well
as the name of every existing property in the UML were changed. 99% of
the modification that caused an update of actually validated constraints were

processed in less than 180ms and 0.1% took more than 1,000ms. For the modification of elements we observed a correlation coefficient of 0.734 between the required processing time and the number of validations.

Category II. Model Evolution. The incremental consistency checker that is used by the Cross-Layer Modeler, the Model/Analyzer, is highly scalable [16]. We previously evaluated the approach on 34 models with model sizes of up to 162,237 model elements and 24 types of consistency rules (constraints). Empirical evaluation showed that the consistency checking part requires only 1.4ms to re-evaluate the consistency of the model after a change for typical UML consistency and well-formedness constraints [22]. The data indicates that the additional change processing infrastructure does not impose a significant performance penalty.

Category III. Template Addition and Removal. Even though adding, removing, or changing a template is a task performed less often than metamodel evolutions, we still investigated this aspect. Since the addition of a new template requires a full scan of the metamodel to create all possible constraints and a complete initial validation of the model we expected this task to be more time consuming than processing changes incrementally. The processing times for the addition and removal of the templates we used in Category I to the UML metamodel that caused the generation or removal of different numbers of constraint instances are shown in Fig. 4b. Adding a template took less than 5,700ms in 90% of our tests, in only 8% of the tests it took more than 10s. On average, the addition of a template took 2,818ms and created constraints that were validated 31,936 times. Removing a template does not require validations of constraints, thus this task is performed in less than 1,600ms in 90% of our tests. Only 5% of template removals take more than 3s.

Summary. The results of the representative metamodel evolutions clearly indicate that our approach is applicable to large and complex metamodels and that it is fast enough to deliver instant feedback about model consistency after metamodel changes. Processing changes that occur frequently during early development phases takes only milliseconds with our approach in most cases and even the worst case values are acceptable considering the fact that they were still below 16s and were reached in less than 1% of all changes. Although changing templates is slightly more expensive because of the inevitable processing of the entire model, the values are still acceptable for a rarely performed task.

4.3   Applicability

In the presented examples, we have illustrated how our approach performs co-evolution of model constraints when metamodel changes occur. However, our approach is not limited to metamodels as the source of constraints. Quite the contrary, any model can be used to trigger template instantiation and the generated constraints may restrict any kind of model – even metamodels [23]. To date, various sample templates for different metamodels and models are available [11], thus we are confident that the approach is generally applicable.

Note that evolving constraints also enables repair technologies that fix detected inconsistencies (e.g., [24–26]). Therefore, our approach provides a foundation for providing guided or even automatic co-evolution of metamodels and models based on evolved constraints.

5   Related Work

There has been an extensive research activity in models and their evolution. Here we focused on those closest to our work and grouped them in three themes.

Metamodel and Model (Co-)evolution. The efficient, and ideally automated, (tool-)support for metamodel evolution and the corresponding co-evolution of conforming models was identified by Mens et al. in 2005 as one of the major challenges in software evolution [27]. Since then, various approaches have been proposed to deal with this challenge. Wachsmuth addresses the issue of metamodel changes by describing them as transformational adaptations that are performed stepwise instead of big, manually performed ad hoc changes [21]. Changes to the metamodel become traceable and can be qualified according to semantics- or instance-preservation. He further proposes the use of transformation patterns that are instantiated with metamodel transformations to create co-transformations for models. Cicchetti et al. classify possible metamodel changes and decompose differences between model versions into sets of changes of the same modification-class [28]. They identify possible dependencies that can occur between different kinds of modifications and provide an approach to handle these dependencies and to automate model co-evolution.

Herrmannsdoerfer et al. also classified coupled metamodel changes and investigated how far different adaptations are automatable [29]. One aspect that these approaches have in common is that they are based on decomposing evolution steps into atomic modification for deriving co-adaptations. Our approach is also based on atomic modifications that are handled individually to perform necessary adaptations incrementally. However, we do not try to automate co-evolution of metamodels and models in the first place. Instead, the co-evolution of metamodels and constraints enables tool users to perform adaptations of a model with guidance based on specific constraints and their own domain knowledge.

Wimmer et al. follow a different approach by merging two versions of a metamodel to a *unified metamodel* and then applying co-evolution rules to the models [30]. They instantiate new metaclasses and remove existing elements that are no longer needed. At first, they encountered problems regarding typecasts and instantiation so they had to change some co-evolution rules. XLM can handle the instantiation of created metaclasses as well as arbitrary typecasts of instances.

In terms of constraint co-evolution, Büttner et al. discuss various metamodel modifications and how they affected constraints [13]. They describe how OCL expressions can be transformed to reflect metamodel evolution. We encountered some of the issues they identified during the evolution of our running example, for example the transition from single-object to collection values and vice versa because of multiplicity changes which is handled automatically in XLM.

Flexible and Multilevel Modeling. Atkinson and Kühne identified several issues in the field of multilevel (meta-)modeling, namely the so-called *shallow instantiation* of the UML [31] that forced us to use a graph-oriented model in XLM. They discussed different approaches to overcome these issues like the concept of *deep instantiation* where instances can be types at the same time; an approach we used in our tool's graph model. Ossher et al. lately presented the *BITKit* tool [3] that allows domain-agnostic modeling and on-the-fly assignment of visual notations to dynamically defined domain types. This approach is also implemented in our tool where the type of a model element can be changed at any time.

6   Conclusions and Future Work

This paper presented an approach that uses constraint templates and an automated template engine to address the issue of co-evolving metamodels and constraints. We illustrated how constraint templates can be written and constraints are generated from them. Moreover, we discussed how automatic co-evolution of constraints is achieved and developed a prototype implementation. We performed a case study with UML as an example of a sophisticated metamodel and 21 industrial UML models that clearly showed that our approach is applicable for complex metamodels. The approach is scalable and processing times for co-evolution are primarily affected by the number of required validations after constraint generation or update.

For future work, we plan to investigate the possible benefits of using the approach not only for metamodel-dependent constraints but also for constraints that primarily rely on domain-knowledge. Moreover, we want to expand the approach so that not only constraints but also new templates can be generated through template instantiation.

Acknowledgments. The research was funded by the Austrian Science Fund (FWF): P21321-N15, the EU Marie Curie Actions – Intra European Fellowship (IEF) through project number 254965, and FWF Lise-Meitner Fellowship M1421-N15.

References

1. Schmidt, D.C.: Guest editor's introduction: Model-driven engineering. IEEE Computer 39(2), 25–31 (2006)
2. Manders, E.-J., Biswas, G., Mahadevan, N., Karsai, G.: Component-oriented modeling of hybrid dynamic systems using the generic modeling environment. In: MOMPES 2012, pp. 159–168 (2006)

3. Ossher, H., Bellamy, R.K.E., Simmonds, I., Amid, D., Anaby-Tavor, A., Callery, M., Desmond, M., de Vries, J., Fisher, A., Krasikov, S.: Flexible modeling tools for pre-requirements analysis: conceptual architecture and research challenges. In: OOPSLA, pp. 848–864 (2010)
4. Herrmannsdoerfer, M., Benz, S., Juergens, E.: COPE - automating coupled evolution of metamodels and models. In: Drossopoulou, S. (ed.) ECOOP 2009. LNCS, vol. 5653, pp. 52–76. Springer, Heidelberg (2009)
5. Object Management Group. Unified Modeling Language (UML), http://www.uml.org/
6. Pardillo, J.: A systematic review on the definition of UML profiles. In: Petriu, D.C., Rouquette, N., Haugen, Ø. (eds.) MODELS 2010, Part I. LNCS, vol. 6394, pp. 407–422. Springer, Heidelberg (2010)
7. Vierhauser, M., Grünbacher, P., Egyed, A., Rabiser, R., Heider, W.: Flexible and scalable consistency checking on product line variability models. In: ASE, pp. 63–72 (2010)
8. Reder, A., Egyed, A.: Model/analyzer: a tool for detecting, visualizing and fixing design errors in UML. In: ASE, pp. 347–348 (2010)
9. Object Management Group. Object Constraint Language (OCL), http://www.omg.org/spec/OCL/
10. Demuth, A., Lopez-Herrejon, R.E., Egyed, A.: Automatically generating and adapting model constraints to support co-evolution of design models. In: ASE, pp. 302–305 (2012)
11. Demuth, A., Lopez-Herrejon, R.E., Egyed, A.: Cross-layer modeler: A tool for flexible multilevel modeling with consistency checking. In: ESEC/SIGSOFT FSE, pp. 452–455 (2011), http://www.sea.jku.at/tools/xlm
12. Eclipse Foundation. Eclipse Modeling Framework (EMF), http://eclipse.org/modeling/emf/
13. Büttner, F., Bauerdick, H., Gogolla, M.: Towards transformation of integrity constraints and database states. In: DEXA Workshops, pp. 823–828 (2005)
14. Egyed, A.: Instant consistency checking for the UML. In: ICSE, pp. 381–390 (2006)
15. Blanc, X., Mougenot, A., Mounier, I., Mens, T.: Incremental detection of model inconsistencies based on model operations. In: van Eck, P., Gordijn, J., Wieringa, R. (eds.) CAiSE 2009. LNCS, vol. 5565, pp. 32–46. Springer, Heidelberg (2009)
16. Egyed, A.: Automatically detecting and tracking inconsistencies in software design models. IEEE Trans. Software Eng. 37(2), 188–204 (2011)
17. Cicchetti, A., Di Ruscio, D., Eramo, R., Pierantonio, A.: Automating co-evolution in model-driven engineering. In: EDOC, pp. 222–231 (2008)
18. Hassam, K., Sadou, S., Gloahec, V.L., Fleurquin, R.: Assistance system for OCL constraints adaptation during metamodel evolution. In: CSMR, pp. 151–160 (2011)
19. Marković, S., Baar, T.: Refactoring OCL annotated UML class diagrams. In: Briand, L.C., Williams, C. (eds.) MoDELS 2005. LNCS, vol. 3713, pp. 280–294. Springer, Heidelberg (2005)
20. Sunyé, G., Pollet, D., Le Traon, Y., Jézéquel, J.-M.: Refactoring UML models. In: Gogolla, M., Kobryn, C. (eds.) UML 2001. LNCS, vol. 2185, pp. 134–148. Springer, Heidelberg (2001)
21. Wachsmuth, G.: Metamodel adaptation and model co-adaptation. In: Ernst, E. (ed.) ECOOP 2007. LNCS, vol. 4609, pp. 600–624. Springer, Heidelberg (2007)
22. Groher, I., Reder, A., Egyed, A.: Incremental consistency checking of dynamic constraints. In: Rosenblum, D.S., Taentzer, G. (eds.) FASE 2010. LNCS, vol. 6013, pp. 203–217. Springer, Heidelberg (2010)

23. Demuth, A., Lopez-Herrejon, R.E., Egyed, A.: Constraint-driven modeling through transformation. In: Hu, Z., de Lara, J. (eds.) ICMT 2012. LNCS, vol. 7307, pp. 248–263. Springer, Heidelberg (2012)
24. Egyed, A., Letier, E., Finkelstein, A.: Generating and evaluating choices for fixing inconsistencies in UML design models. In: ASE, pp. 99–108 (2008)
25. Reder, A., Egyed, A.: Computing repair trees for resolving inconsistencies in design models. In: ASE, pp. 220–229 (2012)
26. Nentwich, C., Emmerich, W., Finkelstein, A.: Consistency management with repair actions. In: ICSE, pp. 455–464 (2003)
27. Mens, T., Wermelinger, M., Ducasse, S., Demeyer, S., Hirschfeld, R., Jazayeri, M.: Challenges in software evolution. In: IWPSE, pp. 13–22 (2005)
28. Cicchetti, A., Ruscio, D.D., Pierantonio, A.: Managing dependent changes in coupled evolution. In: ICMT, pp. 35–51 (2009)
29. Herrmannsdoerfer, M., Benz, S., Juergens, E.: Automatability of coupled evolution of metamodels and models in practice. In: Czarnecki, K., Ober, I., Bruel, J.-M., Uhl, A., Völter, M. (eds.) MODELS 2008. LNCS, vol. 5301, pp. 645–659. Springer, Heidelberg (2008)
30. Wimmer, M., Kusel, A., Schönböck, J., Retschitzegger, W., Schwinger, W., Kappel, G.: On using inplace transformations for model co-evolution. In: MtATL. INRIA & Ecole des Mines de Nantes (2010)
31. Atkinson, C., Kühne, T.: The essence of multilevel metamodeling. In: UML 2001, pp. 19–33 (2001)

Model Checking of UML-RT Models Using Lazy Composition

Karolina Zurowska and Juergen Dingel

Queen's University
School of Computing
Kingston, ON, Canada
{zurowska,dingel}@cs.queensu.ca

Abstract. Formal analysis of models is an important aspect of the Model Driven Development (MDD) paradigm. In this paper we introduce a technique to analyze models with hierarchically organized and asynchronously communicating components as found in, e.g., UML-RT. Typically, the more components are composed during analysis, the less scalable it becomes. In our technique we reduce composition by leveraging the communication topology and the property to be checked. To this end we introduce an extension of Computation Tree Logic (CTL) to express properties of models and we show an algorithm to check such properties. In the algorithm, components are represented by their symbolic execution trees and their composition is lazy, i.e., only performed when necessary. To demonstrate some of the benefits of the technique, its implementation for UML-RT models and case studies are discussed.

1 Introduction

One of the promises of MDD is the opportunity to verify models early on in the development process. This paper presents a technique that takes a step towards fulfilling this promise in the context of UML-RT. UML-RT originated from ROOM [21] and now is a proper profile of UML 2 [6]. It is supported by, e.g., IBM Rational Software Architect Real Time Edition (IBM RSA RTE)[1] [3] and, with some minor differences, in eTrice [1]. As opposed to several approaches to verify statecharts including, e.g., [19,15], our technique avoids translation of models into the input language of an existing model checker, which often introduces additional complexity to the analysis and the interpretation of the results. Instead, UML-RT models are analyzed with the help of a formal language designed to capture the core features of UML-RT, such as modularity, hierarchies and communication.

Many of the state-based MDD modeling languages based on UML 2 [6] support modularity, that is, models are built from components (called, e.g., subsystems, modules or capsules [3,2]). In this work, we present an approach to model checking these models that uses this structure to speed up the analysis.

---

[1] IBM and Rational are trademarks of International Business Machines Corporation, registered in many jurisdictions worldwide.

A. Moreira et al. (Eds.): MODELS 2013, LNCS 8107, pp. 304–319, 2013.

Just as in other state-based modeling notations, UML-RT allows the definition of model structure using containment and connectors: containment shows which capsule contains other capsules and connectors show the communication topology, i.e., which capsule can communicate with which other capsules. Our analysis leverages this information together with the structure of the formula to be checked to improve performance by incorporating components into the search only to the extent that they can influence the satisfaction of the formula. More precisely, only components which can impact the validity of the formula are fully explored; other components are explored only to the extent that they can influence the behavior of these formula-relevant components through connectors. The net result of these optimizations is that in the best case, model structure and formula allow even large models to be checked efficiently. In the worst case (e.g. if all components are mentioned in a formula), though, a full exploration is necessary and our technique brings no savings.

The analysis is based on an on-the-fly symbolic execution of the model with lazy composition as described above. The execution yields a symbolic representation of the state space in the form of a symbolic execution tree (SET) which can be substantially more concise than a concrete one (e.g., an infinite concrete state space may be representable with a finite SET). The execution operates on a formal internal representation of the model, called Functional Finite State Machines (FFSMs), which has been designed to capture key features of state-based modeling languages such as UML-RT including nesting of components, state machines with actions code, and asynchronous communication between components.

The analysis builds on our previous work on the symbolic execution of UML-RT models [26,27]. We note that neither the present, nor our previous work [26,27] is limited to UML-RT, but can be applied to all models that can be represented with FFSMs.

Section 2 briefly discusses UML-RT. Section 3 presents a logic (an extension of Computation Tree Logic [10]) to query symbolic execution trees for UML-RT models. An algorithm to check formulas in this logic and a prototype together with some case studies are described in Sections 4 and 5, respectively. Related work is surveyed in Section 6.

2   UML-RT Models and Their Symbolic Execution

2.1   Overview of the UML-RT Language

The structure of UML-RT models is described in terms of components called *capsules*, which are highly encapsulated active classes. They may be hierarchical (nested), because a capsule may contain instances of other capsules called *parts*. The communication between capsules is signal-driven and uses *ports*. A port has a type that is a *protocol*, which gathers signals sent or received by a capsule through this port.

Example 1. Figure 1(a) presents the structure of a capsule `Controller`. The capsule has 2 parts `carLightsFirst` and `carLightsSecond`, both instances of the

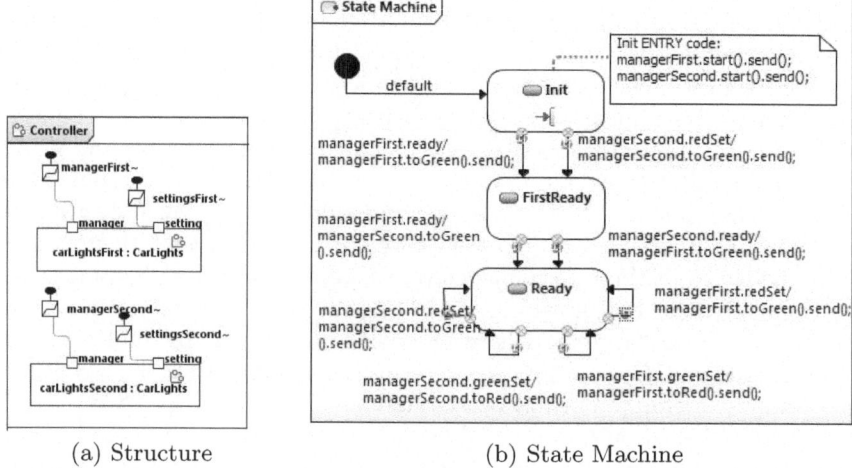

(a) Structure   (b) State Machine

Fig. 1. A structure and behavior of capsule `Controller`. Labels of transitions are of the forms: `port.signal` or `port.signal/action_code`.

`CarLights` capsule. The `CarLights` capsule (structure is omitted here) contains a timer (`lightsTimer`) and two external ports (`manager` and `setting`). The parts communicate with `Controller` through ports `managerFirst`, `managerSecond` and `settingsFirst`, `settingsSecond`, respectively.

The behavior of each capsule is specified with a UML-RT State Machine, which is a variant of UML 2 State Machines [6]. A UML-RT State Machine has *states* and *transitions* which can be guarded and which can contain actions. Transitions are triggered by *signals* received through ports of a capsule. The actions in UML-RT are expressed with the help of *action language*. This language can be C++, Java or UAL (implementation of ALF [7]).

Example 2. Figures 1(b) and 2 show the UML-RT State Machines. The state machine for `Controller` initializes two instances of `CarLights` and then continuously switches between red and green lights without any synchronization, because the lights are supposed to be independent. Several transitions have actions that send signals (action code: `port.signal().send()`). For instance, in the transition triggered by signal `ready()` received on port `managerFirst`, the action is `managerFirst.toGreen().send()`, which sends signal `toGreen` to part `carLightsFirst`, because this part is connected to the port `managerFirst`. The UML-RT State Machine for `CarLights` shown in Figure 2 waits for signal `start` and then cycles through the colours of lights. The cycle is managed with signals `toGreen` and `toRed` received on port `manager`. This capsule uses timers, which are set in action code using the method `informIn(delay)`, where `delay` is the number of seconds after which the timer times out and generates `timeout` signal.

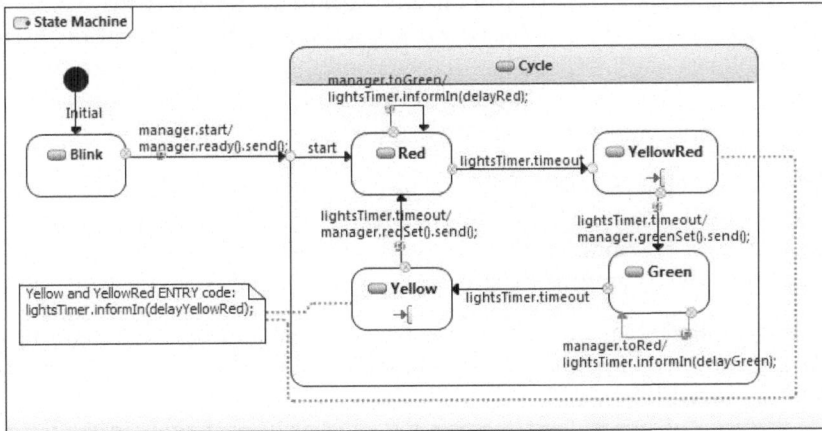

Fig. 2. UML-RT State Machine of CarLights

Formal Representation with Functional Finite State Machines. A Functional Finite State Machine (FFSM) [26,27] represents a UML-RT State Machine with functions used to summarize action code on transition and in states. These functions are obtained through the symbolic execution of the action code. FFSMs describe behaviour of a module (capsule) and its parts. The input/output signals are connected directly with parts (ports are omitted). The work presented in this paper has been defined for FFSMs, so any modeling language that translates to the communicating FFSMs can benefit from the proposed technique.

2.2 Symbolic Execution of UML-RT Models

The technique proposed in [26,27] starts with the symbolic execution of non-composite capsules, realized through the symbolic execution of their UML-RT State Machines [26]. The result is a symbolic execution tree SET, in which states have the structure as in Definition 1.

Definition 1. A *symbolic state* is a tuple $s = (l, v, pc)$, where l is a location (in a UML-RT State Machine), v is a valuation of attributes (variables of a given capsule, which may be accessed at any point of execution) and pc is a set of path constraints, that is, constraints on received inputs, which must be satisfied to reach this state.

Transitions between symbolic states are labeled with input and output actions, which may contain variables. Variables associated with input actions get a symbolic value, which is used later whenever necessary. During symbolic execution similar states which have the same location, the same valuation of variables and the same or stronger constraints, are discovered with the help of a *subsumption relation*, which makes the tree finite.

Non-trivial UML-RT models contain parts, each of which has a behavior given as a UML-RT State Machine. In [27] we showed a technique to compose symbolic execution trees, so that we can symbolically execute composite UML-RT models. The proposed composition is based on asynchronous communication between parts and follows the hierarchical structure of a model, starting at the leaves of the hierarchy (i.e., non-composite capsules). The result of composition is a composite symbolic execution tree with states defined as follows.

Definition 2. Let $\mathbb{C}$ be a set of all capsules in a model. Let $C \in \mathbb{C}$ be a capsule, whose behavior is described by state machine SM; let SET be the symbolic execution tree of SM and let P be the set of parts in C. A *composite symbolic state* is a tuple $css = (s, q, p)$, where:

- s is a symbolic state in SET or a state that resulted from a substitution of some of the variables in C. This substitution models the binding of variables to input variables,
- q is a queue of input signals along with the values of their input variables received by this capsule. The received values may be used later on when creating a new symbolic state for the capsule,
- p is a function $p : P \to \mathbb{S}$, where $\mathbb{S}$ is a set of all composite symbolic execution states for $\mathbb{C}$. The function p maps parts P to their composite symbolic states (in case of non-composite capsules this function is empty).

3   Logic to Query UML-RT Models

In order to define a language that can express properties of executions of FFSMs we will use an extension of Computation Tree Logic (CTL) [10]. This extension starts with Definition 3 of atomic propositions in the logic.

Definition 3. Let C be a capsule with a state machine SM and $css = (s, q, p)$ be a composite symbolic state for C (as in Definition 2). An atomic proposition $ap \in AP$ is:

- l: a location of SM, which is satisfied if s contains that location,
- (cst): a constraint over attributes of SM, which is satisfied if the path constraints in s imply cst,
- <in1(val1),in2(val2),...> : where in1,in2,... are input signals and val1, val2,... are mappings of received input variables to their values. Each input signal (or a value) can be substituted with any, which represents any signal (any value). This proposition is satisfied if the contents of the queue q is as specified,
- in(val_i)[out1(val_o1),...]: where in is an input signal and val_i is a mapping of its variables to their values, out1, out2,... are output signals and val_o1, val_o2, ... are mappings of output variables to expressions that describe their values. As in the previous proposition, signals or mappings can be substituted with any. This proposition is satisfied if there exists an output transition from css with input signal in(val_i) and the sequence of output signals out1(val_o1),...,

---

Algorithm 1. An outline of an algorithm check(f, C).

Require: formula f, a capsule C
Ensure: *true* if f is satisfied in C and *false* otherwise
    init_parts ← init_parts(f, C)
    (*to_explore, rcset*) ← init_exploration(*init_parts*)
3: (*atomic_prop, formulas*) ← translate_and_divide_formula(f)
    while *to_explore* is not empty **do**
       css ← remove an element from *to_explore*
6:     *new_to_explore* ← explore(*top, css, init_parts, init_parts, rcset*)
       add *new_to_explore* to *to_explore*
       result ←label(f, *atomic_prop, formulas, label, rcset, new_to_explore*)
9:    **if** *result* ≠ *null* **then**
       return *result*

- ap @ part: where ap is an atomic proposition and part is a part in C. This proposition is satisfied if ap is satisfied in state p(part), or
- NOT ap, ap1 AND ap2, ap1 OR ap2, ap1 IMPLY ap2: are the usual logical connectives and ap1,ap2,ap are atomic propositions.

In order to relate states and atomic propositions temporally we will use the standard CTL connectives: EF, EG, EU and AF, AG, AU and their compositions with logical connectives. These will constitute a set of formulas F with the standard semantics [10] adapted for symbolic execution trees.

Example 3. The following formulas describe some of the properties of the model introduced in Figure 2 and 1:

- AF(Green @ carLightsFirst): checks whether the first car lights always eventually reaches a state with green lights (is proven true in our tool),
- AF(any(any)[manager.ready()] @ carLightsFirst): checks whether the first car lights always eventually sends the signal ready to the manager (is proven true in our tool).

4   Algorithm to Check Formulas

In this section we will describe an algorithm to check the satisfaction of formulas F expressed in the logic from Section 3. An outline of the algorithm is shown in Algorithm 1.It starts with the initialization (lines 1-3), followed by the exploration loop (line 4). In the loop, a state to be explored is removed from the list *to_explore*. The exploration of this state in line 6 results in a set of new states *new_to_explore*. These states are used during the labeling in line 8. After the labeling step, if formula f can be proved or disproved, the result is returned.

Initialization in Algorithm 1 is performed in three main stages:

1. Collect initial parts (line 1). Gathering initial parts in *init_parts* is achieved by traversing the input formula f until atomic propositions are reached. Parts mentioned in conjunction with @ are included in *init_parts*, as well as parts that, according to the communication topology, generate input actions mentioned in propositions describing queues and input/output.

Algorithm 2. An outline of `explore`(top, css, $init\_parts$, $expl\_parts$, $rcset$).

Require: the top top level part of a composite symbolic state $css = (s, q, p)$, a current reduced composite symbolic tree $rcset$

Require: a set of initial parts $init\_parts$ and a set of currently explored parts $expl\_parts$

Ensure: $new\_to\_explore$ is a set of newly generated states and $rcset$ is a tree updated after exploration

    $new\_to\_explore \leftarrow \emptyset$

    if $top \in expl\_parts$ **then**

3:    **for all** $transition$ in outgoing transitions from s **do**

        $trigger \leftarrow$ get trigger of $transition$

        if $trigger$ is external **then**

6:        $new\_state \leftarrow$ `external`($transition$, css, $rcset$)

        $trigger\_part \leftarrow$ get part generating $trigger$

        if $trigger\_part \in (init\_parts \cup expl\_parts)$ **then**

9:        $new\_state \leftarrow$ `synch`($trigger\_part$, $transition$, css)

        else

          $new\_states \leftarrow$ `pull`($trigger\_part$, top, $trigger$, css, $init\_parts$, $expl\_parts$)

12:      $new\_to\_explore \leftarrow new\_to\_explore \cup new\_states$

    $new\_to\_explore' \leftarrow$ `drop_signal`(css)

    $new\_to\_explore \leftarrow new\_to\_explore \cup new\_to\_explore'$

15: **for all** $part \in$ domain of p **do**

    $new\_to\_explore'' \leftarrow$ `explore`($part$, $p(part)$, $init\_parts$, $expl\_parts$, $rcset$)

    $new\_to\_explore \leftarrow new\_to\_explore \cup new\_to\_explore''$

18: **return** $new\_to\_explore$

---

2. Initialization of a reduced composite symbolic execution tree $rcset$ (line 2). The root of this tree (which is added to the set $to\_explore$ also returned from this procedure) is recursively constructed by taking the root states of all symbolic execution trees generated for parts in the initial set. If a part is not in the initial set the dummy state $null$ is used.

3. Translation of the formula and collection of atomic propositions (line 3). The translation is performed so that a formula includes only AF, EU and EX temporal connectives, since they are sufficient to represent all other temporal formulas [10]. Division of a translated formula into its subformulas is done in the standard way as described in [10] until atomic propositions are reached.

Example 4. Consider the formula AF(Green @ carLightsFirst) (from Example 3). The traversal of this formula returns $init\_parts = \{$carLightsFirst$\}$. The initial state of the reduced composite symbolic tree $rcset$ for the formula and the capsule Controller is given in Figure 3 as the first state. The first two lines in the state describe the top level capsule Controller: the $null$ state (since this part is not in the $init\_parts$) and the contents of the queue, respectively. In the next lines the parts included in Controller are represented in the similar fashion. For the capsule and for the formula, only the part carLightsFirst is initialized, which is represented by a location initial (the initial pseudostate in Figure 2), some initial variable bindings and an empty set of path constraints.

4.1 Exploration Step

Algorithm 2 outlines the main steps of the exploration (in line 6 in Algorithm 1) of a given composite symbolic state $css = (s, q, p)$. First, the exploration is performed for a top level part of css (lines 2 - 14) and then subsequently for the

---

Algorithm 3. pull (*trigger_part, receive_part, trigger, css, init_parts, expl_parts, rcset*).

Require: *trigger* generated by *trigger_part* and received by *receive_part*
Require: a composite symbolic state *css* and sets *init_parts* and *expl_parts*
Ensure: *explored* is a set that, if possible, contains states with generated *trigger* in a queue.

    initial_css ← get current symbolic execution state for *trigger_part* in *css*
    if *initial_css* = *null* **then**
3:      *initial_css* ← initialize part *trigger_part* in *css*
    to_explore_pull ← {*initial_css*}
    explored ← ∅
6: **while** (*to_explore_pull* ≠ ∅) **do**
    current_css ← remove an element from *to_explore_pull*
    new_to_explore ← explore(*top, current_css, init_parts,* {*trigger_part*}, *rcset*)
9:    **for all** *s* ∈ *new_to_explore* **do**
        q ← queue for *receive_part* in *s*
        if *trigger* not in *q* **then**
12:          *to_explore_pull* ← *to_explore_pull* ∪ {*s*}
    explored ← *current_css*
    return *explored* ∩ { leaves of *rcset*}

---

parts in the domain of its p function (the recursive call in line 16). If the top level part *top* is in the initial parts, the full exploration follows.

The full exploration has two phases. In the first phase (lines 4–12) each outgoing transition from a current symbolic state s is considered. If a triggering signal *trigger* for this transition is external (i.e., it connects the top level capsule to its environment), the external procedure is executed. In this procedure a new composite symbolic execution state *new_state* is generated, in which s is changed to the target state of the transition. Since the triggering signal is external, its presence in the queue is not required. Intuitively, the environment is simply assumed to be capable of generating this signal. If *trigger* is not an external signal and the part that can generate it (*trigger_part*) is in the initial set of parts, then the procedure synch is performed (line 9). In this procedure the current queue q is checked for the signal *trigger*, and if the signal is there, a new composite symbolic execution state *new_state* with an updated queue and state is generated. However, if the triggering part is not in *init_parts*, then *trigger* must be pulled from this triggering part, as explained below. In the second phase of the full exploration, the procedure drop_signal is performed. Dropping the input signal happens, if the head of the queue has not been matched with any of the triggers of all outgoing transitions. The details of synch, external and drop_signal realize the composition of symbolic execution trees and are omitted here – they can be found in [27].

The most distinguishing feature of the exploration is the pull operation. This operation, outlined in Algorithm 3, is required if a part needs an input signal from another part that is outside the initial set. First, *trigger_part* is initialized if this is the first time the part is pulled (lines 2–3). Then the exploration of *trigger_part* in lines 6–13 follows. The exploration uses a set *to_explore_pull* and iterates through the composite symbolic execution states in it. Each such state is explored in line 8, which is limited only to the part that is currently pulled, because only *trigger_part* is the parameter to the explore in line 8. Note that this call to explore procedure takes care of possible chain of events, by the recursive calls to pull. Queues in newly generated composite states are checked whether they contain the requested *trigger*, and, if they don't, the composite states are further explored. If there are no more states to explore, the result of the pull, that is, the set of newly explored leaves of the *rcset*, is returned. By returning only leaves of this partial exploration tree, the intermediate states generated when checking for *trigger* are not fully explored later, since they represent interactions of parts that cannot influence the satisfaction of the formula.

Example 5. In Figure 3 the states after an exploration step are shown. The `default()` transition initializes the part `carLightsFirst` to its first location `Blink`, the other parts remain keep the *null* state. The second transition is labeled with `PULL` and this represents the situation in which `Controller` must be checked for the input `managerFirst.start()`. Because this is the first time this part is pulled, it is initialized and the default transition is taken. The code associated with this transition (see entry actions of Figure 1(a)) outputs the required signal `managerFirst.start()`. Because in the next state the signal is in the queue of the `carLightsFirst`, the pull operation is finished.

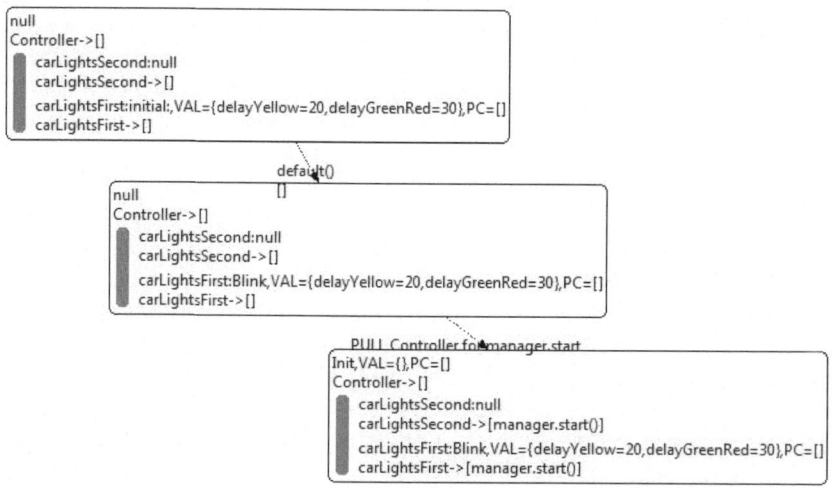

Fig. 3. Exploration step for `Controller` and `AF(Green @ carLightsFirst)`

4.2 Labeling Step

In order to check the satisfiability of formulas introduced in Section 3, we extended the original CTL model checking algorithm [10]. The main goal of this extension is to take advantage of the step-by-step exploration and to check for satisfaction after each step. As in the original algorithm we use the labeling function $label : S \rightarrow \mathbb{P}(F \cup AP)$, which maps each state in a tree to a set of formulas and atomic propositions satisfied in this state.

Algorithm 4. label(f, *atomic_prop, subformulas, label, rcset, discovered*).

Require: a set of atomic propositions *atomic_prop* and formulas *formulas* with a function *label*
Require: a current reduced composite symbolic tree *rcset* and a set of newly discovered states
    discovered,
Ensure: returns **true** or **false** – the satisfaction of a formula f or *null*
    changed ← *discovered*
    for all *state* ∈ *changed* **do**
3:    **for all** p ∈ *atomic_prop* **do**
        check_atomic($st, p, label$)
    while *changed* ≠ ∅ **do**
6:    **for all** st ∈ *changed* **do**
        for all f ∈ *subformulas* **do**
            remove st from *changed*
9:        *changed_state* ← check_formula ($f, st, label$)
        changed ← *changed* ∪ {*changed_state*}
    if f ∈ *label*(root of *rcset*) or (¬f) ∈ *label*(root of *rcset*) **then**
12:    **return true**(or **false**)
    else
        return *null*

The outline of a labeling algorithm, as used in line 8 of Algorithm 1, is shown in Algorithm 4. The algorithm is divided into two main parts. In the first part (lines 2 –4) the satisfaction of atomic propositions only in newly discovered states is checked, because it can be determined right after a composite state is generated. The states with a changed labeling function are gathered in set *changed*. These states are used in the second part of the algorithm to check the satisfaction of formulas (lines 5–10). This check continues until there are no more changes in the labeling functions. After labeling, the labels of the root of the tree are inspected to check whether they contain the main formula or its negation, which determines the satisfaction or dissatisfaction of the whole formula.

Checking the satisfaction of atomic propositions (line 4 in Algorithm 4) is performed for each proposition and for each newly discovered state. If the checked proposition holds, then *label* is updated with this proposition, if not, with its negation. Labeling states with formulas (line 9 in Algorithm 4) is performed for each changed state and is based on the shape of the formula.

Example 6. In case of the reduced composite tree in Figure 3, the truth of AF (Green @ carLightsFirst) for the capsule Controller cannot be determined, because the atomic proposition Green @ carLightsFirst does not hold in any of the shown states and the last state has not been explored yet. However, the satisfaction is proved as soon as state Green is reached in part carLightsFirst along all paths.

4.3 Correctness of the Algorithm

A composite symbolic execution tree of a capsule C, denoted with $\mathcal{CSET}(C)$, is a tree that represents the full composition of C and contains all its execution paths and symbolic execution states. The procedure in Algorithm 1 generates a reduced composite symbolic execution tree $\mathcal{RCSET}(C, f)$ required to check the satisfaction of f in C. This reduced tree may exclude some execution states of C. In order to show the correctness of Algorithm 1 we need to prove the following:

Theorem 1. *Let C be a capsule that has a composite symbolic execution tree $\mathcal{CSET}(C)$ and let f be a formula. Also, let $\mathcal{RCSET}(C, f)$ be the reduced composite symbolic execution tree for C and f as generated by Algorithm 1. We have that f is satisfied in $\mathcal{CSET}(C)$ iff f is satisfied in $\mathcal{RCSET}(C, f)$.*

In the proof of Theorem 1 we must show that states which are not included in $\mathcal{RCSET}(C, f)$ cannot change the satisfaction of f. First, note that the parts of the model mentioned directly or indirectly (as generators of input signals) in the formula f (called initial parts) are included in the construction of $\mathcal{RCSET}(C, f)$. Then, note that the pull operation adds all paths in $\mathcal{RCSET}(M, f)$, which involve communication with non-initial parts as necessary during the execution. In turn, all changes in the satisfaction of atomic propositions in f are included in $\mathcal{RCSET}(C, f)$. This means that if an atomic proposition starts to hold or stops holding along a path in $\mathcal{CSET}(C)$, these changes are reflected in $\mathcal{RCSET}(C, f)$. Moreover, the order of these changes cannot be altered in $\mathcal{RCSET}(C, f)$ and is the same as in $\mathcal{CSET}(C)$. Consequently, omitted states can only duplicate the already existing information about the satisfaction of atomic propositions in f. Removing such states cannot affect the temporal properties of the entire system. For instance, if, while checking `AF p` in some state s, some states "between" s and the first state satisfying `p` are removed, `AF p` will still be found to be satisfied in s. This means that the reduced composite symbolic execution tree $\mathcal{RCSET}(C, f)$ is sufficient to prove or disprove the temporal formulas in the presented logic. Theorem 1 can be formally proven by the induction on the structure of the formula f and is omitted here due to space limitations.

5   Implementation and Illustration

The prototype checker (SAUML 2[2]) has been implemented in IBM RSA RTE as an extension of our previous tool. SAUML 2 consists of a translator of UML-RT models to FFSMs, a symbolic execution engine for non-composite capsules and an implementation of the algorithm from Section 4. We used SAUML 2 on a variety of models with promising results. The results presented in this section were selected to demonstrate, firstly, whether the checker can be used in the context of large UML-RT models and, secondly, how it deals with models of increasing complexity.

5.1   PBX Model Case Study

In order to demonstrate the usability of our method to analyze large models, we used a UML-RT model obtained from our industrial partner. The model is a PBX (private branch exchange) system, that is, a telephone system based on extensions [5]. The model includes several layers, e.g., configuration and telephony components and some more low-level details such as data types and sockets.

---

[2] The tool can be downloaded from `http://research.cs.queensu.ca/`
`~mase/sauml2.html`

The layers contain several subsystems. We experimented with three of them: DeviceManager, CallControl, OAMSubsystem. Each of these subsystems contains up to 6 capsules with state machines with up to 10 states at 3 levels of nesting. After code generation, the subsystems are between 3000 and 6500 lines of code in C++ (which does not include the code for the UML-RT framework). The model uses some advanced UML-RT features that SAUML 2 does not yet support such as the dynamic creation/destruction and binding/unbinding of sub-capsules via optional and plugin roles, multiplicities on ports, and the deferral (and recall) of signals; moreover, our symbolic execution engine currently cannot handle advanced C++ features such as pointers. Some of these features can be replaced by more primitive ones, while leaving the functionality of the model intact. For instance, a port (or part) with multiplicity can be replaced by as many appropriately connected copies of the port (or part) as the multiplicity requires and optional capsules can be replaced by fixed ones.

We used our tool to analyze the subsystems with respect to a number of different properties including:

- DeviceManager: Property 1 (safety property): there is no path leading to a state in which there is an active session for a phone without any extensions (an attribute numExtensions), as expressed in a formula:
  AG (NOT (numExtensions == 0 @ phone1 AND SessionActive @ phone1))
- OAMSubsystem: Property 2 (consuming an input): the assignment of an extension to a device channel (an input signal addSucceeded) is possible : EF (configureDevice.addSucceeded(any)[any] @ gMSC)
- CallControl: Property 3 (sessions can be connected): after ringing (in state Ringing) an originating and terminating sessions (parts sessionOrig and sessionTerm, respectively) will be connected (in state Connected) :
  EF (E [Ringing@call1.sessionTerm U
  (Connected@call1.sessionTerm AND Connected@call1.sessionOrig)])

Table 1 shows the results. Column "Full CSET" contains the results of a full symbolic exploration of subsystems without the use of any property, until the machine resources (standard PC with 4GB of RAM and Intel Core i7 CPU at 2.93 GHz) were exhausted; shown are the number of symbolic states and exploration time. As presented in the "Example property" column, using a property substantially reduces the explored state space in terms of number of states and time. This is due to the lazy composition and, to the lesser extent, due to the on-the-fly labeling. This more substantial effect of the lazy composition is present in all checked properties, because they refer only to a few parts in the model. Although properties 2 and 3 require that a specific state be found, this state has been selected so that it occurs late in the behaviour of the subsystems. In turn the state space explored up to that specific state includes a large part of the entire state space in this reduced, property-driven exploration (meaning that this state will probably not be discovered during the full search without a property for the part of the state space we were able to explore in our experiments). This reduction from the full CSET to the property-driven state space, which is due to the lazy composition, is the most apparent in case of Property 1, which requires

Table 1. Experiments with the subsystems of the PBX model and checking of formulas

Subsystem	Full CSET (without property)		Example property	
	Size	Time	Size	Time
`DeviceManager`	>24000	>4h	2809	3s
`OAMSubsystem`	>32000	>4h	1813	260s
`CallControl`	>48000	>5h	28014	37s

Table 2. Experiments with a UML-RT model (see Section 2) and checking of formulas (size is number of states, time in seconds)

UML-RT model	CSET		Formula 1				Formula 2			
			One		All		One		All	
	Size	Time	Size	Time	Size	Time	Size	Time	Size	Time
2 parts	109	1.9	9	<1	97	<1	4	<1	50	<1
3 parts	1202	2.3	13	<1	681	<1	4	<1	72	< 1
4 parts	13085	39	9	<1	5093	8	4	<1	139	2
5 parts	147820	1799	9	< 1	41447	288	4	<1	238	2

checking all states along all paths, that is, exploring the entire state space. But, since the property mentions only some parts of the model, the lazy composition helps to reduce the searched space. This in turn makes the checking faster, as demonstrated for all the above cases.

5.2   Scalability

In order to check the scalability of the method, we used the examples based on the original traffic lights model introduced in Section 2 with additional traffic lights parts. As shown in Table 2, four UML-RT models are used with 2, 3, 4 and 5 `carLights` parts. In the table, column 'CSET' shows the size of the full composite tree along with the time required to generate it. The results, that is, the sizes of the reduced composite trees and the time required by the analysis are shown in the columns 'Formula 1' and 'Formula 2' using the following formulas:

- Formula 1 is EF (Green @ carLightsFirst AND Green @ carLightsSecond AND ...) and it checks whether it is possible to reach a state in which all mentioned parts are in the Green state. The formula is checked in 2 versions: when only one part is mentioned (so there is no AND clause) and when all parts are mentioned. These formulas are satisfied (due to the lack of dependencies between CarLights parts).
- Formula 2 is AF (Red @ carLightsFirst AND Red @ carLightsSecond AND ...) and it checks whether for all executions the mentioned parts will be in state Red. This formula is also checked in two versions. In case when only one part is mentioned it is satisfied, and if all parts are mentioned it is not satisfied.

We note that for formulas that mention only one part, there is no change in the size of the checked state space and time required by the analysis. On the other hand, formulas referring to many parts, the increasing size of the model affects the complexity of the analysis. However, the increase is not proportional. In case of the first formula, the state that satisfies its atomic proposition is discovered late and the reduced trees are still very large — they grow almost as fast as the whole composite trees. In case of the second formula the state space also increases, but is still substantially smaller than the full composition, because the dissatisfaction is discovered before the state space is fully explored.

The above results show that the proposed checking technique is beneficial for properties that involve a limited number of parts. For properties that require all parts there would likely be no performance improvement. Additionally, the efficiency of the method depends also on the communication-related dependencies between components. Obviously, less communication require fewer pull operations and that makes the tree necessary to check the formula remain small.

6   Related Work

The vast majority of tools for the verification of state-based models translate models to the input language of an existing model checker. For instance, UML State Machines can be analyzed using Spin [20] or Java Pathfinder [17,8], and Stateflow models can be verified using NuSMV and SAL [18]. UML-RT has been translated to Promela [19] and to AsmL used in SpecExlorer [15]. More recently, symbolic execution for UML State Machines has been implemented using Symbolic PathFinder (SPF) [8]. These translational approaches leverage existing analysis tools at the expense of having to capture the semantics of the models in the input languages expected by these tools. However, modern state machine notations as supported by current MDE tools are so sophisticated that the use of Promela or NuSMV seems appropriate only for a small class of models (e.g., those with only boolean and enumeration types [18]). Translation to a high-level language such as Java appears more appropriate, but even then accidental complexity is easily introduced [9]. In contrast, our approach attempts to bring domain-specific model checking to UML-RT and similar languages by using a custom-made intermediate representation (FFSMs) and algorithms which shortens the "semantic gap" and facilitates the exploitation of the model semantics to speed up analysis [24].

Lots of other related work exists in the field of compositional reasoning. The work by Lind-Nielsen et al. [16], e.g., also proposes a "lazy" kind of composition technique that incorporates state machines into the analysis only as needed using a dependency analysis. However, it is formulated in terms of state/event systems which do not appear to support action code of the kind considered here; moreover, our approach not only leverages the communication topology but also the formula being checked. Giese et al. [11] explore compositional reasoning for UML State Machines with parallel composition and synchronous communication and assume-guarantee-style interface constraints expressed in OCL. Our approach does not require the specification of assumptions and analysis is fully automatic. Moreover, the modeling language used in [11] is quite different than UML-RT, focusing on real time aspects of models. Other work [13,25,22,14] has explored the simplification (abstraction) of components during composition while preserving properties of the overall system. In our work, components are also abstracted (using symbolic execution); however, we also employ lazy composition.

Symbolic execution for State Machines has been discussed in [8] and our own work [26,27]. The approach in [8] represents state machines in Java and uses SPF for an analysis that supports different state machine semantics; while our analysis could be adapted to support different state machine dialects, leveraging the semantics of UML-RT for analysis is currently a more important concern. The work in [26,27] presents the symbolic execution routines used in this paper, but does not consider model checking and compositional analysis.

On-the-fly model checking of CTL formulas has been presented previously (e.g., [23]). Our contribution here is that the analysis is implemented for UML-RT with optimizations that take the formula and the structure of the model into account.

Finally, to the best of our knowledge, no tool that analyzes UML-RT models to a comparable extent is currently available.

7   Conclusions

We have presented algorithms and a tool for checking CTL formulas on UML-RT models. The approach is based on previously developed symbolic execution routines [26,27] which can facilitate the analysis of very large state spaces. The checker is domain-specific in that the analysis is performed on a representation of the UML-RT model specifically designed to shorten the semantic gap and leverage the model semantics to speed up the analysis. Speedup is achieved by excluding those components from the analysis that are known to not impact the validity of the checked formula. Performance on our case studies is promising, despite our relatively straight-forward implementation that currently forgoes many optimization opportunities (e.g., using a state-of-the-art symbolic execution engine for action code such as KLEE [4]).

We agree with [24] that the success of model checking in a domain depends on suitable, efficiently analyzable representations for internal models that remain "hidden" from the user. More experimentation and refinement of our prototype on industrial models is necessary before our approach can be judged more definitely in this respect. However, based on the results described in the paper, we consider it a promising step towards the domain-specific verification of industrial UML-RT models that is worth pursuing further.

Apart from refining the prototype, future work will also investigate the use of dynamic symbolic execution [12].

Acknowledgments. This work was partially funded by NSERC, as part of the NECSIS Automotive Partnership with General Motors, IBM Canada and Malina Software Corp.

References

1. eTrice: Real-Time Modeling Tools, http://www.eclipse.org/etrice/
2. IBM Rational Rhapsody,
   http://www.ibm.com/developerworks/rational/products/rhapsody/

3. IBM Rational Software Architect, RealTime Edition, Version 8.0.3,
   http://publib.boulder.ibm.com/infocenter/rsarthlp/v8/index.jsp
4. The KLEE Symbolic Virtual Machine, http://klee.llvm.org
5. Private branch exchange (PBX),
   http://en.wikipedia.org/wiki/Private_branch_exchange
6. Unified Modeling Language (UML 2.0) Superstructure, http://www.uml.org/
7. Action Language for Foundational UML (ALF) (2010)
8. Balasubramanian, D., Pasareanu, C., Whalen, M., Karsai, G., Lowry, M.: Polyglot: Modeling and analysis for multiple statechart formalisms. In: ISSTA 2011 (2011)
9. Balasubramanian, D., Pasareanu, C., Whalen, M., Karsai, G., Lowry, M.: Improving symbolic execution for statechart formalisms. In: MoDeVVa 2012 (2012)
10. Clarke, E.M., Grumberg, O.J., Peled, D.A.: Model checking. MIT Press, Cambridge (1999)
11. Giese, H., Tichy, M., Burmester, S., Schäfer, W., Flake, S.: Towards the compositional verification of real-time UML designs. In: ESEC/FSE 2003, pp. 38–47 (2003)
12. Godefroid, P., Klarlund, N., Sen, K.: Dart: Directed automated random testing. SIGPLAN Not. 40(6), 213–223 (2005)
13. Graf, S., Steffen, B.: Compositional minimization of finite state systems. In: Larsen, K.G., Skou, A. (eds.) CAV 1991. LNCS, vol. 575, Springer, Heidelberg (1992)
14. Jensen, H., Larsen, G., Skou, A.: Scaling up Uppaal. In: Formal Techniques in Real-Time and Fault-Tolerant Systems, pp. 641–678 (2000)
15. Leue, S., Stefanescu, A., Wei, W.: An AsmL Semantics for Dynamic Structures and Run Time Schedulability in UML-RT. Tech. rep., University of Konstanz (2008)
16. Lind-Nielsen, J., Andersen, H.R., Behrmann, G., Hulgaard, H., Kristoffersen, K., Larsen, K.G.: Verification of large state/event systems using compositionality and dependency analysis. In: Steffen, B. (ed.) TACAS 1998. LNCS, vol. 1384, p. 201. Springer, Heidelberg (1998)
17. Mehlitz, P.: Trust your model — verifying aerospace system models with Java JavaPathFinder. In: IEEE Aerospace Conference (2008)
18. Miller, S., Whalen, M., Cofer, D.: Software model checking takes off. CACM 53(2), 58–64 (2010)
19. Saaltink, M., Meisels, I.: Using SPIN to sanalyse RoseRT models. Tech. rep., ORA Canada (1999)
20. Schäfer, T., Knapp, A., Merz, S.: Model checking UML state machines and collaborations. Electronic Notes in Theoret. Comp. Science 55(3), 1–13 (2001)
21. Selic, B., Gullekson, G., Ward, P.T.: Real-time Object Oriented Modeling and Design. Wiley (1994)
22. Valmari, A.: Compositional state space generation. In: Rozenberg, G. (ed.) APN 1993. LNCS, vol. 674, pp. 427–457. Springer, Heidelberg (1993)
23. Vergauwen, B., Lewi, J.: A linear local model checking algorithm for CTL. In: Best, E. (ed.) CONCUR 1993. LNCS, vol. 715, Springer, Heidelberg (1993)
24. Visser, W., Dwyer, M., Whalen, M.: The hidden models of model checking. Software and Systems Modeling 11(4), 541–555 (2012)
25. Zheng, H.: Compositional reachability analysis for efficient modular verification of asynchronous designs. IEEE Transactions on Computer-Aided Design of Integrated Circuits and Systems 29(3), 329–340 (2010)
26. Zurowska, K., Dingel, J.: Symbolic execution of UML-RT state machines. In: SAC-SVT (2012)
27. Zurowska, K., Dingel, J.: Modular Symbolic Execution of Communicating and Hierarchically Composed UML-RT State Machines. In: Goodloe, A.E., Person, S. (eds.) NFM 2012. LNCS, vol. 7226, pp. 39–53. Springer, Heidelberg (2012)

Behavioural Verification in Embedded Software, from Model to Source Code

Anthony Fernandes Pires[1,2], Thomas Polacsek[1], Virginie Wiels[1],
and Stéphane Duprat[2]

[1] ONERA, 2 avenue Edouard Belin,
31055 Toulouse, France
[2] Atos Intégration SAS, 6 impasse Alice Guy, B.P. 43045,
31024 Toulouse cedex 03, France
{anthony.fernandespires,stephane.duprat}@atos.net,
{thomas.polacsek,virginie.wiels,anthony.fernandes_pires}@onera.fr

Abstract. To reduce the verification costs and to be more confident
on software, static program analysis offers ways to prove properties on
source code. Unfortunately, these techniques are difficult to apprehend
and to use for non-specialists. Modelling allows users to specify some
aspects of software in an easy way. More precisely, in embedded software, state machine models are frequently used for behavioural design.
The aim of this paper is to bridge the gap between model and code by
offering automatic generation of annotations from model to source code.
These annotations are then verified by static analysis in order to ensure
that the code behaviour conforms to the model-based design. The models we consider are UML state machines with a formal non-ambiguous
semantics, the annotation generation and verification is implemented in
a tool and applied to a case study.

Keywords: Verification, UML, Formal Methods, Model Driven Engineering.

1 Introduction

Aeronautical software development, and more specifically software for safety
critical applications, is submitted to stringent constraints. DO-178C[1] (certification standard for aeronautical software) specifies development and verification
objectives. Identified verification means are reviews, analyses and test. One of
its supplements, DO-333[2], is dedicated to the use of formal methods. Formal
methods are mathematical techniques which allow performing rigorous verification tasks during software development. Formal methods are already applied in
industry [1].

In an industrial context, at Atos, we notice that the cost of verification activities for embedded software development can sometimes reach 60% of the project

---

[1] DO-178C *Software considerations in airborne systems and equipment certification.*
[2] DO-333 *Formal Methods Supplement to DO-178C and DO-278A.*

A. Moreira et al. (Eds.): MODELS 2013, LNCS 8107, pp. 320–335, 2013.

workload. This is not a new problem, Hoare [2] was already reporting that over half of software development time was dedicated to program testing.

Furthermore, in addition to the increasing complexity of embedded systems, today software is not developed by a single company but by a set of stakeholders. These stakeholders have a common purpose and share some resources and knowledge. In this context, it can be difficult to communicate between all the different stakeholders. It is essential to offer a way for muti-cultural teams to share, to discuss and to work with an unambigous formalism. Model Driven Engineering (MDE) allows us to deal with these difficulties while ensuring the expected level of quality. It suggests using models all along the development lifecycle; models can be used, for instance, for documentation generation, design specification, simulation or code generation.

In this paper, we present an MDE approach to combine the advantages of model-based design and the efficiency of formal methods dedicated to code verification. More specifically, we give a process to support the design, development and verification of the implementation of software for the management of avionic components.

Many modelling languages have been defined through past decades. The UML[3] standard is one of them. UML is widespread and it is currently used in software development teams. The current UML semantics is semi-formal as it is partially expressed in natural language. However, the UML standard has known a significant evolution in its description since version 1.x. The Precise UML group [4] contributed to this evolution. It aimed at investigating a precise semantics for UML. In [3], authors explain that the lack of precise semantics results in, among other, difficulties to rigorously establish the consistency of a model and its implementation.

In our approach, we propose to exploit the UML standard to model the design of embedded software. The design represents all the information needed to directly implement the sofware. The implementation could be done by automatic generation from models or by humans. Both solutions fit and, in this paper, we simply define an implementation pattern for our UML model. We need this pattern to manage an automatic verification task.

The main contribution of this paper is automatic verification of a C code stemming from an UML state machine. We want to prove that a source code implements and only implements its model based design. This verification is done using static analysis. Static analysis allows the detection of bugs and the verification of properties on a program without executing it. It enables effective identification of software defects and allows reducing verification costs. We propose to automatically generate annotations from the model into the code implementation. These annotations represent the behavioural properties of the model. They will be automatically verified by a static analysis tool.

The paper is structured as follows. Section 2 gives the definition of our language, subset of UML state machines, and its formal semantics. Section 3

---

[3] Unified Modeling Language www.uml.org

[4] www.cs.york.ac.uk/puml/

describes our process, gives an implementation pattern for our state machines
and explains the annotations generation. Section 4 presents a prototype that
implements our method. Section 5 reviews existing related work. Lastly, Section
6 concludes the paper and outlines perspectives to this work.

2   State Machine Modelling in Embedded Software Context

2.1   Modelling Language

In [4] we define a UML subset dedicated to embedded software specification and
already used for industrial purpose. In this subset, we use UML state machines
to represent the behavioural specification of software components. We limit the
scope of elements and we define patterns for specific use, without adding new
concepts. These state machines are meant to be driven by a clock and to do a
certain number of actions at each clock *tick*.

Here, we use a limited subset of this language. Our state machines are composed of simple states, which can contain actions defined in their *entry behaviour*.
In UML, an action defined in the *entry behaviour* is executed to completion at
the entry into the state. For the moment, we do not consider hierarchical states
and parallelism behaviour in our language. We have transitions between states.
A transition is composed of a trigger, to manage events received by the state
machine, and a guard, representing the condition to fire the transition. The trigger can be defined by only two events: the tick event and the completion event.
The tick represents our clock tick and the beginning of a new cycle. The completion event is a special event defined in UML, it represents the default event
of the triggers which is automatically generated at the end of all the actions of a
state or at the entry of a state if no action is defined. The guard is represented
by a boolean expression expressed in the OCL standard language[5]. We do not
allow the definition of actions on the transitions, i.e. effects of the transitions.
We authorise a unique pseudostate by state machine: the initial state. These are
the only UML elements used to model our cyclic state machine.

We add two constraints to these state machines. In the first constraint, we
consider that all the actions executed in one cycle end before the end of the cycle.
As we are not interested in time properties, we accept the synchrony hypothesis
defined in [5]. It considers that every reaction of the system is instantaneous. In
the second constraint, we consider that the state machine must be deterministic.
We do not authorise conflicting transitions.

Consider the example of Figure 1. It is based on the example described in [6]
and it illustrates the behaviour of the software controling the landing gear of an
UAV (Unmanned Aerial Vehicle). The landing gear is composed of three gears: a
nose gear, a left gear and a right gear. Each of these gears has an up switch and
a down switch, namely up_switches or down_switches in our example. Each
switch is closed when the gear is respectively up or down. An additional switch

---

[5] http://www.omg.org/spec/OCL/

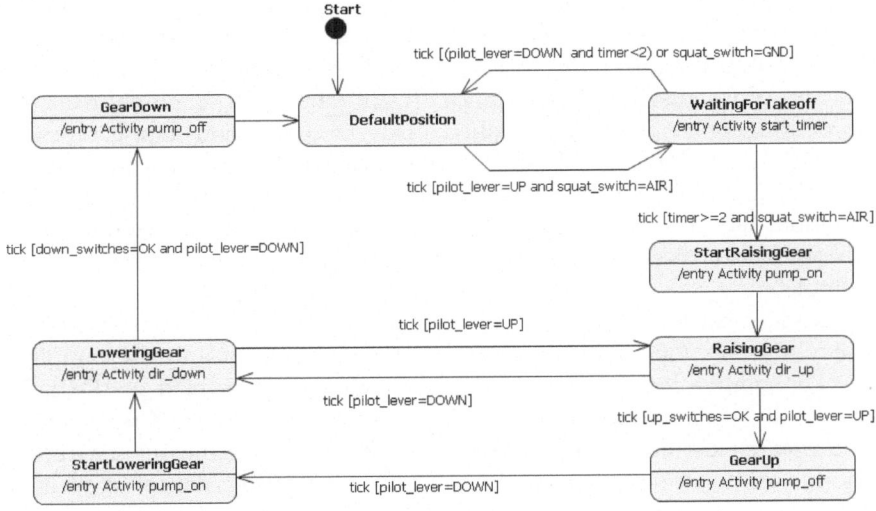

Fig. 1. LandingGear state machine

on the aircraft, named the `squat_switch`, indicates if the weight of the plane is on the nose or not. If the weight is on the nose, corresponding to `squat_switch=GRD` in Figure 1, it means that the plane is still on ground; if not, `squat_switch=AIR`, it means that the plane is in the air. The raising or lowering of the landing gear is managed by an electrically driven hydraulic pump. This pump supplies pressure to the gear actuators. The pressure increases or decreases depending on a computer-driven valve. When the pilot wants to raise the gears, he raises a lever. When the lever is up, `pilot_lever=UP`, the pump is activated and the pressure level is set, corresponding respectively to the actions `Activity pump_on` and `Activity dir_up`. When the pilot wants to lower the gears, he lowers a lever, `pilot_lever=DOWN` the pump is also activated, `Activity pump_on`, and the pressure level is set, `Activity dir_down`.

Starting in the default position, if we look for instance at the takeoff phase, the pilot raises the lever and the aircraft needs to be airborne for two seconds (`timer>2` and `squat_switch=AIR`) before starting raising gears. This allows ensuring the aircraft does not touch the ground during takeoff. After two seconds, the pump is activated and gears are raised. When gears are closed, the pump is deactivated and the gears are in the up position.

2.2 Semantics

We propose to formalise the semantics of our subset, in compliance with the UML semantic basis. To understand it, the reader needs to be familiar with some UML specific concepts.

In UML, state machines behaviour is managed by event processing. Each state machine has an event pool to store events, its politic of dequeuing must be defined by the user. The concept of event processing is called Run-to-Completion which limits the processing of events to one at a time. When an event is taken from the pool, if it enables a transition i.e. it fires a transition according to the correctness of its guard, it is consumed. If not, the event is simply discarded. The processing of a single event is called a Run-to-completion step. It represents the passage between two stable state configurations of a state machine. A state machine is in a stable state configuration when it is in a state where all the state actions have been completed: if a transition is fired at the beginning of the run-to-completion step, this step ends when all the actions of the targeted state are completed.

In our state machine, there are only two types of events, the *tick* event which is an external event periodically given by the environment and the completion event. The completion event is a very particular event defined in UML. It is automatically generated at the end of all the actions of a state and it has priority over all events existing in the event pool. To formally describe our semantics in a very simple way, we decide to make an abstraction of the concept of event and only use the concept of run-to-completion step.

We define S the set of all states of the state machine, VAR the set of variables accessible by the state machine. $s_0 \in S$ is the initial state of the state machine.

We define v as the variable assignment that associates an element of the domain of discourse with each variable of VAR. We define v_0 the variable assignment for s_0 and V the set of all variable assignments.

We define $T : S \times V \to S \cup \{\emptyset\}$, the transition function. For each state, T returns a new state according to the transition guards. A guard condition is simply a first order logic formula, with only constants and free variables and without quantifiers. The only predicate symbols we use are the arithmetic comparison operators: $<, >, \leq, \geq, =, \neq$. In our case, we define two transition functions : T_c which is the transition function for transitions fired by completion event and T_{tick} which is the transition function for transitions fired by *tick* event.

Because we do not have the disjunction of the guards of all outgoing transitions of a state, T_c and T_{tick} could possibly return $\emptyset$ if no guard condition matches. Note that return $\emptyset$ or return the same state as the state passed as a parameter are not the same. Return $\emptyset$ means no transition was taken, return the same state means a reflexive transition was taken. In addition, because a state could have an entry action, to take a reflexive transition causes the execution of the entry action.

We also define $A : S \times V \to V$, the action function. A represents the execution of actions defined in *entry behaviour*. In fact, for each variable assignment and a state, A returns a new variable assignment.

With the definition of the two previous functions, modelling the run-to-completion step (RTC) in our cyclic state machine is quite easy. As we have two kinds of transition functions, we have two kinds of run-to-completion. We define $rtc_c : S \times V \to S \times V$ the run-to-completion step for completion event and $rtc_{tick} : S \times V \to S \times V$ the run-to-completion step for *tick* event. Each of them consists of: first apply T to the current state; second if T returns $\emptyset$ stay in the same state do nothing and return $\emptyset$, else apply A and return the new state and the new variable assignment.

The way to call these two kinds of run-to-completion is specific to the cyclic behaviour of our state machine. We define $Cycle : S \times V \rightarrow S \times V$ the function which represents the behaviour of a state machine in one cycle. At the beginning of $Cycle$, the state machine is in a stable state configuration. $Cycle$ first calls rtc_{tick} to deal with the $tick$ event. If rtc_{tick} returns $\emptyset$, it means that no transition has been fired, so $Cycle$ returns Id, the identity. If it does not return $\emptyset$, it calls rtc_c until there is no more transition with a completion event trigger to fire, i.e. rtc_c return $\emptyset$. In a more formalised way, we have :

$$Cycle = \begin{cases} rtc_{tick} \circ rtc_c^n & \text{with } n \in \mathbb{N} \text{ and } rtc_c^{n+1} \text{ returns } \emptyset \\ Id & \text{if } rtc_{tick} \text{ returns } \emptyset \end{cases}$$

When a cycle begins, the event pool is empty before one unique $tick$ event occurs. If this $tick$ event fired a transition, the $tick$ event is consumed and the run-to-completion step will fill the event pool with one completion event. This completion event is processed by a new run-to-completion step. If this processing leads to the firing of a transition, the event is consumed and the run-to-completion step will fill the event pool with a new completion event. The state machine will repeat the same mecanism until no completion event is present in the pool (it corresponds to the iterative call of the RTC_c function in our semantics). Indeed, if no transition is fired, the completion event is discarded and the pool is left empty until the next cycle. Thanks to the synchrony hypothesis described in the previous section, we are sure that this chain of run-to-completion steps will end before the next cycle i.e. before a new $tick$ event occurs. Consequently, at the beginning of a cycle, the event pool is always empty before the $tick$ event occurs and the completion event will only occur after the processing of this $tick$ event. For example, Figure 2 describes two consecutive cycles in a state machine. Note that it is a particular case, since there is at least one rtc_c for each cycle.

The initial state s_0 is a particular state in UML. It is a pseudostate. As defined in the UML semantics, this state has no trigger and guard defined on its unique outgoing transition. As it is particular in UML, its processing will be defined separetely of the other states in our semantics. We define a function $Cycle_0 : \{s_0\} \times \{v_0\} \rightarrow S \times V$. We have $Cycle_0 = rtc_c^n$ with $n \in \mathbb{N}^*$ where rtc_c^{n+1} returns $\emptyset$. This function is only called once at the very beginning of the execution of the state machine.

A cyclic state machine is defined by a $6-$tuple $\langle s_0, v_0, Cycle_0, S, V, Cycle \rangle$.

3 Formal Verification from Model to Code

3.1 Our Method

In MDE, models are used all along the development chain and allow users to generate the source code implementation. Although a part of our work takes

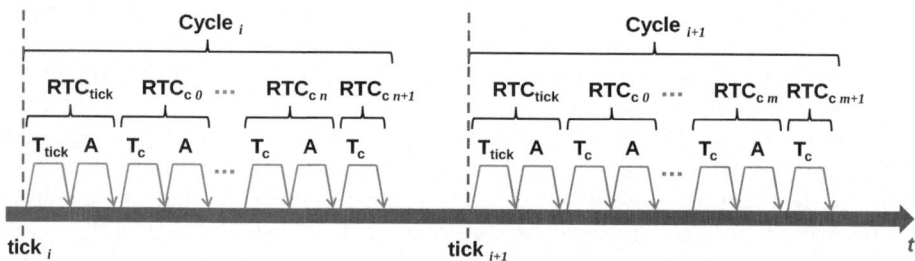

Fig. 2. Example of two consecutive cycles within a state machine

place at the code level, our contribution does not deal with code generation. We want to verify the behaviour of a C program, written by humans or machines, according to its model based design. We will only give the implementation pattern of a state machine, since information is needed on the code structure to manage our verification. Our method focuses on the use of the semantics of UML state machines to derive annotations to verify the code using static analysis.

Regarding the whole process in which we propose our verification method, we can compare our method with a code generation method. At a technical level, automation of properties generation for verification purpose is similar to automation of code generation. But, placed in a certification context like DO-178C for the aeronautical domain, the qualification constraints of a verification tool are much lighter than those of a code generator tool. If the verification tool fails, it does not introduce errors in the target software while a code generator might. A code generator must be qualified at least at the same level of criticality than the target software; it is not the case for a verification tool.

To conduct static analysis we use the Frama-C[6] framework. It is an open-source and modular environment which groups many different techniques and tools to conduct such analysis on C code. It is based on the ACSL language [7] (ANSI/ISO C Specification Language). ACSL is a specification language to express behavioural properties on C code. It is based on first order logic and allows to specify function contracts, invariants, variants, loop specifications, logic specifications and ghost codes. ACSL annotations are represented as comments in C code, using specific tags to be recognised by Frama-C. These annotations are without side effect on the program.

We use our cyclic UML state machine model to generate the corresponding ACSL function contracts to verify the code behaviour. An overview of our process is given Figure 3.

A function contract is composed of preconditions and postconditions. The function contract is: if the preconditions are true when the function is called then the postconditions must be true after the function execution. We use a Frama-C plugin named WP[7] to verify function contracts. WP is based on the Weakest

---

[6] http://frama-c.com/

[7] http://frama-c.com/wp.html

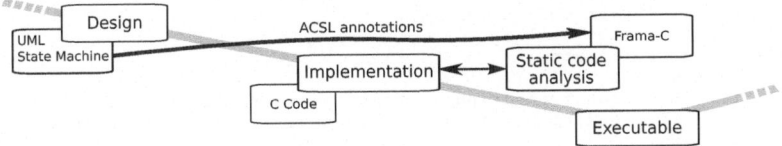

Fig. 3. Our process: verification from model to source code

Precondition calculus introduced in [8]. The Weakest Precondition calculus consists in computing the weakest precondition ensuring the postconditions. WP computes the weakest precondition of the function contracts and generates proof obligations for the verification of the implication of the weakest precondition by the initial preconditions. These proof obligations are discharged by solvers available through Frama-C.

In this work, we only focus on the verification of the transition functions implementation. They represent the core of a state machine behaviour.

3.2 State Machine Implementation Pattern

To generate function contracts on the source code, we need to know: the prototype of functions; the name and the type of the variables of the program. In addition, function contracts are also linked to the structure of the implementation. Therefore, we propose a code design pattern for the implementation of our state machines.

Although we only focus on the transition functions, we give a global code design pattern in order to give an overview of the implementation. This implementation pattern is based on a representation of the states as an enumeration type named `State`. The enumeration possible values of `State` are all the possible states of the state machine and one value named `Null`. This value will represent the $\emptyset$ used in our semantics. In addition, all the variables used in the model retain their names in the implementation.

The other parts of the implementation pattern of our state machine is composed of the following functions.

- Two transition functions, one for the tick event, namely `T_tick`, and one for the completion event, namely `T_c`. They represent the choice of the transition that will be fired according to the transition guards. It returns the targeted state if a transition has been fired, the `Null` value if not. Transition functions are, at top level, a `switch/case` structure to match with the current state. For each case, a conditional structure `if/else` is implemented for each outgoing transition of the state triggered by the corresponding event. It represents the guard of the outgoing transition. The code design pattern for the `T_tick` is given in listing 1.1 (`T_c` is based on the same pattern).

```
State T_tick (State current_state) {
  State output_state=Null;
  switch(current_state) {
    case state1 :
      if (condition_transition1) output_state=targeted_state;
      else if (condition_transition2) output_state=other_targeted_state;
    break;
  }
  return output_state;
}
```

Listing 1.1. T_tick function pattern

- An action function, namely A, which, for each state, executes the entry actions of the state. Note that, according to the semantics, A will only be executed if a transition has been fired (we do not give the code pattern of A).
- Two run-to-completion functions, namely RTC_tick and RTC_c, one for each possible event. Each one calls its corresponding transition function. The code pattern of RTC_tick is given in listing 1.2 (RTC_c is based on the same pattern).

```
State RTC_tick (State current_state) {
  State compute_state=T_tick(current_state);
  if (compute_state!=Null) {
    A(compute_state);
    return compute_state;
  } else return Null;
}
```

Listing 1.2. RTC_tick function pattern

- A function Cycle which implements the running of a state machine during one cycle. It first calls the run-to-completion function for the tick event. If the return is not the Null value: first it calls the run-to-completion function for the completion event until the return of Null and then it returns the new state computed. Note that, the termination of the function must be ensured at the model level, not here at the code level, i.e. the model based design must guarantee that there exists a point where no further completion transition can be fired during the cycle. The code pattern of Cycle is given in listing 1.3. According to the semantics, we define, on the same pattern, a function Cycle_0 which only calls the RTC_c function.

```
State Cycle (State current_state) {
  State compute_state=RTC_tick(current_state);
  if (compute_state!=Null) {
    State last_state;
    while(compute_state!=Null){
      last_state=compute_state;
      compute_state=RTC_c(last_state);
    }
    return last_state;
  } else return current_state;
}
```

Listing 1.3. Cycle function pattern

The running of the state machine is represented by a while loop. In each loop, the program waits until the next cycle and calls the cycle function (the code pattern is given in Listing 1.4).

```
current_state=Cycle_0(starting_state);
while(1) {
  wait_tick();
  current_state=Cycle(current_state);
}
```

Listing 1.4. while loop pattern

The application of the implementation pattern on the T_tick transition function of the example in Figure 1 is given in Listing 1.5.

```
State T_tick(State current_state){
  State output_state=Null;
  switch(current_state) {
    case DefaultPosition:
            if (pilot_lever==UP && squat_switch==AIR)
                output_state=WaitingForTakeoff;
    break;
    case WaitingForTakeoff:
            if (timer>=2 && squat_switch==AIR)
                output_state=StartRaisingGear;
            else if ((pilot_lever==DOWN && timer<2)||squat_switch==GND)
                    output_state=DefaultPosition;
    break;
    case RaisingGear:
            if (pilot_lever==DOWN) output_state=LoweringGear;
            else if (pilot_lever==UP && up_switches==OK)
                    output_state=GearUp;
    break;
    case GearUp:
        if (pilot_lever==DOWN) output_state=StartLoweringGear;
    break;
    case LoweringGear:
            if (pilot_lever==UP) output_state=RaisingGear;
            else if (pilot_lever==DOWN && down_switches==OK)
                output_state=GearDown;
    break;
  }
  return output_state;
}
```

Listing 1.5. T_tick implementation for the LandingGear example

3.3   Behavioural Properties as Function Contract

The source code behavioural verification aims at proving properties stemming from the UML state machine specification. For that, we generate ACSL function contracts on the implementation.

The behavioural properties are divided in two categories: first, the specification completeness, "the specification is fully implemented"; second the specification soundness, "only the specification is implemented".

To ensure the specification completeness at the transition functions level, the implementation must ensure the following properties:

(a) for the current state of the state machine, if the transition guard is true, the transition function returns the specified targeted state;

(b) the transition function is without effect on state machine variables.

Property (a) is represented as one ACSL *ensures* clause for each possible outgoing transition of the current state. An *ensures* clause represents a property that must be true after the program execution. It corresponds to a postcondition. In fact, we generate a set of *ensures* clauses for each state, on each transition function (T_tick and T_c) depending on whether the state is handled by the transition function or not. Following the transition function prototype, the pattern for this property for a state is given in Listing 1.6. Note that the return of a function is defined by the keyword \result in ACSL.

```
ensures <guard of outgoing transition 1>
   .   ==> \result == <target state of outgoing transition 1>;
   .
   .
ensures <guard of outgoing transition N>
       ==> \result == <target state of outgoing transition N>;
```

Listing 1.6. Property (a) pattern

Property (b) is represented by an ACSL *assigns* clause. The *assigns* clause is used to specify exhaustively the memory allocations possibly modified by the C program. So if it is specified with the keyword \nothing, the clause guarantees that no memory allocation has been modified. Following the transition function prototype, the pattern for this property is given in Listing 1.7.

```
assigns \nothing;
```

Listing 1.7. Property (b) pattern

Specification soundness means that nothing else except the specified transitions is implemented in the program. To ensure soundness, the implementation must verify the following properties:

(c) for the target state resulting of the firing of a transition and its specified source state, the guard of the corresponding transition must be true;
(d) if no guard of the outgoing transitions of the current state is true, no transition is fired i.e. the transition function returns ∅.

Property (c) allows to verify that no unspecified transition exists between two states linked by a specified transition. As for property (a), it corresponds to one *ensures* clause for each possible outgoing transition of each state, according to the event handled by the transition function. The pattern for this property is given in Listing 1.8.

```
ensures \result == <target state of outgoing transition 1>
   .           ==> <guard of outgoing transition 1>;
   .
   .
ensures \result == <target state of outgoing transition N>
               ==> <guard of outgoing transition N>;
```

Listing 1.8. Property (c) pattern

Property (d) allows to verify that for a given state, there is no other possible target state than the specified ones. It is also represented as an *ensures* clause. The pattern for this property is given in Listing 1.9. The negation is expressed as the "!" symbol in ACSL.

```
ensures (!<guard of outgoing transition 1>
         && ...
         && !<guard of outgoing transition N>)
                  ==> \result == Null;
```

Listing 1.9. Property (d) pattern

All postconditions presented must be defined for each possible state. ACSL gives the possibility to define multiple named function contracts, called *behavior*, for a function. Therefore, we define, for the global function contract of each transition function, as many *behavior* as there are states with outgoing transitions triggered by the event handled by the transition function. In these *behavior*, the precondition deals with the current state. It is expressed as an *assumes* clause in ACSL. An *assumes* clause represents the property that must be true for applying the *behavior*. For instance, Listing 1.10 gives the ACSL *behavior* for the state RaisingGear of the T_tick function.

```
behavior RaisingGear:
    assumes current_state==RaisingGear;
    assigns \nothing;
    ensures (pilot_lever==DOWN) <==> \result==LoweringGear;
    ensures (pilot_lever==UP && up_switches==OK) <==> \result==GearUp;
    ensures (!(pilot_lever==DOWN) && !(pilot_lever==UP && up_switches==OK))
                 ==> \result==Null;
```

Listing 1.10. The *behavior* for the state RaisingGear in the T_tick function

In addition, we need to add a property in the soundness category:

(e) if a state is not handled by the verified transition function (i.e. this state has no outgoing transition triggered by the event handled by the transition function), the transition function does not fire any transition.

Property (e) means that the return value of the transition function must be $\emptyset$ for all unhandled states. In ACSL, it is represented by a *behavior* composed of an *assumes* clause representing all the states not handled by the transition function and an *ensures* clause representing the Null value returned by the function. The example for the T_tick function of the example in Figure 1 is given in Listing 1.11.

```
behavior OtherStates:
    assumes current_state!=LoweringGear
            && current_state!=DefaultPosition
            && current_state!=WaitingForTakeoff
            && current_state!=RaisingGear
            && current_state!=GearUp;
    assigns \nothing;
    ensures \result==Null;
```

Listing 1.11. property (e) for the T_tick function

All the *behavior* described below represent the global function contract of a transition function. Each global function contract allows to check the conformity of each transition function with the behaviour expressed in the state machine. But, although we are able to detect unspecified transitions, we cannot detect dead code i.e. transitions that never happen at execution or states never reached.

4 Our Tool

We have implemented our approach in a prototype in Java. It comes as an Eclipse[8] plugin depending on the Topcased[9] framework. It allows, from the model explorer of a Papyrus[10] UML model, to choose a state machine and to generate ACSL contracts from it. Users only have to give the path to the C file they want to annotate in order to generate the annotated file. We implement for each ACSL clause and ACSL structure we use, a corresponding object for which we implement its string representation. For instance, in our case an ACSL *behavior* is composed of an object AssumesClause, an object AssignsClause and a collection of objects EnsuresClause.

The generation is done in 4 steps. First, we check that the selected state machine is well formed according to our model rules. Indeed, the Topcased Papyrus editor allows the creation of UML models based on the whole standard, but our language is only a subset. Secondly, we check that the C file contains the transition functions. We use the Eclipse CDT API[11] to parse the C file and to retrieve the corresponding function to annotate. Thirdly, we parse the state machine and we create all the behaviours for each state. Finally we generate a C file, corresponding to the C code and the annotations generated at the right places in the code.

For the example described in Figure 1, we are able to generate 55 lines of function contracts for more than 40 lines of C code for the two transition functions. All the function contracts have been verified in a few seconds thanks to Frama-C and its plugin WP.

5 Related Work

Some work exists on the verification of source code using annotations generated from a model specification.

[9] proposes a way to automatically annotate C code according to a specification composed of SAM (Structured Automata Model) automata. SAM is a domain specific language for the behavioural representation of avionic components. The authors present an algorithm to generate annotations from SAM automata to verify the code behaviour. The approach is similar to our own since it consists in generating function contracts on the transition function implementing the SAM automaton and they also present an industrial experimentation with promising results. By contrast, the SAM automaton and generated function contracts are less complex than our UML state machine and our annotations.

---

[8] www.eclipse.org

[9] Toolkit in OPen-source for Critical Application and SystEms Development. It offers Model Driven Engineering activities and it is based on the Eclipse environment. www.topcased.org

[10] It is tool for modelling in UML. The current Topcased model editor are based on Papyrus version 0.8. www.papyrusuml.org

[11] C/C++ Development Tooling. www.eclipse.org/cdt/

The Aorai plugin of Frama-C [10] allows to generate ACSL annotations from an automaton specification expressed in LTL (Linear Temporal Logic). Aorai automatically annotates the targeted source code and the verification is performed using the solvers available from Frama-C. Actually, the automaton specification represents a chain of function calls and function returns. Each of them can be associated to properties on the program variables. At the end, if the annotations are verified, then the source code conforms to the specification. Aorai focuses on function calls at global program level while our method focuses on function behaviour. Moreover, the specification in LTL is more complex and less intuitive than a specification modelled with state machine diagrams for users non-familiar with temporal logic.

In [11], authors propose the theoretical foundations of a toolset to generate annotations on the software implementation from control theory properties and proof expressed in a control systems design. The goal is to obtain an autocoder with proofs. The source language is an open-source alternative of Matlab[12], Scilab[13] and the target code is implemented in C language. The properties annotated in the design are translated in ACSL annotations in the code. The ACSL annotations are then verified using Frama-C. The authors present two methods. One is a direct mapping of the annotations on the design and the semantics of Scilab operators to annotations on the code. The other uses a gateway language, Lustre [12] in order to take into account different front end languages for the design. The spirit of the approach is close to ours. It differs by the type of systems to verify, the design language and the properties to verify.

In our approach, we use a part of the UML language version 2.4.1 limited to state machine modelling as source for the design. As the current UML semantics is semiformal, we needed to formalise its semantics in order to avoid any ambiguities and to use formal methods in a rigorous way. In the particular case of UML state machines, there is a lot of work on the formalisation of their semantics. [13] aims at giving an overview of the state of the art. It lists 26 semantic approaches structured in three categories. First, it lists work which is based on standard mathematical concepts and notations. For instance, [14] uses Labelled Transition Systems (LTS) expressed in an algebraic specification language for the representation of the semantics and [15] uses Abstract State Machines (ASM). Secondly, it lists the approaches expressing the semantics as a set of rewriting rules. For example, [16] and [17] use graph transformations and [18] defines translation rules to map an UML specification to high-level Petri nets. Finally, it groups approaches based on the translation of UML state machines into other formal languages. For instance, [19] defines the semantics in PVS (Prototype Verification System) and [20] presents a global semantics which is implemented in PROMELA for model checking. Note that none of the approaches supports all the UML state machines concepts. Our work is clearly in the first category. We define a very simple mathematical semantics dedicated to the needed concepts. Our semantics uses new concepts (like cycle, transition

---

[12] www.mathworks.fr/products/matlab/

[13] www.scilab.org

functions, etc.), but it is fully compliant with the semantics described in the UML standard.

6 Conclusion

We presented a method to automatically verify the behaviour of a C source code with respect to its UML design model. The main advantage is to have a full MDE process which gives access to formal methods and associated tools for non-expert users. The main drawback of the approach we presented is that the implementation is very close to the semantics of our state machines. This work was motivated by multiple reasons. It allows users to be more confident about their implementation in a simpler way: as the annotations are automatically generated from the model and automatically verified, users do not need to change their technical know-how. Furthermore, although MDE already permits to generate tests on the code, static analysis is more exhaustive than software testing. Indeed, static analysis does not just test the code, it proves it i.e the results of the verification are valid for all possible executions.

The results of our method are promising but it needs to be improved and experimented on more complex models. For the moment, we only tested it on small examples. Moreover, we are thinking about applying it on other implementation patterns. In further work, the feedback of the verification must be adapted to help the user correct the implementation errors. Currently, the user relies on the verification results of each annotation to determine where the problem is on the code. We could express this feedback in a more detailed and user-friendly way or present it at model level. Furthermore, we plan to extend the UML subset we used. Our state machines are limited to simple states. We would like to take into account hierarchical states such as composite states or submachine states, as defined in the UML standard. We also need to define the formal semantics of the subset in a more complete way since we only presented here the key concepts useful for our method. Therefore, we limited our contribution for this paper to the behavioural verification of transition functions. In future work, we will verify the other functions defined in our semantics, as this point is mandatory to obtain a complete proof of the compliance of the implementation with the state machine behaviour. Finally, we plan to make the annotation generator we presented available online to get the feedback of the community.

References

1. Souyris, J., Wiels, V., Delmas, D., Delseny, H.: Formal verification of avionics software products. In: Cavalcanti, A., Dams, D.R. (eds.) FM 2009. LNCS, vol. 5850, pp. 532–546. Springer, Heidelberg (2009)
2. Hoare, C.A.R.: An axiomatic basis for computer programming. Commun. ACM 12(10), 576–580 (1969)
3. France, R., Evans, A., Lano, K., Rumpe, B.: The uml as a formal modeling notation. Comput. Stand. Interfaces 19(7), 325–334 (1998)

4. Fernandes Pires, A., Duprat, S., Faure, T., Besseyre, C., Beringuier, J., Rolland, J.F.: Use of modelling methods and tools in an industrial embedded system project: works and feedback. In: ERTS, France (2012)
5. Berry, G., Gonthier, G.: The esterel synchronous programming language: design, semantics, implementation. Science of Computer Programming 19(2), 87–152 (1992)
6. Gomez, M.: Embedded state machine implementation. Embedded Systems Programming 41 (2000)
7. Baudin, P., Cuoq, P., Filliâtre, J., Marché, C., Monate, B., Moy, Y., Prevosto, V.: ACSL Version 1.6. (2012)
8. Dijkstra, E.W.: Guarded commands, nondeterminacy and formal derivation of programs. Commun. ACM 18(8), 453–457 (1975)
9. Duprat, S., Gaufillet, P., Moya Lamiel, V., Passarello, F.: Formal verification of sam state machine implementation. In: ERTS, France (2010)
10. Stouls, N., Prevosto, V.: Aoraï Plug-in Tutorial
11. Jobredeaux, R., Wang, T., Feron, E.: Autocoding control software with proofs i: Annotation translation. In: 2011 IEEE/AIAA 30th Digital Avionics Systems Conference (DASC), pp. 7C1-1–7C1-13 (October 2011)
12. Halbwachs, N., Caspi, P., Raymond, P., Pilaud, D.: The synchronous data flow programming language lustre. Proceedings of the IEEE 79(9), 1305–1320 (1991)
13. Crane, M.L., Dingel, J.: On the semantics of uml state machines: Categorization and comparison. In: Technical Report 2005-501, School of Computing, Queen's University (2005)
14. Reggio, G., Astesiano, E., Choppy, C., Hussmann, H.: Analysing uml active classes and associated state machines - a lightweight formal approach. In: Maibaum, T. (ed.) FASE 2000. LNCS, vol. 1783, pp. 127–146. Springer, Heidelberg (2000)
15. Börger, E., Cavarra, A., Riccobene, E.: Modeling the dynamics of uml state machines. In: Gurevich, Y., Kutter, P.W., Odersky, M., Thiele, L. (eds.) ASM 2000. LNCS, vol. 1912, pp. 223–241. Springer, Heidelberg (2000)
16. Varró, D.: A formal semantics of uml statecharts by model transition systems. In: Corradini, A., Ehrig, H., Kreowski, H.J., Rozenberg, G. (eds.) ICGT 2002. LNCS, vol. 2505, pp. 378–392. Springer, Heidelberg (2002)
17. Gogolla, M., Presicce, F.P.: State diagrams in uml: A formal semantics using graph transformations - or diagrams are nice, but graphs are worth their price. In: University of Munich, pp. 55–72 (1998)
18. Baresi, L., Pezzè, M.: On formalizing uml with high-level petri nets. In: Agha, G., De Cindio, F., Rozenberg, G. (eds.) APN 2001. LNCS, vol. 2001, pp. 276–304. Springer, Heidelberg (2001)
19. Aredo, D.B.: Semantics of uml statecharts in pvs. In: Proc. of the 12th Nordic Workshop on Programming Theory (NWPT 2000) (2001)
20. Lilius, J., Paltor, I.P.: Formalising uml state machines for model checking. In: France, R.B. (ed.) UML 1999. LNCS, vol. 1723, pp. 430–444. Springer, Heidelberg (1999)

Formal Verification Integration Approach for DSML[*]

Faiez Zalila, Xavier Crégut, and Marc Pantel

Université de Toulouse, IRIT, France
firstname.lastname@enseeiht.fr

Abstract. The application of formal methods (especially, model checking and static analysis techniques) for the verification of safety critical embedded systems has produced very good results and raised the interest of system designers up to the application of these technologies in real size projects. However, these methods usually rely on specific verification oriented formal languages that most designers do not master. It is thus mandatory to embed the associated tools in automated verification toolchains that allow designers to rely on their usual domain-specific modeling languages (DSMLs) while enjoying the benefits of these powerful methods. More precisely, we propose a language to formally express system requirements and interpret verification results so that system designers (DSML end-users) avoid the burden of learning some formal verification technologies. Formal verification is achieved through translational semantics. This work is based on a metamodeling pattern for executable DSML that favors the definition of generative tools and thus eases the integration of tools for new DSMLs.

Keywords: Domain specific modeling language, Formal verification, Model checking, Translational semantics, Traceability, Verification feedback.

1 Introduction

Domain-Specific Modeling Languages (DSMLs) are a major asset in the development of complex systems. In particular, they are widely used in the early phases of the development of safety critical systems. In this context, model validation and verification (V&V) activities are key features to assess the conformance of the future system to its safety and liveness requirements. They require the introduction of an execution semantics for the DSMLs. It is usually provided as a mapping from the abstract syntax (metamodel) of the DSML to an existing semantic domain, generally a formal language, in order to reuse powerful tools (simulator or model-checker) available for this domain [1,2].

One key issue is that system designers (DSML end-users) should not be required to have a solid knowledge on formal languages and associated tools.

[*] This works was funded by the french Ministry of Industry through the ITEA2 project OPEES and the french ANR project GEMOC.

A. Moreira et al. (Eds.): MODELS 2013, LNCS 8107, pp. 336–351, 2013.
© Springer-Verlag Berlin Heidelberg 2013

The challenge is thus to leverage formal tools so that the system designer has not to burden with formal aspects and to integrate them in traditional CASE tools, like the Eclipse platform. Model Driven Engineering (MDE) already provides means to define metamodels, static properties, textual and graphical syntaxes. What should be addressed is thus 1) providing the system designer with a user-friendly language to formalize system requirements, 2) defining a translational semantics from the DSML to a formal language, 3) translating formal requirements into formal language logic formulae according to the translational semantics, and eventually, 4) bringing back formal verification results back at the DSML level so that they are understandable by the system designer.

Our contribution is on the tooling and methodological side as we propose an approach to integrate formal verification through model-checking for a DSML. We rely on the Executable DSML pattern [3] to define all concerns involved in the definition of DSML semantics. We have fully tooled the Temporal OCL (TOCL) language proposed by Gogolla et al. [4], including the expression of formal properties on a specific model and their translation to the logic formulae of the target language (Linear Temporal Logic (LTL) formulae at the moment). We define guidelines to validate the translational semantics to the formal domain. Finally, the feedback is largely automated thanks to mappings identified while defining the translation semantics.

To illustrate this paper, we consider as a running example the xSPEM executable extension of the SPEM process modeling language [5]. It was designed in order to experiment V&V in the TopCased toolkit using an MDE approach.

The paper is organized as follows. Section 2 presents different manipulated elements by the system designer (models to be verified, verification requests and expected verification results). Section 3 presents the work to be done at DSML level on the running use-case. Section 4 introduces the proposed verification methodology with a translational semantics of xSPEM into the Fiacre formal language [6]. Section 5 explains various steps in order to provide verification results from formal tools to the xSPEM level through Fiacre. Section 6 gives some related work in the domain of user level verification results. Finally, we conclude and presents future work in Section 7.

2   DSML End-User Requirements

This section presents the domain – process modeling – considered in the case study and the requirements of system designers, the DSML end-users. We first present the kind of process models the DSML end-users want to build and the properties they want to check on their models. Finally, we describe the feedbacks expected from verification tools in order to get insights on the errors the models may contain.

2.1   DSML End-User Models

Fig. 1 shows an example of a process model. It corresponds to a simplified development process composed of three activities, each represented in an ellipse: *wd1*,

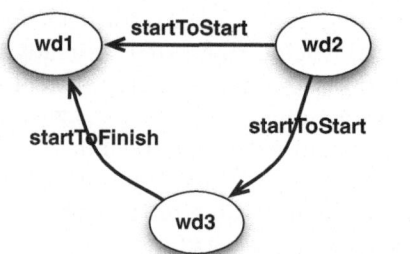

Start wd2
Start wd1
Finish wd2
Start wd3
Finish wd1
Finish wd3

Listing 1.1. A terminating scenario

Fig. 1. a xSPEM model

wd2 and *wd3*. Arrows between activities indicate dependencies: the target activity depends on the source activity. The label specifies the kind of dependency. The word before the "To" indicates the state that must have been reached by the source activity in order to perform on the target activity the action, which appears after the "To". For example, the "startToFinish" dependency between *wd3* and *wd1* means that *wd1* can only be finished when *wd3* has been started. To keep this example simple, we have not represented the resources that are required to perform an activity.

2.2 DSML End-User Verifications

To validate or to verify a model, the DSML end-user generally checks that properties derived from the system requirements hold on that model. We focus on *behavioral properties*, that is properties that concern the evolution of the model over time.

The DSML end-user may be interested in general properties not specific to a given process model. For example, he may want to check whether a process model may finish (we call it P_1 requirement). A process finishes if all its activities finish while respecting constraints imposed by dependencies and resource allocation. If this property holds, the DSML end-users may want to get a terminating scenario and use it to pilot the process execution. Listing 1.1 is an example of terminating scenario for the model of Fig. 1.

Another kind of properties can be targeted which is specific properties. The DSML end-user may also want to verify properties that are specific to a particular process model. As an example, he might want to check whether it is required that *wd1* is finished before *wd2* is finished (we call it P_2 requirement).

2.3 Verification Feedback

Once system designers have defined their models and formalized their requirements through properties, they want to have feedbacks on the assessment of those properties. Obviously, these feedbacks (named also counter-example or scenario) should be expressed at the domain-specific level.

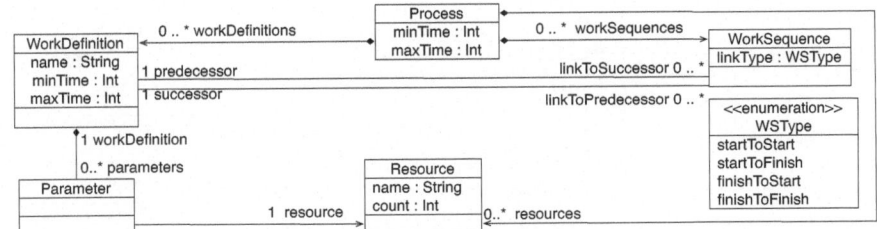

Fig. 2. An extract of the xSPEM Metamodel

For instance, using the example shown in Fig. 1, property P_1 holds and the process may finish. The DSML end-user can be provided with a scenario that describes a possible execution which leads to a finished process. Listing 1.1 is an example of such a terminating scenario. It lists actions (start or finish) applied on activities.

The DSML end-user will be able to play those scenarios using a model animator like the one developed in the TopCased project [7].

3   MDE for V&V CASE Tools

MDE provides powerful techniques and tools to define a metamodel for the considered domain (using Ecore for example), completed with static properties (e.g. OCL) and to generate either textual syntactic editors (e.g. Xtext) or graphical editors (e.g. GMF). The metamodel of xSPEM is shown in Fig. 2. It defines the concepts of *Process* composed of (1) *WorkDefinitions* that model the activities performed during the process, (2) *WorkSequences* that define temporal dependency relations (causality constraints) between activities and (3) *Resources* allocated to activities (*Parameter*).

The DSML end-user is thus able to design models and check whether static properties hold or not. Nevertheless, expressing properties which deal with the evolution of the model over time is not that easy because the metamodel does not usually provide all the required information. For instance, the xSPEM end-user wants to check whether workdefinitions may finish or not but the concept of "finished workdefinition" is not part of the xSPEM metamodel.

3.1   The *Executable DSML pattern*

As part of the TopCased [8] project, Combemale et al. have defined a metamodeling pattern called the *Executable DSML pattern* [3] that describes a way to define and structure the concerns required to make a DSML executable. The original metamodel, called the DDMM (Domain Definition MetaModel) is extended with three other metamodels (Fig. 3). The first metamodel describes stimuli that make the model evolve. They are modeled as events. *Start a WorkDefinition* or *Finish a WorkDefinition* are examples of xSPEM events. These events are modeled in the EDMM (Event Definition MetaModel), top left of Fig. 3. A second metamodel

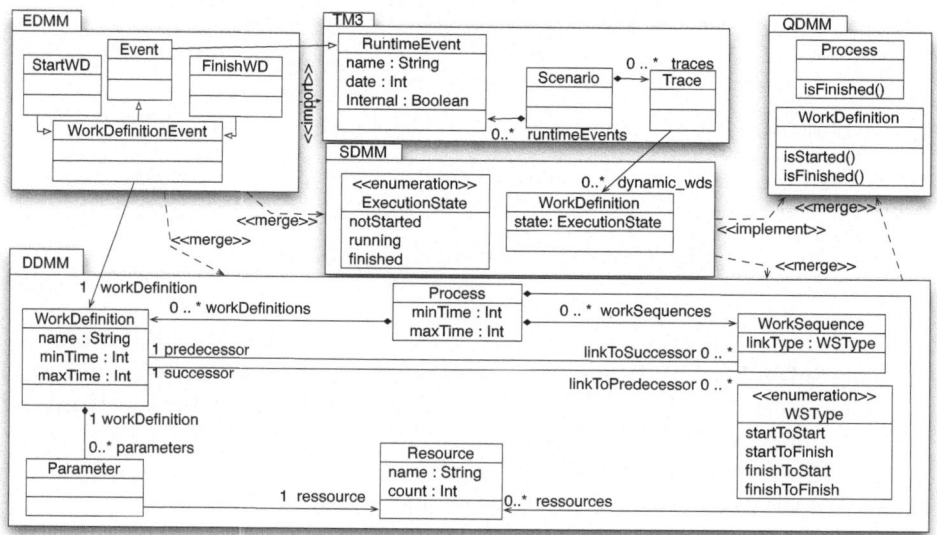

Fig. 3. xSPEM Metamodel

defines elements to model a scenario (either an input scenario or the trace of a particular execution) as a sequence of event occurrences. It is called TM3 (Trace Management MetaModel), top middle of Fig. 3. TM3 is not specific to one particular DSML as it only relies on the abstract *Event* concept. These two extensions allow to generate the scenario, which is a succession of events, that we want to feedback. The third metamodel defines the runtime information, that is data that model the state of the model at runtime and that are not part of the DDMM. This metamodel is called SDMM (State Definition MetaModel), middle of Fig. 3. On the xSPEM example, the SDMM includes the achievement state of a workdefinition which is either *not started*, *running* or *finished*.

Fig 3 shows a fourth metamodel aside the three metamodels obtained by applying the *Executable DSML pattern* to xSPEM. This additional metamodel is called QDMM (Query Definition Metamodel), top right of Fig. 3. It is a kind of an abstract view of the SDMM: it defines queries that may be asked on the model. SDMM may be seen as a way to implement the QDMM by choosing a set of attributes (like a Java class implements a Java inteface). For example, on Fig. 3, the SDMM of WorkDefinition defines an attribute *state* that can be used to implement the queries *isStarted* and *isFinished* from QDMM. Obviously, several SDMM are possible for one QDMM.

3.2 Formalizing Behavioral Properties

The properties of interest for the xSPEM end-user are behavioral properties relying on temporal operators. We have chosen to reuse the TOCL language [4]. TOCL is an extension of OCL that introduces usual future-oriented temporal operators such as *always, sometimes, next, existsNext* as well as their past-oriented duals.

One first step to formalize the properties of interest to the DSML end-user is to analyze the properties in order to identify the queries of interest. The QDMM can then be defined. Considering the properties the DSML end-user wants to assess on xSPEM models, we have identified three queries *isStarted* and *isFinished* on WorkDefinition and *isFinished* on Process. The queries on WorkDefinition are primitive (as we are not able to evaluate them at the moment) whereas *isFinished* on Process may be defined from the other ones. Here is its TOCL definition.

> **context** Process
> **def**: isFinished () : **Boolean** =
> self .workDefinitions
>   −>forAll(a:WorkDefinition| a.isFinished ())

The following property states that a process can never finish (it is the negation of the P_1 property):

> **context** Process   *−− negation of P_1 requirement*
> **inv** isNeverFinished:
>   **always** (**not** self . isFinished ())

If this condition is not satisfied, it means the process can finish and the DSML end-user expects that a model checker would exhibit a counter example that corresponds to a scenario that finishes the process and thus all its activities. This scenario would be obtained on the formal language used by the model checker and would have to be leveraged to the DSML end-user's domain.

We have built a TOCL syntactical editor integrated to the Eclipse platform. It has been defined using the Xtext tool[1].

4   Verification Methodology

One common way to verify a DSML consists in mapping its abstract syntax, defined by a metamodel, to a semantic domain [2]. It is called a translational semantics. The main advantage is to reuse tools available on this semantic domain like simulators or model-checkers. One common drawback is the semantic gap that may exists between the DSML and the semantics domain. To fill this gap, we target the FIACRE formal language [6] because of its high level concepts. FIACRE is a front end language to several verification toolboxes (TINA [9] and CADP [10] currently). This work focuses on the TINA toolbox.

Fig. 4 depicts the main steps and resources implied in the formal V&V of a DSML's model. The yellow part (top of the figure) shows resources manipulated by the DSML end-user: the model conforming to the DSML (Process.xspem), the behavioral requirements formalized using the TOCL editor (Property.tocl) as well as the scenario obtained when one property is not satisfied (Process.xspemscn).

---

[1] http://www.eclipse.org/Xtext/

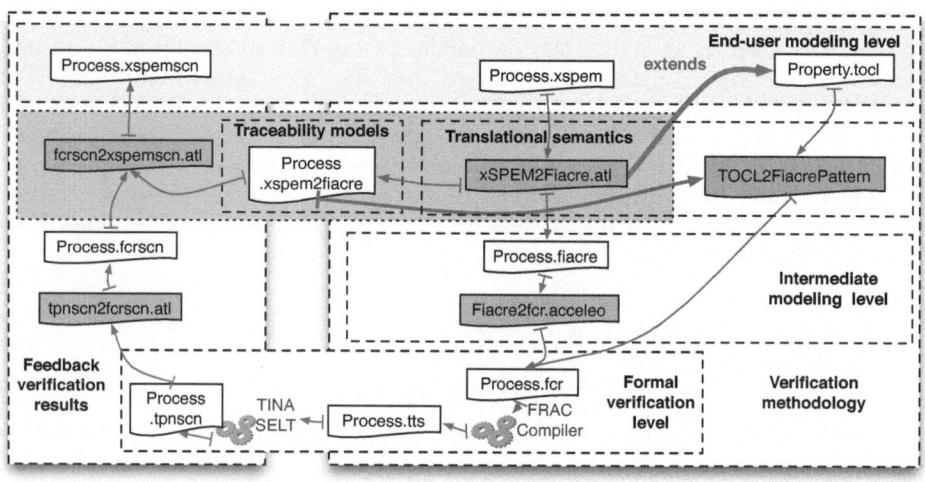

Fig. 4. General approach of DSML V&V

The blue part depicts the DSML designer task. It consists of implementing a translational semantics from the DSML to the FIACRE formal language and, based on this semantics, a backward transformation in order to feedback verification results.

4.1   Fiacre Formal Language

FIACRE [6] is a french acronym for an Intermediate Format for Embedded Distributed Components Architectures. It was designed as the target language for model transformations from different DSMLs such as AADL [11] or PLC [12].

FIACRE is a formal language to represent both the behavioral and timing aspects of systems, in particular embedded and distributed systems, for formal verification and simulation purposes. Fiacre is built around two notions:

- Processes describe the behavioral of sequential components. A process is defined by a set of control states, each associated with a piece of program built from deterministic constructs available in classical programming languages (assignments, if-then-else conditionals, while loops, and sequential compositions), non deterministic constructs (non deterministic choice and non deterministic assignments), communication events on ports, and jumps to next state.
- Components describe the composition of processes, possibly in a hierarchical manner. A component is defined as a parallel composition of instantiated components and/or processes communicating through ports and shared variables. The notion of component also allows to restrict the access mode and visibility of shared variables and ports, to associate timing constraints with communications, and to define priority between communication events.

4.2   Translational Semantics xSPEM2Fiacre

Translational semantics consists in defining the mapping from the DSML to the formal language.

For xSPEM, the translational semantics consists in transforming a xSPEM model into a FIACRE specification. It is performed with a model to model (M2M) transformation expressed in ATL [13] (xSPEM2FIACRE.atl at center of Fig. 4) and then an ACCELEO [14] module generates the FIACRE textual syntax (named Fiacre2fcr.acceleo).

Here are some rationale behind this translational semantics. We illustrate it with some elements in the FIACRE program corresponding to the xSPEM example of Fig. 3.

Based on the QDMM, a FIACRE type called WDQueries was defined to represent the two queries on *WorkDefinition* of interest for the xSPEM end-user and also for causality constraints. It is a record type composed of the two boolean fields isStarted and isFinished.

```
type WDQueries is record   // from QDMM
     isStarted : bool,
     isFinished : bool
end
```

WDsQueries defines an array of WDQueries storing the state of all workdefinitions of an xSPEM process. It is an argument for every workdefinition process.

```
type WDsQueries is array 3 of WDQueries end
```

Named constants are defined to ease the reading of the FIACRE program by avoiding the use of meaningless integers to identify a workdefinition.

```
const wd1Id: int is 0
const wd2Id: int is 1
const wd3Id: int is 2
```

Each workdefinition is translated into one FIACRE process with the same name. Such a process is composed of three states (*notStarted*, *running* and *finished*) and two transitions (from *notStarted* to *running* and then from *running* to *finished*). It is parametrized by two ports (*Start* and *Finish*). They are mainly used to synchronize with resources used by the workdefinition (not presented in this paper) but also ease the identification of xSPEM events for the feedback.

Each transition includes an assignment to update variables which store the state of the activities. They were necessary to implement dependencies because a FIACRE process cannot inspect the current state of other processes.

xSPEM causality constraints are thus mapped into a FIACRE conditional statement that checks whether the FIACRE processes corresponding to the previous activities have reached the expected state. For example, because of the *start2Start* constraint between *wd2* and *wd1*, conditional statement checks whether activity *wd2* is started. If true the current state becomes *running* and it is recorded that this activity has been updated (was updated). Otherwise, nothing happens (loop statement). The following process shows the *wd1* workdefinition translated into FIACRE specification.

```
process wd1 [Start:sync, Finish:sync] (& wds: WDsQueries) is
    states notStarted, Running, finished
    from notStarted
    if (wds[$(wd2Id)].isStarted) then
        Start;
        wds[$(wd1Id)].isStarted := true;
        to Running
    else loop
    end if
    from Running
    if (wds[$(wd3Id)].isStarted) then
        Finish;
        wds[$(wd1Id)].isFinished := true;
        to finished
    else loop
    end if
```

The FIACRE component Process consists in instantiating the three processes
wd1, *wd2* and *wd3* with the actual ports and the array that stores activities'
states (initially all activities are not started and not finished):

```
component Process is
var
    wds: WDsQueries :=
        [ {isStarted=false, isFinished=false},
          {isStarted=false, isFinished=false},
          {isStarted=false, isFinished=false} ]
port
    wd1Start, wd1Finish: sync,
    wd2Start, wd2Finish: sync,
    wd3Start, wd3Finish: sync,
par * in
    wd1[wd1Start, wd1Finish](&wds)
    || wd2[wd2Start, wd2Finish](&wds)
    || wd3[wd3Start, wd3Finish](&wds)
end
```

4.3 Translating TOCL Properties

The key point is then to translate the properties as formulae on the formal
model. Obviously, this translation is done at the metamodel level and thus has
only to be written once for every DSML. As our purpose is to facilitate the
development of CASE tools for new DSML, we focus on generic and generative
approaches advocated by MDE.

We have written a generic tool to translate a TOCL property expressed on
the *xDSML* (using QDMM queries) to a LTL formulae on the formal language.
Technically, TOCL operators, including OCL ones, are translated in a first
transformation that generates a second transformation which handles queries
from QDMM. These transformations have been written using the ATL transformation language. The second transformation only depends on the way primitive
queries from QDMM are evaluated on the formal language. An ATL module
must be provided to describe the LTL fragments that corresponds to the primitive queries of QDMM. According to the formal language, it may correspond

to a process' state in a FIACRE model. Each query appears in that module as a helper method that returns the corresponding LTL fragment as a string. Implementing all these queries is a kind of checklist that ensures that all aspects of interest for the DSML end-user are indeed modeled on the formal side.

Here is the helper that corresponds to the primitive query *isFinished* identified on WorkDefinition in the context of XSPEM to FIACRE transformation.

```
context WorkDefinition
def isFinished (): String =
    self .getFiacreId() +
        "/value wds[(" + self.name + "id)].isFinished"
```

The property body is built according to FIACRE properties [15]. A FIACRE property is composed of two elements[2]: a path and an observable. A path defines the context of applying the observable. For example, the *"Process/2/1"* path identifies the *first* instance in the *second* composition in the main component named *Process*. Observables play the role of atomic proposition in the properties. It can be an instance state change, a communication through a port, a communication through shared variables or the execution of a transition.

The operation getFiacreId() is a helper method which consists of identifying the FIACRE instance – generated by the transformation – corresponding to the current workdefinition (*self*).

The second part in this query corresponds to the predicate to be verified, that is the observable. In the *isFinished()* definition, we check the shared variable wds that stores the state of each WorkDefinition instance.

Based on the translational semantics defined in section 4.2, the property P_1 applied on the the the XSPEM model of Fig. 1 generates the following FIACRE property.

```
property isNeverFinished is ltl
( [] ( not (     Process/1/value wds[ $(wd1Id) ].isFinished
        and Process/2/value wds[ $(wd2Id) ].isFinished
        and Process/3/value wds[ $(wd3Id) ].isFinished )))
```

4.4   Guidelines for Validating the Translation Semantics

Defining a translational semantics is a highly creative activity which requires high skills both in the formal language and in the DSML to find an efficient mapping between both languages as well as in transformation techniques. We thus only provide guidelines to favor the definition of a correct transformation.

The first guideline is the obligation to define for each QDMM primitive query the corresponding LTL fragment. QDMM queries are thus a kind of checklist that ensures that all aspects of interest for the DSML end-user have indeed been modeled on the formal side.

A second way to validate the translational semantics consists in formalizing invariants on the DSML using TOCL and then automatically translating them

---

[2] http://projects.laas.fr/fiacre/properties.html

on the formal side. If they fail, an error is detected (either in the translation, the invariants or the queries implementations).

4.5   Formal Verification

An ACCELEO[3] module generator (named Fiacre2fcr.acceleo) produces the FIACRE specification enriched with generated FIACRE properties.

The complete FIACRE specification (Process.fcr in the Fig. 4) containing both the FIACRE model specification and the properties to check represents the verification entry point shown in the **Formal verification level** part of Fig. 4. It is translated by the FRAC compiler[4] (the FIACRE compiler for the TINA toolbox) into a Timed Transition Systems (TTS) specification, the accepted input by TINA toolbox (Process.tts in Fig. 4).

This TTS specification is verified using SELT[5], the TINA model-checker for a State-Event version of LTL. When the property fails, SELT generates a counter-example as a succession of Petri net transitions. The generated counter-example — also named scenario and verifications results — is not easy to understand for the DSML end-user. So, we have to feedback it at the FIACRE level so that the DSML designer can use them to generate DSML verification results.

5   Feedback Verification Results

Verification results are obtained at the formal level and must be leveraged at the DSML level. This feedback is made easier thanks to the *Executable DSML pattern* [3] applied not only at the DSML level but also at the formal one. Results at the FIACRE level are obtained by analysing textual outputs of the TINA toolbox [16]. Xtext is used to parse textual outputs and model transformations generate the corresponding FIACRE events and scenarios.

FIACRE EDMM contains specific events [17]: an instance of a process entering or leaving a state, a variable changing value, a communication through a port.

In a previous work [18], we relied on the naming convention used when transforming the domain model to the formal one to translate verification results up to the DSML level. String analysis and parsing were used. However this method is tricky and cannot be applied on more complex DSMLs and cannot be generalized.

A more general solution consists in relying on a traceability metamodel which connects both metamodels (the DSML and the formal level). It corresponds to the traceability approach defined in [19]: trace information is considered as an additional model generated when the translational semantics is run.

---

[3] http://www.acceleo.org/pages/home/en

[4] http://projects.laas.fr/fiacre/manuals/frac.html

[5] http://projects.laas.fr/tina/manuals/selt.html

5.1   DSML-Fiacre Traceability Links

Based on the *Executable DSML pattern* applied on each DSML and on FIACRE
metamodel, the DSML designer is invited to define the traceability metamodel
with the appropriate information in order to capture information required to
feedback verification results.

The traceability metamodel depends on the defined translational semantics
and what kind of information would be traced back into the DSML level.
Typically, this information consists of triggering DSML events into the formal
language.

For the xSPEM example, two kinds of events are included *Start a WorkDefinition* and *Finish a WorkDefinition*. As shown in the previous section, the
DSML designer has mapped a workdefinition into a FIACRE instance. Events
are triggered using port signals (*Start* port and *Finish* port).

Fig. 5 shows the traceability metamodel, xSPEM2FIACRE, inspired from the
translational semantics which links xSPEM metamodel (bottom) and FIACRE
one (top).

The *xSPEM2Fiacre* model (shown in Fig. 4 as Process.xspem2fiacre) is
conforms to this metamodel. To find back xSPEM events from FIACRE ones,
we have defined two metaclasses *WDStart2Fiacre* and *WDFinish2Fiacre* that
correspond to the two xSPEM events (start a workdefinition and finish a
workdefinition). They are respectively linked to the *Start* and *Finish* port signal
statements.

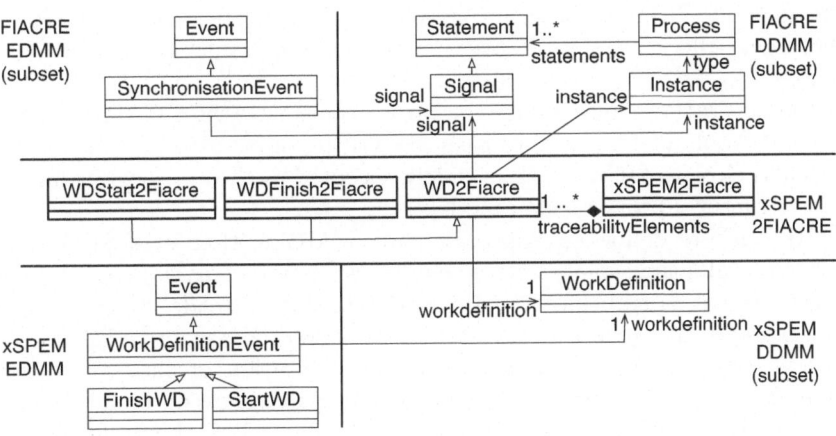

Fig. 5. Defining a traceability meta model

5.2   Feedback Verification Results at DSML Level

The generated FIACRE scenario, Process.fcrscn in Fig. 4, (that only contains FIACRE events) has to be leveraged at the DSML level, xSPEM in our case. An xSPEM scenario only contains events which are instances of the xSPEM's EDMM. Obtaining xSPEM events is done from FIACRE events thanks to the traceability links generated while the translational semantics runs.

Fig. 5 shows the relations between the EDMMs of FIACRE and xSPEM on the one hand (left) and their DDMMs on the other hand (right) through the traceability metamodel (middle). Only the *SynchronisationEvent* is represented because other events are not used for xSPEM. According to the signal and the instance of this event, the corresponding element can be found in the traceability model, and then the workdefinition identified as well as the kind of xSPEM event — either start or finish that workdefinition. Applying our approach on xSPEM model shown in Fig. 1 and TOCL property, negation of P_1 requirement, constructs the scenario presented in the Listing 1.1.

6   Related Work

The problem of integrating formal verification into the design of DSMLs has been widely addressed by the MDE community. In order to tackle property-based verification problem, authors of [20] present the Metropolis design framework for embedded systems.

Their verification approach is based on formal properties specified in Linear Temporal Logic (LTL) and Logic of Constraints (LOC). They have different domains of expressiveness and indeed complement each other quite well. The formal verification methodology of Metropolis consists in translating the Metropolis specification into Promela description, and the LTL properties are checked using the model checker Spin. Translating verification results is done in ad hoc manner.

On the contrary, in our approach, we introduce for the DSML designer a user-friendly tool, TOCL, used to ease the writing of behavioral properties and which is also close to OCL. OCL is widely accepted as the appropriate language to verify structural properties on models.

In [21], authors define an approach named Arcade that uses SPIN model checker for evaluating safety and liveness properties of a Domain Reference Architecture that is translated to Promela language. Arcade interprets SPIN counter-example and generates an Architecture Trace Diagram (ATD).

Nevertheless, the ATD is a graphical representation of the spin counter-example. They do not define a high-level abstraction between model level and formal level. In our work, we separate the two domains (DSML and formal ones) and we hide all formal aspects by translating formal results to domain-specific results.

Hegedüs et al. [22] propose a method to verify BPEL models. It relies on a relation between elements of the source (BPEL) and the target (Petri nets) metamodels, implemented by means of annotations in the transformation's source code. The authors propose a technique for the back-annotation of simulation traces from traces generated by the model checker to the specific animator named BPEL Animation Controller. This approach is based on change-driven model transformations. This choice can be a restriction for DSML designers which are not familiarized with this specific model transformations technique.

In [23], authors introduce an algorithm requiring the DSML's semantics to be defined formally, and a relation R to be defined between states of the DSML and states of the target language. The DSML designer must provide as input a natural-number bound n, which estimates a difference of granularity between the semantics of the DSML and the semantics of the target language.

However, we don't think that DSML designer, for who it it difficult to use formal methods and verification, can define this important information to feedback verification results.

The most important difference between our approach and all the previously quoted approaches is on the fact that we are defining a structured model-based approach allowing to model different steps: defining the model using DDMM, introducing behavioral properties using a TOCL editor and a QDMM extension and capturing runtime information using TM3, EDMM and SDMM extensions.

7   Conclusion

We have presented an approach to integrate verification tools on a DSML in order to assist system designer into the verification of safety and liveness properties on executable models.

It has been illustrated on XSPEM as DSML and FIACRE as the formal language. We introduce a user-friendly language, TOCL, to system designer which allows to specify behavioral properties because it is close to OCL. However, the use of OCL and TOCL have shown that it is still not well suited to many system designers. Therefore, we might need to investigate a more suited user-oriented language for expressing behavioral constraints. So, TOCL can be considered as an intermediate language between LTL and the high-level property language.

To ease feedback verification results, relying on the executable DSML pattern and traceability models, we assist DSML designer to define a traceability metamodel used after to define the backward transformation to feedback verification results at the DSML level.

This approach has been designed for domain specific languages. It is currently being experimented for several significantly different DSMLs. But, it is still to be shown if it can scale up to more complex languages or to languages combining different models of computation.

As future works, we propose to further facilitate the DSML designer task by providing automatically the backward transformation which feedbacks verification results into the DSML level. It can be inspired from the previously defined translational semantics.

References

1. Merilinna, J., Pärssinen, J.: Verification and validation in the context of domain-specific modelling. In: Proceedings of the 10th Workshop on Domain-Specific Modeling, ser. DSM 2010, pp. 9:1–9:6. ACM, New York (2010), http://doi.acm.org/10.1145/2060329.2060351
2. Harel, D., Rumpe, B.: Meaningful Modeling: What's the Semantics of "Semantics"? Computer 37(10), 64–72 (2004)
3. Combemale, B., Crégut, X., Pantel, M.: A Design Pattern to Build Executable DSMLs and associated V&V tools (short paper). In: Asia-Pacific Software Engineering Conference (APSEC), Hong Kong, China (2012)
4. Ziemann, P., Gogolla, M.: An Extension of OCL with Temporal Logic. In: Critical Systems Development with UML – Proceedings of the UML 2002 Workshop, vol. TUM-I0208, pp. 53–62 (September 2002)
5. Software & Systems Process Engineering Metamodel (SPEM) 2.0. Object Management Group, Inc. (October 2007)
6. Berthomieu, B., Bodeveix, J.-P., Filali, M., Farail, P., Gaufillet, P., Garavel, H., Lang, F.: FIACRE: an Intermediate Language for Model Verification in the TOPCASED Environment. In: ERTS 2008 (January 2008)
7. Combemale, B., Crégut, X., Giacometti, J.-P., Michel, P., Pantel, M.: Introducing Simulation and Model Animation in the MDE TOPCASED Toolkit. In: Proceedings of the 4th European Congress Embedded Real Time Software (ERTS), Toulouse, France (January 2008)
8. Farail, P., Gaufillet, P., Canals, A., Camus, C.L., Sciamma, D., Michel, P., Crégut, X., Pantel, M.: The TOPCASED project: a toolkit in open source for critical aeronautic systems design. In: Embedded Real Time Software (ERTS), Toulouse, France (January 2006)
9. Berthomieu, B., Ribet, P.-O., Vernadat, F.: The tool TINA – construction of abstract state spaces for Petri nets and time Petri nets. Int. Journal of Production Research 42(14), 2741–2756 (2004)
10. Garavel, H., Lang, F., Mateescu, R., Serwe, W.: CADP 2010: A toolbox for the construction and analysis of distributed processes. In: Abdulla, P.A., Leino, K.R.M. (eds.) TACAS 2011. LNCS, vol. 6605, pp. 372–387. Springer, Heidelberg (2011)
11. Correa, T., Becker, L., Farines, J.-M., Bodeveix, J.-P., Filali, M., Vernadat, F.: Supporting the Design of Safety Critical Systems Using AADL. In: 2010 15th IEEE International Conference on Engineering of Complex Computer Systems (ICECCS), pp. 331–336 (March 2010)
12. Farines, J.-M., De Queiroz, M.H., De Rocha, V., Carpes, A.M., Vernadat, F., Crégut, X.: A model-driven engineering approach to formal verification of PLC programs (regular paper). In: Emerging Technologies and Factory Automation (ETFA), Toulouse, France, pp. 1–8. IEEE (2011)
13. Jouault, F., Kurtev, I.: Transforming Models with ATL. In: Bruel, J.-M. (ed.) MoDELS 2005. LNCS, vol. 3844, pp. 128–138. Springer, Heidelberg (2006)
14. Eclipse, Acceleo (2012), http://www.eclipse.org/acceleo/
15. Abid, N., Dal-Zilio, S., Botlan, D.L.: A verified approach for checking real-time specification patterns. CoRR, vol. abs/1301.7531 (2013)

16. Zalila, F., Crégut, X., Pantel, M.: Verification results feedback for FIACRE intermediate language. In: Confrence en Ingnierie du Logiciel, CIEL (June 2012), http://gpl2012.irisa.fr/?q=node/31

17. Abid, N., Dal Zilio, S.: Real-time Extensions for the FIACRE modeling language (2010), http://automata.rwth--aachen.de/movep2010/index.php?page=about, http://hal.archives-ouvertes.fr/hal-00593958

18. Zalila, F., Crégut, X., Pantel, M.: Leveraging formal verification tools for DSML users: a process modeling case study. In: Margaria, T., Steffen, B. (eds.) ISoLA 2012, Part II. LNCS, vol. 7610, pp. 329–343. Springer, Heidelberg (2012), http://hal.archives-ouvertes.fr/hal-00720917

19. Jouault, F.: Loosely coupled traceability for ATL. In: Proceedings of the European Conference on Model Driven Architecture (ECMDA) Workshop on Traceability (2005)

20. Chen, X., Hsieh, H., Balarin, F.: Verification approach of metropolis design framework for embedded systems. International Journal of Parallel Programming 34(1), 3–27 (2006)

21. Barber, K.S., Graser, T., Holt, J.: Providing early feedback in the development cycle through automated application of model checking to software architectures. In: Proceedings of the 16th IEEE international conference on ASE 2001, Washington, DC, USA (2001)

22. Hegedüs, Á., Bergmann, G., Ráth, I., Varró, D.: Back-annotation of simulation traces with change-driven model transformations. In: SEFM 2010, pp. 145–155 (2010)

23. Combemale, B., Gonnord, L., Rusu, V.: A generic tool for tracing executions back to a dSML's operational semantics. In: France, R.B., Kuester, J.M., Bordbar, B., Paige, R.F. (eds.) ECMFA 2011. LNCS, vol. 6698, pp. 35–51. Springer, Heidelberg (2011)

Composing Your Compositions
of Variability Models

Mathieu Acher[1], Benoit Combemale[1], Philippe Collet[2], Olivier Barais[1],
Philippe Lahire[2], and Robert B. France[3]

[1] University of Rennes 1, Inria/Irisa, France
`firstname.lastname@irisa.fr`
[2] I3S Laboratory CNRS, University of Nice Sophia Antipolis, France
`firstname.lastname@i3s.unice.fr`
[3] Colorado State University, USA
`france@cs.colostate.edu`

Abstract. Modeling and managing variability is a key activity in a
growing number of software engineering contexts. Support for composing
variability models is arising in many engineering scenarios, for instance,
when several subsystems or modeling artifacts, each coming with their
own variability and possibly developed by different stakeholders, should
be combined together. In this paper, we consider the problem of composing feature models (FMs), a widely used formalism for representing
and reasoning about a set of variability choices. We show that several
composition operators can actually be defined, depending on both match-
ing/merging strategies and semantic properties expected in the composed
FM. We present four alternative forms and their implementations. We
discuss their relative trade-offs w.r.t. reasoning, customizability, traceability, composability and quality of the resulting feature diagram. We
summarize these findings in a reading grid which is validated by revisiting
some relevant existing works. Our contribution should assist developers
in choosing and implementing the right composition operators.

1 Introduction

Designing, developing and maintaining software systems for one customer, one
hardware device, one operating system, one user interface or one execution context is no longer an option. Numerous organizations rather need to efficiently
produce a large variety of similar software products, for satisfying the requirements of a particular domain. Variability, defined as *"the ability of a software
system or artifact to be efficiently extended, changed, customized or configured
for use in a particular context"* [1], is pervasive in a growing number of systems,
from software product lines (SPLs) [2] to dynamic adaptive systems [3]. When
properly managed, variability can lead to order-of-magnitude improvements in
cost, time-to-market, and productivity of products.

Models are traditionally employed to formally identify, organize and configure features of a system, automate the generation of products as well as their

A. Moreira et al. (Eds.): MODELS 2013, LNCS 8107, pp. 352–369, 2013.
© Springer-Verlag Berlin Heidelberg 2013

verification. A variety of models may be used for different development activities and artifacts – ranging from requirements, source codes, certifications and tests to user interfaces. In an increasing number of scenarios, support for composing models and their variability is becoming more and more crucial [4–16].

Multiple systems. When a multitude of subsystems (modular systems such as software components or services) or artifacts must be combined, several variability descriptions are to be related, organized and finally composed to form a consistent result. This context of use is broad, with first needs on organizing several software product lines with shared variabilities [5], evolving to compositional software product lines [4], in which a complex domain is captured and organized [14] into multiple product lines [8,11] with relations between input product lines' variability models. Handling these relations really lead to both reasoning on the represented configuration sets and maintaining a understandable organization (i.e. a feature hierarchy) for the organizations. The same situation arises when extracting FMs from different software artifacts [12,17–19]. However these various usages necessitate different interpretations of the FM composition operation to reflect the captured variable assets.

Multiple stakeholders. Together with multiple product lines comes the need to handle different stakeholders on one or several SPLs. Researchers developed techniques for FMs that reflect organisational structures and tasks. For example, Reiser et al. [6] address the problem of representing and managing FMs in SPLs that are developed by several companies in the automotive domain. Several FMs are used and structured hierarchically, so that they can be managed separately by suppliers. The FM composition is then concerned with the propagation of local changes through the hierarchy. In a similar situation, Hartmann et al. [7] used an FM in the context of a multiple SPL supporting several dimensions. It requires the definition of a merging process of FMs during their pre-configurations.

Multiple perspectives. The need for reasoning on FM compositions while manipulating a consistent FM hierarchy is also emphasized by the separation of concerns on variability models. With their increasing complexities and usages, practitioners may define different viewpoints according to different criteria or concerns. The most used viewpoints are the ones defining the user-oriented view (external variability) from the technical features (internal one) [2]. These views have many usages [10,20,21], i.e. defining abstraction layers, reflecting organizational structure with specific stakeholders [22], supporting collaborative design [23] or multi-level staged configurations [24]. Separation of these views also means that some relations and compositions must be done at some point to reason over the whole SPL, with references, constraints [25], a reduced form of composite model, and even in a semi-automatic way to synthesize an integrated model [11,15].

As a result, several modeling artifacts, each coming with their own variability and possibly developed by different stakeholders, should be combined together. In this paper, we first consider the problem of composing feature models (FMs), a widely used formalism (see Section 2) for representing and reasoning about a set of variability choices (a.k.a. features). We show that several salient variants of composition operators can actually be defined, depending on the semantic properties expected in the composed FM (Section 3). We present four variants with their respective implementations using the FAMILIAR language [15] (Section 4). We also study the different realized trade-offs w.r.t. reasoning, customizability, traceability and composability capacities, as well as quality of the resulting feature diagram (Section 5). We show that existing works [6, 8, 26] and our past attempts [15, 25] can benefit from the new proposed techniques when reasoning, synthesizing feature diagrams, aligning FMs or simply devising new composition-based operators. As a result, the contributions of this paper are:

- the identification of composition mechanisms and semantic properties for building more complex composition-based operators on FMs.
- the survey of four possible variant implementations of such composition-based operators including two new realizations in comparison with previous work [15, 25].
- a reading framework to help on selecting the right composition according to their respective qualities.
- its validation by instantiating some representative existing works.

Our contribution should both assist developers in *i)* choosing or devising composition-based operators for FMs and *ii)* choosing the most adequate tool-supported technique to realize these operators.

2   Background

Feature Models (FMs) are a widely used formalism for modeling and reasoning about commonality and variability of a system [27]. A recent survey of variability modeling showed that FMs are by far the most frequently reported notation in industry [28].

An FM is a hierarchical organization of features that aims to represent the constraints under which features occur together in products configurations. When decomposing a feature into subfeatures, the subfeatures may be optional or mandatory or may form *Xor-* or *Or*-groups (see Fig. 1a for a visual representation of an FM). Not all combinations of features (*configurations*) are authorized by an FM. Importantly, the hierarchy imposes some constraints: the presence of a *child* feature in a configuration logically implies the presence of its *parent* (e.g., the selection of F5 implies the selection of F2). The hierarchy also helps to conceptually organize the features into different levels of increasing detail, thus defining an *ontological semantics*.

A *valid* (or legal) configuration is obtained by selecting features in a manner that respects the hierarchy and the following rules: *i)* If a parent is selected, the following features must also be selected - all the mandatory subfeatures, exactly one subfeature in each of its Xor-groups, and at least one of its subfeatures in each of its Or-groups; *ii)* propositional constraints must hold. An FM defines a

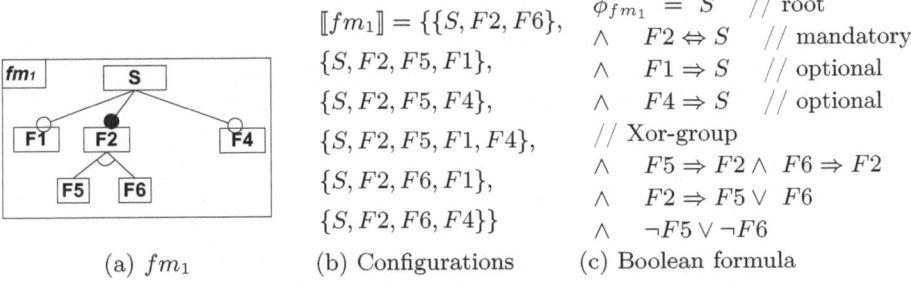

(a) fm_1 (b) Configurations   (c) Boolean formula

Fig. 1. FM, set of configurations and Boolean logic encoding

set of valid feature configurations (see Definition 1). Fig. 1b displays the set of valid configurations characterized by the FM of Fig. 1a.

Definition 1 (Configuration Semantics). *A configuration of an FM fm_1 is defined as a set of selected features. $\llbracket fm_1 \rrbracket$ denotes the set of valid configurations of fm_1 and is a set of sets of features.*

An FM is usually encoded as a propositional formula, denoted ϕ, and defined over a set of Boolean variables, where each variable corresponds to a feature [29] (see Fig. 1c for the propositional formula corresponding to the FM of Fig. 1a). The terms FM and *feature diagram* are employed in the literature, usually to denote the same concept. In this paper, we make a distinction. We consider that a feature diagram (see Definition 2) includes a feature hierarchy (tree), a set of feature groups, as well as human readable constraints (implies, excludes). The syntactical constructs offered by such feature diagrams are not expressively complete w.r.t propositional logics. Similar to [17], we thus consider that an FM is composed of a feature diagram *plus* a propositional formula ψ (see Definition 3).

Definition 2 (Feature Diagram). *A feature diagram $FD = \langle G, E_{MAND}, G_{XOR}, G_{OR}, I, EX \rangle$ is defined as follows: $G = (\mathcal{F}, E, r)$ is a rooted, labeled tree where $\mathcal{F}$ is a finite set of features, $E \subseteq \mathcal{F} \times \mathcal{F}$ is a finite set of edges and $r \in \mathcal{F}$ is the root feature ; $E_{MAND} \subseteq E$ is a set of edges that define mandatory features with their parents ; $G_{XOR} \subseteq \mathcal{P}(\mathcal{F}) \times \mathcal{F}$ and $G_{OR} \subseteq \mathcal{P}(\mathcal{F}) \times \mathcal{F}$ define feature groups and are sets of pairs of child features together with their common parent feature ; I a set of implies constraints whose form is $A \Rightarrow B$, EX is a set of excludes constraints whose form is $A \Rightarrow \neg B$ ($A \in \mathcal{F}$ and $B \in \mathcal{F}$).*

Definition 3 (Feature Model). *An FM is a tuple $\langle FD, \psi \rangle$ where FD is a feature diagram and ψ is a propositional formula over the set of features $\mathcal{F}$.*

3   Meanings of Composition-Based Operators

In an increasing number of contexts, a multiplicity of FMs have somehow to be combined, merged or confronted (i.e., *composed*), for instance, to synthesize an integrated view or reason globally about a system.

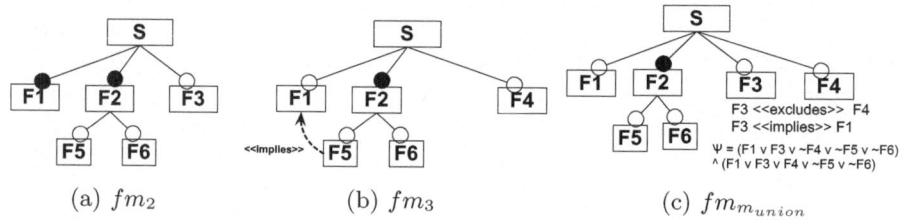

(a) fm_2 (b) fm_3 (c) $fm_{m_{union}}$

Fig. 2. A possible composition ($fm_{m_{union}}$) of fm_1, fm_2, and fm_3

A First Illustrative Example. Let us consider the composition of fm_1, fm_2 and fm_3 (see Fig. 1a, Fig. 2a and Fig. 2b). We denote by ○ a composition operator over FM that computes a new FM. In our specific example, we consider that the composed FM, denoted $fm_{m_{union}}$, should represent the *union* of input sets of configurations of fm_1, fm_2 and fm_3, that is: $[\![fm_{m_{union}}]\!] = [\![fm_1]\!] \cup [\![fm_2]\!] \cup [\![fm_3]\!]$. Such a composition is typically used to build a new SPL offering all the possible configurations supported in at least one of the products or SPLs of an organization or a supplier. Two possible resulting FMs are depicted in Fig. 2c and Fig. 3. Intuitively, when features are selected in the composed FM, it means that the selection of corresponding features (i.e., with the same names) are also valid and both supported in either fm_1 or fm_2 or fm_3. For instance, a partial configuration involving the selections of features F1, F2, and F3 is valid in $fm_{m_{union}}$ since the combination of features F1, F2, and F3 is also valid in fm_2. However it is not possible to both select features F3 and F4 in $fm_{m_{union}}$ since no valid configurations of fm_1, fm_2 and fm_3 are supporting this combination.

Meanings. Obviously, the semantics of the previous composition can be in contradiction with the intentions, requirements or simply modeling objectives of a practitioner. First there are different ways of interpreting the way features *match* and are related to each other (e.g., the mapping is not necessarily one-to-one). Second the *configuration semantics* expressed in the composed FM may differ (stakeholders may want to compute the intersection, the reduced product, the difference, etc. of configuration sets instead of the union). Finally the conceptual organization of the features in the resulting FM is another variation. Due to the variety of compositional scenarios exposed in the introduction, there is no one-size-fits-all interpretation when FM have to be composed. In order to address the variations' meanings, we identify common mechanisms and present a generic framework to devise (new) composition-based operators.

3.1 Different Strategies for Matching and Merging

The composition process exposed in the previous example is in line with many works on model composition that consists in two main phases [30, 31]: *i)* the **matching** phase identifies model elements that describe the same concepts in the input models to be composed; *ii)* the **merging** phase where matched elements are grouped together (i.e., merged) to create new elements in the resulting model.

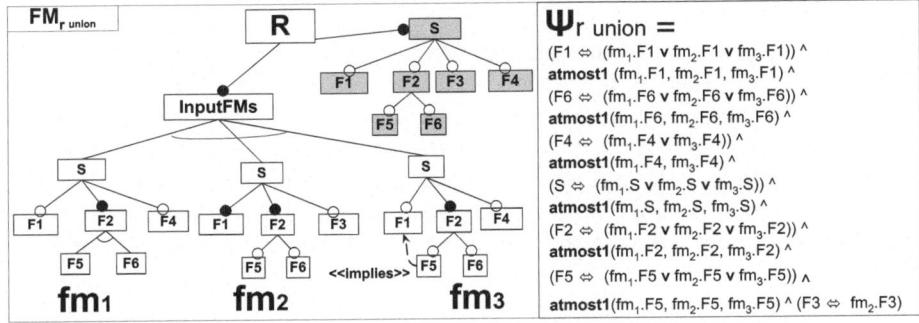

Fig. 3. Composition of fm_1, fm_2, and fm_3, somehow equivalent to $fm_{m_{union}}$. The term atmost1 $(F_1, \ldots, F_n)$ is equivalent to $\wedge_{i<j}(\neg F_i \vee \neg F_j)$

The previous strategy for matching/merging FMs is rather basic and straight-forward: features match if they have the same names while the merging consists in simply creating new features with the same names S, F1, ..., F6. However more sophisticated matching and merging mechanisms are needed especially when input FMs are coming from different sources (e.g., suppliers) or when the composed FM should reflect a *view* of the system that does not necessarily include all the original details or feature names.

We give an example in Fig. 4 ($\psi_{r_{other}}$ will be explained in detail in the next section). Firstly, F56 is mapped to features F5 and F6 of input FMs. The intuition is that either selecting F5 or F6 is sufficient to realize the feature F56. In a sense, F56 *abstracts* features F5 and F6 since no distinction is made between F5 and F6 at the level of abstraction of the view (coloured features). Secondly, F1 is no longer present in the composed view. It is another form of abstraction: unnecessary details are removed. Thirdly another feature, named F8, is present in the view and aims to better structure the FM, considering that features F3 and F4 are ontologically closed.

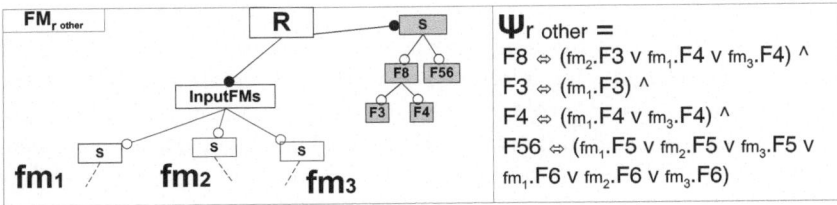

Fig. 4. Another composition of fm_1, fm_2, and fm_3 with different matching/merging strategies and semantic properties

3.2   Different Semantic Properties

The matching and merging mechanisms are the basics for devising a composition operator. However they do not state what are the properties of the composed FM in terms of *configuration semantics* and *ontological semantics*. Let us consider once again the composition of fm_1, fm_2, fm_3 and assume that features F3 match in the three FMs and are merged as a new feature F3 in the composed FMs. There is still need to establish the meaning of the new feature F3 in terms of configuration, i.e., what is the impact of a selection and deselection of F3 in the composed FM?

Configuration Semantics. A first interpretation is that the selection of F3 in the composed FM involves the selection of F3 in *one and only one* input FM. (It corresponds to the *union* of configuration sets as considered in the first illustrative example.) The direct impact of this specific semantics is that the selection of F3 induces in turn the selection of F1 (see Fig. 2c and Fig. 3), since there is no SPL that supports F3 without F1. Another more restrictive interpretation is that the selection of F3 in the composed FM forces the selection of *all* features named F3 in input FMs. If this interpretation is applied on all features, the composition intuitively corresponds to the *intersection* of configuration sets. Yet another (less restrictive) interpretation is that the selection of F3 in the composed FM forces the selection of *at least one* features named F3 in input FMs, etc.

Ontological Semantics. Another important aspect of FMs is the way features are conceptually organized in the tree-based hierarchy. Given a set of configurations, there still exists different candidate FMs yet with different hierarchies [17]. Therefore what the most appropriate feature hierarchy is should be part of the composition. For instance, a practitioner may consider that the feature F3 is more appropriately located below the feature F1 than below the root S in Fig. 3.

4   Variations in the Compositions of Feature Models

A composition operator ∘ takes as input a set of FMs and can be customized for supporting different matching/merging strategies and semantic properties (being related to configuration or ontological aspects) in the resulting FM. The following section addresses another important and related problem: How to implement these compositions? Different variants are indeed worth to consider, each having strengths and weaknesses.

4.1   Denotational-Based Composition (Logic-Based)

The logic-based implementation consists in *i)* encoding the expected configuration set of the composed FM as a Boolean formula ϕ_c *ii)* synthesizing the feature diagram from ϕ_c. Fig. 5a summarizes the process. The first step is to compute ϕ_c. All input FMs (resp. fm_1 and fm_2) are encoded as Boolean formula (resp. ϕ_1 and ϕ_2). Then the composition operator is *denoted* (or translated) in the Boolean logic. If we consider the case of *union* (see the first illustrative example), the denotational operator roughly corresponds to a *disjunction* of formulae (details have been given in [25]). Similar denotations can be applied for computing the intersection, diff, reduced product, etc. of configurations sets. The second step determines an appropriate hierarchy and synthesizes variability information. First we compute the binary implication graph of ϕ_c. It is a directed graph $BIG_c = (V, E)$, V being the set of nodes corresponding to variables of the formula, while the set of edges is formally defined as $E = \{(f_i, f_j) \mid \phi \wedge f_i \Rightarrow f_j\}$. BIG_c is a representation of all logical implications between two variables in ϕ_c and corresponds intuitively to all possible hierarchies of fm_c. Second we compute a directed *minimum spanning tree (MST)* of BIG_c that maximises the parent-child relationships of input FM hierarchies. Finally, other components of the feature diagrams can be synthesized [19, 32]. In Fig. 2c, the resulting synthesized FM corresponds to the first illustrative composition of fm_1, fm_2 and fm_3 (union mode, name-based matching strategy).

4.2   Operational-Based Composition (Reference-Based)

Another radically different implementation is to *reference* input FMs. The key idea is to build a separated FM (i.e., a *view*) that typically contains features with the same names of the input FMs. The features of the view are then related to input features through a set of logical constraints. The result is an FM that both aggregates the input FMs, the view, and the constraints. Fig. 3 depicts the resulting FM on the same kind of composition (union) than previously considered. Other kinds of configuration semantics (e.g., intersection) can be realized by defining another view and logical mapping.

The main difference is that features of input FMs are still present (i.e, the merging strategy differs compared to the denotation-based implementation). Yet it is worth to observe that the configuration semantics expressed in $fm_{r_{union}}$ (see Fig. 3) is *equivalent* to $fm_{m_{union}}$ (see Fig. 2c). The equivalence is defined as follows:

$$[\![fm_{m_{union}}]\!] = [\![fm_{r_{union}}]\!]_{|\mathcal{F}_{r_{view}}}$$

where $\mathcal{F}_{r_{view}}$ is the set of features in the view (coloured features in Fig. 3) and $A_{|B}$ denotes the projection of for two given sets A and B such that: $A_{|B} \stackrel{\triangle}{=} \{a' \mid a \in A \wedge a' = a \cap B\} = \{a \cap B \mid a \in A\}$. Intuitively it means that the exact same combinations of $S, F1, \ldots, F6$ are authorized in $fm_{r_{union}}$ and $fm_{m_{union}}$. This is due to $\psi_{r_{union}}$ that constraints the way features $S, F1, \ldots, F6$ of $fm_{r_{union}}$ can be combined. For instance, $\psi_{r_{union}}$ states that the selection of F2 should correspond to at least and at most one of the following features: $fm1.F2$, $fm2.F2$, or $fm3.F2$. Therefore F2 is actually mandatory in $\psi_{r_{union}}$ (as in $\psi_{m_{union}}$).

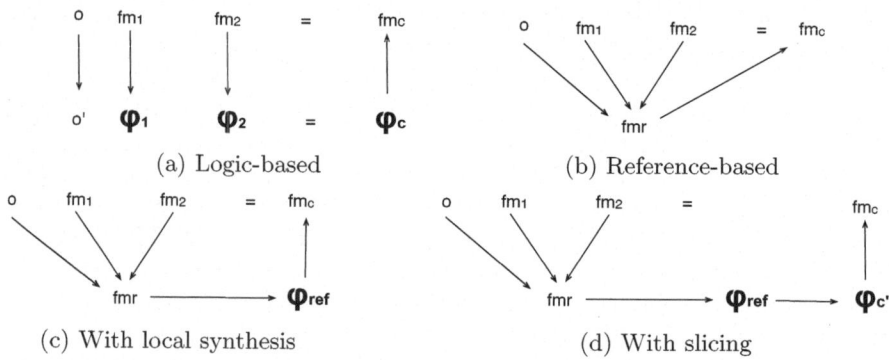

Fig. 5. Variants of composition-based operator implementation

4.3 Hybrid

The semantic equivalence of the denotational and operational-based implementations and the last remarks give the idea of going further by *correcting* the view of the reference-based FM. Two equivalent solutions are considered. In both cases, the principle is to *i)* denote the reference-based FM as a formula ϕ_{ref} and then *ii)* synthesize a new feature diagram and FM (see Fig. 5c and Fig. 5d).

Reference-Based and Local Synthesis. Our goal is to synthesize a new FM that only contains features of $\mathcal{F}_{r_{view}}$. However ϕ_{ref} contains many Boolean variables that may disturb the algorithm. In particular the computation of the implication graph is likely to contain nodes and edges that are not relevant. Furthermore considering all variables of ϕ_{ref} will dramatically increase the computation time. We thus adapt the synthesis procedure so that reasoning operations are only applied *over relevant variables*. For instance, the computation of the implication graph can be realized by checking possible implications only between features of interest. The synthesis of the variability information leads to the same exact feature diagram depicted in Fig. 2c on the previous example.

Reference-Based and Slicing. Another variant is to eliminate disturbing variables in ϕ_{ref} and obtain a new formula $\phi_{c'}$. Intuitively, non relevant variables are removed by existential quantification in ϕ_{ref}.

Definition 4 (Existential Quantification). *Let v be a Boolean variable occurring in ϕ. $\phi_{|v}$ (resp. $\phi_{|\bar{v}}$) is ϕ where variable v is assigned the value True (resp. False). Existential quantification is then defined as $\exists v\ \phi =_{def} \phi_{|v} \lor \phi_{|\bar{v}}$.*

In case of union, intersection, etc., $\phi_{c'}$ is equal to ϕ_c (the formula obtained with a denotational-based approach), i.e., the formula logically represents the exact same valid configurations and the set of variables is exactly the same. Therefore $\phi_{c'}$ can be used afterwards to synthesize an FM: the feature diagram obtained is the same as Fig. 2c.

4.4 Tooling Support

We rely on FAMILIAR (for FeAture Model scrIpt Language for manIpulation and Automatic Reasoning) [15]. The language already includes facilities for importing/exporting, editing, reasoning about FMs and their configurations. Two reasoning back-ends (SAT solvers using SAT4J and BDDs using JavaBDD) are internally used and perform over propositional formulae. Compared to our previous effort [15,19], we extend the language and integrate the new compositional techniques developed in the paper through the form of operations over FMs (aggregateMerge, ksynthesis "over" , etc.). We adapt the Tarjan's algorithm based on corrections reported in [33] to compute the directed MST of binary implication graphs. The code snippet below illustrates how to use the four implementation variants on the illustrative example of the paper. The reference [34] provides a comprehensive tutorial and numerous examples.

```
fm1 = FM (S : ..) fm2 = FM (S : ..) fm3 = FM (S : ..) // input feature models

fmMUnion = merge union { fm1 fm2 fm3 } // logic-based
fmRUnion = aggregateMerge union { fm1 fm2 fm3 } // reference-based

fm6 = extract fmRUnion.S // basic extraction (features are all optionals)
fm7 = slice fmRUnion including fmRUnion.S* // slicing (same FD + formula than fmMUnion)
fm8 = ksynthesis fmRUnion over fm5.S* // local synthesis (same FD but formula differs)
```

5 A Framework for Composing your Compositions

Users of composition operators for FMs have to define a specific semantics (or reuse an existing one, see left part of Fig. 6) and then select an appropriate implementation (see right part of Fig. 6). In this section, we provide a *reading grid* and *practical illustrations* in order to assist users in customizing a composition adapted to their requirements.

5.1 Comparison Framework and Reading Grid

We first discuss and compare the pros and cons of each implementation variant.

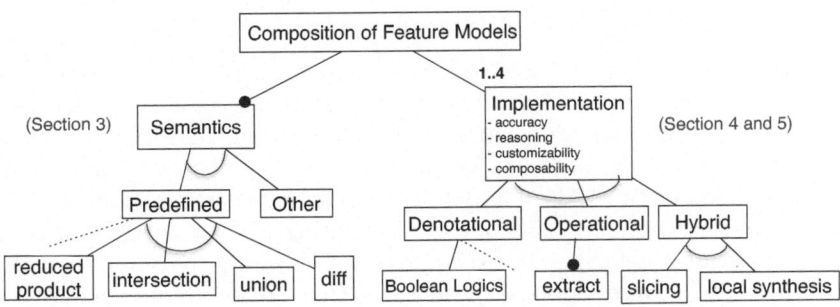

Fig. 6. Composing your Compositions

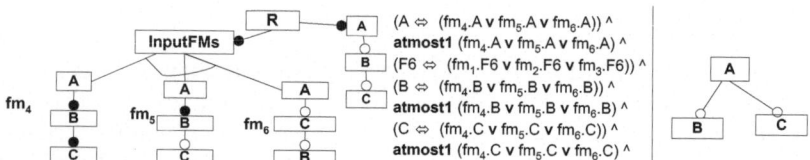

Fig. 7. Composition of fm_4, fm_5, and fm_6 (union): in left-part, the hierarchy leads to an incomplete FM ; in the right-part, a complete and sound FM.

Quality of the Feature Diagram. The feature diagram (see Definition 2) can be seen as a syntactical view of the configuration set that practitioners or automated tools usually exploit in a forward engineering phase. Given a set of configurations (say s), there may not exist a feature diagram FD such that $[\![FD]\!] = s$. In both cases, as much information as possible should be represented in the resulting feature diagram to approximate or fully represent s. It is known as the property of *maximality* [29]. A violation of maximality can have severe consequences, since in this case the syntactical information may contradict the actual meaning of the FM. For instance, the operational-based composition has the worst maximality since the resulting feature diagram is a super-set of all combinations of features and is a very rough over-approximation of s. In particular, the feature F2 is optional in the feature diagram whereas it is always included in every configuration. The other variants have the best possible maximality since they all rely on the logical synthesis technique that is known to produce a maximal feature diagram [32].

Another expected quality of a feature diagram is its *soundness* and *completeness*. In the reference-based FM, the feature hierarchy of the view is chosen without *a priori* considering the configuration set. Therefore it may happen that the retained hierarchy is not a spanning tree of the implication graph, with the consequence of either precluding some valid configurations (incomplete) or all possible configuration (unsound). We give an example in Fig. 7 (the FM is incomplete). Hybrid techniques (i.e., local synthesis and slicing), that rely on the reference-based FM, could be adapted to fix the problem. The idea is to first set a basic and very flattened hierarchy (i.e., all features are child features of the root) that could not violate any configurations. Then a safe hierarchy could be determined from the implication graph and replaced afterwards.

Reasoning. A composition-based operator computes a FM that can be exploited afterwards for *reasoning*, for example, when performing assisted configurations (decision verification and propagation, auto-completion, scheduling of configuration tasks, etc.), when automating analysis over the FMs (e.g., debugging of FMs, comparison of two FMs) [35, 36]. The question we address here is: how to reason about the configurations *once* the resulting FM has been synthesized? The drawback of a reference-based approach is that the reasoning should be performed over (a large amount of) features that are sometimes not relevant. For instance, if we want to perform a configuration over the features F1, F2, ..., F6, it necessarily involves considering the referenced features fm_1.F1, fm_1.F2,

..., fm_3.F6. As a result, the relevant *view* (coloured features of Fig. 3) of the composition is not independent of the other FMs. Furthermore, reasoning operations, usually implemented with SAT solvers or BDD, are not directly usable as such and rather have to be adapted to deal with unnecessary Boolean variables. On the contrary, the denotational-based technique or the use of slicing overcome such limitations since the computed formula only contains relevant Boolean variables and can be exploited independently. The local synthesis is not adequate for simplifying the formula since it calculates a feature diagram that is likely to express an over-approximation of the actual formula. For example, the local synthesis will generate the same feature diagram of Fig. 2c but not $\psi_{m_{union}}$, thus precluding its use for a correct reasoning.

Traceability. Features are usually mapped to development artefacts, such as components, models and user documentation . The preservation of the *traceability* between the FM and the artefacts is essential for automatic derivation of products from the configuration of the composed FM. In the case of a denotational-based technique, the mapping between the input FMs is not kept intact because they are replaced by a merged FM. As a result, the selections of features in the composed model may correspond to as many corresponding features in the input FMs. In the case of reference-based FM, the traceability is kept intact so that it is straightforward and immediate to determine the impact of a selection or a deselection on inputs.

Customizability. In the previous section, we have shown that there are different mechanisms that can be customized to specify the meaning of a composition. The denotational-based strategy is the most rigid since the matching strategy is assumed to be one-to-one and based on feature names while the merging process creates a new feature with the same name. It can be argued that some preprocessing steps and post-processing steps (renaming, removal of unnecessary features, etc.) can be applied to implicitly implement a matching and merging strategy. However the user effort can be very arduous and error-prone. The task is even more complex when the configuration semantics should be defined. The reference-based techniques are more general since any kinds of logical mappings between *i)* the features planned to be present in the composed FM and *ii)* the features in the input FMs can be defined. A last aspect is the customization of the ontological semantics. Denotational or hybrid techniques provide to users the means to select a sound feature hierarchy through the implication graph. The operational-based approach does not permit such scenarios and therefore the specification of the hierarchy is more error-prone.

Composability. Let us consider the composition in union mode and a matching strategy based on feature names (as the example explained in Section 3). The reference-based technique is neither associative nor commutative, e.g., $\circ(\circ(fm_1, fm_2), fm_3) \neq \circ(\circ(fm_1, fm_3), fm_2) \neq \circ(fm_1, fm_2, fm_3)$. Though the configuration set represented is the same, the feature diagrams are different. On the contrary the denotational-based and hybrid techniques are associative and commutative (in the case of union) since the Boolean formulas obtained are the same as previously and the logical operations do have the properties. Finally, it should be noted that a reference-based composition is hardly composable with a denotational-based composition since they are not operating over the same set of features, leading to counter intuitive results. In this case it is needed to slice the reference-based FM in order to align their domains.

	Denotational	Operational	Local Synthesis	Slicing
Diagram quality	A	C	A	A
Reasoning	A	C	C	A
Customizability	C	B	A	A
Traceability	C	A	A	A
Composability	A	C	B	A

Fig. 8. Comparison of approaches (A: best ; C: worst)

Table 8 summarizes the discussions and results by classifying the *best* and the *worst* solution in a given dimension. Some implementation variants are equivalent for some criteria (e.g., denotational and hybrid techniques compute the same feature diagram). The slicing-based technique fulfils all the criterion and, as such, can be considered as the most suited in the general case. Yet, its *performance* has to be confronted to other composition variants in practical settings (with different kinds of input FMs, matching and semantic properties, etc.). We leave it as future work since it is a *knowledge compilation problem* [37] that deserves a focused and careful attention.

5.2   Instantiating the Framework

We revisit some existing works that target different variability modeling scenarios. The goal is to illustrate the tradeoffs and validate the reading grid.

Devising Web Configurators from Product Descriptions. In [12], we extract FMs from product descriptions with the ultimate goal of devising product configurators. In this scenario the requirements are as follows. First, the reasoning facilities are crucial to assist end-users in configuring the products. Second, there are no alignment issues since the product descriptions are semi-structured in a tabular data that defines the vocabulary. Third, the FM has to be transformed (e.g., into widgets such as check boxes, lists, images, etc.). The transformation strategy is both automatic (mandatory features are hidden while Xor-groups are transformed as lists of configuration options) and manual (an expert overrides or defines some specific strategies to transform features into widgets). Given all these requirements, the best solution is to rely on a denotational-based implementation that has good reasoning capabilities, computes a high-quality feature diagram, while other criteria (e.g., composability) are not as important.

Modular Model Checking. In order to implement parallel composition of feature transition systems, Classen et al. proposed to compute the *intersection* of two FMs [38]. The composition consists in computing a FM characterizing the intersection of the two configuration sets. (The matching strategy is based on feature names while the merging strategy is to create a new feature with a same name.) The denotational-based strategy is again the best solution since reasoning is crucial – model checking techniques based on the formula of the composed FM are applied afterwards – the matching strategy is basic while the semantic properties (intersection) can be easily denoted in Boolean logic.

Managing Variability of Independent Suppliers. More and more organizations are developing software based on commercially available components from the marketplace and implemented by external suppliers. In such supply chains, variability coming from different sources has to be integrated (see, e.g., [8, 24]). Specifically, Hartman et al. [8] presented the problem in the domain of wireless solutions. They introduced the Supplier Independent FM (SIFM) in order to select products among the set of products described by several Supplier Specific FMs (SSFM). The key benefits, already given [8], are as follows *i)* the traceability with suppliers is kept intact ; *ii)* the mappings with suppliers' features can be easily customized. This corresponds exactly to the use of a reference-based FM that exhibits such property.

Moreover our tool-supported proposal can raise two limitations. First, the choice of the feature hierarchy in the SIFM is ad-hoc with the risk of being unsafe (precluding some valid configurations). Second, all features in the SIFM are optionals. In both cases, the hybrid techniques can be used to synthesize a better feature diagram (maximal and sound by construction).

Variability Modeling in Large-Scale Organizations. Reiser and Weber presented an approach to cope with large diagrams and large-scale organizations in the car industry [6]. The hierarchical organization of product sublines leads naturally to have an integrated view of the system referring to other features. The traceability with the different departments of the organization is crucial. The mappings can be arbitrarily complex since some features of input FMs are either not referenced by the view features (abstraction) or related through complex logical relationships. A denotational-based approach is therefore too rigid. The reference-based approach is the most appropriate solution while the local synthesis or the slicing techniques can be used for correcting the view.

Impact of FM Composition on Modeling Assets. An FM is usually associated to an asset (e.g., models) [2, 38]. Based on a selection of desired features, a customized model product can be automatically obtained through transformations. Composing such model-based SPLs is naturally emerging (e.g., [4, 38]). Given FMs (e.g., fm_1 and fm_2), their respective (sets of) assets (resp. $A1$ and $A2$), and their bindings (materialized as arrows in Fig. 9), the challenge is to compute a new model-based SPL (fm_c, Ac, and a new binding). The major difficulty is that that the resulting composed triplet should be consistent with $[\![fm_c]\!]$. Mirroring the semantics of the composition-based operators on the triplet raises two main challenges (see Fig. 9): *i)* the composition (Ob) of the bindings (see [39] for the underlying challenges) ; *ii)* the composition (Oa) of the assets.

The semantics and implementation is obvious if the rules of the binding are simple (e.g., one-to-one mapping), and the composition operator used to assemble the assets is the law of a mathematical group composed of the assets (closure, associativity, identity and invertibility). Unfortunately, this is in practice seldom

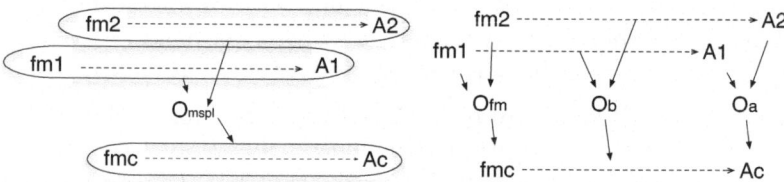

Fig. 9. Composing model-based SPL (left-part) is mirroring the semantics of the composition-based operators on the bindings and the assets (right-part)

the case, e.g., the Common Variability Language provides a powerful action language to express the binding [40], and can be arbitrarily complex. Moreover, most of the composition operators used to derive concrete products by assembling assets do not ensure the properties of the law of a group (e.g., invertibility). Though numerous approaches to model composition have been proposed [30,31], the problem of composing model-based SPLs has not yet deserved enough attention. The trade-offs discussed in the paper are a first step towards automatically mirroring the semantics of compositions operators for model-based SPLs.

6   Conclusion and Perspectives

Composing different variability descriptions from different sources is now a strong need in many engineering contexts. In this paper we have studied the different forms of feature model (FM) compositions, establishing the differences in feature matching and relations, as well as in the expressed configuration and ontological semantics. We have also detailed four different implementations of the composition operation, being based either on the underlying logic or some references between composed FMs. Two implementations are revisited versions from [25] while the two others are new and use forms of slicing and local synthesis over the FMs. We discussed the benefits and drawbacks of each variant using different criteria: the quality of the resulting FM, its customizability, as well as the provided capability of reasoning over the FM and of composing different implementations together. Different practical scenarios of use [6, 8, 12, 24, 38] were presented and a reading grid synthesizes these findings, in the aim of assisting developers choosing and implementing the right compositions.

Our immediate concern is to address one of the challenges opened by our contribution: the impact of the FM composition over the related modeling assets. The tradeoffs made explicit in the proposed reading grid should be reused to identify how to automate a mirroring of the FM composition semantics for model-based product lines.

Acknowledgements. This work was developed in the VaryMDE project (a bilateral collaboration between the Triskell team at INRIA and the Thales Research & Technology) and the CNRS PICS project MBSAR.

References

1. Svahnberg, M., van Gurp, J., Bosch, J.: A taxonomy of variability realization techniques: Research articles. Softw. Pract. Exper. 35(8), 705–754 (2005)
2. Pohl, K., Böckle, G., van der Linden, F.J.: Software Product Line Engineering: Foundations, Principles and Techniques. Springer (2005)
3. Morin, B., Barais, O., Nain, G., Jézéquel, J.M.: Taming dynamically adaptive systems using models and aspects. In: ICSE 2009, pp. 122–132. IEEE (2009)
4. Bosch, J.: Toward compositional software product lines. IEEE Software 27, 29–34 (2010)
5. Buhne, S., Lauenroth, K., Pohl, K.: Modelling requirements variability across product lines. In: RE 2005: Proceedings of the 13th International Conference on Requirements Engineering, pp. 41–52. IEEE (2005)
6. Reiser, M.O., Weber, M.: Multi-level feature trees: A pragmatic approach to managing highly complex product families. Requir. Eng. 12(2), 57–75 (2007)
7. Hartmann, H., Trew, T.: Using feature diagrams with context variability to model multiple product lines for software supply chains. In: SPLC 2008, pp. 12–21. IEEE (2008)
8. Hartmann, H., Trew, T., Matsinger, A.: Supplier independent feature modelling. In: SPLC 2009, pp. 191–200. IEEE (2009)
9. Bošković, M., Mussbacher, G., Bagheri, E., Amyot, D., Gašević, D., Hatala, M.: Aspect-oriented feature models. In: Dingel, J., Solberg, A. (eds.) MODELS 2010. LNCS, vol. 6627, pp. 110–124. Springer, Heidelberg (2011)
10. Hubaux, A., Heymans, P., Schobbens, P.Y., Deridder, D., Abbasi, E.K.: Supporting multiple perspectives in feature-based configuration. In: Software and Systems Modeling, pp. 1–23 (2011)
11. Rosenmüller, M., Siegmund, N., Thüm, T., Saake, G.: Multi-dimensional variability modeling. In: VaMoS 2011, pp. 11–20. ACM (2011)
12. Acher, M., Cleve, A., Perrouin, G., Heymans, P., Vanbeneden, C., Collet, P., Lahire, P.: On extracting feature models from product descriptions. In: VaMoS 2012, pp. 45–54. ACM (2012)
13. Clarke, D., Proença, J.: Towards a Theory of Views for Feature Models. In: Proceedings of the First Intl. Workshop on Formal Methods in Software Product Line Engineering (FMSPLE 2010), pp. 91–100 (2010)
14. Holl, G., Grünbacher, P., Rabiser, R.: A systematic review and an expert survey on capabilities supporting multi product lines. Information and Software Technology 54(8), 828–852 (2012)
15. Acher, M., Collet, P., Lahire, P., France, R.: Familiar: A domain-specific language for large scale management of feature models. Science of Computer Programming (SCP) Special Issue on Programming Languages 78(6), 657–681 (2013)
16. Schobbens, P.Y., Heymans, P., Trigaux, J.C., Bontemps, Y.: Generic semantics of feature diagrams. Comput. Netw. 51(2), 456–479 (2007)
17. She, S., Lotufo, R., Berger, T., Wasowski, A., Czarnecki, K.: Reverse engineering feature models. In: ICSE 2011, pp. 461–470. ACM (2011)
18. Haslinger, E.N., Lopez-Herrejon, R.E., Egyed, A.: On extracting feature models from sets of valid feature combinations. In: Cortellessa, V., Varró, D. (eds.) FASE 2013 (ETAPS 2013). LNCS, vol. 7793, pp. 53–67. Springer, Heidelberg (2013)

19. Acher, M., Heymans, P., Cleve, A., Hainaut, J.L., Baudry, B.: Support for reverse engineering and maintaining feature models. In: VaMoS 2013. ACM (2013)
20. Hubaux, A., Acher, M., Tun, T.T., Heymans, P., Collet, P., Lahire, P.: Separating Concerns in Feature Models: Retrospective and Multi-View Support. In: Domain Engineering: Product Lines, Conceptual Models, and Languages. Springer (2013)
21. Schroeter, J., Lochau, M., Winkelmann, T.: Multi-perspectives on feature models. In: France, R.B., Kazmeier, J., Breu, R., Atkinson, C. (eds.) MODELS 2012. LNCS, vol. 7590, pp. 252–268. Springer, Heidelberg (2012)
22. Mannion, M., Savolainen, J., Asikainen, T.: Viewpoint-oriented variability modeling. In: Proceedings of the 33rd International Computer Software and Applications Conference (COMPSAC 2009), pp. 67–72. IEEE (2009)
23. Mendonca, M., Cowan, D.: Decision-making coordination and efficient reasoning techniques for feature-based configuration. Science of Computer Programming 75(5), 311–332 (2010)
24. Czarnecki, K., Helsen, S., Eisenecker, U.: Staged configuration through specialization and multilevel configuration of feature models. Software Process: Improvement and Practice 10(2), 143–169 (2005)
25. Acher, M., Collet, P., Lahire, P., France, R.: Comparing approaches to implement feature model composition. In: Kühne, T., Selic, B., Gervais, M.-P., Terrier, F. (eds.) ECMFA 2010. LNCS, vol. 6138, pp. 3–19. Springer, Heidelberg (2010)
26. Abo Zaid, L., Kleinermann, F., De Troyer, O.: Feature assembly: A new feature modeling technique. In: Parsons, J., Saeki, M., Shoval, P., Woo, C., Wand, Y. (eds.) ER 2010. LNCS, vol. 6412, pp. 233–246. Springer, Heidelberg (2010)
27. Czarnecki, K., Grünbacher, P., Rabiser, R., Schmid, K., Wąsowski, A.: Cool features and tough decisions: a comparison of variability modeling approaches. In: Proceedings of VaMoS 2012, pp. 173–182. ACM (2012)
28. Berger, T., Rublack, R., Nair, D., Atlee, J.M., Becker, M., Czarnecki, K., Wąsowski, A.: A survey of variability modeling in industrial practice. In: Proceedings of VaMoS 2013. ACM (2013)
29. Czarnecki, K., Wasowski, A.: Feature diagrams and logics: There and back again. In: SPLC 2007, pp. 23–34. IEEE (2007)
30. Wimmer, M., Schauerhuber, A., Kappel, G., Retschitzegger, W., Schwinger, W., Kapsammer, E.: A survey on uml-based aspect-oriented design modeling. ACM Comput. Surv. 43(4), 28:1–28:33 (2011)
31. Jeanneret, C., France, R., Baudry, B.: A reference process for model composition. In: AOM 2008: Proceedings of the 2008 AOSD Workshop on Aspect-Oriented Modeling, pp. 1–6. ACM, New York (2008)
32. Andersen, N., Czarnecki, K., She, S., Wasowski, A.: Efficient synthesis of feature models. In: Proceedings of SPLC 2012, pp. 97–106. ACM Press (2012)
33. Camerini, P.M., Fratta, L., Maffioli, F.: A note on finding optimum branchings. Networks 9(4), 309–312 (1979)
34. Companion web page, https://github.com/FAMILIAR-project/familiar-documentation/blob/master/manual/composition.md
35. Benavides, D., Segura, S., Ruiz-Cortes, A.: Automated analysis of feature models 20 years later: a literature review. Information Systems 35(6) (2010)

36. Thüm, T., Batory, D., Kästner, C.: Reasoning about edits to feature models. In: ICSE 2009, pp. 254–264. ACM (2009)
37. Darwiche, A., Marquis, P.: A knowledge compilation map. J. Artif. Intell. Res (JAIR) 17, 229–264 (2002)
38. Classen, A., Cordy, M., Schobbens, P.Y., Heymans, P., Legay, A., Raskin, J.F.: Featured transition systems: Foundations for verifying variability-intensive systems and their application to LTL model checking. IEEE Trans. Software Eng, TSE (2012)
39. Diskin, Z., Maibaum, T., Czarnecki, K.: Intermodeling, queries, and kleisli categories. In: de Lara, J., Zisman, A. (eds.) Fundamental Approaches to Software Engineering. LNCS, vol. 7212, pp. 163–177. Springer, Heidelberg (2012)
40. Filho, J.B.F., Barais, O., Acher, M., Le Noir, J., Baudry, B.: Generating counterexamples of model-based software product lines: An exploratory study. In: 17th International Conference on Software Product Lines (SPLC 2013) (2013)

Constraints: The Core of Supporting Automated Product Configuration of Cyber-Physical Systems[*]

Kunming Nie[1], Tao Yue[2], Shaukat Ali[2], Li Zhang[1], and Zhiqiang Fan[1]

[1] Software Engineering Institute, Beihang University, Beijing, China
{niekunming,lily,fanzhiqiang}@cse.buaa.edu.cn
[2] Certus Software V&V Center, Simula Research Laboratory, Oslo Norway
{tao,shaukat}@simula.no

Abstract. In the context of product line engineering of cyber-physical systems, there exists a large number of constraints to support, for example, consistency checking of design decisions made in hardware and software components during configuration. Manual configuration is not feasible in this context considering that managing and manipulating all these constraints in a real industrial context is very complicated and thus warrants an automated solution. Typical automation activities in this context include automated configuration value inference, optimizing configuration steps and consistency checking. However, to this end, relevant constraints have to be well-specified and characterized in the way such that automated configuration can be enabled. In this paper, we classify and characterize constraints that are required to be specified to support most of the key functionalities of any automated product configuration solution, based on our experience of studying three industrial product lines.

Keywords: Product Line Engineering, Configuration, Constraints, Classification, Industrial Case Studies, Cyber-Physical Systems.

1 Introduction

Product Line Engineering (PLE) has gained significant attention in the recent years in both academia and industry because of its capability to deal with the ever increasing complexity and variation in software product lines [1]. Using PLE has shown to be effective for enhancing quality and productivity in product development, and speeding up time-to-market in many organizations such as Boeing, Lucent, and Nokia [2]. Modern society is increasingly dependent on Cyber-Physical Systems (CPSs), which rely on software to control many individual systems and complicated coordination of those systems [3]. Such systems include communications and control systems, interacting medical devices, and oil and gas production platforms, with the common characteristics such as large-scale, complex, inter-dependency and collaborative. Therefore, many CPS producers adopted PLE to enhance the reusability, thereby improving the overall quality and productivity of the development process of their products.

---

[*] We thank the Research Council of Norway under the Certus SFI project, the Ministry of Industry and Trade of Norway, and the National Natural Science Foundation of China (No. 61170087) for funding the research.

A. Moreira et al. (Eds.): MODELS 2013, LNCS 8107, pp. 370–387, 2013.

Effectiveness of a PLE approach for CPS is characterized by its support for abstraction and automation. Abstraction plays a central role in software and system reuse, which is required to capture all relevant information (e.g., commonalities and variabilities) in a concise and expressive manner to support automated configuration. Automation, on the other hand, is required for effective selection and customization of reusable components. Due to the inherent complexity of CPS, a large number of reusable components (e.g., electronic, software or network component) are typically configured by stakeholders working at different organizations or different departments of the same organization. A particular configuration process composed of a set of configuration tasks performed sequentially or concurrently by the stakeholders should be followed to configure a large-scale CPS. Consistency checking among all artifacts, particularly configuration files of different components configured by different stakeholders should be performed. Therefore automated support based on concise abstraction of reusable artifacts becomes crucial to configuring CPSs. Moreover, the characteristics of CPSs [4], including strong energy restrictions, being distributed, heterogeneity and software adaptability, bring new challenges for adopting PLE in CPSs. Among them, *Dynamic Configuration (also called Runtime Configuration)* [4], *Temporal Variability* [5], *Feature Interaction* and *Subsystem/Component Interaction* [6] are four important characteristics of PLE of CPSs.

Such an automated configuration solution heavily relies on a large number of constraints that should be formally specified using e.g., the Object Constraint Language (OCL) [7] to facilitate e.g., automated decision inference based on dependencies of variation points, the optimization of configuration orders based on user-defined constraints according to their preferences, or consistency checking among configuration files of the same or different products. Therefore a classification of such constraints according to how they are specified, manipulated and enforced, and relate them in a systematic manner to the functionalities (e.g., decision ordering) of such an automated solution is required. Constraints management has been one of the most challenging and complex problems that practitioners are facing with variability modeling as suggested by Creff *et al.* [8]: precisely specifying constraints among modeling artifacts and clarifying their use in PLE is very necessary. Classifications of feature dependencies were also proposed in [9-11]. However, these works do not particularly put their focus on PLE of CPSs and the current literature and practice still lack a reasonably complete classification to support main functionalities of an automated configuration solution in CPSs: inferring decisions, consistency checking, decision ordering, collaborative configuration and reverting decision.

Based on our experience of working on three commercial CPS product lines (i.e., Subsea Production Systems (SPSs), Video Conferencing Systems (VCSs) and Vessel Prognostics and Health Management Systems (VPHMS)), in this paper, we propose a classification of constraints required to support the five main functionalities we mentioned above. We use a conceptual model to structure and specify all the classification categories, each of which is explained with examples. We also report our experiences of classifying constraints using our classification with three industrial case studies. Note that, in this paper, we only aim to provide such a classification, but not focusing on how to specify them and how to manipulate them to realize the functionalities. In other words, we are not trying to provide a solution. Instead, our objective is to clarify the problems upfront such that researchers and practitioners facing similar kinds of problems can benefit from the classification we propose in this paper. The classification will also be used to guide us in the future to devise an automated configuration solution for CPSs.

The rest of paper is organized as follows. Section 2 provides the background. Section 3 discusses the constraints classification. In Section 4, we present the results of applying our classification to classify constraints of our case studies. Section 5 discusses the related work and we conclude the paper in Section 6.

2   Background

2.1   Key PLE Terminologies

We use a small conceptual model as shown in Fig. 1 to clarify several key PLE concepts and their relationships. *SystemSpecification* is a general concept representing a description of a system at a high level of abstraction. A *ProductLineSpecification* captures all the commonalities and variabilities of a product line family. Examples of *ProductLineSpecification* includes, e.g., feature model [12] and decision model [13]. A *ProductSpecification*, on the other hand, captures the specification of a specific product of the product line family. *VariationPoint* (VP) is a configurable element of *ProductLineSpecification*. It defines the place of the specification that specific customization to be applied to during product configuration. A *variant* (VA) is one of the possible choices or values to be bound for a variation point. Variation points can be specified in different ways, including value range, constraints, or enumeration literals, depending on applications. When resolving a variation point, a variant is bound to the respective variation point (configurable element). A *Constraint*, in our context, is an element of *SystemSpecification*, constraining one or more other elements to support automated product configuration.

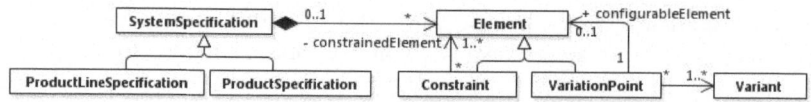

Fig. 1. Conceptual Model

2.2   Industrial Applications

CPSs are documented with characteristics of heterogeneity, being distributed, tight environmental coupling, and strong energy restrictions [4, 14]. CPS product lines commonly have hundreds and thousands of variation points and constraints. In CPS product lines, there exist many different hardware and software components containing variation points at different levels of abstraction. These variation points are typically resolved, as part of the configuration process, by different specialists at different phases of the product development lifecycle to support various activities such as testing and operation. In the rest of the section, we discuss the three CPS product lines used as our industrial case studies.

The first case study is Subsea Production Systems (SPSs) that are large-scale systems-of-systems, in which software controls and monitors the operation of electrical and mechanical instruments. A SPS has up to hundreds of control modules and thousands of instruments. In a family of SPSs, the hardware topology can vary from one product to another, with each topology being a specific configuration of the generic family design. Hardware is configured based on customer requirements, environmental conditions, and different regulations and standards. Members of a family of SPSs share the same software code base configured differently for each product, mainly based on the hardware topology. For example, the number of electrical and mechanical instruments, as well as their properties (e.g., resolution of a sensor) affects the number and values of run-time objects in the software configured for a specific product instance. Constraints between the hardware and software should be captured and accounted for during the configuration process.

Software and hardware variation points occur at different levels of detail and are typically resolved by different specialists in different phases of the product development lifecycle. For example, high-level hardware decisions (e.g., number of wells) are made by domain experts after tendering and front-end engineering design phases. Low-level variation points (e.g., the operating range of a device) are typically configured by configuration engineers or software engineers during the configuration, testing, or operation phases.

The second case study is a commercial Video Conferencing Systems (VCSs) product line family called *Saturn Product Line*. The core functionality of *Saturn* manages establishing and disconnecting video conferences. In total, *Saturn* consists of 20 subsystems such as audio and video subsystems. Each subsystem can run in parallel to the subsystem implementing the core functionality dealing with establishing videoconferences. *Saturn's* implementation consists of more than three million lines of C code. The Saturn family consists of various hardware codecs ranging from C20 to C90. C20 is the lowest end product with minimum hardware and has lowest performance in the family.

The third case study is a family of Vessel Prognostics and Health Management Systems (VPHMSs), which concern fault diagnosis and health evaluation of important ship equipment. A VPHMS contains more than dozens of hardware and software subsystems with regular work processes. Different sensors are installed on the monitored equipment to collect data for parameters of fault prognostics and health evaluation algorithms, which calculate the overall health condition of the equipment. Different equipment requires different sensors, algorithmic models and information display in user interfaces. Taking *Fault Diagnostic* as an example, to diagnose faults of different equipment (e.g., diesel engines), different fault diagnosis algorithms should be selected. Another important characteristic of VPHMS is that hardware components to be monitored and required sensors for monitoring the selected hardware components should be configured. Then the software system should be configured according to the corresponding hardware configuration. This system adopts PLE because the system functionality is relatively stable and the workflow of the system rarely changes. Each product of the product line family is configured, mainly based on the characteristics of monitored equipment—different monitored equipment implies the selection and deployment of different monitoring devices and the selection and configuration of different monitoring algorithms.

3   Constraints Classification Framework

In this section, we discuss the main contribution of the paper, the classification of constraints for supporting automated product configuration in the context of system/software PLE. We use a conceptual model, as shown in Fig. 2, to structure and specify all the classification categories, which were derived, based on our experience of working with three product lines (Section 2.2). We first in Section 3.1 provide the definition of the five functionalities of automated configuration solutions, and then present the constraint classification in Section 3.2.

3.1   Main Functionalities of Automated Configuration Solutions

For an automated product configuration solution, it mainly contains five functionalities: *InferringDecison, ConsistencyChecking, DecisionOrdering, CollaborativeConfiguration* and *RevertingDecision*, among which *InferringDecision* and *ConsistencyChecking* are mostly implemented functionalities in existing configuration tools such as Dopler [13] and Pure::Variants [15].

InferringDecision. Some configuration decisions can be automatically inferred based on existing configuration-relevant information such as constraints (dependencies as part of them) among variation points and variants, and previously made decisions during the configuration process. Such constraints enable the automated configuration of some decisions by evaluating and solving them. Benefits of this functionality is that it reduces the manual configuration effort and improves the quality of configuration by reducing inconsistencies among configuration data (e.g., decisions) [16]. All the product configuration tools we are aware of support the inferring decision functionality, indicating that it is one of the most important functionalities of an automated configuration solution.

ConsistencyChecking. In a general context, consistency checking verifies that certain conditions or properties hold in a group of software artifacts . In the context of CPS PLE, consistency checking is very important and difficult as there are more types of artifacts than a general context. For example, consistency between models belonging to different views (e.g., hardware and software views) of product line architecture models of CPS and consistency between decisions (or configuration data) made within the scope of a product or across products of the same product line. To enable the automated consistency checking, consistency checking rules should be specified as the first class artifacts of an automated configuration tool. These consistency checking rules can be generalized as constraints in our context. This functionality is available in all the configuration tools we have investigated: Pure::Variants [15], Dopler [13], Covamof [18], SPLOT [19], FMP [12] and Questionnaire [20].

DecisionOrdering. For a configuration tool, decision ordering is the functionality that provides users guidance on in which sequence a set of decisions (or configuration parameters) should be configured, by taking into account constraints coming from different sources such as user defined configuration priorities, dependencies between variation points and constraints on a particular product development process of an organization. Guiding users throughout the product configuration process by directing the order of resolving variation points offers benefits such as reducing configuration effort by finding an order which is optimal in the sense that the total number of manual configuration steps is minimized [21]. Existing tools such as Dopler [13], Covamof [18], SPLOT [19], FMP [12] and Questionnaire [20] support this functionality.

CollaborativeConfiguration. This functionality is required as CPS systems are usually composed of subsystems and configuring one subsystem might depend on the configuration of other sub-systems. In addition, typically these subsystems are developed and configured by different organizations, groups, or individuals. Coordinating the configuration process of such a system is not trivial and constraints among required configuration tasks performed by different stakeholders in a valid sequence should be clearly specified to realize this functionality. Some configuration tools (e.g., Pure::Variants [15], Dopler [13], SPLOT [19] and FMP [12]) support the collaborative configuration to various extents.

RevertingDecision: In practice, it is very common that a user goes back to modify configurations she/he made previously. Therefore a configuration tool needs to provide a functionality allowing a user to make changes on any part of the history. This is not trivial considering that some of decisions or configurations are automatically inferred based on constraints (as we discussed in *InferringDecision*). Reverting a decision implies a re-evaluation and re-solving some of these constraints and maintaining the consistency of decisions based on consistency checking rules. Configuration tools Dopler [13] and SPLOT [19] support "undo" and "redo" the most recent configuration a user made. Questionnaire [20] supports rollback to the state when some of previous decisions were not made.

3.2   Classification of Constraints

As discussed previously, all the five functionalities of an automated configuration solution depend on constraints. These constraints are specified for different functionalities, at different PLE (Domain and Application) phases, coming from different sources. Therefore, it is very crucial to classify them in a way that implementing these functionalities can then be facilitated. In this section, we present such a classification of constraints, which was derived based on our direct hand-on experience of studying three product lines from three different domains (Section 2.2). We use a UML class diagram (Fig. 2) to graphically present the classification and its relationships with the five functionalities.

Constraint. As shown in Fig. 2, `Constraint`, as a general concept, is characterized by `ConstrainingScope`, `SystemSpecificationType` and whether or not it is derived (`isDerived`) from other artifacts. CPSs are distributed systems with subsystems connected via network. Such subsystems are often composed of hardware and software components. Therefore, the architecture of such systems is often view-based design. A constraint can be specified as `WithinView` or `CrossView`. To characterize a constraint in this way provides support on consistency checking as constraints within a view are only used to check consistency of a view while constraints across views are for consistency checking among views. In most cases, constraints are enforced on the structural specification of a system, e.g., dependencies among variation points and variants specified as part of UML class diagrams or feature models. There are certain cases that constraints are specified on the behavioral specification of the system (e.g., the state invariant of a state in a UML state machine) and these constraints must be configured for a product. For example, in the context of Saturn Product Line (Section 2.2), hardware configuration (e.g., video port) is used to configure functional state machines related to establishing a videoconference and sending video from camera to the remote participant through the configured video port.

Some constraints can be derived from existing artifacts (attribute `isDerived` of class `Constraint`). For example, the resolution of a variation point *A* depends on the resolution of another variation point *B*, which provides restrictions on the configuration of variation point *C*. Therefore, a constraint can be derived from these dependencies by saying that *B* should be configured before *A* and *C*.

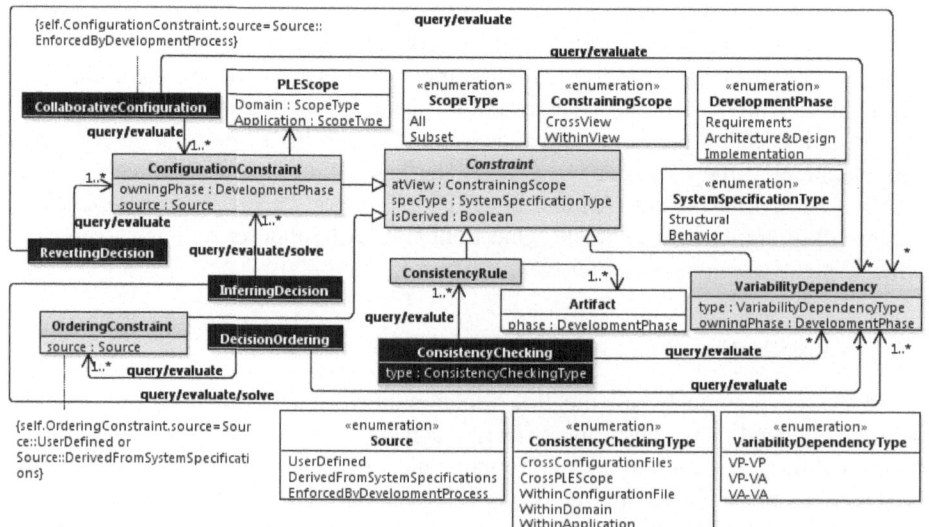

Fig. 2. Constraints classification and its relationships with the five functionalities

We classify constraints into four categories (highlighted as classes with the gray background in Fig. 2): ConfigurationConstraint, OrderingConstraint, ConsistencyRule and VaraibilityDependency. Below, we discuss them one by one.

ConfigurationConstraint. This type of constraints is required by functionalities InferringDecision, RevertingDecision and CollaborativeConfiguration, and includes all the constraints that are required to completely configure a product except dependencies among variation points and variants (VariabilityDependency). Such a constraint might belong to different development phases (DevelopmentPhase). For example, in the context of SPS, configuring a product starts when specifying product requirements, during which high-level decisions (e.g., how many subsea control modules to deploy according to the number of wells to exploit) are often made. In the architecture and design level, configurable parameters such as ranges of temperature sensors should be specified.

We also characterize ConfiguratonConstraint according to where they belong (PLEScope): either PLE domain engineering or application engineering. Domain constraints are the ones that are specified at the product line level and enforced to resolve variation points. Such a constraint can be applied when configuring each product of the product line family or a subset of it (ScopeType). Application constraints, on the other hand, are the constraints that are applied after all the variation points of a product are resolved and when they are operational. For example, after a SPS is deployed offshore, an operator needs to perform some "runtime" configuration on the configurable parameters (e.g., engineering unit of a valve) of the control software deployed to the system. The runtime changes of the values of the configuration parameters typically have crosscutting effects on the base behavior of the systems. Another example is in the context of the *Saturn* product line, where when a VCS product (e.g., C20) is configured with the support of the H323 videoconference protocol, we further need to configure settings for the H323 protocol (e.g., the H323 gateway) at the product level to enable model-based testing. During these "post" configuration activities, some constraints should be specified to enable the three functionalities associated with class ConfigurationContraint. As for domain constraints, application constraints also have enforcement scopes: all configured products or a subset.

OrderingConstraint. It is a particular category of constraints for facilitating the DecisionOrdering functionality. There are mainly two types of sources to obtain this type of constraints: UserDefined and DerivedFromSystemSpecification. A user can define their priorities of configuring a subsystem, a component or even a configurable parameter, based on her/his preference or business requirements. Such user-defined constraints should not violate constraints that have to be satisfied to configure a correct product. Ordering constraints can also be derived from the system specification. For example, an implied order of configuring two variation points can be derived from existing dependencies of them.

ConsistencyRule. It is a very important and complex in the context of PLE, as we discussed in Section 3.1. Typically, to enable this functionality, a set of

ConsistencyRules have to be specified for constraining different Artifacts (derived during different phases of the product line and product development lifecycles) and their relationships. We classify consistency checking in the context of PLE into various types, as shown in enumeration ConsistencyCheckingType. For example, consistency checking can be performed to check the consistency of configuration files developed during different product development phases (e.g., testing, deployment and operation) of a product, or the consistency of the topology configuration of a hardware component and a configuration of a configurable software component deployed to the hardware component. Note that ConsistencyRule is a subclass of Constraint; therefore consistency checking rules are can be classified according to ConstrainingScope and SystemSpecificationType. Therefore, consistency checking within and cross views and specification types can be enabled.

Note that this functionality might need to be invoked by other functionalities, e.g., RevertingDecision, InferringDecision and CollaborativeConfiguration as instant verification of configuration decisions might be needed to ensure the correctness and consistency of configuration decisions with respect to interdependencies of configurable parameters and other consistency rules governing the product line family.

VariabilityDependency. This is the mostly used type of constraints, as it is required by all the five functionalities as shown in Fig. 2. We classify variability dependencies into three types: VP-VP, VP-VA and VA-VA. Dependency VP-VP means that to resolve a variation point (vp_1) another variation point (vp_2) should be configured first. For example, as we discussed in Section 2.2, SPSs are highly-hierarchical, implying that e.g., making a decision on which type of hardware components (e.g., XmasTree[1]of a SPS) to select typically leads to configuring a set of variation points corresponding to the devices (e.g., valve, pressure sensor) owned by a component with this type. Another example is that resolving a hardware variation point (e.g., selecting a specify type of pressure sensors) need the correspond resolving of a software variation point (e.g., the range in the physical unit of a pressure sensor with the selected specific type). Dependency VP-VA means that if one variation point is resolved, then another variation point should be resolved by binding one of its variants. Dependency VA-VA means that if one variation point is resolved by binding one of its variants, then another variation point should be resolved by binding one of its variants.

As we discussed in Section 3.1, configuring a CPS starts from making high-level decisions (e.g., the number of subsea oil and gas wells to exploit for a SPS product) at the requirements engineering phase, then proceeds to the architecture and design of the system by selecting and assigning values of configurable parameters (e.g., engineering unit of a sensor), and all the way through implementation. Variation points exist in all these development phases and therefore dependencies among them should be clearly captured such that the functionalities of an automated configuration solution can be enabled.

---

[1] XmasTree in the context of SPSs is a mechanical component that physically contains a set of instruments such as values, chokes and pressure and temperature sensors.

Relationships among Configuration Functionalities and Constraints. All the five functionalities need to `query` and `evaluate` constraints. `DecisionOrdering` and `InferringDecision` need to solve constraints. `DecisionOrdering` and `RevertingDecision` are all related to `InferringDecision`. `InferringDecision` can be used to obtain the importance degree of a decision, which indicates the impact of configuring one decision on the automated resolution of other decisions based on `ConfigurationConstraints` and decision propagation. Thus, `DecisionOrdering` is related to `InferringDecision` because the most constraining decision(s) can be calculated by comparing the importance degree of decisions, which therefore helps to determine an optimal ordering of making decisions. `RevertingDecision` is related to `InferringDecision` because when reverting a decision, its subsequent decision(s) automatically inferred may need to be also rolled back. This possibly leads to invalid or obsolete configuration and users should be informed of changes and issues raised. To do so, constraints that were used for inferring the decision may need to be reevaluated. When inferring a decision, the consistency with all the decisions already made should be kept, which implies that consistency checking is required to ensure this. Therefore, `InferringDecision` depends on `ConsistencyChecking` functionality.

4   Industrial Case Studies

In this section, we report three industrial case studies based on which we derived our classification. The objective of this section is to show how many instances of constraints were identified for each case study and in which categories of our classification they fall into. At the end of the section, we summarize our observations.

4.1   Subsea Production System (SPS)

The current practice of the organization involves a series of refinements of their products to adapt them to the specific needs of a particular customer. The adaption process is actually a product configuration process, which includes: 1) configuring the hardware topology (e.g., making decisions such as how many wells to construct and how they are connected), and 2) configuring the software that is deployed on the hardware computing resources. The software controls and monitors the oil and gas production process, given a specific set of values for the configurable parameters of the software. These values are different from product to product and are jointly referred to as configuration data. The configurable parameters have to be properly configured before the software is loaded and executed to operate hardware devices.

In the current practice of the organization, their product development process has a set of distinguishable phases (e.g., tender, design, operation) and involves different stakeholders (e.g., customers, hardware engineers, software engineers, test engineers and off shore operators). Different stakeholders might have different configuration rights. By configuration rights, we mean that not everyone has the knowledge required for all configurations and, therefore, we need to restrict certain configuration decisions to stakeholders who have the appropriate expertise. For example, hardware engineers might not have configuration rights to configure the software. The configuration process is integrated with the product development process. The configuration process has multiple configuration phases corresponding to different configuration purposes such as testing and operation.

4.2   Video Conferencing System (VCS)

Our aim in this project was to devise an adequate product line modeling and configuration methodology to support systematic testing and more specifically model-based testing (MBT) of VCS product lines. MBT has shown to be cost-effective in many industry sectors but at the expense of building models of the system under test (SUT). However, the modeling effort to support MBT can significantly be reduced if an adequate product line modeling and configuration methodology is followed. Our case study in this project is *Saturn* product line. *Saturn* has 20 subsystems and each subsystem has at least one configurable state machine specifying its functionality and on average such state machine has five states and 11 transitions. The biggest subsystem state machine has nine hierarchical state machines with 22 states and 63 transitions. Saturn product family models for non-functional behaviors consist of five aspect class diagrams and five configurable aspect state machines modeling various robustness behaviors. The largest aspect state machine specifying robustness behavior has three states and ten transitions, which would translate into 1604 transitions in standard UML state machines [22]. Saturn product line family models also consist of 124 hardware configuration parameters and 99 software configuration parameters.

4.3   Vessel Prognostics and Health Management System (VPHMS)

Our industry partner is facing the following challenges: 1) handling different types of variation points (e.g., selection, value, cardinality), thereby introducing different types of variability dependencies, 2) integrating (through configuration) software components of different versions, developed with different programming languages by different organizations, 3) maintaining the consistency of hardware and software component configurations, and 4) coordinating the collaborative configuration process during which a large number of engineers involved.

A VPHMS needs to monitor up to tens of hardware components and different hardware components require various types of sensors installed. Taking an electromechanical subsystem for example, it monitors 30 equipment with 160 diagnosis algorithms. These algorithms, grouped as the algorithm component, contain hundreds of configurable parameters. Feature model is used to capture the variation points of the product line for the purpose of supporting configuration at the requirements level. At the architecture and design level, UML class, component and deployment diagrams were developed to specify the system architecture and design, on top of which variabilities were specified using stereotypes.

4.4   Summary of Constraint Instances Collected

We summarize the number of instances of applicable constraint categories of each case study in Table 1. It is important to notice that some of the data were directly obtained by counting the number of constraints specified using OCL as part of the architecture and design models we developed before. Some of them were derived based on domain knowledge that was gained via reading documents, studying their current configuration practice, meeting and brainstorming with domain experts of the organizations. These constraints, distinguished from the OCL constraints using italics, were collected as English sentences and were not formally specified using any particular constraint specification language.

From Table 1, one can observe that for SPS, all the five functionalities are important to the organization. Therefore, almost each category of constraints obtained one or more instances. For different categories, various numbers of constraints were either specified in OCL in our previous work [16] or identified based on our domain knowledge for different categories and captured in English. All the constraints were specified on the structural specification of the system and were all directly captured. Consistency checking among configuration files is a very important feature for the organization as we mentioned in Section 2.2, configuration files are generated by configuration engineers for different purposes such as testing and operation, which is not the case for the VCS case study.

Table 1. Classification Coverage by Case Studies

	Categories	SPS	VCS	VPHMS
Configuration Constraint	Domain-All	*15*	*24*	22
	Domain-Subset	*5*	*9*	5
	Application-All	8	0	28
	Application-Subset	4	*266* (C90), *185* (C40 and C60), and *172* (C20)	500
	Requirements	*5*	0	13
	Architecture&Design	27	0	20
	Implementation	0	*33*	22
	EnforcedByDevelopmentProcess	6	N/A	10
Ordering Constraint	UserDefined	8	N/A	10
	DerivedFromSystemSpecifications	10		36
Consistency Rule	CrossConfigurationFiles	25	N/A	0
	CrossPLEScope	3		15
	WithinConfigurationFile	69		14
	WithinDomain	*16*		58
	WithinApplication	0		0
Variability Dependency	Requirements	8	N/A	6
	Architecture&Design	28	N/A	20
	Implementation	0	N/A	22
	VP-VP/ VP-VA/ VA-VA	26	0	48
Basic Property	Structural	241	*33*	49
	Behavioral	0	*33*	5
	isDerived	0	0	20
	CrossView	26	0	20
	WithinView	46	*33*	36

For VCS, we have 24 configurable OCL constraints (13 for functional state machine configuration and 11 for aspect state machine (ASM) configuration) for *Domain-All*. To configure a product (e.g., C20), each of these constraints need to be configured and as a result the corresponding state machines are configured, which in turn are used for MBT. For VCS, we have further nine (bold value in Table 1) ASMs in *Domain-Subset*. One ASM configures an OCL constraint (constraining hardware and software configuration parameters) and the configured constraints configure a subset of state machines. In *Application-Subset*, we show the number of configurable parameters for each VCS product. For example, C90 has 266 configurable parameters that need to be configured at the product level once C90 has been configured. All of our OCL constraints 33 (24 from *Domain-All* plus nine constraints in nine ASMs) are at the *Implementation* level since all the variables constrained using OCL corresponds to VCS's implementation. All of our 33 constraints fall into both *Structural* and *Behavioral* categories as we used UML class diagrams, state machines, and aspect state machines. All of our 33 constraints are in *Within View* and we have four distinct views in VCS: Functional, Non-Functional, Software, and Hardware.

For VPHMS, all the five functionalities are expected to be implemented for automated configuration. There are 22 constraints in *Domain-All* category and five *Domain-Subset* constraints. In the *Application-Subset* category, a subset of products has more than 500 configurable parameters, which are used to set valid ranges for equipment status checking and fault diagnosis. We had 10 constraints defined by users and 36 constraints derived from the architecture model, which are all related to ordering decisions. As for consistency rules, 58 rules were defined to check the consistency of the variability model and 14 rules were defined to keep the consistency of the configuration files. Besides, 15 rules were defined at the *CrossPLEScope* category to keep the consistency of the product line model and product model. We have 48 dependencies among VP and VA. Structural constraints are defined on product line model (e.g., class, component and deployment diagrams) based on UML extension. Five constraints are defined on sequence diagrams that model the variability of workflows of the system. There are 36 constraints following into the *WithView* category while 20 were classified as *CrossView* constraints. Notice that for this case study, so far we are just able to identify all the constraints and captured them in sentences.

The difference of the specified constraints between VCS and the others is that VCS is mainly used for testing, while SPS and VPHMS are used for configuring products. SPS and VPHMS both support the five functionalities and configuration at the requirements and architecture levels. Thus, the constraint categories covered by these two systems have similarities. However, due to the domain difference, there are still some constraints categories different. For example, there are some CrossConfigurationFiles constraints in SPS, while behavior constraints exist in VPHMS.

5   Related Work

Since our motivation is to classify constraints for the purpose of supporting automated configuration for CPSs, we reviewed seven mostly-reported configuration tools: Pure::Variants [15], Dopler [13], Covamof [18], SPLOT [19], Kumbang [23], FMP [12] and Questionnaire [20]. Apart from FMP and Questionnaire, the other five tools are used in the context of PLE of CPSs such as communication systems, intelligent traffic systems, industrial automation systems, aerospace industry, and distributed weather station network respectively. We mapped their current implementation of constraints-relevant functionalities to our classification. Results are presented in Table 2. In addition, we also include research papers [8, 10, 11, 24-35] reporting constraints classifications in the PLE context but not related to tools or at least not mentioned explicitly in the papers.

In Table 2, the rows are the constraint categories and the columns are the functionalities. The blocks in gray are constraint categories specified for each functionality. References in italic are research papers and the rest are configuration tools. One can easily notice that one or more categories of each functionality are not

Table 2. Classification Coverage by Related Work

	Categories	Inferring Decision	Consistency Checking	Decision Ordering	Collaborative Configuration	Reverting Decision
	Domain-All	[18, 19]				[20]
	Domain-Subset					
	Application-All					
C	Application-Subset					
C	Requirements	[12, 15, 18, 19]			[13] [19]	[19]
	Architecture Design	[15, 18, 20, 23]			[13]	
	Implementation	[13, 18]			[24] [13]	[13]
	EnforcedBy DevelopmentProcess				[12]	
O	UserDefined			[12, 18]		
C	DerivedFrom SystemSpecifications			[12, 13, 15]		
	CrossConfigurationFiles					
	CrossPLEScope		[8, 10, 25-27, 35] [12,13,15,18-20,23]			
C	WithinConfigurationFile		[15]			
K	WithinDomain		[13, 19, 20]			
	WithinApplication					
	Requirements	[28, 29] [12, 18, 19]	[25, 30] [12]	[31,32] [12,13,18]	[13] [19]	
V	Architecture&Design	[15, 18, 20, 23]	[15, 18, 20, 23]	[33] [13, 18, 20]	[13]	
D	Implementation		[13, 18]	[13, 18]	[24] [13]	
	VP-VP/VP-VA/VA-VA	[25,27-29] [13,18-20]	[11] [12, 13, 18-20]	[32] [18-20]		[34]
	Structural		[26]			
B	Behavioral	[20]	[20]	[20]		[20]
P	isDerived			[18-20]		
	CrossView		[25] [13]		[24] [12, 13, 19]	
	WithinView		[13]	[13]	[13, 19]	

BP: Basic Property; VD: Variability Dependency; CK: Consistency Rule; OC: Ordering Constraint; CC: Configuration Constraint.

covered by the related work. On the other hand, most of the categories are covered by one or more related work, implying that our classification derived based on our experience of working with three product lines, is quite consistent with what have been reported in the literature and what have been implemented in the tools.

InferringDecision. As shown in the column "InferringDecision" of Table 2, all the tools implement this functionality. Approaches reported in [25, 27-29] define the dependency between VP and VA, including *require, exclude, impact,* and *discourages.* However, these methods mostly focus on the requirements level. Rule engine was used in Dopler tool to execute the IF-THEN rules, while the other tools user constraint solvers (i.e., SAT Solver, BDD Solver and Prolog Solver) to infer decision.

ConsistencyChecking. As shown in the fourth column of Table 2, all the categories we specified are covered by the related work except CrossConfigurationFiles, WithinApplication and isDerived. All tools provide CrossPLEScope consistency checking between the product line and product specifications, either during the configuration process or after. In addition, three tools focus on the inconsistencies detection of variability models (WithinDomain) while only one tools focus on the consistency checking of product specifications (WithinConfigurationFile, WithinApplication).

DecisionOrdering. As shown in the fifth column of Table 2, three research papers [31-33] discuss constraints related to decision ordering, Nohrer *et al.* [32] discusses VP-VP and VA-VA variability dependency. Covamof [18] and FMP [12] rely on user defined configuration priorities, while the others derive configuration priorities from system specifications. Questionnaire [20] introduces order dependency to enforce a partial ordering between VP and VP. There is no related work that discusses ordering constraints based on CrossView constraints, although CPSs usually have many this kind of constraints due to their heterogeneous characteristic (Section 3.2). Dopler [13] implemented DecisionOrdering relying on WithinView constraints. Covamof is used for configuring intelligent traffic systems, which are typical CPSs, and it has implemented the decision ordering functionality.

CollaborativeConfiguration. As shown in the sixth column of Table 2, only one research paper and three tools discuss this functionality. Dhungana *et al.* [24] uses inter-model dependencies to define the relationship between variability models and other models. As for the tools, SPLOT [19] provides multi-view feature model collaborative configuration, FMP [12] supports stage configuration, while Dopler [13] supports role based collaborative configuration. Note that CPSs are often heterogeneous systems and collaborative configuration is very necessary.

RevertingDecision. From Table 2, we can see that only few related work implemented this functionality. Nohrer *et al.* [34] supports selective "undo" to cancel specific decision made before. Dopler [13] and SPLOT [19] supports "undo" and "redo" (simplest reverting decision method) while Questionnaire [20] supports rollback to the state when some of previous decisions were not made. Although this functionality is very important for any practical application of an automated configuration solution, it has not received enough attention.

6   Conclusion

In large scale Cyber-Physical Systems (CPSs) product lines, due to the existence of numerous variation points and constraints, product configuration is a challenging task and thus automation is required. Constraints play an important role in such automated configuration. However, to support automation, a precise classification of constraints is required. With this aim in mind, we present a comprehensive classification of constraints required for supporting automated configuration of large scale CPSs. We identified five main functionalities of automated configuration solution and associate various types of constraints to each of the functionalities based on studying three industrial systems belonging to the CPS domain. We provided results from the three industrial case studies capturing all types of constraints related to automatic configuration. Moreover, we classified existing work using our classification with the aim to provide insights to researchers and practitioners from our experience that can help them to systematically devise their own automated configuration solution.

References

1. Frakes, W.B., Kang, K.: Software reuse research: Status and future. IEEE Transactions on Software Engineering 31, 529–536 (2005)
2. Ali, S., Yue, T., Briand, L., Walawege, S.: A Product Line Modeling and Configuration Methodology to Support Model-Based Testing: An Industrial Case Study. In: France, R.B., Kazmeier, J., Breu, R., Atkinson, C. (eds.) MODELS 2012. LNCS, vol. 7590, pp. 726–742. Springer, Heidelberg (2012)
3. Cyber-Physical Systems, http://cyberphysicalsystems.org/
4. Ortiz, Ó., García, A.B., Capilla, R., Bosch, J., Hinchey, M.: Runtime variability for dynamic reconfiguration in wireless sensor network product lines. In: Proceedings of the 16th International Software Product Line Conference, vol. 2, pp. 143–150. ACM, New York (2012)
5. Haber, A., Rendel, H., Rumpe, B., Schaefer, I.: Evolving delta-oriented software product line architectures. In: Calinescu, R., Garlan, D. (eds.) Monterey Workshop 2012. LNCS, vol. 7539, pp. 183–208. Springer, Heidelberg (2012)
6. Juarez-Dominguez, A.L., Day, N.A., Joyce, J.J.: Modelling feature interactions in the automotive domain. In: Proceedings of the 2008 International Workshop on Models in Software Engineering, pp. 45–50. ACM, New York (2008)
7. Object Constraint Language (OCL), http://www.omg.org/spec/OCL/2.2/
8. Creff, S., Champeau, J., Monégier, A., Jézéquel, J.-M.: Relationships Formalization for Model-Based Product Lines. In: Proceedings of the 2012 19th Asia-Pacific Software Engineering Conference, vol. 1, pp. 158–163. IEEE Press, Washington, DC (2012)
9. Ferber, S., Haag, J., Savolainen, J.: Feature interaction and dependencies: Modeling features for reengineering a legacy product line. In: Chastek, G.J. (ed.) SPLC 2002. LNCS, vol. 2379, pp. 235–256. Springer, Heidelberg (2002)
10. Mei, H., Zhang, W., Zhao, H.: A metamodel for modeling system features and their refinement, constraint and interaction relationships. Software and Systems Modeling 5, 172–186 (2006)

11. Jaring, M., Bosch, J.: A taxonomy and hierarchy of variability dependencies in software product family engineering. In: Proceedings of the 28th Annual International Computer Software and Applications Conference, vol. 1, pp. 356–361. IEEE, Washington, DC (2004)

12. Czarnecki, K., Antkiewicz, M., Kim, C.H.P., Lau, S., Pietroszek, K.: fmp and fmp2rsm: eclipse plug-ins for modeling features using model templates. In: OOPSLA 2005 Companion, pp. 200–201. ACM, New York (2005)

13. DOPLER, Decision Oriented Product Line Engineering for effective Reuse, http://ase.jku.at/dopler/

14. Wan, K., Man, K., Hughes, D.: Specification, analyzing challenges and approaches for cyber-physical systems (CPS). Engineering Letters 18, 308 (2010)

15. Pure Systems website, http://www.pure-systems.com

16. Behjati, R., Yue, T., Briand, L., Selic, B.: SimPL: A Product-Line Modeling Methodology for Families of Integrated Control Systems. Information and Software Technology 55, 607–629 (2013)

17. Visualizing Consistency Checking in Software Product Lines, http://www.jku.at/sea/content/e104861/e170007/e177920/

18. Sinnema, M., Deelstra, S., Nijhuis, J., Bosch, J.: COVAMOF: A framework for modeling variability in software product families. In: Nord, R.L. (ed.) SPLC 2004. LNCS, vol. 3154, pp. 197–213. Springer, Heidelberg (2004)

19. Mendonca, M., Branco, M., Cowan, D.: SPLOT: software product lines online tools. In: Proceedings of the 24th ACM SIGPLAN Conference Companion on Object Oriented Programming Systems Languages and Applications, pp. 761–762. ACM, New York (2009)

20. La Rosa, M., van der Aalst, W.M., Dumas, M., ter Hofstede, A.H.: Questionnaire-based variability modeling for system configuration. Software & Systems Modeling 8, 251–274 (2009)

21. El-Sharkawy, S., Schmid, K.: Supporting the effective configuration of software product lines. In: Proceedings of the 16th International Software Product Line Conference, pp. 119–126. ACM, New York (2012)

22. Ali, S., Briand, L.C., Hemmati, H.: Modeling robustness behavior using aspect-oriented modeling to support robustness testing of industrial systems. Software & Systems Modeling 11, 633–670 (2012)

23. Myllärniemi, V., Asikainen, T., Männistö, T., Soininen, T.: Kumbang configurator–a configuration tool for software product families. In: 19th International Joint Conference on Artificial Intelligence, pp. 51–57. Citeseer, Edinburgh-Scotland (2005)

24. Dhungana, D., Seichter, D., Botterweck, G., Rabiser, R., Grunbacher, P., Benavides, D., Galindo, J.A.: Configuration of multi product lines by bridging heterogeneous variability modeling approaches. In: 15th International Software Product Line Conference, pp. 120–129. IEEE, New York (2011)

25. Silva Filho, R.S., Redmiles, D.F.: Managing Feature Interaction by Documenting and Enforcing Dependencies in Software Product Lines. Feature Interactions in Software and Communication Systems IX 33 (2008)

26. Ziadi, T., Hëlouët, L., Jézéquel, J.-M.: Towards a UML profile for software product lines. In: van der Linden, F.J. (ed.) PFE 2003. LNCS, vol. 3014, pp. 129–139. Springer, Heidelberg (2004)

27. Silva Filho, R.S., Redmiles, D.F.: Towards the Use of Dependencies to Manage Variability in Software Product Lines. Variability Management–Working with Variability Mechanisms 4 (2006)

28. Ye, H., Liu, H.: Approach to modelling feature variability and dependencies in software product lines. In: IEE Software Proceedings, vol. 152, pp. 101–109. IET, UK (2005)
29. Streitferdt, D., Riebisch, M., Philippow, K.: Details of formalized relations in feature models using OCL. In: 10th IEEE International Conference and Workshop on the Engineering of Computer-Based Systems, pp. 297–304. IEEE, New York (2003)
30. Oster, S.: Feature Model-based Software Product Line Testing. PH.D Thesis. University of Namur, Belgium (2012)
31. Lee, Y., Yang, C., Zhu, C., Zhao, W.: An approach to managing feature dependencies for product releasing in software product lines. Reuse of Off-the-Shelf Components, 127-141 (2006)
32. Nohrer, A., Egyed, A.: Optimizing user guidance during decision-making. In: 15th International Software Product Line Conference, pp. 25–34. IEEE, Washington, DC (2011)
33. Zimmermann, O., Koehler, J., Leymann, F., Polley, R., Schuster, N.: Managing architectural decision models with dependency relations, integrity constraints, and production rules. Journal of Systems and Software 82, 1249–1267 (2009)
34. Nöhrer, A., Egyed, A.: Conflict resolution strategies during product configuration. In: International Workshop on Variability Modelling of Software-intensive Systems, vol. 37, pp. 107–114 (2010)
35. Rosenmüller, M., Siegmund, N., Kästner, C., Ur Rahman, S.S.: Modeling dependent software product lines. In: GPCE Workshop on Modularization, Composition and Generative Techniques for Product Line Engineering (McGPLE), pp. 13–18 (2008)

Defining and Validating a Multimodel Approach for Product Architecture Derivation and Improvement

Javier González-Huerta, Emilio Insfrán, and Silvia Abrahão

ISSI Research Group, Universitat Politècnica de València
Camino de Vera, s/n, 46022, Valencia, Spain
{jagonzalez,einsfran,sabrahao}@dsic.upv.es

Abstract. Software architectures are the key to achieving the non-functional requirements (NFRs) in any software project. In software product line (SPL) development, it is crucial to identify whether the NFRs for a specific product can be attained with the built-in architectural variation mechanisms of the product line architecture, or whether additional architectural transformations are required. This paper presents a multimodel approach for quality-driven product architecture derivation and improvement (QuaDAI). A controlled experiment is also presented with the objective of comparing the effectiveness, efficiency, perceived ease of use, intention to use and perceived usefulness with regard to participants using QuaDAI as opposed to the Architecture Tradeoff Analysis Method (ATAM). The results show that QuaDAI is more efficient and perceived as easier to use than ATAM, from the perspective of novice software architecture evaluators. However, the other variables were not found to be statistically significant. Further replications are needed to obtain more conclusive results.

Keywords: Software Product Lines, Architectural Patterns, Quality Attributes, Model Transformations, Controlled Experiment.

1 Introduction

The quality attributes of a software system (e.g., performance, modifiability, and availability) are, to a great extent, permitted or precluded by its architecture [9]. In the case of Software Product Line (SPL) development, in which a set of software-intensive systems sharing a common set of features are developed by taking advantage of the massive reuse of software assets, the product line architecture should have variation mechanisms that help to achieve a set of explicitly allowed variations [9]. These variations may include structural, behavioral and of course quality concerns. The product line architecture should therefore be designed to cover the whole set of variations within the product line. The product architecture can thus be derived from the product line architecture by exercising its built-in architectural variation mechanisms, which support both the functional and non-functional requirements[1] (NFRs) for a specific product.

---

[1] Non-Functional Requirements can be defined as the qualities that a product must have, such as an appearance, or a property of speed or accuracy [30].

A. Moreira et al. (Eds.): MODELS 2013, LNCS 8107, pp. 388–404, 2013.
© Springer-Verlag Berlin Heidelberg 2013

Once it has been derived, the product architecture should be evaluated in order to guarantee that it meets the specific requirements of the product under development [9]. However, in those cases in which levels of quality attributes that fall outside the original specification of the product line are needed (and cannot be attained by using product line variation mechanisms), certain architectural transformations may be applied to the product architecture to ensure that these NFRs are met [5].

Although several methods for architecture derivation and improvement in SPL development have been proposed over the last few years (e.g., [23], [28], [19], [31], [6], [8], [29]), there is still a need for approaches that model the impact between architectural design decisions and quality attributes and use this information to enhance the quality attribute levels of product architectures. We have addressed this problem, in previous works [17] [18] [20], by proposing an approach with which to ensure the desired quality attribute levels for a product by applying architectural transformations to a product architecture derived from a product line architecture using a multimodel. This multimodel represents a set of interrelated viewpoints of the product line and the semantic relationships among elements in each viewpoint. It also allows the product line architecture, the metrics for its evaluation and the relationships among architectural transformations and NFRs to be represented.

In this paper, we present the quality-driven product architecture derivation and improvement (QuaDAI) method, which uses the multimodel to guide the software architect in the derivation, evaluation and improvement of product architectures in a model-driven software product line development process. Since in the software architecture field there is a lack of empirical evidences that support the claimed benefits and capabilities of methods, techniques and tools [1], we also present the results of its empirical validation through a controlled experiment. The objective of this paper is the following: i) to present a method, consisting of a set of activities carried out by model transformation processes, thus allowing us to derive product architectures from the product line architecture, to evaluate the product architecture obtained and, when required, to improve the architectures' quality attribute levels by applying pattern-based architectural transformations; and ii) to evaluate the effectiveness, efficiency, perceived ease of use, usefulness and intention to use of the method in comparison with the Architecture Trade-Off Analysis Method (ATAM) [22]. This evaluation was done by conducting a controlled experiment with fifth year Computer Science students.

The remainder of the paper is structured as follows. Section 2 discusses existing approaches that deal with the derivation, evaluation and improvement of software architectures when following a product line approach. Section 3 presents our multimodel approach for the derivation, evaluation and improvement of product architectures with the desired quality attributes. Section 4 presents the preliminary results of the validation of the approach through a controlled experiment. Finally, the conclusions and future work are presented in Section 5.

2   Related Work

Several approaches for the quality evaluation and analysis of SPL architectures have been proposed over the last few years (e.g., [23], [28], [19], [31]). Among them, Kim et al. [23] and Olumofin and Misic [28] propose two extensions of ATAM (i.e., EATAM [23] and HoPLAA [28]) with which to assess the quality of both product line and product architectures. Both methods extend ATAM with the qualitative analytical treatment of variation points.. Although HoPLAA and EATAM consider the architectural variation points during the architecture design, they lack a systematic mechanism that can be used to deal with those cases in which the NFRs of the product under development are not within the range of values permitted by the architectural variability. In addition, they do not explicitly represent the relationships between the architectural improvements and the quality attributes. These relationships could be reused during the application engineering stage each time a new product architecture needs to be improved, thus facilitating the evaluator task. Neither EATAM nor HoPLAA have been empirically validated. HoPLAA had been compared with ATAM in a running example and the validation of EATAM has not yet taken place.

Guana and Correal [19] proposed an approach that generates an evaluation report with the possible architectural configuration that meets the required quality attributes of the product under development. They defined relationships between a variability feature tree and the functional components, and associated these relationships with a quality scenario, which is analyzed at evaluation time. Roos-Frantz et al. [31] present an approach that automates the quality analysis of SPLs. This automation is performed by associating quality information with the variability view (expressed by means of orthogonal variability models), and by using constraint programming to perform the analysis tasks. The problem is partially addressed by the approaches presented in both [31] and [19]. They explicitly define the relationships amongst system views and use the information to predict the quality attribute levels of the product under development. However, they do not provide mechanisms to measure whether these quality attribute levels are present in the software artifacts. These approaches can also predict the quality attributes of a configuration, but they cannot deal with products with quality attribute levels that are not allowed by the product architecture variation mechanisms. With regard to validation, the approach in [31] has been theoretically but not empirically validated.

Several other approaches deal with the automatic derivation of product architectures in SPL development (e.g., [6], [8], [29]). In the approach by Botterweck et al. [6], the product architectures are produced by means of an ATL model transformation process, which takes as input a domain architecture model and an application feature model and generates an application architecture model, by simply copying the software components. Similarly, Cabello et al. [8] produce application architectural models by means of a QVT transformation. The transformation takes as input the variability view expressed in a feature model and the modular view of the architecture, and generates the PRISMA component and connector architectural view. Finally, Perovich et al. [29], automate the derivation of product architectures by taking as input a feature configuration model. The transformation encapsulates the knowledge of how to build the product architecture when the corresponding feature is present in the feature configuration model. However, when deriving the product architecture these approaches do not take into account quality attribute requirements and they do not consider the application of patterns or architectural transformations to improve the product architectures obtained. None of the aforementioned approaches has been empirically validated.

In summary, there is a need for empirically validated approaches that model the impact between architectural design decisions and quality attributes and use this information to derive the product architectures and to evaluate and enhance their quality attribute levels. The use of the multimodel in these tasks allows the knowledge to be reused in order to facilitate the evaluation tasks, providing mechanisms that automate the selection of the architectural transformations that best fit the NFRs.

3   QuaDAI: Architecture Derivation and Improvement

QuaDAI is a method for the derivation, evaluation and improvement of product architecture that defines an artifact (the multimodel) and a process consisting of a set of activities conducted by model transformations. QuaDAI relies on a multimodel [17] that allows the explicit representation of different viewpoints of a software product line and the relationships among them.

3.1   A Multimodel for Specifying SPLs

A multimodel is a set of interrelated models that represents the different viewpoints of a particular system. A viewpoint is an abstraction that yields the specification of the whole system restricted to a particular set of concerns and it is created with a specific purpose in mind. In any given viewpoint it is possible to make a model of the system that contains only the objects that are visible from that viewpoint [4]. Such a model is known as a viewpoint model, or a view of the system from that viewpoint. The multimodel also allows the definition of relationships among model elements in those viewpoints, which captures the missing information that the separation of concerns could lead to. The multimodel can be used for the specification of single systems, families of systems and in this work is used for the representation of an SPL. The multimodel plays two different roles in SPL development: i) in the *domain engineering phase,* in which the core asset base is created, the multimodel explicitly represents the different viewpoints of the SPL and the relationships among these views; ii) in the *application engineering phase,* in which the final product is derived, the relationships drive the different model transformation processes that constitute the production plan used to produce the final product. The concepts introduced in this section are illustrated through the use of a running example: a software product line from the automotive domain which comprises the safety-critical embedded software systems responsible for controlling a car.

The multimodel used to specify SPLs is composed of (at least) four interrelated viewpoints: *functional, variability, quality,* and *transformation*:

- The **variability viewpoint** expresses the commonalities and variability within the product line. Its main element is the feature, which is a user-visible aspect or characteristic of a system [9]. The variability view of the multimodel has been defined using a variant [11] of the cardinality-based feature model [16], defined specifically for application in a model-driven product line development context (see Fig. 1 top left).

- The **functional viewpoint** expresses the structure of a family of systems represented by the SPL architecture and the core assets (e.g., software components) that satisfy the requirements of the different features (see Fig. 1 top right). The functional view has been defined using the Architectural Analysis and Design Language (AADL) [15]. AADL defines a textual and graphical representation of the runtime architecture of software systems as a component-based model in terms of tasks, their interactions and the hardware platform on which the systems are executed.

- The **quality viewpoint** expresses the decomposition of quality characteristics for SPL into sub-characteristics, quality attributes, and metrics as well as the impacts and constraints among quality attributes. It is represented by a quality model for software product lines [18]. This model extends the ISO/IEC 25010 (SQuaRE) standard [21], thus providing the quality assurance and evaluation activities in SPL development (see Fig. 1 bottom left). The multimodel also allows the specification of product line NFRs as constraints defined over the quality model, affecting characteristics, sub-characteristics and quality attributes [17]. The definition of NFRs as constraints in the quality model provides a mechanism for the automatic validation of their fulfillment once the software artifacts have been obtained.

- The **transformation viewpoint** contains the explicit representation of the design decisions realized by the different model transformation processes that integrate the production plan for a model-driven SPL (see Fig. 1 bottom right). Alternatives appear in a model transformation process when a set of constructs in the source model admits different representations in the target model. The application of each alternative transformation could generate alternative target models that may have the same functionality but might differ in their quality attributes. In this work, we focus on architectural patterns [14], [25]. Architectural patterns specify solutions to recurrent problems that occur in specific contexts [7]. They also specify how the system will deal with one aspect of its functionality, impacting directly on the product quality attributes. Architectural patterns can be represented as architectural transformations, as a means to ensure the quality attributes attained by the product architectures.

In addition to the viewpoints, the multimodel also allows the definition of relationships among elements on each viewpoint with different semantics such as composition, impact or constraint relationships [17]. The composition relationship allows a model element A in a viewpoint to be decomposed into elements B, C... in other viewpoints. The impact relationship allows a model element A in a viewpoint impact on an element B in other viewpoint (e.g., an entity in a viewpoint impacts positively or negatively on a quality attribute from the quality viewpoint). These impact relationships may require additional attributes in which to store their quantification. Finally, constraint relationships allow more complex relationships at multimodel level to be expressed using an OCL-like syntax.

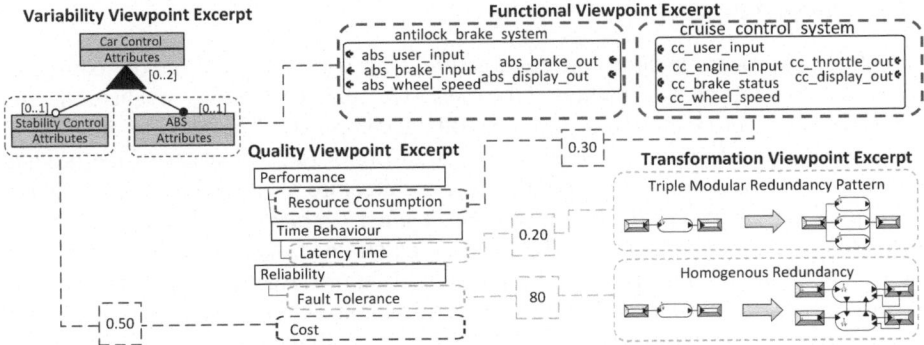

Fig. 1. SPL multimodel overview

In particular, the following types of relationships among elements in the different viewpoints can be defined in the multimodel:

- **Composition relationship:** A composition relationship can be defined between elements in the functional and variability viewpoints. A set of elements in the functional viewpoint can be combined in order to fulfill the requirements of one or more features (in Fig. 1 the *ABS* feature in a car is fulfilled by the *antilock_braking_system* component).

- **Impact relationship:** A composition relationship can be defined between elements in the transformation and quality viewpoints. The selection of a particular transformation in the transformation viewpoint may affect one or more NFRs defined over the quality model (in Fig. 1 the application of the *Homogenous Redundancy pattern* impacts positively on the product fault tolerance). A domain expert therefore establishes the relationship among alternative transformation and quality attributes by determining how a given transformation supports a given quality attribute, based on empirical evidence or on his/her experience. This tradeoff analysis is performed by applying the Analytic Hierarchy Process (AHP) [32]. AHP is a decision-making technique used to resolve conflicts in which it is necessary to address multi-criteria comparisons. The result of the AHP is a weight that shows the relative support of an alternative with regard to a given quality attribute, and it is stored in the quantification attributes of the impact relationship (e.g., in Fig. 1, the *triple modular redundancy pattern* supports *latency time* with a relative weight of 0.20).

On the one hand, the relationships among the functional, variability, and quality viewpoints can be used to drive the product configuration, the core asset selection and the product architecture derivation processes. On the other hand, the relationships defined between the transformation and quality viewpoints allow the use of the quality attributes as a decision factor when choosing from alternative pattern-based architectural transformations.

3.2   QuaDAI Process

The QuaDAI process includes different activities in which the multimodel is used to drive the model transformation processes for the derivation, evaluation and improvement of product architectures in SPL development. The activity diagram of the process supporting the approach is shown in Fig. 2 (a). It consists of the product architecture derivation from the product line architecture in the *Product Architecture Derivation* activity, its evaluation using the *Product Architecture Evaluation* activity and, in those cases in which the NFRs cannot be attained, its transformation through the application of pattern-based architectural transformations in the *Product Architecture Transformation* activity. Once this latter activity has been carried out, the resulting architecture must be evaluated again using the *Product Architecture Evaluation Activity.*

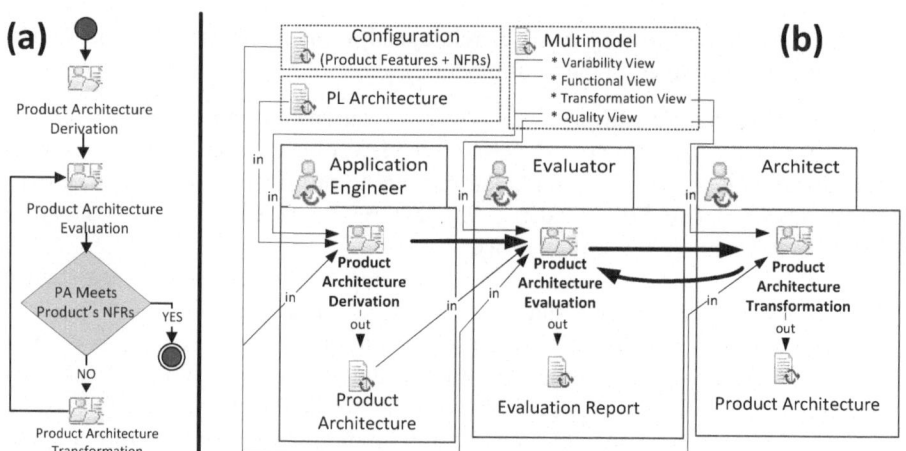

Fig. 2. Overview of the QuaDAI process

Product Architecture Derivation. The product architecture is derived from the product line architecture in the *Product Architecture Derivation* activity, taking as input the product line architecture, the variability and functional viewpoints of the multimodel, and the product configuration, containing both the product specific features and the product-specific NFRs selected by the application engineer (see Fig. 2(b)). In this activity, the decision as to which functional components should be deployed in the product architecture is made by considering the following: i) the composition relationships between features and functional components; ii) the impact relationships between functional components and NFRs; and iii) the impact relationships between features and NFRs. The output of this activity is a first version of the product architecture which must be evaluated in order to analyze the attainment of non-functional requirements.

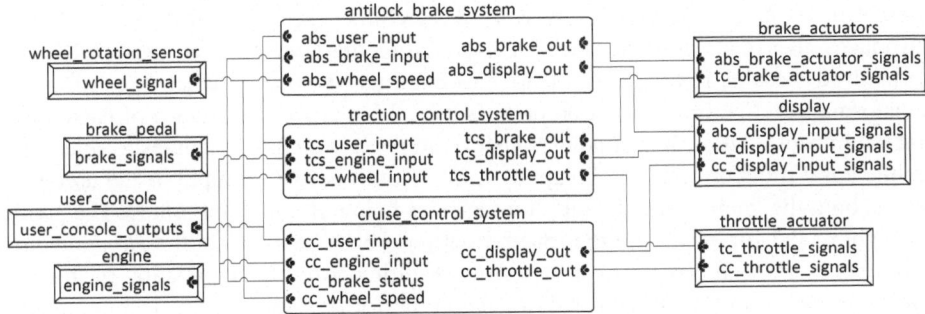

Fig. 3. Excerpt of the Product Line Architecture

Fig. 4 shows the product architecture generated by the product architecture derived from the product line architecture (shown in Fig. 3) for the automotive example when the application engineer selects only the ABS feature and introduces the product specific NFRs, which come from the system's requirements, demanding a fault tolerance of the ABS greater than 99.5% and restricting the ABS latency time to 5ms.

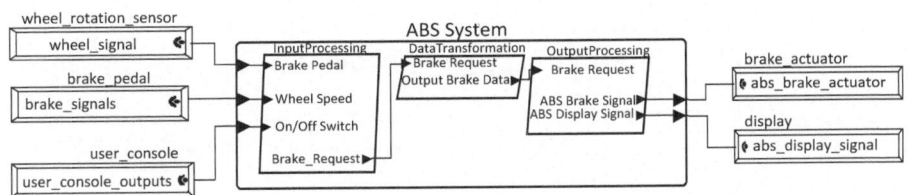

Fig. 4. Portion of the Product Architecture showing the ABS system

Product Architecture Evaluation. In the second model transformation process, the *Product Architecture Evaluation* applies the software measures contained in the quality viewpoint of the multimodel to a product architecture in order to evaluate whether or not it satisfies the desired NFRs. This transformation takes as input the product architecture derived, the product specific NFRs and the quality viewpoint of the multimodel (quality model) containing the metrics to be applied in order to measure the NFRs, generating as output an evaluation report (see Fig. 2(b)). The evaluation for the example architecture shown in Fig. 4 may conclude that the architecture meets the latency NFR but that the fault tolerance NFR is not achieved, and architectural transformations may thus be required.

Product Architecture Transformation. Finally, in those cases in which the non-functional requirements cannot be achieved by exercising the architectural variability mechanisms, in the third activity, the *Product Architecture Transformation* applies pattern-based architectural transformations to the product architecture. The inputs for this activity are the product architecture, the relative importance of the different NFRs and the transformation viewpoint of the multimodel, containing the representation of the transformations to be applied. It generates a product architecture as output in an attempt to cover the NFRs prioritized by the architect (see Fig. 2(b)). The architect introduces the relative importance of each NFR that the product must fulfill as normalized weights ranging from 0 to 1 as external parameters when executing the transformation. The transformation process uses the relative importance of each NFR and the impact relationships among transformations and quality attributes to select the architectural transformation to be applied. In the automotive example, if the architect selects both the latency and the fault tolerance as being of equal importance (i.e., with a weight of 0.5 for each one) the transformation process will select the *Homogenous Redundancy Pattern (HR)*. The architecture resulting from the application of the HR pattern is shown in Fig. 5. This activity can be performed until all the desired quality attributes for the product are fulfilled.

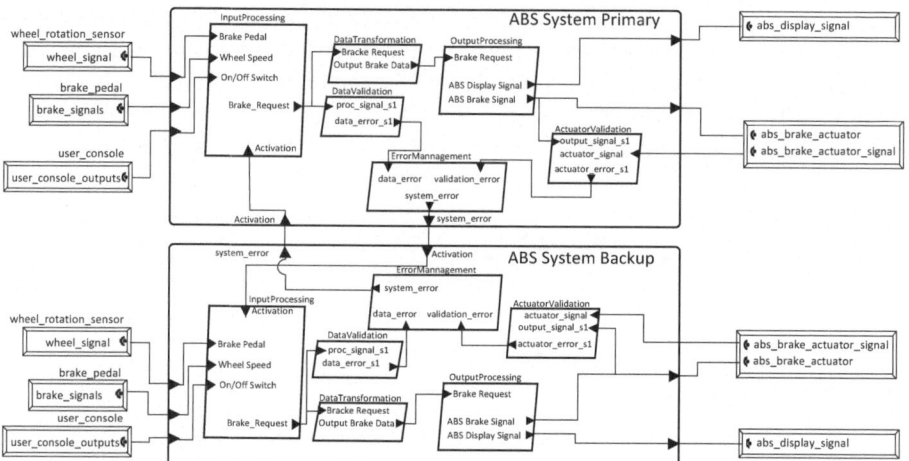

Fig. 5. Product architecture after applying the HR pattern

4   Validation

A controlled experiment was conducted to empirically validate QuaDAI comparing the efficiency, effectiveness and perceived satisfaction of participants using this method against ATAM, a well-known and widely-used software architecture evaluation method [26]. We focus on two activities from the QuaDAI process that occur after deriving the product architecture: *Product Architecture Evaluation* and *Product Transformation*. These activities deal with the evaluation and improvement of product architectures, which are aligned with the main purpose of ATAM.

4.1   Experiment Planning

The controlled experiment was designed by considering the guidelines proposed by Wohlin et al. [34]. According to the Goal-Question Metric (GQM) paradigm [3], the goal of the experiment is to **analyze** the Quality-Driven Architectural Improvement method (QuaDAI) and ATAM **for the purpose** of comparing them **with respect to** their effectiveness, efficiency, ease of use, usefulness and intention of use in order to obtain software architectures that meet a given set of quality requirements **from the viewpoint** of novice software architecture evaluators.

The context of the experiment is the quality evaluation of two software architectures carried out by novice evaluators. This context is determined by the software architectures to be evaluated, the architecture evaluation methods to be applied and the subject selection.

The *software architectures* to be evaluated are the software architecture of an Antilock Braking System *(ABS System)* from an automotive control system and the software architecture of the *Savi* application (http://goo.gl/1Q49O), a mobile application for emergency notifications. The architecture of the *ABS System,* represented through its component and connector view, was selected as experimental object O1, and the *Savi* architecture, represented through the deployment view, was selected as experimental object O2. We also selected a set of four architectural patterns that can be applied to improve the quality attribute levels of interest in each of the product architectures. The experimental tasks include the evaluation of these quality attributes by means of two software metrics in each experimental object before and after applying the architecture evaluation methods. Thirty-one subjects were selected from a group of fifth-year Computer Science students at the Universitat Politècnica de València who were enrolled on an Advanced Software Engineering course from September 2012 to January 2013, where they acquire knowledge and skills on software architecture evaluation. In particular, they received a training of eight hours on this topic before the experiment took place. The evaluation methods being compared are, on the one hand our proposal described in Section 3 (QuADAI) and on the other, the Architecture Trade-Off Analysis Method (ATAM). ATAM is used to assess the consequences of architectural design decisions in the light of quality attributes [22]. The main goals of ATAM are to elicit and refine the architecture's quality goals; to elicit and refine the architectural design decisions and to evaluate the architectural design decisions in order to determine whether they address the quality attribute requirements satisfactorily. ATAM has been selected for comparison with QuaDAI since i) it is a widely used software architecture evaluation method ii) it is able to deal with multi-attribute analysis [1] and iii) it can be used to evaluate both product line and product architectures at various stages of SPL development (conceptual, before code, during development, or after deployment) [9].

The **independent variable** of interest in the study is the use of each method (ATAM or QuaDAI). There are two **objective dependent variables:** *effectiveness* of the method, which is calculated as a function of the *Euclidean Distances* between the NFR values attained by the architecture being evaluated by the subject and the optimal NFR values that can be attained; and *efficiency*, which is calculated as the ratio between the effectiveness and the total time spent on applying the evaluation method. There are also three **subjective dependent variables:** *perceived ease of use,* which refers to the degree to which evaluators believe that learning and using a particular method will be effort-free, *perceived usefulness,* which refers to the degree to which evaluators believe that using a specific method will increase their job performance within an organizational context and *intention to use,* the extent to which a evaluator intends to use a particular method. This last variable represents a perceptual judgment of the method's efficacy – that is, whether it is cost-effective and is commonly used to predict the likelihood of acceptance of a method in practice. These three subjective variables were measured by using a *Likert* scale questionnaire with a set of specific closed questions related to each variable. The aggregated value of each subjective variable was calculated as the mean of the answers to the variable-related questions.

Effectiveness is calculated by applying the formula (1) to normalized *euclidean distances*. The normalization is calculated by applying the formula (2) to the *euclidean distances* calculated by applying the formula (3) and returns a value ranging from 0 to 1. The normalization is required for avoiding the effects of the scales of the metrics that measure each NFR. The *optimal* function in formulas (1) and (2) returns the optimal values of the NFRs that can be achieved for a given experimental object. The *Max* function returns the maximal distance D observed for a given experimental object.

$$Effectiveness(p) = 1 - Norm\big(D(p, optimal(Object))\big) \tag{1}$$

$$Norm\big(D(p, Optimal(Object))\big) = \frac{D(p, Optimal(Object))}{Max(Object)} \tag{2}$$

$$D(p, q) = \sqrt{\sum_{i=1}^{n} (p_i - q_i)^2} \tag{3}$$

The **hypotheses** of this experiment are:

- **H1$_0$:** There is no significant difference between the effectiveness of QuaDAI and ATAM / **H1$_a$:** QuaDAI is significantly more effective than ATAM.
- **H2$_0$:** There is no significant difference between the efficiency of QuaDAI and ATAM / **H2$_a$:** QuaDAI is significantly more efficient than ATAM.
- **H3$_0$:** There is no significant difference between the perceived ease of use of evaluators applying QuaDAI and ATAM / **H3$_a$:** QuaDAI is perceived as easier to use than ATAM.
- **H4$_0$:** There is no significant difference between the perceived usefulness of QuaDAI and ATAM / **H4$_a$:** QuaDAI is perceived as more useful than ATAM.
- **H5$_0$:** There is no significant difference between the intention to use of QuaDAI and ATAM / **H5$_a$:** QuaDAI is perceived as more likely to be used than ATAM.

4.2   Experiment Operation and Execution

The experiment was planned as a balanced within-subject design with a confounding effect, signifying that the same subjects executed both methods with both experimental objects in different order. We established four groups (each group applying one method with one object) and the subjects were randomly assigned to each group. Table 1 shows the schedule of the experiment in more detail.

Several documents were designed as instrumentation for the experiment: slides for training session, an explanation of the methods, forms for gathering data, the patterns description, the metrics documentation, and two questionnaires. Excel spread sheets were also designed in order to automate the metrics calculation and the QuaDAI's trade-off among architectural transformations. The instrumentation of this experiment is available at http://www.dsic.upv.es/~jagonzalez/MODELS2013/instrumentation.

A pilot experiment was conducted beforehand to assess the experimental material and to estimate the time required to accomplish the tasks. This took place with four Computer Science PhD students from the Universitat Politecnica de Valencia. The students completed the experimental tasks in less than an hour. This pilot experiment also allowed us to collect information on how to improve the instrumentation.

The experiment was planned to be conducted in three sessions, Table 1 shows the details for each day. On the first day, the subjects were given the complete training on the methods to be applied and also on the tasks to be performed in the execution of the experiment. On the second and third days the subjects were given an overview of the complete training before applying one evaluation method on an experimental object (O1 or O2). We established a slot of 60 minutes without a time limit for each of the methods to be applied.

The experiment took place in a single room, and no interaction between subjects was allowed. The questions that arose during the session were clarified by the same conductors during the experiment.

With regard to the data validation, we verified that one of the subjects had not completed the 2nd session and that it was therefore necessary to eliminate his first exercise. Since we had 30 subjects distributed in four groups, it was necessary to discard two subjects (which were selected randomly) in order to maintain the balanced design, consisting of a total of 28 subjects, seven in each group.

Table 1. Schedule of the controlled experiment

1st session (120 min)	Training on Software Architecture Evaluation using ATAM and QuaDAI			
2nd session	Software Architecture Evaluation using ATAM and QuaDAI (short training)			
(60 + 60 minutes)	QuaDAI in O1	QuaDAI in O2	ATAM in O1	ATAM in O2
	QuaDAI Questionnaire		ATAM Questionnaire	
2nd session	Software Architecture Evaluation using ATAM and QuaDAI (short training)			
(60 + 60 minutes)	ATAM in O2	ATAM in O1	QuaDAI in O2	QuaDAI in O1
	ATAM Questionnaire		QuaDAI Questionnaire	

4.3   Data Analysis

The quantitative analysis was performed by using the SPSS v16 statistical tool using an $\alpha=0.05$. A summary of the results of the evaluation is shown in Table 2. Mean and standard deviations have also been used as descriptive statistics for the qualitative subjective variables *Perceived Ease of Use (PEOU), Perceived Usefulness (PU)* and *Intention to Use (ITU)*. The five-point *Likert* scale ranging from 1 to 5 adopted for the measurement of the subjective variables has also been considered as an interval scale [9]. The cells highlighted in bold type in Table 2 show the best values for each of the statistics. These results can be used to interpret that the subjects' best performance was with QuaDAI in almost all the variables.

Table 2. Descriptive results

	Effectiveness		Efficiency		Duration (min)	
	Mean	Std. Dev.	Mean	Std. Dev.	Mean	Std. Dev.
QuaDAI	**0.68**	0.39	**0.029**	0.018	**25.36**	7.26
ATAM	0.63	0.36	0.020	0.013	31.11	9.15

	Perceived Ease of Use (PEOU)		Perceived Usefulness (PU)		Intention to Use (ITU)	
	Mean	Std. Dev.	Mean	Std. Dev.	Mean	Std. Dev.
QuaDAI	**3.98**	0.88	**3.80**	0.83	**3.65**	0.84
ATAM	3.50	0.82	3.72	0.73	3.55	0.70

The sample size (<50) indicated that it was necessary to apply the Shapiro-Wilk test to check whether the data was normally distributed so as to select which tests were needed to test the five hypotheses. Table 3 shows the results of the normality test. The variables that are normally distributed for a given architecture evaluation method are shown in bold type.

Table 3. Shapiro-Wilk normality test results

	Effect.	Effic.	PEOU	PU	ITU
QuaDAI	0.000	**0.362**	0.014	0.027	0.024
ATAM	0.000	**0.379**	0.027	0.04	**0.894**

The boxplots in Fig. 6 containing the distribution of each dependent variable per subject per method show that QuaDAI was more effective and efficient, and also that it was perceived as being easier to use, more useful and more likely to be used by the subjects than ATAM.

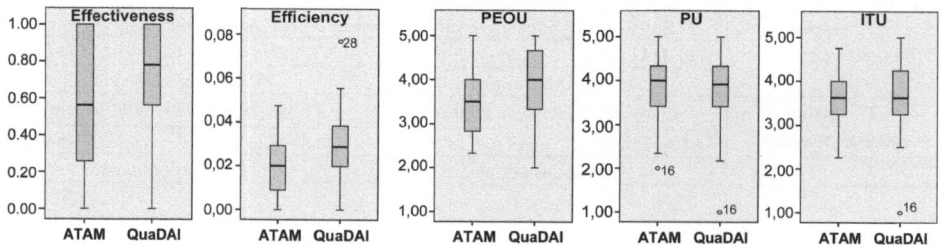

Fig. 6. Boxplots for the various dependent variables

In order to check the statistical significance of these tests we performed the Mann-Withney non-parametric test so as to verify H1, H3, H4, since they are not normally distributed, and H5 and the 1-tailed t-test for independent samples to verify H2. The Mann-Whitney test results were 0.906 for *Effectiveness*, 0.030 for *PEOU*, 0.941 for *PU* and 0.767 for *ITU*. The p-value obtained from the 1-tailed t-test for *Efficiency* was

0.015. These results led us to conclude that the difference in terms of *Efficiency* and *PEOU* is statistically significant, thus allowing us to reject the null hypotheses $H1_0$ and $H3_0$ and accept their respective alternative hypotheses. However, with regard to the *Effectiveness*, *PU* and *ITU*, although the subjects achieved their best results with QuaDAI, we found that the differences were not statistically significant (> 0.05).

4.4   Threats to the Validity

The main threats to the **internal validity** are: learning effect, subjects' experience, information exchange among participants, author's bias, author influence, the order of methods in the training and understandability of the documents. Two experimental objects were used to deal with the learning effect, such as ensuring that each subject applied each method in a different system and considering all the possible combinations of both the method order and the experimental objects. There were no differences on the subjects' experience since none of them had experience in architecture evaluations. The subjects were introduced to the tasks and the problems they would have to solve via their participation in training sessions on both methods. Information exchange was alleviated by using different experimental objects at the same time, and monitoring the subjects while they performed the tasks. Since the experiment was designed to take place in two sessions, the subjects might have been able to exchange information during the time between the sessions, but this was alleviated by asking the participants to return the material at the end of each session. The author's bias in this experiment may have influenced the results since the training sessions were conducted by an author of the method. The author influence was alleviated by not disclosing to the subjects the authorship of the QuaDAI method. The order of methods during the training and experimental sessions could have also influenced the results since it was the same in each session. This issue will be investigated in future replications of this experiment. The understandability of the material was alleviated by clearing up all the misunderstandings that appeared in the pilot experiment and experimental sessions.

The main threat to **external validity** is the representativeness of the results. The representativeness of the results might be affected by the evaluation design and the participant context selected. The evaluation design might have had an impact on the results owing to the kind of architectural models and quality attributes to be evaluated. We selected two different architectures, from two different domains, two different NFRs and four different patterns for each experimental object. The experiment was conducted with students with no experience in architectural evaluations, and who received only limited training on the evaluation methods. However, since they were final year students they can be considered as novice users of architectural evaluation methods, and the next generation of practitioners [24]. The results could thus be considered as representative of novice evaluators.

The main threats to the **construct validity** are the measures used to quantify the dependent variables. Effectiveness was measured using the Euclidean distance which has commonly been used to measure the goodness of a solution with regard to a set of opposed NFRs with different purposes [12] [33]. The subjective variables are based on the Technology Acceptance Method (TAM) [13], a well-known and empirically validated model for the evaluation of information technologies. The reliability of the questionnaire was tested by applying the Cronbach test. Questions related to PEOU, PU and ITU obtained a Cronbach's alpha of 0.824, 0.870 and 0.831, which is higher than the acceptable minimum (0.70) [27]. The main threat to the **conclusion validity** is the validity of the statistical tests applied. This threat was alleviated by applying a set of commonly accepted tests employed in the empirical SE community [27]. However, more replications are needed in order to confirm these results.

5   Conclusions and Future Work

In this paper, we have presented QuaDAI, a method for the derivation, evaluation and improvement of product architectures. This method relies on a multimodel that represents the different viewpoints of the SPL (functional, quality, variability, and transformation), allowing the representation of the product line architecture, the metrics for its evaluation, and the relationships among architectural transformations and NFRs. The approach has three major benefits: i) it is aimed to automate the derivation and improvement of product architectures; ii) it provides a systematic mechanism for dealing with the cases in which the NFRs of the product under development are not within the range of values permitted by the architectural variability; iii) and finally, it takes advantage of the reuse of the architectural knowledge stored in the multimodel for helping designers to decide which architectural patterns should be applied each time a product architecture needs to be improved. We believe that QuaDAI is useful to guide novice architects in performing evaluations as the multimodel explicitly represents the domain expert's knowledge.

We have also validated our method by means of a controlled experiment in which QuaDAI were compared with a widely-used architecture evaluation method (ATAM). The results show that QuaDAI is more efficient and is perceived to be easier to use than ATAM. However, with regard to the effectiveness, PU and ITU, although QuaDAI achieved better results, we found that the differences were not statistically significant. This may be because the lack of experience of the subjects in architecture evaluation. This issue will be examined in future replications of this study.

As future work, we plan to characterize those cases in which the variability mechanisms are not sufficient to achieve the NFRs for a given product. We also plan to study other mechanisms for introducing the relative importance (weights) for the NFRs. Currently, we are using only numbers but we are aware that they may not capture the full range of real-world impact relationships. We will explore the definition of functions that could express conditions on such numbers. In addition, we are aware that not only architectural patterns can be applied to improve a quality attribute. Our approach may also allow managing other complementary architectural transformations that may be needed.

We also plan to conduct replications of this experiment by considering a larger number of subjects with different subject profiles (e.g., practitioners or students with a higher level of knowledge and skills on architecture evaluation) and different experimental objects in order to improve the representativeness of our results.

Acknowledgements. This research is supported by the MULTIPLE project (MICINN TIN2009-13838) and the ValI+D fellowship program (ACIF/2011/235).

References

1. Ali-Babar, M., Lago, P., Van Deursen, A.: Empirical research in software architecture: opportunities, challenges, and approaches. Empirical Software Engineering 16(5), 539–543 (2011)
2. Ali-Babar, M., Zhu, L., Jeffery, R.: A Framework for Classifying and Comparing Software Architecture Evaluation Methods. In: 15th Australian Software Engineering Conference, Melbourne, Australia, pp. 309–318 (2004)
3. Basili, V.R., Rombach, H.D.: The TAME project: towards improvement-oriented software environments. IEEE Transactions on Software Engineering 14(6), 758–773 (1988)
4. Barkmeyer, E.J., Feeney, A.B., Denno, P., Flater, D.W., Libes, D.E., Steves, M.P., Wallace, E.K.: Concepts for Automating Systems Integration NISTIR 6928. National Institute of Standards and Technology, U.S. Dept. of Commerce (2003)
5. Bosch, J.: Design and Use of Software Architectures. Adopting and Evolving Product-Line Approach. Addison-Wesley, Harlow (2000)
6. Botterweck, G., O'Brien, L., Thiel, S.: Model-driven derivation of product architectures. In: 22th Int. Conf. on Automated Software Engineering, New York, USA, pp. 469–472 (2007)
7. Buschmann, F., Meunier, R., Rohnert, H., Sommerlad, P., Stal, M.: Pattern-Oriented software architecture, vol. 1: A System of Patterns. Wiley (1996)
8. Cabello, M.E., Ramos, I., Gómez, A., Limón, R.: Baseline-Oriented Modeling: An MDA Approach Based on Software Product Lines for the Expert Systems Development. In: 1st Asia Conference on Intelligent Information and Database Systems, Vietnam (2009)
9. Carifio, J., Perla, R.J.: Ten Common Misunderstandings, Misconceptions, Persistent Myths and Urban Legends about Likert Scales and Likert Response Formats and their Antidotes. Journal of Social Sciences 3(3), 106–116 (2007)
10. Clements, P., Northrop, L.: Software Product Lines: Practices and Patterns. Addison-Wesley, Boston (2007)
11. Czarnecki, K., Kim, C.H.: Cardinality-based feature modeling and constraints: A progress report. In: Int. Workshop on Software Factories, San Diego-CA (2005)
12. Datorro, J.: Convex Optimization & Euclidean Distance Geometry. Meboo Publishing (2005)
13. Davis, F.D.: Perceived usefulness, perceived ease of use and user acceptance of information technology. MIS Quarterly 13(3), 319–340 (1989)
14. Douglass, B.P.: Real-Time Design Patterns: Robust Scalable Architecture for Real-Time Systems. Addison-Wesley, Boston (2002)
15. Feiler, P.H., Gluch, D.P., Hudak, J.: The Architecture Analysis & Design Language (AADL): An Introduction. Tech. Report CMU/SEI-2006-TN-011. SEI, Carnegie Mellon University (2006)
16. Gómez, A., Ramos, I.: Cardinality-based feature modeling and model-driven engineering: Fitting them together. In: 4th Int. Workshop on Variability Modeling of Software Intensive Systems, Linz, Austria (2010)
17. Gonzalez-Huerta, J., Insfran, E., Abrahao, S.: A Multimodel for Integrating Quality Assessment in Model-Driven Engineering. In: 8th International Conference on the Quality of Information and Communications Technology (QUATIC 2012), Lisbon, Portugal, September 3-6 (2012)
18. Gonzalez-Huerta, J., Insfran, E., Abrahao, S., McGregor, J.D.: Non-functional Requirements in Model-Driven Software Product Line Engineering. In: 4th Int. Workshop on Non-functional System Properties in Domain Specific Modeling Languages, Insbruck, Austria (2012)

19. Guana, V., Correal, V.: Variability quality evaluation on component-based software product lines. In: 15th Int. Software Product Line Conference, Munich, Germany, vol. 2, pp. 19.1–19.8 (2011)
20. Insfrán, E., Abrahão, S., González-Huerta, J., McGregor, J.D., Ramos, I.: A Multimodeling Approach for Quality-Driven Architecture Derivation. In: 21st Int. Conf. on Information Systems Development (ISD 2012), Prato, Italy (2012)
21. ISO/IEC 25000:2005, Software Engineering. Software product Quality Requirements and Evaluation SQuaRE (2005)
22. Kazman, R., Klein, M., Clements, P.: ATAM: Method for Architecture Evaluation (CMU/SEI-2000-TR-004, ADA382629). Software Engineering Institute, Carnegie Mellon University, Pittsburgh (2000), http://www.sei.cmu.edu/publications/documents/00.reports/00tr004.html
23. Kim, T., Ko, I., Kang, S., Lee, D.: Extending ATAM to assess product line architecture. In: 8th IEEE Int. Conference on Computer and Information Technology, Sydney, Australia, pp. 790–797 (2008)
24. Kitchenham, B.A., Pfleeger, S.L., Hoaglin, D.C., Rosenber, J.: Preliminary Guidelines for Empirical Research in Software Engineering. IEEE Transactions on Software Engineering 28(8) (2002)
25. Kruchten, P.B.: The Rational Unified Process: An Introduction. Addison-Wesley (1999)
26. Martensson, F.: Software Architecture Quality Evaluation. Approaches in an Industrial Context. Ph. D. thesis, Blekinge Institute of Technology, Karlskrona, Sweden (2006)
27. Maxwell, K.: Applied Statistics for Software Managers. Software Quality Institute Series. Prentice-Hall (2002)
28. Olumofin, F.G., Mišic, V.B.: A holistic architecture assessment method for software product lines. Information and Software Technology 49, 309–323 (2007)
29. Perovich, D., Rossel, P.O., Bastarrica, M.C.: Feature model to product architectures: Applying MDE to Software Product Lines. In: IEEE/IFIP & European Conference on Software Architecture, Helsinki, Findland, pp. 201–210 (2009)
30. Robertson, S., Robertson, J.: Mastering the requirements process. ACM Press, New York (1999)
31. Roos-Frantz, F., Benavides, D., Ruiz-Cortés, A., Heuer, A., Lauenroth, K.: Quality-aware analysis in product line engineering with the orthogonal variability model. Software Quality Journal (2011), doi:10.1007/s11219-011-9156-5
32. Saaty, T.L.: The Analytical Hierarchical Process. McGraw- Hill, New York (1990)
33. Taher, L., Khatib, H.E., Basha, R.: A framework and QoS matchmaking algorithm for dynamic web services selection. In: 2nd Int. Conference on Innovations in Information Technology, Dubai, UAE (2005)
34. Wohlin, C., Runeson, P., Host, M., Ohlsson, M.C., Regnell, B., Weslen, A.: Experimentation in Software Engineering - An Introduction. Kluwer (2000)

Evolution of the UML Interactions Metamodel

Marc-Florian Wendland[1], Martin Schneider[1], and Øystein Haugen[2]

[1] Fraunhofer Institut FOKUS
Kaiserin-Augusta-Allee 31, 10589 Berlin, Germany
[2] SINTEF, Norway
{marc-florian.wendland,martin.schneider}@fokus.fraunhofer.de,
Oystein.haugen@sintef.no

Abstract. UML Interactions represent one of the three different behavior kinds of the UML. In general, they specify the exchange of messages among parts of a system. Although UML Interactions can reside on different level of abstractions, they seem to be sufficiently elaborated for a higher-level of abstraction where they are used for sketching the communication among parts. Its metamodel reveals some fuzziness and imprecision where definitions should be accurate and concise, though.

In this paper, we propose improvements to the UML Interactions' metamodel for Message arguments and Loop CombinedFragments that make them more versatile. We will justify the needs for the improvements by precisely showing the shortcomings of the related parts of the metamodel. We demonstrate the expressiveness of the improvements by applying them to examples that current Interactions definition handles awkwardly.

Keywords: UML, Interactions, Sequence Diagram, Messages, CombinedFragments.

1 Introduction

UML Interactions are one of the three behavior kinds of UML 2 [1] and describe information exchange among parts of a system via messages. Graphically, UML Interactions are most commonly depicted as sequence diagrams.

UML 1 Interactions originated from a proprietary dialect of sequence charts which came from Siemens. When UML 2 was initiated in 1999 some of the driving forces from the telecom industry had already applied sequence diagrams for many years and were well acquainted with Message Sequence Charts (MSC) [2]. Ericsson, Motorola and Alcatel, supplemented also by tool vendor Telelogic, collaborated to formalize UML in the direction of MSC and SDL (Specification and Description Language, recommended in Z.100 by ITU). This resulted in trying to harmonize the MSC-2000 with UML 2 and still keep most of what had been in UML 1 sequence diagrams as well. While MSC was defined as a stand-alone language, Interactions of UML 2 should be well harmonized and integrated with the rest of UML. However, the telecom companies were not satisfied with informal relations between elements, but

A. Moreira et al. (Eds.): MODELS 2013, LNCS 8107, pp. 405–421, 2013.
© Springer-Verlag Berlin Heidelberg 2013

wanted a UML language that was as precise as what they were used to from SDL and MSC. Other stakeholders of UML were not convinced that UML should be that precise. A lot of compromises were made, though. The concept of *semantic variation points* was introduced and still remains central to the definition of UML. The overall metamodel, however, was supposed to tie the different parts of UML together and in some respects it did that, but in other respects the unification of different concepts was not done with rigor and the language became unnecessary complicated.

Since their advent sequence diagrams were used a lot, however, their use was mostly of descriptive nature. The communication between system parts was sketched rather than precisely defined. When the UML Testing Profile (UTP) ([3] and [4]) appeared, there was emphasis on being able to use sequence diagrams for defining test specifications. Even the data of the messages had to be defined more accurately. In Interactions, exchange of data is expressed as arguments of a message related to a certain element of the message's signature. Due to the compromises made in UML, several issues appear when message arguments need to be precisely specified.

This paper summarizes the most relevant issues for message arguments, explains how they manifest in the metamodel and suggests improvements to the relevant parts of the metamodel to overcome those issues. This paper does not question the general architecture of UML or the rigor of the integration of its parts (such as Activities and Interactions), but rather treat Interactions as a self-sufficient concept space with respect to its features for describing precise message exchange. The motivation for this work stems from the development of an UTP-based tool for model-based testing, called Fokus!MBT [20], and from the application of Interactions for test case specification in industrial and research projects. Thus, the presented work is not a mere theoretical consideration, but has been used for and proven its applicability to real use cases.

As typographical convention, all metaclasses of the UML metamodel are written in camel-case and start with a capital letter. Association ends and properties of metaclasses are written in camel-case, start with a lower case letter and are set to italic. For the sake of comprehensibility, the presented figures do not mention every aspect of the UML abstract syntax (e.g., names of non-navigable association ends are omitted). Introduced concepts are set italic the first time they are mentioned. In case the index of an ordered association ends is relevant for understanding, it is surrounded by square brackets (e.g., [1] indicating the first object). This notation is not standardized for UML object diagrams.

The remainder of this paper is structured as follows: Section 2 summarizes previous work in the area of Interactions. Section 3 presents the relevant parts of the metamodel regarding abstract syntax and semantics. Section 4 represents the main part of our contribution and describes metamodel improvement suggestions for Messages and CombinedFragments. Section 5 proposes two recommendations for the development of metamodels derived from the improvement suggestions presented in section 4. Finally, section 6 summarizes our work and provides an outlook on future considerations of the Interactions metamodel.

2   Related Work

Haugen compares UML Interactions and Message Sequence Charts [5] showing that Interactions and MSCs are similar down to small details.

Haugen, Stolen, Husa, and Runde have written a series of paper on the compositional development of UML Interactions supporting the specification of mandatory and potential behavior, called STAIRS approach ([6], [7], [8], and [9]). Although the compositional idea is reflected throughout the series, a special interest is dedicated to a fine-grained differentiation of event reception, consumption and timing [7] and the refinement of Interactions with regard to underspecification and nondeterminism [9]. Lund and Stolen have presented an operational semantics for UML sequence diagrams in the context of STAIRS [10].

Formal semantics of UML Interactions and sequence diagrams were several times discussed. Störrle presented a formal specification of UML Interactions and a comparison of UML 2.0 and UML 1.4 Interactions [11] and [12]). A similar work was done by Knapp and Cengarle ([13] and [14]), Li and Ruan [15] and Shen et al. [16]. Special attention was set to the semantics of assert and negative CombinedFragments ([17] and [18]), though.

An approach to model checking based upon a formal trace semantics of Interactions was described by Knapp and Wuttke [19].

Our paper is different from the work described above. These publications were mostly dedicated to the trace semantics of Message reception and consumption within UML Interactions, but they did not focus on precisely specifying data transmitted by Messages. Furthermore, the complete metamodel of UML Interactions has not been considered and improved. Our work addresses the precise specification of Message arguments as well as revised parts of the UML Interactions metamodel to make them more robust and manageable by subsequent tooling.

3   Relevant Parts of the UML Interactions Metamodel

This chapter briefly summarizes those parts of the UML Interactions metamodel that are relevant for understanding the focal point of this paper. A full description of the semantics can be found in the current UML specification [1] our work is based on. For the sake of comprehensibility, the necessary parts of the metamodel are shown in Fig. 1. nevertheless. The left-hand side shows the relevant parts of Messages, the right hand side those of CombinedFragments.

Interactions describe the communication between (potentially loosely coupled) parts of a system. The most important building blocks of Interactions are Messages that constitute information exchange between different parts, and Lifelines that represent those communicating parts.

A *Message* represents either the invocation of an Operation or the sending and reception of a Signal. The first kind represents either an *asynchronous* or *synchronous* call, or a *reply* in case of a preceding synchronous call. The second kind (i.e., the sending of a Signal) is by definition always asynchronous. Messages commonly convey data in terms of its *actual arguments* to the receiver. The actual arguments of Message have to correspond to the elements determined by its *signature*. These *signature elements* can manifest as Parameters, in case of an Operation signature, or Properties, in case of a Signal signature. Consistency between actual argument and signature element requires that the actual argument (identified by its index in *Message.argument*) is type compliant with the corresponding signature element (identified by the very same index as the actual arguments, either in *Operation.ownedParameter* or *Signal.ownedAttribute*). The consistency definition implies that both lists must be of equal size.

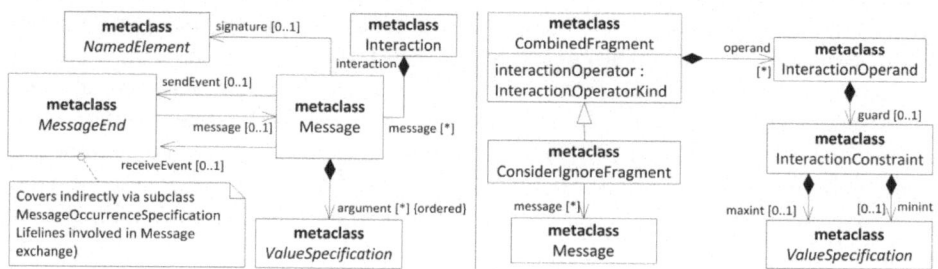

Fig. 1. Relevant parts of the UML Interactions metamodel regarding Messages (left) and CombinedFragments (right)

CombinedFragments were introduced in UML 2 to enable more expressive Interactions. The semantics of a CombinedFragment is determined by its InteractionOperatorKind that also implies the number of InteractionOperands a CombinedFragment may possess. Each InteractionOperand may be guarded by an InteractionConstraint that defines what that must hold to activate the InteractionOperand. Some kinds of CombinedFragments are supplemented with additional information required in their semantic context. These are Loop-kind CombinedFragments (henceforth called Loops) and *ConsiderIgnoreFragments*. Loops represent repetitions of the events enclosed in its InteractionOperand. The number of repetitions can be omitted (any number of repetitions is valid), restricted to a single number of repetitions or specified as an interval for a minimally and maximally intended repetition.

4   Improving Messages and CombinedFragments

The following sections represent the main contribution of our work, i.e., improvement suggestions for the UML Interactions metamodel regarding a precise specification of Message arguments and CombinedFragments. UML is a language of compromises so there are most likely several opinions why the issues[1], being described subsequently,

---

[1] The issues we will discuss and mitigate are already filed in the OMG issue database (see `http://www.omg.org/issues/uml2-rtf.open.html`): #8786, #8899, #16569 and #16571.

actually appear and how they ought to be resolved in the first place. Our improvements are strictly defined from an Interactions point of view. All suggested modifications are local to the Interactions metamodel to make them more robust and as expressive regarding the specification of arguments as Activities, for example. Resolving more fundamental and maybe philosophic or politic issues in the essence of UML is out of scope of this paper, though.

4.1   Precise and Robust Specification of Message Arguments

A Message's actual arguments and the signature elements they need to correspond to are implicitly related via their indices in two distinct lists. This is not problematic as long as the signature elements have just a single, non-optional multiplicity (i.e., lower and upper bounds equals 1) or only the last signature element is optional. In any other case, specifying actual arguments may lead to ambiguities due to UML's inability to model standalone collections of ValueSpecifications and the implicit relation of members of two independent lists based on the respective indices. A discussion whether ValueSpecification collections should be made available in UML is not in the scope of this paper.

For better illustration, we consider an Operation with a single Integer collection Parameter of an unbound size. Fig. 2 illustrates the corresponding object model for a scenario where a user specifies an actual argument list with the values (*1, 2, 3*).

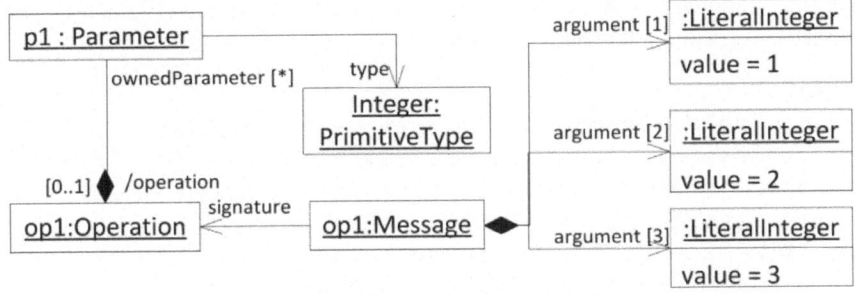

Fig. 2. Object model of ill-formed Message

The Message *op1* contains three actual arguments what would imply that its signature offers three signature elements as well. In fact, it just offers one (see Parameter *p1*), so referring to UML [1] the model presented above is invalid by definition. Activities, for example, can handle collections of actual arguments for a single signature element with the Pin metaclass and we believe Interactions should also provide a *native* concept to be able to handle actual arguments for collections. We emphasize the term *native*, because there are some metamodeling workarounds that misuse metaclasses to ensure syntactical correctness. The issue depicted in Fig. 2 might be solved by misusing the metaclass Expression as pseudo-collection of ValueSpecifications. As long as the metamodel of UML will not be enhanced with dedicated concepts for ValueSpecification collections, Expressions are actually the most elegant (but semantically disputable) way to specify them. Nevertheless, this is kind of a metamodeling trick, since Expressions are intended to specify expression trees in a sense of an Abstract Syntax Tree (AST). As an improvement, we suggest introducing a dedicated concept with clear semantics and syntax for the purpose of precise specification of a Message's actual arguments, called *MessageArgumentSpecification* (see Fig. 3).

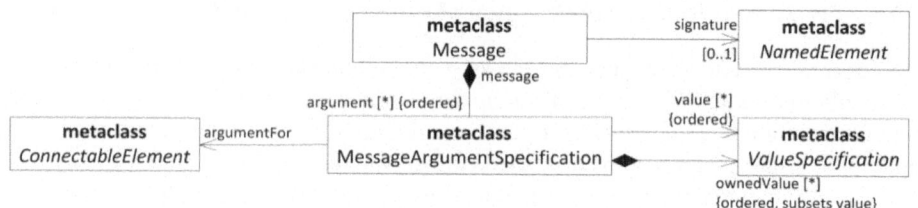

Fig. 3. Explicit relation between a Message's signature element and actual arguments

A MessageArgumentSpecification makes the correspondence of a set of actual arguments to its respective signature element explicit through the association end *argumentFor* that points to the related signature element (ConnectableElement represents the closest common metaclass of both possible signature elements Parameter and Property). The corresponding constraint expressed with the Object Constraint Language (OCL) for restricting what ConnectableElements can be addressed as signature element, is:

```
context MessageArgumentSpecification
inv: not self.message.oclIsUndefined() implies
if self.message.signature.oclIsTypeOf(Operation) then
self.message.signature.oclAsType(Operation).ownedParamete
r->exists(self.argumentFor)
else if self.message.signature.oclIsTypeOf(Signal) then
self.message.signature.oclAsType(Signal).attributes-
>exists(self.argumentFor)
else
false
end if
end if
```

Literally, the ConnectableElement referenced by MessageArgumentSpecification must either be a Parameter of an Operation or a Property owned by Signal. Both Operation and Signal are to be associated with the MessageArgumentSpecification's owning Message (association end *message*) through the association end *signature*. The explicit relation *argumentFor* between an actual argument and signature element eliminates the need for matching by indices of independent lists. Thus, there is no longer the need for collection ValueSpecifications, since the actual arguments for a certain signature element can be easily retrieved by gathering all MessageArgumentSpecifications that point to that signature element via *argumentFor* association end. This does not only simplify the processing of Messages, but also gives rise for more robust models in case of changes to the order of signature elements. As an example, we consider an Operation with two Parameters whose Types are non-compatible. If the user decides to alter the order of the Operation's Parameters, all Messages would have to reflect that change to not become invalid. If there is a large number of Messages that have set the Operation as their signature, and that already have correctly specified actual arguments, reflecting the changes might be a tedious task for the user. With the solution presented above, changing the order did not affect the validity of the Message at all due to the explicit coupling via *argumentFor*. Fig. 4 shows the relevant parts of the improved object model of Fig. 2.

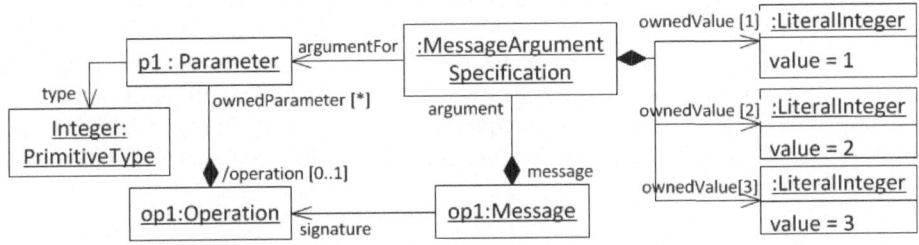

Fig. 4. Object model of well-formed model through improvements

4.2   Using References as Message Arguments

The sole use of ValueSpecifications as actual arguments is sufficient for expressing literal arguments or references to InstanceSpecifications. ValueSpecifications are, however, not capable to reference ConnectableElements (as superclass of Parameter and Property) directly. As a downside, it is not possible to reference values contained in data sources such as formal Parameters of the Interaction (or the corresponding BehavioralFeature the Interactions represents an implementation of) or Properties accessible to the sending Lifeline (such as local attributes of the Type the Lifeline represents, global attributes of the Classifier the Interaction is embedded in or local attributes of the Interaction itself). For the remainder of this paper, we call these values *reference arguments*. To motivate the improvement to the metamodel, the following Java code snippet shows a fundamental concept of using formal parameters of a surrounding Operation as actual parameter for a subsequent procedure call.

```java
public class S { //context classifier of Interaction
  private C c; //offers op3(int i, String s)
  public void op2(int p1){
    c.op3(p1, "That works"); //realized as Interaction
  }
}
```

A realization of this snippet with the concepts offered by Interactions is only possible by either using an OCL navigation expression or again misusing other metaclasses like, e.g., OpaqueExpression (a subclass of ValueSpecification) as reference argument. Even though these workarounds would do the job, they are not satisfying because they impose additional parsing and execution facilities (e.g., in terms of OCL engine or any proprietary engine that evaluates the provided reference argument) being available. In Activities, there is a dedicated means to express data flow among actions (i.e., ObjectFlow and ObjectNode), for example. A native concept of Interactions is lacking, though. In preparation for this paper, we also checked the tools Rational Software Architect (RSA), MagicDraw and Enterprise Architect (EA). Except for the OCL variant, there is no mechanism offered to conveniently allow the user to specify reference arguments. OCL, however, is another language that needs to be learned by a user. Although OCL is highly recommend in the context of UML, for such fundamental concepts like referencing values in an accessible data source, we believe no additional language should be needed.

Unfortunately, the solution we presented in Fig. 3 suffers from the same deficiency as the current metamodel. A MessageArgumentSpecification still refers to ValueSpecifications solely, so consequently, we have to further elaborate our improvement to cope with the needs described above. Fig. 5 depicts our suggestion for such an improvement.

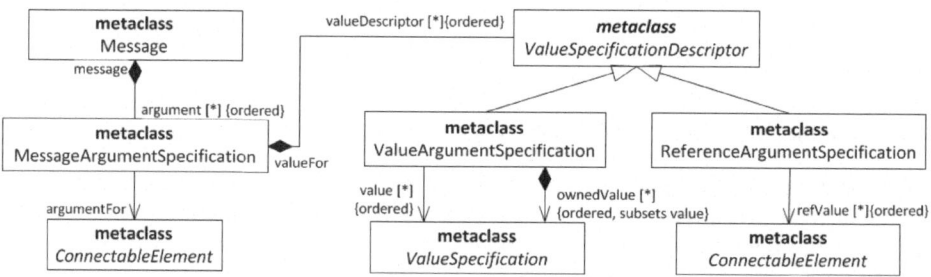

Fig. 5. Extended metamodel to cope with referenced arguments

The improved abstract syntax shown above introduces three new metaclasses. The abstract metaclass *ValueSpecificationDescriptor* replaces ValueSpecification as direct actual argument of a Message. ValueSpecificationDescriptor acts as a placeholder for the actual arguments, and knows two concrete subclasses *ValueArgumentSpecification* and *ReferenceArgumentSpecification*. The first one keeps the ability to use ValueSpecifications as actual arguments. The second one introduces the required facility to access reference arguments.

The extended metamodel now provides the required concepts to select reference arguments accessible from the sending Lifeline as actual arguments. The rules of what is actually accessible by a sending Lifeline are already defined in the current UML specification (see clause 5 of subsection Constraint of section 14.3.18) [1]. Furthermore, both ValueSpecificationDescriptor subclasses can be mixed with each other in a MessageArgumentSpecification. The Java snippet mentioned above stressed the need for mixing value and reference arguments.

A reference argument (*MessageArgument.valueDescriptor.refValue*) and its corresponding signature element (*MessageArgumentSpecification.argumentFor*) are interrelated by the fact that the reference argument needs to be type-compliant with and a subset of the multiplicity of the signature element. A multiplicity subset is defined as follows: Let M be the set of all MessageArgumentSpecifications in an Interaction. Furthermore, let s be a signature element, s_{low} its lower bound and s_{up} its upper bound. Let r be the reference argument corresponding to the signature element s, r_{low} the lower bound and r_{up} the upper bound of the reference argument, and $R_m(r,s)$ the relation of a concrete reference argument and signature element in the context of m (i.e., the concrete arguments are identified by the navigation expressions *m.valueDescriptor.refValue* and *m.argumentFor*). Then the following must hold during runtime:

$$\forall m \in M : R_m(r,s) \rightarrow r_{low} \geq s_{low} \wedge r_{up} \leq s_{up} \tag{1}$$

In Fig. 6, the object model according to the Java code snippet is shown. The grey-shaded objects represent the parts of the specification of the Interaction. The bold-faced object is related to the reference argument concept. The association between MessageArgumentSpecification *ma1* and Parameter *i* as well as the association between ReferenceArgumentSpecification *vd1* and Parameter *p1* (marked by thick arrows) visualize how signature elements and reference elements belong together.

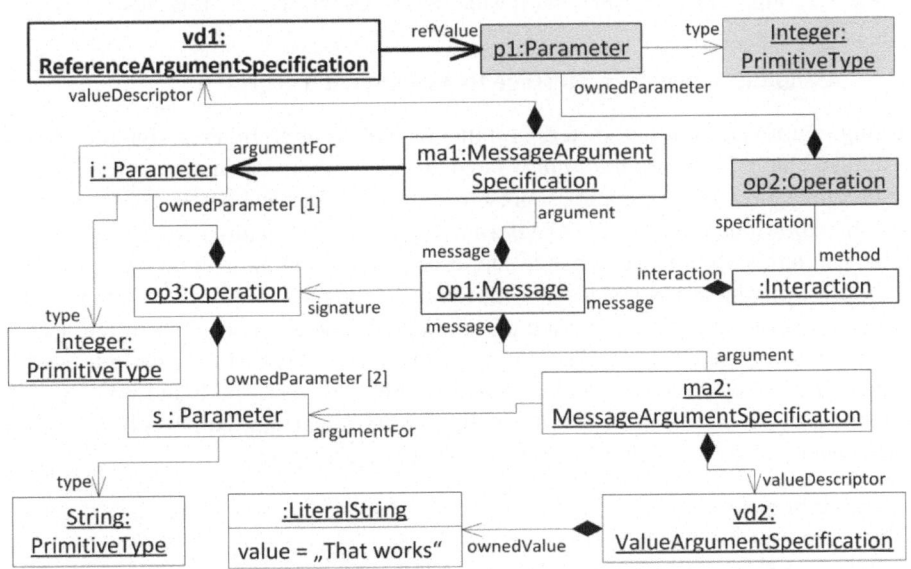

Fig. 6. Corresponding object model of improved Interactions metamodel

Still a problem appears in the solution, if the reference argument is a collection and has wider bounds than the corresponding signature element. There is currently no concept for extracting a subset of values from a reference argument collection. What is required is a facility for specifying such a subset of values that can be used by a reference argument. Therefore, the solution needs to be enhanced with a new metaclass *ReferenceValueSelector*. A ReferenceValueSelector is in charge of specifying that subset, if needed (see Fig. 7).

The subset of values for an actual argument is determined by one or more indices (expressed as Intervals) of the collection identified by ReferenceArgumentSpecification. An Interval allows specifying a minimal and maximal value. Since the association end *index* is unbound, it is possible to specify any number of subsets of elements, identified by their respective indices that shall be extracted from the reference argument collection. The flag *isIndexSetComplement* is a convenient way to specify what indices must not be taken over into the actual argument subset, whereas all indices which are not specified shall be actually considered. Runtime compliance of the index descriptions used in a ReferenceValueSelector cannot be ensured, of course.

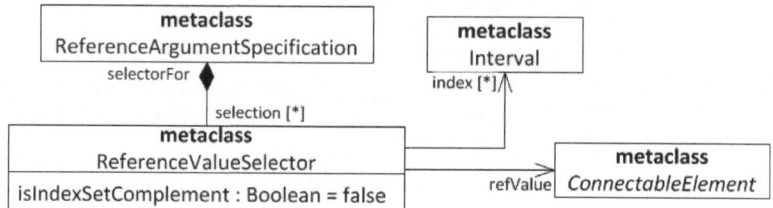

Fig. 7. Metamodel extended with ReferenceValueSelector metaclass

4.3   Assigning Values of a Message to Assignment Targets

Storing return values or parameters of a method call in appropriate assignment targets is rather natural in programming languages. A more complex (probably not meaningful) Java code snippet is presented below. The snippet is solely used for demonstration purposes of the *ArgumentAssignmentSpecification* metaclass we will introduce in this section. The code is supposed to represent parts of an operation body of the class *S*, which was already introduced in Section 4.2. *S* owns two Integer-typed lists (i.e., *piList1* and *piList2*) which are initialized. The actual content of the lists are not relevant for the example. The code simply selects a subset of a list retrieved by calling of c2's operation op4 and adds this subset to piList1 and piList2 of instance s of class S. In this section, we discuss the actual shortcomings of the current UML specification for such constructs and propose a solution.

```
List<Integer> list = c2.op4(); //actual size of list:999
List<Integer> tempList = new
List<Integer>(list.sublist(3,14)); //tempList size: 12
tempList.add(list.get(15)); //tempList size: 13
tempList.add(list.sublist(92,654)); //tempList size: 576
s.piList1.clear():
s.piList1.addAll(tempList);
s.piList2.addAll(tempList);
```

In a model, actual arguments of a Message shall be stored in assignment targets, which manifest in Properties or out-kind Parameters (i.e., Parameter with a ParameterDirectionKind *out, inout* or *reply*) of the surrounding Interaction accessible by the receiving Lifeline. Henceforth, we refer to an assignment target as data sink.

Even though argument assignment is reflected in the textual syntax of Messages in the current UML specification [1], there is no indication how this should be done with respect to the metamodel. The only statement in the notation subsection of Messages (see section 14.3.18) about assignment is that Actions are foreseen to describe the assignment. No further explanations or object model examples are given for clarification of how the connection between such an Action and an actual argument shall be established, nor what concrete Action to ultimately use. Furthermore, an Action needs to be integrated via an *ActionExecutionSpecification* covering the receiving Lifeline, but it is neither clear from the metamodel nor clarified in the textual specification how Message receptions and a set of conceptually related ActionExecutionSpecifications are linked with each other. In preparation for this paper, we investigated EA, RSA and MagicDraw. None of these most popular tools offered functionality for target assignment, though. Only the EA does have at least a notion for marking arguments for assignment, from the study of the resulting XMI, however, it was not clear to the authors how the assignment specification actually manifests.

Another rather conceptual shortcoming is that argument assignment is limited to the return Parameter of a Message solely, so that in-kind signature elements (i.e., either a Parameter with ParameterDirectionKind *in, inout*, or an attribute of a Signal) cannot be stored by a receiving Lifeline in a data sink. This ought to be possible, since in-kind signature elements represent information determined by the sending Lifeline and accessible by a receiving Lifeline. Therefore, actual arguments for in-kind signature elements should be further usable throughout the execution of the receiving Lifeline's behavior. This holds also true for out-kind signature elements of reply Messages, consequently, for sending Lifelines.

To cope with the needs for assigning actual arguments to data sinks accessible by Lifelines, we suggest introducing a similar concept as WriteStructuralFeatureAction from Activities (see clause 11.3.55 of UML [1]) for Interactions, called *ArgumentAssignmentSpecification* (see Fig. 8).

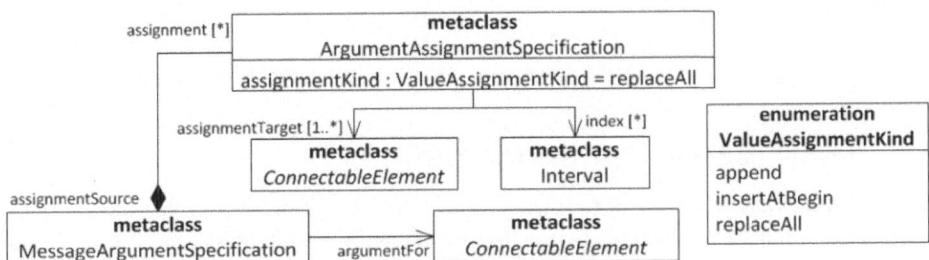

Fig. 8. Adding target assignment facilities to the metamodel

A MessageArgumentSpecification may contain a number of ArgumentAssignmentSpecifications, which, in turn, may specify a number of *assignment targets*. An assignment target represents a data sink that is intended to incorporate the actual arguments. In case the same actual arguments shall be assigned to several data sinks at the same time, the association end *assignmentTarget* is specified to be unbounded. Similar to ReferenceValueSelector, a number of Intervals can be used to specify what actual values at runtime shall be assigned to the assignment targets with respect to their indices, if the corresponding signature element represents a collection. However, the semantics in ArgumentAssignmentSpecification is converse, since it specifies what actual arguments shall be assigned to a data sink, in contrast to what reference arguments shall be taken from a data source as actual argument. However, as with ReferenceValueSelector, runtime compliance cannot be ensured at that point in time.

A *ValueAssignmentKind* specifies the treatment of already existing data in the assignment target in case the data sink represents a collection. Values of the actual argument at runtime will be either

- Added to existing contents of the data sink (*append*),
- Inserted at index 0 of data sink (*insertAtBegin*), or
- Replace all existing contents in the data sink (*replaceAll*).

Fig. 9 shows object model of the improved Interactions metamodel corresponding to the code snippet at the beginning of this section.

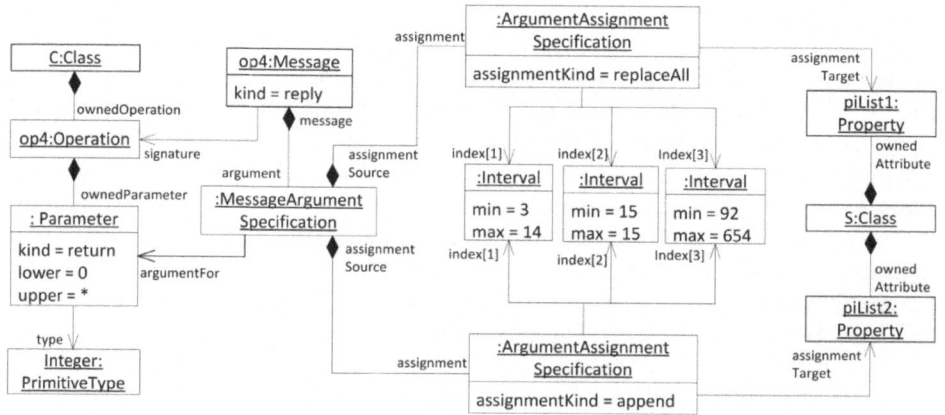

Fig. 9. Complex target assignment statements using collection indices

4.4   Improving Loop CombinedFragments

The semantics for CombinedFragments determined by their respective InteractionOperatorKind, but there are only two actual metaclasses for CombinedFragments in the Interaction's metamodel: CombinedFragment and ConsiderIgnoreFragment, a specialization of CombinedFragment. The reason for a specialization of CombinedFragment by ConsiderIgnoreFragment is the additional information necessary to specify the messages to be considered or ignored. Additional information is also required for Loops to define the number of repetitions of the loop, however, in contrast to ConsiderIgnoreFragment, the repetition bounds have simply been added to the general CombinedFragment via the *InteractionConstraint* metaclass. It has two associations for specifying the bounds of a loop (*minint* and *maxint*). Anyway, it would be possible to specify meaningless combinations of CombinedFragments and repetition bounds, like Alternative CombinedFragment with explicit repetition bounds. To avoid these meaningless constructs, informal constraints were defined that disallow specifying repetition bounds in a different context than Loops. In the case of ConsiderIgnoreFragment the additional information is actually located in the metaclass that requires the information (i.e., ConsiderIgnoreFragment), for Loops, the information is located in the InteractionConstraint instead. This seems to be inconsistent when comparing Loop and ConsiderIgnoreFragment.

Our proposal treats Loops similar to ConsiderIgnoreFragment by introducing a new subclass of CombinedFragment called *LoopFragment* (see Fig. 10). This allows supplementing LoopFragment with the information required to specify the repetition bounds of the loop. Furthermore, the metaclass InteractionConstraint becomes obsolete, since the LoopFragment itself is now in charge of specifying the repetition bounds. By doing so, the only need for InteractionConstraint has vanished.

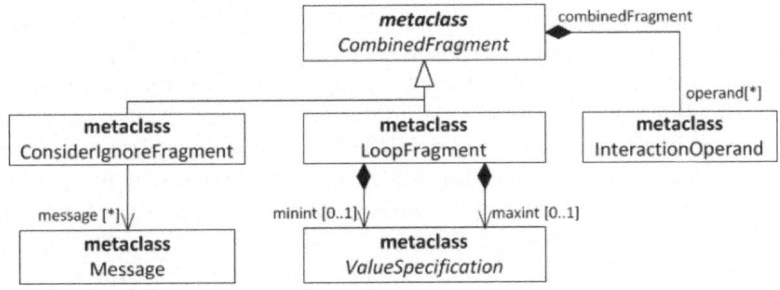

Fig. 10. Improved metamodel for *loop* Combined Fragments

Further considerations regarding CombinedFragments led to the conviction that the different kind of CombinedFragments, determined by the InteractionOperatorKind, should be resolved into concrete subclasses consequently. The reason for this lies in the too strong syntactical influence the InteractionOperatorKind impose on the structure of CombinedFragments. Applying a different InteractionOperatorKind to a CombinedFragment may enforce the removal of all but one InteractionOperand. For example, a CombinedFragment with two InteractionOperands and InteractionOperatorKind *alt* was defined and has been subsequently altered to *opt*, one of the InteractionOperands would have to be removed from the CombinedFragment. Therefore, we further refine the CombinedFragments metamodel in Fig. 11. Due to page limitations the figure does not show all specialized CombinedFragments that would ultimately result. The *...Fragment* metaclasses are placeholder for all remaining CombinedFragments with one or multiple InteractionOperands.

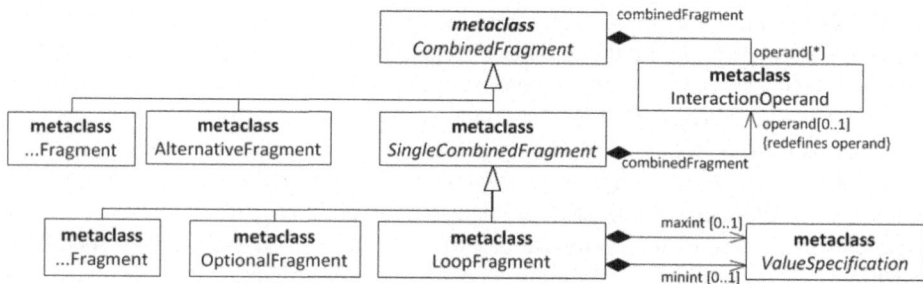

Fig. 11. Further refined CombinedFragment metamodel

5   Lessons Learned

The work presented led to two guidelines infor metamodel development activities. The first one refers to avoiding implicitly related elements; the second one provides an indicator when to use enumerations and when to use multiple metaclasses instead.

5.1   Avoid Implicitly Related Elements

This recommendation is accompanied by Einstein's famous simplicity principle: "Everything should be made as simple as possible, but not simpler." The UML Interactions metamodel counteracted this principle by simply reusing ValueSpecifications for a Message's arguments, instead of introducing a new metaclass that should have actually established a unidirectional link to the signature element. This gave rise to a situation where the list members of two semantically related lists were just implicitly related with each other via their respective indices. A new metaclass *MessageArgumentSpecification,* as we have suggested it, would have made the relation explicit and, the metamodel itself more robust regarding changes done by the user. The problem of implicitly related elements holds also true for other parts of the UML metamodel, though. InvocationAction, for example, exhibits the same issue as Messages in the relation of actual arguments and signature elements.

Our guideline for the creation of more robust metamodels is: Avoid implicitly related elements. The assumed benefits of saving the metaclass that formalizes the relation are paid off by increased efforts for future maintenance, comprehension and metamodel processing.

5.2   Enumeration vs. Metaclass

A question that is still not sufficiently answered, at least to the knowledge of the authors, is when to use enumerations and when to use several specialized metaclasses? Doubtlessly, the underlying semantics will not be influenced either way. Enumerations allow reducing the actual number of metaclasses in a metamodel. For example, every NamedElement defines a visibility within the Namespace it is contained in. The possible visibilities a NamedElement can declare are defined in the enumeration

VisibilityKind as *public*, *private*, *protected* and *package*. Each subclass of NamedElement inherits the visibility feature and its semantics, thus, the design of visibility throughout the entire inheritance hierarchy of NamedElement was well chosen. Specialized metaclasses instead (e.g., NamedElementPublic, NamedElementPrivate etc.) would have resulted in an unnecessarily complex metamodel.

So, using enumerations seems to be adequate and accurate if the EnumerationLiterals merely affect the semantics of the metaclass they are referenced from. Furthermore, enumerations can keep the inheritance hierarchy of the metaclass concise.

With respect to the CombinedFragment's *interactionOperator* (and in few other metaclasses in UML such as Pseudostate), the situation is different. The various literals of InteractionOperatorKind do affect not only the semantics, but the syntactical structure of CombinedFragments as well. In this case, changing the enumeration may require changing the instance of the metaclass as well. The problem of varying syntax due to enumerations is that the understanding of the metamodel becomes unnecessarily complicated and its maintenance prone to errors. Even though the solution we presented in Fig. 11 results in a larger number of similar metaclasses, the metamodel becomes more comprehensible and the actual syntactical differences of the specialized metaclasses become obvious.

Our guideline for metamodels regarding enumerations or specialized subclasses is: If different literals of an Enumeration may turn the model into a syntactically ill-formed model, one should use specialized metaclasses instead.

6   Conclusion and Outlook

In this paper, we have presented improvement suggestions for parts of the UML Interactions metamodel regarding Message arguments and CombinedFragments. We stressed that the current metamodel of Message arguments reveals some issues of precise specification of actual arguments, usage of reference arguments as actual arguments and assignment of actual arguments to data sinks accessible by the receiving Lifeline. Whether these issues originate from the UML Interactions metamodel or ought to be solved by general concepts of the UML metamodel is not in scope of this paper. We assumed the view of a user of UML who is wondering that actual argument handling is possible in UML Activities, but only inconveniently (if ever) supported by Interactions. From that perspective, we suggested improvements limited to the Interactions' Message metamodel to overcome these issues. The improved metamodel was the result of the development of a tool for test modeling, called Fokus!MBT that relies on the UML Testing Profile and leverages UML Interactions as test case behavior [20]. In the scope of Fokus!MBT, a minimalistic profile was created that realizes the metamodel improvements we described with stereotypes. So, the metamodel improvements have been applied to real situations and are not just theoretical considerations.

Finally, we extracted two guidelines to metamodeling for more robust metamodels.

The fact that UML Activities and Interactions do provide different approaches for the very same logical concept gives rise to the considerations that these behavior kinds should be more tightly integrated with each other in future. There is actually an issue submitted for this[2] need. We support that need, which would result in a more concise and comprehensible metamodel for UML. As a result, it might turn out that the issues discussed in the paper rather belong to the fundamental parts of the UML metamodel. However, as long as Activities and Interactions are treated as separate parts, the improvements we presented are most minimalistic, since they do not affect any other part of the UML metamodel. An integration of both behavior kinds is not a trivial task, though, and not in scope of this paper.

Acknowledgements. This work was partially funded by the EU FP 7 projects REMICS (no. 257793) and MIDAS (no. 318786) and ARTEMIS project VARIES.

References

1. OMG UML: OMG Unified Modeling Language (OMG UML), Superstructure, Version 2.4.1, #formal/2011-08-06 (2011), http://www.omg.org/spec/UML/2.4.1/
2. Grabowski, J., Rudolph, E.: Message Sequence Chart (MSC) - A Survey of the new CCITT Language for the Description of Traces within Communication Systems. CCITT SDL Newsletter (16), 30–48 (1993)
3. OMG UTP: OMG UML Testing Profile (UTP), Version 1.2, #ptc/2012-09-13 (2012), http://www.omg.org/spec/UTP
4. Baker, P., Dai, Z.R., Grabowski, J., Haugen, Ø., Schieferdecker, I., Williams, C.: Model-driven testing – using the UML testing profile. Springer (2007)
5. Haugen, Ø.: Comparing UML 2.0 interactions and MSC-2000. In: Amyot, D., Williams, A.W. (eds.) SAM 2004. LNCS, vol. 3319, pp. 65–79. Springer, Heidelberg (2005)
6. Haugen, Ø., Stølen, K.: STAIRS – steps to analyze interactions with refinement semantics. In: Stevens, P., Whittle, J., Booch, G. (eds.) UML 2003. LNCS, vol. 2863, pp. 388–402. Springer, Heidelberg (2003)
7. Haugen, Ø., Husa, K.E., Runde, R.K., Stølen, K.: Why timed sequence diagrams require three-event semantics. In: Leue, S., Systä, T.J. (eds.) Scenarios. LNCS, vol. 3466, pp. 1–25. Springer, Heidelberg (2005)
8. Haugen, Ø., Husa, K.E., Runde, R.K., Stølen, K.: STAIRS towards formal design with sequence diagrams. Journal of Software and Systems Modeling, 349–458 (2005)
9. Runde, R.K., Haugen, Ø., Stølen, K.: Refining UML interactions with underspecification and nondeterminism. Nordic Journal of Computing 12(2), 157–188 (2005)
10. Lund, M.S., Stølen, K.: A fully general operational semantics for UML 2.0 sequence diagrams with potential and mandatory choice. In: Misra, J., Nipkow, T., Sekerinski, E. (eds.) FM 2006. LNCS, vol. 4085, pp. 380–395. Springer, Heidelberg (2006)
11. Störrle, H.: Semantics of interactions in UML 2.0. In: Proceedings of IEEE Symposium on Human Centric Computing Languages and Environments (2003)
12. Störrle, H.: Trace Semantics of UML 2.0 Interactions. Technical report, University of Munich (2004)

---

[2] http://www.omg.org/issues/uml2-rtf.open.html#Issue6441

13. Knapp, A.: A Formal Semantics for UML Interactions. In: France, R.B. (ed.) UML 1999. LNCS, vol. 1723, pp. 116–130. Springer, Heidelberg (1999)
14. Cengarle, M., Knapp, A.: UML 2.0 Interactions: Semantics and Refinement. In: Jürjens, J., Fernàndez, E.B., France, R., Rumpe, B. (eds.) 3rd Int. Workshop on Critical Systems Development with UML (CSDUML 2004), pp. 85–99 (2004)
15. Li, M., Ruan, Y.: Approach to Formalizing UML Sequence Diagrams. In: Proc. 3rd International Workshop on Intelligent Systems and Applications (ISA), pp. 28–29 (2011)
16. Shen, H., Virani, A., Niu, J.: Formalize UML 2 Sequence Diagrams. In: Proc. 11th IEEE High Assurance Systems Engineering Symposium (HASE), pp. 437–440 (2008)
17. Störrle, H.: Assert, Negate and Refinement in UML-22 Interactions. In: Jürjens, J., Rumpe, B., France, R., Fernandez, E.B. (eds.) Proc. Wsh. Critical Systems Development with UML (CSDUML 2003), San Francisco (2003)
18. Harel, D., Maoz, S.: Assert and negate revisited: modal semantics for UML sequence diagrams. In: Proc. International Workshop on Scenarios and State Machines: Models, Algorithms, and Tools (SCESM 2006) (2006)
19. Knapp, A., Wuttke, J.: Model Checking of UML 2.0 Interactions. In: Kühne, T. (ed.) MoDELS 2006. LNCS, vol. 4364, pp. 42–51. Springer, Heidelberg (2007)
20. Wendland, M.-F., Hoffmann, A., Schieferdecker, I.: Fokus!MBT – A Multi-Paradigmatic Test Modeling Environment. To appear in Proceedings of: Academics Tooling with Eclipse Workshop (ACME), In Conjunction with the Joint Conferences ECMFA/ECSA/ECOOP, Montpellier, France (2013) ISBN 978-1-4503-2036-8

A Graph-Pattern Based Approach for Meta-Model Specific Conflict Detection in a General-Purpose Model Versioning System

Asha Rajbhoj and Sreedhar Reddy

Tata Consultancy Services
54B, Industrial Estate, Hadapsar
Pune, 411013 India
{asha.rajbhoj,sreedhar.reddy}@tcs.com

Abstract. Model driven engineering is the key paradigm in many large system development efforts today. A good versioning system for models is essential for change management and coordinated development of these systems. Support for conflict detection and reconciliation is one of the key functionalities of a versioning system. A large system uses a large number of different kinds of models, each specifying a different aspect of the system. The notion of conflict is relative to the semantics of a meta-model. Hence conflicts should be detected and reported in a meta-model specific way. In this paper we discuss a general purpose model versioning system that can work with models of any meta-model, and a graph-pattern based approach for specifying conflicts in a meta-model specific way. We also present an efficient algorithm that uses these graph-patterns to detect conflicts at the right level of abstraction.

Keywords: Model driven engineering, Model versioning, Meta-model.

1 Introduction

Model driven engineering plays a central role in many large system development efforts today. In these systems, models are used for specifying and controlling all the aspects of a development life-cycle. In our own organization, over the past 17 years, we have extensively used MDE to develop several large business critical applications [1, 2]. We use a large number of different kinds of models, viz., UML, ER, BPMN, GUI models, batch processing models, product-line models and so on. These modeling requirements evolved over a period of time to keep pace with changing business and technology needs. Our experience shows that this evolutionary trend is likely to continue into the future as well. Therefore we provide a general purpose modeling framework where meta-models are first class artifacts. We can define new meta-models, extend exiting meta-models and integrate them as required. For instance, each of the above mentioned models has its own meta-model. We integrate these meta-models into one unified meta-model. The meta-models and their model instances are stored in a model repository. The repository is designed for efficient life-cycle management of large models by a large team of users. A repository with hundreds of components and thousands of classes, supporting a team of 100+

A. Moreira et al. (Eds.): MODELS 2013, LNCS 8107, pp. 422–435, 2013.

members is a common scenario. One of our larger projects had a repository of around a million objects, 22 million properties and around a million links.

Given the size and variety of models, and given the dynamics of a large team where changes keep happening continuously, a robust model versioning system is an absolute must for orderly change management. Conflict detection and reconciliation (or diff and merge) is one of the key functions of change management. The notion of conflict is relative to the semantics of a meta-model and depends on the usage context. For instance, suppose we change the type of a parameter of an operation in a class model. This has to be presented as a conflict in the right context – conflict in the class definition at the outer level, conflict in the operation definition at the next level, and then the specific change in parameter type. Just reporting the change in parameter type does not provide the right context. Conflicts have to be detected and reported in a manner that is intuitive to the modeler so as to reduce the chances of reconciliation errors. Different users may be interested in different modeling contexts. For instance, a data modeler may only be interested in conflicts that occur in the data models, and not, say conflicts that occur in the screen definitions of a GUI model. Hence it should be possible to specify multiple, stakeholder specific, *conflict contexts* or views on the underlying model. We provide meta-model graph patterns as a means to specify such *conflict contexts*. A graph pattern specifies a hierarchically structured view on a subset of the meta-model that is relevant to a given context.

Scale-up is another important concern in a repository that supports large models. In order to scale up, the time it takes to perform various life-cycle operations such as export, check-in, check-out, diff, merge, etc must be proportional to the size of the change between successive operations and not vary much with the absolute size of the model. Similarly the time for conflict detection must also be proportional to the size of the change. This is trivial when conflicts are to be detected and reported at the level of atomic operations; we only have to process the contents of change logs. However, to construct context specific conflict reports we have to go beyond the change logs; we have to consult the base model as well. We present an algorithm that computes context specific conflict reports efficiently, starting from primitive operations recorded in the change log.

The rest of the paper is organized as follows. Section 2 gives an overview of our modeling framework. Section 3 presents our versioning model. Section 4 presents our delta model, the model we use for recording changes. Section 5 presents our *diff and merge* approach, the graph pattern model for specifying *conflict contexts* and the *diff* algorithm to detect conflicts using these graph patterns. Section 6 discusses related work. Section 7 concludes with discussion and results.

2   Modeling Framework

An information system can be seen as a collection of parts and their relationships. A model of an information system is a description of these parts and relationships in a language such as UML. The modeling language itself can be described as a model in another language. The latter language is the meta-model for the former as shown in Fig 1.

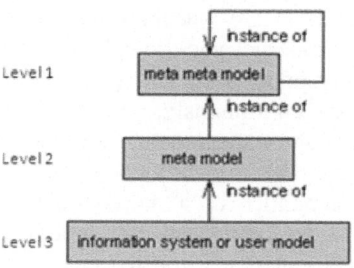

Fig. 1. Modeling layers

We use a reflexive modeling language [2] that is compatible with OMG MOF [8] to define models at all levels. A model at each level is an instance of the model at the previous level. The model at level 1, the meta meta-model, is an instance of itself. The meta meta-model shown in Fig. 2 is the base model. It is the schema for describing meta-models. The meta meta-model is capable of describing itself, i.e., it can model itself.

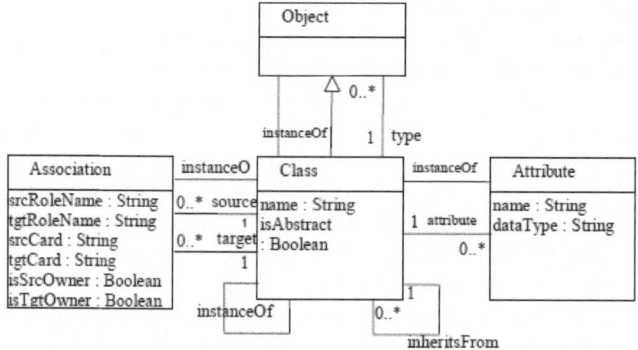

Fig. 2. Reflexive Meta Meta-model

Everything in a model is an object. An object is described by its class. A class is specified in terms of a set of attributes and associations. An object is an instance of a class that has attribute values and links to other objects as specified by its class. Since everything is an object, a class is also an object that is specified by another class called metaclass. In Fig. 2, the class *class* is a metaclass which is an instance of itself. A meta model specification consists of: a model schema which is an instance of the meta meta-model, a diagramming notation to edit its instance models, and a set of constraints and rules to specify consistency and completeness checks on its instance models. We provide a reflexive modeling language aware generic model editor for creating models as well as their meta-models. We use OCL [16] to specify well-formed-ness constraints over models. Cardinality and optionality constraints are supported by the reflexive model itself. We provide a diagram definition workbench to define visual notations and map them onto meta-model elements. Having a meta-modeling framework enabled us to extend modeling languages as per need. We use an industrial-strength relational database as a storage mechanism for managing large scale models. Storage schema reflects the structure of models.

3   Versioning Model

Fig. 3 presents our versioning model. The model repository contains a set of *configuration items*. A configuration item has a number of *configuration item versions*. A configuration item version is the container of model *objects*. A configuration item version can have one or more versions derived from it (as indicated by the *next* association), and a configuration item version may be derived from one or more previous versions. A configuration item version may be composed of other configuration item versions. A configuration item version may have dangling links, i.e. association links with one end missing. The dangling ends are automatically bound to the missing objects (based on object IDs) when two configuration item versions that contain the required objects are placed together in a container configuration item version. A *configuration* is a special configuration item whose versions must always be complete, i.e. they should not have any dangling links pointing to objects outside their boundaries. *Configurations* are used for modeling deliverables that must be complete in all respects.

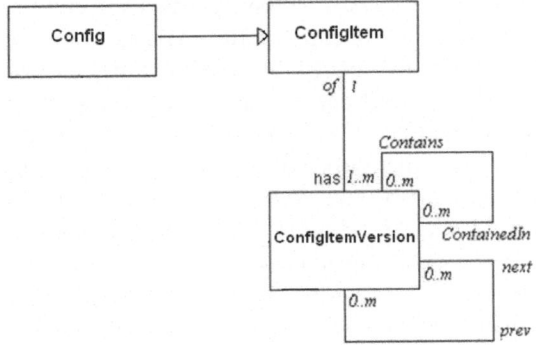

Fig. 3. Meta-model of Versioning

4   Delta Model

A model version may exist in one of two states: materialized state or delta state. A materialized version stores a fully materialized model, whereas a delta version only records changes with respect to its parent version. We use the model shown in Fig. 4 for recording changes.   Please note that even a materialized version has an associated delta model, which serves as a record of all the changes in that version with respect to its parent. The change logs can be exploited to implement life-cycle operations such as model export, code generation, etc, more efficiently.

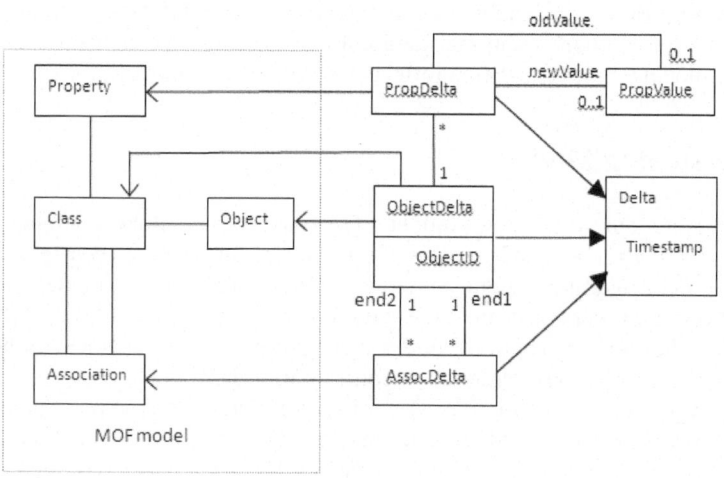

Fig. 4. Delta Model

Referring to the model in Fig. 4, a *Delta* is a record of a single change in the model. It has a timestamp property that records the time of the change and an *opCode* property that records the operation causing the change, which is one of ADD/MODIFY/DELETE. *ObjectDelta* records changes to objects; *PropDelta* records changes to properties; and *AssocDelta* records changes to associations. *ObjectDelta* has an association to *Object* to identify the object that has changed; it also stores the ID (UUID) of the object. *PropDelta* has an association to *Property* to identify the property that has changed, and records two values – new and old (if any). *AssociationDelta* identifies the association that has changed, and has two links to *ObjectDelta* to identify the two end objects. An *AssociationDelta* is owned by the owner (navigable) end of the *Association*. When a property or an association changes, its owner object is also recorded as modified. The associations between *ObjectDelta, PropDelta* and *AssocDelta* mirror the associations between *Class, Property* and *Association* in the meta meta-model, and thus record the same structure. From the delta model one can retrieve all the changes that have occurred. Delta model is used for various purposes like tracking changes, optimizing storage for model versioning, model comparison, model validation, model based code generation, etc.

4.1   Delta Optimizations

Objects, property values and association links can undergo changes multiple times. As a result there could be multiple deltas recorded for the same object. For example within a single version the value of a property may be modified multiple times or an object may be created and then deleted. A delta compaction operation removes such redundant operations. Table 1 gives the compaction rules which are self-explanatory.

Table 1. Compaction rules

Change 1	Change 2	Optimized Change
ADD	DELETE	Nullified
ADD	MODIFY	ADD
MODIFY	MODIFY	MODIFY
MODIFY	DELETE	DELETE
DELETE	ADD	Not Possible
DELETE	MODIFY	Not Possible

5   Diff-Merge

In a large team, development is usually carried out concurrently by different sub teams. For example, a development team needs to work on a new release while continuing to fix bugs in an older released version. This necessitates branch version creation and reconciliation on a frequent basis. A large system uses a large number of different kinds of models, each specifying a different aspect of the system. The notion of conflict is relative to the semantics of a meta-model. Hence conflicts need to be detected and reported in a meta-model specific way. Typically such reconciliation needs to be carried out in a step by step manner by different groups that are responsible for different aspects, e.g. database group doing data model reconciliation, GUI team doing GUI model reconciliation and so on. Thus the process of conflict detection and reconciliation is not only meta-model specific but also usage context specific. For example when one compares class models of two UML models, one wants to see the conflicts in a structured manner. One wants to know which classes are in conflict, and within each of those classes which attributes are in conflict, which operations are in conflict and so on. This is the structure in which one wants to view the conflict even when the change is only minor, say type change in a parameter of an operation in a class. Same observation holds for other aspects of the system as well such as screens in a GUI model, tables in a database model, and so on. Experience shows that if the change is not presented as a conflict at the right level, in the right context, the scope for making mistakes in reconciliation increases significantly, especially in a large team comprising of heterogeneous groups working on different aspects. To address this need we use meta-model graph patterns to specify contexts of interest. These patterns can then guide how conflicts should be detected and presented in a structured manner.

5.1   Pattern Model

We define a model pattern as a graph of object nodes, their properties and associations. Pattern provides a means to specify conflict contexts. It is specified in terms of a meta-model, as shown in Fig. 5. A pattern node maps to a meta-model class; properties of interest are specified by a set of property items (*PProp* in the figure) that map to the corresponding meta-model properties; a pattern edge maps to a meta-model association. A pattern has a root node (i.e., number of 'in' edges = 0). A pattern is essentially a connected, directed acyclic sub graph of a meta-model graph. Given a model that conforms to the meta-model, a pattern selects a set of matching sub graphs of the model. Thus a pattern can also be seen as specifying a view over the model.

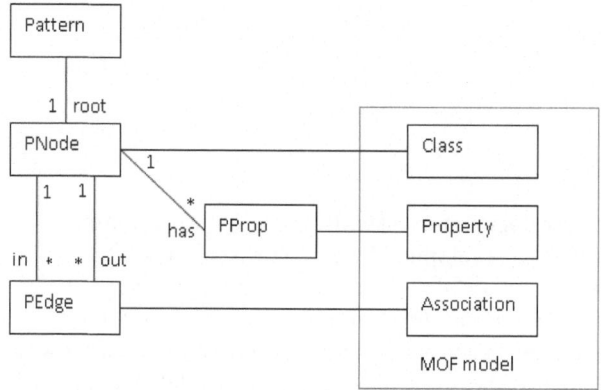

Fig. 5. Pattern Model

Let's take UML model as an example. Suppose in a specific context we are only interested in classes and their operations. A pattern such as the one shown in Fig. 6 can be specified.

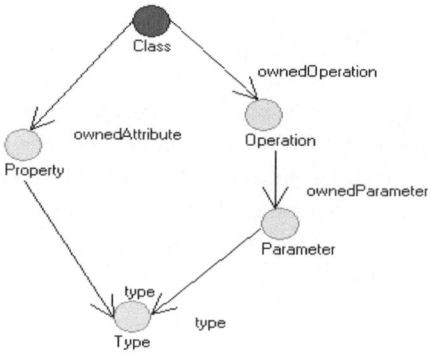

Fig. 6. Class Pattern

Similarly we can use patterns to specify other contexts that are of interest to different stakeholders.

5.2   *Diff* Algorithm

There are stages in the life cycle of a project such as during testing and bug fixing where many small changes are made by different teams and these have to be reconciled quickly. At the same time, conflicts should be presented in a structured context, as we discussed earlier, to minimize the reconciliation errors. The following are therefore the issues the diff algorithm needs to address:

- Diff performance should be proportional to the size of the delta model and not be affected by the size of the base model. Base models can be quite large. Delta models in comparison are quite small.
- Diff should be constructed as per the context specified by the pattern graph. This means only those changes recorded in the delta models are relevant that match the types specified in the pattern graph. Also, of these matching changes only those changes are relevant that can form valid paths from the root of the pattern graph. For example, with respect to the pattern given in Fig 6, suppose the name of a Type object changes. This change is only relevant to the pattern if it happens to be the type of an attribute or operation parameter of some class in the model.

The algorithm uses the following strategies to address these issues:

- Delta-driven, bottom-up computation: The algorithm uses post-order traversal on the pattern graph to compute differences bottom-up, starting from changes recorded in the delta model. At each node, it computes all the differences corresponding to that node as recorded in the source and target delta models. Difference computations of objects that do not have the specified association path to an object of a parent node are dropped. Existence of parent object and the corresponding association are first checked in the delta model and then in the base model. This ensures two things: 1) only those parts of the base model are accessed that have paths from changes recorded in the delta model, and 2) changes not relevant to the context are excluded from the computation.
- Symmetric, two-way diff: In bottom-up diff, we complete all diffs at a node before moving to the next node up in the hierarchy. As we do this, we need to drop objects that have no path to the parent node in the graph. But this should be done only when an object has no path in both source and target delta models. To ensure this, at each node, we compute diff by scanning both source and target delta models. Objects on the two sides are correlated by UUIDs stored in object deltas. The output of the algorithm is a diff model as shown in Fig. 7. Diff model is essentially a pair of correlated hierarchical structures. For every DiffObject node in the source hierarchy there is a corresponding DiffObject node in the target hierarchy and vice versa. Similarly for every edge in the source hierarchy there is a corresponding edge in the target hierarchy and vice versa. The diff model is built up bottom-up as we traverse the pattern graph bottom-up. For the pattern shown in Fig. 6, diff is computed for Type, Property, Parameter, Operation and Class in that order. As shown in Fig. 8, change in type name from BankUser to Bank_User is propagated to parameter p_user then to the operation getAccount and finally to the root class Account.

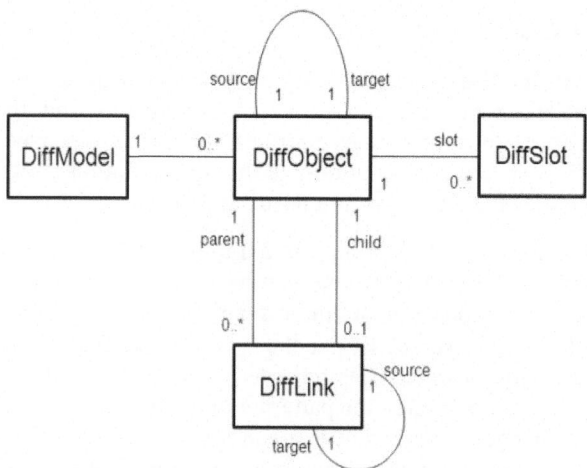

Fig. 7. Diff Model

The algorithm is presented in more detail below. The algorithm assumes the *diff* is being computed between two branch versions whose parent version is available in a materialized form (called base model in the algorithm). It can be easily extended to the case where the parent model also exists only in the delta form.

Algorithm ComputeDiff

Input: Model baseModel, Pattern P, DeltaModel deltaSrc, DeltaModel deltaTgt
Output: DiffModel diffSrc, DiffModel diffTgt
Begin

        Initialise diffSrc, diffTgt   //These store computed diff tree.
        PNode rNode = root of pattern P;
        DoDiff(rNode, baseModel, deltaSrc, deltaTgt, diffSrc, diffTgt)
        Display diffSrc, diffTgt
End

Algorithm DoDiff

Input: PNode rNode, Model baseModel, DeltaModel deltaSrc, DeltaModel deltaTgt,
      DiffModel diffSrc, DiffModel diffTgt
Begin

// **Step 1**: Recursively invoke DoDiff to compute differences bottom up, in a post-order traversal.
For each cNode ∈ rNode.child
 Do
   DoDiff(cNode, baseModel, deltaSrc, deltaTgt, diffSrc, diffTgt)
Done

// **Step 2**: Find all differences at this level, i.e. at the level of rNode in the pattern graph. This
// involves finding differences w.r.t. ADD/DELETE of objects of the given type as well as their
// property value differences. These need to be computed from source as well as target deltas. Note

// that differences with respect to associated child node hierarchies would already have been
// completed by the time we reach here.
For each deltaObject in source delta whose type matches the type of rNode
Do

    a)   Get the corresponding delta object, if any, from the target delta model using matching object ID.

    b)   If both delta objects record DELETE operations, continue with the next object.

    c)   Otherwise create corresponding DiffObject nodes in source and target diff models and link them up.

    d)   If source delta records an ADD operation, then mark the corresponding target diff model object DUMMY.

    e)   Do property value diff on the corresponding objects in source and target w.r.t base model object (if any) and record these differences in DiffSlot elements in the diff models. Properties of type *blob* are treated as different if their binaries are different.

Done
For each deltaObject in target delta whose type matches the type of rNode
Do

    // Do steps (a) to (e) above, but with respect to the target delta
Done

// **Step 3**: Filter out all those diff tree nodes at this level that do not have a path to the parent node in
// the pattern graph. Such nodes do not belong to the context under consideration. For those nodes
// that do have a path to the parent, record the corresponding association path in the diff model via
// DiffLink elements.

If (rNode is the root, i.e. does not have a parent in the pattern graph) **then return**;

For each diffObject that belongs to the source diff model whose type matches the type of rNode
Do

    a)   Check if the corresponding model object has an associated parent object as specified by the edge to the parent node in the pattern graph. Parent object and association may exist fully in the delta model, partly in the delta model (association in delta, object in base) or fully in the base model. If they do not exist in the source delta model, check if they exist in the   target delta model. It is sufficient that they exist at least in one of the models; they need not exist in both.

    b)   If there is no path to the parent, then purge the diff tree rooted at the diffObject. Purge also the diff tree rooted at the corresponding linked diffObject in the target diff model.

    c)   Else, create requisite parent diffObject, DiffLink elements and link them to the child diffObject. Do this in both source and target diff models and create corresponding links.

    Done
  End

Fig. 8 shows a graphical rendering of a sample *diff model* computed by the algorithm. Left hand side shows the source hierarchy and the right hand side shows the corresponding target hierarchy. Name change is directly shown in display, whereas other property changes are indicated by a property change icon placed before the object. On selection of the object, property differences are shown in the properties pane at the bottom. Blob properties differences can be seen by using appropriate editor. Association order change is indicated by a suitable icon, on selection of which the source and target object order lists are shown in the bottom pane. Dummy nodes are inserted where appropriate to make up for missing nodes. For example, when a new object is created in the source version but not in the target, the algorithm inserts a dummy node at the corresponding place in the target hierarchy. The *diff* display only shows changed parts in this hierarchical context. The structure can be folded or unfolded as required, and merge can be performed at an appropriate level.

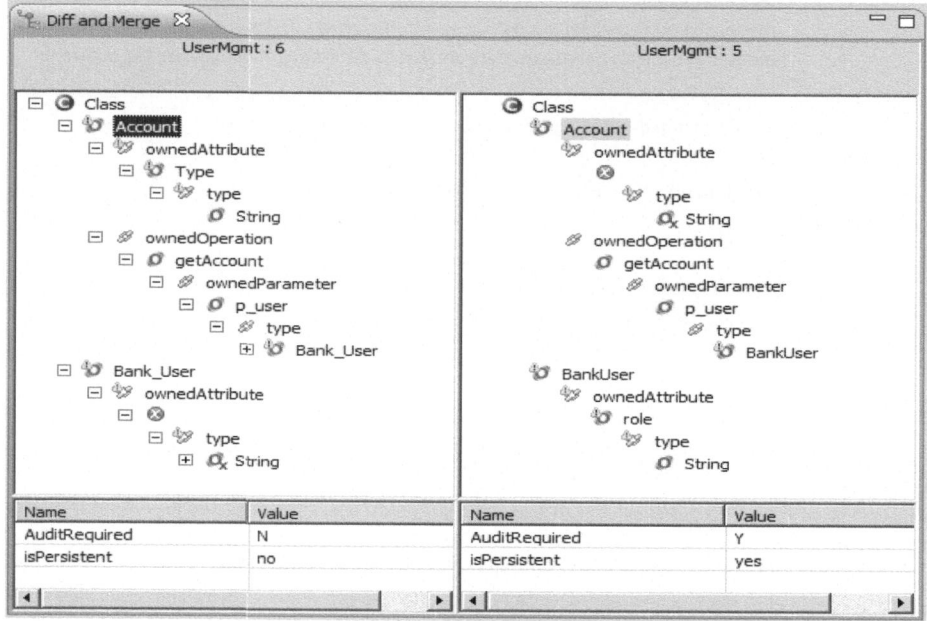

Fig. 8. Diff display

5.3   Merge Operation

Merge operation is guided by the *diff model*. It involves selecting diff nodes from the source or target hierarchy and performing operations such as 'copy' or 'delete' on those nodes until the diff model becomes completely empty. A copy operation is performed when we want to overwrite the contents of one side by the contents of the other. The operation copies properties and associations from one workspace to the other. When the copy is performed at an aggregate node, the operation is performed recursively down the sub tree in a bottom-up manner. A 'delete' operation is allowed on a node only when the corresponding node on the other side is a dummy. As the merge operation proceeds and the nodes are reconciled, the diff model is automatically kept consistent by propagating the reconciliation information to other dependent parts of the diff model, without having to re-compute the diff.

6   Related Work

Modeling tools such as Enterprise Architect [15], Rational Software Architect [3] and so on relied traditionally on file-based version control systems to provide model versioning. While file based version control systems are mature, their notion of change is limited to text lines. A text line does not always map to a meaningful modeling unit, at the right level of abstraction. To compute context specific conflicts of the kind we are discussing, these files have to be first loaded into modeling workspaces and the models completely reconstructed. This obviously does not scale well for large sized models.

More recently, several new approaches have been reported that support versioning directly in the model repository. Many of these are meant for specific meta-models such as UML. For example Odyssey-VCS [5] support versioning of UML models. Some of them are more generic. They can support versioning on models of any meta-model. For example EMFStore [6] can support versioning on any EMF based model. However none of these approaches, to the best of our knowledge, supports the notion of conflict contexts as first class artifacts in the versioning system. Also in our tests we discovered that EMFStore does not scale well for large models -- the size of the model it can support seems to be limited by the amount of memory available. EMFCompare [14] can display comparison results in a meta-model specific way, as per the composition hierarchy specified in the meta-model. But this only provides one static view on the conflicts. There is no support for multiple context specific views. For example when an operation signature changes, the change is relevant not only in the context of a class, but also in the context of a screen definition (in the GUI model) that maps its fields to the operation parameters. Also in our tests we discovered that the diff performance of EMFCompare deteriorates with the model size – it seems to depend on the base model size rather than the delta size.

7   Discussion and Results

The proposed model versioning approach and the *diff and merge* algorithm have been extensively used within our organization over 5 years in several large projects. The approach has significantly reduced the cycle times for change management, especially during time-critical life-cycle stages such as acceptance testing. The pattern-based, context sensitive *diff and merge* approach has significantly reduced change reconciliation errors compared with our earlier context-agnostic *diff and merge* approach. The new delta driven *diff and merge* algorithm has also contributed significantly to the reduction in turn-around times.

We share some results collected from one of our larger repositories with a model size of around 1 million objects, 22 million slots and 1 million links. Table 2 shows performance results for components of various sizes but with a fixed delta size. It can be seen that the performance of check-out and diff operations hardly varies with the base model size. Check-in operation time slightly increases with increase in base model size. This is due to additional model validations carried out on the model before checking in.

Table 2. Performance results

Overall Application Size 1 million objects, 22 million slots, and 1 million links					
with delta for 11 objects, 200 slots , 10 links					
Component Size			Check in (seconds)	Check out (seconds)	Diff (seconds)
Objects	Slots	Links			
5556	53121	154422	15	3	4
7244	84926	156746	16	3	6
12727	197716	163400	18	3	6
21422	347878	177082	23	3	6
23395	370233	176426	25	3	6

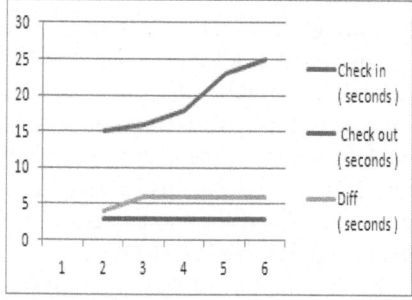

Table 3 show the results for different sizes of delta, keeping the base model size constant for one of the largest components in this repository having 23395 objects, 370233 slots and 176426 links. It is observed that check-in, check-out and diff times grow linearly with delta size. Combining the results from tables 2 and 3, we can see that the time taken for these operations depends only the delta size and remains largely independent of the base model size.

Table 3. Performance results with delta sizes

Overall Application Size 1 million objects, 22 million slots, and 1 million links			
Component having 23395 objects, 370233 slots, 176426 links			
Delta for	Check in (seconds)	Check out (seconds)	Diff (seconds)
11 objects, 200 slots, 10 links	25	3	6
22 objects, 200 slots, 20 links	26	3	7
44 objects, 400 slots, 40 links	30	5	8
66 objects, 600 slots, 60 links	31	7	10
88 objects, 800 slots, 80 links	32	9	15
110 objects, 1000 slots, 100 links	35	16	20

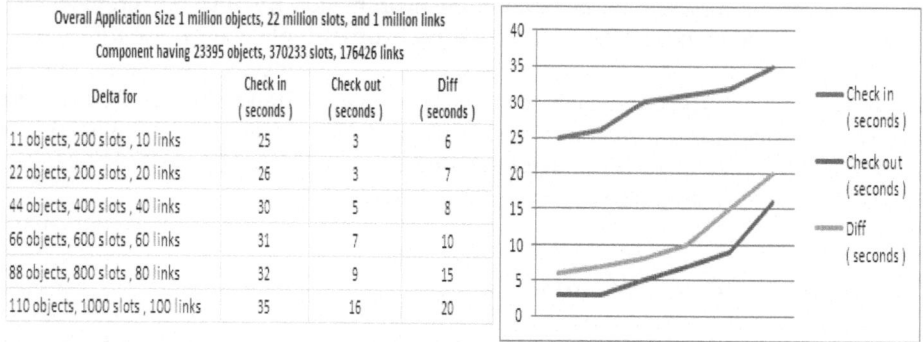

For the sake of comparison we tried creating models of similar size using EMF and version them using EMFStore [6]. However we could not proceed beyond a model file size of about 13 MB having around 0.4 millon objects. Hence we could not compare results with similar model sizes with EMFStore. AMOR has shared results in [12]. Its is clear from the results that its execution time grows significantly with increasing model size.

References

1. Kulkarni, V., Venkatesh, R., Reddy, S.: Generating Enterprise Applications from Models. In: Bruel, J.-M., Bellahsène, Z. (eds.) OOIS 2002. LNCS, vol. 2426, pp. 270–279. Springer, Heidelberg (2002)

2. Kulkarni, V., Reddy, S., Rajbhoj, A.: Scaling Up Model Driven Engineering – Experience and Lessons Learnt. In: Petriu, D.C., Rouquette, N., Haugen, Ø. (eds.) MODELS 2010, Part II. LNCS, vol. 6395, pp. 331–345. Springer, Heidelberg (2010)
3. Letkeman, K.: Comparing and merging UML models in IBM Rational Software Architect: Part 3—a deeper understanding of model merging. Technical report, IBM Rational (2005)
4. Altmanninger, K., Seidl, M., Wimmer, M.: A survey on model versioning approaches. Int. J.Web Inf. Syst. 5(3), 271–304 (2009)
5. Murta, L., Corrêa, C., Prudêncio, J.G., Werner, C.: Towards Odyssey-VCS 2: improvements over a UML-based version control system. In: Proceedings of the 2nd International Workshop on Comparison and Versioning of Software Models at ICSE 2008, pp. 25–30. ACM, New York (2008)
6. Kögel, M., Helming, J.: EMFStore: a model repository for EMF models. In: Proceedings of the 32nd International Conference on Software Engineering (ICSE 2010), vol. 2, pp. 307–308. ACM, New York (2010)
7. Altmanninger, K., Kappel, G., Kusel, A., Retschitzegger, W., Schwinger, W., Seidl, M., Wimmer, M.: AMOR– towards adaptable model versioning. In: 1st International Workshop on Model Co-Evolution and Consistency Management, In Conjunction with MODELS 2008 (2008)
8. Model Object Facility, http://www.omg.org/spec/MOF/2.0
9. Unified Modeling Language, http://www.omg.org/spec/UML/2.2/
10. Eclipse. Eclipse Modeling Framework, http://www.eclipse.org/emf
11. Helming, J., Koegel, M.: UNICASE, http://unicase.org
12. http://code.google.com/a/eclipselabs.org/p/model-versioning-benchmarks/wiki/PerformanceResultsofAMOR
13. OMG (2010): BPMN 2.0, OMG document - dtc/10-06-04., http://www.bpmn.org
14. EMF Compare, http://www.eclipse.org/emf/compare/
15. Enterprise Architect from sparx systems, http://www.sparxsystems.com/
16. Object Constraint Language, http://www.omg.org/spec/OCL/2.2

On the Complex Nature of MDE Evolution

Regina Hebig[1], Holger Giese[1], Florian Stallmann[2], and Andreas Seibel[1]

[1] Hasso Plattner Institute at the University of Potsdam
Prof.-Dr.-Helmert-Str. 2-3, D-14482 Potsdam, Germany
{forename.surname}@hpi.uni-potsdam.de
[2] SAP AG, Hasso-Plattner-Ring 7, D-69190 Walldorf, Germany
florian.stallmann@sap.com

Abstract. In Model-Driven Engineering (MDE) the employed setting of languages as well as automated and manual activities has major impact on productivity. Furthermore, such settings for MDE evolve over time. However, currently only the evolution of (modeling) languages, tools, and transformations is studied in research. It is not clear whether these are the only relevant changes that characterize MDE evolution in practice. In this paper we address this lack of knowledge. We first discuss possible changes and then report on a first study that demonstrates that these forms of evolution can be commonly observed in practice. To investigate the complex nature of MDE evolution in more depth, we captured the evolution of three MDE settings from practice and derive eight observations concerning reasons for MDE evolution. Based on the observations we then identify open research challenge concerning MDE evolution.

1 Introduction

Model-driven engineering (MDE) is used in many domains for software development today to improve productivity, quality, and time-to-market by using (modeling) languages and automated development activities, such as code generation or model transformations. Besides these automated activities also manual activities play a major role. This is captured by the notion of an *MDE setting* that refers to the manual and automated activities that are employed during development, the set of artifacts that are consumed or produced by these activities, the set of languages used to describe the artifacts, as well as the set of tools that allow editing used languages or implement automated activities. The artifacts that are consumed and produced lead to implicit constraints on the order of the different activities. In Model-Driven Engineering (MDE) the employed setting has major impact on productivity (e.g., on changeability [13]).

Similarly to software, MDE settings evolve over time as well. Currently only the evolution of (modeling) languages, tools, and transformations is studied in research (e.g., [12,28,2,36,15,22], or [34]). However, it is not clear whether these are the only relevant changes that characterize MDE evolution in practice. There is also no detailed knowledge about motivations for MDE evolution in practice.

In this paper we address this lack of knowledge. We first discuss the possible changes that can occur in MDE settings. Then, we report on a first study

A. Moreira et al. (Eds.): MODELS 2013, LNCS 8107, pp. 436–453, 2013.

that demonstrates that not only forms discussed in literature but all discussed forms can be commonly observed in practice. To investigate the complex nature of MDE evolution in more depth, we captured the evolution of additional three MDE settings from practice over a longer period of time and derive eight observations concerning the reasons for MDE evolution. For example, whole sequences of changes are driven by trade-offs between issues such as productivity, cost of ownership, and complexity. Based on a review of the state-of-the-art and the observations we identify open research challenge concerning MDE evolution.

The paper is organized as follows: We first discuss change types that may occur in an evolution step (Section 2). Then, we use two independent data sources (a number of industrial case studies and reports from literature) in Section 3 to reveal that all theoretically possible change types can be observed rather commonly. In Section 4, we report on three more detailed case studies addressing the evolution over a longer period and the resulting observations on the nature of MDE evolution. Finally, we provide an overview on what change types are supported by approaches in the literature (Section 5) and discuss the implications of our findings for research and practice.

2   Possible Change Types

Following we identify possible types of changes for MDE settings and discuss impacts that can be caused by these change types.

Change Types. When considering possible change types, all aspects of an MDE setting need to be taken into account. The involved technical assets are implementations of automated activities and the used (modeling) languages (including supporting tools). Both can be exchanged without affecting the order of activities or the number of elements. Therefore, we call these changes *non-structural*. We refer to exchange or evolution of an automated activity (e.g., any model operation or code generation) as change type $C1$ and to exchange or evolution of a used language as change type $C2$. Further, changes can affect the number of elements in an MDE setting. Possible changes concern the number of artifacts (referred to as $C3$), the number of languages (referred to as $C4$), the number of manual activities (referred to as $C5$), the number of automated activities (referred to as $C7$), as well as the number of tools (referred to as $C6$). The latter two changes might occur independently, since tools can support multiple automated or manual activities. Each change in the number of automated ($C7$) or manual activities ($C5$) leads to a change in the order of activities. Thereby, we call the relative positioning of automated activities within (and behind) the manual activities *order of manual and automated activities*. Only some changes in the number of manual or automated activities also change this order of manual and automated activities (e.g., an automated activity might be introduced between two manual activities). Therefore, we refer to this special case as change type $C8$. We call changes that affect the order of activities or the number of elements in an MDE setting ($C3$-$C8$) *structural changes*.

Discussion of Impact. Changing an MDE setting leads to changes for developers and a company. This can affect the *degree of automation* of development, the *complexity* of work, and the *changeability and maintainability* of the software under construction (i.e., the software that is built with an MDE setting). Further, the effort for *integration* and *maintenance of consistency* when working with different tools is affected. Finally, tools and automated activities that are used need to be maintained and, therefore, affect the *cost of ownership* for a company. Since these aspects imply potentials and risks for the productivity, we call them *productivity dimensions* in the following. Changes in an automated activity ($C1$) and changes in the number of automated activities ($C7$) can affect the *degree of automation*. Changing a used (modeling) language ($C2$) or the number of used languages ($C4$) can have benefits concerning the degree of abstraction, but yields the risk that the developers lack the know how to use that language (affecting the *complexity* of the MDE setting) [3]. Similarly, a growing number of models ($C3$), necessary manual activities ($C5$), or tools ($C6$) increases *complexity* for developers. In addition, a change in the number of models affects the need to *maintain the consistency* of different models [17]. Further, new tools can lead to additional activities to move artifacts between them (increasing the *integration effort*). As tools and implementations of automated activities have to be maintained, changes in either number of tools $C6$ or automated activities $C7$ can affect the *cost of ownership*. Finally, a main risk results from the addition of automated or manual activities if this leads to a change of the order of manual and automated activities ($C5$, $C7$, and $C8$). This can introduce constellations where automatically created artifacts are touched manually (which imply risks for *changeability and maintainability*).

To summarize, the main risks and potentials for non-structural changes concern the *degree of automation* and the *complexity* of the MDE settings. In contrast, structural changes imply some important additional risk and potentials, such as changes in the effort required to maintain consistency of all required artifacts or changes in the *cost of ownership*. Further, structural changes can have stronger effects on the different domains of productivity than non-structural changes. For example, increasing the number of used languages ($C4$) has a worse impact on the required know how than just applying changes to a used language ($C2$) in most cases. Finally, there is a group of structural changes ($C5$, $C7$, and $C8$) that can affect the *changeability and maintainability* of the software under construction. This group of changes has the potential to introduce or eliminate risky constellations from MDE settings. Therefore, we call these structural changes *substantial structural changes* in the following.

Structural Evolution. We distinguish between the terms *change*, *evolution step*, and *evolution*. A *change* is a local modification of a MDE setting, an *evolution step* combines all changes leading from an MDE setting to a next one, and *evolution* describes how an MDE setting evolves over time due to evolution steps. We call an evolution step a *structural evolution step*, if the set of changes contains at least one structural change. Similarly, we call an evolution step *substantial structural evolution step* if the set of changes contains at least one substantial structural change. We call an *evolution* that contains a least one (substantial) structural evolution step *(substantial) structural evolution.*

3   Existence and Relevance of Structural Evolution

We have discussed and categorized the possible changes to MDE settings above. However, there is currently little knowledge whether the structural changes actually occur in practice. We formulate the following hypotheses:

$H_{existence}$: *Structural and substantial structural evolution occurs in practice.*
H_{common}: *Structural and substantial structural evolution is common in practice.*

3.1   Data Collection and Analysis

To evaluate the hypotheses, data about evolution in practice is required. However, such data is rare. For making justifiable and generalizable statements we use the concept of triangulation (as described in [32]) and combine the data from two independent sources, each with its own advantages and disadvantages. As the first data source, we use data records from an exploratory and descriptive field study that we performed with the focus on capturing the structure of MDE settings in practice. The observed cases were not chosen with the topic of evolution in mind, which reduces the selection bias. However, the disadvantage of this first data set is that all case studies stem from a single company and that all data was collected by our team only. As the second data source, we use reports about MDE in practice that can be found in literature. Although a selection bias cannot be excluded for literature studies, the advantage of this data source is that it provides us with a broader spectrum of companies and domains and that the reports are captured by different research teams. Thus, the second data source does not suffer from the problems of the first data source and vice versa.

SAP Case Studies. We performed an exploratory and descriptive field study ([4]) in cooperation with SAP AG. The focus of the study was to learn about the characteristics of MDE in practice. The choice of the six captured case studies was made by our contact persons within the company. We used semi-structured interviews. In contrast to questionnaires, interviews have the advantage that misunderstandings can be better identified and compensated ([30]). This allowed us to combine the collection of complex MDE settings with more open questions about the motivations and reasons for the use of MDE techniques.

For each case study, we performed two telephone interviews, which lasted between 30 and 60 minutes each. The interviewees were developers that participated in the creation of tools for the MDE setting or used it. Between the initial and the final interview, we performed several rounds of feedback to ensure correctness of the captured data. More details about this field study can be found in [14]. As result we gained a descriptive model of each MDE setting as well as records from the more exploratory parts of the interviews.

We systematically went through these records, searching for hints or more concrete information on evolution. Where possible, we assigned concrete change types to these hints or rated them as structural or non-structural.

Literature Reports. As a second data source we performed a small meta study. We systematically searched through the proceedings of the MODELS conference from 2007 to 2011 and ECMFA, respectively ECMDA-FA conferences from 2007 to 2012, the proceedings of the Workshop on Models and Evolution ME, as well as its predecessors MCCM (Workshop on Model Co-Evolution and Consistency Management) and MoDSE (Workshop on Model-Driven Software Evolution) from 2007 to 2011, the proceedings of the OOPSLA Workshops on Domain-Specific Modeling from 2007 to 2011, as well as the Software and Systems Modeling journal (SoSyM) from 2007 to 2012, including papers published online first until end of July 2012. In addition, we performed online key word search and followed references in reviewed papers. In particular we used the ACM digital library for keyword search in the proceedings of the ICSE conference.

We searched for reports on the application of model-driven techniques or domain-specific modeling languages in practice. Note that we focused on no-purchase tool chains. We identified thirteen reports that describe MDE introduction or usage ([27,10,35,23,8,31,1,33,19,3] and three case studies in [16]). We filtered the reports to ensure that the captured period of time that is long enough to be able to observe evolution. Thus, reports that focus only on the initial introduction of MDE or on settings that were used for a single project only, were not suitable. Therefore, we excluded five reports ([35,23,8,31,1] as well as the telecom case study in [16], where the described example was only used during one project). Finally, we chose seven reports ([27,10,33,19,3], as well as the case studies of the printer company (CsP) and the car company (CsC) [16]), which stem from different domains, such as the telecommunication industry, financial organizations, and development of control systems.

Again, we systematically went through the reports and annotated hints or concrete information about evolution with change types where possible.

3.2   Threats to Validity

The two data sources provide us with information about only 13 MDE settings. Of course a bigger number of cases would allow making more accurate statements how often structural changes occur in practice. However, the fact that we use data from two different data source helps to minimize selection bias as well as biases due to corporate culture. Thus, although larger scaled empirical studies may help obtain more accurate information in future, the data is sufficient to answer the question whether structural changes are sufficiently common in practice to be a relevant object for further research.

Due to the character of the data sources, the information about change types that occurred is not necessarily complete. It is thus likely that we even underestimate the number of occurrences of structural evolution in practice.

Finally, it is questionable whether the results can be generalized for all domains of software engineering. Without having data about multiple MDE settings for each domain, it is not possible to say whether differences are specific to the setting or to the whole domain. However, due to the data from literature reports, which stem from different domains, it is possible to conclude that structural evolution is not a phenomenon that is specific to a single domain.

3.3   Data

Following, an overview about the changes identified for MDE settings from the SAP case studies and the literature reports is given (summarized in Table 1).

SAP Case Studies. For the case study Cs6, we found no hints about evolution in the records. For the case studies Cs1, Cs2, and Cs5, we found hints on evolution in the records. Such hints are often short descriptions of the improvements reached by the introduction of the current setting. For example, we recorded the statement that the development functionality now provided by one tool was split between several tools before in case study Cs2. We can thus conclude that the number of tools changed (*C6*).

For the case studies Cs3 and Cs4, we have more precise information. On the one hand, we further investigated the evolution history of the case study Cs3 later on. It is included in detail in this paper (see Section 4.4). On the other hand, our records for case study Cs4 included a more detailed description of

Table 1. Identified change types (○ = hints on changes; ● = documented changes)

| | SAP Case Studies | | | | | | Meta-Study | | | | | | |
	Cs1	Cs2	Cs3	Cs4	Cs5	Cs6	[33]	[19]	[10]	[27]	[3]	CsP [16]	CsC [16]
Changes in general	○	○	●	●	○		○	●	●	●	●	○	●
Non-Structural Changes			●	●				●	●		●		●
[C1]exchange automated activity			●	●				●	●	●			
[C2]exchange language		●						●	●		●		●
Structural Changes	○	○	●	●	○		○	●	●	●	●		
[C3]change number of artifacts			●		○			●	●	●			
[C4]change number of languages			●		○			●	●	●			
[C5]change number of manual activities			●	●	○			●	●				
[C6]change number of tools	○	○	●		○		○	●	●		●		
[C7]change number of automated activities	○	○	●	●	○		○	●	●	●	●		
[C8]change order of manual / automated activities	○		●					●	●	●			

a former version of this MDE setting. Therefore, we can use the difference to this former version to derive information about the evolution that happened. In these two cases, we also have information about non-structural evolution.

Literature Reports. In [33], the adoption of MDE in a financial organization is reported. The report ends with a note that better integration of different tools (*C6*) and more automation of the construction phase (*C7*) are planned in future.

In [19], a tool vendor reports how the language FBL together with its engineering environment changed. Starting with an editor and a code generator, they later introduced the tool function test to enable developers to debug FBL (*C6*). Thereby, the introduction of automated verification or debugging operations changes the order of manual and automated tasks. As result manual programming is followed by automated debugging and further manual correction before the automated generation is applied (*C7,C8*). Further they report on, the introduction of templates to allow programming on a higher level of abstraction. Thus, language (templates instead of FBL) and generation implementation (transformation plus generation) changed (*C1,C2*).

Fleurey et al. present a process for the migration of systems to new platforms in [10]. To apply the process it is proposed to substitute the used transformations to fit the current use case. In addition, they describe how they actually did adapt the process to apply it for the migration of a banking application. Interestingly, the changes actually applied differ strongly from the proposed changes. In this special case, it was necessary that the resulting system conforms to the development standards of the customer. Thus, it was not sufficient to produce code, but to provide corresponding models that were synchronized with the code, such that round-trip engineering on the migrated system was possible. Therefore, they replaced the code generation with an automated UML extraction. They integrated the Rational Rose code generator used by the customer to generate code skeletons out of the models (*C6*). Further, they added a generation to migrate the remaining code from the platform-independent model (extracted from the original code) into the code skeletons (*C1, C2, C3,C4*). Conforming to the round trip engineering, some manual migration tasks have to be applied to the models (*C5*). The corresponding reapplication of the Rational Rose code generation adds an additional automated step to the MDE settings (*C7*). Thus, instead of being only followed by manual migration, the automated migration is followed by manual migration activities on the Rational Rose model, a generation of code and further manual migration activities on the code (*C8*).

For the Telefónica case study in [27] it is reported that the developed DSML for the generation of configuration files was changed later on. Thereby, the verification language EVL to incrementally check the correctness of the models during development was integrated. This intermixes manual modeling activities with an automated analysis for correctness (*C7,C8*). Further, the generation of the configuration files was exchanged: the number of input models and languages changed from one to a flexible number (*C3,C4*). Also the number of manual activities changes for the developer, who creates the different DSL models (*C5*).

In [3], Baker et al. report about changing tools ($C6$) and a changing number of languages and used models ($C3$, $C4$) with the introduction of Message Sequence Charts (MSC) and SDL. Further, they report about changes in MSC ($C2$) that enabled automated generation of test cases ($C7$).

Although the report about the printer company (CsP) in [16] includes hints that the studied MDE setting changed, the information is not sufficient to make assumption about actual types of change. Similarly, the report about the car company (CsC) in [16] includes no detailed information about the actual change. However, this report informs us about a change of the used modeling language.

3.4 Summary on Hypotheses

As summarized in Table 1, all types of structural evolution and non-structural evolution that we identified in Section 2 actually occur in practice. This validates our first hypothesis $H_{existence}$. Furthermore, per data source, we found hints on structural changes for more than 70% of the MDE settings, respectively. All in all, this concerns more than three-quarter of the considered case studies. In all cases where structural changes could be identified, substantial structural changes ($C5$, $C7$, or $C8$) occurred as well. A change of the order of manual and automated activities ($C8$) occurred in 5 of 13 MDE settings (at least one third in each data source). Although a higher number than 13 case studies would allow more reliable statements about the actual relevance of structural changes, the data from both data sources supports the hypothesis that structural evolution is common (H_{common}).

4 Case Studies on Structural Evolution Steps

So far we have shown that structural changes and substantial structural changes occur commonly in practice. However, there is still a lack of knowledge about structural evolution and motivations that drive structural evolution. To address these issues, we extended our descriptive and exploratory field study to also capture information about the evolution history of MDE settings.

4.1 Data Collection and Analysis

We extended our field study from Section 3.1, such that also historical structural evolution steps where in focus[1]. Thereby, we took a conscious decision to go on with research that bases on a few detailed case studies. This form of research has some important advantages when it comes to understanding complex phenomena and their drivers. To address the new issues we changed the method of eliciting the case studies, by substituting the rounds of feedback that where performed per email with a third interview. In addition, we included questions on how the

---

[1] Project's home pages: http://www.hpi.uni-potsdam.de/giese/
projects/mde_in_practice.html?L=1

MDE settings evolved over time and asked for motivations and responsibilities for the captured changes. All captured evolution step were initiated and performed before we captured them. As result we gain models from different historical versions of the MDE settings together with records from the interviews.

We systematically went through the records and coded them following the constant comparison method described in [32]. Therefore, we started with a set of preformed codes. These codes referred to the motivation for an evolution step, the institution or role that triggered the evolution step, and the institution or role that implemented the evolution step. As we went through the records we added codes when necessary (e.g., for external influences on the evolution). Based on these codes we derived several observations.

4.2   Threats to Validity

It is always difficult to draw general conclusions from a few case studies. Thus, a broader set of data that captures more domains of software engineering and different companies would be helpful to further substantiate the outcomes of this study. Despite the small number of case studies, we are lucky that indeed different companies are under study. All observations presented here are based on at least two of the case studies, which is adequate for this initial stage of research on structural evolution in practice. The data was not only captured to study evolution but also other aspects of MDE settings in practice. It cannot be excluded that this leads to a selection bias. However, all parts of the study were observational. Therefore, we do not expect that capturing the MDE settings as explicit models influences our results on the captured evolution histories.

4.3   Case Studies

In cooperation with SAP AG, Ableton AG, and Capgemini, we captured three case studies for MDE settings that are subject to structural evolution. The SAP case study Cs3 was already chosen and captured in the initial stage of this field study. However, after extending the focus, we further investigated this case study to also capture the evolution in detail. All in all, the three case studies span 15 evolution steps. The observed structural changes are summarized in Table 2. The SAP case study was already subject to seven structural evolution steps in a period of around 6 years. The Capgemini case study was subject to seven structural evolution steps in a period of around 4 years. For the Ableton case study, we captured one structural evolution step. Due to space reasons, we only provide details for the SAP case study.

4.4   Business Object Modeling in SAP Business ByDesign

SAP Business ByDesign[2] is a hosted ERP solution for small and medium enterprises. It was built on top of a newly designed platform that has introduced

---

[2] SAP Business ByDesign http://www.sap.com/solutions/technology/cloud/
business-by-design/highlights/index.epx

Table 2. Structural evolution steps in the case studies (• = documented change)

Structural Changes	SAP (Cs3)							Ableton	Capgemini						
	S1	S2	S3	S4	S5	S6	S7		S1	S2	S3	S4	S5	S6	S7
[C3]change number of artifacts	•	•			•	•	•	•		•	•		•	•	
[C4]change number of languages	•	•	•		•	•	•	•		•	•		•		
[C5]change number of manual activities	•	•	•	•	•	•	•					•	•		
[C6]change number of tools	•	•	•	•	•	•	•			•	•	•		•	•	•
[C7]change number of automated activities	•	•	•	•	•	•	•	•		•	•	•		•	•	•
[C8]change order of manual / automated activities	•		•		•	•		•		•	•	•	•	•	•	•

numerous new architecture and modeling concepts into the development process. We focus on a very specific aspect, namely the design and implementation of *business objects*, the main building blocks of the system. Business ByDesign is primarily built using a proprietary programming language and runtime (ABAP), with a tool chain that is necessarily also largely proprietary. The ABAP infrastructure has been a major success factor for SAP, as it enables customers to modify and extend SAP's software. The origin of object modeling at SAP lies in the Data Modeler, a graphical design tool for creating entity-relationship diagrams using the SAP SERM notation. It has no generation capabilities, but as it is part of the ABAP infrastructure, it is possible to navigate directly from an entity or relationship to the implementing table (provided that the link has been manually maintained in the model).

A New Architecture. Business ByDesign is based on a modular service-oriented architecture (SOA). In this context, the Data Modeler was used as a conceptual modeling tool for designing the structural aspects of business objects. An important design goal was to provide a set of consistently designed services with harmonized signatures. The chosen solution was to make the object models available in a service repository, which was done by manually reentering them in a different tool. From there, skeletons for the business objects were generated and subsequently fleshed out manually.

S1: Code Generation (*C3 – C8*). To improve development efficiency, architects in different teams began to develop frameworks that automated and standardized the generic parts of the object implementation. This typically covered the generation of elementary services and table structures during development, but also extended to runtime libraries. The generation process used the generated skeletons as input, but required specification of additional model parameters.

To increase homogeneity in the platform, one of the frameworks was ultimately selected over the others as the mandated standard (*C4*, *C6*).

S2: Behavioral Modeling (*C3 – C7*). Business ByDesign introduced a concept called Status and Action Management (SAM) for constraining when and in which sequence basic services can be invoked on an object. The constraints were evaluated at runtime by a dedicated engine and models were created in Maestro, a proprietary, standalone (non-ABAP) tool providing a graphical editor with simulation capabilities. The goal was to make object behavior more transparent and to ensure correctness of the implementation by eliminating the need to manually write checks for preconditions.

S3: Model Integration (*C2*, *C4 – C8*). Conceptual SOA modeling was done in ARIS, a commercial business modeling tool, using a custom visual DSL. As many of these models contained references to business objects, it seemed advantageous to consolidate the conceptual models and move the detailed design of object structure and data types into ARIS, eliminating the potential for inconsistencies. While this move further severed the link between model and implementation, it enabled additional validation activities in ARIS.

S4: Model Quality (*C5*, *C6*, *C7*). To meet external quality standards, it became necessary to demonstrably *prove* that models in ARIS and the service repository were consistent. Therefore, an infrastructure for replicating models from ARIS into the system hosting the service repository was created. This allowed cross-checking manually created content against the replicated conceptual models. The introduction of the checks revealed how strongly conceptual modeling and implementation frameworks had evolved in different directions.

S5: A New Infrastructure (*C3 – C8*). Several releases later, development efficiency and total cost of ownership became a major focus while the importance of conceptual modeling declined. In a bold move, ARIS, Maestro, and the service repository were eliminated and replaced by a new metadata repository that was built using the business object runtime infrastructure itself. The new repository was closer to the implementation and provided a *single source of truth* by consolidating multiple tools and databases. However, this also came at a cost. There initially were no graphical modeling capabilities, the ability to simulate status models was lost, and the modeling of design alternatives or future evolutions of existing objects was not supported.

S6: A Simpler Alternative (*C1 – C8*). In parallel with the new repository, a new Visual Studio-based tool targeting third-party developers was developed, allowing them to define and program business objects using a script language. As its focus was simplicity, the supported feature set was reduced. In return, the editor acts as a facade that completely hides the underlying tools from the user, thus allowing for very efficient development – within the set limits.

S7: Optimization (*C3 – C7*). Finally, the latest release has brought a redesign of the underlying frameworks. The motivation for this was primarily runtime efficiency, as the existing set of independently developed frameworks proved to generate a significant overhead in their interactions. It was therefore decided to merge features such as Status and Action Management directly into the business object runtime, which was in turn made an integral part of the basic service infrastructure. For the first time, all modeling activities for business objects were gathered in a single tool.

The history of business object development provides multiple examples for structural changes to the development process. The case study illustrates how the weight given to different productivity dimension changes. While initially automation was the key driver of the change (*S1*), the reduction of cost of ownership became more important later on (*S5*). Finally, this case study shows that a sequence of structural evolution steps with changing priorities can transform even a code-centric development approach into a complex MDE setting.

4.5   Observations

The case studies provide us with some observations on the occurrence and combination of evolution steps based on the documented data (*O1* - *O3*). In addition, we derived observations on motivations and drivers for structural evolution from the coded records of the interviews (*O4* - *O8*).

O1: Structural evolution steps are not necessarily exceptions, but can occur in sequence several times (e.g., SAP and Capgemini case studies).

O2: Structural evolution steps are most often combinations of multiple different structural changes (see Table 2).

O3: Substantial structural changes occur in a major part of observed structural evolution steps. We observed change type *C8* in 10 of the 15 evolution steps of our case studies. A minor observation in that context is that just one of the occurrences of *C8* was caused by improving an existing automated activity such that a manual activity was no longer necessary (*C5*). In most cases *C8* was caused by the introduction of additional automated activities (*C7*).

O4: Structural changes are often trade-offs, e.g. w.r.t costs and manageability. For example, implementing a smaller new generation step is easier to manage than applying a change to an existing automated activity. A further factor in such a trade-off is the weight that is given to the different productivity dimensions. In many of the observed cases it was decided to increase the *degree of automation* or tool support by adding new automated activities instead of adapting existing automated activities like transformation steps. Thus, a substantial structural change that might lead to drawbacks for the changeability is accepted in favor of costs and manageability of the structural evolution step.

O5: The factors involved in such trade-offs change over time. For example, costs that can be invested in a change can differ strongly. We even captured cases where developers implemented evolution steps in their leisure time. The weight that is given to different productivity dimensions can also change. For example, while evolution step *S1* in the SAP case study was mainly driven by the desire to increase the *degree of automation*, a priority that led to evolution step *S5* was the desire to decrease *cost of ownership* and *complexity* by decreasing the number of involved tools (see Section 4.4).

O6: Changes in an MDE setting can be driven by the need to take other MDE settings into account (e.g., the evolution in [10] or evolution steps *S3* and *S5* in the Capgemini case study). This can happen, when models or other artifacts in software development are supplied by one company and used the other. Then changes in the MDE setting of one company can lead to new opportunities for integration of both settings.

O7: Some evolution steps are motivated by preceding evolution steps. They reduce the complexity of MDE settings, which can be considered as 'refactoring', after several preceding evolution steps were applied. An example of this is the introduction of the new repository in business object development (evolution step *S5* in the SAP case study).

O8: Some evolution steps are not planned centrally, but are caused by developers who add automation steps to ease their daily work. Examples are evolution steps *S4* and *S6* in the Capgemini case study as well as the solutions added for code generation in evolution step *S1* in the SAP case study (see Section 4.4).

5   Literature on Support for Evolution

Below, an overview is given how evolution of languages, tools, or transformations is addressed in literature (summarized in Table 3). First there are approaches that support specific changes of model operations (*C1*), e.g., MDPE workbench ([11,27]) capsules the application of an extensible set of performance analysis techniques on models. Another example for a specific supported change is the MasterCraft code generator presented in [20]. The generator is built such that it can easily be configured to implement architectural decisions taken within a project. Other approaches address the change of automated activities in a more general form. For example, in [21], a method for incremental development of a transformation chain is discussed and Yie et al. [36] approach the adaption of a fully automated transformation chain. Both approaches work for automated activities that are implemented in form of a transformation chain.

Some approaches deal with language evolution and migration of models, such that they become valid for a new version of the language (*C2*). For example, in [12] the differences between two metamodels are used to generate a transformation that migrates the corresponding models. Further examples are the Modif metamodel [2], Model Change Language (MCL) [28], or the usage of higher-order model transformations for metamode model co-evolution ([6,26,5]). All these approaches only address the evolution of modeling languages.

Some MDE approaches expect specific simultaneous changes of used languages and transformations. For example, the OMG's MDA [29] and the migration process presented in [10] expect exchange of languages and transformations to address a new target platform for a software system.

Other approaches deal with systematically adapting transformations according to language evolution (*C1* and *C2*). For example, in [15] a systematic strategy and in [22] semi-automated support for the adaption of the model transformation according to changes in a metamodel are proposed. Vermolen et al. lift the semi-automated adaption of transformations to modeling languages on a more technology-independent layer by allowing also migrations of programming languages or data structures [34]. Meyers et al. subdivide metamodel- and model evolution into four primitive scenarios, describing how evolution of models, metamodels, or transformations enforces co-evolution among each other [25,24]. The resulting scenarios are combinations of the change types *C1* and *C2*.

Finally, there are approaches that lead to an addition of input models to an automated activity, which is exchanged or evolved. Specific side effects are an increasing number of models (*C3*) and potentially modeling languages (*C4*). Further, in most cases the introduction of a new input model leads to an additional manual modeling activity for creating this new model (*C5*). An example is presented in [18], where a system of DSLs that are used in combination can be extended due to the hierarchical structure of the DSLs. Similarly, in [9] a modifiable interpreter is presented. Here a composition model is used to define how different domain-specific models are related.

To summarize, none of the approaches provides support for substantial structural evolution and support for structural evolution that is not substantial is provided by two approaches for specific changes only. This is also reflected by the focus of change classifications in literature about MDE. For example in [7], change types *C1* and *C2* are categorized more in detail.

Table 3. Supported and used change types in literature (. = specific changes covered; o = approach provides solution with assumptions on the language or implementation to be changed; • = approach with a general coverage of the change type)

Kind of Changes\Approaches	[27] [20]	[21] [36]	[12] [2] [26]	[28] [6] [5]	[29] [10]	[15] [22]	[34]	[25] [24]	[18]	[9]
Non-Structural Changes										
[*C1*]exchange automated activity	.	o		.	.	.		o	o	o
[*C2*]exchange language			o	.	o		•	o		o
Structural Changes										
[*C3*]change number of artifacts									.	.
[*C4*]change number of languages									.	.
[*C5*]change number of manual activities									.	.
[*C6*]change number of tools										
[*C7*]change number of automated activities										
[*C8*]change order of manual / automated activities										

6 Conclusion and Implications

In this paper we report on two studies that we performed on the occurrence of structural evolution of MDE settings. The results revealed that all identified types of structural evolution actually commonly occur in practice. Further, we made a set of interesting observations about the way structural changes are combined in the same or subsequent evolution steps and on the trade-offs behind and motivations for structural evolution. An overview of literature surprisingly showed that only rare special cases of structural evolution are so far addressed by researchers. This indicates that there is still a lack of knowledge and support for evolution of MDE settings in practice. To conclude, we discuss what implications for research and practice arise from our results.

Implications for Research: The observations O1, O2, and O3 indicate that properties of an MDE setting, like its support for changeability, might be changed in complex ways multiple times. Consequently, methods and techniques to actively plan steer evolution into the right direction are necessary.

This situation is reinforced by the fact that evolution seems to be poorly predictable. As observations O4 and O5 indicate, the needs on an MDE setting change over time due to organizational factors. Further, external changes, e.g., in other MDE settings, might lead to new unexpected opportunities or forces (O6). Consequently, it is also almost impossible to predict a set of possible versions of the MDE setting which might be used for an upfront evaluation. Therefore, research needs to provide a better understanding how MDE settings influence productivity factors like the degree of automation, costs of ownership, changeability, and maintainability. Techniques are required that allow analyzing these influences. Such techniques can then be used by practitioners to predict risks when balancing trade-offs to plan the next evolution step.

Observation O7 indicates that there is a need for manageability, which indicates that research needs to support the identification of potentials for refactoring MDE settings. Further, we need to collect best practices for implementing new requirements on MDE settings, such that for example the extent of structural changes can be reduced. E.g., frameworks for combining and extending DSLs, like the one presented in [18], might be a first step in this direction.

Implications for Practice: Observation O8 indicates that sometimes developers trigger and implement evolution steps on their own initiative. Considering the risks and potential that are associated with substantial structural changes, methods and techniques are required that permit to identify the cause of currently observed problems and estimate the impact of planned changes. Also a proper management of the change requests has to be established such that developers can contribute to improve MDE settings with their know-how without the risk of uncoordinated and inefficient evolution.

Acknowledgments. We are grateful to the participants of our studies with SAP, Ableton, and Capgemini. Especially we want to thank Axel Uhl, Cafer Tosun, Gregor Engels, and Marion Kremer for their support in choosing the case studies and for making this research possible. Further we thank the HPI Research School on Service-Oriented Systems Engineering for funding parts of this research.

References

1. Aschauer, T., Dauenhauer, G., Pree, W.: A modeling language's evolution driven by tight interaction between academia and industry. In: Proceedings of the 32nd ACM/IEEE International Conference on Software Engineering, ICSE 2010, vol. 2, pp. 49–58. ACM, New York (2010)
2. Babau, J.-P., Kerboeuf, M.: Domain Specific Language Modeling Facilities. In: Proceedings of the 5th MoDELS Workshop on Models and Evolution, Wellington, Nouvelle-Zélande, pp. 1–6 (October 2011)
3. Baker, P., Loh, S., Weil, F.: Model-Driven Engineering in a Large Industrial Context — Motorola Case Study. In: Briand, L.C., Williams, C. (eds.) MoDELS 2005. LNCS, vol. 3713, pp. 476–491. Springer, Heidelberg (2005)
4. Basili, V.R.: The role of experimentation in software engineering: past, current, and future. In: Proceedings of the 18th International Conference on Software Engineering, ICSE 1996. IEEE Computer Society, Washington, DC (1996)
5. van den Brand, M., Protić, Z., Verhoeff, T.: A Generic Solution for Syntax-Driven Model Co-evolution. In: Bishop, J., Vallecillo, A. (eds.) TOOLS 2011. LNCS, vol. 6705, pp. 36–51. Springer, Heidelberg (2011)
6. Cicchetti, A., Ruscio, D.D., Eramo, R., Pierantonio, A.: Automating Co-evolution in Model-Driven Engineering. In: Proceedings of the 2008 12th International IEEE Enterprise Distributed Object Computing Conference, pp. 222–231. IEEE Computer Society, Washington, DC (2008)
7. Corrêa, C.K.F., Oliveira, T.C., Werner, C.M.L.: An analysis of change operations to achieve consistency in model-driven software product lines. In: Proceedings of the 15th International Software Product Line Conference, SPLC 2011, vol. 2, pp. 24:1–24:4. ACM, New York (2011)
8. Deng, G., Lu, T., Turkay, E., Gokhale, A., Schmidt, D.C., Nechypurenko, A.: Model Driven Development of Inventory Tracking System (2003)
9. Estublier, J., Vega, G., Ionita, A.D.: Composing Domain-Specific Languages for Wide-Scope Software Engineering Applications. In: Briand, L.C., Williams, C. (eds.) MoDELS 2005. LNCS, vol. 3713, pp. 69–83. Springer, Heidelberg (2005)
10. Fleurey, F., Breton, E., Baudry, B., Nicolas, A., Jézéquel, J.-M.: Model-Driven Engineering for Software Migration in a Large Industrial Context. In: Engels, G., Opdyke, B., Schmidt, D.C., Weil, F. (eds.) MODELS 2007. LNCS, vol. 4735, pp. 482–497. Springer, Heidelberg (2007)
11. Fritzsche, M., Johannes, J.: Putting Performance Engineering into Model-Driven Engineering: Model-Driven Performance Engineering. In: Giese, H. (ed.) MODELS 2008. LNCS, vol. 5002, pp. 164–175. Springer, Heidelberg (2008)
12. Garcés, K., Jouault, F., Cointe, P., Bézivin, J.: Managing Model Adaptation by Precise Detection of Metamodel Changes. In: Paige, R.F., Hartman, A., Rensink, A. (eds.) ECMDA-FA 2009. LNCS, vol. 5562, pp. 34–49. Springer, Heidelberg (2009)
13. Hebig, R., Gabrysiak, G., Giese, H.: Towards Patterns for MDE-Related Processes to Detect and Handle Changeability Risks. In: Proceedings of the 2012 International Conference on on Software and Systems Process (2012)
14. Hebig, R., Giese, H.: MDE Settings in SAP. A Descriptive Field Study. Tech. Rep. 58, Hasso-Plattner Institut at the University of Potsdam (2012)

15. Herrmannsdoerfer, M., Ratiu, D., Wachsmuth, G.: Language Evolution in Practice: The History of GMF. In: van den Brand, M., Gašević, D., Gray, J. (eds.) SLE 2009. LNCS, vol. 5969, pp. 3–22. Springer, Heidelberg (2010)

16. Hutchinson, J., Rouncefield, M., Whittle, J.: Model-driven engineering practices in industry. In: Proceeding of the 33rd International Conference on Software Engineering, ICSE 2011, pp. 633–642. ACM, Waikiki (2011)

17. Hutchinson, J., Whittle, J., Rouncefield, M., Kristoffersen, S.: Empirical assessment of MDE in industry. In: Proceeding of the 33rd International Conference on Software Engineering, ICSE 2011, pp. 471–480. ACM, New York (2011)

18. Johannes, J., Fernández, M.A.: Adding Abstraction and Reuse to a Network Modelling Tool Using the Reuseware Composition Framework. In: Kühne, T., Selic, B., Gervais, M.-P., Terrier, F. (eds.) ECMFA 2010. LNCS, vol. 6138, pp. 132–143. Springer, Heidelberg (2010)

19. Karaila, M.: Evolution of a Domain Specific Language and its engineering environment – Lehman's laws revisited. In: Proceedings of the 9th OOPSLA Workshop on Domain-Specific Modeling (2009)

20. Kulkarni, V., Barat, S., Ramteerthkar, U.: Early Experience with Agile Methodology in a Model-Driven Approach. In: Whittle, J., Clark, T., Kühne, T. (eds.) MODELS 2011. LNCS, vol. 6981, pp. 578–590. Springer, Heidelberg (2011)

21. Küster, J.M., Gschwind, T., Zimmermann, O.: Incremental Development of Model Transformation Chains Using Automated Testing. In: Schürr, A., Selic, B. (eds.) MODELS 2009. LNCS, vol. 5795, pp. 733–747. Springer, Heidelberg (2009)

22. Levendovszky, T., Balasubramanian, D., Narayanan, A., Karsai, G.: A Novel Approach to Semi-automated Evolution of DSML Model Transformation. In: van den Brand, M., Gašević, D., Gray, J. (eds.) SLE 2009. LNCS, vol. 5969, pp. 23–41. Springer, Heidelberg (2010)

23. Mansurov, N., Campara, D.: Managed Architecture of Existing Code as a Practical Transition Towards MDA. In: Jardim Nunes, N., Selic, B., Rodrigues da Silva, A., Toval Alvarez, A. (eds.) UML 2004 Satellite Activities. LNCS, vol. 3297, pp. 219–233. Springer, Heidelberg (2005)

24. Meyers, B., Mannadiar, R., Vangheluwe, H.: Evolution of Modelling Languages. In: 8th BElgian-NEtherlands Software eVOLution Seminar, BENEVOL (2009)

25. Meyers, B., Vangheluwe, H.: A framework for evolution of modelling languages. Science of Computer Programming, Special Issue on Software Evolution, Adaptability and Variability 76(12), 1223–1246 (2011)

26. Meyers, B., Wimmer, M., Cicchetti, A., Sprinkle, J.: A generic in-place transformation-based approach to structured model co-evolution. In: Proceedings of the 4th International Workshop on Multi-Paradigm Modeling (MPM 2010) @ MoDELS 2010. Electronic Communications of the EASST (2010)

27. Mohagheghi, P., Gilani, W., Stefanescu, A., Fernandez, M., Nordmoen, B., Fritzsche, M.: Where does model-driven engineering help? Experiences from three industrial cases. Software and Systems Modeling

28. Narayanan, A., Levendovszky, T., Balasubramanian, D., Karsai, G.: Automatic Domain Model Migration to Manage Metamodel Evolution. In: Schürr, A., Selic, B. (eds.) MODELS 2009. LNCS, vol. 5795, pp. 706–711. Springer, Heidelberg (2009)

29. Object Management Group: MDA Guide Version 1.0.1 (June 2003)

30. Runeson, P., Host, M., Ohlsson, M.C.: Experimentation in Software Engineering : An Introduction. Kluwer Academic Publishers (November 1999)
31. Sadovykh, A., Vigier, L., Gomez, E., Hoffmann, A., Grossmann, J., Estekhin, O.: On Study Results: Round Trip Engineering of Space Systems. In: Paige, R.F., Hartman, A., Rensink, A. (eds.) ECMDA-FA 2009. LNCS, vol. 5562, pp. 265–276. Springer, Heidelberg (2009)
32. Seaman, C.: Qualitative methods in empirical studies of software engineering. IEEE Transactions on Software Engineering 25(4), 557–572 (1999)
33. Shirtz, D., Kazakov, M., Shaham-Gafni, Y.: Adopting model driven development in a large financial organization. In: Akehurst, D.H., Vogel, R., Paige, R.F. (eds.) ECMDA-FA. LNCS, vol. 4530, pp. 172–183. Springer, Heidelberg (2007)
34. Vermolen, S., Visser, E.: Heterogeneous Coupled Evolution of Software Languages. In: Czarnecki, K., Ober, I., Bruel, J.-M., Uhl, A., Völter, M. (eds.) MODELS 2008. LNCS, vol. 5301, pp. 630–644. Springer, Heidelberg (2008)
35. Vogel, R.: Practical case study of MDD infusion in a SME: Final Results. In: Tamzalit, D., Deridder, D., Schätz, B. (eds.) Models and Evolution Joint MODELS 2009 Workshop on Model-Driven Software Evolution (MoDSE) and Model Co-Evolution and Consistency Management (MCCM), pp. 68–78 (2009)
36. Yie, A., Casallas, R., Wagelaar, D., Deridder, D.: An Approach for Evolving Transformation Chains. In: Schürr, A., Selic, B. (eds.) MODELS 2009. LNCS, vol. 5795, pp. 551–555. Springer, Heidelberg (2009)

Simplification and Correctness of UML Class Diagrams – Focusing on Multiplicity and Aggregation/Composition Constraints

Mira Balaban[1,*] and Azzam Maraee[1,2,**]

[1] Computer Science Department, Ben-Gurion University of the Negev, Israel
[2] Deutsche Telekom Laboratories, Ben-Gurion University of the Negev, Israel
{mari,mira}@cs.bgu.ac.il

Abstract. Model-driven Engineering requires efficient powerful methods for verifying model correctness and quality. Class Diagram is the central language within UML. Its main problems involve *correctness* problems, which include the *consistency* and the *finite satisfiability* problems, and *quality* problems, which include the *redundancy* and *incomplete design* problems. Two central constraints in class diagrams are the *multiplicity* and the *aggregation/composition* constraints. They are essential in modeling configuration management, features, biology, computer-aided design and database systems.

The contribution of this paper involves efficient algorithms for tightening multiplicity constraints that cannot be realized, and for identification of correctness problems that are caused by aggregation/composition constraints. The algorithms are analyzed, and their soundness and completeness properties are proved. We show that these constraints are inter-related, and that the combination of these algorithms strengthens their results.

1 Introduction

The central role of models in the emerging *Model-driven Engineering* approach calls for deep formal study of models, so that tools can provide an inclusive support to users. It is essential to have precise, consistent and correct models. Models should provide reliable support for the designed systems, and be subject to stringent quality verification and control criteria.

Class Diagrams are probably the most important and best understood model among all UML models. The Class Diagrams language allows complex constraints on its components. But the interaction among these constraints can create correctness and quality problems that users cannot observe without some assistance. For example, the class diagram in Figure 1 includes (redundant) multiplicity constraints that cannot be realized, i.e., are not used in any legal

---

* Supported in part by the Paul Ivanir Center for Robotics and Production Management at Ben- Gurion University of the Negev.
** Supported by the Lynn and William Frankel Center for Computer Sciences.

A. Moreira et al. (Eds.): MODELS 2013, LNCS 8107, pp. 454–470, 2013.

instance. The interaction of the multiplicity constraints on the association cycle r_1, r_2, r_3 entails that the minimum multiplicity constraints on the properties (association ends) p_1, p_3, p_6 and the maximum multiplicity constraints on the properties p_2, p_4, p_5 are not exploited in any legal instance, and therefore are redundant. Figure 1b presents an equivalent class diagram without redundancy of multiplicity constraints: All multiplicity constraints are either raised to meet the corresponding maximum, or decreased to meet the corresponding minimum. In order to develop tool support for class diagrams there is a need for a formal detailed study of the constraints and their interactions.

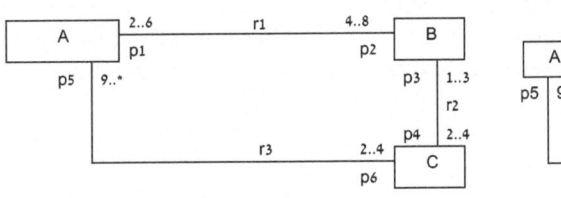 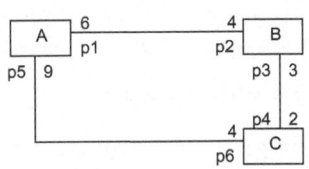

(a) A class diagram with redundant multiplicity constraints

(b) A tight class diagram

Fig. 1. Class diagram with redundant multiplicity constraint and its tightened equivalent version

This paper focuses on two central constraints that are imposed on properties in class diagrams: *Multiplicity* and *aggregation/composition* constraints. They are heavily used in modeling configuration management, features, biology, computer-aided design and database systems. Multiplicity constraints restrict the number of objects of one class that can be associated with an object from another class. Aggregation/composition constraints specify whole-part relationships between an object (the assembly) to its parts (the components).

Correctness of class diagrams has been studied in quite a few works, but there is very little research on class-diagram constraints [1–5]. This paper continues our previous work [4, 6, 7, 3], and presents efficient algorithms for (1) tightening multiplicity constraints that cannot be realized; (2) identification of correctness problems that are caused by aggregation/composition constraints. The algorithms are analyzed, and their soundness and completeness properties are proved. We show that these constraints are inter-related, and that the combination of these algorithms strengthens their results.

Section 2 formally defines the UML class diagram model. Section 3 presents a method for tightening multiplicity constraints. Section 4 presents methods for identification incorrectness caused by aggregation/composition constraints. Section 5 shortly surveys related work and Section 6 concludes the paper.

2 Background

2.1 Abstract Syntax and Semantics of Class Diagrams

The subset of UML2.0 class diagrams considered in this paper includes *classes* (without attributes), *properties* (association-ends), *binary associations*, and the constraints *multiplicity, aggregation, composition, class hierarchy, generalization set (GS)* and *subsetting*. The formulation is based on the meta-model notion of *Property* [8, 9]. The semantics is set-theoretic.

Abstract Syntax: A class diagram is a tuple $\langle \mathcal{C}, \mathcal{P}, \mathcal{A}, \mathcal{M}, \mathcal{M}appings, \mathcal{R}elations \rangle$, where $\mathcal{C}$ is a set of *class* symbols, $\mathcal{P}$ is a set of *property* (*association end*) symbols, $\mathcal{A}$ is a set of *association* symbols, and $\mathcal{M}$ is a set of *multiplicity* symbols.

The $\mathcal{M}$**appings Are:**

- **Property mappings:**
  1. *inverse* : $\mathcal{P} \rightarrow \mathcal{P}$ is a bijective mapping, that assigns to every property p its unique inverse, denoted p^{-1}. It satisfies: $invers = invers^{-1}$ and for every property p, $inverse(p) \neq p$.
  2. *source*: $\mathcal{P} \rightarrow \mathcal{C}$ and *target*: $\mathcal{P} \rightarrow \mathcal{C}$ are injections of properties to classes such that for a property $p \in \mathcal{P}$, $target(p) = source(p^{-1})$. In Figure 1a, p_1 is p_2^{-1}, $target(p_2) = source(p_1) = B$, and $source(p_2) = target(p_1) = A$.
- **Association mapping:** *props*: $\mathcal{A} \rightarrow \mathcal{P} \times \mathcal{P}$ is an injection that satisfies $props(a) = \langle p, p^{-1} \rangle$ (arbitrary ordering). Notation: $assoc(p_1)$ or $assoc(p_1, p_2)$ (where $p_2 = p_1^{-1}$) denote the association of p_1 or of $\langle p_1, p_2 \rangle$, and $props_1(a)$, $props_2(a)$ (arbitrary ordering) denote the two properties of a. Note that for a property p, $assoc(p)$ is unique. In Figure 1a, $props(r_1) = \langle p_1, p_2 \rangle$ and $assoc(p_1) = assoc(p_2) = assoc(p_1, p_2) = r_1$.
- **Multiplicity mappingss:**
  1. *mul*: $\mathcal{P} \rightarrow \mathcal{M} \times \mathcal{M}$ is an assignment of two multiplicities to every property symbol, where the first denotes the *minimum multiplicity*, and the second denotes the *maximum multiplicity*.
  2. *val*: $\mathcal{M} \rightarrow \mathbb{N} \cup \{0\} \cup \{*\}$ is an assignment of values to multiplicities. A compact notation for the values of the multiplicities of a property: $minMul(p) = val(mul(p)_1)$, $maxMul(p) = val(mul(p)_2)$.
  For simplicity we use a compact symbolic notation that captures all symbols related to an association. For example, the association r_1 in figure 1a is denoted $r_1(p_1 : A[2..6], \; p_2 : B[4..8])$.

The $\mathcal{R}$**elations Are:**

- **Aggregation and Composition:** Predicates on $\mathcal{P}$, such that composition is a refinement of aggregation, i.e., for $p \in \mathcal{P}$, $composition(p) \Rightarrow aggregation(p)$. Aggregate/composite properties are denoted p^a and p^c respectively. Visually, aggregate/composition properties are marked by diamonds, with an empty diamond for aggregation and a solid diamond for composition.

- **Class-hierarchy:** A non-circular binary relationship $\prec$ on the set of class symbols: $\prec\ \subseteq\ \mathcal{C} \times \mathcal{C}$. Henceforth $C_2 \prec C_1$, stands for C_2 is a subclass of C_1. $\prec^*$ is the transitive closure of $\prec$, and $C_2 \preceq^* C_1$ stands for $C_2 = C_1$ or $C_2 \prec^* C_1$.
- **Generalization-set:** An $(n+1)$-ary $n \geq 2$ relationship on $\mathcal{C}$. Its elements $\langle C, C_1, \ldots, C_n \rangle$, called *GS* constraints, must satisfy: For $i, j = 1..n$ (1) $C \neq C_i$; (2) $C_i \neq C_j$; (3) $C_i \prec C$. C is called the *superclass* and the C_i-s are called the *subclasses*. *GS* constraints may be associated with *disjoint/overlapping* and *complete/incomplete* constraints. A *GS* constraint is denoted $GS(C, C_1, \ldots, C_n; Const)$.
- **Subsetting:** A binary relation $\prec$ [1] on the set of property symbols: $\prec\ \subseteq\ \mathcal{P} \times \mathcal{P}$. $p_1 \prec p_2$, stands for "p_1 subsets p_2", where p_1 is *the subsetting property*, and p_2 is *the subsetted property*. The UML specification requires that $source(p_1) \prec^* source(p_2)$, $target(p_1) \prec^* target(p_2)$ and $maxMul(p_1) \leq maxMul(p_2)$. As for class hierarchies, $\prec^*$ is the transitive closure of $\prec$, and $p_1 \preceq^* p_2$ stands for $p_1 = p_2$ or $p_1 \prec^* p_2$.

Semantics: The standard set theoretic semantics of class diagrams associates a class diagram with *instances I*, that have a semantic domain and an *extension mapping*, that associates syntactic symbols with elements over the semantic domain. Classes are mapped to sets of objects in the domain, and associations are mapped to relationships between these sets. The denotation of classes and associations are called *extensions*. For a symbol x, x^I is its denotation in I.

Symbol Denotation

1. **Classes:** For $C \in \mathcal{C}$, C^I, the extension of C in I, is a set of elements in the semantic domain. The elements of class extensions are called *objects*.
2. **Properties:** For $p \in \mathcal{P}$, p^I is a multi-valued function from its source class to its target class: $p^I : source(p)^I \rightarrow target(p)^I$.
3. **Associations:** For $a \in \mathcal{A}$, a^I is a binary relationship on the extensions of the classes of a. If $props(a) = \langle p_1, p_2 \rangle$, then p_1^I and p_2^I are restricted to be inverse functions of each other: $p_1^I = (p_2^I)^{-1}$. The association denotes all object pairs that are related by its properties: $a^I = \{(e, e') \mid e \in target(p_1)^I,\ e' \in target(p_2)^I,\ p_2^I(e) = e'\}$. Elements of association extensions are *links*.

Constraints

1. **Multiplicity Constraints:** For every $e \in source(p)^I$, $minMul(p) \leq |p^I(e)| \leq maxMul(p)$. The upper bound is ignored if $maxMul(p) = *$.
2. **Aggregation Constraints:** Aggregation denotes *part-whole* relationships. Therefore, cycles of aggregated objects are not allowed: For aggregation properties $p_1^a, \ldots, p_n^a$, such that $target(p_i^a) = source(p_{i+1}^a), i = 1, n - 1$, if $e \in source(p_1^a)^I$, then $e \notin p_n^{a\,I}(p_{n-1}^{a\,I}(\ldots(p_1^{a\,I}(e))))$.

---

[1] We use the same symbol as for class hierarchy. Distinction is made by context.

3. **Composition Constraints:** A composition is an aggregation which is not multi-valued, and satisfies the *Multi-composition* constraint:
   For composite properties p^c, q^c such that $source(p^c) = source(q^c)$, $e \in source(p^c)^I$ implies that either $p^c(e) = q^c(e)$ or there are properties $p = p_1^c, \ldots, p_n^c$, such that $target(p_i^c) = source(p_{i+1}^c), i = 1, n-1$, and
   $$p_n^{c\,I}(p_{n-1}^{c\,I}(\ldots(p_1^{c\,I}(e)))) = q^c(e).$$

4. **Class-hierarchy Constraints:** A constraint $C_1 \prec C_2$ denotes a subset relations between the class extension: ${C_1}^I \subseteq {C_2}^I$.

5. **GS Constraints** have the following meaning: *disjoint:* $C_i^I \cap C_j^I = \emptyset, \forall i, j$; *overlapping:* For some i, j, it might be $C_i^I \cap C_j^I \neq \emptyset$; *complete:* $C^I = \bigcup_{i=1}^{n} C_i^I$; *incomplete:* $\bigcup_{i=1}^{n} C_i^I \subseteq C^I$.

6. **Subsetting Constraint:** For $p_1, p_2 \in \mathcal{P}$, $p_1 \prec p_2$ states that p_1 is a sub-mapping of p_2, i.e., for $e \in source(p_1)^I$, ${p_1}^I(e) \subseteq {p_2}^I(e)$.

A *legal instance* of a class diagram is an instance that satisfies all constraints; it is empty if all class extensions are empty, and is infinite if some class extension is not finite. Class diagrams CD, CD' are *equivalent*, denoted $CD \equiv CD'$, if they have the same legal instances.

2.2   Semantic Problems in Class Diagrams

This paper focuses on the problem of multiplicity constraint redundancy as shown in Figure 1a, and on two *correctness* problems: *consistency* [10] and *finite satisfiability* [3].

Consistency deals with necessarily empty classes, and finite satisfiability deals with necessarily empty or infinite classes. Figure 2a presents a consistency problem due to the interaction between the *subsetting* constraint on property p_1, and the two composition constraints. The multiplicity and the *subsetting* constraints on p_1 imply that in a legal instance I every object of D^I is a component of two different objects (of B^I and C^I), in violation to the multi-composition constraint. Therefore the class diagram is inconsistent.

Figure 2b shows a finite satisfiability problem due to the interaction between its multiplicity and composition constraints. The multiplicity constraints on p_1, q_2 imply that in every legal instance I, either C_1^I, C_2^I are infinite or they include a cycle of linked objects. But since p_1, q_2 are composition properties the no aggregation/composition object cycle constraint is violated. Therefore, a legal instance must be empty or infinite.

3   Identification of Redundancy Problems Caused by Non Tight Multiplicity Constraints

This section presents a method for tightening multiplicity constraints so that they specify only realizable multiplicity values. Following [11, 3, 7], the method is based on construction of a directed graph with labeled edges, whose nodes

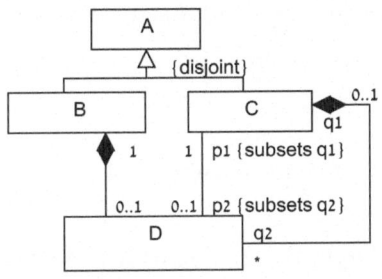
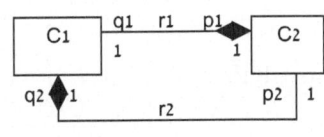

(a) A class diagram with a consistency problem

(b) A class diagram with a finite
satisfiability problem

Fig. 2. Class diagrams with finite satisfiability and consistency problems

represent classes, and edges represent multiplicity constraints between them. The method identifies cycles in the graph, whose edges correspond to redundant multiplicity constraints, and suggests how to tighten these constraints.

Definition 1 (Tight Property and Tight Class Diagram)

1. *A property p is tight if for m being one of its multiplicity constraints, i.e., $minMul(p)$ or $maxMul(p)$, there exists an instance I and an object $e \in source(p)^I$, such that $|p^I(e)| = m$.*
2. *A class diagram is tight if all of its properties are tight.*

Algorithm 1. *Identification Graph Construction*

Input: A class diagram CD
Output: A directed graph, $graph(CD)$, with labeled edges.
begin
    1. Initialize $graph(CD)$ by a node $n(C)$ for every class C.
    2. For every association $a(p_1 : C_1[min_1, max_1], p_2 : C_2[min_2, max_2])$
       connect nodes $n(C_1), n(C_2)$ by an edge labeled $\langle p_1, p_2 \rangle$ directed from
       $n(C_1)$ to $n(C_2)$, and a dual edge labeled $\langle p_2, p_1 \rangle$ directed from $n(C_2)$ to
       $n(C_1)$. For a label $\langle p, q \rangle$, if $maxMul(q) = *$ or $minMul(p) = 0$, drop
       the edge.
    3. For every class hierarchy constraint $C_1 \prec C_2$, connect nodes $n(C_1), n(C_2)$
       by an edge labeled 1 from $n(C_1)$ to $n(C_2)$.
    4. For every GS constraint $G = GS(C, C_1, \ldots, C_n; const)$, create edges
       for the n class hierarchy constraints $C_i \prec C$, for $i = 1..n$.

end

For an edge e and path π in $graph(CD)$, their source and target nodes are denoted $source(e)$, $target(e)$, $source(\pi)$ and $target(\pi)$, respectively.

Definition 2 (Edge and Path Weights)

1. *The weight of an edge e in $graph(CD)$, with label $\langle p, q \rangle$, is denoted $weight(e)$ and defined as $weight(e) = \frac{maxMul(q)}{minMul(p)}$. For an edge e with label 1 (derived from an hierarchy constraints), $weight(e) = label(e) = 1$.*

2. *The weight of a path* $\pi = e_1, \ldots, e_n$ *in graph(CD) is denoted weight(π) and defined as* $weight(\pi) = \prod\limits_{i=1}^{n} weight(e_i)$.

In [11, 3, 7] it is shown:

Proposition 1. *For every non-empty finite legal instance I of CD: For every path π in graph(CD),* $\frac{|target(\pi)^I|}{|source(\pi)^I|} \leq weight(\pi)$.

In particular, the claim applies to edges in the graph. For a cycle with weight 1, the inequality is strengthened into an equality:

Proposition 2. *If γ is a cycle with weight 1 in graph(CD), then for every non-empty finite legal instance I, every edge e in γ satisfies* $\frac{|target(e)^I|}{|source(e)^I|} = weight(e)$.

The following claim shows that a cycle with weight 1 in $graph(CD)$ determines the actual number of links between objects of classes in the cycle. The tightening of multiplicity constraints follows from this result.

Claim 1. *If γ is a cycle in graph(CD) such that weight(γ) = 1, then for every edge e in γ, with label(e) = $\langle p_1, p_2 \rangle$, and for every finite legal instance I of CD:*

1. *For every object* $e \in C_1^I$, $|p_2^I(e)| = maxMul(p_2)$.
2. *For every object* $e \in C_2^I$, $|p_1^I(e)| = minMul(p_1)$.

Proof. (sketched) Based on Proposition 2, we get that for $assoc(p_1, p_2) = a(p_1 : C_1[min_1, max_1], \ p_2 : C_2[min_2, max_2])$, $|a^I| = max_2 \cdot |C_1^I|$. But $|a^I| = \sum\limits_{e_i \in C_1^I} |p_2^I(e_i)|$, while $|p_2^I(e_i)| \leq max_2$. Similarly for the other equality. □

This claim has the following conclusion:
For an edge labeled $\langle p_1, p_2 \rangle$ in $graph(CD)$, if a weight 1 cycle goes through the edge, then $minMul(p_2) \neq maxMul(p_2)$ implies that p_1 is not tight. Moreover, p_2 can be tightened by setting $minMul(p_2)$ to be $maxMul(p_2)$ and p_1 can be tightened by setting $maxMul(p_1)$ to be $minMul(p_1)$. Algorithm 2 is based on these results:

Algorithm 2. *Multiplicity Tightening*

   Input: A class diagram CD
   Output: A modified class diagram
   for *each edge* $e \in graph(CD)$. *with label(e)* = $\langle p_1, p_2 \rangle$ **do**
      If there is a cycle γ through e, with $weight(\gamma) = 1$,
         set: $minMul(p_2) := maxMul(p_2)$ and $maxMul(p_1) := minMul(p_1)$
   end

Example 1. *Consider the class diagram in Figure 1a. Its identification graph in Figure 3 includes the cycle shown in bold, from A to C to B and to A with weight 1. Figure 1b presents the tightened class diagram, obtained as follows:*

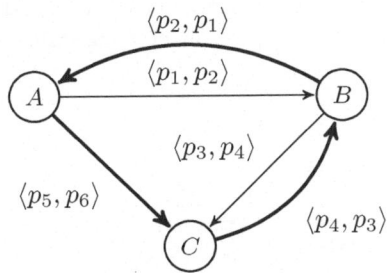

Fig. 3. The identification graph of the class diagram in Figure 1a

1. *The edge from A to C: This edge is labeled $\langle p_5, p_6 \rangle$. The tightening:*
   $maxMul(p_5) = 9$, $minMul(p_6) = 4$.
2. *The edge from C to B: This edge is labeled $\langle p_4, p_3 \rangle$. The tightening:*
   $maxMul(p_4) = 2$, $minMul(p_3) = 3$.
3. *The edge from B to A: This edge is labeled $\langle p_2, p_1 \rangle$. The tightening:*
   $maxMul(p_2) = 4$, $minMul(p_1) = 6$.

Properties and Correctness of Algorithm 2

Based on Claim 1, if algorithm 2 modifies a class diagram CD, then its output
is a class diagram that is equivalent to CD but more tight. We show that for
class diagrams that include only multiplicity, and hierarchy constraints (denoted
$CD_{mul,\prec}$), the algorithm yields a tight class diagram, i.e., all properties in the
output class diagram are tight. This result is based on Proposition 3, below.

Proposition 3. *In a finitely satisfiable class diagram $CD \in CD_{mul,\prec}$, a property p with $minMul(p) \neq maxMul(p)$ is tight if and only if all cycles in
graph(CD) through an edge labeled $\langle p, \_ \rangle$ or $\langle \_, p \rangle$ (_ being a wild card) have
weight greater than 1.*

Proof. (sketched) The harder **if** direction is proved by constructing instances
that realize the multiplicities $minMul(p)$ and $maxMul(p)$ of p. The construction
follows similar constructions in [11, 3]. The correctness of the construction relies
on showing that there exist finite legal instances I, J that satisfy the stronger
forms of the multiplicity constraints.   □

This proposition implies the following completeness result for Algorithm 2:

Theorem 1. *For a class diagram in $CD_{mul,\prec}$, Algorithm 2 computes an equivalent, tight class diagram.*

The **Multiplicity Tightening** algorithm is not complete for class diagrams
with additional constraints. Figure 4 presents class diagrams that the algorithm cannot fully tighten. In Figure 4a, property p should be tightened into
$maxMul(p) = 1$, due to the interaction between the *subsetting, multiplicity*
and *GS* constraints. But the non-tight status is not reflected in the cycles of the
identification graph. Similarly, in Figure 4b, property p_2 should be tightened into

$maxMul(p) = 2$, due to the interaction between the multiplicity and the GS constraints. The catalog in [6, 12] present simplification patterns for constraint interactions of this kind.

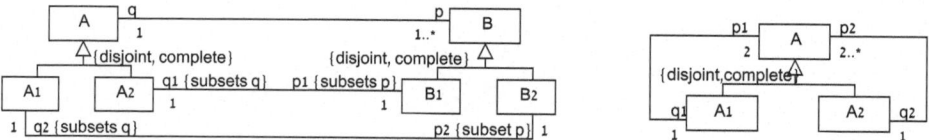

Fig. 4. Non tight class diagrams due to interaction of multiplicity, subsetting and GS constraint

3.1   Heuristics for the *Multiplicity Tightening* Algorithm

Finding multiple cycles in a graph is a hard problem. Breaking the graph into smaller not connected sub-graphs, or reducing its size can greatly improve the operation. We present heuristics and guidelines for achieving these goals.

Achieving Smaller Not Connected Sub-graphs: Class diagrams are naturally structured by *package* hierarchy, aiming at small class diagrams for packages. Since the *Multiplicity Tightening* algorithm ignores trivial multiplicity constraints (*o* for minimum and * for maximum), it is recommended to have only trivial multiplicity constraints between classes in different packages. This way identification graphs will have the sizes of the inside packages class diagrams, which is ideally small.

Reducing the Size of the Graph: Reducing a class diagram by composing *adjacent associations* yields a smaller identification graph. The idea is to compose associations that have a common end class, tighten the resulting smaller class diagram, and restore a full size class diagram that is equivalent but possibly tighter than the input diagram.

The *composition of properties* is an operation that composes properties into a single property. For properties $p_1, \ldots, p_n$, $n > 1$, such that $target(p_i) = source(p_{i+1})$, $i = 1, n-1$, their composition is a property $p_1 \circ p_2 \ldots \circ p_n$ whose source is $source(p_1)$, target is $target(p_n)$, $minMul$ is $\prod_{i=1}^{n} minMul(p_i)$ and $maxMul$ is $\prod_{i=1}^{n} maxMul(p_i)$. The *composition of associ-* ations $aassoc(p_1), \ldots, assoc(p_n)$ where $target(p_i) = source(p_{i+1})$, $i = 1, n-1$, is a new association $assoc(p_1^{-1} \circ \ldots p_n^{-1}, p_1 \circ \ldots p_n)$. Note that property and association composition preserve the weights in cycles of the identification graph[2].

---

[2] But the composition does not preserve equivalence. In [2] an equivalence preserving composition is used.

The heuristics for class diagram reduction suggests finding classes that participate in multiple non-trivial multiplicity constraints[3], compose associations between these classes, tighten the reduced class diagram, and restore the full size class diagram. For example, consider the class diagram in Figure 5a. Assume that the selected classes are the ones marked in gray. Composition of the associations between these classes, i.e., $assoc(p_5, p_6)$, $assoc(p_7, p_8)$, $assoc(p_9, p_{10})$, implies removing classes D, E. The reduced class diagram is the one given in Figure 1a, whose tightened diagram appears in Figure 1b. In the restored class diagram (Figure 5b), the associations that have not been composed are tightened. The composed associations are not tightened, but their multiplicity products are constrained as follows: $minMul(p_9) \cdot minMul(p_7) \cdot minMul(p_5) = maxMul(p_9) \cdot maxMul(p_7) \cdot maxMul(p_5) = 4$, $minMul(p_{10}) \cdot minMul(p_8) \cdot minMul(p_6) = maxMul(p_{10}) \cdot maxMul(p_8) \cdot maxnMul(p_6) = 9$. Following Proposition 3, the fully tightened class diagram is given in Figure 5c.

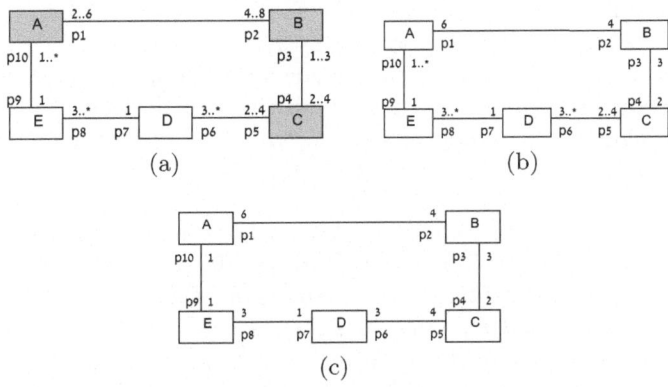

Fig. 5. A class diagram before abstraction

4   Correctness of Aggregation/Composition Constraints

Aggregation/composition constraints impose complex restrictions on object interaction. The combination with multiplicity constraints, and especially with the inter-association *subsetting* constraint might cause correctness problems that are hard to detect and identify. We describe first possible correctness problems, followed by identification methods.

Finite-Satisfiability Problems due to Aggregation/Composition Cycles
Figure 6a presents a finite satisfiability problem: The multiplicity constraints on r_1, r_2 dictate that in every non-empty legal instance, if classes A, B are finite, then they include a cycle of linked objects. The {*subsets q*}, {*subsets p*} constraints entail an illegal r, r_2 composition object cycle (see Figure 6b). Therefore, this class diagram has only empty or infinite legal instances.

---

[3] This abstraction heuristics reminds the *abstraction rules* of [13, 14], although these works have different goals.

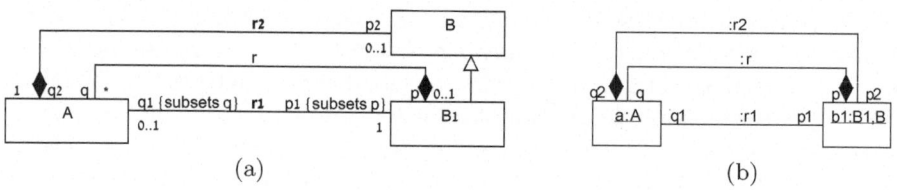

Fig. 6. Indirect composition cycles

A sequence of associations $assoc(p_1), assoc(p_2), \ldots, assoc(p_n)$ forms (1) an *association cycle* if $target(p_i) = source(p_{i+1})$ for $i = 1, n-1$, and $target(p_n) = source(p_1)$; (2) an *association-hierarchy cycle* if $target(p_i) \preceq source(p_{i+1})$ for $i = 1, n-1$, and $target(p_n) \preceq source(p_1)$ (recall that $C_1 \preceq C_2$ means that either $C_1 = C_2$ or $C_1 \prec C_2$). An association cycle is a special case of an association-hierarchy cycle. Below we always refer to the latter, unless we mean only an association cycle. For example, in Figure 6a, the associations $assoc(p_1), assoc(p_2), assoc(q_1)$ form an association-hierarchy cycle.

The following Lemma characterizes association-hierarchy cycles that impose object cycles on their finite legal instances. Claim 2 then characterizes combinations with aggregation/composition constraints as in Figure 6a, that enforce illegal aggregation/composition object cycles.

Lemma 1. *Let CD be an association-hierarchy cycle $assoc(p_1), assoc(p_2), \ldots, assoc(p_n)$. Then if for $i = 1, n$, $minMul(p_i) > 0$, then every non-empty legal instance of CD is either infinite, or includes a cycle of linked entities. That is, for a non-empty legal instance I, either it is infinite, or there exists $e \in source(p_i)^I, i = 1, n$ such that $e \in (p_{i-1}^I \circ \ldots p_1^I \circ p_n^I \cdots \circ p_i^I)^k(e), k \geq 1$, where $(p \circ q)^k$ denotes k applications of the composition of p and q.*

Proof. (sketched) If I is a non-empty finite legal instance, then since its classes are finite and all multiplicity constraints require at least one link, then cyclic repeated applications of the properties must reach repeated objects.   □

Note that the Lemma does not require that the involved classes are disjoint. Therefore, the cycle of linked objects can include an object several times.

Claim 2. *Let $assoc(p_1), assoc(p_2), \ldots, assoc(p_n)$ be an association-hierarchy cycle, $minMul(p_i) > 0$, for $i = 1, n$, and one of the following conditions holds.*

1. *for each i, there exists an aggregation/composition property q_i such that $p_i \preceq^* q_i$ (i.e., either p_i is an aggregation/composition property or it subsets such a property);*
2. *for each i, there exists an aggregation/composition property q_i such that $p_i^{-1} \preceq^* q_i$;*

Then every finite instance of the association cycle, includes a cycle of objects that are related by aggregation/composition properties.

Proof. (Sketched) In both cases, by Lemma 1, every finite instance I has a cycle of objects $e_1, \ldots, e_n, \ldots, e_1$, $e_i \in source(p_i)^I$, that are related by these properties. If the properties satisfy the first condition, then every e_i is a q_i aggregation/composition component of e_{i+1} (for $i = n$ replace $i + 1$ by 1). Therefore, $e_1, \ldots, e_n, \ldots, e_1$ is an aggregation/composition cycle. A similar argument holds for the second condition, but in the opposite direction.   □

Correctness Problems due to the Multi Composition Constraint

Figures 7a and 7b present a class A that plays the component role in two different composition constraints with classes B and C. In Figure 7a, class B, being a subclass of class D, is also a component of C. The multi-composition constraint requires that an object is not a physical part of two different objects that are not related by composition (the transitivity of composition implies that every part is transitively a component of all of its composition ancestors). Therefore, in Figure 7a the multi-composition between classes A, B, C is "benign", and there might be a legal finite instance in which class A is not empty.

Figure 7b presents a different case, where an object of class A that is linked via properties q'_1, q'_2 to objects of the disjoint classes C and B, respectively, violates the multi-composition constraint. Yet, properties p_1, p_2, p_3 form an association-hierarchy cycle and by Lemma 1, every finite instance of this class diagram has a cycle of related objects from classes A, B, C. The subsetting constraints imply violation of the multi-composition constraint. Therefore, this class diagram does not have a finite non-empty instance.

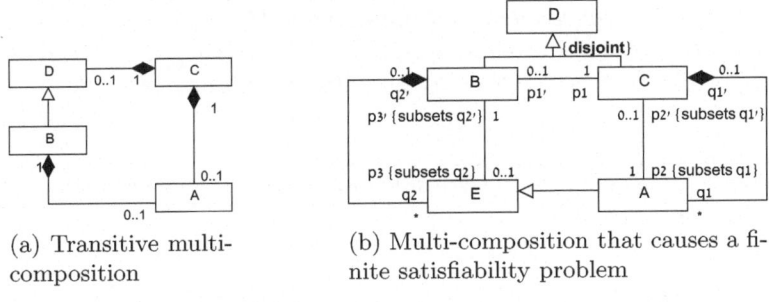

(a) Transitive multi-composition

(b) Multi-composition that causes a finite satisfiability problem

Fig. 7. Class diagrams with multi-composition

Claim 3 generalizes this observation. It characterizes a situation where an object in a mandatory object cycle must be a component of two other objects that are not composition related. The claim relies on two relations between classes: The syntactic *Composition-related* relation, and the semantic *necessarily-disjoint* relation. Classes A and B are *composition-related* if they are connected by a sequence of composition properties. Classes A and B are *necessarily-disjoint* if in every legal instance of the class diagram they denote disjoint sets of objects. Explicit disjoint GS constraints point on a necessarily-disjoint relation, but there can be more involved indirect cases as well.[4]

---

[4] An incomplete algorithm for deciding this relation appears in [3].

Claim 3. *Let $assoc(p_1), assoc(p_2), \ldots, assoc(p_n)$ be an association-hierarchy cycle, $minMul(p_i) > 0$, for $i = 1, n$, and for some $p_i, i = 1..n$, such that $target(p_i^{-1}), target(p_{i+1})$ are not composition related and are necessarily disjoint, $p_i^{-1} \preceq^* q^c$ and $p_{i+1} \preceq^* r^c$ for composition properties q^c, r^c. Then every finite instance of the association cycle violates the multi-composition constraint.*

Proof. (Sketched) By Lemma 1, every finite instance I has a cycle of n objects related by these properties. Since p_i^{-1} and $p_{i+1} \preceq^*$ composition properties, the object $e \in source(p_{i+1})^I$ in this cycle, is a component of an object in $target(p_i^{-1})^I$ and an object in $target(p_{i+1})^I$, and these objects are not composition related and are different since the classes are necessarily disjoint.   □

Claim 4 characterizes a situation where due to subsetting of composition properties, an object is a component of two different objects, as in Figure 2a:

Claim 4. *Let p_1, p_2 be properties with a common source, $minMul(p_i) > 0$, for $i = 1, 2$, and where $target(q^c), target(r^c)$ are not composition related and are necessarily disjoint. Then if $p_1 \preceq^* q^c$ and $p_2 \preceq^* r^c$ for composition properties q^c and r^c, then the class diagram violates the multi-composition constraint.*

4.1   Identification Methods

We present identification methods that are based on construction of directed graphs that capture relevant multiplicity, subsetting, aggregation/composition and class-hierarchy constraints in a class diagram.

Identification of Aggregation/Composition Cycles

Algorithm 3 constructs a directed graph denoted $graph_{agg/comp}(CD)$. Claim 5 shows that cycles in this graph point to finite satisfiability problems.

Algorithm 3. *Aggregation/composition-graph-construction*

Input: A class diagram CD
Output: A directed graph $graph_{agg/comp}(CD)$, with $+$ or $-$ labeled edges
begin

    1. Initialize $graph_{agg/comp}(CD)$ by a node $n(C)$ for every class/association-class C
    2. For each property p: If $p \preceq^* q$ for an aggregation/composition property q, add edges as follows:
       (a) If $minMul(p) > 0$, then create an edge labeled $\langle +, p, q \rangle$ from $n(source(p))$ to $n(target(p))$
       (b) If $minMul(p^{-1}) > 0$, create an edge labeled $\langle -, p, q \rangle$ from $n(target(p))$ to $n(source(p))$
    3. For each class hierarchy $B \prec A$, create an edge from $n(B)$ to $n(A)$

end

Claim 5. *A cycle of either all $+$ labeled edges or all $-$ labeled edges in $graph_{agg/comp}(CD)$ identifies a finite satisfiability problem caused by the involved properties.*

Proof. (sketched) Graph edges correspond to $\preceq^*$ constraints with aggregation/-composition properties that satisfy the conditions of Claim 2.   □

Example 2. *Figure 8 presents the aggregation/composition graph of the class diagram in Figure 6a. The cycle identifies the association-hierarchy cycle r_1, r_2 through properties p_1, q_2, with the subsetting constraints $p_1 \preceq^* p^c$, and $q_2^c \preceq^* q_2^c$. The cycle has $+$ labeled edges since both properties have non-zero minimum multiplicities. By Claim 2 the cycle identifies a finite satisfiability problem.*

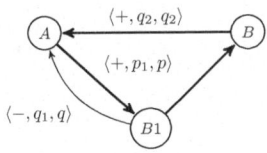

Fig. 8. Aggregation/composition graph of Figure 6a

Identification of multi-composition problems

Claim 3 describes finite satisfiability problems caused by violation of the multi-composition constraint. Such problems are characterized by two composition properties that have a common source class, and necessarily-disjoint classes that are not composition-related, as their targets. Algorithm 4 constructs a directed graph denoted $graph_{multi-comp}(CD)$. Claim 6 characterize cases where finite satisfiability problems are caused by cycles in this graph, following Claim 3.

Algorithm 4. *Multi-composition-graph-construction*

Input: A class diagram CD

Output: A directed labeled graph $graph_{multi-comp}(CD)$

begin

    1. Initialize $graph_{multi-comp}(CD)$ by a node $n(C)$ for every class/ association-class C

    2. For each property p with $minMul(p) > 0$ add an edge labeled p from $source(p)$ to $target(p)$.

    3. For each class hierarchy constraint $C_1 \prec C_2$ add an edge labeled $\prec$ from C_1 to C_2.

end

Claim 6. *If a cycle in $graph_{multi-comp}(CD)$ includes edges e_1, e_2, labeled p_1, p_2, respectively, such that (1) $p_1^{-1} \preceq^* q^c$ and $p_2 \preceq^* r^c$ for composition properties q^c, r^c; (2) $target(p_1) \preceq source(p_2)$ (there is a $\preceq$ labeled path in the graph); (3) classes $target(p_1^{-1}), target(p_2)$ are not composition related and are necessarily disjoint, then the cycle identifies a finite satisfiability problem caused by the involved properties and their constraints.*

Combining simplification with incorrectness identification

Multiplicity constraints affect all other constraints in class diagrams. Figure 9 shows a class diagram (9a) that is not finitely satisfiable, but the problem cannot be identified by Algorithm 3, since $graph_{agg/comp}(CD)$ (9b) does not include cycles. However, applying Algorithm 2 to this class diagram yields an equivalent tight class diagram (9c), on which Algorithm 3 succeeds, since its $graph_{agg/comp}(CD)$ (Figure 9d) includes a composition cycle.

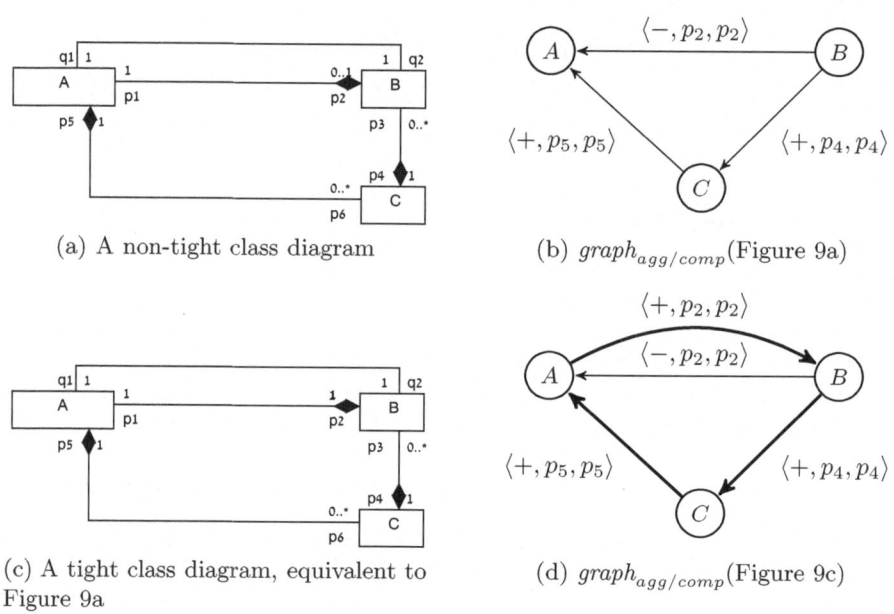

(a) A non-tight class diagram

(b) $graph_{agg/comp}$(Figure 9a)

(c) A tight class diagram, equivalent to Figure 9a

(d) $graph_{agg/comp}$(Figure 9c)

Fig. 9.

5   Related Work

Most works on class diagram correctness focus on *consistency* [10, 15, 16] and *finite satisfiability* problems [11, 17–21, 7, 3, 5]. There is a limited amount of works investigating class-diagram constraints, including their impact on correctness and quality [1, 22, 2–5]. But the impact of aggregation/composition constraints on the finite satisfiability problem have not been investigated yet. In our previous work [4], we investigate semantic implications of the inter-association constraints, their interaction with other constraints, and implied correctness and quality problems. The catalog in [6, 12] presents simplification patterns for constraint interactions of this kind.

Hartmann [23] presents a graph-based method for tightening multiplicity constraints with gaps (e.g. {1, 4, 5}) in Entity-Relationship Diagrams (ERDs) with functional dependencies and without hierarchy constraints. Similarly to our method, his method is also based on finding cycles in a directed graph. Feinerer et al. [2] investigate multiplicity constraint redundancies in class diagrams with multiplicity, uniqueness and *equation* constraints. The latter are imposed on association cycles (like OCL constraints). They present tightening rules that are based on equivalence preserving association composition. Their method has been implemented in their *CLEWS* prototype.

6   Conclusion and Future Work

The paper continues our previous work on correctness and quality problems that result from interaction of a variety of constraints of the class diagram language. The identification algorithms are implemented in the *FiniteSatUSE* tool [24], as part of our ongoing effort for constructing a model level integrated development environment. We intend to extend the simplification and correctness methods to additional constraints, and strengthen completeness result.

References

1. Costal, D., Gómez, C.: On the use of Association Redefinition in UML Class Diagrams. In: Embley, D.W., Olivé, A., Ram, S. (eds.) ER 2006. LNCS, vol. 4215, pp. 513–527. Springer, Heidelberg (2006)
2. Feinerer, I., Salzer, G., Sisel, T.: Reducing Multiplicities in Class Diagrams. In: Whittle, J., Clark, T., Kühne, T. (eds.) MODELS 2011. LNCS, vol. 6981, pp. 379–393. Springer, Heidelberg (2011)
3. Balaban, M., Maraee, A.: Finite Satisfiability of UML Class Diagrams with Constrained Class Hierarchy. ACM Transactions on Software Engineering and Methodology, SEM (to appear)
4. Maraee, A., Balaban, M.: Inter-association Constraints in UML2: Comparative Analysis, Usage Recommendations, and Modeling Guidelines. In: France, R.B., Kazmeier, J., Breu, R., Atkinson, C. (eds.) MODELS 2012. LNCS, vol. 7590, pp. 302–318. Springer, Heidelberg (2012)
5. Feinerer, I., Salzer, G.: Numeric Semantics of Class Diagrams with Multiplicity and Uniqueness Constraints. Software and Systems Modeling, SoSyM (2013)
6. Balaban, M., Jelnov, P., Maraee, A., Sturm, A.: A Pattern-Based Approach for Improving Model Design Quality (submitted)
7. Maraee, A.: UML Class Diagrams–Semantics, Correctness and Quality. PhD thesis, Ben Gurion University of the Negev (2012)
8. OMG: UML 2.4 Superstructure Specification. Specification Version 2.4.1. Object Management Group (2011)
9. Kleppe, A., Rensink, A.: On a Graph-Based Semantics for UML Class and Object Diagrams. In: Ermel, C., Lara, J.D., Heckel, R. (eds.) Graph Transformation and Visual Modelling Techniques. Electronic Communications of the EASST, vol. 10. EASST (2008)
10. Berardi, D., Calvanese, D., Giacomo, D.: Reasoning on UML Class Diagrams. Artificial Intelligence 168, 70–118 (2005)

11. Lenzerini, M., Nobili, P.: On the Satisfiability of Dependency Constraints in Entity-Relationship Schemata. Information Systems 15, 453–461 (1990)
12. BGU Modeling Group: UML Class Diagram Anti-Patterns (2010), http://www.cs.bgu.ac.il/~cd-patterns/
13. Alexander, E.: Automated Abstraction of Class Diagrams. ACM Transactions on Software Engineering and Methodology, TOSEM 11, 449–491 (2002)
14. Shoval, P., Danoch, R., Balaban, M.: Hierarchical ER diagrams (HERD)–the Method and Experimental Evaluation. Advanced Conceptual Modeling Techniques, 264–274 (2003)
15. Queralt, A., Teniente, E.: Verification and Validation of UML Conceptual Schemas with OCL Constraints. ACM Transactions on Software Engineering and Methodology T 21, 13:1–13:41 (2012)
16. Kaneiwa, K., Satoh, K.: On the Complexities of Consistency Checking for Restricted UML Class Diagrams. Theor. Comput. Sci. 411, 301–323 (2010)
17. Thalheim, B.: Entity Relationship Modeling, Foundation of Database Technology. Springer (2000)
18. Calvanese, D., Lenzerini, M.: On the Interaction between ISA and Cardinality Constraints. In: The 10th IEEE Int. Conf. on Data Engineering (1994)
19. Hartmann, S.: Coping with Inconsistent Constraint Specifications. In: Kunii, H.S., Jajodia, S., Sølvberg, A. (eds.) ER 2001. LNCS, vol. 2224, p. 241. Springer, Heidelberg (2001)
20. Boufares, F., Bennaceur, H.: Consistency Problems in ER-schemas for Database Systems. Information Sciences, 263–274 (2004)
21. Shaikh, A., Clarisó, R., Wiil, U., Memon, N.: Verification-driven Slicing of UML/OCL Models. In: Proceedings of the IEEE/ACM International Conference on Automated Software Engineering, pp. 185–194. ACM (2010)
22. Alanen, M., Porres, I.: A Metamodeling Language Supporting Subset and Union Properties. Software and Systems Modeling 7, 103–124 (2008)
23. Hartmann, S.: On the Implication Problem for Cardinality Constraints and Functional Dependencies. Annals of Mathematics and Artificial Intelligence 33, 253–307 (2001)
24. BGU Modeling Group: FiniteSatUSE – A Class Diagram Correctness Tool (2011), http://sourceforge.net/projects/usefsverif/

Specification of Cyber-Physical Components with Formal Semantics – Integration and Composition

Gabor Simko, David Lindecker, Tihamer Levendovszky, Sandeep Neema, and Janos Sztipanovits

Institute for Software Integrated Systems
Vanderbilt University
Nashville, TN

Abstract. Model-Based Engineering of Cyber-Physical Systems (CPS) needs correct-by-construction design methodologies, hence CPS modeling languages require mathematically rigorous, unambiguous, and sound specifications of their semantics. The main challenge is the formalization of the heterogeneous composition and interactions of CPS systems. Creating modeling languages that support both the acausal and causal modeling approaches, and which has well-defined and sound behavior across the heterogeneous time domains is a challenging task. In this paper, we discuss the difficulties and as an example develop the formal semantics of a CPS-specific modeling language called CyPhyML. We formalize the structural semantics of CyPhyML by means of constraint rules and its behavioral semantics by defining a semantic mapping to a language for differential algebraic equations. The specification language is based on an executable subset of first-order logic, which facilitates model conformance checking, model checking and model synthesis.

Keywords: Cyber-Physical Systems, formalization, formal specification, Model-Based Engineering, heterogeneous composition.

1 Introduction

Model-Based Engineering of Cyber-Physical Systems (CPS) needs correct-by-construction design methodologies, hence CPS modeling languages require mathematically rigorous, unambiguous, and sound specifications of their semantics. Cyber-physical systems are software-integrated physical systems often used in safety-critical and mission critical applications, for example in automotive, avionics, chemical plants, or medical applications. In these applications sound, unambiguous, and formally specified modeling languages can help developing reliable and correct solutions.

Traditional systems engineering is based on *causal modeling* (e.g., Simulink), in which components are functional and a well-defined causal dependency exists between the inputs and outputs. It is known that such a causal modeling

A. Moreira et al. (Eds.): MODELS 2013, LNCS 8107, pp. 471–487, 2013.

paradigm is imperfect for physical systems and CPS modeling [31] since physical laws are inherently acausal.

Recently, *acausal modeling* has gained traction and several languages have been introduced for acausal modeling (e.g., Modelica, bond graphs). Every time a new language is introduced, there is a natural demand to extend it to support as many features as possible. Unfortunately, this often leads to enormously large and generic languages, which have many interpretations and variants without a clear, unambiguous semantics. Because of the size of these languages, there is not much hope for complete formalization of their semantics.

A fundamental problem is that generic languages provides support for way more features than a specific problem needs, still they often lack support for some essential functions that would be otherwise needed. Thus, in most cases it is more feasible to use Domain Specific Modeling Languages (DSML), which are designed to support exactly the necessary functions. Additionally, because DSMLs are usually significantly smaller than generic languages, their formal specification is feasible.

In this paper, we focus on the semantic specifications of heterogeneous CPS languages using our CyPhyML DSML as an illustrative example. Our main contribution is an executable specification for CPS languages with a logic-based language for both the structural and behavioral (operational and denotational) semantic specifications, which lends itself to model conformance checking, model finding and Linear Temporal Logic (LTL) model checking. Using the same language for both structural and behavioral semantic specifications is an important step towards better understanding CPS DSMLs and their composition. In previous practices, structure and behavior were formalized in different languages (e.g., OCL and Abstract State Machines) and they were completely separated. Since in our formalism they are represented using the same logic-based formalism, understanding their relations becomes a matter of deductive reasoning. While in this paper we discuss the key concepts for developing the specifications, leveraging these specifications to reason about the connections between structure and behavior remains a matter of future work.

Our working example will be our Cyber-Physical Modeling Language (CyPhyML), an integration language for composing heterogeneous CPS DSMLs. In DARPA's AVM (Adaptive Vehicle Make) program, we required a CPS modeling language that supports the integration of acausal physical modeling, data-flow modeling, CAD models, bidirectional parameter propagation and Design Space Exploration (DSE). While there are several DSMLs that can tackle these problems individually, we needed an integration language to compose them. Therefore, we defined the component-based language CyPhyML, which is capable of representing the integration of heterogeneous components defined in third-party DSMLs. This allows us to compose heterogeneous physical, data-flow and other models designed in external languages and tools such as Modelica, our bond graph language variant or the Embedded Systems Modeling Language (ESMoL).

The organization of the paper is the following: Section 2 describes related work, while Section 3 provides an overview of the background for CPS design, semantics and the formal language that we use. In Section 4 we discuss the meta-model for the compositional sub-language of CyPhyML. Section 5 describes the structural and behavioral semantics of this sub-language and Section 6 discusses the formalization of the integration of third-party DSMLs. Section 7 is devoted to the evaluation and validation of our approach, and Section 8 draws our conclusion.

2 Related Work

The logic-based language FORMULA was first proposed by Jackson [13] as a formal language for specifying the structural semantics of DSMLs and later for specifying their operational semantics [14]. Our research can be considered the continuation of these initiatives. In [29, 30], we used FORMULA for specifying the structural and denotational semantics of a physical modeling language and in [21], we specified the operational semantics of a state-chart language variant. FORMULA provides tools for executing these specifications, in particular they can be used for automated model finding, model conformance checking and LTL model checking.

A different line of research discussed by Rivera [24, 26] uses Maude, an equational logic and term rewriting-based language to specify the operational behavioral and structural semantics of DSMLs. Using Maude's rewriting engine, this representation can be used for LTL model checking, and by leveraging the Real-Time Maude framework it can be used for real-time simulations and analysis [25]. Furthermore, research by Romero [27], Egea [8], and Rusu [28] uses Maude-based formalizations for arguing about model sub-typing, type inference, model conformance and operational semantics of model transformations.

In [6], we introduce a translational approach using the Abstract State Machines (ASM) and a semantic anchoring framework, and in [7], we show how such a semantic anchoring framework can be used for compositional behavioral specifications. Gargantini [10] also introduces an ASM-based semantic framework that includes translational approaches, semantic mapping, semantic hooking and semantic meta-hooking, and a weaving approach for semantic specifications.

Esfahasin [9] uses the Z notation to formally specify the behavioral semantics of an activity-oriented DSML modeled in GME. While Z is not executable, the formal specification provides an unambiguous guideline for automated code generation for their models.

There are several languages for integrating heterogeneous languages, with major emphasis on the composition of heterogeneous computational languages. For example, Ptolemy [11] [12] provides a framework for composing heterogeneous actors described by a variety of Models of Computation (MoC), e.g. finite-state machines, synchronous and dynamic data flows, process networks, discrete events, continuous-time and synchronous-reactive systems. While Ptolemy does support continuous-time dynamics, it lacks support for acausal physical systems modeling.

BIP (Behavior, Interaction and Priority) [2] is a framework that supports the composition of heterogeneous computational systems. The key idea is the separation of component behaviors from component interactions. Such a separation of concerns facilitates the correct composition of components. In [4], the algebra of BIP is formulated, and in [5], the SOS style formalization of glue operators is described.

In this paper, we address the formal semantics of CPS composition languages, which brings additional challenges because of the integration of acausal physical models and causal computational models.

3   Background

3.1   Cyber-Physical Systems

There are significant differences between physical and computational systems. Computational systems are traditionally modeled with the causal modeling approach: components, blocks, software are functional entities, which produce outputs given some inputs. In contrast, physical systems are acausal and the appropriate approach to model them is the acausal modeling approach [31]: interactions are non-directional and there are no input and output ports. Instead, interactions establish simultaneous constraints on the behavior of the connected components by means of *variable sharing*.

For instance, a resistor can be modeled as a two port element, where each port represents a voltage and a current, and the behavior of the resistor is defined by the equations $U_1 - U_2 = R \cdot I_1$ and $I_1 = I_2$. Here, it is unreasonable to talk about the directions of the ports because such a direction is not part of the model: a resistor can be equally driven by a source of current or a source of voltage.

A different problem of CPS modeling is the semantics of time. Physical system models are based on continuous-time (*real* time), while computational systems are inherently discrete-time (e.g., discrete event, periodic discrete time, etc.). The merge of heterogeneous time domains is non-trivial and raises several questions.

If the system uses the notion of events, at any *real* time instant several events may happen simultaneously. To track the causality of these events, we must expand the time domain: super-dense time and non-standard real time [3] have been proposed as expansions of the real time for this purpose. Often, such causally related simultaneous events are the results of the synchronous approach (i.e., the abstraction that computation and communication take zero time).

Another problem is that algebraic loops (loops without delays or integrators) in synchronous systems may have ambiguous semantics: there might be no solutions or several solutions for the system equations. There are several approaches to tackle the problem of algebraic loops: (i) avoid algebraic loops by structural constraints (e.g., Lustre), (ii) do not consider algebraic loops at the design phase, detect problems during simulation (does not support correct-by-construction), (iii) define the least fix-point semantics (Scott semantics) [22].

3.2   Structural and Behavioral Semantics

In general, models represent a structure and associated behaviors. Accordingly, specification of modeling languages requires support for specifying both structural and behavioral semantics [14].

Structural semantics (also known as static semantics) describes the meaning of model instances in terms of their structure [6]. Structural semantics is described by a mapping from model instances into a two-valued domain, which distinguishes well-formed models from ill-formed models.

Behavioral semantics is represented as a mapping of the model into a mathematical domain that is sufficiently rich for capturing essential aspects of the behavior [7]. In other words, the explicit representation of behavioral semantics of a DSML requires two distinct components: (i) a mathematical domain and a formal language for specifying behaviors and (ii) a formal language for specifying transformation between domains. Different types of behavioral semantics can be distinguished based on the formalism of the description, for instance, denotational semantics or operational semantics.

Denotational semantics describes the semantics of the language by mapping its syntactic elements to some well-defined (mathematical) semantic domain. The key advantage of denotational semantics is its composability.

Operational semantics describes the step-wise execution of models of the language by an abstract machine. The operational semantics can be formalized as a transformation that specifies how the system evolves through its states.

3.3   FORMULA Notation

FORMULA is a constraint logic programming tool developed at Microsoft Research [1] based on first-order logic and fixed-point semantics [15, 16]. It has found many application in Model-Based Engineering such as reasoning about meta-modeling [17] or finding specification errors by constraints [18]. Furthermore, it has been proposed as a formal language for specifying the structural and behavioral semantics of DSMLs as discussed in the related work.

Although we use the newer syntax of FORMULA 2.0, the general principles of the language are unchanged and described in more detail in [15, 16].

The `domain` keyword specifies a domain (analogous to a meta-model) which is composed of type definitions, data constructors and rules. A model of the domain consists of a set of *facts* (also called initial knowledge) that are defined using the data constructors of the domain, and the well-formed models of the domain are distinguished from the ill-formed models by the conformance rules.

FORMULA has a complex type system based on built-in types (e.g., `Natural`, `Integer`, `Real`, `String`, `Bool`), enumerations, data constructors and union types. Enumerations are sets of constants defined by enumerating all their elements, for example, `bool ::= {true,false}` denotes the usual 2-valued Boolean type.

Data constructors can be used for constructing algebraic data types. Such terms can represent sets, relations, partial and total functions, injections, surjections and bijections. Consider the following type definitions:

```
A ::= new (x:Integer, y:String).
B ::= fun (x:Integer -> y:String).
C ::= fun (x:A => y:String).
D ::= inj (x:Integer -> y:String).
E ::= bij (x:A => y:B).
F ::= (x:Integer, y:String).
```

Data constructor A is used for defining A-terms by pairing Integers and Strings, where the optional x and y are the accessors for the respective values (for example, A(5,"f") is an A-term). Data constructor B is used for defining a partial function (functional relation) from the domain of Integers to the codomain of Strings. Similarly, C is used to define a total function from A-terms to Strings, D is used to define a partial injective function, and E is used to define a bijective function between A-terms and B-terms.

While the previous data constructors are used for defining initial facts in models, derived data constructors are used for representing facts derived from the initial knowledge by means of rules. For example, derived data constructor F defines a term over pairs of Integers and Strings.

Union types are unions of types in the set-theoretical sense, i.e., the elements of a union type are defined by the union of the elements of the constituent types. FORMULA uses the notation of T ::= A + B to define type T as the union of type A and type B.

FORMULA supports the notation of set comprehension in the form of {head|body}, which denotes the set of elements formed by head that satisfies body. Set comprehension is most useful when using built-in operators such as count or max. For instance, given a relation Pair ::= new (State,State), the expression State(X), n = count({Y|Pair(X,Y)}) counts the number of states paired with state X.

Rules allow information to be deduced. They have the form:

$$A_0(X) \; :\!- \; A_1(X), \; \cdots, \; A_n(X), \; no \; B_1(X), \; \cdots, \; no \; B_m(X).$$

Whenever these is a substitution for X where all $A_1, \cdots, A_n$ are derivable and all $B_1, \cdots, B_m$ are not derivable, then $A_0(X)$ becomes derivable. The use of negation (no) is stratified, which implies that rules generate a unique minimal set of derivations, i.e., a least-fix point.

To help writing multiple rules with the same left-hand side term, the semicolon operator is used, whose meaning is logical disjunction. For instance, in A(X) :- S(X); T(X). any substitution for X, such that S(X) or T(X) is derivable, makes A(X) derivable.

Type constraint x:A is true if and only if variable x is of type A, while x is A is satisfied for all derivations of type A. The special symbol _ denotes an anonymous variable, which cannot be referred to elsewhere.

The well-formed models of a domain *conforms* to the domain specifications. Each FORMULA domain contains a special `conforms` rule, which determines its well-formed models.

Domain composition is supported through the keywords `extends` and `includes`. Both denote the inheritance of all types, data constructors and rules, but while `domain A extends B` ensures that all the well-formed models of A are well-formed models of B, definition `domain A includes B` might contain well-formed models in A which are ill-formed models of B.

Finally, FORMULA transformations define rules for creating output models from input models and parameters. Transformations are specified as sets of rules, where the left-hand side terms are the data constructors of the output domain, whereas the right-hand side of the rules can contain a mixture of the terms from the input and output domains, and the transformation parameters. The semantics of these transformation rules is simple: if a data constructor term of the output domain is deducible using the transformation rules, it will be a fact in the output domain.

4   A Cyber-Physical Modeling Language

A CPS modeling language should, at least, contain structures for defining components with physical and computational behaviors, support both acausal and causal modeling and facilitate hierarchical composition. The Cyber-Physical Modeling Language (CyPhyML) we introduce in this section is a minimal language with support for these functions, therefore it serves as a case study for building such languages. The GME meta-model [20] of CyPhyML is shown in Fig. 1.

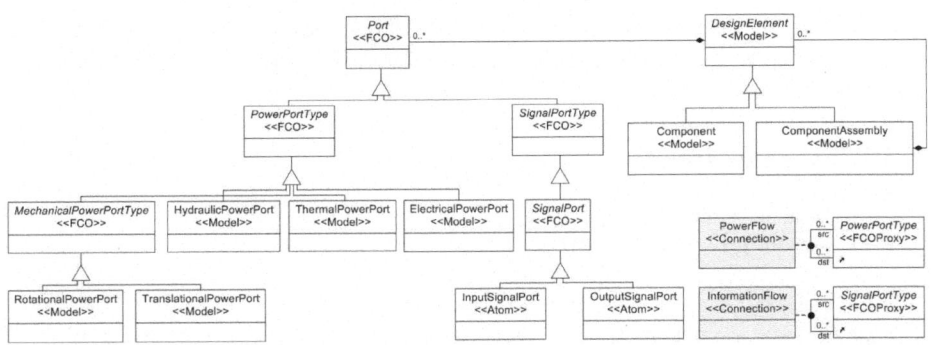

Fig. 1. GME meta-model for the composition sub-language of CyPhyML

Components are the main building blocks of CyPhyML. A CPS component represents a physical or computational element with a number of exposed ports. Hierarchical composition is provided by means of component assemblies, which also facilitate component encapsulation and port hiding. There are two types of ports: acausal power ports, denoting the interaction points through which physical energy flows and signal ports, through which causal information flows. CyPhyML is interpreted in continuous (physical) time, thus signals are continuous-time functions. CyPhyML distinguishes several types of power ports, such as electrical power ports, mechanical power ports, hydraulic power ports and thermal power ports.

We can formalize CyPhyML the following way. A CyPhyML model $\mathcal{M}$ is a tuple $\mathcal{M} = \langle C, A, P, parent, portOf, E_P, E_S \rangle$ with the following interpretation:

- C is a set of components,
- A is a set of component assemblies,
- ($D = C \cup A$ is the set of design elements),
- P is the union of the following sets of ports: $P_{rotMech}$ is a set of rotational mechanical power ports, $P_{transMech}$ is a set of translational mechanical power ports, $P_{multibody}$ is a set of multi-body power ports, $P_{hydraulic}$ is a set of hydraulic power ports, $P_{thermal}$ is a set of thermal power ports, $P_{electrical}$ is a set of electrical power ports, P_{in} is a set of continuous time input signal ports, P_{out} is a set of continuous time output signal ports. Furthermore, P_P is the union of all the power ports and P_S is the union of all the signal ports,
- $parent: D \rightarrow A^*$ is a containment function, whose range is $A^* = A \cup \{root\}$, the set of design elements extended with a special root element $root$,
- $portOf: P \rightarrow D$ is a port containment function, which uniquely determines the container of any port,
- $E_P \subseteq P_P \times P_P$ is the set of *power flow* connections between power ports,
- $E_S \subseteq P_S \times P_S$ is the set of *information flow* connections between signal ports.

We can model these concepts with FORMULA using data constructors and union data types. Thus, the abstract syntax for CyPhyML in FORMULA is the following:

```
C ::= new (id:UID).
A ::= new (id:UID).
D ::= C + A.
P_rotMech ::= new (id:UID).
P_transMech ::= new (id:UID).
...
P_mechanical ::= P_rotMech + P_transMech.
P_power ::= P_mechanical + P_electrical + P_thermal + P_hydraulic.
P_signal ::= P_in + P_out.
P ::= P_power + P_signal.
parent ::= fun (D => A + {root}).
portOf ::= fun (P => D).
Ep ::= new (P_power,P_power).
Es ::= new (P_signal,P_signal).
```

Note that UID stands for a unique identifier, which is needed for distinguishing individual members of the sets.

5   Formalization of Semantics

5.1   Structural Semantics

The structural semantics of a language describes the well-formedness rules for its models. We can define the structural semantics of a language using logic rules: the two-valued semantic domain that distinguishes well-formed and ill-formed models is then equivalent to the deducibility of a special `conforms` constant. To develop the structural semantics of CyPhyML, we define some helper data constructors: Dangling ports are not connected to any other ports:

```
dangling(X) :- X is P_power, no Ep(X,_), no Ep(_,X).
dangling(X) :- X is P_signal, no Es(X,_), no Es(_,X).
```

A distant connection connects two ports belonging to different components, such that the components have different parents, and neither component is parent of the other one:

```
distant(E) :- E is Es(X,Y), portOf(X,PX), portOf(Y,PY), PX != PY,
    Parent(PX,PPX), Parent(PY,PPY), PPX != PPY, PPX != PY, PX != PPY.
distant(E) :- E is Ep(X,Y), portOf(X,PX), portOf(Y,PY), PX != PY,
    Parent(PX,PPX), Parent(PY,PPY), PPX != PPY, PPX != PY, PX != PPY.
```

A power port connection is valid if it connects power ports of same types:

```
validEp(E) :- E is Ep(X,Y), X:P_rotMech, Y:P_rotMech.
...
invalidEp :- E is Ep, no validEp(E).
```

A signal port connection is *invalid* if a signal port receives signals from multiple sources, or an input port is the source of an output port:

```
invalidEs :- E is Es(X,Y), Es(Z,Y), X!=Z.
invalidEs :- E is Es(X,Y), X:P_in, Y:P_out.
```

Note that output ports can be connected to output ports.

Finally, we can express the well-formedness of a CyPhyML model: a model is structurally valid if and only if it does not contain any dangling ports, distant connections and invalid port connections, hence it `conforms` to the domain:

```
conforms :- no dangling(_), no distant(_), no invalidEp, no invalidEs.
```

5.2   Denotational Semantics

The denotational semantics of a language is described by a semantic domain and a mapping that maps the syntactic elements of the language to this semantic domain. In this section, we define a semantic domain for CPS, and specify the semantic mapping from CyPhyML to this domain.

Semantic Domain. Continuing our example, the denotational semantics of CyPhyML is described by a semantic mapping from the domain of CyPhyML models to a well-defined mathematical domain, the domain of differential algebraic equations (DAE) extended with periodic discrete-time variables.

Such a semantic domain is reusable: for any CPS language that combines continuous-time physical systems with periodic discrete-time controllers, it can be used as a semantic domain. Furthermore, it facilitates the composition of such languages by establishing a common semantic domain.

We represent the domain of (semi-explicit) differential algebraic equations using the following signature:

```
domain DAEs
{
    term ::= cvar + Real + op.
    op   ::= neg + inv + mul + sum.
    equation ::= eq + diffEq.
    cvar ::= new (UID).
    neg ::= new (term).
    inv ::= new (term).
    mul ::= new (term, term).
    // sum and its addends
    sum     ::= new (UID).
    addend ::= new (sum, term).
    // predicates
    eq      ::= new (term, term).
    diffEq ::= new (cvar, term).
}
```

A `term` is a (continuous time) variable, a `real` number, or the application of an operator on a term. We define two unary operators: `negation` and `inversion`; a binary operator, `multiplication`; and an n-ary operator, `summation`. The `addends` of sums are represented as relations between `sums` and `terms`. An `equation` is either a predicate `eq` that denotes the equality of the left-hand side and the right-hand side, or a predicate `diffEq` that denotes the differential equation where the derivative of the left-hand side variable equals the right-hand side term.

We extend the DAE domain by adding periodic discrete-time variables, and sample and zero-order hold operators:

```
domain Hybrid extends DAEs
{
    dvar   ::= new (UID,Real,Real).
    sample ::= new (dvar,cvar).
    hold   ::= new (cvar,dvar).
}
```

A hybrid equation extends the differential algebraic equations by periodic discrete-time variables $D \in \text{UID} \times \mathbb{R} \times \mathbb{R}$. A discrete-time variable has a unique identifier, a sampling period p and an initial phase p_0. The discrete-time variable has a well-defined value at *real* times $\{p_0 + n \cdot p \mid n \in \mathbb{N}\}$, everywhere else it is absent.

A model of the hybrid domain is a set of equations E, which represents a set of trajectories over the variables: a trajectory is a function ν that assigns a value to each variable in the system such that $\nu \models E$, i.e., ν simultaneously satisfies all the equations of E. In particular, trajectory ν assigns a real number

$\nu(t, x) \in \mathbb{R}$ to each continuous variable x and continuous time t, and ν assigns a value $\nu(t, x) \in \mathbb{R} \cup \bot$ to each discrete variable x, such that $\nu(t, x) = \bot$ when x is absent.

We can extend the valuation function ν to terms: $\nu(t, \texttt{neg(u)}) \overset{def}{=} -\nu(t, \texttt{u})$ and $\nu(t, \texttt{inv(u)}) \overset{def}{=} 1/\nu(t, \texttt{u})$ and $\nu(t, \texttt{mul(u,v)}) \overset{def}{=} \nu(t, \texttt{u}) \cdot \nu(t, \texttt{u})$ and $\nu(t, \texttt{sum(i)}) \overset{def}{=} \sum \nu(t, \texttt{x})$, where the sum is over each $\texttt{x}$ for which $\texttt{addend(sum(i),x)}$ is a fact.

Finally, the interpretation for the predicates are the following:

$$\nu \models \texttt{eq(u,v)} \quad \text{if } \nu(t, \texttt{u}) = \nu(t, \texttt{v}) \text{ for all } t$$
$$\nu \models \texttt{diffEq(u,v)} \text{ if } \tfrac{d}{dt}(\nu(t, \texttt{u})) = \nu(t, \texttt{v}) \text{ for all } t$$
$$\nu \models \texttt{sample(u,v)} \text{ if } \begin{cases} \nu(t, \texttt{u}) = \nu(t, \texttt{v}) & \text{if } t = p + n \cdot p_0 \text{ for some } n \in \mathbb{N} \\ \nu(t, \texttt{u}) = \bot & \text{otherwise} \end{cases}$$
$$\nu \models \texttt{hold(u,v)} \quad \text{if } \nu(t, \texttt{u}) = \nu(t_0, \texttt{v})$$

where p, p_0 are the period and initial phase of the discrete variable and t_0 is the greatest upper bound such that $t_0 \leq t$ and $t_0 = p + n \cdot p_0$ for some $n \in \mathbb{N}$.

Semantic Mapping. Acausal CPS modeling languages distinguish acausal power ports and causal signal ports. In CyPhyML, each *power port* contributes two variables to the equations, and the denotational semantics of CyPhyML is defined as equations over these variables. *Signal ports* transmit signals with strict causality. Consequently, if we associate a signal variable with each signal port, the variable of a destination port is *enforced* to denote the same value as the variable of the corresponding source port. This relationship is one-way: the value of the variable at the destination port cannot affect the source variable along the connection in question.

Next, we create helper functions to generate unique identifiers for variables and summations in the DAE domain:

```
pV(P,cvar(ID("e",P.id)),cvar(ID("f",P.id))) :- P is P_power.
sV(P,cvar(ID("s",P.id))) :- P is P_signal.
sumName(P,sum(ID("sum",P.id))) :- P is P_power.
```

Relation `pV` maps each power port to a pair of continuous-time variables, `sV` maps signal ports to continuous-time variables and `sumName` assigns a summation operator to each power port. Note the usage of `ID` that is a data constructor for UIDs; its first argument is a string and its second argument is another UID.

Denotational Semantics of Power Port Connections. The semantics of power port connections is defined through their transitive closure. Using fixed-point logic, we can easily express the transitive closure of connections as the least fixed point solution for `Ept`:

```
EpT(X,Y) :- Ep(X,Y); Ep(Y,X).
EpT(X,Y) :- EpT(X,Z), Ep(Z,Y), X!=Y;
            EpT(X,Z), Ep(Y,Z), X!=Y.
```

Using `Ept`, we can express the denotational semantics of power ports: power port connections make the effort variables equal and make the flow variables to sum up to zero across the transitively connected power ports (but only those power ports which are contained within a component).

```
eq(S,0), addend(S,F1), addend(S,F2),
eq(E1,E2) :- EpT(P1,P2),
             portOf(P1,C1), C1:Component,
             portOf(P2,C2), C2:Component,
             pV(P1,E1,F1), pV(P2,E2,F2), sumName(P1,S).
```

The explanation, why such a pair of power variables (effort and flow) is used for describing physical connections, is out of scope in this paper, but the interested reader can find a great introduction to the topic in [31].

Denotational Semantics of Signal Port Connections. A signal connection path (EsT) is a directed path along signal connections. We can use fixed-point logic to find the transitive closure by solving for the least fixed point of EsT:

```
EsT(X,Y) :- Es(X,Y).
EsT(X,Y) :- EsT(X,Z), Es(Z,Y).
```

A signal path (SP) is a signal connection path EsT such that its end-points are signal ports of components (therefore leaving out any signal ports that are ports of component assemblies).

```
SP(X,Y) :- EsT(X,Y), portOf(X,CX), portOf(Y,CY), CX:C, CY:C.
```

The semantics of signal connection is simply the equality of signal variables:

```
eq(S1,S2) :- EsT(P1,P2), sV(P1,S1), sV(P2,S2).
```

6   Formalization of Language Integration

In the previous section, we have formally defined the semantics of CyPhyML composition, but we have not specified, how components are integrated into CyPhyML. In this section, we develop the semantics for the integration of external languages: a bond graph language and the SignalFlow (ESMoL) language. Note that in the future we can easily augment the list by additional languages (for example, we have developed the integration of a subset of the Modelica language).

Bond Graphs are multi-domain graphical representations for physical systems describing the structure of power flows [19]. Regardless of the domain – electrical, mechanical, thermal, magnetic or hydraulic – the same graphical representation is used to describe the flows. A bond graph contains nodes and bonds (links) between the nodes, where bonds represent the flow of energy between components. This energy flow is represented by power variables: the effort and the flow variables, which are bijectively associated with bonds. Note that these effort and flow variables are different from the effort and flow variables of CyPhyML: they denote different entities in different domains.

Previously, we have introduced a bond graph language along with its formal semantics [30]. In this work, we consider a bond graph language that defines power ports in addition: these are ports through which a bond graph component interacts with its environment. Each power port is connected through exactly one bond, therefore a power port represents a pair of power variables: the power variables of its bond. Our bond graph language also contains output signal ports for measuring effort and flows at bond graph junctions, and modulated bond graph elements that are controlled by input signals through input signal ports.

SignalFlow (ESMoL [23]) is a language and tool-suite for designing and implementing computational and communication models. SignalFlow is based on a periodic time-triggered execution, and its components expose periodic discrete-time signal ports on their interface.

Structural Integration

The role of CyPhyML in the integration process is to establish semantic matching between the languages. Component integration is an error-prone task because of the slight differences between different languages. During the formalization we found the following issues: (i) power ports have different meaning in different modeling languages, (ii) even if the semantics is the same, there are differences in the naming conventions, (iii) the discrete-time signals of SignalFlow must be aligned with the continuous-time CyPhyML signals.

To formalize the integration of external languages, we have to extend Cy-PhyML with the *semantic interfaces* of these languages. Hence, we need language elements for representing the external models and their containment in CyPhyML, the ports of these external models, and the port mapping between the ports and the CyPhyML ports. The models and their containment are represented by the following data constructors:

```
BondGraphModel  ::= new (id:UID).
SignalFlowModel ::= new (id:UID, rate:Real).
Model ::= BondGraphModel + SignalFlowModel.
ModelContainer ::= fun (Model => Component).
```

Note the second argument of `SignalFlowModel`: since SignalFlow models are periodic, they have a real value describing their period. The interface ports and port mappings are the following:

```
BG_mechanicalRPort ::= new (id:UID).
...
Model_power  ::= BG_powerPort.
Model_signal ::= BG_signalPort + SF_signalPort.
ModelPortOf  ::= fun (Model_power+Model_signal => Model).
ModelPortMap ::= fun (Model_power+Model_signal, String ->
     P_power+P_signal).
```

Here, the second argument of `ModelPortMap` is the *role* of the port mapping. It is used for denoting special port mappings, such as the positive and negative pins of an electrical connector.

Finally, the following elements are added to the well-formedness rules of Cy-PhyML:

```
// tm(M) denotes that port mapping M is valid (port types are matched)
tm(M) :- M is ModelPortMap(X,_,Y), X:BG_mechanicalRPort, Y:P_rotMech.
...
// invalid, if port mappings are not within same CyPhyMl component:
inv :- ModelPortMap(X,_,Y), ModelPortOf(X,Z), PortOf(Y,W),
       no ModelContainer(Z,W).
// or invalid type matching for any port mapping
inv :- M is ModelPortMap, no tm(M).
// conforms, if both CyPhyML conforms AND port mappings are not ill−formed
conforms :- CyPhyML.conforms, no inv.
```

We also need to extend the definition of our helper functions with the following rules:

```
pV(P,cvar(ID("e",P.id)),cvar(ID("f",P.id))) :- P is Model_power.
sV(P,cvar(ID("s",P.id))) :- P is BG_signalPort.
sV(P,dvar(ID("s",P.id),M.rate,0)) :- P is SF_signalPort,
                                     ModelPortOf(P,M).
```

Note that the SignalFlow ports are converted to discrete-time variables, where the sampling rate is determined by the containing model, and the initial phase defaults to zero.

Bond Graph Integration

For hydraulic and thermal power ports the effort and flow variables of bond graphs and CyPhyML denote the same quantities:

```
eq(E1,E2), eq(F1,F2) :- ModelPortMap(X,_,Y), X:BG_hydraulicThermal,
                        pV(X,E1,F1), pV(Y,E2,F2).
```

In mechanical domains, bond graph efforts denote force and torque and bond graph flows denote velocity and angular velocity. In the CyPhyML language, efforts are position and angular position, flows are force and torque. Therefore, for mechanical power ports, the role of effort and flow is swapped and the derivative of the CyPhyML effort variable is the flow variable of the bond graph:

```
eq(E1,F2), diffEq(E2,F1) :- ModelPortMap(X,_,Y), X:BG_mechanicalPort,
                            pV(X,E1,F1), pV(Y,E2,F2).
```

For the electrical domain, bond graph electrical power ports denote a pair of physical terminals (electrical pins). They are connected to pairs of CyPhyML ports, one to the negative, and the other to the positive pin, which are represented with a plus and minus sign in ModelPortMap.

```
eq(F1,F2), eq(F1,F3),
eq(add(E1,E2),E3) :- ModelPortMap(X,"-",Y), ModelPortMap(X,"+",Z),
    X:BG_electricalPort, pV(X,E1,F1), pV(Y,E2,F2), pV(Z,E3,F3).
```

Finally, bond graph and CyPhyML signal ports are semantically matching:

```
eq(U,V) :- ModelPortMap(X,_,Y), sV(X,U), sV(Y,V).
```

SignalFlow Integration

The discrete signals of SignalFlow output ports are converted to continuous-time signals in CyPhyML by means of hold:

```
hold(V,U) :- ModelPortMap(X,_,Y), X:SF_outSignal, sV(X,U), sV(Y,V).
```

Continuous-time signals of CyPhyML input ports are sampled, when mapped to SignalFlow input ports:

```
sample(U,V) :- ModelPortMap(X,_,Y), X:SF_inSignal, sV(X,U), sV(Y,V).
```

7 Semantic Backplane

The presented approach was used for developing the formal specifications for a suite of languages in DARPA's AVM program. These specifications are collectively called the *semantic backplane*. In this section, we provide some details about the size of the languages and the specifications.

The evaluation and validation of the languages are performed through DARPA's on-going FANG challenge (http://vehicleforge.org), during which more than 1000 systems engineers and 200 design teams are using our tools for building vehicle designs. It is interesting to see the complexity of this semantic backplane in terms of its size: CyPhyML, the integration language contains 4121 model elements, which gets compiled into a FORMULA domain with 1635 lines of code (63 enumerated types, 437 union types, 670 primitive data constructors with 2768 attributes). We have developed a code generator that performs this step automatically. The structural and behavioral specifications of the language consists of 1113 lines of code. Furthermore, the complete infrastructure specification adds an additional 2499 lines of code. Altogether, the specifications for the complete system consist of 21 domains, 6 transformations, 647 rules, 262 derived data constructors and 3612 lines of manually written code. On one hand, these numbers indicate the non-trivial size of the project, and on the other hand, it shows that the approach still results in a reasonably compact specification, which – we believe – is comprehensible and relatively easily maintainable.

8 Conclusion

Safety-critical CPS applications call for sound modeling languages, hence we need mathematically rigorous and unambiguous formal specifications for the structural and behavioral semantics of CPS DSMLs. In this paper, we discussed how a logic-based language can be used for specifying both the structural and the denotational behavioral semantics of a CPS language. Our approach has two advantages: (i) we used an executable formal specification language, which lends itself to model conformance checking, model checking and model synthesis; (ii) both the structural and behavioral specifications are written using the same logic-based language, therefore both can be used for deductive reasoning: in particular, structure-based proofs about behaviors become feasible.

So far, we have formally specified the structural and behavioral semantics for CyPhyML, Hybrid Bond Graphs and ESMoL. However, it remains a matter of future work to use these formalizations for model checking, deductive reasoning and correctness proofs.

Acknowledgement. We are grateful for the comments and suggestions received from three anonymous referees, which proved to be very useful. This work was supported by the National Science Foundation under grant number CNS-1035655.

References

1. FORMULA, http://research.microsoft.com/en-us/projects/formula
2. Basu, A., Bozga, M., Sifakis, J.: Modeling heterogeneous real-time components in BIP. In: SEFM, pp. 3–12 (September 2006)
3. Benveniste, A., Bourke, T., Caillaud, B., Pouzet, M.: Non-standard semantics of hybrid systems modelers. Journal of Computer and System Sciences 78(3), 877–910 (2012)
4. Bliudze, S., Sifakis, J.: The algebra of connectors – structuring interaction in BIP. IEEE Transactions on Computers 57(10), 1315–1330 (2008)
5. Bliudze, S., Sifakis, J.: A notion of glue expressiveness for Component-Based systems. In: van Breugel, F., Chechik, M. (eds.) CONCUR 2008. LNCS, vol. 5201, pp. 508–522. Springer, Heidelberg (2008)
6. Chen, K., Sztipanovits, J., Abdelwalhed, S., Jackson, E.: Semantic anchoring with model transformations. In: Hartman, A., Kreische, D. (eds.) ECMDA-FA 2005. LNCS, vol. 3748, pp. 115–129. Springer, Heidelberg (2005)
7. Chen, K., Sztipanovits, J., Neema, S.: Compositional specification of behavioral semantics. In: Proceedings of the Conference on Design, Automation and Test in Europe, DATE 2007, San Jose, CA, USA, pp. 906–911. EDA Consortium (2007)
8. Egea, M., Rusu, V.: Formal executable semantics for conformance in the MDE framework. Innovations in Systems and Software Engineering 6(1-2), 73–81 (2010)
9. Esfahani, N., Malek, S., Sousa, J.P., Gomaa, H., Menascé, D.A.: A modeling language for activity-oriented composition of service-oriented software systems. In: Schürr, A., Selic, B. (eds.) MODELS 2009. LNCS, vol. 5795, pp. 591–605. Springer, Heidelberg (2009)
10. Gargantini, A., Riccobene, E., Scandurra, P.: A semantic framework for metamodel-based languages. Automated Software Engineering 16(3-4), 415–454 (2009)
11. Goderis, A., Brooks, C., Altintas, I., Lee, E.A., Goble, C.: Composing different models of computation in kepler and ptolemy II. In: Shi, Y., van Albada, G.D., Dongarra, J., Sloot, P.M.A. (eds.) ICCS 2007, Part III. LNCS, vol. 4489, pp. 182–190. Springer, Heidelberg (2007)
12. Goderis, A., Brooks, C., Altintas, I., Lee, E., Goble, C.: Heterogeneous composition of models of computation. Future Generation Computer Systems 25(5), 552–560 (2009)
13. Jackson, E., Sztipanovits, J.: Formalizing the structural semantics of domain-specific modeling languages. Software and Systems Modeling 8(4), 451–478 (2009)

14. Jackson, E., Thibodeaux, R., Porter, J., Sztipanovits, J.: Semantics of domain-specific modeling languages. Model-Based Design for Embedded Systems 1, 437 (2009)
15. Jackson, E.K., Bjørner, N., Schulte, W.: Canonical regular types. ICLP (Technical Communications), 73–83 (2011)
16. Jackson, E.K., Kang, E., Dahlweid, M., Seifert, D., Santen, T.: Components, platforms and possibilities: towards generic automation for MDA. In: Proceedings of the Tenth ACM International Conference on Embedded Software, EMSOFT 2010, pp. 39–48. ACM, New York (2010)
17. Jackson, E.K., Levendovszky, T., Balasubramanian, D.: Reasoning about meta-modeling with formal specifications and automatic proofs. In: Whittle, J., Clark, T., Kühne, T. (eds.) MODELS 2011. LNCS, vol. 6981, pp. 653–667. Springer, Heidelberg (2011)
18. Jackson, E.K., Schulte, W., Bjørner, N.: Detecting specification errors in declarative languages with constraints. In: France, R.B., Kazmeier, J., Breu, R., Atkinson, C. (eds.) MODELS 2012. LNCS, vol. 7590, pp. 399–414. Springer, Heidelberg (2012)
19. Karnopp, D., Margolis, D.L., Rosenberg, R.C.: System dynamics modeling, simulation, and control of mechatronic systems. John Wiley & Sons, Hoboken (2012)
20. Ledeczi, A., Maroti, M., Bakay, A., Karsai, G., Garrett, J., Thomason, C., Nordstrom, G., Sprinkle, J., Volgyesi, P.: The generic modeling environment. In: Workshop on Intelligent Signal Processing, Budapest, Hungary, vol. 17 (2001)
21. Lindecker, D., Simko, G., Madari, I., Levendovszky, T., Sztipanovits, J.: Multi-way semantic specification of domain-specific modeling languages. In: ECBS (2013)
22. Liu, X., Lee, E.A.: CPO semantics of timed interactive actor networks. Theoretical Computer Science 409(1), 110–125 (2008)
23. Porter, J., Hemingway, G., Nine, H., van Buskirk, C., Kottenstette, N., Karsai, G., Sztipanovits, J.: The ESMoL language and tools for high-confidence distributed control systems design. part 1: Design language, modeling framework, and analysis. Tech. Report ISIS-10-109, ISIS, Vanderbilt Univ., Nashville, TN (2010)
24. Rivera, J.E., Duran, F., Vallecillo, A.: Formal specification and analysis of domain specific models using maude. Simulation 85(11-12), 778–792 (2009)
25. Rivera, J.E., Durán, F., Vallecillo, A.: On the behavioral semantics of real-time domain specific visual languages. In: Ölveczky, P.C. (ed.) WRLA 2010. LNCS, vol. 6381, pp. 174–190. Springer, Heidelberg (2010)
26. Rivera, J.E., Vallecillo, A.: Adding behavior to models. In: EDOC, p. 169. IEEE (October 2007)
27. Romero, J.R., Rivera, J.E., Duran, F., Vallecillo, A.: Formal and tool support for model driven engineering with maude. Journal of Object Technology 6(9), 187–207 (2007)
28. Rusu, V.: Embedding domain-specific modelling languages in maude specifications. ACM SIGSOFT Software Engineering Notes 36(1), 1–8 (2011)
29. Simko, G., Levendovszky, T., Neema, S., Jackson, E., Bapty, T., Porter, J., Sztipanovits, J.: Foundation for model integration: Semantic backplane. In: IDETC/CIE (2012)
30. Simko, G., Lindecker, D., Levendovszky, T., Jackson, E., Neema, S., Sztipanovits, J.: A framework for unambiguous and extensible specification of DSMLs for cyber-physical systems. In: ECBS (2013)
31. Willems, J.: The behavioral approach to open and interconnected systems. IEEE Control Systems 27(6), 46–99 (2007)

Endogenous Metamodeling Semantics for Structural UML 2 Concepts

Lars Hamann and Martin Gogolla

University of Bremen, Computer Science Department
Database Systems Group, D-28334 Bremen, Germany
{lhamann,gogolla}@informatik.uni-bremen.de
http://www.db.informatik.uni-bremen.de

Abstract. A lot of work has been done in order to put the Unified Modeling Language (UML) on a formal basis by translating concepts into various formal languages, e.g., set theory or graph transformation. While the abstract UML syntax is defined by using an endogenous approach, i. e., UML describes its abstract syntax using UML, this approach is rarely used for its semantics. This paper shows how to apply an endogenous approach called metamodeling semantics for central parts of the UML standard. To this end, we enrich existing UML language elements with constraints specified in the Object Constraint Language (OCL) in order to describe a semantic domain model. The UML specification explicitly states that complete runtime semantics is not included in the standard because it would be a major amount of work. However, we believe that certain central concepts, like the ones used in the UML standard and in particular property features as subsets, union and derived, need to be explicitly modeled to enforce a common understanding. Using such an endogenous approach enables the validation and verification of the UML standard by using off-the-shelf UML and OCL tools.

Keywords: Metamodeling, Semantics, Validation, UML, OCL.

1 Introduction

In order to describe the abstract syntax of modeling languages, well-known concepts like classes, associations, and inheritance are used to express the structure of a language. These elements are commonly used in combination with a textual language to express further well-formedness rules which cannot be expressed using a graphical syntax. To improve the expressiveness of graphical modeling languages, especially when using complex inheritance relations, additional annotations have been developed to express more detailed information about the relation between model elements. Examples of these annotations are the subsets relations between properties and tagging a property as a derived union. The abstract syntax definition of the UML [23,26] uses these newer modeling elements

A. Moreira et al. (Eds.): MODELS 2013, LNCS 8107, pp. 488–504, 2013.

since UML 2. Such a distinguished usage calls for the need of a precise definition at the syntax level (design time) and also on the semantic level (runtime)[1].

In this paper, we present an endogenous approach to specify the syntax and the semantics of central concepts of modeling languages. To this end, we use the same formalism, i. e., class diagrams enriched with constraints expressed in the Object Constraint Language (OCL) [24,32], as used currently for the syntax description of modeling languages. To demonstrate our approach we choose particular UML language features (subsets, union and derived), but the same method may be applied to all UML language elements. The language features we choose are also important on their own, because they are used in MOF (i. e. as a description language for UML) without having a proper formal semantics currently. Our work is different to other approaches, like for example [1,19], that define a formal semantics for the modeling elements mentioned above, in the sense, that we use the same languages to describe the syntax and the semantics instead of translating syntactical elements into a different formalism.

The rest of this work is structured as follows: In the next section we describe the concept of metamodeling semantics. In Sect. 3 we explain our approach for metamodeling the runtime semantics of modeling elements by using well-known examples. Section 4 identifies benefits arising when using tool-based validation of modeling concepts. Before the paper ends with a conclusion and future work, we discuss related approaches in Sect. 5.

2 Metamodeling Semantics

The notion *Metamodeling Semantics* can be explained well by quoting a statement from [16]:

> Metamodeling semantics is a way to describe semantics that is similar to the way in which popular languages like UML are defined. In metamodeling semantics, not only the abstract syntax of the language, but also the semantic domain, is specified using a model.

Metamodeling a language by defining the abstract syntax using a graphical modeling language combined with a formal textual language to express well-formedness rules is a well-known technique. The UML specification for example uses UML (or MOF which itself uses UML) in combination with the Object Constraint Language (OCL) to define its abstract syntax. In [16] this is called the *Abstract Syntax Model (ASM)*, which defines the valid structures in a model. The same technique is rarely used to define the semantics of a language, i. e., to specify a *Semantic Domain Model (SDM)* of a modeling language. A *semantic domain* defines the meaning of a particular language feature, whereas a semantic domain model describes this meaning by modeling the runtime behavior of a (syntactically) valid model using its runtime values and applying meaning to

---

[1] In this work, we distinguish between design time and runtime by using classes and objects. Note, that this distinction is not always appropriate.

them. For example, later we will see that in the UML there is the class `Class` in the abstract syntax part, and there is the class `InstancesSpecification` in the semantic domain part which together can describe (through an appropriate association) that a class (introduced at design time) is interpreted (at runtime) by a set of objects, formally captured as instance specifications. Another publicly available example for metamodeling semantics can be found in Section 10 of the OCL specification [24]. It defines constraints on values, i.e., runtime instances, which are part of the SDM. For example, the runtime value of a set is constrained as follows:

```
context SetTypeValue inv: self.element->isUnique(e : Element | e.value)
```

The central idea behind the approach in [24] is to describe the runtime behavior of OCL using OCL, which is similar to the UML metamodel described by UML models. While this is done in the UML to constrain the metamodel level M1, i.e., the valid structure of models, very little formal information is given for the level M0. Nearly only, the structure for the runtime snapshots is specified, but little use is made of defining runtime constraints in a formal language like OCL. An excerpt of the UML metamodel which shows important elements for our work is shown in Fig. 1. The diagram combines elements from roughly six syntax diagrams of the UML metamodel. On the left side, the ASM (syntax) of the UML is shown. On the right, the SDM (semantics) elements are given as they are present in the current specification. In the next section we define runtime constraints on the semantic domain model for several modeling constructs which are frequently used in the definition of the UML metamodel, but are only defined in an informal way with verbal descriptions in the current UML.

3   OCL-Based Instance and Value Semantics

In this section we describe our approach of metamodeling semantics for different language features. We start with commonly used constraints on properties and how they can be described without leaving the technology space. Next we explain the semantics for evaluating derived properties.

3.1   Subsetting and Derived Unions

We explain our proposal by starting with a basic class diagram, which uses subsetting and union constraints on attributes of classes. Later on, we extend this diagram by using subsetting and union on associations. Subsetting and union constraints on properties (a property can be an attribute or an association end) define a relation between these two properties. The values of a subsetting property must be a subset of the values for the subsetted property. Union can be used on a single property. Its usage defines that the values of a property are the union of all its subsetting properties.

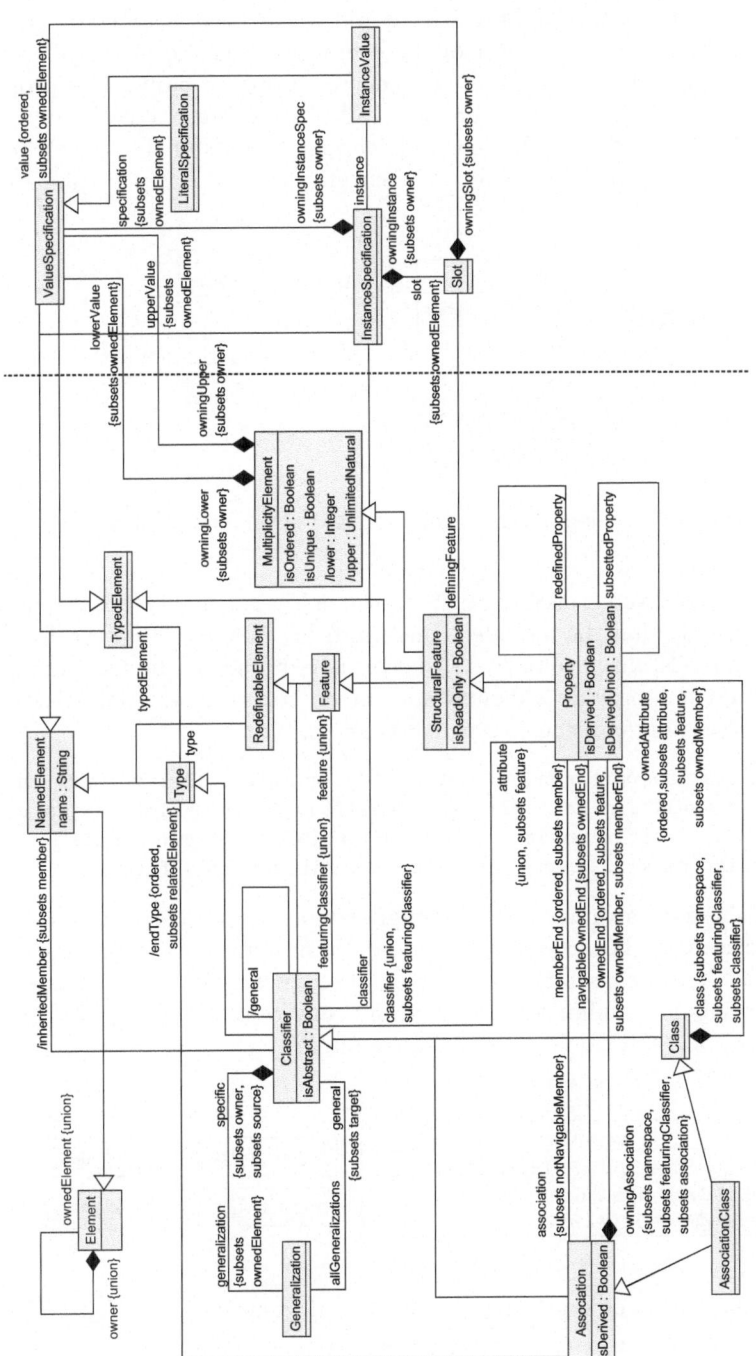

Fig. 1. Combined view of UML metamodel elements important for our work

Figure 2 shows a simple model of vehicles (c. f. [4]). A vehicle consists of vehicle parts. For a car, information about the front and back wheels is added to the class Car. Because these wheels are part of the overall vehicle, the properties `front` and `back` are marked as subsets of the general property `part`. The property `part` itself is marked as a derived `union` of all of its subsets. Furthermore, the subsetting properties restrict the lower and upper bounds of the wheels to the common number of wheels for a car (2 is equivalent to 2..2). A valid object

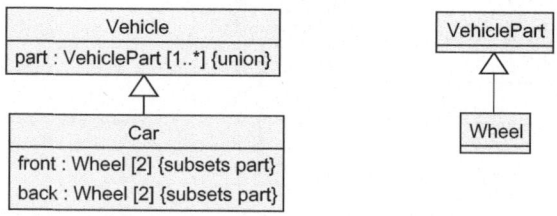

Fig. 2. Class diagram using `subsets` and `union` on attributes

diagram w. r. t. the given class diagram is shown in Fig 3. For this simple diagram, one can see directly that the intended constraints are fulfilled. However, for more complicated models, an automatic validation is required. If the used modeling language would not provide `subsets` and `union` constraints, a modeler could still specify constraints on the classes `Vehicle` and `Car`:

```
context Vehicle inv partIsUnion: let selfCar = self.oclAsType(Car) in
    selfCar <> null implies self.part = selfCar.front->union(selfCar.back)
context Car inv frontIsSubset: self.part->includesAll(self.front)
context Car inv backIsSubset:  self.part->includesAll(self.back)
```

However, these constraints would strongly couple the abstract class `Vehicle` and its subclass `Car`, because `Vehicle` needs information about its subclasses to validate the union constraint. This breaks well-known design guidelines. The above constraints are similar to the generated constraints from [20]. Using such an automatic approach would reduce the coupling.

Fig. 3. A valid object diagram of the class diagram shown in Fig. 2

To allow a generic usage of these constraints the UML provides the ability to specify subset relations between properties using a reflexive association on

Property (which represents class attributes and association ends) and to mark a property as a derived union (see Fig. 1). Further, several well-formedness OCL rules are given, to ensure the syntactical correctness of the usage. For example, the type of the subsetting property must conform to the type of the subsetted end [23, p. 126]. However, information about the semantics of the UML language element subsets is only provided textually, not in a formal way. We propose to add (what we call) runtime semantics by means of OCL constraints to the already present elements describing runtime elements. For the above example, a constraint describing the runtime semantics of subsets can be specified on the UML metaclass Slot (a slot allows, for example, to assign an attribute value to an attribute):

```
context Slot inv subsettingIsValid:
let prop = self.definingFeature.oclAsType(Property) in
(prop <> null and prop.owner.oclIsKindOf(Class)) implies
 prop.subsettedProperty->forAll(subsettedProp |
   let subsettedValues = self.owningInstance.slot->
    any(definingFeature=subsettedProp).value.getValue()->asSet() in
   let currentValues = self.value.getValue()->asSet() in
   subsettedValues->includesAll(currentValues))
```

This constraint checks for each slot that defines a value or values for an attribute of a class, if it is a subset of the values defined by the slots of the subsetted properties. Because this constraint only considers attributes of classes, the navigation to the slots of the owning instance of the context slot is enough. For associations, and especially for associations with more than two ends, the calculation of the values to be considered is more complicated.

A class diagram which makes use of subsets and union on association ends is given in Fig. 4. The previously specified attributes part and front are changed to association ends, while the attribute back is left out in order to keep the following examples at a moderate size.

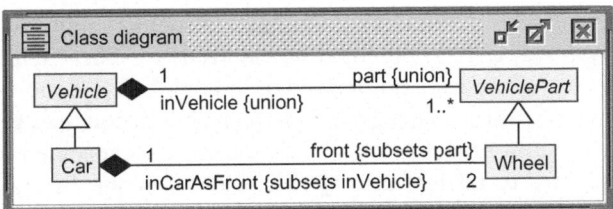

Fig. 4. Class diagram using subsets and union on association ends

Figure 5 shows an example instantiation of the class diagram. The links shown as a solid line are inserted by the user, while the dashed links are automatically calculated by our tool, because they are part of a derived union. In our tool, all

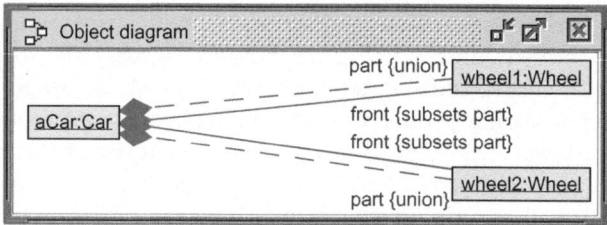

Fig. 5. A valid object diagram of the class diagram shown in Fig. 4

derived links (either established through a derived union or through an explicit derived association end) are shown as dashed links.

The object diagram in Fig. 6 shows an instantiation of the UML metamodel representing the class diagram of Fig. 4 at the top and the object diagram shown in Fig. 5 at the bottom. This figure intentionally includes so many dashed lines and compositions, in order to show the inherent complexity of the UML metamodel. This complexity can automatically be revealed by using our tool. In Sect. 4 we are going to explain these so-called virtual links in more detail. On the other side, these virtual links allow us to suppress certain elements in the object diagram to make it easier to be read. For example, the generalization relationships are only shown as derived links between the classes leaving out the generalization instance. To be more concrete, in the left upper part of Fig. 6 the dashed link between Class3 (Vehicle) and Class4 (Car) corresponds to the left generalization arrow in Fig. 4. We use this diagram in the following to explain an extended runtime semantics which also covers associations.

A runtime semantics for subsetting that covers attributes and association ends must consider all tuples of instances which are linked to a subsetted property and the set of instances linked to this tuple at the subsetting end. For the previously shown example on attributes, this tuple contains only one element, namely the defining instance, whereas for association ends of an association with n ends, this tuple contains $n - 1$ elements. We accomplish this by using a query operation called getConnectedObjects() which is similar to the operation Extent::linkedObjects(...) defined in the MOF specification[22], but covers n-ary associations, properties, and derived unions. We do not show the operation in detail, because it is rather lengthy[2]. The query operation uses the metaclasses of the semantic domain model to obtain all connections specified for a property. For this, it navigates to all instance specifications to consider and their owned slots. If a property is defined as a derived union, this operation is recursively invoked on all properties subsetting the derived union property and collects all connected values in a single set, i. e., it builds the union of the values. To give a more detailed view of the usage of this central operation, Fig. 7 shows the result of invoking it on the property part using the state shown in Fig. 6.

---

[2] Interested readers are referred to the USE distribution which contains a well-defined subset of the UML metamodel including this operation.

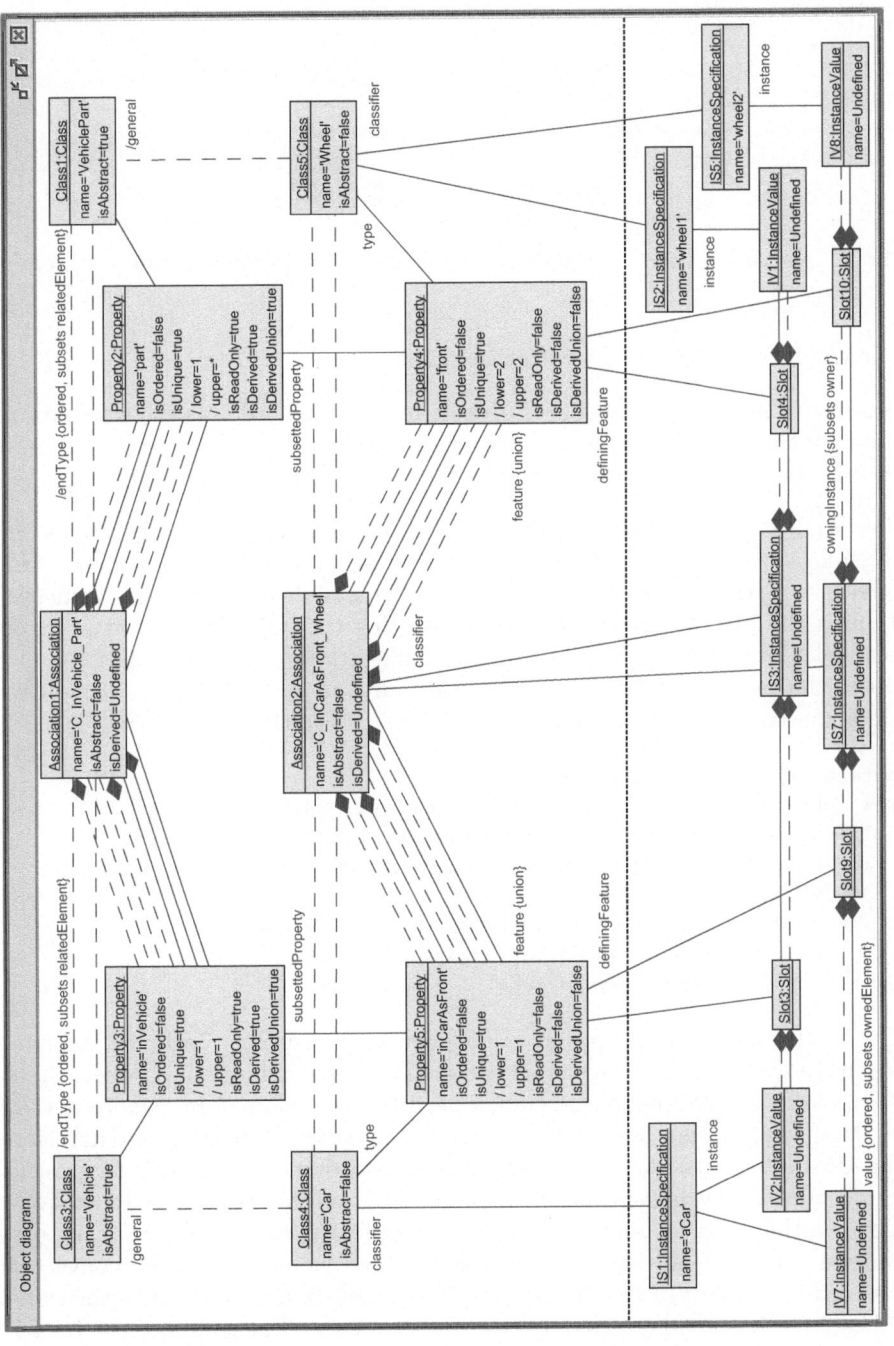

Fig. 6. The diagrams shown in Fig. 4 and 5 as an instantiation of the UML metamodel

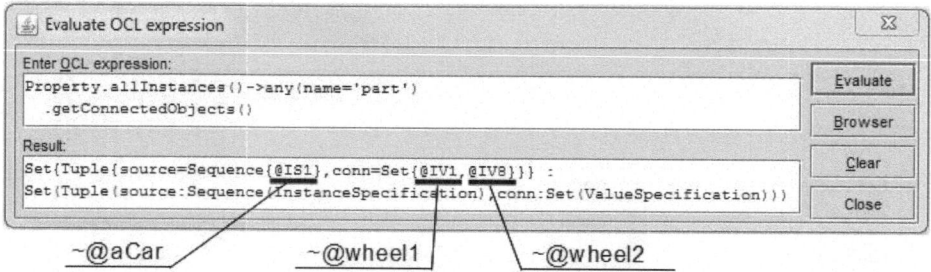

Fig. 7. Querying runtime values by using the operation `getConnectedObjects()`

The result is a set of tuples with two parts:

1. **source**: The sequence of source objects in the same order as the association ends, if the property is owned by an association.
2. **conn**: The objects connected to the source objects at the property.

The result of the evaluation is the calculated union of the property values for all possible source objects. Because only one vehicle (named `aCar`), is present in the given state, the set contains a single tuple. This tuple consists of the sequence containing the instance specification representing the object `aCar` and a set of values which are linked to this instance via subsetting properties of `part`.

Given the previously described operation `getConnectedObjects()`, we can define a constraint which ensures the subsetting semantics:

```
1 context Property inv subsettingIsValid:
2   let subsetLinks = self.getConnectedObjects() in
3   self.subsettedProperty->forAll(supersetProperty |
4     let supersetLinks = supersetProperty.getConnectedObjects() in
5     subsetLinks->forAll(t1 |
6       supersetLinks->one(t2 | t1.source=t2.source and
7         t2.conn.getValue()->asSet()->includesAll(
8           t1.conn.getValue()->asSet()))))
```

The central part of the given invariant can be seen on line 7 where the operation `includesAll` is used, which is the OCL way to validate, if a collection is a superset of another one. Some things need to be explained in a more detail. First, the usage of the operation `getValue():OclAny`, which is an extension to the UML metaclass `ValueSpecification`, is required to be able to get the concrete value of a value specification. The UML metamodel defines several operations on this class for retrieving basic types like `stringValue():String` but excludes a generic definition. Second, the collected values need to be converted to a set using `->asSet()` (see lines 7 and 8) because values can map to the same specifications. It should be mentioned, that if evaluated at runtime, the invariant only validates the union calculation if subsets is used in the context of a derived union. If subsets is used on a property which is not a derived union, the constraint validates the user defined structure. Including the described invariant and similar invariants for other runtime elements, adds a precise definition of its semantics to the modeling language.

3.2   Derived Properties

Derived properties are widely used during the specification of models and meta-models, because they allow to shorten certain expressions and to assign associated elements an exact meaning by naming them. If a formal expression is given which describes how to calculate the values of the derived properties, the definition of the metamodel is even stronger. If the derived property is marked as read only, a query language can be used to evaluate these derive expressions. Writable derived properties are allowed for example in the UML, but we exclude this type of properties, because the computational overhead of computing the inverse values would be too high. Furthermore, only bijective derive expressions can be used. For example, an attribute `weight` for the class `Car` used in the example could be derived as follows:

```
context Car::weight:Integer derive: self.part.weight->sum()
```

Assigning a value to the attribute weight of a car cannot lead to a single result in the weights of the parts. A common way to overcome this issue is to use a declarative approach like it is done in the UML specification by using invariants for a derive expression [23, p. 128]. This transfers the responsibility to set the correct derived values or the inverse direction to an implementation. Therefore, the UML metamodel excludes the ability to add a derive expression to a property like it is done with default values. Whereas, the OCL specification links to the UML metamodel for the placement of derive expressions [24, p. 182]. We propose to add such a possibility, to allow the specification of the runtime semantics of derived read only properties. For this, we extend the metamodel by defining an additional association between `Property` and `ValueSpecification`. To ensure, that a derived expression is only used on read only properties, the following well-formedness rule needs to be added:

```
context Property inv: self.derivedValue <> null implies self.readOnly
```

The context of such a derive expression used during evaluation is related to the previously explained semantics of `subsets` and `union`. To recapitulate the essentials, for a generic solution it is necessary to consider the combinations of source objects and their connected objects. Only this allows to use derived association ends on associations with more than two association ends and further allows the evaluation of backward navigations, i. e., from a derived end to an opposite end. The major difference to the validation of subsetting is, that only if a derived association end of a binary association or an attribute are the target of a navigation, the source objects are known. If a navigation uses instead the derived end as the source, for all possible combinations of the connected end types the expression needs to be evaluated and checked if the source object of the navigation is in the result. As an example consider the derived association end /general of the reflexive association defined on the class Classifier shown in Fig. 1. The UML specification defines the derived end using a constraint on classifier as follows [23, p. 52][3]:

```
general = self.generalization.general->asSet()
```

Used as a derive expression, the result for a navigation from a classifier instance to the association end general can be calculated using the source instance as the context object self. For the opposite direction of the navigation, i. e., navigating from a classifier instance to its subclasses, the derive expression needs to be evaluated for all instances of Classifier:

```
superclass = Classifier.allInstances()->select(general->includes(self))
```

For n-ary associations navigating to the derived association end, the derive expression needs to be evaluated with each combination of the source object and all possible instances at the other ends (excluding the derived end). The resulting set is the union of all evaluation results. If a navigation starts at the derived end of an n-ary association, the calculation is similar to the case of navigating backward in a binary association. Except, that the evaluation is performed for the cross product of all instances which can participate in the association. This means all instances of the end types except the derived end.

4   Tool Based Validation

Because of the endogenous nature of the semantics described in the previous chapter, they were developed in parallel to extensions to a modeling tool. To validate the structural constraints used inside the UML metamodel, these were added to the tool, which allowed us to represent greater parts of the metamodel. Using a tool based validation approach and extending it in a step-wise manner added a reverse link to the specification of the runtime semantics. Without a validation tool, it is rather hopeless to bring a metamodel including well-defined semantics for a modeling language to a consistent state. Using a modeling tool to validate its modeling language, like the bootstrapping approach used for compilers, allows to discover issues beyond syntactical errors in an early state. For example, only after using derived unions in combination with derived association ends we discovered an infinite recursive definitions at the metamodel level in the current UML standard. In this particular case, a derived association end was used inside a union and the derive expression used this union. In the following parts of this section, we explain some beneficial features supporting the definition of (meta-)models which are integrated in our modeling tool USE [11,30]. Additional supporting features are beyond the scope of this paper, but can be

---

[3] The constraint has slightly been modified to be more expressive. In detail, the body of the operation Classifier::parent() was embedded into the constraint. Further, asSet() was added to establish type soundness.

found in several publications of our group, e. g., [13,14,12]. Such a left out feature is the possibility to evaluate the specified constraints on a model instance, which was used to validate the invariants presented in this paper.

During the development of a metamodel, already on the syntactical level the usage of automatically generated dynamic views can support the user. While the size of a model increases, the usage of the modeling elements discussed in this paper (subsets, union and derived properties) can get unmanageable without adequate support by a tool. USE provides a comprehensive view which provides information about these elements defined for an association. An example of this view is presented in Fig. 8. It shows the derived union association specified between the metaclasses `Classifier` and `Feature` in the UML metamodel. A user can directly see which associations are related to the selected one and what kind of relations are defined. Implicit information, like for example a missing subsets on the opposite end is highlighted.

⟨— Association ends info													
Association			A_Classifier_FeaturingClassifier_Feature_Feature										▼
Rolename	Type	Mul	Union	Derived	Subsets	... ...	Subsets	Derived	Union	Mul.	Type	Rolename
featuringClassifier	Classifier	*	✔	□		...		□	✔	*	Feature	feature
interface	Interface	0..1	□	□	featuringClassifier	...	feature	□	□	*	Operation	ownedOperation
datatype	DataType	0..1	□	□	featuringClassifier	...	feature	□	□	*	Operation	ownedOperation
datatype	DataType	0..1	□	□	classifier, featuringClassifier	...	attribute, feature	□	□	*	Property	ownedAttribute
classifier	Classifier	0..1	□	✔	featuringClassifier	...	feature	□	✔	*	Property	attribute
owningAssociation	Association	0..1	□	□	featuringClassifier	...	feature	□	□	*	Property	ownedEnd
notNavigableOw...	interface	0..1	□	□	featuringClassifier, classifier	...	attribute, feature	□	□	*	Property	ownedAttribute
Legend: green: end of selected association; blue: end is directly redefined/subsetted; red: end redefines/subsets implicitly another end													

Fig. 8. Information about association relations available in USE

Another valuable functionality, which was touched slightly while explaining Fig. 5 and 6 is the automatic calculation and presentation of virtual links (presented as dashed lines) which result from associations that include a derived expression or derived unions. In Fig. 9 an in-depth view on the defined and derived links between the instances representing the composition `C_InCarAsFront` and its owned end `front` is shown. While the three lower links are specified by the user, the upper four links are automatically presented to the user because they are part of a derived union. Another usage of virtual links is to compress diagrams as it was done in Fig. 6 by excluding the generalization instances, but still showing the generalization link between classes using the derived end `/general`.

Furthermore, using derived associations allows a user to model information in a different way which may be more suitable to express her intention. The USE session presented in Fig. 10 shows an example, which uses a derived ternary association to show the direct relation of associated objects. The example defines a small library model composed of classes for users, copies and books. The fact that a user can borrow copies of books is modeled by two binary associations which together link all three classes. A third association is defined, that is derived

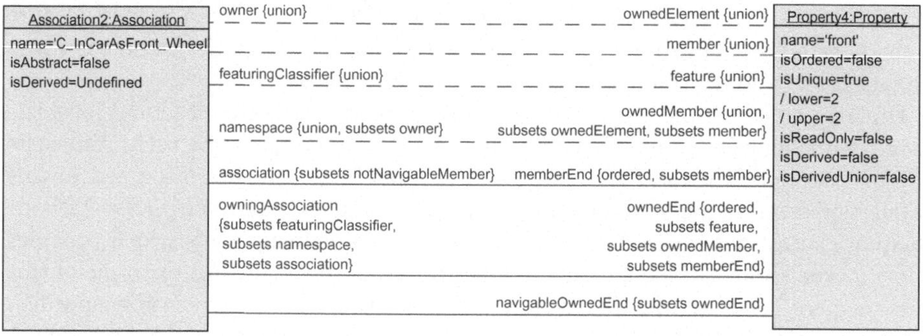

Association2:Association	owner {union}	ownedElement {union}	Property4:Property
name='C_InCarAsFront_Wheel' isAbstract=false isDerived=Undefined	member {union}	name='front' isOrdered=false
	featuringClassifier {union}	feature {union}	isUnique=true / lower=2
	namespace {union, subsets owner}	ownedMember {union, subsets ownedElement, subsets member}	/ upper=2 isReadOnly=false isDerived=false
	association {subsets notNavigableMember}	memberEnd {ordered, subsets member}	isDerivedUnion=false
	owningAssociation {subsets featuringClassifier, subsets namespace, subsets association}	ownedEnd {ordered, subsets feature, subsets ownedMember, subsets memberEnd}	
		navigableOwnedEnd {subsets ownedEnd}	

Fig. 9. A detailed view on virtual links present in the UML metamodel instance (Fig. 6)

and combines the aforementioned associations into a single ternary one. The definition of the derived association in the concrete syntax of USE is as follows:

```
association BorrowsCombined between
  User[*] role dUser
  Copy[0..1] role dCopy derived(aUser:User,aBook:Book) =
    aUser.copy->select(c | c.book=aBook)
  Book[*] role dBook
end
```

The shown textual language is an excerpt of the language used to define UML models in USE. It is comparable to HUTN (UML Human-Usable Textual Notation) of the OMG [21]. To be able to show derived links, our language defines the keyword derive to mark an an association end as derived. The derive keyword requires an OCL expression which defines the derived links. For n-ary associations, also the naming of the parts of a combination is required to be able to evaluate an arbitrary OCL expression. In contrast to this, a derived expression on a binary association can use a single context variable self, because there is no combination of instances at association ends.

For example, to calculate the links for the association BorrowsCombined the derive expression at the association end dCopy is evaluated for all pairs of User and Book objects (these pairs are expressed by the signature (aUser:User, aBook:Book) of the derive definition shown above. The derive expression returns all copies associated with a given pair of a user and a book. For each Copy object in the result set a link connected to the input pair and the copy object is shown in the object diagram. In addition, the example shows how one can use a multiplicity constraint on derived associations. In this example, the multiplicity constraint 0..1 in the association end dCopy excludes double borrowings (a user borrows more than one copy of the same book). The multiplicity violation of the example state is reported to the user, as can be seen at the bottom of Fig. 10.

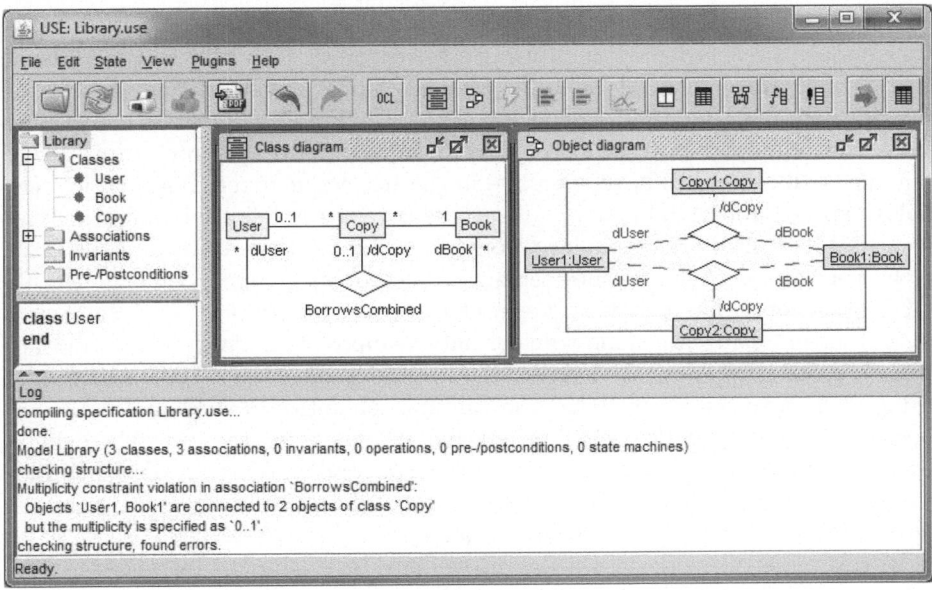

Fig. 10. Screenshot of USE while validating a snapshot with derived ternary association

5   Related Work

Metamodeling semantics has been used in areas not focused in this paper. In [8] it is applied to define the semantics of multiple inheritance using a set-theoretic based metamodel. [16] shows its application to specify the semantics of OCL, whereas [9,15] cover a detailed view on the overall topic of metamodeling semantics. A combined view of different metamodeling levels is used in [10] to specify the semantics of entity relationship diagrams and their transformation into the domain of relational schemata.

As examples for the ongoing discussion about the need of a formal semantics for UML and to what extend it should be defined, we refer to [27] and [5]. The authors of [5] discuss the benefits and drawbacks of a precise UML specification including runtime semantics from several points of view. Furthermore, the problems arising by trying to be a general purpose language for different domains implying semantic variation points is explained. We believe, that both points of view are valid, but the viewpoints change during the development process. At an early stage of design, the used modeling language could allow to violate the precise semantics. While the process continues, these violations should be more and more forbidden until a state is reached where no violation is allowed.

Beside the vast amount of publications defining the semantics of UML, e. g. [18,31,28], work covering the UML language elements presented in this paper has been done. [4] gives a descriptive insight of using union and subsets and shows its relation to composite structures.

Exogenous definitions of the semantics for subset and union properties have, for example, been provided in [1] using a set-theoretic formalization, [3,2] using graph transformations, and [19] using a so-called property oriented abstract syntax to define the semantics of what the authors call inter-association constraints (these include subsets and union). These examples of exogenous definitions of semantics all require to have expertise in the respective external semantic technology space. [20] introduces a UML profile covering redefinition and other elements. While the work is similar to ours in the sense that it stays in the same technological space, the runtime semantics is enforced generating model specific OCL constraints, like the ones shown at the beginning of Sect. 3. A semantics for subsetting using the same transformation approach is given in [7]. Another transformation approach to describe the runtime semantics of UML constraints using OCL is shown in [6]. Here, the runtime semantics implied by UML compositions are translated to OCL constrains, i.e. the semantics must be defined by a transformation into a specific application model. Whereas our semantics works in a universal way, where constraints are formulated on the metamodel level without the need for transformation.

In this paper we presented a way to validate (meta-)model instances by creating snapshots, i.e., instantiations, of these models and by examining their behavior, for example, by checking the multiplicity constraints on an instance or by examining the current states of the defined invariants. Other approaches use automatic techniques to reason about models specified in UML/OCL. An approach like [17] could, for example, be used to find valid configurations of writable derived properties as discussed earlier in this paper. In addition, it can be used like the ones in [29] and [25] to answer questions about the satisfiability and other properties of a model.

6   Conclusion and Future Work

We presented a proposal to specify the runtime semantics of a modeling language using a metamodel describing syntax and semantics in the same language. Using the same technology space reduces the overall complexity of the language description, because knowledge of other languages is not required. Furthermore, the process of specifying the language is improved, if this self describing technique is used in combination with tool-supported validation. As we have shown in Sect. 4, bringing models into being by creating snapshots can give insights into the model which are rather vague if only the static specification is used.

As future work, the application of our approach to other areas of modeling languages, for example property redefinition and association generalization, seem to be promising directions to extend our work. The covered elements of the UML metamodel for validation and the options on the user interface in our tool USE can be strengthened as well. Larger case studies with other modeling language, for example domain-specific languages, will give further feedback on the usability of the approach.

References

1. Alanen, M., Porres, I.: A metamodeling language supporting subset and union properties. Software and Systems Modeling 7(1), 103–124 (2008)
2. Amelunxen, C.: Metamodel-based Design Rule Checking and Enforcement. Ph.D. thesis, Technische Universität Darmstadt (2009), dissertation
3. Amelunxen, C., Schürr, A.: Formalizing Model Transformation Rules for UML/MOF 2. IET Software Journal 2(3), 204–222 (2008); Special Issue: Language Engineering
4. Bock, C.: UML 2 Composition Model. Journal of Object Technology 3(10), 47–73 (2004), http://www.jot.fm/issues/issue_2004_11/column5
5. Broy, M., Cengarle, M.V.: UML formal semantics: lessons learned. Software and System Modeling 10(4), 441–446 (2011)
6. Chavez, H.M., Shen, W.: Formalization of UML Composition in OCL. In: Miao, H., Lee, R.Y., Zeng, H., Baik, J. (eds.) ACIS-ICIS, pp. 675–680. IEEE (2012)
7. Costal, D., Gómez, C., Guizzardi, G.: Formal Semantics and Ontological Analysis for Understanding Subsetting, Specialization and Redefinition of Associations in UML. In: Jeusfeld, M., Delcambre, L., Ling, T.-W. (eds.) ER 2011. LNCS, vol. 6998, pp. 189–203. Springer, Heidelberg (2011)
8. Ducournau, R., Privat, J.: Metamodeling semantics of multiple inheritance. Science of Computer Programming 76(7), 555–586 (2011)
9. Engels, G., Hausmann, J.H., Heckel, R., Sauer, S.: Dynamic Meta Modeling: A Graphical Approach to the Operational Semantics of Behavioral Diagrams in UML. In: Evans, A., Caskurlu, B., Selic, B. (eds.) UML 2000. LNCS, vol. 1939, pp. 323–337. Springer, Heidelberg (2000)
10. Gogolla, M.: Exploring ER and RE Syntax and Semantics with Metamodel Object Diagrams. In: Nürnberg, P.J. (ed.) Proc. Metainformatics Symposium (MIS 2005). ACM Int. Conf. Proceeding Series, vol. 214, 12 pages. ACM Press, New York (2005)
11. Gogolla, M., Büttner, F., Richters, M.: USE: A UML-Based Specification Environment for Validating UML and OCL. Science of Computer Programming 69, 27–34 (2007)
12. Gogolla, M., Hamann, L., Xu, J., Zhang, J.: Exploring (Meta-)Model Snapshots by Combining Visual and Textual Techniques. In: Gadducci, F., Mariani, L. (eds.) Proc. Workshop Graph Transformation and Visual Modeling Techniques (GTVMT 2011). ECEASST, Electronic Communications (2011), journal.ub.tu-berlin.de/eceasst/issue/view/53
13. Hamann, L., Hofrichter, O., Gogolla, M.: OCL-Based Runtime Monitoring of Applications with Protocol State Machines. In: Vallecillo, A., Tolvanen, J.-P., Kindler, E., Störrle, H., Kolovos, D. (eds.) ECMFA 2012. LNCS, vol. 7349, pp. 384–399. Springer, Heidelberg (2012)
14. Hamann, L., Hofrichter, O., Gogolla, M.: On Integrating Structure and Behavior Modeling with OCL. In: France, R.B., Kazmeier, J., Breu, R., Atkinson, C. (eds.) MoDELS 2012. LNCS, vol. 7590, pp. 235–251. Springer, Heidelberg (2012)
15. Hausmann, J.H.: Dynamic META modeling: a semantics description technique for visual modeling languages. Ph.D. thesis, University of Paderborn (2005)
16. Kleppe, A.: Object constraint language: Metamodeling semantics. In: Lano, K. (ed.) UML 2 Semantics and Applications, pp. 163–178. John Wiley & Sons, Inc. (2009)

17. Kuhlmann, M., Hamann, L., Gogolla, M.: Extensive Validation of OCL Models by Integrating SAT Solving into USE. In: Bishop, J., Vallecillo, A. (eds.) TOOLS 2011. LNCS, vol. 6705, pp. 290–306. Springer, Heidelberg (2011)

18. Lano, K.: UML 2 Semantics and Applications. John Wiley & Sons, Inc. (2009)

19. Maraee, A., Balaban, M.: Inter-association Constraints in UML2: Comparative Analysis, Usage Recommendations, and Modeling Guidelines. In: France, R.B., Kazmeier, J., Breu, R., Atkinson, C. (eds.) MoDELS 2012. LNCS, vol. 7590, pp. 302–318. Springer, Heidelberg (2012)

20. Nieto, P., Costal, D., Gómez, C.: Enhancing the semantics of UML association redefinition. Data Knowl. Eng. 70(2), 182–207 (2011)

21. OMG (ed.): UML Human-Usable Textual Notation (HUTN). Object Management Group (OMG) (August 2004), http://www.omg.org/spec/HUTN/

22. OMG (ed.): Meta Object Facility (MOF) Core Specification 2.4.1. Object Management Group (OMG) (August 2011), http://www.omg.org/spec/MOF/2.4.1

23. OMG (ed.): UML Superstructure 2.4.1. Object Management Group (OMG) (August 2011), http://www.omg.org/spec/UML/2.4.1/Superstructure/PDF

24. OMG (ed.): Object Constraint Language 2.3.1. Object Management Group (OMG) (January 2012), http://www.omg.org/spec/OCL/2.3.1/

25. Queralt, A., Teniente, E.: Verification and Validation of UML Conceptual Schemas with OCL Constraints. ACM Trans. Softw. Eng. Methodol. 21(2), 13 (2012)

26. Rumbaugh, J., Jacobson, I., Booch, G.: The Unified Modeling Language - Reference Manual, 2nd edn. Addison-Wesley (2004)

27. Rumpe, B., France, R.B.: Variability in UML language and semantics. Software and System Modeling 10(4), 439–440 (2011)

28. Shan, L., Zhu, H.: Unifying the Semantics of Models and Meta-Models in the Multi-Layered UML Meta-Modelling Hierarchy. Int. J. Software and Informatics 6(2), 163–200 (2012)

29. Soeken, M., Wille, R., Drechsler, R.: Encoding OCL Data Types for SAT-Based Verification of UML/OCL Models. In: Gogolla, M., Wolff, B. (eds.) TAP 2011. LNCS, vol. 6706, pp. 152–170. Springer, Heidelberg (2011)

30. A UML-based Specification Environment. Internet, http://sourceforge.net/projects/useocl/

31. Varró, D., Pataricza, A.: Metamodeling Mathematics: A Precise and Visual Framework for Describing Semantics Domains of UML Models. In: Jézéquel, J.-M., Hussmann, H., Cook, S. (eds.) UML 2002. LNCS, vol. 2460, pp. 18–33. Springer, Heidelberg (2002)

32. Warmer, J., Kleppe, A.: The Object Constraint Language: Getting Your Models Ready for MDA. Object Technology Series. Addison-Wesley, Reading (2003)

Computer Assisted Integration of Domain-Specific Modeling Languages Using Text Analysis Techniques

Florian Noyrit, Sébastien Gérard, and François Terrier

CEA, LIST, Laboratory of Model Driven Engineering for Embedded Systems,
Point Courrier 174, Gif-sur-Yvette, 91191, France
{florian.noyrit,sebastien.gerard,francois.terrier}@cea.fr

Abstract. Following the principle of separation of concerns, the Model-driven Engineering field has developed Domain-Specific Modeling Languages (DSML) to address the increasing complexity of the systems design. In this context of heterogeneous modeling languages, engineers and language designers are facing the critical problem of language integration. To address this problem, instead of doing a syntactic analysis based on the domain models or metamodels as it is common practice today, we propose to adopt natural language processing techniques to do a semantic analysis of the language specifications. We evaluate empirically our approach on seven real test cases and compare our results with five state of the art tools. Results show that the semantic analysis of textual descriptions that accompany DSMLs can efficiently assist engineers to make well-informed integration choices.

1 Introduction

The principle of separating concerns is widely used in engineering to address complexity. In the field of Model-Driven Engineering (MDE), this principle notably led to the development of Domain-Specific Modeling Languages (DSML). Those languages provide constructs that are directly aligned with the concepts of the domain in question. A specific domain, in the broad sense, can be an application domain (e.g. automotive) or a specific concern (e.g. requirement modeling).

Even though the principle of separation of concerns has demonstrated its practical effectiveness, it also implies heterogeneity issues within the development process. Indeed, once the problems of the various concerns have been solved separately, one must reintegrate them to build the global system. The integration must be done by taking into consideration the semantic relationships that may exist between the various DSML. This problem is recognized as the problem of finding correspondences [1] to define an architectural framework. Identifying correspondences between DSMLs is required to define a sound integration and to maintain the consistency of the architecture.

Also, when designing a DSML, it is good practice to first capture the conceptualization of the desired DSML with a domain model [2]. This domain model may be concretized with a metamodel and thereby define a pure-DSL. Alternatively, it may be used to design a UML profile: an extension of UML. In this case, the domain

A. Moreira et al. (Eds.): MODELS 2013, LNCS 8107, pp. 505–521, 2013.

model must be integrated with UML by projecting it on the UML metamodel. To design a UML profile, the language designers must look for the appropriate UML concept to extend: the base metaclass. An appropriate base metaclass is one that can host, on a semantic basis, the stereotype that will extend UML for a specific concern or domain.

Those two integration problems are usual for languages designers, methodologists and integrators in MDE. In both cases, the heart of the integration process is to analyze the semantic similarities that may exist between the concepts of different languages descriptions (DSML/DSML in the first integration problem, UML/DSML in the second integration problem). Unfortunately, the analysis of those semantic relationships is mostly a manual activity intensively relying on the knowledge of engineers who are experts in the languages to integrate, i.e., in the related domains and concerns. Consequently, it is not only a time consuming task but also an error-prone process. The purpose of this paper is to propose solutions to assist engineers in finding semantic similarities between DSMLs.

To achieve this purpose, we propose to use Natural Language Processing (NLP) and more precisely text analysis techniques to find the semantic similarities between language descriptions. The purpose of this paper is to define how to apply advanced results coming from the text analysis domain in the context of MDE. The main contribution is that we have adapted text analysis techniques for our application domain and added heuristics to improve their practical results in our specific context.

After detailing the problem of integrating DSMLs in section 2, we introduce the related work in section 3. Then, in section 4, we present the SemAnalysis approach we developed. In section 5, we introduce the test set used to evaluate our approach and we compare our results with five state of the art tools. In the meantime, we also analyze briefly two key success factors in our approach. Finally, we discuss future work and we give a summary of the paper in section 6.

2   Challenges to Integrate DSML

Before presenting our approach, we first detail the complexity of the integration problems we want to address. Then, we show shortcomings of using only domain models or metamodels to find an appropriate integration. Finally, we discuss the complexity of the integration of domain models with UML to define UML profiles.

2.1   Complexity of the Integration Cases: There Are Many Pairs to Evaluate

The complexity of finding semantic relationships between DSMLs procedure implies a $n \times m$ algorithmic complexity if we consider only 1-1 correspondences (and 2^{n+m} if we consider n-m correspondences). We will consider only 1-1 correspondences because it is sufficient for our test set. The language designer must evaluate the semantic similarity of all possible mappings. For instance, finding correspondences between SysML [3] (a DSML dedicated to the design and development of complex heterogeneous systems or systems of systems) and MARTE [4] (which is dedicated to model-driven development of real-time and embedded systems) requires going through 9000 pairs.

As mentioned, the main difficulty in designing a UML profile is to find the best UML base metaclasses that can host the specific domain concepts. The outline of the usual procedure to find the most appropriate base metaclasses can be formulated as following: *for each, concept in the domain model and for each UML metaclass, compare the semantics of the metaclass with the semantics of the domain concept. If there is a metaclass that envelops completely the domain concept then do nothing. If there are one or many metaclasses that can be the bases for the domain concept, then create a stereotype that extends those metaclasses. If there is no metaclass that can be the base for the domain concept, then either redefine the semantics of the domain concept or give up on doing a UML profile.* Analyzing this procedure led us to consider that the problem essentially relies on finding semantic similarities too. Even though this approach is a little bit naïve, it gives a sense of the complexity of the task. This procedure implies a $n \times m$ algorithmic complexity. Knowing that UML is about 250 metaclasses, for MARTE there are 75000 pairs to evaluate. Once again, if we consider n-m correspondences, complexity will be greater.

Thanks to their knowledge on the UML metamodel or specific domains, experts would most probably be able to focus on good candidates instead of going through all pairs, reducing this way the complexity of the task. However, this is too dependent on the knowledge the experts have in the different domains. This can lead to missing or inadequate integration and hard review and verification tasks. To reduce the efforts, a technique that provides automatically an ordered list of candidates would be of great help for engineers and would assist them in their decision making.

2.2   Domain Models Don't Contain Much Information

The definition of a DSML, be it implemented as a UML profile or a pure-DSL, consists of: (1) its abstract syntax which defines the rules for constructing well-formed language statements. It is usually defined using a metamodel, (2) one or several concrete syntaxes which is/are the physical rendering of symbols, (3) the semantics that assign meanings to symbols and statements. The semantics can be defined formally but they are most of the time informally given using a textual description in some natural language.

Thus, domain models (defined with a metamodel) only define the abstract syntax and the domain terminology. However the terminology only gives some clues on the actual semantics of a concept: domain models as such don't provide enough information to make appropriate integration decision. Consider, for instance, the FlowPort concept we represented in Fig. 1, which appears in both SysML and MARTE:

Fig. 1. The FlowPort definition in SysML and MARTE

At first glance, both concepts seem to be identical. However, if we look at their semantics, we can observe important differences between them. Namely, the semantics of SysML state that a "FlowPort is an interaction point through which input and/or output of items such as data, material, or energy may flow". In MARTE, "FlowPorts have been introduced to enable dataflow-oriented communications between components, where messages that flow across ports represent data items". MARTE's FlowPort is actually a specialization of SysML's FlowPort. On the contrary, concepts which seem to be different may be equivalent. For example, we can mention the "StructuredComponent" concept introduced in MARTE and the "Block" concept defined in SysML. Even though their syntactic definitions are rather different, those two concepts are almost equivalent semantically.

In [5], Kappel G. et al. evaluated the possibility to integrate metamodels using state of the art techniques from the ontology alignment community and reached a similar conclusion: domain models/metamodels are probably not enough. We need to look at another source of information. Domain models usually don't come alone. The semantics of the specific language is usually attached to the domain model: the specifications. As mentioned, the semantics are most often defined informally using a textual description in some natural language. Thus, in practice, the semantics of every concept is defined with a textual description. The key intuition is that semantic similarities can be more accurately found using this untapped source of information. After all, language designers that manually integrate DSMLs or design UML profiles actually read the specifications to make appropriate integration choices.

2.3   UML Particularities

UML is a relatively complex language that contains several subtleties. As a consequence, when projecting domain model on UML, language designers who have UML expertise choose base metaclasses that may seem counter intuitive to non-experts. For instance, we can mention the Assign stereotype in MARTE. Assign is used to allocate application elements to execution platform elements. Choosing the Dependency as base metaclass can appear as natural choice. However dependencies appear in the client (source of the dependency). This contradicts the platform independence required in MARTE. As a consequence, the semantically neutral metaclass Comment has been chosen.

There are several UML profiles readily available [6]. Some are even widely spread standards (MARTE and SysML are good examples but we could also mention CCM [7], EAST-ADL [8], or UTP [9] etc.). These UML profiles are frequently revised and improved. They are a very interesting source of expertise because the language designers of these UML profiles have already made appropriate choices for the base metaclass for their specific domain. The intuition is that this source of expertise is a kind of good Practice and common sense that should be used to find base metaclasses.

3   Related Work

The field of Schema/Ontology Alignment developed several matching techniques [10] to find correspondences between concepts. These techniques are those usually applied to our problems. We will especially consider the Alignment API [11], FOAM [12], CROSI [13] and Lily [14] tools. They are mainly based on finding terminological or structural similarities (e.g. Levenshtein distance and similarity flooding [15]). A few try to go beyond by trying to find semantic similarities, e.g., S-match [16]. In addition, while some techniques only use the input ontologies, some rely on external source of information such as lexical databases (most notably WordNet [17]) or upper ontologies. Some tools use the formal semantics of OWL [18] ontologies to infer similarities on a logical basis, e.g., LogMap [19]. In the MDE field, AMW [20] is a framework that can be used to implement heuristics mostly base on the syntax to generate weaving models using metamodels as inputs. The results from our first experiments with these approaches were aligned with those reported in [5]: if the terminologies are too far apart, results on finding similarities are very low. Still, on average, Alignment API offers the best results on our test sets.

To address the problem of mapping a domain model on UML, Giachetti [21] proposes an approach where language designers must name domain concepts with the name of the corresponding UML metaclasses so that the UML profile can be generated automatically. This assumption is not reasonable because it assumes that the language designer already knows how the domain is projected on UML.

4   The SemAnalysis Approach

Compared to the aforementioned techniques, SemAnalysis proposes to exploit semantic information available in the form of short texts in a natural language. Instead of analyzing the domain model itself, we analyze the specifications in natural language that accompany the domain model. To do that, we use NLP techniques that will quantify the semantic similarity between textual descriptions of concepts. The key rationale is that specifications that "talk" about the same things are somehow related.

The point of our research is to study the applicability of NLP techniques to find semantic similarity that are not identified by techniques that only use domain models as input. We adapted the Explicit Semantic Analysis [22] technique for our use cases because it demonstrates good practical results [23]. We adapted this technique to our specific context.

4.1   From Domain Model to UML

The objective is to find the semantic similarities that may exist between the domain concepts and the UML metaclasses in order to design a UML profile. The inputs for this integration case are:

— The domain model we want to project on UML where each specific concept is commented by its textual description extracted from the specification.
— The UML metamodel with a comment per metaclass that contains the description extracted from the specification.

— A set of well-known and widely adopted UML profiles that will constitute the training set. Each stereotype is commented by the textual description extracted from the specification.

Fig. 2 depicts the algorithm of the approach we propose to address this problem:

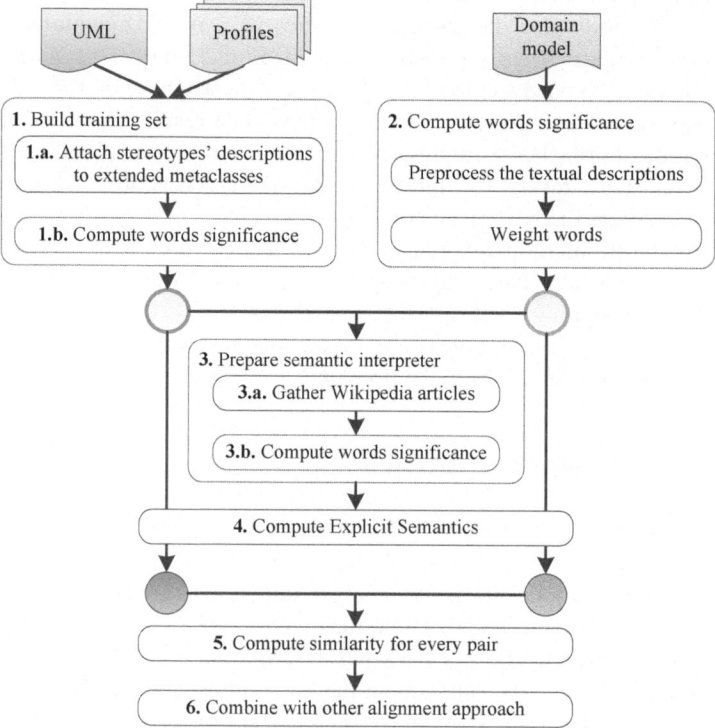

Fig. 2. Outline of the algorithm to find UML base metaclasses

Standard UML profiles contain expertise that is interesting to use to build a training set (step 1). This is done by concatenating the stereotypes' description with the description of the extended metaclasses (step 1.a). This step outputs a UML metamodel with metaclasses commented with the UML specifications supplemented with the specifications of the UML profiles. The rationale is that a stereotype is somehow a refinement of the base metaclasses with domain-specific semantics.

This artifact is then preprocessed to remove stop words and to stem [24] the useful words. Then, each word is weighted using TF-IDF [25] measure (step 1.b, detailed in step 2). This measure weights more words that appear frequently in a text while not appearing frequently in other texts. The domain model's textual descriptions are processed similarly (step 2): stop words are removed and remaining words are stemmed and weighted using TF-IDF.

The semantic interpreter is prepared on the basis of Wikipedia (step 3). However, we don't use the entire Wikipedia database (which contains more than 4.1 million articles on March 12, 2013). For each UML metaclass and domain concept, we gather only 10 Wikipedia articles using the 10 most significant words computed in previous steps (step 3.a.). Those 10 Wikipedia articles are the 10 first results returned by the search engine of Wikipedia. Therefore for each concept, we gather at most 100 Wikipedia articles. It is usually less because some words are significant for multiple concepts (in this case, Wikipedia search is done only once) and because Wikipedia search can give less than 10 results. This is a practical choice that helps to speed up the whole process yet maintaining a representative shortened Wikipedia database. The gathered Wikipedia articles are processed similarly to the inputs: stop words are removed and remaining words are stemmed and weighted using TF-IDF (step 3.b.).

The interpretation is done by computing the Explicit Semantics of every textual description (step 4). The Explicit Semantics is the weighted vector of Wikipedia articles ordered by their relevance to the textual description. This vector is the interpretation vector. For each Wikipedia article the weight is computed as follows: $\sum_{word_i \in TextualDescription} v_i \times k_j$ where v is the vector of weighted words from the textual descriptions (of either the training set or the domain model) and k the weighted words from the Wikipedia articles. For more details the reader can refer to [22]. Intuitively the more a word is significant to both the textual description of a domain concept and the Wikipedia article, the more the Wikipedia article is relevant to this textual description and therefore must be more weighted.

Now that domain concepts and UML metaclasses have an interpretation vector to represent them, similarities can be computed. Every possible pair $(Domain\ Construct, UML\ metaclass)$ is evaluated by computing the cosine similarity (step 5). This similarity measure ranges from -1 to 1 where -1 means that the domain concept and the metaclass are exactly opposites, 1 means that they are exactly the same and 0 means they are independent. The cosine similarity measure is used to order the UML metaclasses: the similarity vector. The closer the value is to 1, the more likely the metaclass is a good candidate for the extension. In practice, domain concepts that are sub-concepts of another rarely extend a base metaclass directly. This heuristic helps to identify the domain concepts that will probably extend a base metaclass. Concretely, for each domain concept that may extend a base metaclass (i.e. no super-concept), if s denotes the similarity vector then, the similarity $s_i = s_i / max(s)$.

We mentioned in the related work that existing techniques provide good results when terminologies are close. Thus, if terminologies are close, instead of using our results directly, the language designer can decide, a priori, to combine our semantic analysis with the terminological/syntactical similarities provided by other alignment tools (step 6).

4.2   Find Semantic Similarities between DSMLs

The inputs for this problem are the two domain models where concepts are commented by the corresponding textual description extracted from the specifications. Fig. 3 depicts the algorithm.

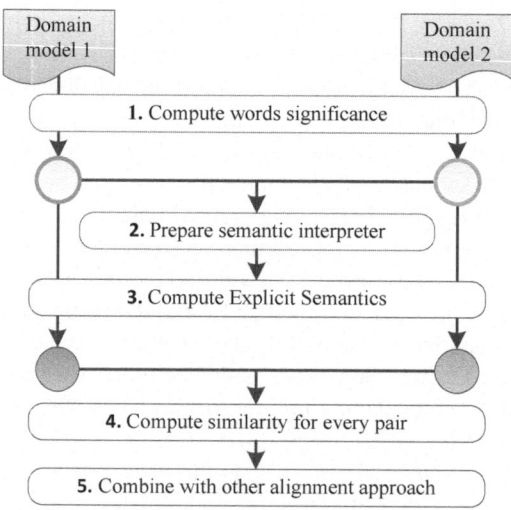

Fig. 3. Outline of the algorithm to find semantic similarities between DSMLs

The two domain models are preprocessed to remove stop words and stem remaining words from textual descriptions. Then, each word is weighted using TF-IDF (step 1).

As in the previous algorithm, the semantic interpreter is prepared (step 2) by gathering Wikipedia articles on the basis of the most significant words. Wikipedia articles are processed similarly to the domain models: stop words are removed and remaining words are stemmed and weighted using TF-IDF. The semantic interpretation is done by computing the Explicit Semantics of each textual description: a weighted vector of Wikipedia articles ordered by their relevance to the concept (step 3). Every possible pair $(Domain\ Construct\ 1, Domain\ Construct\ 2)$ is evaluated by computing the cosine similarity (step 4).

As in the previous problem, if terminologies are close the language designer can combine our semantic analysis with the terminological/syntactical similarities provided by other alignment tools (step 5).

5 Evaluation

In this section, we evaluate our approach. First, we introduce the test set used for the evaluation. Then we present the empirical results. The language specifications of all the cases we use in our test set are publically available.

5.1 Test Set

Concerning the problem of finding the base metaclasses, we applied our approach on EAST-ADL [8], MARTE [4], SysML [3], UTP [9] and SoaML [26] domain-specific languages. The four latter are standard UML profiles recommended by the Object Management Group.

- *EAST-ADL* is dedicated to the development of automotive electronic systems. EAST-ADL provides both a UML profile and a metamodel. The latter can be considered as domain model. It defines about 100 concepts.
- *MARTE* provides both a domain model and a UML profile.
- *SysML* doesn't provide a domain model. Still it defines a subset of UML (known as UML4SysML). This subset supplemented with the stereotypes can be considered as a domain model.
- The *UML Testing Profile (UTP)* provides concepts for the design, visualization, specification, analysis, and documentation of the artifacts involved in testing. It defines a little bit less than 30 concepts. Unfortunately doesn't provide with the domain model. We created one on the basis of the profile. Even though it is not ideal domain model, it is still representative.
- The *Service oriented architecture Modeling Language (SoaML)* is dedicated to modeling and design of services within a Service-Oriented Architecture. It provides both a domain model and a UML profile. It defines a little bit less than 30 concepts.

For each test case, the training set consists of all those languages but the one we try to integrate. For all these test cases, we haven't combined our semantic analysis with syntactic analysis.

Concerning the problem of finding semantic similarities between DSMLs, we tested the approach on the two following cases:

- *MARTE/SysML*. These two DSMLs have significant overlaps and their combination is highly likely in the design of complex technical systems [27]. The main overlaps are: components modeling, allocation definition and quantitative analysis. For the rest, these languages are either independent or complementary. For concepts that match, the terminologies are really close.
- *MOF (EMOF)* [28]*/EMF Ecore* [29]. They serve the same purpose: both are dedicated to the specification of metamodels. EMF Ecore is a variant of EMOF developed as part of the Eclipse Modeling Framework. They are mostly aligned and the terminologies are very similar.

For all these test cases, we have combined our semantic analysis with syntactic analysis.

Even though computation in our approach is polynomial in time, it should be noted that in practice this will not raise scalability issues because DSMLs have a limited number of concepts and therefore the computation time is satisfactory. To the best of our knowledge, DSMLs with more than 300 concepts like MARTE are exceptional. On our test cases, computation time was under 1 minute.

5.2   Evaluation Procedure

In addition to SemAnalysis, the test set has been used with the Alignment API, FOAM, CROSI, LogMap and Lily tools. Those tools use OWL as input format. Therefore domain models have been translated to OWL ontologies by applying the transformations recommended in ODM [30]. All the tools we used in the evaluation (including ours) give, for each pair, the confidence that the pair matches. The value ranges from 0 (low confidence) to 1 (high confidence). Some tools focus only on equivalence and some also consider the subsumption relationship. Whatever the kind of relationship, we consider that the elements are semantically related. We didn't use results from S-Match and AMW because these tools output results without confidence values. Thus, it would have been hard to fairly compare them with the others.

The evaluation is done by comparing the alignment proposed by the tools with a reference alignment. For the problem of finding the UML base metaclasses when designing a UML profile, the reference is given by the mapping that exists between the domain model and the actual UML profile. This mapping was already defined in the standard for MARTE. For East-ADL, SoaML, SysML and UTP the mapping is trivial. For the problem of finding semantic similarities between DSMLs, we manually defined the references. For MOF/EMF ECore, the mapping is trivial. For MARTE/SysML, we defined a reference that follows the alignment guidelines proposed in [27].

We use the precision, recall and F-Measure to assess the quality of the alignments. The complete results for the different test cases are given at the end of this paper in Table 4-Table 10. They present the precision (Pre.), recall (Rec.) and F-Measure (F) measures.

Otherwise, we evaluated the terminology similarity of our test cases. To do so, we compute the Levenshtein distance of each pair that appears in the reference alignment. We compare the average Levenshtein distance (ALD) with the average length of names (ALN) of concepts that appear in the reference alignment. We consider that terminologies are similar when $ALD/ALN \leq 0.5$. Table 1 reports the terminology similarity of our test cases. It confirms that tests cases for the problem of finding semantic similarity between DSMLs have very similar terminologies.

Table 1. Terminology similarity analysis

	Average length of names (ALN)	Average Levenshtein distance (ALD)	ALD/ALN
East-ADL	11.72	12.81	**1.09**
MARTE	13.90	11.31	**0.81**
SysML	10.49	9.31	**0.89**
UTP	13.28	11.10	**0.84**
SoaML	9.67	8.04	**0.83**
SysML/MARTE	11.20	3.60	**0.32**
MOF/Ecore	9.46	3.69	**0.39**

5.3   Analysis and Interpretation of the Results

Table 2 gives the synthesis of F-measures with a threshold to 0.9 for the different test cases and the different tools. SemAnalysis provides clear progress to the problem of finding the base metaclass and only slight improvements to the problem of finding semantic similarities between DSMLs.

Table 2. Synthesis of F-Measure with threshold to 0.9

	SemAnalysis	Crosi	Align. API	FOAM	Lily	LogMap
EAST-ADL	0.34	0.03	0.03	0.00	0.03	0.00
SysML	0.52	0.00	0.00	0.00	0.00	0.00
MARTE	0.14	0.00	0.00	0.02	0.02	0.00
UTP	0.44	0.00	0.00	0.00	0.00	0.00
SoaML	0.48	0.30	0.30	0.30	0.30	0.00
SysML-MARTE	0.80	0.71	0.71	0.20	0.80	0.00
MOF-Ecore	0.76	0.00	0.76	0.54	0.76	0.00
Arithmetic mean	**0.50**	**0.15**	**0.26**	**0.15**	**0.27**	**0.00**

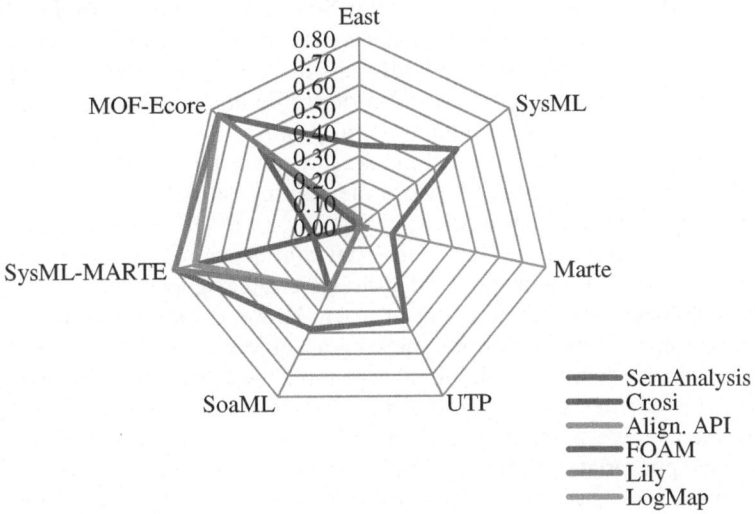

Alignment API and Lily provide results which are comparable to those from SemAnalysis so that improvements from SemAnalysis are not obvious. To test the significance of the improvement of our tool, a t-test can be used [31]. The null hypothesis that we want to reject is that SemAnalysis provides, on average, an F-Measure that is lower or equal to those provided by Alignment API or by Lily. To be significant, the two-tailed p-value must be ≤ 0.05. The t-test can be used only on normal distributions. Shapiro-Wilk test confirms the normality ($W = 0.953$ for SemAnalysis, 0.752 for Alignment API and 0.749 for Lily). The t-test gives a two-tailed p-value of 0.0113 for Alignment API and 0.0207 for Lily. We can therefore reject the null hypothesis and conclude that improvements provided by SemAnalysis are significant. Note that improvements from SemAnalysis start to be insignificant with a threshold to 0.5 on confidence.

All those results confirm what we mentioned in the related work section and our first intuition: *if the terminology of matching concepts is similar, tools based only on metamodels/domain models offer rather good integration results. If the terminologies are far apart, the domain models don't contain enough information.* The results show that the syntactic similarity heuristic is not sufficient and that the semantic analysis we propose can provide significant improvements. More important, results confirm the hypothesis that specifications contain semantic information that is exploitable. Its use can complete the analysis based on syntactic information.

To illustrate this, in the MOF-ECore test case, most of the concepts in Ecore correspond to MOF ones prefixed with an 'E' (e.g. Class ≍ EClass, NamedElement ≍ ENamedElement, Operation ≍ EOperation). Interestingly, one match that is not trivial in this test case is the Comment ≍ EAnnotation match. Alignment API, Lily, FOAM and LogMap give a confidence of 0 and CROSI gives 0.19 while SemAnalysis gives 1. For the aforementioned match that exists between Block and StructuredComponent in the SysML-MARTE test case, Alignment API, LogMap, Lily and FOAM give a confidence of 0 and CROSI gives 0.11 while SemAnalysis gives 0.56. In other words, results from other tools are very/too influenced by the similarity of the terminologies.

To test the intuition that existing UML profiles are a good source of expertise, we studied the correlation between the number of profile in the training set and the evolution of the F-Measure. We found a high positive Spearman's rank correlation. Although encouraging, this correlation measure must be considered very carefully because the number of profiles we put in the training set is low and because we may face overfitting issues on large scale.

If we consider only the matches with 1-0.9 confidence, i.e., the matching pairs we are the most confident about, the F-Measures are rather good. The evaluation shows that fully automated integration is out of reach. However, we can assist the language designers during the integration by showing an ordered short list of candidates. To evaluate to which extent the ordering is appropriate and therefore to which extent the tool assists the engineers, we measured the average ranking of the appropriate candidate (i.e. the average number of candidates that must be reviewed manually before reaching the appropriate candidate). Table 3 reports these values for each test case (- means that the tool gave a confidence of 0 to all the candidates and therefore no ordering is provided).

Table 3. Arithmetic mean number of candidate to review manually (σ: standard derivation)

	SemAnalysis		Crosi		Align. API		FOAM		Lily		LogMap	
	Mean	σ	Mean	σ	Mean	σ	Mean	σ	Mean	σ	Mean	σ
EAST-ADL	5	6.6	145	79.2	44	43.0	-	-	49	42.9	51	43.5
SysML	3	2.4	102	88.9	86	80.8	-	-	89	79.6	-	-
MARTE	9	16.0	105	87.0	106	76.7	109	73.7	107	75.4	-	-
UTP	3	4.0	110	65.9	92	79.5	-	-	93	78.3	99	78.0
SoaML	4	6.6	101	91.4	44	47.4	47	47.5	43	47.5	56	58.1
SysML-MARTE	5	0.7	26	73.3	48	101.2	191	91.2	33	96.0	75	118.0
MOF-Ecore	3	0.6	2	2.8	5	6.7	7	7.4	3	5.1	-	-

Those results confirm that our tool provides a very useful assistance. For example, in the SysML test case, on average, the appropriate match is the third in the list (of 247 UML metaclasses) proposed by SemAnalysis while it is the 86th for Alignment API. SemAnalysis provides very significant improvements in terms of assistance. By "reading" the specifications like human agent would have done, SemAnalysis can "understand" the domain concepts and therefore propose more appropriate correspondences than tools that only consider the information encoded in the domain models.

5.4   Analysis of Two Success Factors

As the textual description of each concept is at the heart of our approach, we must analyze to which extent the length of textual descriptions is important in our approach. Therefore we decided to check if there was a correlation between the number of words in the textual description of a concept and the F-Measure for this concept. On our test set, on average, we find a low positive Pearson product-moment correlation of 0.12 and a low positive Spearman's rank correlation of 0.13. We think these results follow the well-known principle: *it is not so much the length of a text as what it actually says that makes it meaningful.*

To speed up the process of preparing the semantic interpreter, we don't process the entire Wikipedia database and gather only a limited number of articles. We must analyze to which extent this practical choice impacts our results. We informally tested this practice by increasing the number of gathered articles. On our test set, we haven't observed clear improvements on the results by gathering more articles. However we have observed some improvements when we gathered manually the articles from Wikipedia categories related to the domain of the DSML e.g. "Systems_engineering", "Automotive_industry" categories. We interpret this in a similar way than for the length of the textual descriptions: *it is not so much the number of articles as the adequacy of the articles with the domain of the DSML to integrate that is important.*

6   Summary and Future Work

We considered two usual DSML integration problems in MDE; namely the problem of finding the integration between a domain model and UML and the problem of finding semantic similarities between DSMLs. We showed that these problems are inherently hard to address because domain models contain limited information and because UML is complex. We followed the intuition that textual descriptions that accompany the domain model and the existing UML profiles could be exploited to find more accurately semantic similarities. We developed an approach based on text analysis techniques that reads and interprets language specifications written in natural language to assist the integration process. We evaluated this approach on seven real test cases and compared our results with five state of the art tools. On our test set, our approach provides significant improvements and really useful assistance. Our results confirm the intuition: if the domain models don't contain enough information (i.e. when terminologies are too far apart), textual descriptions can be exploited to assist the engineers to integrate DSMLs.

The results are very encouraging but our approach should be tested with a larger test set. One of the main reasons for the limited size of our test set is that specifications are hard to process because they are only available in PDF or PS formats. Today, the preparation of specifications for automatic processing is very laborious. It requires transforming plain text into structured data. We think there is a real need to define or use standards to transform today's specifications into actual models [32]. This would enable information retrieval and various kinds of computations on the content of the specifications. In addition, it would help to improve the consistency and the overall quality of specifications.

The point of our research was to assess the applicability of NLP techniques to address usual integration problems in MDE. We chose one technique that demonstrates good practical results. Now that we have shown how NLP techniques can be used in our context and how useful they can be, we shall try other techniques (e.g. Latent Semantic Analysis [33], Corpus-based and Knowledge-based [34], Kullback–Leibler divergence for text categorization [35]).

Table 4. Measures for the EAST-ADL test case

	1-0.9			1-0.8			1-0.7			1-0.6			1-0.5		
	Pre.	Rec.	F	Pre.	Rec.	F	Pre.	Rec.	F	Pre.	Rec.	F	Pre.	Rec.	F
SemAnalysis	0.31	0.40	**0.34**	0.30	0.40	**0.34**	0.25	0.50	**0.34**	0.24	0.59	**0.34**	0.20	0.67	**0.31**
Crosi	0.40	0.02	**0.03**	0.40	0.02	**0.03**	0.40	0.02	**0.03**	0.33	0.02	**0.03**	0.35	0.05	**0.08**
Align-API	0.40	0.02	**0.03**	0.38	0.02	**0.04**	0.50	0.08	**0.13**	0.40	0.11	**0.17**	0.33	0.12	**0.17**
FOAM	0.00	0.00	**0.00**	0.00	0.00	**0.00**	0.00	0.00	**0.00**	0.00	0.00	**0.00**	0.00	0.00	**0.00**
Lily	0.29	0.02	**0.03**	0.30	0.02	**0.04**	0.27	0.03	**0.06**	0.20	0.03	**0.05**	0.20	0.04	**0.06**
LogMap	0.00	0.00	**0.00**	0.00	0.00	**0.00**	0.00	0.00	**0.00**	0.40	0.02	**0.03**	0.29	0.02	**0.03**

Table 5. Measures for the SysML test case

	1-0.9			1-0.8			1-0.7			1-0.6			1-0.5		
	Pre.	Rec.	F	Pre.	Rec.	F	Pre.	Rec.	F	Pre.	Rec.	F	Pre.	Rec.	F
SemAnalysis	0.43	0.67	**0.52**	0.43	0.69	**0.53**	0.35	0.72	**0.47**	0.27	0.78	**0.40**	0.23	0.86	**0.37**
Crosi	0.00	0.00	**0.00**	0.00	0.00	**0.00**	0.00	0.00	**0.00**	0.00	0.00	**0.00**	0.44	0.11	**0.18**
Align-API	0.00	0.00	**0.00**	1.00	0.08	**0.15**	0.50	0.11	**0.18**	0.45	0.14	**0.21**	0.35	0.19	**0.25**
FOAM	0.00	0.00	**0.00**	0.00	0.00	**0.00**	0.00	0.00	**0.00**	0.00	0.00	**0.00**	0.00	0.00	**0.00**
Lily	0.00	0.00	**0.00**	1.00	0.03	**0.05**	0.43	0.08	**0.14**	0.36	0.11	**0.17**	0.29	0.11	**0.16**
LogMap	0.00	0.00	**0.00**	0.00	0.00	**0.00**	0.00	0.00	**0.00**	0.00	0.00	**0.00**	0.00	0.00	**0.00**

Table 6. Measures for the MARTE test case

	1-0.9			1-0.8			1-0.7			1-0.6			1-0.5		
	Pre.	Rec.	F	Pre.	Rec.	F	Pre.	Rec.	F	Pre.	Rec.	F	Pre.	Rec.	F
SemAnalysis	0.10	0.27	**0.14**	0.09	0.29	**0.13**	0.07	0.37	**0.12**	0.06	0.41	**0.10**	0.04	0.43	**0.08**
Crosi	0.00	0.00	**0.00**	0.00	0.00	**0.00**	0.00	0.00	**0.00**	0.00	0.00	**0.00**	0.03	0.06	**0.04**
Align-API	0.00	0.00	**0.00**	0.06	0.06	**0.06**	0.04	0.06	**0.05**	0.03	0.08	**0.04**	0.02	0.08	**0.04**
FOAM	0.03	0.02	**0.02**	0.02	0.02	**0.02**	0.02	0.02	**0.02**	0.02	0.02	**0.02**	0.02	0.02	**0.02**
Lily	0.03	0.02	**0.02**	0.02	0.02	**0.02**	0.04	0.04	**0.04**	0.03	0.04	**0.04**	0.03	0.04	**0.03**
LogMap	0.00	0.00	**0.00**	0.00	0.00	**0.00**	0.00	0.00	**0.00**	0.00	0.00	**0.00**	0.00	0.00	**0.00**

Table 7. Measures for the UTP test case

	1-0.9			1-0.8			1-0.7			1-0.6			1-0.5		
	Pre.	Rec.	F	Pre.	Rec.	F	Pre.	Rec.	F	Pre.	Rec.	F	Pre.	Rec.	F
SemAnalysis	0.39	0.52	**0.44**	0.39	0.52	**0.44**	0.35	0.61	**0.45**	0.26	0.68	**0.38**	0.23	0.74	**0.35**
Crosi	0.00	0.00	**0.00**	0.00	0.00	**0.00**	0.00	0.00	**0.00**	0.00	0.00	**0.00**	0.00	0.00	**0.00**
Align-API	0.00	0.00	**0.00**	0.00	0.00	**0.00**	0.00	0.00	**0.00**	0.17	0.06	**0.09**	0.10	0.06	**0.08**
FOAM	0.00	0.00	**0.00**	0.00	0.00	**0.00**	0.00	0.00	**0.00**	0.00	0.00	**0.00**	0.00	0.00	**0.00**
Lily	0.00	0.00	**0.00**	0.00	0.00	**0.00**	0.25	0.03	**0.06**	0.17	0.03	**0.05**	0.08	0.03	**0.05**
LogMap	0.00	0.00	**0.00**	0.00	0.00	**0.00**	0.00	0.00	**0.00**	0.00	0.00	**0.00**	0.00	0.00	**0.00**

Table 8. Measures for the SoaML test case

	1-0.9			1-0.8			1-0.7			1-0.6			1-0.5		
	Pre.	Rec.	F	Pre.	Rec.	F	Pre.	Rec.	F	Pre.	Rec.	F	Pre.	Rec.	F
SemAnalysis	0.40	0.61	**0.48**	0.39	0.61	**0.47**	0.28	0.65	**0.39**	0.22	0.78	**0.35**	0.17	0.87	**0.29**
Crosi	1.00	0.17	**0.30**	1.00	0.17	**0.30**	1.00	0.17	**0.30**	1.00	0.17	**0.30**	0.80	0.17	**0.29**
Align-API	1.00	0.17	**0.30**	1.00	0.17	**0.30**	0.83	0.22	**0.34**	0.71	0.22	**0.33**	0.63	0.22	**0.32**
FOAM	1.00	0.17	**0.30**	1.00	0.17	**0.30**	1.00	0.17	**0.30**	1.00	0.17	**0.30**	1.00	0.17	**0.30**
Lily	1.00	0.17	**0.30**	1.00	0.17	**0.30**	0.83	0.22	**0.34**	0.83	0.22	**0.34**	0.83	0.22	**0.34**
LogMap	0.00	0.00	**0.00**	0.00	0.00	**0.00**	0.00	0.00	**0.00**	1.00	0.13	**0.23**	1.00	0.13	**0.23**

Table 9. Measures for the SysML/MARTE test case

	1-0.9			1-0.8			1-0.7			1-0.6			1-0.5		
	Pre.	Rec.	F	Pre.	Rec.	F	Pre.	Rec.	F	Pre.	Rec.	F	Pre.	Rec.	F
SemAnalysis	1.00	0.67	**0.80**	1.00	0.67	**0.80**	0.88	0.78	**0.82**	0.89	0.89	**0.89**	0.57	0.89	**0.70**
Crosi	1.00	0.56	**0.71**	1.00	0.56	**0.71**	0.83	0.56	**0.67**	0.63	0.56	**0.59**	0.50	0.78	**0.61**
Align-API	1.00	0.56	**0.71**	0.75	0.67	**0.71**	0.64	0.78	**0.70**	0.50	0.78	**0.61**	0.29	0.78	**0.42**
FOAM	1.00	0.11	**0.20**	0.50	0.11	**0.18**	0.50	0.11	**0.18**	0.50	0.11	**0.18**	0.50	0.11	**0.18**
Lily	1.00	0.67	**0.80**	1.00	0.67	**0.80**	0.88	0.78	**0.82**	0.67	0.89	**0.76**	0.57	0.89	**0.70**
LogMap	0.00	0.00	**0.00**	0.00	0.00	**0.00**	0.00	0.00	**0.00**	1.00	0.67	**0.80**	1.00	0.67	**0.80**

Table 10. Measures for the MOF/Ecore test case

	1-0.9			1-0.8			1-0.7			1-0.6			1-0.5		
	Pre.	Rec.	F	Pre.	Rec.	F	Pre.	Rec.	F	Pre.	Rec.	F	Pre.	Rec.	F
SemAnalysis	1.00	0.62	**0.76**	1.00	0.62	**0.76**	1.00	0.62	**0.76**	1.00	0.62	**0.76**	1.00	0.62	**0.76**
Crosi	0.00	0.00	**0.00**	0.00	0.00	**0.00**	1.00	0.08	**0.14**	1.00	0.38	**0.56**	0.89	0.62	**0.73**
Align-API	1.00	0.62	**0.76**	1.00	0.62	**0.76**	0.89	0.62	**0.73**	0.73	0.62	**0.67**	0.67	0.62	**0.64**
FOAM	0.70	0.44	**0.54**	0.58	0.44	**0.50**	0.58	0.44	**0.50**	0.58	0.44	**0.50**	0.58	0.44	**0.50**
Lily	1.00	0.62	**0.76**	1.00	0.62	**0.76**	1.00	0.62	**0.76**	1.00	0.62	**0.76**	0.89	0.62	**0.73**
LogMap	0.00	0.00	**0.00**	0.00	0.00	**0.00**	0.00	0.00	**0.00**	0.00	0.00	**0.00**	0.00	0.00	**0.00**

References

1. ISO/IEC/IEEE: ISO/IEC/IEEE 42010 - Systems and software engineering - Architecture description (2011)
2. Selic, B.: A Systematic Approach to Domain-Specific Language Design Using UML. In: International Symposium on Object and Component-Oriented Real-Time Distributed Computing (2007)
3. Object Management Group: Systems Modeling Language (SysML) - Version 1.2 - formal/2010-06-01 (2010), http://www.omg.org/spec/SysML/1.2/
4. Object Management Group: UML Profile for MARTE: Modeling and Analysis of Real-Time Embedded Systems - Version 1.1 - formal/2011-06-02 (2011), http://www.omg.org/spec/MARTE/1.1/
5. Kappel, G., Kargl, H., Kramler, G., Schauerhuber, A., Seidl, M., Strommer, M., Wimmer, M.: Matching Metamodels with Semantic Systems - An Experience Report. In: BTW 2007 Workshop Model Management und Metadaten-Verwaltung, Aachen (2007)
6. Pardillo, J.: A Systematic Review on the Definition of UML Profiles. In: Petriu, D.C., Rouquette, N., Haugen, Ø. (eds.) MODELS 2010, Part I. LNCS, vol. 6394, pp. 407–422. Springer, Heidelberg (2010)

7. Object Management Group: CORBA Component Model (CCM) - Version 4.0 - formal/06-04-01 (2006), http://www.omg.org/spec/CCM/4.0/
8. ATESST: EAST-ADL 2.1 RC3 Specification (2010), http://www.atesst.org/
9. Object Management Group: UML Testing Profile (UTP) - Version 1.0 - formal/2005-07-07 (2005), http://www.omg.org/spec/UTP/1.0/
10. Ontology Matching, http://www.ontologymatching.org/
11. David, J., Euzenat, J., Scharffe, F., Trojahn dos Santos, C.: The Alignment API 4.0. Semantic Web Journal 2, 3–10 (2011)
12. Ehrig, M., Sure, Y.: FOAM–Framework for Ontology Alignment and Mapping Results of the Ontology Alignment Evaluation Initiative. In: Integrating Ontologies Workshop Proceedings (2005)
13. Kalfoglou, Y., Hu, B.: CROSI Mapping System (CMS), results of the 2005 ontology alignment contest. In: Integrating Ontologies Workshop Proceedings (2005)
14. Wang, P., Xu, B.: Lily: Ontology alignment results for oaei 2008. In: Proceedings of the Third International Workshop on Ontology Matching, pp. 167–175 (2008)
15. Melnik, S., Garcia-Molina, H., Rahm, E.: Similarity flooding: A versatile graph matching algorithm and its application to schema matching. In: International Conference on Data Engineering (2002)
16. Giunchiglia, F., Shvaiko, P., Yatskevich, M.: S-match: an algorithm and an implementation of semantic matching. In: Bussler, C.J., Davies, J., Fensel, D., Studer, R. (eds.) ESWS 2004. LNCS, vol. 3053, pp. 61–75. Springer, Heidelberg (2004)
17. Miller, G.A.: WordNet: a lexical database for English. Communications of the ACM 38 (1995)
18. W3C: OWL2 Web Ontology Language, http://www.w3.org/TR/2009/REC-owl2-overview-20091027/
19. Jiménez-Ruiz, E., Cuenca Grau, B.: LogMap: Logic-based and scalable ontology matching. In: Aroyo, L., Welty, C., Alani, H., Taylor, J., Bernstein, A., Kagal, L., Noy, N., Blomqvist, E. (eds.) ISWC 2011, Part I. LNCS, vol. 7031, pp. 273–288. Springer, Heidelberg (2011)
20. Atlas Model Weaver (AMW), http://www.eclipse.org/gmt/amw/
21. Giachetti, G., Marín, B., Pastor, O.: Using UML as a Domain-Specific Modeling Language: A Proposal for Automatic Generation of UML Profiles. Advanced Information Systems Engineering (2009)
22. Gabrilovich, E., Markovitch, S.: Computing Semantic Relatedness using Wikipedia-based Explicit Semantic Analysis. In: Proceedings of the 20th International Joint Conference on Artifical Intelligence (2007)
23. Gottron, T., Anderka, M., Stein, B.: Insights into explicit semantic analysis. In: Proceedings of the 20th ACM International Conference on Information and Knowledge Management, pp. 1961–1964 (2011)
24. Porter Stemming Algorithm, http://tartarus.org/~martin/PorterStemmer/
25. McGill, M.J., Salton, G.: Introduction to Modern Information Retrieval. McGraw-Hill (1983)
26. Object Management Group: Service oriented architecture Modeling Language (SoaML) - Version 1.0 - formal/2012-03-01 (2012), http://www.omg.org/spec/SoaML/1.0/
27. Espinoza, H., Cancila, D., Selic, B., Gérard, S.: Challenges in combining sysML and MARTE for model-based design of embedded systems. In: Paige, R.F., Hartman, A., Rensink, A. (eds.) ECMDA-FA 2009. LNCS, vol. 5562, pp. 98–113. Springer, Heidelberg (2009)

28. Object Management Group: Meta Object Facility (MOF) - Version 2.4.1 - formal/2011-08-07 (2011), http://www.omg.org/spec/MOF/2.4.1/
29. Eclipse Modeling Framework (EMF), http://www.eclipse.org/modeling/emf/
30. Object Management Group: Ontology Definition Metamodel (ODM) - Version 1.0 - formal/2009-05-01 (2009), http://www.omg.org/spec/ODM/1.0/
31. Wohlin, C., Runeson, P., Höst, M., Ohlsson, M.C., Regnell, B., Wesslén, A.: Experimentation in Software Engineering: an Introduction. Kluwer Academic Publishers (2000)
32. Skene, J., Emmerich, W.: Specifications, not meta-models. In: Proceedings of the 2006 International Workshop on Global Integrated Model Management, pp. 47–54. ACM, New York (2006)
33. Deerwester, S., Dumais, S.T., Furnas, G.W., Landauer, T.K., Harshman, R.: Indexing by Latent Semantic Analysis. Journal of the American Society for Information Science (1990)
34. Mihalcea, R., Corley, C., Strapparava, C.: Corpus-based and Knowledge-based Measures of Text Semantic Similarity. In: Proceedings of the National Conference on Artificial Intelligence (2006)
35. Bigi, B.: Using Kullback-Leibler Distance for Text Categorization. Advances in Information Retrieval (2003)

Towards the Notation-Driven Development of DSMLs

Laurent Wouters

Université Pierre et Marie Curie, France
Laboratoire d'Informatique de Paris 6 (LIP6)
Commissariat à l'Énergie Atomique, France
laurent.wouters@cea.fr

Abstract. Domain-Specific Modeling Languages (DSML) enable domain experts to leverage Model-Driven Engineering methods and tools through concepts and notations from their own domain. The notation of a DSML is critical because it is the sole interface domain experts will have with their tool. Unfortunately, the current process for the development of DSMLs strongly emphasizes the abstract syntaxes and often treats the notations (concrete syntaxes) as byproducts. Focusing on the case of *visual* DSMLs, this paper proposes to automatically generate a DSML's abstract syntax from the specification of its concrete syntax. This shift towards the notation-driven development of DSMLs is expected to enable the production of DSMLs closer to domain experts' expectations. This approach is validated by its implementation in a prototype, its application on an industrial case and the results of an empirical study.

Keywords: Domain-Specific Modeling, Visual Languages.

1 Introduction

Domain-Specific Modeling Languages (DSMLs) enable domain experts to model and design products by only manipulating concepts from their own domain. For example, a DSML for Electrical Engineering enables the engineers to design electrical circuits using concepts such as Capacitor, Resistor, Diode, etc. Unfortunately, DSMLs are still difficult to produce and software engineers are contracted for this purpose. They usually have to interact with the domain experts in order to elicit a part of their knowledge so that they can produce a DSML that fit the experts' expectations.

The acceptance of a DSML can be compared to the acceptance of any new technology by a class of users, a field that has been heavily studied [4,8,22]. Models of the user acceptance have been proposed in [9]. Two of the most prominent factors for acceptance are the perceived ease of use and the perceived usefulness of the new technology [8]. The notation (concrete syntax) is the first contact of domain experts with their DSML and thus plays a crucial role in its acceptance. This raises the issue of the definition of notations answering well domain experts' expectations. The notations are parts of the DSMLs that are built through

A. Moreira et al. (Eds.): MODELS 2013, LNCS 8107, pp. 522–537, 2013.

specific development processes. These processes must ensure the quality of the DSMLs produced with them and in particular their notations.

Because the domain experts' expectations naturally tend to focus on the notation, software engineers tasked to produce a DSML may want to emphasize this aspect. However, the current approaches and tools for the design and implementation of DSMLs strongly emphasize the abstract syntaxes. For example, using the Eclipse EMF and GMF platform, a software engineer must first define its abstract syntax using ECORE and then assign visual symbols to the elements of this metamodel. In this way, the development of a DSML is driven by its metamodel. This approach has several issues, most notably its rigidity as identified in [1, 12, 16], which hinders the optimal development of the DSMLs' concrete syntaxes.

To alleviate this issue, we propose to shift the focus of the software engineers onto the concrete syntaxes, thus phasing in a notation-driven approach to the development of DSMLs. In this new approach, a software engineer would first build and validate the concrete syntax of a DSML with the domain experts in order to maximize their acceptance, and then take care of the underlying concepts, i.e. the abstract syntax. To make possible this approach we rely on existing approaches for the specification of DSMLs' concrete syntaxes in the form of visual grammars, focusing solely on DSMLs with *visual* concrete syntaxes. This paper then proposes a way to automatically generate the DSMLs' abstract syntaxes from the visual grammars.

To give a better understanding of this approach, this paper summarizes the relevant state of the art in Section 2, including existing approaches for the specification of DSMLs' concrete syntaxes. Section 3 then presents how a DSML's abstract syntax can be derived from the specification of its concrete syntax. This approach is validated in Section 4 by its application on a use case coming from the aeronautic industry, as well as an empirical study. The results are discussed in Section 5. We finally conclude in Section 6.

2   State of the Art

In order to focus the attention of the software developers onto the DSMLs' concrete syntaxes, the notation-driven development of DSMLs needs an approach for the direct specification of the concrete syntaxes detached from any abstract syntax. Interestingly, visual DSMLs' concrete syntaxes are in fact visual languages that can be specified in varied ways. As defined in [6], a visual notation is a visual language noted L formed over an alphabet of visual symbols noted S. A diagram expressed in this language is then a visual sentence, a set of related visual symbols from S. An example of visual language is shown in Figure 1 where the rounded rectangles and the arrows constitute visual symbols. The visual symbols are characterized by attributes categorised as follow:

– Graphical attributes are related to the visual appearance of a symbol, e.g. the size, shape and color of the rounded rectangles in Figure 1.

- Syntactic attributes define the relations of a visual symbol with other symbols in order to determine the correctness of a visual sentence. For example, arrows in Figure 1 are only permited to have the rounded rectangles as origin and target.
- Semantic attributes are related to how the visual symbols are to be interpreted. In the context of this work, semantic attributes are how the visual symbols are mapped to the abstract syntax of a modeling language. For example, Figure 1 is to be interpreted as a state-machine with rounded rectangles representing the states and the arrows the transitions. State-machine, states and transitions are all terms of the abstract syntax.

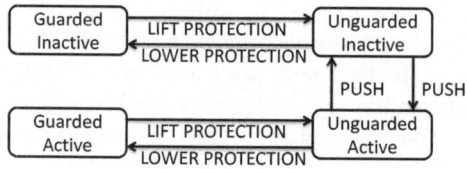

Fig. 1. Example of visual language

Hereafter are summarized some of the existing approaches for the specification of visual languages.

2.1 Grammar-Based Approaches

Grammar-based approaches to the specification of visual languages are close to the specification approaches for string grammars. String grammars can be formally specified through well-known approaches such as BNF (Backus-Naur Form) and EBNF (Extended Backus-Naur Form), to the point where the EBNF notation is an ISO standard [14]. Grammar-based specifications of visual languages, also called visual grammars, follow the same philosophy in that they enable the specification of visual languages through grammar rules defining the valid visual sentences. Furthermore, these approaches usually come with dedicated parsing approaches and algorithms sometimes derived from string-based parsing algorithms. For example, the Extended Positional Grammars [5] approach presented below includes the XpLR parsing technique derived from the LR (Left to right Rightmost derivation) family of parsing methods [15].

A first category of approaches are based on graph grammars. A graph grammar is composed of rules that have a left-hand side and a right-hand side. For context-free graph grammars, the left-hand side consists in a single node and the right-hand side is an arbitrary graph. The meaning of the rules is that the left-hand side node can be replaced by the right-hand side graph. It is possible to use graph grammars for the specification of valid graphs, as well as the specification of graph transformations [10].

For example, the small visual language for state-machines in Figure 1 can be defined with the grammar shown in Figure 2. In this grammar, $R1$ is the axiom (the top-level rule) and specifies how to add a single rectangle. The rule $R2$ can then be used to add a new rectangle connected by an arrow to an existing rectangle. Finally, the rule $R3$ is used to connect by a new arrow two existing rectangles.

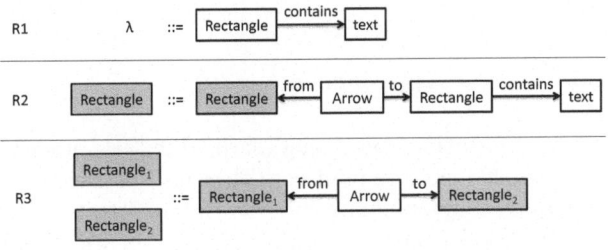

Fig. 2. Graph Grammar for the visual language in Fig. 1

Notable approaches based on graph-grammars include:

- Layered Graph Grammars introduced in [19] splits the definition of a visual language into the "physical layout" for the visual symbols' graphical attributes, and the "spatial relation graph" for their syntactic attributes, i.e. their relative positionning.
- Reserved Graph Grammars introduced in [23] improve over Layered Graph Grammars by simplifying the writing of rules and removing ambiguities.
- Contextual Layered Graph Grammars introduced in [3] improve Layered Graph Grammars by allowing the expression of positive and negative conditions for the application of the rules.
- Positional Grammars introduced in [7].
- Extended Positional Grammars introduced in [5].

Conversely, Picture Layout Grammars introduced in [13] are not based on graph-grammars. Their terminal symbols are attributed drawing elements such as the rectangles, ellipses, texts, etc. The non-terminal symbols are defined by the grammar rules organizing the spatial relationships between the constitutive terminals and non-terminals. The small visual language for state-machines in Figure 1 can be specified with the following grammar given in [13]:

Listing 1.1. Picture Layout Grammar for State Machines

```
1 FSDiagram -> StateList
2 StateList -> State
3 StateList -> (State, StateList)
4 State -> contains(rectangle, text)
5 State -> leaves (State, Transition)
6 Transition -> labels(arrow, text)
```

In this grammar, the first rule is the top-level one and correspond to the entire picture of Fig. 1. Each rounded rectangle in Fig. 1 corresponds to a State, as defined in rule 4. It defines the State symbol as a rectangle containing a text element. The arrows in Fig. 1 are defined as the Transitions symbols in rule 6. Their relation to the States is defined in rule 5. With rich composition rules and support for connectors, Picture Layout Grammars can be used for the specification of complex visual languages well beyond simple nodes and connectors.

2.2   Metamodel-Based Approaches

The abstract syntax annotation approach described in [21] consists in introducing elements of a language's concrete syntax within its abstract syntax. More precisely, a visual language's symbols are directly mapped to the DSML's abstract syntax by annotating its concepts. It is a metamodel-based approach because a language's abstract syntax is directly mapped to its concrete syntax. It serves as the definition of the visual notation. This approach is prominently used by the tools based on Eclipse GMF (Graphical Modeling Framework), such as EuGENia [20]; however it is not suited for our purpose where a specification of the concrete syntax independent from the abstract syntax is desired.

In order to enable the exchange of UML diagrams between tools, a core metamodel for diagrams has been proposed in [2]. It is a precursor to the Diagram Definition [17] and Diagram Interchange metamodel, now an OMG standard. This metamodel contains concepts such as Node and Edge, but also other elements. It is general enough by enabling the use of any SVG (Scalable Vector Graphic) shape, for example rectangles and ellipses. Visual symbols can be composed and their relations are specified using absolute positioning. Using this metamodel, a software engineer is able to describe any diagram, corresponding to a connection-based or geometric-based visual language. However, this is a metamodel for diagrams and as such cannot be used for the expression of visual languages themselves.

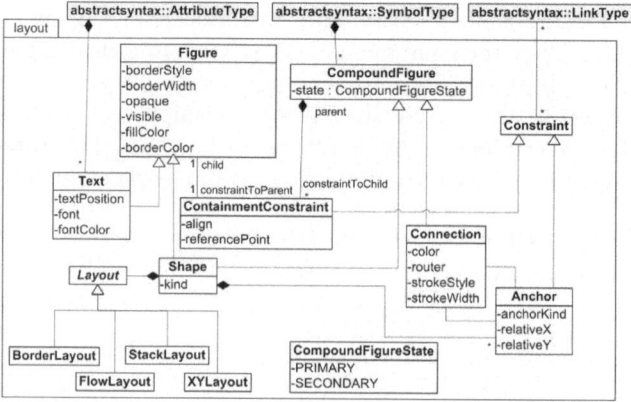

Fig. 3. Metamodel of Visual Languages by [11]

The metamodel for concrete syntaxes proposed in [18] contains simple concepts such as NodeFigure and EdgeFigure. These can be nested within each other. This approach leverages the metamodel representation of the visual notation in the definition of mappings between the abstract and concrete syntax elements. However, the authors do not specify how the graphical and syntactic attributes of the visual symbols will be defined. The drawbacks are that this approach does not specify how the elements in the concrete syntax are to be visualized. It is missing the definition of graphical and syntactic attributes. It also focuses on connection-based visual languages. Looking at the concrete syntax's metamodel, geometric-based visual languages are not supported. The metamodel for concrete syntaxes proposed in [11] is much more complete than the one proposed in [18]. In fact, it explicitly targets the representation of visual languages in the form of a model. It contains concepts such as VLSpec (Visual Language Specification), Alphabet and SymbolType, in addition to those shown in Figure 3.

2.3 Conclusion

As shown in this section, it is possible to specify the concrete syntax of a DSML, in the form of a visual language, independently from its abstract syntax. The specification of a visual language can be achieved in multiple ways with different strengths and weaknesses. However, the forced proximity of the specification of a visual language with the underlying abstract syntax in metamodel-based approaches is symptomatic. On the other end of the spectrum, some grammar-based approaches such as the Picture Layout Grammars are completely detached in addition to their offering of great visual expressiveness.

Because we precisely aim at focusing the attention of the software engineers onto the concrete syntaxes and thus produce visual languages very close to the experts' expectations, it is logical to lean toward some of the grammar-based approaches. In this way, the software engineers would not be tempted to spend time on the abstract syntax. For these reasons, we chose to base our work on Picture Layout Grammars [13]. As will be discussed in Section 5, this does not mean that the following would not be applicable to other approaches for the specification of visual languages.

3 Generating Abstract Syntaxes from Visual Languages

Based on the Picture Layout Grammars approach for the specification of visual languages, this section presents how abstract syntaxes can be derived from them. For this purpose, we first introduce a refinement of the Picture Layout Grammars that allows the expression of a great deal of details about visual symbols.

3.1 Concrete Visual Syntax Specification Language

This refinement will be hereon referred to as the Concrete Visual Syntax Specification Language (CVSSL). A complete specification with the CVSSL contains two parts:

- The specification of the visual symbols using grammar rules similar to Picture Layout Grammar rules.
- The specification of the toolboxes that will be available to the domain experts. This part lists the visual symbols that the domain experts will be manipulating. It is necessary because a visual symbol may be too complex to be expressed with only one grammar rule, as will be demonstrated in the following sub-section.

As introduced above, the core of a CVSSL specification is specified using grammar rules that have a visual interpretation. These rules are similar to grammar rules for string-based languages expressed in the BNF or EBNF notations. A rule is composed of a head and a body. The semantic is that the rule's head (a symbol) can be replaced by the rule's body. The visual interpretation is that the rule's head is a visual symbol defined by the rule's body, i.e. the visual elements in it. In this context, a rule's head is called a variable and is referred to by its name. A rule's body can be composed of multiple elements, called terminals. Supported terminals include shapes (rectangles, ellipses, etc.), images, labels (text), and placeholders for inputs and pieces of data. For example, a white rectangle with black borders is noted:

Listing 1.2. White rectangle with a black border of size 3

```
1  [[]  150*50  |white|black:3]
```

They are called terminals because they are not defined by other grammar rules. Terminals can be aggregated with operators in a rule's body. Supported operators are the concatenation, the union, the repetition and the special graph operator.

As an example, using the CVSSL, the visual symbol for the "Air Traffic Controller" element in Figure 4 can be specified as follow:

Listing 1.3. Grammar rules for the "Air Traffic Controller" element

```
1  Operator -> {OperatorInner  [[]  200*90  |white|black:1]}:stack;
2  OperatorInner -> {OperatorName OperatorSkills OperatorStates}:
       vertical;
3  OperatorName -> {<s "Name" 198*20>  [[]  200*22  |white|black:1]}:stack;
4  OperatorSkills -> {Skill*:vertical  [[]  200*22]}:stack;
5  OperatorStates -> {{StateWorkload StateStress}:vertical  [[]  200*50  |
       white|black:1]}:stack;
```

3.2   Abstract Syntax Generation

When a DSML's concrete syntax is specified using the CVSSL, it is possible to generate a default abstract syntax corresponding to it. The main reasoning for this purpose is that the visual symbols described in the concrete syntax will become concepts within the abstract syntax in the form of classes and relations. As a help to the reader, the following vocabulary will be used:

- The "application" of the rule "$R \to s$" is the replacement of the variable R by the visual sentence s.

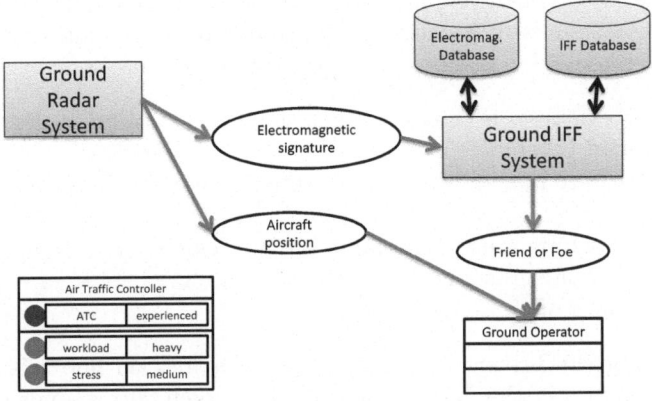

Fig. 4. Example of visual sentence

- A variable R "produces" a visual sentence w when the recursive application of the grammar's rules allows the variable R to be replaced by w. For example, with the rules "$A \rightarrow aBc$" and "$B \rightarrow b$", then A produces the "abc" visual sentence by the replacement of the variable B by its definition.
- The "minimal production" of a variable R is the smallest visual sentence that can be produced by R. It is obtained by the application of empty rules whenever possible, i.e. whenever an optional operator or a zero-or-more operator is used.

Primary Classes. If the variable R is used in the notation specification as a toolbox element, it means that the domain experts will be able to manipulate visual symbols defined by R. Then, a class named R is created in the default abstract syntax. For example, considering the Listing 1.3 above, as well as the Listing 1.4, the "Operator" variable is defined as a toolbox element, then a class named "Operator" will be created. Conversely, the variables "OperatorName", and "OperatorSkills" from the same listing are not toolbox elements and no class corresponding to them will be created.

Listing 1.4. Toolboxes for the example

```
1 toolbox "Elements" {
2     element Data "Data"
3     element System "System"
4     element Operator "Operator"
5     element Database "Database"
6     element Skill "Operator Skill"
7 }
```

Primitive Attributes. In the CVSSL it is possible to denote an area where an expert will be able to input some data. These areas, called data placeholders, have special notations, an example of which is given on line 3 of the Listing 1.3.

The rationale is to generate class attributes for the data placeholders. If the variable R corresponds to a class and its minimal production contains a data placeholder with the description p and the type t, then:

- An attribute name n is constructed as the concatenation of the words found in p, preceded by "has".
- A class attribute named n of type t is created for the class corresponding to R.
- If a class attribute with that name already exists, then a unique name is created based on n (usually by appending an incremented integer).
- The cardinality of the attribute is always 0..1.

Still considering the Listing 1.3, the data placeholder on line 3 is part of the minimal production of the "Operator" symbol, which corresponds to a class in the abstract syntax being built. Hence, an attribute named "hasName" of type "String" and cardinality 0..1 is added to the class named "Operator".

Relations from Grammar Operators. If the variable R can produce a visual sentence that contains the variable C and both are toolbox elements, then:

- If the variable C can only occur at most one time at the targeted location, then the cardinality is functional (0..1), otherwise it is unbounded (0..*).
- A name n is constructed as the concatenation of the string "has" and the name of C. If the cardinality is unbounded, the name n is turned into its plural form by appending "s" to it or turning the final "y" into "ies".
- If no relation named n starting from R exists in the abstract syntax it is created with the identified cardinality. The range of the relation is the class corresponding to C.
- If a relation or attribute with the same name n already exists for R, then a unique one is created.

For example in the Listing 1.3, the "Operator" symbol can produce zero or more "Skill" symbols (on line 4). Because the symbol "Skill" is also a toolbox element, a relation between the two classes will be created. It will be named "hasSkills" and have an unbounded cardinality.

Relations from Graph Connectors. In a visual notation, the special "graph" construct can be used to express graph-based sub visual languages containing nodes and connectors that may bear some legend. In principle, nodes are visual symbols defined by grammar rules that must also be toolbox elements to specify the fact that domain experts can interact with them and are thus compiled into classes in the default abstract syntax. The rationale is that the connectors may represent relations between these nodes. Hence, when a transition does not bear any legend, it is compiled into a relation in the default abstract syntax. This relation always has an unbounded cardinality on both sides and its name is the concatenation of "link" with the name of the connector. It can start from each class corresponding to the nodes from which the connector can originate. Conversely, it can end on each class corresponding to nodes to which the connector can go. For example, considering the following excerpt also corresponding to the visual language for Figure 4

Listing 1.5. Example of visual graph in CVSSL

```
1 CommandPost -> graph {
2    nodes Data, System, Operator, Database
3    <DataExport #0000FF:1 {Operator, System simple} {Data arrow}>
4    <DataImport #FF0000:1 {Data simple} {Operator, System arrow}>
5    <Connection {System simple} {Database arrow}>
6 } ;
```

Here the connector "DataExport" will be used to create a relation from the classes "Operator" and "System" to the class "Data", as each of them are identified as toolbox elements in Listing 1.4. The same process is applied for the connectors "DataImport" and "Connection".

Association Classes from Graph Connectors. In the case where a legend is attached to the connector, an association class is needed in the default abstract syntax in order to attach the abstract syntax elements corresponding to the legend directly to it. Consider the following example corresponding to the visual language shown in Figure 1 where the connector "Transition" has a legend defined by the "Legend" variable. This variable is defined by a rule that can produce the "Interaction" variable, which is here assumed to be a toolbox element.

Listing 1.6. Grammar for state machines

```
1 StateMachine -> graph {
2    node State
3    <Transition black:1 ^Legend {State simple} {State arrow}>
4 } ;
5 Legend -> Interaction? ;
```

The produced default abstract syntax for this sample then contains an association class named "Transition". The symbol "Transition" is also a toolbox element and treated as such, it will have attributes and/or relations corresponding to its legend.

3.3   Limitations

Using the CVSSL to express a concrete syntax, the rules presented above can be used to produce a complete abstract syntax corresponding to a default interpretation as concepts of the visual symbols specified in it. However several limitations have been identified.

First and foremost, the rules are not able to derive the classes' hierarchy, i.e. their subclassing relations. This is because the information is not present in the visual languages. However, one could define a set of rules for the automatic inference of the subclassing relations, based on the existence of common attributes for example. One remaining difficulty would still be the naming of the super-classes. Building the corresponding rules constitutes future works.

A second limitation is the difficulty to identify the true nature of the relations between the classes in the abstract syntaxes. Could a specific relation be a composition or an aggregation? It is hard to derive this information from the visual language.

A third limitation is the identification of the navigability of the relations. The visual language does not hold any information that could be leveraged in this regard.

3.4   Conclusion

This section presented rules for the automatic derivation of an abstract syntax in the form of a metamodel from the specification of a visual language. Some limitations have been identified that will require software engineers to adapt the produced metamodels after the generation process. However, this methodology is expected to effectively shift their focus onto the concrete syntaxes of the DSMLs they are tasked to produce for the domain experts. In this way, DSMLs' concrete syntaxes closer to the expert's expectations could be produced, thus maximizing their acceptance.

4   Validation

The validation of the approach proposed here is three-fold. First, the derivation rules presented in the previous section have been implemented into a compiler available under the LGPL licence at http://xowl.org. Second, it has been applied on a use case coming from the aeronautic industry. Third, an empirical study has been conducted in order to assess whether the concrete syntaxes produced in this way are indeed closer to the experts' expectations.

4.1   Industrial Use Case

In the context of the building of a military command post, experts in human-machine interactions are tasked to verify the procedures that operators will have to execute. For example, a given procedure must still be achievable for operators under stressful conditions. The representation of the information flow would enable the experts to better analyze the interactions between the operators and potentially to propose new procedures. The experts are facing an issue with the increasing number of procedures that must be analyzed; they cannot manually analyze them all and need to automate this task. To achieve this, the experts require a DSML for them to represent the information flows in the form of models, so that they can be automatically analyzed. Fortunately, the experts are able to provide some examples of the drawings they produce using informal tools such as Microsoft Visio, Powerpoint, or even simple pen and paper. The Figure 4 is one example.

Using our approach, we built using the CVSSL the complete visual language for this domain. The visual language cannot be fully shown here but is available at http://xowl.org. Then, a default abstract syntax has been derived using the rules described in Section 3. The resulting metamodel is shown in Figure 5.

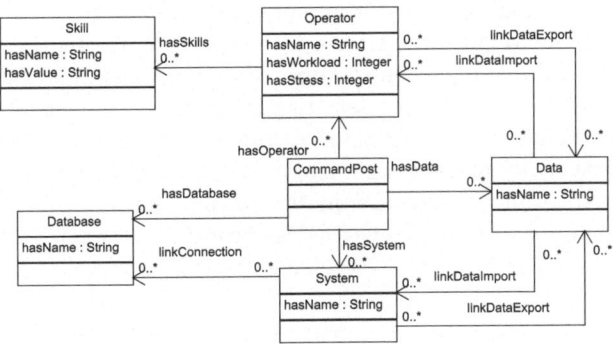

Fig. 5. Metamodel derived from the concrete syntax

This application case demonstrates that we are indeed able to derive a complete abstract syntax from the specification of a visual language (expressed in the CVSSL). As noted in Section 3, the derivation process has some limitations that are illustrated here. It is not able to infer some sub-classing relationships. A software engineer would probably have created an abstract class "Agent" and made the "Operator" and "System" classes inherit from it. In addition, he/she would arguably have turned the relation "hasSkills" into a composition. Some naviguability and cardinality issues could also be addressed; but overall, the Figure 5 shows a good starting point.

4.2 Empirical Study

In order to assess whether the concrete syntaxes produced are indeed closer to the experts' expectations, we realized an empirical study. Its definition is summarized as follow: The goal of the empirical study is to analyze the building of a DSML for the purpose of evaluating the used approach with respect to the proximity of the concrete syntax with the domain experts' expectations in the context of novice software engineers. The subjects are master students in their last year majoring in Computer Science. For the purpose of this experiment, the previous application case is reused. We measure the proximity of the notations produced by subjects with respect to the provided pre-existing domain schemas on a 0 to 100 scale. For this purpose, we defined in advance a set of 61 objective criteria that have to be met by the notations produced by the subjects. The criteria themselves are designed so that the perfect score can be achieved regardless of the used approach. A few examples are given hereafter:

- Systems are rectangles
- Systems are colored in grey
- Databases are cylinders

A set of criteria are defined for each of the notational element. They include the shape, color and outline of the elements, as well as how they are composed. For example the rectangles representing systems have the systems' name within them. We attributed weights to criteria in order to represent the fact that the shape of a notational symbol is more important than the color of its outline. In addition, these criteria are not necessarily pass or fail. It is possible for subjects to get half the points of a criteria for example. It is also important to note that these criteria really measure the proximity of the subjects' implementation with the expected result and not the quality of the result. Subjects that deviate from the expected notation but nevertheless produced a coherent notation with unambiguous and visually distinctive elements will be penalized. The point of this metric is really to favor results closest to the expectations.

In this experiment the variable A representing the approach for building the DSML is defined with one dependent variable: Q for the concrete syntax's proximity. There are then two treatments of this study, one for the Metamodel-Driven approach (A_m) and one for the Notation-Driven approach (A_n). During the implementation of this study, the experimenters play the role of the domain experts. Experimenters will have the perspective of domain experts in regard to their evaluation of the subjects' notations.

A population of 55 subjects plays the role of software engineers hired to implement a DSML. Each subject individually performs the whole task. In order for the population to be representative and unbiased, the subjects are all master students in their last year majoring in Computer Science. In this way, all subjects have roughly the same level of experience and expertise. Implementing a DSML is a task they can be expected to perform in a professional environment right after their graduation.

In this study, the following null hypothesis evaluating the produced concrete syntaxes' proximity is defined. It specifies that the use of a Notation-Driven approach for building a DSML does not improve the concrete syntax' proximity with the domain experts' expectations. If the hypothesis is rejected, it means the use of a Notation-Driven approach has an impact on the corresponding proximity. The impact can be positive or negative and is obtained by comparing the distribution of the results in each group. Then, H_0 is defined as: "The proximity of the concrete syntax using the Metamodel-Driven approach is equal to the proximity using the Notation-Driven approach."

The results are aggregated by quartile and group in Figure 6. The statistics by group are summarized in Table 1. We then used the ANOVA statistical test to determine whether the H_0 hypothesis should be rejected. The value of F is 23.01 whereas the value of F_{crit} is 3.89. With these results ($F \geq F_{crit}$), we reject H_0. This means that the Notation-Driven approach has an impact on the proximity of the produced concrete syntaxes with the domain experts' expectations.

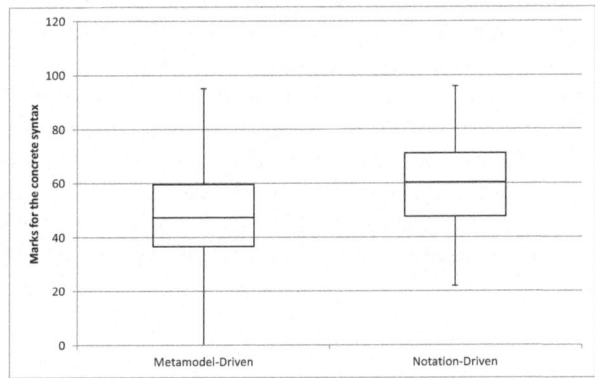

Fig. 6. Marks by group

Table 1. Statistics by group for the concrete syntaxes

	Metamodel-Driven	Notation-Driven
MIN	0.00	22.00
MEDIAN	47.36	60.24
MAX	95.00	96.00
MEAN	47.32	59.31
STANDARD DEVIATION	19.54	15.60

Looking at Figure 6, we can see that the concrete syntaxes produced using the Notation-Driven approach are indeed closer to the domain experts' expectations.

5 Discussion

Regarding the validation of our approach by the presented empirical study, some possible threats to its validity have been identified: The experiment's subjects are master students and not (yet) professional software engineers. This potential bias is mitigated by the fact that all subjects were close to graduation at the time of the study and could be expected to perform the work described in this experiment in their immediate line of work. Also, the experimenters took part in the evaluation process of the subjects' submissions. This potential bias is mitigated by the fact that objective criteria were used for this purpose.

The approach described in this paper relies on Picture Layout Grammars for the specification of visual languages. A legitimate question is then, how is it still applicable with other specification methods, in particular metamodel-based ones. In this regard, it has to be noted that the derivation rules described in Section 3 are general enough so that they can be transposed and/or adapted to other methods. For example, it should be possible to implement them as model transformation rules that can be applied to models representing visual notations in a metamodel-based specification approach. The only provision is that it must be possible to identify the visual symbols that correspond to interaction points for the domain experts, i.e. elements they can manipulate.

Furthermore, this paper focused solely on the case of *visual* DSMLs. Another legitimate question is how is it applicable to DSMLs with a *textual* DSMLs. An element of answer lies in the fact that the Picture Layout Grammars are very similar to the context-free grammars used for the specification of textual languages, in particular the EBNF notation. Provided that the same extensions are defined in order to identify the interaction points for the domain experts, the same set of derivation rules could be used. An interesting point is that the XText [1] Eclipse plugin also goes into this direction with an approach for the mixed specification of the abstract and concrete syntaxes of DSMLs at the same time.

6   Conclusion

The paper presented an approach for the automatic derivation of an abstract syntax from the specification of a DSML's concrete syntax. It has been validated by its implementation, its application to an industrial use case and its evaluation in an empirical study. The conclusion is that it is indeed possible to automatically derive a DSML's abstract syntax from the specification of its concrete syntax, provided some extension to the visual language's specification approach. This approach still has some limitations (e.g. class hierarchies) that can be seen as possible future works. Future works also include the replication of the approach for textual DSMLs.

Leveraging this approach, software engineers are able to work efficiently with domain experts in order to build a domain's visual language without caring about the underlying concepts. This notation-driven approach focusing the efforts of the software engineers onto what the domain experts are actually caring about is expected to improve the acceptability of the produced DSMLs. The empirical study presented in Section 4 certainly points toward that direction.

References

1. Amyot, D., Farah, H., Roy, J.-F.: Evaluation of development tools for domain-specific modeling languages. In: Gotzhein, R., Reed, R. (eds.) SAM 2006. LNCS, vol. 4320, pp. 183–197. Springer, Heidelberg (2006)
2. Boger, M., Jeckle, M., Müller, S., Fransson, J.: Diagram interchange for UML. In: Jézéquel, J.-M., Hussmann, H., Cook, S. (eds.) UML 2002. LNCS, vol. 2460, pp. 398–411. Springer, Heidelberg (2002)
3. Bottoni, P., Taentzer, G., Schürr, A.: Efficient parsing of visual languages based on critical pair analysis and contextual layered graph transformation. In: Visual Languages (2000)
4. Brown, S.A., Massey, A.P., Montoya-Weiss, M.M., Burman, J.R.: Do i really have to? user acceptance of mandated technology. European Journal of Information Systems 11, 283–295 (2002)

---

[1] http://www.eclipse.org/Xtext/

 5. Costagliola, G., Deufemia, V., Polese, G.: A framework for modeling and implementing visual notations with applications to software engineering. ACM Transations on Software Engineering Methodologies 13, 431–487 (2004)
 6. Costagliola, G., Lucia, A.D., Orefice, S., Polese, G.: A classification framework to support the design of visual languages. Journal of Visual Languages Computing 13, 573–600 (2002)
 7. Costagliola, G., Lucia, A.D., Orefice, S., Tortora, G.: A parsing methodology for the implementation of visual systems. IEEE Transactions on Software Engineering 23, 777–799 (1997)
 8. Davis, F.D.: Perceived usefulness, perceived ease of use and user acceptance of information technology. MIS Quaterly 13, 319–340 (1989)
 9. Davis, F.D., Bagozzi, R.P., Warshaw, P.R.: User acceptance of computer technology: A comparison of two theoretical models. Management Science 35, 982–1003 (1989)
10. de Lara, J., Vangheluwe, H., Alfonseca, M.: Meta-modelling and graph grammars for multi-paradigm modelling in atom 3. Software and Systems Modeling 3, 194–209 (2004)
11. Ermel, C., Ehrig, K., Taentzer, G., Weiss, E.: Object oriented and rule-based design of visual languages using tiger. European Association of Software Science and Technology Journal 1 (2006)
12. Evans, A., Fernández, M.A., Mohagheghi, P.: Experiences of developing a network modeling tool using the eclipse environment. In: Paige, R.F., Hartman, A., Rensink, A. (eds.) ECMDA-FA 2009. LNCS, vol. 5562, pp. 301–312. Springer, Heidelberg (2009)
13. Golin, A.J.: Parsing visual languages with picture layout grammars. Journal of Visual Languages Computing 2, 371–393 (1991)
14. ISO/IEC. Syntactic metalanguage - extended bnf (1996)
15. Knuth, D.E.: On the translation of languages from left to right. Information and Control 8, 607–639 (1965)
16. Kolovos, D.S., Rose, L.M., Paige, R.F., Polak, F.A.C.: Raising the level of abstraction in the development of gmf-based graphical model editors. In: Proceedings of the 2009 ICSE Workshop on Modeling in Software Engineering, MISE 2009, pp. 13–19. IEEE Computer Society (2009)
17. OMG. Diagram Definition (2012)
18. Ráth, A., Ökrös, A., Varró, D.: Synchronization of abstract and concrete syntax in domain-specific modeling languages. Software and Systems Modeling 9, 453–471 (2010)
19. Rekers, J., Schürr, A.: Defining and parsing visual languages with layered graph grammars. Journal of Visual Languages Computing 8 (1997)
20. E. Team. Eclipse eugenia (October 2012)
21. Temate, S., Broto, L., Tchana, A., Hagimont, D.: A high level approach for generating model's graphical editors. In: Information Technology: New Generations (2011)
22. Venkatesh, V., Morris, M.G., Davis, G.B., Davis, F.D.: User acceptance of information technology: Toward a unified view. MIS Quaterly 27, 425–478 (2003)
23. Zhang, D.-Q., Zhang, K., Cao, J.: A context-sensitive graph grammar formalism for the specification of visual languages. Computer Journal 44, 186–200 (2001)

Validation of Derived Features
and Well-Formedness Constraints in DSLs*
By Mapping Graph Queries to an SMT-Solver

Oszkár Semeráth, Ákos Horváth, and Dániel Varró

Budapest University of Technology and Economics,
Department of Measurement and Information Systems,
1117 Budapest, Magyar tudósok krt. 2.
so765@hszk.bme.hu, {ahorvath,varro}@mit.bme.hu

Abstract. Despite the wide range of existing generative tool support,
constructing a design environment for a complex domain-specific language (DSL) is still a tedious task as the large number of derived features
and well-formedness constraints complementing the domain metamodel
necessitate special handling. Incremental model queries as provided by
the EMF-IncQuery framework can (i) uniformly specify derived features
and well-formedness constraints and (ii) automatically refresh their result set upon model changes. However, for complex domains, derived
features and constraints can be formalized incorrectly resulting in incomplete, ambiguous or inconsistent DSL specifications. To detect such
issues, we propose an automated mapping of EMF metamodels enriched
with derived features and well-formedness constraints captured as graph
queries in EMF-IncQuery into an effectively propositional fragment of
first-order logic which can be efficiently analyzed by the Z3 SMT-solver.
Moreover, overapproximations are proposed for complex query features
(like transitive closure and recursive calls). Our approach will be illustrated on analyzing a DSL being developed for the avionics domain.

Keywords: model validation, model queries, SMT-solvers.

1 Introduction

The design of integrated development environments (IDEs) for complex domain-
specific languages (DSL) is still a challenging task nowadays. Generative environments like the Eclipse Modeling Framework (EMF) [1], Xtext or the Graphical
Modeling Framework (GMF) significantly improve productivity by automating
the production of rich editor features (e.g. syntax highlighting, auto-completion,
etc.) to enhance modeling for domain experts. Furthermore, there is efficient tool
support for validating well-formedness constraints and design rules over large

---

* This work was partially supported by the CERTIMOT (ERC_HU-09-01-2010-0003),
  the TÁMOP (4.2.2.C-11/1/KONV-2012-0001) projects, a collaborative project with
  Embraer and the János Bolyai Scholarship.

A. Moreira et al. (Eds.): MODELS 2013, LNCS 8107, pp. 538–554, 2013.

model instances of the DSL using tools like Eclipse OCL [2] or EMF-INCQUERY [3]. As a result, Eclipse-based IDEs are widely used in the industry in various domains including business modeling, avionics or automotive.

However, in case of complex, standardized industrial domains (like ARINC 653 [4] for avionics or AUTOSAR [5] in automotive), the sheer complexity of the DSL is a major challenge itself. (1) First, there are hundreds of well-formedness constraints and design rules defined by those standards, and due to the lack of validation, there is no guarantee for their consistency or unambiguity. (2) Moreover, domain metamodels are frequently extended by derived features, which serve as automatically calculated shortcuts for accessing or navigating models in a more straightforward way. In many practical cases, these features are not defined by the underlying standards but introduced during the construction of the DSL environment for efficiency reasons. Anyhow, the specification of derived features can also be inconsistent, ambiguous or incomplete.

As model-driven tools are frequently used in critical systems design to detect conceptual flaws of the system model early in the development process to decrease verification and validation (V&V) costs, those tools should be validated with the same level of scrutiny as the underlying system tools as part of a software tool qualification process issues in order to provide trust in their output. Therefore software tool qualification raises several challenges for building trusted DSL tools in a specific domain.

In the current paper, we aim to validate DSL tools by proposing an automated mapping from their high-level specification to the state-of-the-art Z3 SMT-solver [6]. We assume that DSL tools are specified by their respective EMF metamodels extended with derived features and well-formedness constraints captured (and implemented) by graph queries within the EMF-INCQUERY framework [7,8]. We define a validation process, which gradually investigates derived features and well-formedness constraints to pinpoint inconsistency, ambiguity or incompleteness issues. We identify constraints and derived features which can be mapped to effectively propositional logic formula [9], which are a decidable fragment of first order logic with effective reasoning support. Moreover, we provide several approximations for constraints which lie outside of this fragment to enable formal analysis of a practically relevant set of constraints.

The main innovation of our approach is to provide a *combined validation* of metamodels, derived features and well-formedness constraints *defined by an advanced graph query language* (instead of OCL) using *approximations to cover complex query features.* Our approach is illustrated on validating several DSL tool features taken from an ongoing industrial project in the avionics domain.

The rest of the paper is structured as follows. Sec. 2 provides an overview of EMF metamodels enriched with derived features and well-formedness constraints captured by graph queries of the EMF-INCQUERY language in the scope of a DSL from the avionics domain. Sec. 3 describes a high-level overview of mapping DSLs to logic formula and validation scenarios from a domain expert's viewpoint. Details of the mapping are elaborated in Sec. 4, while Sec. 5 includes an initial

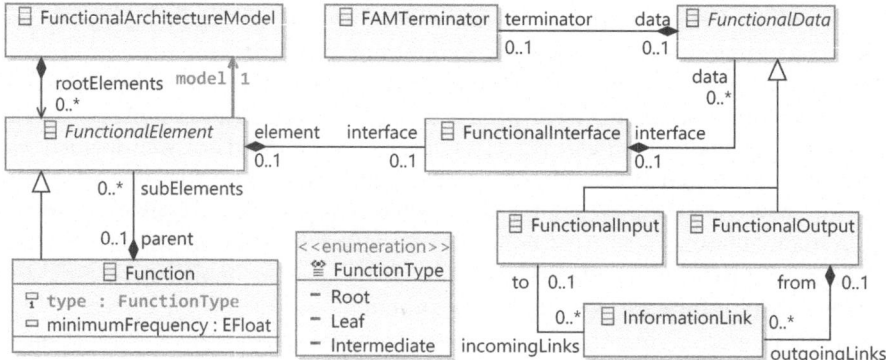

Fig. 1. Metamodel of the Functional Architecture

evaluation of expressiveness and preliminary execution results. Related work is assessed in Sec. 6 while finally, Sec. 7 concludes our paper.

2   Preliminaries: Domain Modeling

To illustrate the proposed V&V technique, this paper elaborates a case study from DSL tool development for avionics systems. To create an advanced modeling environment, we augment the metamodel with *query-based derived features* and *well-formedness validation rules*. Both of these advanced features are defined using model queries. Within the paper, we use the language of the EMF-INCQUERY [10] framework to define these queries over EMF metamodels.

2.1   Metamodel of the Case Study

In model-driven development of avionics systems, the *functional architecture* and the *platform description* of the system are often developed separately to increase reusability. The former defines the services performed by the system and links between functions to indicate dependencies and communication, while the latter describes platform-specific hardware and software components and their interactions. The functional architecture is usually partially imported from industry accepted tools and languages like AADL [11] or Matlab Simulink [12].

A simplified metamodel for functional architecture is shown in Fig. 1. The FunctionalArchitectureModel element represents the root of a model, which contains each Function (subtype of the FunctionalElement). Functions have a minimumFrequency, a type attribute and multiple FunctionalInterfaces, where each functional data is either an FunctionalOutput (for invoking other functions) or an FunctionalInput (for accepting invocations). An output can be connected to an input through an InformationLink. Finally, if an input or output is not connected to an other Function then they must be terminated in a FAMTerminator.

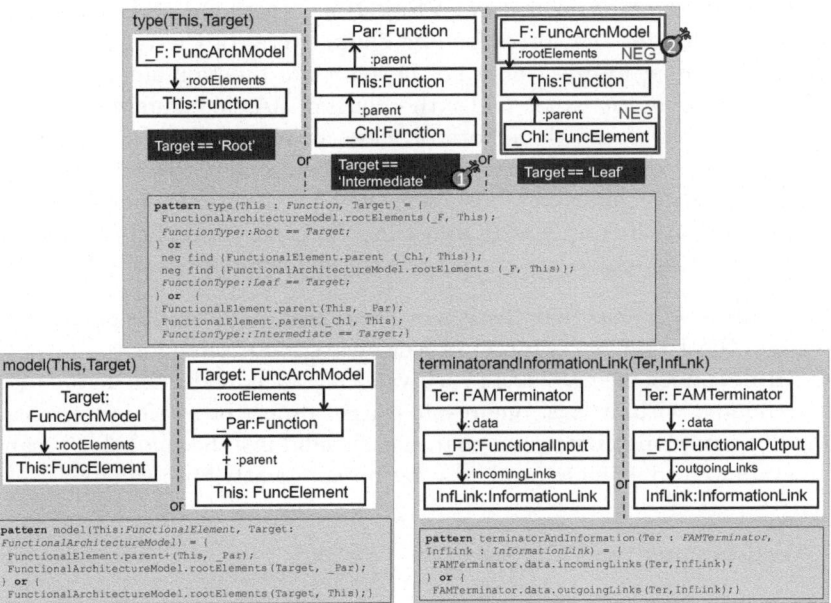

Fig. 2. The model and type DF and the terminatorandInformationLink WF constraint

2.2   Derived Features

Derived features (DF) are often essential extensions of metamodels to improve navigation, provide path compression or compute derived attributes. The value of these *features* can be computed from other parts of the model by a *model query* [7,13]. Such queries have two parameters, in case of (i) *derived EReferences* one parameter represents the source and another the target EObjects of the reference while in case of (ii) *derived EAttributes* one parameter represents the container EObject while the other one the computed value of its attribute.

FunctionalElements are augmented with the model derived EReference (highlighted in blue in Fig. 1) that represents a reference to the container FunctionalArchitctureModel EObject from any FunctionalElement within the containment hierarchy. Additionally, for the type EAttribute of the Function EObject a derived attribute is defined, which takes a value from the enumeration literals: Leaf, Root, Intermediate.

In Fig. 2 we use a custom graphical and the EMF-INCQUERY textual notation [3] to illustrate the queries defined for these derived features. On the graphical notation each rectangle is a named variable with a declared type, e.g. the variable _Par is a Function, while arrows represent references of the given EReference between the variables, e.g. the function This has the _Par function as its parent. A special reference between variables is the transitive closure depicted by an arrow with a + symbol, e.g., the parent reference between the This and _Par variables in the model query. Finally, the OR pattern bodies represent that the matches of the query is the union of the matches of its or bodies.

For example, the type query (see in Fig. 2) has three OR pattern bodies each defining the value for the corresponding enum literal of the type attribute: (i) Leaf if the container EObject does not have a child function along the subFunctions EReference and it is not under the FunctionalArchitectureModel along the rootElements EReference, where both of these constraints are defined using negative application conditions (NEG), (ii) Root if container EObject is directly under the FunctionalArchitectureModel connected by the rootElements EReference or (iii) Intermediate if container EObject has both parent and child functions. *Validation challenges:* We aim to validate the following properties for DFs:

- **Consistency** means that there is at least one valid instance model containing an object that has a target object or attribute value for the DF.
- **Completeness** means that in each valid instance model the derived feature is evaluated with at least one result (target object or attribute value).
- Finally, **unambiguity** means that in each valid instance model, DF can only be evaluated to a single result (target object or attribute value).

2.3   Well-Formedness Constraints

We also define some structural well-formedness (WF) constraints (usually derived from design rules and guidelines) to be validated on functional architecture models. In our current approach WF constraints define ill-formed model structures and thus they cannot have a match in a valid model. In our running example, a design rule captures that a FunctionalData EObject with a FAMterminator cannot also be connected to an InformationLink. It is specified by the terminatorandInformationLink query (see in Fig. 2) that has two OR pattern bodies, one for the FunctionalInputs and one for the FunctionalOutputs with their corresponding incomingLinks and outgoingLinks, respectively.

The aim of our case study is to demonstrate that its derived features and well-formedness constraints can be effectively validated using our mapping method (see in Sec. 4) to the Z3 SMT solver.
Validation challenges:

- **Consistency** of WFs can only be interpreted over the complete DSL specification, which in our understanding means that there is at least one valid instance model that satisfies all constraints.
- The **subsumption** property of a DSL is defined over its set of well-formedness constraints. If a WF constraint is subsumed by the set, then such a WF constraint does not express any additional restriction over the DSL. Therefore, it can be removed without changing the set of the valid instance models.

3   Overview of the Approach

Our approach (illustrated in Fig. 3) aims at validating complex DSL languages by automatically mapping from their high-level specification to the Z3 [6] SMT-solver. These complex DSLs are assumed to be defined by (i) a metamodel

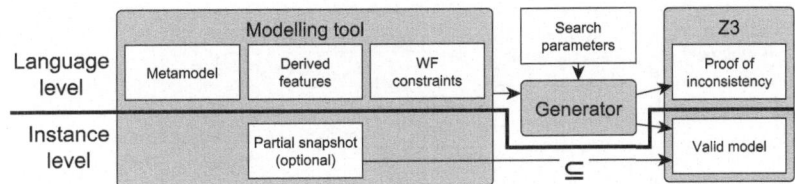

Fig. 3. Overview of DSL validation: Inputs and outputs

specified in EMF and augmented with both (ii) derived features and (iii) well-formedness (WF) constraints captured by model queries within the EMF-INCQUERY framework. These three artifacts form the input for our generator to provide the logical formulas that is fed into the Z3 solver. The output of the solver is either a proof of inconsistency or a valid model that satisfies all given constraints generated from the input artifacts.

Additionally, search parameters can be defined to impose additional restrictions or specific overapproximations to reduce the complexity of the formula to be proved. Moreover, as an optional input for the generator the user can define – based on the counter examples and proves provided by the solver – specific instance level constraints in the form of a partial snapshot [14,15] (also called input model) to restrict the domain of possible instance model and thus prune trivial valid models (e.g., empty model) provided by the Z3 solver.

End User Validation Workflow. Our iterative validation workflow for complex DSLs (see Fig. 4) assumes the existence of the metamodel (captured in EMF), its derived features and well-formedness constraints (captured as graph queries).

First, each DF is investigated by adding them to the formal DSL specification (extending it with one new DF at a time in a predefined order), and then by validating this specification in Z3. Then, WF constraints are validated similarly, by incrementally adding a single WF constraint at each validation step.

The validation fails, if the compiled set of formulas are inconsistent (formally, no models can be constructed within a given search limit). In such a case, the designer needs to either (i) fine-tune the search parameters, (ii) provide a new partial snapshot or (iii) modify the DSL specification itself based on the proof outcome. If the formal DSL specification with all DF and WF constraints is validated, then it is valid under the assumptions imposed by the search parameters and the partial snapshot.

The separation to start the iterative validation process with the derived features and then continue with the WF constraints is based on the observation that each derived feature eliminates a large set of trivial, non-conforming instance models (which are not valid instances of the DSL). Adding a single constraint at a time to the validation problem helps identify the location of errors the solver provides only very restricted traceability information.

Example DSL Validation Scenario. To illustrate the execution of our validation workflow Fig. 5 shows a possible scenario for our running example. As the input

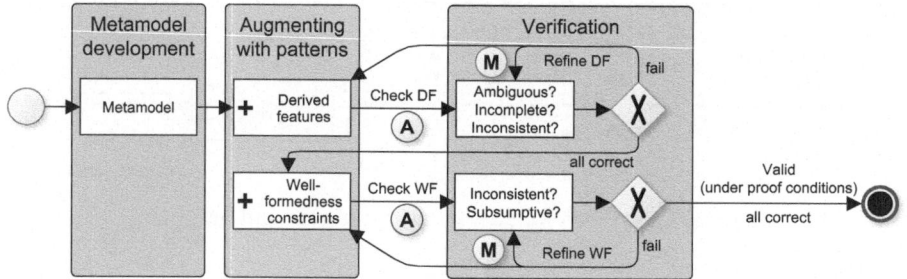

Fig. 4. End user workflow of validation of DSLs

for the validation scenario we use the metamodel, DFs and WF constraints as defined in Sec. 2 with three modifications (to inject hypothetical conceptual flaws into the queries):

1. the second pattern body (marked as 1 in Fig. 2) is missing from the DF query `type`, which defines `Function` elements of `Intermediate` type,
2. the third body of query `type` specifying the `Leaf` type is also changed: it forgets to define a NAC condition over the `rootElements` EReference (bomb2).
3. one WF constraint is added to the DSL specification expressed by the `IL2T` query, which prohibits that a `InformationLink` is connected to a `FAMTerminator`. This constraint only differs from the first body of the original WF constraint that it uses the inverse edges and thus it is a redundant.

Sec. 3 describes how the DFs and WF constraints are added one by one during the validation process (assuming that the metamodel is already validated). Some instance models are depicted on the right side, which illustrate counter examples retrieved by the solver (`CE_i`) and a partial snapshot (`PS`) used for initializing a solver run. Each row in Fig. 5 describes the validation step in the current iteration, its *outcome* and the *action* taken by the user to continue validation.

First (Step 1) we add the `type` DF to the formal specification and validate its consistency by setting the default overapproximation for the transitive acyclicity constraint (see in Section 4.1) to a maximum of 2 levels. Then (Step 2), the completeness of the `type` DF is checked resulting in a failure illustrated by the counter example `CE1` showing a function without an `Intermediate` type. This is fixed by adding the second pattern body with the `Intermediate` definition to the `type` pattern. By correcting it, the validation is successfully executed. After this the ambiguity of the attribute is tested (Step 3), which fails again (with a function node that is both a `Leaf` and a `Root` as a counter example). This is fixed by adding the missing NAC condition on the `rootElements` to the third pattern body of `type`. Step 4 adds the `model` DF and is followed in Step 5 with its completeness validation, which fails as pointed out in `CE3` since it does not have a `model` EReference. A partial snapshot is defined with a `FunctionalArchitecutreModel` object to prune the search space and avoid such counter examples, however, its

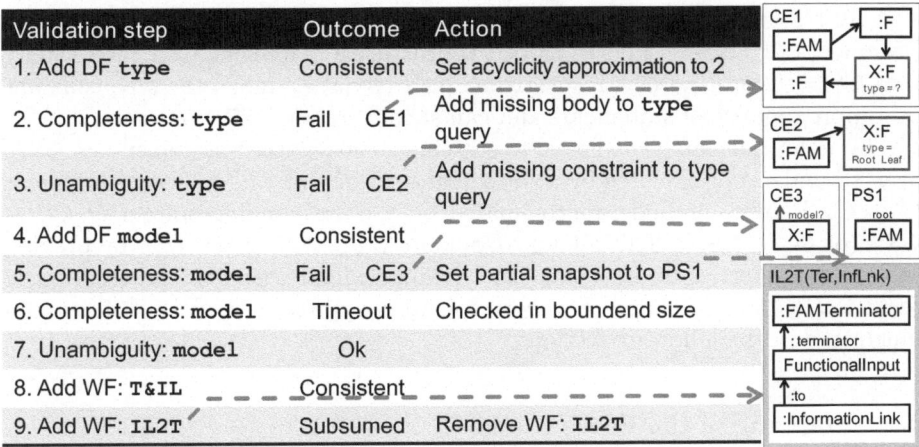

Validation step	Outcome		Action
1. Add DF `type`	Consistent		Set acyclicity approximation to 2
2. Completeness: `type`	Fail	CE1	Add missing body to `type` query
3. Unambiguity: `type`	Fail	CE2	Add missing constraint to type query
4. Add DF `model`	Consistent		
5. Completeness: `model`	Fail	CE3	Set partial snapshot to PS1
6. Completeness: `model`	Timeout		Checked in boundend size
7. Unambiguity: `model`	Ok		
8. Add WF: `T&IL`	Consistent		
9. Add WF: `IL2T`	Subsumed		Remove WF: `IL2T`

Fig. 5. Example DSL validation scenario

revalidation (Step 6) ends in a `Timeout` (more than 2 minutes) and thus this feature can only be validated on a concrete bounded domain of a maximum of 5 model objects. In Step 7, the unambiguity of the `model` DF is validated without a problem. Followed by the consistency validation of the WF constraint `terminatorandInformationLink` (Step 8). Finally, WF constraint `IL2T` is checked for subsumption (Step 9) and found positive; thus it is already expressed by the DSL specification and thus it can be deleted from the set of WF constraints.

4   Mapping DSLs to FOL Formulae

In this section, we demonstrate how Ecore metamodels augmented with derived features and well-formedness constraints captured as model queries (namely, EMF-INCQUERY graph patterns) are mapped to first order logical (FOL) formulae. Our idea is to map all DSL concepts to the effectively propositional fragment (EPR) [9] of FOL to guarantee decidability and efficient automated validation using the Z3 [6] solver. EPR formulae are written in prenex normal form, and contain only constants, universal quantifiers, and functions that return boolean values (aka predicates). If the mapping of a language features leads out of EPR formulae, then the specification is handled as a general FOL problem or it is approximated by EPR statements (as in case of transitive closure, which is inexpressible in FOL).

Mapping Structure for DSL. In order to represent a DSL specification in FOL we use the following structure: $DSL = META \wedge DFs \wedge WFs$, where $META$ represents the set of FOL statements defined by the metamodel (e.g., type hierarchy), DFs symbolizes the statement set specified by the derived features and finally, WFs represents the set of statements for the well-formedness constraints.

A FOL statement can be handled using under- or overapproximations, where statements C^U or C^O under- or overapproximate statement C if they satisfy that $C^U \Rightarrow C$ or $C \Rightarrow C^O$, respectively. As a trivial example, the *true* constant overapproximates all statements and can substitute any DSL constraint.

This definition can be extended to statement sets, where a statement set CS is over- or underapproximated by a statement set CS^O (or CS^U), if each statement $C \in CS$ is over- or underapproximated by a corresponding statement $C^O \in CS^O$ (or $C^U \in CS^U$). This allows to validate properties of the *DSL* by proving the same properties on its under- or overapproximations. The construction of *META*, *DFs* and *WFs* and their corresponding approximations are defined and illustrated in the following sections.

4.1 Mapping of the Ecore Model

The different features of the target DSL captured as an Ecore metamodel are mapped to FOL formulae in the following way. Each generated statement is added to the *META* set.

Type Hierarchy. The elements of the output instance model are uniformly mapped to a Z3 type *object* declared by the compiler. Type indicator predicates are used to describe that an *object* is an instance of an EClassifier. Additionally, to interpret supertype relations, a disjunction d of conjunctions c_i of type predicates are constructed, formally $d = c_1 \vee c_2 \vee \ldots \vee c_n$. For each non-abstract type in the metamodel one $c_i = type_1 \wedge type_2 \wedge \ldots \wedge type_m$ is constructed where exactly those type predicates $type_i$ appear as positive literals that are direct or indirect types of c_i. This way only one c_i can be true in d for any objects that conforms to the metamodel.

For example, the `Function` class in Table 1 is mapped to a formula where only the `Function(f)` and the `FunctionalElement(f)` predicates are positive literals.

References and Attributes. An *EReference* between two EObjects is a directed relation represented as binary *reference predicates* (boolean functions) and its target type is explicitly asserted to restrict their range to the specific EObject types. E.g. the FOL formula generated for `parent` EReference in Table 1 ensures that the source object `e` is a `FunctionalElement` while the target end `f` is a `Function`.

An *inverse reference* in Ecore is mapped to two separate predicates defined in the opposite direction and an additional equivalence operation is defined between them to assert their inverse nature. For instance, `parent(e,f)` is defined as an inverse of `subElements(f,e)` in Table 1.

The objects of an EMF model are arranged into a directed tree hierarchy along the *containment* EReferences, which is mapped into two constraints: (i) The acyclicity constraint is defined as a transitive closure stating that any object is unreachable from itself (see the example in Section 4.2) and (ii) the singular

Table 1. Examples of mapping the features of an Ecore metamodel

EObject	$\mapsto$ Object
f : Function [Function] ——▷ [FunctionalElement]	**Type:** $Function(f)$ $\mathbf{c}_{function}$: $Function(f) \wedge FunctionalElement(f)$ $\mapsto$ $\wedge \neg FAMTerminator(f) \wedge \neg InformationLink(f)$ $\wedge \ldots \wedge \neg FunctionalInterface(f)$
e.getParent == f 0..1 parent 0..* subElements [Function] ◆—— [FunctionalElement]	**Reference predicate** $Parent(e,f)$ **End types:** $\forall e, f : Parent(e,f) \Rightarrow$ $\mapsto$ $(FunctionalElement(e) \wedge Function(f))$ **Inverse edges:** $\forall e, f :$ $Parent(e,f) \Leftrightarrow subElements(f,e)$ **At most one multiplicity:** $\forall e, f_1, f_{extra} :$ $Parent(e,f_1) \wedge Parent(e,f_{extra}) \Rightarrow f_1 = f_{extra}$
f.type : FunctionalType [Function] [type : FunctionType] <<enumeration>> [FunctionType] – Root – Leaf – Intermediate	**Attribute type:** $\mapsto$ $Type = \{Root, Intermediate, Leaf\}$ **Attribute value:** $type(f, Leaf)$

root constraint expresses that there is exactly one object in the model without a parent.

Our approach currently supports *EAttributes* with enumeration types only, where the enum literals are mapped to constants and the EAttribute is represented as a predicate with the source as the container object and the target as the value of corresponding constant. For example, the type(f,Leaf) defines that the value of the type EAttribute is a Leaf in Table 1. We plan to investigate [16] to extend to other types.

By default, predicates derived Ecore links assume the most general 0..* *multiplicity*. An upper bound can be mapped to an EPR by assuring there that the number of different target objects are less than it defines, however, a lower bound cannot be expressed without existential quantifiers and thus leads out of EPR. Without going into details, an example mapping of cardinality constraints is demonstrated in Row 2 of Table 1.

4.2   Mapping of the Graph Queries

In the current section we highlight how different features of the EMF-INCQUERY graph query language are mapped to FOL formulae.

Structure of a Query. On the top level, a graph query consists of: (i) a parameter list, which is a fixed size vector of variables over the objects of the instance model and (ii) one or more disjunctive (*OR*) pattern bodies, which define constraints over its parameters and additional existentially quantified internal variables. A query in our mapping is defined as a disjunction of its bodies, where the bodies are the conjunction of its constraints.

In Table 2, the mapping of the query of the `type` DF is exemplified, where the first row defines how its pattern bodies are mapped to three separate `body_i` predicates. The second row demonstrates how the second body of the query is mapped to a FOL formula, where the `_Par` and `_Chl` are its inner variables. Simple constraints in a pattern body are handled as follows:

- *Attribute check* conditions are mapped to their corresponding equivalent in FOL as only the equivalence and non-equivalence relations are defined over enum literals. For instance, in Table 2 the third row defines an equivalence relation between the `Target` variable and the `Intermediate` constant.
- An *EClassifier* constraint defines the type of the object that is bound to a variable, which is simply mapped to its corresponding type predicate. E.g., in the fourth row in Table 2, the `This` variable can only be of type `Function`.
- *EReference* constraints are compiled into their corresponding reference predicates, for example, in Table 2 the `parent` EReference is mapped to the its corresponding `parent(_Chl,This)` reference predicate.
- Finally, a *negative application condition* is mapped to (i) a subpattern definition for the negative pattern identically to how a pattern body is constructed and a (ii) pattern call constraint. If the formula of the subpattern is satisfied, the latter invalidates the caller pattern along the given parameter substitution. For instance, in Table 2 the `nacSubPattern(Child,Parent)` is constructed and it is called using the ¬`nacSubPattern(_Chl,This)` formula with the `_Chl` and `This` variables as defined by in the third pattern body of the `type` query.

Constraint Approximation. The EMF-INCQUERY graph query language is more expressive than the EPR fragment of FOL thus some constraints (like recursively called patterns, transitive closures) cannot be expressed within its boundaries. Our approach derives over- and underapproximations to handle such problematic language features. Below, we sketch the overapproximation of the transitive closure feature of the query language, while more technical details are available in [17].

We use an overapproximation on the maximum iteration of the traversal on the transitive reference. The idea is to define unique transitive predicates for each iteration that defines how many more references it can traverse along the transitive reference, where finally the last predicate is substituted with the *true* predicate (overapproximation). Additionally, to force acyclic traversal, the predicates also specify uniqueness constraints over the visited objects.

For example, predicate $parentMatch(This, P) \Rightarrow parent2Match(This, P)$ defines an overapproximation of length 2 for the transitive closure of the `parent` EReference in the second pattern body of the `model` query, in the following way:

2: $parent2Match(This, P) \Rightarrow parent(This, P) \lor \exists m1 : parent(This, m1) \land parent1Match(m1, P, This)$

1: $parent1Match(This, P, d1) \Rightarrow parent(This, P) \lor \exists m2(m2 \neq d1) : parent(This, m2) \land parent0Match(m2, P, d1, This)$

0: $parent0Match(This, P, d1, d2) \Rightarrow parent(This, P) \lor \exists m3(m3 \neq d1, m3 \neq d2) : parent(This, m3) \land \textbf{true}$

Table 2. Mapping of graph query features

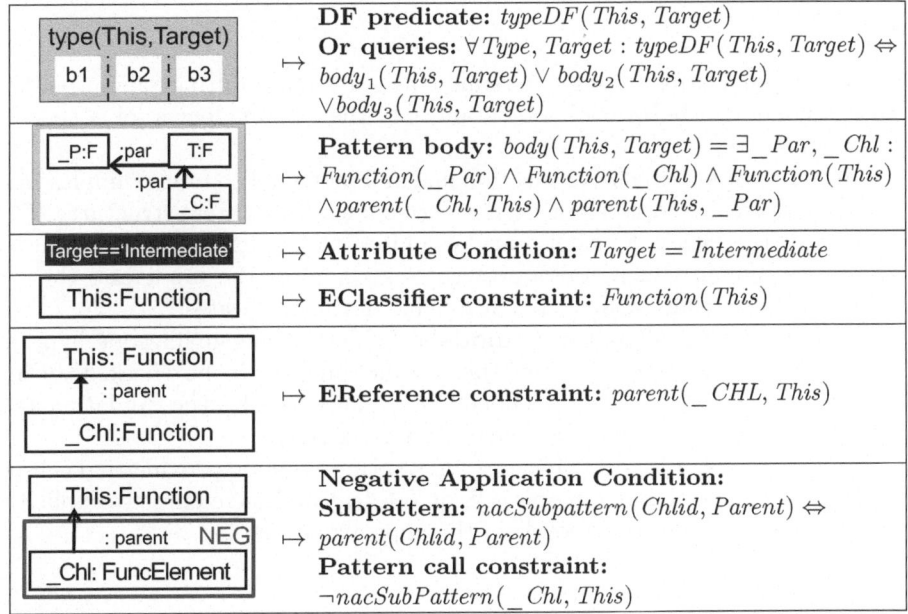

type(This,Target) b1 ┊ b2 ┊ b3	**DF predicate:** $typeDF(This, Target)$ **Or queries:** $\forall Type, Target : typeDF(This, Target) \Leftrightarrow$ $body_1(This, Target) \vee body_2(This, Target)$ $\vee body_3(This, Target)$
_P:F ←:par T:F :par _C:F	**Pattern body:** $body(This, Target) = \exists\_Par, \_Chl :$ $Function(\_Par) \wedge Function(\_Chl) \wedge Function(This)$ $\wedge parent(\_Chl, This) \wedge parent(This, \_Par)$
Target=='Intermediate'	$\mapsto$ **Attribute Condition:** $Target = Intermediate$
This:Function	$\mapsto$ **EClassifier constraint:** $Function(This)$
This: Function ↑ : parent _Chl:Function	$\mapsto$ **EReference constraint:** $parent(\_CHL, This)$
This:Function ↑ : parent NEG _Chl: FuncElement	**Negative Application Condition:** **Subpattern:** $nacSubpattern(Chlid, Parent) \Leftrightarrow$ $parent(Chlid, Parent)$ **Pattern call constraint:** $\neg nacSubPattern(\_Chl, This)$

Note that a similar idea is used in case of recursive pattern calls, where (1) the call hierarchy is flattened first, and then (2) only recursive calls are needed to be overapproximated based on the maximum number of allowed calls.

Patterns as DF and WF. When constructing the set of axioms for a DSL from graph patterns, derived features and well-formedness constraints need to be handled differently. In case of DFs, we need to guarantee that the evaluation of the predicate of the derived feature and its graph query definition is equivalent. For example, in case of type of a Function where *type* is the attribute predicate and *typeDF* is a pattern it looks like this: $\forall src, trg : type(src, trg) \Leftrightarrow typeDF(src, trg)$. This statement is added to the statement set DFs to be validated next.

In most cases, a pattern captures a WF constraint to highlight problematic locations, thus it is essentially an ill-formedness constraint which is not allowed to have any match in a valid model. Therefore, the axiom needs to be quantified accordingly. For instance, for pattern terminatorandInformationLink we add to the WF set: $\forall Ter, InfLink : \neg terminatorandInformationLink(Ter, InfLink)$.

4.3   Search Parameters

The validation run can be parameterized by different (optional) search parameters:

- **Target partition:** In order to reduce the state space during validation, the metamodel can be pruned to contain only the relevant parts for a specific validation run.
- **Partial snapshot:** The verification may fail on trivial counterexamples that are theoretically correct but do not corresponds to the real structures. The range of the checked models can be limited to the extension of an initial instance model, which constitutes the constants of the input and the assumptions partially define the truth-value of the predicates.
- **Maximum size of instance models:** Following the small scope hypothesis [18], the maximum size of the instance models to be checked during validation can be optionally defined. This allows to solve the validation as a SAT problem or provide a minimal counter example.
- **Approximation level:** Whenever an over- and underapproximation is used to describe a certain metamodel, DF or WF feature it is required to explicitly define the boundaries (or level) of the approximation.

5   Evaluation

The aim of our evaluation is to illustrate that our mapping approach is capable of expressing and validating complex metamodel and query features either by directly mapping them to EPR (denoted as +), solve them as a general FOL proving problem (–) or approximate the general problem by relaxing it to an ERP (e.g. overapproximate the containment hierarchy by neglecting it). The Table 3 summarizes all relevant features of both the Ecore metamodels and the EMF-INCQUERY model query languages that can (+) or cannot (–) be mapped directly to EPR, needs approximation (A) to define it in FOL or is inexpressible (X) in FOL. As the DF and WF constraints in overall are validated using different polarity the quantifications of their variables will differ and thus they cannot be mapped the same way (e.g., the same query may not be validated as DF or WF over the same properties). Detailed discussion about the mapping of these features is available in [17].

The runtime performance[1] of our approach is negligible in cases when the mapping can be kept in EPR and then is usually under 1 sec for example, in our running example it was less than 100 ms for all feature validation except for the completeness validation of the model DF (timeout). However, whenever the mapped features are outside of EPR the outcome of the validation relies on the underlying automated theorem prover, which may be able to validate the feature but there are no guarantees that it will ever produce a proof or refutation due to undecidability of FOL in general.

---

[1] Average PC with 4 Gb RAM, running Win 7.

Table 3. Expressing Ecore and EMF-INCQUERY language features in Z3

Features of the metamodel			DF	Features of model query	WF
EClasses	E +		E +	Classifier constraint	E +
Class hierarchy	E +		E −	EReference constraint	E +
EEnums	E +		E −	Acyclic pattern call	E +
EReferences	E +		E −	Negative pattern call	E −
EAttributes	E +		A −	Transitive closure	A +
Multiplicity upper bound	E +		A −	(Positive) pattern call recursion	A +
Multiplicity lower bound	E −		A −	Arbitrary call graph	A −
Inverse edges	E +		X	Aggregate (eg. Count, Sum)	X
Containment hierarchy	A −		X	Check expressions	X
Partial snapshot	E +				

E: Expressible A: Approximable X: Inexpressible +: in EPR −: not in EPR

6   Related Work

There are several approaches and tools aiming to validate UML models enriched with OCL constraints [19] relying upon different logic formalisms such as constraint logic programming [20,21,16], SAT-based model finders (like Alloy) [22,23,24,25], first-order logic [26,27], constructive query containment [28], higher-order logic [29,30], or rewriting logics [31]. Some of these approaches (like e.g. [21,23,24]) offer bounded validation (where the user needs to explicitly restrict the search space), others (like [27,29,26]) allows unbounded verification (which normally results in increased level of user interaction and decidability issues).

SMT-solvers have also been used to verify declarative ATL transformations [32] allowing the use of an efficiently analyzable fragment of OCL [27]. The FORMULA tool also uses the Z3 SMT-solver as underlying engine, e.g. to reason about metamodeling frameworks [15] where proof goals are encoded as CLP satisfiability problem. The main advantage of using SMT solvers is that it is refutationally complete for quantified formulas of uninterpreted and almost uninterpreted functions and efficiently solvable for a rich subset of logic. Our approach uses SMT-solvers both in a constructive way to find counter examples (model finding) as well as for proving theorems. In case of using approximations for rich query features, our approach converges to bounded verification techniques.

Graph constraints are used in [33] as means to formalize a restricted class of OCL constraints in order to find valid model instances by graph grammars. An inverse approach is taken in [34] to formalize graph transformation rules by OCL constraints as an intermediate language and carry out verification of transformations in UML-to-CSP tool. These approaches mainly focus on mapping core graph transformation semantics, but does not cover many rich query features of the EMF-IncQuery language (such as transitive closure and recursive pattern calls). Many ideas are shared with approaches aiming to verify model transformations [34,35,32], as they built upon the semantics of source and target languages to prove or refute properties of the model transformation.

The idea of using *partial models*, which are extended to valid models during verification also appears in [14,15,36]. These initial hints are provided manually to the verification process, while in our approach, these models are assembled from a previous (failed) verification run in an iterative way (and not fully manually). *Approximations* are used in [37] to propose a type system and type inference algorithm for assigning semantic types to constraint variables to detect specification errors in declarative languages with constraints.

Our approach is different from existing approaches as it uses a graph based query language instead of OCL for capturing derived features and well-formedness constraints. Up to our best knowledge, this is the first approach aiming to validate queries captured within the EMF-IncQuery framework, and the handling of derived features is rarely considered. Furthermore, we sketch an iterative validation process how DSL specifications can be carried out. Finally, we also cover the validation of rich language features (such as recursive patterns or transitive closure) which is not covered by existing (OCL-based) approaches.

7   Conclusion

In the paper, we addressed the validation of DSL tools specified by a combination of EMF metamodels and graph queries (of EMF-INCQUERY) capturing derived features and well-formedness rules. For that purpose, we defined an iterative (and semi-automated) validation workflow and a mapping of metamodels and queries to the effectively propositional (EPR) fragment of first-order logic, which can be efficiently analyzed by the Z3 SMT solver. In order to cover rich language features (such as transitive closure and recursion), we proposed constraint approximations to yield formulae that fall into EPR. Moreover, validation can be guided by the designer in the form of initial (partial) model snapshots, which need to be included in valid instance models. We illustrated our approach on a running example extracted from an ongoing research project in the avionics domain.

Our future work is intended to be directed to improve the level of query feature coverage and raise the level of automation of our system. For instance, our current approach is restricted to handle attributes of enumeration values only, while real metamodels contain attributes of integers, strings, etc. For this purpose, we may build upon [16] where reasoning is provided for string attributes in OCL constraints or other decision procedures for numeric domains.

In our current framework, automation is restricted to forward mappings, while refinements are carried out manually by the domain engineer. It would be advantageous to shift our framework towards a black-box solution as much as possible, which immediately raises several challenges. On the tooling level, counterexamples derived by Z3 should be back-annotated to the DSL tooling (as model instances). On the validation level, an interesting direction is to develop counterexample guided refinement of approximations where false positive counterexamples obtained as a result of approximations can be filtered by instance-level validation techniques.

References

1. The Eclipse Project: Eclipse Modeling Framework, http://www.eclipse.org/emf
2. Willink, E.D.: An extensible OCL virtual machine and code generator. In: Proc. of the 12th Workshop on OCL and Textual Modelling, pp. 13–18. ACM (2012)
3. Bergmann, G., Horváth, Á., Ráth, I., Varró, D., Balogh, A., Balogh, Z., Ökrös, A.: Incremental Evaluation of Model Queries over EMF Models. In: Petriu, D.C., Rouquette, N., Haugen, Ø. (eds.) MODELS 2010, Part I. LNCS, vol. 6394, pp. 76–90. Springer, Heidelberg (2010)
4. ARINC - Aeronautical Radio, Incorporated: A653 - Avionics Application Software Standard Interface
5. AUTOSAR Consortium: The AUTOSAR Standard, http://www.autosar.org/
6. De Moura, L., Bjørner, N.: Z3: an efficient SMT solver. In: Ramakrishnan, C.R., Rehof, J. (eds.) TACAS 2008. LNCS, vol. 4963, pp. 337–340. Springer, Heidelberg (2008)
7. Ráth, I., Hegedüs, Á., Varró, D.: Derived features for EMF by integrating advanced model queries. In: Vallecillo, A., Tolvanen, J.-P., Kindler, E., Störrle, H., Kolovos, D. (eds.) ECMFA 2012. LNCS, vol. 7349, pp. 102–117. Springer, Heidelberg (2012)
8. Hegedüs, Á., Horváth, Á., Ráth, I., Varró, D.: Query-driven soft interconnection of EMF models. In: France, R.B., Kazmeier, J., Breu, R., Atkinson, C. (eds.) MODELS 2012. LNCS, vol. 7590, pp. 134–150. Springer, Heidelberg (2012)
9. Piskac, R., de Moura, L., Bjorner, N.: Deciding effectively propositional logic with equality, Microsoft Research, MSR-TR-2008-181 Technical Report (2008)
10. Bergmann, G., Ujhelyi, Z., Ráth, I., Varró, D.: A graph query language for emf models. In: Cabot, J., Visser, E. (eds.) ICMT 2011. LNCS, vol. 6707, pp. 167–182. Springer, Heidelberg (2011)
11. SAE - Radio Technical Commission for Aeronautic: Architecture Analysis & Design Language (AADL) v2, AS-5506A, SAE International (2009)
12. Mathworks: Matlab Simulink - Simulation and Model-Based Design, http://www.mathworks.com/products/simulink/
13. The Object Management Group: Object Constraint Language, v2.0 (May 2006), http://www.omg.org/spec/OCL/2.0/
14. Sen, S., Mottu, J.M., Tisi, M., Cabot, J.: Using models of partial knowledge to test model transformations. In: Hu, Z., de Lara, J. (eds.) ICMT 2012. LNCS, vol. 7307, pp. 24–39. Springer, Heidelberg (2012)
15. Jackson, E.K., Tiham, Balasubramanian, D.: Reasoning about metamodeling with formal specifications and automatic proofs. In: Whittle, J., Clark, T., Kühne, T. (eds.) MODELS 2011. LNCS, vol. 6981, pp. 653–667. Springer, Heidelberg (2011)
16. Büttner, F., Cabot, J.: Lightweight string reasoning for OCL. In: Vallecillo, A., Tolvanen, J.-P., Kindler, E., Störrle, H., Kolovos, D. (eds.) ECMFA 2012. LNCS, vol. 7349, pp. 244–258. Springer, Heidelberg (2012)
17. Semeráth, O.: Validation of Domain Specific Languages, Technical Report (2013), https://incquery.net/publications/dslvalid
18. Jackson, D.: Software Abstractions: Logic, Language, and Analysis. The MIT Press (2006)
19. Gogolla, M., Bohling, J., Richters, M.: Validating UML and OCL models in USE by automatic snapshot generation. Softw. Syst. Model. 4(4), 386–398 (2005)
20. Cabot, J., Clarisó, R., Riera, D.: UMLtoCSP: a tool for the formal verification of UML/OCL models using constraint programming. In: Proc. of the 22nd IEEE/ACM International Conference on Automated Software Engineering (ASE 2007), pp. 547–548. ACM, New York (2007)

21. Cabot, J., Clarisó, R., Riera, D.: First international conference on software testing verification and validation. In: Verification of UML/OCL Class Diagrams using Constraint Programming, pp. 73–80. IEEE (2008)
22. Anastasakis, K., Bordbar, B., Georg, G., Ray, I.: On challenges of model transformation from UML to Alloy. Softw. Syst. Model. 9(1), 69–86 (2010)
23. Büttner, F., Egea, M., Cabot, J., Gogolla, M.: Verification of ATL transformations using transformation models and model finders. In: Aoki, T., Taguchi, K. (eds.) ICFEM 2012. LNCS, vol. 7635, pp. 198–213. Springer, Heidelberg (2012)
24. Kuhlmann, M., Hamann, L., Gogolla, M.: Extensive validation of OCL models by integrating SAT solving into USE. In: Bishop, J., Vallecillo, A. (eds.) TOOLS 2011. LNCS, vol. 6705, pp. 290–306. Springer, Heidelberg (2011)
25. Soeken, M., Wille, R., Kuhlmann, M., Gogolla, M., Drechsler, R.: Verifying UML/OCL models using boolean satisfiability. In: Design, Automation and Test in Europe (DATE 2010), pp. 1341–1344. IEEE (2010)
26. Beckert, B., Keller, U., Schmitt, P.H.: Translating the Object Constraint Language into first-order predicate logic. In: Proc of the VERIFY, Workshop at Federated Logic Conferences (FLoC), Copenhagen, Denmark (2002)
27. Clavel, M., Egea, M., de Dios, M.A.G.: Checking unsatisfiability for OCL constraints. ECEASST 24 (2009)
28. Queralt, A., Artale, A., Calvanese, D., Teniente, E.: OCL-Lite: Finite reasoning on UML/OCL conceptual schemas. Data Knowl. Eng. 73, 1–22 (2012)
29. Brucker, A.D., Wolff, B.: The HOL-OCL tool (2007), http://www.brucker.ch/
30. Grönniger, H., Ringert, J.O., Rumpe, B.: System model-based definition of modeling language semantics. In: Lee, D., Lopes, A., Poetzsch-Heffter, A. (eds.) FMOODS 2009. LNCS, vol. 5522, pp. 152–166. Springer, Heidelberg (2009)
31. Clavel, M., Egea, M.: The ITP/OCL tool (2008), http://maude.sip.ucm.es/itp/ocl/
32. Büttner, F., Egea, M., Cabot, J.: On verifying ATL transformations using 'off-the-shelf' SMT solvers. In: France, R.B., Kazmeier, J., Breu, R., Atkinson, C. (eds.) MODELS 2012. LNCS, vol. 7590, pp. 432–448. Springer, Heidelberg (2012)
33. Winkelmann, J., Taentzer, G., Ehrig, K., Küster, J.M.: Translation of restricted OCL constraints into graph constraints for generating meta model instances by graph grammars. ENTCS 211, 159–170 (2008), Proc. of the 5th Int. Workshop on Graph Transformation and Visual Modeling Techniques (GT-VMT 2006) (2006)
34. Cabot, J., Clarisó, R., Guerra, E., de Lara, J.: A UML/OCL framework for the analysis of graph transformation rules. Softw. Syst. Model. 9(3), 335–357 (2010)
35. Lúcio, L., Barroca, B., Amaral, V.: A technique for automatic validation of model transformations. In: Petriu, D.C., Rouquette, N., Haugen, Ø. (eds.) MODELS 2010, Part I. LNCS, vol. 6394, pp. 136–150. Springer, Heidelberg (2010)
36. Kuhlmann, M., Gogolla, M.: Strengthening SAT-based validation of UML/OCL models by representing collections as relations. In: Vallecillo, A., Tolvanen, J.-P., Kindler, E., Störrle, H., Kolovos, D. (eds.) ECMFA 2012. LNCS, vol. 7349, pp. 32–48. Springer, Heidelberg (2012)
37. Jackson, E.K., Schulte, W., Bjørner, N.: Detecting specification errors in declarative languages with constraints. In: France, R.B., Kazmeier, J., Breu, R., Atkinson, C. (eds.) MODELS 2012. LNCS, vol. 7590, pp. 399–414. Springer, Heidelberg (2012)

Self-adaptation with End-User Preferences: Using Run-Time Models and Constraint Solving[*]

Hui Song[1], Stephen Barrett[1], Aidan Clarke[2], and Siobhán Clarke[1]

[1] Lero: The Irish Software Engineering Research Centre
SCSS, Trinity College Dublin, College Green, Dublin 2, Ireland
[2] Software Group, IBM Ireland, Dublin 15, Ireland
firstname.lastname@scss.tcd.ie, aidan_clarke@ie.ibm.com

Abstract. This paper presents an approach to developing self-adaptive systems that takes the end users' preferences into account for adaptation planning, while tolerating incomplete and conflicting adaptation goals. The approach transforms adaptation goals, together with the run-time model that describes current system contexts and configurations, into a constraint satisfaction problem. From that, it diagnoses the conflicting adaptation goals to ignore, and determines the required re-configuration that satisfies all remaining goals. If users do not agree with the solution, they can revise some configuration values. The approach records their preferences embedded in the revisions by tuning the weights of existing goals, so that subsequent adaptation results will be closer to the users' preferences. The experiments on a medium-sized simulated smart home system show that the approach is effective and scalable.

1 Introduction

Self-adaptability is an important feature of modern software-based systems. In adaptive systems, an adaptation agent monitors changes on a system or its environment, plans an appropriate configuration, and reconfigures the system accordingly [1–3]. Adaptation planning is guided by a set of policies, which specifies the desired system configuration under different contexts [4].

Adaptation policies are likely to be *incomplete* and *conflicting*: Under some particular context, either there may be multiple configurations that fit the goals, or no configuration can satisfy all the goals simultaneously. Such *imperfect* policies are practically unavoidable. Firstly, it is difficult for developers to eliminate all incompleteness and conflicts by enumerating every possible composition of the contexts to add extra policies. Secondly, the system may be constructed from existing components, each of which carries separately developed, and thus potentially conflicting, policies. At runtime, imperfect policies will result in multiple possible adaptation solutions. An adaptation agent has to choose one solution from them, but which one is the best may depend on who is using the system.

---

[*] This work was supported, in part, by Science Foundation Ireland grant 10/CE/I1855 to Lero - the Irish Software Engineering Research Centre (www.lero.ie)

A. Moreira et al. (Eds.): MODELS 2013, LNCS 8107, pp. 555–571, 2013.

A promising improvement on self-adaptation is to tolerate imperfect policies, and do adaptation planning while considering end user preferences [1, 5, 6]. This paper takes such an approach, building the method over approaches based on models at runtime. [2, 7, 8]. By wrapping heterogeneous target systems as standard run-time models, we implement adaptations on top of model reading and writing, guided by model constraints in the form of OCL invariants. The challenges of this approach are threefold: 1) How could adaptation on run-time models and declarative model constraints be solved automatically; 2) How should user preferences be coded and utilized in adaptation planning; 3) What is an appropriate interface for end users to express their preferences?

The contributions of this paper can be summarized as follows.

- We design a partial evaluation semantics on OCL to automatically transform a run-time model into a constraint satisfaction problem (CSP) [9]. The variables of CSP are the context and configuration attributes, and constraints are from the current values of these attributes and the OCL invariants.
- We provide a novel approach to planning adaptations on CSP. We use *constraint diagnosing* to determine the optimal set of constraints to ignore, and then use *constraint solving* to assign new configuration values that satisfy the remaining constraints. User preference is reified as different weights of the constraints, and a constraint with higher weight will more probably be satisfied.
- We provide a straightforward way for end users to express their preference: After each round of adaptation, we allow users to directly redress the adaptation result, and in the background, we tune the weights of existing constraints according to the user's revision.

We evaluated the approach on a simulated smart home system. The adaptation significantly reduced the number of violated goals, and after a few rounds of preference tuning, the adaptation results became much closer to the simulated user preferences. The approach scales to medium-sized systems: An adaptation with 2000 constraints took 2 seconds on average. All implementation code and experiment results are available on-line [10].

The rest of the paper is structured as follows. Section 2 gives an overview of the approach, with a simplified running example. Sections 3 to 5 present the three technical contributions. Section 6 shows the experiments and results. Section 7 introduces related approaches, and Section 8 concludes the paper.

2   Approach Overview

2.1   Background and Terminology

A *run-time model* is a model that presents a view of some aspect of an executing system [11]. In this paper we focus on structural run-time models [7] that present the structural composition of a system, and the attribute values of different compositional elements. Some of these attributes describe an observation of a system, such as room temperature, while some others describe ways to manipulate a system, such as the state of an electronically controllable switch. We name these *contexts* and *configurations*, respectively. A run-time model is dynamically synchronized with the executing system, which means that the model state $s \in S$ (the elements and all their attribute values), at any time point, is the snapshot of the system at this time point, and transferring the state to s' (by giving new values to some configuration attributes) will cause the system to change accordingly. The set of all the possible model states S is defined by a meta-model. System adaptation based on a run-time model is a process to read the model state s, and then plan a new state s'.

We use model constraints on run-time models as the *adaptation policies* to guide the adaptation planning [1]. A model constraint is a function $cons : S \to \mathbb{B}$. For a model state $s \in S$, if $cons(s) = \top$ (we use $\top$ for *true* and $\bot$ for *false*) we say s satisfies $cons$. The objective of an adaptation is to make the model satisfy as many constraints as possible. From this perspective, the role played by model constraints in our approach conforms to the definition of *goal policies*, as they "directly specify desired system states" rather than "define how to achieve them" [1, 5]. In the rest of this paper, we call these model constraints *adaptation goals* in order to avoid ambiguity with the concept of constraints in CSP, as follows.

A *constraint satisfaction problem* (CSP) [9], or in particular a *satisfiability modulo theory* (SMT), is composed of a set of variables V and a set of first order logic constraints C over these variables. A constraint solver checks if there exists a labelling function $f : V \to D$ that assigns a value to each variable and these values satisfy all the constraints. If so, we say the CSP (V, C) is satisfiable, and the solver returns such an f. Some solvers divide constraints into *hard* and *weak* ones, i.e., $C = C_h \cup C_w$, and weak constraints can be ignored when necessary. For an unsatisfiable problem, the solver returns a sample of conflicting constraints from C_w. From the samples, we can construct a *diagnosis* $C_d \subseteq C_w$, such that $(V, C - C_d)$ is satisfiable. This process is called constraint diagnosing [12].

2.2   Motivating Example

We use a simple smart home system as a running example throughout this paper. Cheap but powerful sensors are now available, which collect a diversity of data from our living environment, and devices are frequently employed to make many household items electronically controllable. This enables and requires dynamic adaptation of an entire home when the environment changes, in order to improve living qualities and to save resources. At the same time, such a smart home is a highly personalized system. For the same context, different users may expect different adaptation effects.

Figure 1 describes a simplified domain model of smart home. The left part is a meta-model defining the types of system elements, the context information such as electricity price, time, room temperature, and the configuration points such as turning on or off the water heater. The heating system can work on different settings: 0 for off, 5 for fairly hot and 10 for very hot, etc. The right part of Figure 1 lists five adaptation goals, i.e., "when it is cold, the heatings should

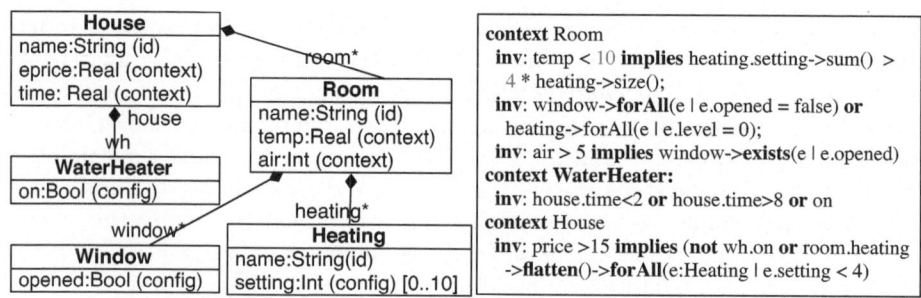

Fig. 1. Sample smart home meta-model and adaptation goals

be at sufficient settings for comfort", "do not open window when the heating is on", "do open window when air quality is bad", "keep water heater on in the early morning", and "when the electricity is expensive do not use water heater and strong heating together". The five sample goals are both *incomplete* and *conflicting*: The first does not point out a specific value for the heating settings. Alternatively, when it is cold and the air is bad, we can never satisfy the first three goals simultaneously.

Guided by such goals, there may not be a single perfect adaptation decision, and our solution is to take user preferences into account. For example, if we know the user prefers "heating 1 to work in setting 10", then we can choose setting 10 for this heating whenever it is one of the choices. For another example, if the user regards the third goal has a lower priority than others (he is more tolerable of smelly air), then when this goal conflicts with others, we sacrifice it first.

Since the smart home system targets end users who are probably without a computer science background, it is a burden for them to add new goals or tune the goal weights manually. Therefore, we provide a simplified interface: after each time of adaptation, the users can further *revise* the configuration by changing some of the attributes with the values they prefer. According to the revision, the approach generates goals or tunes the weights in the background.

2.3   The Adaptation Approach with User Preference

This paper presents a dynamic adaptation approach guided by the domain model and user preferences. Figure 2 shows the approach architecture, where solid arrows indicate the main adaptation loop at runtime, and dashed arrows are the post-adaptation reference recording. The trident lines are the user intervention.

The system context and configuration are captured by a run-time model [7], such as the one shown in the left part of Figure 3. The construction and mainte-nance of run-time models are out of the scope of this paper, and some techniques can be found elsewhere [8, 13, 14]. Adaptation planning and preference tuning based on runtime models have the following three activities.

The approach first transforms the current run-time model into a CSP, such as the one shown on the right of Figure 3. It transforms each context or config-

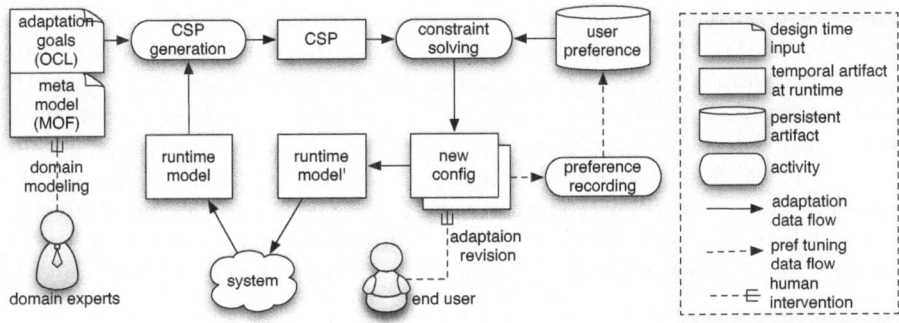

Fig. 2. Approach overview

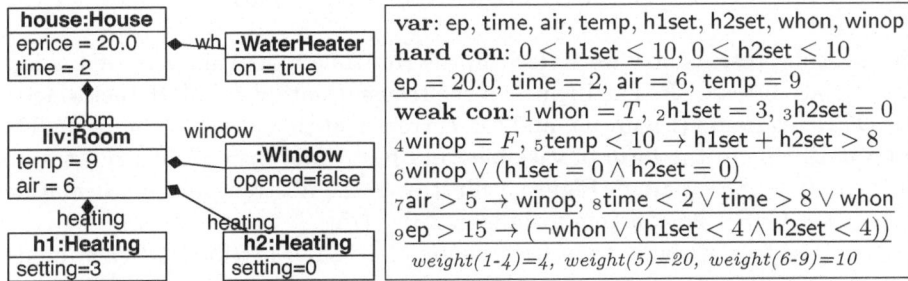

Fig. 3. Sample smart home runtime model and the generated CSP

uration attribute from each model element into a variable. The *hard constraints* are generated from configuration domains and current context values, as they cannot be violated after adaptation. The *weak constraints* are generated from configuration values and adaptation goals. The key technical idea here is a partial evaluation of the OCL language to identify the mapping from the attributes mentioned in OCL rules to the variables, which we will explain in Section 3.

Based on the generated CSP, the adaptation planning is to change the values of some of the configuration variables, so that the new configuration values, together with the current context, satisfy as many goals as possible. The planning begins by deciding which configuration variables to change, and which goals to ignore. This step boils down to finding an optimal *diagnosis* of the CSP. For example, from the CSP in Figure 3, we can find a diagnosis (2,7,9), such that if we change the value of h1set, we can find a solution(h1set = 9) to satisfy all the goals except 7 and 9. Since different diagnoses lead to different adaptation solutions, to help grade diagnoses (and the adaptation results), we assign each weak constraint a weight, and a constraint with bigger weight is more likely to be satisfied. The adaptation result is the one corresponding to the diagnosis with the minimal total weight. Under the weights shown in the bottom of Figure 3, diagnosis (2,7,9) has the minimal total weight 24. Section 4 presents our constraint diagnosing and solving approaches.

After each automated adaptation, if users change some of the configuration attributes, we record their preferences by tuning the weights of existing goals or generating new ones. Following our running example, if the user revises the adaptation result by increasing h1set to 10, we will generate a new constraint h1set = 10. Now if in any case the adaptation engine needs to choose a value for h1set, it will first consider the value 10. As another example, if the user also opens the window, we will decrease the weights of 4 and 6, and increase the weight of 7 (as will be shown in Section 5). Next time under the same circumstance, we would find a different optimal diagnosis (2,4,6,9), and the window would be automatically opened.

3   Transforming a Run-Time Model to CSP

This section presents how we transform the run-time model and the OCL adaptation goals into a CSP. The **inputs** of the transformation are MOF meta-model and OCL invariants (Figure 1), and the current run-time model (Figure 3). The **output** CSP is in the form of variables and first order logic (FOL) constraints on them. The right part of Figure 3 illustrates the abstract and mathematical form of the CSP (the concrete form is in Z3Py [15]).

We generate a variable from each context or config attribute of each model element, i.e., $genvar : M \times Elem \times Attr \rightharpoonup V$. For an element e from the current run-time model m, and an attribute $a \in e.Class.AllAttributes$ that is annotated as context or config, we get a variable $v = genvar(m, e, a)$. From the model instance as shown in Figure 3, we generate 8 variables listed on the right. The constraints are generated from the domains of configuration attributes, the current context and configuration values, and the adaptation goals. Except for goals, the generation is straightforward, with self-explainable samples in Figure 3.

To transform the goals into FOL constraints, we replace the context and config attributes in the OCL invariants by the corresponding variables, resolve the static values in the run-time model, and maintain the operations between them. The challenge is that the OCL invariants are defined in the meta-model level, without concretely mentioning any model instances, whereas the FOL constraints are based on the variables that are generated from a particular model instance. We implement the transformation by defining a new *partial evaluation* [16] semantics on the OCL expressions, i.e., $[\![expr]\!]_{env} : M \rightarrow C$. The semantics on each expression *expr* is a function from a run-time model $m \in M$ to a constraint $c \in C$. Here env is an environment recording the mapping from OCL variables to values or model elements. As a simple example, if m is the model instance in Figure 3, then $[\![\texttt{self.temp < 10}]\!]_{\{self \mapsto liv1\}}(m) = t < 10$, where $t = genvar(m, \texttt{liv1}, \texttt{temp})$.

Figure 4 lists an excerpt of the partial evaluation semantics on some typical forms of OCL expressions. For a data value in type of boolean, integer or real, we directly generate the value literal (1). For an OCL variable, we find its value from the environment and continue to evaluate this value (2). If the expression does not mention any context or configuration properties, we execute the OCL

1. $[\![\mathsf{val}]\!]_c(m) = \texttt{literal}(\mathsf{val})$; 2. $[\![\mathsf{var}]\!]_c(m) = [\![c(\mathsf{var})]\!]_c(m)$;
3. $[\![\mathsf{expr}]\!]_c(m) = [\![\texttt{ocleval}(m, \mathsf{expr}, c)]\!]_c(m)$
if expr does not mention any context/config attributes
4. $[\![\mathsf{expr}.\mathsf{attr}]\!]_c(m) = \texttt{genvar}(m, \texttt{ocleval}(\mathsf{expr}, c), \mathsf{attr})$; *if attr is context/config*
5. $[\![\mathsf{expr}_1 + \mathsf{expr}_2]\!]_c(m) = [\![\mathsf{expr}_1]\!]_c(m) + [\![\mathsf{expr}_2]\!]_c(m)$;
6. $[\![\mathsf{expr}_1 \textbf{ and } \mathsf{expr}_2]\!]_c(m) = \texttt{And}([\![\mathsf{expr}_1]\!]_c(m), [\![\mathsf{expr}_2]\!]_c(m))$;
7. $[\![\mathsf{expr}\text{->}\textbf{sum}]\!](m) = [\![v_1]\!]_c(m) + ... + [\![v_n]\!]_c(m), v_1...v_i \in \texttt{ocleval}(m, \mathsf{expr}, c)$;
8. $[\![\mathsf{expr}_1\text{->}\textbf{forAll}(e|\mathsf{expr}_2)]\!]_c(m) =$
$\texttt{And}([\![\mathsf{expr}_2]\!]_{c\cup\{e\mapsto v_i\}}(m),...), v_i \in \texttt{ocleval}(m, \mathsf{expr}_1, c)$;
9. $[\![\textbf{let } e = \mathsf{expr}_1\textbf{ in } \mathsf{expr}_2]\!]_c(m) = [\![\mathsf{expr}_2]\!]_{c\cup\{e\mapsto\texttt{ocleval}(\mathsf{expr}_1,c)\}}(m)$;

Fig. 4. The partial evaluation semantics on OCL to generate constraints

query to get its result (normally a value), and then evaluate the result (3). If the expression is to access a context or configuration property, we obtain the host model element and use its accessed attribute to locate the variable in CSP (4). For the mathematical and logical OCL operations, we generate the corresponding FOL operation (5 and 6), following the Z3Py format (e.g., it uses `And(a,b)` for conjunction). For an operation on collection, we obtain the host collection first, and then combine the partial evaluation of each collection item (7, 8). For `let` or iteration expressions where new variables are introduced (8, 9), we resolve the variable value first and put it to the environment before evaluating the sub expressions. Using this semantics, we transform the OCL invariants by traversing all the model elements in the current run-time model.

4 Adaptation Planning Based on CSP

This section presents the adaptation planning based on a generated CSP $(V, C_h \cup C_w)$. If the CSP is satisfiable we do not need to do anything for adaptation. Otherwise, we plan the adaptation by *constraint diagnosing* and *constraint solving*.

In order to grade the diagnoses, we attach each weak constraint a weight, $\mathsf{weight} : C_w \to \mathbb{N}$, and the target of adaptation planning is to find the diagnosis with the minimal total weight. From C_d, we perform constraint solving on $(V, C_h \cup C_w - C_d)$, and obtain a new configuration f which is a mapping from each config variable to a value, where $f \vdash (C_h \cup C_w - C_d)$.

Our algorithm to search for the optimal diagnosis is inspired by the work of Reiter [17] and Greiner et al. [12] on non-weighted CSPs, which is essentially a breadth-first searching for minimal hitting sets, each of which covers all the sample conflicting sets returned by the solvers. With the help of the constraint weights, we leverage a dynamic programming approach similar to the Dijkstra shortest path algorithm.

We illustrate the basic idea of our algorithm using the sample CSP in Figure 3, and its execution process is shown in Figure 5. We first ask the solver for an arbitrary sample set of conflicting constraints, and it returns $\{4,7\}$, meaning

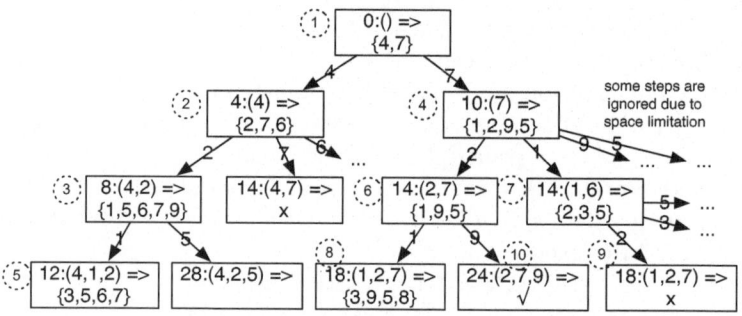

Fig. 5. Sample diagnosing process

that the closed window conflicts with the "should open window" goal. To make the CSP satisfiable, we must open the window or ignore the goal, and thus we make (4) and (7) as two candidate diagnoses, and pick the one with the lowest total weight to check (i.e., (4) weights 4). Here *checking a candidate* means that we remove the constraints in this candidate from the original CSP, and ask the solver for a new sample conflict set. By checking (4), we get a sample set {2,7,6}, that means if we remove 4, there is still a conflict between 2, 7 and 6 ("bad air, open window" conflicts with "heating on, close window"). So we extend the candidate by each of the conflicting constraints, and get three new candidates. Now we have four unchecked candidates, i.e., (4,2), (4,7), (4,6), and (7). We also pick the one with the lowest total weight (i.e., (4,2)) to check and expand. After no candidates weighted 10 left unchecked, we check (7) and get {1,2,9,5}, which leads to four new candidates. After having all the candidates under 24 checked, we check (2,7,9), and the solver returns "satisfiable". Its intuitive meaning is to change the first heating, ignore the bad air and high electricity price.

Algorithm 1 lists the steps of the diagnosing algorithm. We maintain a set cands of all the unchecked candidates, and put an empty set as the initial diagnosis (Line 1). The main part of the algorithm is a loop (Lines 3-17). Each time, we take out the candidate diagnosis curr which has the minimal total weight (Line 4). Then we check whether removing curr will make the CSP satisfiable (Line 10, we skip Lines 5-10 first as they are related to optimization). If the check succeeds, we return curr as the final diagnosis, and terminate the algorithm (line 10), otherwise, we ask the solver to provide a new sample(Line 12). If the solver cannot find any (this only happens when the hard constraints are conflicting), we terminate the algorithm without a solution (Line 13). After having the new sample newsamp, we take each constraint c from it (Line 15), expand the current candidate by adding c into it and push it into the pool (16).

We employ the following optimization. Firstly, since the diagnosis should have an intersection with every conflicting sample [17], we cache all the samples returned by the solver (Line 14). When dealing with any candidate, we first check if it covers all the cached samples (Line 9), and if not, we use one uncovered sample from the cache to extend the candidate instead of bothering the solvers to

---

Algorithm 1. Weight-based constraint diagnosing

In: Variables V, hard constraints C_h, weak constraints C_w, and weight
Out: A diagnosis $C_d \subseteq C_w$, with the lowest total cost

1 cands←$\{\phi\}$;
2 cache←$\{\}$, visited←$\{\}$, lastweight←-1 ;
3 **while** cands *is not empty* **do**
4   curr ← pop (cands) **where** currweight←$\sum_{c\in\text{curr}}$ weight(c) is minimal ;
5   **if** lastweight = currweight **then**
6   **if** curr ∈ visited **then continue**;
7   **else** visited←visited $\cup$ {curr}
8   **else** lastweight←currweight, visited←$\{\}$;
9   **if** $\exists(s \in$ cache$)[s \cap$ curr $= \phi]$ **then** newsamp←s ;
10   **else if** satis$(V, C_h, C_w -$ curr$) = T$ **then return** curr as C_d;
11   **else**
12   newsamp ← sample$(V, C_h, C_w -$ curr$)$;
13   **if** newsamp $= \phi$ **then throw** *'conflicts in hard constraints'*;
14   **else** cache←cache $\cup$ {newsamp} ;
15   **foreach** $c \in$ newsamp **do**
16   newcand←curr $\cup$ $\{c\}$; push(cands, $NewCand$) ;

---

produce one. The second goal is to accelerate the set operations. We implement cands as a heap queue, so that we can push an item or pop the smallest one in $O(\log n)$. Since it is hard to filter identical items in a heap queue, we maintain a list of recently visited candidates with the same particular total weight, and use it to check if the current candidate has been visited (Lines 5-7).

5 End User Preference Recording

If users revise an adaptation result, we reify their preferences by tuning the weights of existing constraints or generating new ones, so that the subsequent adaptation results will be closer to the one that users preferred.

In order to tune the CSP, the first task is to identify the user's *preferred diagnosis* corresponding to the revised configuration they provide. Formally speaking, for a revised configuration f', the preferred diagnosis $C'_d \subseteq C_w$ holds that $f' \vdash (C_h \cup C_w - C'_d)$. From the configuration f', it is straightforward to reversely derive the diagnosis C'_d: Just find all the original weak constraints that cannot be satisfied by the current configuration f', i.e., $C'_d = \{c \in C_w | \neg(f' \vdash c)\}$.

We handle the weight tuning separately for the two different containment relationships between C_d and C'_d, as shown in Figure 6.

Firstly, if $\neg(C_d \subseteq C'_d)$, as shown in Figure 6(a), we have three subsets namely I: $C_d - C'_d$, II: $C'_d - C_d$ and III: $C_d \cap C'_d$. III can be empty, but I and II can

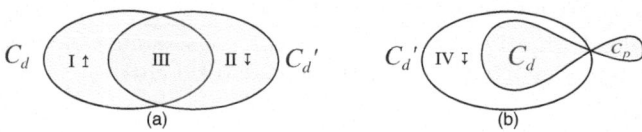

Fig. 6. Two different conditions for constraint weight tuning

not[1]. We increase the weight of each constraint in I, and decrease II. In particular, $\mathsf{weight}'(c \in \mathrm{I}) = \mathsf{weight}(c) \times (\sum_{i \in \mathrm{II}} \mathsf{weight}(i) / \sum_{j \in \mathrm{I}} \mathsf{weight}(j))$, $\mathsf{weight}'(c \in \mathrm{II}) = \mathsf{weight}(c) \times (\sum_{i \in \mathrm{I}} \mathsf{weight}(i) / \sum_{j \in \mathrm{II}} \mathsf{weight}(j))$. In this way, we change all the weights in proportion, and switch the total weight of C_d and C_d'. The intuitive meaning of this tuning can be illustrated by the following example. The adaptation result in the last section $h1set = 9$ corresponds to $C_d = \{2, 7, 9\}$. Suppose the user further modify the configuration by opening the window ($winop = T$), and this new f' corresponds to $C_d' = \{2, 4, 6, 9\}$. Now we have I= $\{7\}$ and II= $\{4, 6\}$. We get $\mathsf{weight}'(7) = 10 * (4 + 10)/10 = 14$, which means that the user is reluctant to break constraint 7 (bad air -> open window), and we get $\mathsf{weight}'(4) = 2$ and $\mathsf{weight}'(6) = 6$, indicating he does not care about 4 (keep the window's status) and 6 (do not open window when heating).

Secondly, if $C_d \subseteq C_d'$, as shown in Figure 6(b). We also decrease the weights in IV=$C_d' - C_d$. However, since the weight is not negative, we cannot make the total weight of C_d' less than that of C_d. Therefore, we introduce a set of new constraints C_p: for each variable $v \in V$, if user modified it with a new value d, then $v = d$ is a constraint in C_p. Now under the new CSP $(V, C_d, C_w \cup C_p)$, the original configuration f corresponds to diagnosis $C_d \cup C_p$, whereas the user's preferred configuration f' still corresponds to C_d'. We make $\mathsf{weight}'(c \in \mathrm{IV}) = \mathsf{weight}(c)/2$, and $\mathsf{weight}'(c \in C_p) = \max(\sum_{i \in IV} \mathsf{weight}(i)/|C_p|, \mathtt{default})$. For example, from the same f and $C_d = \{2, 7, 9\}$, if the users modify the result by further set $h2set = 5$, then this new f' corresponds to $C_d' = \{2, 3, 7, 9\}$. So we have IV=$\{3\}$, $C_p = \{10 : h2set = 5\}$. The intuitive meaning is that the user would like to turn h2 to setting 5 when possible. This condition also covers $C_d = C_d'$, where we only generate new constraints, without tuning any weights.

6   Evaluation

The implementation of the whole approach has two parts. We implement the CSP generation engine by Xtend [18], reusing the Eclipse OCL library for the parsing of OCL texts. We choose Microsoft Z3 [15] as the constraint solver, and implement the adaptation planning and preference tuning in Python.

We use a simulated smart home system to evaluate the effect and performance of the approach. The target system simulates a typical home similar to the example described in Section 2, but much more complex. The setting of

---

[1] $C_d' \subseteq C_d$ never happens, otherwise C_d cannot be a minimal diagnosis.

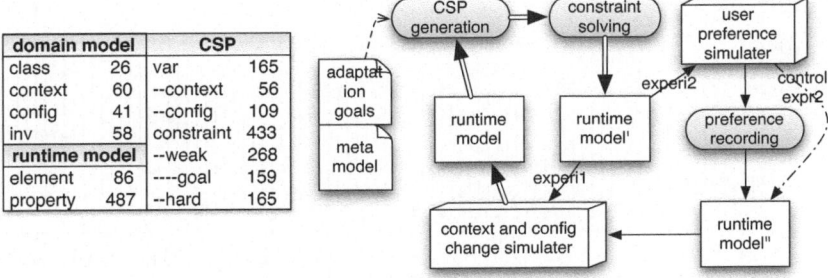

domain model		CSP	
class	26	var	165
context	60	--context	56
config	41	--config	109
inv	58	constraint	433
runtime model		--weak	268
element	86	----goal	159
property	487	--hard	165

Fig. 7. Experiment setting

this simulated system is based on existing smart home projects, especially the "Adaptive House" from University of Colorado [19], and the household level smart grid research from our own group [20]. The table in Figure 7 summarizes the sample system. The main run-time model corresponds to a fictitious 10-room house with full equipments. From this run-time model, we generate a CSP that contains 165 variables and 433 constraints.

All the implementation source code, the experiment artefacts, and the results mentioned in this section can be found in our GitHub repository [10].

6.1   Effectiveness

On this target system, we perform two experiments to answer the following two questions: 1) Does the adaptation make the system more consistent with adaptation goals? 2) Will the adaptation results more closely match users' preferences, after users revise the adaptation outcome over a few iterations.

The first experiment follows the small central circle in Figure 7. We implement "change simulator" to randomly modify the attributes in the run-time model to simulate the system evolution. We perform adaptation planning on model with state s, and get a new model state s' as the adaptation result. After that, s' is fed to the simulator, which randomly modifies the attributes again and starts the next round of adaptation. For each round of adaptation, we care about how s' is *improved* compared to s, in terms of what proportion of the goals violated by s are satisfied by s'.

Figure 8(a) shows the results. We run the adaptation 100 times, each of which is represented by a vertical arrow. The start and end points of an arrow corresponds to the numbers of violated goals before and after an adaptation, respectively. The x axis describes how many configuration variables are changed by the adaptation (The adaptations with 0 changes are not displayed). We can see that in most cases, the adaptation has a significant improvement, reducing the number of violated goals from 10-20 to 1-4, and these improvements are mostly achieved by modifying 6-12 configuration values.

The second experiment evaluates the effect of preference tuning. We implement another simulator to act as an imitated user, and embedded 11 preference

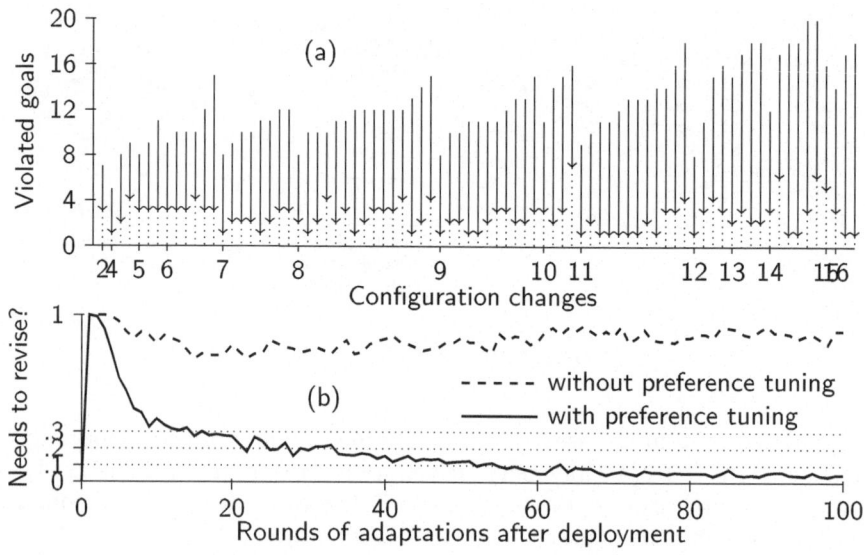

Fig. 8. Effects of adaptation and user preference tuning

rules in the simulator, in the form of `condition->config=value` ("under a special `condition`, I prefer the value of a `config` variable to be equal to the a
specific `value`"). Such a rule is either a refinement to an adaptation goal (e.g.,
"if a heating setting is greater than 0, then it should be 10"), or an insistence to
a particular goal (e.g., "whenever the air condition is bad, the window should be
opened"). As shown by the bigger circle in Figure 7, after each adaptation, the
user simulator evaluates the results. If any preference rule is violated, it picks
one and only one from them, changes the configuration value according to the
`config=value` part, yielding a new model s''. After that, the system simulator
will randomly change context and configuration on s'', and start the next round
of adaptation. Ideally, after more revisions, the automated adaptation result s'
will be less probable to violate any preference.

Figure 8(b) illustrates the results. We run the experiment 1000 times, each
time with 100 rounds of the adaptation/tuning loop as shown in Figure 7. The
solid line illustrates that for the xth round of adaptation after initialization, the
adaptation output has y possibility to violate one or more preference rules (i.e.,
1000*y times of violation is observed in the 1000 times of experiments). We can
see that the possibility of preference violation goes down very quickly. After only
10 rounds (each round with at most one refinement on one configuration!), there
is only 30% possibility to violate any preference, and after about 60 rounds, it
is less than 10%. As a comparison, we run another 1000 times of experiments
bypassing the preference tuning, and the possibility of preference violation is
shown by the dashed line. The experiment shows that the preference tuning
has a good effect even on such an exaggerated situation (almost every time the
adaptation will violate a preference rule).

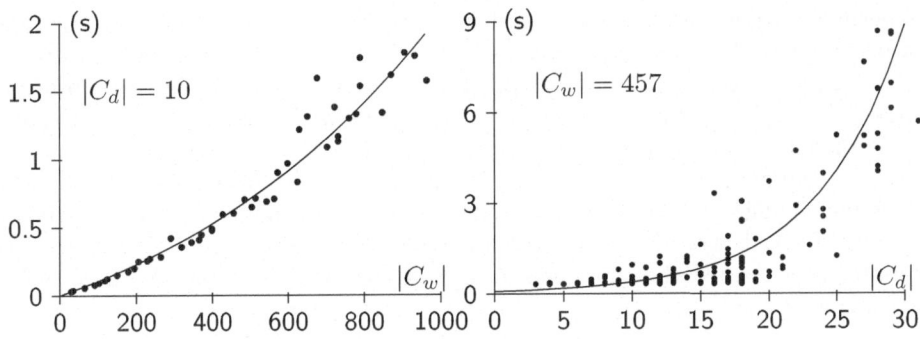

Fig. 9. Experiment results on performance

6.2   Scalability

The scalability of the whole approach mainly depends on the execution time of the adaptation planning step, because the other two only have a linear time complexity with the scale of run-time models. There are two main factors influencing the performance of this step, i.e., the size of the weak constraints $|C_w|$, and the size of the resulting diagnosis $|C_d|$. We show the influence of these factors respectively. The experiment processes are the same as the experi1 in Figure 7. All the experiments are performed on a MacBook Pro laptop with Intel i5 2.0GHz CPU and 4GB memory. The software environment includes MacOS X 10.5, Microsoft Z3, and Python 2.7.3. The weights of constraints from current configurations are randomly chosen between 200 to 300, and for goals, the range is 2000 to 3000.

To evaluate the influence of $|C_w|$, we keep adding elements to the runtime model, and this leads $|C_w|$ growing from 30 to 957. For each run-time model, we run the experiment for 100 times, and select the adaptation whose diagnosis size equals to 10. The left part of Figure 9 shows the average time on each run-time model. According to the approximate fitting curve, the time still grows exponentially with the size of constraints, but in a quite flat way.

To evaluate the influence of $|C_d|$, we choose one run-time model with $|C_w| = 457$, and control $|C_d|$ by making the simulator change more context and configurations variables, sometimes with extreme values. We run 1000 rounds of adaptations, and record the size of diagnosis and the execution time of each round in the right part of Figure 9: The execution time ascends quite fast with the increase of $|C_d|$, reaching a maximal 9 seconds when $|C_d| = 29$, though 96% of the adaptations finished within 2 seconds.

6.3   Threats and Discussion

All the experiments are performed on the same domain model, and similar run-time models with different sizes. Therefore the effectiveness and performance can be affected by some specific features of this experiment system. To alleviate this threat, we defined the run-time model and the goals independently before the experiments. The effectiveness of preference tuning strongly depends on the type of preferences. A "refinement preference" rule can be only violated once on the same element, whereas an "insistence to a goal" rule may be violated multiple times. We designed the imitated preference rules with a balance of both types. Note that if the preference rules themselves have conflicts, the preference tuning is not convergent. We avoid such conflicts, imitating a "firm-minded" user who does not change his mind on preference. The size of diagnosis currently has a ceiling of 30. A well designed domain model with fewer conflicting goals will significantly reduce the diagnosis size, and therefore increase the adaptation performance.

7   Related Work

Models at runtime are widely used to support dynamic system adaptation. Garlan et al. [2] and Sicard et al. [14] execute action policies on run-time architecture models to achieve self-optimization and self-repair, respectively. Morin et al. support dynamic adaptation by executing the "aspect-oriented rules" defined on run-time models [8, 21]. We follow the same idea, executing adaptation policies on a basic type of run-time models that present only the structural system aspects [7]. Our innovation is to tolerate conflicting policies, with the consideration of end user preference. This paper is also an attempt of a novel way to leverage models at runtime for adaptation: Based on the fact that run-time models are formal descriptions of run-time system states, we utilize a mathematical tool, constraint solving, to achieve automated adaptation planning guided by declarative OCL constraints defined on the models.

Salehie and Tahvildari [1] regard the consideration of user preference as an essential aspect of self-adaptive software, but also note that the research in this direction is still in an early stage. Maximilien et al. [6] utilize a set of user preference policies in addition to the business policies, to improve the automated service selection. Kephart [5] proposes to support user preference by a *flexible interpretation of adaptation policies*. Our approach follows this direction by using tunable weighted goal policies. We support a straightforward interface for end users, conforming to Russell et al.'s principle on user experience of autonomic computing, i.e., only showing users the understandable actions [22].

This approach has a similar motivation with goal-based adaptation approaches [23–25], i.e., to increase the abstraction level of adaptation, but the two branches of work address different concerns. Those approaches focus on the modelling of adaptive systems, from a requirement perspective, and achieve this by adopting and extending a requirement modelling concept, the *goals*. To implement the adaptive systems, they link goals to lower-level modelling elements, such as tasks [25] or operations [23], or statically calculate the potential target systems for different contexts [24, 26]. Our approach is focused on how to plan the adaptation at runtime from a declarative specification about the desired system. As a first attempt, we choose model constraints as such a specification. We also name them *goals* for short as they conform to the definition of "goal policy" from adaptive system literature, but they do not have as strong expression power as requirement goals, such as the goal decomposition hierarchy. From this point of view, the two branches are complementary: We will investigate how to utilize requirement goal-based models as an input to our approach, and by doing this, we can provide a possible way to execute the requirement goal models at runtime without mapping them to imperative specifications.

Adaptation planning on a run-time model is similar to inconsistency fixing on a static model under editing. Recent approaches seek the automated inference of fixing updates by designing extra fixing semantics on the constraint languages [27], or analysing the relation between previous editing and fixing actions with the constraint rules [28]. Xiong et al. use constraint solving to construct the recommended fix ranges for configuration models at runtime [29]. Instead of a range, adaptation requires a specific value for each configuration item, and we choose such a value with the help of user preferences.

Constraint solving has been used by others for self-adaptation. Sun et al. use constraint solving to verify the role based access control policies [30]. White et al. use constraint solving to guide the system configuration on feature models [31]. Sawyer et al. [26] do constraint solving on the requirement-level goals to solve out proper configurations for all the possible contexts, and use the result to guide run-time adaptation. Instead of analysis in advance, we use constraint solvers at runtime, while the target model is still changing. Neema et al. [32] present a similar constraint guided adaptation framework but our work is focused more on the technical solution about how to solve constraints. This work is related to the generation of CSP from class diagrams [33, 34] or OCL constraints [35]. However, we do not perform verification merely on meta-models, but also use a model instance as a seed, based on a new partial evaluation mechanism.

8   Conclusion and Future Work

This paper reports our initial attempt towards automated system adaptation with the consideration of end user preferences. We transform run-time models into a CSP, and perform constraint diagnosing and solving to plan the new system configuration. If users revise the automated calculated configurations, we record their preferences by tuning the constraint weights, and subsequent adaptations will then yield results closer to the users preferences.

Our future plan is to apply the approach to different domains, and evaluate the experience from real users. Instead of supporting only the adaptation of attribute values, we will investigate how to transform the more complicated model changes into CSP, such as changing references between elements. In order to improve the scalability, we are now investigating the usage of AI search techniques on constraint diagnosis. Another important direction is to enhance the interface of this work to both developers and end users: For developers, we will investigate how to derive model constraints from higher-level models, such as requirement goals; For end users, we will provide a more interactive graphical user interface for them to revise the adaptation results.

References

1. Salehie, M., Tahvildari, L.: Self-adaptive software: Landscape and research challenges. ACM Transactions on Autonomous and Adaptive Systems (TAAS) 4(2), 14 (2009)
2. Garlan, D., Cheng, S., Huang, A., Schmerl, B., Steenkiste, P.: Rainbow: Architecture-based self-adaptation with reusable infrastructure. Computer 37(10), 46–54 (2004)
3. de Lemos, R., Giese, H., Müller, H.A., Shaw, M., Andersson, J., Litoiu, M., Schmerl, B., Tamura, G., Villegas, N.M., Vogel, T., Weyns, D., Baresi, L., Becker, B., Bencomo, N., Brun, Y., Cukic, B., Desmarais, R., Dustdar, S., Engels, G., Geihs, K., Göschka, K.M., Gorla, A., Grassi, V., Inverardi, P., Karsai, G., Kramer, J., Lopes, A., Magee, J., Malek, S., Mankovskii, S., Mirandola, R., Mylopoulos, J., Nierstrasz, O., Pezzè, M., Prehofer, C., Schäfer, W., Schlichting, R., Smith, D.B., Sousa, J.P., Tahvildari, L., Wong, K., Wuttke, J.: Software engineering for self-adaptive systems: A second research roadmap. In: de Lemos, R., Giese, H., Müller, H.A., Shaw, M. (eds.) Software Engineering for Self-Adaptive Systems. LNCS, vol. 7475, pp. 1–32. Springer, Heidelberg (2013)
4. Kephart, J., Walsh, W.: An artificial intelligence perspective on autonomic computing policies. In: IEEE International Workshop on Policies for Distributed Systems and Networks, pp. 3–12. IEEE (2004)
5. Kephart, J.: Research challenges of autonomic computing. In: ICSE, pp. 15–22. IEEE (2005)
6. Maximilien, E., Singh, M.: Toward autonomic web services trust and selection. In: Proceedings of the 2nd international conference on Service Oriented Computing, pp. 212–221. ACM (2004)
7. Blair, G., Bencomo, N., France, R.: Models@ run. time. Computer 42(10), 22–27 (2009)
8. Morin, B., Barais, O., Nain, G., Jezequel, J.: Taming dynamically adaptive systems using models and aspects. In: ICSE, pp. 122–132. IEEE Computer Society (2009)
9. Kumar, V.: Algorithms for constraint-satisfaction problems: A survey. AI Magazine 13(1), 32 (1992)
10. Song, H.: All the source code, experiment resource, and results mentioned in this paper, hosted by github, https://github.com/songhui/cspadapt
11. France, R., Rumpe, B.: Model-driven development of complex software: A research roadmap. In: 2007 Future of Software Engineering, pp. 37–54. IEEE Computer Society (2007)
12. Greiner, R., Smith, B., Wilkerson, R.: A correction to the algorithm in reiter's theory of diagnosis. Artificial Intelligence 41(1), 79–88 (1989)
13. Song, H., Xiong, Y., Chauvel, F., Huang, G., Hu, Z., Mei, H.: Generating synchronization engines between running systems and their model-based views. In: Ghosh, S. (ed.) MODELS 2009. LNCS, vol. 6002, pp. 140–154. Springer, Heidelberg (2010)
14. Sicard, S., Boyer, F., De Palma, N.: Using components for architecture-based management: the self-repair case. In: ICSE, pp. 101–110. ACM (2008)
15. Microsoft Research: Z3: a high-performance theorem prover, http://z3.codeplex.com
16. Jones, N.D., Gomard, C.K., Sestoft, P.: Partial evaluation and automatic program generation. Prentice-Hall, New York (1993)
17. Reiter, R.: A theory of diagnosis from first principles. Artificial Intelligence 32(1), 57–95 (1987)

18. Xtend: a statically-typed programming language which compiles to comprehensible java source code, http://www.eclipse.org/xtend/

19. Mozer, M.: The adaptive house, http://www.cs.colorado.edu/~mozer/nnh/

20. Galvan, E., Harris, C., Dusparic, I., Clarke, S., Cahill, V.: Reducing electricity costs in a dynamic pricing environment. In: IEEE SmartGridComm, pp. 169–174. IEEE

21. Morin, B., Mouelhi, T., Fleurey, F., Le Traon, Y., Barais, O., Jézéquel, J.: Security-driven model-based dynamic adaptation. In: ASE, pp. 205–214. ACM (2010)

22. Russell, D., Maglio, P., Dordick, R., Neti, C.: Dealing with ghosts: Managing the user experience of autonomic computing. IBM Systems Journal 42(1), 177–188 (2003)

23. Baresi, L., Pasquale, L., Spoletini, P.: Fuzzy goals for requirements-driven adaptation. In: RE, pp. 125–134. IEEE (2010)

24. Cheng, B.H.C., Sawyer, P., Bencomo, N., Whittle, J.: A goal-based modeling approach to develop requirements of an adaptive system with environmental uncertainty. In: Schürr, A., Selic, B. (eds.) MODELS 2009. LNCS, vol. 5795, pp. 468–483. Springer, Heidelberg (2009)

25. Dalpiaz, F., Giorgini, P., Mylopoulos, J.: An architecture for requirements-driven self-reconfiguration. In: van Eck, P., Gordijn, J., Wieringa, R. (eds.) CAiSE 2009. LNCS, vol. 5565, pp. 246–260. Springer, Heidelberg (2009)

26. Sawyer, P., Mazo, R., Diaz, D., Salinesi, C., Hughes, D.: Using constraint programming to manage configurations in self-adaptive systems. Computer 45(10), 56–63 (2012)

27. Nentwich, C., Emmerich, W., Finkelstein, A.: Consistency management with repair actions. In: ICSE, pp. 455–464. IEEE (2003)

28. Egyed, A., Letier, E., Finkelstein, A.: Generating and evaluating choices for fixing inconsistencies in uml design models. In: ASE, pp. 99–108. IEEE (2008)

29. Xiong, Y., Hubaux, A., She, S., Czarnecki, K.: Generating range fixes for software configuration. In: ICSE, pp. 58–68. IEEE (2012)

30. Sun, W., France, R., Ray, I.: Rigorous analysis of uml access control policy models. In: 2011 IEEE International Symposium on Policies for Distributed Systems and Networks (POLICY), pp. 9–16. IEEE (2011)

31. White, J., Dougherty, B., Schmidt, D., Benavides, D.: Automated reasoning for multi-step feature model configuration problems. In: Proceedings of the 13th International Software Product Line Conference, pp. 11–20. Carnegie Mellon University (2009)

32. Neema, S., Ledeczi, A.: Constraint-guided self-adaptation. Self-Adaptive Software: Applications, 325–327 (2003)

33. Maoz, S., Ringert, J.O., Rumpe, B.: CD2Alloy: Class diagrams analysis using alloy revisited. In: Whittle, J., Clark, T., Kühne, T. (eds.) MODELS 2011. LNCS, vol. 6981, pp. 592–607. Springer, Heidelberg (2011)

34. Cabot, J., Clarisó, R., Riera, D.: Verification of UML/OCL class diagrams using constraint programming. In: Software Testing Verification and Validation Workshop, pp. 73–80. IEEE (2008)

35. Cabot, J., Clarisó, R., Riera, D.: UMLtoCSP: a tool for the formal verification of uml/ocl models using constraint programming. In: ASE, pp. 547–548. ACM (2007)

Runtime Model Based Management
of Diverse Cloud Resources

Xiaodong Zhang[1,2], Xing Chen[1,2,4], Ying Zhang[1,2], Yihan Wu[1,2], Wei Yao[3],
Gang Huang[1,2,*], and Qiang Lin[5]

[1] Key Laboratory of High Confidence Software Technologies (Ministry of Education)
[2] School of Electronics Engineering and Computer Science, Peking University, Beijing, China
[3] Bona Information Technology Co., Ltd, Guangzhou, China
[4] College of Mathematics and Computer Science, Fuzhou University, Fuzhou 350108, China
[5] Information Center of Guangdong Power Grid Corporation, China
{zhangxd10,chenxing08,zhangying06,wuyh10}@sei.pku.edu.cn,
wei.yao@bonait.com, hg@pku.edu.cn, linqiang@gdxx.csg.cn

Abstract. Due to the diversity of resources and different management requirements, Cloud management is faced with great challenges in complexity and difficulty. For constructing a management system to satisfy a specific management
requirement, a redevelopment solution based on existing system is usually more
practicable than developing the system from scratch. However, the difficulty
and workload of redevelopment are very high. In this paper, we present a runtime model based approach to managing diverse Cloud resources. First, we construct the runtime model of each kind of Cloud resources. Second, we construct
the composite runtime model of all managed resources through model merge.
Third, we make Cloud management meet personalized requirements through
model transformation from the composite model to the customized models. Finally, all the management tasks can be carried out through executing operating
programs on the customized model. The feasibility and efficiency of the approach are validated through a real case study.

Keywords: runtime model, Cloud management, diverse Cloud resources.

1   Introduction

Cloud computing is a model for enabling ubiquitous, convenient, on-demand network
access to a shared pool of configurable computing resources that can be rapidly provisioned and released with minimal management effort or service provider interaction
[1]. With the rapid development of Cloud computing, it brings unprecedented challenges to management of diverse Cloud resources, which mainly comes from the following two aspects:

First, there are many different kinds of hardware and software resources in Cloud,
which include CPU, memory, storage, network, virtual machines and various software

---

* Corresponding author.

A. Moreira et al. (Eds.): MODELS 2013, LNCS 8107, pp. 572–588, 2013.

such as web servers, application servers, and Database servers. All these resources have to be managed well, which brings a huge challenge to Cloud management.

Second, there are different management requirements consisting of specific management scenarios and appropriate management styles. In some scenarios, administrators need to manage specific kind of resource; while in other scenarios, administrators have to manage different kinds of resources together.

In fact, from the view of system implementation, Cloud management is the execution of a group of management tasks. A management task is a group of management operations on one or more kinds of Cloud resources. A management operation is an invocation of a management interface provided by Cloud resources themselves or a third-party management service. Due to the specificity and large scale of Cloud, the management tasks of different Clouds are not the same. (For instance, Amazon EC2 [2] mainly manages infrastructure level Cloud resources such as virtual machines, while Google App Engine [3] manages platform level Cloud resources in addition to infrastructure, which includes operating systems, programming language execution environment and web servers.) To satisfy the personalized management requirements, Cloud administrators usually conduct redevelopment based on the existing management systems. However, due to the diversity of Cloud resources and personality of Cloud management requirements, the difficulty and workload of redevelopment are very high, which have to understand the existing systems first and have to invoke and organize many kinds of heterogeneous management interfaces of Cloud resources and third-party management services to satisfy a given management requirement.

Addressing the issues above, we try to leverage runtime model for the management of diverse Cloud resources. A runtime model is a causally connected self-representation of the associated system that emphasizes the structure, behavior, or goals of the system from a problem space perspective [4]. It has been broadly adopted in the runtime management of software systems [5][6][7][8]. With the help of runtime models, administrators can obtain a better understanding of their systems and write model-level programs for management. We have developed a model-based runtime management tool called SM@RT (Supporting Model AT Run Time [9][10][11]), which provides the synchronization engine between a runtime model and its corresponding running system. SM@RT makes any state of the running system reflected to the runtime model, as well as any change to the runtime model applied to the running system in an on-the-fly fashion.

In this paper, we present a runtime model based approach to managing diverse Cloud resources. First, we construct the runtime model of each kind of Cloud resource (Cloud resource runtime model) automatically based on its architecture meta-model and management interfaces. Second, According to the Cloud management requirements, we construct the composite runtime model spreading all of the corresponding Cloud resources and their management interfaces through model merge. Third, according to personalized management requirements, we customize different parts of the composite model to get different kinds of customized models through model transformation. Thus, Cloud management tasks can be carried out through executing operating programs on the customized model, which benefits from many model-centric analyzing or planning methods and mechanisms such as model checkers.

The whole approach only needs to define a group of meta-models, mapping rules and model-level operating programs, thus greatly reduces the hand coding workload. Particularly, the Cloud resource runtime models are able to shield the heterogeneity of the management interfaces of homogeneous resource instances, and the composite runtime model shields the distribution of Cloud resources. The model operating programs not only simplify the implementation of Cloud management system, but also improve the correctness, effectiveness and automaticity of Cloud management by introducing model analysis, model checking, model simulation, and model reasoning.

The contributions of this paper can be summarized as follows. Firstly, we present a runtime model based approach to managing diverse Cloud resources, which can meet the personalized management requirements while avoiding the difficulty and heavy workload of redevelopment. Secondly, we apply the runtime model to a real Cloud system, which to our knowledge, is a first practical evaluation on runtime model based management of diverse Cloud resources. The results are promising.

The rest of this paper is organized as follows: Section 2 gives an overview of the runtime model based approach to managing diverse Cloud resources. Section 3 presents the construction of Cloud resource runtime models. Section 4 introduces the construction of the Composite runtime model. Section 5 describes model transformation from the composite model to the customized model. Section 6 illustrates a real case study and reports the evaluation. Section 7 discusses the related work. Section 8 concludes this paper and indicates our future work.

2   A Brief Overview of the Approach

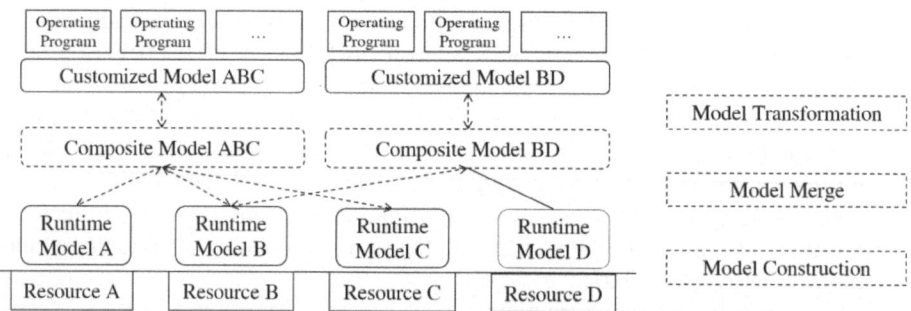

Fig. 1. Overview of the runtime model based approach to managing diverse Cloud resources

Fig. 1 is an overview of the runtime model based approach to managing diverse Cloud resources.

First, we present an approach to constructing the runtime models of Cloud resources. There are many different kinds of resources in Cloud. For example, there are virtual machine platforms such as Xen, VMware and KVM, operating systems such as Windows and Linux, application servers such as JOnAS, JBoss, Websphere and WebLogic, web servers such as Apache, IIS and Nginx, database servers such as MySQL, SQL server and Oracle. The Cloud resource runtime model in our approach is abstracted from the architecture of this kind of resources in a semi-automatic way with the help of SM@RT.

Second, we propose a model merge mechanism which aims to build the composite runtime model of diverse Cloud resources. Management of the Cloud actually is management of the Cloud resources. Our approach allows the Cloud administrators to customize any group of resources to construct the composite runtime model through merging the runtime models of each kind of resources.

Third, we present a model transformation mechanism which transforms the composite models to customized models. Cloud administrators just need to write some mapping rules according to the personalized management requirements, and the model transformation will be automatically completed.

After the three steps above are done, Cloud management tasks can be carried out through executing different kinds of model operating programs, while without considering the management interfaces of underlying Cloud resources. Further, we can improve the correctness, effectiveness and automaticity of Cloud management through introducing model analysis, model checking, model simulation, and model reasoning.

3   The Construction of Cloud Resource Runtime Models

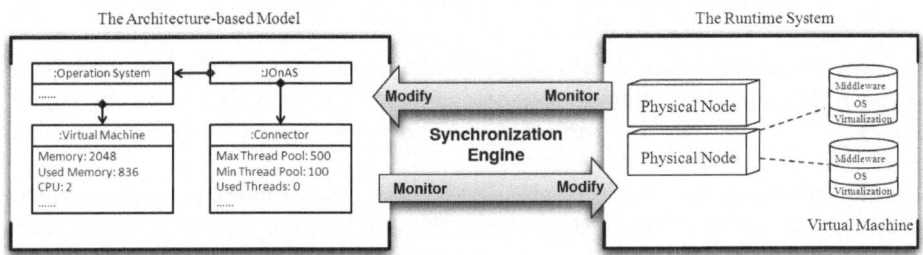

Fig. 2. Synchronization between the runtime model and the running system

As we introduced in section 2, the construction of Cloud resource runtime models can be easily done with the help of SM@RT, which is proposed in our previous work [9][10][11]. SM@RT consists of a domain-specific modeling language (called SM@RT language) and a code generator (called SM@RT generator) to support model-based runtime system management. The SM@RT language allows developers to specify: (1) the structure of the running system by a UML-compliant meta-model; (2) how to manipulate the system's elements by an access model. With these two models, the SM@RT generator can automatically generate the synchronization engine to reflect the running system to the runtime model. The synchronization engine not only enables any states of the system to be monitored by the runtime model, but also any changes to the runtime model to be applied on the running system. For instance, in Fig. 2, the synchronization engine builds a model element in the runtime model for the JOnAS platform. When the model element of JOnAS is deleted, the synchronization engine is able to detect this change, identify which platform this removed element stands for, and finally invoke the script to shut down the JOnAS platform.

With the help of SM@RT, developers or administrators are able to leverage the existing model-based tools (Like OCL, ATL, GMF etc.) to manage running systems. Due to page limitation, more details of the runtime model construction with SM@RT can be found in [9][10][11].

4   The Construction of the Composite Runtime Model

In a Cloud environment, diverse resources usually need to run collaboratively to support the Cloud applications. So the unified management of these resources is necessary to guarantee the applications working correctly. Particularly, different Cloud administrators may focus on different kinds of resources. For instance, some focus on the management of the infrastructure, while others focus on the management of software in Cloud. Therefore, we propose a model merge mechanism. According to the specific management requirements, Cloud administrators can choose and integrate managed elements and management methods of different kinds of resources in the form of the composite runtime model. Thus administrators can manage diverse Cloud resources through operations on the composite model.

After getting the composite runtime model, we have to guarantee the data synchronization between the composite runtime model and the Cloud resource runtime models. On the one hand, when Cloud administrators operate on the composite runtime model, the model operations are transferred to the corresponding Cloud resource runtime models. On the other hand, changes of the Cloud resource runtime models are automatically discovered through periodic comparisons with their previous copies. And then the changes are transformed to model operations, which will be executed on the composite runtime model.

Particularly, only the "Set", "Add" and "Remove" operations can lead to changes of the runtime models. Table 1 shows three different kinds of model operations and a specific example is shown in the section of case study.

Table 1. Three kinds of model operations.

Name	Description	Post Condition
Add	\<action node="ToAddNode" type="add"\> \<query node="FatherNode" condition="Constraint" /\> \<set key="attr1" value="val1" /\> \<set key="attr2" value="val2" /\> \</action\>	$\exists$ *ToAddNode* $n1$,$\exists$ *FatherNode* $n2$, $n1$ is child node of $n2$ $\wedge n2$ *match Constraint* $\wedge attrs \subseteq n1.attributes$
Set	\<action key="attr" value="val" type="set"\> \<query node=TargetNode" condition="Constraint" /\> \</action\>	$\exists$ *TargetNode* n, n *match Constrint* $\wedge$ *TargetAttr* $\in n.attributes$
Remove	\<action node="TargetNode" condition="Constraint" type="remove" /\>	$\forall$ *TargetNode* n, n *notmatch Constraint*

Fig. 3 shows an example of runtime model merge. There are two kinds of resources in the example: Application Servers and Virtual Machines. We now want to manage the two kinds of resources in a unified way. We have constructed the runtime models of both virtual machines and application servers, which can manage the two kinds of resources separately. We just need to construct the composite model through merging the two resource runtime models. And Cloud administrators can manage both kinds of resources through operating on the composite model.

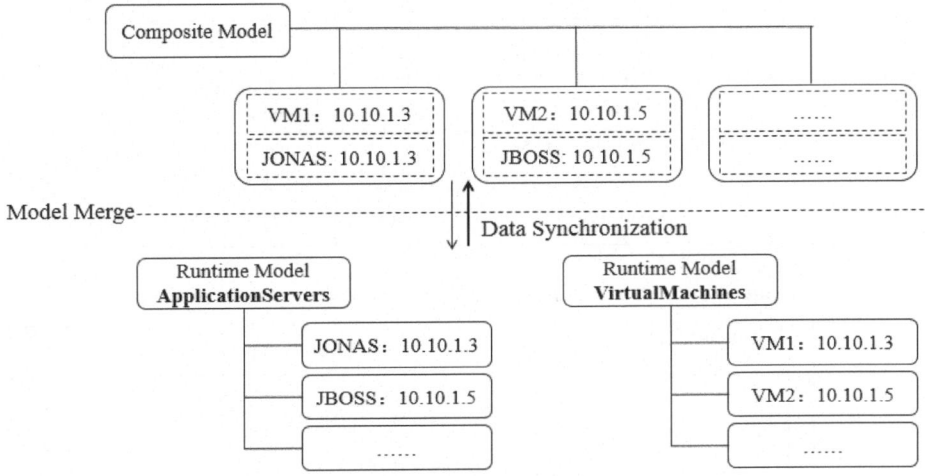

Fig. 3. An example of runtime model merge

5   Model Transformation from the Composite Model to the Customized Model

In Cloud environment, there are different management requirements consisting of specific management scenarios and appropriate management styles. To better meet the personalized management requirements of Cloud, we define the customized models. The composite model is an aggregation of the runtime models of diverse Cloud resources and the customized model is constructed through model transformation from the composite model according to the personalized management requirements. The transformation is based on a set of mapping rules between the two models. The mapping rules describe the mapping relationship between the elements of two models. Every attribute of the element in the customized model is related with one of the element in the composite model. All changes on the customized model will be transformed to operations on the composite model, vice versa. We define the description methods of mapping rules and some keywords are shown in Table 2. We implement a model transformation approach based on SM@RT, which can generate transformation codes (written in QVT [12]) automatically based on the mapping rules. Table 3 presents three types of basic mapping relationships between model elements. A more detailed example of model transformation is shown in the case study section.

Table 2. Keywords of the description of mapping rules

Keywords	Descriptions	Keywords	Descriptions
helper	Mapping Rules	**type**	Types of Mapping Rules
mapper	There is a mapping relationship between the attributes of the objective element and the source element.	**query**	There is a mapping relationship between the attributes of the objective element and the element that is related to the source element.
key	Elements or Attributes of Source Models	**value**	Elements or Attributes of Objective Models
condition	Preconditions	**node**	Types of Objective Elements

Table 3. Three types of basic mapping rules between model elements

	One-to-One Mapping Relationship	Many-to-One Mapping Relationship	One-to-Many Mapping Relationship
Classes in Source Model	**MachineType** -kind -id -creationTimestamp -name -description -guestCpus -memoryMb -imageSpaceGb	**Image** -kind -id -creationTimestamp -name -description -sourceType -preferredKernel **Kernel** -kind -id -creationTimestamp -name -description	**VM** -id -tenantId -name -flavorId -imageId -ip -status
Classes in Objective Model	**Flavor** -id -name -ram -disk -vcpus	**Image** -id -name -status -progress -minDisk -minRam -rawDiskSource -kernelDescription	**Apache** -id -applianceId -name -ip **JOnAS** -id -applianceId -name -ip **MySQL** -id -applianceId -name -ip
Examples of Transformation Code	vcpus:=self.guestCpus	kernelDescription := gccloud.objectsOfType(Kernel) ->select(id=self.preferredKernel) ->selectOne(true).description	if(self.imageId="MYSQLTYPE"){ return object MySQL}

One-to-One Mapping Relationship: One element in the customized model is related to a certain element in the composite model. Particularly, the attributes of the elements in the customized model are also corresponding to the ones of related elements in the composite model. For instance, in Table 3, the *MachineType* element in the composite model and the *Flavor* element in the customized model both reflect the configurations of virtual machines. And the attributes of "id", "name", "ram", "disk" and "vcpus" of the *MachineType* element in the composite model are corresponding to the attributes of "id", "name", "memoryMb", "imageSpaceGb" and "guestCpus" of the *Flavor* element in the customized model. It is one-to-one mapping relationship between the *MachineType* and *Flavor* elements.

Many-to-One Mapping Relationship: One type of elements in the customized model is related to two or more types of elements in the composite model. Particularly, the attributes of a certain type of the element in the customized model are corresponding to the attributes of different types of elements in the composite model. For instance, the *Image* element in the composite model and the *Image* element in the customized model both reflect the types of virtual machines. But there is no attribute of the *Image* element in the composite model which is corresponding to the "kernelDescription" attribute of the *Image* element in the customized model. And the related one is in the *Kernel* element in the composite model, whose "id" attribute is equal to the "preferredKernel" attribute of the *Image* element in the composite model.

One-to-Many Mapping Relationship: One type of elements in the composite model is related to two or more types of elements in the customized model. For instance, the *VM* elements in the composite model represent virtual machines, and the elements of *Apache*, *JOnAS* and *MySQL* represent virtual machines with specific software. During model transformation, any *VM* element will be mapped to one of the elements of *Apache*, *JOnAS* and *MySQL*.

Table 3 also shows some sample transformation codes of the three basic mapping relationships. In one-to-one mapping relationship, mapping is fulfilled with an assignment. In many-to-one mapping relationship, the related elements in the source model need to be selected and integrated. In one-to-many mapping relationship, the type of the objective element needs to be determined. Any mapping relationship between the customized model and the composite model can be demonstrated as the combination of the three relationships above.

By using our approach, Cloud management can be carried out through executing different types of model operating programs. The programs can be written based on technologies like model query, model view and model transformation, while without considering the management interfaces of underlying Cloud resources. For example, monitoring is very important in Cloud management. Through model query, we can easily get and modify the running states and attributes of all resource units in Cloud.

Further, based on the runtime model, we can improve the correctness, effectiveness and automaticity of Cloud management through introducing model analysis, model checking, model simulation and model reasoning. For example, we can use SBRA-based [13] algorithm to evaluate the reliability of each resource units and find out the key units which have crucial influence on the Cloud. We can also use Capacity Planning [14] technology to improve the elasticity of the Cloud.

6   Case Study

Most of current Cloud management systems provide solutions to managing specific sets of resources. For instance, OpenStack [15] is an open source product which is aimed to manage Cloud infrastructure. Hyperic [16] is another product which manages different kinds of software including web servers, application servers, database servers, and so on. However, to the best of our knowledge, there is currently no product which can manage both of the infrastructure and software resources in a unified manner. In our cooperation program with China Southern Power Grid Corporation [17] on Cloud management, we found that the industry has a strong demand for the unified management of both kinds of resources.

In order to validate the feasibility and efficiency of our approach, we present a case study on a real Cloud system, which   satisfies the above management requirement through runtime model construction, model merge and model transformation. We now present the evaluations from three aspects.

6.1   Runtime Model Construction of Cloud Resources

As described in Section 3, we only need to define the architecture-based meta-model and the access model of one kind of Cloud resource, then the Cloud resource runtime model can be constructed automatically with the help of SM@RT. Due to the page limitation, we don't introduce more on the working principle of SM@RT, which has been presented clearly in our previous work [9][10][11].

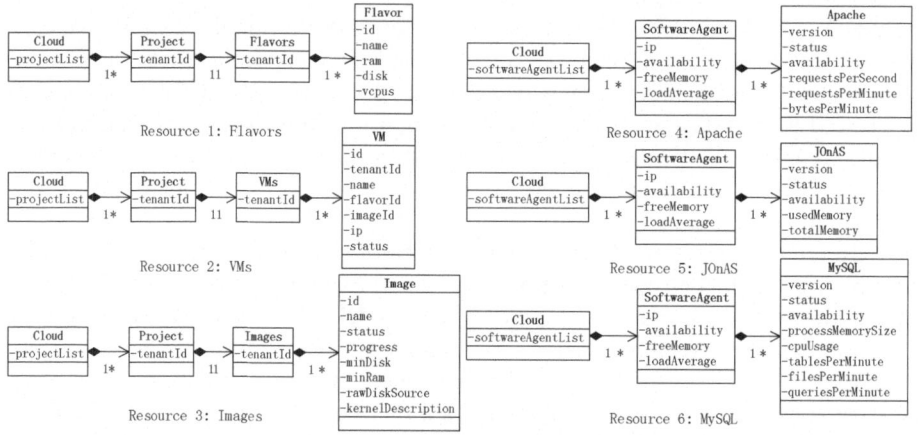

Fig. 4. Architecture-based meta-models of Cloud resources

Fig. 4 shows the architecture-based meta-models of each kind of resources in the Cloud we used in this case study. In the Cloud, virtual machines are the smallest units of resource allocation, each of which is included in a project. The resources of Cloud infrastructure are divided into several projects and each project belongs to a tenant. The configuration of the virtual machine contains the image and the flavor. The image describes the system type and pre-install software (for instance, "Ubuntu 12.04 MySQL" image and "Windows Server 2008 Apache" image). The flavor describes the hardware resource configuration (for instance, small-flavor: CPU 2 x 2.4G Hz, memory 1024MB, disk 10GB; large-flavor: CPU 8 x 2.4G Hz, memory 16384MB, disk 100GB) of the virtual machine. (Please note, we borrow the terms like project, tenant, image and flavor from OpenStack). The Cloud vendor provides many different kinds of software products such as Apache, JOnAS and MySQL for Cloud users to deploy on the virtual machines. For managing the software products, a software agent runs on each VM to monitor and control the software product.

Although there are hundreds of management APIs of different kinds of resources in the Cloud, we can model them into the access model through specifying how to invoke the APIs to manipulate each type of elements. Table 4 summarizes all types of manipulations of the Cloud resources and the management interfaces of the resources can be mapped to the manipulations on their runtime models. For instance, the creation and deletion of the VM are mapped to "Add" and "Remove" manipulations of the element of the *VM* class; the starting up and shutting down of Apache are mapped to "Set" manipulation of the "status" attribute in the element of the *Apache* class.

Table 4. Summary of the manipulations of the Cloud resources

Name	Meta Element	Parameter	Description
Get	Property(1)	-	Get the value of the property
Set	Property(2)	newValue	Set the property to *newValue*
List	Property(*)	-	Get a list of values of this property
Add	Property(*)	toAdd	Add *toAdd* into the value list of this property
Remove	Property(*)	toRemove	Remove *toRemove* from the list of this property
Query	Class	Condition	Find an element according to *Condition*
Identify	Class	Other	Check if this element equals to *Other*
Auxiliary	Package	-	User-defined auxiliary operations

6.2   The Composite Runtime Model of Diverse Cloud Resources

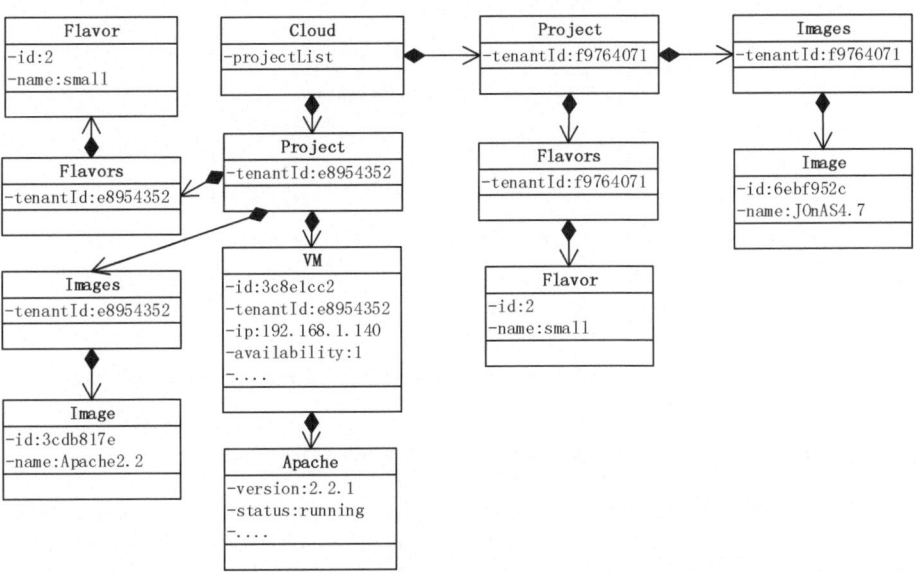

Fig. 5. The composite runtime model of diverse Cloud resources

After the Cloud resource runtime models are constructed, we construct different composite models through merging different ones of them according to different requirements. If the Cloud administrator focuses on the management of virtual machines, he or she can merge the runtime models of flavors, images and VMs to manage these resources in a unified manner. If the administrator pays attention to the management of software, he or she can merge the runtime models of Apache, JOnAS and MySQL to manage them in a unified manner. Sometimes, the Cloud administrators want to manage both the hardware and software resources, and then all the resource runtime models can be merged to generate a composite model spreading all these resources.

Fig. 5 shows the composite runtime model which is merged of six kinds of resources. There are two projects in the runtime model, one of which contains one VM and the other contains none.

After the composite model is constructed, we must guarantee the data synchronization between the composite model and distributed resource models. Fig. 6 shows how the action of creating a virtual machine is transferred from the composite model to the runtime model of VMs and executed on the runtime model. The file transferred to the runtime model details the action to be executed:

1. Query: Find the parent element - a project whose "tenantId" is "f9764071".
2. Add: Create an element, whose type is *VM*.
3. Set: Carry out the configuration of the new *VM* element.

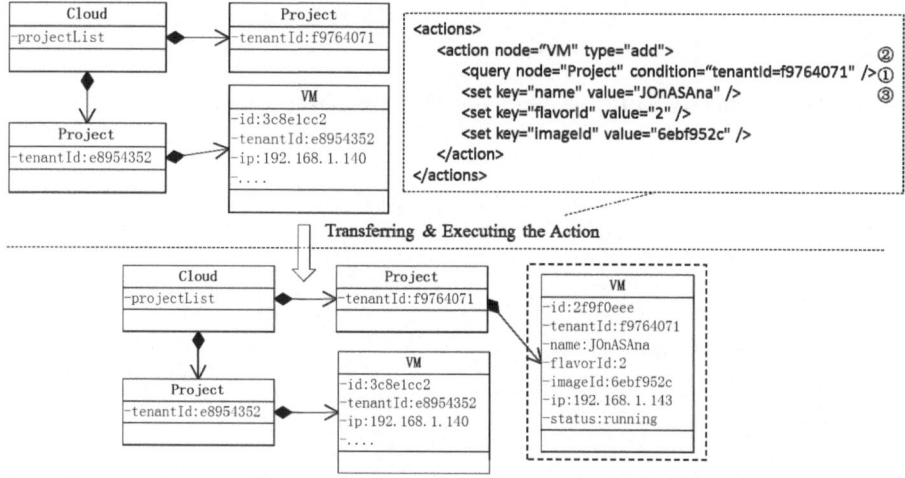

Fig. 6. The operation of VM creation is transferred to the runtime model of VMs

6.3   Transformation from the Composite Model to the Customized Model

In a Cloud environment, the hardware and software resources of virtual machines need to be managed together in order to optimize the allocation of resources. The virtual machine and the software deployed can be regarded as an appliance [18], which is the basic managed unit. Several appliances compose a project. The resources of the infrastructure are divided into many projects. According to this management requirement, we construct the customized model. Fig. 7 shows the main elements in the customized model. The root element is the *Cloud* element, which contains a list of projects. The *Project* element contains an *Appliances* element, which is regarded as a list of appliances. The *Appliances* element contains a list of Apache systems, a list of JOnAS systems and a list of MySQL systems, which are all regarded as appliances. The elements of each appliance contain configurations of the hardware and software resources. For instance, the *Apache* element contains an *ApacheSwConfig* element and a *HwConfig* element. So management actions can be described by the operations on the customized model.

In order to construct the customized model through transformation from the composite model, we define the mapping rules between the two models. The key challenge is the mapping from the *VM* elements and one of *Apache, JOnAS* and *MySQL* elements in the composite model to one of *Apache, JOnAS* and *MySQL* elements in the customized model. There are two difficult points in this process.

1.   The *VM* element is mapped to the element of *Apache, JOnAS* or *MySQL*, which is determined by the attribute of "imageId" of the *VM* element. This is the one-to-many mapping relationship.

2.   It also needs to find the element of *Apache, JOnAS* or *MySQL* and achieve the configurations of software resources in the composite model. The related element of *Apache, JOnAS* or *MySQL* is determined by the attribute of "ip" of the *VM* element. Then the hardware and software information from the *VM* element and element of *Apache, JOnAS* or *MySQL* are transformed to the attributes of the element of each appliance. This is the many-to-one mapping relationship.

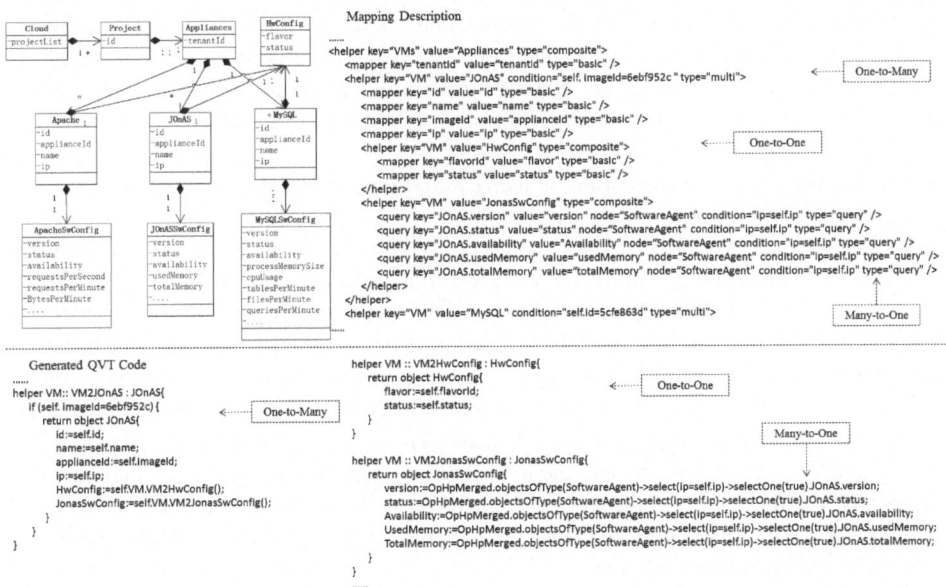

Fig. 7. The main elements of the customized model, mapping description and code snippets

Fig. 7 shows the description and the code snippets of the mapping relationship from the *VM* and *JOnAS* elements in the composite model to the *JOnAS* elements in the customized model.

6.4   Evaluation

We evaluate our approach from three aspects.

A.   Construction and merge of Cloud resource runtime models.
For constructing the runtime models of Cloud resources, we just need define the architecture-based meta-model and the manipulations of the resources on the Eclipse Modeling Framework (EMF) [19]. The runtime model will be generated automatically by our SM@RT tool. So the construction of Cloud resource runtime models is one-off work, which is acceptable for Cloud administrators.

The existing form of runtime models is a document in XML format. The process of model merge is the merging of several documents in XML format based on some rules. The time cost of such a process is in seconds. What's more, for the management of a set of Cloud resources, model merge only needs to be conducted once. So the time cost of model merge can almost be ignored in the runtime model based approach.

B.   Comparison of the programming difficulty of using management interfaces   with using runtime models.
According to our previous work [20], for the same management tasks, the programs using runtime models like QVT [12] programs are simpler to write compared with programs using management interfaces like Java programs. With the help of the architecture-based model, Cloud administrators can focus on the logics of management tasks without handling the different types of low-level management interfaces. In addition, the modeling language provides operations such as "select", "sum" and so on in the model level, which makes it simpler to do programming.

C.   Comparison of execution time of using management interfaces with using runtime model for the same management tasks.
We manage a Cloud infrastructure, which consists of 11 physical servers and supports about 150 appliances, through our runtime model based approach. To evaluate its performance, we develop Java programs by using management interfaces and QVT programs by using runtime models to execute five groups of management tasks respectively. The five groups of management tasks include: creating appliances, deleting appliances, getting the "usedMemory" attribute of appliances, setting the "name" attribute of appliances and restarting Apache. The execution results are shown in Table 5. The execution time means the average time cost of each group of management tasks, and the data delay is the average delayed time to obtain the data. For instance, if the data delay is 30 seconds, the time delay between the returned result and the actual values is 30 seconds on average.

For the "create new appliances", "delete appliances", "set 'name' attribute" and "restart Apache" management tasks, the execution time of Java programs is less than the QVT ones. The main reason is that the two sets of programs are based on the same management APIs and there are some extra operations in runtime model based approach, which ensure the synchronization between the runtime model and real system. However, the difference is small and completely acceptable for Cloud management.

For the "get 'used-memory' attribute" management tasks, the execution time of Java programs is longer than the QVT ones, but the data delay of QVT programs is longer than the Java ones. The reasons include two folds. On the one hand, the Java programs query the attributes of appliances through directly invoking the management interfaces, so the execution time increases linearly with the number of the appliances and the data delay is very little. On the other hand, the runtime model is equivalent to the snapshot of system metrics and getting the attributes of appliances just needs a reading operation, so the execution time of the QVT programs is shorter. The runtime model is synchronized with the running system with traversing all the metrics of the running system, so the data delay increases linearly with the size of the model. In this test, the data delay of the "get" operation is 30 seconds, which is acceptable for system monitoring. It is important to note that we can control the data delay within the accepted limits through splitting the runtime model into small models, which will be implemented in our future work.

Table 5. The performance test result of the unified managment

Management Tasks	Number of Appliances	Using Management Interfaces		Using Runtime Model	
		Execution Time (second)	Data Delay (second)	Execution Time (second)	Data Delay (second)
Create new appliances	1	22.9	-	24.1	-
	5	43.4	-	45.5	-
	10	58.7	-	62.1	-
Delete appliances	1	11.2	-	13.8	-
	5	29.7	-	30.1	-
	10	41.4	-	45.6	-
Get "usedMemory" attribute	5	1.2	0.6	0.6	30
	20	4.2	2.2	0.8	30
	100	18.6	11.4	1.6	30
Set "name" attribute	5	2.1	-	4.1	-
	20	8.3	-	11.7	-
	100	39.7	-	44.2	-
Restart Apache	5	9.1	-	12.3	-
	20	37.6	-	41.2	-
	100	192.4	-	207.3	-

7   Related Work

Due to the diversity of Cloud resources and specific management requirements, there are many management systems which are aimed to manage different types of resources and provide different kinds of services. For instance, Eucalyptus [21], OpenStack [15], Tivoli [22] and Hyperic [16] are aimed to provide the solution to shield the heterogeneity and distribution of Cloud resources. The systems above help Cloud administrators manage specific resources in a unified manner. However, they cannot customize, integrate and extend existing management systems of resources efficiently and flexibly to satisfy different management requirements and the difficulty and workload of redevelopment is high.

There are some research work which try to integrate management systems based on service-oriented architecture. Heiko Ludwig et al. [23] propose a solution to the system management in a distributed environment, which encapsulates management functions into RESTful services [24] and makes them subscribed by administrators. In our previous work [25], we propose the solution of "Management as a Service (MaaS)" from the reuse point of view. We encapsulate functions, processes, rules and experiments in IT management into web services and regard them as reusable assets, which are to be presented, used and collaborate in a service-oriented style. In general, it is feasible to integrate management function based on service-oriented architecture. However, management services are not as good as system parameters for reflecting the states of running systems, and service subscription and composition are also more complicated, which may lead to extra difficulties in system management.

Runtime models have been widely used on different systems to support self-repair [26], dynamic adaption [27], data manipulation [28], etc. We also have made lots of research in the area of runtime model based system management. In our previous work [9][10][11], SM@RT (Supporting Models AT Runtime) is proposed. Given the meta-model specifying the structure of the running system and an access model specifying how to manipulate the system's elements, the SM@RT tool can automatically generate the synchronization engine to reflect the running system to the runtime model. The experimentation on application servers such as JOnAS has shown good runtime performance. Our another work [8] applies the runtime model to system fault tolerance and presents a runtime model based configuration of fault tolerance solution for component-based system. However, to the best of our knowledge, there is no existing work which applies the runtime model to managing a real Cloud system.

8   Conclusion and Future Work

In this paper, we proposed a runtime model based approach to managing diverse Cloud resources. Through runtime model construction of different kinds of Cloud resources, model merge of the runtime models of customized resources and model transformation from composite model to customized model, personalized Cloud management requirements can be satisfied with executing a set of model operating programs. We firstly applied the runtime model to a real Cloud system and the evaluation shows promising results.

For future work, firstly, we plan to apply the approach in production environment. Secondly, we will add some more advanced management functions with the help of model analysis and reasoning techniques to ease the tasks of Cloud management. Thirdly, we will do more work on the specification of the domain model.

Acknowledgment. This work is supported by the National Basic Research Program of China (973) under Grant No. 2009CB320703; the National Natural Science Foundation of China under Grant No. 61222203, 61361120097, 60933003; the Postdoctoral Funding No. 2013M530011, and the NCET.

References

1. Mell, P., Grance, T.: NIST definition of cloud computing. National Institute of Standards and Technology (October 7, 2009)
2. Amazon EC2, http://aws.amazon.com/ec2/
3. Google App Engine, https://appengine.google.com/
4. Blair, G., Bencomo, N., France, R.B.: Models@ run.time. Computer 42(10), 22–27 (2009)
5. Huang, G., Mei, H., Yang, F.Q.: Runtime recovery and manipulation of software architecture of component-based systems. Auto. Soft. Eng. 13(2), 257–281 (2006)
6. France, R., Rumpe, B.: Model-driven Development of Complex Software: A Research Roadmap. In: Future of Software Engineering, FOSE 2007 (2007)
7. Occello, A., Dery-Pinna, A., Riveill, M.: A Runtime Model for Monitoring Software Adaptation Safety and its Concretisation as a Service. Models@ runtime (2008)
8. Wu, Y., Huang, G., Song, H., Zhang, Y.: Model driven configuration of fault tolerance solutions for component-based software system. In: France, R.B., Kazmeier, J., Breu, R., Atkinson, C. (eds.) MODELS 2012. LNCS, vol. 7590, pp. 514–530. Springer, Heidelberg (2012)
9. Song, H., Xiong, Y., Chauvel, F., Huang, G., Hu, Z., Mei, H.: Generating synchronization engines between running systems and their model-based views. In: Ghosh, S. (ed.) MODELS 2009. LNCS, vol. 6002, pp. 140–154. Springer, Heidelberg (2010)
10. Song, H., Huang, G., Xiong, Y., Chauvel, F., Sun, Y., Mei, H.: Inferring Meta-models for Runtime System Data from the Clients of Management APIs. In: Petriu, D.C., Rouquette, N., Haugen, Ø. (eds.) MODELS 2010, Part II. LNCS, vol. 6395, pp. 168–182. Springer, Heidelberg (2010)
11. Song, H., Huang, G., Chauvel, F., Zhang, W., Sun, Y., Shao, W., Mei, H.: Instant and Incremental QVT Transformation for Runtime Models. In: Whittle, J., Clark, T., Kühne, T. (eds.) MODELS 2011. LNCS, vol. 6981, pp. 273–288. Springer, Heidelberg (2011)
12. Object Management Group. Meta Object Facility (MOF) 2.0 Query/View/Transformation (QVT) (retrieved May 9, 2011)
13. Sherif, Y., Bojan, C., Hany, H.: A Scenario-Based Reliability Analysis Approach for Component-Based Software. IEEE Transactions on Reliability 53 (2004)
14. Gunther, N.J.: Guerrilla Capacity Planning. Springer (2007) ISBN 3-540-26138-9
15. OpenStack, http://www.openstack.org/
16. Hyperic, http://www.hyperic.com/
17. China Southern Power Grid Corporation, http://eng.csg.cn/
18. Sapuntzakis, C.P., Brumley, D., Chandra, R., Zeldovich, N., Chow, J., Lam, M.S., Rosenblum, M.: Virtual Appliances for Deploying and Maintaining Software. In: LISA, vol. 3, pp. 181–194 (2003)
19. Eclipse Modeling Framework, http://www.eclipse.org/modeling/emf/
20. Huang, G., Chen, X., Zhang, Y., Zhang, X.: Towards architecture-based management of platforms in the cloud. Frontiers of Computer Science 6(4), 388–397 (2012)
21. Eucalyptus, http://www.eucalyptus.com/
22. IBM Tivoli Software, http://www-01.ibm.com/software/tivoli/
23. Ludwig, H., Laredo, J., Bhattacharya, K.: Rest-based management of loosely coupled services. In: Proc. of the 18th International Conference on World Wide Web, pp. 931–940. ACM Press, New York (2009)
24. Restful Web Services, http://en.wikipedia.org/wiki/Representational_state_transfer

25. Chen, X., Liu, X., Fang, F., Zhang, X., Huang, G.: Management as a Service: An Empirical Case Study in the Internetware Cloud. In: Proc. of the 7th IEEE International Conference on E-Business Engineering, pp. 470–473 (2010)
26. Sicard, S., Boyer, F., De Palma, N.: Using components for architecture-based management: the self-repair case. In: ICSE, pp. 101–110 (2008)
27. Morin, B., Barais, O., Nain, G., Jezequel, J.M.: Taming dynamically adaptive systems using models and aspects. In: ICSE, pp. 122–132 (2009)
28. MoDisco Project, http://www.eclipse.org/gmt/modisco/

The Semantic Web as a Software Modeling Tool: An Application to Citizen Relationship Management

Borislav Iordanov, Assia Alexandrova, Syed Abbas,
Thomas Hilpold, and Phani Upadrasta

Miami-Dade County, Community Information and Outreach
Department, Florida, USA
{boris,assia,sabbas,hilpold,phani}@miamidade.gov
http://www.sharegov.org

Abstract. The choice of a modeling language in software engineering is traditionally restricted to the tools and meta-models invented specifically for that purpose. On the other hand, semantic web standards are intended mainly for modeling data, to be consumed or produced by software. However, both spaces share enough commonality to warrant an attempt at a unified solution. In this paper, we describe our experience using Web Ontology Language (OWL) as the language for Model-Driven Development (MDD). We argue that there are benefits of using OWL to formally describe both data and software within an integrated modeling approach by showcasing an e-Government platform that we have built for citizen relationship management. We describe the platform architecture, development process and model enactment. In addition, we explain some of the limitations of OWL as an MDD formalism as well as the shortcomings of current tools and suggest practical ways to overcome them.

Keywords: semantic web, owl, model-driven development, e-government, live system, executable models.

1 Introduction

1.1 Motivation

The promise of model-driven development (MDD) is justifiably attractive for any organization supporting its constantly evolving business processes with software that must adapt as quickly and in a cost effective way. We use the term MDD in the general sense of *a software development process where the primary artifact is the model*. We are not referring to any particular specification, technology stack or categorization of the artifacts produced. In adopting an MDD approach one would expect business changes to be absorbed more easily, with much fewer code changes. E-Government aims at replacing a heavy bureaucracy and manual paperwork with lean software for improved efficiency of service, accountability

A. Moreira et al. (Eds.): MODELS 2013, LNCS 8107, pp. 589–603, 2013.

and transparency. There is a modern trend towards government openness and open data ([6], [7]) which relies heavily on semantic web (SW) technologies such as RDF ([11]) and OWL ([12]). Based on e-government application development experience at our local government organization, we have come to the realization that there is a fundamental similarity between MDD technologies on one side and SW standards and tools on the other. In both cases, a high-level language is used to create domain models. The difference is in how those models are being put to use in software and it comes mainly from the intended applications of MDD, and respectively the SW. The languages and tools used for MDD are predominantly software-centric as evidenced by the historical development of the OMG stack ([1]). The domain models are used in various model transformations in order to automatically generate artifacts pertaining to the software development process otherwise obtained through manual labor, such as code, documentation and tests. By contrast, in the SW the domain models are used to describe structured data in a formal machine processable way and are usually interpreted as visual presentations for human consumption, data analysis, or mapping to other data formats, but are not constitutive of the software end-product per se.

1.2   The OWL MDD Landscape

The idea of marrying MDD with OWL has been around for a while ([3], [18], [19]). However, such marriages always aim at bridging a conventional MDA technology stack with OWL by expressing UML models in OWL or vice-versa, so that tools from both can be leveraged simultaneously. We are not aware of actual practical production uses of such approaches, but we believe that mixing several meta-models would significantly contribute to the complexity of the development process and should be done only when a clear benefit is demonstrated. Therefore, we have opted to drop the conventional MDD technology stack and build exclusively with OWL (more on why OWL vs. UML in section 4.1). Furthermore, since we are not aware of other attempts to use only OWL for MDD, we have had to establish one ab initio.

1.3   Structure of the Paper

First, we describe our problem domain, *Citizen Relationship Management* and the overall requirements for the project. Then we outline the platform architecture and main technological choices. Next, we describe our modeling approach: what is being modeled, how models are interpreted. Finally, we discuss some implementation details.

2   The Problem

The business user of the software described herein is a municipal call center which has been using a legacy case management system for over 10 years. Due to technical constraints, and limitations with configuration of workflows, permissions and business rules, the call center specialists and the fieldworkers using the system (e.g. Animal Services officers, Public Works field personnel) have had to establish numerous workarounds in their work process, and essentially adjust the way they do business based on the configuration options available in the legacy software. As the call center operation grew, however, the system could not match the emerging business requirements without extensive customization. Changes to workflows, notifications, and data fields required an extended amount of time to complete. Additionally, the user interface did not have the necessary flexibility to accommodate emerging business rules, and call center staff required extensive training on the multiple steps needed to complete essential tasks.

The underlying case management model of the system did not match the more dynamic business model of the call center. It was necessary to develop a citizen relationship management system with an architecture that more dynamically reflects changes to the business model, and helps the call center operate more efficiently when providing information and services to constituents.

2.1 Domain

Citizen Relationship Management (CiRM) is based on the CRM (Customer Relationship Management) concept, except that there are no profit-oriented activities ([9]). A CiRM system is built to support services to citizens in a wide variety of areas, from requesting basic information, to paying bills, to picking up garbage, to the filling of potholes. A key aspect is reporting non-emergency problems, such as abandoned vehicles or stray animals on the street. These types of non-emergency issues are increasingly handled by city or county-wide call centers in the US, accessed through the 311 phone number. A CiRM is therefore more *case-centric*, with emphasis places on incidents, problem situations and discrete services rather than *customer-centric*, where the focus is on customers, their accounts and their preferences. In CiRM, the focal point of a business process is always a service case which once completed, is archived and accessed only for audit or reporting purposes.

2.2 General Requirements

A key requirement we have had to fullfill is the porting of current case models from the legacy vendor system to our new CiRM system. Another requirement is the integration with applications by other agencies. Frequently there is overlap in functionality with such departmental systems, where both serve similar case management purposes. Enterprise requirements, however, dictate that the systems must be synchronized, and that data and transaction mapping needs to be performed between the two. Yet another critical requirement, particularly important for e-government is traceability/accountability. It is necessary to maintain detailed case histories both to satisfy public records laws, but also to improve customer service and conduct service trends analysis. An additional requirement was the ability to adjust case models at runtime-this is one of the crucial reasons for an MDD approach was adopted.

3   Platform Architecture

3.1   Overview

Due to lack of semantic web-based MDD tools, in the course of the system's
development effort we created a generic platform where most of the important
back-end components are not related to the CiRM domain per se. This project's
motivation in adopting MDD is to a large degree for the software to be model-
driven *at runtime*, in addition to the usual advantages of having an explicit
model and writing less code. Consequently, we write software that interpets our
OWL models rather generating code from them. This makes live modifications
possible which has tremendous benefits. The architecture outlined here pertains
to the platform with application-specific artifacts being plugged into the various
architectural components. A detailed architecture was developed following the
TOGAF process ([13]) with all relevant documents produced over a period of
several months. A basic outline is depicted in Figure 1.

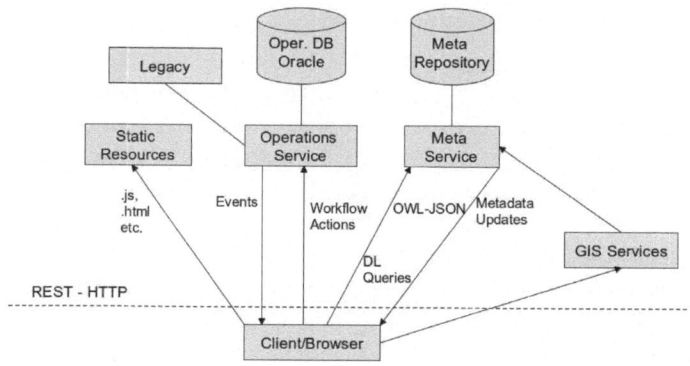

Fig. 1. Architecture Outline

According to the architecture, the divide between data and metadata leads to
two sets of services: operational services, handling operations data (e.g. actual
service cases) and meta services that handle purely metadata related functions
such streaming models, generating blueprints, generating UI components. The
meta services are the core the of architecture as this is were all models, including
application domain models and software component models, reside. Models (i.e.
ontologies) are persisted in a data store referred to as the *Metadata Repository*
or *metabase* for short. The *operations services* on the other hand manage data
in an Oracle RDBMS and handle integration with external/legacy systems. The
end-user application is based on the latest web technologies - HTML5, JavaScript
and related standards.

3.2   Meta Services

Instead of static code generation, we have opted to build the software around the idea of executable models. Both the problem domain and the solution domain are expressed in a formal model that is accessible and modifiable at runtime. The model is then interpreted at runtime by an execution engine comprised of several collaborating components. It is an OWL graph database with full versioning support at the axiom level[1]. Versioning at the axiom level means that change sets are defined in terms of additions and removals of logical OWL statements, which is the natural granularity for managing changes in OWL. There is one and only one metadata repository available for querying. Both server-side and client-side components consume metadata to perform their functions.

The meta services employ OWL description logic reasoning to answer queries using the convenient Manchester DL syntax. Any metadata is returned in JSON format. We employ an ad hoc JSON representation of OWL (there is no standard JSON serialization) that we have defined in due course. Our representation doesn't follow the axiomatic view of OWL. Rather it is more object centric (rather than "fact centric") - we serialize an individual and then all of its properties recursively.

The responsibility of the meta services is to manage all aspects of the model. Many administrative tasks amount to changing certain configurations or tuning a business process or case model, or to adjusting access authorization rules. All those activities are entirely within the realm of metadata management. Thus many modifications that traditionally would require restart of servers or even recompilation and redeployment are entirely handled at runtime. This is where we have found the true benefit of the MDD approach.

3.3   Operation Services

The operation services implement the management of business data and the enactment of business process workflows. Just like the meta services, some of the operation services are purely platform-oriented (i.e. domain-independent) while others are really specific to the application. What defines a service as being operations vs. meta oriented is the fact that it is manipulating concrete business data. The volume of data is much higher, and the data itself is repetitive following structural patterns (i.e. records) in the case of operations services. Alternatively, entities that configure application behavior in some way are not operational data. This, combined with our organization's investment in RDBMs and RDBMs-based reporting technology, led us to chose an Oracle cluster as the backing store. We note, however, that conceptually the line between operational data and metadata becomes fuzzy. In fact, the relational database holds OWL data just like the metabase - some of it in the form of triples, other under a classical relational schema via an ORM-like mapping between OWL and SQL. As with the meta services, historical information is preserved - every time an entity

---

[1] To be described in a future publication, available at http://sharegov.gov

is modified, its current version is time stamped and archived. The services are implemented in Java as a REST API with the application-specific ones isolated under a separate relative path. The API endpoints are referred as action points or workflow steps within the model which is how the model embeds business process behaviors.

3.4   Client-Side Components

Much of the application hand-coding was done using browser-based technologies - JavaScript, HTML/CSS. Because all server-side APIs are stateless and given the capabilities of modern browsers, the bulk of the logic of the application is implemented in JavaScript. We consider JavaScript to be a highly expressive, dynamic language that complements well our late bound use of the models. In fact, JavaScript code can be easily re-generated from a model at runtime, as an administrative task, without the need for compilation or re-deployment. Granted, we lose the benefits of statics checks. However, our development and deployment processes incorporate tests and the ability to rollback any deployment in case of discovered errors, until they are fixed. Serializing OWL ontologies, or a part thereof, in JSON already provides the structural portion of a JavaScript dynamic object, which is then complemented with additional functions.

Besides regular business logic, client-side components naturally implement UI interaction. Synthesis of UI interfaces is based on an association between UI components and certain high-level abstractions in the domain model. For instance items that are a list, are displayed with a table viewer. Things that are a string are edited with an input box. The model execution engine is capable of doing something sensible in terms of UI, given a business object. It will display a form to edit the object or show a list of its properties to view it, but the layout may not be appealing. To accomodate specifics, HTML templates are used. Such templates are stored in the model together with other software artifacts. Editing a UI template then becomes an administrative task rather than a development task and business users can be empowered to perform it.

4   Modeling with OWL

The flagship modeling language in the MDD world is arguably UML. However several factors, the least of which was a taste for adventure, tilted our decision towards OWL. In deciding on the OWL variant to use, we were not presented with much of a dilemma since the variant promoted and exlcusively supported by the most popular tool (Protege, [15]) is OWL 2.0, formerly known as OWL DL (Description Logic). The standard API for working with OWL in Java is the OWLAPI ([16]) which is also exclusively based on OWL 2.0.

4.1   Why OWL?

Admittedly, the choice of OWL as a modeling language for software development may seem unconventional. While there has been previous work in that direction, such work still ultimately targets the OMG MDA ecosystem and mindset. By contrast, our entire architecture is built around OWL, so let us summarize the key driving forces behind this decision, in increasing order of importance:

1. Open Linked Data - By using a SW standard for all our data and metadata, we are positioned to expose it in the context of the whole Semantic Web following the example of an increasing number of government agencies. There is no need for a contrived translation into logical form of a data structure shifting to meet frequent requirements changes.
2. Simplicity - Conceptually, the core of OWL is rather simple. It looks like a small subset of an object-oriented language. While Description Logic in its full power can be difficult to master, working with a handful of concepts like *individuals*, *classes* and *properties* is something well within the grasp of business analysts, especially if provided a foundation and some examples to imitate.
3. Inference - Unlike the core of UML, OWL is not an object-oriented modeling tool. It is in fact a logical language with logical semantics and reasoning capabilities not available in mainstream software modeling tools. As a result, OWL comes with inference capabilities and it supports Horn-style if-then rules, making it possible to express non-trivial business logic directly within the model itself. As an example, in UML one has to explicitly declare that a class is a subclass of another. In OWL this can be done as well, of course, but in addition one can ask the system to try and prove it as a consequence of other logical axioms.
4. Knowledge Engineering vs. Software Development - We have adopted an expert system philosophy of sorts where the application behavior is driven by a rich domain description rather than by a detailed software-only model. Our goal was to separate facts about the problem domain (*world ontology*) from facts about the solution domain (*software platform ontology*) from facts about the application itself (*application ontology*). As OWL is much less about *data structures* and much more about factual information, it was the better choice for this frame of mind. Moreover, OWL and its ecosystem are developed with the expectation that ontologies will be manipulated by end-user software in a pervasive way, unlike UML which is mainly for engineering tools that produce software artifacts.

Note that, in the last point above, the stated conceptual division of the ontological space does not align naturally with the different types of models in the standard MDA world, namely the CIM (computation independent model), PIM (platform independent model), PSM (platform specific model), see [2]. The CIM, PIM and PSM models correspond to the usual waterfall development steps of analysis, design and coding. All three revolve around the software artifact being produced. Even the most abstract and the most business-centric of the three, the CIM, is still about the target application. By contrast, our world ontology is both application and platform-agnostic. Our software platform ontology is also application-agnostic - it covers both concepts that come as part of UML, such as activities, state etc. and platform-specific concepts such as RDBMs notions, UI components and the like. Finally, only our application ontology, building on the previous two, is about the application and the model is expressed directly in terms of platform-specific entities.

The world ontology serves the dual purpose of formalizing knowledge about the organization, its function, the environment etc. on one hand, and as the basis for software on the other. Also, as noted above, OWL is used for both data and metadata which yields a very smooth transition from one to the other and makes it easier to create a more dynamic, live system. Business rules can be expressed in SWRL where rules that are exclusive to the model are left to an OWL reasoner to interpret while rules that apply to business objects are run through our own ad hoc inferencing. There are several aspects/dimensions to the model and for development purposes we employ different namespaces and different ontologies (i.e. modules), but the end result at runtime is a single big ontology with all the knowledge the application requires.

One key feature missing from OWL 2.0 are meta classes - it is impossible to describe ("talk about") a class. That is, one cannot assign a property to a class like one would to an instance (or an individual in OWL lingo). Also, it is possible to constrain the domain and range of a property, but one cannot make a property be a member of a class. For example, to specify that a property is required, one can use a logical statement saying that class C is a subclass of the class of individuals that all have that property.

Lack of meta classes poses difficulties in particular when modeling the solution domain since the software is described in terms of component types, how they relate to each other, what can be done with them etc. In other words, when modeling the solution domain we frequently have to create descriptions at the meta level as well. In OWL this limitation is overcome by relying on the fact that classes and individuals are disjoint logically, and therefore one is allowed to use the same name for both a class and an individual. So to talk about a class X, we simply declare an individual with the same name X. The reasoner knows nothing about the connection between the class X and the instance X, but this is not an issue as the platform execution engine does recognize that connection. This technique is called *punning* ([5]). It makes the creation of models more verbose due to such duplicate declarations. UML's meta-level is defined analogously to punning, however in OWL the important consequence is the indecidability of reasoning with meta-models and the need to tweak the semantics to make inference work ([8]) .

Finally, we note that UML is not actually directly comparable to OWL. More likely, it is comparable to OWL together with a software-centric *upper ontology* as evidenced by core concepts such as activities, sequences, state etc.

4.2   Upper Ontologies

A common practice in the semantic web world when modeling a concrete domain is to find (or define) some very general conceptualization-an *upper ontology* and use it as a starting point. Such conceptualizations have been published and

Fig. 2. Ontology Snapshot

standardized ([10]), but every organization is free to do its own metaphysics. Because at our organization we already had developed such an upper ontology for another project (a semantic search application, where OWL was used for knowledge representation), that ontology was adopted. The top level classes are shown in Figure 2 (a).

There are few, if any, concrete software implications of this upper categorization of the world. It mainly serves as an abstraction aid to a modeler/developer. It also facilitates understanding, documentation, providing opportunities for integration with other in-house software that shares the same upper ontology. For example, now we are in a better position to integrate our online knowledge resources (semantic search) with the government services (CiRM) modeled in their full detail. And this is yet another aspect that sets our approach appart from conventional MDD. Only the relevant abstractions layers can be used as needed, without complete code generation from the whole model.

4.3   Domain Model

The domain (or world) model is an ontology that describes the problem domain in a software implementation neutral way. Among the aspects of the problem domain is the complete structure of the government organization, with useful information about each department such as phone numbers, office hours of various service points, the list of services it provides. Note that this information is a generally useful and searchable semantic knowledge base, ready to be published online. It is also part of our CiRM domain model used as runtime metadata.

However, the predominant type of business entity in the CiRM world is the service case. A service case is created based on a problem reported by a citizen. Different types of problems require the collection of different information, the engagement of different types of actors and a unique workflow. A given type of problem thus has its own *case model*. Much of the domain modeling revolves around creating and maintaing models of the various types of cases.

Each type of case is an OWL class, but also a (punned) OWL individual so that metadata about that class can be stated. The case type individual has properties describing (among others):

1. Questions that need to be answered to assess the situation (e.g. "approximately how far is the pothole from the sidewalk?")
2. The location of the case (e.g. street address or GIS xy coordinates)
3. The workflow for handling such a case until it is marked as *closed*

All case models also share a common set of attributes such as the location of the case, the date/time when it was opened, who opened it and current status. However because there's no notion of inheritance or subsumption between OWL individuals, and because case type metadata is associated with a punned individual, this commonality has to be handled in a special way by the execution engine. On the other hand, since data in the CiRM platform is represented as OWL ontologies too, the connection between the case model and the case occurrences is immediate and natural. There is no need to translate from one meta model to another (e.g. UML to Java), hence no mismatch is possible, no unnatural representations in the target language warranted.

4.4   Software Model

Software artifacts are modeled in OWL by treating the application software as a domain to be described like any other domain. Model elements range from top-level entities like `Software_Application` to simple name-value `ConfigParam` entities. Since the runtime representation of the domain model remains in OWL (no separate Java object model needed), and since we do not do code generation for back-end components, only those that must be dynamically found in some way are modeled, like SOAP and REST services or Java implementation classes that must be linked depending on the context. Nevertheless, some parts of our system are driven in an entirely generic way by the model. Figure 2 (b) depicts a sample from the software model portion of the ontology.

We mentioned above the synthesis of user interfaces. To achieve this, we have created a set of UI components as a client-side JavaScript library and we have described them in our ontology. Just like case models lead to JavaScript business objects, descriptions of the UI components are first JSON-serialized and then augmented behaviorally as browser-based UI components. A UI component can be as simple as an HTML template rendered contextually from some data, e.g. top-level UI components like a whole page. Or, it can be something with much richer functionality. For instance, a familiar type of component is the *data table* component for interacting with data in tabular format, with the ability to sort by column or filter out certain rows. We can create an OWL individual description of a data table with a particular configuration, associate it with an operational data query and plug it in, say, an HTML template. In other words, the software model contains concrete instantiations of software components, bound to the domain model and ready to be assembled for end use in addition to abstract descriptions of components types. This is possible because of our universal usage of OWL.

Another illustrative example of the benefits of the integration of domain and solution models within a single ontology repository is access control: notions such as business actions and access policies are part of the solution domain (as they pertain to application behavior) while a case type is part of the problem domain. But we can directly associate a case type with a set of access policies for the various actions available without ever leaving the world of our OWL repository. We can use Description Logic queries to find out what the access policies are. Furthermore, we can use SWRL if-then rules to automatically create access policies based on some properties of the resource being protected.

In general, the inferencing capabilities of OWL have proven to be a very powerful tool, but there are several practical limitations in addition to the lack of meta-modeling that we have had to deal with.

4.5   Problems with OWL

While the experience of using OWL as an MDD foundation has been overwelcomingly positive, it was not without roadblocks, mostly resulting from the relative immaturity of SW technologies:

- The main obstacle is the lack of solid, high performance reasoner[2] implementation. There is currently no reasoner that supports all possible inferences.
- Reasoners are not designed to work in a multi-threaded concurrent environment.
- No reasoner supports any sort of contextualized inferencing where a query is performed within the context of a set of extra assumptions/axioms. This would be valuable in reasoning with the operational data entities which, compared to the large meta ontology, are just small sets of axioms that could be assumed just for the context of a given reasoning task.
- Punning provides a workable solution for the lack of meta classes, but in order to express inheritence and other meta properties we would have to develop or adopt an ad hoc framework on top of OWL to recover the lost expressiveness of OWL Full (which has meta classes).
- OWL lacks some basic data structures such as arrays and lists which are difficult to express ([4]).
- Lack of MDD tooling means that some dependencies are harder to track. When an ontology entity is referred directly in code, those references can easily become invalid and undetected. Therefore, we have learned to keep such cases to a minimum. We simply consider this as part of the general drawback of dynamic languages vs. static compilation.

---

[2] This is how OWL inference engines are called.

– The fact the OWL is fist and foremost a mathematical logic language that just shares some of the notions behind object-oriented programming (without its constructs or semantics) has led occasionally to unexpected inference results or to overly verbose models. In particular, consequences of the Open World Assumption and Non-Unique Name Assumption ([17]) challenged the team.

The list is not exhaustive, but it covers the most unexpected problems faced in the course of the project. The technical issues related to reasoning over the models were the biggest hurdle. They were avoided either through aggressive caching or by hand-coding ad hoc inference procedures within the meta services.

5   Model Change Management and Operational Data – Two Implementation Highlights

In this section we present a few details about the implementation and our development process relevant to MDD.

5.1   Model Change Management

Following our guiding vision of a model-driven live system where the software is modified at runtime, we needed a reliable change management process and tools. Nearly all business aspects are represented in the model. There are virtually no configuration files, except for a few bootstraping parameters like the location of the metabase. Therefore, a lot of software changes amount to meta repository updates and a crucial aspect of the architecture is the ability to manage those updates just like source code updates within a version control system (VCS). The lack of a native VCS is a frequent problem with modeling tools since file-based versioning is too coarse grained and leads to merging problems due to the usually non-deterministic model serialization. But versioning is crucial to the agile development process we have put in place. Since models essentially compress information, changes are potentially high impact, hence the importance of the ability to go back in time .

As part of our platform development effort, we created a distributed versioning system similar to GIT, but for OWL and that is at the level of the language itself, rather then the textual representation. The units being tracked and versioned are the logical axioms of OWL. The implementation relies on a hypergraph database ([14]) which acts both as the VCS and the meta repository. A software model update is enacted as a push of an ontology changeset which triggers clearing of caches and updates of other runtime structures within the meta services. Rolling back an update triggers the exact same set of events to adjust the runtime state.

Model updates in this setup are akin to component deployments in a traditional architecture. We use Protege to work with the model via a plugin integrated to our infrastructure. The idealized model development process looks very much like a standard programming process:

1. Make model changes on local machine.
2. Push changeset to local development environment.
3. Test locally, then push same changes to test environment.
4. Potentially multiple team members push to test environment - changesets get automatically merged.
5. Check OWL consistency with reasoner, run application-specific test suite in the test environment.
6. Push from merged changeset from test to production.
7. Rollback last changeset from production in case of problems.

In cases where business users need to work with the model, but find it difficult to learn Protege and OWL, a simplified web-based UI was developed. However, model modifications through that UI go through the same change management process via the same VCS. A similar process is put in place for the static web resources. It would be easy to store those resources inside the model as well, but we have not done so due to lack of tool support. Finally, note that only updates to the Java-based core components, i.e. the server-side of the model execution engine, force an interruption of service, but such updates are much rarer.

5.2 Operational Data as Ontologies

We refer to top level entities in our operational data as *business objects*. Those are the enterprise entities that one finds in any enterprise framework and the things that we persist in our relational database. Even though they are stored in an RDBMs, our runtime system manipulates them as OWL ontologies. Each business object is represented as a small ontology following a few naming conventions enforced by the execution engine, such as its IRI[3] format and the presence of a top-level individual representing the entity. We refer to such ontologies as *business ontologies* or *BOs* for short. The typical BO type is of course the *ServiceCase*. Two notable aspects of our relational storage are: (1) the ability to store BOs in a generic way as sets of axioms or store them in a more efficient way by mapping a given BO type to an SQL table; and (2) the auto-versioning of all BOs, using the customary valid_from/valid_to timestamp mechanism. That is, a modification of a business entity creates a new version of that entity instead of overwriting the existing data. Previous data can be retrieved for auditing purposes.

As with metadata ontologies, BOs are manipulated mostly through their JSON representation which is object-like and very natural to programmers. As noted in section 3.4, JSON serialization is akin to code generation at runtime - when functions are merged into the JSON representation, we have a complete JavaScript object entity, dynamically synthesized from metadata and operational data, in the true spirit of MDD. To create a brand new entity, we use metadata information to construct a prototypical blueprint instead of existing operational data. In particular, a case model is also used as a prototype to construct a new

---

[3] International Resource Identifier.

case. This is more in tune with the object-based nature of JavaScript, as opposed to class-based nature of Java and other static languages traditionally the target of MDD.

Finally, note that the perennial problem of model evolution that entails changes to the structure of operational data is solved by matching versioned data with the appropriate versioned metadata. For instance, when a property is added or removed from a BO type, only newly created data will have the correct blueprint. Because of the auditing requirement, updating all existing data is not an option, regardless of whether it is feasible or not. So whenever the latest metadata is incompatible with some older BO (e.g. after a property removal), the meta repository has to be queried for the corresponding older version of the BO type with which to interpret the operational data. Only in case of updates of the BO is any synchronization triggered, the user alerted in case of merge conflicts or other inconsistencies and given the opportunity to manually correct them.

6 Conclusion

Some of the advantages of using OWL for MDD are the simplicity and universality of OWL. When metadata and data, domain and solution all share the same underlying formalism, many design problems are minimized or eliminated. When administrative tasks amount to adjustments of a live application model, many development tasks are dispensed with. On the other hand, we have experienced difficulties with the level of maturity of SW supporting tools, given the unorthodox use we made of them. We are hopeful that our practical experience has contributed to bridging the largely historical gap between the classical AI techniques of knowledge representation and the modern sofware engineering approach of model-driven development.

References

1. Watson, A.: A brief history of MDA. Upgrade, the European Journal for the Informatics Professional 9.2, 7–11 (2008)
2. Truyen, F.: The Fast Guide to Model Driven Architecture The Basics of Model Driven Architecture (January 2006),
   http://www.omg.org/mda/presentations.htm
3. Parreiras, F.S.: Semantic Web and Model-Driven Engineering, ISBN: 978-1-1180-0417-3
4. Drummond, N., Rector, A.L., Stevens, R., Moulton, G., Horridge, M., Wang, H., Seidenberg, J.: Putting OWL in Order: Patterns for Sequences in OWL. In: OWLED (2006)
5. Grau, B.C., Horrocks, I., Motik, B., Parsia, B., Patel-Schneider, P., Sattler, U.: OWL 2: The Next Step for OWL (2008)
6. Bertot, J.C., Jaeger, P.T., Grimes, J.M.: Using ICTs to create a culture of transparency: E-government and social media as openness and anticorruption tools for societies. Government Information Quarterly 27(3), 264–271 (2010)

7. Janssen, K.: The influence of the PSI directive on open government data: An overview of recent developments. Government Information Quarterly 28(4), 446–456 (2011)
8. Motik, B.: On the Properties of Metamodeling in OWL. Journal of Logic and Computation 17(4), 617–637
9. Schellong, A.: Citizen Relationship Management. Peter Lang Publishing, Brussels (2008)
10. Niles, I., Pease, A.: Towards a standard upper ontology. In: Proceedings of the International Conference on Formal Ontology in Information Systems (FOIS), 29 p. (2001)
11. Miller, E., Manola, F.: RDF Primer. W3C Recommendation (2004)
12. W3C OWL Working Group. OWL 2 Web Ontology Language Document Overview. W3C (2009)
13. Josey, A., Harrison, R., Homan, P., Rouse, M., van Sante, T., Turner, M., van der Merwe, P.: TOGAF Version 9.1 - A Pocket Guide, 1st edn. van Haren Publishing, Amersfoort (2011)
14. Iordanov, B.: HyperGraphDB: A Generalized Graph Database. In: Proceedings of the 2010 International Conference on Web-age Information Management (2010), http://www.hypergraphdb.org/docs/hypergraphdb.pdf
15. http://protege.stanford.edu/
16. http://owlapi.sourceforge.net/
17. Baader, F. (ed.): The description logic handbook: theory, implementation, and applications. Cambridge university press (2003)
18. Gaevi, D., Djuri, D., Devedi, V.: Model driven architecture and ontology development. Springer (2006)
19. Staab, S., Walter, T., Gröner, G., Parreiras, F.S.: Model driven engineering with ontology technologies. In: Aßmann, U., Bartho, A., Wende, C. (eds.) Reasoning Web. LNCS, vol. 6325, pp. 62–98. Springer, Heidelberg (2010)

Concern-Oriented Software Design

Omar Alam[1], Jörg Kienzle[1], and Gunter Mussbacher[2]

[1] School of Computer Science, McGill University, Montreal, Canada
Omar.Alam@mail.mcgill.ca, Joerg.Kienzle@mcgill.ca
[2] University of Ottawa, Ottawa, Canada
gunterm@eecs.uottawa.ca

Abstract. There exist many solutions to solve a given design problem, and it is difficult to capture the essence of a solution and make it reusable for future designs. Furthermore, many variations of a given solution may exist, and choosing the best alternative depends on application-specific high-level goals and non-functional requirements. This paper proposes Concern-Oriented Software Design, a modelling technique that focuses on concerns as units of reuse. A concern groups related models serving the same purpose, and provides three interfaces to facilitate reuse. The variation interface presents the design alternatives and their impact on non-functional requirements. The customization interface of the selected alternative details how to adapt the generic solution to a specific context. Finally, the usage interface specifies the provided behaviour. We illustrate our approach by presenting the concern models of variations of the *Observer* design pattern, which internally depends on the *Association* concern to link observers and subjects.

1 Introduction

In the early phases of software development, the requirements of the software to be built are elaborated. Typically, these requirements specify what functionality the application is supposed to provide, as well as the high-level goals the different stakeholders have and the qualities, i.e., non-functional requirements, they expect from the application. The software design phase then consists of coming up with a *good* software design that provides the specified functionality and satisfies the identified high-level goals.

What makes software design so difficult is that there are many ways to solve a specific design problem, each solution having advantages and disadvantages. The designer must carefully consider how each solution positively or negatively affects the stakeholders high-level goals and the non-functional properties of the application before making her choice. This typically requires a high level of expertise from the designer, as software design approaches currently provide only little support for trade-off analysis. Whereas many approaches provide mechanisms for reusing design (classes, components, patterns, frameworks), there are to the best of our knowledge no current approaches that provide the designer with insight on the commonalities and variations among different reusable design solutions to a given problem, and how those solutions impact high-level goals.

A. Moreira et al. (Eds.): MODELS 2013, LNCS 8107, pp. 604–621, 2013.

To overcome these limitations, this exploratory paper proposes *concern-oriented software design*. Section 2 reviews some existing units of software design reuse, and motivates the need for a broader unit that encompasses different design alternatives. Section 3 presents this unit – the *concern* – and it's most important interface – the *variation interface,* which describes the available design variations of the concern and their impact on high-level goals and qualities. Section 3.2 shows how we extended the *Reusable Aspect Models* approach to support concern-orientation, and 3.3 presents the example design concern *Association*. The concern reuse process with impact analysis of the chosen variants is described in 3.4. Section 4 highlights the need to support concern dependencies, section 5 briefly discusses related work and the last section concludes the paper.

2   Motivation

Software reuse is a powerful concept that originated in the sixties, and is defined as the process of creating new software using existing software artifacts. To make software reuse applicable, reusing an artifact should be easier than constructing it from scratch. This entails that the reusable artifacts are easy to understand, find, and apply [17]. There are characteristics of software artifacts that facilitate reuse, e.g., grouping, encapsulation, information hiding, and well-defined interfaces.

2.1   Units of Reuse

This subsection reviews some of the most popular units of reuse for software designs, and gives a very brief introduction to Reusable Aspect Models, the modelling approach we are using to illustrate concern-oriented software design.

Classes: Classes are the most common unit of reuse in the object-oriented world. They group related state and behaviour (attributes and operations), and allow to reuse these properties in different contexts. Classes can nicely encapsulate a "local" design solution, where design state and behaviour fits into one entity. They fail when the design behaviour crosscuts several application entities.

Components: Components are more coarse grained entities that package related functionalities behind well-defined interfaces. They are very popular in some application domains, e.g., web services, where dynamic configuration is desired. Whereas components are designed for reuse, they fail just like classes to encapsulate designs that crosscut the application architectural structure. Also, most component-based approaches do not provide information about how a component impacts non-functional application properties.

Design patterns: Design patterns [9] are abstract design descriptions of solutions to recurring design problems. They capture interactions between classes, and explain tradeoffs/impacts of the interaction pattern on high-level goals. However, design patterns are usually described informally in textual format or using incomplete UML diagrams or code examples that cannot be reused as such in an application design without substantial development effort.

Frameworks: Frameworks are software application platforms that are usually big in size and offer many features. Due to their size, they are usually difficult to

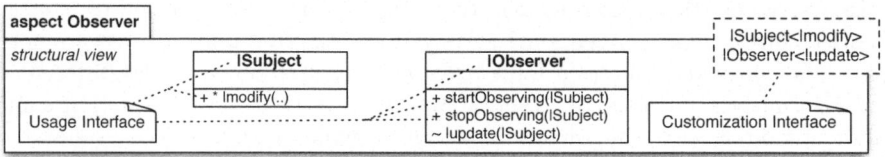

Fig. 1. Observer RAM Model Interface (Customization and Usage)

configure/customize for a specific need. Frameworks often define a limited set of extension points, and dictate the control flow of the application that uses them. This makes it hard to reuse several frameworks in the same application.

Software Product Lines (SPLs): SPLs [23] specify the variabilities and commonalities in a family of products and are an example of large-scale reuse. The focus, however, is on products and not on describing a generic, possibly crosscutting, concern which is applied to many products.

Reusable Aspect Models: Reusable Aspect Models (RAM) [16] is an aspect-oriented multi-view modelling approach for software design modelling. A RAM model consists of a UML package specifying the structure and the behaviour of a software design using class, sequence, and state diagrams.

Reusability is a key element in RAM. Each model has a well-defined *model interface* [2] (explained in more detail in the next subsection), which specifies how the design can be (re)used within other models. Having an explicit model interface makes it possible to apply proper information hiding principles [22] by concealing internal design details from the rest of the application. Thanks to aspect-oriented techniques, this is possible even if the encapsulated design details crosscut the rest of the application design. RAM also offers the modeller the possibility to create *model hierarchies*, which allows one RAM model to reuse the structure and behaviour of another RAM model within its design. Model composition techniques are used to flatten aspect hierarchies to create the final software design model.

2.2 Interfaces

Units of reuse such as the ones listed above typically either explicitly or implicitly define *interfaces* that detail *how* the unit is supposed to be reused. We classify these interfaces here into two kinds: *usage* and *customization interfaces*.

Usage Interface: *The usage interface* for units that are used in software design *specifies the design structure and behaviour that the unit provides* to the rest of the application. In other words, the usage interface presents an abstraction of the functionality encapsulated within the unit to the developer. It describes *how* the application can trigger the functionality provided by the unit.

For instance, for classes the usage interface is the set of all *public* class properties, i.e., the attributes and the operations that are visible and accessible from the outside. For components, the usage interface is the set of services that the component provides (i.e., the *provided interface*). For frameworks, design patterns, and SPLs, the usage interface is comprised of the usage interfaces of all the classes that the framework/pattern/SPL offers.

The *usage interface* of a RAM model is comprised of all the *public* model elements, i.e., the structural and behavioural properties that the classes within the design model expose to the outside. To illustrate this, the usage interface of the RAM design of the *Observer* design pattern is shown in Fig. 1. The *Observer* design pattern [9] is a software design pattern in which an object, called the *subject*, maintains a list of dependents, called *observers*. The functionality provided by the pattern is to make sure that, whenever the subject's state changes, all observers are notified. The structural view of the *Observer* RAM model specifies that there is a |Subject class that provides a public operation that modifies its state (|modify) that can be called by the rest of the application. In addition, the |Observer class provides two operations, namely startObserving and stopObserving, that allow the application to register/unregister an observer instance with a subject instance.

Customization Interface: Typically, a unit of reuse has been purposely created to be as general as possible so that it can be applied to many different contexts. As a result it is often necessary to tailor the general design to a specific application context. *The customization interface* of a reusable software design unit *specifies how to adapt the reusable unit to* the *specific needs* of the application under development.

For example, the customization interface of generic or template classes allows a developer to customize the class by instantiating it with application-specific types. For components, the customization interface is comprised of the set of services that the component expects from the rest of the application to function properly (i.e., the *required interface*). The developer can use this information at configuration time to plug in the appropriate application-specific services. The customization interface for frameworks and design patterns is often comprised of interfaces/abstract classes that the developer has to implement/subclass to adapt the framework to perform application-specific behaviour.

The *customization interface* of a RAM model specifies how a generic design model needs to be adapted to be used within a specific application. To increase reusability of models, a RAM modeller is encouraged to develop models that are as general as possible. As a result, many classes and methods of a RAM model are only partially defined. For classes, for example, it is possible to define them without constructors and to only define attributes relevant to the current design concern. Likewise, methods can be defined with empty or only partial behaviour specifications. The idea of the customization interface is to clearly highlight those model elements of the design that need to be completed/composed with application-specific model elements before a generic design can be used for a specific purpose. These model elements are called *mandatory instantiation parameters*, and are highlighted visually by prefixing the model element name with a |, and by exposing all model elements at the top right of the RAM model similar to UML template parameters. Fig. 1 shows that the customization interface for the *Observer* model comprises the class |Subject with a |modify operation, and the class |Observer class with an |update operation.

2.3 The Need for a Broader Unit of Reuse

Typically, there are many ways to solve a specific design problem, each solution having advantages and disadvantages. There are, for example, families of algorithms for achieving similar behaviour that have varying run-time resource requirements, and different ways of organizing information into data structures. The choice of data structures and algorithms has an effect on application performance and memory usage. The existence of a multitude of sorting algorithms, for example, shows clearly that there is no one good way of sorting. A more complex example is *transactions* [11], a design concept for fault tolerance that emerged in the database community. A transaction groups together a set of operations on data objects, ensuring atomicity, consistency, isolation, and durability of data updates. There are many ways of designing support for transactions, including pessimistic/optimistic and strict/semantic-based concurrency control, in-place/deferred update, and logical/physical and forward/backward recovery. Again, each technique has advantages and disadvantages.

Because of the multitude of possible designs, before a developer can focus on choosing a specific solution, she must carefully consider how each possible solution positively or negatively affects the stakeholders high-level goals and the non-functional properties of the application. This design decision is arguably the most important activity of the design process, and has a crucial impact on the quality of the entire application design. Ultimately it is the capability of choosing the most appropriate design that distinguishes a good designer from a bad one.

Unfortunately, none of the units of reuse discussed above makes this important design activity easy for the developer. Even if the unit is accompanied with documentation that describes the impact of the design solution, the documentation usually does not mention other alternative design solutions.

For example, a class typically only provides one solution to a specific problem. At best, the class comes with documentation that describes the impact of the encapsulated design. For example, the `ArrayList` class provided as part of the Java standard class library [10] implements a queue, i.e., a data structure that stores a sequence of elements and provides operations to insert and remove elements from the sequence, and iterate over the elements in the sequence. However, there is no support in Java to capture the impact of a class on the non-functional properties of an application that uses it. This is not a problem for an experienced Java developer, since she has probably used the class before. If not, other sources of information, i.e., the (textual) Java documentation or Java developer websites, need to be consulted to discover the impact of the class on non-functional application properties. Likewise, there are many ways to store a sequence of elements in Java, i.e., using the `CopyOnWriteArrayList` class, the `Vector` class, the `LinkedList` class, or simply a standard array. Each way has a different impact on performance and memory requirements. Again, there is no direct support in Java to capture this information. The only way to find this information is to assume that all classes that implement a sequence are located in the same Java package (`java.util` for `ArrayList`), and that they all implement the `List<E>` interface.

Similar arguments can be made for other units of reuse, i.e., components. The situation is different, however, for patterns, frameworks, and SPLs. A description of a design pattern, for example, is required to contain a *Consequences* section that contains a description of the results, side effects, and trade offs caused by using the pattern. There is also a *Related Patterns* section, which mentions other patterns that have some relationship with the pattern that is being described and discusses the differences between this pattern and similar patterns. Unfortunately, these textual descriptions are very informal.

Sophisticated frameworks are often designed in such a way that they provide a variation of similar functionalities to the developer. Typically, the choices are presented to the developer in form of class hierarchies from which the developer can instantiate the class that fits her requirements best. Whereas the functional impact of the different options is usually explained well, the impact on non-functional application properties is rarely documented rigorously. As a result, using a framework in the most appropriate way for a specific application still requires considerable expertise.

SPLs inherently describe variations, and, consequently, SPL techniques are certainly applicable to some aspects of concern-oriented software design. The crucial difference is that SPLs are focused on producing a product instead of specifying a possibly crosscutting concern. SPLs typically lack rigorous interfaces that have been designed to support composition of crosscutting concerns, allowing many concerns to be combined for one product and a single concern to be applied to many products.

Based on the arguments presented in this section we suggest that in order for reuse to be maximally effective, a new, broader unit of reuse that encompasses all design solutions targeted at solving a design problem is needed. We call this new unit of reuse a *concern*. To make reuse simple and straightforward, a concern must provide an interface that clearly describes the different variations of the designs it encapsulates, as well as their impact on non-functional application properties. The following section presents how we envision such a *variation interface* to look like.

3   Reusable Software Design Concerns

In order to be able to show a concrete example of a variation interface, we introduce here a simple, low-level design concern called *Association*.

It happens very frequently in object-oriented designs that an object of class A needs to be associated with other objects of class B. This situation occurs so commonly that object-oriented modelling languages such as UML [20] have a graphical way of representing associations, namely with a line connecting class A and class B. At both ends of the line, multiplicities can be shown that specify for a given instance of A, how many instances of B can minimally and maximally be associated with it. Optionally, an association end can also be annotated as being {ordered}, or qualified using a key.

Implementing associations with multiplicity 0..1 or 1 is easy, since it simply requires the class A to store a reference to an instance of class B. Implementing

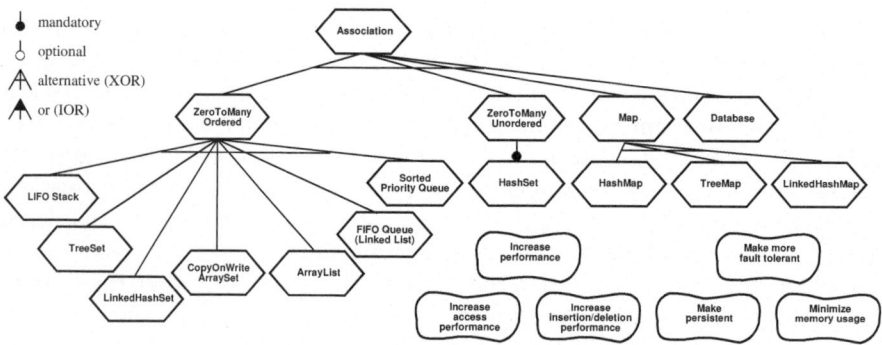

Fig. 2. Association Variation Interface

an association where the upper bound of the multiplicity is greater than 1, e.g., 0..*, can be done in many ways, and it is the job of a designer to determine the most appropriate way. Typically, the design has to introduce an intermediate collection data structure that stores the instances of B and refer to it from within class A. Operations need to be provided that add and remove instances of B from the collection contained in the object of class A.

What kind of collection to use depends on the functional requirements of the association. For example, an {ordered} association has to be designed with a collection that orders the elements it contains, e.g., a queue (FIFO), a stack (LIFO), or a priority queue (sorted using some criteria). A qualified association has to be designed with some sort of dictionary or map that allows to find objects by means of a key. But even for a given abstract data structure there are many different internal implementations possible. For example, a queue can be structured internally as an array or a linked list, the choice of which affects the algorithms for insertion, deletion, and iteration. This ultimately impacts the non-functional properties of the application, e.g., memory usage and performance.

In this section we will show how we envision a variation interface for the *Association* concern. We then present how we introduced concerns into RAM, show some detailed designs of associations with RAM, and how a developer can generate a model for a specific association design by selecting the desired variation from the variation interface.

3.1   Specifying a Variation Interface

As argued previously, the variation interface needs to capture the variations offered by a concern as well as the impact of a selection of variations on high-level goals such as non-functional application properties. Variations are best expressed at a high level of abstraction, where details of the variation can be ignored and the focus can be on the relationships among offered variations. Feature modelling and goal modelling have addressed these modelling requirements, and hence we make use of feature and goal modelling techniques in the specification of the variation interface. As an example, the variation interface for the *Association* concern is shown in Fig. 2.

Feature Models: Kang et al. [15] introduced feature models to capture the problem space of a software product line (SPL) [23]. In our context, a concern can be seen as a specific kind of SPL. A feature model captures the potential features of members of an SPL in a tree structure, containing those features that are common to all members and those that vary from one member to the next. A particular member is defined by selecting the desired features from the feature model, resulting in a feature model configuration [7]. A node in a feature model represents a feature of the SPL (e.g., *ZeroToManyOrdered* in Fig. 2). A set of inter-feature relationships allows to specify (i) mandatory and optional parent-child feature relationships, (ii) alternative (XOR) feature groups and (iii) or (IOR) feature groups (see legend in Fig. 2). A mandatory parent-child relationship specifies that the child is included in a feature model configuration if the parent is included. In an optional parent-child relationship, the child does not have to be included if the parent is included. Exactly one feature must be selected in an alternative (XOR) feature group if its parent feature is selected, while at least one feature must be selected in an or (IOR) feature group if its parent feature is selected. Often, *includes* and *excludes* integrity constraints are also specified, which cannot be captured with the tree structure of the feature model alone. An *includes* constraint ensures that one feature is included if another one is. An *excludes* constraint, on the other hand, specifies that one feature must not be selected if another one is. Note that integrity constraints are not required to express the variation interface of the *Association* concern.

Goal Models: Goal modelling is typically applied in early requirements engineering activities to capture stakeholder and business objectives, alternative ways of satisfying these objectives and the positive/negative impacts of these alternatives on various high-level goals and quality aspects. The analysis of goal models guides the decision-making process, which seeks to find the best suited alternative for a particular situation. These principles also apply in our context, where an impact model is a type of goal model that describes the advantages and disadvantages of features offered by a concern and gives an indication of the impact of a selection of features on high-level goals that are important to the user of the concern. Several different goal modelling techniques exist, e.g., i* [25], KAOS [8], GRL which is part of the User Requirements Notation (URN) standard [13], and the NFR framework [6]. Common concepts among these techniques are (i) stakeholders which are the holders of intentions, (ii) intentional elements, i.e., goals which stakeholders want to achieve (e.g., *Make more fault tolerant* in Fig. 2) and tasks which represent alternative ways of achieving the goals (e.g., *ZeroToManyOrdered* in Fig. 2) and (iii) a set of links between intentional elements including contributions (positive/negative impact of one intentional element on another; see Fig. 3 for examples of positive contributions), AND/OR/XOR decompositions and dependencies. In GRL goal modelling, the concept of strategy refers to a selection of intentional elements (typically tasks) with initial satisfaction values. When the goal model is evaluated, these initial values are propagated in the goal model using the links and weights associated with the links, leading to an assessment of the high-level goals in the goal model.

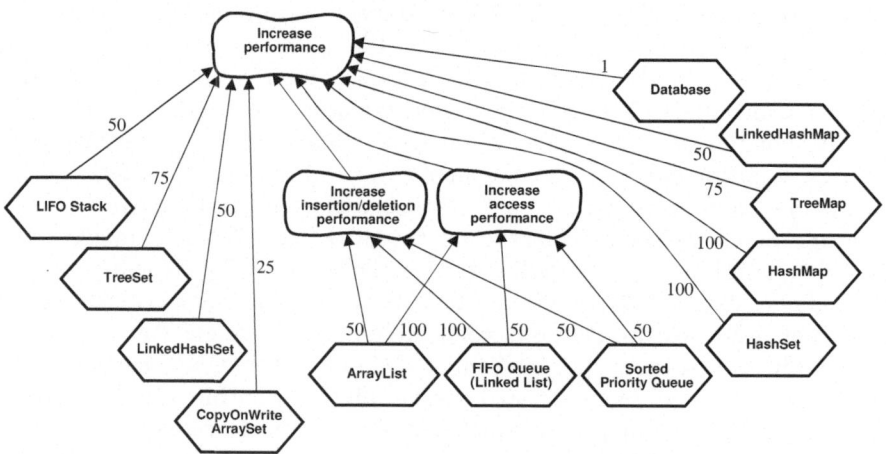

Fig. 3. Impact Model for Performance for the Association Concern

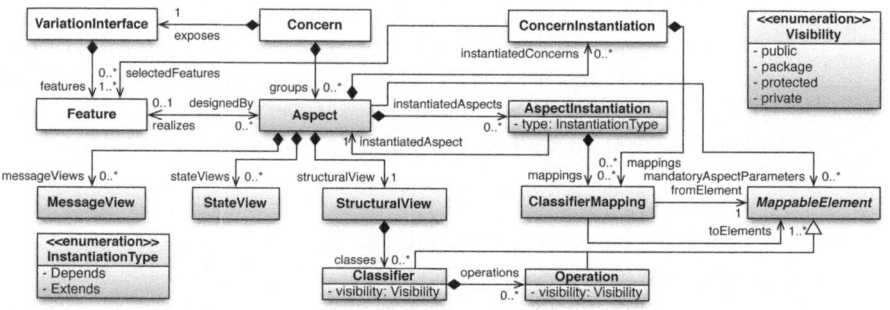

Fig. 4. The Concern-Oriented RAM Metamodel

Various strategies may be compared with each other, enabling trade-off analysis and the discovery of the best suited alternative.

AoURN/SPL [19] is an aspect-oriented extension of URN that integrates feature models and aspect-oriented goal models to enable combined reasoning about feature configurations and impact on high-level goals. It is hence an ideal modelling notation to express variation interfaces for design concerns.

The impact model in Fig. 3 shows how the different features of *Association* impact performance. The impact model is an intrinsic part of the *Association* concern. Those features contributing 100 (e.g., *HashSet*) to the main goal of increasing performance are the best choice in terms of performance. All other features are worse in terms of performance relative to the features contributing 100, e.g., *TreeMap* (contributes 75) is less desirable in terms of performance than *HashSet*, but better than *LinkedHashSet* (contributes 50). *Database* is the worst choice with a contribution of only 1.

3.2   Integrating Concern-Oriented Reuse with RAM

This subsection describes how we integrated concerns and variation interfaces with RAM. The detailed design of an individual feature can be described within a RAM model. The variation interface for a concern is described using AoURN/SPL, and it is therefore not necessary to add this capability to RAM itself. However, the RAM models that specify the detailed design of each variation of a concern must be packaged together with the variation interface, and a mapping between RAM models and the concern features that they implement must be specified.

Fig. 4 shows the updated RAM metamodel supporting concern-oriented reuse. The old metamodel entities are depicted in light grey, whereas the new entities are shown in white. The old entities specify that an aspect is composed of a structural view, message views, and state views. The *mandatoryAspectParameters* designate all elements that are part of the customization interface of the aspect, and the classifiers and operations contained in the structural view that have *public* visibility constitute the aspect's usage interface. The *Concern* is added as a new root model element that groups together one or more aspects. The concern exposes a *VariationInterface*, which defines a set of *Features*. Each feature is associated with the RAM aspects that specify its design, if any.

The concrete syntax of RAM has been adapted as a consequence. An aspect model must now specify the concern to which it belongs by declaring its name in the aspect header: `ConcernName.AspectName`. The mapping between a RAM model and the feature of the concern that it designs, if any, is specified in the aspect header using the keyword *realizes* followed by the name of the feature.

3.3   RAM Design of the Association Concern

This subsection presents parts of the detailed design of the *Association* concern using RAM, namely the RAM models *CommonDesign, Ordered,* and *ArrayList*.

CommonDesign: Fig. 5 shows the *CommonDesign* RAM aspect that encapsulates the structure and behaviour shared by all design variations of the *Association* concern. It provides three partial classes: |Data, |Collection, and |Associated. |Data is the class of the object that is to be associated with potentially many instances of the class |Associated. |Collection is some kind of collection that is contained within |Data that aggregates many |Associated objects. The class |Data defines two public methods: |forwardingMethod and getAssociated. As shown in the corresponding message view, |forwardingMethod forwards any received calls to |targetMethod in |Collection. getAssociated() provides access to the |Collection object contained in |Data. Finally, the initCollection message view specifies that whenever a constructor of |Data is invoked, a |Collection instance is also created and stored in the reference myCollection. The customization interface of *Association* exposes |Data, |Collection, |Associated as well as |forwardingMethod and |targetMethod, since these are the generic model elements that need to be made specific before the aspect can be used.

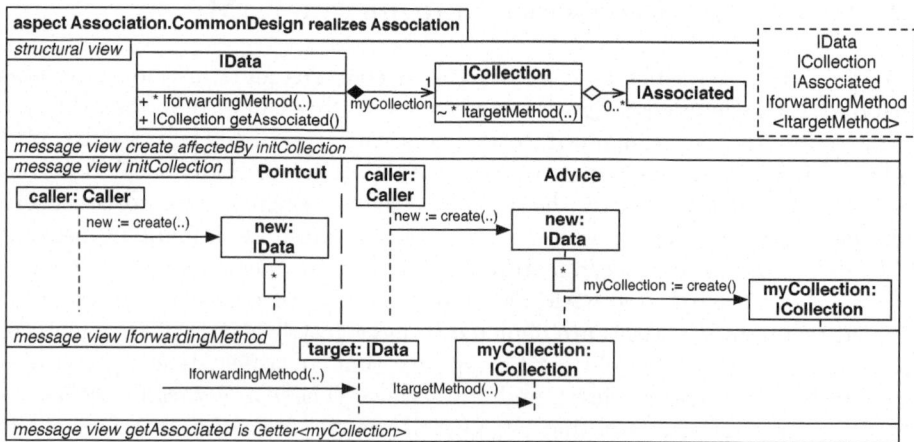

Fig. 5. The *CommonDesign* RAM Model of the *Association* Concern

Ordered: Fig. 6 shows the RAM model for ordered associations. It extends *CommonDesign*, and specifies that the |Collection is now a |Sequence. It completes the usage interface for |Data by adding all operations that are relevant for ordered associations, e.g., adding/removing elements to/from a specific position. The behaviour of these operations is to forward the call to the contained |Sequence class. This is achieved by instantiating the |forwardingMethod behaviour for each operation (see instantiation compartment).

Since *Ordered* has made the *CommonDesign* more concrete, the customization interface has shrunk: only the |Data and |Associated classes, and the implementation class |Sequence are still partial and need to be adapted further before the aspect can be used in a concrete application.

ArrayList: *ArrayList* (also shown in Fig. 6) is a very small aspect that simply specifies that the Java class ArrayList is supposed to be used as an implementation class for |Sequence. Now, only the |Data and |Associated classes are left in the customization interface.

3.4   Concern Reuse Process

The process of reusing a design concern is straightforward:

1. Use the variation interface of the concern to select the most appropriate feature, i.e., the feature that provides the desired functionality and maximizes positive impact on relevant non-functional application properties. This generates the detailed design for the selected feature of the concern.
2. Use the customization interface of the generated design to adapt the generic design elements to the application-specific context. This generates the application-specific usage interface for the selected feature of the concern.
3. Use the selected concern feature within the application design according to the usage interface.

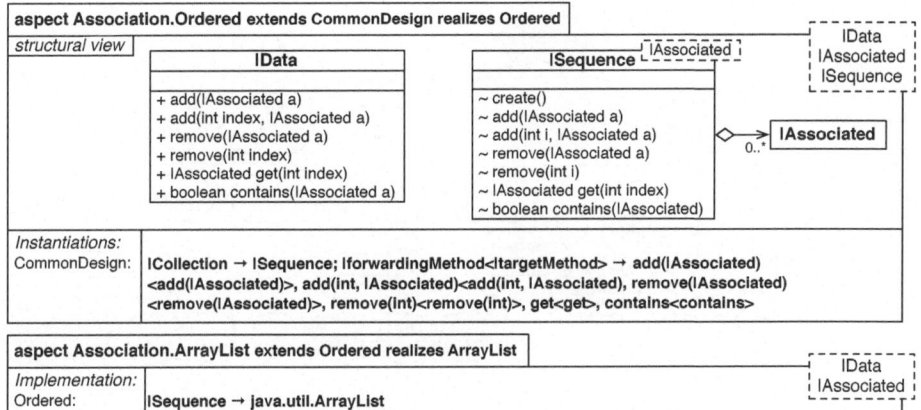

Fig. 6. The *Ordered* and *ArrayList* RAM Model

For instance, when reusing the *Association* concern, the developer looks at the available features (see Fig. 2) and determines functionality-wise that she needs an *ordered* association. The variation interface tells her that there are many possible design choices, ranging from *LIFO Stack* to *Sorted Priority Queue*. She then uses the impact analysis tool to evaluate the impact of the different choices on non-functional application properties. For example, Fig. 7 shows the impact of selecting the *ArrayList* feature. The initial satisfaction value for the selected feature is set to the maximum of 100, the others are set to 0. The evaluation mechanism [3] calculates satisfaction values for the high-level goals/non-functional application properties for which impact models have been defined. Many different evaluation mechanism exists [3] for goal models. They range from simple bottom-up evaluations that propagate satisfaction values towards the root(s) of the goal model to more sophisticated, constraint-based evaluation mechanisms that search the goal model for a set of leaf elements that satisfies desired satisfaction value(s) at the root(s) [18].

The evaluated feature and impact model in Fig. 7 shows that the configuration is valid, since the selection of *ArrayList* resulted in the root of the feature model to be positively evaluated with 100. An invalid feature configuration would result in the root feature to be evaluated with 0 [19]. In addition, the evaluation mechanism shows the impact of the feature configuration on several high level goals: access performance is maximized (100) and insertion/removal performance is average (50), which overall results in good performance (75). Memory usage is very good (80), but fault tolerance and persistence are minimal (1). A different feature selection would result in a different impact assessment. If a feature configuration is valid, then its assessment can be compared with those of other valid feature configurations to decide on the most suitable feature selection.

Once the developer decides to go with a choice, the RAM weaver assembles all RAM models that realize the selected features and combines them according to the instantiation directives specified within the models. In the case of the feature *ArrayList*, the RAM models *ArrayList*, *Ordered*, and *CommonDesign* are woven

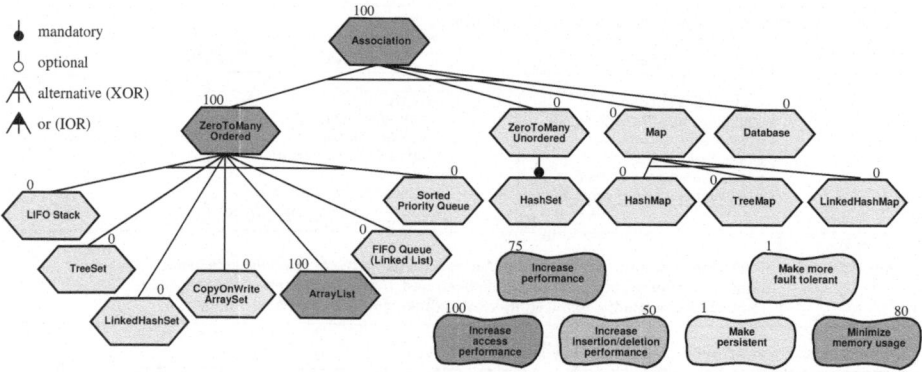

Fig. 7. Evaluation of the Feature Selection "ArrayList" for the Association Concern

together, thus generating a new RAM model that contains the detailed design for the chosen feature. The customization interface and usage interface of the resulting model are shown in Fig. 8.

The last thing that is left to do is to customize the generated design to the application. For example, the instantiation directive |Data → User; |Associated → Account; add → addAccount would associate the User class with multiple Account classes using an ArrayList, and allow the application to associate Account objects with a User by calling addAccount on a User.

4   Concerns Dependencies

The *Association* concern is an example of a low-level design concern. A real-world application typically contains many design concerns at different levels of abstraction and of varying complexity. Whereas many high-level concerns are application-specific, a great number are nevertheless of general nature, e.g., design concerns related to security (authentication, encryption, etc.), distribution (serialization, network communication, replication), graphical user interfaces (widgets, event handlers), etc. Internally, the designs of the features of such higher-level concerns require design infrastructure that again can be very general. For example, the *observer design pattern* introduced in section 2 is a general design technique that allows objects to register with some interesting data object and receive notifications whenever the state of the data object changes. Certain variants of graphical user interface designs use the observer design pattern to update graphical views whenever the visualized data changes. Likewise, certain variants of designs for replication use the observer design pattern to ensure that a state change executed on one replica is reflected on all other replicas.

Based on this observation we argue that in order for concern-oriented reuse to be effective, concern dependencies need to be supported. In other words, the realization of a feature of a concern can reuse other concerns within its design, thus creating a *concern hierarchy*. To this end, the feature realization selects the specific variant of the concern that is the most appropriate. If the most appropriate feature cannot be determined at the level of the current concern, then the

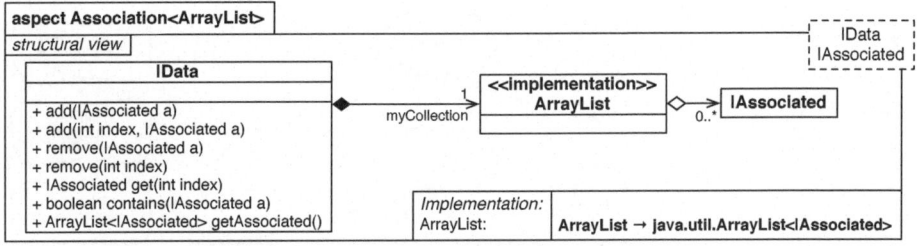

Fig. 8. Generated Detailed Design for the Association<ArrayList> Selection

set of possible features is selected, and as a result re-exposed as subfeatures of the feature of the current concern.

To support concern dependencies, we had to add another element to the RAM metamodel (Fig. 4). In addition to aspect instantiations, every aspect model now has a set of *ConcernInstantiations* (CI). A CI selects a set of features of an external concern, and specifies mappings of the elements in the customization interface of the generated design model to elements in the current model.

4.1 Observer Concern Design Using RAM

This subsection illustrates concern dependencies by means of the *Observer* concern. There exist many different designs of the observer pattern in the literature. For instance, the notification message sent to the observers when the state of the subject changes can include the modified state (*Push*), or no data at all, and hence it is the responsibility of the observer to query the subject to get the changes (*Pull*). *Push* reduces the number of messages exchanged, whereas *Pull* can reduce the amount of data that is transferred. Also, in a single threaded design, in the case where there are a significant number of observers or when update operations require lengthy computations, state updates on subjects are slow. In that case, a multi-threaded implementation that executes notifications concurrently is a good alternative design that increases the speed at which a change is executed. Finally, there is an extended design of the observer pattern called model-view-controller (MVC) that defines additional *Controller* objects that react to events and then request state changes on the subject (here called *Model*), which in turn notifies the observer of the change (here called *View*). MVC has again two possible design strategies – *Active* and *Passive* – which differ in the way the control flow passes through the related controller, model, and view objects. Fig. 9 shows the basic variation interface of the *Observer* concern.

Several of the RAM models that specify the detailed design of the features of the *Observer* concern need to associate classes with each other. For example, a subject is associated with observers, and views are associated with controllers. If we assume here that the order in which the observers are notified matters, the RAM model would therefore instantiate the *Association* concern as follows: `Association<Ordered>: |Data →` `|Subject; |Associated →` `|Observer; add → registerObserver;` etc. Which specific ordered association design from the seven available choices in *Association* is ultimately used is left

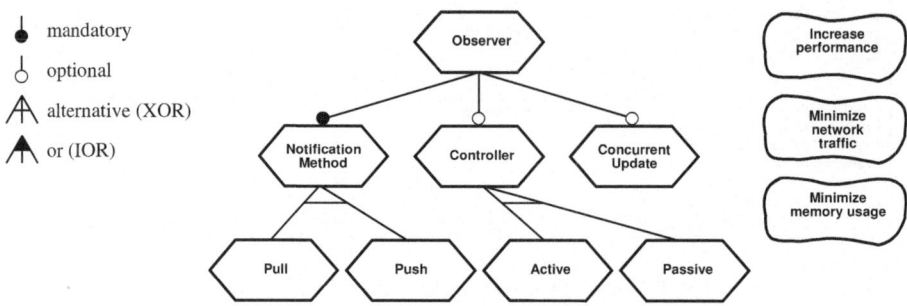

Fig. 9. The *Observer Concern* Variation Interface

unspecified. As a result, the choices are transferred to the variation interface of the *Observer* concern, so that the user of the *Observer* can choose the design that fits his application requirements best. In other words, another mandatory sub-feature of Observer called *OrderedObservers* is added to the variation interface of *Observer*; this new feature corresponds to the *ZeroToManyOrdered* feature of the *Association* concern and hence also has the same seven subfeatures.

5   Relation to Related Research

Reuse is the main focus in the context of software product line (SPL) develop-ment [24,5], and since software design concerns are very close to SPLs we intend to incorporate best practices from this field. However, reuse within an SPL is of limited scope, i.e., within the product line, and is not intended to cover generic concerns that are applicable to many products. Concern-orientation is about reuse in a broader sense, i.e., within contexts that are not envisioned when the concern is created. Concern dependencies – which translates to inter SPL depen-dencies – requires composition support for crosscutting concerns which has only recently attracted attention in the SPL community [4]. We argue that generic reuse of, e.g., Java libraries has a greater impact than product-specific reuse with SPL. The vision of concern-oriented development is to provide *generic* but coordinated reuse across all software development phases.

Because our RAM implementation of concern-oriented software design sup-ports modularization of crosscutting design concerns, it has similarities with ModelSoC [14], a MDE approach in which models of concerns are expressed in orthogonal views, and composed based on Reuseware [12], a generic frame-work to add modularization support to any modelling language. However, it is an abstract framework, it does not define model/concern interfaces, nor does it consider variability within a concern.

6   Conclusion and Outlook

This exploratory paper presents concerns, a new unit of reuse for software de-signs. A concern provides three interfaces – variation, customization, and usage interface – that describe a) the available design variations of the concern and the impact the different variants have on high-level goals, qualities, and non-functional requirements, b) how a given variant can be adapted to the needs of a specific application, and c) how the application can finally access the behaviour provided by the concern. Consequently, to reuse a concern, the developer must 1) select the feature with the best impact on relevant non-functional properties from the variation interface based on provided impact analysis, then 2) adapt the generated detailed design model to the application context by mapping the model elements from the customization interface to application-specific model elements, to finally 3) use the behaviour provided by the selected concern features through the usage interface. We outlined how concern dependencies enable the reuse of low-level design concerns within high-level ones, and how unresolved variations of the low-level concern are propagated into the variation interface of the high-level one.

Technically, we showed how we extended our own Reusable Aspect Models design modelling approach to support concern-oriented reuse, explained how the variation interface for concerns was modelled and evaluated using AoURN/SPL, and outlined how the RAM weaver generates the detailed design model based on the selected features. We illustrated our approach with the *Association* concern, and outlined how the *Association* concern is reused by the *Observer* concern.

In future work, we plan to more tightly couple the AoURN/SPL tool jUCM-Nav [21] and the RAM tool TouchRAM [1], so that feature configurations selected in jUCMNav are automatically communicated to the RAM weaver. Furthermore, we are investigating how to automate the generation of the combined variation interface of two concerns (e.g., when an aspect of one concern reuses features of another concern). We are also working on larger case studies involving transaction and security concerns, and plan to undertake controlled experiments with designers regarding the usability and cost-effectiveness of concern-oriented software design.

If adopted on a large scale, we believe that concern-orientation has the potential to revolutionize software design reuse. It enables the creation of standard design concern libraries. Vendors can sell design concerns that target specific domains. Developers can become specialists responsible for the maintenance and evolution of specific design concern libraries. Ultimately, libraries, reuse, and specialization would provide a clear structure to software development, and as a result align the practice of software engineering closer to what is done in other engineering disciplines.

References

1. Al Abed, W., Bonnet, V., Schöttle, M., Yildirim, E., Alam, O., Kienzle, J.: TouchRAM: A multitouch-enabled tool for aspect-oriented software design. In: Czarnecki, K., Hedin, G. (eds.) SLE 2012. LNCS, vol. 7745, pp. 275–285. Springer, Heidelberg (2013)
2. Al Abed, W., Kienzle, J.: Information Hiding and Aspect-Oriented Modeling. In: 14th Aspect-Oriented Modeling Workshop, Denver, CO, USA, pp. 1–6 (October 4, 2009)

3. Amyot, D., Ghanavati, S., Horkoff, J., Mussbacher, G., Peyton, L., Yu, E.S.K.: Evaluating goal models within the goal-oriented requirement language. International Journal of Intelligent Systems 25(8), 841–877 (2010)
4. Bošković, M., Mussbacher, G., Bagheri, E., Amyot, D., Gašević, D., Hatala, M.: Aspect-oriented feature models. In: Dingel, J., Solberg, A. (eds.) MODELS 2010. LNCS, vol. 6627, pp. 110–124. Springer, Heidelberg (2011)
5. Chen, L., Ali Babar, M.: A systematic review of evaluation of variability management approaches in software product lines. Information and Software Technology 53(4), 344–362 (2011)
6. Chung, L., Nixon, B.A., Yu, E., Mylopoulos, J.: Non-Functional Requirements in Software Engineering. Springer (2000)
7. Czarnecki, K., Helsen, S., Eisenecker, U.W.: Staged configuration through specialization and multilevel configuration of feature models. Software Process: Improvement and Practice 10(2), 143–169 (2005)
8. Dardenne, A., van Lamsweerde, A., Fickas, S.: Goal-directed requirements acquisition. Science of Computer Programming 20, 3–50 (1993)
9. Gamma, E., Helm, R., Johnson, R., Vlissides, J.: Design Patterns. Addison Wesley, Reading (1995)
10. Gosling, J., Joy, B., Steele, G., Bracha, G.: The Java Language Specification, 3rd edn. The Java Series. Addison-Wesley, Boston (2005)
11. Gray, J., Reuter, A.: Transaction Processing: Concepts and Techniques. Morgan Kaufmann Publishers, San Mateo (1993)
12. Henriksson, J., Johannes, J., Zschaler, S., Aßmann, U.: Reuseware - adding modularity to your language of choice. Journal of Object Technology 6(9), 127–146 (2007)
13. International Telecommunication Union (ITU-T): Recommendation Z.151 (10/12): User Requirements Notation (URN) - Language Definition (approved October 2012)
14. Johannes, J., Aßmann, U.: Concern-based (de)composition of model-driven software development processes. In: Petriu, D.C., Rouquette, N., Haugen, Ø. (eds.) MODELS 2010, Part II. LNCS, vol. 6395, pp. 47–62. Springer, Heidelberg (2010)
15. Kang, K., Cohen, S., Hess, J., Novak, W., Peterson, S.: Feature-oriented domain analysis (FODA) feasibility study. Tech. Rep. CMU/SEI-90-TR-21, Software Engineering Institute, Carnegie Mellon University (November 1990)
16. Kienzle, J., Al Abed, W., Klein, J.: Aspect-Oriented Multi-View Modeling. In: AOSD 2009, pp. 87–98. ACM Press (March 2009)
17. Krueger: Software reuse. CSURV: Computing Surveys 24 (1992)
18. Luo, H., Amyot, D.: Towards a declarative, constraint-oriented semantics with a generic evaluation algorithm for GRL. In: de Castro, J.B., Franch, X., Mylopoulos, J., Yu, E.S.K. (eds.) Proceedings of the 5th International i * Workshop 2011, Trento, Italy, August 28-29. CEUR Workshop Proceedings, vol. 766, pp. 26–31. CEUR-WS.org (2011)
19. Mussbacher, G., Araújo, J., Moreira, A., Amyot, D.: AoURN-based modeling and analysis of software product lines. Software Quality Journal 20(3-4), 645–687 (2012)
20. Object Management Group: Unified Modeling Language: Superstructure (v 2.4.1)
21. University of Ottawa: jUCMNav website (2013), http://softwareengineering.ca/jucmnav
22. Parnas, D.L.: On the criteria to be used in decomposing systems into modules. Communications of the Association of Computing Machinery 15(12), 1053–1058 (1972)

23. Pohl, K., Böckle, G., van der Linden, F.J.: Software Product Line Engineering: Foundations, Principles and Techniques. Springer-Verlag New York, Inc., Secaucus (2005)
24. Pohl, K., Metzger, A.: Variability management in software product line engineering. In: Proceedings of the 28th International Conference on Software Engineering (ICSE 2006), pp. 1049–1050. ACM (2006)
25. Yu, E.: Modelling strategic relationships for process reengineering. Ph.D. thesis, Department of Computer Science, University of Toronto (1995)

Analyzing Enterprise Models
Using Enterprise Architecture-Based Ontology

Sagar Sunkle, Vinay Kulkarni, and Suman Roychoudhury

Tata Research Development and Design Center
Tata Consultancy Services
54B, Industrial Estate, Hadapsar
Pune, 411013 India
{sagar.sunkle,vinay.vkulkarni,suman.roychoudhury}@tcs.com

Abstract. Development and maintenance of enterprise systems is becoming more difficult due to change drivers along multiple interconnected dimensions. It is advisable to model the enterprise first and analyze it for potential concerns. For modeling enterprises, ontologies have been considered apt and have been used in the past for the same, but application of ontologies for EA analysis based on concepts of enterprise and relations between them have been scarce. We present our ongoing work on analyzing enterprise models using EA-based ontological representation of enterprise. Our contributions are twofold: first, we show how an existing EA modeling language can be leveraged to create EA ontology and second, we show how two known EA analyses can be realized using this ontology. Initial results suggest that ontology representation facilitates basic EA analysis prototyping due to right mix of representation and inference functionalities and is extensible for more involved EA analyses.

Keywords: Ontology, Enterprise Models, Analysis, Enterprise Architecture.

1 Introduction

From our past experience in delivering 70+ large business-critical enterprise applications with model-driven [1–3] and also product line approaches [4,5], we have observed that enterprises are getting larger in size and becoming increasingly connected. They are evolving into complex *system-of-systems* that are characterized by high dynamics and glaring absence of a know-all oracle. The cost of incorrect decision in building these systems is becoming prohibitively high in spite of cost benefits brought about by abstraction and automation in model-driven [6] and product line-based development [4]. It is deemed prudent therefore to put more emphasis on understanding the target organization environment or in other words, modeling the whole enterprise and using this model to know more about the real enterprise [7, 8].

Apart from providing a coherent vision of the complex enterprise, it is possible to use enterprise models to conduct analyses that reveal how an enterprise is structured and how it behaves. For instance, change impact analysis [9] of EA deals with finding out ripple effects of a change to a concept based on the kind of relations it has with other concepts. Landscape mapping analysis [10] of EA deals with deriving relations

A. Moreira et al. (Eds.): MODELS 2013, LNCS 8107, pp. 622–638, 2013.

between unrelated concepts to get an estimate on mutual dependence of concepts. A proper modeling mechanism is needed that provides both core representation abilities to model an enterprise as well as reasoning abilities to conduct analyses on this model.

For this purpose, ontologies are considered as one of the most versatile mechanisms available. Enterprise ontologies have been used to find answers to common sense questions using deductive capabilities [11], as a communication medium [12] and for task management in enterprises [13]. Owing to the lesser maturity of ontology building and reasoning tools at the time, enterprise ontologies were restricted in their use to non-analysis purposes for models like shared representation of enterprise knowledge [14], semantic gel for integrating disparate set of modeling techniques and tools [13], and discovery of implicit facts in enterprise models [15] etc., with little or no focus on analyzing these models. In this paper, we detail an attempt to show how this can be achieved.

Our approach is to show that ontological representations can be leveraged effectively for modeling and analyzing enterprises. For this we create an EA ontology that is based on concepts and entities in ArchiMate [16] and model the well-known case study of post-merger of three insurance companies [17]. Our specific contribution is the demonstration of how the existing ontology tools can be used to perform EA analyses, particularly change impact analysis [9] and landscape mapping analysis [10] of EA with reference to concepts and relations in this case study using our EA ontology. The main components in our implementation are inference rule execution and exploitation of graph structure of ontology. Our initial implementation of these analyses suggests that ontologies and ontology tools provide the right mix of representation and reasoning abilities for modeling enterprises and quickly prototyping various interesting analyses.

The paper is structured as follows. Section 2 elaborates our motivation and outlines our approach. Section 3 describes our EA ontology based on ArchiMate concepts and relations and how we model the case study using this ontology. In Section 4, we detail two EA analyses, namely change impact analysis and landscape mapping analysis and present their implementation with ontology tools based on the model of the case study described in Section 3. We then discuss some pertinent issues and related work in Section 5 and Section 6 concludes the paper.

2   Motivation and Outline

While developing a number of enterprise applications in banking, insurance, and other domains, we found that for long, the underlying assumption with enterprise systems has been that requirements of IT systems are known a priori and they are unlikely to change drastically in foreseeable near future. Under this hypothesis, it was possible to encode knowledge about implementation of IT systems with models as high level specifications and generate platform-specific implementations. Yet recently we have observed that multiple change drivers are active along the business dimension with dynamic supply chains, mergers and acquisitions, globalization and regulatory compliances, etc.; along IT and infrastructure dimensions, we see changes brought about by cloud and mobile technology. In the presence of these change drivers, it is becoming imperative that business, IT, and infrastructure dimensions are treated holistically. Essentially, a model of enterprise should be used to make sense of entities individually and from the point of view of the entire enterprise [18].

Such a model of enterprise is generally created based on the principles of what is known as *enterprise architecture* (EA). It is defined as the process of translating business vision and strategy into effective enterprise change[1]; or the organizing logic for business process and IT infrastructure that can be targeted at a company's operating model to address its standardization and integration requirements[2]. We wanted to create model of enterprise as a computational representation of business, IT, and infrastructure dimensions and capture structural and behavioral aspects across these dimensions. This is illustrated on the left of Figure 1.

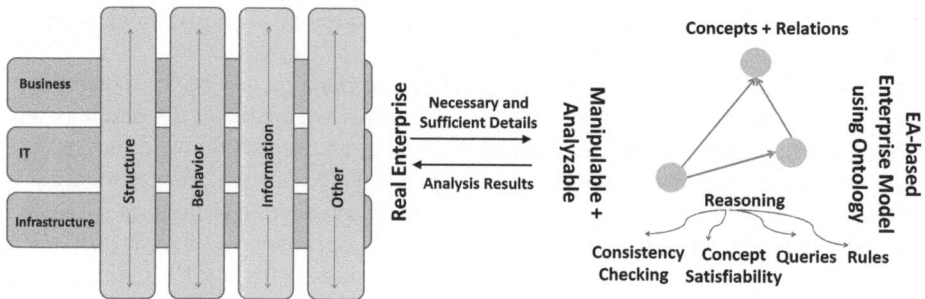

Fig. 1. Machine-processable and Analyzable Enterprise Models using Ontology [7]

As a first step in creating such an enterprise model we looked into EA frameworks which assist in the process of creating, maintaining, and leveraging architecture of an enterprise [19], for instance, Zachman Framework, the Open Group Architecture Framework (TOGAF), Federal Architecture Framework (FEA), Gartner, and ArchiMate. Our initial reviews of these frameworks suggested that irrespective of the architectural methodology used by these frameworks, architectural artifacts used in these frameworks are *documents used as reference material* and are *non-machine-processable* [8]. These frameworks lack self assessment mechanism, i.e., what is modeled cannot be checked for consistency but is correct by definition making them *blue-print* frameworks [20]. Experienced enterprise architects and other personnel are supposed to use their judgment in this regard.

In contrast, representing enterprise models using ontology provides both machine-processability and a number of reasoning services including consistency checking with specialized reasoners [21]. It is possible therefore to make application of EA frameworks and techniques more or less person-independent. These models could be used to conduct various analyses of the real enterprise that they capture and translate the results back to the real enterprise. This is shown on the right of Figure 1.

In the following section, we show how we use ArchiMate EA modeling language as the basis of our EA ontology.

---

[1] http://www.gartner.com/it-glossary/enterprise-architecture-ea/ Gartner IT Glossary.

[2] http://cisr.mit.edu/research/research-overview/classic-topics/ enterprise-architecture/ MIT Center for Information Systems Research.

3   EA Ontology

In this section, we show how our EA ontology is constructed and how Archisurance entities can be represented as individuals of this ontology.

3.1   Enterprise Metamodel

To create our enterprise ontology, we chose ArchiMate as the EA framework to refer to because its set of core concepts and relations provide good starting points for all that we intend to model in an enterprise. We mainly refer to the generic metamodel of ArchiMate. This generic metamodel is inspired from the *subject - verb - object* nature of natural language sentences [22]. Main concepts are active and passive structure concepts and behavior concepts. Interface and Service are structural and behavioral concepts respectively, but they are organized separately due to service-oriented roots of ArchiMate [16]. Note that in ArchiMate parlance what we referred to as dimensions is called layers and IT layer is referred to as Application layer. On the left of Figure 2, the generic EA metamodel of ArchiMate is illustrated.

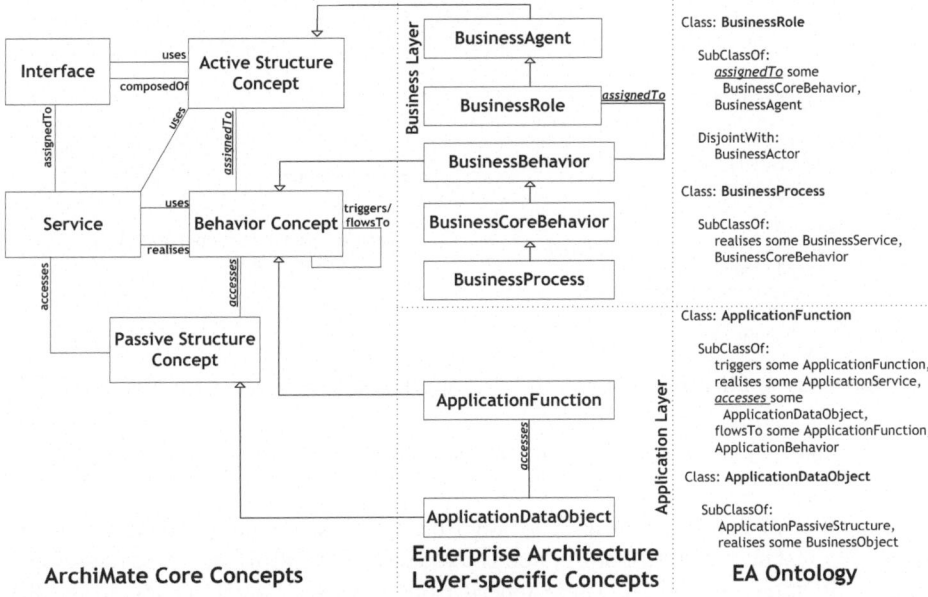

Fig. 2. Expressing Business and Application Layer Concepts in terms of ArchiMate Core Concepts

The relations between generic concepts reflect in each of business, application, and infrastructure layers. This is shown in the middle of Figure 2 with two example concepts each in business and application layers. An active structure concept is assignedTo a behavior concept. In the business layer, a BusinessRole is assignedTo a BusinessProcess. A behavior concept accesses a passive structure concept. In the application layer, an ApplicationFunction accesses an ApplicationDataObject.

A total of 9 structural relations including ones shown in the generic metamodel and other structural object-oriented relations such as specialization, aggregation, a very generic association relation, grouping relation for facilitating grouping of concepts are possible. Similarly, 3 behavioral relations are available including ones shown in the generic metamodel and junction relation used for modeling splits or joins of triggering or flow relations.

The core concepts and relations in the generic EA metamodel form the top level hierarchy in the EA ontology. Further distinction is made between business, application, and infrastructure layers and structural and behavioral concepts[3]. Concepts in a specific layer thus inherit from more generic concepts up the hierarchy. Thus an ApplicationFunction is subclass of ApplicationBehavior which is defined as a class that is equivalent to ApplicationLayer and Behavior. Other application layer concepts are similarly defined and then relations between them are defined as shown on the right of Figure 2. The some quantifier indicates one or more individuals. EA ontology concept definition are shown here using Manchester Syntax[4].

Class: **ApplicationService**

EquivalentTo:
  ApplicationLayer
  and Service

SubClassOf:
  accesses some *ApplicationDataObject*,
  usedBy some
    (ApplicationComponent
    or ApplicationFunction
    or **BusinessCoreBehavior**)

Class: **InfraArtifact**

SubClassOf:
  realises some **ApplicationDataObject**,
  InfraPassiveStructure

Business-Application Alignment   **Application-Infrastructure Alignment**

Fig. 3. Expressing Business-Application and Application-Infrastructure Alignment Concepts

A number of concepts are used to align business, application, and infrastructure layers. For instance, ApplicationService is usedBy BusinessProcess, BusinessFunction, or BusinessInteraction. These inherit from BusinessCoreBehavior. In the EA ontology, an ApplicationService is defined as shown on the left of Figure 3. Similarly, between application and infrastructure layers, an InfraArtifact realises an ApplicationDataObject. This is shown on the right of Figure 3.

---

[3] This distinction is useful in one of the two analyses described later in Section 4.2. Unlike distinctions in ArchiMate, other EA frameworks may represent a different notion of structure and behavior [23].

[4] http://www.w3.org/TR/owl2-manchester-syntax/ OWL 2 Web Ontology Language Manchester Syntax.

3.2   Case Study and Instantiated EA Ontology

Archisurance is an enterprise architecture and modeling case study referred to in [9, 16, 17, 24, 25]. It concerns a recent merger of three insurance companies dealing in homeowners' and travel insurance, auto insurance, and legal expense insurance formed to take advantage of synergies between three organizations. The new company offers all the insurance products of the previous companies and intends to adjust its offerings in response to changing market conditions. Like its constituents, Archisurance sells directly to customers via web, email, telephone, and postal mail channels.

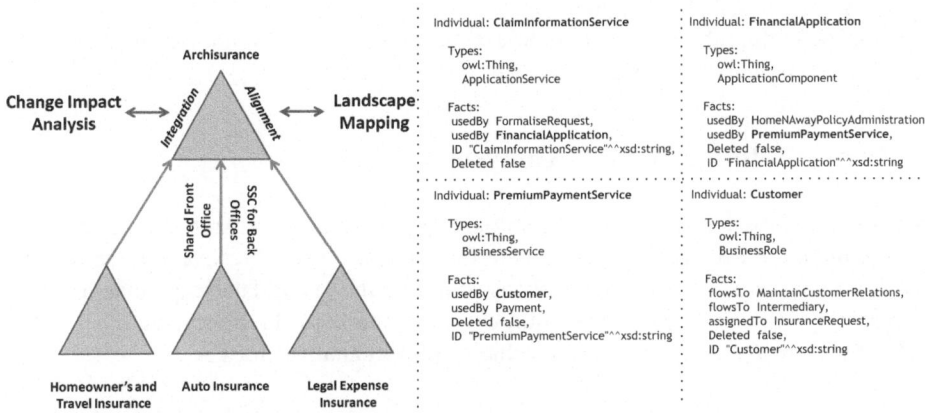

Fig. 4. Archisurance Case Study and Individuals Definitions using EA Ontology

After the merger, Archisurance has set up a shared front-office as a multi-channel contact center. A shared service center has been established to handle document processing at back-offices of the three previous companies. Key business functions of Archisurance include customer relations, claims, finance, and document processing among others. Main concerns in this merger are integration and alignment for the new companies' business processes and applications. Two EA analysis approaches could be used to address these issues to some extent. For instance, change impact analysis [9] can be conducted to find out how different entities in Archisurance affect each other due to new integration efforts and landscape mapping [10] can be used to help business and IT alignment efforts. This is illustrated on the left of Figure 4.

For these analyses, we created individuals representing Archisurance entities using our EA ontology concepts and relations. On the right of Figure 4, two business layer and application layer individuals capturing a small functionality of Archisurance are shown. An ApplicationService ClaimInformationService is usedBy FinancialApplication which is an ApplicationComponent. It is in turn usedBy a BusinessService called PremiumPaymentService which is usedBy a BusinessRole called Customer to obtain information about some claim. A total of 109 individuals are defined similarly to capture most of Archisurance case study from several resources [9, 16, 17, 24, 25].

Ontology Tools. We used the open source ontology editor Protégé[5] to build our EA ontology and to instantiate Archisurance model. While Protégé makes ontology building quite easy, when requiring programmatic access to manipulate the model properties or the ontology, it is better use an API. We use Apache Jena[6] for this purpose which is a semantic web application framework that provides an ontology API for handling ontologies specified in the web ontology language (OWL).

To programmatically invoke reasoner services, we use Pellet[7] API. Pellet is an OWL 2 reasoner that provides various reasoning services earlier shown in Figure 1.

For querying as well as executing rules over Archisurance model, we rely on SPARQL[8] which is a query language for resource description framework (RDF - Serialization format for OWL ontologies).

We show in the following section, how these ontology APIs come together to create EA analysis implementations.

4   Using Ontology for EA Analysis

In this section, we describe how the ontological representation of Archisurance detailed so far can be used to specify and execute EA analyses. Our objective is to show how two EA analyses, change impact analysis proposed in [9] and landscape map analysis proposed in [10], can be prototyped quickly using ontological representation[9].

In the following, we begin with the change impact analysis for EA.

4.1   Change Impact Analysis for EA

Change impact analysis for EA is concerned with computing the effects of change in any part of an enterprise on the rest of the enterprise [9]. For instance, changes in an enterprise's strategy can have multiple significant consequences in all three layers of an enterprise including business processes, organization structure, data management and technical infrastructure. First change may trigger changes that further trigger more changes creating a *ripple effect* in all of an enterprise. The basic use of change impact analysis is to find out what would happen if a change occurs before it actually happens. This is particularly relevant in the integration effort in Archisurance, as indicators of what can be integrated and what needs to remain same as before [7, 9].

The basic idea of change impact analysis in EA is centered around a set of heuristic rules based on the nature of relations that connect concepts. With regards to ArchiMate relations shown earlier in Figure 2, a number of heuristic rules are defined in [9], which

---

[5] http://protege.stanford.edu/ Protégé Ontology Editor.

[6] http://jena.apache.org/ Apache Jena.

[7] http://clarkparsia.com/pellet/features Pellet Reasoner.

[8] http://www.w3.org/TR/rdf-sparql-query/ SPARQL RDF Query Language.

[9] Formalization of these analyses based on description logics is not the focus of this paper. We rely on Pellet for soundness of inference rule execution [21] based on facts expressed in EA ontology. Formalization of landscape map analysis is provided in [24]. Change impact analysis in [9] is based on object-oriented change impact identification, formalization of which is presented in [26].

take the form of *'If there is a relation of kind X between concepts A and B, then when A is deleted/modified B needs to be deleted/modified/is going to be dangled.'*, where X is an ArchiMate relation. Changes to A may lead to changes in B. These changes may trigger further changes in concepts that B is related to and so on, creating a ripple effect. Table 1 shows the heuristic rules for various ArchiMate relations.

Except for the rules for composedOf relation, rules for the rest of the relations are specified as in [9]. We show in the next section how our ontological representation makes it easy to examine the ripple effect.

Table 1. Heuristic Rules Capturing Change in EA [7]

Relation X	When Concept A <X> Concept B	Notes
accesses	*A.Deleted >> #*	Generally, A is a behavioral concept accessing data object B
	A.Modified >> B.Modified	To maintain integrity of model, B *may* need to be modified
	B.Deleted >> A.Dangled	Signal to enterprise architect to adjust model
	B.Modified >> A.Modified	The way A accesses B *may* need to be modified
assignedTo	*A.Deleted/Modified >> B.Dangled*	Deleting/modifying A may result in dangled B, for which enterprise
	B.Deleted >> A.Modified	architect needs to be signaled
	B.Modified >> A.Modified	
usedBy	*A.Deleted >> B.Dangled*	B is generally declared to the environment. If A is deleted, B cannot use
	A.Modified >> B.Modified	it anymore; A should be replaced by something that will satisfy B's
	B.Deleted >> #	requirement
	B.Modified >> A.Modified	
realises	***A.Deleted >> B.Deleted***	B is generally a logical entity while a concrete entity A realizes it
	A.Modified >> B.Modified	
	B.Deleted >> #	
	B.Modified >> A.Modified	
triggers	*A.Modified/B.Modified >> #*	Since B starts *after* A, they are isolated and changes in either do not
	A.Deleted >> B.Dangled	affect the other
	B.Deleted >> #	If after deleting A, there is no trigger left for B, enterprise architect
		needs to be signaled
composedOf	***A.Deleted >> B.Deleted***	B cannot exist without A
	A.Modified >> B.Modified	A's modification may need modifying B; similarly change in B may
	B.Deleted >> A.Modified	require change in A
	B.Modified >> A.Modified	

>> - Implies, # - Don't Care

EA Change Impact Analysis with Ontology. A rule can be specified in SPARQL using the CONSTRUCT query form. CONSTRUCT generates new facts based on existing facts that match patterns specified in the WHERE clause. The facts generated by CONSTRUCT are nevertheless not updated in the base ontology. For this we can use the INSERT query form.

Listing 1.1. INSERTQuery Form for composedOf relation in SPARQL

```
1  INSERT
2     { ?b :Deleted true . } # Then b is deleted as well.
3  WHERE
4     {
5     # If a is composed of b
6     ?a :composedOf ?b .
7     # and a is deleted
8     ?a :Deleted true .
9     };
```

Listing 1.1 shows that when a is composed of b and a is deleted, then so should be b. This SPARQL query is in *Terp* format which is a combination of Turtle and Manchester syntax for RDF serialization[10]. The WHERE clause specifies *if* part and CONSTRUCT clause specifies the *then* part of a rule. Unlike CONSTRUCT, INSERT actually updates the boolean datatype property *Deleted* to true. Note that similar to INSERT there is a query form called DELETE, but we do not want to delete anything from the underlying ontology, only indicate using a boolean flag that a concept is deleted.

Executing such rules over an ontology is achieved by loading the ontology (.owl file created, say in Protégé) as an Apache Jena ontology model via Pellet reasoner factory. If any inconsistencies are present in the ontology being used, they are reported immediately[11]. Then, a GraphStore is created with this model which acts as a container for graphs of triples to be updated in the underlying ontology. The INSERT rule for instance can then be executed over this ontology and the updated ontology is returned via updated GraphStore. When talking about updating ontology, we are referring only to individuals rather than classes. Only the model is updated, not the metamodel.

Implementation Results. To see the effect of executing such rules over the representation of entire enterprise, we refer the reader to Figure 5 which shows a snapshot of Archisurance with concepts that are related to the *ApplicationComponent* **HomeNAwayPolicyAdministration**. We wish to know what would happen if this concept is deleted. As shown in Table 1, deleting concepts leads to deleting concepts they are related to when relations are *realises* and *composedOf*. Deletion of a concept is treated as a trigger for a change ripple.

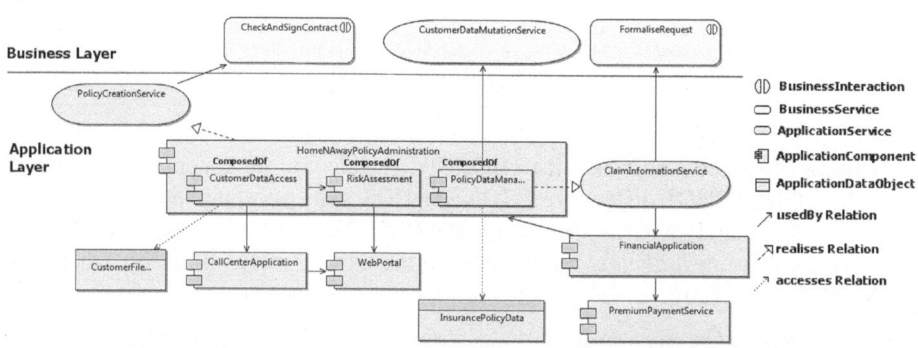

Fig. 5. A Snapshot of Business and Application Layer Concepts in Archisurance

To actually affect change ripples, we have to execute INSERT for all relations as enumerated in Table 1 in one iteration. The iterations continue, until no new nodes (concepts) in the GraphStore have their *Deleted* property updated to true. This is shown in

---

[10] www.w3.org/2007/02/turtle/primer/ Turtle Syntax for SPARQL.

[11] Note that versions of Protégé come equipped with various reasoners which can be used to correct inconsistencies while building the ontology itself.

Listing 1.2. All the *Update strings are essentially INSERT queries similar to Listing 1.1. Once the iterations stop, we get all nodes (concepts) that are deleted (i.e., need to be deleted) or have been dangled (i.e., are potentially dangling) due to deletion of **HomeNAwayPolicyAdministration**.

Upon executing, we find that concepts that are deleted are {**PolicyDataManagement, CustomerDataAccess, RiskAssessment, ClaimInformationService, PolicyCreationService**}. Similarly concepts whose relations could now be potentially dangling are {**FinancialApplication, CheckAndSignContract, WebPortal, CallCenterApplication, FormaliseRequest, CustomerDataMutationService**}. Note that effects of this deletion reach from the application layer to the business layer due to relations between affected concepts. Deletion of **HomeNAwayPolicyAdministration** results in making the relations of all business layer concepts shown in Figure 5 to be potentially dangling. Only the accesses relations to concepts {**CustomerFileData, InsurancePolicyData**} and usedBy relation to {**PremiumPaymentService**} remain unaffected.

It is possible in this way to represent effects of any change specified in Table 1. Since we do not actually delete a concept in the ontology, we do not have to order the updates. For instance, **RiskAssessment** application component is both deleted (because **HomeNAwayPolicyAdministration** is deleted) and dangled (because **CustomerDataAccess** is usedBy **RiskAssessment** and **CustomerDataAccess** is deleted because **HomeNAwayPolicyAdministration** is deleted). We simply indicate that both deletion and dangling is possible for the concept **RiskAssessment**.

Listing 1.2. Ripple Effect Computation due to Deletion of a Concept

```
1  public void affectRipples(String startConcept) {
2    ...
3    while (rippleOut){
4      UpdateAction.parseExecute(prefix + accessUpdate , graphStore) ;
5      UpdateAction.parseExecute(prefix + assignedToUpdate , graphStore) ;
6      UpdateAction.parseExecute(prefix + usedByUpdate , graphStore) ;
7      // also execute usedBy, realises, triggers, & composedOf over graphStore
8      ...
9      resultsNumNodes = com.clarkparsia.pellet.sparqldl.jena.
              SparqlDLExecutionFactory.
10       create(numNodesUpdated, model ).execSelect();
11       while (resultsNumNodes.hasNext()) {
12         QuerySolution row= resultsNumNodes.next();
13         RDFNode concept= row.get("updatedConcepts");
14         ... // Collect concepts that changed
15       }
16       ... // Continue until no new concepts change
17    }
18  }
```

With this implementation infrastructure, it is easily possible to see which concepts of a given kind in a given layer are most important and any change to these should be treated with care. It is also possible to go from a coarser level of changes (i.e., deletion or modification or concepts) to finer levels where value of a specific property changes for a given concept leading to similar changes in properties of other concepts. The point we want to stress is that with the ontological representation and rule execution, variants of change can be easily conceptualized and tested for impact analysis of EA.

4.2   Landscape Mapping Analysis for EA

Landscape mapping analysis of EA is basically concerned with providing non-technical stakeholders such as managers with a high level overview. Landscape maps can be used both visually and non-visually. Their most general use is in finding mutual dependence of three different kinds of entities in EA. For instance, to show which IT systems support operations of a company, a three-dimensional map could be imagined which captures the mutual dependence of business functions and business products of that company on application components [10].

It might be the case that kinds of entities of which mutual dependence is to be checked are not directly connected in the EA metamodel. For instance, while business functions and business products are connected by *assignedTo* relation in the meta-model, business products and application components are not directly related but there could be indirect relations between them. For instance, a business product may aggre-gate some business service which use application components (i.e., there is relation *usedBy* between application components and business services). The most important element of landscape map generation is therefore the derivation of indirect relationships between concepts of different kinds.

Components of EA Landscape Mapping Analysis. A composition operator has been defined in [24], that allows for composition of relations in any architecture de-scription language. This operator is also applicable to EA description language such as ArchiMate. The composition is essentially folding of intermediate relations between two concepts of kinds which are not related in the metamodel. This is illustrated in Figure 6.

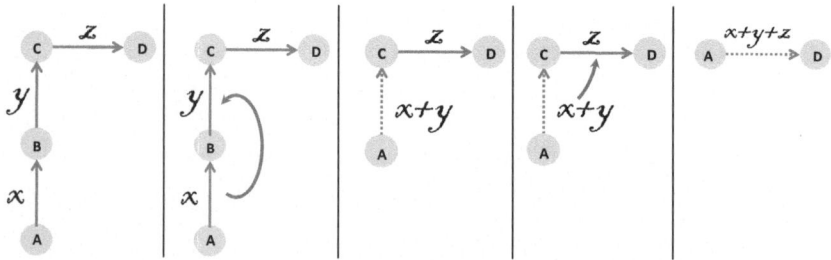

Fig. 6. Composition of Relations to Derive Indirect Relation between Concepts

Figure 6 shows that concepts A and D are related indirectly via concepts B and C. The + operator is the composition operator defined in [24] that specifies how two relations such x and y are supposed to be composed. In each succession, a two-step relation is derived such as x + y, until A and D are directly connected.

With regards to ArchiMate relations shown earlier in Figure 2, composition of each pair of these relations has been computed in [24], resulting in weight assignment for each of these relations as shown in Table 2. The composition is thus defined as the relation with minimum of weights of two relations. For instance, between *usedBy* and

Table 2. Weight Assignment to Relations for Composition [24]

Relation	Weight
associatedWith	1
accesses	2
usedBy	3
realises	4
assignedTo	5
aggregates	6
composedOf	7

realises, usedBy has lesser weight meaning that their composition leads to *usedBy* as the composed relation.

A landscape map is a mutual dependence of two kinds of concepts with the third kind of concept. When concepts of two different kinds are not directly related, composition operator can be used to derive a relationship. For instance, to find out mutual dependence of business services and business processes on application components, a landscape map could be defined as *'Set of application components C, given business processes P and business services S such that (1) C is* usedBy *P* ***and*** *(2) P* realises *S'*. In this case, while metamodel specifies *realises* relation between *BusinessProcess* and *BusinessService*, to find out whether *ApplicationComponent* and *BusinessProcess* are related by *usedBy* relation, we can use the composition operator.

EA Landscape Mapping Analysis with Ontology. There are two components to creating a landscape map. One component is executing rules of a landscape map (such as *'If C is* usedBy *P*, then-', seen in the previous section) while the other component is composing relations when concepts of two kinds are not directly related.

To compose relations between two concepts related indirectly, we need to find a path of relations. For instance, with respect to Figure 6, this path between concepts A and D is x - y - z, which we compose as pairs {x,y} and {{x,y},z}. In SPARQL parlance, this is tantamount to replacing chain of relations of arbitrary length with single relation for which it provides a mechanism called property paths[12]. An example of such a path encoding the rule of composition for **realises** relation based on weights in Table 2 is shown in Listing 1.3.

Listing 1.3. Property Path to Replace Chain Starting with realises Relation in SPARQL

```
1  INSERT
2      { ?a :realises ?d . } # Then replace the chain by realises relation
3  WHERE
4      {
5      # If between concept a and d, a chain starts with realises which is
6      # followed by one or more occurances of any of composedOf,
7      # aggregates, assignedT, or itself,
8      ?a :realises/(:composedOf|:aggregates|:assignedTo|:realises)+ ?d .
9      };
```

---

[12] http://www.w3.org/TR/sparql11-property-paths/ SPARQL Property Paths.

It is possible thus to use SPARQL property path queries to compute and replace paths of relations according to composition rules. Once a path is obtained, it can be very easily composed with the help of weights shown in Table 2.

Another important consideration is of the fact that all relations considered in Table 2 are structural relations as shown in Figure 2 earlier. For behavioral relations *triggers* and *flowsTo*, composition takes place in a different manner, rules for which are specified in ArchiMate specification 7.5[13]. For instance, if two concepts a and b are related to other concepts x and y via structural relations p and q respectively and x and y are related by a behavioral relation r, then a is related to b via r. The composition of chain of structural relations and chain of behavioral relations need to be distinguished from each other which becomes possible due to distinction made earlier between structural and behavioral concepts and relations in Section 3.1.

Implementation Results. Once relations are derived between concept of kinds that are unrelated to each other, rules of landscape maps can be executed similar to as shown in Section 4.1.

With the mechanisms of rule execution and composition specified earlier and path computation, we found the relation **usedBy** to be the most frequent derived relation considering purely structural relations. It was found between concepts of a number of pairs. Examples of these pairs include {**ApplicationComponent, BusinessActivity**}, {**ApplicationService, BusinessService**}, {**ApplicationService, BusinessActivity**}, {**ApplicationService, BusinessRole**}, {**ApplicationComponent, Business-Role**}, and {**InfraService, BusinessService**} with the model we created as individuals as described in Section 3.2. Note that these entities are not directly related in the EA metamodel. Landscape maps generally require deriving relations between concepts belonging to different layers that may be different from inter-layer relations specified in the metamodel.

We also computed landscape maps similar to one described in Section 4.2, i.e., between application components, business functions, and business services. These are not shown here for the want of space. Suffice it to say that with our infrastructure in place, it was quite easy to select any three ontology classes and check for individuals that satisfied the conditions of the landscape map. Also while checking three kinds of concepts is prevalent, it is possible to obtain mutual dependence of any number of kinds of concepts. Note that landscape maps are an ideal visualization mechanism for EA [10]. We only cover their computation using ontology in this paper.

5   Discussion and Related Work

In this section, we provide a brief review of work in ontological representations of enterprises while discussing some pertinent issues.

Further Change Impact Analysis in EA. Change impact analysis suggested in [9] essentially reduces change impact computation to change propagation defined over ArchiMate relations. There are two issues that need to be addressed. Firstly, apart

---

[13] http://pubs.opengroup.org/architecture/archimate2-doc/chap07.html Derived Dynamic Relationship in ArchiMate Specification- Section 7.5.

from key heuristics guiding change propagation, it is possible that some sort of decision making is involved when affecting change one way or the other. In an ongoing work [27,28], we take the stance that such decision making essentially captures *whys* of enterprise [29]. This is to say that response to any change in enterprise may take place in multiple alternative ways with explicit decisions as to which alternative is better from what perspective. This approach of change impact computation based on *intentions* differs from exemplified change impact analysis which gives semantics to specific set of relations. Change impact analysis with intentions is carried out with forward evaluation [30], which is similar in nature to change propagation. We have extended our EA ontology with intentional concepts and in the ongoing work; we are implementing forward evaluation over this ontology with mechanisms of concept and relation definitions and rule execution that we have demonstrated in this paper.

Secondly, giving semantics to specific relations (here to those in ArchiMate) means, that this analysis approach is not immediately usable if enterprise model is created using EA ontology that is based on some other EA framework or modeling language other than ArchiMate. Again, due to very generic nature of relations in ArchiMate, it might be possible to establish correspondence between kinds of relations in ArchiMate and other EA frameworks, but this is out of the scope of this paper. First steps toward this are suggested in [23].

Application to other EA Frameworks and Enterprise Models. Our message in this paper is that ontological representation of enterprise models is suitable for quick prototyping of EA-based analyses. We are actively applying the proposed EA ontology to case studies in our organization. For organizations already using other EA frameworks, it is possible to construct an ontology in a manner similar to one proposed here by using concepts and relations of given EA framework or modeling language and utilizing rich ecosystem of ontology tools. Enterprise models based on these EA frameworks can then be created in terms of collection of individuals representing actual enterprise entities and EA analyses can be executed over these.

Utility of Ontological Representation. Machine-processability comes naturally with standardized ontology representation. We also found that classification, contradictory fact checking, and concept satisfiability for inconsistency were quite helpful both when constructing the EA ontology as well as modeling the case study, as reasoners for OWL-DL, specifically Pellet support reasoning with individuals and user-defined datatypes [21]. All contradictory changes to both metamodel and model were immediately brought to notice which we corrected. This itself was considered as one of the most important benefits of ontological representation in major works in enterprise ontology [11–13].

It is natural to think that purely graph like representation of enterprise model with EA-based metamodel would suffice for EA analysis instead of using ontological representation. As a matter of fact, GraphStore used in Section 4.1 earlier is essentially a graph of triples that is updated with INSERT operation. The only shortcoming of purely graph-like representation seems to be reasoning support for integrity constraints, procedural rules, etc. [21]. Reasoning support for graph representation has been proposed [31], but lack of tools like Pellet reasoner for OWL-DL ontologies is a concern with purely graph representation of enterprise models. Further research for comparing different kinds of knowledge representation techniques for creating and analyzing enterprise models is needed.

Other Ontology Approaches for Enterprises. As seen previously, the focus in previous ontology approaches was not on EA analysis. These approaches targeted specific aspects of enterprises rather than taking a holistic view of it, for instance activities and resources [11, 14], tasks and workflows [13], organization [15], and strategy and marketing [12] etc., with key stress on views of enterprise models which are essentially stakeholder-specific projection of information. Our basic motivation for enterprise modeling is that point views are insufficient to tackle rising complexities. This is where EA frameworks come into play. While we based our ontology on EA framework and modeling language ArchiMate, it is equally possible to do the same using other frameworks as suggested earlier.

Applicability to other EA Analyses. A number of other analyses could be readily prototyped with our EA ontology such as EA data accuracy analysis that uses an abstract model of read/write relations between structural and behavioral concepts [32] and quantitative analysis of EA that uses attributes of both concepts and relations for quantification [33]. Analyses geared toward decision-making based on intentions mentioned in this section [29] and based on quantitative measures for chosen quality attributes of enterprise [34] use strategic dependency and rationale models and extended influence diagram-based models respectively on the top of enterprise concepts and relations. Testing applicability of our approach and extending it to take care of additional structures such as these is part of our ongoing work.

6   Conclusion

Apart from automation, models could be used to capture reality and understand it by analyzing these models. EA frameworks provide holistic treatment of enterprise systems but lack machine-processability, modeling assessment, and analyzability. Ontologies help in addressing these issues in general and we showed in this paper how current ontology tools can be utilized in concert to create machine-processable and analyzable enterprise models based on ArchiMate EA framework. We also showed that various existing EA analyses that are based on the nature of concepts and relations can be readily prototyped with this infrastructure. The same advantages can be obtained if EA ontology was based on any other EA framework. Our ultimate objective is to transfer the result of EA analyses back to the actual enterprise. This would require considerable human intervention and automating this to the maximum extent possible constitutes part of our ongoing work. Yet we believe that using ontologies to address these issues as shown in this paper takes a small step in that direction.

References

1. Kulkarni, V., Venkatesh, R., Reddy, S.: Generating Enterprise Applications from Models. In: Bruel, J.-M., Bellahsène, Z. (eds.) OOIS 2002. LNCS, vol. 2426, pp. 270–315. Springer, Heidelberg (2002)

2. Kulkarni, V., Reddy, S.: Introducing MDA in Large IT Consultancy Organization. In: APSEC, pp. 419–426. IEEE Computer Society (2006)
3. Kulkarni, V., Reddy, S., Rajbhoj, A.: Scaling Up Model Driven Engineering – Experience and Lessons Learnt. In: Petriu, D.C., Rouquette, N., Haugen, Ø. (eds.) MODELS 2010, Part II. LNCS, vol. 6395, pp. 331–345. Springer, Heidelberg (2010)
4. Kulkarni, V.: Raising Family is a Good Practice. In: Apel, S., Batory, D.S., Czarnecki, K., Heidenreich, F., Kästner, C., Nierstrasz, O. (eds.) FOSD, pp. 72–79. ACM (2010)
5. Kulkarni, V., Barat, S., Roychoudhury, S.: Towards Business Application Product Lines. In: [35], pp. 285–301
6. Sunkle, S., Kulkarni, V.: Cost Estimation For Model-driven Engineering. In: [35], pp. 659–675
7. Sunkle, S., Kulkarni, V., Roychoudhury, S.: Analyzable Enterprise Models Using Ontology. In: Deneckère, R., Proper, H.A. (eds.) CAiSE Forum. CEUR Workshop Proceedings, vol. 998, pp. 33–40. CEUR-WS.org (2013)
8. Kulkarni, V., Roychoudhury, S., Sunkle, S., Clark, T., Barn, B.: Modeling and Enterprises - The Past, the Present, and the Future. In: MODELSWARD 2013 (accepted, 2013)
9. de Boer, F.S., Bonsangue, M.M., Groenewegen, L., Stam, A., Stevens, S., van der Torre, L.W.N.: Change Impact Analysis Of Enterprise Architectures. In: Zhang, D., Khoshgoftaar, T.M., Shyu, M.L. (eds.) IRI, pp. 177–181. IEEE Systems, Man, and Cybernetics Society (2005)
10. van der Torre, L.W.N., Lankhorst, M.M., ter Doest, H., Campschroer, J.T.P., Arbab, F.: Landscape Maps for Enterprise Architectures. In: Martinez, F.H., Pohl, K. (eds.) CAiSE 2006. LNCS, vol. 4001, pp. 351–366. Springer, Heidelberg (2006)
11. Fox, M.S.: The TOVE Project Towards a Common-sense Model of the Enterprise. In: Belli, F., Radermacher, F.J. (eds.) IEA/AIE 1992. LNCS, vol. 604, pp. 25–34. Springer, Heidelberg (1992)
12. Uschold, M., King, M., House, R., Moralee, S., Zorgios, Y.: The Enterprise Ontology. The Knowledge Engineering Review 13, 31–89 (1998)
13. Fraser, J., Tate, A., Bridge, S.: The Enterprise Tool Set - An Open Enterprise Architecture (1995)
14. Gruninger, M., Fox, M.S.: An Activity Ontology for Enterprise Modelling (June 1994), http://www.eil.utoronto.ca/tove/active/active.html
15. Fox, M.S., Barbuceanu, M., Gruninger, M.: An Organisation Ontology For Enterprise Modelling: Preliminary Concepts For Linking Structure And Behaviour. In: Proceedings of the 4th Workshop on Enabling Technologies: Infrastructure for Collaborative Enterprises (WET-ICE 1995), p. 71. IEEE Computer Society, Washington, DC (1995)
16. Lankhorst, M.: Enterprise Architecture at Work: Modelling. Communication and Analysis. Springer (2005)
17. Jonkers, H., Lankhorst, M.M., van Buuren, R., Hoppenbrouwers, S., Bonsangue, M.M., van der Torre, L.W.N.: Concepts For Modeling Enterprise Architectures. Int. J. Cooperative Inf. Syst. 13(3), 257–287 (2004)
18. Kulkarni, V., Sunkle, S.: Next Wave of Servicing Enterprise IT Needs. In: IEEE Conference on Business Informatics, CBI (accepted, 2013)
19. IEEE: Recommended Practice for Architectural Description of Software-Intensive Systems. IEEE Std 1471-2000 (2000)
20. Wagter, R. (Erik) Proper, H.A., Witte, D.: A Practice-Based Framework for Enterprise Coherence. In: Proper, E., Gaaloul, K., Harmsen, F., Wrycza, S. (eds.) PRET 2012. LNBIP, vol. 120, pp. 77–95. Springer, Heidelberg (2012)
21. Sirin, E., Parsia, B., Grau, B.C., Kalyanpur, A., Katz, Y.: Pellet: A Practical OWL-DL Reasoner. Web Semant. 5(2), 51–53 (2007)

22. Haren, V., Publishing, V.H.: ArchiMate 2. 0 Specification. Van Haren Publishing Series. Bernan Assoc. (2012)
23. Berrisford, G., Lankhorst, M.: Using ArchiMate with an Architecture Method. Via Nova Architectura (June 2009)
24. van Buuren, R., Jonkers, H., Iacob, M.-E., Strating, P.: Composition of Relations in Enterprise Architecture Models. In: Ehrig, H., Engels, G., Parisi-Presicce, F., Rozenberg, G. (eds.) ICGT 2004. LNCS, vol. 3256, pp. 39–53. Springer, Heidelberg (2004)
25. Jonkers, H., Band, I., Quartel, D.: Archisurance Case Study. The Open Group Case Study (Document Number Y121) (January 2012)
26. Kung, D., Gao, J., Hsia, P., Wen, F., Toyoshima, Y., Chen, C.: Change Impact Identification in Object Oriented Software Maintenance. In: Proceedings of the International Conference on Software Maintenance, pp. 202–211 (September 1994)
27. Sunkle, S., Kulkarni, V., Roychoudhury, S.: Intentional Modeling for Problem Solving in Enterprise Architecture. In: Proceedings of International Conference on Enterprise Information Systems, ICEIS (accepted, 2013)
28. Sunkle, S., Roychoudhury, S., Kulkarni, V.: Using Intentional and System Dynamics Modeling to Address WHYs in Enterprise Architecture. In: International Conference on Software Engineering and Applications (ICSOFT-EA) (accepted, 2013)
29. Yu, E.S.K., Strohmaier, M., Deng, X.: Exploring Intentional Modeling and Analysis for Enterprise Architecture. In: Tenth IEEE International Enterprise Distributed Object Computing Conference (EDOC) Workshops, p. 32 (2006)
30. Horkoff, J., Yu, E.: Evaluating Goal Achievement in Enterprise Modeling – An Interactive Procedure and Experiences. In: Persson, A., Stirna, J. (eds.) PoEM 2009. LNBIP, vol. 39, pp. 145–160. Springer, Heidelberg (2009)
31. de Freitas, R.P., Veloso, P.A.S., Veloso, S.R.M., Viana, P.: Reasoning with Graphs. Electron. Notes Theor. Comput. Sci. 165, 201–212 (2006)
32. Närman, P., Johnson, P., Ekstedt, M., Chenine, M., König, J.: Enterprise Architecture Analysis for Data Accuracy Assessments. In: EDOC, pp. 24–33. IEEE Computer Society (2009)
33. Iacob, M., Jonkers, H.: Quantitative Analysis of Enterprise Architectures. In: Proceedings of the First International Conference on Interoperability of Enterprise Software and Applications, INTEROP-ESA (February 2005)
34. Johnson, P., Lagerström, R., Närman, P., Simonsson, M.: Enterprise Architecture Analysis With Extended Influence Diagrams. Information Systems Frontiers 9(2-3), 163–180 (2007)
35. France, R.B., Kazmeier, J., Breu, R., Atkinson, C. (eds.): MODELS 2012. LNCS, vol. 7590. Springer, Heidelberg (2012)

Analyzing the Effort of Composing Design Models of Large-Scale Software in Industrial Case Studies

Kleinner Farias[1], Alessandro Garcia[2], Jon Whittle[3], and Carlos Lucena[2]

[1] PIPCA, University of Vale do Rio dos Sinos (Unisinos), São Leopoldo, RS, Brazil
kleinnerfarias@unisinos.br
[2] OPUS Research Group/LES, Informatics Department, PUC-Rio, RJ, Brazil
{afgarcia,lucena}@inf.puc-rio.br
[3] School of Computing and Communications, Lancaster University, UK
whittle@comp.lancs.ac.uk

Abstract. The importance of model composition in model-centric software development is well recognized by researchers and practitioners. However, little is known about the critical factors influencing the effort that developers invest to combine design models, detect and resolve inconsistencies in practice. This paper, therefore, reports on five industrial case studies where the model composition was used to evolve and reconcile large-scale design models. These studies aim at: (1) gathering empirical evidence about the extent of composition effort when realizing different categories of changes, and (2) identifying and analyzing their influential factors. A series of 297 evolution scenarios was performed on the target systems, leading to more than 2 million compositions of model elements. Our findings suggest that: the inconsistency resolution effort is much higher than the upfront effort to apply the composition technique and detect inconsistencies; the developer's reputation significantly influences the resolution of conflicting changes; and the evolutions dominated by additions required less effort.

Keywords: Model composition effort, empirical studies, effort measurement.

1 Introduction

Model composition plays a central role in many software engineering activities, e.g. reconciling models developed in parallel by different development teams [11][18][33], and evolving models to add new features [14][15][32]. In collaborative software development [30], for example, separate development teams may concurrently work on a partial model of an overall design model to allow them to concentrate more effectively on parts of the model relevant to them. However, at some point, it is necessary to bring these models together to generate a "big picture" view of the overall design model. So, there has been a significant body of research into defining model composition techniques in the area of governance and management of enterprise design models [9], software configuration management [11], and the composition of software product lines [25][28].

A. Moreira et al. (Eds.): MODELS 2013, LNCS 8107, pp. 639–655, 2013.

Consequently, both academia and industry are increasingly concerned in developing effective techniques for composing design models (e.g. [3-8][10-17]). Unfortunately, both commercial and academic model composition techniques suffer from composition conflict problems [10][11][12]. That is, models to-be composed conflict with each other and developers are usually unable to deal with the conflicting changes. Hence, these conflicts may be transformed into inconsistencies in the output composed model [24][26].

The current composition techniques cannot automatically resolve these inconsistencies [24][27][29]. The reason is that the inconsistency resolution relies on an understanding of what the models actually mean. This semantic information is typically not included in any formal way in the design models. Consequently, developers must invest some effort to manually detect and resolve these inconsistencies. The problem is that high effort compromises the potential benefits of using model composition techniques, such as gains in productivity. To date, however, nothing has been done to *quantify* the composition effort and *characterize* the factors that can influence the developers' effort in practice. Hence, developers cannot adopt or assess model composition based on practical, evidence-based knowledge from experimental studies.

The goal of this paper, therefore, is to report on five industrial exploratory case studies that aimed at (1) providing empirical evidence about model composition effort, and (2) describing the influential factors that affected the developers' effort. These studies were performed in the context of using model composition to evolve design models of five large-scale software systems. During 56 weeks, 297 evolution scenarios were performed, leading to 2.288.393 compositions between modules, classes, interfaces, and their relationships. We draw the conclusions from quantitative and qualitative investigations including the use of metrics, interviews, and observational studies. We investigate the composition phenomena in their context, stressing the use of multiple sources of evidence, and making clear the boundary between the identified phenomenon and its context.

The remainder of the paper is organized as follows. Section 2 introduces the main concepts used throughout the paper. Section 3 presents the empirical methodology. Section 4 discusses the study results. Section 5 contrasts our study with related work. Finally, Section 6 presents some concluding remarks and future work.

2   Background

2.1   Model Composition Tasks and Effort

The term model composition refers to a set of activities that should be performed over two (or more) input models, M_A and M_B, in order to produce an output intended model, M_{AB}. M_A is the base model while M_B is the delta model that has the needed changes to transform M_A into M_{AB}. Developers use composition algorithms to produce M_{AB}. These algorithms are responsible for defining the model composition semantics. In practice, these algorithms are unable to generate M_{AB} in all cases due to some influential factors (Section 4.2). Consequently, an output composed model, M_{CM}, is produced instead of M_{AB}.

We use M_{CM} and M_{AB} to differentiate between the output composed model, which has inconsistencies and the model desired by developers, respectively. In practice, these models do not often match ($M_{CM} \neq M_{AB}$) because the input models, M_A and M_B, have some conflicting changes. However, usually it is not always possible to deal with all conflicts properly given the problem at hand [12][32][33]. The problem is that syntactic and semantic information should be considered, but they are rarely represented in a formal way. Rather, they are represented in natural language. Consequently, some conflicting changes are transformed into inconsistencies in M_{CM}.

With this in mind, the model composition effort can be defined, as the effort required to produce M_{AB} from M_A and M_B. Fig. 1 states the effort equation. The equation makes it explicit that the composition effort is based on the effort to perform three key composition tasks such as: (i) $f(M_A, M_B)$: the effort to apply a model composition technique; (ii) $diff(M_{CM}, M_{AB})$: the effort to detect inconsistencies in the composed model; (iii) $g(M_{CM})$: the effort to resolve inconsistencies i.e., the effort to transform M_{CM} into the intended model (M_{AB}). Note that if M_{CM} is equal to M_{AB}, then $diff(M_{CM}, M_{AB}) = 0$ and $g(M_{CM}) = 0$. Otherwise, $diff(M_{CM}, M_{AB}) > 0$ and $g(M_{CM}) > 0$. These variables are counted in minutes in our study.

Composition Effort: $f(M_A, M_B) + diff(M_{CM}, M_{AB}) + g(M_{CM})$

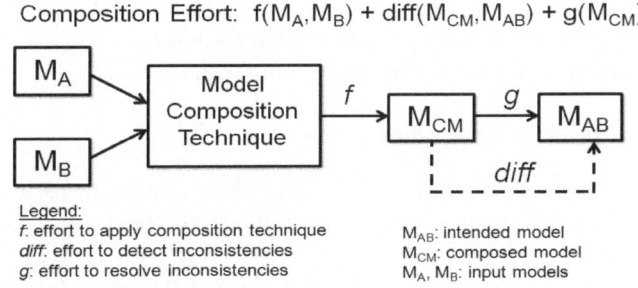

Legend:
f: effort to apply composition technique
diff: effort to detect inconsistencies
g: effort to resolve inconsistencies

M_{AB}: intended model
M_{CM}: composed model
M_A, M_B: input models

Fig. 1. Model composition effort: an equation

2.2   Composition Conflict and Inconsistency

Composition conflicts arise when contradicting values are assigned to model element's properties. Usually these contractions happen when teamwork members edit such properties in parallel and they are not aware of the changes. Two types of properties can be affected: *syntactic* and *semantic* properties. While the syntactic properties are defined in the modeling language's metamodel [36], the developers are ought to specify the (static and behavioral) semantic properties. Developers should determine which contradicting values assigned to these properties will remain. For example, a developer should define if a class A will be concrete (i.e. *A.isAbstarct* = false) or abstract (i.e. *A.isAbstarct* = true). The output intended class A will be produced, if and only if, this decision is done correctly; otherwise, the output composed class A will be inconsistent. In practical terms, these inconsistencies are unexpected values attributed to model element's properties e.g., A.isAbstract = false instead of the expected value true. Two broad categories of inconsistencies are usually present in output models of our study, namely syntactic and semantic inconsistencies.

Syntactic inconsistencies emerged when any output composed model elements did not conform to the rules defined in the modeling language's metamodel. For example, a package UML cannot have UML classes with the same name. Another example would be all relationship should have the client and supplier defined. Semantic inconsistencies emerged when the meaning of the composed model elements does not match with the meaning of the elements of the intended model. For instance, an inconsistency occurs when functionalities found in M_{CM} are not found in M_{AB}, or when model elements assume a meaning that is no longer expected or valid. The presence of both types of inconsistencies affects the correctness of the composed model.

3   Study Methodology

3.1   Objective and Research Questions

This study aims at gathering knowledge about the values that the composition effort's variables (Fig. 1) can assume in real-world settings. As these variables may be affected by some influential factors, this work also attempts to reveal and characterize these factors. With these aims in mind, we formulate two research questions:

- RQ1: What is the effort to compose design models?
- RQ2: What are the factors that affect composition effort?

3.2   Context and Case Studies

As previously mentioned, during 56 weeks, 297 evolution scenarios were performed leading to 2.288.393 compositions between modules, classes, interfaces, and relationships. All five cases differ in terms of their size, number of participants, and application domain. We present a brief description of the five systems used as follows:

1. *System AL (SysAL)*: controls and manages the importation and exportation of products.
2. *System Band (SysBand)*: a logistics system that manages the flow of goods.
3. *System GR (SysGR)*: supports weather forecast and controls environmental catastrophes.
4. *System Mar (SysMar)*: simulates the extraction of oil from deep ocean areas.
5. *System PR (SysPR)*: a logistics system for refineries.

They were chosen based on some reasons presented in the following. First, they are characterized as typical, revelatory [2], and encompassed UML class and sequence diagrams, use case specifications, architectural diagrams, glossary of domain terms, and business rules. Still, they are representative of complex software systems, which were initially unknown by the developers. This characterizes a typical situation where maintainers are not the initial developers of the system.

Second, the subjects used IBM Rational Software Architect (RSA) [16], a robust modeling tool to create and compose design models. The IBM RSA was used due to: (1) the implementation robustness of its composition algorithms; (2) the tight integration with the Eclipse IDE; and (3) the tool had been already adopted in previous successful projects. Additionally, all cases used a bug tracking system, i.e., JIRA [37], with which it was possible to coordinate the developers' tasks, specifically during the creation of the design models and review of the models.

Finally, industrial case studies avoid one of the main criticisms of case studies in software engineering regarding the degree of realism of the studies. Thus, we believe that the collected data are representative of developers with industrial skills.

3.3   Subjects

In total, 12 subjects were recruited based on convenience [2]. Table 1 describes the subjects' background. We analyzed the level of *theoretical knowledge* and practical experience of these subjects. The subjects had, on average, 120 hours of courses (lecture and laboratory) considering theoretical issues about software engineering, including object-oriented programming, software architecture, and software modeling using UML. This can be seen, in part, as an intensive UML-specific training. The subjects also had a considerable practical experience, which was acquired from previous software development projects. The data show that the subjects fulfil the requirements in terms of age, education, and experience. The knowledge and experience sharing help subjects solve the composition problems more properly. All subjects were familiar with IBM RSA. Therefore, we are confident that the subjects had the required training, theoretical knowledge and practical experience about model composition to get rid of any threat to the vitality of our findings.

Table 1. Descriptive statistics: subjects' background

Variables	Mean	SD	Min	25th	Med	75th	Max
Age	25.3	4.47	21	22	24.5	27	38
Degree	2.16	1.06	1	1	2	3	4
Graduation year	2006.4	4.8	1992	2005.25	2006.5	2010	2010
Years of study at university	5.75	2.8	3	3	5	7.5	12
YOEW UML	1	1.4	1	1.25	3	4.75	5
YOEW Java	4.5	1.84	2	2.5	4	6.75	7
Used IBM RSA (1 or 0)	1	1	1	1	1	1	1
YOEW software development	5	3.6	2	2.25	4.5	5.75	16
Hours of software modeling	98.33	40.38	60	60	90	120	180
Hours of OO programming	156.66	89	80	80	130	225	360
Hours of software design	130	53.85	80	80	120	190	220

Degree: 1 = Student, 2 = Bachelors, 3 = Masters, 4 = PhD, YOEW = Years of experience with, Med: Median, SD = Standard Deviation, 25th = lower quartile, 75th = upper quartile

3.4   Study Design

The study design is characterized as a *holistic case study* [1][2], where contemporary phenomena of model composition are studied as a whole in their real-life contexts. Five industrial case studies were performed to investigate RQ1 and RQ2. The subjects were *randomly* and *equally* distributed to the five studies, following a within-subjects design [1]. The study had a set of activities that were organized in three phases. In each study, the subjects used the IBM Rational Sofwtare Architect to create and combine the design models. Fig. 2 shows through an experimental process how the three phases were organized. The activities are further described as follows.

Firstly, the issues are created and submitted to JIRA, an issue tracking system. After opening an issue, the developers may perform three activities, including the creation of design models, detection and resolution of inconsistencies.

Training. All subjects received training to ensure they acquired the needed familiarity with the   model composition technique.

Apply Composition Technique. The models used in our study were UML class and sequence diagrams. Table 2 shows some metrics about the models used. The subjects create UML class and sequence diagrams using IBM RSA. Both diagrams were elaborated regarding the specifications of use cases and following the best modeling practices. Thus, the participants composed M_A and M_B taking into account the use case specifications. Note that M_B (delta model) represented the changes to be submitted to the repository. The measure of application effort (time in minutes) was collected during this activity. In addition, the composed model, video and audio records represent the outputs of this activity. The video and audio records were later used during the qualitative analyses (Section 4). It is important to point out that a participant (subject x) that produced an M_{CM} was discouraged from detecting inconsistencies in it to avoid bias; thus, another participant (subject n-x) was responsible for detecting and resolving the inconsistencies in M_{CM} in order to produce M_{AB}.

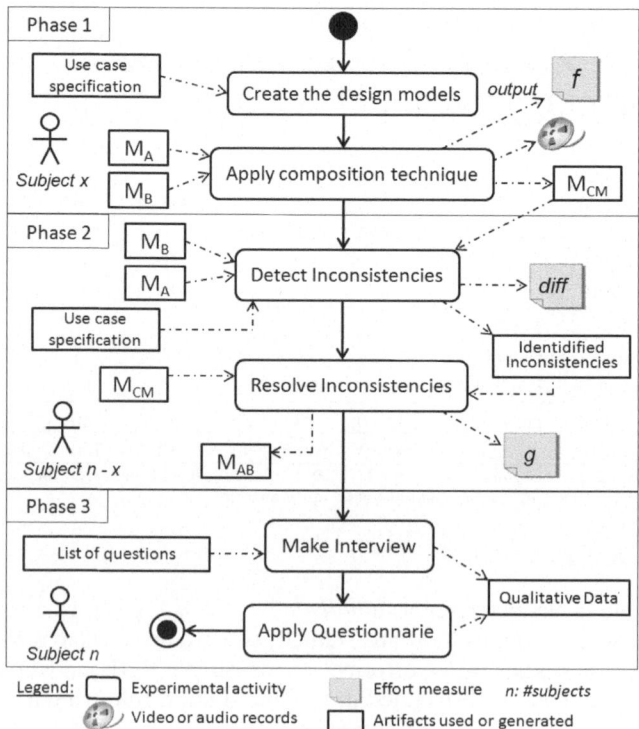

Fig. 2. The experimental process

Detect Inconsistencies. Subjects reviewed M_{CM} for detecting inconsistencies. To this end, they checked if M_{CM} had the changes described in the use case specification. They used the IBM RSA's model validation mechanism to identify syntactic inconsistencies. As a result of this activity, we have the measure of detection effort (time in minutes), and video and audio records.

Resolve Inconsistencies. The subjects resolved the inconsistencies localized in order to produce M_{AB}. In practical terms, they added, removed, or modified some existing model elements to solve them. The resolution effort was also measured (time in minutes) and the video and audios were recorded. After addressing the model inconsistencies, the developers submitted the intended model to the repository. Thus, the compositions were executed in two moments: after the original creation of the models and after resolving the inconsistencies. All model versions were registered using a version control system, thereby allowing a systematic historical analysis of the compositions, M_{CM}.

Make Interview and Answer Questionnaire. Some interviews were conducted with the purpose of collecting qualitative data. The subjects also filled out a questionnaire. These procedures allowed us to collect information about their background (i.e., their academic background and work experience) and apply some inquisitive questions.

Table 2. The collected measures of the design models used

Metrics	SysAL	SysBand	SysGR	SysMar	SysPR
#classes	316	892	1394	2828	1173
#attributes	1732	3349	8424	9689	3808
#operations	3479	7590	10608	23722	9111
#interfaces	18	83	143	223	93
#packages	34	166	175	345	187
#afferent coupling of the packages	278	1147	1632	4044	2329
#efferent coupling of the packages	235	996	1278	2723	1451
#abstractness of the packages.	9.58	50.45	36.9	66.5	51.9
#weeks	6	15	8	17	10
#developers	3	7	2	7	4
#evolutions scenarios	6	95	55	64	77

#: the number of or degree of all, Sys: system

4   Study Results

This section presents the study results about the composition effort variables (RQ1) and explains the factors that we found to influence the composition effort in our study (RQ2).

4.1   RQ1: Composition Effort Analysis

Application Effort. Table 3 shows a descriptive statistics about the application effort. The results indicate that effort to compose models was, on average, 3.17 minutes and 4.43 minutes in SysBand and SysMar projects, respectively. Given the complexity and the size of the design models in question, these central tendency measures are in fact low values. For example, a developer spent just around 4 minutes to submit the most complex evolving changes to the repository in the SysMar project. In addition, the median measures follow these trends: 3 minutes and 3.12 minutes into the SysBand and Marlin project, respectively. Thus, these measures imply *that the required effort to apply the semi-automated composition technique is low even for large-scale models*. Consequently, it is possible to advocate model composition as appropriate to support collaborative software modeling in which resources and time are usually tight.

In general, we observed that there was no significant variation on developers' application effort. *Developers' effort tends to be similar rather than spreading out over a large range of values*. There were a few exceptions as we are going to discuss below. With 1.55 and 1.58 minutes, the standard deviation measures indicate that in the majority of the model composition sessions the developers spent an effort near 3.17 minutes or 4.43 minutes. These results can help developers to better estimate the effort by establishing thresholds, and check if the effort spent by developers is an expected value (or not).

Table 3. Descriptive statistics for application effort

Cases	N	Mean	SD	Min	25th	Med	75th	Max
SysMar	40	4.73	4.52	0.25	2	3.2	6.79	22
SysBand	69	3.29	1.93	0.83	2	3	4	14.2

N = number of compositions, SD = standard deviation, Min = minimum,
25th = first quartile; Med = median, 75th: third quartile, Max: maximum.

Fig. 3 distributes the collected sample in six effort ranges. These ranges in the histogram systematically group the cases of application effort. The axis-y of the histogram represents the number of compositions, while the axis-x captures the ranges of effort. The main feature is that: *the presence of a distribution pattern of the application effort through the ranges of effort*. The three low-effort categories (i.e., t < 2, 2 ≤ t < 4, and 4 ≤ t < 6) represent the most likely ranges of effort that developers invest to compose the input models. The number of cases falling into these categories is equal to 29 (in SysMar) and 64 (in SysBand), representing 72.5% and 92.75% of the composition cases, respectively.

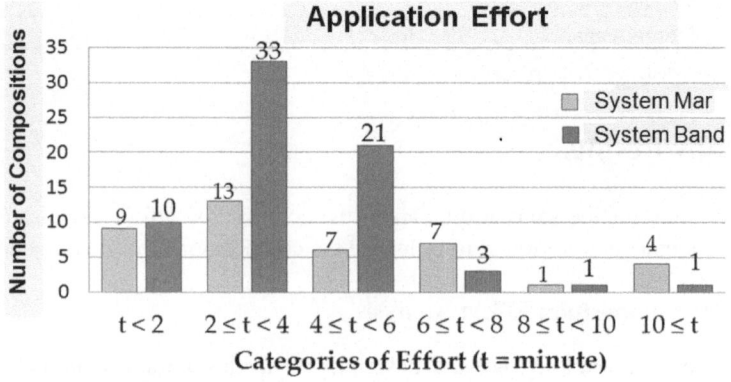

Fig. 3. Histogram of the application effort measures

On the other hand, the number of cases in the high-effort categories (i.e., $6 \leq t < 8$, $8 \leq t < 10$ and $10 \leq t$) is equal to 12 (in Marlin) and 5 (in SysBand), comprising 17.39 % and 12.5% of the cases respectively. The number of composition cases in the low-effort categories outnumbers the amount of cases in the high-effort categories, comprising more than 70% and 90% of the cases in the SysMar and SysBand projects, respectively. On the other hand, the number of cases in the high-effort categories was by around 30% (in Marlin) and 7.25 % (in SysBand). In practice, these results mean that developers spent less than 6 minutes in 85.32% of the full set of composition cases, and only 14.68% of the cases required more than 6 minutes.

Detection Effort. Table 4 shows a descriptive statistics about the effort spent to detect inconsistencies. A careful analysis indicated that some interesting features were observed. First, *the most experienced developers spent 23.2% less effort to detect inconsistencies than less experienced developers.* This observation was derived from the comparison of the medians in the SysMar and SysBand cases. This observation is also confirmed by the means' values. In this case, the most experienced developers invested 38.57% less effort to detect inconsistencies than less experienced developers.

Second, we also found that *the higher the number of teamwork members, the higher the effort to localize inconsistencies.* Comparing the number of teamwork members of the projects, we could observe that the developers of the SysMar and SysBand projects, both with 7 developers, invested a higher amount of effort to detect inconsistencies than the developers of the SysGR and SysPR systems (with 2 and 4 developers, respectively). For example, the developers spent 49.46% more effort (by about 3.45) to detect inconsistencies in the SysMar project than in SysGR project, by taking the medians 6.55 and 3.31 into account. This observation was also reinforced when we compare the SysMar and SysPR projects. That is, SysMar's developers spent 64.27% more effort (by about 4.21) to localize the inconsistencies; this difference is observed by comparing the medians 6.55 and 2.34, respectively. Therefore, the projects with a higher number of developers had to invest the double of effort to localize the inconsistencies.

Third, *the higher the number of inconsistencies in behavioral models, the higher the effort to detect inconsistencies.* Even though certain projects (e.g., System A) had a lower number of developers, a number of inconsistencies were concentrated on behavioral models, i.e. sequence diagrams in our case. The key problem highlighted by developers was that the behavioral models require an additional effort to go through the execution flows. An association in a structural model (e.g., class diagram) represents essentially one relationship between two classes. On the other hand, in a sequence diagram, which represents the interaction between the instances of these classes, the counterpart of the simple association is represented by n interactions (i.e. several messages exchanged between the objects). The problem is that developers must check each interaction.

Another finding is that *the higher the distribution of inconsistencies in different models, the higher the effort to identify them.* In the case studies, the systems were strongly decomposed in different concerns. These concerns were called "conceptual areas" by the developers. This unit of modularization brings together application domain concerns in a same package. The biggest problem arises when the inconsistencies in a conceptual area give rise to several inconsistencies, and hence affecting many other model elements located in other conceptual areas, thereby leading to ripple effects. This propagation is inevitable as there are usually some relationships between these units of modularization. Hence, developers often had to identify inconsistencies in the model elements of the conceptual areas they have from limited to none knowledge. Note that during the case studies the developers created diagrams related to a specific concern of the system (specified in use cases), and these diagrams were grouped in a conceptual area (similar to a package). Thus, the lack of knowledge about the model elements in the unknown conceptual area led developers to invest an extra effort to detect and resolve the inconsistencies.

Table 4. Descriptive statistics for detection effort

Cases	N	Mean	SD	Min	25th	Med	75th	Max
SysMar	63	7.57	5.1	0.54	2.45	6.55	12.49	16.54
SysBand	86	4.65	2.39	0.36	2.37	5.03	6.38	9.21
SysGR	24	3.66	1.52	1.32	2.67	3.31	4.16	7.39
SysPR	44	2.91	1.75	1.04	1.39	2.34	4.12	7.15
System A	6	12.37	4.2	5.26	8.25	13.15	16.36	17.37

N = number of compositions, SD = standard deviation, Min = minimum,
25th = first quartile; Med = median, 75th: third quartile, Max: maximum.

Resolution Effort (g). Table 5 shows a descriptive statistics of the inconsistency resolution effort. A key finding is that *the developers invest more effort to resolve inconsistencies than to both apply the model composition technique and detect the inconsistencies.* This can be explained based on several observations. First, in the SysMar project, for example, the teamwork members spent 64.91% more effort resolving inconsistencies than applying the model composition technique. This difference comprises the comparison between the medians 3.2 (application) and 9.12 (resolution). This difference becomes more explicit when we consider the values of the mean. This evidence is reinforced by the SysBand project. The resolution of inconsistencies consumes almost three times more effort than the application of the composition technique, if we compare the medians 3.2 (application) and 9.12 (resolution). The difference between the application and resolution effort becomes higher when we consider the value of the mean, i.e. jumping significantly their values from 64.91% to 88.40% (in SysMar) and from 80.31% to 88.35% (in SysBand).

Second, in SysMar project, the inconsistency resolution consumed 28.17% more effort than the inconsistency detection. This comprises the difference between the medians 6.55 and 9.12. The results in the SysBand project followed the same trend. Developers spent 66.99 percent more effort with inconsistency resolution than with inconsistency detection, when compared with the medians 5.03 and 15.24. Considering the mean, this difference of effort becomes more evident, leaping abruptly from 28.17 percent to 81.44 percent (in SysMar) and from 66.99 percent to 83.42 percent (in SysBand). Analyzing the collected data from the *SysGR* and *SysAL* projects, this observation is also confirmed. For example, the resolution effort is 82.98 percent and 54.96 percent higher than the detection effort in *SysGR* and *SysAL*, respectively. On the other hand, in *SysAL* project, the resolution and detection effort were practically equal. Therefore, the collected data suggest that teamwork members tend to spend more effort resolving inconsistency rather than applying the model composition technique and detecting inconsistencies.

Table 5. Descriptive statistics for resolution effort

Cases	N	Mean	SD	Min	25th	Med	75th	Max
SysMar	31	40.79	74.79	3.09	4.13	9.12	11.33	246.25
SysBand	8	28.06	28.04	5.55	8.17	15.24	41.44	95.44
SysGR	16	25.86	13.75	5.12	17.70	19.45	42.5	53.33
SysPR	44	2.86	1.92	1.2	2.03	2.33	2.52	10.41
SysAL	5	31.04	12.75	16.21	16.21	29.20	46.8	55.4

N = number of compositions, SD = standard deviation, Min = minimum,
25th = first quartile; Med = median, 75th: third quartile, Max: maximum.

Another finding is that *the experience acquired by the developers did not help to significantly reduce the inconsistency resolution effort*. Although more experienced developers have invested less effort to compose the input models and detect inconsistencies, their additional experience did not help significantly to reduce the inconsistency resolution effort. For example, in SysBand project, more experienced developers spent 40.15 percent more effort to resolve inconsistency than less experienced developers from SysMar project, compared the medians 9.12 and 15.24. The main reason is that most experienced developers tend to be more cautious than less experienced ones, and hence they tend to invest more time analyzing the impact of the resolution of each inconsistency.

4.2   RQ2: Influential Factors on Composition Effort

Some factors influence the effort of composing large-scale design models in real-world settings. This section analyzes the side effects of these factors on the composition effort variables.

The Effects of Conflicting Changes. A careful analysis of the results has pointed out that the production of the intended model is strictly affected by the presence of different types of change categories in the delta model. These changes would be: *addition*, model elements are inserted into base model; *removal*, a model element in the base model is removed; *modification*, a model element has some properties modified; *derivation*: model elements are refined for accommodating new changes and/or moved to other ones, commonly seen as a 1:N modification. We have also observed that the current composition algorithms are not able to effectively accommodate these changes in the base model, in particular when they occur simultaneously.

Developers and researchers recognize that software should adhere to the Open-Closed principle [31] as the evolutions become more straightforward. This principle states "software should be open for extensions, but closed for modifications." However, this observation did not occur in all the cases as modifications and derivations of model elements happened as well. In our study, the open-closed principle was more closely adhered by the evolutions dominated by additions rather than any other one. In this case, developers invested low effort compared to other cases. This suggests that the closer to the *Open-Closed* principle the change, the lower the composition effort.

On the other hand, evolution scenarios that do not follow the Open-Closed principle required more effort to produce the intended model, M_{AB}. This finding was identified when the change categories simultaneously occur in the delta model; hence, compromising the composition for some extent. This extra effort was due to the inca-pability of the matching algorithm to identify the similarities between the input model elements given the presence of widely scoped changes. In the SysMar project, for example, the composition techniques were not able to execute the compositions by about 17 percent (11/64) of the evolution scenarios. This required developers to recreate the models manually. In the SysBand project, by about 10 percent (10/95) of the composition cases did not produce an output model as well; or the composed model produced had to be thrown away due to the high amount of inconsistencies.

In particular, we also observed that the refinement (1:N) of model elements in the delta model caused more severe problems. This problematic scenario was noticed during the refinement of some classes belonging to the MVC (Model-View-Controller) architecture style into a set of more specialized ones. In both cases, the name-based, structural model comparison was unable to recognize the 1:N composi-tion relations between the input model elements. However, we have observed these conflicts do not only happen when developers perform modifications, removals, or refinements in parallel, but also when developers insert new model elements. This finding was noted from the fact that although evolutions following the Open-Closed principle had reduced the developers' effort, they still caused too frequent undetected inconsistencies.

Conflict Management. The detection of all possible semantic conflicts between two versions of a model is an undecidable problem [10]; as many false positive conflicts can appear. To alleviate this problem, some previous works recommend to reduce the size of the delta model to minimize the number of conflicts [11]. However, this ap-proach does not ameliorate in fact the complexity of the changes. The problem is not the number of conflicts that the size of the delta can cause, but the complexity of the conflicts. To alleviate the effort to tame the conflicts, we narrowed down the scope of the conflicts. For this, the delta model now represented one or two functionalities of a particular use case. Hence, the conflicts became more manageable and reasonable. The compositions had a smaller scope.

On the other hand, sometimes the presence of more widely scope changes was in-evitable in the delta model. This was, for example, the case when the models (e.g., class and sequence diagrams) were reviewed and meliorated for assuring quality is-sues. Unfortunately, this led to decrease the precision of the compositions due to the presence of non-trivial compositions. It is known that the domain independent com-position algorithms cannot rely on the detailed semantics of the models being com-posed or on the meaning of changes. Instead of being able to identify all possible conflicts, the algorithms detect as many conflicts as possible, assuming an approx-imate approach. Consequently, developers need to deal with many false positive con-flicts.

In practice, we noted that if the composition generates many conflicts, developers prefer throwing the models away (and investing more effort to recreate it after) to resolving all conflicts. Although the composition algorithm detects the conflicting changes created by developers in parallel, developers are unable to understand and proactively resolve these conflicts generated from non-trivial compositions. This can be explained by two reasons. First, the complexity of the conflicts affected the model elements. Second, the difficulty of understanding the meaning of the changes per-formed by other developers. More importantly, developers were unable to foresee the ripple effects of their actions. This is linked to two very interesting findings. First, developers have a tacit assumption that the models to-be-composed will not conflict with each other, and a common expectation is that little effort must be spent to integrate models. Hence, the developer tends to invest low effort to check whether the composition produced inconsistencies or not. Therefore, we can conclude that the need to throw the model away in order to recreate it after demonstrates the complexity of the problem.

Conflict Resolution and Developer Reputation. We have observed that when two changes in the input models (M_A and M_B) contradict each other, the one created by the more experienced developer tends to remain in the output composed model. In other words, the reputation of the developers influences the resolution of conflicting changes. It is important to recall that a developer can accept and reject the conflicting change of another developer. We observed this finding during the observational study, interviews, and analyzing the change history in the repository. This was particularly observed when novice developers reject the changes performed by them, and accept the ones carried out by senior developers. That is, if a novice developer modifies a design model, and this change conflicts with another one performed by a more experienced developer, the novice tends to consider the change carried out by the latter.

An additional interesting finding was that the effort of taming the conflicting changes tended to be less when the reputations of the developers were particularly opposite, one much high and another one too low. A careful analysis of the changes in the model elements reveals some interesting insights. We have noted that the implementation of the new changes (via M_A) by more experienced developers for encapsulating new evolutions are more oblivious to the modifications being implemented in the delta model. This observation holds for both structural and behavioral models i.e., class and sequence diagrams, respectively. As a consequence, the modifications realized by more experienced developers tended to help novice developers find an answer for the conflicts more quickly, thereby reducing the composition effort. Still, these modifications usually stay unchanged for a longer time, when compared with those realized by novice developers.

Reputation can be seen as the opinion (or a social evaluation) of a member of the development team toward other developer. We have identified two types of reputation: *technical* and *social*. The technical reputation refers to the level of knowledge considering issues related to the technology and tools used in the company such as the composition tool, IDEs, CASE tools, and version control systems. This type of reputation is acquired mainly solving daily problems. On the other hand, the social reputation refers to the position assumed by a member of the development team e.g., senior developer. After interviewing 8 developers, the data collected suggests that the technical reputation caused more influence for resolving conflicts than the social reputation. That is, 75 percent of the developers (6/8) reported that the technical reputation has a higher influence than the social one. We have concluded that the developer reputation indeed affects the way that conflicts are resolved. In particular, the changes performed by the subjects with high reputation tend to remain in the output composed model when ones conflict with other changes implemented by less experienced developers.

5   Related Work

Model composition is a very active research field in many research areas [34][35] such as synthesis of state charts [13][18], weaving of aspect-oriented models [19][20][21], governance and management of enterprise design models [9], software configuration management [30], and composition of software product lines [25][28]. For this reason, several academic and industrial composition techniques have been proposed such as MATA [19], Kompose [23], Epsilon [22], IBM RSA [16], and so on. With this in mind, some observations can be done.

First, these initiatives focus only on proposing the techniques instead of also dem-onstrate their effectiveness. Consequently, qualitative and quantitative indicators con-sidering these techniques are still incipient. In addition, the situation is accentuated considering effort indicators. This lack hinders mainly the understanding of their side effects. Second, their chief motivation is to provide programming languages to ex-press composition logic. Unfortunately, these approaches do not offer any insights or empirical evidences whether developers might reach the potential benefits claimed by using composition techniques in practice. Although some techniques are interesting approaches, sometimes they are used in practice because of the large number of false positives that they can produce in real-world settings. Nevertheless, the effort required for the user to under-stand and correct composition inconsistencies will ultimately prove to be too great. The current article takes a different approach. It aims to provide a precise assessment of composition effort in real life context, quantifying effort and identifying the influential effort.

Moreover, current works tend to investigate on the proactive detection and earlier resolution of conflicts. Most recently, Brun et al. [33] proposes an approach, namely Crystal, to help developers identify and resolve conflicts early. The key contributions are that conflicts are very common than would be expected, appearing over-lapping textual edits but also as subsequent build and test failures. In a similar way, Sarma et al. [32] proposes a new approach, named Palantír, based on the precept of workspace awareness, to detection and earlier resolution of a larger number of conflicts. Based on two laboratory experiments, the authors confirmed that the use of the Palantír re-duced of the number of unresolved conflicts. Although these two approaches are in-teresting studies, the earlier detection does alleviate the problem of model composi-tion. The problem is the same, but is only reported more quickly. In addition, they appear to be overly restrictive to the code, not leading to broader generalizations at the modeling level. Lastly, they neither make consideration about the effort to com-pose of the artefacts used nor investigate the research questions in five case studies.

6   Concluding Remarks and Future Work

This paper represented the first in vivo exploratory study to evaluate the effort that developers invest to compose design models (RQ1) and to analyze the factors that affect developers' effort (RQ2). In our study, a best-of-breed model composition technique was applied to evolve industrial design models along 297 evolution scena-rios. The works were conducted during 56 weeks producing more than 2 million of compositions of model elements. We investigated the composition effort in this sample, and analyzed the side effects of key factors that affected the effort of applying the composition technique as well as detecting and resolving inconsistencies.

We summarize the findings related to RQ1 as follows: (1) the application effort measures do not follow an ad hoc distribution and, rather, it assumed a distribution pattern; (2) the application effort tends to reduce as developers become more familiar with technical issues rather than application domain issues; (3) the more experienced developers spend 23.2 percent less effort to detect inconsistencies than less experienced developers; and (4) the more the number of inconsistencies in behavioral models, the higher the effort to detect inconsistencies. Additionally, we also present four findings with respect to RQ2 as follows: (1) the production of the intended model is strictly affected by the presence of different types of change categories in the delta model; (2) the closer to the Open-Closed principle the change, the lower the composition effort. That is, evolutions dominated by additions reduce the composition effort. On the other hand, the refinement (1:N) of model elements in the delta model caused severe composition problems and hence increased the composition effort.

Although we gathered quantitative and qualitative evidence to supporting the aforementioned findings, further empirical studies are still required to check whether they are observed in other contexts and with different subjects. Future investigation points would be to answer some questions such as: (1) Do developers invest much more effort to compose behavioral models (e.g. sequence diagrams) than structural models (e.g. component diagrams)? Are the influential factors in composition effort similar in these two contexts? (2) How different are the findings similar or different with respect to code merge (i.e. implementation-level composition)? (3) Do developers invest more effort to resolve semantic inconsistencies than syntactic ones? It is by no means obvious that, for example, developers invest less effort to resolve inconsistencies related to the well-formedness rules of the language metamodel than to resolve inconsistencies considering the meaning of the model elements. Finally, we hope that the issues outlined throughout the paper encourage other researchers to replicate our study in the future under different circumstances. Moreover, we also hope that this work represents a first step in a more ambitious agenda on better supporting model composition tasks.

References

1. Runeson, P., Höst, M.: Guidelines for Conducting and Reporting Case Study Research in Software Engineering. Empirical Software Engineering 14, 131–164 (2009)
2. Wohlin, C., Runeson, P., Höst, M., Ohlsson, M., Regnell, B., Wesslén, A.: Experimentation Software Engineering - An Introduction. Kluwer Academic Publishers (2000)
3. Kitchenham, B., Al-Khilidar, H., Babar, M., Berry, M., Cox, K., Keung, J., Kurniawati, F., Staples, M., Zhang, H., Zhu, L.: Evaluating Guidelines for Reporting Empirical Software Engineering Studies. Empirical Software Engineering 13(1), 97–12 (2008)
4. Boisvert, R., Tang, P. (eds.): The Architecture of Scientific Software. Kluwer Academic (2001)
5. Kelly, D.: A Study of Design Characteristics in Evolving Software Using Stability as a Criterion. IEEE Transactions on Software Engineering 32(5), 315–329 (2006)
6. Camtasia Studio Pro. (2011), http://www.techsmith.com/camtasia/

7. Farias, K.: Analyzing the Effort on Composing Design Models in Industrial Case Studies. In: 10th International Conference on Aspect-Oriented Software Development Companion, Porto de Galinhas, Brazil, pp. 79–80 (2011)

8. Farias, K., Garcia, A., Whittle, J.: Assessing the Impact of Aspects on Model Composition Effort. In: 9th International Conference on Aspect-Oriented Software Development Companion, Saint Malo, France, pp. 73–84 (2010)

9. Norris, N., Letkeman, K.: Governing and Managing Enterprise Models: Part 1. Introduction and Concepts. IBM Developer Works (2011), http://www.ibm.com/developerworks/rational/library/09/0113_letkeman-norris

10. Mens, T.: A State-of-the-Art Survey on Software Merging. IEEE Transactions on Software Engineering 28(5), 449–462 (2002)

11. Perry, D., Siy, H., Votta, L.: Parallel Changes in Large-Scale Software Development: an Observational Case Study. Journal ACM Transactions on Software Engineering and Methodology (TOSEM) 10(3), 308–337 (2001)

12. Keith, E.: Flexible Conflict Detection and Management in Collaborative Applications. In: 10th Annual ACM Symposium on User Interface Software and Technology, pp. 139–148 (1997)

13. Ellis, C., Gibbs, S.: Concurrency Control in Groupware Systems. ACM SIGMOD, 399–407 (1989)

14. Berzins, V.: Software Merge: Semantics of Combining Changes to Programs. Journal ACM Transactions on Programming Languages and Systems 16(6), 1875–1903 (1994)

15. Berzins, V., Dampier, D.: Software merge: Combining Changes to Decompositions. Journal of Systems Integration 6(1-2), 135–150 (1996)

16. IBM Rational Software Architecture (2011), http://www.ibm.com/developerworks/rational/products/rsa/

17. Berzins, V.: On Merging Software Extensions. Acta Informatica 23, 607–619 (1986)

18. Gerth, C., Küster, J.M., Luckey, M., Engels, G.: Precise Detection of Conflicting Change Operations Using Process Model Terms. In: Petriu, D.C., Rouquette, N., Haugen, Ø. (eds.) MODELS 2010, Part II. LNCS, vol. 6395, pp. 93–107. Springer, Heidelberg (2010)

19. Whittle, J., Jayaraman, P., Elkhodary, A., Moreira, A., Araújo, J.: MATA: A unified approach for composing UML aspect models based on graph transformation. In: Katz, S., Ossher, H., France, R., Jézéquel, J.-M. (eds.) Transactions on AOSD VI. LNCS, vol. 5560, pp. 191–237. Springer, Heidelberg (2009)

20. Whittle, J., Jayaraman, P.: Synthesizing Hierarchical State Machines from Expressive Scenario Descriptions. ACM TOSEM 19(3) (January 2010)

21. Klein, J., Hélouët, L., Jézéquel, J.: Semantic-based Weaving of Scenarios. In: 5th AOSD 2006, Bonn, Germany (March 2006)

22. Epsilon Project (2011), http://www.eclipse.org/gmt/epsilon/

23. Kompose: A generic model composition tool (2011), http://www.kermeta.org/kompose

24. Sabetzadeh, M., Nejati, S., Chechik, M., Easterbrook, S.: Reasoning about Consistency in Model Merging. In: 3rd Workshop on Living With Inconsistency in Software Development (September 2010)

25. Jayaraman, P., Whittle, J., Elkhodary, A.M., Gomaa, H.: Model Composition in Product Lines and Feature Interaction Detection Using Critical Pair Analysis. In: Engels, G., Opdyke, B., Schmidt, D.C., Weil, F. (eds.) MODELS 2007. LNCS, vol. 4735, pp. 151–165. Springer, Heidelberg (2007)

26. Diskin, Z., Xiong, Y., Czarnecki, K.: Specifying Overlaps of Heterogeneous Models for Global Consistency Checking. In: Dingel, J., Solberg, A. (eds.) MODELS 2010. LNCS, vol. 6627, pp. 165–179. Springer, Heidelberg (2011)
27. Egyed, A.: Fixing Inconsistencies in UML Design Models. In: 29th International Conference on Software Engineering, pp. 292–301 (2007)
28. Thaker, S., Batory, D., Kitchin, D., Cook, W.: Safe Composition of Product Lines. In: 6th GPCE 2007, Salzburg, Austria, pp. 95–104 (2007)
29. Egyed, A.: Automatically Detecting and Tracking Inconsistencies in Software Design Models. IEEE Transactions on Software Engineering 37(2), 188–204 (2010)
30. Whitehead, J.: Collaboration in Software Engineering: A Roadmap. In: Future of Software Engineering at ICSE, pp. 214–225 (2007)
31. Meyer, B.: Object-Oriented Software Construction, 1st edn. Prentice-Meyer, Hall, Englewood Cliffs (1988)
32. Sarma, A., Redmiles, D., van Der Hoek, A.: Palantír: Early Detection of Development Conflicts Arising from Parallel Code Changes. IEEE TSE 99(6) (2011)
33. Brun, Y., Holmes, R., Ernst, M., Notkin, D.: Proactive Detection of Collaboration Conflicts. In: 8th SIGSOFT ESEC/FSE, Szeged, Hungary, pp. 168–178 (2011)
34. France, R., Rumpe, B.: Model-Driven Development of Complex Software: A Research Roadmap. In: FuSE at ICSE 2007, 37–54 (2007)
35. Apel, S., Liebig, J., Brandl, B., Lengauer, C., Kästner, C.: Semistructured Merge: Rethinking Merge in Revision Control Systems. In: 8th SIGSOFT ESEC/FSE, pp. 190–200 (2011)
36. OMG, Unified Modeling Language: Infrastructure, version 2.2, Object Management Group (February 2011)
37. JIRA, http://www.atlassian.com/software/jira/overview

Parallel Execution of ATL Transformation Rules

Massimo Tisi, Salvador Martínez, and Hassene Choura

AtlanMod, École des Mines de Nantes - INRIA, LINA, Nantes, France
`firstname.lastname@inria.fr`

Abstract. Industrial environments that make use of Model-Driven Engineering (MDE) are starting to see the appearance of very large models, made by millions of elements. Such models are produced automatically (e.g., by reverse engineering complex systems) or manually by a large number of users (e.g., from social networks). The success of MDE in these application scenarios strongly depends on the scalability of model manipulation tools. While parallelization is one of the traditional ways of making computation systems scalable, developing parallel model transformations in a general-purpose language is a complex and error-prone task. In this paper we show that rule-based languages like ATL have strong parallelization properties. Transformations can be developed without taking into account concurrency concerns, and a transformation engine can automatically parallelize execution. We describe the implementation of a parallel transformation engine for the current version of the ATL language and experimentally evaluate the consequent gain in scalability.

1 Introduction

Part of the industrial landscape looks at tools based on Model-Driven Engineering (MDE) to handle in a uniform way a plethora of software engineering tasks at development/maintenance time. Some examples are the development of critical systems [8], reverse engineering and modernization [20], artifact management [5]. MDE tools are also used at runtime, in systems built around the manipulation of model-based abstractions during system execution [6]. The most popular MDE frameworks, like the Eclipse Modeling Framework (EMF), are inspired by the OMG's Meta-Object Facility (MOF), and provide facilities to define and manipulate metamodels and conforming models. Model manipulation operations on these frameworks can be developed using APIs in general-purpose languages (the most popular approach) or by specific model-transformation languages (MTLs) originally designed to ease development, analysis and maintenance of the model-manipulation code.

Some of the companies that embraced (or want to embrace) MDE need to handle huge amounts of data. In MDE terms this reflects in the need to manipulate very large models (VLMs), e.g. models made by millions of model elements. Examples of such models appear in a wide range of domains as shown in industrial cases provided by literature: in [4] the authors work over industrial

A. Moreira et al. (Eds.): MODELS 2013, LNCS 8107, pp. 656–672, 2013.

AUTOSAR[2] models with over 1 million model elements; [18] analyses civil-engineering related models with more that 7 million computational objects; in the area of model-driven software product lines, [17] handles product families with up to 10 million model elements. Reverse engineering tasks may also produce large models as shown in [3], where our team obtains large models with up to 5 million model elements from the Eclipse JDT sources.

Due to the physical constraints preventing frequency scaling in modern CPUs, multi-core architectures are very popular today, making parallelism a cost-effective solution to improve computation times for VLMs. However, using a general-purpose language, parallel programs are more difficult to write with respect to sequential programs [16], mainly because of: 1) new classes of potential bugs introduced by concurrency (e.g., race conditions); 2) the difficulty in getting good parallelization while handling communication and synchronization between the different concurrent tasks; 3) increased difficulty in debugging the parallel code. One of the well-known approaches to simplify parallel programming is relying on implicitly parallel languages, and several such languages are available[1]. Using implicit parallelism, the developer does not need to worry about dividing the computation and handling communication and synchronization. The language implementation takes care of these aspects and the development of parallel programs is substantially simplified, which results in a significant productivity gain.

In this paper we want to show that ATL (the AtlanMod Transformation Language [14]), a rule-based model-transformation language designed with the principle of rule independence can be overloaded with implicit parallelism. By running on a parallelized engine, the execution time of ATL model transformations can scale well on the number of processors. While implicit parallelism had a limited success in general-purpose languages, we argue that the specific task of model transformation on VLMs may greatly benefit from it.

We provide the following contributions:

- We study the parallelization of the ATL language, separating it in two indipendent problems of transformation language parallelization and query language parallelization and we address the first analyzing decomposition and synchronization aspects.
- We provide a multi-threaded implementation of the ATL engine by adapting the standard engine. The resulting compiler and virtual machine are publicly available[2] and we plan to merge them in the next default version of ATL.
- We experimentally measure the improvement in scalability, by comparing the execution times of the same transformation in three semantically equivalent implementations: 1) a Java implementation, 2) an ATL implementation running on the standard engine, 3) the same ATL implementation running on the multi-threaded engine. Since no other change is performed to ATL, this experimentation gives an idea of the net effect of the parallelization.

---

[1] http://en.wikipedia.org/wiki/Implicit_parallelism
[2] http://www.emn.fr/z-info/atlanmod/index.php/Parallel_ATL, EPL licence.

In this paper we apply our approach to the development of a multi-threaded version of ATL with the aim of improving scalability on multi-core and multi-processor computers. However we plan in future work to adapt our automatic parallelization approach and apply it to distributed environments, with the aim to implement a distributed engine for ATL.

The paper is structured in the following way: Section 2 introduces the ATL transformation language and the running case whereas Section 3 details the parallelization problem and the proposed approach. Section 4 describes the implementation of the parallel engine for ATL and Section 5 presents the results of its performance evaluation. Section 6 discusses related work before the final Section 7 that summarizes conclusions and future works.

2   The ATL Language

To briefly illustrate the ATL language we rely on a small example on which we base also the experimentation section, i.e. the Class2Relational transformation[3] that transforms class diagrams into relational models. In Listing 1.1 we show an excerpt of this transformation (the full code can be found on the paper's website) and Fig. 1 illustrates its application to a very small model.

Listing 1.1. ATL Class2Relational transformation (excerpt)

```
1  rule Class2Table {
2    from
3      c : ClassDiagram!Class
4    to
5      out : Relational!Table (
6        name <- c.name,
7        cols <- c.attr->select(e | not e.multiValued),
8        key <- Set {key}
9      ),
10     key : Relational!Column (
11       name <- 'objectId',
12       type <- thisModule.objectIdType()
13     )
14 }
15
16 rule DataTypeAttribute2Column {
17   from
18     a : ClassDiagram!Attribute (
19       a.type.oclIsKindOf(ClassDiagram!DataType) and not a.multiValued
20     )
21   to
22     out : Relational!Column (
23       name <- a.name,
24       type <- a.type
25     )
26 }
```

The listing shows two rules, respectively responsible of transforming Classes into Tables with their respective Key column (Class2Table) and single-valued primitive-type Attributes into Columns (DataTypeAttribute2Column). Rules transform occurrences of the *input pattern (from)* in occurrences of the *output pattern (to)*. Occurrences of the input pattern may be filtered by introducing a *guard*, a boolean condition that source model elements must satisfy (e.g. line 19). Elements of the output pattern can have their features initialized through the use of *bindings*, expressions computing the values to assign to each feature (lines

---

[3] http://www.eclipse.org/atl/atlTransformations/#Class2Relational

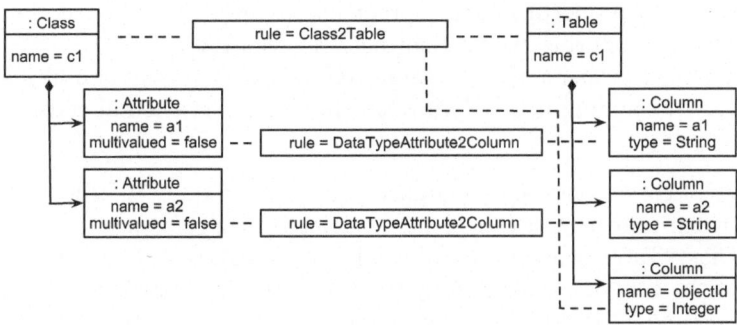

Fig. 1. Application of Class2Relational to a minimal model. For each rule application a trace link is generated labeled with the name of the applied rule.

6-8, 11-12, 23-24). For expressing guards and bindings, ATL relies on a separate *query language*, the OMG's Object Constraint Language (OCL). To help in factorizing OCL code ATL allows the definition of OCL functions, named *helpers*. For instance the binding at line 16 calls the objectIdType() helper (not included in the excerpt) that looks in the source model for a usable datatype for identifiers. The two rules in the Listing 1.1 are examples of *matched* rules, declarative rules that are spontaneously triggered when they match elements in the source model. The language allows also the definition of *lazy* rules, that need to be explicitly triggered by other rules.

Two features of the ATL language are not considered in the rest of the paper and are left to future work: 1) ATL includes an imperative part that does not increase the expressive power of the language, but is designed to simplify the implementation in complex cases, that would be verbose to encode in declarative rules; 2) ATL includes a separate execution mode called refining mode, in which transformation rules are applied in-place for the refinement of the source model. In the following we implicitly refer to the declarative part of ATL in standard execution mode.

The standard execution mode of ATL imposes a few constraints that result important for parallelization, since they strongly limit the possible dependencies between rules:

- During the matching phase, output elements of transformation rules are immediately instantiated and added to the target model, and are not subject to following matches. This means that the output of a rule cannot be used as intermediate[4] data and cannot be transformed or deleted by another rule[4]. This constraint is one of the main differences between ATL and typical MTLs based on graph transformations.
- OCL expressions are never allowed to navigate the target model. The consequence is that the OCL expression that calculates a binding cannot use the output of another rule.

---

[4] Lazy rules can be triggered recursively, but they always match over the source model and not over the target elements previously generated.

- Single-valued properties in the target model are assigned once and are not updated again during the transformation execution.
- Multi-valued properties in the target model can be updated multiple times, but only for adding new values (this allows for incremental construction of the property).

Because of these constraints matched rules depend on each other only in one case, i.e. when they generate elements connected by a reference. In the example the rule Class2Table generates a Table whose reference *cols* has to be connected to some of the columns generated by the rule DataTypeAttribute2Column. The connection (line 7) is made by calculating the set of Attributes in the source model that correspond to the Columns to connect (in the example all the attributes of the matched Class that are not multivalued). ATL will implicitly fill the *cols* reference with all the Columns that are generated by any rule matching the Attributes calculated at line 7. This mechanism is called *implicit resolution algorithm*.

ATL transformations are compiled in a bytecode format called ASM, interpreted by the ASM virtual machine. The ATL architecture together with the full execution algorithm for ATL transformations is described in [14].

3   ATL Parallelization

As several other transformation languages, the ATL language embeds a separate query language that allows to define expressions over the models under transformation. In the ATL case the query language is the functional language OCL, and ATL restricts its use on computations over the source model. This constraint makes the execution of ATL and OCL two independent phases: 1) ATL launches the execution of OCL code from guards or bindings; 2) OCL calculates a result in a side-effect free way, by navigating the source model and possibly calling other OCL functions (helpers), and returns the result to ATL.

This separation makes the two problems of parallelizing ATL and OCL completely independent. The automatic parallelization of OCL code is a typical problem of parallelization of a functional language, and it is already studied in literature [21]. For this reason in the following we will deal only with the parallelization of the rule execution language. Our resulting engine will of course support OCL expressions but they will be executed in the same task of the rule application that launches them. A parallel engine for OCL may be integrated in future, and it will not require changes to the parallelization mechanism discussed in this paper.

In the next two sections we consider the parallelization of the transformation execution language as a problem composed by two orthogonal subproblems.

1. Decomposition, i.e., how to decompose the transformation computation to parallelize the calculation.
2. Synchronization, i.e., how to coordinate the dispatched tasks and manage their inter-communication. As we are using shared memory structures, con-

current access to these data structures has to be optimized to maximize parallelism.

3.1   Decomposition

The computation of a model transformation is composed of 1) a set of expression evaluation over source model elements (matchings), 2) a set of rule applications, one for each match found in the first set. A significant part of the computation of each rule application seems to be independent from other rule applications, suggesting the possibility of executing each rule application and each match in a different thread. While the approach would be probably suitable to small models, VLMs would force the engine to instantiate millions of tasks per transformation. Even with the support of an efficient job scheduler, responsible of assigning the jobs to a limited fixed set of threads, the cost of instantiating, keeping in memory and synchronizing between millions of jobs would overtake the benefits of parallelism.

For this reason we look to a more coarse-grained decomposition for the transformation computation. Traditional literature on parallelism distinguishes two opposite approaches (and a set of intermediates between the two): task parallelism and data parallelism.

Task Parallelism. In task parallelism, each task contains a different set of operations, but works on the same data set. The approach is especially convenient when the fact of working on the same data does not introduce dependencies among the execution threads.

In our model transformation scenario, an example of task parallelism is grouping the computation *by rule* so that: 1) each task executes a different rule, including the OCL expressions for guards and bindings; 2) each task works on the full source and target models.

In this paper we will follow this approach, motivated by our main argument: the ATL language structures the computation in rules, that the language constraints (see Section 2) make highly independent from each other. As we will see in the next section, the manipulation of shared data will introduce synchronization issues that we will need to address relying on the ATL specificities.

After dividing the computation by rule, we have the option to further decompose the rule in two execution threads for the two well-defined phases of a rule execution: matching and rule application. Since every rule application needs to rely on the output of its matching phase, the strong dependency between the two threads hampers a direct improvement in parallelization. However, as we will see in the next section, dividing matching and rule application provides a better flexibility that we can exploit for improving synchronization.

In summary we instantiate two jobs for rule. For instance, the execution of the limited excerpt in Listing 1.1 results in four jobs:

- a *match* job for Class2Table looks for elements of type Class, and for each one it instantiates a trace Link, together with an empty Table and an empty Column as placeholders for the next job.

- an *apply* job for Class2Table computes and assigns the properties of the Tables and the Columns created by the corresponding matcher.
- a *match* job for DataTypeAttribute2Column looks for elements of type Attribute that satisfy the condition at line 19, and for each one it instantiates an empty Column.
- an *apply* job for DataTypeAttribute2Column computes and assigns the properties of the Columns created by the corresponding matcher.

Data Parallelism. In pure data-parallelism approaches, the input domain is partitioned and each task executes the same operations on a different partition. In model transformations terms, source and optionally target models are divided in submodels and each transformation task is responsible for transforming its assigned chunk. The approach in general reduces inter-thread communication, by eliminating shared data, and by concentrating collaboration issues in a final merging step of the generated partial results.

While we did not address this kind of parallelism in this paper we recognize its importance, especially when moving to distributed environments, where communication cost is higher. We plan in future work of studying this possibility and the interaction with task parallelism in model transformations.

3.2   Task Synchronization

A decomposition of a model transformation in parallel tasks may in general introduce synchronization issues for accessing shared data structures. Fig. 2 visualizing this problem by representing the Parallel Transformation, a read-only source model, and a set of read-write data structures, that comprise the Target Model, a set of Trace Links to store information about rule executions, and other generic runtime data structures used by the transformation code, or the transformation execution algorithm.

Dashed ellipses in Fig. 2 represent possible synchronization issues:

- the source model is read-only, hence concurrent reads do not require a synchronization mechanism;
- CRUD operations on the target model may require synchronization. This is true for CRUDs on model elements, or on single properties (for the sake of the discussion in Fig. 2 we distinguish operations on single-valued properties from operations on multi-valued properties). Moreover operations on properties may need to be synchronized with operations on elements. E.g., one thread may need to finish creating an element, before another thread tries to set a contained property.
- CRUD operations on trace links may require synchronization. For instance trace links may be stored in a collection that does not allow link creations to interleave. Moreover CRUDs on trace links need to be synchronized with CRUDs on model elements. E.g., a target element creation needs to be complete before the corresponding trace link can be connected to the element.
- finally the engine may require synchronization on other runtime data, coming from the transformation code or the internal engine implementation.

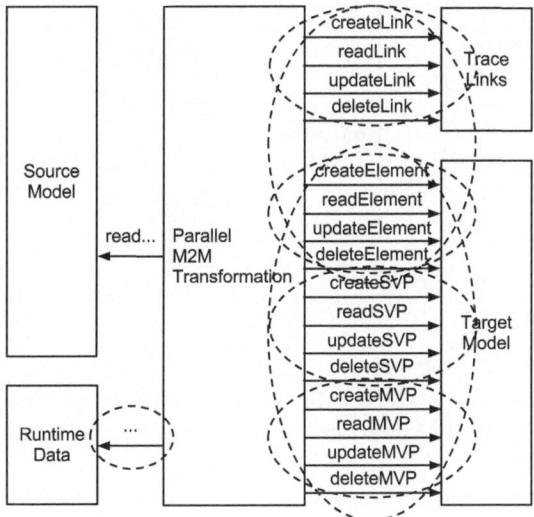

Fig. 2. Synchronization for concurrent data access in parallel transformations

All these possible synchronization points make parallelization a difficult task for model transformations in a general purpose language and risk to hamper the actual gain in scalability. In the next section we will try to reduce the synchronization points by exploiting the specific constraints of ATL.

One Task per ATL Rule. When the transformation is written in ATL and we decide to assign a different task to each ATL rule, the number of operations that may require synchronization results strongly reduced w.r.t. the general case, as shown in Fig. 3:

- On the target model:
    - After they are created, model elements are not further modified by the ATL engine (but their properties are). However, element creations need to be synchronized, since they operate on the collections used by the EMF framework, that does not offer any support to concurrent access.
    - Single-valued properties are only created and contextually associated to a value. Since they are stored in EMF as Java references and they are not subject to modifications, they do not need synchronization.
    - Multi-valued properties are created and updated by adding elements during the transformation. EMF stores multi-valued properties in Java Lists that do not support concurrent update.
    - No synchronization is needed between operations on properties and operations on elements, since in ATL a property can be assigned only by the rule that creates the element. Hence, element creation and property assignment always happen in the same thread.

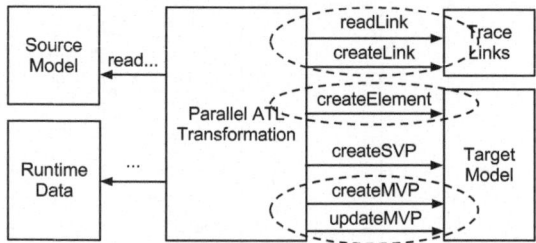

Fig. 3. Synchronization in parallel ATL transformations

- On trace links:
  - Trace links can be created by some rule, and only read by other rules, requiring a synchronization method. However no update or deletion is allowed.
  - No synchronization is needed between element creation and link creation, since they always happen in the same rule/thread.
- On runtime data:
  - ATL supports the definition of runtime data structures in the OCL part, but being OCL side-effect free they do not require synchronization.
  - The engine does not introduce internal data structures that need synchronization.

While the synchronization in ATL results simplified w.r.t. Fig. 2, it still may represent a significant overhead. Critical sections for each one of the operations are short, since they consist in a single elementary operation on a collection, but the number of passages by a critical section is proportional to model size.

In the next section we will try to optimize the synchronization of operations over trace links. Instead, unfortunately, not much can be optimized about operations on the target model, since the creation of elements and properties cannot be avoided and EMF takes charge of this creation by using standard collections. An optimization in this sense should be done on the modeling framework side: EMF may provide non-blocking operations for element and property creation.

One Task per Match/Apply. We can strongly reduce lock contention on accessing trace links by dividing each rule in two separate threads, as explained in Section 3.1, and organizing job dispatching in two phases (Fig. 4).

In a first *matching phase* all the matching jobs are executed. The jobs are responsible for creating elements and creating trace links and these two operations still need synchronization, since they involve concurrent matchers modifying the same collections.

A second *apply phase* is activated when all the matchers have completed execution. The *launch* message in Fig. 4 represents a hard synchronization point, and it negatively affects the total computation time especially when matchers have very different execution time. In the worst case of one matcher much slower than the others, the hard barrier prevents other threads to be launched and the

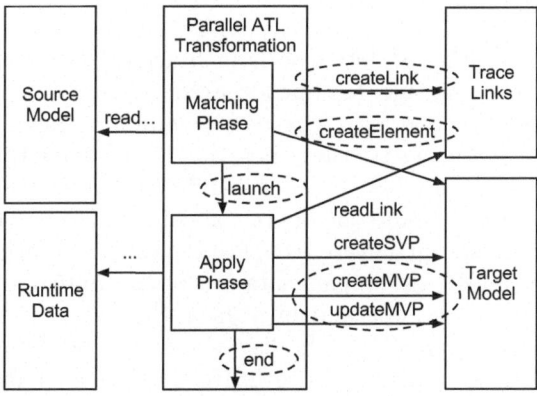

Fig. 4. Synchronization in two-phases parallel ATL transformations

other cores stay idle. An analogous behavior happens at the end of the transformation (but it is common to the previous approaches): the transformation termination is determined by the end of the slowest parallel job.

The gain in this wait stands in the fact that the trace link list at this point is read-only and no synchronization is needed during all the apply phase. To have an idea of the impact of this change, we have to consider that an ATL transformation executes a readLink operation each time it fills a reference in the target element, if the reference involves more rules (the most common case). In other words the number of readLink operations is of the same order of magnitude of the number of references in the target model. In Section5 we will provide experimental evidence of the resulting speed-up.

4   The Parallel ATL Engine

We have adapted the ATL compiler and virtual machine (VM) to implement automatic parallelization. The new engine has full support for declarative ATL and parallelizes computation based on matches rules, following the approach described in the previous section.

One of the criteria for the engine adaptation is to maintain the separation of concerns between compiler and VM: 1) the VM provides basic primitives to enable parallelization and guarantees the absence of race conditions on concurrent access; 2) the compiler defines the parallel tasks by translating ATL rules in low-level primitives.

In this model, decomposition (Section 3.1) is implemented in the compiler together with the division in phases, and synchronization of concurrent access (Section 3.2) is implemented in the virtual machine. A consequence is that other transformation languages that can compile towards our virtual machine, can in principle implement their own parallelization mechanism by using our primitives.

4.1   Virtual Machine

The main virtual machine primitive to launch a parallel task is a new opcode in the ASM bytecode language: the opcode *FORK* spawns a new job containing the operation passed as operand. The new primitive is analogous to the pre-existing *CALL* that launches another operation in the same thread. The *CALL* opcode takes an operation reference as operand and derives the program control in order to execute the opcodes the operation contains. When the processing of the opcodes terminates, control is returned to the caller operation that continues its execution. Conversely, the implementation of the *FORK* opcode wraps the operation referenced as its operand in a Java *Runnable*. Then, it calls a job executor to add this *Runnable* to the list of tasks to be launched. After this, the program control is immediately returned to the caller operation. A Java *ExecutorService* allocates the transformation tasks to a fixed number of threads passed as parameter at the transformation launch.

For thread coordination, the VM adds to the native library another data type, the integer semaphore, mapped to a Java Semaphore. In this way the compiler can instantiate semaphores and call primitives for initializing it, acquiring and releasing tokens. Token acquisition blocks the caller until a token becomes available (i.e. the integer semaphore contains a value $>= 0$). Integer semaphores are used by the compiler to synchronize threads at the end of each phase.

Finally, as discussed in Section 3.2 a set of operations on trace links and target models need to be made thread safe. In the VM implementation, a synchronized block is added to the VM operations for creating new model elements and updating multivalued properties in the target model. The same approach is followed for the operation in charge of adding new links to the hash registry of transformation tracelinks.

4.2   Compiler

The default ATL compiler has been subject to the minimal modifications necessary to implement our parallelization algorithm. With respect to the old one, the new compiler:

- Adds to the beginning of the transformation the initialization of two integer semaphores with a negative number of tokens, equal to the number of rules.
- Creates a *match operation* for each rule and calls them sequentially using the *FORK* opcode.
- Creates a single *applyPhase operation* and calls it using a *FORK*.
- Adds as first instruction of the *applyPhase operation* a request for a token from the first semaphore. The request is refused until enough tasks have released a token on the semaphore.
- Adds as last instruction of each *match operation* a release instruction on the first semaphore.
- Creates in the *applyPhase operation*, an *apply operation* for each rule and calls them sequentially with *FORK*.

- Adds as last instruction of the main task a request for a token on the second semaphore.
- Adds as last instruction of each *apply operation* a release instruction on the second semaphore.

5   Experimental Evaluation

In this section we assess the performance of the parallel ATL engine by running two experimentations.

In the first experimentation we compare three equivalent implementations of the simple Class2Relational transformation, part of which has been presented in Listing 1.1: a Java implementation using the EMF Java API, an ATL implementation running on the standard ATL engine and the same ATL implementation running on the parallel ATL engine. The purpose is comparing execution time of parallel ATL over normal ATL and Java in a typical system. The ATL implementations have been developed by simplifying the Class2Relational transformation from the ATL Transformation Zoo [1]. For developing the Java implementation we provided an EMF expert with the specification of the ATL transformation.

We execute the three transformations feeding them with large class models generated by a stochastic metamodel instantiator that we developed adapting a publicly available tool from Obeo[5]. The tool allows us to define probability distributions for all the element types and properties of the metamodel and use them to drive instantiation. In our experimentation we define a single uniform probability distribution, and we use it for the number of Packages to generate, the number of Classes of each Package, the number of Attributes for each Class.

We use the instantiator to generate two sets of 10 models. For the first set the distribution is designed to produce models with an average of 10,000 elements, for the second the average is 1,000,000 elements. Given one of the two sets, and one of the three implementations, we produce 100 observations by running 10 times the transformation of the 10 models in the set. We summarize the results in Fig. 5 where each box represents 100 observations. The leftmost plot refers to models of 10,000 elements, the rightmost to models of 1,000,000 elements.

The tests have been performed on an environment with the following characteristics: 8-cores processor Intel Core i7-2760QM CPU @ 2.40GHz, with 8GB of physical memory, and running Ubuntu Linux (64 bits) version 12.10 (quantal) with Linux kernel 3.5.0-25-generic. As application environment, tests where performed on the Eclipse Platform version 4.2.1 on top of the OpenJDK Java Virtual Machine version 1.7.0_15. Note that the i7 CPU has only 4 physical cores, while it presents 8 cores to the OS by using hyper-threading.

In measurement, model loading and model serialization times were not taken into account. Loading and serialization are time-consuming tasks that also impact scalability when working with very big models. However, dealing with such problems lies out of the scope of the present work.

---

[5] https://github.com/Obeo/emf.specimen

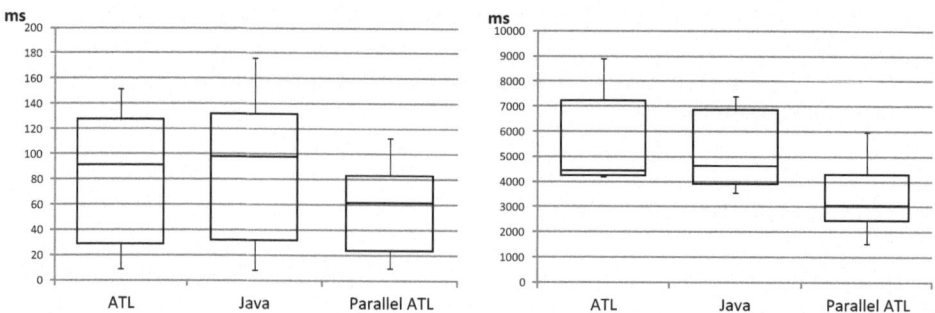

Fig. 5. Box plots summarizing the execution times of the same transformation on 4 cores. The leftmost plot refers to models of 10,000 elements, the rightmost to models of 1,000,000 elements.

From Fig. 5 we can observe that on the multi-core processor the ATL transformation on the parallel engine performs significantly better then the Java and standard ATL versions. The performance improvement is independent on the size of the models, resulting in a speed-up respectively of 1.49 and 1.48 (w.r.t. normal ATL) for the 10,000 and 1,000,000 elements model sets. We can see also that values have a lower dispersion with the parallel approach, that appears more robust (for 1,000,000 elements, the standard deviation is 1990ms for standard ATL, 2053ms for Java, and 1319ms for parallel ATL). While in this experiment we limited the processor to use always 4 cores, in the second experimentation we intend to measure the speed-up of the approach w.r.t. the number of cores.

Fig. 6 presents for each number of cores the correspondent speed-up of the parallel ATL engine over the default one. Tests are run in the same configuration as above but to stress the system and obtain more significant values we use a more complete and computationally expensive version of the Class2Relational transformation. While the original ATL implementation of Class2Relational counts only 6 rules, in order to keep all 8 virtual cores occupied during the transformation computation we have developed a new version that includes rules to translate super-classes, abstract classes and their attributes. The complete implementation is available in the paper's website.

To better evaluate the effect of model size on the speed-up, we run the test over 4 model sets of 10 models each. Model sets are generated as above and their respective average model size is 1000, 10000, 100000 and one million elements. Table 1 shows the average execution times in the different configurations.

The test shows a higher speed-up w.r.t. the previous experimentation, proving that the second version of Class2Relational is more parallelizable than the first. The speed-up curve, apart from small fluctuations shows a constant increase exhibiting good scalability on the number of cores. On the other side the graph shows that the speed-up is negatively influenced by model size, at least for small models. Parallelism on models of 1,000 elements perform significantly better than on models of 10,000 elements. However from a certain size the speed-up stays constant and does not deteriorate even for VLMs. The speed-up over VLMs

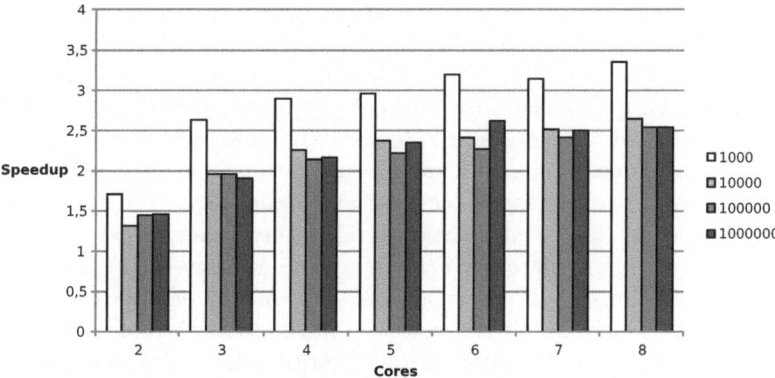

Fig. 6. Speed Up

is more than 2.5, from which we can derive that the transformation over the parallel engine contains at least a 60% of parallelized code. The fact that only the first 4 cores are physical explains the little gain in speedup obtained from 4 cores (2.2) to 8 cores (2.5).

6   Related Work

Automatic parallelization is an under-studied subject in model transformations, and the parallelization properties of the most popular model transformation languages (QVT, ATL, ETL, Kermeta, ...) are still unknown. Conversely parallelization is a deeply studied subject in the graph-transformation community. A seminal work is [7], where the authors describe the concept of amalgamation as a generalization of the theorem of parallel graph transformation. Basically common parts of rule derivations are joined (amalgamated) in a single derivation. This allows to relax the requirement of parallel independence so that rules do not need to be independent anymore as long as the common part is amalgamated and executed first. [12] studies parallel independence in hierarchical graph transformations. The problem of parallelizing graph transformations is however very different (and more difficult) than parallelizing model transformations, especially because of need to handle rule recursion and convergence. Traditionally the attention of graph transformations is more directed on optimizing the matching phase, that is an NP task and the typical bottleneck for transformation performances.

Table 1. Average execution times (in milliseconds) and speed-up (between parenthesis) per model size and number of cores

# Elem.	Std. ATL	Parallel ATL						
		2 cores	3 cores	4 cores	5 cores	6 cores	7 cores	8 cores
1000	83.4	48.9(1.7)	31.7(2.6)	28.8 (2.8)	28.2(2.9)	26.1(3.1)	26.5(3.1)	24.9(3.3)
10000	1338.8	1013.4(1.3)	685(1.9)	592.8(2.2)	565(2.3)	556.2(2.4)	532(2.5)	505.3(2.5)
100000	34942	24137(1.4)	17849(1.9)	16312(2.1)	15742(2.2)	15367(2.2)	14483(2.4)	13732(2.5)
1000000	308290	211032(1.4)	162487(1.9)	142262(2.1)	131393(2.3)	117439(2.6)	123122(2.5)	121341(2.5)

In [13] the authors implement parallel graph transformations on multicore system with the VMTS tool. Similarly to our approach, the authors divide execution into two phases. The matching phase is parallelized but the apply phase is executed sequentially. In [15] the same authors distinguisg between transformation-level (i.e., paralellizing rules) and rule-level (i.e. parallelizing matching) parallelism and contribute an algorithm for the latter. but they do not provide concrete estimations of performance gain and scalability. Our approach would mostly be located at the transformation-level. Some authors apply parallel graph transformation to manipulate EMF models. The authors in [11] study parallel graph transformations on EMF based on the concept of amalgamated graph transformations. Viatra 2 [22] can rewrite multiple matches of a rewriting rule in parallel, but it does not support parallelization among different rules.

A related work on ATL is [9], where authors propose some early research ideas about parallelizing and distributing the language. They propose a distributed implementation based on MapReduce [10]. MapReduce is a programming model for expressing distributed computations on massive amounts of data and an execution framework for large-scale data processing on clusters of commodity servers. Programs written in this functional style are automatically parallelized and executed on a large cluster of commodity machines. Our work may help in distributing ATL with the aim of making it a transformation language for distributed computation.

The work in [19] for parallelizing the XSLT language has many analogies to ours. The authors study the implicit parallelism of XSLT transformations, with different execution models, task and data parallelism, and they provide an engine implementation designed to work on multicore systems. They also show in a performance evaluation the speedup and scalability gains.

7   Conclusions and Future Work

In this article we added an implicit parallelization mechanism to the ATL language, and we studied how the structure of the language helps in overcoming some typical synchronization problems of parallelization. We believe that automatic parallelization may result beneficial to the general acceptance of MDE in industries handling big data.

While in this work we focused on task parallelism, in future we plan to study data parallelism for ATL and possible intermediate approaches. A study on static analysis of rule dependencies may help in anticipating some rule applications, without the need to re-introduce locks on data access. Finally implicit parallelism has its own drawbacks (difficulties in debugging, reduced control by the programmer over the parallel execution) that still need to be studied for ATL.

References

1. ATL Transformation ZOO, http://www.eclipse.org/atl/atlTransformations/
2. AUTOSAR Consortium: The AUTOSAR Standard, http://www.autosar.org/
3. GraBaTs 2009 Case Study,
   http://www.emn.fr/z-info/atlanmod/index.php/GraBaTs_2009_Case_Study.
4. Bergmann, G., Horváth, Á., Ráth, I., Varró, D., Balogh, A., Balogh, Z., Ökrös, A.: Incremental evaluation of model queries over EMF models. In: Petriu, D.C., Rouquette, N., Haugen, Ø. (eds.) MODELS 2010, Part I. LNCS, vol. 6394, pp. 76–90. Springer, Heidelberg (2010)
5. Bézivin, J., Jouault, F., Valduriez, P.: On the Need for Megamodels. In: Proceedings of Workshop on Best Practices for Model-Driven Software Development at the 19th Annual ACM Conference on Object-Oriented Programming, Systems, Languages, and Applications (October 2004)
6. Blair, G., Bencomo, N., France, R.B.: Models@ run. time. Computer 42(10), 22–27 (2009)
7. Boehm, P., Fonio, H.-R., Habel, A.: Amalgamation of graph transformations: a synchronization mechanism. J. Comput. Syst. Sci. 34(2-3), 377–408 (1987)
8. Burmester, S., Giese, H., Hirsch, M., Schilling, D., Tichy, M.: The fujaba real-time tool suite: model-driven development of safety-critical, real-time systems. In: Proceedings of the 27th International Conference on Software Engineering, pp. 670–671. ACM (2005)
9. Clasen, C., Del Fabro, M.D., Tisi, M., et al.: Transforming very large models in the cloud: a research roadmap. In: First International Workshop on Model-Driven Engineering on and for the Cloud (2012)
10. Dean, J., Ghemawat, S.: Mapreduce: simplified data processing on large clusters. Communications of the ACM 51(1), 107–113 (2008)
11. Ehrig, H., Golas, U., Taentzer, G., Ermel, C., Biermann, E.: Parallel independence of amalgamated graph transformations applied to model transformation. In: Graph Transformations and Modeldriven Engineering, pp. 1–21 (2010)
12. Habel, A., Hoffmann, B.: Parallel independence in hierarchical graph transformation. In: Ehrig, H., Engels, G., Parisi-Presicce, F., Rozenberg, G. (eds.) ICGT 2004. LNCS, vol. 3256, pp. 178–193. Springer, Heidelberg (2004)
13. Imre, G., Mezei, G.: Parallel graph transformations on multicore systems. In: Pankratius, V., Philippsen, M. (eds.) MSEPT 2012. LNCS, vol. 7303, pp. 86–89. Springer, Heidelberg (2012)
14. Jouault, F., Allilaire, F., Bézivin, J., Kurtev, I.: Atl: A model transformation tool. Science of Computer Programming 72(1), 31–39 (2008)
15. Mezei, G., Levendovszky, T., Mészáros, T., Madari, I.: Towards truly parallel model transformations: A distributed pattern matching approach. In: IEEE EUROCON 2009, pp. 403–410. IEEE (2009)
16. Patterson, D.A., Hennessy, J.L.: Computer organization and design: the hardware/-software interface. Morgan Kaufmann (2009)
17. Pohjonen, R., Tolvanen, J.-P., Consulting, M.: Automated production of family members: Lessons learned. In: Proceedings of the Second International Workshop on Product Line Engineering-The Early Steps: Planning, Modeling, and Managing (PLEES 2002), pp. 49–57. Citeseer (2002)
18. Steel, J., Drogemuller, R., Toth, B.: Model interoperability in building information modelling. Software & Systems Modeling 11(1), 99–109 (2012)

19. Sun, Y., Li, T., Zhang, Q., Yang, J., Liao, S.-W.: Parallel xml transformations on multi-core processors. In: IEEE International Conference on e-Business Engineering, ICEBE 2007, pp. 701–708. IEEE (2007)
20. Ulrich, W.M., Newcomb, P.: Information Systems Transformation: Architecture-Driven Modernization Case Studies. Morgan Kaufmann (2010)
21. Vajk, T., Dávid, Z., Asztalos, M., Mezei, G., Levendovszky, T.: Runtime model validation with parallel object constraint language. In: Proceedings of the 8th International Workshop on Model-Driven Engineering, Verification and Validation. ACM (2011)
22. Varró, D., Balogh, A.: The model transformation language of the viatra2 framework. Science of Computer Programming 68(3), 214–234 (2007)

Transformation of Models Containing Uncertainty

Michalis Famelis, Rick Salay, Alessio Di Sandro, and Marsha Chechik

University of Toronto
Toronto, Canada
{famelis,rsalay,adisandro,chechik}@cs.toronto.edu

Abstract. Model transformation techniques typically operate under the assumption that models do not contain uncertainty. In the presence of uncertainty, this forces modelers to either postpone working or to artificially remove it, with negative impacts on software cost and quality. Instead, we propose a technique to adapt existing model transformations so that they can be applied to models even if they contain uncertainty, thus enabling the use of transformations earlier. Building on earlier work, we show how to adapt graph rewrite-based model transformations to correctly operate on May uncertainty, a technique that allows explicit uncertainty to be expressed in any modeling language. We evaluate our approach on the classic Object-Relational Mapping use case, experimenting with models of varying levels of uncertainty.

1   Introduction

Model Driven Engineering (MDE) promises to accelerate and improve the quality of software development: software is described using high-level models which are easy to reason with. These models are then transformed into lower-level designs through a series of model transformations. Finally, low-level designs are used for effective code generation.

One of the factors prevalent within software engineering is *model uncertainty* which exists whenever a modeler is unsure about the information in the model. Uncertainty stems from a variety of causes including stakeholder conflicts [16], incomplete information [28], alternative design decisions [25], etc. Existing MDE solutions do not handle models with uncertainty. So when uncertainty is unresolved, the modeler should either delay the application of transformations until more information becomes available, or make premature resolutions in order to apply transformations, thus creating a risk that these resolutions are incorrect. In either case, uncertainty diminishes the benefits of MDE.

In this paper, we propose an approach that allows applying *existing* transformations to models containing uncertainty. The essence of the approach involves automatically modifying – "lifting" – transformations so they operate on models with uncertainty and correctly transform both the content of the model and the uncertainty about it. As a result of our approach, transformations can be applied early in the model development lifecycle, tolerating the uncertainty and allowing

A. Moreira et al. (Eds.): MODELS 2013, LNCS 8107, pp. 673–689, 2013.

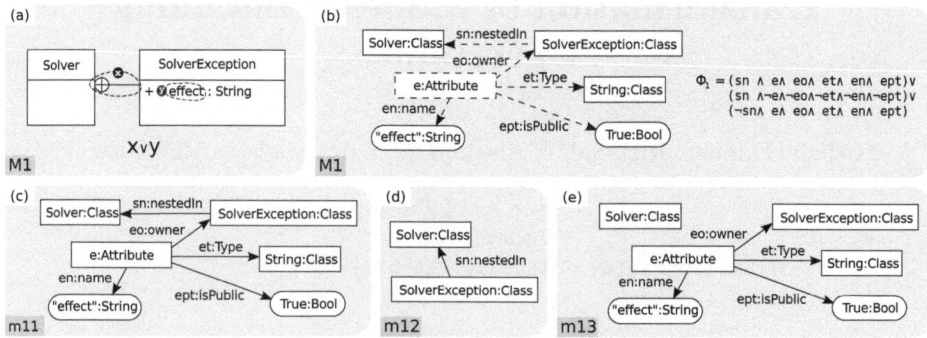

Fig. 1. (a) May model M_1, showing points of uncertainty. (b) M_1 as a typed graph (UML abstract syntax). (c-e) Concretizations m_{11}, m_{12}, m_{13} of M_1.

modelers to defer its resolution until extra information is available. This eliminates the need to delay transformation application and removes the pressure to potentially compromise model quality by resolving the uncertainty prematurely.

Uncertainty has been studied in different contexts including requirements engineering [6], adaptive systems [21] and software processes [13] but there has been little work specifically on *model* uncertainty. To address this gap, we have proposed a language-independent method of expressing uncertainty within models [10], through *May models*. May models allow a modeler to specify whether an element *should* be present, or its presence is *unknown*. Optional *May formulas* specify constraints over presence/absense of elements, in order to disallow infeasible or undesired uncertainty resolutions.

In this paper, we develop an approach for automatic "lifting" of transformations *specified as graph rewrite rules* so they *apply to models containing May uncertainty*. Specifically, the paper makes the following contributions:

1. an approach for transforming models that contain uncertainty, centered around the notion of lifting;
2. an automated method for creating lifted versions of existing transformation rules, so that they apply to May models;
3. an application of the approach to the classic Object-Relational Mapping (ORM) problem to assess its feasibility.

Relation to Previous Work. We first introduced the notion of lifting model transformations in [11]. In that approach, lifting is accomplished purely in propositional logic, via the use of *transfer predicates*. Rules are first turned into "template predicates" which, given a match in the input model, are instantiated with the propositional variables of the input model. This approach has a number of problems: (a) Transfer predicates need to be constructed ad-hoc, separately for each rule. On the other hand, the lifting approach proposed in this paper can be used for *arbitrary* rules. (b) Instantiation of the templates requires a-priori knowledge of the vocabulary of the input model, making it awkward to handle expanding/contracting vocabularies via additive/deleting rules. Instead, lifting is not dependent on the input model or the matching site. (c) The transfer predicates approach cannot handle NACs. (d) The May models resulting from applying the transfer predicates approach are expressed as propositional formulas over the set of both the input and the output model variables: in effect, the new model was expressed as a delta from the old. Thus, obtaining the new model required quantifying the old variables out – a computationally expensive process. (e) The transfer predicate approach requires a separate testing step to verify that the transformation was applied correctly. Moreover, testing entails enumerating *all* concretizations! Instead, the lifting presented here is guaranteed to be correct by construction.

In [10], we studied a different form of May model transformation: uncertainty-reducing refinement. The goal of this transformation is to reduce the number of possible concretizations of a given model with uncertainty, by specifying additional information. Work in [19,18] expanded the scope of the problem to additional uncertainty types, comprising the *MAVO* uncertainty framework described in [20]. The objective of this work is different: lifted transformations do not change the level of uncertainty by removing concretizations. Moreover, we aim to adapt classical transformations to May models instead of developing and checking transformations developed specifically for models with uncertainty.

The rest of this paper is organized as follows: We introduce a motivating example in Sec. 2. In Sec. 3, we give the necessary background. We describe the lifting process in Sec. 4 and evaluate it in Section 5. After comparing our approach with related work in Sec. 6, we conclude in Sec. 7 with a summary and a discussion of follow-on research.

2   Motivating Example

In this section, we introduce a running example to motivate and illustrate the key points of our approach. Suppose a modeler is creating a UML class diagram for an automated reasoning engine. The modeler has decided that there should exist a class `Solver` which throws exceptions, objects of type `SolverException`, whenever it reaches an error state. However, the modeler has yet to make the following design decisions: (a) whether `SolverException` should be an inner class of `Solver`, and (b) whether `SolverException` should have a `String` attribute called `effect` that would record an estimation of the effect of the exception on the reasoning process. In addition, the modeler expects that at least one of these features will be present in her model.

The resulting UML class diagram with uncertainty is encoded as a May model M_1 in Fig. 1(a). In this model, "⊕" is the UML symbol for a "nested class" and used here to indicate that `SolverException` is an inner class of `Solver`. The syntax for capturing uncertainty in M_1 is described in [14]. This model has two *points of uncertainty* – the relationship between the classes `Solver` and `SolverException` (denoted by x) and the presence of the `effect` attribute in class `SolverException` (denoted by y). *Maybe* elements that make up each point of uncertainty are enclosed in dashed ellipses. To better illustrate the details of each point of uncertainty, we show M_1 as a type graph (a simplified version of the

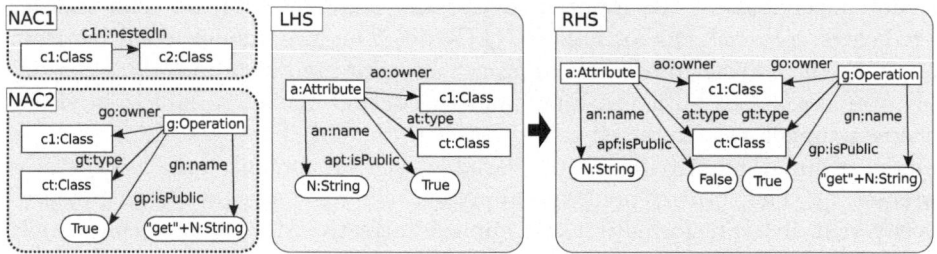

Fig. 2. Transformation rule R_{EV} for doing the *Encapsulate Variable* refactoring

UML abstract syntax) in Fig. 1(b). The node e and the edges sn, eo, et, en, ept are annotated with Maybe and thus indicated using dashed lines. An additional *May formula* Φ_1, also shown in Fig. 1(b), constrains the possible combinations of Maybe elements, defining the possible ways in which uncertainty can be resolved. Specifically, each Maybe element is represented by a propositional variable of the same name in the May formula. Thus, allowable configurations of the May model correspond to valuations of the variables that satisfy the May formula. In our scenario, the modeler's uncertainty can be resolved in one of three possible ways, corresponding to the models m_{11}, m_{12}, m_{13} shown in Figs. 1(c-e), respectively. These models are called *concretizations* of M_1.

Assume that the modeler notices that her model has an anti-pattern, namely, that the attribute effect is public. She decides that, unless SolverException is an inner class, effect should be made private for security reasons, and be accessed through a getter method. This can be accomplished by performing the *Encapsulate Variable* refactoring [3]. A generic method for implementing this refactoring using graph transformations was described by Mens et al. [15]. A simplified version of this rule, called R_{EV}, is shown in Fig. 2. The left-hand side (LHS) of the rule matches a node a (and its associated edges such as ao:owner) that represents a public attribute . The right-hand side (RHS) makes it private (by deleting the isPublic edge apt from a to True and adding a new isPublic edge apf from a to False). It also creates a public getter operation ge and its associated edges. In addition, the rule has two negative application conditions (NACs), i.e., conditions under which the rule should not be applied. These are: NAC$_1$, specifying the case when the class containing the public attribute is an inner class, and NAC$_2$, specifying the case when the class already has a getter.

Rule R_{EV} cannot be directly applied to the May model M_1 because it contains uncertainty. Our goal is thus to create its "lifted" version, $\mathcal{R}_{EV}$ that can be applied directly to M_1. The intuition behind such a lifting is as follows [11]: take the three concretizations, m_{11}, m_{12}, m_{13}, of M_1; apply R_{EV} to each of them, resulting in models $m_{21}, _{22}, m_{23}$ in Fig. 3(a-c); represent the resulting models as a May model M_2 in Fig. 3(d). That is, applying the lifted rule to a May model should be equivalent to a representation of the result of applying the original rule to each of the concretizations of the May model. So, applying the lifted version $\mathcal{R}_{EV}$ of R_{EV} to M_1 should produce the May model M_2 directly, without having to produce and transform individual concretizations. In this paper, we

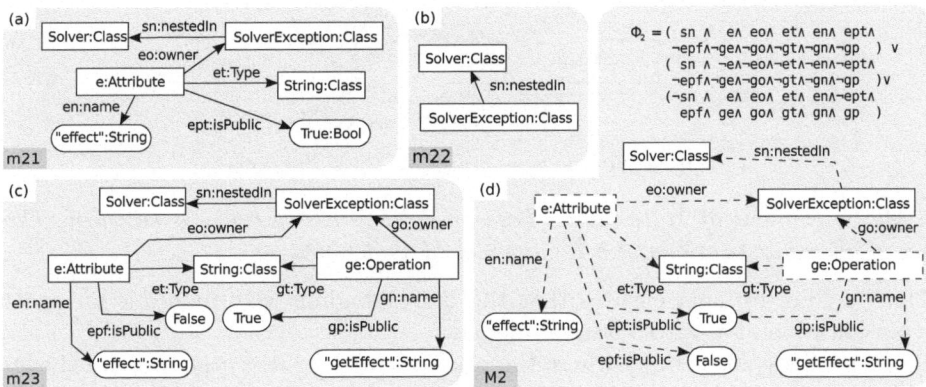

Fig. 3. (a-c) Classical models resulting from applying R_{EV} to the classical models in Fig. 1(c-e). (d) The result of applying the lifted version $\mathcal{R}_{EV}$ to M_1 directly: the May model M_2.

use this example to describe our technique for lifting transformations expressed as graph rewrite rules to correctly handle May models.

3 Background

In this section, we provide the background necessary for the rest of the paper and fix the notation.

May Models. The formal definition and semantics of May models is given in [12]. In this section, we give an informal definition and illustrate it using the motivating example.

Definition 1 (May model). *A* May model M *is a tuple* $\langle G, ann, \Phi_M \rangle$, *where* G *is a typed graph called a* base graph, *ann is a function that annotates a subset* S_M *of elements of* G *with* Maybe, *and* Φ_M *is the* May formula. *The tuple* $\langle G, ann \rangle$ *representing the* Maybe-*annotated typed graph* G *is called the* May graph. S_M *is denotes the set of all* Maybe *elements of* M.

The base graph is typed by a metamodel, represented by a *type graph*. A simplified type graph for class diagrams is shown in Fig. 4. M_1 is shown as an instance of this type graph in Fig. 1(b) Annotating an element with Maybe indicates the uncertainty of the modeler about whether that element should be part of the model or not. In Fig. 1(b), Maybe-annotated elements such as the attribute node e are shown with dashed lines.

Each Maybe element is represented by a propositional variable which expresses the proposition *"the element is part of the model"*. The May formula is expressed over this vocabulary of variables. Allowable configurations of Maybe elements are thus specified by the satisfying assignments of the May formula.

Definition 2 (Concretization). *A concretization of a May model* $\langle G, ann, \Phi_M \rangle$ *is a classical model derived from M by assigning each propositional variable for*

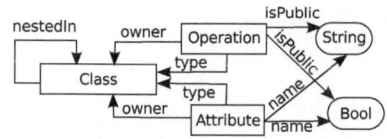

Fig. 4. Simple type graph for class diagrams

a *Maybe* element of M to either *True* or *False*, such that Φ_M is satisfied. The set of all concretizations of a May model M is denoted by $[M]$.

Thus, a May formula ensures that the corresponding May model is an *exact* representation of a set of classical models.

$[M_1] = \{m_{11}, m_{12}, m_{13}\}$ where the classical models m_{11}, m_{12}, m_{13} are shown in Fig. 1(c-e). Each of them represents a case where all uncertainty is resolved, i.e., all variables corresponding to Maybe elements have been set to either True or False. For example, model m_{13} in Fig. 1(e) can be obtained by satisfying the last disjunctive clause of Φ_1, i.e., by setting sn to False and e, eo, etc. to True.

For example, consider a May model M_1' in which the class Solver is also annotated with Maybe, but whose May formula is changed so that each clause contains the non-negated term Solver. Even though Solver is annotated with Maybe in M_1', all concretizations of M_1' must contain it and thus $[M_1] = [M_1']$. We call models that have the same set of concretizations *equivalent*. A May model M is said to be in the *graphical reduced form* (GRF) iff an element is annotated with Maybe in the May graph iff it is not common to all of M's concretizations. In [12] we give an algorithm for transforming any May model to a GRF equivalent model. M_1 is given in GRF.

Model Transformations. We focus on *graph transformations* [9]. Such transformations apply to models that do not contain uncertainty, e.g., m_{11} in Fig. 1(c). They are implemented by executing a set of graphical rules defined as follows:

Definition 3 (Transformation rule). *A transformation rule R is a tuple $R = \langle\{NAC\}, LHS, RHS\rangle$, where the typed graphs LHS and RHS are respectively called the* left-hand *and the* right-hand *sides of the rule, and $\{NAC\}$ represents a (potentially empty) set of typed graphs, called* negative application conditions.

We show the RHS and LHS of the rule R_{EV} in Fig. 2. In addition, R_{EV} contains two NACs (NAC$_1$ and NAC$_2$), indicated by a dotted border.

The LHS, RHS and NACs of a rule consist of different *parts*, i.e., sets of model elements which do not necessarily form proper graphs. These parts play different roles during the rule application:

$\mathbf{C}^r$: The set of model elements that are present both in the LHS and the RHS, i.e., remain unaffected by the rule.
$\mathbf{D}^r$: The set of elements in the LHS that are absent in the RHS, i.e., deleted by the rule.
$\mathbf{A}^r$: The set of elements present in the RHS but absent in the LHS, i.e., added by the rule.
$\mathbf{N}^r$: The set of elements present in any NAC, excluding those included in $\mathbf{C}^r$.

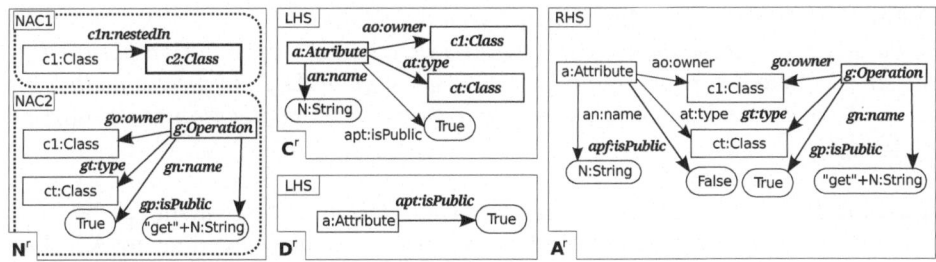

Fig. 5. Parts of the rule R_{EV}. Each rule part contains only those elements whose label appears ***in bold serif font***[1]

The parts of the example rule R_{EV} from Fig. 2 are shown in Fig. 5. Specifically, $\mathbf{C}^r$ is the set[1] $\{a, ao, an, at, c1, ct\}$, $\mathbf{D}^r$ is the (unary) set $\{apt\}$, $\mathbf{A}^r$ is $\{g, go, gn, gp, gt, apf\}$, and $\mathbf{N}^r$ is $\{g, gn, go, gt, cln, c2\}$.

A rule R is *applied* to a model m by finding a *matching site* of its LHS in m:

Definition 4 (Matching site). *A matching site of a transformation rule R in a model m is a tuple $K = \langle \overline{\mathbf{N}}, \mathbf{C}, \mathbf{D} \rangle$, where $\mathbf{C}$ and $\mathbf{D}$ are matches of the parts $\mathbf{C}^r$ and $\mathbf{D}^r$ of the LHS of R in m, and $\overline{\mathbf{N}}$ is the set of all matches of NACs in m that are anchored at the matches $\mathbf{C}$ and $\mathbf{D}$.*

For example, a matching site K_1 for the rule R_{EV} in the model m_{11} in Fig. 1(c) is $\langle \mathbf{C}_1, \overline{\mathbf{N}}_1, \mathbf{D}_1 \rangle$, where $\mathbf{C}_1 = \{e, eo, en, et, \mathtt{SolverException}, \mathtt{String}\}$, $\overline{\mathbf{N}}_1 = \{\{\mathtt{Solver}, sn\}\}$, and $\mathbf{D}_1 = \{ept\}$.

In the above definition, $\overline{\mathbf{N}}$ denotes the set of all matches within m of the NACs of R. given the match of $\mathbf{C}^r$ and $\mathbf{D}^r$. If the same NAC can match multiple ways, then all of them are included in $\overline{\mathbf{N}}$ as separate matches. For example, if the model in Fig. 1(c) had another class $\mathtt{Solver2}$ that also nested $\mathtt{SolverException}$ via an edge $sn2$, then $\overline{\mathbf{N}}$ would contain two matches for NAC_1: $\overline{\mathbf{N}} = \{\{\mathtt{Solver}, sn\}, \{\mathtt{Solver2}, sn2\}\}$. The set of matching sites define the places in the model m where the rule can potentially be applied.

Definition 5 (Applicability condition). *Given a transformation rule R, a model m, and matching site $K = \langle \overline{\mathbf{N}}, \mathbf{C}, \mathbf{D} \rangle$, the rule R is applicable at K iff $\overline{\mathbf{N}}$ is empty*[2].

The above definition ensures that the rule can only be applied at a given site if no NAC matches. For R_{EV}, the matching site K_1 in m_{11} does not satisfy the applicability condition as $\overline{\mathbf{N}}_1 \neq \emptyset$. On the other hand, the model m_{13} in Fig. 1(e) contains a matching site $K_2 = \langle \emptyset, \mathbf{C}_1, \mathbf{D}_1 \rangle$, which does satisfy this condition. Then, the rule can be applied:

---

[1] Nodes that represent values (e.g., boolean True, the string N, etc.) are also considered to be part of $\mathbf{C}^r$ but are omitted here for brevity.

[2] The theory of graph transformation requires some additional formal preconditions, most notably the *gluing condition* [9]. These are not discussed here for brevity.

Definition 6 (Rule application). *Given a transformation rule R, a model m, and a matching site K in m for which the rule applicability condition is satisfied, rule R is* applied, *producing a model m′, by removing* **D** *from m and adding* **A**, *where* **A** *is a match of the part* $\mathbf{A}^r$ *of R in m. Rule application is denoted as* $m \stackrel{R}{\Longrightarrow} m'$.

Applying R_{EV} to m_{13} at K_2 thus requires the deletion of the element ept because it is contained in **D**, and the addition of new elements according to $\mathbf{A}^r$. The resulting model m_{23} is shown in Fig. 3(c), where **A** is the set {ge, go, gn, gp, gt, epf}.

We refer to rules such as the ones described above as "classical" to differentiate them from their "lifted" counterparts which can be applied to May models.

4 Lifting Transformations

In this section, we describe the process of lifting a transformation rule to apply to May models. A classical rule R adapted to apply to May models is called *lifted* and is denoted by $\mathcal{R}$.

May models are intended to be exact representations of sets of models and lifted transformations should preserve this. Therefore, applying a lifted transformation rule $\mathcal{R}$ to a May model M_{in} should be equivalent to applying its classical version R to each of the concretizations of M_{in} and building a May model from the result. We refer to this principle, defined in [11], as the *Correctness Criterion* for lifting transformations and define it formally below.

Definition 7. *Let a rule R, a May model M_{in} with a set of concretizations* $[M_{in}] = \{m_{in}^1, \ldots, m_{in}^n\}$, *and the set* $U = \{m_{out}^i \mid \forall m_{in}^i \in [M_{in}] \cdot m_{in}^i \stackrel{R}{\Longrightarrow} m_{out}^i\}$ *be given.* $\mathcal{R}$ *is a* correct lifting *of R iff for any production* $M_{in} \stackrel{\mathcal{R}}{\Longrightarrow} M_{out}$, *the set of concretizations of the resulting May model M_{out} satisfies the condition* $[M_{out}] = U$.

In the motivating example, we aim to compute a lifted version $\mathcal{R}_{EV}$ of R_{EV} s.t. for the May models M_1 and M_2 in Figs. 1(a) and 3(a), $M_1 \stackrel{\mathcal{R}_{EV}}{\Longrightarrow} M_2$.

In traditional rule application during graph transformation, it is sufficient to find a graph match of the LHS of the rule and then check whether the NACs are applicable. However, a May model also has a propositional component, the May formula which constrains the possible combinations of Maybe elements. Thus, doing the graphical match for the May graph is not sufficient to guarantee correctness and needs to be augmented with manipulation of the May, to ensure that the appropriate concretizations get transformed. We illustrate both parts of the transformation on our running example in Sec. 4.1 and then generalize in Sec. 4.2. In Sec. 4.3, we prove correctness of this approach.

4.1   Lifting Example

We illustrate the transformation of the graph and the formula using our running example where the rule R_{EV} in Fig. 2 is applied to the May model M_1, shown in Fig. 1(b), to produce M_2 in Fig. 3(d). Fig. 6 summarizes the application of this rule for the single existing matching site, showing the May graphs and the truth tables of the May formulas Φ_1 and Φ_2 of M_1 and M_2, respectively. Each column of the truth tables is a Maybe element. Each row corresponds to an allowable configuration of Maybe elements, denoted by 1, and thus defines a concretization. The truth tables also show which Maybe elements are matched by each of the rule's parts. For example, the edges eo and ept are both matched by the rule's LHS, where eo is found in the match **C** of the $\mathbf{C}^r$ part of the rule, and ept in **D** match of $\mathbf{D}^r$. Our objective is to construct the lifted transformation $\mathcal{R}_{EV}$ that produces M_2 when applied to M_1. We begin by constructing the graphical part of $\mathcal{R}_{EV}$ first, followed by the propositional part.

Graphical Part. Consider applying R_{EV} to M_1 by directly applying it to M_b, M_1's base graph. Clearly, this approach does not produce the correct outcome. First, NAC_1 matches in M_b and thus the rule does not apply at all! Yet, there exists a concretization of M_1, m_{13}, for which neither of R_{EV}'s NACs match and thus R_{EV} should be applicable. We therefore expect it to be applicable to M_1 as well. Second, the RHS of the rule does not specify which elements in the output model should become Maybe, whereas M_2 clearly has them.

Thus, the classical strategy for rule application is not sufficient and needs to be augmented by the uncertainty in the model, i.e., the Maybe annotations of its elements. The presence of Maybe elements in the match of NAC_1 and in the match of the LHS of R_{EV} are both indications that R_{EV} applies to *some* concretizations but not others. We thus need to change the May model M_1 so that it represents both those concretizations that are unchanged by R_{EV} and those where the rule has been applied. Applying R_{EV} to a concretization of M_1 entails (1) deleting the edge ept, because it is included in the match **D** of $\mathbf{D}^r$, and (2) adding the elements of **A**: ge, gn, go, gt, gp, and epf. However, we cannot altogether delete ept from M_1 because it should still remain in the unchanged concretization m_{11}. Instead, we must keep it annotated with Maybe to indicate that it is part of some concretizations but not others. Similarly, the newly added elements should be annotated with Maybe to indicate that they are added in m_{13} but not M_{11} or m_{12}.

We summarize the application of the graphical part of $\mathcal{R}_{EV}$ to M_1 as follows: (a) Apply R_{EV} to the base graph M_b of M_1 even though NAC_1 matches because the match contains a Maybe element. (b) Include both **D** and **A** in the base graph of M_2 and annotate all of their elements with Maybe because the match of the LHS in M_1 contains a Maybe element.

Propositional Part. We now define the propositional part of $\mathcal{R}_{EV}$ that transforms the May formula Φ_1 of M_1 into Φ_2 of M_2. We achieve this by defining an operation on Φ_1 that has the effect of transforming the truth table of Φ_1 into the truth table of Φ_2. First note that the truth tables can be split into two parts:

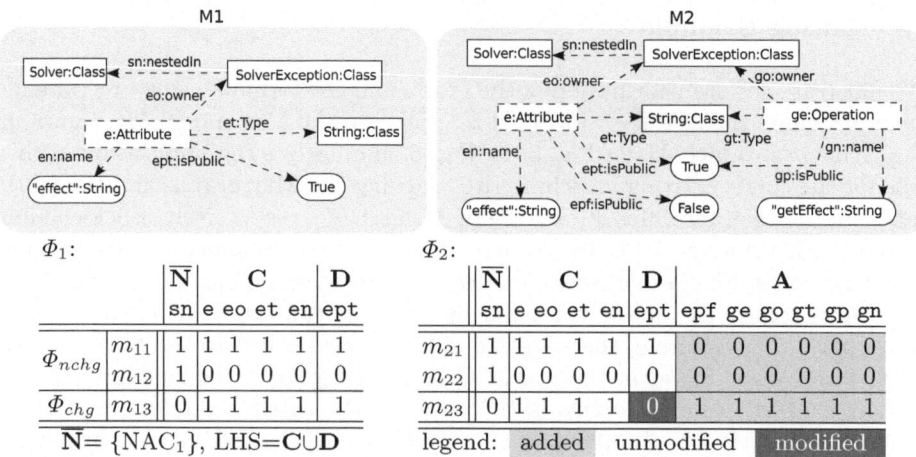

Fig. 6. Applying the lifted version of R_{EV} to the motivating example. Left: input model M_1, May graph and truth table of the May formula. Right: output model M_2, May graph and truth table of the May formula.

(a) The concretizations where R_{EV} does not apply (i.e., m_{11} and m_{12}). The corresponding rows m_{21} and m_{22} in Φ_2 remain unchanged, and the variables in **A** are set to False (denoted by 0) to indicate that $\mathbf{A}^r$ is not added. We denote the formula representing the unchanged part by Φ_{nchg}.

(b) The concretizations where R_{EV} does apply (i.e., m_{13}). The corresponding row m_{23} has the variables of **D** set to 0 to indicate that $\mathbf{D}^r$ is deleted and the variables of **A** set to 1 to indicate that $\mathbf{A}^r$ is added. We denote the formula representing the changed part by Φ_{chg}.

Thus, $\Phi_2 = \Phi_{nchg} \vee \Phi_{chg}$.

To obtain the unchanged part, we begin by specifying a condition, over elements of M_1, under which the rule R_{EV} applies, i.e., when its NAC $\mathbf{N}^r$ does not match in M_b and both $\mathbf{C}^r$ and $\mathbf{D}^r$ do match: $\Phi_{apply} = \neg\phi_{\mathbf{N}}^{and} \wedge \phi_{\mathbf{C}}^{and} \wedge \phi_{\mathbf{D}}^{and}$. Let $\phi_{\mathbf{X}}^{and}$ where $\mathbf{X} \in \{\mathbf{N},\mathbf{C},\mathbf{D}\}$ denote the conjunction of all variables in $\mathbf{X}$ that represent elements that are Maybe. Restricting Φ_1 to those concretizations of M_1 where R_{EV} does not apply ($\neg\Phi_{apply}$) and forcing the variables of **A** to become False produces the unchanged part: $\Phi_{nchg} = (\Phi_1 \wedge \neg\Phi_{apply}) \wedge \neg\phi_{\mathbf{A}}^{or}$, where $\phi_{\mathbf{A}}^{or}$ indicates the disjunction of all variables in **A** that represent elements that are Maybe.

For the changed part Φ_{chg}, we restrict Φ_1 to those concretizations of M_1 where R_{EV} does apply and force the variables of **D** to become False and those of **A** to become True: $\Phi_{chg} = (\Phi_1 \wedge \Phi_{apply})|^{\exists\mathbf{D}} \wedge \neg\phi_{\mathbf{D}}^{or} \wedge \phi_{\mathbf{A}}^{and}$. Here, $(\Phi_1 \wedge \Phi_{apply})|^{\exists\mathbf{D}}$ indicates *existential quantification* of all variables in **D** that occur in formula $\Phi_1 \wedge \Phi_{apply}$. In our example, $\mathbf{D} = \{\mathtt{ept}\}$, so it becomes $(\Phi_1 \wedge \Phi_{apply})|_{\mathtt{ept}=T} \vee (\Phi_1 \wedge \Phi_{apply})|_{\mathtt{ept}=F}$. That is, we eliminate each variable in **D** from $\Phi_1 \wedge \Phi_{apply}$ by taking the disjunction of the cases where it is set to False and to True. Quantifying out variables in **D** is done before forcing them to become False (using $\neg\phi_{\mathbf{D}}^{or}$) because we are changing the values of existing variables (the variables of **D** already occur in Φ_{apply}) and not just setting the value for new variables as we are for $\mathbf{A}$. Otherwise, we get an inconsistency because $\Phi_{apply} \Rightarrow \phi_{\mathbf{D}}^{and}$ by definition.

Substituting the variables from the example and simplifying gives:

$$\Phi_{nchg} = (\text{sn} \wedge \text{e} \wedge \text{eo} \wedge \text{et} \wedge \text{en} \wedge \text{ept} \wedge \neg\text{epf} \wedge \neg\text{ge} \wedge \neg\text{go} \wedge \neg\text{gt} \wedge \neg\text{gt} \wedge \neg\text{gp} \wedge \neg\text{gn}) \vee$$
$$(\text{sn} \wedge \neg\text{e} \wedge \neg\text{eo} \wedge \neg\text{et} \wedge \neg\text{en} \wedge \neg\text{ept} \wedge \neg\text{epf} \wedge \neg\text{ge} \wedge \neg\text{go} \wedge \neg\text{gt} \wedge \neg\text{gt} \wedge \neg\text{gp} \wedge \neg\text{gn})$$
$$\Phi_{chg} = (\neg\text{sn} \wedge \text{e} \wedge \text{eo} \wedge \text{et} \wedge \text{en} \wedge \neg\text{ept} \wedge \text{epf} \wedge \text{ge} \wedge \text{go} \wedge \text{gt} \wedge \text{gt} \wedge \text{gp} \wedge \text{gn})$$

The resulting formula $\Phi_2 = \Phi_{nchg} \vee \Phi_{chg}$ is the same as the May formula in Fig. 3(d) and has the same truth table as the one shown in Fig. 6.

4.2   General Case

We can generalize the above process to an arbitrary rule R and define how the graphical part of its lifted version $\mathcal{R}$ is applied to a May model M to produce a May model M'. As with the running example, we define this in terms of applying R to the base graph of M and then making modifications. Following Definition 4, the matching site for $\mathcal{R}$ is a matching site for R in the base graph of M.

Definition 8 (Lifted rule applicability conditions). *Given a May model M with a May formula Φ_M, a transformation rule $R = \langle \{NAC\}, LHS, RHS \rangle$, and a matching site $K = \langle \overline{\mathbf{N}}, \mathbf{C}, \mathbf{D} \rangle$, the lifted rule $\mathcal{R}$ is applicable at K iff the following conditions hold:*

1. *For all $N \in \overline{\mathbf{N}}$, N contains a Maybe element*
2. *$\Phi_M \wedge \Phi_{apply}$ is satisfiable, where $\Phi_{apply} = \neg \bigvee \{\phi_{\mathbf{N}}^{and} | N \in \overline{\mathbf{N}}\} \wedge \phi_{\mathbf{C}}^{and} \wedge \phi_{\mathbf{D}}^{and}$.*

In this definition, Condition 1 ensures that there is no NAC match without Maybe elements; otherwise the NAC match would necessarily occur in every concretization and so R would not apply to *any* concretization of M. Condition 2 uses the constraints in the May formula to ensure that at this matching site, the rule R matches in at least one concretization of M. Specifically, this checks that there exists a concretization in which all f the Maybe elements of $\mathbf{C}$ and $\mathbf{D}$ are True and not all of the Maybe elements in any NAC match are set to True.

We now give the general definition of a rule application for a lifted rule.

Definition 9 (Lifted rule application). *Given a May model M with a May formula Φ_M, a transformation rule $R = \langle \{NAC\}, LHS, RHS \rangle$ and matching site $K = \langle \overline{\mathbf{N}}, \mathbf{C}, \mathbf{D} \rangle$ in M for which the rule applicability conditions are satisfied, the lifted rule $\mathcal{R}$ is applied to produce a May model M' as follows:*

1. *if K contains no Maybe elements, apply R in the classical way to produce the base graph of M' and set $\phi_{M'} = \phi_M$.*
2. *otherwise,*
   (a) *set $M' = M$;*
   (b) *add the elements $\mathbf{A}$ of the $\mathbf{A}^r$ part of the RHS to M';*
   (c) *annotate all elements of $\mathbf{A}$ and $\mathbf{D}$ with Maybe;*
   (d) *set $\Phi_{M'} = [(\Phi_M \wedge \neg\Phi_{apply}) \wedge \neg\phi_{\mathbf{A}}^{or}] \vee [(\Phi_M \wedge \Phi_{apply})|^{\exists \mathbf{D}} \wedge \neg\phi_{\mathbf{D}}^{or} \wedge \phi_{\mathbf{A}}^{and}]$.*

In this definition, Case 1 captures the situation when there are no Maybe elements at the matching site and so the rule can be applied in the classical way and the May model is unaffected. Case 2 captures the situation when there are Maybe elements in parts of the matching site so that R may apply in some concretizations but not in others. This case mirrors the discussion of $\mathcal{R}_{EV}$ in Section 4.1. In particular, in the graphical part, $\mathbf{D}^r$ is not deleted (step a) but $\mathbf{A}^r$ is still added (step b) and all of the elements in $\mathbf{A}$ and $\mathbf{D}$ are set to Maybe (step c). The propositional part (step d) is the same as for the $\mathcal{R}_{EV}$ example except that $\varPhi_{nchg}$ and $\varPhi_{chg}$ are inlined and the more general case of $\overline{\mathbf{N}}$ is used in $\varPhi_{apply}$ (from Definition 8) to account for multiple NAC matches that could exist in the base graph of M.

As with a classical rule system, lifted rules continue to be applied until no rule is applicable. Note that the resulting model M' may not necessarily be in GRF after every rule application. That is, M' can contain redundant Maybe elements. If M' is intended for human consumption (as opposed to automated reasoning) then the additional step of putting it into GRF is advisable. However, this step is optional since it does not affect the set of concretizations that the May model represents.

4.3   Analysis

In this section, we discuss some key properties of lifted rules such as their correctness, termination and confluence. The resulting properties apply to *arbitrary* transformations being lifted, whether they are injective, endogenous, exogenous and so on.

Correctness. We now show that lifting described by Definitions 8 and 9 satisfies the correctness condition in Definition 7. Specifically, we show that if a lifted rule $\mathcal{R}$ is applied to a May model M to produce a May model M', then the concretizations of M' must be exactly the set obtained by applying the classical rule R to each concretization of M. We focus our argument on a specific matching site $K = \langle \overline{\mathbf{N}}, \mathbf{C}, \mathbf{D} \rangle$ since by transitivity, if the rule is correct when applied to each site, then the application to any sequence of sites is also correct.

We begin with checking correctness of the applicability condition (Definition 8) of the lifted rule $\mathcal{R}$: whenever R is applicable for some concretization of M at K, then $\mathcal{R}$ is also applicable, i.e., $\mathcal{R}$ it does not miss any sites where a concretization can be affected by R. By Condition 1 of Definition 8, if there is a NAC in $\overline{\mathbf{N}}$ that has no Maybe elements then $\mathcal{R}$ does not apply at K. But a NAC without Maybe in the base graph of M means that this NAC appears in every concretization of M and thus the classical rule R does not apply to any concretization either and thus applying the lifted rule does not miss any classical rule applications.

Condition 2 says that $\varPhi_M \wedge \varPhi_{apply}$ must be satisfiable for $\mathcal{R}$ to apply, which happens iff there exists a concretization of M where $\mathbf{C}^r$ and $\mathbf{D}^r$ are present and no NAC in $\overline{\mathbf{N}}$ is present – exactly the classical applicability condition in Definition 5. If this condition does not hold, there are no classical rule applications in any concretization, therefore the lifted rule applicability condition is correct.

We now argue that the lifted rule application in Definition 9 is correct. To do this, we show that if $\mathcal{R}$ satisfies the applicability conditions, then applying $\mathcal{R}$ at a site K has the same effect as applying R at K in each concretization. Case 1 says that when K contains no Maybe elements, we apply the rule classically to the base graph of M. Without Maybe elements, K occurs in every concretization of M and so the classical application of R in every concretization would be identical to applying $\mathcal{R}$.

Case 2 applies when K has some Maybe elements. In this case, the concretizations are split into those where R does not apply and those where it does. We then aim to show that the steps (a-d) for constructing the graphical and propositional effect of applying $\mathcal{R}$ are "correct by construction". We do not repeat this argument, described in Sec. 4.1, here, for brevity. Thus, we conclude that the lifted rule application is also correct. Since both the applicability condition and the effect of application are correct, we conclude that $\mathcal{R}$ satisfies the specification of correct lifting in Definition 7.

Termination. To prove termination, we show that if an application of a set of classical rules on an input model always terminates than so does the set of the corresponding lifted rules. Without loss of generality, we restrict ourselves to a rule set containing a single classical rule R which we assume is terminating. Since $\mathcal{R}$ is correct according to Definition 7, repeatedly applying it to a May model M has the same effect as repeatedly applying R to each concretization of M. Since R is terminating, it eventually is no longer applicable to any concretization of M. At this point, Φ_{apply} which encodes classical applicability is False and thus $\Phi_M \wedge \Phi_{apply}$ is not satisfiable, and, by Condition 2 of Definition 8, $\mathcal{R}$ does not apply. Thus, when the application of R terminates, the application of $\mathcal{R}$ terminates as well. Therefore, if R is terminating, so is $\mathcal{R}$.

Confluence. We argue that if a set of classical rules is confluent then the corresponding set of lifted rules is also confluent "up to an equivalence", that is, when the process terminates, the resulting May model has the same set of concretizations, regardless of the order in which the rules have been applied. Repeatedly applying lifted rules to a May model M has the same effect as repeatedly applying the corresponding classical rules to each concretization of M. Since the classical rules are confluent and terminating, the process over lifted rules reaches the same final set of concretizations. Thus, the lifted rule set is confluent "up to an equivalence".

5   Evaluation

We applied our lifting approach to the problem of mapping simple UML class diagrams to relational database schemas. This problem is called "Object-Relational Mapping" (ORM) and is often used as a benchmark for model transformations [2]. Our aim was to gather evidence about how the lifting approach scales as uncertainty increases. We thus measured the runtime of performing ORM with lifted rules while increasing levels of uncertainty and compared it with the baseline runtime of performing ORM for a classical model. The ORM transformation

Table 1. Results of applying the ORM rules to the Ecore metamodel

Number of concretizations:	1	24	48	108	144	192	256
Number of Maybe elements:	0	5	6	8	10	12	14
Time (sec):	32.6	32.8	32.7	32.9	32.6	33.0	48.4
Size of May formula (KiB):	0	27.9	14.0	1,080.9	1,153.4	19,361.9	320,570.7

rules we used came from [26] and consist of 5 layered transformation rules that, given a class diagram, create a relational schema and traceability links.

We used the class diagram specification of the Ecore metamodel [24] as input to the ORM rules. Serializing Ecore models in a database is an important technical problem that has resulted in the establishment of two Eclipse projects, *CDO* [7] and *Teneo* [8], both of which implement ORM for Ecore. We manually flattened the Ecore metamodel and adapted it to the type graph used by the ORM rules in [26]. The resulting model consisted of 65 model elements: 17 classes, 17 associations, 6 generalization links and 25 attributes. Starting with a May model with a single concretization (no uncertainty), we gradually increased the degree of uncertainty by adding more concretizations, by a step of roughly 50, thus creating models with 1, 24, 48, 108, 144, 192, and 256 concretizations. To accomplish that we incrementally injected points of uncertainty, annotating elements with Maybe and creating the corresponding May formulas. The most uncertain case (256 concretizations) contained 8 points of uncertainty, expressed across a total of 14 Maybe elements.

We implemented the lifting of the ORM rules using Henshin [1]. For the satisfiability check required in Definition 8, we used the Z3 SMT solver [5]. We used the Model Management Tool Framework [17] as the integration platform. We executed the case study on a computer with Intel Core i7-2600 3.40GHz×4 cores (8 logical) and 8GB RAM, running Ubuntu-64 12.10. We applied the set of lifted rules to each input May model and recorded the total runtime and the size of the resulting May formula. Our observations are shown in Table 1.

The results show that the total runtime remains almost constant at roughly 32.8 seconds, except for the largest category where it increases to 48.4 seconds. On the other hand, we see a dramatic increase in the size of the May formula, from 27.9 KiB for the smallest category, to approx. 320.6 MiB for the largest. This exponential growth in size is reasonable, given (Definition 9). Overall, the results suggest that lifting scales reasonably with respect to time, whereas the increasing size of the May formula may be a problem. However, we note that our implementation did not attempt to incorporate any formula simplification heuristics, and therefore there is room for optimization.

6   Related Work

The notion of uncertainty addressed by May models captures the scenario of having multiple possible alternative design solutions, with the modeler being unsure about which one to pick. Discussion of work related to representing sets of models is out of scope of the current paper; a thorough comparison of May models with related formalisms can be found in [12]. May models encode a set of classical models, and lifted rules are rules that can transform entire sets of models simultaneously. In the following, we discuss work related to transformations that apply to modeling formalisms that represent sets of models.

Different variants of feature models have been proposed in the literature to encode a set of possible configurations of a software product line [22]. Transformations of feature models, i.e., the creation of a feature model representing a subset of the original, have been studied in [4] under the name of *feature model specialization*. This process is described as a series of operations such as "feature cloning" and "reference unfolding" and resembles the uncertainty-reducing transformation of [10]. Graph transformations have also been applied to feature models, e.g., in [23], they are used to refactor product lines via feature model merging. Transformations that apply to metamodel definitions also transform sets of models, i.e., the set of possible instances of the metamodel. The Object-to-Relational Mapping transformation [26] in Sec. 6 is one such example. Similarly, special purpose transformation languages have been built to transform ontologies, such as a rule based language based on xOWL [27].

The main difference between these transformations and the lifting approach presented here is that they are tailored to specific tasks, whereas lifting applies to *arbitrary* transformation rules. Moreover, these techniques only indirectly affect the classical models (e.g., variants or instances) represented by the abstraction formalism. On the other hand, lifted transformations match and transform the alternatives directly, via the propositional part of the lifted rules.

7   Conclusion

In this paper, we have shown how to adapt existing model transformations to May models, a formalism that allows uncertainty to be explicated in software artifacts. To achieve this, we have introduced the process of *lifting* graph transformation rules and proved its correctness of application to May models. We have implemented our approach and applied it to the Object-Relational Mapping benchmark. Our experience showed that the overhead of applying lifted transformations is reasonable, so we feel that the approach is feasible for transforming realistic models with uncertainty. In the future, we are planning to implement lifting as a higher-order transformation (HOT). We expect the approach to lift a classical rule to a layered graph grammar of classical rules, allowing us to implement a dedicated tool by reusing existing graph grammar implementations such as Henshin [1]. We also intend to evaluate our approach further and expand our lifting technique to models containing other types of uncertainty [20].

References

1. Arendt, T., Biermann, E., Jurack, S., Krause, C., Taentzer, G.: Henshin: Advanced concepts and tools for in-place EMF model transformations. In: Petriu, D.C., Rouquette, N., Haugen, Ø. (eds.) MODELS 2010, Part I. LNCS, vol. 6394, pp. 121–135. Springer, Heidelberg (2010)
2. Bézivin, J., Schürr, A., Tratt, L.: Model Transformations in Practice Workshop. In: Bruel, J.-M. (ed.) MoDELS 2005. LNCS, vol. 3844, pp. 120–127. Springer, Heidelberg (2006)
3. Casais, E.: The Automatic Reorganization of Object Oriented Hierarchies – A Case Study. Object Oriented Systems 1, 95–115 (1994)
4. Czarnecki, K., Helsen, S.: Staged Configuration Using Feature Models. In: Nord, R.L. (ed.) SPLC 2004. LNCS, vol. 3154, pp. 266–283. Springer, Heidelberg (2004)
5. De Moura, L., Bjørner, N.: Satisfiability Modulo Theories: Introduction and Applications. Commun. ACM 54(9), 69–77 (2011)
6. Ebert, C., De Man, J.: Requirements Uncertainty: Influencing Factors and Concrete Improvements. In: Proc. of ICSE 2005, pp. 553–560 (2005)
7. Eclipse, CDO website: http://www.eclipse.org/cdo/ (accessed March 16, 2013)
8. Eclipse, Teneo website: http://wiki.eclipse.org/Teneo/ (accessed March 16, 2013)
9. Ehrig, H., Ehrig, K., Prange, U., Taentzer, G.: Fundamentals of Algebraic Graph Transformation, 1st edn. Monographs in Theoretical Computer Science. An EATCS Series. Springer (2006)
10. Famelis, M., Chechik, M., Salay, R.: Partial Models: Towards Modeling and Reasoning with Uncertainty. In: Proc. of ICSE 2012 (2012)
11. Famelis, M., Chechik, M., Salay, R.: The Semantics of Partial Model Transformations. In: Proc. of MiSE 2012 (2012)
12. Famelis, M., Chechik, M., Salay, R.: Towards Modeling and Reasoning with Uncertainty (submitted, 2013)
13. Ibrahim, H., Far, B.H., Eberlein, A., Daradkeh, Y.: Uncertainty Management in Software Engineering: Past, Present, and Future. In: Proc. of CCECE 2009, pp. 7–12 (2009)
14. Famelis, M., Santosa, S.: MAV-Vis: a Notation for Model Uncertainty. In: Proc. of MiSE 2013 (2013)
15. Mens, T., Van Eetvelde, N., Demeyer, S., Janssens, D.: Formalizing Refactorings with Graph Transformations. Journal of Software Maintenance and Evolution: Research and Practice 17(4), 247–276 (2005)
16. Sabetzadeh, M., Nejati, S., Chechik, M., Easterbrook, S.: Reasoning about Consistency in Model Merging. In: Proc. LWI 2010 (2010)
17. Salay, R., Chechik, M., Easterbrook, S., Diskin, Z., McCormick, P., Nejati, S., Sabetzadeh, M., Viriyakattiyaporn, P.: An Eclipse-Based Tool Framework for Software Model Management. In: Proc. of Eclipse 2007, pp. 55–59 (2007)
18. Salay, R., Chechik, M., Famelis, M., Gorzny, J.: Verification of Uncertainty Reducing Model Transformations (submitted, 2013)
19. Salay, R., Chechik, M., Gorzny, J.: Towards a Methodology for Verifying Partial Model Refinements. In: Proc. of VOLT 2012 (2012)
20. Salay, R., Famelis, M., Chechik, M.: Language Independent Refinement using Partial Modeling. In: de Lara, J., Zisman, A. (eds.) FASE 2012. LNCS, vol. 7212, pp. 224–239. Springer, Heidelberg (2012)

21. Sawyer, P., Bencomo, N., Whittle, J., Letier, E., Finkelstein, A.: Requirements-Aware Systems: A Research Agenda for RE for Self-adaptive Systems. In: Proc. of RE 2010, pp. 95–103 (2010)
22. Schobbens, P.Y., Heymans, P., Trigaux, J.C.: Feature diagrams: A survey and a formal semantics. In: Proc. of RE 2006, pp. 139–148 (2006)
23. Segura, S., Benavides, D., Ruiz-Cortés, A., Trinidad, P.: Automated Merging of Feature Models Using Graph Transformations. In: Lämmel, R., Visser, J., Saraiva, J. (eds.) GTTSE 2007. LNCS, vol. 5235, pp. 489–505. Springer, Heidelberg (2008)
24. Steinberg, D., Budinsky, F., Paternostro, M., Merks, E.: EMF: Eclipse Modeling Framework, 2nd edn. Addison-Wesley (2009)
25. van Lamsweerde, A.: Requirements Engineering - From System Goals to UML Models to Software Specifications. Wiley (2009)
26. Varró, D., Varró–Gyapay, S., Ehrig, H., Prange, U., Taentzer, G.: Termination Analysis of Model Transformations by Petri Nets. In: Corradini, A., Ehrig, H., Montanari, U., Ribeiro, L., Rozenberg, G. (eds.) ICGT 2006. LNCS, vol. 4178, pp. 260–274. Springer, Heidelberg (2006)
27. Wouters, L., Gervais, M.P.: Ontology Transformations. In: Proc of EDOC 2012, pp. 71–80 (2012)
28. Ziv, H., Richardson, D.J., Klösch, R.: The Uncertainty Principle in Software Engineering (1996) (unpublished)

Automated Verification of Model Transformations in the Automotive Industry*

Gehan M.K. Selim[1], Fabian Büttner[2], James R. Cordy[1],
Juergen Dingel[1], and Shige Wang[3]

[1] School of Computing, Queen's University, Kingston, Ontario, Canada
[2] AtlanMod, École des Mines de Nantes - INRIA, LINA, Nantes, France
[3] Electrical and Controls Integration Lab.,
General Motors Research and Development, Warren, Michigan, USA

Abstract. Many companies have adopted MDD for developing their software systems. Several studies have reported on such industrial experiences by discussing the effects of MDD and the issues that still need to be addressed. However, only a few studies have discussed using automated verification of industrial model transformations. We previously demonstrated how transformations can be used to migrate GM legacy models to AUTOSAR models. In this study, we investigate using automated verification for such industrial transformations. We report on applying an automated verification approach to the GM-to-AUTOSAR transformation that is based on checking the satisfiability of a relational transformation representation, or a transformation model, with respect to well-formedness OCL constraints. An implementation of this approach is available as a prototype for the ATL language. We present the verification results of this transformation and discuss the practicality of using such tools on industrial size problems.

Keywords: Model Transformation, Automated Verification, Automotive Industry.

1 Introduction

Model Driven Development (MDD) has been increasingly used in the last decade for software development and, in many cases, has replaced traditional, code-centric approaches. In MDD, *models* or software abstractions are the basic building blocks in the software development life cycle and *model transformations* are the technology used to map between models conforming to different metamodels. Transformations are used for different purposes in MDD, e.g., refactoring, migration, and code generation. Since transformations are essential in MDD, transformation testing and verification is essential to the success of MDD.

---

* This work was partially funded by the Nouvelles Équipes Program of the Pays de la Loire Region (France), and by NSERC (Canada), as part of the NECSIS Automotive Partnership with General Motors, IBM Canada and Malina Software Corp.

A. Moreira et al. (Eds.): MODELS 2013, LNCS 8107, pp. 690–706, 2013.

Several studies have reported on industrial experiences in adopting MDD [13,25]. However, only a few of them have specifically discussed using model transformations in industry. Daghsen *et al.* [14] used transformations to map AUTOSAR timing models to classical scheduling models to perform timing analysis. Giese *et al.* [15] used triple graph grammars to synchronize SysML system engineering models with AUTOSAR software engineering models. Studies reporting on automated verification of industrial transformations have also been limited.

In this study, we report on using a light-weight, automated verification prototype to reason about the correctness of an ATL [22] transformation developed for the automotive industry [29]. More specifically, we check the correctness of the transformation with respect to OCL well-formedness constraints after translating the ATL transformation into a logical satisfiability problem. The basic approach has been presented in previous work [10] but to our knowledge we are the first reporting on its application to an industrial-sized verification problem.

While the transformation itself is not exceptionally large (in the number of transformation rules), the corresponding metamodels are. Together, they comprise 1586 classes, 897 associations, and 371 multiplicity constraints. Since even types not directly touched by the transformation are relevant for the verification (due to constraints that relate them), we have to deal with large potential instances. To verify our transformation, we have successfully checked models of up to 20000 potential elements with reasonable runtimes (although all counter examples found contained much fewer elements and were found quite quickly). Hence we claim that the verification approach is applicable to realistic verification scenarios.

The rest of this paper is organized as follows: Section 2 gives an overview of the GM-to-AUTOSAR transformation previously presented in [29]; Section 3 introduces the applied verification approach and prototype; Section 4 describes the case study conducted to verify the GM-to-AUTOSAR transformation using the aforementioned prototype; Section 5 summarizes the results of the case study and investigates the performance of the used approach; Section 6 discusses its strengths and limitations; Section 7 summarizes related work in the literature and Section 8 concludes and discusses future work.

2   Background: Model Transformation in the Automotive Industry

We now review the GM-to-AUTOSAR transformation presented in [29] which was used to migrate GM legacy models to the AUTOSAR standard.

2.1   Overview of the Model Transformation Problem

As one of the leading automotive companies, General Motors has been adopting MDD for the develoment of automotive software. GM engineers have been using a domain-specific metamodel for the development of vehicle control software (VCS). We refer to their domain-specific metamodel as the *GM metamodel*.

AUTOSAR (the AUTomotive Open System ARchitecture) [2] has been developed and adopted by many organizations as an automotive industry standard that is meant to facilitate the development and integration of software components from different vendors. AUTOSAR specifies requirements for software that is meant to conform to the standard. Further, AUTOSAR has its own metamodel with a well-defined architecture and interfaces.

Since the majority of organizations in the automotive industry are migrating to AUTOSAR, transforming models conforming to the GM metamodel to their equivalent AUTOSAR models is an important goal. Thus, we have previously developed and reported on a transformation that maps between subsets of the GM metamodel and the AUTOSAR metamodel as its source and target metamodels. In that work, we focused on subsets of the two metamodels that represent the deployment and interaction of software components.

2.2 The GM Metamodel

Fig. 1 illustrates the subset of the GM metamodel that we manipulated in our transformation in [29][1]. The *PhysicalNode* models a physical node on which software is deployed. A *PhysicalNode* may contain multiple *Partitions* (i.e., processing units or memory partitions) on which software is deployed. Multiple *Modules* can be deployed on a single *Partition*. A *Module* is an atomic, deployable, and reusable element in a product line and can contain multiple *Schedulers*. A *Scheduler* is the basic unit for software scheduling. It contains behavior-encapsulating entities, and is responsible for managing services provided or required by the behavior-encapsulating entities. Each *Scheduler* may provide and/or require *Services*, which model the services provided or required by the *Scheduler*.

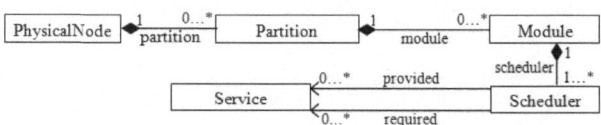

Fig. 1. Subset of the GM metamodel directly used by our transformation in [29]

2.3 The AUTOSAR Metamodel

The AUTOSAR metamodel is defined as a set of templates. Each template specifies an AUTOSAR artifact such as software components. Among the defined templates, the *System* template [1] models the configuration of a system or an Electronic Component Unit (ECU). An ECU is a physical unit on which software is deployed. When used for modeling the configuration of an ECU, the System template is referred to as the *ECU Extract*. Fig. 2 shows the subset of the ECU Extract manipulated by our transformation. The ECU extract is modeled using the *System* type that aggregates *SoftwareComposition* and *SystemMapping*

---

[1] In this study, we follow the same obfuscated naming conventions that we used for the GM metamodel in [29] for reasons of confidentiality.

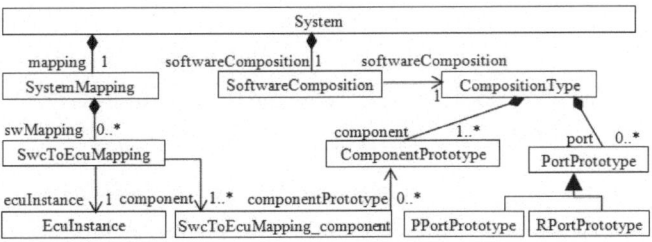

Fig. 2. Subset of the AUTOSAR System Template directly used by our transformation

elements. The *SoftwareComposition* type points to the *CompositionType* type
which eliminates any nested software components in a *SoftwareComposition*. The
SoftwareComposition type models the architecture of the software components
deployed on an ECU, the ports of these software components and the ports'
connectors. Each Software component is modeled using the *ComponentPrototype* type, which defines the structure and attributes of a software component;
each port is modeled using the *PortPrototype* type (i.e., a *PPortPrototype* or a
RPortPrototype) for providing or requiring data and services.

The *SystemMapping* type binds the software components to ECUs and
the data elements to signals and frames (not shown). The *SystemMapping*
type aggregates the *SwcToEcuMapping* type, which assigns *SwcToEcuMap-
ping_components* to an *EcuInstance*. *SwcToEcuMapping_components* in turn,
refer to *ComponentPrototype* elements. According to AUTOSAR, only one *Swc-
ToEcuMapping* should be created for each processing unit or memory partition
in an ECU.

3   Verification Methodology

We apply the automated verification approach presented in [10] to the GM-to-
AUTOSAR transformation. In short, we translate the ATL transformation T,
its source metamodel MM_{src}, and its target metamodel MM_{tar} into a combined
model, or a *transformation model*, consisting of MM_{src} and MM_{tar} and additional model elements that represent the transformation rules. Additionally, a
set *Sem* of OCL constraints is generated for the combined model that characterizes the execution semantics of the ATL rules. For declarative ATL rules
without recursion, the constraints describe the ATL semantics one-to-one, i.e.,
each valid instance of the transformation model corresponds to an execution of
the transformation and vice versa.

Using this representation we can check partial correctness of the transformation with respect to properties specified as OCL constraints over the source
and/or the target model, by checking if there exists a counterexample within
a specific scope (i.e., maximum number of objects per class). More specifically,
for a set of transformation preconditions (or assumptions) $Pre_1, \ldots, Pre_n$ and a
set of postconditions (or assertions) $Post_1, \ldots, Post_m$, we want to show that for
each instance M of the transformation model,

$$\begin{aligned} &(Sem_1 \text{ and } Sem_2 \text{ and } \dots \text{ and } Sem_k \text{ and} \\ &\ Pre_1 \text{ and } Pre_2 \text{ and } \dots \text{ and } Pre_n) \text{ implies} \\ &(Post_1 \text{ and } Post_2 \text{ and } \dots \text{ and } Post_m) \end{aligned} \qquad (1)$$

holds. This can be expressed equivalently as follows: For each postcondition $Post_i$ $(1 \le i \le m)$, the following formula must be unsatisfiable (i.e., there is no model M under which the formula is true):

$$Sem_1 \text{ and } \dots \text{ and } Sem_k \text{ and } Pre_1 \text{ and } \dots \text{ and } Pre_n \text{ and } not(Post_i) \qquad (2)$$

Fig. 3 illustrates this using a simple example. In the upper part we have an ATL transformation (c) over the shown source and target metamodels (a) and (b). The transformation copies the A-B structure to the C-D structure, but creates an additional D object when copying an 'empty' A object. The middle part shows the transformation model of this transformation. In the class diagram (d), each of the three rules is translated into a trace class and connected to the source and target classes according to the *from* and *to* patterns of the rule. The OCL constraints (e) capture the execution semantics of the transformation such as the matching of rule R1, the binding of primitive and object-typed properties, and the controlled creation of target objects. Some pre-/post- conditions are shown in (f) and (g), respectively.

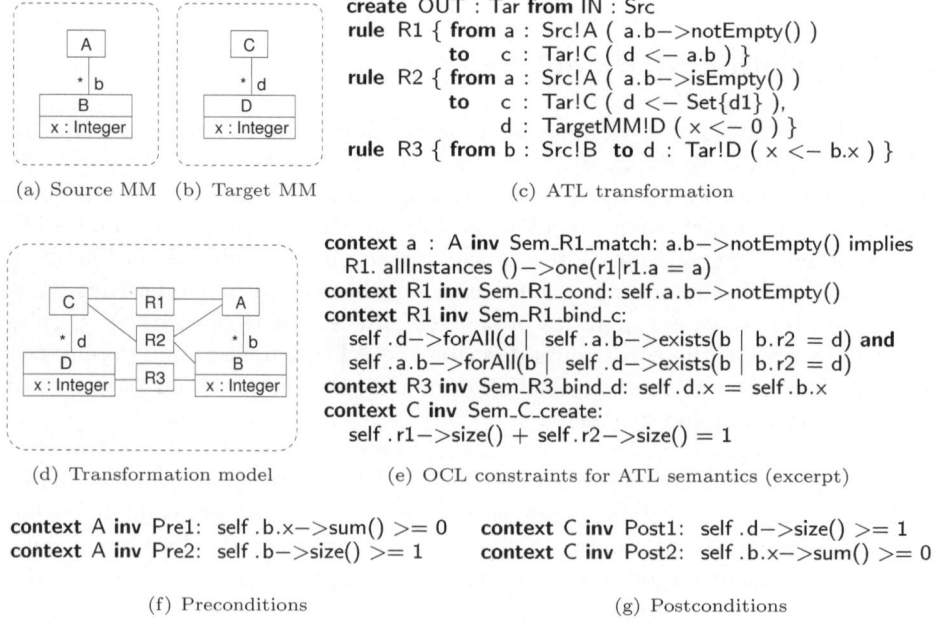

(a) Source MM   (b) Target MM

```
create OUT : Tar from IN : Src
rule R1 { from a : Src!A ( a.b->notEmpty() )
          to   c : Tar!C ( d <- a.b ) }
rule R2 { from a : Src!A ( a.b->isEmpty() )
          to   c : Tar!C ( d <- Set{d1} ),
               d : TargetMM!D ( x <- 0 ) }
rule R3 { from b : Src!B to d : Tar!D ( x <- b.x ) }
```

(c) ATL transformation

(d) Transformation model

```
context a : A inv Sem_R1_match: a.b->notEmpty() implies
       R1. allInstances ()->one(r1|r1.a = a)
context R1 inv Sem_R1_cond: self.a.b->notEmpty()
context R1 inv Sem_R1_bind_c:
       self .d->forAll(d |  self .a.b->exists(b | b.r2 = d) and
       self .a.b->forAll(b |  self .d->exists(b | b.r2 = d))
context R3 inv Sem_R3_bind_d: self .d.x = self .b.x
context C inv Sem_C_create:
       self .r1->size() + self.r2->size() = 1
```

(e) OCL constraints for ATL semantics (excerpt)

```
context A inv Pre1: self .b.x->sum() >= 0        context C inv Post1: self .d->size() >= 1
context A inv Pre2: self .b->size() >= 1         context C inv Post2: self .b.x->sum() >= 0
```

(f) Preconditions

(g) Postconditions

Fig. 3. Transformation model example

To verify that, for example, postcondition $Post_i$ is implied by the transformation (given the preconditions), we have to check that Eq. (2) is unsatisfiable. This can be tested using metamodel satisfiability checkers, or *model finders*, such as the USE Validator [23] which is publicly available [35]. The USE Validator translates the UML model and the OCL constraints into a relational logic formula and employs the SAT-based solver Kodkod [33] to check the unsatisfiability of Eq. (2) for each of the post-conditions $Post_i$ within a given scope. Thus, we have four different representations of the problem space, (i) ATL + OCL, (ii) OCL, (iii) relational logic, and (iv) propositional logic (for the SAT solver).

We have implemented the whole chain as an verification prototype (Fig. 4). We have implemented the ATL-to-OCL transformation [10] as a higher-order ATL transformation [32], i.e., a transformation from Ecore and ATL metamodels to Ecore metamodels (where the Ecore model can contain OCL constraints as annotations). Our implementation automatically generates the *Sem* constraints from the ATL transformation as well as *Pre* and *Post* constraints from the structural constraints in the source and target metamodels (further constraints to be verified can be added manually). Since the USE validator has a proprietary metamodel syntax, we have created a converter from Ecore to generate a *USE specification*. We also generate a default search space configuration, which is a file specifying the scopes and ranges for the attribute values. In the search configuration, we can disable or negate individual invariants or constraints.

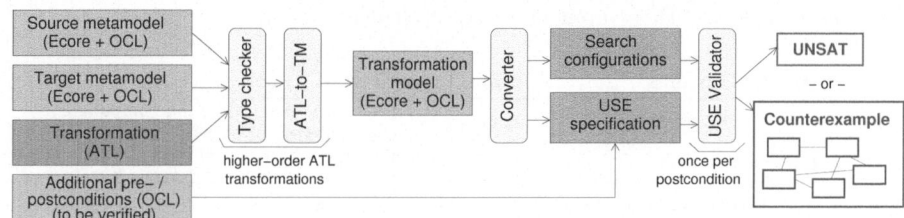

Fig. 4. The tool chain used to perform the transformation verification

Steps to Verify a Postcondition Using the Prototype: To check Eq. (2) for a postcondition, we have to negate the respective postcondition and disable all other postconditions in the generated *search configuration* (Fig. 4) and then run USE. If USE reports 'unsat', this implies that there is no input model in the search space for which the transformation can produce an output model that violates the postcondition. If there exists a counterexample, USE provides the object diagram of the counterexample which can be analyzed using many browsing features of the tool. Although the implementation is a prototype, it is not specific to the GM-to-AUTOSAR transformation.

4   Case Study: Evaluating Transformations in the Automotive Industry Using Automated Verification

We use the prototype described in Section 3 to verify our GM-to-AUTOSAR transformation. However, the verification prototype can only verify ATL transformations composed of declarative matched rules and non-recursive lazy rules. Thus we have changed the implementation described in [29] to be completely declarative and compatible with the format required by the prototype. The final reimplementation is intended to achieve the same mapping as the original implementation described in [29].

In this section, we describe the constructs used to re-implement our transformation and the different kinds of constraints formulated for verification.

4.1 Reimplementation of the GM-to-AUTOSAR Model Transformation

In the first implementation of the GM-to-AUTOSAR transformation, we used two ATL matched rules, 9 functional helpers and 6 attribute helpers to implement the required mapping between the two metamodels. After reimplementing the transformation to be completely declarative, the new transformation was composed of three matched rules and two lazy rules. Although we had to reimplement the transformation to use the verification prototype, we point out that the new declarative implementation is simpler and more readable. The rules implemented are listed in Table 1 together with the types of the rules, the input element matched by the rule, and the output elements generated by the rule.

Table 1. The types of ATL constructs used to reimplement the transformation, their designated names, and their input and output element types

Rule Type	Rule Name	Input Types	Output Types
Matched Rule	createComponent	*Module*	*SwCompToEcuMapping_component, ComponentPrototype*
Matched Rule	initSysTemp	*PhysicalNode*	*System, SystemMapping, SoftwareComposition, CompositionType, EcuInstance*
Matched Rule	initSingleSwc2EcuMapping	*Partition*	*SwcToEcuMapping*
Lazy Rule	createPPort	*Scheduler*	*PPortPrototype*
Lazy Rule	createRPort	*Scheduler*	*RPortPrototype*

As described in [29], the relationships between the outputs of the matched rules are built using the ATL predefined function `resolveTemp`. The `resolveTemp` function allows a rule to reference the elements that are yet to be generated by another rule at runtime. For example, the `resolveTemp` function was used to connect the *SwcToEcuMapping* elements created by the `initSingleSwc2EcuMapping` matched rule to the *SystemMapping* element created by the `initSysTemp` matched rule. Further, the matched rule `initSysTemp` calls the two lazy rules and assigns the union of the lazy rules' outputs to the *ports* of the *CompositionType* produced by the `initSysTemp` rule.

4.2 Formulation of OCL Pre- and Postconditions

In general, the OCL postconditions in our approach can be either defined on elements of the target metamodel only (then we call them *target invariants*), or they can relate the elements of the source and target metamodels (then we call them *transformation contracts*). Usually, a transformation contract specifies an implication 'when an input has a property then it's corresponding output has a property'. The OCL preconditions are propositions about the input that we assume to always hold.

In our case study, the preconditions were given by the multiplicity and composition constraints automatically extracted from the GM metamodel as OCL constraints. The formulated OCL postconditions are summarized in Table 2. We divide the formulated postconditions into four categories: *Multiplicity Invariants*, *Uniqueness Contracts*, *Security Invariants*, and *Pattern Contracts*. For each constraint in Table 2, we add to the beginning of its formulation an abbreviation (e.g., $(M1)$, $(U2)$) that will be used in the rest of the paper to refer to the constraint. The Multiplicity Invariants were automatically generated by the prototype. All the other postconditions were manually formulated.

Table 2. Formulated OCL Constraints

Multiplicity Invariants:

- $(M1)$ **Context** CompositionType **inv** CompositionType_component: self.component→**size()** ≥ 1
- $(M2)$ **Context** SoftwareComposition **inv** SoftwareComposition_softwareComposition: self.softwareComposition $\neq$ **null**
- $(M3)$ **Context** SwcToEcuMapping **inv** SwcToEcuMapping_component: self.component→**size()** ≥ 1
- $(M4)$ **Context** SwcToEcuMapping **inv** SwcToEcuMapping_ecuInstance: self.ecuInstance $\neq$ **null**
- $(M5)$ **Context** System **inv** System_softwareComposition: self.softwareComposition $\neq$ **null**
- $(M6)$ **Context** System **inv** System_mapping: self.mapping $\neq$ **null**

Uniqueness Contracts: Let Unique (invName, X, Y) be
Context Global **inv** invName: (X.**allInstances()**→**forAll**(x1:X, x2:X| x1.Name=x2.Name **implies** x1=x2)) **implies** (Y.**allInstances()**→ **forAll**(y1:Y, y2:Y| y1.shortName = y2.shortName **implies** y1=y2))

- $(U1)$ UnqCompName= Unique (UNQCOMPNAME, Module, ComponentPrototype)
- $(U2)$ UnqSysMName= Unique (UNQSYSMNAME, PhysicalNode, SystemMapping)
- $(U3)$ UnqSysName= Unique (UNQSYSNAME, PhysicalNode, System)
- $(U4)$ UnqSwcmpsName= Unique (UNQSWCMPSNAME, PhysicalNode, SoftwareComposition)
- $(U5)$ UnqCmpstyName= Unique (UNQCMPSTYNAME, PhysicalNode, CompositionType)
- $(U6)$ UnqEcuiName= Unique (UNQECUINAME, PhysicalNode, EcuInstance)
- $(U7)$ UnqS2EName= Unique (UNQS2ENAME, Partition, SwcToEcuMapping)
- $(U8)$ UnqPpName= Unique (UNQPPNAME, Scheduler, PPortPrototype)
- $(U9)$ UnqRpName= Unique (UNQRPNAME, Scheduler, RPortPrototype)

Security Invariant:

- $(S1)$ **Context** System **inv** Self_Cont: mapping.swMapping→**forAll**(swc2ecumap: SwcToEcuMapping| swc2ecumap.component → **forAll**(mapcomp : SwCompToEcuMapping_component| mapcomp.componentPrototype→**forAll**(comppro: ComponentPrototype| softwareComposition.softwareComposition.component→ **exists**(c: ComponentPrototype| c=comppro))))

Pattern Contracts:

- $(P1)$ **Context** Global **inv** Sig2P: PhysicalNode.**allInstances()**→ **forAll**(e1:PhysicalNode| e1.partition→ **forAll**(vd: Partition| vd.module→ **forAll**(di: Module| di.scheduler→ **forAll**(ef:Scheduler| (ef.provided→**notEmpty()**) **implies** (System.**allInstances()**→**one**(sy:System| (sy.shortName=e1.Name) **and** (sy.softwareComposition.softwareComposition.port→ **one**(pp:PortPrototype| pp.shortName=ef.Name) **and** (pp.**oclIsTypeOf**(PPortPrototype)))))))))))
- $(P2)$ **Context** Global **inv** Sig2R: PhysicalNode.**allInstances()**→ **forAll**(e1:PhysicalNode| e1.partition→ **forAll**(vd:Partition| vd.module→ **forAll**(di: Module| di.scheduler→ **forAll**(ef:Scheduler| (ef.required→**notEmpty()**) **implies** (System.**allInstances()**→ **one**(sy:System| (sy.shortName=e1.Name) **and** (sy.softwareComposition.softwareComposition.port→ **one**(rp:PortPrototype| (rp.shortName=ef.Name) **and** (rp.**oclIsTypeOf**(RPortPrototype)))))))))))

Multiplicity Invariants ensure that the transformation does not produce an output that violates the multiplicities in the AUTOSAR metamodel (Fig. 2). As described in Section 3, the prototype generates a USE specification with a multiplicity invariant for each multiplicity in the AUTOSAR metamodel. Ideally, we would check the satisfiability of all the multiplicity invariants generated for the AUTOSAR metamodel. Since our transformation manipulates a subset of the metamodels, we only check multiplicity invariants for output elements affected by our transformation. We have identified six of the generated multiplicity invariants that are affected by our transformation. ($M1$) ensures that each *CompositionType* is associated to more than one *ComponentPrototype* through the *component* association. ($M2$) ensures that each *SoftwareComposition* is associated with one *CompositionType* through the *softwareComposition* association. The rest of the multiplicity invariants can be interpreted in a similar way.

Uniqueness Contracts require the output element (of type Y) generated by a rule to be uniquely named (by the *shortName* attribute) within its respective scope if the corresponding input element (of type X) matched by the rule is uniquely named (by the *Name* attribute) within its scope too. For example, in Section 4.1, we discussed that the matched rule `createComponent` maps *Modules* to *ComponentPrototypes*. Thus, *U1* mandates that the *ComponentPrototypes* generated by the transformation are uniquely named, if the corresponding *Modules* are uniquely named too. The rest of the uniqueness contracts are similar and ensure uniqueness of the output elements of each rule described in Section 4.1 if their corresponding input elements are unique too.

The only security invariant defined, *S1*, mandates that within any *System* element, all its composite *SwcToEcuMappings* must refer to *ComponentPrototypes* that are contained within the *CompositionType* lying under the same *System* element (refer to Fig. 2). Thus, this invariant assures that any ECU configuration (modeled by a *System* element) is self contained and does not refer to any *ComponentPrototype* that is not allocated in that ECU configuration.

Pattern contracts require that if a certain pattern of elements is found in the input model, then a corresponding pattern of elements must be found in the output model. Pattern contracts also mandate that corresponding elements in the input and output patterns must have the same name. *P1* mandates that if a *PhysicalNode* is connected to a *Service* through the *provided* association (in the input model), then the corresponding *System* element will eventually be connected to a *PPortPrototype*. *P1* also ensures that the names of the *PhysicalNode* and the *System* are equivalent and that the names of the *Scheduler* (containing the *Service*) and the *PPortPrototype* are equivalent. The contract *P2* is similar to *P1* but manipulates *required Services* and *RPortPrototypes* instead.

Since invariants are constraints on target metamodel elements, the Multiplicity and Security invariants are specified within the *context* of their respective AUTOSAR elements. Since contracts are constraints on the relationships between the source and target metamodel elements, they do not relate to an AUTOSAR element per se. Thus, we add a class to the USE specification file, *Global*, which is used as the context of the Uniqueness and Pattern contracts.

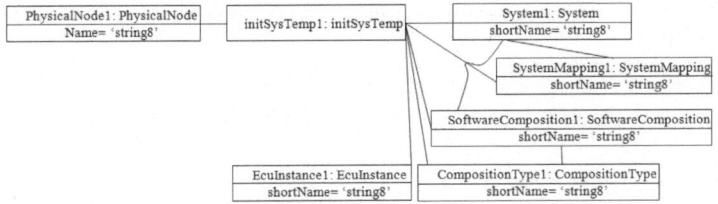

Fig. 5. Counterexample generated for the mult. inv. `CompositionType_component`

5   Results

In this section, we discuss the results of verifying the OCL contraints defined in Section 4.2 using the verification prototype. We show how the verification prototype was able to uncover bugs in the GM-to-AUTOSAR transformation that were fixed and re-verified. We also describe the results of a study to determine the performance of the used verification approach.

5.1   Verifying the Formulated OCL Constraints

Using the verification prototype, we generated a USE specification and a search configuration as shown in Fig. 4. After adding the constraints (Table 2) to the USE specification, we ran the USE tool once for each constraint.

Out of the 18 constraints defined in Table 2, two multiplicity invariants were found to be violated by the transformation: `CompositionType_component` and `SwcToEcuMapping_component`. In other words, our transformation can generate a *CompositionType* with no *ComponentPrototypes* and/or a *SwcToEcuMapping* with no *ComponentPrototypes*. Both of these possible outputs violate the multiplicities defined in the AUTOSAR metamodel (Fig. 2). The counterexamples were found by USE even within a scope of just one object per concrete class.

Due to the page limit, we only show an excerpt of the counterexample generated for the invariant `CompositionType_component` in Fig. 5. The counterexample shows that the rule `initSysTemp` maps a *PhysicalNode* to five elements, one of which is *CompositionType*. Since the rule does not have any restrictions on the generated *CompositionType*, it was created without associating it to any *ComponentPrototype* through the *component* association. The counterexample for the `SwcToEcuMapping_component` invariant was similar showing that the `initSingleSwc2EcuMapping` rule creates a *SwcToEcuMapping* element without mandating that it is associated to any *SwCompToEcuMapping_component* element through the *component* association.

After examining the two counterexamples generated by USE for the two violated multiplicity invariants, we identified two bugs in two rules shown in Table 3: `initSysTemp` and `initSingleSwc2EcuMapping`. The bold, underlined text are the updates to the rules that fix the two bugs. `initSysTemp` initially mapped a *PhysicalNode* to many elements, including a *CompositionType* that must contain at least one *ComponentPrototype*. If the *PhysicalNode* did not have any

Table 3. The two rules that required updates to address the two violations of multiplicity invariants

```
rule initSysTemp{
from ph: GM!PhysicalNode (ph.partition→exists(p|p.Module→notEmpty()))
to
    . . .
    compostype:autosar!CompositionType(
    . . .
    component ←ph.partition→collect(p|p.Module)→flatten()→collect(m|
    thisModule.resolveTemp(m, 'comp'))) }
```
```
rule initSingleSwc2EcuMapping {
from p:GM!Partition((GM!PhysicalNode.allInstances()→one(ph|ph.partition→includes(p)))
    and(p.module→notEmpty()))
to
    mapping:autosar!SwcToEcuMapping (
    shortName ← p.Name,
    component ← p.Module→collect(m|thisModule.resolveTemp(m, 'mapComp')),
    ecuInstance ←thisModule.resolveTemp((GM!PhysicalNode.allInstances()→select(ph|
    ph.partition→includes(p)))→first(),'EcuInst'))}
```

Module in any of its *Partition*s, then the created *CompositionType* will not contain any *ComponentPrototype*s. Thus we added a matching constraint to the *PhysicalNode* matched by the rule to ensure that any of its *Partition*s must contain at least one *Module*. Similarly, `initSingleSwc2EcuMapping` initially mapped a *Partition* to a *SwcToEcuMapping* that must contain at least one *SwCompToEcuMapping_component*. If the *Partition* did not have any *Module*, then the created *SwcToEcuMapping* will not contain any *SwCompToEcuMapping_component*. Thus we added a matching constraint to the *Partition* matched by the rule to ensure that it must contain at least one *Module*.

The 18 constraints were reverified on the updated transformation, and were all found to be satisfied.

5.2   Performance of the Verification Approach

To explore the performance of our approach, we used the verification prototype to verify the 18 constraints (Table 2) for different scopes. We ran the verification with scopes between one and 12. We only show the results for scopes 6, 8, 10, and 12 due to the page limit. The scope determines the maximum number of objects per concrete class in the search space. In our tests, we used the same scope for all classes, although it could be set individually. Since our transformation model has 1586 classes, a scope of n generates a model with $1586n$ potential elements (and their corresponding links and attribute values). All experiments where run on a standard laptop at 2.50 GHz and 16 GB of memory, using Java 7, Kodkod 2.0, and Glucose 2.1.

For each combination of constraint and scope, the prototype generates two time values: the time the prototype takes to translate the relational logic formula into a propositional formula (i.e., *translation time*) and the time the SAT solver takes to solve the formula (i.e., *constraint solving time*).

We show these two time values (in seconds) in Table 4. Each column represents the time intervals for each of the 18 constraints, where the *Constraint*

Abbreviation is the abbreviation given to each constraint in Table 2 (e.g., (M1) and (U5)). Each row represents the time intervals for a different scope. Thus, each cell within the table shows the translation time and the constraint solving time of a certain constraint at a specific scope.

Table 4. Translation\Constraint Solving times (seconds) for the 18 constraints on different scopes. For a scope of 12, the verification of S1 did not terminate in a week.

		Constraint Abbreviation (from Table 2)								
		U1	U2	U3	U4	U5	U6	U7	U8	U9
Scope	6	76\25	76\19	76\22	76\7	77\19	76\24	76\7	76\7	74\5
	8	169\74	165\79	168\106	165\37	168\85	171\68	167\38	166\57	169\45
	10	279\165	280\188	279\210	281\114	277\211	280\207	281\147	282\170	279\206
	12	455\976	434\643	431\623	428\322	426\827	428\616	425\584	427\604	430\501

		Constraint Abbreviation (from Table 2)								
		M1	M2	M3	M4	M5	M6	S1	P1	P2
Scope	6	74\2	73\0.4	74\1	74\1	75\0.5	74\0.5	74\40	242\14	244\7
	8	162\2	162\1	164\2	163\2	164\1	166\1	168\429	1453\37	1422\65
	10	280\12	281\1	277\6	281\3	275\1	274\1	277\3619	6225\80	6178\249
	12	426\18	425\1	421\25	424\4	422\1	425\1	*	21312\710	21092\814

Two observations can be made from Table 4. First, despite the exponential complexity of checking boolean satisfiability, we could verify the postconditions for scopes up to 12 in most of the cases; only the analysis of S1 did not finish for scope 12; the constraint solving time of S1 in scope 10 was the longest (just over an hour). Although we have no proof that no bugs will appear for bigger scopes, we are confident that a scope of 12 was sufficient to uncover any bugs in our transformation with respect to the defined constraints. In fact, the two bugs that were uncovered and fixed were found at a scope of one.

Second, the translation times are larger than expected and grow mostly polynomially. This can be attributed to the approach used by Kodkod to unfold a first-order relational formula into a set of clauses in conjunctive normal form (CNF), given an upper bound for the relation extents [33]. While transforming a formula into CNF grows exponentially with the length of the formula, it only grows polynomially with the scope in our case (as the formula's length does not change significantly). For example, each pair of nested quantifiers will generate a number of clauses that grows quadratically with the scope. The relational logic constraints generated implicitly by USE for all associations expand similarly. This justifies why the two pattern contracts (i.e., P1 and P2) show the highest translation times; they have the most quantifiers of the 18 constraints.

Using an incremental SAT solver would improve the performance of the prototype. Since most of the generated Boolean formula is the same for all the 18 constraints (i.e., the encoding of classes, associations, multiplicities, and preconditions), we expect that the translation (i.e., the first number in each cell of Table 4) can be done once for the entire verification process; except for P1 and P2 which differ in their high number of nested quantifiers.

6   Discussion

6.1   Strengths of the Verification Approach

We claim that the verification approach is practical to use for two reasons. First, the used approach provides a fully automated translation from ATL transformations and their constrained metamodels to OCL and relational logic. The approach further provides a fully automated verification of the generated translation. Even when applied to a realistic case study, the approach scaled to a scope that was large enough to strongly suggest that the analysis did not overlook a bug in the transformation due to the boundedness of the underlying satisfiability solving approach. If we wanted to perform the same verification on a Java implementation of the transformation, we would require equally rich class and operation contracts for, say, Ecore in JML [21]. To the best of our knowledge, no research has explored automatically inferring such contracts. Even then, we expect that the user would have to explicitly specify loop invariants as soon as the transformation contains non-trivial loops, like the loops in our transformation.

Second, the study translates a substantial subset of ATL for verification, i.e., all rules except for imperative blocks, recursive lazy rules and recursive query operations other than relational closures. Thus, the approach takes advantage of the ways declarative, rule-based transformation languages (e.g., ATL) provide to iterate over the input model without requiring recursion or looping. This simplifies verification by, for instance, obviating the need for loop invariants. Although this subset of ATL is not Turing-complete, it can be used to implement many non-trivial transformations. We have statically checked the 131 transformations (comprising 2825 individual rules) in the ATL transformation zoo [36], and 83 of them fall into the described fragment, i.e., neither use recursive rules nor imperative features. Of the remaining 48 transformations, 24 of them that use imperative blocks but no recursion could be expressed declaratively, too.

We conclude that our verification approach greatly benefited from the conceptual simplicity of the declarative fragment of ATL compared to, e.g., a general-purpose programming language such as Java.

6.2   Limitations of the Verification Approach

We identify two limitations of the verification approach.

Correctness of ATL-to-Relational-Logic Translation: Extensive testing and inspection was used to ensure that all steps involved in the translation of ATL and OCL to first-order relational logic are correct. However, in the absence of a formal semantics of ATL and OCL, a formal correctness proof is impossible and the possibility of a bug in the translation remains. This should be taken into account before our approach is used in the context of safety-critical systems.

Bounded Search Approach: All verification approaches based on a bounded search space cannot guarantee correctness of a transformation because the scopes experimented with may have been too small. The maximum scope sufficient to show bugs in a transformation is transformation-dependent. For example, a transformation with a multiplicity invariant that requires a multiplicity to be 10, will require a scope of 11 to generate a counterexample for that invariant, if any. With respect to our case study, we are confident that a scope of 5 is sufficient to detect violations of the given constraints; we ran analyses with scopes up to 12, because we wanted to study the performance of the approach. Real proofs of unsatisfiability can be created using SMT solvers and quantifier reasoning [9], but the problem is generally undecidable (i.e., the SAT solver does not terminate on all transformations), and the mapping presented in [9] does not yet cover all language features used in our case study. Further, we have not yet applied any a priori optimizations of the search problem, e.g., metamodel pruning [30], which we plan to apply for future work.

7 Related Work

There are several approaches that translate declarative model transformations into some logic or logic-like language to perform automated verification. Anastasakis *et al.* [3] and Baresi and Spoletini [5] use relational logic and the Alloy analyzer to check for inconsistencies in a transformation. Inaba *et al.* [19] verify the typing of transformations with respect to a metamodel using second-order monadic logic and the MONA solver. Troya and Vallecillo [34] define an encoding of ATL in rewriting logic, that can be used to check the possible executions of a transformation in Maude. Cabot *et al.* [11] translated QVT-R and triple graph grammar transformations into OCL contracts, requiring an OCL model finder to conduct the counterexample checking. Our translation of ATL into OCL (based on [10]) closely resembles this approach. In another previous work [9], we have presented a mapping of ATL directly into first-order logic, using quantifier reasoning to prove transformation properties with SMT solvers.

Asztalos *et al.* [4] formulated transformations and their properties as assertions in first-order logic. A deduction system was implemented to deduce the properties from the rules. Lucio *et al.* [24] verified correctness constraints for transformations in DSLTrans language using a model checker implemented in Prolog. Rensink [28] checked first-order linear temporal properties for graph transformation systems. Becker *et al.* [6] verified a metamodel refactoring implemented as a graph rewriting system by extending the metamodel with predicate structures which were used to specify well-formedness graph constraints. Stenzel *et al.* [31] implemented an algebraic formalization of a subset of operational QVT in the KIV theorem prover.

There are also several approaches that use OCL constraints to specify contracts for model transformations. Guerra *et al.* [18], Gogolla and Vallecillo [16], Braga *et al.* [7], and Cariou *et al.* [12] discussed testing transformations against contracts. In the same vein, Narayanan *et al.* [26] discuss a methodology to specify structural correspondence rules between source and target. Our constraints presented in Sect. 4.2 can be considered a transformation contract in this sense, although we do not use the contracts to test the actual transformation implementation but use them to verify the transformation independent of any input.

Regarding the used approach to check the satisfiability of OCL-constrained models, there are several potential alternatives to the USE Model Validator [23] that we employed. Gonzalez *et al.* [17] implemented the EMFtoCSP model finder that encodes metamodels and OCL constraints as constraint-logic programs (performing bounded verification). Queralt and Teniente [27] implemented a symbolic reasoning procedure for OCL constraints, based on predicate calculus. Brucker *et al.* [8] implemented the HOL-OCL theorem prover to interactively prove correctness constraints. Jackson *et al.* [20] used the FORMULA tool to reason about metamodels, but they did not support OCL.

The novel aspect of our study is two-fold: First, we have applied an automated verification methodology to an industrial model transformation implemented in the ATL transformation language. Second, we have shown the applicability of this approach to realistic search spaces and discussed the performance of our approach. Most of the referenced research papers evaluate their verification approach on small examples and do not address the performance aspect.

8   Conclusion and Future Work

In this study, we demonstrated how automated verification can be useful in verifying industrial transformations. First, we described the GM-to-AUTOSAR transformation that we have developed for General Motors [29]. We also discussed an automated transformation verification prototype that works on the declarative, non-recursive subset of ATL and its application to our transformation. The prototype was able to uncover two bugs in the transformation that violated two multiplicities in the AUTOSAR metamodel. We further discussed the performance of the verification prototype by showing the translation and constraint solving times for all the constraints over different scopes. The numbers showed that both the Translation times and the Constraint Solving times grow exponentially with the scope. Nonetheless, analysis of the transformation in sufficiently large scopes (up to 12) was possible. We conclude that the application of our verification approach to the case study was successful and provides evidence for its practicality, even in industrial contexts.

For future work, this study can be extended in several ways. First, other industrial transformations should be incorporated in the case study to have a better idea of the practicality of using automated verification on such transformations. Our case study explored a transformation that manipulates metamodels that are considered large on an industrial scale. The transformation, although far from being trivial, does not fully manipulate the two metamodels. We conducted a couple of experiments that show that the verification problem scales almost linearly when more independent rules are added. However, we still need to investigate the performance on larger and more complex transformations. As a result of our demonstration of the effectiveness of our approach in migrating a subset of the GM metamodel to its AUTOSAR equivalent, engineers at General Motors have expressed interest in extending the transformation to the full scope of the GM metamodel. Second, incremental SAT solvers can be used in the bounded search approach to improve the performance and the execution time of the approach, as suggested in Section 5.2. Third, pruning of the manipulated metamodels or the transformation model can be applied before executing the bounded search, as suggested in Section 6.2.

References

1. AUTOSAR Consortium. AUTOSAR System Template,
   http://AUTOSAR.org/index.php?p=3&up=1&uup=3&uuup=3&uuuup=0&uuuuup=0/
   AUTOSAR_TPS_SstemTemplate.pdf (2007)
2. AUTOSAR Consortium. AUTOSAR (2007), http://{AUTOSAR}.org/
3. Anastasakis, K., Bordbar, B., Küster, J.: Analysis of Model Transformations via Alloy. MoDeVVa, pp. 47–56 (2007)
4. Asztalos, M., Lengyel, L., Levendovszky, T.: Towards Automated, Formal Verification of Model Transformations. In: ICST, Paris, France, pp. 15–24 (2010)
5. Baresi, L., Spoletini, P.: On the Use of Alloy to Analyze Graph Transformation Systems. In: Corradini, A., Ehrig, H., Montanari, U., Ribeiro, L., Rozenberg, G. (eds.) ICGT 2006. LNCS, vol. 4178, pp. 306–320. Springer, Heidelberg (2006)
6. Becker, B., Lambers, L., Dyck, J., Birth, S., Giese, H.: Iterative Development of Consistency-Preserving Rule-Based Refactorings. In: Cabot, J., Visser, E. (eds.) ICMT 2011. LNCS, vol. 6707, pp. 123–137. Springer, Heidelberg (2011)
7. Braga, C., Menezes, R., Comicio, T., Santos, C., Landim, E.: On the Specification, Verification and Implementation of Model Transformations with Transformation Contracts. In: Simao, A., Morgan, C. (eds.) SBMF 2011. LNCS, vol. 7021, pp. 108–123. Springer, Heidelberg (2011)
8. Brucker, A.D., Wolff, B.: Semantics, Calculi, and Analysis for Object-Oriented Specifications. Acta Informatica 46(4), 255–284 (2009)
9. Büttner, F., Egea, M., Cabot, J.: On verifying ATL Transformations Using 'Off-the-Shelf' SMT Solvers. In: France, R.B., Kazmeier, J., Breu, R., Atkinson, C. (eds.) MODELS 2012. LNCS, vol. 7590, pp. 432–448. Springer, Heidelberg (2012)
10. Büttner, F., Egea, M., Cabot, J., Gogolla, M.: Verification of ATL Transformations Using Transformation Models and Model Finders. In: Aoki, T., Taguchi, K. (eds.) ICFEM 2012. LNCS, vol. 7635, pp. 198–213. Springer, Heidelberg (2012)
11. Cabot, J., Clarisó, R., Guerra, E., de Lara, J.: Verification and Validation of Declarative Model-to-Model Transformations Through Invariants. Systems and Software 83(2), 283–302 (2010)
12. Cariou, E., Belloir, N., Barbier, F., Djemam, N.: OCL Contracts for the Verification of Model Transformations. EASST 24 (2009)
13. Cottenier, T., Van Den Berg, A., Elrad, T.: The Motorola WEAVR: Model Weaving in a Large Industrial Context. In: AOSD, Vancouver, Canada, vol. 32 (2007)
14. Daghsen, A., Chaaban, K., Saudrais, S., Leserf, P.: Applying Holistic Distributed Scheduling to AUTOSAR Methodology. In: ERTSS, Toulouse, France (2010)
15. Giese, H., Hildebrandt, S., Neumann, S.: Model Synchronization at Work: Keeping sysML and AUTOSAR Models Consistent. In: Engels, G., Lewerentz, C., Schäfer, W., Schürr, A., Westfechtel, B. (eds.) Nagl Festschrift. LNCS, vol. 5765, pp. 555–579. Springer, Heidelberg (2010)
16. Gogolla, M., Vallecillo, A.: Tractable Model Transformation Testing. In: France, R.B., Kuester, J.M., Bordbar, B., Paige, R.F. (eds.) ECMFA 2011. LNCS, vol. 6698, pp. 221–235. Springer, Heidelberg (2011)

17. González Pérez, C.A., Büttner, F., Clarisó, R., Cabot, J.: EMFtoCSP: A Tool for the Lightweight Verification of EMF Models. In: FormSERA, Zurich, Switzerland, pp. 44–50 (2012)
18. Guerra, E., de Lara, J., Wimmer, M., Kappel, G., Kusel, A., Retschitzegger, W., Schönböck, J., Schwinger, W.: Automated Verification of Model Transformations Based on Visual Contracts. Automated Software Engineering 20(1), 5–46 (2013)
19. Inaba, K., Hidaka, S., Hu, Z., Kato, H., Nakano, K.: Graph-Transformation Verification Using Monadic Second-Order Logic. In: PPDP, pp. 17–28 (2011)
20. Jackson, E., Levendovszky, T., Balasubramanian, D.: Automatically reasoning about metamodeling. SoSyM, pp. 1–15 (2013)
21. Jacobs, B., Poll, E.: A Logic for the Java Modeling Language JML. In: Hussmann, H. (ed.) FASE 2001. LNCS, vol. 2029, pp. 284–299. Springer, Heidelberg (2001)
22. Jouault, F., Allilaire, F., Bézivin, J., Kurtev, I.: ATL: A Model Transformation Tool. Sci. Comput. Program. 72(1-2), 31–39 (2008)
23. Kuhlmann, M., Hamann, L., Gogolla, M.: Extensive Validation of OCL Models by Integrating SAT Solving into USE. In: Bishop, J., Vallecillo, A. (eds.) TOOLS 2011. LNCS, vol. 6705, pp. 290–306. Springer, Heidelberg (2011)
24. Lúcio, L., Barroca, B., Amaral, V.: A Technique for Automatic Validation of Model Transformations. In: Petriu, D.C., Rouquette, N., Haugen, Ø. (eds.) MODELS 2010, Part I. LNCS, vol. 6394, pp. 136–150. Springer, Heidelberg (2010)
25. Mohagheghi, P., Dehlen, V.: Where is the Proof? - A Review of Experiences from Applying MDE in Industry. In: Schieferdecker, I., Hartman, A. (eds.) ECMDA-FA 2008. LNCS, vol. 5095, pp. 432–443. Springer, Heidelberg (2008)
26. Narayanan, A., Karsai, G.: Verifying Model Transformations by Structural Correspondence. EASST 10 (2008)
27. Queralt, A., Teniente, E.: Verification and Validation of UML Conceptual Schemas with OCL Constraints. TOSEM 21(2), 13 (2012)
28. Rensink, A.: Explicit State Model Checking for Graph Grammars. In: Degano, P., De Nicola, R., Meseguer, J. (eds.) Concurrency, Graphs and Models. LNCS, vol. 5065, pp. 114–132. Springer, Heidelberg (2008)
29. Selim, G.M.K., Wang, S., Cordy, J.R., Dingel, J.: Model Transformations for Migrating Legacy Models: An Industrial Case Study. In: Vallecillo, A., Tolvanen, J.-P., Kindler, E., Störrle, H., Kolovos, D. (eds.) ECMFA 2012. LNCS, vol. 7349, pp. 90–101. Springer, Heidelberg (2012)
30. Sen, S., Moha, N., Baudry, B., Jézéquel, J.-M.: Meta-model Pruning. In: Schürr, A., Selic, B. (eds.) MODELS 2009. LNCS, vol. 5795, pp. 32–46. Springer, Heidelberg (2009)
31. Stenzel, K., Moebius, N., Reif, W.: Formal Verification of QVT Transformations for Code Generation. In: Whittle, J., Clark, T., Kühne, T. (eds.) MODELS 2011. LNCS, vol. 6981, pp. 533–547. Springer, Heidelberg (2011)
32. Tisi, M., Jouault, F., Fraternali, P., Ceri, S., Bézivin, J.: On the Use of Higher-Order Model Transformations. In: Paige, R.F., Hartman, A., Rensink, A. (eds.) ECMDA-FA 2009. LNCS, vol. 5562, pp. 18–33. Springer, Heidelberg (2009)
33. Torlak, E., Jackson, D.: Kodkod: A Relational Model Finder. In: Grumberg, O., Huth, M. (eds.) TACAS 2007. LNCS, vol. 4424, pp. 632–647. Springer, Heidelberg (2007)
34. Troya, J., Vallecillo, A.: A Rewriting Logic Semantics for ATL. Journal of Object Technology 10(5), 1–29 (2011)
35. The USE Validator,
   http://sourceforge.net/projects/useocl/files/Plugins/ModelValidator/
36. The ATL Transformation Zoo,
   http://www.eclipse.org/atl/atlTransformations/.

Data-Flow Based Model Analysis
and Its Applications

Christian Saad and Bernhard Bauer

University of Augsburg, Germany
{saad,bauer}@informatik.uni-augsburg.de

Abstract. In this paper we present a data-flow based approach to static model analysis to address the problem of current methods being either limited in their expressiveness or employing formalisms which complicate seamless integration with standards and tools in the modeling domain.

By applying data-flow analysis - a technique widely used for static program analysis - to models, we realize what can be considered a generic "programming language" for context-sensitive model analysis through declarative specifications. This is achieved by enriching meta models with data-flow attributes which are afterward instantiated for models. The resulting equation system is subjected to a fixed-point computation that yields a static approximation of the model's dynamic behavior as specified by the analysis. The applicability of the approach is evaluated in the context of a running example, the examination of viable application domains and a statistical review of the algorithm's performance.

1 Introduction and Motivation

Modeling languages have become a prominent instrument in the field of computer science as they enable the formalization of an application domain's concepts, their properties and the relationships between them. An abstract syntax given in the form of a meta model allows to validate and enforce structural constraints and fosters automated processing of the formalized information, e.g. through code generation or model transformations. In addition, the rise of modeling techniques has lead to new approaches to software engineering such as the Model-driven Architecture [1] and Model-based Testing [2].

Since their introduction, the OMG's [3] Meta-Object Facility (MOF) and derived languages like the Unified Modeling Language (UML) have become the de-facto standard in industry and research alike. Building upon a common meta meta model, the MOF's *M3* layer, a family of *M2* languages has evolved with applications ranging from software engineering to business process management.

An important factor for the popularity of modeling techniques is that they are often perceived to provide an intuitive way for practitioners to formalize application domains. However, the less rigorous theoretical framework can also be a serious drawback when attempting to assert a model's correctness: Although the basic form of the language expressions (models) is given by the abstract syntax (meta model), it is often necessary to enforce additional constraints on

A. Moreira et al. (Eds.): MODELS 2013, LNCS 8107, pp. 707–723, 2013.

the language's structural layout. The subset of these constraints that can be statically verified is known as the static semantics or the well-formedness rules of a language. To formalize these rules, a technique is required that allows to enrich meta model elements with a specification of their static semantics.

Over time, existing formal approaches have been proposed for the purpose of model analysis. However, this usually involves a translation of (meta) models into logic-based representations [4, 5] resulting in a gap between the two domains that can be difficult to manage on a technical level but may also lead to problems on a conceptual level as model-specific semantics have to be mapped to the logic-based systems on which the analyses are defined and executed.

This issue is addressed by the OMG's Object Constraint Language (OCL) which allows to annotate constraints at meta model elements and to evaluate them for models. However, limitations of its expressiveness due to its static navigational expressions are the subject of ongoing discussion [6, 7]. The `closure()` operator[1] introduced in version *2.3.1* (January 2012) of the specification only applies to `Set` types and is limited to calculating the transitive closure of a relationship. Finally, it has been argued that OCL itself lacks a proper formalization [8] and multiple proposals have been made to address this problem [9–11].

The approach detailed in this paper represents a generic, declarative method for computing properties that can be derived from the structural layout of a model. It is based on attribute grammars (AG) and data-flow analysis (DFA), two well-understood and well-defined methods from the field of compiler construction used to validate static semantics and to derive optimizations from a program's control-flow respectively. Data-flow analysis is a powerful method that implicitly provides support for transitive declarations. For example, the following (recursive) definition computes the transitive closure of the parent relationship: `allParents = directParent ∪ directParent.allParents`. Since DFA applies fixed-point semantics to resolve cyclic dependencies, analyses can derive static approximations of dynamic behavior, e.g. by computing which nodes will be visited on all paths leading to an action in an activity diagram.

In this paper we detail the approach initially outlined in [12]. Its intended target audience are language engineers responsible for developing (model-based) domain-specific languages (DSL) and tooling as opposed to users of the implemented languages (who may also be developers in their respective domain).

The presented methodology allows to attach data-flow attributes to elements of MOF-based meta models in a fashion similar to OCL's derived attributes. These attributes can then be automatically instantiated and evaluated for derived models. Result computation consists of the execution of data-flow rules, applying fixed-point evaluation semantics when necessary. Structural differences between modeling and formal languages required an adaption of the worklist algorithm commonly employed to solve DFA equation systems.

The proposed analysis specification language is a textual DSL which itself is based on a meta model that is tied to the MOF. On a technical level, the

---

[1] An example use case would be the enforcement of non-cyclic generalization hierarchies for Classifiers: `self->closure(superClass)->excludes(self)`.

presented approach therefore integrates with standards, languages and tools in the modeling domain, avoiding the inherent difficulties in the application of formal methods. Its applicability is evaluated in the context of several use cases.

This paper is structured as follows: In Section 2, we outline basic principles of data-flow analysis and attribute grammars. Their suitability for model analysis is examined in Section 3.1 through a comparison of the domains of modeling and formal languages. Section 3.2 describes the structure and semantics of the specification language while Section 3.3 demonstrates how resulting equation systems can be computed taking into account the adjustments made to traditional DFA. The approach is evaluated in Section 4 and its versatility is exemplified through several use cases in Section 5. We conclude with a survey of related work and a summary of the approach along with an outlook on future developments.

2   Background

Data-flow analysis (DFA, [13]) is a method commonly used in compiler construction in order to derive context-sensitive information from a program's control-flow, usually for optimization purposes. Canonical examples for this approach include the calculation of reaching definitions or variable liveness analysis.

Data-flow equations are annotated at control-flow nodes $n \in N$ and operate on sets containing values from a specific value domain: Applying a join operator $\Delta \in \{\cap, \cup\}$ to the output values calculated at neighboring nodes in the flow graph yields the input value for each node: $in(n) = \Delta_{m \in \Theta(n)} out(m)$ where Θ is either the direct predecessor or successor relationship. By using values at preceding nodes as input, information is propagated in a forward direction[2]. Inserting the intersection operator for Δ retains only values which are contained in any incoming set, i.e. information which reaches a node on all of its incoming paths, while the use of the union operator aggregates results "arriving" on any incoming path. The result $out(n)$ is determined by removing (*kill*) information which is locally destroyed and adding (*gen*) information which is locally generated: $out(n) = gen(n) \cup (in(n) - kill(n))$. The equation system formed by the entirety of all equation instances induces a global information flow throughout the graph as local results are distributed along outgoing paths.

In the presence of back edges in the control-flow, the equation system contains cyclic dependencies. This case is handled by applying fixed-point evaluation semantics: First, all nodes are initialized with either the empty set in the case of $\Delta = \cup$, or the complete value domain for $\Delta = \cap$. Then, the equations are evaluated repeatedly until all values are stable. This indicates that the most accurate approximation, a minimal or maximal fixed-point, has been detected. The existence of a fixed-point itself is guaranteed if operations are monotonic and performed on values which have a partial order with finite height.

---

[2] Some analyses, for example the detection of live variables, require information flow in a backwards direction in which case the process is reversed, i.e. results calculated at successor nodes are used as the equations' arguments.

A canonical optimization is the worklist algorithm: Starting with the execution of the flow-equation at the entry node, each time the (re)calculation of an equation yields a value that differs from its previous result, the equations at the depending nodes are added to the worklist since they are the ones affected by the new input. This process is repeated until the worklist is empty.

A second technique for static analysis used in compiler construction are attribute grammars. Introduced by [14], they are used to analyze context-sensitive information - e.g. the set of defined variables - depending on the layout of the language expression's syntax tree. Traditional AGs extend a context-free grammar G with a set of attributes A, each of which is assigned to a (non) terminal symbol $X \in N \cup T$ and is either of the type Inh (inherited) or Syn (synthesized). The attributes can be thought of as property fields of the nodes in the syntax trees, their values being calculated by semantic rules R assigned to the productions that describe how an attribute value can be calculated from the values of other attributes in the same production. Semantic rules are given in the form $X_i.a = f(...)$, where a is an attribute assigned to X_i and f is an arbitrary function that calculates a result for a based on its arguments. This leads to information being transported from one place in the AST to another, either bottom-up (synthesized) or top-down (inherited). Therefore, attribute grammars can be considered to be form of data-flow analysis [15] and support the definition of regular DFA if supplemented with fixed-point semantics [16, 17].

3   Data-Flow Based Model Analysis

3.1   Applying Data-Flow Analysis to Models

Transferring DFA to the modeling area requires a careful consideration of conceptual similarities and differences between the domains of formal languages and modeling. As discussed in [18, 19], relationships between these technical spaces can be identified by aligning their respective layers of abstraction.

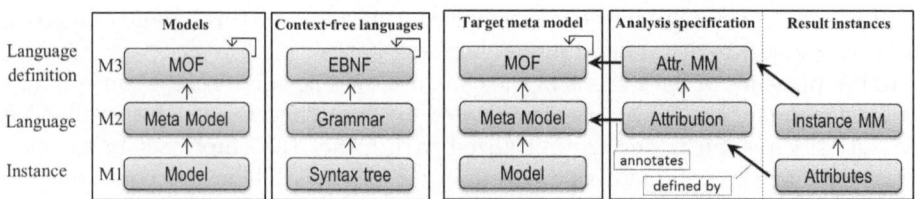

Fig. 1. Alignment of abstraction layers   **Fig. 2.** Analysis specification/instances

Figure 1 illustrates how MOF employs a common meta meta model on the *M3* abstraction layer to implement capabilities for defining *M2* meta models which represent the abstract syntax of a modeling language. Prominent examples include the Unified Modeling Language (UML) and the Business Process Modeling

Notation (BPMN). In MOF terminology models, e.g. UML diagrams or BPMN processes, are located on *M1*. A model is syntactically valid if it complies with the syntactic restrictions defined in its meta model. A similar hierarchy is used by formal languages, more specifically context-free grammars, which are used for programming language specification. In addition to enforcing syntactic correctness, the integrity of static semantic constraints can be validated by extending the grammar with semantic attributes as described in Section 2.

From a conceptual view point, the analysis of instances (models / syntax trees) therefore requires analysis specification on the language level which has to be supported by appropriate constructs on the *M3*/language definition layer. In the DFA context, a method is required which enables to assign flow equations to meta model elements $Model_{M1} \lhd MetaModel_{M2}$ alongside semantics for instantiating and solving the analysis for arbitrary models ($\lhd$ signifies *instanceof*).

To accomplish this, an approach was chosen that mirrors the concept of attribute grammars to assign semantic attributes to meta model elements. While this could be achieved by either extending the *M3* layer or the meta model with constructs for analysis specification, this would lead to incompatibilities with standards and tools that depend on compliance to MOF. Instead, attributes and their instantiations are defined separately (Figure 2), allowing all artifacts to remain unaware of the analyses. The language for analysis specifications - termed *Attributions* is given by an attribution meta model (*Attr.MM*) while their instantiations are defined by a separate meta model (*Instance MM*).

Computing flow-based analyses for models requires adaptations of the traditional algorithms for evaluating attribute grammars and DFA. The reason for that is that edges in model graphs - which are instances of associations or references defined in its meta model - denote relationships between objects which may possess arbitrary semantics depending on the domain for which the meta model was defined. In fact, associations between elements are often not directed, and if they are, two elements may be connected via multiple paths with undefined semantics in the context of flow-analysis. As such, they cannot be aligned with edges in flow graphs which carry the implicit semantics of a control flow, making it safe to automatically route information along incoming/outgoing paths.

In attribute grammars, attributes in syntax trees depend on results from the same grammatical production as input. This means that different rules may apply in different contexts depending on the production instance's respective neighbors in the syntax tree. In that, productions compare to classifiers in the meta model while the occurrences of productions in the syntax tree correspond to objects in the model. However, compared to syntax trees, the graph structure of models does not offer an easily identifiable direction for inheritance/synthesis.

In summary, information flow in models is highly specific to an application domain and an analysis since they don't possess an inherent flow direction as exists for control-flow graphs and syntax trees. This problem can be circumvented by ensuring that information is routed only along relevant, analysis-dependent paths: To provide maximal flexibility, rather than flow-equations being automatically supplied with input values depending on the context in which they

appear, they must be able to request required input as needed. Input/output
dependencies between attribute instances are therefore encoded inside the flow-
equations, thereby superimposing the model with a (dynamically constructed)
data-flow graph. The work-list algorithm must be adapted to record dependencies as they become visible through the execution of the rules and to schedule
the re-computation of unstable attribute values using this information.

3.2   Analysis Specification and Instantiation

In this section we describe the language for analysis specification and the instantiation semantics in the context of a running example. They are based on
and comply to the Essential MOF (EMOF) subset of MOF and have been implemented using the Eclipse Modeling Framework (EMF, [20]).

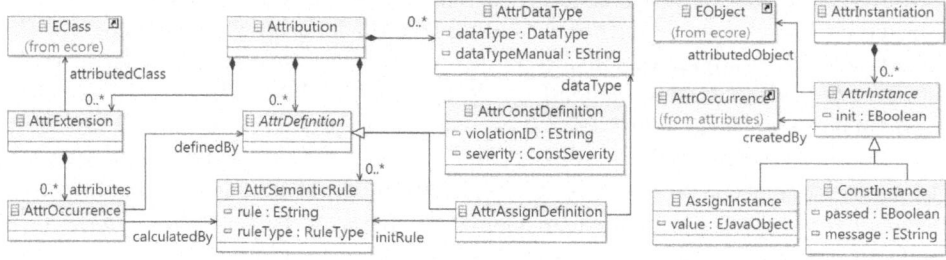

Fig. 3. Analysis meta model (*Attr.MM*)   **Fig. 4.** Instantiation MM

Figure 3 shows the elementary concepts of the analysis specification meta
model: In the notion of attribute grammars, *attribute occurrences* indicate the
presence of *attribute definitions* (of the type *assignment* or *constraint*) at classes
(*EClass*) in the target meta model. *Attribute extension* containers connect these
occurrences to meta model classes through the *attributedClass* relationship. Attached to the *definitions* and *occurrences* are *semantics rules* (corresponding to
data-flow equations) that calculate the fixed-point initialization and iteration
values respectively. They may be defined in an arbitrary language for which the
language interpreter implements an interface to the DFA solver (cf. Section 3.3).

The instantiation meta model (cf. Figure 2) is shown in Figure 4. Each *attribute instance* links to the *occurrence* from which it was instantiated and to
the model object for which it was created. Depending on the *attribute definition*
type, it is either an *assignment instance*, returning a result value complying to
the definition's *data type*, or a *constraint instance* of type `boolean` indicating
whether a constraint/well-formedness rule was violated.

This is exemplified in Figure 5(a) which shows a reachability analysis annotated at a control-flow graph meta model. It is assumed that an *attribute
definition* with the id `is_reachable`, the type `boolean` and the initialization
value `false` was specified. Two *occurrences* of this *definition* have been assigned
to the classes `node` and `startnode`, the latter overwriting the first to always

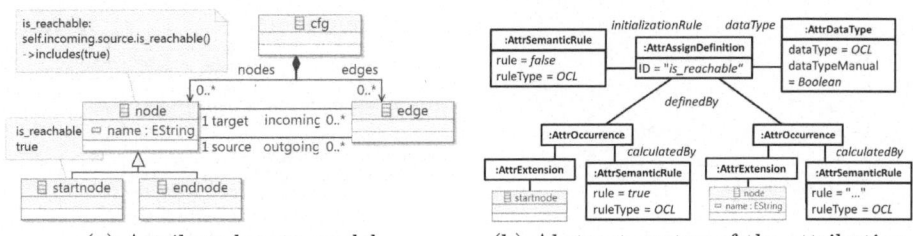

(a) Attributed meta model   (b) Abstract syntax of the attribution

Fig. 5. Reachability analysis defined for control-flow graph meta model

return `true` at instances of `startnode`. The abstract syntax of the attributed
meta model can be seen in Figure 5(b). The OCL rule uses the injected operation
`is_reachable()`[3] to request the value of this attribute at the respective predecessor nodes from the DFA solver, resulting in a recursive definition in which a
node is considered to be reachable if at least one of its predecessors is reachable.

The instantiation semantics for attributes follows the EMOF semantics for the
instantiation of meta model classes: An attribution $AT(MM, AT_{DEF}, AT_{RULE},$
$AT_{OCC}, AT_{DT}, AT_{TYPE}, AT_{ANN})$[4] extends a meta model $MM(MM_{CL},$
$MM_{GEN})$ given by the set of classes MM_{CL} and their generalization relationships MM_{GEN} indicating inheritance of structural and behavioral features in
accordance to EMOF semantics. The attribution consists of attribute definitions AT_{DEF}, each possessing a data type (AT_{DT}) and an initialization rule
(AT_{RULE}) assigned by the relation AT_{TYPE}. Furthermore, the annotation relation AT_{ANN} ties each occurrence in AT_{OCC} to a class $c \in MM_{CL}$ and an
iteration rule in AT_{RULE}.

An instantiation $INST(AT, M, INST_{AT}, INST_{LINK})$ contains attribute instances $INST_{AT}$ for an attribution AT and a model M $\triangleleft$ MM with objects M_{OBJ}
and a relation M_{TYPEOF} denoting their class type. For each $obj \in M_{OBJ}$, an
attribute instance $i \in INST$ exists *iff* there are ≥ 1 occurrences $occ \in AT_{OCC}$
for the class type of obj or its super-types. To realize overwriting at subtypes the
most specialized type is used. This can be implemented by starting at a model
object's concrete type and traversing the generalization hierarchy upwards. For
the first occurrence of each distinct attribute definition which is encountered an
instance is created. Multiple inheritance is only supported if generalization relations are diamond-shaped and a unique occurrence candidate can be identified.

The control-flow model in Figure 6 depicts the instances of the attribute
`is_reachable` which are attached to the corresponding model elements. The
dashed lines indicate the implicit dependencies encoded in the flow equations.
The corresponding abstract syntax representation is shown in Figure 7.

The meta model is complemented by a concrete syntax using the Eclipse
Xtext parser/editor generator which maps grammatical symbols to meta model

---

[3] Attribute access operations can be automatically injected into an OCL environment:
For all *attribute definitions* connected to a class through *occurrences*, an operation
is added to the class with the id of the *definition* and the *data type* as return type.

[4] Multiple attributions can be merged if they extend the same meta model.

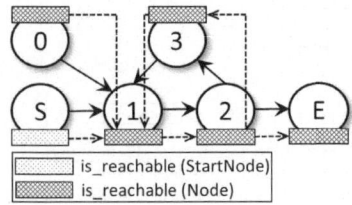

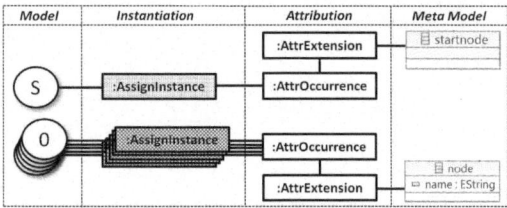

Fig. 6. Attributed model   **Fig. 7.** Abstract syntax

elements. The syntax comprises all relevant artifacts: *Attribute definitions, attribute extensions, semantic rules* and *datatypes.* Except *attribute extensions* (and the therein contained *attribute occurrences*), all objects can be cross-referenced by other parts of the attribution. This excerpt from the language's grammar defines the declaration syntax for *assignments* and *occurrences* and their connection to the targeted meta model classes:

```
Attribution returns attribution::Attribution:
  'attribution' id=ID '{' ( ( (attrDefinitions+=AttributeDefinition)* &
                             (attrSemanticRules+=SemanticRule)* &
                             (attrDataTypes+=AttrDataType)* &
                             (attrExtensions+=AttrExtension)* ) '}' ;

AttributeDefinition returns attributes::AttrDefinition:
  'attribute' (AttrAssignDefinition | AttrConstDefinition) ;

AttrAssignDefinition returns attributes::AttrAssignDefinition:
  'assignment' id=ID (name=STRING)? ("[" description=STRING"]")? ':'
    dataType=[datatypes::AttrDataType]
    'initWith' initializationRule=[semanticrules::AttrSemanticRule] ';' ;

AttrExtension returns attributes::AttrExtension:
  'extend' attributedClass=[ecore::EClass] 'with' '{' (attributes += AttrOccurrence)* '}' ;

AttrOccurrence returns attributes::AttrOccurrence:
  'occurrenceOf' definedBy=[attributes::AttrDefinition]
  'calculateWith' calculatedBy=[semanticrules::AttrSemanticRule] ';' ;
```

The following example[5] specifies the attributes `is_reachable`, `all_predecessors` and `scc_id` which perform reachability analysis and calculate a node's transitive predecessors as well as strongly connected component (SCC) membership.

```
attribution flowanalysis {
  - attribute definitions (consisting of id, data type and initialization rule)
  attribute assignment is_reachable : OCLBoolean initWith boolean_false;
  attribute assignment all_predecessors : OCLSet initWith set_empty;
  attribute assignment scc_id : OCLBoolean initWith int_zero;

  - semantic rules (ocl rules using helper operations injected into OCL environment)
  rule ocl isreachable_node : standard
    " self . incoming.source. is_reachable()->includes(true)";
  rule ocl allpredecessors_node : imperative
    " self . incoming.source ∪ self . incoming.source. all_predecessors ()";
```

---

[5] Common types (e.g. `OCLBoolean`) and rules for trivial calculations such as `boolean_true` are contained in a "standard library" omitted here for lack of space. For the same reason, imperative OCL statements were converted to formula.

```
rule ocl sccid_node : imperative
  " self ∪ self . all_predecessors () == self.incoming.source. all_predecessors ()";

– attribute occurrences (define occurrences and bind them to classes)
extend node with {
occurrenceOf is_reachable calculateWith isreachable_node;
occurrenceOf all_predecessors calculateWith allpredecessors_node;
occurrenceOf scc_id calculateWith sccid_node;
}
extend startnode with {
occurrenceOf is_reachable calculateWith boolean_true;
}
}
```

3.3   Dynamic, Demand-Driven Fixed-Point Analysis

Compared to an exhaustive algorithm, a demand-driven DFA solver limits computation to a subset of requested results [21]. In this context, this subset corresponds to a set of requested instances $INST_{AT(REQ)} \subseteq INST_{AT}$, e.g. all instances of a specific attribute, all attributes located at a given class etc. However, unknown to the solver, transitive dependencies to instances $INST_{AT} \setminus INST_{AT(REQ)}$ may exist. For example, scc_id relies on all_predecessors. $INST_{AT(REQ)}$ must therefore be expanded dynamically on discovery of these dependencies.

Because dependencies between attribute instances are "hidden" inside flow-equations, traditional methods for call-graph construction [22, 23] are not applicable. The dependency graph that superimposes the attributed model therefore has to be constructed on-the-fly during the fixed-point computation using dynamic dependency discovery. As a side-effect, support for the inclusion of transitive dependencies as described above is implicitly provided by such an algorithm.

The adapted worklist algorithm carries out the following steps: The requested instances $INST_{AT(REQ)}$ are initialized before their associated iteration rules are executed. If a rule requests another instance's value as input, this access is relayed to the solver which is thereby able to record the dependency between the calling and the called instance and at the same time can discover calls to attributes not in $INST_{AT(REQ)}$. A new iteration starts at the leaves of the constructed dependency graph, i.e. at instances without input dependencies, and at cyclic dependencies whose values are updated after each iteration.

As an optimization for this method in the context of flow-based model analysis, we propose a demand-driven, iterative algorithm that constructs and operates on a directed acyclic dependency graph with multiple root and leaf nodes. Each root node represents an attribute instance not required as input by other instances. Leaves are either instances which themselves do not depend on input or so-called reference nodes that indicate the presence of cyclic dependencies and are used to trigger the fixed-point computation. This method compensates for the absence of a CFG structure by maintaining a set of starting points for the fixed-point iterations (the leaf nodes) while the identification of independent branches enables parallelized computation. It also provides a comprehensive representation of the computation process useful for debugging purposes.

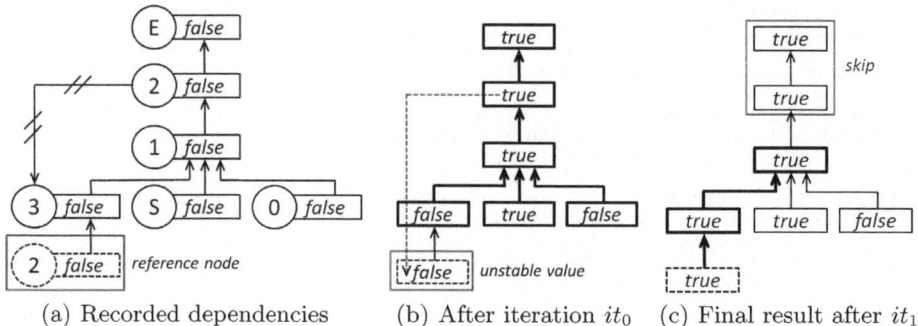

(a) Recorded dependencies   (b) After iteration it_0 (c) Final result after it_1

Fig. 8. Dependency discovery and result computation

In the first phase of the evaluation process, the DFA equations corresponding to the instances from $\mathrm{INST}_{AT(REQ)}$ are executed. By monitoring the input requests during the rules' execution, the solver is able to construct an initial dependency graph from the recorded data-flow dependencies. The graph is then converted into an acyclic representation by identifying cyclic dependencies through a depth-first traversal strategy and replacing back edges with *reference nodes*. Finally, all instances in are reset to their respective initialization value. This is demonstrated in Figure 8(a) for the example presented in Figure 6: The back edge between is_reachable instances at nodes *3* and *2* has been replaced by a reference node and all values have been reset to false.

In the second phase, the graph is traversed repeatedly in a bottom-up fashion, starting at unstable leaf nodes. Each instance node's iteration rule can be executed once its input dependencies have been satisfied, i.e. all of its children have been either executed or do not have an unstable node in their transitive children set. Parallelization is possible if rules are executed through a working queue to which the parents of traversed nodes are added once the aforementioned condition applies. Since rules are free of side effects, it is safe to stop traversal at nodes if their execution yields the same result for an instance as in the last iteration. This avoids unnecessary recalculations of stable results. After the traversal, unstable instances at cyclic dependencies can be detected: A reference node is classified as unstable if its result from the previous iteration $it_{(n-1)}$ is different from the current iteration (it_n) value at the referenced node. As long as instances with values that differ between iteration $it_{(n-1)}$ and it_n are identified, a new fixed-point iteration $it_{(n+1)}$ is triggered starting with the parents of the unstable reference nodes. For the first iteration it_0, all leaves are classified as unstable with the DFA initialization values representing $it_{(n-1)}$.

Figure 8(b) shows the result after the initial iteration with the highlighted nodes representing the executed rules. Since is_reachable at the model object *2* now differs from its previous value, the new result is transferred to the reference node. Its predecessor, the instance at model node *3*, is scheduled as starting point for bottom-up traversal in it_1. The stable fixed point is reached after iteration it_1, shown in Figure 8(c). Since the value for model object 1 has not changed, the traversal can be aborted without recalculation of 2 and E.

The discovery of new dependencies during the evaluation process can result in the introduction of additional nodes, the reconnection of existing nodes or the merging of previously separate graphs. To handle this case, the required modifications are postponed until after the current iteration it_n finishes. Then, an intermediate step $it_{n'}$ is carried out in which the existing graphs are extended by repeating the chain-building steps of phase 1 for the discovered attribute instances. For iteration $it_{(n+1)}$, re-evaluation is scheduled to start at the smallest set of leaf nodes that includes all newly created instances and nodes which introduced new dependencies to existing instances as parents.

4 Evaluation

In this section we present our findings in the evaluation of the scalability of the fixed-point computation for models. Both the number of rule executions in relation to the amount of instances and the time for the analysis are indicators for its performance aspects. The goal is a qualitative assessment of the applicability of the approach for the analysis of large models. The evaluation employs the attributes defined in Section 3.2 - is_reachable, all_predecessors and scc_id - as well as all_predecessors_min which calculates the dominating sets, using equivalent bitvector-based implementations of the semantic rules. To evaluate the scalability with respect to the amount of instances, five models have been generated randomly to contain 50, 100, 500, 1000 and 2000 nodes. Except the start and the final node, each node has exactly two outgoing connections to arbitrary targets. Because each attribute is calculated for each node, the number of results therefore amounts to four times the number of nodes. The computation has been carried out with the algorithm described in Section 3.3 and a modified worklist algorithm that does not construct a dependency graph to demonstrate the unoptimized application of traditional DFA to the modeling context. The values represent the median of 90 of 100 analysis runs (to eliminate caching issues, the first 10% have been discarded) on an Intel i7 2,20GHz computer.

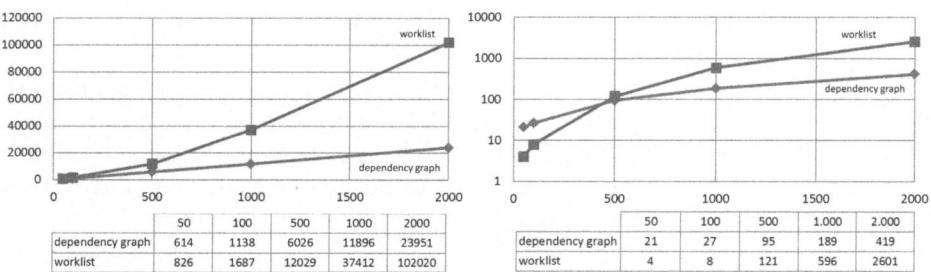

	50	100	500	1000	2000
dependency graph	614	1138	6026	11896	23951
worklist	826	1687	12029	37412	102020

	50	100	500	1.000	2.000
dependency graph	21	27	95	189	419
worklist	4	8	121	596	2601

Fig. 9. Number of rule executions   **Fig. 10.** Analysis time in ms (log. scale)

Figure 9 shows the total amount of rules executed in the fixed-point iterations. The time in milliseconds is pictured in Figure 10 using a logarithmic scale. From the results it can be deduced that while the worklist method is faster at a lower number of instances, it is soon outperformed by the dependency graph approach. This can be explained by the overhead induced by the complex data structures maintained by the graph-based algorithm. The dependency graph algorithm breaks even between 100 and 500 nodes (400-2000 instances) as the time and the amount of rule executions scales with the total number of results.

In the master thesis [24] our approach has been applied to detect illegal backward data dependencies in AUTOSAR[6] models. The author concludes that with an execution time of 2.4 seconds (including pre-analysis steps) for the TIMMO-2-USE breaking system use case, the "case study shows that the analysis tool is able to cope with medium sized systems".

5   Applications

The presented approach has been applied to different domains to verify its viability and versatility as a technique that supports a wide range of use cases. The open source Model Analysis Framework[7] (MAF, [25]), was developed as a proof-of-concept platform and a reference implementation. The tooling suite is built on top of Eclipse technology such as the Eclipse Modeling Framework, Xtext, MDT OCL and M2M QVT. It contains a DFA solver module which can be integrated into third party applications and an IDE that supports analysis specification, configuration and debugging.

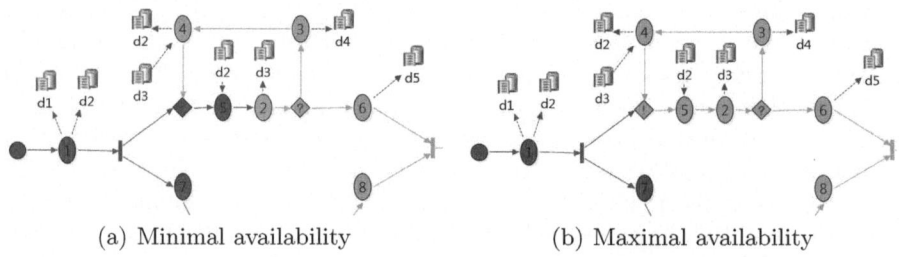

(a) Minimal availability   (b) Maximal availability

Fig. 11. Minimal and maximal availability of *d3*

Multiple analyses (available from the MAF repository) have been implemented for Eclipse's Java Workflow Tooling[8] (JWT) project - a tooling suite for modeling executable business processes. In the process shown in Figures 11(a) and 11(b), resource objects have been assigned to business actions, outgoing arrows denoting the production and incoming arrows the use of a resource.

---

[6] http://www.autosar.org, http://www.timmo-2-use.org/

[7] http://code.google.com/a/eclipselabs.org/p/model-analysis-framework/

[8] http://www.eclipse.org/jwt/

Flow-analysis can now be used to detect whether resources will be available at steps where they are required as input. Fixed-point computation yields two results: We can track the propagation of resources assuming that all paths are taken ($\Delta = \bigcup$, maximal availability) and the case where only information is regarded arriving on all paths at once ($\Delta = \bigcap$, minimal availability). The latter case differs from the former if resources are created inside cycles or in diamond-shaped (i.e. alternative) paths because not every execution of such a process will traverse these paths. In the figures the availability of the resource $d3$ is highlighted in green. The notable difference lies in node 5 where $d3$ will only be available after the cycle has been traversed at least once. This is reflected in the minimal availability result depicted in Figure 11(a). It indicates that it cannot be guaranteed that the resource will be available at 5 on all executions of this process. On the other hand, from Figure 11(b) we can deduce that there is at least one path on which $d3$ will have been created once we arrive at this point.

By combining this information with the local input/output of each node, the user can be given an indication about the validity of the process with respect to resource availability. This use case can be extended in multiple ways, e.g. to approximate how many instances of a resource must be provisioned if it can be accessed multiple times at once in parallel execution paths.

Additional use cases which are currently being evaluated include the detection of structural clones, the formalization of modeling guidelines and the computation of model metrics for different application domains (cf. [26]).

Currently, the Model Analysis Framework is also used in several research projects, including the ITEA2 project VERDE[9] and WEMUCS[10] (IuK Bayern).

VERDE employs state-machines to derive test cases in the notion of model-based testing (cf. Deliverables 5.3.1, 5.4.2). Subjecting them to static analysis therefore enables early feedback to the developer on whether a model conforms to its intended behavior. Specifically, DFA is used to compute edge coverage information to drive test path generation and to perform a variable analysis in the notion of compiler construction on the code embedded in the state machine's states and transitions. Results of static analysis are used to detect relevant test cases, e.g. paths where variables are accessed that might not have been initialized or adopt border case values. Applying static analysis to state machine models presents a unified approach that enables early violation detection and indication of potential problems as well as a focused test case generation.

The goal of the ongoing WEMUCS project is to provide methods and tools for the development, optimization and testing of software for embedded multi-core systems. The analysis of AUTOSAR models (cf. Section 4) is used to identify dependencies between functions (RunnableEntities) incurred by their data accesses. The dependencies detected using DFA are used to derive a valid execution order for the entities (or to ask for manual problem resolution if this is not

---

[9] Validation-driven design for component-based architectures, http://www.itea-verde.org/

[10] Methods and tools for iterative development and optimization of software for embedded multicore systems, http://www.multicore-tools.de

possible). Afterward, a DFA implementation of the token flow algorithm [27] is applied to the constructed control-flow graph to cluster the entities into single-entry-single-exit (SESE) components. These components represent parallelizable blocks and can subsequently be used as input for a scheduling algorithm.

6   Related Work

The canonical method for formalizing the static semantics of modeling languages is the Object Constraint Language which was recently extended with the ability to handle transitive closures[11]. However, as a constraint language it is not well suited for the derivation and approximation of context-sensitive information - a limitation removed by the fixed-point semantics of the data-flow method.

Several attempts were made to convert UML models with annotated OCL constraints to other technical spaces by translating constraints into satisfiability problems [28–30]. With the existence of powerful OCL interpreters, these methods are not strictly required for constraint evaluation, however in some cases they provide additional features, e.g. snapshot generation [31], to validate whether the semantics of the modeling language are preserved.

The relevance of flow-based analysis is evident from the amount of research work that employs DFA: The authors of [32] convert UML sequence diagrams to control-flow graphs for validation purposes while [33, 34] attempt to improve test case generation from statecharts. Def-use relationships for UML Action Semantics are derived in [35] and [36] applies DFA to identify patterns for translating graph-oriented BPMN models into block-oriented BPEL code. While originally given as an imperative algorithm, the SESE decomposition proposed in [27] was easily converted to a declarative flow analysis (cf. Section 5). It can be assumed that these methods could have profited from the presented approach as a unified method for defining flow-based analyses in their respective domains.

Although there are many usage scenarios for DFA in the modeling area, there exists - to our knowledge - only one approach that is directly comparable in that it provides a generalized technique for analysis specification and evaluation: JastEMF [37] translates meta models to circular reference attribute grammars (CRAG) [38], an extension of traditional attribute grammars, by mapping the containment hierarchy of the meta model to grammatical productions. Both the cross-references between meta model elements and semantic specifications (comparable to flow equations) are then defined as semantic attributes. CRAGs support fixed-point evaluation semantics through designated remote and circular attributes. Compared to the flow-analysis, this method strongly relies on the formalism of formal languages and attribute grammars, substituting the syntax tree with the model's containment tree to which the notion of attribute inheritance/synthesis is applied while the graph structure of the model has to be specified as part of the analysis in form of reference attributes.

---

[11] http://www.omg.org/issues/issue13944.txt

7   Conclusions and Outlook

In this paper we presented an approach for static model analysis in the notion of data-flow analysis, a well-understood technique from the field of compiler construction. The stated goal was to provide language engineers with a unified method for complementing (existing) model-based DSLs with static analysis capabilities. By validating well-formedness constraints and deriving static approximations of behavioral properties based on contextual, flow-sensitive information, many aspects of modeled systems can be evaluated on a conceptual level.

To motivate the applicability of flow analysis, we studied the relationships between the area of formal languages, in which this method is traditionally applied, and the field of modeling. Based on an alignment of the respective abstraction layers, we proposed an analysis specification DSL that transfers the underlying principles to the modeling domain. Because this language itself is model-based, it closely integrates with the target domain, eliminating the need for transformations between different technological and conceptual backgrounds and thus reducing the effort for implementation and usage. Since analyses are defined nonintrusively and arbitrary languages can be used to specify DFA equations, full compatibility with existing modeling languages and tools is retained and flexibility is provided with regard to adaption to diverse technological ecosystems.

As opposed to traditional DFA where dependencies between flow-equation instances are derived from the control flow itself, the ambiguous edge semantics in model graphs make the automatic propagation of results along these paths impractical. To overcome this problem, we use a demand-driven, iterative algorithm supporting the dynamic discovery of dependencies during solving. It allows for partial parallelization and its performance has been evaluated experimentally.

In conclusion, this approach provides the capabilities and the versatility required to implement sophisticated analyses - as demonstrated in the context of several use cases - along with a close integration with modeling concepts, namely the widely-used OMG standards. It provides a generic "programming language" for specifying declarative analyses that rely on an examination of flow-sensitive properties. The application range also extends to structural models, e.g. computing metrics for UML class diagrams such as the Attribute Inheritance Factor (AIF) relating the inherited attributes at a class to all available attributes [39].

Next steps include the examination of additional application areas and an evaluation of practical experiences with relation to the specification process. The solving algorithm will be complemented with a formalized description and in-depth evaluation. A "standard library" containing common flow analyses will be defined to serve as starting point for custom implementations.

References

1. Object Management Group. Model-Driven Architecture (June 2003), http://www.omg.org/mda/
2. Apfelbaum, L., Doyle, J.: Model based testing. In: Software Quality Week Conference, pp. 296–300 (1997)

3. Object Management Group (OMG) specifications, http://www.omg.org/spec
4. Malgouyres, H., Motet, G.: A UML model consistency verification approach based on meta-modeling formalization. In: Proceedings of the 2006 ACM Symposium on Applied Computing, pp. 1804–1809. ACM (2006)
5. Shah, S.M.A., Anastasakis, K., Bordbar, B.: From UML to alloy and back again. In: Ghosh, S. (ed.) MODELS 2009. LNCS, vol. 6002, pp. 158–171. Springer, Heidelberg (2010)
6. Mandel, L., Cengarle, M.V.: On the expressive power of OCL. In: Wing, J.M., Woodcock, J. (eds.) FM 1999. LNCS, vol. 1708, p. 854. Springer, Heidelberg (1999)
7. Baar, T.: The definition of transitive closure with OCL – limitations and applications. In: Broy, M., Zamulin, A.V. (eds.) PSI 2003. LNCS, vol. 2890, pp. 358–365. Springer, Heidelberg (2004)
8. Brucker, A.D., Doser, J., Wolff, B.: Semantic issues of OCL: Past, present, and future. Electronic Communications of the EASST 5 (2007)
9. Cengarle, M.V., Knapp, A.: A formal semantics for OCL 1.4. In: Gogolla, M., Kobryn, C. (eds.) UML 2001. LNCS, vol. 2185, pp. 118–133. Springer, Heidelberg (2001)
10. Marković, S., Baar, T.: An OCL semantics specified with QVT. In: Wang, J., Whittle, J., Harel, D., Reggio, G. (eds.) MoDELS 2006. LNCS, vol. 4199, pp. 661–675. Springer, Heidelberg (2006)
11. Brucker, A.D., Wolff, B.: A proposal for a formal OCL semantics in isabelle/HOL. In: Carreño, V.A., Muñoz, C.A., Tahar, S. (eds.) TPHOLs 2002. LNCS, vol. 2410, pp. 99–114. Springer, Heidelberg (2002)
12. Saad, C., Bauer, B.: Data-flow based model analysis. In: Proceedings of the Second NASA Formal Methods Symposium (NFM 2010), NASA/CP-2010-216215, pp. 227–231. NASA (April 2010)
13. Kildall, G.A.: A unified approach to global program optimization. pp. 194–206 (1973)
14. Knuth, D.E.: Semantics of context-free languages. Theory of Computing Systems 2(2), 127–145 (1968)
15. Babich, W.A., Jazayeri, M.: The Method of Attributes for Data Flow Analysis. Acta Inf. 10, 245–264 (1978)
16. Rodney, F.: Automatic generation of fixed-point-finding evaluators for circular, but well-defined, attribute grammars. In: Proceedings of the 1986 SIGPLAN Symposium on Compiler Construction, SIGPLAN 1986, pp. 85–98. ACM, New York (1986)
17. Jones, L.G.: Efficient evaluation of circular attribute grammars. ACM Trans. Program. Lang. Syst. 12(3), 429–462 (1990)
18. Wimmer, M., Kramler, G.: Bridging Grammarware and Modelware. In: Bruel, J.-M. (ed.) MoDELS 2005. LNCS, vol. 3844, pp. 159–168. Springer, Heidelberg (2006)
19. Alanen, M., Porres, I.: A Relation between Context-Free Grammars and Meta Object Facility Metamodels. Technical report, TUCS (2004)
20. Steinberg, D., Budinsky, F., Paternostro, M., Merks, E.: EMF: Eclipse Modeling Framework, 2nd edn. Addison-Wesley, Boston (2009)
21. Horwitz, S., Reps, T., Sagiv, M.: Demand interprocedural dataflow analysis. In: Proceedings of the 3rd ACM SIGSOFT Symposium on Foundations of Software Engineering, SIGSOFT 1995, pp. 104–115. ACM, NY (1995)
22. Ryder, B.G.: Constructing the call graph of a program. IEEE Transactions on Software Engineering (3), 216–226 (1979)
23. Jahromi, S.A.H.M., Honar, E.: A framework for call graph construction (2010)

24. Minnerup, P.: Models in the development process for parallelizing embedded systems. Master's thesis, Augsburg University, 86159 Augsburg, Germany (2012)
25. Saad, C., Bauer, B.: The Model Analysis Framework An IDE for Static Model Analysis. In: Industry Track of Software Language Engineering (ITSLE), 4th International Conference on Software Language Engineering (SLE 2011) (May 2011)
26. Baroni, A.L., Abreu, O.B.E.: An OCL-based formalization of the MOOSE metric suite. In: Proceedings of ECOOP Workshop on Quantative Approaches in Object-Oriented Software Engineering (2003)
27. Götz, M., Roser, S., Lautenbacher, F., Bauer, B.: Token Analysis of Graph-Oriented Process Models. In: New Zealand Second International Workshop on Dynamic and Declarative Business Processes (DDBP), 13th IEEE International EDOC Conference (EDOC 2009) (September 2009)
28. Cabot, J., Clarisó, R., Riera, D.: Verification of UML/OCL class diagrams using constraint programming. In: IEEE International Conference on Software Testing Verification and Validation Workshop, ICSTW 2008, pp. 73–80. IEEE (2008)
29. Anastasakis, K., Bordbar, B., Georg, G., Ray, I.: On challenges of model transformation from UML to Alloy. Software and Systems Modeling 9(1), 69–86 (2010)
30. Soeken, M., Wille, R., Kuhlmann, M., Gogolla, M., Drechsler, R.: Verifying UML/OCL models using Boolean satisfiability. In: Proceedings of the Conference on Design, Automation and Test in Europe, pp. 1341–1344. European Design and Automation Association (2010)
31. Gogolla, M., Bohling, J., Richters, M.: Validation of UML and OCL Models by Automatic Snapshot Generation. In: Stevens, P., Whittle, J., Booch, G. (eds.) UML 2003. LNCS, vol. 2863, pp. 265–279. Springer, Heidelberg (2003)
32. Garousi, V., Bri, L., Labiche, Y.: Control Flow Analysis of UML 2.0 Sequence Diagrams (2005)
33. Briand, L., Labiche, Y., Lin, Q.: Improving the coverage criteria of uml state machines using data flow analysis. Software Testing, Verification and Reliability 20(3), 177–207 (2010)
34. Kim, Y.G., Hong, H.S., Bae, D.-H., Cha, S.-D.: Test cases generation from uml state diagrams. IEEE Proceedings Software 146, 187–192 (1999)
35. Waheed, T., Iqbal, M.Z.Z., Malik, Z.I.: Data Flow Analysis of UML Action Semantics for Executable Models. In: Schieferdecker, I., Hartman, A. (eds.) ECMDA-FA 2008. LNCS, vol. 5095, pp. 79–93. Springer, Heidelberg (2008)
36. García-Bañuelos, L.: Pattern Identification and Classification in the Translation from BPMN to BPEL. In: Meersman, R., Tari, Z. (eds.) OTM 2008, Part I. LNCS, vol. 5331, pp. 436–444. Springer, Heidelberg (2008)
37. Bürger, C., Karol, S., Wende, C., Aßmann, U.: Reference Attribute Grammars for Metamodel Semantics. In: Malloy, B., Staab, S., van den Brand, M. (eds.) SLE 2010. LNCS, vol. 6563, pp. 22–41. Springer, Heidelberg (2011)
38. Magnusson, E., Hedin, G.: Circular Reference Attributed Grammars - Their Evaluation and Applications. ENTCS 82(3) (2003)
39. Abreu, F.B., Carapuça, R.: Object-oriented software engineering: Measuring and controlling the development process. In: Proceedings of the 4th International Conference on Software Quality (1994)

Contract-Aware Slicing of UML Class Models

Wuliang Sun, Robert B. France, and Indrakshi Ray

Colorado State University, Fort Collins, USA

Abstract. Slicing is a reduction technique that has been applied to class models to support model comprehension, analysis, and other modeling activities. In particular, slicing techniques can be used to produce class model fragments that include only those elements needed to analyze semantic properties of interest. In this paper we describe a class model slicing approach that takes into consideration invariants and operation contracts expressed in the Object Constraint Language (OCL). The approach is used to produce model fragments, each of which consists of only the model elements needed to analyze specified properties. We use the slicing approach to support a technique for analyzing sequences of operation invocations to uncover invariant violations. The slicing technique is used to produce model fragments that can be analyzed separately. The preliminary evaluation we performed provides evidence that the proposed slicing technique can significantly reduce the time to perform the analysis.

Keywords: Class model slicing, UML/OCL, Contract.

1 Introduction

Slicing techniques [22] produce reduced forms of artifacts that can be used to support, for example, analysis of artifact properties. *Slicing criteria* are used to determine the elements that are included in slices. Slicing techniques have been proposed for different software artifacts, including programs (e.g., see [5][22]), and models (e.g., see [1][2][4][9][10]). In the model-driven development (MDD) arena, model slicing techniques have been used to support a variety of modeling tasks, including model comprehension [1][2][10], analysis [7][11][12], and verification [4][17][18].

Rigorous analysis of structural invariants and operation contracts expressed in the Object Constraint Language (OCL) [19] can be expensive when the class models are large. Model slicing techniques can be used in these situations to reduce large models to just those fragments needed to perform the analysis. This reduction can help minimize the cost of analysis. However, many of the existing class model slicing techniques do not take constraints and operation contracts expressed in auxiliary constraint languages into consideration when producing model slices. Their applicability is thus limited to situations in which the determination of slices does not require information found in constraints. There are a few slicing approaches that take into consideration class model constraints expressed in the OCL, but either they handle only invariants [17] or only operation

A. Moreira et al. (Eds.): MODELS 2013, LNCS 8107, pp. 724–739, 2013.

contracts [7], or they can only be used to slice a single class (e.g., see [11]). In this paper we describe a class model slicing approach that takes into consideration both structural invariants and operation contracts expressed in the OCL.

We developed the approach to improve the efficiency of a model analysis technique we created to check that operation contracts do not allow invariant violations when sequences of conforming operations are invoked [21]. The slicing technique is used to reduce the problem of analyzing a large model with many invariants to smaller subproblems that involve analyzing a model fragment against a subset of invariants and operation contracts. Each model fragment can be analyzed independently of other fragments.

Given a class model with OCL constraints, the slicing approach automatically generates slicing criteria consisting of a subset of invariants and operation contracts, and uses the criteria to extract model fragments. Each model fragment is obtained by identifying and analyzing relationships between model elements and the constraints (invariants and operation contracts) included in a generated slicing criterion.

The analysis results are preserved by the slicing technique. This assertion is based on the observation that the technique produces the fragments by identifying the model elements that are directly referenced by OCL expressions and analyzing their dependencies with other model elements. The preliminary evaluation also provides some evidence (albeit, not formal) that the analysis results are preserved by the slicing technique.

The rest of the paper is organized as follows. Section 2 presents an example that will be used to illustrate the slicing approach in the rest of the paper. Section 3 describes the model slicing approach, and Section 4 describes the results of a preliminary evaluation of the approach. Section 5 discusses related work, and Section 6 concludes the paper with an overview of plans for future related work.

2   Background

We will use the Location-aware Role-Based Access Control (LRBAC) model, proposed by Ray et al. [13] [14] [15], to illustrate the contract-aware model slicing approach. LRBAC is an extension of Role-Based Access Control (RBAC) [16] that takes location into consideration when determining whether a user has permission to access a protected resource.

In LRBAC, roles can be assigned to, or deassigned from users. A role can be associated with a set of locations in which it can be assigned to, or activated by users. A role that is associated with locations can be assigned to a user only if the user is in a location in which the role can be assigned. A user can create a session and activate his assigned roles in the session. A role can be activated in a session only if the user that creates the session is in a location in which the role can be activated. Figure 1 shows part of a design class model that describes LRBAC features.

Permissions are granted to roles, and determine the resources (*objects*) that a user can access (*read*, *write* or *execute*) via his activated roles. Permissions are

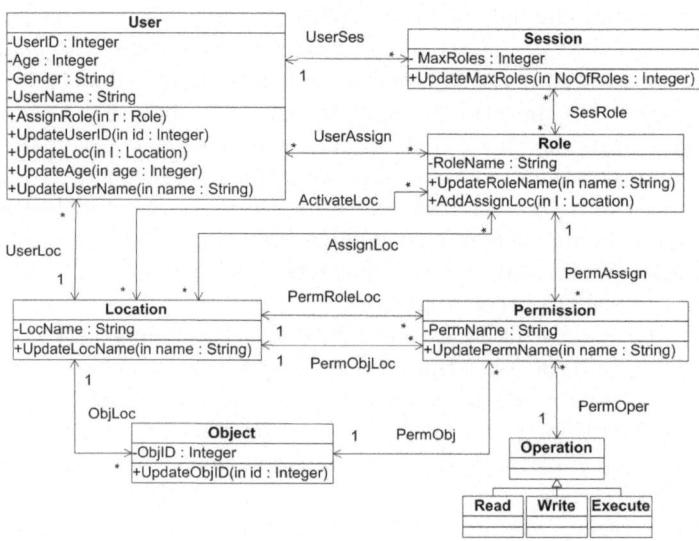

Fig. 1. A Partial LRBAC Class Model

associated with locations via two relationships: *PermRoleLoc* and *PermObjLoc*. *PermRoleLoc* links a permission to its set of allowable locations for the role associated with the permission, and *PermObjLoc* links a permission to its set of allowable locations for the object associated with the permission.

Operation contracts and invariants in the LRBAC model are specified using the OCL. For example, the OCL contracts for operations *UpdateUserID*, *AssignRole* and *UpdateLoc* are given below:

```
// Update a user's ID
Context User::UpdateUserID(id:Int)
Pre: self.UserID != id
Post: self.UserID = id
```

```
// Assign a role r to user u
Context User::AssignRole(r:Role)
Pre: self.UserAssign→excludes(r) and r.AssignLoc→includes(self.UserLoc)
Post: self.UserAssign = self.UserAssign@pre→including(r)
```

```
// Move a user into a new location l
Context User::UpdateLoc(l:Location)
Pre: self.UserLoc→excludes(l) and self.UserAssign→isEmpty()
Post: self.UserLoc→includes(l)
```

Examples of OCL invariants for the LRBAC model are given below:

// *Each user has a unique ID.*
Context *User* **inv UniqueUserID::**
User.allInstances()→forAll(u1, u2:User|u1.UserID = u2.UserID

// *For every role r that is assigned to a user, the user's location belongs to*
// *the set of locations in which role r can be assigned.*
Context *User* **inv CorrectRoleAssignment:**
self.UserAssign→forAll(r|r.AssignLoc→includes(self.UserLoc))

// *The number of roles a user can activate in a session cannot exceed the value*
// *of the session's attribute, MaxRoles.*
Context *Session* **inv MaxActivatedRoles:**
self.MaxRoles >= self.SesRole→size()

For the LRBAC model, one may want to determine if there is a scenario in which the operation contracts allow the system to move into a state in which a user has unauthorized access to resources. In previous work [21], we developed a class model analysis technique that uses the Alloy Analyzer [6] to find scenarios (sequences of operation invocations) that start in valid states (states that satisfy the invariants in the class model) and end in an invalid state. The analysis uses the operation contracts to determine the effects operations have on the state. If analysis uncovers a sequence of operation calls that moves the system from a valid state to an invalid state, then the designer uses the trace information provided by the analysis to determine how the operation contracts should be changed to avoid this scenario. Like other constraint solving approaches, performance degrades as the size of the model increases. The slicing technique described in the paper can improve the scalability of the analysis approach by reducing the problem to one of separately analyzing smaller model fragments.

3   The Slicing Approach

The model slicing approach described in this paper is used to decompose a large model into fragments, where each fragment contains model elements needed to analyze a subset of the invariants and operation contracts in the model. Fig. 2 shows an overview of the slicing approach.

The input to the approach is a UML class model with invariants and operation contracts expressed in the OCL. The approach has two major steps. In the first step, the input class model with OCL constraints is analyzed to produce a dependency graph that relates (1) invariants to their referenced model elements, and (2) operation contracts to their containing classes and other referenced classes and class properties. The dependencies among model elements are determined by relationships defined in the UML metamodel.

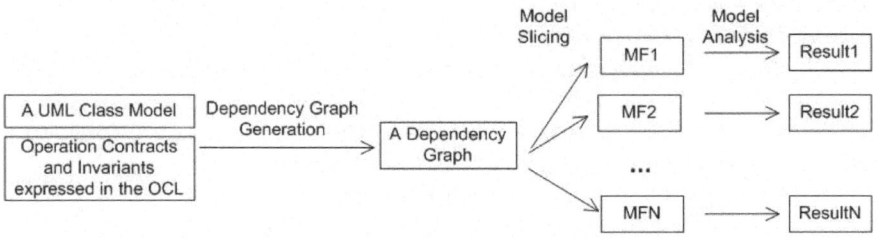

Fig. 2. Approach Overview

Table 1. Referenced Classes and Attributes for Each Operation Contract/Invariant Defined in the LRBAC model

Operation Contract/Invariant	Referenced Classes	Referenced Attributes
Op1 AssignRole	User, Role, Location	None
Op2 UpdateUserID	User	UserID
Op3 UpdateLoc	User, Role, Location	None
Op4 UpdateAge	User	Age
Op5 UpdateUserName	User	UserName
Op6 UpdateMaxRoles	Session	MaxRoles
Op7 UpdateRoleName	Role	RoleName
Op8 AddAssignLoc	Role, Location	None
Op9 UpdateLocName	Location	LocName
Op10 UpdatePermName	Permission	PermName
Op11 UpdateObjID	Object	ObjID
Inv1 NonNegativeAge	User	Age
Inv2 UniqueUserID	User	UserID
Inv3 GenderConstraint	User	Gender
Inv4 CorrectRoleAssignment	User, Role, Location	None
Inv5 MaxActivatedRoles	Session, Role	MaxRoles
Inv6 UniqueObjectID	Object	ObjID

In the second step of the approach, the dependency graph is used to generate slicing criteria, and the criteria are then used to extract one or more model fragments from the class model. The generated model fragments can be analyzed separately.

In the remainder of this section we describe the process for generating a dependency graph and the slicing algorithm used to decompose the class model into model fragments.

3.1   Constructing a Dependency Graph

Dependencies among invariants, operation contracts and model elements are computed by traversing the syntax tree of the OCL invariants and operation contracts. For example, consider the analysis of the operation contract for *AssignRole* (the contract is given in Section 2). The expression $self.UserAssign$ is an association end call expression and it returns a set of roles assigned to the user (referred to by

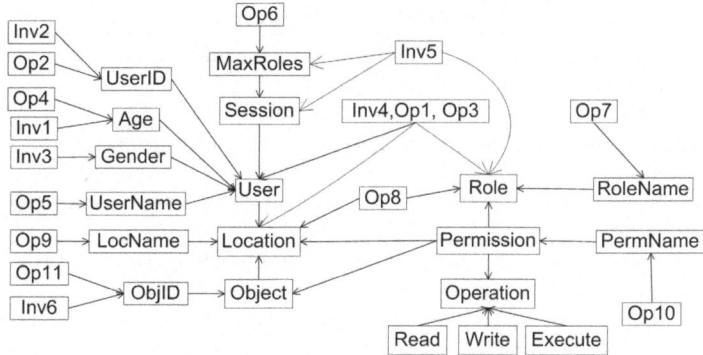

Fig. 3. A Dependency Graph

$self$). There is thus a dependency between this contract and the class $Role$. The expression $self.AssignLoc$ returns a user's current location, and thus there is a dependency with the class $Location$. The parameter r refers to an instance of class $Role$, and $r.AssignLoc$ returns a set of locations in which role r can be assigned to any user. The analysis thus reveals the operation contract for $AssignRole$ references and thus depends on, the following classes: $User$, $Role$ and $Location$. If an OCL constraint involves a statement like $Role.allInstances()$, then the OCL constraint references class Role. A similar analysis is done for each OCL contract and invariant. Table 1 lists the referenced classes and attributes for the contracts and invariants defined in the LRBAC model.

The computed dependencies and relationships defined in the UML metamodel are used to build a dependency graph. A dependency graph consists of nodes and edges, where each node represents a model element (e.g., classes, attributes, operations and invariants), and each edge represents a dependency between two elements. For example, if a class model has only one class that includes only one attribute, the generated dependency graph consists of two nodes, a node representing the class and a node representing the attribute, and one edge that represents the relationship between the attribute and its containing class.

Figure 3 shows a graph that describes the dependency relationship among classes, attributes, operations and invariants of the LRBAC class model described in Fig. 1. Algorithm 1 describes the process used to generate the graph.

Steps 1 to 5 describe how the metamodel relationships and computed dependencies between OCL invariants and contracts and their referenced model elements are used to build an initial dependency graph. In step 6 of the algorithm, if an operation contract (op) or invariant (inv) only references its context class, cls, and an attribute in cls, $attr$, the edge that points to vertex cls from vertex op (or inv), can be removed because the dependency can be inferred from the dependency between the vertex cls and the vertex $attr$. For example, Table 1 shows that operation $UpdateUserID$'s ($Op2$) only references class $User$ and its attribute $UserID$ in its specification. The edge pointing to vertex $User$ from vertex $Op2$ is redundant, and is thus removed from the dependency graph shown in

---

Algorithm 1. Dependency Graph Generation Algorithm

Input: A UML Class Model + OCL Operation Contracts/Invariants
Output: A Dependency Graph
Algorithm Steps:

Step 1. Create a vertex for each class, attribute, operation contract and invariant of the class model in the dependency graph.

Step 2. For every attribute, *attr* defined in a class, *cls*, create a directed edge from vertex *attr* to vertex *cls*.

Step 3. For every class, *sub*, that is a subclass of a class, *super*, create a directed edge from vertex *sub* to vertex *super*.

Step 4. For every class that is part of a container class (i.e., a class in a composition relationship), create a directed edge to a container class vertex from a contained class vertex.

Step 5. If there is an association between class x and y, and the lower bound of the multiplicity of the association end in y is equal to or greater than 1, create a directed edge to vertex y from vertex x.

Step 6. For every referenced class (or attribute, *attr*), *cls*, of an operation contract (or invariant, *inv*), *op*, create a directed edge to vertex *cls* (or *attr*) from vertex *op* (or *inv*). If the operation contract (or invariant) only references its context class, *cls*, and its context class's attribute (or attributes) in its specification, the edge that points to vertex *cls* from vertex *op* (or *inv*), is removed.

Fig. 3. Invariant *Inv*5 in Table 1 references its context class, *Session*, and class *Session*'s attribute, *MaxRoles*, in the specification. But the edge pointing to vertex *Session* from vertex *Inv*5 cannot be removed from Fig. 3 since invariant *Inv*5 also references class *Role* in its specification through the navigation from class *Session* to class *Role*.

3.2   Slicing a Class Model

The generated dependency graph is used to guide the decomposition of a model into fragments that can be analyzed separately. The first step is to identify model elements that are not involved in the analysis. These are referred to as *irrelevant model elements*. The intuition behind this step is based on the following observation: If the classes and attributes that are referenced by an operation, are not referenced by any invariant, the operation as well as its referenced classes and attributes (i.e., analysis-irrelevant model elements) can be removed from the class model because a system state change triggered by the operation invocation will not violate any invariant defined in the model. Similarly, if the classes and attributes that are referenced by an invariant, are not referenced by any operation, the invariant as well as its referenced classes and attributes (i.e., analysis-irrelevant model elements) can be removed from the class model because any operation invocation that starts in a valid state will not violate the invariant. *Irrelevant model elements* are identified using the process described in Algorithm 2, and are removed from the class model.

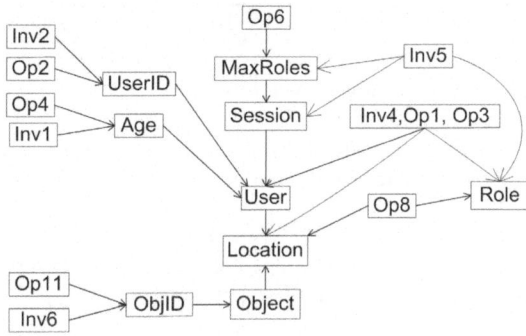

Fig. 4. A Dependency Graph Representing a LRBAC Model with the *Irrelevant Model Elements* Removed

The second step is to identify model elements that are involved in a *local* analysis problem. A *local* analysis problem refers to an analysis that can be performed within the boundary of a class [17]. Model elements that are involved in a *local* analysis problem are referred to as *local analysis model elements*. For example, operation *UpdateUserID* in Fig. 1 is used to modify the value of attribute *UserID* in class *User*, and invariant *Inv2* defines the uniqueness constraint on *UserID*. The invocation of operation *UpdateUserID* may or may not violate the constraint specified in *Inv2*, but it will not violate other invariants because *UserID* is not referenced by other operations or invariants. Thus an analysis that involves checking if an invocation of *UpdateUserID* violates *Inv2* can be performed within the boundary of *User*. Model elements that are involved in *local* analysis problems are identified using the process described in Algorithm 3. Note that in the above example, *UpdateUserID*, *UserID* and *Inv2* are identified *local analysis model elements*. Thus these model elements and their dependent model elements (*User* and *User*'s dependent class *Location*) can be extracted from the LRBAC model and analyzed separately.

In the third step, the class model is further decomposed into a list of model fragments using Algorithm 4.

Identifying *Irrelevant Model Elements*: Algorithm 2 is used to remove analysis-irrelevant model elements. The algorithm first computes *ARClsAttrVSet*, a set of analysis relevant class and attribute vertices, where each vertex is directly dependent on at least one operation vertex and at least one invariant vertex. The algorithm then computes *AROpInvVSet*, a set of analysis relevant operation and invariant vertices, where each vertex has a directly dependent vertex that belongs to *ARClsAttrVSet*. The algorithm then performs a Depth-First Search (DFS) from each vertex in *AROpInvVSet*, and labels all the analysis-relevant vertices, *ARVSet*. The vertices not in *ARVSet* represent the *irrelevant model elements* that need to be removed from the class model.

Algorithm 2. Irrelevant Model Elements Identification Algorithm

---

1: Input: A dependency graph
2: Output: A set of analysis-irrelevant vertices
3: Algorithm Steps:
4: Set $OpVSet$ = a set of operation vertices, $InvVSet$ = a set of invariant vertices;
5: Set $VSet$ = all the vertices in the dependency graph, $OpDVSet$ = {}, $InvDVSet$ = {};
6: **for** each operation vertex OpV in $OpVSet$ **do**
7:     Get a set of OpV's directly dependent vertices, $OpVDDSet$;
8:     $OpDVSet = OpDVSet \cup OpVDDSet$;
9: **end for**
10: **for** each invariant vertex $InvV$ in $InvVSet$ **do**
11:     Get a set of $InvV$'s directly dependent vertices, $InvVDDSet$;
12:     $InvDVSet = InvDVSet \cup InvVDDSet$;
13: **end for**
14: Set $ARClsAttrVSet = OpDVSet \cap InvDVSet$, Set $AROpInvVSet$ = {};
15: **for** each vertex V in $OpVSet \cup InvVSet$ **do**
16:     **if** one of V's directly dependent vertex is in $ARClsAttrVSet$ **then**
17:         $AROpInvVSet = AROpInvVSet \cup V$; Break;
18:     **end if**
19: **end for**
20: Set $ARVSet$ = {};
21: **for** each vertex V in $AROpInvVSet$ **do**
22:     Perform a Depth-First Search (DFS) from vertex V;
23:     Get a set of labeling vertices, $VDFSSet$, from vertex V's DFS tree;
24:     $ARVSet = ARVSet \cup VDFSSet$;
25: **end for**
26: Return ($VSet$ - $ARVSet$);

Figure 4 shows a dependency graph representing a LRBAC model with the analysis irrelevant model elements removed. Lines 6-14 of Algorithm 2 compute $ARClsAttrVSet$. Lines 6-9 compute $OpDVSet$, a set of directly dependent attribute and class vertices from each operation vertex. Similarly, lines 10-13 compute $InvDVSet$, a set of directly dependent attribute and class vertices from each invariant vertex. $ARClsAttrVSet$ is the intersection of $OpDVSet$ and $InvDVSet$.

Lines 15-19 compute $AROpInvVSet$. For example, vertex $Op4$ is an analysis-relevant operation vertex because its directly dependent vertex, Age, is an analysis-relevant attribute vertex, while vertex $Op5$ is analysis-irrelevant because $UserName$ is not an analysis-relevant vertex. Lines 21-25 compute $ARVSet$.

Identifying *Local Analysis Model Elements*: Algorithm 3 is used to identify fragments representing local analysis problems. The algorithm first computes a set of attribute and class vertices, $LocalVSet$, that are involved in the local analysis problems. A vertex, $ClsAttrV$, is added to $LocalVSet$ only if (1) the vertex is a member of $ARClsAttrVSet$ (indicated by Line 6), and (2) all vertices directly dependent on $ClsAttr$ have no other directly dependent vertices

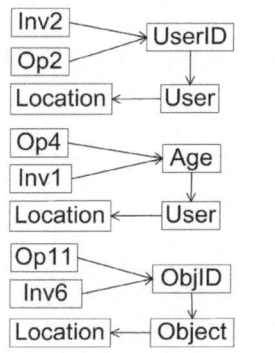

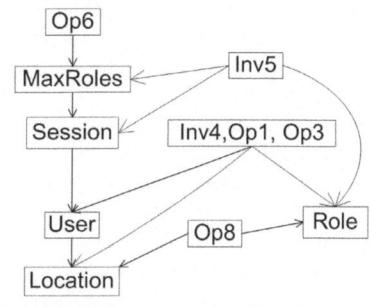

(a) Local Analysis Model Elements identified by Algorithm 3

(b) Reduced Dependency Graph with Local Analysis Model Elements Removed

Fig. 5. Dependency Graphs Representing Model Fragments Extracted from the LRBAC Model in Fig. 1

(indicated by Lines 7-15). The algorithm then uses the vertices in $LocalVSet$ to construct new dependency graphs, where each graph represents a model fragment involved in a local analysis problem.

The dependency graph in Fig. 4 is decomposed into several subgraphs, as shown in Fig. 5a and Fig. 5b, using Algorithm 3. Each dependency graph in Fig. 5a represents a model fragment involved in a local analysis problem.

For example, $\{UserID, Age, ObjID\}$ is the $LocalVSet$ set of the dependency graph in Fig. 4. The vertices that directly depend on vertex $ObjID$ are $Op11$ and $Inv6$, and they are moved from DG to a new dependency graph. Vertex $ObjID$'s DFS tree consists of $ObjID$, $Object$ and $Location$, and they are copied from DG to the new dependency graph. $ObjID$ is then removed from DG. Note that vertex $Object$ becomes analysis-irrelevant in DG after vertex $ObjID$, $Op11$, and $Inv6$ have been removed from DG. Thus it is necessary to perform Algorithm 2 on DG to remove the analysis-irrelevant vertices, as indicated by Line 25.

Decomposing the Dependency Graph: Algorithm 4 is used to decompose a dependency graph without analysis-irrelevant vertices and local analysis problem related vertices. The algorithm computes a set of slicing criteria where each criterion consists of a set of operation and invariant vertices. Each slicing criterion is then used to generate a new dependency graph that represents a model fragment.

For example, for each vertex, v, in $ARClsAttrVSet$, Line 5 of Algorithm 4 computes a collection Col, where each member of Col is a set of operation and invariant vertices that directly depend on v. $ARClsAttrVSet$ (see Algorithm 2) is a set of class and attributes vertices on which both operation and invariant vertices directly depend. For example, $ARClsAttrVSet$ for the graph shown in Fig. 5b is $\{MaxRoles, User, Location, Role\}$. Thus Col for the graph is $\{\{Op6, In5\}, \{In4, Op1, Op3\}, \{In4, Op1, Op3, Op8\}, \{In4, Op1, Op3, Op8, In5\}\}$.

Algorithm 3. Local Analysis Problem Identification Algorithm

1: Input: A dependency graph, DG, produced from the original graph after removing the irrelevant vertices produced by Algorithm 2
2: Output: A set of dependency graphs
3: Algorithm Steps:
4: Reuse $ARClsAttrVSet$ in Algorithm 2;
5: Set $LocalVSet = \{\}$;
6: **for** each vertex, $ClsAttrV$, in $ARClsAttrVSet$ **do**
7:    Set $Flag = $ TRUE;
8:    **for** each vertex, V, that is directly dependent on $ClsAttrV$ **do**
9:        **if** V has other directly dependent vertices **then**
10:           Set $Flag = $ FALSE; Break;
11:       **end if**
12:    **end for**
13:    **if** $Flag == $ TRUE **then**
14:       $LocVSet = LocVSet \cup ClsAttrV$;
15:    **end if**
16: **end for**
17: **for** each vertex, $LocalV$, in $LocalVSet$ **do**
18:    Create an empty dependency graph, $SubDG$;
19:    Move the operation and invariant vertices that directly depend on $LocalV$, from DG to $SubDG$;
20:    Perform a DFS from vertex $LocalV$;
21:    Get a set of labeling vertices, $LocalVDFSSet$, from vertex $LocalV$'s DFS tree;
22:    Copy $LocalVDFSSet$ from DG to $SubDG$;
23:    Remove $LocalV$ from DG;
24: **end for**
25: Perform Algorithm 2 on DG to remove analysis-irrelevant vertices;

Line 6 uses the union-find algorithm described in [3] to merge the non-disjoint sets in Col, and produce a collection of sets with disjoint operation and invariant vertices. For example, Col for the graph shown in Fig. 5b becomes $\{Op6, In5, In4, Op1, Op3, Op8, In5\}$ with the union-find algorithm being used.

Lines 7-16 use each disjoint set, S, in Col to construct a new dependency graph from the input dependency graph DG. Lines 8-13 build a forest for S from each DFS tree of a vertex in S. Lines 14-15 create a new dependency graph that consists of all vertices in the forest. Since Col for the graph shown in Fig. 5b has only one disjoint set, the forest generated from the disjoint set consists of all the vertices in the dependency graph, indicating that the graph in Fig. 5b is the minimum dependency graph that cannot be decomposed further.

4   Preliminary Evaluation

We developed a research prototype to investigate the feasibility of developing tool support for the slicing approach. The prototype was developed using Kermeta [8], an aspect-oriented metamodeling tool. The inputs to the prototype are

Algorithm 4. Dependency Graph Decomposition Algorithm

1: Input: A dependency graph, DG, produced from the original graph by Algorithm 3
2: Output: A set of dependency graphs
3: Algorithm Steps:
4: Recompute $ARClsAttrVSet$ for DG using Algorithm 2;
5: Compute a collection $Col = S_1, S_2,...,S_v$ of operation and invariant vertex sets, where S_v represents a set of operation and invariant vertices that directly depend on vertex v, a member of $ARClsAttrVSet$;
6: Use the *disjoint-set data structure and algorithm* described in [3] to merge the nondisjoint-sets in Col;
7: **for** each set, S, in Col **do**
8:     Set $SubVSet = \{\}$;
9:     **for** each vertex, V, in S **do**
10:         Perform a DFS from vertex V;
11:         Get a set of labeling vertices, $VDFSSet$, from vertex V's DFS tree;
12:         $SubVSet = SubVSet \cup VDFSSet$;
13:     **end for**
14:     Create an empty dependency graph, $SubDG$;
15:     Copy all the vertices in $SubVSet$, from DG to $SubDG$;
16: **end for**
17: Delete DG;

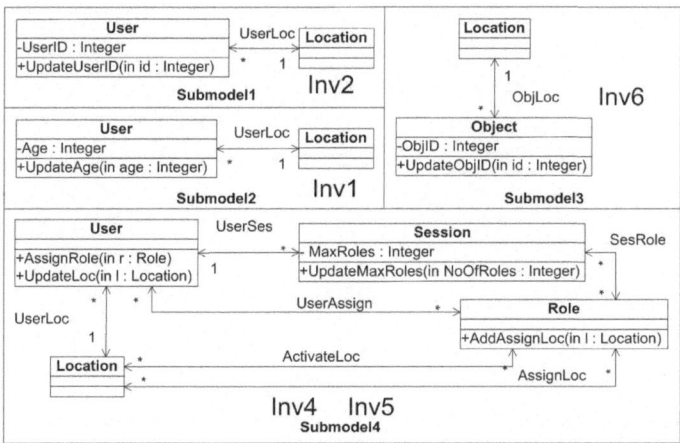

Fig. 6. A List of Model Fragments Generated from the LRBAC Model in Fig. 1

(1) an EMF Ecore [20] file that describes a UML design class model, and (2) a textual file that contains the OCL invariants and operation specifications. The prototype produces a list of model fragments extracted from the input model. The prototype implementation uses a visitor pattern based transformation approach to generate a dependency graph from a UML class model with OCL invariants and operation specifications.

Figure 6 shows four model fragments extracted from the LRBAC model in Fig. 1. Each model fragment corresponds to a dependency graph in Fig. 5. The model

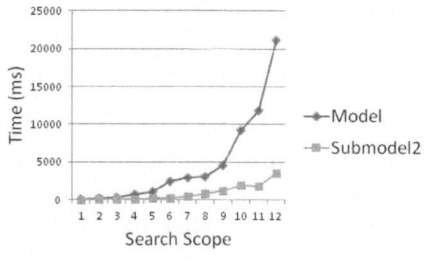

(a) Analyzing Model Fragment against Inv1

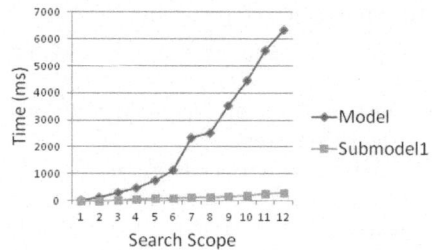

(b) Analyzing Model Fragment against Inv2

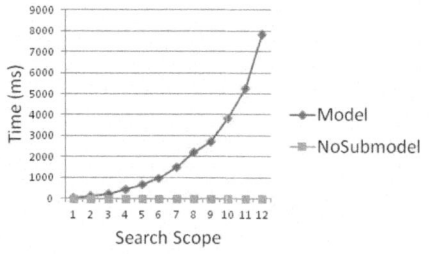

(c) Analyzing Model Fragment against Inv3

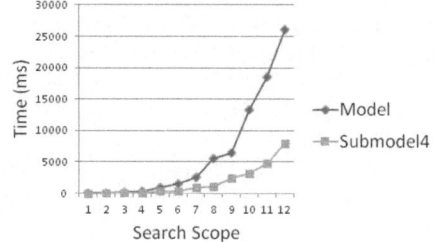

(d) Analyzing Model Fragment against Inv4

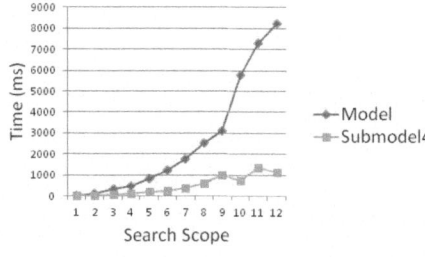

(e) Analyzing Model Fragment against Inv5

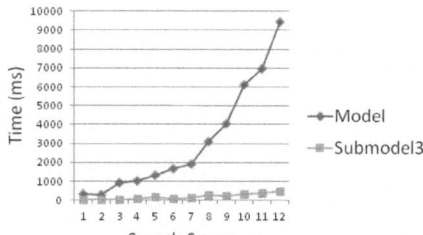

(f) Analyzing Model Fragment against Inv6

Fig. 7. Analyzing Unsliced Model and Model Fragments against each Invariant of Table 1

fragments and the unsliced model were analyzed against the invariants defined in Table 1 by the Alloy Analyzer (version 4.2 with SAT4J), on a laptop computer with 2.17 GHz Intel Dual Core CPU, 3 GB RAM and Windows 7.

Figure 7 shows the results of a preliminary evaluation we performed on the unsliced model and the model fragments. Each subfigure in 7 has an x axis, namely *SearchScope*, indicating the maximum number of instances the Alloy Analyzer can produce for a class, and a y axis, namely *Time*, showing the total analysis time (in millisecond) for building the SAT formula and finding an Alloy instance.

For example, Fig. 7a shows the time used to analyze the unsliced model $Model$ and the model fragment $Submodel2$ against the invariant $Inv1$. The difference between the time used for analyzing $Model$ and that for $Submodel2$ is relatively small when the Alloy search scope is below 5. For a search scope above 10, the time used for analyzing $Model$ becomes significantly large while that for $Submodel2$ is still below 5000 ms. Fig. 7c shows that the invariant $Inv3$ was not analyzed in any model fragment (the analysis time remains at 0). This is because $Inv3$ was removed after the dependency analysis identified the invariant as an analysis-irrelevant element.

Note that the four algorithms described in the paper use set addition/deletion operations, a depth-first-search algorithm, and a disjoint-set algorithm. Thus the execution time for implementations of these four algorithms should not increase significantly as the size of the class model increases. Since the execution time of SAT solver-based tools (e.g., Alloy) could be exponential on the size of the class model, the slicing algorithm described in the paper could speed up the verification process for large models.

The preliminary evaluation also showed that the analysis results are preserved by the slicing technique. For example, the analysis performed on the unsliced model and the model fragments both found that the constraints specified in invariant $Inv2$, $Inv5$ and $Inv6$ were violated by operation $UpdateUserID$, $UpdateMaxRoles$ and $UpdateObjID$ respectively. The analysis of the full model also revealed that Inv3 is not violated by operation invocations; this is consistent with the identification of Inv3 as an analysis-irrelevant element.

Note that the approach is limited in its ability to produce smaller model fragments from a larger model w.r.t. the slicing criteria. There may be properties that require all model elements to be present when analyzed (reflecting a very tight coupling across all model elements). The slicing approach described in this paper does not guarantee that more than one independently analyzable fragments will be produced from a model.

5   Related Work

Kagdi et al. [9] proposed an approach to slicing UML class models. The slices are applicable to models that do not require a context (e.g., a set of scenarios in which objects are involved) for the computation of a model slice. OCL invariants and operations are not considered in their slicing approach. Blouin et al. [2] described a modeling language, $Kompren$, for modeling model slicers for different domain specific modeling languages. The slicer produced by $Kompren$, however, requires a modeler to specify a slicing criterion. In the approach described in this paper the criteria is automatically generated.

Shaiky et al. [17][18] proposed a slicing approach for UML class models with OCL invariants, and utilized the approach to improve the scalability of verifying the satisfiability property. The model partitioning process is guided by the following rule: All constraints restricting the same model element should be verified together and therefore must be contained in the same slice. Unlike the slicing technique described in the paper, their approach cannot be used to decompose a model with both OCL invariants and operation specifications.

Lano et al. [11][12] presented an approach to slicing a UML class with operation specifications and OCL invariants. Their approach uses a state machine to specify a sequence of operation invocations on an instance of a class. If a class feature (e.g., an attribute) does not occur in any operation defined in the class, it can be removed together with any invariants that refer to it. Compared with their approach, our slicing approach focuses on a class model rather than a class, and does not require a state machine to guide the slicing process.

6   Conclusion

We presented a slicing approach for UML class models that includes OCL invariants and operation contracts. The slicing approach is used to improve the efficiency of a model analysis technique that involves checking a sequence of operation invocations to uncover violations in specified invariants. The approach takes as input a UML class model with operation contracts and OCL invariants, and decomposes the model into model fragments with disjoint operations and invariants. The results of the preliminary evaluation we performed showed that the proposed slicing technique can significantly reduce the time to perform the analysis. We are currently using large models (e.g., UML metamodels) that have a substantial number of invariants and operation contracts to evaluate the slicing approach.

Acknowledgment. The work described in this report was supported by the National Science Foundation grant CCF-1018711.

References

1. Androutsopoulos, K., Binkley, D., Clark, D., Gold, N., Harman, M., Lano, K., Li, Z.: Model projection: simplifying models in response to restricting the environment. In: 2011 33rd International Conference on Software Engineering (ICSE), pp. 291–300. IEEE (2011)
2. Blouin, A., Combemale, B., Baudry, B., Beaudoux, O.: Modeling model slicers. In: Whittle, J., Clark, T., Kühne, T. (eds.) MODELS 2011. LNCS, vol. 6981, pp. 62–76. Springer, Heidelberg (2011)
3. Cormen, T.H.: Introduction to algorithms. The MIT press (2001)
4. Eshuis, R., Wieringa, R.: Tool support for verifying UML activity diagrams. IEEE Transactions on Software Engineering 30(7), 437–447 (2004)
5. Gallagher, K.B., Lyle, J.R.: Using program slicing in software maintenance. IEEE Transactions on Software Engineering 17(8), 751–761 (1991)
6. Jackson, D.: Alloy: a lightweight object modelling notation. ACM Transactions on Software Engineering and Methodology (TOSEM) 11(2), 256–290 (2002)
7. Jeanneret, C., Glinz, M., Baudry, B.: Estimating footprints of model operations. In: 2011 33rd International Conference on Software Engineering (ICSE), pp. 601–610. IEEE (2011)

8. Jézéquel, J.-M., Barais, O., Fleurey, F.: Model driven language engineering with kermeta. In: Fernandes, J.M., Lämmel, R., Visser, J., Saraiva, J. (eds.) Generative and Transformational Techniques in Software Engineering III. LNCS, vol. 6491, pp. 201–221. Springer, Heidelberg (2011)

9. Kagdi, H., Maletic, J.I., Sutton, A.: Context-free slicing of UML class models. In: Proceedings of the 21st IEEE International Conference on Software Maintenance, ICSM 2005, pp. 635–638. IEEE (2005)

10. Korel, B., Singh, I., Tahat, L., Vaysburg, B.: Slicing of state-based models. In: Proceedings of the International Conference on Software Maintenance, ICSM 2003, pp. 34–43. IEEE (2003)

11. Lano, K., Kolahdouz-Rahimi, S.: Slicing of UML models using model transformations. In: Petriu, D.C., Rouquette, N., Haugen, Ø. (eds.) MODELS 2010, Part II. LNCS, vol. 6395, pp. 228–242. Springer, Heidelberg (2010)

12. Lano, K., Kolahdouz-Rahimi, S.: Slicing techniques for UML models. Journal of Object Technology, 10 (2011)

13. Ray, I., Kumar, M.: Towards a location-based mandatory access control model. Computers & Security 25(1), 36–44 (2006)

14. Ray, I., Kumar, M., Yu, L.: Lrbac: A location-aware role-based access control model. Information Systems Security, 147–161 (2006)

15. Ray, I., Yu, L.: Short paper: Towards a location-aware role-based access control model. In: First International Conference on Security and Privacy for Emerging Areas in Communications Networks, SecureComm 2005, pp. 234–236. IEEE (2005)

16. Sandhu, R.S., Coyne, E.J., Feinstein, H.L., Youman, C.E.: Role-based access control models. Computer 29(2), 38–47 (1996)

17. Shaikh, A., Clarisó, R., Wiil, U.K., Memon, N.: Verification-driven slicing of UML/OCL models. In: Proceedings of the IEEE/ACM International Conference on Automated Software Engineering, pp. 185–194. ACM (2010)

18. Shaikh, A., Wiil, U.K., Memon, N.: Evaluation of tools and slicing techniques for efficient verification of UML/OCL class diagrams. Advances in Software Engineering (2011)

19. O.M.G.A. Specification. Object constraint language (2007)

20. Steinberg, D., Budinsky, F., Merks, E., Paternostro, M.: EMF: Eclipse Modeling Framework. Addison-Wesley Professional (2008)

21. Sun, W., France, R., Ray, I.: Rigorous analysis of UML access control policy models. In: IEEE International Symposium on Policies for Distributed Systems and Networks (POLICY), pp. 9–16. IEEE (2011)

22. Weiser, M.: Program slicing. In: Proceedings of the 5th International Conference on Software Engineering, pp. 439–449. IEEE Press (1981)

Usability Inspection in Model-Driven Web Development: Empirical Validation in WebML

Adrian Fernandez[1], Silvia Abrahão[1], Emilio Insfrán[1], and Maristella Matera[2]

[1] ISSI Research Group, Universitat Politècnica de València, Spain
{afernandez,sabrahao,einsfran}@dsic.upv.es
[2] Politecnico di Milano, Italy
matera@elet.polimi.it

Abstract. There is a lack of empirically validated usability evaluation methods that can be applied to models in model-driven Web development. Evaluation of these models allows an early detection of usability problems perceived by the end-user. This motivated us to propose WUEP, a usability inspection method which can be integrated into different model-driven Web development processes. We previously demonstrated how WUEP can effectively be used when following the Object-Oriented Hypermedia method. In order to provide evidences about WUEP's generalizability, this paper presents the operationalization and empirical validation of WUEP into another well-known method: WebML. The effectiveness, efficiency, perceived ease of use, and satisfaction of WUEP were evaluated in comparison to Heuristic Evaluation (HE) from the viewpoint of novice inspectors. The results show that WUEP was more effective and efficient than HE when detecting usability problems on models. Also, inspectors were satisfied when applying WUEP, and found it easier to use than HE.

Keywords: Model-driven Web development, Usability inspections, Measure operationalization, Empirical validation, WebML.

1 Introduction

Usability is considered as one of the most important quality factors for Web applications: the ease or difficulty experienced by users largely determines their success or failure [26]. The challenge of developing more usable Web applications has promoted the emergence of a large number of usability evaluation methods [24]. However, most of these approaches only consider usability evaluations after the Web application is fully implemented and deployed. Studies such as that of Matera et al. [20] and Juristo et al. [18] however claim that usability evaluations should also be performed at early stages of the Web development (e.g., at modeling time) in order to detect early how to improve the user experience and decrease maintenance costs. This is in line with the results of a recently performed systematic mapping study on usability evaluation methods for Web applications [9], which revealed a lack of usability evaluation methods that have been empirically validated and that can be properly used to evaluate analysis and design models of a Web application under development.

A. Moreira et al. (Eds.): MODELS 2013, LNCS 8107, pp. 740–756, 2013.

In order to address these issues, we have proposed a usability inspection method (Web Usability Evaluation Process – WUEP [10]), which can be instantiated and integrated into different *model-driven Web development processes*. The peculiarity of these development processes is that Platforms-Independent Models (PIMs) and Platform-Specific Models (PSMs) are built to represent the different views of a Web application (e.g., content, navigation, presentation); finally, the source code (Code Model - CM) is obtained from these models using model-to-text automatic transformations. In this context, inspections of the PIMs and PSMs can provide early *usability evaluation reports* to identify potential usability problems that can be corrected prior to the generation of the source code.

In our view, comparative empirical studies are useful to evaluate and improve any newly proposed evaluation method, since valuable information can be achieved when a method is compared to others. Several empirical studies for validating Web usability evaluation methods have been reported in literature (e.g., [8]). However, they focus on traditional Web development processes, while only few studies address model-driven Web development processes (e.g., [1][19][27]). Among these studies, we presented in [12] an operationalization and validation of WUEP in a specific process based on the Object-Oriented Hypermedia (OO-H) method. In this study, WUEP was compared against Heuristic Evaluation (HE) [25]. The results showed that WUEP is more effective and efficient than HE in supporting the detection of usability problems.

In order to verify the generalization of WUEP into another process, we also operationalized WUEP for its application to the Web Modeling Language (WebML) [6], one of the most well-known industrial model-driven Web development process. We adapted generic measures, taken from the Web Usability Model [10] on which WUEP is based, to specific WebML modeling constructs, as a means to *predict* and *improve* the usability of Web applications generated from these models. A pilot experiment was conducted to analyze the feasibility and validity of this operationalization [11]. In this paper, we present the results of an experiment replication aimed at providing further analysis about its effectiveness, efficiency, perceived ease of use, and satisfaction in comparison to HE.

This paper is structured as follows. Section 2 discusses existing work that addresses usability evaluations in model-driven Web development. Section 3 provides an overview of WUEP. Section 4 describes how WUEP has been instantiated for use with WebML. Section 5 describes the experiments designed to empirically validate WUEP. Section 6 shows the analysis of the results obtained and discusses threats to the validity. Finally, Section 7 presents our conclusions and further work.

2   Related Work

Despite the fact that several model-driven development (MDD) methods have been proposed since late 2000 for developing Web-based interactive applications, few work address usability evaluations in this type of processes (e.g., [2],[13],[22]).

Atterer and Schmidt [2] proposed a prototype of a model-based usability validator. The aim was to perform an analysis of operative Web applications by previously tagging its sections in order to build a page model. This model is then compared by patterns extracted from usability guidelines.

Fraternali et al. [13] presented the Web Quality Analyzer, a framework which is able to automatically analyze the XML specification of Web applications designed through WebML for identifying the occurrence of some design patterns, and calculating metrics revealing if they are used consistently throughout the application.

Molina and Toval [22] presented a method to integrate usability goals in model-driven Web development by extending the expressiveness of navigation models to incorporate these usability goals. A meta-model was defined in order to describe the requirements to be achieved for these navigational models.

These works represent the first steps to incorporate usability evaluation in model-driven Web development, however from them it does not emerge any systematic process. Furthermore, only few of them have been validated through empirical studies to show evidence about the effectiveness of performing usability evaluations on models (e.g., [1] [19] [27]).

There are some studies in literature that compare usability evaluation methods through empirical studies. Abrahão et al. [1] present an empirical study which evaluates the user interfaces generated automatically by a model-driven development tool. This study applies two usability evaluation methods: an inspection method (Action Analysis) and an empirical method (User Testing) with the aim of comparing what types of usability problems the two methods are able to detect in the user interfaces, and what their implications are for transformations rules and PIMs.

Matera et al. [19] presented the empirical validation of the Systematic Usability Evaluation (SUE) method for hypermedia applications based on the adoption of operational guidelines called Abstract Tasks. The experiment showed the major effectiveness and efficiency of the inspection method with respect to traditional heuristic evaluation techniques.

Panach et al. [27] provided metrics to evaluate the understandability attributes of Web applications (i.e., a usability sub-characteristic) as result of a model-driven development process. Metrics values were aggregated to obtain indexes which were compared to the perception of these same attributes by end users. However, the study did not consider any performance measure of method usage. As indicated by Hornbæk [14], for assessing the quality of usability evaluation methods it is important to consider not only the evaluators' observations and satisfaction with the methods under evaluation but also the performance of the methods (e.g., in terms of number of usability detected problems).

The analysis of the previous works highlights a lack of empirical validations of usability inspection methods for model-driven Web development processes. This motivated us to conduct a family of experiments to validate our usability inspection method when it was applied to the Object-Oriented Hypermedia (OO-H) method [12]. However, generalizations about the usefulness of WUEP require it to be instantiated and validated in other model-driven Web development methods. Hence, this paper focuses on the operationalization of WUEP to another method, WebML, and on its validation through an experimental study.

3   Web Usability Evaluation Process

The Web Usability Evaluation Process (WUEP) has been defined by extending and refining the quality evaluation process that is proposed in the ISO 25000 standard [16]. The aim of WUEP is to integrate usability evaluation into model-driven Web development processes by employing a Web Usability Model as the principal input artifact. This model breaks down the usability concept into 16 sub-characteristics and 66 measurable attributes, which are then associated with 106 measures in order to quantify them. These measures provide a generic definition, which should be operationalized in order to be applied to models obtained at different abstraction levels (PIMs, PSMs, and, CMs) in different MDWD processes (e.g., WebML, OO-H).

The aim of applying measures is to reduce the subjectivity inherent to existing inspection methods. It is important to remark that by applying measures, the evaluators inspect models in order to predict usability problems (i.e., to detect problems that would be experienced by end-users when using the generated Web application). We are not intended to evaluate the usability of the models themselves. Therefore, inspection of these models (by considering the traceability among them) allows us to discover the source of the detected usability problems and facilitates the provision of recommendations to correct these problems at earlier stages of the Web development process.

We are aware that not all usability problems can be detected based on the evaluation of models since they are limited by their own expressiveness and, most importantly, they may not predict the user behavior or preferences. However, studies such as that of Hwang and Salvendy [15] claim that usability inspections, applying well-known usability principles on software artifacts, may find around 80% of usability problems. In addition, the use of inspection methods for detecting usability problems in models can be complemented with other evaluation methods performed with end-users before releasing a Web application to the public.

The main stages of WUEP are:

1. In the *establishment of the evaluation requirements* stage, the evaluation designer defines the scope of the evaluation by (a) establishing the purpose of the evaluation; (b) specifying the evaluation profiles (type of Web application, Web development method employed, context of use); (c) selecting the Web artifacts (models) to be inspected; and (d) selecting the usability attributes from the Web usability model which are going to be evaluated.
2. In the *specification of the evaluation* stage, the evaluation designer operationalizes the measures associated with the selected attributes in order for them to be applied to the models to be evaluated. This operationalization consists of establishing a mapping between the generic definition of the measure and the concepts that are represented in the Web artifacts (modeling primitives of models or UI elements in the final Web application). In addition, thresholds are established for ranges of values obtained for each measure by considering their scale type and the guidelines related to each measure whenever possible. These thresholds provide a usability problem classification based on their severity: low, medium, or critical. It is important to note that the operationalization needs to be performed once within a specific model-driven Web development method, and can be reused in further evaluations that involve Web applications developed using the same method.

3. In the *design of the evaluation* stage, the template for usability reports is defined and the evaluation plan is elaborated (e.g., number of evaluators, evaluation constraints).
4. In the *execution of the evaluation* stage, the evaluator applies the operationalized measures to the selected Web artifacts (i.e., models) in order to detect usability problems by considering the rating levels established for each measure.
5. In the *analysis of changes* stage, the Web developer analyzes all the usability problems in order to propose changes with which to correct the affected artifacts from a specific stage of the Web development process. The changes are applicable to the previous intermediate artifacts (i.e., PIMs, PSMs and model transformations if the evaluation is performed on the final Web user interface).

4   Instantiation in WebML

This section presents how WUEP can be instantiated for evaluating the usability of Web applications developed using the Web Modeling Language (WebML) method. This method is complemented by the WebRatio tool, which offers visual editors for the definition of the models and transformation techniques for code generation in different platforms. WebML was selected because: i) it is a well-known model-driven Web development method in industry with several success stories reported [28], ii) it offers conceptual models of real Web applications and their corresponding generated source code, and iii) it can be considered a representative method of the whole set of model-driven Web development methods [23] .

In the rest of this section, we first give a short overview about WebML to present its main modeling primitives. Secondly, we provide some examples of how some generic measures were operationalized in WebML models. Finally, we also provide a proof of concept about how WUEP can be applied in a WebML-based Web application in order to detect and report usability problems at early stages of the Web development process.

4.1   Overview of WebML

WebML is a domain-specific language for specifying the content structure of Web applications (i.e., Data Model) and the organization and presentation of their contents in one or more hypertexts (i.e., Hypertext Model). Considering that the Hypertext Model is obtained early in the Web development process, it plays a relevant role in ensuring the usability of the final Web application since it describes how data resources are assembled, interconnected and presented into information units and pages. Table 1 shows some of the most representative modeling primitives provided by the Hypertext Model. These primitives are classified according to three perspectives: a) Composition, defining pages and their internal organization in terms of elementary interconnected units; b) Navigation, describing links between pages and content units to be provided to facilitate information location and browsing; and c) Operation, specifying the invocation of external operations for managing and updating content.

Composition primitives are based on containers called *Pages* (which can be grouped by *Areas*) and a set of building blocks called Content units. *Pages* and *Areas* can be marked as *Homepage (H)*, *Landmark (L)*, or *Default (D)*. The content units represent one or more instances of the entities of the structural schema, typically selected by means of queries over the entity attributes or over their relationships. In particular, they allow representing a set of attributes for an entity instance (*DataUnits*), and list of properties of a given set of entity instances (*IndexUnits*).

Navigation primitives are based on links that connect units and pages, thus forming the hypertext. Links connect units in several configurations, yielding to composite navigation mechanisms. They can be activated by a user action (*Normal Link*); the Web application (*OK or KO Link*); or even can be employed only as transport of parameters between modeling primitives (*Transport Link*).

Table 1. WebML Hypertext modeling primitives

Operation primitives enable managing the messages that are prompted to the user after any operation (*MultiMessageUnit*), expressing built-in update operations, such as creating, deleting or modifying an instance of an entity (respectively represented through the *CreateUnit*, *DeleteUnit* and *ModifyUnit*), and collecting input values into fields (*EntryUnits*). From the user point of view the execution of an operation is a side effect of navigating a contextual link. Operations may have different incoming links, but only one is the activating-one.

The Data Model and Hypertext Model are taken as input of a model compiler that is able to automatically generate the Web application source code. This is supported by the WebRatio tool which also provides predefined presentation templates to customize the presentation of the final Web application.

4.2   Operationalizing Measures for WebML

The operationalization of measures is a mean to establish a mapping between the generic definition of the measure and the modeling primitives that are represented in a specific model defined during a specific MDWD process.

For WebML, we have operationalized a total of 16 measures for the Hypertext model (http://www.dsic.upv.es/~afernandez/MODELS13/operationalization). As an example, Table 2 presents two measures (i.e., PAE and UOC) from the Web Usability Model and shows their operationalization for the WebML Hypertext Model. The details regarding the generic definition of the measure are provided by the five first rows: *name, attached usability attribute, generic description, measurement scale*, and *interpretation*. The details regarding the operationalization of the measure are provided in the last two rows: *operationalization* and *thresholds* established in order to detect a usability problem (UP). In these examples, thresholds were established by dividing the range of obtained values in convenient intervals. However, other examples of measures provide empirically validated thresholds (e.g., navigation depth). Domain experts (Web designers) have validated these values. The mapping between each element from the generic measure definition and the modeling primitives is highlighted in bold and marked with asterisks (*).

Table 2. Examples of operationalized measures to be applied in WebML

Measure Name	**Proportion of actions with error messages associated (PAE)**
Usability Attribute	Appropriateness recognizability / User guidance / Message availability
Generic Description	Ratio between the number of **user actions** (*) without an **error message** (**) to provide feedback and the total number of user actions.
Scale	Ratio between 0 and 1
Interpretation	The higher the value worse is the guidance (in terms of messages) that is provided to the user..
Operationalization	Let HM : Hypertext Model $$PAE(HM) = \frac{\text{Number of \textbf{Operation Units} (*) that not provide a KO link leading to a \textbf{MultiMessage Unit} (**)}}{\text{Total number of \textbf{Operation Units} (*)}} \quad (1)$$ Where Operation Units can be any CreateUnit, ModifyUnit and DeleteUnit
Thresholds	[PAE = 0]: No UP [0.3 < PAE ≤ 0.6]: Medium UP [0 < PAE ≤ 0.3]: Low UP [0.6 < PAE ≤ 1]: Critical UP

Measure Name	**User operation cancellability (UOC)**
Usability Attribute	Operability / Controllability / Cancel support
Generic Description	Proportion between the number of **implemented functions** (*) that cannot be **cancelled by the user** (**) prior to completion and the total number of functions requiring the pre-cancellation capability.
Scale	Ratio between 0 and 1.
Interpretation	The higher the value the worse controllability the WebApp presents due to the fact that it is necessary to use external operations (i.e., browser actions) in order to go back to a previous state if user wants to cancel the current operation.
Operationalization	Let HM : Hypertext Model $$OUC(HM) = \frac{\text{Number of \textbf{Operation Units} (*) reached by a unit which has not a \textbf{Normal Link} (**) to its predecessor unit}}{\text{Total number of \textbf{Operation Units} (*)}} \quad (2)$$ Where *Operation Units* can be any *CreateUnit, ModifyUnit* and *DeleteUnit*
Thresholds	[UOC = 0]: No UP [0.3 < UOC ≤ 0.6]: Medium UP [0 < UOC ≤ 0.3]: Low UP [0.6 < UOC ≤ 1]: Critical UP

4.3   Applying WUEP into Practice with WebML

We here show a proof of concept about the feasibility of WUEP by applying it to evaluate the usability of a WebML-based Web application. We follow the steps introduced in Section 3.

Establishment of Evaluation Requirements. The purpose of the evaluation is to perform an early usability evaluation during the development of an e-commerce Web application. The application selected is a furniture online store aimed at supporting two types of users: potential customers, and the website administrator. The Web artifact to be evaluated is the Hypertext Model HM0 (see Figure 1), which covers the Store editing functionality issued by the administrator. The Area *Store editing* allows the administrator to access all the stores (IndexUnit *All Stores*) and their details (Normal Link *expand* and DataUnit *Store details*), adding new stores (Normal Link *new*, EntryUnit *New Store*, and CreateUnit Create store); removing existing stores (Normal Link *drop* and DeleteUnit *Delete store*), and modifying existing stores (EntryUnit *Modify Store*, Normal Link *apply*, and CreateUnit *Create store*). All the operations include their OK and KO links after its completion.

The usability attributes to be evaluated are *Message availability* and *Cancel support*. These attributes were selected because of their relevance for any data-intensive Web applications [7].

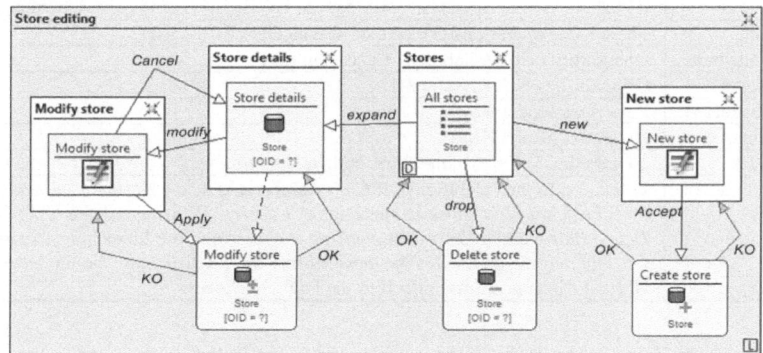

Fig. 1. Hypertext Model HM0

Specification of the Evaluation. The generic measures selected were the ones presented in Table 2.

Design of the Evaluation. A template for reporting usability problems (UP) is defined by considering the following fields: ID, description of the UP, affected usability attribute, severity level, artifact evaluated, source of the problem, occurrences, and recommendations.

Execution of the Evaluation. The operationalized measures are applied in the Web artifacts in order to detect usability problems:

Proportion of Actions with Error Messages Associated (PAE). Applying this measure (Table 2, Equation 1), we obtain the value 3/3 = 1 since from a total of three Operation Units (*Create Store*, *Modify Store*, and *Delete Store*) none of them has its KO link connected to a MultiMessageUnit. This means that a critical usability problem was detected (and reported as UP01 in Table 3(a)) since the value obtained is in the threshold [0.6 < PAE ≤ 1].

User Operation Cancellability (UOC). Applying this measure (Table 2, Equation 2), we obtain the value 2/3 = 0.66 since from the total of three Operation Units (*Create Store*, *Modify Store*, and *Delete Store*) only two OperationUnits (*Create Store*, and *Delete Store*) are not reached by a unit with a return link to its predecessor. This means that a critical usability problem was detected (and reported as UP02 in Table 3(b)) since the value obtained is in the threshold [0.6 < UOC ≤ 1].

Table 3. Usability report

a) ID	UP01
Description	There are no messages that help Web designers to identify which types of errors have occurred during performing operations
Affected attribute	Appropriateness recognisability / User guidance / Message availability
Severity level	Critical: [0.6 < PAE=1 ≤ 1]:
Artifact evaluated	Hypertext Model HM0
Problem source	Hypertext Model HM0
Occurrences	3 Operation Units: *Create Store*, *Modify Store*, and *Delete Store*.
Recommendations	Connect a MultiMessage Unit to the KO link for each Operation Unit.

b) ID	UP02
Description	There some operations that cannot be cancelled by the user
Affected attribute	Operability / Controllability / Cancel support
Severity level	Critical: [0.6 < UOC=0.66 ≤ 1].
Artifact evaluated	Hypertext Model HM0
Problem source	Hypertext Model HM0
Occurrences	2 Operation Units: *Create Store*, and *Delete Store*.
Recommendations	In relation to the OperationUnit *Create Store*: add a new Normal Link *cancel* from the EntryUnit *New Store* to the Page *All Stores*. With regard the OperationUnit *Delete Store*: add a EntryUnit *confirmation* between the IndexUnit *All stores* and the OperationUnit itself. The new EntryUnit *confirmation* would have a new Normal Link *cancel* from itself to the Page *All Stores*.

Analysis of Changes. The changes proposed by this report are analyzed by the Web developers (e.g., cost, impact, difficulty) and lately corrected. Figure 2 shows the Hypertext Model which was manually corrected by the Web developer considering the usability report. However, we aim at automatizing the application of changes. By considering the traceability between the Hypertext Model and the final Web application, the corrections proposed are aimed at obtaining a more usable Web application by construction [1], where each model of a Web application is inspected and improved before the source code is generated.

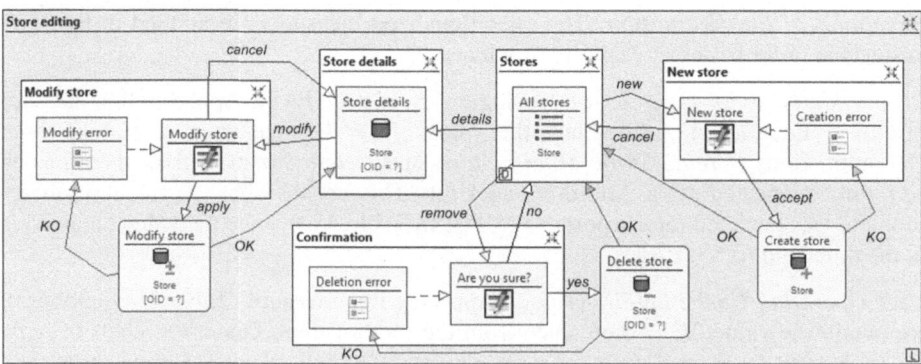

Fig. 2. Hypertext Models corrected after the usability evaluation

5   Empirical Validation

This section first presents an overview of the original experiment, then the design and execution of the experiment replication. The results obtained in both experiments are also presented and discussed. We followed the guidelines proposed by Wohlin et al. [29] and Juristo and Moreno [17].

5.1   Overview of the Original Experiment (EXP)

According to the Goal-Question-Metric (GQM) paradigm [3], the goal of the experiment was to analyze the WUEP operationalization for the WebML development process, for the purpose of evaluating it with regard to its effectiveness, efficiency, perceived ease of use, and the evaluators' perceived satisfaction of it in comparison to Heuristic Evaluation (HE) from the viewpoint of a group of novice usability evaluators. The context of the experiment is the evaluation of two Web applications performed by novice inspectors. This context is determined by the Web applications to be evaluated, the usability evaluation methods to be applied and the subject selection.

The Web applications selected were a Web Calendar for meeting appointment management, and an e-commerce application for a Book Store. They were developed by the WebRatio company using the WebML model-driven development process. Two different functionalities of the Web Calendar application (appointment management and user comments support) were selected for defining the experimental object O1, whereas two different functionalities of the Book Store application (search and shopping) were selected for defining the experimental object O2. Each experimental object contains two Web artifacts: a Hypertext model (HM) and a Final User Interface (FUI) generated from the model. We selected these four functionalities since they are relevant to the end-users and similar in size and complexity.

The usability inspection methods to be evaluated were WUEP and HE. Since the context of the experiments was from the viewpoint of a group of usability inspectors, we evaluated the execution stages of both methods. Two of the authors therefore performed the evaluation designer role in both methods in order to design an evaluation plan. In critical activities such as the selection of usability attributes in WUEP, we required the help of two external Web usability experts. In the case of the HE, all 10 heuristics were selected. In the case of the WUEP, a set of 20 usability attributes were selected as candidates from the Web Usability Model through the consensus reached by the two evaluator designers and other two Web usability experts. The attributes were selected by considering the evaluation profiles (i.e., which of them would be more relevant to the type of Web application and the context in which it is going to be used). Only 12 out of 20 attributes were randomly selected in order to maintain a balance in the number of measures and heuristics to be applied. The associated measures from the 12 attributes were operationalized to be applied at the selected Web artifacts (6 measures for HMs and 6 measures for FUIs).

The experiment was conducted in the context of an Advanced Software Engineering course from September 2011 to January 2012 at the Universitat Politècnica de València (UPV). Specifically, the subjects were 30 fifth-year students enrolled in the undergraduate program in Computer Science.

The experiment has two independent variables: the evaluation method (WUEP and HE) and the experimental objects (O1 and O2). There are two objective dependent variables: effectiveness, which is calculated as the ratio between the number of usability problems detected and the total number of existing (known) usability problems; and efficiency, which is calculated as the ratio between the number of usability problems detected and the total time spent on the inspection process. There are also two subjective dependent variables: perceived ease of use and evaluators' perceived satisfaction. Both were calculated by closed questions from a five-point Likert-scale questionnaire (i.e., arithmetic mean from 5 questions assigned to each variable), which also includes open-questions to obtain feedback from the evaluators.

The hypotheses of the experiment were the following:

- $H1_0$: There is no significant difference between the effectiveness of WUEP and HE / $H1_a$: WUEP is significantly more effective than HE.
- $H2_0$: There is no significant difference between the efficiency of WUEP and HE / $H2_a$: WUEP is significantly more efficient than HE.
- $H3_0$: There is no significant difference between the perceived ease of use of WUEP and HE / $H3_a$: WUEP is perceived to be significantly easier to use than HE.
- $H4_0$: There is no significant difference between the evaluators' perceived satisfaction of applying WUEP and HE / $H4_a$: WUEP is perceived to be significantly more satisfactory to use than HE.

The results of the experiment show that WUEP was more effective and efficient than HE in the detection of usability problems in artifacts obtained using a specific model-driven Web development process. In addition, the evaluators were satisfied when they applied WUEP, and found it easier to use than HE. Preliminary results of this experiment have been reported in [11]. The experimental material is available for download at http://www.dsic.upv.es/~afernandez/MODELS13/instrumentation.

5.2   The Experiment Replication (REP)

We conducted a strict replication of the experiment using a group of more experienced students in software modeling (i.e., Master students). The same materials used in the original experiment were used in the replication experiment. Strict replications are needed to increase confidence in the conclusion validity of the experiment. The subjects were 24 students enrolled on the "Quality of Web Information Systems" course on the Masters in Software Engineering, Formal Methods and Information Systems at the UPV. The alternative hypotheses tested were the same as the original experiment. It also was analyzed the order influence of the method and the two experimental objects employed.

The experiment was planned as a balanced within-subject design with a confounding effect, signifying that the same subjects use both methods in a different order and with different experimental objects (the subjects' assignation was random). Table 4 shows the schedule of the experiment operation in more detail. In addition, before the controlled experiment, a control group was created in order to provide an initial list of usability problems by applying an ad-hoc inspection method, and to determine whether the usability problems reported by the subjects were real or false positives. This group was formed of two independent evaluators who are experts in usability evaluations, and one of the authors of this paper. Several documents were designed as instrumentation for the experiment: slides for training session, an explanation of the methods, gathering data forms, and two questionnaires.

Table 4. Schedule of the replication experiment

	Group 1 (6 subjects)	Group 2 (6 subjects)	Group 3 (6 subjects)	Group 4 (6 subjects)
1st Day (120 min)	1st: WebML Introduction; 2nd: Training with HE; and 3rd: Training with WUEP			
2nd Day (30 + 90 min)	1st:WebML Introduction; 2nd:Training with WUEP; and 3rd Training with HE			
	WUEP in O1	WUEP in O2	HE in O1	HE in O2
	Questionnaire for WUEP		Questionnaire for HE	
3rd Day (30 + 90 min)	1st: WebML Introduction; 2nd: Training with HE; and 3rd: Training with WUEP			
	HE in O2	HE in O1	WUEP in O2	WUEP in O1
	Questionnaire for HE		Questionnaire for WUEP	

6   Analysis of Results

After the execution of each experiment, the control group analyzed all the usability problems detected by the subjects. If a usability problem was not in the initial list, this group determined whether it could be considered as a real usability problem or a false positive. Replicated problems were considered only once. Discrepancies in this analysis were solved by consensus.

6.1   Quantitative and Qualitative Results

The quantitative analysis was performed by using the SPSS v16 statistical tool and $\alpha = 0.05$. Table 5 summarizes the overall results of the usability evaluations. Mean and standard deviation were used also for the subjective variables being the five-point Likert scale adopted for their measurement as an interval scale [5].

Table 5. Overall results of the usability evaluations from both experiments

Statistics	Method	EXP (N=30)		REP (N=24)	
		Mean	SD	Mean	SD
Number of problems per subject	HE	3.29	1.08	4.29	0.99
	WUEP	**6.50**	1.14	**6.91**	1.24
False positives per subject	HE	1.38	1.24	1.91	1.24
	WUEP	**0.54**	0.66	**0.29**	0.46
Replicated problems per subject	HE	0.88	0.80	1.50	0.93
	WUEP	**0.00**	0.00	**0.00**	0.00
Duration (min)	HE	**70.13**	13.52	**67.66**	14.01
	WUEP	80.88	18.46	72.75	11.14
Effectiveness (%)	HE	33.04	10.85	37.24	8.04
	WUEP	**65.32**	11.54	**60.16**	10.32
Efficiency (Problems / min)	HE	0.05	0.02	0.06	0.02
	WUEP	**0.08**	0.02	**0.09**	0.02
Perceived Ease of Use	HE	3.38	0.73	3.73	0.76
	WUEP	**3.80**	0.72	**3.94**	0.65
Perceived Satisfaction of Use	HE	3.63	0.67	3.74	0.73
	WUEP	**3.92**	0.75	**4.08**	0.53

The overall results obtained have allowed us to interpret that WUEP has achieved the subjects' best performance in about all the analyzed statistics (see cells in bold), The only exception is the duration of the evaluation session, which however was longer for WUEP due to the longer time required to read the material containing the WUEP description. As indicated by the results, WUEP tends to provide a low degree of false positives and replicated problems. The lack of false positives can be explained by the fact that WUEP tends to minimize the subjectivity of the evaluation. The lack of replicated problems can be explained by the fact that WUEP provides operationalized measures that are classified to be applied in one type of Web artifact.

The boxplots with the distribution of each dependent variable per subject per method (see Figure 3) show that WUEP was more effective and efficient than HE, and WUEP was also perceived by the evaluators as being easier to use and more satisfactory than HE.

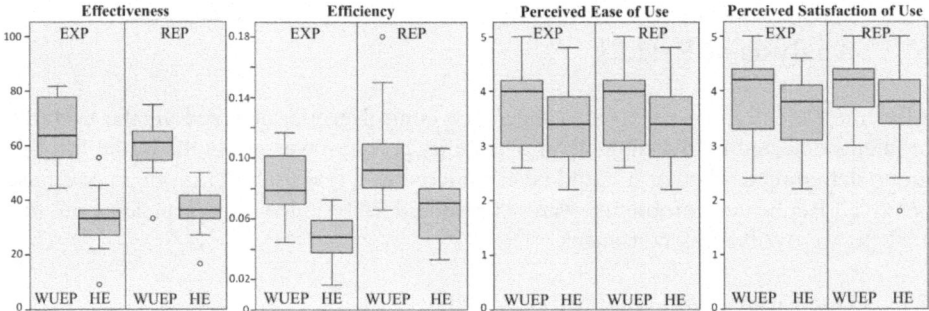

Fig. 3. Boxplots for each dependent variable in both experiments

We applied the Shapiro-Wilk test to verify whether the data was normally distributed with the aim to select which tests are needed in order to determine whether or not these results were significant. Table 6 provides the results of all the hypothesis verifications. We applied the Mann-Whitney non-parametric test for variables that resulted not normally distributed (i.e., In EXP: Effectiveness(WUEP) with p-value 0.021; and in REP: Efficiency(WUEP) with p-value 0.011, and Perceived Ease of Use(HE) with p-value 0.012). We applied the 1-tailed t-test for variables that resulted normally distributed. All the alternative hypotheses were accepted except H4 in EXP and H3 in REP. We believe this may be caused owing the subjects would need more training with WebML artifacts in order to perceived it more useful.

Table 6. p-values obtained for the test of hypothesis

		Significance Test	p-value	Accept Alternative Hypothesis?
EXP	**H1**	Mann-Whitney	**0.000** (< 0.05)	**YES** *(WUEP more effective than HE)*
	H2	1-tailed t-test	**0.000** (< 0.05)	**YES** *(WUEP more efficient than HE)*
	H3	1-tailed t-test	**0.026** (< 0.05)	**YES** *(WUEP more easier to use than HE)*
	H4	1-tailed t-test	0.086 (> 0.05)	NO *(no significant differences in satisfaction)*
REP	**H1**	1-tailed t-test	**0.000** (< 0.05)	**YES** *(WUEP more effective than HE)*
	H2	Mann-Whitney	**0.000** (< 0.05)	**YES** *(WUEP more efficient than HE)*
	H3	Mann-Whitney	0.202 (> 0.05)	NO *(no significant differences in ease of use)*
	H4	1-tailed t-test	**0.036** (< 0.05)	**YES** *(WUEP more satisfactory than HE)*

In order to strengthen our analysis, we used the method suggested in [4] to test the effect of the order of both independent variables (usability evaluation methods and experimental objects). We used the Diff function: $Diff_x$ = $observation_x(A)$ - $observation_x(B)$, where x denotes a particular subject, and A, B are the two possible values of one independent variable. We created Diffs variables from each dependent variable. Finally, we verified that there were no significant differences between Diff functions since that would signify that there was no influence in the order of the independent variables (all the p-values obtained were > 0.05).

Finally, a qualitative analysis was performed by analyzing the open-questions that were included in the questionnaire. This analysis revealed some important issues which can be considered to improve WUEP (e.g., *"WUEP might be more useful if it were automated by a tool, especially the calculation of certain metrics"*), and it also collected positive impressions from the participants (e.g., *"I was surprised because I was able to systematically detect usability problems without previous experience"*).

6.2   Threats to the Validity

The main threats to the internal validity of the experiment are: learning effect, evaluation design, subject experience, method authorship, and information exchange among evaluators. The learning effect was alleviated by ensuring that each subject applied each method to different experimental objects, and all the possible order combinations were considered. The evaluation design might have affected the results owing to the selection of attributes to be evaluated during the design stage of WUEP. We attempted to alleviate this threat by considering relevant usability attributes involving experts. Subject experience was alleviated due to the fact that none of the subjects had any experience in usability evaluations. The possibility of students knowing about our WUEP's authorship might have biased the results. We attempted to alleviate this threat by not disclosing more information; we also intend to conduct external replications with different conductors. Information exchange might have affected the results since the experiment took place over two days, and it is difficult to be certain whether the subjects exchanged any information with each other.

The main threats to the external validity of the experiment are: representativeness of the results, and duration of the experiment. Despite the fact that the experiment was performed in an academic context, the results could be representative with regard to novice evaluators with no experience in usability evaluations. However, the previous selection of usability attributes with their operationalized measures and the selection of the Web application might have affected the representativeness. To alleviate these issues, we intend to carry out a survey with Web designers to determine the relative importance of the usability attributes for different categories of Web applications. Since the duration of the experiment was limited to 90 min, only 2 representative software artifacts were selected from the different available types , although WUEP can be instantiated in more artifacts such as layout position-grids and style-templates.

The main threats to the construct validity of the experiment are: measures that are applied in the quantitative analysis and the reliability of the questionnaire. Measures that are commonly employed in this kind of experiment were used in the quantitative analysis [8]. The reliability of the questionnaire was tested by applying the Cronbach test. Questions related to the Perceived Ease of Use obtained a Cronbach's alpha of

0.80 and 0.82, in EXP and REP respectively, whereas Perceived Satisfaction of Use obtained a Cronbach's alpha of 0.78 and 0.75, in EXP and REP respectively. These values are higher than the acceptable minimum (0.70) [21].

The main threat to the conclusion validity of the experiment is the validity of the statistical tests applied. This was alleviated by applying the most common tests that are employed in the empirical software engineering field [17].

7   Discussion and Outlook

This paper presented the operationalization and empirical validation of a usability inspection method (WUEP) for its use within the WebML development process. From a practical point of view, our usability inspection strategy enables the development of more usable Web applications *by construction* [1]. Usability by construction means that each model built at different stages of a model-driven Web development process (PIM, PSM, Code) satisfies a certain level of usability of the corresponding Web application, thereby reducing the effort of fixing usability problems when the Web application is generated.

The effectiveness, efficiency, perceived ease of use and satisfaction of WUEP were compared in two experiments against a widely-used inspection method: Heuristic Evaluation (HE). The results show that WUEP was more effective and efficient than HE in the detection of usability problems in WebML models. Although the evaluators found it easier to use than HE and they were also more satisfied when applying WUEP, these variables resulted not statistically significant in some cases. These results confirmed our previous findings [12] when an instantiation of WUEP into the OO-H method was compared against HE, strengthening the case for using WUEP rather than HE, at least in contexts with fairly inexperienced usability evaluators. Although the experimental results provided good results on the usefulness of WUEP as a usability inspection method for Web applications developed through MDWD processes, we are aware that more experimentation is needed to confirm these results, since they need to be interpreted with caution being them only valid within the context established in these experiments. However, the replication presented here significantly adds to the existing validation of WUEP. We also obtained valuable feedback from these experiments based on which we can improve our proposal.

As future work, we plan to replicate this experiment with practitioners with different level of experience in usability evaluations, and to analyze in depth the empirical evidences collected by identifying which type of usability problems are most detected in models in order to suggest new mechanisms (modeling primitives, model-transformations, or patterns) to directly support some usability attributes. We also plan to validate the completeness of problem prediction through experiments in which the results of the evaluations obtained at the model level will be compared to the ones obtained when users interact with the generated Web applications.

Acknowledgements. This paper has been funded by the MULTIPLE project (MICINN TIN2009-13838) and the Erasmus Mundus Programme of the European Commission under the Transatlantic Partnership for Excellence in Engineering – TEE Project.

References

1. Abrahão, S., Iborra, E., Vanderdonckt, J.: Usability Evaluation of User Interfaces Generated with a Model-Driven Architecture Tool. In: Maturing Usability: Quality in Software, Interaction and Value, pp. 3–32. Springer (2007)
2. Atterer, R., Schmidt, A.: Adding Usability to Web Engineering Models and Tools. In: Lowe, D.G., Gaedke, M. (eds.) ICWE 2005. LNCS, vol. 3579, pp. 36–41. Springer, Heidelberg (2005)
3. Basili, V., Rombach, H.: The TAME Project: Towards Improvement-Oriented Software Environments. IEEE Transactions on Software Engineering 14(6), 758–773 (1988)
4. Briand, L., Labiche, Y., Di Penta, M., Yan-Bondoc, H.: An experimental investigation of formality in UML-based development. IEEE TSE 31(10), 833–849 (2005)
5. Carifio, J., Perla, R.: Ten Common Misunderstandings, Misconceptions, Persistent Myths and Urban Legends about Likert Scales and Likert Response Formats and their Antidotes. Journal of Social Sciences 3(3), 106–116 (2007)
6. Ceri, S., Fraternali, P., Bongio, A.: Web modeling language (WebML): a modeling language for designing Web sites. In: 9th International World Wide Web Conference, pp. 137–157 (2000)
7. Ceri, S., Fraternali, P., Acerbis, R., Bongio, A., Butti, S., Ciapessoni, F., Conserva, C., Elli, R., Greppi, C., Tagliasacchi, M., Toffetti, G.: Architectural issues and solutions in the development of data-intensive Web applications. In: Proceedings of the 1st Biennial Conference on Innovative Data Systems Research, Asilomar, CA (2003)
8. Conte, T., Massollar, J., Mendes, E., Travassos, G.H.: Usability Evaluation Based on Web Design Perspectives. In: Proceedings of the International Symposium on Empirical Software Engineering and Measurement (ESEM 2007), pp. 146–155 (2007)
9. Fernandez, A., Insfran, E., Abrahão, S.: Usability evaluation methods for the Web: a systematic mapping study. Information and Software Technology 53, 789–817 (2011)
10. Fernandez, A., Abrahão, S., Insfran, E.: A Web usability evaluation process for model-driven Web development. In: Mouratidis, H., Rolland, C. (eds.) CAiSE 2011. LNCS, vol. 6741, pp. 108–122. Springer, Heidelberg (2011)
11. Fernandez, A., Abrahão, S., Insfran, E., Matera, M.: Further Analysis on the Validation of a Usability Inspection Method for Model-Driven Web Development. In: 6th International Symposium on Empirical Software Engineering and Measurement (ESEM 2012), pp. 153–156 (2012)
12. Fernandez, A., Abrahão, S., Insfran, E.: Empirical Validation of a Usability Inspection Method for Model-Driven Web Development. Journal of Systems and Software 86, 161–186 (2013)
13. Fraternali, P., Matera, M., Maurino, A.: WQA: an XSL Framework for Analyzing the Quality of Web Applications. In: Proceedings of IWWOST 2002 - ECOOP 2002 Workshop, Malaga, Spain (2002)
14. Hornbæk, K.: Dogmas in the assessment of usability evaluation methods. Behaviour & Information Technology 29(1), 97–111 (2010)
15. Hwang, W., Salvendy, G.: Number of people required for usability evaluation: the 10±2 rule. Communications of the ACM 53(5), 130–113 (2010)
16. International Organization for Standardization: ISO/IEC 25000, Software Engineering – Software Product Quality Requirements and Evaluation (SQuaRE) – Guide to SQuaRE (2005)
17. Juristo, N., Moreno, A.M.: Basics of Software Engineering Experimentation. Kluwer Academic Publishers (2001)

18. Juristo, N., Moreno, A., Sanchez-Segura, M.I.: Guidelines for eliciting usability functionalities. IEEE Transactions on Software Engineering 33(11), 744–758 (2007)
19. Matera, M., Costabile, M.F., Garzotto, F., Paolini, P.: SUE inspection: an effective method for systematic usability evaluation of hypermedia. IEEE Transactions on Systems, Man, and Cybernetics, Part A 32(1), 93–103 (2002)
20. Matera, M., Rizzo, F., Carughi, G.: Web Usability: Principles and Evaluation Methods. In: Web Engineering, pp. 143–180. Springer (2006)
21. Maxwell, K.: Applied Statistics for Software Managers. Software Quality Institute Series. Prentice Hall (2002)
22. Molina, F., Toval, A.: Integrating usability requirements that can be evaluated in design time into Model Driven Engineering of Web Information Systems. Advances in Engineering Software 40(12), 1306–1317 (2009)
23. Moreno, N., Vallecillo, A.: Towards interoperable Web engineering methods. Journal of the American Society for Information Science and Technolog 59(7), 1073–1092 (2008)
24. Neuwirth, C.M., Regli, S.H.: IEEE Internet Computing Special Issue on Usability and the Web 6(2) (2002)
25. Nielsen, J.: Heuristic evaluation. In: Usability Inspection Methods. John Wiley & Sons, NY (1994)
26. Offutt, J.: Quality attributes of Web software applications. IEEE Software: Special Issue on Software Engineering of Internet Software, 25–32 (2002)
27. Panach, I., Condori, N., Valverde, F., Aquino, N., Pastor, O.: Understandability measurement in an early usability evaluation for MDD. In: International Symposium on Empirical Software Engineering (ESEM 2008), pp. 354–356 (2008)
28. Webratio. Success stories, Online article,
    http://www.webratio.com/portal/content/en/success-stories
29. Wohlin, C., Runeson, P., Host, M., Ohlsson, M.C., Regnell, B., Weslen, A.: Experimentation in Software Engineering - An Introduction. Kluwer (2000)

Model-Driven Approach
for Supporting the Mapping of Parallel Algorithms
to Parallel Computing Platforms

Ethem Arkın[1], Bedir Tekinerdogan[2], and Kayhan M. İmre[1]

[1] HacettepeUniversity, Dept. of Computer Engineering, Ankara, Turkey
{earkin,ki}@hacettepe.edu.tr
[2] BilkentUniversity, Dept. of Computer Engineering, Ankara, Turkey
bedir@cs.bilkent.edu.tr

Abstract. The trend from single processor to parallel computer architectures
has increased the importance of parallel computing. To support parallel computing it is important to map parallel algorithms to a computing platform that
consists of multiple parallel processing nodes. In general different alternative
mappings can be defined that perform differently with respect to the quality requirements for power consumption, efficiency and memory usage. The mapping
process can be carried out manually for platforms with a limited number of processing nodes. However, for exascale computing in which hundreds of thousands of processing nodes are applied, the mapping process soon becomes intractable. To assist the parallel computing engineer we provide a model-driven
approach to analyze, model, and select feasible mappings. We describe the developed toolset that implements the corresponding approach together with the
required metamodels and model transformations. We illustrate our approach for
the well-known complete exchange algorithm in parallel computing.

Keywords: Model Driven Software Development, Parallel Computing, High
Performance Computing, Domain Specific Language, Tool Support.

1 Introduction

The famous Moore's law states that the number of transistors on integrated circuits
and likewise the performance of processors doubles approximately every eighteen
months [1]. Since the introduction of the law in 1965, the law seems to have quite
accurately described and predicted the developments of the processing power of components in the semiconductor industry [2]. Although Moore's law is still in effect,
currently it is recognized that increasing the processing power of a single processor
has reached the physical limitations [3]. Hence, to increase the performance the current trend is towards applying parallel computing on multiple nodes. Here, unlike
serial computing in which instructions are executed serially, multiple processing elements are used to execute the program instructions simultaneously.

To benefit from the parallel computing power usually parallel algorithms are defined that can be executed simultaneously on multiple nodes. As such, increasing the

A. Moreira et al. (Eds.): MODELS 2013, LNCS 8107, pp. 757–773, 2013.

processing nodes will increase the performance of the parallel programs [4][5][6]. An important challenge in this context is the mapping of parallel algorithms on a computing platform that consists of multiple parallel processing nodes. In general a parallel algorithm can be mapped in different alternative ways to the processing nodes. Further, each mapping alternative will perform differently with respect to the quality requirements for speedup, efficiency and memory usage that are important in parallel computing [7]. The mapping process can be carried out manually for platforms with a limited number of processing nodes. However, over the last decade the number of processing nodes has increased dramatically to tens and hundreds of thousands of nodes providing processing performance from petascale to exascale levels [8]. As a consequence selecting a feasible mapping of parallel algorithm to computing platforms has become intractable for the human parallel computing engineer. Once the feasible mapping is selected the parallel algorithm needs to be transformed to the target parallel computing platform such as MPI, OpenMP, MPL, and CILK [15]. Due to the complexity and size of the parallel computing platform usually it is not easy to implement the algorithm manually on these platforms based on the selected mapping. Moreover, in case of requirements for changing the implementation platform porting the system to a new platform will be cumbersome.

In this paper we provide a model-driven approach to analyze, model, and select feasible mappings of parallel algorithms to a parallel computing platform. In the approach we provide the steps for defining models of the computing platform and the parallel algorithm. Based on the analysis of the algorithm and the computing platform feasible mappings are generated. The approach is supported by a corresponding toolset that builds on a predefined metamodel. Using model-to-model and model-to-text transformations we provide a solution to the code generation and portability problems. We provide an evaluation of our approach for the well-known complete exchange algorithm in parallel computing. The evaluation considers both the time to generate the alternative mappings, and the feasibility of the generated alternative on a real computing platform with respect to speedup and efficiency performance quality attributes.

The remainder of the paper is organized as follows. In section 2, we describe the problem statement. Section 3 presents the metamodel which is used by the approach that is described in section 4. Section 5 presents the tool that implements the approach. In section 6 we describe the evaluation of the approach. Section 7 presents the related work and finally we conclude the paper in section 8.

2   Problem Statement

In this section we will describe the problem statement in more detail by considering the mapping of the complete exchange parallel algorithm to a parallel computing platform. Fig. 1 shows the complete exchange algorithm which purpose is to collect all data from all nodes and to distribute data to all nodes [9][10][11]. This algorithm is a commonly used parallel algorithm that is often used as part of a bigger parallel algorithm. For instance, in simulation of molecular dynamics, the data of all particles are exchanged with each other to calculate some values like affinity between molecules. The complete exchange algorithm refers to nodes of a computing platform on which the algorithm will run. Hereby, some nodes are selected as *dominating nodes* [12] that collect data, exchange data with each other and distribute the data to the other nodes.

```
Procedure Complete-Exchange:
For i=1 to n-1
   Collect data to the dominating nodes from the dominated nodes
Endfor
For i=n-1 downto 1
   Exchange the selected data between dominating nodes
   Distribute data from dominating nodes to the dominated nodes
Endfor
```

Fig. 1. Pseudo code for Complete Exchange Algorithm

The algorithm is mapped to a computation platform that is defined as a *configuration* of nodes. We distinguish among the *physical configuration* and *logical configuration*. The physical configuration defines the actual physical configuration of the system with the physical communication links among the processing units. We assume a distributed memory model in which each node has its own memory unit. The *logical configuration* is a view of the physical configuration that defines the logical communication structure among the physical nodes. Typically, for the same physical configuration we can have many different logical configurations. An example of a physical configuration and its logical configurations is shown in Fig. 2.

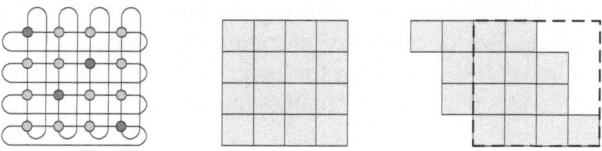

Fig. 2. Physical configuration of a topology (left) with two different logical configurations (middle and right)

Given a parallel algorithm like the complete exchange algorithm, it is important to define a feasible mapping of the algorithm steps to the logical configuration. The feasibility of a mapping is defined by the extent to which it supports the performance quality attributes of *speedup* with respect to serial computing and *efficiency* [7]. Speedup S_p is defined by the following formula:

$$S_p = \frac{T_s}{T_p} \qquad (1)$$

where   Ts is the execution time of the serial algorithm.
          Tp is the execution time of the parallel algorithm with p processors.

Efficiency metric defines how well the processors are utilized in executing the algorithm. The formula for Efficiency Ep is as follows:

$$E_p = \frac{S_p}{p} \qquad (2)$$

where   Sp is the speed up as defined in equation (1) above and p is the number of processors.

760   E. Arkın, B. Tekinerdogan, and K.M. İmre

To measure speedup and efficiency the following metrics are applied:

- *Number of Cores Used*- the number of cores that are used in the computing platform for executing the algorithm.
- *Port Count Used* - the total number of ports of all cores that are used in the communication among the cores.
- *Communication Length* - the total number of communication links among cores that are needed to realize the execution of the algorithm.

To define a feasible mapping of the parallel algorithm to the computing platform the values for the above metrics should be minimized as much as possible to increase speedup and efficiency [7][13][14].

We can now refer to these metrics to discuss the feasibility of the mapping of the algorithm to the computing platform. Fig. 3 shows, for example, three different alternative logical configurations of the computing platform to execute the complete exchange algorithm. Each given logical configuration consists of 12x12 cores and represents actually a mapping alternative. The realization of the configurations will differ with respect to the assignment of dominating nodes, the number of cores used, the port count used and the communication length. Hence each logical configuration of the computing platform will result in a different speedup and efficiency. Similar to the example logical configurations in Fig. 3 we can identify many other different logical configurations. Selecting the optimal logical configuration with respect to speedup and efficiency is an important challenge for the parallel computing engineer. For smaller computing platforms with a limited number of cores the generation and selection of feasible alternative could be done to some extent. However, for larger multicore platform with thousand or tens of thousands of nodes this process becomes intractable.

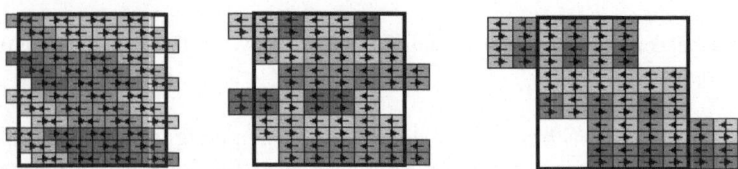

Fig. 3. Three alternative mapping of complete-exchange algorithm

Here we focus on two important and related problems. First of all, for a given parallel algorithm and physical configuration we need to define and generate the possible logical configurations and accordingly the mapping alternatives. Secondly, once a feasible mapping alternative is selected the required code for the parallel computing platform needs to be provided to realize the parallel algorithm. Due to the complexity and size of the mapping problem it is not easy to implement the parallel algorithm manually on the parallel computing platforms. Moreover, in case the implementation platform requires changing, porting the system to a new platform will be cumbersome and require considerable time [15]. Obviously, a systematic approach that is supported by tools is necessary to analyze the parallel algorithm, model the logical configuration, select feasible mapping alternatives and generate the code for the computing platform.

3   Approach

Fig. 4 shows the approach for supporting the mapping of a parallel algorithm for a parallel computing platform, and the generation of the code for the parallel computing platform. The approach consists of two basic sub-processes, *library definition* and *parallel algorithm mapping and model transformations*. The main purpose of the *library definition* sub-process is to define reusable assets including primitive tiles, communication patterns and operation definitions, which will be explained in subsequent sections. The activities of the library definition process include *Define Logical Configuration, Define Communication Patterns* and *Define Operations*. The created reusable assets are stored in the Parallel Algorithm Mapping Library (PAML). The parallel algorithm mapping and model transformations sub-process consists of the activities *Analyze Algorithm, Select Logical Configuration Size, Generate Alternative Models, Select Feasible Model,* and *Model Transformation*. This sub-process reuses the PAML assets to analyze the parallel algorithm and generate the alternative mapping models. The metrics for speedup and efficiency are calculated for each model and a feasible model is selected to be used on transformation and generation of artifacts. In the following subsections we will describe the metamodel and each step of the approach.

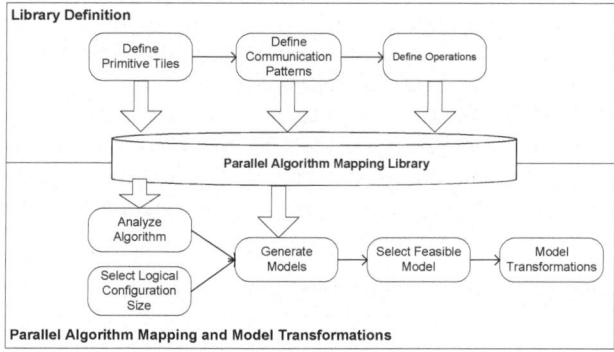

Fig. 4. Approach for mapping of parallel algorithm to parallel computing platforms

3.1   Metamodel

Fig. 5 shows the abstract syntax of the metamodel that is used by the approach in Fig. 4. The metamodel integrates the concepts for parallel algorithms (upper part of figure) with the concepts of parallel computing platforms (lower part of figure). In the metamodel, *Algorithm* includes one or more *Sections*. *Section* can be either *Serial Section* or *Parallel Section* and can be composed of other sections. Each section maps to one *Operation*. *Logical Configuration* defines the configuration that we have defined in section 2, and is composed of a number of *Tiles*. *Tile* can be either a (single) *Core*, or *Pattern* that represents a composition of tiles. Patterns are shaped by the operations of the sections in the algorithm. *Pattern* includes also the communication links among the cores.

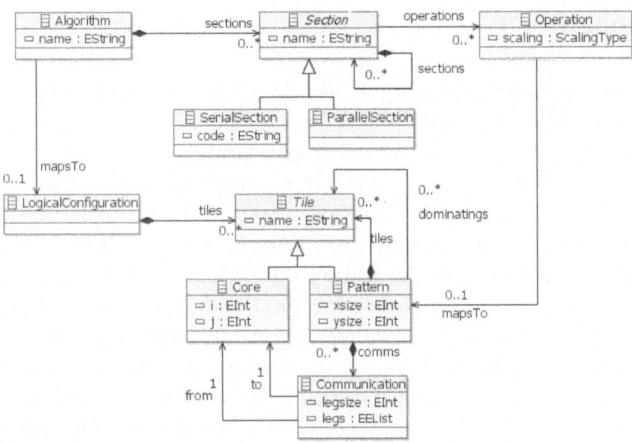

Fig. 5. Abstract Syntax of the Parallel Algorithm Mapping Metamodel (PAMM)

3.2   Define Primitive Tiles

As shown in Fig. 4, the first step of the definition of the library is the definition of primitive tiles. As stated before, we distinguish among the *physical configuration* and *logical configuration* of the topology. For very large topologies including a large number of cores, as in the case of exascale computing, the logical topology cannot be drawn on the same scale. Instead, for representing the topology in a more succinct way the topology can be defined as a regular pattern that can be built using *tiles*. Tiles as such can be considered as the basic building blocks of the logical configuration. The tile notation is used for addressing group of processing elements that form a neighborhood region on which processes and communication links are mapped. The smallest part of a tile is a *processing element* (core).

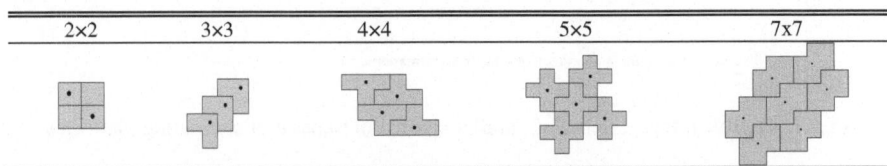

Fig. 6. Primitive tiling examples

Tiles can be used to construct the logical configuration using *scaling* that can be defined as the composition of the larger structure from the smaller tiles. In general we can distinguish among different primitive tiles which can be constructed in different ways. The selected tiling configuration will be dependent on the required communication patterns of the algorithm that will be explained in the next sub-section. Examples of primitive tiles are shown in Fig. 6 [16][17][9].

3.3   Define Communication Patterns

Each primitive tile defines the structure among the nodes but initially does not describe the dynamic behavior among these nodes. Hence, after defining the primitive tiles, we need to define the dynamic behavior among the nodes. This is defined using communication patterns for each tile configuration. A communication pattern includes communication paths that consist of a source node, a target node and a route between the source and target nodes. An example communication pattern is shown in Fig. 7.

Communication Paths	Tile	Communication Pattern

Fig. 7. Communication patterns constructed with tile and matching communication paths

3.4   Define Operations

To define the mapping of an algorithm to a computing platform we consider an algorithm as consisting of a number of sections that include either parallel or serial code. As shown in the metamodel in Fig. 5 each section is mapped to a primitive operation that represents a reusable abstraction of recurring instructions in parallel algorithms. We can identify for example the following primitive operations: *Scatter* that distributes a set of data to nodes; *Gather* that collects data from nodes; *Reduce* that confines a mapped data. To realize an operation a corresponding communication pattern will be needed in the logical configuration. In general, one operation could be realized using different communication patterns. Fig. 8 shows, for example, some of the possible communication patterns for the *scatter* primitive operation.

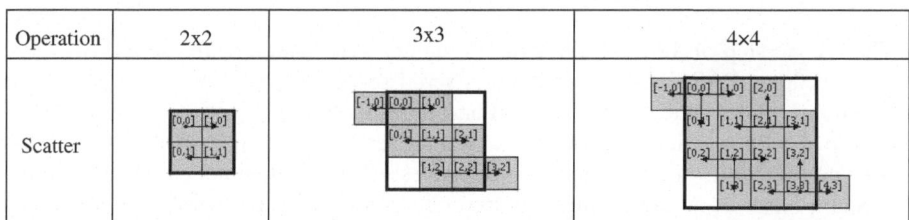

Fig. 8. Example communication patterns on different tiles for selected primitive operations

Each operation will in the end run on the tiles of the logical configuration. To compose the logical configuration using the primitive tiles, the tiles must be scaled to larger dimensions. When the tiles are scaled to a larger size, the operations, in other words the communication patterns assigned to operations, must also be scaled to larger logical configuration. Hereby, the scaling strategy of the operation affects the order of communication patterns when scaling the operations. Scaling strategy is the order of communication pattern generation for operation as bottom up or top down.

3.5   Analyze Algorithm

In the previous steps we composed our reusable library with the primitive tiles, communication patterns and operation. Hereby, to support the mapping of the algorithm to parallel computing platform, first we need to analyze the parallel algorithm. In this paper, the complete-exchange algorithm is selected for demonstrating the approach. Since the inherent complexity of the algorithm is relatively high for large input size, providing parallel implementations of these algorithms is usually considered to be important.

First of all we identify the separate sections of the algorithm. This is typically defined by considering separate code blocks which form a coherent set of steps to perform a computation. For example in Fig. 9 we have identified three separate sections for the complete exchange algorithm. The first section defines the transfer process of the data from the dominated nodes to the dominating nodes. The second section defines the exchange of the selected messages between the dominating nodes. Finally the third section defines the distribution of the data from dominating nodes to the dominated nodes. Note that the second and third sections belong to the same for loop, but they have been distinguished as separate sections since they form two separate coherent set of steps.

NO	PAR/SER	Algorithm Section
1	PAR	**Procedure** Complete-Exchange: **For** i=1 **to** n-1 Collect data to the dominating nodes from the dominated nodes **Endfor**
2	PAR	**For** i=n-1 **downto** 1 Exchange the selected data between dominating nodes
3	PAR	Distribute data from dominating nodes to the dominated nodes **Endfor**

Fig. 9. Sections of Complete Exchange Algorithm

The second step of the analysis includes the characterization of the serial (SER) and parallel sections (PAR) of the algorithm. A serial section is a part of the algorithm that will run on a single node, for instance an arithmetic operation. Typically a serial section is identified with a serial code block. A parallel section is the part of the algorithm to coordinate data with communications to be processed on different nodes. The decision of the section types of an algorithm is carried out manually by the parallel programming engineer. This is because the automatic analysis of the parallel algorithms is not trivial and no tool support has been provided for this yet. Moreover, the manual approach enables the parallel programming engineer to support different selection decisions, if this is possible with respect to the properties of the analyzed algorithm.

3.6   Select Logical Configuration Size

The selected algorithm will run on a number of processors that together form the logical configuration. The logical configuration size states the number of processors and determines which primitive tiles and communication patterns will be selected from the reusable library to construct the logical configuration. The primitive tiles and communication patterns are selected based on the *scale factors* that are calculated using the logical configuration size. The scale factor is the ratio of a logical configuration size to another logical configuration size. For example a 6x6 logical configuration has a scale factor of 3 to a 2x2 logical configuration. Hereby, we can construct a 6x6 logical configuration using a 3x3 logical configuration each node consisting of 2x2 logical configuration.

To calculate all the scale factors of a logical configuration we adopt *prime factorization* [18]. Prime factorization is the decomposition of a composite number into smaller primitive numbers. The primitive tiles with the primitive size numbers can be scaled to larger logical configuration by using prime factors as scale factors. For example if we have a 12x12 torus topology, the prime factors of 12 are 2, 2 and 3. As such, we can use a 3x3, and two 2x2 primitive tiles to construct the entire logical topology.

3.7   Generate Alternative Models

After finding the scale factors of logical configuration and decomposing the algorithm to parallel and serial sections, we can now generate the alternative mapping models. Since we labeled each algorithm section as PAR or SER, we need to select communication patterns assigned to operations from parallel domain library.

For complete-exchange example, gather, scatter and exchange operations are defined for various primitive tiles. Fig. 10 shows the example 2x2 (named as A2) and 3x3 (named as A3) size primitive tiles and patterns.

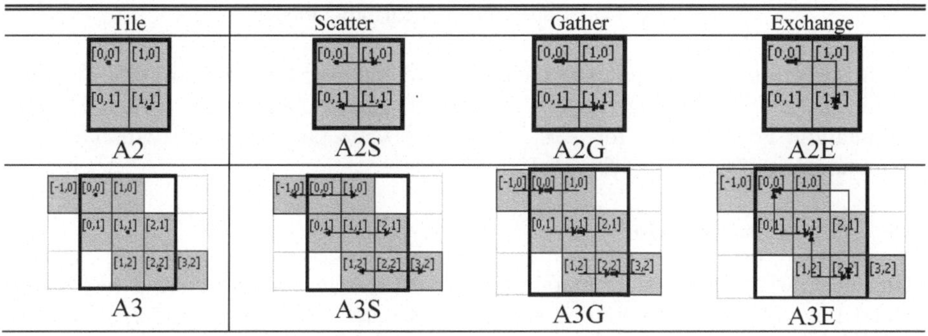

Tile	Scatter	Gather	Exchange
A2	A2S	A2G	A2E
A3	A3S	A3G	A3E

Fig. 10. Complete Exchange Operations

To generate the Parallel Algorithm Mapping Model (PAMMO), the patterns that are assigned to operations are scaled according to scale factors that are found by prime factorization. For example for 12x12 topology, the scale factors are found as 3, 2 and 2. A3S, A2S and A2S patterns are selected from the library to generate scatter operation. After selection of patterns, a sequence of patterns for each scale factor is generated. Fig. 11 shows this generated sequence of scatter operation patterns for 12x12 logical configuration.

The model generation algorithm is given in Fig. 12. Hereby, if the section is serial, than the serial code part is directly gathered to the mapping model. If the section is parallel, the pattern for the operation is generated whether the scaling strategy is UP or DOWN.

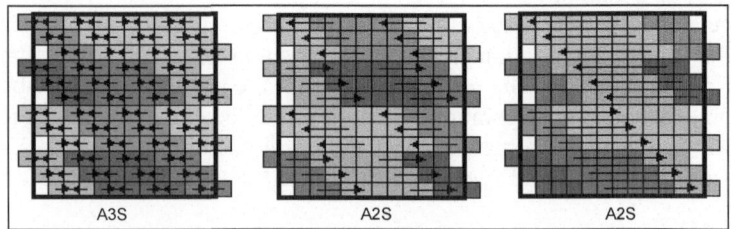

Fig. 11. Scatter operation patterns for a 12x12 topology

```
Procedure GenerateModel (section, size)
if typeof(section) = SER then Add section with code endif
if typeof(section) = PAR then
   Get the operation pattern from PAML
if scaling = UP then create pattern bottom up endif
if scaling = DOWN then create pattern top down endif
   ScalePattern(pattern, size)
endif
for each subsection in section GenerateModel(subsection) endfor
end
```

Fig. 12. Pseudo code for generating models

The algorithm just generates the one possible mapping for the algorithm. To generate all alternative mapping models, all variants of scale factors are found by using permutation. For example for 12x12 topology, scale factors [3,2,2] will have three permutations of [3,2,2], [2,3,2] and [2,2,3].

3.8   Select Feasible Model

After generating the possible mapping alternatives a feasible alternative needs to be selected by the parallel computing engineer. As stated before in section 2, alternatives will be selected based on the performance metric values for the number of cores used, port count used, and communication length. The calculation of the number of cores used is defined by summing all the cores that appear in the communications for executing the algorithm. The calculation of the number of ports is defined by summing the ports of the source and target nodes in the communications. Finally, the communication length is calculated by summing up the paths that occur within the communications for executing the algorithm.

3.9   Model Transformations

The previous steps have focused on analyzing the parallel algorithm and selecting a feasible mapping alternative. Subsequently, the algorithm needs to be implemented on the computing platform that is represented by the logical configuration. In practice there are several computing platforms to implement the mapping such as, MPI, OpenMP, MPL, and CILK [15]. For different purposes different platforms might need to be selected. For example, if the parallel computing platform is built using distributed memory architecture then the MPI implementation platform needs to be chosen. In case shared memory architecture is used then OpenMP will be typically preferred. Other considerations for choosing the implementation platform can be driven by performance of these platforms.

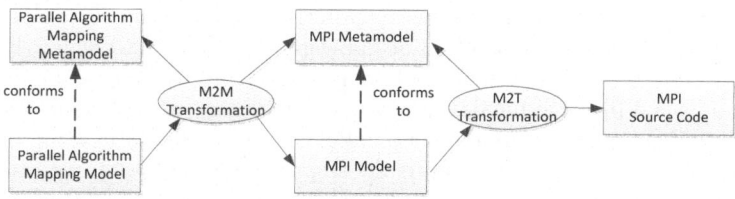

Fig. 13. Example model transformation chain of selected parallel algorithm mapping model in which a MPI implementation platform is chosen

To support the required platform independence requirement we apply the concepts of Model-Driven Architecture [19] in which a distinction is made between platform independent models (PIM), platform specific models (PSM) and code. In our case the PIM is represented by the logical configuration on which the parallel algorithm is mapped. We term this as Parallel Algorithm Mapping Model (PAM). The PSMs can be defined based on the existing parallel computing platforms. In Fig. 13 we show an example transformation chain for mapping the PAM to the MPI Model [20]. The mapping is defined by the M2M Transformation. MPI [20] is a popular and widely used parallel programming framework that adopts language-independent specifications to program parallel computers.

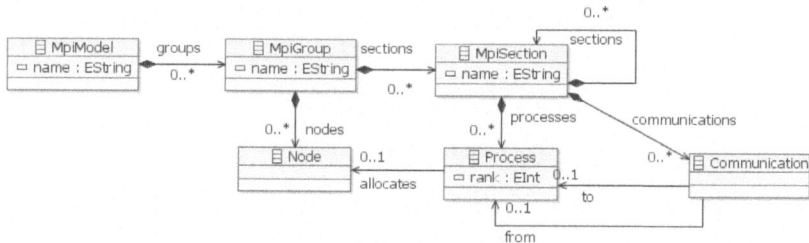

Fig. 14. MPI metamodel

Fig. 14 shows the metamodel for the MPI platform, which is used in the model transformation chain in Fig. 13. A typical MPI model defines the abstract processes and the communications that will run on the nodes, which together realize the parallel algorithm. An MPI model consists of a number of *MPIGroup* objects that define the selection and configuration of physical nodes. *MPIGroup* includes *MPISections*, which are composed of *Processes*. *Process* has *Communication* structures for message passing between the nodes.

From the final MPI model eventually the required code will be generated using M2T transformation techniques [21]. The details about the transformation will be explained in the next section in which we describe the tool that implements the approach.

4   Tool

For supporting the process as defined in the previous sections we have developed the tool ParMapper[1]. This tool is a Java based application that can run on any Java Virtual Machine. The conceptual architecture of ParMapper is shown in Fig. 15. ParMapper includes two different types of tools including (1) tools for defining and preparing the configurations and likewise the development of the library, and (2) tools for defining the mapping of an algorithm to a given parallel computing platform using the library. The Library Definition Toolset supports the steps for defining primitive tiles (section 3.2), defining patterns (section 3.3), and defining the corresponding operations (section 3.4). The remaining steps of the process are supported by the Parallel Algorithm Mapping Toolset for analyzing algorithm (section 3.5), selecting topology size (section 3.6), generating alternative models (section 3.7), and selecting the feasible model (section 3.8). The last step of the process, model transformations, (section 3.9) is supported by third party transformation tools like ATL [22] and XPand [23].

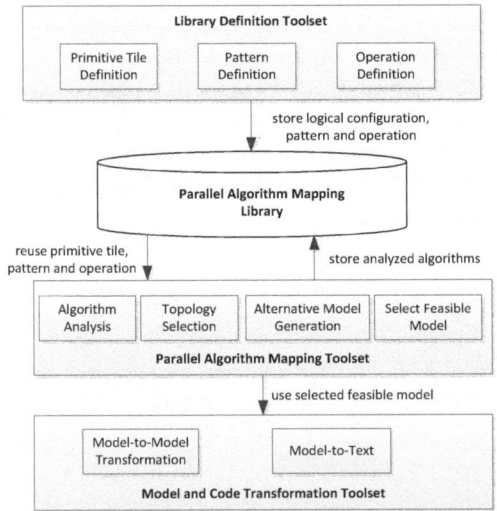

Fig. 15. Conceptual Architecture of the ParMapper Tool

The *Model and Code Transformation Toolset* are implemented in the *Eclipse* Development environment. For M2M and M2T transformations we used ATL and XPand, respectively. Fig. 16 shows part of the transformation rules from PAMM to

---

[1] The tool can be downloaded from
http://web.cs.hacettepe.edu.tr/~earkin/parmapper/

MPI metamodel. The transformation rules define the mapping of the communication patterns to MPI sections, cores to processes and communications to MPI communications. Fig. 17 shows part of the XPand code templates that we implemented to transform a MPI model to C code. In the first part of the template the MPI initializations and type definitions are provided (not shown). Subsequently, for each section the data initialization and the communication between the processes are defined. Each section is finalized with a barrier command that triggers the next step in the control flow of the parallel algorithm.

```
rule Algorithm2MpiModel {
   from algorithm: ParallelModel!Algorithm
   to application: MpiModel!MpiModel (
       name<- algorithm.name, groups <- OrderedSet{mpiGroup}),
     mpiGroup: MpiModel!MpiGroup (
       name <- algorithm.name,sections<- algorithm.getPatterns()  )}
rule Pattern2Section {
   from pattern: ParallelModel!Pattern
   to section: MpiModel!MpiSection (
     name<- pattern.name,  processes <- pattern.getCores(),
     communications <- pattern.getCommunications())}
rule Core2Process {
   from core: ParallelModel!Core
   to process: MpiModel!Process (
     rank<- core.i.mod(core.getGlobalSize()) * core.getGlobalSize() +
           core.mod(core.getGlobalSize()), data <- core.data   )}
rule Comm2Comm {
   fromp_communication : ParallelModel!Communication
   to communication : MpiModel!Communication (
       from<- p_communication.from,  to <- p_communication.to,
       fromData<- p_communication.fromData,)}
```

Fig. 16. Transformation rules from PAMM to MPI metamodel

```
«IMPORT mpi»
… // MPI initializations and type definitions
  «FOREACH groups AS group»
    «FOREACH group.sections AS section»
      «FOREACH section.processes AS process»
        «FOREACH process.data AS data»
          «data.type»* «data.name»;
if(rank == «process.rank») «data.name» = («data.type»*)
                malloc(«data.size»*sizeof(«data.type»));
        «ENDFOREACH»
      «ENDFOREACH»
      «FOREACH section.communications AS comm»
if(rank == «comm.from.rank») {
MPI_Isend(«comm.fromData.name», «comm.fromData.size», MPI_«comm.fromData.type»,
«comm.to.rank», «comm.from.rank», MPI_COMM_WORLD, &request);          }
if(rank == «comm.to.rank») {
MPI_Irecv(«comm.toData.name»+«(comm.toData.size/4) * 0», «comm.fromData.size»,
MPI_«comm.toData.type», «comm.from.rank», MPI_ANY_TAG, MPI_COMM_WORLD, &request);
       }
      «ENDFOREACH»
MPI_Barrier(MPI_COMM_WORLD);
    «ENDFOREACH»
  «ENDFOREACH»
… // Final code
```

Fig. 17. Transformation template from MPI metamodel to MPI source code

5   Evaluation

In the previous sections we have provided a model-driven development approach for generating the mapping alternatives. Obviously, for large scale multi core platform the question is whether the alternatives are generated in feasible time. We have evaluated the generation process by considering various logical configuration sizes for the mapping alternatives of the complete exchange algorithm that is defined in the problem statement section. The mapping alternatives have been generated on a multicore PC with 12 core Intel Xeon 2.67Ghz processor and 40 GB of RAM.

Table 1 shows the result of the evaluation. The left column of the table shows the adopted logical configuration size which range from 36x36 to 1296x1296. The latter configuration size is typical for exascale computing. The middle column shows the number of generated mapping alternatives. The right column shows the time-to-generate the total number of alternatives. For the largest logical configuration size (1296x1296) the overall time to generate the alternatives took around 3 hours, which we consider to be feasible for that scale. We could reduce the time further by running the program on an even more powerful machine.

Table 1. Mapping model generation times

Logical Configuration Size		# Mapping Alternatives	Time To Generate
1296	(36x36)	6	00:00:02
5184	(72x72)	10	00:00:05
46656	(216x216)	20	00:00:55
419904	(648x648)	35	00:16:44
944784	(972x972)	21	00:22:19
1679616	(1296x1296)	70	02:45:43

Table 2. Metric and time to run values for alternative mappings for complete exchange algorithm

Mapping	Calculated Metric Values			Measured Values		
	Ports Used	Communication Length	Core Used	Time To Run(ms)	Speedup*	Efficiency* (for 144 cores)
Alternative 1	792	880	516	200.07980	4.9980t	0.0347t
Alternative 2	792	952	516	202.37916	4.9412t	0.0343t
Alternative 3	792	1024	516	205.23701	4.8724t	0.0338t
Alternative 4	792	1024	588	203.90900	4.9041t	0.0340t
Alternative 5	792	1024	624	209.87113	4.7648t	0.0330t

*t is the total time for the computation running on single processing unit.

Besides of the evaluation of the generation time that is needed in model-driven transformations we have also looked at the speedup and efficiency measures for the generated alternatives. Since we used a PC with 12 cores we run the generated five alternatives from a 12x12 logical configuration size. Table 2 shows the measurement results of the parallel application that uses the complete exchange algorithm (5 mapping alternatives) for exchanging data while executing the parallel computations. The columns Port Number, Communication Length and Core Used are computed by ParMapper tool. The column Time To Run is measured, based on which the Speedup and Efficiency values are calculated (See equations (1) and (2) in section 2). To achieve reliable results we have in fact run the program 1000 times for each alternative and took the mean value of these 1000 runs.

From Table 2, we can derive that calculated metric values of ParMapper seem to directly correlate with the measured values. For example, in the table it appears that

Alternative 1 has the minimal time to run value and as such will perform the most optimal with respect to the speedup and efficiency metrics. If we look at the calculated metric values on the left of the table then we can see that these are also minimal values with respect to the other alternatives.

6   Related Work

Optimizing the mapping of parallel algorithms to parallel computing platforms has been addressed before and several tools have been introduced. These tools very often support the optimization of the mapping process by tracing or profiling the applications during run-time. Examples of these tools are TAU [24], HPC Toolkit [25], Open|Speedshop[26], and Scalasca[27]. Since the optimization is done at run-time these tools usually require that the implementation of the algorithm is completed before the analysis. However, for large scale parallel computing platforms the effort for the implementation is usually substantially high and as such an early analysis approach as defined in ParMapper is needed. Integration of ParMapper with existing profiling tools can be helpful to achieve an optimization after running the feasible alternative. Tools such as CUDA-CHiLL[28] and hiCUDA [29], support code generation and also include mechanism to auto tune the code. But the analysis is again done after the implementation. Moreover, the space of different implementation alternatives and the reasoning with respect to metrics of speedup and efficiency is not directly supported.

ParMapper supports a model-driven approach to support different platform specific parallel programming frameworks and code generation. Similarly Gamatié et al. [30] present the so-called GASPARD design framework for massively parallel embedded systems. In GASPARD, high-level specifications of an embedded system are defined with the MARTE standard profile [31]. The resulting models are then automatically refined into low-level implementations. Different from ParMapper the approach as used in Gaspard does neither provide early analysis nor the design space generation and exploration of feasible mappings. Sussman [32] explains a model-driven mapping approach for distributed memory parallel computers. But this approach provides a running framework and does not support code transformation.

7   Conclusion

In this paper we have provided a systematic approach and the corresponding tool support for mapping parallel algorithms to parallel computing platforms. We have illustrated the approach for the complete exchange algorithm. With the tool we could generate the logical configurations for even large scale multi core applications such as in exascale computing. We have evaluated the approach by considering the required time for generating the models, as well as the reliability of the generated alternatives with respect to the actually measured values. Our study shows that ParMapper is reliable and can be used by parallel computing engineers to generate alternative mappings, provide an early analysis of these with respect to speedup and efficiency, and generate the platform specific model and the source code.

The tool is publicly made available to share our results and get feedback from the parallel computing community. Although we have applied the approach for one parallel computing algorithm, we believe that the approach is general and can be applied to other algorithms as well. In our approach we have assumed a parallel computing platform based on a distributed memory model. Further we assume a physical configuration that can be organized as mesh or torus that is widely used in parallel computing platforms. In our future work we will also consider the analysis of other parallel algorithms and execute ParMapper program on large scale multi core computers. In this context, we will enhance the analysis approach by considering various other quality factors such as power consumption and memory consumption and we will consider possible extensions to metamodels and approach.

References

1. Moore, G.E.: Cramming More Components Onto Integrated Circuits. Proceedings of the IEEE 86(1), 82–85 (1998)
2. Aizcorbe, A.M., Kortum, S.S.: Moore's Law and the Semiconductor Industry: A Vintage Model. Scandinavian Journal of Economics 107(4), 603–630 (2005)
3. Frank, M.P.: The physical limits of computing. Computing in Science & Engineering 4(3), 16–26 (2002)
4. Amdahl, G.M.: Validity of the Single Processor Approach to Achieving Large Scale Computing Capabilities. Reprinted from the AFIPS Conference Proceedings, Atlantic City, N.J., April 18-20, vol. 30, pp. 483–485. AFIPS Press, Reston (1967); when Dr. Amdahl was at International Business Machines Corporation, Sunnyvale, California. IEEE Solid-State Circuits Newsletter 12(3), 19–20 (Summer 2007)
5. Gustafson, J.L.: Reevaluating Amdahl's law. Communications of the ACM 31(5), 532–533 (1988)
6. Hill, M.D., Marty, M.R.: Amdahl's Law in the Multicore Era. Computer 41(7), 33–38 (2008)
7. Karp, A.H., Flatt, H.P.: Measuring parallel processor performance. Commun. ACM 33(5), 539–543 (1990)
8. Kogge, P., Bergman, K., Borkar, S., Campbell, D., Carlson, W., Dally, W., Denneau, M., Franzon, P., Harrod, W., Hiller, J., Karp, S., Keckler, S., Klein, D., Lucas, R., Richards, M., Scarpelli, A., Scott, S., Snavely, A., Sterling, T., Williams, R.S., Yelick, K., Bergman, K., Borkar, S., Campbell, D., Carlson, W., Dally, W., Denneau, M., Franzon, P., Harrod, W., Hiller, J., Keckler, S., Klein, D., Williams, R.S., Yelick, K.: Exascale Computing Study: Technology Challenges in Achieving Exascale Systems. DARPA (2008)
9. İmre, K.M., Baransel, C., Artuner, H.: Efficient and Scalable Routing Algorithms for Collective Communication Operations on 2D All–Port Torus Networks. International Journal of Parallel Programming 39(6), 746–782 (2011) ISSN: 0885-7458
10. Kim, S.-G., Maeng, S.-R., Cho, J.-W.: Complete exchange algorithms in wormhole-routed torus networks: a divide-and-conquer strategy. In: Proceedings of the Fourth International Symposium on Parallel Architectures, Algorithms, and Networks (I-SPAN 1999), pp. 296–301 (1999)
11. Suh, Y.-J., Shin, K.G.: All-to-all personalized communication in multidimensional torus and mesh networks. IEEE Transactions on Parallel and Distributed Systems 12(1), 38–59 (2001)

12. Tsai, Y.J., McKinley, P.K.: An extended dominating node approach to collective commu-nication in all-port wormhole-routed 2D meshes. In: Proceedings of the Scalable High-Performance Computing Conference, pp. 199–206 (1994)
13. Chien, A.A., Konstantinidou, M.: Workloads and Performance Metrics for Evaluating Parallel Interconnects, pp. 23–27. Morgan-Kaufmann (Summer-Fall 1994)
14. Zhang, X.D., Yan, Y., He, K.Q.: Latency Metric: An Experimental Method for Measuring and Evaluating Parallel Program and Architecture Scalability. Journal of Parallel and Distributed Computing 22(3), 392–410 (1994) ISSN 0743-7315, 10.1006/jpdc.1994.1100
15. Talia, D.: Models and Trends in Parallel Programming. Parallel Algorithms and Applica-tions 16(2), 145–180 (2001)
16. Baransel, C., İmre, K.M.: A Parallel Implementation of Strassen's Matrix Multiplication Algorithm for Wormhole-Routed All-Port 2D Torus Networks. Journal of Supercomputing 62(1), 486–509 (2012)
17. Peters, J.G., Syska, M.: Circuit-Switched Broadcasting in Torus Networks. IEEE Transac-tions on Parallel and Distributed Systems 7(3), 246–255 (1996)
18. Lenstra, H.W., Pomerance, C.: A Rigorous Time Bound for Factoring Integers. Journal of the American Mathematical Society 5(3), 483–516 (1992)
19. Object Management Group (OMG), Model Driven Architecture (MDA), ormsc/2001-07-01 (2001)
20. MPI: A Message-Passing Interface Standart, version 1.1 (2013), http://www.mpi-forum.org/docs/mpi-11-html/mpi-report.html
21. Czarnecki, K., Helsen, S.: Feature-based survey of model transformation approaches. IBM Syst. J. 45(3), 621–645 (2006)
22. ATL: ATL Transformation Language (2013), http://www.eclipse.org/atl/
23. Xpand, Open Architectureware (2013), http://wiki.eclipse.org/Xpand
24. Shende, S.S., Malony, A.D.: The Tau Parallel Performance System. Int. J. High Perform. Comput. Appl. 20(2), 287–311 (2006)
25. Adhianto, L., Banerjee, S., Fagan, M., Krentel, M., Marin, G., Mellor-Crummey, J., Tallent, N.R.: HPCToolkit: Tools for performance analysis of optimized parallel programs. Concurrency and Computation: Practice and Experience 22(6), 685–701 (2010)
26. Krell Institute, Open|Speedshop (2013), http://www.openspeedshop.org
27. Geimer, M., Saviankou, P., Strube, A., Szebenyi, Z., Wolf, F., Wylie, B.J.N.: Further Im-proving the Scalability of the Scalasca Toolset. In: Jónasson, K. (ed.) PARA 2010, Part II. LNCS, vol. 7134, pp. 463–473. Springer, Heidelberg (2012)
28. Rudy, G., Khan, M.M., Hall, M., Chen, C., Chame, J.: A programming language interface to describe transformations and code generation. In: Cooper, K., Mellor-Crummey, J., Sarkar, V. (eds.) LCPC 2010. LNCS, vol. 6548, pp. 136–150. Springer, Heidelberg (2011)
29. Han, T.D., Abdelrahman, T.S.: hiCUDA: High-Level GPGPU Programming. IEEE Trans-actions on Parallel and Distributed Systems 22(1), 78–90 (2011)
30. Gamatié, A., Le Beux, S., Piel, É., Ben Atitallah, R., Etien, A., Marquet, P., Dekeyser, J.-L.: A Model-Driven Design Framework for Massively Parallel Embedded Systems. ACM Transactions on Embedded Computing Systems 10(4), 1–36 (2011)
31. Object Management Group. A UML profile for MARTE (2009), http://www.omgmarte.org
32. Sussman, A.: Model-driven mapping onto distributed memory parallel computers. In: Proceedings Supercomputing 1992, pp. 818–829 (1992)

Compositional Synthesis of Controllers from Scenario-Based Assume-Guarantee Specifications

Joel Greenyer[1] and Ekkart Kindler[2]

[1] Software Engineering Group, Leibniz Universität Hannover, Germany
greenyer@inf.uni-hannover.de
[2] DTU Compute, Technical University of Denmark, Denmark
ekki@dtu.dk

Abstract. Modern software-intensive systems often consist of multiple components that interact to fulfill complex functions in sometimes safety-critical situations. During the design, it is crucial to specify the system's requirements formally and to detect inconsistencies as early as possible in order to avoid flaws in the product or costly iterations during its development. We propose to use Modal Sequence Diagrams (MSDs), a formal, yet intuitive formalism for specifying the interaction of a system with its environment, and developed a formal synthesis approach that allows us to detect inconsistencies and even to automatically synthesize controllers from MSD specifications. The technique is suited for specifications of technical systems with real-time constraints and environment assumptions. However, synthesis is computationally expensive. In order to employ synthesis also for larger specifications, we present, in this paper, a novel assume-guarantee-style compositional synthesis technique for MSD specifications. We provide evaluation results underlining the benefit of our approach and formally justify its correctness.

Keywords: Scenario-Based Specification, Compositional Controller Synthesis, Consistency Checking, Assume-Guarantee.

1 Introduction

Modern software-intensive systems in areas like transportation or production often consist of many components that interact to provide complex functionality in sometimes safety-critical situations. In the early design, interactions are typically specified by scenarios. We propose a model-based approach and use Modal Sequence Diagrams (MSDs), introduced by Harel and Maoz [8], to specify interaction scenarios. MSDs are a formal interpretation of UML sequence diagrams, based on the concepts of Live Sequence Charts (LSCs) [6], and allow engineers to specify which sequences of events may, must, or must not happen in a system that reacts to events in its environment. We extended MSDs to support real-time constraints and assumptions on the environment. These extensions are important for the specification of mechatronic systems where the software interacts with physical/mechanical parts of the system. Furthermore, we developed

A. Moreira et al. (Eds.): MODELS 2013, LNCS 8107, pp. 774–789, 2013.

a technique for synthesizing controllers from such specifications and for showing their consistency [7].

Formal scenario-based modeling and synthesis techniques have the potential to immensely aid engineers in the development of modern technical systems, but unfortunately, synthesis is computationally complex. To make synthesis feasible also for bigger specifications, we present, in this paper, a novel technique that for certain kinds of specifications, allows engineers to decompose the synthesis problem into two parts that can be solved more efficiently.

The technique comprises of four manual steps that require the engineer to (1) subdivide the component structure of the system in two parts, (2) possibly splitting components in two, and (3) subdividing the MSD specification accordingly. Last (4), additional MSDs may be introduced as additional requirements that one part of the system can assume about the other, in order to help it realize its part specification. If controllers can be successfully synthesized for the resulting part specifications, the composition of these controllers forms an implementation of the overall specification. We present a formal justification for the soundness of our technique, which was inspired by Stark [18].

The technique presented in this paper is the first that allows for the decomposition of the synthesis problem for LSC/MSD specifications into two synthesis tasks that can be solved independently. Kugler and Segall also proposed a compositional synthesis approach for LSC specifications [13] that improves the synthesis' efficiency. In their approach, controllers are also synthesized for specification parts. Ultimately, however, always a last synthesis step is required to obtain a controller for the complete specification from the controllers for the specification parts. This is not the case with our technique, and thus we can often more drastically reduce the complexity of the synthesis problem. Also Maoz and Sa'ar recently proposed a technique for synthesizing controllers from LSC specifications with environment assumptions [16], but they do not address the decomposition of the synthesis problem.

Our technique requires the creativity of the engineer in finding a viable decomposition of the specification as well as assume/guarantee properties that are small enough so that the compositional synthesis is of advantage. If, for a chosen decomposition of the specification, no controllers could be synthesized, this does not imply that there does not exist a controller for the global specification. There might be other decompositions for which synthesizing controllers was possible. In this sense, our technique is not complete. Another limitation of our approach is that, in the decomposition, the second part specification can make assumptions about the first, but not vice versa. Supporting assumptions in both directions would require extra mechanisms, which we plan to investigate in future work.

This paper is structured as follows. We introduce an example in Sect. 2 and explain the foundations in Sect. 3. We describe our compositional synthesis technique in Sect. 4. Here we focus mainly on the technical aspects of creating a correct specification decomposition, but give a brief discussion on the methodology for using our technique. We then present realization details and evaluation results in Sect. 5, discuss related work in Sect. 6, and conclude in Sect. 7.

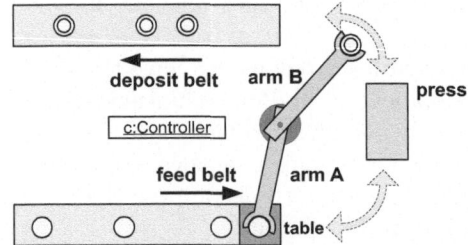

Environment Assumptions:

A1) The interarrival time of plates on the table is greater FMIN.

A2) The time for moving arm A from the table to the press or from the press to the table is between AMIN and AMAX.

A3) The time for moving arm B from the press to the deposit belt or from the deposit belt to the press is between BMIN and BMAX.

A4) The time for the press to press a blank plate is between PMIN and PMAX.

Requirements:

R1) When a blank plate arrives at the table, arm A must pick it up, move it to the press, and release it into the press. The arm then has to move back to the table, where it must arrive before the next blank arrives.

R2) When arm A has released the blank into the press, the press must press it, and then arm B must pick up the plate.

R3) When arm B has picked up the processed plate, it must transport the plate to the deposit belt.

R4) When arm B has arrived at the deposit belt, it must release the processed plate and then move back to the press.

R5) Arm A must only release a blank into the press if arm B has picked up the processed plate from the press.

R6) Arm A must not attempt to pick up the next blank before having returned to the table.

R7) Arm B must not attempt to pick up the pressed plate before having returned to the press.

Fig. 1. A sketch of the production cell system and its textual specification

2   Example

As an example, we consider a simplified specification of a production cell [14], an industrial production robot with two arms. One arm, *arm A*, picks up metal blanks that arrive from a *feed belt* on a *table* and places them into a *press*, where they are pressed into plates. The other arm, *arm B*, picks up the pressed plates and places them on a *deposit belt*, where they are transported off again. Figure 1 shows the system with its requirements and environment assumptions in plain text. Initially, arm A is located at the table, and arm B is located at the press.

After formalizing the above requirements and assumptions into an MSD specification MS for a single controller component $\underline{c}$, the technique described in this paper will allow us to

1. split the controller component $\underline{c}$ into two components, $\underline{c1}$ for arm A, and $\underline{c2}$ for arm B and the press,
2. split MS into two part specifications MS_1 and MS_2 for $\underline{c1}$ resp. $\underline{c2}$,
3. introduce additional properties as assumptions to MS_2 and as requirements to MS_1, with the aim of helping $\underline{c2}$ in being able to realize MS_2, while not making it impossible for $\underline{c1}$ to realize MS_1,

so that finally, if controllers $\underline{c1}$ and $\underline{c2}$ can be synthesized, they together form an implementation for the global specification MS.

3   Foundations

As foundations, we first formalize a notion of components that interact via messages. Then we introduce controllers and MSDs. As time is relevant in our example, we consider a timed setting. Our technique, however, is also applicable in an untimed setting.

3.1   Object Systems, Message Events, Runs

We consider systems of *objects* that interact via messages. Our definitions are based on Harel and Marelly [9]. For brevity, we consider synchronous messages only. Our technique would in principle also work for asynchronous communication, but this would need to be formalized.

Definition 1 (Object system, message, messages event, alphabet). *An* object system *consists of a set of objects O that exchange* messages. *A message has a name (from a set of names $Name$) and a sending and receiving object. The sending and receiving of a message in an object system is a single* message event, *or simply* event, *$e \in O \times Name \times O$. The set of possible message events is called the* alphabet, *denoted with $\Sigma \subseteq O \times Name \times O$.*

We consider a timed setting where message events occur at certain points in time. The progress of time is represented by a sequence of positive, increasing real values [1]. A message event itself does not take any time.

Definition 2 (Timed event, timed words, timed language). *A* timed event *is a pair $(e, r) \in (\Sigma \times \mathbb{R}^{\geq 0})$ where e is a message event occurring at time r. A* timed word *$\pi \in (\Sigma \times \mathbb{R}^{\geq 0})^{\omega}$ is an infinite sequence of timed events. For every two subsequent timed events in a timed word $\pi = \ldots, (e_i, r_i), (e_{i+1}, r_{i+1}), \ldots$, we require that $r_i \leq r_{i+1}$. Furthermore, for every $r \in \mathbb{R}^{\geq 0}$, we require that there exists a timed event (e_i, r_i) such that $r_i > r$, i.e., time must progress. The set of all timed words is denoted by $\mathcal{L}$ and a subset $L \subseteq \mathcal{L}$ is called a* timed language. *The complement of a language L is denoted by $\overline{L}$ and defined as $\overline{L} = \mathcal{L} \setminus L$.*

3.2   Controllers and Parallel Composition

Subsets of objects in the object system can be controlled by a *controller*. There can be multiple controllers, but the objects controlled by different controllers must be disjoint. We consider a controller to be a timed automaton [1] with some additional constraints, which will be described shortly. We rely on the usual definitions [1,5], and only briefly and informally explain the essential concepts, since the concrete controller formalism is not important for our approach.

A *timed automaton* $TA = (\Sigma, S, S_0, X, I, T)$ is an automaton with a finite set of *locations* S, $S_0 \subseteq S$ being *start locations*, and a finite set of real-valued variables X, called *clocks*, which increase synchronously and monotonically over time. I are *invariants* for locations, which specify that a timed automaton must not be in a location at a certain time. A timed automaton has *edges* between locations, which are defined through a relation $T \subseteq S \times \Sigma \times \mathcal{C}(X) \times 2^X \times S$. An edge $(s_s, e, \psi, \lambda, s_t)$ goes from location s_s to location s_t and is labeled by an event e. The element $\psi \in \mathcal{C}(X)$ is called a *constraint* on clock variables that is the *guard* of an edge, permitting it to be taken only at certain times. $\lambda \in 2^X$ is a subset of clocks that are *reset* when the edge is taken. A timed automaton *accepts* a timed language. For an automaton TA, we denote the accepted timed language as $L(TA)$.

If two timed automata share some events but have a disjoint set of clocks, we can form the *parallel composition* of the two automata, which is defined through the construction of the product of the two automata. For two timed automata TA_1 and TA_2, the parallel composition is denoted as $TA_1 \| TA_2$.

For a controller of a subset of objects in the object system, we require that for each message event not sent or received by an object that is controlled by the controller, each location has unguarded self-edges labelled with that event and without any clock reset. This requirement reflects the fact that a controller for a particular subset of objects should not be able to block the sending or receiving of messages among objects that it does not control.

Definition 3 (Controller). *We define a controller C as an extended timed automaton: $C = (\Sigma, S, S_0, X, I, T, O_C)$, where $O_C \subseteq O$ is a subset of objects in an object system O controlled by C. Let $\Sigma_C = \Sigma \cap ((O_C \times Name \times O) \cup (O \times Name \times O_C))$ be the messages sent and received by the objects in O_C. Then for every controller C we require that for every location $s \in S$ and every event $e \in \Sigma \setminus \Sigma_C$, there is an edge $(s, e, true, \emptyset, s) \in T$ (unguarded, no clocks reset). If $C1$ and $C2$ are controllers for objects O_{C1} and O_{C2}, we require that $O_{C1} \cap O_{C2} = \emptyset$.*

The additional self-edge for all the message events sent and received by the object not controlled by a controller allow us to infer the following.

Lemma 1 (Composition is conjunction). *Let C_1 and C_2 be two controllers accepting the languages $L(C_1)$ and $L(C_2)$. Then $L(C_1 \| C_2) = L(C_1) \cap L(C_2)$.*

We assume an open-world setting where the object system is subdivided into *system objects* and *environment objects*. System objects are *controllable*, i.e., the objects we seek an implementation for. Environment objects are *uncontrollable*; they represent for example sensors and actuators by which a software controller monitors and acts upon the physical world.

In this setting, we assume that if an environment event occurs, the system objects can immediately take any finite number of steps to react to this event before the next environment event occurs (in accordance with Harel and Marelly [9]). If the system waits for time to pass, environment events may occur again. This behavior can be ensured by formulating certain restrictions for the controllers of the environment and system objects, but we omit these restrictions for brevity.

3.3   MSD Specifications

An MSD specification specifies the valid interaction behavior in an object system [8]. We consider MSD specifications that not only formulate requirements on the system, but also formulate assumptions on how the environment behaves. The requirements and assumptions are two sets of MSDs.

Furthermore, MSDs can be *existential* or *universal*. Existential diagrams specify sequences of events that must be possible to occur in the object system and universal diagrams specify requirements that must be satisfied by all the sequences of events. We consider only universal MSDs in this paper.

MSDs, Lifelines, and Messages. An MSD is a sequence diagram where each lifeline represents an object in the object system. A message in an MSD represents a message event. Furthermore, a message has a *temperature* and an *execution kind*. The temperature can be either *hot* or *cold*; the execution kind can be either *monitored* or *executed*. Figure 2 shows two MSDs ArmATransportBlankToPress and PressPlateAfterArmAReleasesBlankPlate from the production cell specification. They formalize the requirements $R1$ and $R2$ and refer to the object system sketched at the top of Fig. 1. The temperature and execution kind are indicated by a label (e.g., h,c, e,m). The hot or cold temperature is also represented by red or blue color of the arrows. Monitored messages also have a dashed arrow; executed messages have a solid arrow.

Intuitively, a monitored message says that something may happen whereas an executed message says that something must eventually happen (liveness). A hot message says that no event expected at another point in the scenario must occur (safety) before the event represented by that message occurs. A cold message, by contrast, says that this may happen. We assume that an MSD has only one first message, which must be cold and monitored.

For example, consider the MSD ArmATransportBlankToPress in Fig. 2: The hot and executed message `pickUp` says that after `blankArrived` occurred, `pickUp` must eventually occur and no other event represented by a message in the diagram is allowed to occur. Then, likewise, `moveToPress` must occur. The hot, but monitored message `arrivedAtPress` means that `arrivedAtPress` may occur, but as long as it does not occur, no other message event in the diagram must occur. Then `releaseBlank` must occur, etc. This interpretation of the message temperature and execution kind extends the original definition [8] where the temperature alone reflects both the safety and liveness requirements.

More specifically, the semantics of these messages is as follows: When an event occurs in the system that is represented by the first message in an MSD, an *active copy* of the MSD or *active MSD* is created. As further events occur that are represented by the subsequent messages in the diagram, the active MSD progresses. This progress is captured by the *cut*, which marks for every lifeline the locations where the occurred messages are attached to the lifeline. If the cut reaches the end of an active MSD, the active copy is terminated.

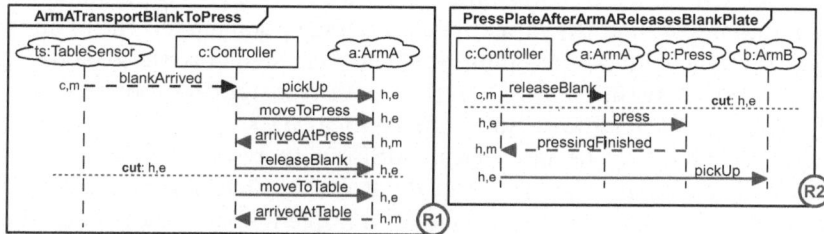

Fig. 2. The MSDs of the production cell specification for requirements R1 and R2

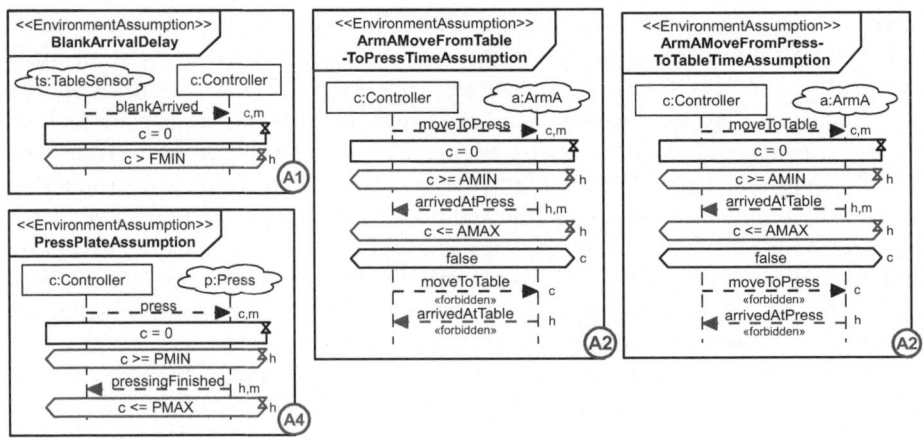

Fig. 3. The MSDs of the production cell specification for assumptions A1, A2, and A4

If the cut is in front of a message on its sending and receiving lifeline, the message is *enabled*. If a hot message is enabled, the cut is also *hot*; otherwise the cut is *cold*. Similarly, if an executed message is enabled, the cut is also *executed*; otherwise the cut is *monitored*.

A *safety violation* occurs if, in a hot cut, a message event occurs that is represented by a message in the MSD that is not currently enabled. If the same situation occurs in a cold cut, it is called a *cold violation*. Safety violations must never happen, while cold violations may occur and result in terminating the active copy of the MSD. If the cut is executed, this means that the active MSD must progress and it is a *liveness violation* if an active MSD never terminates or progresses to a monitored cut.

There can be multiple active copies of MSDs at a time. Figure 2 shows a reachable configuration of cuts for (active copies of) the MSDs ArmATransport-BlankToPress and PressPlateAfterArmAReleasesBlankPlate.

Environment Assumptions, Time, and Forbidden Messages. We model environment assumptions by MSDs that have an additional label «Environment-Assumption». Figure 3 shows assumption MSDs from the production cell example. BlankArrivalDelay models the assumption $A1$. The MSDs ArmAMoveFromPress-ToTableTimeAssumption and ArmAMoveFromTableToPressTimeAssumption model the assumptions $A2$, and the MSD PressPlateAssumption models the assumption $A4$. The MSDs modeling the assumption $A3$ are very similar to those modeling assumption $A2$, and are thus omitted. In these MSDs, we find additional constructs, namely *clock resets*, *conditions*, and *forbidden messages*.

Time constraints can be modeled in MSDs with resets of real-valued clock variables and conditions, similar to timed automata. Clock resets and conditions are boxes resp. hexagons that span one or multiple lifelines. If the cut is immediately before a clock reset or condition on all the lifelines it spans, the clock reset or condition is *enabled*. If a clock reset is enabled, then immediately, and before any other message event occurs, the clock variable is reset to zero and the cut progresses beyond the clock reset.

Conditions have a temperature (hot or cold), represented by a red resp. blue border color. In our figures, they have an additional label (h/c). We distinguish *timed* and *untimed* conditions. In this paper, untimed conditions have only the expression *true* or *false*. Timed conditions have an attached hour-glass symbol and can have expressions of the form $x \bowtie expr$ where x is a clock variable, *expr* is an integer constant, and $\bowtie$ is an operator $<, \leq, >, \geq$.

If a condition is enabled, and its expression evaluates to true, the cut progresses immediately and before any other message event occurs. If the expression of a cold condition evaluates to false, the active MSD is terminated. If the expression of a hot condition evaluates to false, the cut cannot progress, but at the same time it is a liveness violation if the cut never progresses. From this follows that it is a liveness violation if a hot untimed *false* condition is enabled.

For hot timed conditions, we distinguish *minimal delays* ($\bowtie \in \{>, \geq\}$) and *maximal delays* ($\bowtie \in \{<, \leq\}$). If a minimal delay evaluates to false, the cut progresses as soon as it becomes true. Meanwhile the cut is hot, i.e., no message that is not currently enabled in the active MSD is allowed to occur. If a maximal delay evaluates to false, this is a liveness violation of the MSD.

In the MSD BlankArrivalDelay, for example, a clock reset followed by a minimal delay is used to formalize the assumption that blanks arrive on the table with a certain minimal delay: after `blankArrived` occurred, the clock c is immediately reset to zero and then the minimal delay will be enabled until $FMIN$ time units have passed. In this time `blankArrived` must not occur.

At the end of an MSD, separated by a terminal cold *false* condition, there can be hot or cold *forbidden messages*. If there is an active MSD and a message event occurs that is represented in the MSD by a cold forbidden message, this is a cold violation, and the active MSD terminates. If a message event occurs that is represented by a hot forbidden message, this is a safety violation.

In the MSD ArmAMoveFromTableToPressTimeAssumption a clock reset and hot time conditions are used to express that after `moveToPress`, the event `arrivedAtPress` must occur within a certain interval. The hot forbidden message states that, in this interval, also `arrivedAtTable` must not occur. The cold forbidden message `moveToTable` states that `moveToTable` is allowed to occur, but, since this leads to the termination of the active MSD, then it cannot be assumed that the arm will arrive at the press in the specified interval.

To complete the example, Fig. 4 shows the MSDs for the requirements $R3$-$R7$.

Satisfying and Implementing a Specification, and Consistency. Without giving a more formal definition on the MSD semantics, we denote the (timed) language accepted by an MSD D as $L(D)$.

Definition 4 (Language accepted by a set of MSDs). *For an object system O and a set of message events Σ, Let $M = \{D_1, \ldots, D_n\}$ be a finite set of MSDs. We define the language accepted by M as $L(M) = \bigcap_{i=1}^{n} L(D_i)$.*

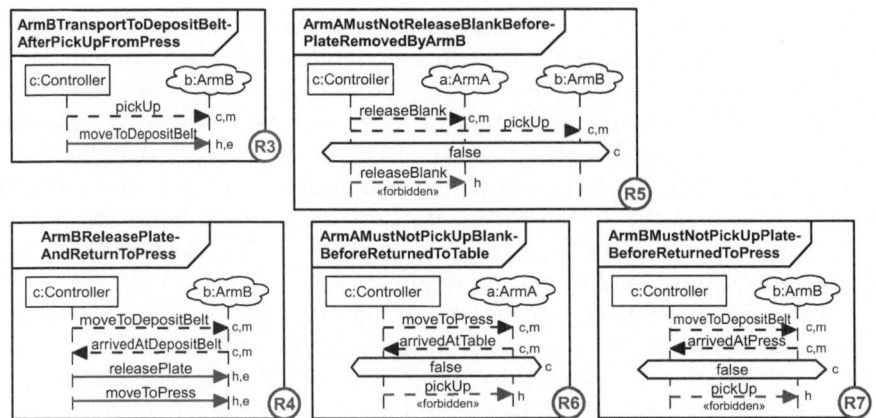

Fig. 4. The MSDs of the production cell specification for requirements R3–R7

A (timed) word *satisfies* an MSD specification if it is accepted by the requirement MSDs or not accepted by the assumption MSDs[1].

Definition 5 (Satisfying an MSD specification). *For an object system O and a set of message events Σ, $MS = (A, G, O_E, O_S)$ is an MSD specification where A and G are sets of MSDs. A is called the* assumptions *and G is called the* requirements *or* guarantees. *O_E are the environment objects and O_S are the system objects, $O_E \cup O_S = O$, $O_E \cap O_S = \emptyset$. The language satisfying MS, denoted with $L(MS)$, is defined as $L(MS) = \overline{L(A)} \cup L(G)$. A controller C for all objects O* satisfies *an MSD specification MS iff $L(C) \subseteq L(MS)$.*

A system controller for all the system objects *implements* an MSD specification if the controller that results from the composition with any possible environment controller satisfies the specification.

Definition 6 (Implementing an MSD specification, consistency). *Given an MSD specification $MS = (A, G, O_E, O_S)$, a system controller C_S for O_S* implements *MS if, for the closed system formed by the composition with every possible environment controller C_E for O_E holds $L(C_E \| C_S) \subseteq L(MS)$. From Lemma 1 and our definition of environment controllers, this is equivalent to $L(C_S) \subseteq L(MS)$. An MSD specification is* consistent *if there exists a system controller for all the system objects O_S that implements the specification.*

4   The Assume-Guarantee Synthesis Approach

Given an MSD specification MS, called the *global specification* in the following, this section explains how to decompose this specification into two specifications

---

[1] Of course, we expect the environment to satisfy the assumptions, but in environments that do not, the system is not required to satisfy the requirements.

MS_1 and MS_2, called *part specifications*, possibly adding MSDs as requirements to MS_1 and assumptions to MS_2, so that the consistency of the global specification follows from the consistency of the part specifications.

4.1   Decomposing the Global Specification

Assume a given MSD specification $MS = (A, G, O_E, O_S)$ for the objects O. Then, we can decompose this specification as follows.

Step 1 (Subdivide the set of system objects). We subdivide the objects O_S into two disjoint sets O_{S1} and O_{S2} with $O_{S1} \cup O_{S2} = O_S$ and $O_{S1} \cap O_{S2} = \emptyset$ with the respective environment objects $O_{E1} = O \setminus O_{S1}$ and $O_{E2} = O \setminus O_{S2}$.

Step 2 (Create subsets of MSDs for the part specifications). We create two part specifications $MS_1 = (A_1, G_1, O_{E1}, O_{S1})$ and $MS_2 = (A_2, G_2, O_{E2}, O_{S2})$ such that $G_1 \cup G_2 = G$ and each part specification may contain any subset of the assumption MSDs in the global specification: i.e. $A_1, A_2 \subseteq A$.

If we can now successfully synthesize system controllers from the part specifications, this means that these controllers implement their part specification regardless of the behavior of their opposite controller. It may be, however, that one controller must assume additional properties about the other controller, which, in turn, must guarantee these properties.

Step 3 (Add assume/guarantee properties to the part specifications). A set of MSDs, called AG^+, can be added as additional assumptions to part specification MS_2 and as additional requirements to part specification MS_1, i.e., $MS_1 = (A_1, G_1 \cup AG^+, O_{E1}, O_{S1})$ and $MS_2 = (A_2 \cup AG^+, G_2, O_{E2}, O_{S2})$

Now the implementation of the second part specification makes assumptions on the implementation of the first. Currently, we allow this only in one direction. Otherwise, we could always easily construct two part specifications that are consistent only because both controllers can mutually violate their assumptions, but then fail to implement the global specification.

4.2   Decomposing System Objects

In many cases, as in our production cell, it is necessary to decompose a system object into two objects that fulfill distinct functions in the two part specifications. This requires also to change the MSD specification such that for the two resulting objects an equivalent behavior is specified as for the initial object.

The goal is to split up the modified specification in such a way that one part of the specification specifies the behavior of the first object and another part of the specification specifies the behavior of the second object. In order to successfully apply the described compositional synthesis technique, the behavior of the first object must be independent from the behavior of the second, i.e., there may remain MSDs that specify how the second object must react to events involving the first object, but not vice versa. An example follows in Sect. 4.3.

Decomposing a system object is done before Step 1; thus, we call it "Step 0":

Step 0 (Decomposing system objects). An object that is a system object in the global specification can be decomposed into two system objects. This implies the following changes:

1. The events that the initial object sends and receives have to be separated into the message events that the resulting objects send and receive.
2. In each MSD of the specification where a lifeline represents the initial object, this lifeline must be split into two lifelines that represent the two objects resulting from the decomposition.
3. Also the diagram messages attached to the original lifelines must be attached to one of the resulting lifelines according to the changed message events. In MSDs where the effect is that one of the lifelines does not send or receive any messages, this lifeline can then be removed. Otherwise,
4. the lifelines must be synchronized so that the order of the events as in the original MSD is preserved. This can be achieved by introducing conditions with the expression **true** that cover both lifelines. These conditions must always be introduced between two messages where a message attached to one lifeline is followed by a message attached to the other lifeline. (We assume that the specified synchronization can always be realized in the final implementation.)

4.3 The Decomposition of the Production Cell Specification

For our production cell example, we first decompose the system object $\underline{c}$ into the objects $\underline{c1}$ and $\underline{c2}$ as already explained in Sect. 2: $\underline{c1}$ interacts with the table sensor and arm A, $\underline{c2}$ with the press and arm B. With an according separation of message events, the MSDs shown previously must be altered as follows:

1. The MSDs representing the requirements $R1$ and $R6$ and assumptions $A1$ and $A2$ are changed so that the lifeline representing object $\underline{c}$ is replaced by one lifeline representing the object $\underline{c1}$.
2. The MSDs representing the requirements $R3$, $R4$, and $R7$ as well as the assumptions $A3$ and $A4$ are changed so that the lifeline representing object $\underline{c}$ is replaced by one lifeline representing the object $\underline{c2}$.
3. The MSDs for the requirements $R2$ and $R5$ are replaced as shown in Fig. 5.

The part specifications are created such that $\underline{c1}$ is the system object in the first part specification and $\underline{c2}$ is the system object in the second part specification. Then the MSDs (as modified in Step 0) are split up so that the first part specification is made up of the requirements MSDs for $R1$ and $R6$ and the assumption MSDs for $A1$ and $A2$. The second part specification is made up of the MSDs for $R2 - R5$, $R7$, and $A3$ and $A4$.

Finally, the MSD BlankArrivalAtPressDelay as shown in Fig. 6 is added as an additional assumption to the second part specification and as an additional requirement to the first part specification. The MSD specifies that controller $\underline{c1}$ must order arm A to release blank plates into the press with a minimal time delay of $RMIN$. For certain values for $RMIN$ and the other constants, Sect. 5 documents the results of the controllers synthesized for the global specification and the part specifications.

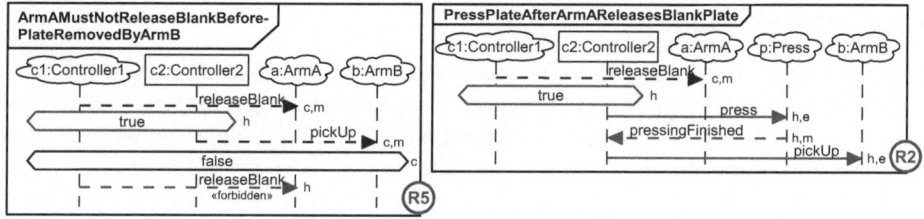

Fig. 5. The MSDs for the requirements R2 and R5 after decomposing the controller

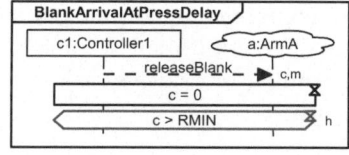

Fig. 6. The MSDs representing the additional assume-guarantee property

4.4 Soundness of the Compositional Synthesis Technique

For proving the soundness of the composition, we assume that we have specifications MS, MS_1 and MS_2 as defined in Sect. 4.1. And we assume that we have two system controllers C_1 and C_2 which implement MS_1 and MS_2 respectively:

$$L(C_1) \subseteq L(MS_1) \tag{1}$$

$$L(C_2) \subseteq L(MS_2) \tag{2}$$

In order to show $L(C_1 \| C_2) \subseteq L(MS)$, we use the following properties, which can be derived from Def. 4, 5, and 6, and the definition of MS, MS_1 and MS_2:

$$L(MS_1) = \overline{L(A_1)} \cup (L(G_1) \cap L(AG^+)) \tag{3}$$

$$L(MS_2) = \overline{L(A_2)} \cup \overline{L(AG^+)} \cup L(G_2) \tag{4}$$

$$L(MS) = \overline{L(A_1)} \cup \overline{L(A_2)} \cup (L(G_1) \cap L(G_2)) \tag{5}$$

Combining these properties we obtain

$L(C_1 \| C_2)$	= by Lemma 1
$L(C_1) \cap L(C_2)$	$\subseteq$ by (1) and (2)
$L(MS_1) \cap L(MS_2)$	= by (3) and (4)
$(\overline{L(A_1)} \cup (L(G_1) \cap L(AG^+))) \cap$	
$\quad (\overline{L(A_2)} \cup \overline{L(AG^+)} \cup L(G_2))$	= laws of boolean algebra
$(\overline{L(A_1)} \cap \overline{L(A_2)}) \cup (\overline{L(A_1)} \cap \overline{L(AG^+)}) \cup$	
$\quad (\overline{L(A_1)} \cap L(G_2)) \cup$	
$\quad (L(G_1) \cap L(AG^+) \cap \overline{L(A_2)}) \cup$	
$\quad (L(G_1) \cap L(AG^+) \cap \overline{L(AG^+)}) \cup$	
$\quad (L(G_1) \cap L(AG^+) \cap L(G_2))$	$\subseteq$ laws of boolean algebra
$\overline{L(A_1)} \cup \overline{L(A_2)} \cup (L(G_1) \cap L(G_2))$	= by (5)
$L(MS)$	

4.5 Methodology

Once an engineer has decomposed a specification in such a way that the technical conditions of Sect. 4.1 are met, the presented approach is fully automatic. The question remains how an engineer can come up with such a decomposition. This is a question of methodology, which we can only address briefly here.

We argue that engineers who design a complex system typically have a good idea of how to split up the system in order to keep on top of its complexity. The split into components would follow this "mindset".

Our approach works for systems where we can identify components that build on each other, so that later components can make assumptions on earlier ones, avoiding cyclic assumptions. The additional assume-guarantee properties $AG+$ can be used to restrict the timing or relative order of message events that one component shares with an other.

5 Realization and Evaluation

In SCENARIOTOOLS[2] [7], we implemented a synthesis technique for timed MSD specifications by a mapping from a UML-based MSD specifications in ECLIPSE to Timed Game Automata (TGA) that are input for UPPAAL TIGA [3,2], an extension of the UPPAAL model checker for solving two-player games.

With this mapping, we formulate a winning condition that checks whether there is a strategy for the system to always eventually reach a state where all cuts of requirement MSDs are monitored and no safety violation occurred in any requirement MSDs, or there is an executed cut in an assumption MSD, or a safety violation occurred in an assumption MSD. We call this the $AGAF$ condition. We also check a weaker condition for which strategies can be synthesized more quickly: here we only check that never safety violations occur in requirement MSDs or they occur in assumption MSDs. We call this the AG condition. If the winning condition is satisfied, the tool generates a winning strategy for the system; if not, a winning strategy for the environment is generated. From the winning strategy, a controller can be derived.

In our MSD-to-TGA mapping, we can also specify different degrees of freedom for the system: Either it can always choose to send any system message and also consider to wait for environment events, or we can restrict it to immediately send only system messages that correspond to an executed message in a requirement MSD that is enabled in a current cut. The latter corresponds to the behavior of the *play-out* algorithm, an executable semantics for LSCs/MSDs [10,15], and can drastically simplify the synthesis. If a strategy could be synthesized in the latter setting, the specification is called *consistently executable*.

Figure 7 shows the synthesis times and results from checking the consistent executability of the part specifications and the global specification for the production cell example with different values for $FMIN$, $RMIN$, etc. $RMIN$ is irrelevant for the global specification, since it was only added with the MSD

---

[2] http://www.cs.uni-paderborn.de/index.php?id=scenariotools

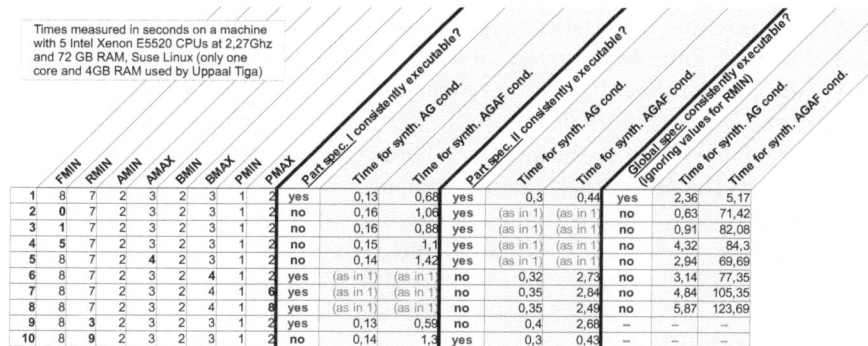

Times measured in seconds on a machine with 5 Intel Xenon E5520 CPUs at 2,27Ghz and 72 GB RAM, Suse Linux (only one core and 4GB RAM used by Uppaal Tiga)

	FMIN	RMIN	AMIN	AMAX	BMIN	BMAX	PMIN	PMAX	Part spec. I consistently executable?	Time for synth. AG cond.	Time for synth. AGAF cond.	Part spec. II consistently executable?	Time for synth. AG cond.	Time for synth. AGAF cond.	Global spec. consistently executable? (ignoring values for RMIN)	Time for synth. AG cond.	Time for synth. AGAF cond.
1	8	7	2	3	2	3	1	2	yes	0,13	0,68	yes	0,3	0,44	yes	2,36	5,17
2	0	7	2	3	2	3	1	2	no	0,16	1,06	yes	(as in 1)	(as in 1)	no	0,63	71,42
3	1	7	2	3	2	3	1	2	no	0,16	0,88	yes	(as in 1)	(as in 1)	no	0,91	82,08
4	5	7	2	3	2	3	1	2	no	0,15	1,1	yes	(as in 1)	(as in 1)	no	4,32	84,3
5	8	7	2	4	2	3	1	2	no	0,14	1,42	yes	(as in 1)	(as in 1)	no	2,94	69,69
6	8	7	2	3	2	4	1	2	yes	(as in 1)	(as in 1)	no	0,32	2,73	no	3,14	77,35
7	8	7	2	3	2	4	1	6	yes	(as in 1)	(as in 1)	no	0,35	2,84	no	4,84	105,35
8	8	7	2	3	2	4	1	8	yes	(as in 1)	(as in 1)	no	0,35	2,49	no	5,87	123,69
9	8	3	2	3	2	3	1	2	yes	0,13	0,59	no	0,4	2,68	–	–	–
10	8	9	2	3	2	3	1	2	no	0,14	1,3	yes	0,3	0,43	–	–	–

Fig. 7. The synthesis times for the part specifications vs. the global specification of the production cell with different values for the constants $FMIN$, $RMIN$, etc

PressPlateAssumption, see Fig. 6. The table shows that in the case of consistent constant values the sum of the time needed to synthesize a strategy for the part specifications (0.68 seconds + 0.44 seconds = 1.12 seconds) is only one fifth of the time needed for synthesizing a strategy for the global specification (5.17 seconds). For more evaluation results and discussion, see [7, Appendix C].

6   Related Work

Our technique is the first that allows for the decomposition of the synthesis problem for LSCs/MSDs into two problems that can be solved independently.

Kugler and Segall also proposed a compositional approach for synthesizing controllers from LSC specifications [13]. With their approach, however, the synthesis problem cannot be split into two separate parts. They first do synthesize controllers for subsets of LSC in a specification—the resulting controllers, however, are then input for a subsequent synthesis step. Ultimately, a controller for the whole specification must be synthesized, which is not the case in our approach. While their approach may be more flexibly applicable, our approach can often more drastically reduce the time required by the synthesis.

Maoz and Sa'ar recently proposed a technique for synthesizing controllers from LSC specifications with environment assumptions [16], but they do not address the decomposition of the synthesis problem. Their approach also differs from ours in the way that assumptions are formulated. They propose to model environment assumptions by specially labeled environment messages in LSCs. We instead propose to model assumptions by specially labeled MSDs. Only this makes it possible to model the same property as requirements in one specifications and assumptions in another, which is the key to our technique.

Chatterjee and Henzinger also present a compositional assume-guarantee synthesis approach from specifications in temporal logic [4]. They, however, regard a different problem: translated into our terminology, they regard the problem of synthesizing controllers for two system objects that interact with an environment and have local, possibly interdependent specifications. The goal is to synthesize two controllers that fulfill each system object's local specification without violating the specification of the other system object. This process, called *co-synthesis*, does not aim at being more efficient than synthesizing a global controller—in general the problem is even more complex. They, however, sketch an abstraction approach to make the co-synthesis more efficient.

Nejati et al. present a compositional approach for synthesizing sequential compositions of *features*. Features are units of functionality that are modeled with state machines, to fulfill certain requirements [17]. They, however, are only considering to find a viable composition of features and do not consider the synthesis of state machines themselves.

Krüger proposes a mapping from (High-Level) Message Sequence Charts to assume-guarantee specifications of components [12]. The scenario language regarded by Krüger, however, does not allow for flexible overlappings of scenarios as it is allowed for LSCs or MSDs. So the resulting synthesis problem is more simple than the MSD/LSC synthesis problem that we consider.

7   Conclusion and Outlook

We presented a novel compositional synthesis technique for scenario-based specifications, which makes use of the assume-guarantee paradigm. The technique allows engineers to decompose the problem of synthesizing a controller for an MSD specification into two synthesis problems that can be solved independently from each other. This can significantly reduce the overall computation time for synthesizing the controllers. We provided a soundness proof and some evaluation results that document the benefit of our technique.

A limitation of our technique is that we currently allow only for one controller to make assumptions about the other. The reasons for this lies in the nature of liveness properties: a violation of a liveness property cannot be pinpointed to a specific point of the run at which it is violated. Therefore, if both controllers violate some assumptions which are liveness properties, it is not clear which one violated its assumption first. If there were cyclic assumptions and guarantees concerning liveness properties, each controller could blame the violation on the other. Therefore, no component would need to guarantee anything.

There are different ways of dealing with this problem. One idea is applying a concept for composing controllers proposed in [11]. This concept relies on explicit dependency graphs between the involved assume-guarantee properties of a components, which need to stay acyclic when combining components. Another idea would be to apply the compositional synthesis technique of Chatterjee and Henzinger [4] (see also Sect. 6), if by using the described abstraction techniques the co-synthesis problem can be sufficiently simplified.

References

1. Alur, R., Dill, D.L.: A Theory of Timed Automata. Theoretical Computer Science 126(2), 183–235 (1994)

2. Behrmann, G., Cougnard, A., David, A., Fleury, E., Larsen, K.G., Lime, D.: UPPAAL-Tiga: Time for playing games! In: Damm, W., Hermanns, H. (eds.) CAV 2007. LNCS, vol. 4590, pp. 121–125. Springer, Heidelberg (2007)

3. Cassez, F., David, A., Fleury, E., Larsen, K.G., Lime, D.: Efficient on-the-fly algorithms for the analysis of timed games. In: Abadi, M., de Alfaro, L. (eds.) CONCUR 2005. LNCS, vol. 3653, pp. 66–80. Springer, Heidelberg (2005)

4. Chatterjee, K., Henzinger, T.A.: Assume-Guarantee Synthesis. In: Grumberg, O., Huth, M. (eds.) TACAS 2007. LNCS, vol. 4424, pp. 261–275. Springer, Heidelberg (2007)

5. Clarke Jr. E.M., Grumberg, O., Peled, D.A.: Model Checking. The MIT Press (1999)

6. Damm, W., Harel, D.: LSCs: Breathing life into message sequence charts. In: Formal Methods in System Design, vol. 19, pp. 45–80. Kluwer Academic Publishers (2001)

7. Greenyer, J.: Scenario-based Design of Mechatronic Systems. Ph.D. thesis, University of Paderborn (October 2011)

8. Harel, D., Maoz, S.: Assert and negate revisited: Modal semantics for UML sequence diagrams. Software and Systems Modeling (SoSyM) 7(2), 237–252 (2008)

9. Harel, D., Marelly, R.: Come, Let's Play: Scenario-Based Programming Using LSCs and the Play-Engine. Springer (August 2003)

10. Harel, D., Marelly, R.: Playing with time: On the specification and execution of time-enriched LSCs. In: Proc. 10th Int. Symp. on Modeling, Analysis and Simulation of Computer and Telecommunication Systems, pp. 193–202 (2002)

11. Kindler, E.: Modularer Entwurf verteilter Systeme mit Petrinetzen, Edition Versal, vol. 1. Bertz Verlag, dissertation, Technische Universität München (December 1995)

12. Krüger, I.: Distributed System Design with Message Sequence Charts. Ph.D. thesis, Technische Universität München, Institut für Informatik (2000)

13. Kugler, H., Segall, I.: Compositional synthesis of reactive systems from live sequence chart specifications. In: Kowalewski, S., Philippou, A. (eds.) TACAS 2009. LNCS, vol. 5505, pp. 77–91. Springer, Heidelberg (2009)

14. Lewerentz, C., Lindner, T.: KORSO: Methods, Languages, and Tools for the Construction of Correct Software. In: Jähnichen, S., Broy, M. (eds.) KORSO 1995. LNCS, vol. 1009, pp. 388–416. Springer, Heidelberg (1995)

15. Maoz, S., Harel, D.: From multi-modal scenarios to code: Compiling LSCs into AspectJ. In: Proc. Int. 14th Symp. on Foundations of Software Engineering (FSE 2005), pp. 219–230. ACM (2006)

16. Maoz, S., Sa'ar, Y.: Assume-guarantee scenarios: Semantics and synthesis. In: France, R.B., Kazmeier, J., Breu, R., Atkinson, C. (eds.) MODELS 2012. LNCS, vol. 7590, pp. 335–351. Springer, Heidelberg (2012)

17. Nejati, S., Sabetzadeh, M., Chechik, M., Uchitel, S., Zave, P.: Towards compositional synthesis of evolving systems. In: Harrold, M.J., Murphy, G.C. (eds.) Proc. 16th Int. Symp. on Foundations of Software Engineering, pp. 285–296. ACM (2008)

18. Stark, E.W.: A proof technique for rely/guarantee properties. In: Maheshwari, S.N. (ed.) FSTTCS 1985. LNCS, vol. 206, pp. 369–391. Springer, Heidelberg (1985)

Author Index